THE WORLD
of the
Battleship

THE WORLD
of the
Battleship

◆

*The Lives and Careers of
Twenty-One Capital Ships from the
World's Navies, 1880–1990*

Edited by
BRUCE TAYLOR

NAVAL INSTITUTE PRESS
ANNAPOLIS, MARYLAND

Frontispiece: The three units of the Sverige class execute a turn in line ahead in the spring of 1940. This photo, which was taken from *Sverige*, shows *Gustaf V* leading *Drottning Victoria*. Note the paravane awaiting use on the forecastle. *(Krigsarkivet – Military Archives, Stockholm)*

In memory of
Professor Sir Peter Russell (1913–2006)
once my mentor and always master of those who study maritime history

First published in Great Britain in 2018 by
Seaforth Publishing,
A division of Pen & Sword Books Ltd,
47 Church Street,
Barnsley S70 2AS

www.seaforthpublishing.com

Published and distributed in the
United States of America and Canada by the
Naval Institute Press,
291 Wood Road, Annapolis,
Maryland 21402-5034

www.nip.org

Library of Congress Control Number: 2018948313

ISBN 978 0 87021 906 1

Printed and bound in India

Contents

The Contributors   6

Editor's Acknowledgments   8

Editor's Note   8

General Bibliography   8

Abbreviations   9

Introduction   Bruce Taylor   10

China   *Chen Yuen* (1882)   Qing Feng   20
Argentina   *Garibaldi* (1895)   Guillermo Andrés Oyarzábal   38
France   *Iéna* (1898)   Philippe Caresse   53
Norway   *Eidsvold* (1900)   Jacob Børresen   73
Russia   *Slava* (1903)   Sergei Vinogradov with Stephen McLaughlin   91
Denmark   *Peder Skram* (1908)   Tom Wismann   113
Brazil   *Minas Geraes* (1908)   João Roberto Martins Filho   129
The Netherlands   *De Zeven Provinciën* (1909)   Leon Homburg   153
Greece   *Georgios Averof* (1910)   Zisis Fotakis   170
Turkey   *Yavuz Sultan Selim* (1911)   Gökhan Atmaca   183
Austria-Hungary   *Viribus Unitis* (1911)   Lawrence Sondhaus   202
Australia   *Australia* (1911)   Richard Pelvin   219
Chile   *Almirante Latorre* (1913)   Carlos Tromben Corbalán & Fernando Wilson Lazo   247
Spain   *Alfonso XIII* (1913)   Agustín Ramón Rodríguez González   268
Sweden   *Sverige* (1915)   Ulf Sundberg   290
Great Britain   *Hood* (1918)   Bruce Taylor   308
Japan   *Nagato* (1919)   Hans Lengerer & Lars Ahlberg   336
Finland   *Väinämöinen* (1930)   Jari Aromaa   357
Germany   *Scharnhorst* (1936)   Thomas Schmid   374
Italy   *Littorio* (1937)   Arrigo Velicogna   393
United States   *Missouri* (1944)   Paul Stillwell   409

Index   434

The Contributors

Lars Ahlberg was born in Sweden in 1955 and joined the Swedish Army in 1975. The latter part of his service career was spent in staff positions and finally with the Swedish Air Defence Regiment in Halmstad from which he retired in the rank of major in 2016. He has published on the Halland Regiment and with Hans Lengerer (see below) is co-author of a two-part monograph on the carrier *Taihō* (2004–8) and *Capital Ships of the Imperial Japanese Navy 1868–1945: The Yamato Class and Subsequent Planning* (2014), the product of a lifelong interest in naval history. He lives in the port of Halmstad in southwestern Sweden.

Jari Aromaa was born in Finland in 1960. He studied Metallurgy at the Helsinki University of Technology and received a doctorate in Science in 1994. His interest in Finnish military history was kindled by his grandfathers who served in the Navy and Coastal Artillery respectively from the late 1920s to the 1950s. He lives in the Helsinki area and works as a senior lecturer in Chemical Engineering at Aalto University.

Gökhan Atmaca was born in Ankara in 1976 and graduated from Ankara University in 1998, in which year he joined the Turkish Naval Forces as a history instructor. In 2009 he was appointed Director of the Piri Reis Research Centre of the Istanbul Naval Museum and has since become Director of Naval History Archives at that institution. He has published numerous works on nineteenth- and twentieth-century Ottoman and Turkish naval history including *Türk Deniz Harp Tarihi Atlası* (An Historical Atlas of Turkish Naval Warfare) (2008) and *Barbaros Hayrettin Zırhlısı: Üç Savaş Bir Gemi* (The Battleship *Barbaros Hayrettin*: Three Wars, One Ship) (2015). He lives with his family in Istanbul and currently holds the rank of lieutenant commander.

Jacob Børresen was born into a prominent Norwegian naval family in 1943. The grandson of Rear Admiral Jacob Børresen (1857–1943), he made his career in the Royal Norwegian Navy in which he commanded submarines and frigates and served as a planner and director of exercises and operations both nationally and as part of NATO, retiring in 2000 in the rank of Commodore. He is author of *The Norwegian Navy: A Brief History* (2012) together with numerous books and publications on strategy, defence policy and security policy in Norwegian and international journals. He lives in the port of Horten on the Oslofjord.

Philippe Caresse was born into a naval family in France in 1964 and joined the Marine Nationale in 1982, serving in the destroyer *d'Estrées*. He has published an extensive range of ship monographs on the French, German, US and Japanese navies from the late-nineteenth century to the Second World War, is co-author with John Jordan of *French Battleships of World War One* (2017), and author of the forthcoming *Battleships of the Iowa Class*. A diving instructor, he is the harbourmaster of a marina on the Côte d'Azur.

Zisis Fotakis was born in Volos and received a BA in History from Athens University in 1995 before going to Oxford where he was awarded an MSc in Economic and Social History (1997) and a doctorate in Modern History (2003). He has published extensively in Greek naval and maritime affairs including *Greek Naval Strategy and Policy, 1910–1919* (2005) and is currently lecturer in Naval History at the Hellenic Naval Academy in Piraeus.

Leon Homburg was born in the Netherlands in 1967 and studied Maritime History at the University of Leiden. He joined the Koninklijke Marine as an enlisted officer in 1992 since when he has worked as registrar and latterly as curator at the Dutch Navy Museum in Den Helder. Returning to civilian status in 1997, he has published several ship monographs and articles on the Dutch navy from 1850, and in 1993 was involved in locating the wreck of Hr. Ms. submarine O 22 which disappeared in the Skagerrak in November 1940.

Hans Lengerer was born in Germany in 1940 and joined the executive branch of the civil service in 1962. His interest in the Imperial Japanese Navy was fostered by the late historians Erich Gröner and Prof. Jürgen Rohwer, and he has published over fifty articles and eight books since 1969. Among his collaborations with Lars Ahlberg (see above) since retiring in 2000 are the privately published *Contributions to the History of Imperial Japanese Warships* of which fifteen papers have so far been issued. He lives in the state of Baden-Württemberg.

Stephen McLaughlin was born in New York City in 1957 and graduated with a bachelor's degree in History from the University of California, Berkeley in 1979, followed by a master's degree in Library Science from the same university in 1981. He worked as a librarian for the San Francisco Public Library for thirty-five years before retiring in June 2017. Interested in naval history, and battleships, since his teenage years, he has published many articles and is author of *Russian and Soviet Battleships* (2003). He lives in Richmond, California.

João Roberto Martins Filho was born in the state of São Paulo in 1953 and has a doctorate in Political Science from the Universidade Estadual de Campinas. He is senior lecturer at the Universidade Federal de São Carlos and was a founding member and first president of the Brazilian Defence Studies Association. He is author of *A Marinha brasileira na era dos encouraçados, 1895–1910* (The Brazilian Navy in the Age of the Battleship, 1895–1910) (2010) and lives in the city of Campinas in his home state.

Guillermo Andrés Oyarzábal was born in Argentina in 1958 and entered the Argentine navy as an officer cadet in 1975. A veteran of the Falklands War, he held a succession of seagoing and shore-based appointments in the Armada before joining the Department of Naval History in 1999, of which he was director from 2002–12. He has published over a hundred books and articles on Argentine naval and maritime affairs including *William Brown: An Irish Seaman in the River Plate* (2008). Currently in the rank of captain, he is Director of the Research Department of the Naval War College and a professor of history at the Pontificia Universidad Católica Argentina in Buenos Aires.

Qing Feng (馮青) was born in China and graduated with a BA in History from Fujian Normal University before receiving a doctorate in Political Science from Chuo University in Tokyo. She is author of *Chugoku Kaigun to Kindai Nicchu Kankei* (The Chinese Navy and Japanese-Chinese Relations in the Modern Era) (2011) and an editor of *Gunji Shigaku* (The Journal of Military History). She lives in Tokyo and lectures at Meiji University.

Richard Pelvin was born in Australia in 1947 and has degrees in Arts and Defence Studies from Monash University and the University of New South Wales. After ten years at the Australian Defence Department, including in the Naval and Army Historical Sections, he became Curator of Official Records at the Australian War Memorial. Since resigning in 2002 he has worked on contract as a researcher and writer in military history and as a historical consultant to various Government authorities. He is author of three illustrated histories of Australia in the First and Second World Wars and the Vietnam War as well as articles for various journals, and is currently Archival Consultant to the Australian Army History Unit. He lives in Canberra.

Agustín Ramón Rodríguez González was born in Madrid in 1955 and received his doctorate in History from the Universidad Complutense in 1986. A fellow of the Spanish Royal Academy of History, he has published over forty volumes on Spanish naval and maritime affairs from the fifteenth to the twentieth centuries with particular emphasis on the decades around the Spanish-American War of 1898. He is on the advisory board of the Naval Museum of Madrid and was awarded the Cross of Naval Merit by the Armada for services to history in 2001.

Thomas Schmid was born in Germany in 1964 and received a degree in Computer Science at the Augsburg University of Applied Sciences. An outstanding computer graphic artist, he has been able to apply his art to a lifelong passion for naval and maritime history, including collaborations with James Cameron on *Titanic* (1997) and his expedition to the wreck of the *Bismarck* (2002). He has also participated in the salvage of the *Admiral Graf Spee* off Montevideo (2004) and in the search for Vizeadmiral von Spee's lost fleet off the Falkland Islands (2014).

Lawrence Sondhaus is Professor of History at the University of Indianapolis where he is Director of the Institute for the Study of War and Diplomacy. Among his many publications in military and naval history are *The Naval Policy of Austria-Hungary, 1867–1918* (1994), *Naval Warfare, 1815–1914* (2001), *Strategic Culture and Ways of War* (2006), *World War One: The Global Revolution* (2011) and *The Great War at Sea: A Naval History of the First World War* (2014).

Paul Stillwell was born in Dayton, Ohio and has a bachelor's degree in History from Drury College and a master's in Journalism from the University of Missouri-Colombia. A member of the U.S. Naval Reserve from 1962 to 1992, he was on active duty during the Vietnam War from 1966–9, including service in the battleship *New Jersey*, being recalled to active duty to document the role of the U.S. Navy during the Iran-Iraq War in 1988. Joining the staff of the U.S. Naval Institute in 1974, he held a succession of positions culminating in Director of History. His many publications include illustrated histories of the battleships *New Jersey* (1986), *Arizona* (1991) and *Missouri* (1996), and *The Golden Thirteen: Recollections of the First Black Naval Officers* (1993) which was named one of *The New York Times*' notable history books for that year. He is a recipient of the Naval Historical Foundation's Knox Naval History Award and lives in Maryland.

Ulf Sundberg was born in Sweden in 1956. A lieutenant in the Swedish naval reserve, he graduated in Economics from the Stockholm School of Economics and has a master's degree in History from Åbo Akademi University in Turku, Finland where he is currently completing a doctorate in fortress warfare in the Great Northern War. He has published several books and articles on Swedish political and military history from the Middle Ages to 1814 and is author of *A Short Guide to British Battleships in World War II* (2008).

Bruce Taylor was born in Chile in 1967 and educated at the University of Manchester and at Oxford where he received a doctorate in Modern History in 1996. Among other publications he is author of *The Battlecruiser HMS* Hood: *An Illustrated Biography, 1916–1941* (2005) and co-author with Daniel Morgan of *U-Boat Attack Logs: A Complete Record of Warship Sinkings from Original Sources, 1939–1945* (2011). He lives in Southern California and makes his living as a freelance translator.

Carlos Tromben Corbalán holds a master's degree in History from the Pontificia Universidad Católica de Valparaíso and a doctorate in Maritime History from the University of Exeter. He is author of numerous books and articles on nineteenth- and twentieth-century Chilean naval history including monographs on the Armada's engineering, aviation and electrical branches as well as the first in the two-volume study *La Armada de Chile, una historia de dos siglos* (The Chilean Navy: Two Centuries of History) (2017). He is currently a research fellow at the Centre for Strategic Studies of the Chilean navy in which he holds the rank of retired captain.

Arrigo Velicogna was born in Italy in 1974 and earned a BA in History from the University of Bologna before being awarded an MA and a doctorate in War Studies from King's College London. His research interests lie in the US and Japanese navies from 1920–45 and in the Korean and Vietnam War. He is currently working on a new study of US military operations in South Vietnam and has authored articles on military history and military technology. He has lectured at King's College and Wolverhampton University and worked with the British Army.

Sergei Vinogradov was born in Moscow in 1960 and graduated from the Moscow Construction Engineering Institute in 1982. He has worked as a civil engineer and a school teacher and is currently on the staff of the Central Museum of the Armed Forces in Moscow. Many years' research in the naval archives of St Petersburg have yielded numerous books and articles on the battleships of the Imperial Russian Navy, most notably *Poslednie ispoliny Rossiiskogo imperatorskogo flota* (The Last Giants of the Russian Imperial Navy) (1999), *Bronenosets 'Slava'. Nepobezhdennyi geroi Moonzunda* (Battleship *Slava*: The Immovable Hero of the Moonsund) (2011), and most recently *Lineinyi korabl' Imperatritsa Mariia* (The Battleship *Imperatritsa Mariia*) (2017). He lives in Moscow.

Fernando Wilson Lazo was born into a naval family in Chile in 1970, his grandfather having served more than once as an officer in the *Almirante Latorre*. He holds bachelor's and master's degrees in History and International Relations respectively from the Pontificia Universidad Católica de Valparaíso where he is completing his doctorate. He has published numerous articles and chapters on Chilean naval history and maritime affairs and currently teaches at the Universidad Adolfo Ibáñez and at the Chilean Naval War College and Military Academy. He lives with his family in Viña del Mar in central Chile.

Tom Wismann was born into a family with a tradition of service in the Danish navy dating back to 1666. Conscripted into the Kongelige Danske Marine in 1976, he served in the fishery protection frigate *Fylla* and later as a volunteer commanded a flotilla in the Danish Maritime Home Guard in the rank of Lieutenant Commander. A marine engineer by training, he has published numerous monographs and articles on the ships of the Royal Danish Navy, and has for many years been a member of the board of the Danish Naval Historical Society and editor of the Society's journal. He lives in Helsingør, classically known as Elsinore.

Editor's Acknowledgments

THIS VOLUME, years in the making, would not exist without the generous collaboration and assistance of many individuals who are mentioned where applicable in the first footnote of each chapter. Where the volume as a whole is concerned, my first acknowledgment as editor must of course be to my contributors, twenty-three of them aside from myself, who have honoured me with the impressive fruits of their knowledge and labour and shown commendable patience both during the long gestation of this volume and latterly with my interventions, sometimes as translator and always as editor. The quality of their individual contributions speaks for itself and my sincere hope is that they will find the overall product to be worthy of their ship, its navy and their dedication to our subject. In the same vein, I should like to make special acknowledgment to six people who have particularly contributed to the realisation of this project: Christopher McKee for his early encouragement, Olaf Janzen for many invaluable introductions at its inception, Philippe Caresse and Steve McLaughlin for material support and good fellowship through its course, and Lars Ahlberg and Ray Burt who have always been ready with a good photo when it was needed most. Julian Mannering, Stephanie Rudgard-Redsell and Steve Dent at Seaforth have made the completion of this project a pleasure. My lasting thanks to them all for helping me make this cherished dream of mine a reality.

This book has occupied the teenage years of my children Emma and Alex, and as I write these lines I am reminded of the uncomplicated love they never fail to show me and their forbearance with my inexplicable nautical enthusiasms. To them and to Bettina, always beautiful, brilliant and shining, I owe a debt unlikely to be settled ere the seas run dry.

Bruce Taylor
Beverly Hills, Calif., March 2018

Editor's Note

A full listing of the sources consulted (published and unpublished) will be found at the close of each chapter and in the General Bibliography immediately below, citations being referenced in the footnotes where applicable. Credits are given after each photo where it has been possible to establish either the source or the copyright with certainty. Extensive efforts have been made to locate copyright holders in the remaining cases and these are encouraged to contact the editor or the authors with proof of copyright.

General Bibliography

Readers are referred to the Sources section at the close of each chapter for material specific to the vessel in question, but the following general works have been consulted in the selection, preparation or editing of many and in some cases all of the ships treated in this book.

Breyer, Siegfried, *Battleships and Battle Cruisers, 1905–1970* (London: Macdonald & Jane's, 1973)

Campbell, N. J. M., *Naval Weapons of World War Two* (London: Conway Maritime Press, 1985)

Friedman, Norman, *Naval Weapons of World War One: Guns, Torpedoes, Mines and ASW Weapons of All Nations: An Illustrated Directory* (Barnsley, S. Yorks.: Seaforth Publishing, 2011)

Gardiner, Robert, gen. ed., *Conway's All the World's Fighting Ships*, 4 vols. I: *1860–1905*; II: *1906–1921*; III: *1922–1946*; IV: *1947–1995* (London: Conway Maritime Press, 1979–95)

Silverstone, Paul, *Directory of the World's Capital Ships* (London: Ian Allan, 1984)

Wilson, H. W., *Battleships in Action*, 2 vols. (London: Sampson Low, 1926)

Abbreviations

AA Anti-Aircraft
ABT Ansaldo-Belluzzo-Tosi (consortium)
ACM Archive Centrale de la Marine, Paris
ACNB Australian Commonwealth Naval Board
AGNA Archivo General de la Nación Argentina, Buenos Aires
AHA Archivo Histórico de la Armada, Valparaíso, Chile
ANMEF Australian Naval and Military Expeditionary Force
AO1 Artilleriofficer 1 (principal gunnery officer), Svenska marinen
AP Armour Piercing
AWM Australian War Memorial, Canberra
BCF Battle Cruiser Fleet; Battle Cruiser Force (from December 1916); Royal Navy
BCS Battle Cruiser Squadron, Royal Navy
BS Battle Squadron, Royal Navy
Capt. Captain, Capitán
Cdr Commander
Cdre Commodore
CNF Commonwealth Naval Forces
CNM Central Naval Museum, St Petersburg
CO Commanding Officer
CPO Chief Petty Officer
C.R.D.A. Cantieri Riuniti dell'Adriatico, Trieste
DEHN Departamento de Estudios Históricos Navales, Buenos Aires
DPHDM Diretoria do Patrimônio Histórico e Documentação da Marinha, Rio de Janeiro
ELIA Elliniko Logotechniko kai Istoriko Archeio (Hellenic Literary and Historical Archive), Athens
Fregkpt. Fregattenkapitän (Commander, Kaiserliche Marine/Reichsmarine/Kriegsmarine)
grt gross register tons
HA High-Angle
HE High Explosive
HMAS His Majesty's Australian Ship (Royal Australian Navy)
HMM Hellenic Maritime Museum, Piraeus
HMS His Majesty's Ship (Royal Navy)
H.M.S. Hans Majestäts Skepp (Svenska marinen)
HMS/m His Majesty's Submarine (Royal Navy)
HPT high-pressure turbine
Hr. Ms. Hare Majesteits (Koninklijke Marine)
HSHN Historical Service of the Hellenic Navy, Athens
ihp indicated horsepower
INM Istanbul Naval Museum (?stanbul Deniz Müzesi)
I.v.S. Ingenieurskantoor voor Scheepsbouw, The Hague
j.g. junior grade (U.S. Navy)
Kapt.z.S. Kapitän zur See (Captain, Kaiserliche Marine/Reichsmarine/Kriegsmarine)
KIS Kweekschool voor Inlandse Schepelingen (Training Establishment for Native Ratings), Makassar, Dutch East Indies
Kltz Kapitein-luitenant ter zee (Commander, Koninklijke Marine)

Korvkpt. Korvettenkapitän (Lieutenant-Commander, Kaiserliche Marine/Reichsmarine/Kriegsmarine)
Ktz Kapitein ter zee (Captain, Koninklijke Marine)
K.u.K. Kaiserliche und Königliche Kriegsmarine (Austro-Hungarian navy)
LCS Light Cruiser Squadron (Royal Navy)
LPT low-pressure turbine
Lt Lieutenant
Lt Cdr Lieutenant-Commander
LysO Lysofficer (searchlight officer), Svenska marinen
MARICOST Direzione Generale delle Costruzioni Navali e Meccaniche (Naval Construction and Engineering Bureau, Regia Marina)
MARINARMI Direzione Generale delle Armi e degli Armamenti Navali (Naval Weapons and Armaments Bureau, Regia Marina)
MFA Hellenic Ministry of Foreign Affairs, Diplomatic Archive, Athens
MG machine gun
Mid. Midshipman
MMDH Marinemuseum (Dutch Navy Museum), Den Helder, The Netherlands
MMN Museo Marítimo Nacional, Valparaíso, Chile
MS manuscript
MTB Motor Torpedo Boat
NA National Archives, College Park, Md.
NAA National Archives of Australia, Canberra & Melbourne
NBF Night Battle Force (Imperial Japanese Navy)
NCO non-commissioned officer
NHC U.S. Naval Historical Center, Washington D.C.
NHHC Naval History and Heritage Command, U.S. Navy
NIMH Nederlands Instituut voor Militaire Historie (Netherlands Institute for Military History), The Hague
NRS National Records of Scotland, Edinburgh
RAF Royal Air Force
RAN Royal Australian Navy
RN Royal Navy
SECN Sociedad Española de Construcción Naval (consortium)
shp shaft horsepower
SMS Seiner Majestät Schiff (Kaiserliche Marine/Kaiserliche und Königliche Kriegsmarine)
SPC–A Sea Power Centre – Australia, Canberra
TCG Türkiye Cumhuriyeti Gemisi ('Ship of the Turkish Republic')
TF Task Force (U.S. Navy)
TNA The National Archives, Kew, London
   ADM Admiralty Series
   FO Foreign Office Series
TSC Thomas Schmid Collection
UP Unrotated Projectile
USAAF United States Army Air Forces
USS United States Ship
VKK Verein K.u.K. Kriegsmarine – Archiv, Vienna
wl waterline

Introduction

◆

Bruce Taylor

THE AIM OF THIS BOOK is to provide in-depth coverage of a representative vessel from each navy which had a battleship in active commission between 1882 and 1992: one navy, one ship, one chapter, arranged chronologically by launch date. The first point to make is that this volume interprets the word 'battleship' in its broadest sense of a capital ship, the term revived by Admiral Sir Reginald Custance of the Royal Navy in the early twentieth century to describe a vessel mounting at least one big gun, which for the purposes of this work is loosely reckoned as being in excess of 8in (203mm). As readers will soon realise, falling under this description is an extremely large variety of warships – as varied in size and design as the

circumstances under which they were ordered or acquired, the technology that informed their development and the navies which commissioned and operated them for five years or fifty.

The story of the development of the steel capital ship from the mid-nineteenth century has been told many times and in many places and need not be rehearsed here. Suffice to say that practically all the principal developments in that process as they reached the twentieth century find their representative within the pages of this book, including the turret ship *Chen Yuen* (1882); the armoured cruisers *Garibaldi* (1895) and *Georgios Averof* (1910); the pre-dreadnought battleships *Iéna* (1898) and *Slava* (1903); the coastal battleships *Eidsvold* (1900) and *Peder*

Skram (1908), albeit somewhat different interpretations of the type; the dreadnoughts *Minas Geraes* (1908), *Viribus Unitis* (1911) and *Alfonso XIII* (1913); the super dreadnought *Almirante Latorre* (1913); the armoured ships *De Zeven Provinciën* (1909) and *Sverige* (1915); the battlecruisers *Goeben/Yavuz Sultan Selim* (1911), *Australia* (1911) and *Hood* (1918); the coast defence ship *Väinämöinen* (1930); and finally the fast battleships *Nagato* (1919), *Scharnhorst* (1936), *Littorio* (1937) and *Missouri* (1944). The absence will be noted of a representative of the monitor and semi-dreadnought types, but readers interested in the evolution of the capital ship will nonetheless find the staggering range and pace of development laid before them, from *Chen Yuen*, the largest vessel in Asia of her day with her reciprocating engines and ponderous 12in (305mm) guns, through the apogee of the age of navalism as embodied in the turbine-powered dreadnoughts *Viribus Unitis* and *Almirante Latorre*, and culminating in the USS *Missouri* in her role as a fast carrier escort with radar-assisted fire control and, latterly, cruise missiles. The content of the chapters in any case supports the view that, taken all round, the class or type of a vessel is one thing, her career, fortunes and legacy are quite another, and it is the latter which have invariably governed their inclusion in this volume.

Indeed, although the technical characteristics of each vessel are given full coverage in the chapters devoted to them, this volume goes much further in offering an overview of the national, political, financial, diplomatic and naval circumstances under which each came to be ordered or acquired, together with the organisation, nature and tenor of her shipboard life insofar as it can be reconstructed. In doing so the chapters in their

The battlecruiser HMS *Hood* glides into Vancouver, British Columbia to a rapturous welcome on 25 June 1924. Until the early years of the Second World War the battleship was the ultimate expression of a nation's military power and diplomatic authority. *(Bruce Taylor Collection)*

The signing of the Washington Naval Treaty on 6 February 1922, one of the defining moments in the history of the capital ship. *(Library of Congress)*

different ways address the extent to which all these elements represented and in some cases came to symbolise the aspirations, concerns and cultural realities of the states and societies which commissioned and manned them in peace and war. The result serves to reinforce the contention that during much of the era covered by this book the battleship in its various guises was in many cases a nation's greatest public assertion of military strength and the essential prerequisite for it to project or mediate its interests beyond its own shores; the ultimate symbol, in short, of its status as a power of any type until the Second World War, whatever the *ex post facto* justification of that assessment. All of the chapters of which this book is composed contain the threads of these themes, and while no single entry could by the nature of its subject possibly encompass them all, an unprecedented range of information and interpretation is here made available for the first time for even the most prominent navies. What these chapters therefore provide is the deep context and implications of the technical structures and service careers by which most warships are usually assessed. Out of this aggregated context and consequence comes the full panorama of battleship culture, the World of the Battleship of the title.

◆

It is sometimes easy to forget that the age of the battleship was a truly global phenomenon and that in the period covered by this book the world was girt and encinctured by representatives of the type from Chile to China and Austria-Hungary to Australia. Although the twenty-one units covered in these chapters include all of the major and medium-sized navies and several smaller ones, it must at this point be confessed that not every nation which operated a battleship during the period in question is among their number. Strong cases could and should be made under the aforementioned criteria for the inclusion of the British-built coast defence ship *Vasco da Gama* (1876) of the Marinha Portuguesa and one of the two vessels of similar type completed in Japan for the Siamese navy in 1938; perhaps the omission will be rectified in a future edition. Nonetheless, and within the limits of the size and selective nature of the sample, much as the twenty-one ships treated here belonged to navies spread across the world, they were in fact the product of only thirteen states several of which (notably Spain, Finland, Denmark and the

Netherlands) relied to varying degrees on foreign expertise, components and supplies to complete their vessels. Even major navies placed some reliance on foreign technology or manufacturing: *Hood*'s Brown Curtis turbines may have been built in Britain but they were done so to a US design, while *Slava* was commissioned in St Petersburg with 243 tons of armour from the firm of Wm. Beardmore & Co. of Glasgow. This is not to be wondered at since battleships were among the greatest design, construction and engineering challenges of their time, requiring expertise, financing, infrastructure and capital assets enjoyed by few nations.

Until the Washington Treaty of 1922 the major naval powers could build without any restriction beyond those imposed by financing, tactical doctrine, technology and infrastructure. However, smaller entities opting for domestic as against foreign construction tended in addition to be constrained by the ongoing expenditure on operation and maintenance. Add to this the fact that, until eased by the major advances in engine technology of the 1920s and '30s, battleship design presented a delicate balancing act between armament, protection and speed against the changing requirements and interpretations of technical necessity; witness the influence of the Sino-Japanese War of 1894–5 on the design of several of the ships covered in the earlier part of this volume. This state of affairs together with the relentless advance of naval technology and

ship size placed an added burden on smaller powers which had therefore to confront the possibility, even the probability, of *ab initio* technical and tactical obsolescence before their vessels had cleared the fitting-out basin. Just fourteen years and a 130 per cent increase in displacement separate the commissioning of HMS *Dreadnought* in 1906 and that of HMS *Hood* in 1920, and the following lines by the Dutch officer E. P. Westerveld published in 1908 and uncovered by Leon Homburg in the course of his research on *De Zeven Provinciën* perfectly capture the dilemma for smaller navies as it related to a vessel's tactical relevance:

The size of any battleship [...] is directly dependent on a nation's capabilities, on the understanding that the minimum size should be that which permits the fitting of the largest guns possible, because only then may the ship engage at ranges lying within those of the enemy without the ship being destroyed before she is able to show her power.[1]

As can be seen in the chapters on *Sverige* and *Väinämöinen*, even when the appropriate design

[1] E. P. Westerveld, 'Onze marine in de Indische Krijgskundige Vereeniging' in *Marineblad* 22 (1907–8), pp. 897–963; p. 948. Westerveld was Secretary of the Navy from 1922–5.

was selected the endeavour frequently pushed the civilian yards entrusted with their construction into uncharted waters from a technical standpoint while placing a significant strain on both yard and government finances. In several instances this resulted in delayed or prolonged construction, as in the case of *Peder Skram* which was completed thirteen years after the initial order was placed in 1896. Even then budgetary and other constraints might restrict the operational use of what were comparatively new vessels, a state of affairs reflected in the fact that nine of the ships treated in these pages for one reason or another spent lengthy periods idle or inactive before meeting whatever fate lay in store for them.

On the other hand, the construction of these vessels either in home or foreign yards, together with the equipping, commissioning and ongoing maintenance required to make and keep them operational, necessarily entailed a significant transfer of technology for many of the navies involved. The ability of the Orlogsværftet (Naval Dockyard) in Copenhagen to undertake the construction of the series of coast defence units which at length resulted in *Peder Skram* was directly related to the procurement of the turret ship *Rolf Krake* from the Glasgow firm of Robert Napier & Sons in 1862 and the maintenance of her fabric thereafter. In the case of *Almirante Latorre*, the Armada de Chile was given access to

the state of the art of British naval technology not once but twice: on the transfer of the former HMS *Canada* to Chilean service in 1920 and during her subsequent reconstruction at Devonport in 1929–31. This transfer often extended not only to the provision of engine plant, guns and equipment but also the expertise to use them, for let it never be forgotten that the acquisition of *matériel* is one thing and the ability to operate it effectively quite another, especially under battle conditions. Of this *Chen Yuen* with her foreign instructor officers provides the clearest example, but the ultimate exemplar is surely *Goeben/Yavuz* which was handed over to the Ottoman navy in 1914 not only *in toto* but fully manned as well. Sometimes, however, this knowledge transfer might rest in the hands of a single individual. Such is the case of José Toribio Merino, then in the rank of commander but subsequently Commander-in-Chief of the Chilean navy and a member of the ruling military junta, whose service in the light cruiser USS *Raleigh* in the Pacific War equipped him to write *Latorre*'s damage-control and Combat Information Center manuals, later extended fleet-wide.

The endeavour of acquiring and maintaining a meaningful seagoing capability also involved improvements in administration and infrastructure which often constitute an exercise in nation-building of more lasting importance than the

vessels themselves. The development and extent of these capabilities by the leading naval powers is well documented, but the present volume offers the less well known but equally instructive examples of Spain, Brazil and Argentina. Taking *Alfonso XIII* as his subject, Agustín Ramón Rodríguez González explains how the construction of the new Armada was put into the hands of a consortium of British firms in 1909 which established or took over practically the entire Spanish naval and military industrial complex based on its own technology and expertise. The result, fully realised over the course of the next decade, was the creation of a major warship-building capability which survives to this day. As João Roberto Martins Filho shows in his chapter on *Minas Geraes*, the Brazilian government embraced the reconstruction of a Marinha centred on battleships as the great challenge of the age and in doing so found itself grappling with some of the irreducible elements of which naval power is composed at national level: *matériel*, the human factor and strategic considerations in the context of the wider social and political conditions specific to that country. In the case of Argentina, meanwhile, Guillermo Andrés Oyarzábal shows how the purchase of *Garibaldi* as the first unit in a squadron of armoured cruisers required the government to establish the basing and maintenance facilities necessary to support its substantial investment. After prolonged political debate this resulted in the construction of a graving dock as the centrepiece of a new naval base at Bahía Blanca on the Atlantic coast 400 miles south of Buenos Aires and utterly removed from the Armada's traditional sphere of estuarine operations in the River Plate. The procurement of *Garibaldi* and her sisters therefore had a profound influence not only on naval and national infrastructure per se but also on Argentina's conception of herself as a geographical and strategic entity, a development with far-reaching consequences for her foreign policy and self-perception.

Although the acquisition of its namesake vessel by another distant naval entity, Australia, did not entail the same degree of administrative or infrastructural enhancement, the ordering and commissioning of a unit of the first rank elevated

Technology transfer: one of the two vertical triple-expansion engines fitted in the Danish coastal battleship *Olfert Fischer* (1903), seen here with some of those responsible for manufacturing it in the engine building shop of the Naval Dockyard in Copenhagen. This plant, replicas of which were also installed in *Peder Skram* (1908) a few years later, was manufactured under licence from the local firm of Burmeister & Wain. Other examples of technology transfer came from much further afield. (*Forsvarsgalleriet – Danish Armed Forces Photo Archive*)

Schoolgirls of the Escola Normal de Belo Horizonte in the Brazilian state of Minas Geraes sewing a flag for its namesake battleship in 1939. The culture of the battleship was widely embraced in every nation which commissioned them. *(Diretoria do Patrimônio Histórico e Documentação da Marinha (DPHDM)/3926)*

the new nation's sense of herself as an independent state while making good its determination to participate in its own defence and that of the British Empire. In fact, there is not a single ship treated in these pages which was not in its own way regarded as a source of national pride and prestige or viewed as symbolic of its heritage or aspirations, whether it was *Slava* ostentatiously launched before a gathering of foreign dignitaries in August 1903 months prior to the outbreak of the Russo-Japanese War, or Admiral Count Rudolf Montecuccoli's injunction before the Austro-Hungarian Delegations for 'a stronger navy, with which we can assume our proper place among the Mediterranean powers' at the very moment *Viribus Unitis* was entering service in October 1912. The incorporation into the fleet of the products of domestic or foreign construction such as *Garibaldi*, *Minas Geraes*, *Georgios Averof*, *Australia*, *Almirante Latorre* and *Scharnhorst* were therefore not only major public spectacles but might also constitute key national milestones. Nor was this without substance, as in the case of the construction of the España-class battleships which greatly enhanced Spain's strategic and diplomatic position in the Mediterranean. The completion of *Nagato* as fleet flagship, acknowledged both then and now as a major achievement of Japanese design, construction and diplomacy, was greeted with an outpouring of patriotic fervour and celebrated in song and verse. This pride extended into the home as well, with pictures and postcards of Norway's new squadron of battleships adorning almost every coastal household by 1900. Even when these patriotic sentiments were not given visual form in the various elaborate decorations and devices applied to their hulls they often found expression in the choice of name, some of which like *De Zeven Provinciën*, *Australia* and *Sverige* were or evoked those of the nation itself. No greater honour could possibly have been bestowed, and the fact that ships have by ancient tradition borne a public name and with it an individualised, even personified, identity, is a distinguishing feature of naval culture which should never be forgotten.

◆

The national context of these vessels brings us to one of the most significant and least explored dimensions of naval history as it centred on the

battleship. Not only was the staggering expense of building, operating and maintaining a capital ship – to say nothing of the navy of which she formed a part – borne by the taxpayer, but these activities were either directly or indirectly bound up with civilian communities ashore. This extended not only to the construction process which might provide years of employment and support for hundreds or thousands of men and their dependants, but also the political background for the procurement itself. The aggressive campaign orchestrated by Admiral Sir John Fisher in parliament and the media for the construction of eight battleships for the Royal Navy in 1909 is only among the more prominent examples of this phenomenon; another is the £7.5 million raised (unavailingly as it turned out) by public subscription throughout the Ottoman Empire for the purchase of the battleships *Reşadieh* and *Sultan Osman-i Evvel* immediately before the Great War. In January 1912 the outcry created by a government decision to scrap the nascent Swedish armoured ship programme resulted in a national campaign which within a year had raised 17 million kronor in public donations, more than enough to cover the cost of the first unit, *Sverige*. As with knowledge transfer, private citizens could at times play a key role in the procurement process, as in the case of the Greek financier Georgios Averof the provisions of whose will covered the down payment on the armoured cruiser which bears his name.

The ostensible purpose of the battleship was to operate in war, deterrence or defence as circumstances dictated, but the fact that these vessels

were at the same time vested with the symbolic power of a nation state and served by a crew of many hundreds, even thousands, accorded them a public status which has never been equalled by any contrivance of war, a point too easily forgotten after over seventy years in which the most potent weapons in a nation's arsenal have usually been kept out of sight. This circumstance was due in part to the enormous increase in the cost and complexity of building and operating men-of-war thanks to the technological developments of the second half of the nineteenth century, with the effect of greatly reducing the number of commissioned vessels of the first rank. The growing exclusivity of the battleship as a repository of advanced technology, destructive power and national identity together with its ability to make transoceanic voyages in comparative comfort immediately opened the possibility of these vessels being used as instruments of diplomacy in peacetime in a manner that was not only unprecedented but caught the public imagination. Though ostensibly an expression of diplomatic relations, the underlying message was of the projection of naval power, and the selection by the Peiyang Fleet of the name *Chen Yuen* ('Striking from Afar') for one of its first capital ships can have been no coincidence. So it was that practically every vessel covered in this book consciously showed the flag in foreign harbours at one time or another in her career, from *Chen Yuen* at Nagasaki in 1886 to *Missouri* at Rio de Janeiro in 1947, either as part of a planned courtesy visit or official mission or in the course of a major cruise. Sometimes these extended to circumnavigations lasting many months of which the best example is the Great White Fleet of 1907–9, the symbolic arrival of the U.S. Navy as a global force. Even the simple need to refuel and resupply would in the ordinary course of events bring the leviathans to some foreign port or anchorage, their presence offshore announcing the reach of some distant power to the onlooker. The mystique is well captured in an article published in a Lisbon newspaper as *Hood* lay off the city in January 1925:

> The great *Hood*, the most powerful warship in the world [...] has been lying in the waters of the Tagus for a week, rigid, secret and impenetrable. Until yesterday the sleeping monster had kept her decks closed to the curiosity of all who have been passing round her in boats, seeking to discover what there might be within this extraordinary fortress. It was a hopeless task. The *Hood*, in the usual British manner, remained insensible, unapproachable.[2]

Some ships like *Hood* between the world wars and *Missouri* from 1946–9 made a speciality of

[2] *Diário de Notícias*, 29 January 1925.

this activity upon which their reputation as the most famous warships of their time partly rested. This phenomenon, the importance of which is too readily overlooked, afforded battleships a peacetime role and prestige in which they became national and international showpieces without ever ceasing to be recognised as instruments of war under the burnished guns and scrubbed teak. A secondary dimension of this capability was their ability to render meaningful humanitarian aid, as shown by the tireless efforts of *Slava* off Messina in 1907 and by *Hood* while conveying refugees to safety during the Spanish Civil War in 1938. As it turned out, the same power that equipped warships to take life also afforded them the ability to save it.

Naval historians have naturally and rightly focused their attention on the status of the steel battleship as the principal means of waging war at sea together with the technical realities that attended their design, construction and operation, but the mantle placed on the capital ship extends the relevance of these vessels well beyond their specifications and tactical and strategic employment in time of war. Indeed, and with due allowance for the limitations of the sample, the inescapable fact is that even those

vessels treated in this volume which seldom if ever fired their guns in anger fully vindicated and justified the cost and expenditure of acquiring and maintaining them. The commissioning of *Garibaldi* and her sisters from 1896 onwards gave Argentina a balance of power with Chile on the basis of which she could first settle her border disputes with that country on equal terms in 1899 and then negotiate an arms limitation treaty three years later. In the case of Norway, the procurement from Britain of four coastal battleships including *Eidsvold* gave that country the strength and self-confidence to put an end to the century-old union with Sweden and assert her independence in 1905. But whereas *Eidsvold* and her sisters successfully upheld their country's neutrality during the First World War, they proved unable to do so in 1940, and the same is true in both respects of *Peder Skram* and the other coastal battleships of the Danish navy. Equally, whereas *De Zeven*

A cup of tea on the quarterdeck of HMS *Hood* for refugees of the Spanish Civil War in the summer of 1938. The humanitarian work carried out by warships is an overlooked dimension of their record and status. *(HMS Hood Association/Percival Collection)*

The front page of the Rio de Janeiro journal *O Malho* for 3 December 1910, a week after the end of the Revolt of the Lash. Titled 'The Amnesty of Fear', the cartoon shows politicians cowering under the guns of the battleships *Minas Geraes* and *São Paulo*. (*Biblioteca Nacional do Brasil, Rio de Janeiro*)

Comrades: a working party poses for the camera on the forecastle of the Chilean battleship *Almirante Latorre*, c. 1950. Close confinement and mutual reliance bred friendships hard to replicate in civilian life. (*Museo Marítimo Nacional, Valparaíso (MMN)/2679*)

Provinciën was able to preserve the neutrality of the Dutch East Indies during the Great War, she succumbed in her obsolescence to the Japanese onslaught of 1942 along with the rest of the Koninklijke Marine. Things were different for Sweden, and despite being completed too late to have any bearing on the First World War, *Sverige* and the other major units of the Svenska marinen not only secured their country's neutrality during the second conflict but were instrumental in keeping her from German invasion. Similarly, although *Väinämöinen* and (until her loss) her sister *Ilmarinen* could not alter the outcome of Finland's involvement in the Second World War, they nonetheless succeeded in deterring any Soviet or German landing on her southern coast or archipelagos before the Armistice of September 1944. Meanwhile, as Richard Pelvin shows in his chapter on the battlecruiser *Australia*, the presence of that ship not only facilitated the dismantling of the German position in the Pacific, but drove Vizeadmiral Maximilian Graf von Spee's squadron out of Australasian waters and eastward towards South America. In a different vein, several of the vessels treated in this volume also serve as a vehicle for challenging underlying assumptions and conventional wisdom. A case

in point is Arrigo Velicogna's chapter on *Littorio* which questions standard views on the performance of the Regia Marina in the Mediterranean during the Second World War and reminds us how a major vessel can act as a bargaining chip even in defeat.

If these accomplishments were brought about by units many of which had little or no record of combat, so much greater was the public vindication for the massive expenditure and effort in procurement, manning and operation in the case of those which covered themselves in glory, even when the sacrifice ultimately proved unavailing as in the case of *Slava*. As Zisis Fotakis demonstrates in his contribution on *Georgios Averof*, her arrival in the Aegean in September 1911 permitted the Hellenic Navy to take on its Ottoman counterpart practically single-handedly at a critical juncture in the history of modern Greece, the borders of which would have been much smaller but for her feats during the First Balkan War. *Goeben/Yavuz*, meanwhile, served the interests of the Central Powers as a strategic unit of the first importance before providing the focus of the new Turkish navy. Finally, *Scharnhorst* captured the aggressive spirit of the resurgent German navy, a vessel whose signal wartime achievements both from a

material, strategic and propaganda standpoint were matched by the high morale of her crew. As Thomas Schmid shows in his chapter, this spirit they took with them undaunted into their final battle.

However, the unique status and prestige accorded the battleship was a sword which cut both ways. As Qing Feng shows, the capture of *Chen Yuen* by the Japanese was the source of decades of humiliation for the Chinese people while the mutinies in *Minas Geraes*, *Almirante Latorre* and *De Zeven Provinciën* had a devastating effect on their respective navies and on national prestige, as was the case after Invergordon in 1931. If the immolation of *Iéna* shook the confidence of the Marine Nationale and demonstrated the fallibility of the new technology, that of the *Hood*, destroyed with practically her entire company by the leading unit of the German navy, shattered the morale of the nation and raised in the minds of ordinary Britons the spectre of total defeat. But perhaps the greatest damage was reserved for the moment when such ships, once hailed as defenders of the nation, might be turned against their own people, as when *Minas Geraes* and *São Paulo* were unleashed in Guanabara Bay to shell the defenceless city of Rio de Janeiro:

Master Chief Boatswain's Mate John Davidson who joined *Missouri* as a seaman first class in 1946, formed part of her recommissioning crew in 1986 and became the the ship's command master chief before retiring two years later. Senior ratings like him formed the backbone of a ship's company, the essential bridge between sailors and officers. *(Courtesy Rich Pedroncelli)*

social adjustments taking place during the period under review which left no state untouched; the more deferential crews of *Hood*'s commissioning in 1920 were certainly not those of the Hostilities-Only Navy of 1941, and the mutation of attitudes and aspirations in a ship such as HMS *Warspite*, first commissioned in 1915 and stricken in 1946, would have been even greater.

All of the navies treated in this volume required their officers to undergo varying degrees of professional formation with the partial exception of the Peiyang Fleet in which some were graduates of the Fujian Naval Academy but many owed their positions to the system of preferment characteristic of Imperial China. Whatever the nature of this training, all navies exhibit the gamut of class structure and relations, from the seldom-relenting hostility and mutual suspicion typical of the Imperial Russian Navy in the years before the Revolution (from which *Slava* was however exceptionally free), through the simmering social and political tensions afflicting *Georgios Averof* over the course of her career, to the generally stable but occasionally mordant and diffident communities of the Royal Navy, and thence to the more relaxed environment characteristic of the Scandinavian navies and the U.S. Navy, even if the latter was still addressing the issue of race. Indeed, it is hard to imagine any navy of the day other than that of the United States committing the following to paper in an orientation booklet for sailors joining the carrier *Midway* in 1945:

The greatest threat was the presence of those floating fortresses themselves, bristling with guns and powerful turrets training menacingly while cruising at close range off the shores of the city. This terrorising impression assumed even greater proportions thanks to the propaganda that had preceded and accompanied the acquisition of the new Squadron [...]. The news had a devastating effect as it stirred terror in the hearts of the population who now saw all this destructive paraphernalia being turned against them.[3]

home, workplace and weapon of all who sail in her. More than that, she is their only succour and defence against the remorseless power of wind and water. For this reason, as for the large number of those embarked in her and the arduous nature of their service, the life and functioning of a warship has arguably more of the quality of a community than any other military entity. Moreover, a warship community is part of a wider institution – a navy – which in its turn is an expression of the government that directs and supports it and the culture and society from which it emerges. No ship community can therefore be abstracted from the wider context of events, and the period encompassed by this volume saw transcendent social and political changes in which individual vessels sometimes played a major role as reflected, including many of those treated in these pages.

These remarks bring us to what has often been referred to in naval studies as the 'human element' or the 'human factor' and which constitutes a key theme in this volume.[4] One of the distinctive features of naval life is that a ship, however large or small she may be, is at once the

As in the profession of arms generally, the dominant feature of shipboard life was and is the division between officers and men, with varying degrees of status and authority being conferred on senior non-commissioned officers including the intermediary rank of warrant officer or its equivalents. The degree of separation between the various classes in their living conditions and relationships provides an immediate point of comparison between navies, and readers of this volume have an unprecedented opportunity to do just that. In making these assessments, however, due allowance should be made for the major

MILITARY COURTESY
Politeness and thoughtfulness for the other fellow, whether he is your Division Officer or an Apprentice Seaman, go a long way toward making it possible for hundreds of men to live and work cooped up together without getting in each other's hair. Remember that. Be careful about saluting, about giving a cheerful 'Aye-Aye, Sir' – and don't forget the 'Sir.' Uncover in Officer's Country; stand at 'Attention' when you know you should. Take pride in doing these things. The are the mark of a self-respecting bluejacket who knows his job. Your officers, including the Captain, are no better men than you are. They know it. You don't have to prove it by being impolite. We're all Americans and damned proud of it!

---

[3] Hélio Leôncio Martins, *A Revolta dos marinheiros, 1910* (São Paulo: Cia. Editora Nacional; Rio de Janeiro: Serviço de Documentação da Marinha, 1988), pp. 52–3.

[4] See Ronald H. Spector, *At War at Sea: Sailors and Naval Combat in the Twentieth Century* (New York: Viking Press, 2001), and John Reeve & David Stevens, ed., *The Face of Naval Battle: The Human Experience of Modern War at Sea* (St Leonards, NSW: Allen & Unwin, 2003).

Ratings collecting soup from the galley in the battleship *Iéna, c.* 1905. The provision of wholesome food was a significant factor in shipboard morale. *(Philippe Caresse Collection)*

The salute, standing at attention, addressing an officer as 'Sir' are just part of the Navy way of being polite. You had a different way of doing it in civilian life but it amounted to the same thing.[5]

A battleship was nothing if not an organisational expression and great reliance was placed on petty officers to bridge this gap by exerting authority over the men in the most immediate sense. Accordingly, all navies vested their regulating petty officers with significant powers backed up by naval discipline, and in the Royal Navy and Royal Australian Navy the Master-at-Arms was the senior rating afloat, the only enlisted man who enjoyed the privilege both of a cabin and a bunk. Aside from the Master-at-Arms the U.S. Navy embarked a Master Chief Boatswain's Mate who acted as the senior enlisted adviser to both the captain and crew. Acknowledging the status and long service of a very senior rating with privileges, privacy and separation was one thing, but in some cases the

---

[5] *This Is the USS* Midway *(CVB 41): Personal Information Booklet* (n.p., undated but 1945), pp. 24–5.

delegation of authority was truly extensive. In the Dutch navy the *Chef d'équipage* was not only responsible for shipboard discipline but also occupied a key liaison position between the lower deck and the officers and captain which seems to have extended well beyond that of his

Royal Navy and U.S. Navy counterparts. However, these powers pale alongside those wielded by the *rotnyi feldfebel* (Sergeant-Major) commanding each of the eight or so divisions in a Russian battleship, who was responsible not only for the discipline and loyalty of the men in his charge but also their work details, leave, pay and clothing allowances, etc.

Taken as a whole, and mindful of the harsh realities of working-class life ashore, the span of years covered by this volume encompasses an extraordinary evolution in living conditions afloat, though not necessarily in the same navy. In most cases the period opens with arrangements which would not have been unfamiliar to sailors serving a century earlier: cabins with bunks aft for the officers and open messdecks slung with hammocks for the men forward, the former served their meals in a spacious and well-appointed wardroom and the latter eating what were often semi-improvised preparations cheek by jowl with their shipmates in the same confined living space. Improved conditions for the lower deck came through a growing appreciation first of the physical needs of men serving in steam- as against sail-powered vessels and then in respect of their growing social and educational

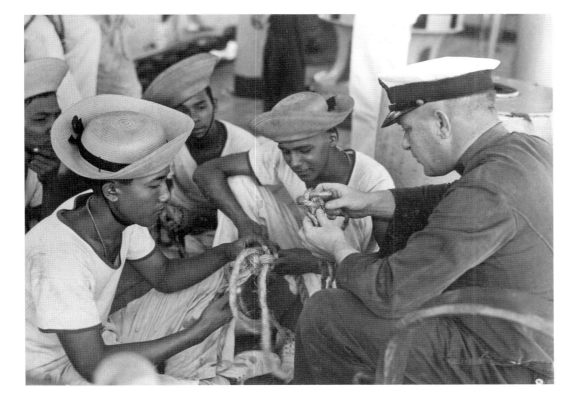

Indonesian ratings being instructed in the splicing of rope by a Dutch petty officer in the armoured ship *De Zeven Provinciën, c.* 1930. The accommodation of mixed crews added depth and complexity to shipboard life. *(Dutch Navy Museum (MMDH))*

aspirations and expectations, all of which were consistent with and in the context of developments ashore. Accordingly, the years around the turn of the twentieth century witnessed significant efforts to improve living conditions particularly with respect to hygiene and food. The discussion between Capt. Voiellaud and Rear Admiral Maquis on bathing facilities for the men in *Iéna* in 1903 related by Philippe Caresse is a case in point of this movement.

The generally poor standard of food served afloat was notoriously a source of unrest and dissatisfaction on the lower deck and naval authorities made efforts to address this during the period under review. The commissioning of *Hood* in 1920 was accompanied by the introduction in the Royal Navy of General Messing in place of the old Canteen or Broadside Messing system in which the galleys had previously only cooked the men's own preparations. Similarly, the cafeteria-style service offered in *Missouri* in 1944 differed from the general messing model which characterised US battleship organisation until the 1930s. Then there were the challenges of satisfying the gustatory needs of mixed crews. In *Chen Yuen* as in the Peiyang Fleet generally separate arrangements had to be made to accommodate the pronounced regional variations in Chinese cuisine. This was mirrored in the Dutch East Indies where *De Zeven Provinciën* provided for the differing tastes of its European and Indonesian ratings, and the same was no doubt true of *Yavuz* with her mixed German and Turkish crew who likewise differed both on cultural and religious grounds. Conversely, it may come as no surprise to learn that the Regia Marina opted to rely on specialist staff from commercial restaurants ashore rather than train its own personnel in the culinary arts. To these meals many navies also offered the complement or consolation as the case may be of alcoholic beverages, from the rum first consumed in the Royal Navy in the seventeenth century, the beer brewed in the larger German vessels, Dutch gin and the wine characteristic of the Mediterranean navies. The U.S. Navy, though famously 'dry' since 1914, was by no means alcohol-free, particularly among the officers, while one of the features of life in *Yavuz* in the 1920s and '30s was the smell of *rakı* issuing through the ship in the evening. Those other consolations of religious practice and shipboard pets and mascots are worthy of detailed treatment in their own right.

Although physical conditions had a significant bearing on welfare and morale, these were of course ultimately dependent on the prevailing regime afloat which frequently mirrored that

ashore. By 1890 the navies treated in these pages had with the exception of Brazil abandoned flogging and settled instead on a penal system based on deprivation of privileges, stoppage of pay and additional duty for minor offences, reinforced by short-term incarceration aboard or prosecution and imprisonment ashore for more serious transgressions. Nonetheless, corporal punishment continued to be administered by both regular and irregular means with the caning of boys and midshipmen in the Royal Navy surviving well into the twentieth century, while the Imperial Japanese Navy developed a culture of casual violence and brutality which originated in the sadistic treatment meted out to officer cadets at the Etajima Naval Academy. Of course, regulation was one thing, enforcement quite another, and the draconian punishments provided for misdemeanours in the Peiyang Fleet were no doubt frequently evaded by recourse to the reigning corruption. Similarly, there is little evidence that much use was made of the array of bloodcurdling instruments discovered by Cdr E. E. Hazlett of the U.S. Navy in the Austro-Hungarian battleship *Zrínyi* in 1918.

Despite the huge risks entailed, the realities of discomfort, grinding work, poor food, harsh or unjust discipline and other factors lent themselves

To serve her all her days: the seated figure is Chief Stoker Harry Watson, 'Double Bottom Chief Stoker' of HMS *Hood* who died on 24 May 1941 after twenty-one years' service in the ship. *(HMS Hood Association)*

to exploitation by political or other agitators, especially under additional pressure, if a line were crossed, or in the event of any deterioration in the wider social and political conjuncture. The result was often mutiny which affected most navies in one form or another in the period under review, including the *Potëmkin* in 1905, Kronshtadt in 1917 and 1921, Cattaro and Kiel in 1918, the French squadron in the Black Sea in 1919, Port Chicago, California in 1944, the Royal Indian Navy in 1946 and the Chinese Nationalist cruiser *Chongqing* in 1949 among many others. Accordingly, it will come as no surprise that eight of the twenty-one vessels covered in this book experienced what is generally termed 'mutiny' in whatever form. These incidents of course occupy a spectrum from the mass disobedience in *Australia* in 1919, the strike action over pay in the Atlantic Fleet including *Hood* at Invergordon in 1931, the political unrest in *Slava* in her early years and thence to the full-scale mutinies, again over pay but in the context of political and social developments, in *Almirante Latorre* and *De Zeven Provinciën* which were eventually put down with violence in 1931 and 1933 respectively. To these we must add the succession of mutinies punctuating the career of *Georgios Averof*, initially on class, patriotic and political grounds but subsequently as a result of poor living conditions as well. But mass disobedience and mutiny was one thing, revolution and revolt quite another, and this volume contains two examples of these in the shape of the unsuccessful uprising in the *España* (formerly *Alfonso XIII*) at Ferrol on the outbreak of the Spanish Civil War in July 1936, and the Revolt of the Lash which originated in the battleship *Minas Geraes* in November 1910 and had lasting implications for Brazilian society as a whole.

The Revolt of the Lash which resulted from the continued use of flogging in the Marinha brasileira provides the clearest example of the extent to which a battleship could serve as a microcosm of the demographic, social and political fabric of a national or transnational entity. Whereas the crew of the *Slava* accurately reflects the class fissures of Imperial Russia and that of *Viribus Unitis* the ethnic composition of the Austro-Hungarian Empire on the eve of the dissolution of both entities, the Revolt of the Lash encapsulates the precarious social balance centred on race which characterised post-emancipation Brazil. Moreover, and quite aside from the issues of discipline and race underpinning it, this incident was brought on by the incorporation of these vast and sophisticated new vessels which not only presented a severe organisational and technical challenge to the Marinha, but elevated the men's perception of themselves and of the

War and remembrance: veterans and survivors of the battleship *Scharnhorst* lay a wreath at the memorial in Wilhelmshaven to the nearly 2,000 sailors lost in her during the Second World War. *(Courtesy Philippe Caresse)*

way they should be treated by it. It is also undeniable that the firepower and symbolic value of *Minas Geraes* and *São Paulo*, fully exercised during the Revolt of the Lash, played a decisive role in the government's decision-making during the episode. No vessel but a battleship could have presented a dilemma on this scale to a government in 1910.

———◆———

The chapters contained in this volume provide an overdue reminder that battleships are not simply or perhaps even chiefly technological expressions, but sophisticated cultural organisms and communities encompassing national values and aspirations at both popular and institutional level. These realities and the internal organisation and leadership of each vessel had a material effect on the functioning and morale of their crews in both peace and war, quite aside from the unique experience and quirks of each as their crewmen recognised them, and which might encapsulate the difference between a vessel's indicated specifications and her actual performance and capabilities. Naval history as it concerns battleships therefore comprehends not only the procurement, design and construction of these vessels together with their service careers against the backdrop of domestic and international

affairs, but also their internal operation at the cellular level as expressed in the actions and perceptions of the communities and individuals of which they were composed. Can any member of the *Hood*'s Engineering Department have thought of the boiler room fan flats without thinking also of the eccentric figure of Chief Mechanician Charles W. Bostock, whose proudest possession was a certificate from the Netley mental asylum attesting to his sanity? Or of Chief Stoker Harry Watson whose twenty-one years of service in the ship were owed to his irreplaceable knowledge of her double bottom compartments, a relationship sundered only by death? Indeed, to study the history of a warship at this human level is to discover a cast of characters at every stage in its creation and existence, from Li Hung-chang, governor general of Zhili province and father of the Peiyang Fleet, General Umberto Pugliese, lead designer of the Littorio class yet persecuted for his Jewish heritage, Menachem Mendel Schneerson, the seventh and last Lubavitcher Rebbe, toiling for months on the wiring diagrams for the USS *Missouri* in full Hasidic dress in the New York Navy Yard,[6] the

impatient figure of Rear Admiral Jacob Børresen on the bridge of his flagship *Eidsvold*, the 'Black Admiral' João Cândido Felisberto, binoculars in hand on the deck of *Minas Geraes*, Boy Seaman William Warner wading through a flooded messdeck to reach his hammock in HMAS *Australia* in the North Sea, and Korvkpt. (Ing.) Otto König urging his men on in the *Scharnhorst*'s hellish engine spaces during her final battle. In these personal experiences and countless others like them rests that special something which sets a ship and its community apart from all others.

While few would dispute the centrality of the human dimension of life afloat, the re-creation of such a community in all its splendour and misery, in its terror and ennui, its structure and subtlety, has rarely proved enticing to historians who in taking on any such project must resign themselves to the possibility, even the likelihood, of only partial success after much labour.[7] The intellectual challenge of piecing together the structure, nature and tenor of life aboard in the face of documentary destruction and oblivion, an unforgiving combination of military, institutional and social history in a technical setting, has caused this dimension of naval life to be pushed into the background and even relegated to the inconsequential in some quarters. Not only is this a disservice to what must by any measure be reckoned among the most imposing, challenging and far-reaching endeavours to which a state and society can lend itself, but the panorama of naval history cannot be regarded as complete without it. This volume with its twenty-one strands reeved through one block is intended as a step towards reversing that neglect.

---

[6] Milton Fechter, 'Wiring the *Missouri*' at http://www.chabad.org/therebbe/article_cdo/aid/141185/jewish/Wiring-the-Missouri.htm [accessed March 2018]

[7] See Serge Dufoulon, *Les Gars de la Marine : Ethnographie d'un navire de guerre* (Paris: Editions Métailié, 1998), and Bruce Taylor, 'Arms and the Man: Some Approaches to the Study of British Naval Communities Afloat, 1900–1950' in Craig C. Felker and Marcus O. Jones, ed., *New Interpretations in Naval History: Selected Papers from the Sixteenth Naval History Symposium Held at the United States Naval Academy, 10–11 September 2009* (Newport, R.I.: Naval War College Press, 2012), pp. 61–72.

———◆———

Peiyang Fleet (北洋艦隊 – Běiyáng Jiànduì)

The Turret Ship *Chen Yuen* (1882)

◆

Qing Feng (馮青)

AT THE TIME of her commissioning in 1885 the turret ship *Chen Yuen* (鎮遠; pinyin: *Zhenyuan*) was not only the largest vessel in China, but also the greatest capital ship in Asia.[1] Over the course of a thirty-year career she served both in the Peiyang Fleet of the Ch'ing Empire and the Japanese Combined Fleet, and in doing so promoted the military and political development of both states. Even after her decommissioning in 1915 *Chen Yuen* continued to cast a long shadow on Sino-Japanese relations and the Asian maritime order which has survived to the present time. This, then, is part of the heritage to which China looks back as she embarks on an ambitious programme of naval development for the twenty-first century, and which from this perspective represents less a birth than a revival of Chinese sea power. To that extent, the career of *Chen Yuen* is not simply an overlooked episode in naval history but one which offers clues both to contemporary Chinese national and navalist sentiment and to the increasingly complex relationship between China and Japan.

Origins

Beset by internal unrest and ruthless foreign intervention, by the mid-nineteenth century the Ch'ing Empire stood on the brink of collapse. Nonetheless, from the early 1860s the Manchus responded by initiating a series of institutional reforms which came to be known as the Self-Strengthening Movement. Central to this was the development of a military-industrial capacity which would allow the Ch'ing dynasty to maintain the internal status quo and defend itself against outside interference through the adoption of Western military technology. In practice this involved the construction of arsenals and shipyards, together with the hiring of foreign advisers to oversee the training of Chinese artisans in the latest manufacturing methods and techniques. The better part of the resources for these initiatives were allocated to military preparedness, but the Ch'ing also established four disparate regional fleets, those of Peiyang, Nanyang, Fujian and Guangdong, based mainly on the ports of Weihaiwei (now Weihai), Shanghai, Foochow (now Fuzhou) and Canton (now Guangzhou) respectively.

Although it traces its origins to 1871, the

Chen Yuen or *Ting Yuen* in a Chinese port in the 1880s or '90s. Note the single 5.9in turret positioned right forward with the ship's dragon emblem beneath. The anchors have been drawn up onto the glacis and the twin 12in guns of the starboard turret are trained on the port beam. *(Bundesarchiv, Koblenz RM 2/1854)*

---

[1] The editor would like to thank Steve McLaughlin, Lars Ahlberg, Ray Burt and Pei Meng for their kindness in connection with this chapter.

Peiyang (Northern Ocean) Fleet took shape in the context of Japanese naval expansion which resulted in the formal annexation of the Ryukyu Islands as the Okinawa Prefecture in 1879. The guiding spirit in its development was the remarkable figure of Li Hung-chang (1823–1901), imperial minister of foreign affairs and trade and governor general of Zhili province from 1870–95, who immediately recognised the threat from across the East China Sea. Rather than operating as the Ch'ing imperial navy per se, the Peiyang Fleet had instead all the characteristics of a private force under the personal control of Li Hung-chang, with responsibility for seaward defence of the region containing the imperial capital, Beijing. Whereas it had earlier been overshadowed by its Nanyang counterpart to the south, Li Hung-chang now diverted the majority of the sea defence fund to the Peiyang Fleet, which he consciously modelled on the Royal Navy. Chinese plans to place orders in British yards were scuppered by Russian pressure, so the first tangible result of this allocation was the cable Li Hung-chang sent in July 1880 to Li Feng-p'ao, the Chinese minister in Berlin, asking him to place an order for the turret ship *Ting Yuen* ('Eternal Peace') with the AG Vulcan shipyard of Stettin. The following year came an order for a second unit with the same specifications – *Chen Yuen* ('Striking from Afar'). Fully fitted, the price for *Ting Yuen* and *Chen Yuen* came to 6.2 million reichsmarks each. What did the Ch'ing Empire get for its money?

Design and Construction

The construction of *Ting Yuen* and *Chen Yuen* was supervised by several graduates of the Fujian Naval Academy sent out from China, notably Liu Pu-ch'an (later commander of *Ting Yuen*) and Wei Han, who were also responsible for procuring the necessary armour and equipment to be fitted in the new vessels. *Ting Yuen* was laid down in March 1881 and launched on 28 December that same year. Construction began on *Chen Yuen*, probably on the vacated slip, in March 1882 with the launch taking place on 28 November 1882. Although designed and built in Germany with hull construction and body lines almost identical to those of the armoured corvette *Sachsen* of 1877, the layout with two large barbettes amidships owed much to the British HMS *Inflexible* (1876) and the smaller *Agamemnon* and *Colossus* classes. *Chen Yuen* had a steel hull fitted with a ram bow giving a total length of 297ft (90.5m), a beam of 63.6ft (19.4m) and 19.4ft (5.9m) of draught at a standard displacement of 7,144 tons. Full-load

Li Hung-chang, imperial minister of foreign affairs and trade, governor general of Zhili province and father of the Peiyang Fleet. Aside from listing his many titles, the inscription around this portrait records it as having been taken in the autumn of 1896. This copy was given to a Captain Mills during Li's visit to General Grant's tomb in New York City that year. *(Library of Congress/122743)*

displacement was 7,335 tons (including 400 tons of coal and 24 tons of grain).

Chen Yuen's scheme of protection centred on a 143ft (43.6m) citadel containing the barbettes, the magazine and the engine spaces, protected by compound armour up to 16.7in (424mm) thick. The turrets were protected by 12in (305mm) of armour, the conning tower and casemates by 9.5in (242mm), with horizontal protection up to 3in (76mm). Waterline protection consisted of a 14in (356mm) armour belt backed by a further 14in of teak. Total weight of armour was 1,461 tons. The ship was powered by two sets of horizontal compound reciprocating engines fed by eight Krupp boilers. The three-cylinder compound engines manufactured by Vulcan were rated for 7,200ihp and delivered a top speed of 15.4 knots during trials, an improvement on *Ting Yuen* whose engines yielded 6,200ihp and could only manage 14.5 knots. *Chen Yuen* had stowage for up to 1,000 tons of coal giving a range of 4,500 nautical miles at 10 knots, though both vessels were rigged with masts and sails for the voyage from the Baltic to the Bohai Sea. However, her steering initially left something to be desired since the positioning of the main

battery forward without sufficient compensating weight aft resulted in the ship trimming by the head. *Chen Yuen* carried three generators producing 70kW of power, used among other functions to light 240 electric lamps and two searchlights. Fresh water was provided by plant capable of supplying the crew of 330 men from twenty holding tanks distributed around the vessel.

Chen Yuen's main armament consisted of four Krupp 12in (305mm) 20-calibre breech-loading guns in twin turrets set *en échelon*, these capable of broadside fire on either beam.[2] However, as demonstrated at the Battle of the Yalu River in September 1894, any attempt to fire a full charge on the forwardmost bearing was liable to demolish the light bridge structure situated on the platform erected over the turrets. The latter were enclosed by a steel shield 1in (25mm) thick. *Ting Yuen* and *Chen Yuen* each had stowage for 197 12in shells weighing 725lb (329kg) apiece. The absolute range was 8,530yds (7,800m). To these were added a pair of Krupp 5.9in (150mm) 40-calibre guns mounted in single turrets traversing on rollers in the bow and stern of the ship and protected by 3.5in (90mm) of vertical armour and 1in (25mm) shields. Secondary armament consisted of eight 1.5in (37.5mm) Maxim-Nordenfeldt quick-firing guns, to which two Hotchkiss 1.85in (47mm) pieces were added shortly before delivery. The armament was completed by three 15in (380mm) torpedo tubes fitted in the bow and the stern and there was stowage for twenty-one torpedoes. As was common at the time, *Chen Yuen* shipped three torpedo boats together with a steam picket boat.

Despite these impressive specifications, the design of *Chen Yuen* was not without its shortcomings, many of which were identified by the Japanese during the Sino-Japanese War of 1894–5. Chief among them was the extremely slow rate of fire of the main armament and the high freeboard which presented a generous target to enemy gunners.[3]

Service in the Peiyang Fleet

Although *Ting Yuen* was completed in May 1883 and *Chen Yuen* in April of the following year, delivery of the ships was delayed by the Sino-French War which broke out over control of the province of Tonkin in August 1884, and it was

---

2 Koichi Takasu, 'Kokai kaisen: Sono sento keika wo tadoru' in *Sekai no Kansen* 486 (September 1994), p. 144, & Pao Tsun-p'eng, Chungkuo *Haichün Shih* (Teipei: Haichün Publishing, 1951), p. 297.

3 'The Defects of the *Ting Yuen* and *Chen Yuen*' in *Tokyo Asahi*, 16 August 1894.

Ting Yuen lying in a state of completion at the Vulcan yard at Stettin, perhaps during the period between 1883 and 1885 when her delivery and that of her sister *Chen Yuen* was delayed by the Sino-French War. Note the torpedo boat stowed amidships. *(NHHC/NH 2088)*

not until 3 July 1885 that they sailed for China under the ensign of the German merchant marine and with German crews. With them sailed another product of the AG Vulcan shipyard, the protected cruiser *Tsi Yuen*, the squadron fetching Taku (now Dagu) Harbour in the port of Tianjin in November.

The completion of its first truly effective units had a transformative effect on the Peiyang Fleet. Already on 24 October 1885 Li Hung-chang had seen to the establishment of the navy department, with Prince I Hsüan installed as minister and himself as vice minister.[4] He then secured the appointment of Ting Ju-chang, an army officer and a member of his circle, as admiral of the Peiyang Fleet. No sooner had the squadron reached Tianjin than Li Hung-chang carried out a personal tour of inspection. Greeting him in the harbour was *Chen Yuen* painted in the manner of the Royal Navy, her black hull broken with a red stripe at the waterline and the superstructure done in white, while the funnels, masts and turrets were finished in buff. Adorning the bow, however, was the symbol of the Ch'ing Empire, a golden dragon, which also featured on the triangular ensign worn by Chinese naval vessels. *Chen Yuen* and *Ting Yuen* were commissioned soon after, becoming the backbone of the Peiyang Fleet which was based at Port Arthur (now Lüshunkou) and Weihai, and gradually settling into an annual routine. In winter the entire Peiyang Fleet left its northern bases for the South China Sea, cruising to Zhejiang, Fujian and Guangdong provinces together with the Nanyang Fleet and occasionally to ports in southeast Asia. In the spring, summer and autumn the Peiyang Fleet, including *Chen Yuen*, cruised in the coastal waters of Shandong, Zhili and Fengtian provinces and occasionally northward to the Russian coast for joint exercises.

Meanwhile, Li Hung-chang continued to press for the expansion of the Peiyang Fleet which placed a succession of orders for new vessels, so that by 1889 it comprised twenty-five ships displacing a total in excess of 37,000 tons. In addition to *Ting Yuen*, *Chen Yuen* and *Tsi Yuen* there were another six protected cruisers, all completed either in Britain or Germany with the

---

4 Ch'ih Chung-hu, 'Haichün Tashihchi' in Shen Yün-lung, ed., *Chindai Chungkuo Shiliao Ts'ungk'an, hsüpien*, no. 18 (Taipei: Wenhai Publishing, 1975), pp. 11–12.

exception of *Ping Yuen* which was built at Mamoi (now Mawei) near Fuzhou. To these were added six earlier gunboats, three training vessels, a transport and six torpedo boats. Some 2,780 officers and sailors were employed.

Shipboard Organisation

No sooner had *Chen Yuen* arrived from Germany than the process began of bringing her to her full complement of 329 men. Her first commanding officer in Chinese service was Lin Tai-tseng, the scion of a distinguished Fujian family whose relatives included the famous imperial official of the First Opium War (1839–42) Lin Tse-hsu, and the shipping minister of Fujian Shen Pao-chen.[5] Born in 1851, after studies at the Fujian Naval Academy and service with the Fujian Fleet on graduation, Lin Tai-tseng travelled to the West and became the first Chinese naval student in Britain between 1876 and 1879, serving in the broadside ship *Achilles*. Returning to China, he joined the Peiyang Fleet in 1880 and was successively in command of the gunboat *Zhenxi*, the cruiser *Chao Yung* and finally *Chen Yuen*, to which Li Hung-chang appointed him in the equivalent rank of rear admiral in 1885. This appointment, in which Lin Tai-tseng remained until 1894, seems to have placed him as Admiral Ting Ju-chang's deputy in command of the Peiyang Fleet.

Assisting Lin was an executive officer in the rank of commander, a chief officer, a gunnery officer, a chief engineer and two senior engineers, together with a number of navigators and other officers, many of whom were graduates of the Fujian Naval Academy and had received training in Europe or the United States. These officers were accommodated in cabins on the main deck aft in the traditional manner with a large suite in the stern for the senior officer embarked. The bulk of the crew, comprising forty seamen first class, fifty seamen second class and fifty seamen third class, in addition to stokers, signalmen, mine specialists, electricians, painters, cooks, clerks and doctors, etc., was accommodated in a series of messes and small cabins on the main deck forward, physically separated from their officers by the engine spaces. The majority of these men were drawn from local army units, older vessels or, in the most extreme cases, press-ganged from the crews of coastal and river steamers. The accountant and his staff charged with managing the financial affairs of the ship reported directly to the captain and were invariably appointed from among his friends and relatives. *Chen Yuen*'s ordinary complement was completed by the sixteen members of Captain Lin's staff, including the cooks and personal servants he brought from his home province of Fujian.

The lack of any centralised manning system in the Peiyang Fleet and widespread use of preferment had a number of obvious drawbacks. Although many high-ranking officers, including Captain Lin, had graduated from the Fujian Naval Academy, studied abroad and enjoyed several years of practical experience, a significant number were appointed based chiefly on personal introduction rather than skill and merit.

Lieutenant-Commander Philo McGiffin (see below), who served in *Chen Yuen* during the Battle of the Yalu River, made no attempt to disguise his contempt for the average Chinese officer:

> The class to which they belong, the Mandarin class, is the very worst in China. It is not a part of their aim or traditions to be brave and manly; but all their thought is to get into a position where they can squeeze and oppress, and live easy, indolent lives on the fruits of their spoil.[6]

Moreover, as was traditional in the Peiyang Fleet, there were strong regional rivalries aboard, with a majority of officers and sailors hailing from Fujian, but a significant proportion of men originating from the province of Guangdong. Aside from linguistic distinctions, the most immediate effect of this was felt in shipboard catering arrangements, with the pronounced regional variations in Chinese cuisine requiring separate preparation of food to ensure palatability.

As the largest unit in the Peiyang Fleet, *Chen Yuen* also played host to a variety of instructors and cadets from the naval academies.[7] Naval instruction at fleet level was under the overall supervision of Captain William Lang, a Royal Navy officer commissioned by Li Hung-chang into the service of the Ch'ing government. Reflecting British practice, in 1888 Lang was responsible for reorganising the Peiyang Fleet into seven functional squadrons, with the seagoing vessels divided into three wings of three ships each, *Ting Yuen* and *Chen Yuen* occupying the right and left wings respectively. The training of the torpedo boat unit was in the hands of another Briton, a Lieutenant Rogers. Needless to say, fleet instruction followed the British model, with commands delivered in English, but orders and drills, etc., were supplied both in English and Chinese. A number of German, British and US specialists also

Ting Yuen with *Chen Yuen* immediately beyond rigged for the journey from Stettin to Tianjin in 1885. They are flying the ensign of the German merchant marine and reached China under German crews. *(Courtesy Ray Burt)*

---

[5] *Nichi-Ro Senso Heiki Jinbutsu Jiten* (Tokyo: Gakken Publishing, 2012), p. 270.

[6] Alfred T. Story, 'Captain M'Giffin – Commander of the "Chen Yuen" at the Battle of Yalu River' in *The Strand Magazine* 10, no. 60 (July–December 1895), pp. 616–24; p. 617.

[7] Kaigun Sanbobu, *Shinkoku Hokuyo Kaigun Jikkyo Ippan*, 1890, Fukushima Prefectural Library, Sato collection, S222.2K.

served aboard, with responsibility for instruction in gunnery, mines, torpedoes and engineering. Most of the engineers were Chinese, with foreign instructors acting in a largely supervisory capacity until the outbreak of the Sino-Japanese War. Aside from Annapolis graduate Lt.-Cdr. Philo McGiffin (see below), who served as her executive officer in 1894, four Western instructors are recorded as having sailed in *Chen Yuen*: H. Plambeck with responsibility for training and seamanship, D. Iffland, a German C. Heckman and one 'Gramraldt' in the engineering department, and a Higgins in charge of gunnery. However, in all operational respects *Chen Yuen* was solely under Chinese command.

Financing and Pay

As with recruitment, the Peiyang Fleet had no centralised financing system and its funds were obtained not from the Ch'ing government but directly from local sources. The fleet was allocated a 40 per cent share of the annual income of seven customs houses, including those of Guangzhou and Fuzhou, 8 per cent of that of the Shanghai customs house, 400,000 silver taels (33,510lb) per annum in domestic duties from Jiangsu and Zhejiang provinces, and 300,000 taels (25,130lb) per annum from Jiangxi, Fujian and Guangdong provinces.[8] *Chen Yuen*'s monthly seagoing budget amounted to 850 taels, which was overseen by the commanding officer.[9] Essential expenditure such as that on coal, propellant, shells and maintenance of the decks, armour and hull below the waterline, rope, flags and assorted stores and equipment manufactured in steel, iron, wood or copper was met by the Ministry of the Navy with coal supplied by the K'aip'ing mine in Guangdong. All expenditure above the waterline had to be covered from the seagoing budget, including paint, oil, paper, cotton waste, emery cloth, flags, as well as fresh water, etc. Also payable from the seagoing budget were pilots' fees and the pay of the captain's private staff and secretaries. The allocation of this budget was the responsibility of a purchasing committee chaired by the captain and charged with procurement from sources reserved exclusively for the Peiyang Fleet, or otherwise obtained directly from the local chamber of commerce.

---

[8] Yixin's memorandum, 12 July 1875, in Chang Hsia, ed., *Ch'ingmo Haichün Shihliao* (Beijing: Haiyang Publishing, 2001), pp. 616–17.

[9] Chung-yüeh Hsieh, ed., *Peiyang Haichün Tzuliao Huipien* (Beijing: China National Microfilming Centre for Library Resources, 1994), pp. 993–7.

A sailor of the Peiyang Fleet poses on the port side of the boat deck beside a 1.5in Maxim-Nordenfeldt gun with one of the Hotchkiss 1.85in pieces behind him, *c.* 1894. The port 12in turret can just be made out in the background. In the foreground is the base of one of the halyards. (*The Strand Magazine*)

Chen Yuen's monthly payroll amounted to 5,387 taels in statutory and seagoing pay. Officers and senior non-commissioned officers (from captain to chief petty officer) received both statutory pay and seagoing pay, the captain drawing 132 and 198 taels per month respectively. Sailors, however, drew only the statutory pay, which in the case of boatswains amounted to 14 taels per month, declining to 10 taels for seamen first class and 9 taels for torpedomen first class. Victualling and uniform allowances were included in official pay and were spent at the recipient's discretion.

Life Aboard

The entire crew served under martial law and any violation by the captain would see him brought before the governor general of Zhili province, Li Hung-chang. Minor infractions would be penalised by loss of a month's salary, but serious offences could result in dismissal or demotion with the gravest being judged by Li Hung-chang himself. Deserters would be condemned to eighty lashes and suffer a month's imprisonment in peacetime, but in time of war were supposed to be summarily executed. Other criminal offences were dealt with by the admiral in accordance with the forty articles of military discipline established in the first year of the reign of the Yungcheng emperor (1723). From these details we might assume that discipline aboard *Chen Yuen* was extremely harsh, but this was not the case in practice since life in the Peiyang Fleet accurately reflected the corruption in wider Chinese society. As Japanese sources subsequently asserted, insubordination and indiscipline aboard were rife, with drunkenness, desertion and criminality habitually receiving slight punishment or none at all, and service aboard

marked by the traditional pursuits of gambling and the smoking of opium among both officers and men.[10]

Much as the vessels of the Peiyang Fleet were of Western design and construction, where uniform was concerned it followed the traditional outlook of the Ch'ing Empire, in which it was customary to dress in long clothing. Although some adjustments were made, the full dress of officers of all ranks matched that of their counterparts in the imperial military and civil service ashore, but with the exception of the captain, the ship's doctors and the accountant staff, officers wore a short-sleeved uniform when serving aboard – albeit with a dragon embroidered on the cuffs. Officers wore a Western-style hat with a brim of wool in winter and of leather in summertime. No standard uniform was issued to crewmen, who donned the customary civilian dress, distinguished by a blue belt and small round cap or traditional brimmed hat, both at sea and ashore.[11]

All the doctors embarked in *Chen Yuen* were schooled in Chinese medicine, with the exception of one trained in Western medicine who was expected to perform surgery and had responsibility both for *Ting Yuen* and *Chen Yuen*, meaning that a majority of ailments were treated using traditional methods. *Chen Yuen*'s yearly medical budget amounted to 300 taels, which was used to cover the expense of treating any officer or enlisted man suffering from disease, illness or injury sustained in the course of duty or in battle.

As in the rest of Chinese society, a majority of *Chen Yuen*'s men subscribed to the ancient religion of the land, which in the case of the Peiyang Fleet centred on the goddess of the seas known as Tianfei or Mazu, whose cult originated in Fujian during the Song dynasty (960–1279) and spread along the Chinese coast. Prayers were offered to Tianfei to deliver the ship from the hazards of the ocean, and the devotional tablets dedicated to her and set up in the officers' quarters were presented by the emperor himself. This observance extended to the flying of red flags bearing one of Tianfei's many appellations – Tianshang shengmu (Heavenly Holy Mother) – from the masts on the first and fifteenth day of each month in the Chinese lunar calendar. Also celebrated was the Buddhist and Taoist Hungry Ghost Festival in July, when sacrifices were offered by the crew to their deceased ancestors.

Japan and the Peiyang Fleet

Before the outbreak of the Sino-Japanese War *Chen Yuen* and the other major units of the

---

[10] *Shinkoku Hokuyo Kaigun Jikkyo Ippan*, p. 42.

[11] *Ibid.*

Peiyang and other Chinese fleets made a succession of training cruises to Japan in 1886, 1891 and 1892 during which visits were made to the ports of Nagasaki, Sasebo, Kobe, Yokohama and Yokosuka. These cruises were prompted by Li Hung-chang who not only wanted the fleet to improve its navigational skills in manoeuvres on the high seas but also to show the flag and promote diplomatic relations, while at the same time leaving the Japanese government under no illusion as to the power of the Peiyang Fleet. In this it was all too successful, and such a blatant display of power at a time when Japan had only one capital ship – the central battery ship *Fuso* (1877) of 3,717 tons – served to contribute to the anti-Chinese feelings shared by a large sector of Japanese society, while also stoking fears of the threat posed to Japan by the Ch'ing Empire.[12]

The first of these cruises, which also took in British Hong Kong, the Korean ports of Busan

[12] Feng Qing, *Chugoku Kaigun to Nicchu Kankei* (Tokyo: Kinseisha, 2011).

and Wonsan and the Russian naval base of Vladivostok, resulted in a notorious incident in August 1886 while *Chen Yuen*, *Ting Yuen* and four cruisers were lying at Nagasaki. Drunken disturbances ashore led to fighting between Chinese sailors and locals, during which eight Chinese officers and sailors were killed and forty-two wounded. The fracas left two policemen dead and twenty-nine other Japanese wounded. Although the Chinese death toll was higher, the local authorities blamed the Peiyang Fleet for the incident and considered the visit nothing less than an attempt to cow the Japanese into submission. Whatever the causes of this episode, voices were immediately raised in Japanese government circles to the effect that it was time for Japan to acquire vessels to defend herself against a Chinese belligerency which could conceivably extend to invasion, and within months orders had been placed for three Matsushima-class protected cruisers designed by the French naval architect Louis-Émile Bertin, the last of which was built in Japan. Although the class displaced just 4,300 tons by comparison with the 7,150 of

Chen Yuen and *Ting Yuen*, the Japanese navy was confident that it could confront the major units of the Ch'ing Empire in a three-against-two situation. In the event, dockyard delays both in France and Japan meant that it was over five years before any were commissioned, but Japan had nonetheless begun her momentous process of naval expansion.

Despite what came to be known as the Nagasaki Incident and deteriorating relations between the two states, Admiral Ting Ju-chang continued to show the flag in Asian waters and a squadron consisting of six warships and 1,460 officers and men paid a second visit to Japan in 1891. The squadron called at Kobe on 30 June and at Yokohama on 14 July where *Ting Yuen* hosted a grand reception attended by 100 members of the imperial family, senior government officials and high-ranking naval and military officers. Among the guests was the then Captain Tōgō Heihachirō, chief of staff of the Kure naval district, who took the opportunity to tour the Chinese squadron during which he formed a high opinion of Captain Lin Tai-tseng

Units of the Peiyang Fleet: *Ting Yuen* with the British-built protected cruiser *Chih Yuen* or *Ching Yuen* beyond, the latter delivered by Armstrongs in 1887. Note the triangular ensign of the Peiyang Fleet flying from *Ting Yuen*'s gaff. (*Musée de la Marine, Paris*)

of *Chen Yuen*, commenting on his height and pale complexion, and describing him as 'the most formidable man in the Peiyang Fleet, like a precious sword, and highly respected by his subordinates'.[13] Judging from McGiffin's description of the gibbering wreck cowering in the lower conning tower of *Chen Yuen*, Capt. Lin's nerve had gone by the time of the Battle of the Yalu River in 1894.[14]

The Sino-Japanese War

On 1 August 1894 two decades of tension over conflicting interests in the Korean Peninsula culminated in the outbreak of the First Sino-Japanese War. The immediate cause was the dispatch by the Ch'ing Empire of 28,000 troops to quell the Donghak peasant revolt in Korea that summer, an action the Japanese regarded as a violation of the Tientsin Convention of 1884, which had essentially established the peninsula as a co-protectorate. The prevailing view among commentators in the West was that Japan would be crushed by the modernised Chinese army and navy but they had not counted on the skill and determination of the Japanese armed forces, which immediately took the offensive to gain command of the sea and enjoyed unbroken victory on land. A portent of this came a week before the formal outbreak of hostilities when the Battle of Pungdo fought off the Korean port of Asan on 25 July led to the sinking or capture of two Chinese gunboats and the chartered transport *Kow-shing* with over 1,100 casualties, but without loss to the Japanese. This debacle was compounded by a mutiny aboard the *Kow-shing*, when her British master attempted to follow Japanese orders to surrender, resulting in fruitless negotiations and the sinking of the vessel with heavy loss of life. Crippled by a failure of centralised command and suffering from budgetary shortfalls and material deficiencies due to administrative corruption, the Peiyang Fleet was in fact in a poor position to prosecute a war against the new Japanese Combined Fleet. To cite the most notorious example, efforts by Li Hung-chang to secure the expenditure of 354,000 taels on six quick-firing guns to improve *Ting Yuen*

Ting Yuen, Admiral Ting Ju-chang's flagship at the Battle of the Yalu River, seen in *c.* 1892. Note the diminutive bridge structure immediately forward of the first funnel which was demolished by the opening salvo of one of the 12in turrets beneath it. (© *National Maritime Museum, Greenwich, London C7441*)

13 Ogasawara Naganari, *Seisho Togo Heihachiro Zenden*, 3 vols. (Tokyo: Kokusho kanokai, 1987), III, pp. 315–16.
14 Story, 'Captain M'Giffin', p. 620.

Admiral Ting Ju-chang (1836–95), commander of the Peiyang Fleet. (*Courtesy Chen Yue*)

and *Chen Yuen*'s offensive capabilities against the new Japanese cruisers were thwarted by diversion of the funds to the Empress Dowager Cixi's sixtieth birthday celebrations, including the erection of a marble paddle steamer in the grounds of the Summer Palace in Beijing.

This, then, was the context of the Battle of the Yalu River, fought in Korea Bay on the afternoon of 17 September 1894. The engagement was brought on when the Combined Fleet under Admiral Itō Sukeyuki decided to intercept the Peiyang Fleet as it sailed for its base at Port Arthur having escorted a convoy to the mouth of the Yalu. With twelve major units each, the two navies had notional parity of strength, albeit with *Ting Yuen* and *Chen Yuen* affording the Chinese superiority in armour and firepower. However, the Japanese enjoyed a clear advantage in rate of fire, speed and manoeuvrability, and in the event also took the tactical initiative. Intending to dispose his force in line abreast, disorganisation as the Peiyang Fleet weighed anchor resulted in Admiral Ting Ju-chang proceeding in a ragged formation with his flagship *Ting Yuen* and *Chen Yuen* – now repainted in a uniform 'invisible grey' – in the centre. Meanwhile, Admiral Itō approached the Chinese formation bow-on in two squadrons sailing in line ahead. *Chen Yuen*'s executive officer Lt.-Cdr. Philo McGiffin has left this description of the atmosphere aboard as battle approached:

Dark-skinned men, with queues tightly coiled around their heads and with arms bare to the elbow, clustered along the decks in groups at the guns, waiting impatiently to kill and be killed. Sand was sprinkled on the decks, and more was kept handy against the time when they might become slippery. In the superstructure and down out of sight in the bowels of the ship were men at the shell-whips and ammunition-hoists, in torpedo-rooms, etc. Here and there a man lay flat on deck, with a charge of powder – fifty pounds or more – in his arms, waiting to spring up and pass it on when it

should be wanted. These men were stationed at intervals to serve the guns quickly; for charges must not be massed along the deck, lest a shell drop in and make trouble. The nerves of the men below deck were in extreme tension. On deck one could see the approaching enemy, but below nothing was known, save that any moment might begin the action, and bring a shell in through the side. Once the battle had begun, they were all right, but at first the strain was intense.

The fleets closed on each other rapidly. My crew was silent. The sublieutenant in the military foretop was taking sextant angles and announcing the range, and exhibiting an appropriate small signal-flag. As each range was called the men at the guns would lower the sight-bars, each gun captain, lanyard in hand, keeping his gun trained on the enemy. Through the ventilators could be heard the beats of the steam-pumps; for all the lines of hose were joined up and spouting water, so that in case of fire no time need be lost. The range was about four miles, and decreasing fast. 'Six thousand meters!' 'Five thousand eight hundred' – 'six hundred' – 'five hundred' – five hundred!' 'Five thousand four hundred!' The crisis was rapidly approaching.[15]

At 1220 the Peiyang Fleet opened fire at 5,300yds (4,850m), well beyond its effective range. However, even before the Japanese had

returned fire, things started badly for the Chinese when *Ting Yuen*'s opening 12in salvo demolished her own bridge, pinning Admiral Ting under the wreckage and putting him and his staff *hors de combat* for the rest of the engagement. Having closed the Peiyang Fleet from ahead, a signal from Admiral Itō brought his flying squadron diagonally across the Chinese right flank followed by the main squadron at closer range, the intention being to rake the Chinese line with a murderous fire before the latter squadron circled behind the enemy in a melee. Itō waited until 1225 to open fire, and within minutes the Armstrong-built protected cruisers *Chao Yuen* and *Yang Wei* were first set on fire and then sunk, to be followed by the protected cruiser *Chih Yuen* and the armoured cruiser *King Yuen* as the battle devolved into a succession of ship-to-ship actions. Two vessels quit the scene at an early stage, the protected cruiser *Tsi Yuen* which made Port Arthur largely unscathed and the corvette *Kuang Chia* which stranded in her haste to get clear of the action and had eventually to be scuttled. As McGiffin recalled, the brunt of the Japanese attack now fell on *Ting Yuen* and *Chen Yuen*:

> The Principal Squadron now seemed to ignore the four smaller Chinese vessels, and its five ships steamed around our two ironclads, pouring in a storm of shell. Time and again fires broke out, but, with one notable excep-

tion, the flames were subdued without much trouble. Some of the enemy's ships used melinite shells, the noxious fumes from which could at once be distinguished from those of powder. One ship, for a time, practised 'broadside firing by director' – i.e. each gun is laid by its crew on the object, and the entire battery, joined in one electric circuit, is fired by pressing a key. This system, though doubtless hard on the structure of the ship using it, was most effective – the result of so many shot striking at once, and producing perhaps several fires, being very annoying.[16]

The worst of these fires was on the forecastle, and as McGiffin recounted these were only brought under control thanks to adroit work with the hoses at huge personal risk:

> I was in the conning-tower, from whence I had been issuing orders, when a fire broke out in the superstructure over the forecastle. It had made considerable headway when I gave orders for a line of hose to be run out. We were then in the hottest of the fight, and the men refused to go unless an officer led them […] so I had to go myself. A number of men volunteered to follow me. We had no sooner reached the forecastle than the awful fire of the enemy's guns began to tell upon us. One after another my men were fairly torn to pieces. A shot from a rapid-firing gun actually passed between my legs, wounding both wrists in its passage, and carrying away the tail of my coat. I was bending over pulling up the hose at the time. A shell hit the tower and as it burst a piece struck me. I had just removed it when I received another wound in almost the same place, and from the same cause.
>
> At this time we were being peppered by three of the enemy's ships at close quarters – one on the port side, one on the starboard, and one right ahead; but the one on the port side was doing the most mischief, and so the men at the two starboard guns had been ordered to turn their guns round and try to silence the ship that was pressing us so hard on the port side. To do this, of course, they

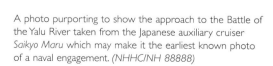

A photo purporting to show the approach to the Battle of the Yalu River taken from the Japanese auxiliary cruiser *Saikyo Maru* which may make it the earliest known photo of a naval engagement. *(NHHC/NH 88888)*

15 Philo N. McGiffin, 'The Battle of Yalu: Personal Recollections by the Commander of the Chinese Ironclad "Chen Yuen"' in *The Century Magazine* 50, no. 4 (August 1895), pp. 585–605; pp. 594–5.
16 *Ibid.*, p. 598.

had to fire across the forecastle. When, therefore, I and the men who had volunteered to go with me to put out the fire were about to go forward, I ordered the head gunner at the starboard battery to cease firing at the vessel on the port side, and direct his guns at the ship right ahead, otherwise they would fire upon us. But the instant after I had turned my back, a shot knocked the head gunner to pieces, and the man who took his place did not know that we had gone forward, and, keeping the guns directed towards the ship on the port side, fired.

The explosion blew all of us who were left off our legs. The man by my side, indeed, was killed. At the same time, a shot from one of the enemy's rapid-firing guns ripped across my body, cutting quite a gash, but not doing any serious injury. I was rendered unconscious, however. Fortunately, I had fallen upon a hose that had been torn by a shot, and the water spurting from the rent fell upon my face and revived me. [...] When I opened my eyes, I saw that I was right in front of the muzzle of the other starboard gun, and that my head was directly in the line of fire. I watched the training of the gun for a second or two; then, realizing that in another instant it would go off and I should be blown to pieces, I threw myself over the side of the superstructure onto the deck below, a depth of some eight feet. As I fell the gun went off.[17]

The ship was later calculated to have taken 220 shell hits, though her 14in belt was not breached and only isolated penetrations of the deck armour to high-trajectory hits were recorded. At 1730, however, the Japanese fleet turned away, leaving *Ting Yuen* in a parlous state and *Chen Yuen* having expended her entire inventory of 5.9in shells and with only twenty-five steel projectiles remaining for her main armament. It is nonetheless a testament to the stoutness of her construction that she had lost only thirteen crewmen killed and twenty-eight wounded, while the Peiyang Fleet as a whole suffered the loss of five ships and over 700 men killed and 120 wounded. Although the Combined Fleet lost no ship outright, it did not escape damage, suffering seventy men killed and 208 wounded, more than half inflicted by two heavy shells from *Chen Yuen*, including one at 1530 which struck the forward barbette of Itō's flagship *Matsushima*.[18]

---

[17] Story, 'Captain M'Giffin', pp. 620–1.

[18] Sugawa Kunihiko, 'Hyocuo kinen *Chin'en* no Ikari' in *Senpaku* (October 1942), pp. 635–9; Koichi Takasu, 'Kokai kaisen', p. 148.

PHILO McGIFFIN

Philo Norton McGiffin was born into a family of Scottish descent in Washington, Pennsylvania in 1860 and entered the U.S. Naval Academy at Annapolis in 1877 where his reputation as a creative practical joker has since elevated him to the status of folk hero. Although McGiffin passed out as a midshipman in 1884, doing so was no guarantee of a commission in the U.S. Navy of the day and he was unsurprisingly discharged with a year's pay. This turn of events brought McGiffin to China where he was commissioned lieutenant in the Ch'ing imperial navy in the spring of 1885 at the height of the Sino-French War. McGiffin spent the next nine years as an instructor at the Chinese naval academy at Tianjin and then at that of Weihai which he was instrumental in founding in 1887, being appointed executive officer of the *Chen Yuen* in 1894. On the outbreak of the Sino-Japanese War in August of that year the Japanese put a 5,000-yen bounty on McGiffin's head; he took to carrying a vial of prussic acid for use in the event of capture. Grievously wounded at the Battle of the Yalu River during which his shipmates regarded him as leading a charmed life, McGiffin returned to the United States but never recovered in mind or body and committed suicide with his own revolver in the New York Postgraduate Hospital on 11 February 1897 at the age of just thirty-six.

A heavily retouched photo of Cdr Philo McGiffin bearing the injuries sustained during the Battle of the Yalu River; from these and the psychological injuries he never recovered. *(The Strand Magazine)*

Philo McGiffin cheats death during the Battle of the Yalu River. *(The Strand Magazine)*

After the battle: nursing an arm wounded during the Battle of the Yalu River, *Chen Yuen*'s German engineer instructor C. Heckman poses beside some of her battle damage in the starboard waist just forward of the mainmast. *Chen Yuen* is calculated to have taken some 220 shell hits during the engagement. *(NHHC/NH 61992)*

Splinter damage to *Chen Yuen*'s superstructure abreast the funnels after the Battle of the Yalu River. Seen in the foreground are signal halyards severed during the engagement. *(NHHC/NH 61993)*

This shell caused a succession of explosions which set *Matsushima* on fire, disabled her 12.6in (320mm) Canet gun, destroyed four of her secondary battery of twelve 4.7in guns and inflicted ninety-six casualties. Although the damage to his flagship required Itō to shift his flag to her sister *Hashidate*, he had nonetheless secured a decisive victory over the Peiyang Fleet whose six battered survivors reached Port Arthur the following day.[19]

The End of the Peiyang Fleet

For a month the survivors of the Peiyang Fleet, and *Chen Yuen* in particular, licked their wounds at Port Arthur, while the Japanese navy kept watch from Korea Bay. In October, however, a deterioration in the military situation ashore resulted in Ting Ju-chang being ordered to withdraw his fleet across the Bohai Strait to Weihai leaving only *Chen Yuen* behind while repairs continued. When by early November it became clear that Port Arthur was unlikely to

hold out much longer against the Japanese army, she too was withdrawn to Weihai, the approaches to which were littered with obstacles to hinder a Japanese surprise attack. It was while negotiating these on 14 November that *Chen Yuen* grounded on a reef, suffering a 20ft (6m) gash in her hull which flooded the port engine room. Only desperate damage-control efforts managed to staunch the entry of water and the ship barely made port. His nerve apparently broken during the Battle of the Yalu River, Captain Lin Tai-tseng took full responsibility for the incident and the following day committed suicide with an overdose of opium, being succeeded in command by Yang Yung-lin. The capture of Port Arthur a week later on the 22nd not only deprived the Peiyang Fleet of its main base but also of the dry-docking and repair facilities needed to restore *Chen Yuen* to a seagoing condition.

On 30 January 1895 the Japanese army launched its attack on Weihai. Confined to harbour, *Chen Yuen* kept the Japanese army and fleet under continual bombardment, firing 119 shells on 1 February alone.[20] On 5 February,

however, *Ting Yuen* fell victim to an audacious night attack by Japanese torpedo boats which broke into the harbour and struck her on the port side, requiring the ship to be grounded. Thereafter *Ting Yuen* joined *Chen Yuen* as a floating battery. By now the Japanese had captured the fortifications commanding the harbour and on 9 February *Ting Yuen* was heavily damaged by shore-based artillery fire. With the Chinese position now hopeless both ashore and afloat, the decision was taken to scuttle *Ting Yuen* inside the port, an event followed by a succession of suicides among the senior figures in the Peiyang Fleet, beginning with Captain Liu Pu-ch'an of *Ting Yuen* on 10 February. Admiral Ting Ju-chang had earlier declined an invitation to surrender, which included the offer of asylum extended to him by Admiral Itō who had come to regard him as a personal friend. As Ting stated in his reply, 'The only thing now left for me to do is die', which he did on the 12th after taking a massive overdose of opium the previous night. *Chen Yuen*'s own service in the Peiyang Fleet was also drawing to a close, her commander Captain Yang Yung-lin committing suicide on the 12th. The following day Captain Ch'eng Pi-kuang raised a white flag in the gunboat *Chen Pei* and sent a letter of

[19] Kaigun Yushukai, *Kinsei Teikoku Kaigun Shiyou* (Tokyo: Hara shobo, 1938), p. 596; Hans Georg Jentschura, *Warships of the Imperial Japanese Navy, 1869–1945* (Annapolis, Md.: U.S. Naval Institute, 1986), p. 96.

[20] *Tokyo Asahi*, 5 February 1905.

Chen Yuen seen after her capture by the Japanese at Weihai on 12 February 1895 with another vessel lying alongside. The damage to the superstructure and fittings has been picked out in white. *(NHHC/NH 88889)*

surrender on Admiral Ting's behalf to his Japanese counterpart, stating 'now I pray for a ceasefire to prevent further loss of life, and I hereby surrender all vessels, batteries and armaments to your country'.[21]

Not until the 17th did the Japanese Combined Fleet enter Weihai, while a landing party occupied Liugongdao Island and proceeded to destroy all military installations ashore. Aware that *Chen Yuen* was largely intact aside from the damage to her hull, the Japanese elected to take her as a prize instead of finishing her off, one of ten vessels, including the protected cruiser *Tsi Yuen*, taken as spoils of war, with an estimated total displacement of over 15,000 tons and a value in excess of 30 million yen.[22] Only the training ship *Tongji* was spared to transport the coffins of those officers who had committed suicide, including that of Admiral Ting, while over 5,000 surrendered Chinese officers, sailors and soldiers were disbanded. Defeat in the Sino-Japanese War also sounded the death knell of the Department of the Navy which was abolished on 12 March just short of its tenth anniversary. Li Hung-chang had been its first and last vice minister.

So ended the Peiyang Fleet. While accepting that 'the Japanese had better ships, more of them, better and larger supplies of ammunition, better officers, and as good men', and freely admitting 'the courage of the Japanese crews and the dash of their commanders', Lt.-Cdr. McGiffin of *Chen Yuen* also took pains to praise the conduct of the men of the Peiyang Fleet, 'the despised Chinese sailor', who yet proved capable of great heroism and fortitude while 'their decks were [...] almost continuously swept by a storm of missiles'.[23] To them and to his erstwhile commander-in-chief McGiffin dedicated this bitter epitaph:

China's fleet is now a thing of the past, and many gallant men have perished with it, striving vainly to save their country's credit,

21 Ch'ih Chung-hu, *Haichün Tashihchi*, p. 63.
22 Japan Centre for Asian Historical Records, C08040497700, no. 2, 'Hokaku moshikuwa shuyo kansentei oyobi sono kaiko iin'.
23 McGiffin, 'The Battle of Yalu', p. 601.

with fate against them, and handicapped by corruption, treachery, and incompetence on shore. Chief among those who have died for their country is Admiral Ting Ju Chang, a gallant soldier and true gentleman. Betrayed by his countrymen, fighting against odds, almost his last official act was to stipulate for the lives of his officers and men. His own he scorned to save, well knowing that his ungrateful country would prove less merciful than his honorable foe. Bitter, indeed, must have been the reflections of the old wounded hero, in that midnight hour, as he drank the poisoned cup that was to give him rest.[24]

Prize of the Japanese Navy

Much as *Chen Yuen*'s career could be regarded as having ended with the annihilation of the Peiyang Fleet at Weihai in February 1895, this was by no means the case, despite the oblivion – intended or otherwise – into which her later years have fallen. Refloated at Weihai, *Chen Yuen* was towed to Port Arthur by the auxiliary cruiser *Saikyo Maru* where temporary repairs were carried out between April and June. This was also the first opportunity for the Japanese to submit *Chen Yuen* to close inspection, with

[24] *Ibid.*, p. 604.

Chen Yuen's starboard waist after her capture at Weihai on 12 February 1895, her battle damage indicated in white paint. Note the 1.5in Maxim-Nordenfeldt gun on the boat deck on the extreme left and the Japanese sentry on the right. *(NHHC/NH 88892)*

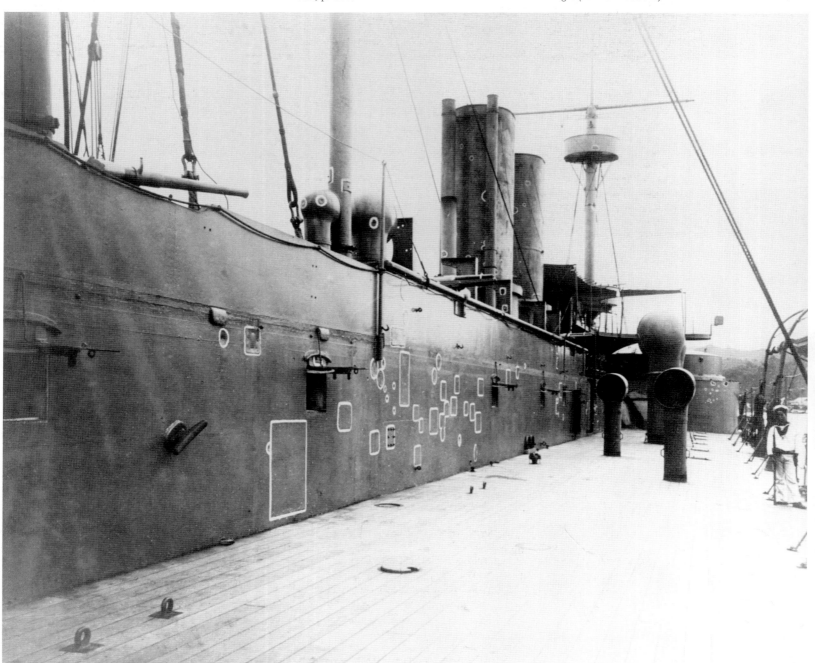

A battered *Chen Yuen* docked and under repair at Port Arthur on 6 May 1895, three months after capture by the Japanese and eight months after the Battle of the Yalu River. *(Courtesy Lars Ahlberg)*

Chen Yuen brought as a prize under the Japanese ensign to Hiroshima where she is seen on around 20 July 1895, still wearing her battle scars from the Yalu River and Weihai. *(Qing Feng)*

much attention being paid to the extent and nature of her battle damage. These observations proved influential on new Japanese construction, with provision being made to increase vertical instead of horizontal protection given the flat trajectory of shells over the battle ranges of the day. The Japanese were also amused to note extensive use of sandbags around the turrets despite the 16.7in of armour protecting them, though this was no doubt a measure against splinters.[25]

On 16 March *Chen Yuen* was commissioned into the Imperial Japanese Navy as *Chin Yen*, becoming at once the largest vessel and the only capital ship serving under the Rising Sun flag. On 5 July 1895 her first Japanese commanding officer, Capt. Arima Shinichi, sailed her from Port Arthur for Japan via Weihai with a reduced complement of fifteen officers, six warrant officers and 176 ratings, anchoring at Nagasaki on 10 July, where the ship remained for six days. Memories of the Nagasaki Incident of 1886 were still fresh and the contrast between the arrogance and pomp of the Ch'ing Empire in former days and its abject defeat and humiliation after the Sino-Japanese War all too apparent, tangible proof if any were needed that the balance of naval power in Asia had experienced a seismic shift in favour of Japan. The intervening years had therefore replaced fear and humiliation with pride and a measure of *Schadenfreude*, a sentiment captured in these words by Hattori Seiichi: 'we remembered that, several years ago, when Ting Ju-chang led *Ting Yuen* and *Chen Yuen*, the

two great ironclads visiting Japan, they displayed an arrogant manner in front of our people … Their insolent words have lingered in our ears'.[26]

Chin Yen next made her way through the Inland Sea from Hiroshima and nearby Kure to Kobe, and finally to Yokohama on 28 July where she received a rapturous welcome from a huge crowd lining the shore. She was subsequently assigned to the Yokosuka naval district and underwent extensive repair and modernisation in the shipyard there. Although director-firing equipment was installed, modifying the main battery presented too challenging a proposition so attention focused instead on the secondary battery. The bow and stern turrets were re-equipped with a 6in (152mm) quick-firing gun, two more being mounted amidships just forward of the mainmast and a further two right aft, a development which had the added benefit of rectifying the tendency of the ship to trim forward thanks to the positioning of the main battery, with a consequent improvement to her steering. Thus refitted, *Chin Yen* – now bearing the chrysanthemum bow emblem of a vessel of the Imperial Japanese Navy – received a visit from the Meiji emperor himself at Yokosuka naval yard on 25 November 1896, before embarking on a cruise which was effectively a triumphal progress through every Japanese port of consequence. By the time it was over *Chin Yen* was a household name in Japan.

Classified as a second-class battleship, *Chin Yen* became flagship of the reserve fleet on

21 March 1898 and resumed her courtesy visits to domestic ports. By the time the emperor reviewed the fleet at Kobe on 9 November that year it was obvious how far the Japanese navy had come within just three years of the end of the Sino-Japanese War, notably the completion of the British-built battleships *Fuji* and *Yashima* which replaced *Chin Yen* as the largest vessel in the fleet. Having disposed of the Peiyang Fleet, the Imperial Japanese Navy was making ready to confront its other regional competitor, the Imperial Russian Navy.

The Russo-Japanese War

The origins of the Russo-Japanese War of 1904–5 lie in the competing ambitions of both countries in Manchuria, and above all Korea, particularly in the aftermath of the Sino-Japanese War. In April 1895 Japan had capped its one-sided campaign against the Ch'ing Empire with the equally lopsided Treaty of Shimonoseki, involving the cession to Japan of the Liaodong Peninsula (including Port Arthur), recognition of Korean independence, and payment of a vast indemnity. However, Russia, France and Germany immediately recognised these terms as a threat to the stability of China and to their own position in the region, particularly Russia, which had long sought an ice-free base to serve its naval and mercantile interests in the Far East and regarded Port Arthur as the ideal solution. These concerns resulted within days of the signing of the Treaty of Shimonoseki in the so-called Triple Intervention by which the aforementioned powers obliged Japan to withdraw from the Liaodong Peninsula in return for an increased indemnity. The humiliation attending this retreat was compounded by Russian occupation of the peninsula and fortification of Port Arthur in 1897. Continued involvement by both countries in Korean affairs

[25] *Tokyo Asahi*, 24 February 1905.

[26] Hattori Seiichi, *Sei Shin dokuenzetsu zokuhen* (Tokyo: Kobayashi Uemon, 1895), p. 214.

Chin Yen participating in a fleet review by the Meiji emperor at Kobe on 9 November 1898. Note the new 6in gun mounted abreast the mainmast on a platform encroaching onto the waist. The scuttles visible in the stern belong to the officers' cabins. *(NHHC/NH 61965)*

and further incursions by Russia in Manchuria prompted the Japanese to begin negotiations with Russia in 1903 in an attempt to stave off war. But whereas Japan was willing to recognise a Russian sphere of influence in Manchuria, St Petersburg was disinclined to do likewise for Tokyo over Korea, and the two countries broke off diplomatic relations on 5 February 1904. Three days later the Japanese Imperial Navy launched a surprise attack on Port Arthur hours before war was declared, to which Russia responded with its own declaration on 10 February.

Although *Chin Yen* was now obsolete, her four 12in guns still offered considerable firepower and she was assigned to the Fifth Squadron of the Third Fleet alongside three of her erstwhile opponents at the Battle of the Yalu River ten years earlier: the protected cruisers *Matsushima*, *Hashidate* and *Itsukushima*, wearing the flag of Vice Admiral Kataoka

Shichiro. On 6 February *Chin Yen* sailed for war from the port of Sasebo near Nagasaki, but it was not until 10 August that she got her first taste of action under the Japanese ensign, participating in the Battle of the Yellow Sea as part of the Main Force under Admiral Tōgō Heihachirō who had commanded the protected cruiser *Naniwa* at the Yalu River in 1894. The engagement was brought on by an attempt by the Russian First Pacific Squadron under Admiral Wilgelm Vitgeft in the battleship *Tsesarevich* to break the six-month Japanese blockade of Port Arthur. After a series of prolonged manoeuvres and engagements, at 1840 that evening *Tsesarevich* was taken under fire by the battleship *Asahi* which scored a hit that killed Vitgeft together with his staff. Not only that, but the shell caused the ship's wheel to be flung over into a sharp turn to port sending *Tsesarevich* in a circle back towards her own line. In the ensuing chaos *Tsesarevich* and three destroyers ended up fleeing to the German treaty port of Tsingtao (now Qingdao) where they were interned and disarmed, while the rest of the Pacific Squadron returned to Port Arthur to be destroyed by artillery bombardment in early December. *Chin Yen* took two shells during the

engagement while scoring several hits on Russian vessels.

The Russian Second Pacific Squadron had meanwhile begun its epic voyage to the Far East which ended in the Strait of Tsushima on 27–28 May 1905. Having sailed from the Korean port of Busan, Admiral Tōgō's Combined Fleet intercepted the Russian fleet on the afternoon of the 27th. By nightfall the better part of Admiral Zinovy Rozhestvenskii's force had been destroyed, with a total of twenty-one ships, including all eight battleships, sunk or captured by the time the last shot had been fired. The Fifth Squadron, including *Chin Yen*, had joined in attacking the rear of the enemy, sinking the supply ship *Kamchatka* while inflicting heavy damage on Rozhestvenskii's flagship *Kniaz Suvorov*. Morning found the Squadron busy mopping up the last of the Russian resistance and escorting some of the seven prizes into Japanese ports. *Chin Yen* herself entered the Japanese naval base on the island of Tsushima on 20 June before being assigned to the Ominato guard district in northern Honshu following a brief refit at Kure. On 4 July she sailed from Ominato to support the landings on Sakhalin three days later. Following the Russian surrender *Chin Yen* escorted the armoured cruiser *Bayan* (subsequently *Aso*) to Japan after she had been salvaged at Port Arthur. On 23 October *Chin Yen* participated in an imperial review of the fleet of 165 vessels held at Yokohama. It was her last act as a front-line unit.

A Long Shadow

On 11 December 1905 *Chin Yen* was relegated to the status of first-class coastal defence ship, spending the next six years as a training vessel for non-commissioned officers and cadets. She was decommissioned in April 1911 and replaced in that role by her old adversary *Itsukushima*, herself redesignated a second-class cruiser. Moved to Yokosuka, that autumn *Chin Yen* became a target for the 8in (203mm) guns of the first-class cruiser *Kurama* before being sold for scrapping at Yokohama in April 1912. With the sanction of the Ministry of Finance, the 152,387 yen raised from the sale was allocated to cover part of the 400,000-yen cost of building the grand hall of the Etajima Naval Academy in Hiroshima Bay, which project broke ground in January 1913.

Chin Yen anchored in a Japanese port, c. 1900. The stern turret has been reequipped with an Armstrong 6in gun, two more of which are mounted aft and amidships just forward of the mainmast. (Courtesy Ray Burt)

This demolition might have been the last of *Chen Yuen* but it was not to be since few ships have coloured the relationship between two countries more than she. Aside from her remarkable career, this significance lay in the fact that her scrapping in 1912 was not absolute. Already in 1896 *Chen Yuen*'s two anchors weighing 4 tons apiece had been unshipped and put on display, together with 120ft (36.5m) of chain and ten 287lb (130kg) shells in Tokyo's Ueno Park. Amidst a specially planted grove of pines a stone was erected between the anchors bearing an inscription written by a veteran of the battles of the Yalu River and Weihai in 1894–5, Admiral Count Kabayama Sukenori: 'Here beside the Shinobazu pond on 25th April 1896 Sukenori enshrines those who were killed in action or died of wounds in the battle for the Penghu Islands, Taiwan, and plants pines in their memory, offering prayers that they may be as immortal as the pine.'[27] To one of the anchors a wooden plaque was affixed describing it as 'An anchor from the captured warship *Chin Yen*'. Nor was this all. On 27 May 1942 a private organisation known as the Kurogane Society erected an 8ft (2.4m) monument as part of an effort to whip up patriotic sentiment during the

27 Sugawa, 'Hyocuo kinen *Chin'en* no Ikari', p. 637.

Pacific War. An inscription explaining why the monument was built and providing a summary of the career of the *Chin Yen* was written by another veteran of the Battle of the Yalu River, Admiral Arima Ryokitsu, subsequently chief priest at the Meiji Shrine. A second plaque positioned in front of one of the anchors recounted the battle history of the Imperial Japanese Navy during the First Sino-Japanese War of 1894–5.

From the beginning China regarded the display of *Chen Yuen*'s anchors as a source of bitter humiliation, one felt particularly strongly among the many Chinese students in Japan. After the end of the Second Sino-Japanese War of 1931–45 Nationalist China made the return of the anchors and cancellation of the humiliation a national priority, and in February 1947 sent Navy Major Chung Han-po at the head of a delegation from the Republic of China to Japan to effect this. Post-war Japan was then governed by the Supreme Commander Allied Powers, Japan, General of the Army Douglas MacArthur, who did not, however, consider this matter to fall within his responsibilities and flatly rejected it. Undeterred, Chung turned to MacArthur's chief of staff, Major General Charles Willoughby, arguing that China had shown restraint and tolerance towards post-war Japan and that recovery of the anchors was an important gesture for the Chinese government and people. Chung's arguments persuaded

Chin Yen dressed overall for a Japanese national celebration on 22 June 1897, the dragon of the Ch'ing dynasty prominent on her bows as a reminder of her Chinese origins. Few vessels have ever been vested with such symbolic importance as *Chen Yuen/Chin Yen*.
(Courtesy Ray Burt)

Willoughby who agreed to review the situation, with the result that it was decided to return these spoils of war to China.

Accordingly, the Ueno Park monument was torn down with the two anchors, shells and chains removed and formally handed over to Chung as the representative of the Republic of China in a ceremony held at Shibaura in Tokyo Harbour on 1 May 1947. By October these items had reached Shanghai where they were transferred to the Qingdao naval college and put on display as an encouragement to officer cadets and sailors. With the establishment of the People's Republic of China these items were moved to Beijing where they have since been housed in the People's Liberation Army Historical Museum. There was, however, one artefact from *Chen Yuen* the Japanese did not return: the ship's bell, which was carried in the Imperial Japanese Navy's cadet ship *Awashima*

and is now displayed in the grounds of Odawara High School in Kanagawa Prefecture.

Although this episode served to assuage the shame of the First Sino-Japanese War, that humiliation was never completely forgotten and remained a source of resentment to add to China's collective memory of her suffering at the hands of Japanese militarism.

Conclusion

The selection by the Ch'ing Empire of the name *Chen Yuen* (Striking from Afar) for one of its battleships was intended to convey the impression that her power could extend far and wide, and this is precisely what she accomplished in the nine years of peace before the First Sino-Japanese War. For the Chinese, the disasters that attended that conflict not only affected Asian strategy and diplomacy, but transformed *Chen Yuen* from a source of national pride and power into one of humiliation, a wound reflected in the determination of the Chinese government to recover her surviving relics after the Second World War. At the same time, the capture of *Chen Yuen* proved to be one of the driving forces behind the rapid expansion of the young

Imperial Japanese Navy. The ceaseless parading of the renamed *Chin Yen* before the army and the general public not as a weapon but as a spoil of war served as a tangible reminder to the Japanese of their ability to defeat China, the immense ageless presence across the sea from which their own civilisation ultimately derived. This same confidence impelled Japan (and *Chin Yen* with her) along an imperial career which eventually led to the Russo-Japanese War whose influence extended beyond Asia to Europe and the United States.

Although *Chen Yuen* occupies first place in this volume for chronological reasons, she is perhaps the only vessel treated in its pages which continues to have a discernible influence in our own time as a symbol of the ongoing relations between China and Japan. Moreover, as much as Western headlines speak of 'the rise of China in Asia and the Pacific', Chinese sources stress that this is less a rise than a revival, one that like all revivals has a keen sense of the past and a long memory. To that extent, it is not hard to interpret the expansion of the People's Liberation Army Navy, including the commissioning of its first aircraft carrier *Liaoning* in 2012, as the restoration of an earlier greatness, to which the completion of a full-size replica of *Ting Yuen* at Weihai serves as a tangible reminder.

Sources

Unpublished Sources

Fukushima Prefectural Library, Fukushima, S222.2K, Sato collection, Kaigun Sanbobu, *Shinkoku Hokuyo Kaigun Jikkyo Ippan*, 1890

Japan Center for Asian Historical Records, Tokyo, C08040497700 no. 2, 'Hokaku moshikuwa shuyo kansentei oyobi sono kaiko iin'

Bibliography

Brook, Peter, 'The Battle of the Yalu, 17 September 1894' in Antony Preston, ed., *Warship 1999–2000*, XXII (London: Conway, 1999), pp. 31–43

Ch'ih Chung-hu, 'Haichün Tashihchi' [Key Events in Modern Chinese Naval History] in Shen Yün-lung, ed., *Chindai Chungkuo Shiliao Ts'ungk'an, hsüpien* [Collected Documents in Modern Chinese History], no. 18 (Taipei: Wenhai Publishing, 1975)

Chu, Samuel C., & Kwang-Ching Liu, *Li Hung-chang and China's Early Modernization* (Armonk, N.Y.: M. E. Sharpe, 1994)

Evans, David C., & Mark R. Peattie, *Kaigun: Strategy, Tactics, and Technology in the Imperial Japanese Navy, 1887–1941* (Annapolis, Md.: Naval Institute Press, 1997)

Feller, A. B., 'Steel and Shot off the Yalu River' in *Military History* 16 (February 2000), pp. 34–40

Hattori Seiichi, *Sei Shin dokuenzetsu zokuhen* [A Sequel to the Speech of the Conquering Ch'ing Empire] (Tokyo: Kobayashi Uemon, 1895)

Hsieh Chung-yüeh, ed., *Peiyang Haichün Tzuliao Huipien* [Documents of the Peiyang Fleet] (Beijing: China National Microfilming Centre for Library Resources, 1994)

Jentschura, Hans Georg, *Warships of the Imperial Japanese Navy, 1869–1945* (Annapolis, Md.: U.S. Naval Institute, 1986)

Kaigun Yushukai, *Kinsei Teikoku Kaigun Shiyou* [A Concise History of the Imperial Japanese Navy] (Tokyo: Hara shobo, 1938)

McGiffin, Lee, *Yankee of the Yalu: Philo Norton McGiffin, American Captain in the Chinese Navy, 1885–1895* (New York: E. P. Dutton, 1968)

McGiffin, Philo N., 'The Battle of Yalu: Personal Recollections by the Commander of the Chinese Ironclad "Chen Yuen"' in *The Century Magazine* 50, no. 4 (August 1895), pp. 585–605; available at: http://ebooks.library.cornell.edu/m/moa/ [accessed September 2017]

Mach, Andrzej, 'The Chinese Battleships' in Randal Gray, ed., *Warship*, VIII (London: Conway, 1984), pp. 9–18

Naganari Ogasawara, *Seisho Togo Heihachiro Zenden* [A Life of Admiral Tōgō Heihachirō], 3 vols. (Tokyo: Kokusho kanokai, 1987)

Nichi-Ro Senso Heiki Jinbutsu Jiten [A Dictionary of Weapons and Protagonists of the Russo-Japanese War] (Tokyo: Gakken Publishing, 2012)

Olender, Piotr, *Sino-Japanese Naval War, 1894–1895* (Petersfield, Hants.: Mushroom Model Publications, 2014)

Paine, S. C. M., *The Sino-Japanese War of 1894–1895: Perception, Power, and Primacy* (Cambridge: Cambridge University Press, 2003)

Pao Tsun-p'eng, *Chungkuo Haichün Shih* [A History of the Chinese Navy] (Teipei: Haichün Publishing, 1951)

Qing Feng, *Chugoku Kaigun to Nicchu Kankei* [The Chinese Navy and Japanese-Chinese Relations in the Modern Era] (Tokyo: Kinseisha, 2011)

Rawlinson, John L., *China's Struggle for Naval Development 1839–1895* (Cambridge, Mass.: Harvard University Press, 1967)

Roberts, Stephen S., 'The Imperial Chinese Steam Navy, 1862–1895' in *Warship International* 11 (1974), no. 1, pp. 19–57

Story, Alfred T., 'Captain M'Giffin – Commander of the "Chen Yuen" at the Battle of Yalu River' in *The Strand Magazine* 10, no. 60 (July–December 1895), pp. 616–24; available at: https://books.google.com/books?id=tM0kAQAAIAAJ [accessed September 2017]

Sugawa Kunihiko, 'Hyocuo kinen *Chin'en* no Ikari' [Commemorating *Chen Yuen*'s Anchor] in *Senpaku* [Ship] (October 1942), pp. 635–9

Takasu Koichi, 'Kokai kaisen: Sono sento keika wo tadoru' [The Battle of Yalu River: The Course of the Engagement] in *Sekai no Kansen* [Ships of the World] 486 (September 1994), p. 144

Tokyo Asahi, 1894, 1905 & 1906

Wilson, H. W., *Battleships in Action*, 2 vols. (London: Sampson Low, Marston & Co., 1926)

Wright, Richard N. J., *The Chinese Steam Navy* (London: Chatham Publishing, 2000)

Armada de la República Argentina

The Armoured Cruiser
Garibaldi (1895)

◆

Guillermo Andrés Oyarzábal

THE ARRIVAL of the Italian-built armoured cruiser *Garibaldi* and her three sisters between 1896 and 1898 marks the coming of age of the Armada Argentina.[1] The commissioning of these vessels had a profound influence not only on naval tactics and infrastructure but also on Argentina's conception of herself as a strategic entity, a development with far-reaching consequences for her foreign policy and national identity. With their capabilities, specifications and the technological advance implied by them, *Garibaldi* and her sisters therefore charted a course towards broader horizons and greater possibilities for the Argentine navy and the nation they represented for half a century.

Relations with Chile and the Development of Naval Power

The Argentine navy traces its origins to the revolutionary squadrons established during the War of Independence which broke out in 1810, and the Armada developed gradually through the nineteenth century in the context of border wars and foreign intervention. The late 1880s found Argentina in the process of settling her frontiers with Brazil and progressing towards definitive agreements with Paraguay following the devastating War of the Triple Alliance (or Paraguayan War) of 1864–70, while at the same time suffering a steady deterioration in her relations with Chile. These centred not only on territorial disputes in the northern Puna de Atacama region

and particularly at the southern tip of the continent, but also on military mistrust and suspicion fuelled by adroit use of journalism which conspired to sour diplomatic relations. Preparedness is a military axiom, and although there was for the most part no belief that the ongoing tensions with Chile and occasionally with Brazil might suddenly lead to war, any military expenditure by those countries was interpreted as a latent threat with the ulterior motive of gaining naval supremacy over the South American continental powers. Of Argentina's two would-be antagonists, her trans-Andean neighbour Chile exhibited a sense of purpose that could not fail to alarm the Argentine government, which at the same time appreciated the heavy financial sacrifices involved in developing her own naval power.[2]

This situation, together with other considerations exercising public opinion, finally resulted in 1889 in the approval by the Argentine Congress of an initial commitment authorising the allocation of 4.7 million pesos for the purchase of naval vessels and ordnance, together with an additional 4.5 million for the construction of a capital ship. These appropriations, which were passed into law in 1891, provided for the funds to be raised from the sale of the Andean railway line joining the towns of Villa María in the province of Córdoba with Villa Mercedes in that of Mendoza, together with the sale of government land at a minimum rate of 5,000 pesos per square league. Meanwhile, and until such time as these transactions were completed, the Executive

Branch was authorised to raise the necessary funds from loan transactions, being also permitted to appropriate a variety of state income sources.

This turn of events confirms the influence on Argentine decision-making of the military policy embarked on by Chile whose navy was significantly larger than that of Argentina. In 1890 the Armada de Chile boasted the British-built central battery ships *Almirante Cochrane* (1874) and *Blanco Encalada* (1875), with the barbette ship *Capitán Prat* (1890) nearing completion in France. These were all larger and better armed than the Argentine navy's only significant oceangoing vessel, the British-built central battery ship *Almirante Brown* (1880). Argentine rearmament policy therefore centred on the addition between 1890 and 1893 of her first oceangoing cruisers, the *25 de Mayo* and the *9 de Julio*, part of a naval programme which nonetheless continued to prioritise riverine vessels by the addition of a significant number of torpedo boats of various sizes.[3] Needless to say, the acquisition of warships was one thing, the evolution of a coherent naval strategy quite another. Until the mid-1890s the Río de la Plata (River Plate), upon whose southern shore lies the city of Buenos Aires, was the only region accorded any importance in national planning, and war dispositions

---

[1] The editor would like to thank Guillermo C. Berger and Ricardo Burzaco of Buenos Aires for kindly supplying images and information for this chapter.

[2] 'Nautilus', 'La Marina de Guerra Nacional. Defensa del Río de la Plata' in *Boletín del Centro Naval* 8 (1890–1), p. 133.

[3] In 1890 some 33 per cent of naval expenditure was allocated to armaments, increasing to 42 per cent in 1891 and no less than 55 per cent of the total over the next two years. By 1895 it stood at 65 per cent. Susana Rato de Sambuccetti, 'Evolución del gasto público en un período de crisis (1889–1895)' in *Temas de historia argentina y americana* 1 (2002), pp. 133–86.

were therefore based largely on the defence of this immense estuary and its tributaries along the Argentine riverine coast. Accordingly, it was torpedoes and torpedo boats which occupied first place in the country's defensive strategy, even if international developments in the area of underwater warfare had left Argentina well astern by comparison with her regional neighbours whose coastlines allowed them to project their influence beyond continental waters.

In Argentina as elsewhere the key debates were carried on in professional journals, in her case the *Boletín del Centro Naval* founded in 1882. Where the effectiveness of point-defence weapons such as the torpedo were concerned, an influential article by Lieutenant de vaisseau (Lieutenant) J. Lephay of the French navy analysing opinions in the British and US press posited that the conventional wisdom that any naval engagement should 'endeavour to capture the enemy rather than destroy him' in fact ran counter to the declared role of the ram and the torpedo, which was to 'dispose of the enemy as a total loss'.[4] According to the author, the gun, though previously only 'fleetingly discussed', had now recovered its former supremacy, but under new principles in the context of complex and integrated weapons systems. Meanwhile, in 1895

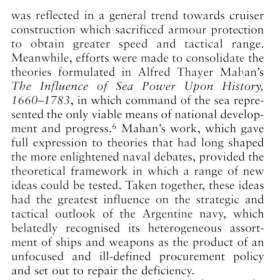

The architect of the new Argentine fleet, Commodore Martín Rivadavia. *(DEHN)*

Garibaldi at Genoa before sailing for Argentina in the autumn of 1896. *(NHHC/NH 88672)*

Lt. Cdr. Richard Wainwright (who later found fame as executive officer of USS *Maine* in 1898) published an article in the United States Naval Institute's *Proceedings* journal which was regarded as a 'faithful expression' of the ideas prevailing in that country's navy.[5] To Wainwright, the eclipse of defensive naval tactics

was reflected in a general trend towards cruiser construction which sacrificed armour protection to obtain greater speed and tactical range. Meanwhile, efforts were made to consolidate the theories formulated in Alfred Thayer Mahan's *The Influence of Sea Power Upon History, 1660–1783*, in which command of the sea represented the only viable means of national development and progress.[6] Mahan's work, which gave full expression to theories that had long shaped the more enlightened naval debates, provided the theoretical framework in which a range of new ideas could be tested. Taken together, these ideas had the greatest influence on the strategic and tactical outlook of the Argentine navy, which belatedly recognised its heterogeneous assortment of ships and weapons as the product of an unfocused and ill-defined procurement policy and set out to repair the deficiency.

By 1895 the evolution of naval doctrine, the need to adjust existing tactical criteria in light of the latest technological developments, and a concern to remedy the parlous state of the Argentine fleet with vessels capable of redressing the balance of power with Chile had coalesced into a coherent naval policy. Accordingly, Argentina now abandoned not only the theories of the French *Jeune école*, which favoured the employment of medium-sized units and torpedo vessels for coastal defence, but also the debate between the proponents of armour and those of gunnery, opting instead to apply the latest technology to her own navy. The leading figure in this movement was the energetic and farsighted figure of Capitán de navío (Captain) Martín Rivadavia (1852–1901). A grandson of Bernardino Rivadavia, one of the founding fathers of the Argentine Republic, the younger Rivadavia was not only the most prominent officer in the Armada but also among the few

4　Originally published in the *Revue Maritime et Coloniale* and published as 'La Táctica naval moderna. Opiniones de la prensa inglesa y americana' in *Revista general de Marina* 37 (1895), pp. 609–20 & 766, reprinted in *Boletín del Centro Naval* 13 (1895–6), pp. 394–402.

5　Originally published in the *Revue Maritime et Coloniale* in August 1895, summarised in *Le Yacht*, and republished therefrom as 'Tactical Problems in Naval Warfare', *United States Naval Institute Proceedings* 21 (1895), no. 74, pp. 217–57; *Boletín del Centro Naval* 13 (1895–6), pp. 424–9.

6　First published by Little, Brown & Co. in Boston in 1890; in Spanish translation in 1901 (El Ferrol: Imprenta del Correo Gallego), and in Argentina in 1935 under the title *Influencia del poder naval en la historia, 1660–1783*, 2 vols. (Buenos Aires: Escuela de Guerra Naval).

Garibaldi lying at the southernmost port of Ushuaia on the island of Tierra del Fuego shortly after delivery in 1896. She and her sisters transformed Argentina's conception of her strategic and geographical possibilities as a naval and maritime power. *(AGNA/Fundación Histarmar)*

capable of reconciling the traditions defended by the older officers, whose concerns focused on the riverine squadrons, and the innovation promoted by the younger generation with a broader perspective and technical formation. Supported by the latter and enjoying the full confidence of the government with the enthusiastic support of Congress which had finally awoken to the dangers of pursuing a half-hearted military policy, Rivadavia opened unprecedented new horizons for the Armada and laid the foundations for its consolidation as a major national and regional institution. The effect was immediate and on a scale that would have been scarcely imaginable just a few years earlier.

Argentina's First Armoured Cruiser

In 1895 the focus turned on the Argentine naval procurement mission in Europe which, as was customary, assessed the bids tendered by the main shipyards in order to find a vessel that would best suit Argentina's needs. Aside from their operational and seagoing capabilities, the perceived threat from Chile meant that much emphasis was placed on cost and quicker delivery times. These concerns resulted in the rejection first of British yards on the former ground, and then of French yards on the latter with their notoriously protracted delivery times. Instead it was in the Italian shipbuilding industry that the Argentine naval mission under Capitán de fragata (Commander) Manuel Domecq García found its ideal vessel: the armoured cruiser *Giuseppe Garibaldi*. The prototype of a class of ships which eventually saw service in four navies, *Giuseppe Garibaldi* was the product of an ambitious design prepared by Edoardo Masdea under the supervision of the naval engineer and Minister of Marine Benedetto Brin, supported by a team at the Ansaldo yard at Genoa.

With 15 per cent of the displacement devoted to armament, 20 per cent to propulsion, 25 per cent to armour and 40 per cent to the hull, the design emphasised speed and manoeuvrability while offering a good balance of protection and armament on a full-load displacement of 6,840 tons.[7] The vessels had an overall length of 328ft (100m), with 59ft 9in (18.2m) in the beam and drawing 23ft 4in (7.1m) at standard load. Propulsion was delivered by eight boilers powering two sets of triple-expansion engines producing 13,000ihp for a best speed of 20 knots. To this was added an impressive tactical range of 6,900 miles at an economical speed of

---

[7] Pablo Arguindeguy, *Apuntes sobre los buques de la Armada Argentina, 1810–1970*, 7 vols. (Buenos Aires: Secretaría General Naval, 1972), IV, p. 1764.

Loading the Armstrong 10in gun in one of *Garibaldi*'s turrets shortly after her delivery to the Argentine navy. *(AGNA/Fundación Histarmar)*

Manning one of *Garibaldi*'s six Armstrong 4.7in guns on the port side of the forecastle deck. *(AGNA/Fundación Histarmar)*

10 knots. There was bunkerage for 1,137 tons of coal. Protection consisted of a 6in (152mm) nickel steel belt, narrowing to 3in (76mm) at the extremities, with horizontal armour of between 1in (25mm) and 2in (51mm) on the main deck at the waterline. Bulkheads, barbettes and the conning tower were protected by 6in (152mm) of armour, with 3in (76mm) gun shields. Although it was never tested in Argentina's case, submerged protection was deficient and contributed to the loss of her Italian namesake and near sister *Giuseppe Garibaldi* (1899) to a single torpedo from the Austro-Hungarian submarine *U-4* in July 1915.

Armament varied from ship to ship within the class, but in the case of the subject of this chapter the main battery consisted of two 10in (254mm) 40-calibre guns mounted in single turrets forward and aft and manufactured at Armstrong's Pozzuoli works near Naples. *Garibaldi* carried an assorted quick-firing secondary armament, ranging from ten Armstrong 6in (152mm) guns disposed in casemates on either side of the upper deck, six Armstrong 4.7in (120mm) guns on the forecastle deck, ten Hotchkiss 2.2in (56mm) and eight Maxim 1.5in (38mm) guns. The armament was completed by four above-water 18in (457mm) torpedo tubes (removed in 1900–1), two Maxim 0.303in (7.7mm) machine guns and a pair of 3in (76mm) landing guns. *Garibaldi* was

essentially an attempt to meet the requirements of a cruiser without entirely subordinating the protection of a battleship. As the *Boletín* put it: 'Battleships capable of 18 knots at standard draught are still very rare, and we can be satisfied at having that specification for our own vessel, without sacrificing those other indispensable capabilities which must be met by a ship in her role as a cruiser.'[8]

Already in 1893 the Regia Marina had ordered two units of the class, *Giuseppe Garibaldi* herself whose keel was laid at Gio. Ansaldo & Co. of Genova-Sestri Ponente on 25 July 1893, and *Varese* laid down at Orlando of Livorno the following year. Helped by close cultural ties between Argentina and Italy and assisted by Ansaldo shareholder Ferdinando María Perrone, who kept an office in Buenos Aires, the Argentine government was not long in registering its interest. By June 1895 discussions were well in hand for the purchase of one of the units under construction for the Regia Marina, with Domecq García (now promoted captain) describing the design as having 'all the features of a warship' and emphasising as its chief merit the opportunity to take delivery of the vessel very quickly – within just four or five months instead of the three years required by an order in any other country. The reason for this urgency was not far to seek as the naval arms race with Chile

began in earnest. As Captain Domecq García explained to the once and future president of Argentina, General Julio Roca, in a letter which constitutes the first mention of the purchase of *Garibaldi*, such an acquisition

> would put us at a distinct advantage with respect to the C... [i.e. Chilean] Fleet which is currently being strengthened with the construction of a 6,000-ton vessel being built by the firm of Armstrong [*Esmeralda*, 7,032 tons] and one of 8,000 tons which may possibly be built in France [*O'Higgins*, 7,500 tons, also built by Armstrong's].[9]

The purchase of *Giuseppe Garibaldi* was formalised in a contract signed with Ansaldo in London worth £752,000 on 14 July 1895, the ship having been launched as recently as 26 June.[10] Although Garibaldi, the 'Hero of the

8 Flavio Gai, 'El *José Garibaldi*' in *Boletín del Centro Naval* 13 (1895–6), pp. 47–9.

9 Departamento de Estudios Históricos Navales [DEHN], Buenos Aires, 5 June 1895.

10 DEHN, 'Informe favorable respecto de la adquisición de un crucero acorazado en la casa Ansaldo de Italia', Buenos Aires, 19 June 1895, signed by Manuel Domecq García, Félix Dufourq, José Durand and Aníbal Carmona.

Above: Decked with Italian flags, *Giuseppe Garibaldi* goes down the ways at Ansaldo of Genova-Sestri Ponente on 25 July 1893. Two years later she was purchased for the Argentine navy. *(DEHN)*

Right: *Garibaldi* at Genoa before sailing for Argentina in the autumn of 1896. *(NHHC/NH 88671)*

Two Worlds', had commanded the Uruguayan fleet against the province of Buenos Aires during the Uruguayan Civil War before returning to lead the Risorgimento in 1848, in an example of political expediency the Argentine government decided to pay Italy and the large Italian expatriate community the compliment of preserving the name – albeit dropping *Giuseppe*.

An Italian-Built Squadron

It is a measure of how anxious the Argentine government was to take possession of its new vessel as the crisis with Chile escalated that *Garibaldi* sailed from Genoa on 13 October 1896 with not a single naval officer embarked and apparently little more than a steaming crew mustered haphazardly in Genoa and other ports in place of her standard complement of twenty-eight officers and 420 men.[11] *Garibaldi* reached Buenos Aires on 10 December where Argentine society generally and military opinion in particular viewed her acquisition as a major coup with far-reaching consequences for the country and the navy. Here was the first in a line of vessels which were intended to redress the balance between Argentina and the other South American naval powers. The point was not lost on this contributor to the *Boletín*:

> So it is that the *Garibaldi* has become ours, and with it this country has committed herself to organising a navy capable of effectively guarding her maritime interests, protecting her rights and, most significantly of all, providing a basis for the progressive development of our sea coasts; an important role has therefore been assigned to our navy, since although the sacrifice made by our country on behalf of its navy has yet to reach its limit, our leaders believe that we shall soon discover the extent to which peace and understanding between the rival powers in this part of the Americas are strengthened through a maritime balance of power.[12]

Meanwhile, the total tonnage of the Argentine fleet which stood at 23,220 tons in 1895 was increased by nearly a third thanks to the addition of *Garibaldi*, with more of her kind to follow.

The enthusiastic reception given to *Garibaldi* even before she joined the Armada in 1896 opened the way to the acquisition of a modern squadron which would allow that country to project her power beyond continental waters. The purchase of *Garibaldi* in July 1895 was therefore followed by that of *Varese* (renamed *San Martín*)

The port battery of *Garibaldi*'s near sister *San Martín* trained on the beam, *c.* 1902. Both vessels shared the same secondary armament of ten Armstrong 6in guns disposed in casemates on either side of the upper deck and six Armstrong 4.7in guns on the forecastle deck. *(DEHN)*

in a deal negotiated by Rivadavia himself and signed in April 1896. Laid down for the Regia Marina in 1894 and launched at Leghorn on 25 May 1896, *San Martín* represented a considerable advance on her sister, both in size and specifications. Aside from a main armament of four 8in (203mm) guns, the forward and after pairs of 6in (152mm) guns were repositioned to engage targets dead ahead and astern. Improvements in armour quality, together with modifications to ammunition supply and provision of searchlights, raised the full-load displacement to 8,100 tons, while the experience of the First Sino-Japanese War (1894–5; see *Chen Yuen*) was brought to bear in the decision to replace all wooden bulkheads with those of steel.[13] Commissioned on 25 April 1898 after successfully completing sea and gunnery trials off La Spezia, *San Martín* reached Argentina on 13 June.

But this was not all. In 1897 Martín Rivadavia, now promoted commodore, was appointed Chief of Staff of the Armada. In the lengthy private letter he wrote to the Minister of War and Marine, General Nicolás Levalle, in February 1898, Rivadavia underlined the pressing need 'to complete the nation's battle-fleet' with the acquisition of a third armoured cruiser

> of a power at least equal to that of *General San Martín* or *Garibaldi*. [...] In making this statement I am taking account not only the inferiority of the nation's maritime power compared with that of Chile [...] but speaking also and most particularly from the perspective of clear necessity from a professional standpoint. [...] As Your Excellency is aware, a battle unit is composed of three vessels which together muster the highest degree of homogeneity, and formations must as a rule have at least that number of ships in order to engage in a squadron-to-squadron action.[14]

Led by General Levalle in the Senate and with Rivadavia appointed Argentina's first Minister of Marine in 1898, obstacles were cleared and resources allocated from Treasury reserves and a series of domestic loans aimed at prioritising defence and strengthening the fleet with further capital ships.[15] As had been the case with *Garibaldi*, an invitation to tender was issued and bids received from the main shipyards of Britain, France and Germany, all of which were rejected on grounds of cost and due to estimated delivery periods of between eighteen and twenty-four months. Inevitably, and just as Rivadavia had hoped, it was the Italian shipbuilding industry which again received orders for two armoured cruisers, this time in the shape of two improved units of the Giuseppe Garibaldi class. These consisted of *Cristóbal Colón*, originally ordered by the Spanish navy from Ansaldo but completed for Argentina as *Pueyrredón*, and *Varese*, ordered by the Regia Marina from Orlando but commissioned into the Armada as *Belgrano*.

Argentine Units of the Giuseppe Garibaldi class

	Garibaldi	San Martín	Pueyrredón	Belgrano
Laid down	1894	1894	1896	1896
Length (overall, ft/m)	328ft (100m)	350ft (106.7m)	350ft (106.7m)	350ft (106.7m)
Beam (ft/m)	59ft 9in (18.2m)	53ft 2in (16.2m)	59ft 9in (18.2m)	53ft 2in (16.2m)
Draught (standard, ft/m)	23ft 4in (7.1m)	25ft (7.6m)	25ft (7.6m)	27ft (8.3m)
Displacement (full load)	6,840	8,100	8,000	7,300
Armour (belt max)	6in (152mm)	6in (152mm)	6in (152mm)	6in (152mm)
Main armament/calibre	2 × 10in (254mm)/40	4 × 8in (203mm)/45	2 × 10in (254mm)/40	2 × 10in (254mm)/40
Speed (max)	20	18	19	18
Endurance (nm/knots)	6,000/10	6,000/10	6,000/10	6,000/10
Power (ihp)	13,000	13,500	13,000	13,000

Source: www.histarmar.com.ar

---

[11] Crónica, 'Marina Argentina' in *Boletín del Centro Naval* 15 (1897–8), p. 499.

[12] Gai, 'El *José Garibaldi*', p. 47.

[13] *Memoria del Ministerio de Guerra y Marina* (1895–6) (Buenos Aires: Departamento de Marina, 1896), pp. 57–9.

[14] DEHN, Donaciones varias, box 6, private letter from Martín Rivadavia to Nicolás Levalle, Buenos Aires, February 1898.

[15] Nicolás Levalle, *Memoria del Ministerio de Guerra y Marina* (1897–8) (Buenos Aires: Departamento de Marina, 1898), II, vi.

Three of the four units of the Garibaldi class lying at the Puerto Militar near Bahía Blanca in 1901. They are *Garibaldi, Pueyrredón* and, furthest from the camera, *San Martín.* (DEHN)

Displacing 8,000 and 7,300 tons respectively, this pair represented a further improvement on *Garibaldi* and *San Martín*, being fitted with large-tube boilers permitting steam to be raised in just forty-five minutes and mounting two 10in (254mm) guns with Armstrong breeches, thereby permitting a considerable increase in the rate of fire. *Pueyrredón* was duly commissioned into the Armada on 4 August 1898, followed by *Belgrano* on 8 October.

This notable transformation in Argentina's naval strength did not go unnoticed in Europe, especially in Italy which was the immediate beneficiary of her rapid procurement policy. On 4 July 1898 the Genoese newspaper *Il Secolo XIX* stated in connection with the preliminary trials of the newly acquired *Pueyrredón* that Argentina, 'persuaded that no nation can be truly strong unless she has gained absolute control of the sea, is endeavouring with all her resources – which are not insubstantial – to modernise her fleet and strengthen it with formidable fighting units.'[16]

New Navy, New Nation

The acquisition of *Garibaldi* and her sisters therefore had consequences which went well beyond the ordinary course of naval procurement, since it not only challenged the strategic theories of the past but initiated a permanent and irreversible evolution which shaped the Armada into an entity capable both of defending Argentina's territorial interests and promoting her national development. The tactical and strategic principles upon which the new Argentine navy was being built are revealed in a lecture given aboard *San Martín* by her executive officer Cdr Félix Dufourq in August 1898.[17] His text began by defining the essential concepts, supported by telling examples from naval history, and concluded by laying down the foundations of maritime strategy in the context of national necessity:

So it is that the strategic aim of naval warfare is to bring one's battlefleet into contact with that of the enemy to the best possible advantage in respect of the number and effectiveness of fighting units, in order that their crews may, based on the instruction received in peacetime training, at the hour of battle extract the utmost from such a complex mechanism and the capabilities of their weapons with courage and discipline, and so gain victory.[18]

Much as these may be universal truths of naval warfare, when taken in context they reflect the consolidation of a new awareness in the Armada Argentina. As such, they not only encompass such incontrovertible principles as the balance of power to which Argentina now aspired, but also a deliberate and continuous process of modernisation of naval assets together with the provision of properly trained crews in specially designed shore establishments to create an ideal fleet. This was composed in the first instance of a homogeneous squadron of capital ships supported by destroyers, since 'history reminds us that almost all naval battles have been fought off the coast'. Dufourq also envisaged the provision of armed

[16] Crónica, 'Las Pruebas preliminares del *Pueyrredón*' in *Boletín del Centro Naval* 16 (1898–9), p. 48.

[17] Félix Dufourq, 'Conferencia dada a bordo del crucero-acorazado *General San Martín* por su 2° Comandante, en Punta Piedras, agosto 30/98' in *Boletín del Centro Naval* 17 (1899–1900), p. 25.

[18] *Ibid.*, 32.

transports capable of supplying coal, the commissioning of a transport fitted out as a repair ship, and even a hospital ship.

Cdr Dufourq's lecture also points to a definitive rupture with Argentina's traditional defensive strategy in favour of the development of land communications, ports and fortifications far removed from the major population centres, together with naval assets capable of projecting her power both on the high seas and on the very threshold of the enemy. It marks official recognition of the secondary role of older units, with the battle squadron to be composed solely of the latest vessels as part of a policy traced out by Levalle and Rivadavia. This strategy was of course entirely consistent with the naval doctrine of the day, especially in Britain, and as an article in the *Boletín* put it, in exercising 'prudent foresight' the Armada had captured the pragmatic spirit of an age in which it was no longer of any concern whether right emerged from good doctrine or from the barrel of a gun.[19]

The debates centring on the acquisition of *Garibaldi* and her sisters were not confined to technical, tactical, strategic and geopolitical considerations, but also to the provision of basing and maintenance facilities for vessels of a size unprecedented in the Argentine navy. The need to refit and repair the major units joining the fleet required the construction of graving docks and facilities at what would effectively constitute the nation's premier naval base. The

question of where this facility would be located was therefore the subject of prolonged debate, with conservative commentators opting for a location on the River Plate in the economic and political heartland of the nation, while the claims of the port of Bahía Blanca on the Atlantic 400 miles south of Buenos Aires were pressed by a younger and more progressive party. Opponents of the River Plate option declared that vessels of *Garibaldi*'s 24ft (7.3m) draught would be unable to navigate its waters, while their counterparts stated that it was scarcely credible to subordinate national strategy to the extent of establishing a port in faraway Bahía Blanca simply because of the draught of the navy's main units. Although the notion of *Garibaldi* as a tool for developing Argentina's Atlantic coast was consistent with the construction of a deep-water port at Bahía Blanca, this alone was not reckoned to warrant the enormous expenditure involved. Moreover, supporters of the River Plate option were soon able to demonstrate that the traditional ports of La Plata or Buenos Aires itself, in the shape of Puerto Madero, were perfectly capable of accommodating *Garibaldi*, but this did not remove the major limitations imposed by navigation of the River Plate with its extensive shallows and sandbanks, which then as now required constant dredging.

The debate also revealed the altered conception of the nation created by Argentina's latest acquisition: 'The *Garibaldi* must go to Puerto

Madero so that she can be seen by the citizens of the Republic,' trumpeted *La Prensa*, one of the leading Buenos Aires newspapers. To this Bahía Blanca (where *Garibaldi* happened to be lying at the time) indignantly retorted that 'By the looks of it the *Garibaldi* is not currently in Argentine waters and Bahía does not form part of the Republic.'[20] In 1896 the Minister of War and Marine Guillermo Villanueva responded by acknowledging that *Garibaldi*'s draught had influenced the government to order a 'broader and more detailed study of the location of the naval base'.[21] The resulting decision to construct the 'Puerto Militar' (later renamed Puerto Belgrano) near Bahía Blanca but far from the industrial and economic centres of the nation no doubt owed as much to *Garibaldi*'s specifications as it did to Cdr Dufourq's advocacy.[22]

The new ships also required a reorganisation of naval assets involving the creation of two divisions, the Río de la Plata Division based in the Buenos Aires Roads and the Bahía Blanca Division with its anchorage at the nearby Puerto Militar, each composed of vessels appropriate to the theatre of operations in question.[23] Whereas the Río de la Plata Division encompassed the old coastal defence craft, river gunboats and protected cruisers, that of Bahía Blanca was responsible for guarding the immense 1,500-mile coastline of Argentine Patagonia with *Garibaldi*, *San Martín*, *Pueyrredón* and *Belgrano*, together with the new British-built protected cruiser *Buenos Aires*. Command of the *Garibaldi* was given to Captain Manuel José García Mansilla, the Argentine navy's leading exponent on battle tactics and naval evolutions on which he wrote an influential volume.[24] These developments were crowned by a naval review off Punta Piedras at the mouth of the River Plate in October 1898, designed as a

[19] 'Williams', 'Los Nuevos buques. Sus características principales' in *Boletín del Centro Naval* 15 (1897–8), p. 51.

[20] Diego Brown, 'El Futuro Puerto Militar. Refutación a *La Prensa*' in *Boletín del Centro Naval* 14 (1896–7), pp. 171–3.

[21] *Memoria del Ministerio de Guerra y Marina* (1895–6), p. 91.

[22] 'J. G.', 'El Acorazado *Garibaldi*' in *Boletín del Centro Naval* 14 (1896–7), p. 431.

[23] Decree of 5 November 1898 on the reorganisation of naval forces in Ercilio Domínguez, ed., *Colección de Leyes y Decretos Militares* (Buenos Aires: Cía. Sudamericana de Billetes de Banco, 1898), V, p. 214.

[24] *Estudio sobre evoluciones navales y táctica de combate* (Buenos Aires: Editorial Guillermo Kraft, 1897).

Garibaldi anchored off Bahía Blanca, the home port of the new Argentine navy. *(DEHN)*

demonstration both to foreign observers and above all to the Argentine people of the high degree of capability and proficiency which had been attained by the Armada in a few short years. Prominent among the twenty-eight vessels gazed on by a large multitude of people and representatives of the domestic and foreign press were the Garibaldi-class armoured cruisers. However, *Garibaldi* herself was in urgent need of refit and repair, and in December 1898 sailed for Genoa where she was taken in hand at Ansaldo for eighteen months at a cost of 90,000 gold pesos.

Although *Garibaldi* remained in dockyard hands in Italy until June 1900, by late 1899 the

GRAVING DOCK AT THE PUERTO MILITAR

On 2 January 1902 *San Martín* became the first vessel to enter the graving dock at the Puerto Militar, which she did to a rapturous welcome.[25] The formal inauguration of the dock in the presence of President Julio Roca was postponed until early March for technical and protocol reasons, and naturally enough it was *Garibaldi*, the vessel which had first prompted the government to undertake this engineering project, which was the focus of the ceremonies on that occasion. These were planned to take place on the afternoon of 7 March, but mechanical problems conspired to delay her entry until the next tide at 0200 on the 8th. By then the weather had taken a turn for the worse and *Garibaldi* was docked in darkness and torrential rain. Nonetheless, the Armada made the best of an awkward situation, one of her officers making bold to declare that '*Garibaldi* is the first warship to enter a graving dock anywhere in South America by night and in inclement weather.'[26] The ceremony finally took place at 1300 that same day, with Roca symbolically scraping *Garibaldi*'s hull in anticipation of her being cleaned and repainted before recalling that his

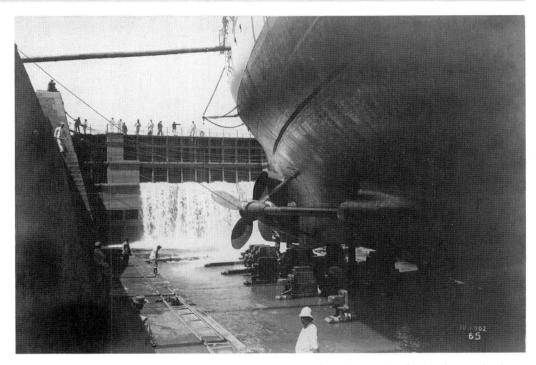

Above: *Garibaldi*'s near sister *San Martín* occupying the new graving dock at the Puerto Militar in January 1902. Its completion that same month made it the finest facility of its kind in the hemisphere south of the United States. *(DEHN)*

Left: The bearded figure of President Julio Roca on *Garibaldi*'s quarterdeck during the dedication of the graving dock at the Puerto Militar on 8 March 1902. *(DEHN)*

own inauguration had taken place aboard her. As Roca informed Luis Luiggi, chief engineer of the works, in a letter expressing his high appreciation, both merchant shipping and the Armada now had the essential element required for them to be properly maintained.[27] In the words of the local press, 'this impressive construction not only demonstrates our vitality, but ensures the integrity and sovereignty of our nation.'[28]

[25] *La Nación*, Buenos Aires, 3 January 1902.
[26] *La Nueva Provincia*, Bahía Blanca, 9 March 1902.
[27] *Ibid.*, 12 January 1902.
[28] *El Porteño*, Bahía Blanca, 9 March 1902.

frontline Argentine fleet consisted of a battle squadron composed of four modern armoured cruisers and four British-built units: the protected cruisers *25 de Mayo* (1890), *9 de Julio* (1892) and *Buenos Aires* (1895), and the gunboat *Patria* (1893), supported by the three transports mentioned above. These eight warships together displaced 44,000 tons and were armed with an aggregate of 276 quick-firing guns and thirty-seven torpedo tubes. They could steam in formation at 20 knots and remain operational for up to two months with the aid of their support vessels.[29] Just as the Armada had hastened to incorporate *Garibaldi* into the fleet in 1896, so now it urged completion of the naval base and large graving dock near Bahía Blanca upon which it would rely in any conflict with Chile. With tensions simmering, in early 1900 the sail training ship *Presidente Sarmiento* reached

---

[29] *Memoria del Ministerio de Guerra y Marina* (1897–8), II, x–xi.

Argentina with a cargo of ammunition for the armoured cruisers purchased in Italy, where orders were placed for the addition of two improved units of the Garibaldi class to the fleet in the shape of the *Mariano Moreno* and *Bernardino Rivadavia* of 7,700 tons displacement, thereby offering the prospect of a squadron of six armoured cruisers.

The Balance of Power and the Pacts of May

The creation of a battle squadron and development of port infrastructure completed the naval defence strategy needed by Argentina to secure a balance of power with Chile, on which basis it could negotiate with that country on equal terms (see *Almirante Latorre*). An early consequence of the acquisition of the squadron of armoured cruisers was the agreement signed between Argentina and Chile in March 1899 over the vexed issue of the mineral-rich desert region of the Puna de Atacama in the north of the two

countries. In January 1899 the newly re-elected President Julio Roca embarked with Rivadavia in *Belgrano* and sailed south to the Chilean city of Punta Arenas on the Magellan Strait where he met his opposite number Federico Errázuriz Echaurren on 15 February. The negotiations culminated in the accord known as the *Abrazo del Estrecho* ('Embrace of the Strait') reached on *Belgrano*'s quarterdeck. The resulting agreement, brokered by US President James Buchanan and signed on 24 March that year, accorded Argentina an 85 per cent share of the territory.

These circumstances, together with the willingness of both countries to reach a peaceful settlement over the main territorial disputes served to clear the way for negotiations, and in March 1902 the Argentine government appointed Dr. José Antonio Terry as its ambas-

Garibaldi lying in the graving dock at the Puerto Militar near Bahía Blanca on 8 March 1902. Astern of her is the British-built steam frigate *Presidente Sarmiento*, since converted to a training ship and now preserved in Buenos Aires. *(DEHN)*

sador to Chile. A series of discussions, including with Chilean president Dr. Germán Riesco, resulted in agreement on the main issues, with progress in the negotiations facilitated by cross-party consensus among Argentina's leading statesmen past and present, including Roca, former presidents Bartolomé Mitre and Carlos Pellegrini, and ministers Amancio Alcorta and Joaquín V. González, all of whom bent their talents and patriotic instincts to secure peace.

These negotiations resulted in the so-called *Pactos de Mayo* (Pacts of May) signed on 28 May 1902, the first naval arms limitation agreement signed between two modern states. Of the three main documents of which it was composed – the Preamble, the Arbitration Treaty, and the Naval Arms Limitation Convention – it is the latter which had the greatest effect on naval assets and operations.

Right: *San Martín* running trials off Leghorn in the summer of 1898. *(NHHC/NH 94366)*

Below: Members of the Argentine delegation gathered on *San Martín*'s quarterdeck en route to Chile for the signing of the Pacts of May in 1902. The figure in the centre is Commodore Rivadavia. *(DEHN)*

Consisting of five articles, the Convention imposed a suspension on all current construction and a five-year moratorium on further naval procurement, to be broken only with eighteen months' notice. The reduction of the respective fleets was to take place within the space of a year and was to continue until these had reached what was referred to as 'a discreet equivalency'. To emphasise the defensive spirit of the agreement, procurement of armaments for coastal fortifications and port defences were explicitly excluded from the Convention.[30]

Garibaldi's sister San Martín was the unit selected to carry the Argentine embassy to Chile, where the Pacts of May were formally signed in great solemnity in the presidential palace in Santiago on 23 September 1902. This event was preceded by a succession of formal visits to the ship by senior figures in the Chilean navy, including Vice Admiral Jorge Montt and President Riesco himself. As San Martín's commanding officer Captain Juan A. Martin recalled, the cruise was all that could be expected of a diplomatic visit:

San Martín received continual visits the entire length of Chile and left the overall impression of being a perfect instrument, from her smart and well-maintained structure to her disciplined and orderly crew unblemished by any incident, while frequently being offered many kind compliments. We for our part returned

home enchanted by the welcome that had been extended to us, which immediately drew us to the Chilean people and reminded us of the age of San Martín and O'Higgins, now celebrated in the names of our two flagships ...[31]

Although the Pacts of May put an end to the Argentine-Chilean naval arms race, the resulting armed peace interpreted military power as a means of avoiding war, via negotiation on the basis of equality or even supremacy. This in turn provided senior officers in the Argentine army and navy with the rationale to uphold the necessity of maintaining powerful and balanced armed forces with respect to those of Chile and Brazil, a notion which would be invoked five years later when Brazil began a programme of battleship construction (see Minas Geraes). The agreement was condemned in some quarters of Argentine society, but the majority view was that military power had ultimately averted war and that it was now time to accept a significant reduction in armaments. Naturally enough, the consequences fell hardest on the Armada, which under the terms of the Pacts of May was required to disarm both Garibaldi and Pueyrredón, while disposing of the two units of the class then under construction by Ansaldo in Italy. These were taken over by Japan as Kasuga and Nisshin in a deal brokered by the British, and in time to see action in the Russo-Japanese War of 1904–5. Meanwhile, the disarmament of Argentina's first

two armoured cruisers resulted in the elimination of the Bahía Blanca Division and the creation of a second division in the River Plate.

Later Career

The ratification of the Pacts of May therefore halted Garibaldi's career as a frontline unit, the ship being disarmed and placed under reduced complement in January 1903. By the time the moratorium had expired in 1907 and steps taken to rearm her and bring her up to full complement, the face of capital ship construction had been transformed by the appearance of HMS Dreadnought. Moreover, the Armada was now beginning to address the possibility of a naval arms race with Brazil which had placed orders for two dreadnoughts from British yards in 1906, eliciting a response from Argentina in the shape of the two Rivadavia-class battleships ordered from the United States in 1908. Facing obsolescence, the Italian armoured cruisers were assigned to instructional duties, and that same year Garibaldi was allocated as a training ship for the Escuela de Artillería (Gunnery School) as well as for deck officers, signalmen and stokers.

The importance of effective training had gone hand in hand with the technological development of the Argentine navy since the 1880s, and it was a former officer of the Regia Marina, Cdr Eduardo Múscari, who first mustered all training facilities in a single ship.[32] The first vessel to serve this purpose had been the elderly steamer General Brown, which was replaced by Garibaldi in 1915 when the battleships

Shipboard photos of the Argentine navy are extremely rare for this period. This one shows crewmen of Garibaldi's near sister Pueyrredón celebrating victory in an inter-ship coaling competition c. 1900. (Courtesy Ricardo Burzaco)

[30] See Carlos Alberto Silva, La Política internacional de la Nación Argentina (Buenos Aires: Imprenta de la Cámara de Diputados, 1946), p. 376, & Enrique González Lonzieme, 'Los Conflictos con Chile (1883–1904)' in Historia Marítima Argentina 8 (1990), pp. 401–5.

[31] Juan A. Martin, 'Viaje del crucero acorazado San Martín a Chile (septiembre de 1902). Canje de los Pactos de Mayo sobre equivalencia naval, paz y amistad' in Boletín del Centro Naval 70 (1952), no. 607, pp. 419–33. The Argentine José de San Martín (1778–1850) and the Chilean Bernardo O'Higgins (1778–1842) were leading figures in South America's struggle for independence from Spain. The British-built armoured cruiser O'Higgins (1897) entered service with the Chilean navy in 1898.

[32] Report of the commission composed of Francisco Beuf, Daniel de Solier and Rafael Blanco, Buenos Aires, 15 January 1882, Memoria del Ministerio de Guerra y Marina de la República Argentina (1881–2) (Buenos Aires: Ministerio de Guerra y Marina, 1882).

Rivadavia and *Moreno* joined the fleet. This did not, however, prevent her participating in the crushing of the violent episode of labour unrest known as the Semana Trágica ('tragic week') in Buenos Aires in January 1919 at the cost of 800 lives. In 1922 *Garibaldi* was selected as the base ship for the Escuela de Maquinistas y Marineros Señaleros (Stokers' and Signalmen's School), imparting training in seamanship along with classes in maths, geometry, physics and Spanish, while signalmen received additional instruction in visual signalling, steering and naval evolutions, including boat-work under oar and sail. Nonetheless, in 1924 *Garibaldi* was on hand to greet an Italian squadron consisting of the armoured cruisers *San Marco* and *San Giorgio* during Crown Prince Umberto's cruise of South America. Together with *San Martín* and *Pueyrredón*, *Garibaldi* was designated a coast-defence ship in 1927 but continued to serve in a training capacity with occasional service as a hydrographic vessel until being decommissioned

in 1933 and subsequently cannibalised for spares. Stricken on 20 March 1934, *Garibaldi* was sold in November 1935 and sailed to Sweden under her own steam where she was scrapped in 1936–7.

Where *Garibaldi*'s sisters were concerned, *San Martín* remained as flagship of the battle squadron until 1911. An extensive refit at Puerto Belgrano in 1926 saw her reboilered for oil firing and the gun mountings and superstructure were reconstructed. She was decommissioned in 1935 but not scrapped until 1947. *Pueyrredón* also served as a training vessel, the highlight of her career being the world cruise manned by cadets of the Escuela Naval (Naval College) on which she embarked in 1918. She was reboilered for oil firing in 1922 but assigned to coastal defence duties in 1927. Based in the River Plate, the years from 1937–40 were spent with the training squadron in coastal waters, with further instructional cruises taking place from 1941–52. Decommissioned in August 1954, she was sold to

the Boston Metals Co. of Baltimore in January 1955, which had her towed to Japan for demolition. *Belgrano*, meanwhile, became the first vessel in the Armada to have a Marconi wireless set fitted in 1907. In October 1927 she represented Argentina at a naval review in Genoa where the crew attended the inauguration of a monument to her namesake, one of the heroes of the Argentine war of independence. After a brief sojourn in Spanish waters she returned to Genoa for reboilering and improvements to her armament and superstructure, the work completed in 1928. In December 1933 *Belgrano* was ordered to Mar del Plata and converted to a submarine depot ship and tender. She was decommissioned on 8 May 1947 and later scrapped at Riachuelo.

Conclusion

The Pacts of May of 1902 dictated what turned out to be a temporary reduction in the strength of the Armada, but the fundamental criteria

Garibaldi's ship's company ranged on the forecastle at Puerto Belgrano in October 1913 by which time she had been assigned to training duties under reduced complement. Note the pair of Hotchkiss 2.2in guns mounted on either side of the 10in turret. *(AGNA/Fundación Histarmar)*

which had underpinned its growth were well established in official circles, and the ensuing detente permitted a gradual consolidation of naval forces and rectification of areas of weakness. At the time the agreement was signed in 1902 the Armada Argentina had twenty-seven fighting ships in commission, many of which reflected the latest in naval development. These vessels were supported by twenty-two auxiliary units designed for riverine, coastal and oceanic operations. The Puerto Militar was the finest naval basing facility in South America, while the naval college and cadet training facilities were firmly established. This capability enabled the full integration of southern Argentina and its adjacent waters into the body of the nation and significantly expanded its sense of itself. Meanwhile, the sail training ship *Presidente Sarmiento* quartered the oceans of the world as an ambassador of Argentina's national and maritime potential. In this process of state and naval projection the addition of *Garibaldi* and her sisters to the fleet had played a decisive role.

Sources

Unpublished Sources

Archivo del Departamento de Estudios Históricos Navales, Buenos Aires (DEHN)
Files and folders (1881–1902)
Family archive donations:
Vicealmirante Manuel Domecq García
Capitán de navío Félix Dufourq
Origins of the Military Port, Puerto Belgrano
Archivo General de la Armada, Buenos Aires
Archivo General de la Nación Argentina, Buenos Aires (AGNA)
Archivo de Relaciones Exteriores de la República Argentina, Buenos Aires

Bibliography

Anon., 'Las Economías en la Armada' in *Boletín del Centro Naval* 2 (1883–4), p. 547
_____, 'Puerto Militar – Proyectado en el Río de La Plata' in *Boletín del Centro Naval* 13 (1895–6), p. 1
_____, 'La Táctica naval moderna. Opiniones de la prensa inglesa y americana' in *Revista General de Marina* 37 (1895), 609 & 766; reprinted in *Boletín del Centro Naval* 13 (1895–6), pp. 394–402 & 424–9
'A. J.', '"La Ciencia del oficial de marina" de la *Revista Marítima Brasileña*' in *Boletín del Centro Naval* 14 (1896–7), p. 553
Arguindeguy, Pablo, *Apuntes sobre los buques de la Armada Argentina, 1810–1970*, 7 vols. (Buenos Aires: Secretaría General Naval, 1972)
Arguindeguy, Pablo, & Horacio Rodríguez, *Buques de la Armada Argentina (1852–1899), sus comandos y operaciones* (Buenos Aires: Instituto Nacional Browniano, 1999)
Braun Menéndez, Armando, 'Roca y los Pactos de Mayo' in *Estrategia* 3 (September–October 1969), p. 95
Brown, Diego, 'El Futuro Puerto Militar' in *Boletín del Centro Naval* 14 (1896–7), p. 79
_____, 'El futuro Puerto Militar. Refutación a *La Prensa*' in *Boletín del Centro Naval* 14 (1896–7), pp. 171–3
Burzaco, Ricardo, *Acorazados y cruceros de la Armada Argentina, 1881–1982* (Buenos Aires: Eugenio B Ediciones, 1997)
Burzio, Humberto F., *Historia del torpedo y sus buques en la Armada Argentina* (Buenos Aires: Departamento de Estudios Históricos Navales, 1968)
Cabral, Luis, *Anales de la Marina de Guerra de la República Argentina* (Buenos Aires: Imprenta de Juan A. Alsina, 1904)
Crónica, 'Marina Argentina' in *Boletín del Centro Naval* 15 (1897–8), p. 499
_____, 'Las Pruebas preliminares del *Pueyrredón*' in *Boletín del Centro Naval* 16 (1898–9), p. 48
Dufourq, Félix, 'Conferencia dada a bordo del crucero-acorazado *San Martín* por su 2º Comandante, en Punta Piedras, agosto 30/98' in *Boletín del Centro Naval* 17 (1899–1900), p. 254
Gai, Flavio, 'El *José Garibaldi*' in *Boletín del Centro Naval* 13 (1895–6), pp. 47–9
González Lonzieme, Enrique, 'Los Conflictos con Chile (1883–1904)' in *Historia Marítima Argentina*, 8 (1990), pp. 401–5
'J. G.', 'El Acorazado *Garibaldi*' in *Boletín del Centro Naval* 14 (1896–7), p. 431
Martin, Juan A., 'Viaje del crucero acorazado *San Martín* a Chile (septiembre de 1902). Canje de los Pactos de Mayo sobre equivalencia naval, paz y amistad' in *Boletín del Centro Naval* 70 (1952), no. 607, pp. 419–33; available at http://www.histarmar.com.ar/InfHistorica-3/ViajeCrAcSanMartin-1902.htm [accessed November 2015]
Memoria del Ministerio de Guerra y Marina (Buenos Aires: Departamento de Marina, 1895–1902)
'Nautilus', 'La Marina de Guerra Nacional. Defensa del Río de la Plata' in *Boletín del Centro Naval* 8 (1890–1), p. 133
Oyarzábal, Guillermo Andrés, *Argentina hacia el sur: la utopía del primer puerto militar (1896–1902)* (Buenos Aires: Instituto de Publicaciones Navales, 2002)
_____, *Los Marinos de la generación del ochenta: evolución y consolidación del poder naval en el Argentina (1872–1902)* (Buenos Aires: Editorial Planeta, 2007)
Rato de Sambuccetti, Susana, 'Evolución del gasto público en un período de crisis (1889–1895)' in *Temas de historia argentina y americana* 1 (2002), pp. 133–86
Scheina, Robert L., *Latin America: A Naval History, 1810–1987* (Annapolis, Md.: Naval Institute Press, 1987)
Silva, Carlos Alberto, *La Política internacional de la Nación Argentina* (Buenos Aires: Imprenta de la Cámara de Diputados, 1946)
'Spectator', 'El Desarme – Limitación de armamentos' in *Boletín del Centro Naval* 19 (1901–02), p. 729
Wainwright, Richard, 'Tactical Problems in Naval Warfare' in *United States Naval Institute Proceedings* 21 (1895), no. 74, pp. 217–57
'Williams', '"El Futuro Puerto Militar" por Diego Brown, examen de sus ideas' in *Boletín del Centro Centro Naval* 14 (1896–7), p. 273
_____, 'Corazas y proyectiles modernos' in *Boletín del Centro Centro Naval* 14 (1896–7), p. 409
_____, 'Los Nuevos buques. Sus características principales' in *Boletín del Centro Centro Naval* 15 (1897–8), p. 451

Boletín del Centro Naval, Buenos Aires, 1882–1904
El Comercio, Punta Arenas, Chile, 1901–2
El Deber, Bahía Blanca, Argentina, 1895–8
La Nación, Buenos Aires, 1872–1902
La Nueva Provincia, Bahía Blanca, Argentina, 1898–1902
La Prensa, Buenos Aires, 1872–1902
Revista del Club Naval y Militar, Buenos Aires, 1884–7

Fundación Histarmar website: www.histarmar.com.ar [accessed November 2017]

Marine Nationale
The Battleship *Iéna* (1898)

Philippe Caresse

ÉNA IS THE FRENCH NAME for the Thuringian town of Jena lying on the banks of the River Saale in central Germany. To naval historians it is the cradle of the renowned optical firm of Carl Zeiss but in France it will always be remembered for Napoleon's crushing defeat of the Prussian Army on 14 October 1806, the battle which prompted the philosopher Hegel to declare 'the end of history'. Small wonder, then,

that France should lose little time in naming a major vessel after one of her greatest victories, in this case the 90-gun ship of the line launched at Rochefort in 1813 which remained on the navy list until 31 December 1864. However, it is the battleship launched in 1898 that provides the subject of this chapter, for which fate had an end in store almost as explosive as Napoleon's victory one hundred years earlier.

Origins

Defeat in the Franco-Prussian War of 1870–1 resulted in a significant reallocation of France's military expenditure.[1] The loss of Alsace and Lorraine obliged the government to prioritise

[1] John Jordan & Philippe Caresse, *French Battleships of World War One* (Barnsley, S. Yorks.: Seaforth Publishing, 2017).

The battleship *Jauréguiberry* (1893), a unit of the notorious *flotte d'échantillons*. (Marius Bar)

the construction of a new line of fortifications at enormous cost and with consequences that were immediately felt in the navy. Moreover, despite its considerable fighting power the reputation of the French fleet had not been enhanced by any significant action during the recent conflict and it was therefore easy for the de facto president of the Third Republic, Adolphe Thiers (1871–3), to declare it an 'instrument de luxe'. This prompted a reassessment of the role of the navy as a whole and in 1880 the so-called *faillite du cuirassé* ('end of the battleship') was declared in favour of more modest vessels such as the cruiser and above all the torpedo boat which were not only faster but required less financial upkeep. These developments and the ongoing naval rivalry with Britain prefigured the ascendancy of the so-called *Jeune École* which eschewed the construction of major units in favour of small, powerfully equipped torpedo vessels intended to engage enemy battlefleets and fast cruisers to attack merchant shipping. The *Jeune École* reached its apogee during the brief tenure of Admiral Théophile Aube as Minister of Marine between 1886 and 1887 during which no effort was spared to halt the development of the battleship and limit its displacement to 11,000 tons. Under a succession of reactionary and counter-reactionary Ministers of Marine this strategy not only obstructed any coherent development of the navy for a generation, but resulted in the parade of hybrid barbette ships of doubtful military value which ploughed France's coastal waters for several decades: *Hoche* (1886), *Neptune* (1887), *Marceau* (1887), *Magenta* (1890) and *Brennus* (1891).

Nonetheless, in 1889 design work began on a class of battleships intended to displace 13,000 tons and mounting two 13.4in (340mm) and two 10.8in (274mm) guns in enclosed turrets which came to be known as the 1890 Programme. The *Jeune École*, however, immediately took fright at this displacement, which in the event did not exceed 12,400 tons, with Minister of Marine Edouard Barbey insisting that the calibre be revised downwards to 12in (305mm). Plans were developed concurrently by no less than five designers and curiously no one in the navy seems to have been concerned about the possibility of commissioning five different battleships, albeit answering to the same design brief. What resulted between 1897 and 1898 was the memorable but flawed *flotte d'échantillons* (sample fleet) consisting of *Masséna*, *Carnot*, *Jauréguiberry*, *Charles Martel* and *Bouvet*. Although the amount of freeboard and tumble-home was reckoned to afford the ships a degree of steadiness as gunnery platforms, stability was in fact severely compromised and the great naval

Iéna lying peacefully at anchor off Toulon in 1905, two years before her brief service career came to a violent end. *(Philippe Caresse Collection)*

constructor Émile Bertin rightly identified them as liable to capsizing. Of these design faults *Bouvet* duly paid the price in the Dardanelles on 18 March 1915, lost in two minutes on a mine in a disaster which left seventy-five survivors out of a complement of 723.

Meanwhile, on 25 August 1892 the Conseil des Travaux (Board of Works) received a note from Minister of Marine Auguste Burdeau requiring it to submit studies for the construction of a new class of battleship. The 1892 Programme was the subject of much discussion with respect to displacement and the disposition of the armament. The project was entrusted to the constructor Alphonse Thibaudier who had participated in designing Yokosuka dockyard in 1867 and had unsuccessfully submitted a design to the 1890 programme. The Charlemagne class which resulted consisted of three homogenous battleships based on the hull design of *Bouvet*. Where the main armament was concerned, not only was the earlier practice of disparity in the calibre of the heavy ordnance discarded, but the lozenge arrangement abandoned in favour of two 12in twin turrets disposed fore and aft in the manner of the British Royal Sovereign class. The armament was completed by ten 5.5in (138.6mm) guns in casemates and on the shelter deck, eight 4in (100mm) and twenty 1.85in (47mm) guns, together with four 17.7in (450mm) torpedo tubes of which two were below the waterline. Protection consisted of an armour belt to a maximum of 15.75in (400mm), along with 3.5in (90mm) on the conning tower and 10.6–13.8in (270–350mm) on the turrets.

The Charlemagne class was completed after the six- or seven-year lapse typical of late nineteenth-century French warship construction and entered service between 1899 and 1900. However, already on 23 December 1896 Thibaudier had, at the request of the minister, submitted the following list of modifications to the designs:

– Improvement of protection by increasing the height of the upper layer of the armour belt from 19.7 to 35.4in (500 to 900mm)
– Belt thickness reduced from 15.75 to 12.6in (400 to 320mm) thanks to the use of Harveyised steel
– Tactical range increased to 5,200nm
– Engine power increased from 14,350 to 15,000ihp.

The armament was unchanged. On 11 February 1897 the Directeur du Matériel (Controller of Procurement), acting on the minister's orders, duly submitted the project for scrutiny by the Construction Committee. These preliminary studies were passed by the minister to the Section

Technique (Technical Department) with orders to assess the consequences of reducing the 12in armament from four guns to three by mounting a single-gun turret aft instead of the twin turret as originally planned. It was also requested that provision be made for substituting the 5.5in guns with 6.5in (164.7mm) weapons. In addition, a note from the Technical Department stating that an armour belt extending only 35in (900mm) above the waterline was not acceptable in a modern vessel resulted in approval being given for incorporation of the system of underwater protection first adopted by the Majestic-class battleships of the Royal Navy.

On the basis of these discussions, Thibaudier prepared a revised design which he submitted on 9 February 1897. The removal of a 12in gun and the replacement of the 5.5in guns by 6.5in weapons permitted the 4.3in (110mm) armour of the conning tower to be restored and the secondary belt extended along the length of the ship. Nonetheless, Thibaudier believed that the removal of the 12in gun would represent a significant reduction in the ship's offensive capabilities in comparison to foreign vessels, and the final studies of the second design, including a restored fourth gun, were subsequently approved at a meeting held on 4 March 1897, the Construction Committee declaring that: 'This design represents a marked improvement on the original scheme, chiefly on account of her defensive strength, stability in action, tactical range and, to a lesser degree, on account of her offensive strength and speed.'[2] The order was placed with Brest Dockyard on 3 April 1897. A revised estimate completed on 31 March 1899 put the cost of building her at 25,582,371 francs.

Hull, Armour and Equipment

The hull had an overall length of 401ft (122.31m) and 396.4ft (120.82m) at the waterline. Maximum beam was 68.4ft (20.84m) and 68.3ft (20.81m) at the waterline, *Iéna* having the pronounced tumblehome typical of French vessels of the era. Maximum draught was 24.3ft (7.42m) forward and 27.8ft (8.46m) aft. The standard displacement was 11,687 tons, rising to 12,104 tons at full load. The main armour belt of Harveyised steel ranged from 9.1–12.6in (232–320mm) and was 7.8ft (2.4m) high. Vertical protection above it consisted of 3in (76mm) in the lower sections and 0.5in (12mm)

<hr>

[2] Cited in Philippe Caresse, *Histoire des cuirassés d'escadre* Iéna et Suffren : *Genèses, caractéristiques et carrières* (Outreau, Pas-de-Calais: Lela Presse, 2009), p. 17; references to this work are henceforth cited in brackets in the text.

Iéna's forward 12in turret, bridge and foremast seen from the eyes of the ship as she lies at Villefranche in 1904 or 1905. Note the 1.85in guns on the foremast platform and the stars on the tompions protecting the muzzles of the main armament. *(Philippe Caresse Collection)*

in the upper. The armoured deck had a maximum thickness of 3in (76mm), the armoured transverse bulkheads fore and aft being of 3.5in (90mm). The conning tower was faced by 11.7in (298mm) of armour, with 10in (254mm) at the rear and a roof consisting of two layers of 1in (25mm) plate. The communications tube received 7.9in (200mm) and the turrets 10.9–12.5in (278–318mm) of armour with a 2in (50mm) roof, while the trunking was of 10in (254mm). Casemate protection was 3.2in (90mm), the gun shields having 4.7in (120mm). Total weight of armour was 4,135 tons.

The enclosed bridge was positioned above the conning tower. It consisted of four bay windows forward and two on each side with a pair of doors giving access from aft. Attached to the after part of the foremast was the lamp room, while a bridge for the admiral and his staff was positioned immediately forward of the mainmast. On 18 May 1902 the squadron commander Rear Admiral René Maquis made a specific request to the Minister of Marine for a wireless to be installed in *Iéna* as a matter of urgency, the equipment being fitted in an extension of the maintop superstructure. The foremast and mainmast, each rising to a height of 130ft (40m) above the waterline, were fitted with platforms carrying 1.85in guns. There were six 23.6in (600mm) 66A searchlights, four positioned in the superstructure and one in each mast. Where ground tackle was concerned, there were two 15-ton Marrel-type anchors in hawsepipes, a reserve Marrel anchor of 7.49 tons to starboard, two kedge anchors of 1.8 tons and another of 705lb (320kg). There were twenty boats, notably a launch, two steam picket boats and five cutters, all of which had mountings for 1.85in (47mm) and/or 1.5in (37mm) guns. Handling of the larger boats was carried out using four swan-necked cranes located to port and starboard of the after funnel.

The hull below the waterline was painted in a dark 'Schweinfurth' green, delineated by a 10in (254mm) boot topping in white. The hull above the waterline was black while the superstructure and masts were painted in a buff colour, with the exception of the 12in guns which were menacingly done in black until shortly before *Iéna* was destroyed when they were made homogenous with the rest of the superstructure. The buff coverage was extended to the level of the waist in 1906. The funnel tops were black.

Armament and Propulsion

Iéna was armed with four 12in (305mm)/40-calibre guns of the 1893/1896 model in two enclosed turrets manufactured by the Société de Construction des Batignolles of Nantes and traversing on bearings. These were provided with three sighting positions under hoods: one for the layer of each of the two guns and a third for the turret captain in the centre. The guns could fire 745lb (338kg) shells to a range of 13,123yds (12,000m) at a maximum elevation of 15 degrees with an initial velocity of 2,559ft/sec (780m/sec) and at the rate of a round per minute. There were 180 rounds in the magazines to give three hours of fire. Fire control consisted of a pair of large

Iéna launched at Brest on 1 September 1898. The letters 'R. F.' stand for 'République Française'. *(Philippe Caresse Collection)*

Brute force employed in one of the engine rooms of the battleship *Charles Martel* (1893) whose plant was similar to that of *Iéna*. *(Philippe Caresse Collection)*

rangefinding tables in the conning tower, but it was not until 1907 that 9ft (2.75m) Barr & Stroud rangefinders were mounted on either side of the bridge.

Secondary armament consisted of eight 6.5in (164.7mm)/45-calibre 1893 model guns mounted in the port and starboard casemates. Each could fire a 114lb (52kg) shell to a range of 9,842yds (9,000m) at 15 degrees elevation with a muzzle velocity of 2,838ft/sec (865m/sec). Theoretical rate of fire was two to three rounds per minute. There were 1,606 shells in the magazines, again

for three hours of fire. There were also eight 4in (100mm)/45-calibre 1893 model guns in shielded mountings on the shelter deck and on the forward and after superstructure. Each gun fired a 56lb (25.5kg) shell with a range of up to 10,390yds (9,500m) at 20 degrees elevation with a muzzle velocity of 2,329ft/sec (710m/sec). The theoretical firing rate was six rounds per minute in rapid fire and three per minute in continuous fire. There were 2,074 shells in the magazines to ensure three hours of fire.

The tertiary armament comprised twenty Hotchkiss 1.85in (47mm)/50-calibre 1885 model guns positioned atop the forward and after superstructure, on the foremast and mainmast platforms and also on the main deck. Each gun fired a 5.4lb (2.46kg) shell to a range of 4,374yds (4,000m) at 24 degrees elevation with a muzzle velocity of 2,001ft/sec (610m/sec). The theoretical firing cycle was fifteen rounds per minute in rapid fire and seven per minute in continuous fire. Magazine capacity was 15,000 shells.

So much for the specifications. Writing in 1903, Rear Admiral René-Julien Marquis, then commanding the 2nd Division of the Mediterranean Fleet, expressed significant reservations as to the likely effectiveness of this battery against the torpedo-boat attacks so feared by the capital ships of the day:

> One could say so much about the division of our 47mm guns into three tiers. However, it would seem that successive reports from gunnery exercises have exhausted the list of

arguments in favour of a better disposition. We shall have to put up with the existing arrangements while regretting that we will never be able to attain the desired level of safety from torpedo-boat attack. The number of ready-use rounds is insufficient and the hoists are desperately slow. It is, in my view, a mistake not to accord more importance to the role of the light armament now that we no longer have the Bullivant nets to protect our ships. The 47mm guns, much more so than the large- and medium-calibre guns, will have to fire at night; yet these are the only guns without a fire-control system designed for night firing. This is a deficiency which needs to be rectified as soon as possible. [34]

There is no evidence it ever was. The armament was rounded off with four 17.7in (450mm) torpedo tubes, two submerged and two above the waterline. The 1889 model torpedoes measured 16.5ft (5.04m) and weighed a total of 968lb (439kg), of which the charge accounted for 176lb (80kg). Twelve spare torpedoes were carried of which four were practice units. Aside from the 1.85in (47mm) and 1.5in (37mm) guns for mounting in the ship's boats, the landing party was equipped with two 2.6in (65mm) 1881 model field guns.

Iéna carried twenty Belleville mixed (coal and oil) boilers disposed in three boiler rooms. Rated at 256psi ($18kg/cm^2$), these supplied steam to three four-cylinder triple-expansion engines built by Forges et Chantiers de la Méditerranée at Le Havre with a designed horsepower of 15,300 on three shafts. The boilers were first flashed up on 31 March 1900 and the ship attained 18.11 knots at 16,589.4ihp during trials on 16 July 1901. Bunker capacity was 770 tons of coal at normal load, rising to 1,164 tons at maximum load for a range of 4,600 nautical miles at 6.3 knots and 3,100 at 14.1 knots. The 80V electricity supply was provided by 600A/82V and 1200A/82V axle-tree dynamos.

Construction

Iéna was laid down at Brest Dockyard on 3 April 1897, built under the supervision of constructors Maugas and Lyasse and launched on the evening tide of 1 September 1898. Five days later the journal *Le Yacht* carried a report of the event:

> One rarely sees so large a crowd at the launch of a ship as that for *Iéna* last Thursday. At two o'clock the dockyard gate was opened and an impatient crowd invaded both banks of the Penfeld. *Iéna*'s hull, longer than that of *Gaulois*, the previous battleship launched, seems to have a less ponderous appearance. However, no difference can be discerned at first sight: here were the same casemates and the same superstructure for medium and light guns. Let us hope that *Iéna*'s lines will not be spoiled by the hideous battlement structures which, rising from the base of the masts, disfigure *Gaulois* and *Charlemagne*. Rear Admiral [Auguste Jean Marie Le Borgne] de Kerambosquer, *Préfet Maritime*,[3] presided

Iéna nearing completion at Brest in December 1898 or January 1899. The after turret awaits its 12in guns but the rest of her armament has been installed including a 1.85in gun on the stern walk and others on the mainmast platform. Note the imposing buildings of the Port Militaire rising beyond. *(Philippe Caresse Collection)*

---

[3] Though invariably a naval officer, the Préfet Maritime (Maritime Prefect) is a civil servant with authority over maritime affairs in a given region and reports directly to the government and the Chief of Staff.

over the ceremony, and Constructor 1st Class Maugas, who supervised the work, directed the launch operations. At 1310 the dockyard workers began knocking out the timber supports and at about 1400 *Iéna* began to slide first slowly and then faster as the massive hull entered the water, stopping almost within her own length. The port authorities then took charge of the hull to guide it to the fitting-out basin. In the meantime the *Préfet* summoned the constructor in charge of the launch and congratulated him warmly. [46–7]

After the ceremony the battleship was towed to the fitting-out basin to receive the various elements of the superstructure, her guns, and the equipment necessary to complete her armament; *Le Yacht*'s hopes for *Iéna*'s appearance were to be dashed as her upper works showed no improvement in this respect. On 8 August 1899 Capitaine de vaisseau (Captain) Duroch was appointed to oversee completion of the work, officially becoming her first commander on 1 November. Already on 9 October he had written a letter demanding the mounting of *Iéna*'s armament and the embarkation of 115 specialist sailors. Turret assembly began on 3 December along with the installation of the engines and boilers. On 22 January 1900 a further 166 men were drafted to the ship and November found her alongside in No. 8 Basin at Salou where preparations were being made to test her submerged torpedo tubes.

Iéna sailed from Brest for the first time on 4 January 1901. Having carried out compass trials off l'Auberlac'h in Brittany she returned to port on the 10th and the following day began engine trials which continued progressively until 19 April. The boilers became operational in May when trials began of the secondary and tertiary armament. High-speed engine trials were successfully completed on 1 July. On the 16th the machinery was dismantled and the ship docked for refitting between 1 and 14 August. Her first commanding officer, Capt. Pailhès, was appointed on 1 November having earlier been responsible for submerged defences in the Brest naval sector.

Service

Iéna entered service on 14 April 1902, five years after being laid down, being assigned to the 2nd Division of the Mediterranean Squadron. Four days later she received orders to make for

Toulon, and the following morning duly weighed anchor and sailed on her maiden voyage as a commissioned vessel of the Marine Nationale. It was to be an eventful trip. No sooner had she cleared Brest than the engines were worked up to ninety revolutions, the ship making for Cap Villano once the Ar-Men light had been rounded. The Bay of Biscay lived up to its reputation and speed had to be reduced to 12 knots. There were also problems of a technical nature with the rudder which jammed on more than one occasion when manoeuvring. The defect was attributed to flooding of the circuit-breakers of the servomotors when the rudder was at maximum angle, requiring intervention from the engineering personnel to avoid the ship having to return to Brest. Then at 1910 on the 24th, as *Iéna* was being battered in a heavy swell in the Gulf of Lyons, a man was ordered to recover the mooring of the port boom but was washed overboard and lost despite efforts to find him. At 2100 *Iéna* resumed her course for Toulon, which she reached at 0800 the following morning. All in all, an inauspicious start.

On 1 May Rear Admiral Marquis shifted his flag from *Charles Martel* to *Iéna* which thereby became flagship of the 2nd Division of the Mediterranean Fleet, the main units of his command now consisting of *Iéna*, *Bouvet* and *Jauréguiberry*. On the same day Capt. Voiellaud succeeded Capt. Pailhès in command of *Iéna*, which was brought to full complement by the drafting of 248 men from *Charles Martel*. *Iéna*'s

officers declared themselves satisfied with the quality of this draft, but less so with a contingent of fifteen hard cases offloaded by the armoured cruiser *Montcalm* before embarking President Émile Loubet on a state visit to Russia: 'As for the *matelots de pont* (seaman ratings), they represent the sweepings of the navy, those whose physical, intellectual and moral qualities kept them from attending school and who are destined to be absorbed at the bottom of the pile by the various branches aboard.' [53] That *Iéna*'s ship's company was nonetheless brought to a high degree of efficiency was demonstrated in May of the following year when the crew succeeded in embarking 612 tons of coal in four hours at an average rate of 153 tons per hour, a performance which earned the congratulations of Vice Admiral Édouard Pottier, by then in command of the Mediterranean Fleet.

With this *Iéna* joined the fleet in the fullest sense and began the round of port visits that was to fill her summer months for the next five years and which no doubt made this the most agreeable naval station in the world: La Ciotat, Port de Bouc, Port Vendres, Sète, Villefranche, Salins d'Hyères, St-Tropez, Marseilles and Golfe Juan on the French Mediterranean coast; Mers el-Kebir, Algiers, Bougie, Philippeville, Bône, Bizerta, La Goulette in North Africa, and Ajaccio in Corsica. Indeed, she rarely left Mediterranean waters for the more challenging conditions of the Atlantic, a point brought home by an incident in

Brest harbour on 11 August 1902. Needing to shift to another mooring, *Iéna* had to rely on the tug *Travailleur* to execute the manoeuvre since she did not have her boilers flashed up. Unfortunately, a powerful gust of wind put the two vessels in difficulty and a collision was narrowly averted. The port commander, Capt. Pissére, sent the following note to the Naval General Staff after the incident:

I believe ships should have their boilers lit when shifting their moorings. This is how things are done at Brest, where in my experience of command over the course of two years in the Northern Fleet two accidents which could have resulted on the first occasion in a collision between the [armoured cruiser] *Bruix* and the [battleship] *Formidable*, and on the second between the [cruiser] *Surcouf* and the same battleship were avoided by judicious use of the ships' engines. I know that at Toulon, where this is not standard practice, they do not need to take the currents which are a feature of Brest into account, but we on the other hand don't

Sailors gather along the port rails as *Iéna* enters Villefranche in 1903. Note the 33ft picket boat on its crutches and the swan-neck crane used to hoist it in and out.
(*Philippe Caresse Collection*)

have an *Indefatigable* [harbour tug] with 1500hp of pulling power. For myself, I have always been of the opinion that lighting boilers is a sensible precaution and I see no disadvantage in the procedure. [54–5]

In June 1903 came *Iéna*'s first exercise in showing the flag when the Mediterranean Fleet sailed for Cartagena under Vice Admiral Pottier to salute King Alfonso XIII on having reached his majority the previous year, part of a rapprochement with Spain in the context of what became the Franco-British Entente Cordiale (see *Alfonso XIII*). The fleet sailed from Toulon and reached Cartagena on 23 June having been joined by the Oran mobile torpedo-boat defence flotilla en route. *Jauréguiberry* and *Carnot* were unable to enter the inner roads but the young king came aboard *Iéna* and commented on her 'splendid appearance' and 'sumptuous orderliness'. Having performed some manoeuvres, the fleet sailed for Alicante before returning to Toulon on the 29th.

The following spring found *Iéna* at Barcelona from 4–10 April, and then at Naples and Genoa between 24 April and 5 May as part of a state visit paid by President Loubet to King Victor Emmanuel III of Italy, including a review off Naples attended by the Italian and French Mediterranean Fleets. The battleships *Suffren*,

Saint Louis and *Gaulois* formed the 1st Division, with the 2nd Division comprising *Iéna* (Rear Admiral Léon Barnaud), *Bouvet* and *Charlemagne*. Loubet was embarked in the armoured cruiser *Marseillaise* accompanied by

LIFE ABOARD

Iéna was designed for a peacetime complement of thirty-three officers and 668 ratings, with accommodation for a staff of fifteen officers and sixty-three men when she was serving as a flagship – a total of 779. Some 50 tons of provisions were embarked for forty-five days at sea, along with 6 tons of wood to fire the galleys. Drinking water was stowed in twenty-two tanks holding between 176 and 660gal (800–3,000l) each. Kept under lock and key was the main libation of the Marine Nationale, no less than 4,207gal (19,126l) of wine, in addition to 62gal (280l) of spirits.

As in other navies, a new emphasis on physical fitness was reflected in the five instructors embarked to lead the men in gymnastics, including provision of a high bar; the fact that eight *prévôts d'armes* (ship's police) were required to supervise this suggests that it was far from popular, but there were also classes in boxing and the sparring game known as *bâton*. Further evidence of concern for the wellbeing of the crew comes in Capt. Voiellaud's report on a general inspection conducted in July 1903:

Another of the modifications required to promote the efficiency of the ship relates to the problems presented by the hygiene of these men. As it is, the crew washbasins are positioned under the forward 305mm turret and cannot handle more than thirty men at once, nor do they have any showers. With respect to the two washplaces reserved for engineering personnel, these are well appointed but lack ventilation. We have suggested that the sailors use individual basins in an effort to abolish communal washing out of the tubs. More than two hundred have been embarked but in vain; the sailors prefer the tub. [56]

Reading this, Rear Admiral Marquis issued Voiellaud this firm reply:

The basin doesn't suit the habits of our men who always keep the upper parts of their bodies very clean. They soap their torsos each morning, taking water from the tub with both hands, and the water splashed over the decks is

Pothau, *Latouche-Tréville* and *Chanzy* of the same type together with an assortment of cruisers and destroyers. The summer cruise that year took the fleet to the Levant with visits to Suda Bay, Beirut, Messina, Smyrna, Mytilene, Salonika and the Piraeus between 17 May and 3 July 1904. Two years later *Iéna*, *Gaulois* and *Bouvet* were back at Naples, dispensing humanitarian aid in the wake of the catastrophic eruption of Mount Vesuvius of 7 April 1906 which destroyed the town of Ottaiano and claimed 216 lives, the French squadron distributing 9,000 rations to some of the 34,000 left homeless. A year later it would be *Iéna*'s turn to receive succour.

removed when the ship is cleaned. The men would have insufficient water in a little basin to wash anything other than their faces. [56]

It was quite another matter where the slop-buckets of the offices and petty officers were concerned. These were of porcelain with a galvanised iron cover. However, the servants charged with emptying them soon discovered the tendency of the handles to slip out of their aperture and that the buckets themselves were none too robust. The Marine, or Royale as it was known, soon adopted a more amenable solution.

The accommodation spaces were heated by steam, but this system cannot have been much utilised since *léna* spent practically her entire career in the Mediterranean. To the contrary, it was the immense heat in the engine spaces which was a matter of concern. In 1904 it was intended to take the opportunity of a cruise to Djibouti to celebrate the opening of the Djibouti–Addis Ababa railway to perform a detailed study, first of the ventilation and refrigeration of the magazines, and then of the ventilation of certain engine spaces, particularly the dynamo and boiler rooms which frequently reached temperatures of between 56 and 62°C (133–143°F). Special permission was requested from the Commander of the 2nd Division of the Mediterranean Fleet for an engineer to embark at Toulon to study the matter. In the event, Emperor Menelik II of Ethiopia cancelled his attendance at the festivities, the voyage was called off and *léna* instead joined the summer cruise to the Levant which cannot have been very much cooler than the Gulf of Aden.

Despite claims that the subsequent destruction of the ship was due to sabotage, such indications as there are suggest that crew morale and *esprit de corps* were good throughout *léna*'s career. The senior officers were popular among the men, the ship had held the squadron coaling record for sixteen months straight and it was generally acknowledged that her living arrangements represented a considerable advance on earlier designs. In fact, the evidence for human agency in the disaster that befell her extends no further than a death threat issued to Sub Lt Boucheron in November 1906, whereas that for material deficiency is overwhelming. [83]

88. MARINE — Le Cuisinier brûle le Café

Brewing coffee on deck during a standeasy. *(Philippe Caresse Collection)*

Men of the *léna* dousing themselves at a washtub on the forecastle deck when coming off duty, a source of some irritation to Capt. Voiellaud in 1903. *(Philippe Caresse Collection)*

Iéna welcomed to Naples in April 1906 while on a humanitarian mission to assist victims of the eruption of Vesuvius earlier that month. *(Philippe Caresse Collection)*

Evaluation

How might we evaluate *Iéna* as a fighting vessel from the evidence of her brief career? On 21 October 1903 *Iéna, Bouvet, Jauréguiberry, Saint Louis, Charlemagne* and *Gaulois* anchored at Palma for a brief courtesy visit to the Balearic Islands. Six days later they made for Ibiza before weighing anchor and sailing for Toulon on the 30th. For two days *Iéna* and the battleships of the 1st and 2nd Division were buffeted by a severe storm north of the Balearics in a swell of up to 26ft (8m). That night *Jauréguiberry* lost formation and it was not until dawn that she sighted *Bouvet* and managed to regain station. Meanwhile, *Iéna* (then commanded by Capt. Voiellaud) held her course and led the battleships in line ahead at two points to the wind and at a speed of 3 knots, pitching heavily but not shipping too much water. To port the cruiser *Galilée* and the torpedo boat destroyers *Épieu* and *Rapière* battled through heavy seas. Although *Iéna*'s seakeeping qualities invited favourable

comment from Capt. Bouxin in the report he prepared on turning over command in November 1905, as with Rear Admiral Marquis

two years earlier her military capabilities received a rather less complimentary verdict:

Iéna is an excellent ship and keeps the sea admirably. Her pitching and rolling movements are light and she rides the waves gently. The navigating bridge is well designed. One might criticise the arrangement of the ground tackle and the mooring bitts. The manoeuvre is a lengthy one and becomes very delicate when mooring in port. But on the whole one gets the feeling of having as seaworthy a ship beneath one's feet as could possibly be expected. Taken all round, the ship performs well, one can handle her as one pleases so long as she is not in shallow water…

From a military standpoint, *Iéna* is a first-class vessel. One could certainly criticise her defects as in all vessels of this type. The armour of the waterline belt has been exaggerated at the expense of that of the superstructure, and it is feared that the casemates – the lower part of which are unprotected – would soon be put out of action. The guns mounted are too few in number and the calibre of the weapons no longer meets combat requirements; this could only be remedied by increasing the rate of fire, but the hoists are quite unarmoured and supply of the guns would be affected. It is essential that the fire-control positions be protected since the conning tower is too small to allow the large numbers of men required by those duties to operate there. The subdivision is well designed; it allows ease of movement and

Iéna's last commanding officer, Capt. Paul Adigard, who perished in his cabin on 12 March 1907. *(Philippe Caresse Collection)*

Rear Admiral Henri-Louis Manceron, commander of the 2nd Division of the Mediterranean Fleet, who barely escaped sharing his flag captain's fate. *(Philippe Caresse Collection)*

effective oversight. Despite these faults, *Iéna* is an excellent warship and could successfully engage the majority of warships in service with foreign powers. [51–2]

Sadly, fate had a different end in store for *Iéna*. Indeed, the principal actors in her great drama were waiting in the wings even as Bouxin penned these lines, the ship still flying the flag of Rear Admiral Henri-Louis Manceron as commander of the 2nd Division of the Mediterranean Fleet, with Capt. Paul Adigard in command and Capitaine de frégate (Commander) Amédée Maire Joseph Van Gaver as her executive officer as dawn broke on Tuesday, 12 March 1907.

Disaster

On 4 March 1907 *Iéna* entered No. 2 Dry Dock in the Missiessy Basin of Toulon harbour for hull maintenance and inspection of the rudder shaft, the seal of which had leaked from the beginning of her service life. The opportunity would also be taken for repairs to the boiler and furnace casings as well as the installation of trunking for the two steam uptakes. Before doing so *Iéna* had landed all her shells and dry gun cotton in line with the requirements set forth in a ministerial order of 6 July 1892. Her immobilisation was not intended to extend beyond the 19th when the fleet was scheduled to sail for five days of manoeuvres, the 2nd Division being required to make for Genoa to attend the launching of the pre-dreadnought battleship *Roma*. Dawn on 12 March found *Suffren* in No. 3 Dock while *Masséna* had vacated No. 1 Dock early that morning. It was a beautiful sunny day with a light mistral blowing to cool the atmosphere. At 1030 the stand-easy sounded aboard *Iéna*, and the crew prepared to rig the messdecks for lunch which was served at 1100 while the dockyard workers made for their refectory ashore. Decks and passageways emptied until 'hands to work' was sounded at 1300. Capt. Adigard was in his cabin preparing to go ashore with Rear Admiral Manceron's chief of staff, Cdr Vertier, and an aide-de-camp, Lieutenant de vaisseau (Lieutenant) Dumesnil. Vertier was giving orders to his *fourrier* (quartermaster sergeant) in his cabin, which was opposite Adigard's. Lt Thomas, who was to assume command while these officers were ashore, was in his cabin. Rear Admiral Manceron himself was seated at his desk in his cabin.

At 1335 Lt Marc was standing on the dock between the two battleships, near *Suffren*'s gangway, his back to *Iéna* while engaged in conversation with the aide-de-camp of Admiral Charles Touchard, Commander-in-Chief of the

Mediterranean Fleet. Suddenly he noticed the expression change on his companion's face. Turning round he saw that *Iéna* was ablaze from the mainmast to the after 12in turret. A succession of explosions ensued, the first muffled, the second much more violent. Fiery gases were propelled upwards via the magazine hoists and debris of all types was hurled into the air as flames roared through vents, portholes and scuttles while the ship began belching forth a yellowish pillar of smoke. Below deck the gases propagated along passageways throughout the ship from frame 78 to frame 61, shattering pipework and ducts as they went and leaving deep burn-marks on the steel itself. Quartier-maître torpilleur (Leading Torpedoman) Degaraby was beside the training engines in the after turret compartment:

I was opening the door to return to my storeroom when the first explosion occurred. I saw a flash come aft like a rocket from where I had just been and there was a cloud of yellow smoke. I heard the detonation immediately after seeing the flame. It wasn't that loud. I smelt an acrid odour that was not ether. I made my way to the steering compartment and climbed a ladder leading to the Admiral's lobby. Reaching it I found the lobby ablaze and descended again, the second explosion occurring while I was halfway down the ladder. I ascended once more to find only smoke without flames and was able to make my way through the Admiral's quarters. About two minutes elapsed between the first and second explosion. [63]

Witnesses counted a total of seven explosions, the times of which were noted aboard the armoured cruiser *Desaix*. The first deflagration was confirmed at 1335, followed by others at 1355, 1410, 1420, 1421, 1422, with the last being registered at about 1425. Paint began to burn and run near the conflagration and the linoleum on the decks ignited in the heat, the upper bridges on the mainmast collapsing towards the stern. Neither plating nor bulkheads offered any resistance and the after superstructure was flung against the flying bridge. The devastation extended from right aft to the forward 12in turret, beyond which the ship was left intact, but the bridge, conning tower and foretop were all heavily damaged. Below the main belt the hull was rent from port to starboard between frame 74 and 84, destroying all the machinery and leaving a hole large enough for a dynamo to tumble down into the dock. Damage in the vicinity was limited by the fact that the Missiessy Basin was at some remove from the main part of the dockyard but the explosions blew the roofs off three dockside workshops. Although the explosions were confined to the after magazines, one need only read an inventory of *Iéna*'s munitions to appreciate the violence of these deflagrations: forty-three high-explosive 12in shells filled with black powder and twenty-four with mélinite (picric acid), thirty-one semi-armour-piercing shells filled with mélinite and thirty-six capped armour-piercing shells. Also stowed were some 633 4in shells of all types, together with 5,298 1.85in rounds and nearly 15 tons of black powder.

Caught like Capt. Adigard in his cabin above

Smoke roils out of *Iéna* as the blaze takes hold in the No. 2 Dry Dock at Toulon on the afternoon of 12 March 1907. The ship visible in the foreground is her near-sister *Suffren* lying in the neighbouring dock in the Missiessy Basin. Only *Iéna*'s mainmast is visible, the foremast having been engulfed in smoke. *(Philippe Caresse Collection)*

the seat of the detonation, Rear Admiral Manceron left this account of his escape from the blast:

> I was seated at my desk in the course of writing a letter. Five minutes earlier Capt Adigard had entered and asked me: 'Admiral, will you have need of the boat? No. Well, I'm going to take it to attend the meeting with the *Préfet*.' Shortly after I felt as if I had been lifted off the deck. I had the impression that the explosion had occurred beneath my feet. When I discovered I was still alive after the explosion I began feeling my way out of my office. I struggled to find the door of my dining cabin because I had been hit by the bulkhead which had been dislodged by the explosion; perhaps it was that which saved my life. Shoving the partitions aside with my arms, I saw my steward streaming with blood. I said to him: 'Don't worry, they're only scratches.'
>
> Capt. Adigard's cabin did not have a fully closing door since so many people came and went through it; it was a door that swung open and shut freely, in other words a simple wooden frame with a padded interior, meaning that he took the full force of the blast without it meeting any resistance. By contrast, although the destructive effect on my cabin was identical, the door was always locked shut and I had entered through the door giving onto the battery with a scuttle facing outboard. Some of the force of the gas had served to dislodge the bulkhead and also rip the door from its hinges which then struck me and so saved my life by acting as a shield.
>
> The effect of the disaster on my office was identical to that of my unfortunate Capt. Adigard and I still wonder how I got out alive.
>
> I had just a few steps to take before reaching my lobby. I got out only with difficulty as it was filled with smoke. My impression is that between 10 and 50 seconds had elapsed. On reaching the lobby I noticed that there were many officers gathered at the entrance to the dock. Having taken hold on the shelter deck it was terrifying how quickly the blaze spread from one end of the ship to the other. It is absolutely necessary that we abandon our abominable painting procedures. It is unacceptable for us to continue painting our ships as we have been doing, and greasing them three or four times a week.
>
> The seat of the disaster was aft and 10 minutes later the fore part of the ship was ablaze. [63]

Also in his cabin was Lt Dumesnil who had a similar tale to tell:

> I felt a terrifying concussion smash through my cabin, an extremely violent shock like the blast of a 305mm gun fired near me. Everything was turned upside down. My cabin was darkened with smoke which entered through a scuttle on *Suffren*'s side. The door was dislodged on the port side; I rushed at it to reach the officers' wardroom; the gangways were on the starboard side. I was hit by the smoke and the vortex of flame. I was slightly asphyxiated. However, I immediately recovered my sang-froid, climbed out of my scuttle and reached dry land. [64]

Mécanicien en chef (Chief Artificer) Borelli was on deck beside the after funnel when the first explosion occurred. He immediately went below via the auxiliary hatch and entered the workshop:

> I was in the workshop within half a minute of the first explosion having occurred. It didn't seem very powerful to me and I attributed it to falling shores striking the hull. It seemed to me that a number of heavy objects were falling at the same time. I had a look to see whether the ship was inclined. At the same time I realised that electric power had failed and I looked to see whether any steam was escaping from the boilers. Then came a second explosion which was very much stronger than the first. 'We must get away from here,' I told the men. We gathered dockside and I looked into the bottom of the dock where I could see that the shores were burning. As the gangway was empty, I returned on board to see whether there was any means of flooding the forward magazines. The gangway was deserted and there were men escaping along a hawser. The flames advanced from the starboard side aft. There was no smoke. At that moment I noticed an artificer who was entirely covered with *terre jaune* [a yellow powder given off by Powder B] grease; his hair was matted with it. He wasn't suffering at all. He came before me and I asked 'Where were you?' I knew he should have been in the after boiler room. 'And the others?' 'I don't believe any were saved.' This artificer had been in the upper part of boiler room; struck by the gases, he was able to escape and believed himself to be completely out of danger; he sent a telegram to his family informing them that he was safe and sound; but he fell ill during the night and succumbed to an infection the following day. [64]

Few were able to escape from the engine rooms where they were claimed by blast, fire, trauma or asphyxiation. Bodies were found at their posts in the starboard engine room and more by the exit ladders both there and in the centre engine room, indicating that they had attempted to escape before being killed. Some stokers had sufficient time to extinguish the boiler fires before making the supreme sacrifice. Meanwhile, Second-maître timonier (Petty Officer Quartermaster 2nd Class) Guillou was gathering his laundry from the fo'c'sle at the moment of the catastrophe. As he recalled,

> I felt a jolt forward. I looked up and noticed flashes to starboard. I took two or three steps as the crew started coming on deck forward, the doors were closed and the gangway manned. I went back, stopped for a moment, gathered a rope which extended from the ship to the dock, and then descended feet first. I don't know how I succeeded in clambering like this since it was very difficult given that the rope was slack. Twelve men came after me and only one fell: the steward. The first to follow me along the sling could get no further. He cried out, I passed him the end of a rope and led him to the dock. I saw an apprentice artificer who was on fire throw himself into the dock. [66]

Another who witnessed some acrobatic efforts to escape the ship was Lt Roland Nepveu:

> Over the gap, clinging to the chains which secured the bows to the dock, were two dozen men who had earlier been reluctant to brave the blazing gangway and now battled against fresh coal-tar to make it across with scant assistance from a smaller chain. One by one they fell ten metres into the void and there were already not less than ten broken bodies scattered at the bottom of the dock. [71]

Lying under the large crane of the Missiessy Basin was the battleship *Patrie* preparing to be refloated. Her commanding officer, Capt. Prat, immediately grasped that the only means of dousing the conflagration was to batter down the dock gates. With the authorisation of the Préfet Maritime of Toulon, Vice Admiral Marquis, he ordered a 6.5in shell fired at the dock gates, but the practice round in question simply rebounded off the gate and came to rest in the dockyard wall. Alongside *Iéna* men rushed to the dock gates to open the sluices in order to flood the dock. Enseigne de vaisseau (Sub Lieutenant) Roux and Premier maître (Chief Petty Officer) Thomas were already there, to be joined by Matelot mécanicien (Mechanician) Dublin of the *Desaix*. Unfortunately, as Borelli's testimony relates, the wrenches needed to open the sluices

Toulon - 5 - La Catastrophe de l'Iéna
C'est au moment où il cherchait à ouvrir la vanne du bassin, à l'endroit marqué d'une croix, que l'enseigne de vaisseau Roux mourut en héros coupé en deux par un éclat d'obus (12 Mars 1907)

Sub Lt Roux's death while attempting to open the sluices of the dock gates commemorated on a postcard, one of many produced in the wake of the disaster. The spot where he died is marked with a cross at the bottom of the photo and *Iéna*'s stern and nameplate can be seen immediately beyond. *(Philippe Caresse Collection)*

were not to hand and there was an agonising wait before a sailor appeared with them and Roux set to work. At that moment *Iéna* erupted in a powerful explosion and splinters of red-hot metal flew in all directions. When those who had flung themselves on their bellies began struggling to their feet it was to find that Sub Lt Roux had been literally cut in two by steel splinters. Chief Artificer Borelli describes the scene:

I was joined by Artificer Faure and we went to the rear of the dock where lay a barge containing a steam pump known as a Pétau used to douse fires. However, the boiler fire had been extinguished; the order had been to flash up in the evening for the night. I told Faure to stay there and returned to the quay. I gave orders to search for the wrenches to flood the dock. Many people went in search of them; at some point I cannot now recall I heard that the wrenches were on their way. The explosions continued; the most violent occurred during this period. Almost immediately after that the wrenches appeared; one was inserted into each sluice and they began to open. We left once they had done so. Mr Roux had been killed, cut in two on the lock gate of the dock. Mr Tiercelin was also wounded. Having opened these two gates we returned to the pump barge.

A whaler arrived and took us in tow; we came alongside the submarine quay and unloaded the wounded. I was unhurt; I said to the whaler: 'Let's go back and see if there's anything more to be done,' perhaps even recover Roux's body. The two men in the whaler and I searched for a way back but the explosions became more numerous and there was nothing more we could do. [64–5]

Another seeking any means of flooding the dock was Sub Lt Clémentel:

I was on watch and the captain had just passed the order to call away his boat. While making my way to the boat station I heard a first explosion. I thought there had been a rupture of scalding water in the dock. I hastened over and saw that the entire after part of the ship was ablaze. I said to myself: the magazine has exploded, the ship needs to be flooded. I had no idea what the detonation of a battleship would be like but I had the feeling that the ship was practically lost. I had 10,000kg [10 tons] of Powder B and 1,000kg [1 ton] of mélinite [under me]. I ran to the end of the dock to call the boat but I never saw it that afternoon. I ran between *Iéna* and *Suffren* crying 'The wrenches!' At that moment I reached the head of the dock where the crew was escaping down the bulwark netting. They were jostling to get down. 'Don't push,' I told them, 'the fire is only aft, you've got plenty of time.' At this point I noticed men near a winch which could have been the sluice of a waste-weir. 'Open it, open it!' I shouted to them. At that moment a naval constructor standing there said to me 'But, lieutenant, there are men in the dock!'

We were to starboard, the side on which all the smoke was issuing; everything was pitch black. At that moment I felt real fear and instinctively retreated. Having put the dock in which *Masséna* was lying between *Iéna* and myself, I saw Mr Tiercelin all covered in blood near the Pétau [pump] and went to him. It was then that the second explosion occurred. Flames issued from the after turret. My eyes were glued to this spectacle and this is what they told me: 'The moment that turret goes up the ship will be done for.' But it stayed put and earned my respect. [65]

This second explosion prompted Vice Admiral Marquis, the Préfet Maritime of Toulon, to order all able to do so to stay clear of the *Iéna* until the dock could be flooded. The officer responsible for shipping movements in the port of Toulon that afternoon was Capt. Dufayot de la Maisonneuve. His report, written three days after the event, records the efforts made to come to *Iéna*'s assistance as the disaster unfolded:

Admiral,
A first explosion was heard on 12 March at 1335. The sailor on watch in the tower having realised that this accident had occurred aboard the *Iéna*, the self-powered pump – the one mounted on the barge – the launches, and tugs with steam raised were sent to Missiessy. The others began flashing up their boilers. The large harbour tug *Travailleur* also made her way over there. The explosions came in quick succession, and Vice Admiral [Marquis] the Préfet Maritime gave the order to keep clear. The boilers of the Pétau pump on the barge, then tied up alongside the gate of the dock, had already been flashed up by Quartier-maître mécanicien [Leading Mechanician] Antoni and Ouvrier mécanicien [Mechanician's Assistant] Pin. However, they evacuated when ordered to do so. The same was true of the self-powered pump which took up a position close to the docks. The tug *Lamalgue* was in the Castigneau tidal basin when the first explosion occurred and her commander Petty Officer Albertini headed for Missiessy at his best speed and positioned himself alongside the gate of the dock in which *Suffren* was lying. He was uncoiling the hoses when a second explosion took place, with which he received the order to withdraw. The other tugs

remained in the southern part of the port awaiting the order to proceed.

On arrival the [Rear Admiral] Major General asked for volunteers to open the sluice-gates of the lock in which *Iéna* was lying.[4] Sub Lieutenant Roux was killed in the attempt, but Petty Officer Lacoste did not hesitate to come forward followed by Petty Officer Fondacci, Leading Seamen Cardi and Giorgi, and Able Seamen Publius, Colombani and Badin. These brave men risked their lives to perform this task and it is thanks to their devotion to duty that the midships and forward magazines were flooded.

[…]

Once the water level in the dock was sufficiently high the Préfet Maritime gave the order to attack the fire. The self-powered pump and that on wheels were installed at each end of the dock, while *Travailleur*, the water tankers and the tugs were positioned around *Iéna* from where their pumps flooded the entire ship. The fire soon died down. As soon as it was possible to walk on the plating a few men were sent to the fore part of the ship to prevent the fire from spreading, and to the after section to extinguish the flames in the cabins; gangways were placed to provide access to the companionways. The men returned that night and pumping continued. A small explosion

---

[4] The identity of the Rear Admiral-Major General is not known.

occurred forward at 0015. The hoses, passed through the scuttles, gushed large quantities of water into the ship. No fires were visible by 0800 but a thick smoke was still issuing from the lower decks.

With the fore topmast threatening to collapse at any time, the sailors lost no time in bringing it down. On the morning of the 13th an inspection began of the bowels of the ship with buckets and jets of water from the pumps were occasionally used to douse any sacks, bedding, etc. that were still smouldering. These operations took a long time. The fire was not completely extinguished until about 3 o'clock that afternoon. At this point an engineer officer of the port authority ordered his men to open the ejectors and intakes to allow the water filling the forward compartments to drain into those aft from which water was escaping through the holes opened in the hull by the explosions. This work was laborious but essential to permit removal of the bodies, and it continued until the 14th.

The artificers and sailors fetched water in buckets since it was impossible to operate the pumps as the water pressure was too low. As always, the staff of this Directorate went about their tasks zealously and with devotion to duty. As you are aware, they spent much of their time in the areas affected by the fire. The deputy director, Commander Reverdit, himself spent many hours standing in water in the bowels of the ship visiting each compartment

in turn to ensure that any furniture still smouldering was doused. [67–8]

At 1435 on the 12th the head of the 3ème Section sent the following telegram to the Préfet Maritime in Paris: 'It is my sad duty to inform you that a fire and explosions have occurred aboard the *Iéna* in the Missiessy Basin resulting in numerous casualties. The ship is severely damaged. I will provide you with further details as soon as I am able.' [66] But how many casualties? The newspapers were quick to exaggerate the figure, *Le Matin* declaring there to have been over four hundred fatalities of a complement of 779. The reality as it was revealed in a roll call of survivors taken at 1700 on the 12th in the 5ème Dépôt was less extreme, but no less awful for that, and each passing day brought further macabre discoveries: Capt. Adigard, his head apparently smashed by a shell detonation in his cabin, Cdr Vertier (the executive officer), Lt Thomas and Sub Lt Roux, engineer officers Gié and Estève, senior medical officer Roustan, together with 111 sailors and workers died in the course of their duty, a total of 118 men. The remains of ninety-nine men were eventually found within the ship itself of whom twenty-nine could not be identified. Thirty-three wounded men were evacuated to the main naval hospital at Saint-Mandrier suffering from third- and, above all, second-degree burns to their faces, heads, hands and forearms, as well as fractures. Nor were the casualties confined to the crewmen and workers: a shell fragment hurled several hundred yards from No. 2 Dock killed a mother and her child in the rue Zoé.

Inquiry

The events of 12 March came as an unprecedented shock to the Marine Nationale. The continued existence of a number of venerable institutions was called into question amid a barrage of criticism, and the episode ultimately led to the resignation first of a minister of marine and subsequently of a prime minister. The naval staff itself was at a loss following the destruction of the *Iéna*. For two years they had weathered a deplorable crisis on the subject of the navy's rate of fire which compared unfavourably with foreign gunnery. To this was added a catalogue of accidents, beginning with the dramas of the submarines *Farfadet* and *Lutin* which were lost off North Africa in July 1905 and October 1906 respectively.

Naturally enough, questions were immediately raised as to the causes of the disaster and how to prevent a repetition. At the suggestion of senator and soon-to-be Minister of Marine Ernest

Iéna after the last fires were put out, the ship gutted from the after funnel to the stern. Note Rear Admiral Manceron's burnt out cabin and the collapsed fore topmast which was soon pulled down. *(Philippe Caresse Collection)*

Shells and debris disgorged from *Iéna*'s ruptured hull litter the bottom of No. 2 dock. *(Philippe Caresse Collection)*

Toulon - 6 - La Catastrophe de l'Iéna
Brèche pratiquée aux flancs du navire par l'explosion des soutes
Dans le fond du bassin, obus non encore éclatés
dont l'enlévement offre de grands dangers

Monis, a senatorial commission consisting of twelve members was appointed on 20 March and arrived in Toulon on 3 April to gather evidence as part of its inquiry. Meanwhile, questions were raised in the Chamber of Deputies by Henri Michel and Admiral Amédée Bienaimé on 21 March, and a week later this body followed the lead of the Senate in appointing a twenty-two-member commission of its own.

From the outset a majority of witnesses regarded Powder B as unquestionably responsible for the entire catastrophe in view of the succession of increasingly massive explosions and above all the clouds of yellowish smoke generated. The experts were unanimous. It was noted that Powder B tended to degrade with the passage of time, and in doing so produced gases which had an oxidising effect, thereby increasing ambient temperature. It was known that the burning of 2.2lb (1kg) of Powder B yielded 30.6gal (139l) of nitrogen dioxide, which turned into a yellow steam of nitric acid on contact with the air. Blood tests subsequently performed on three bodies revealed the presence of carbon monoxide. However, experts from the Service des Poudres et Salpêtres (Powders and Saltpetres Service), which was responsible for manufacturing Powder B, rejected any theory which apportioned sole responsibility to their propellant, resisted any investigation into its properties, and focused their attention on the black powder instead. Although former Minister of Marine Camille Pelletan believed that the explosion had resulted from the detonation of a torpedo, with cases being made for sabotage and an electrical short-circuit, Admiral Bienaimé was in no doubt that the disaster was the result of a spontaneous deflagration of propellant. Meanwhile, the incumbent Minister of Marine Gaston Thomson ventured no opinion at all.

On 31 March Thomson ordered experiments to be carried out at the Gâvres firing range under conditions mirroring those of *Iéna*. Two caissons of similar dimensions were built to represent a 4in magazine on the one hand, and a black powder one on the other. The cartridge cases were duly lit on 6 and 7 August, but the commission was dissatisfied with these tests which took no account of the state of the propellant stowed in the ship. Before these tests had been concluded the Senate Commission of Inquiry had published its own conclusions, while those of the Chamber of Deputies commission received their final review on 29 October. Opinion in the Deputies' commission was divided. Deputy Henri Michel, who had been

appointed Rapporteur Général (Chief Investigator) declared that he himself 'had been led if not to material proof then at least to the moral certainty and unshakeable conviction that it was Powder B which was the primary cause of the disaster so much deplored by the navy and by the nation.' However, the content of the Michel Report, which was submitted on 7 November 1907, was not debated until 16–19 October 1908, with no conclusions being reached: 'The parliamentary commission of enquiry of the Chamber of Deputies finds itself unable to reach any conclusion with absolute certainty as to the initial cause of the *Iéna* disaster.'

Meanwhile, the report of the Senate commission chaired by Ernest Monis was issued on 9 July 1907 and debated between 21 and 26 November. It leant heavily on a report prepared by Capt. Adigard for the fleet commander, Admiral Touchard, on 7 November 1906, in connection with the orders of 1 June and 12 July 1897 requiring stocks of Powder B to be subject to annual inspection, subsequently amended by a circular dated 31 December 1901 requiring evidence to be collected including a sample vial for analysis by the gunnery officers on a quarterly basis. Adigard's November report was based on an inspection of propellant carried out on 14 June 1906 which stated that 67 per cent of the 12in charges were more than six years old, as were 16 per cent of the 6.5in cartridges and 86 per cent of the 4in cartridges. This accumulation had worried Adigard, whose report expressed his concern that such a concentration in *Iéna* might

imperil the ship. Moreover, the magazine in question was adjacent to a black-powder magazine, a danger enhanced by the arrangements for flooding both magazines simultaneously via a communication door in the partition separating them. A fire in No. 5 magazine appears to have caused the detonation of the black-powder magazines, as well as a blaze in the neighbouring magazines in which Powder B was stowed. Predictably enough, the conclusion to Monis' report constituted a damning indictment of Powder B:

Investigation of the role played by Powder B in the explosion of the *Iéna* has revealed no differences between this accident and those that preceded it. The first indication of disaster was the sudden appearance above *Iéna*'s stern of a flame of Powder B. This flame originated in No. '5' (4in) magazine to starboard. The fire in this magazine was not caused by any human intervention, nor did it result from any of the accidental causes which have been considered: explosion of the torpedoes, short-circuiting, radio waves, racing of the Rateau pump and its supposed consequences; it is attributable only to the decomposition of Powder B. This decomposition, which is characteristic of this powder, may have been precipitated by the conjunction of three unfortunate circumstances:

– The magazine was located beneath the dynamo compartment where the temperature is constantly high.

- The magazine had no refrigerating machinery; in order to ventilate it the doors had to be opened for an hour each morning at the risk of introducing air containing varying levels of humidity.
- The stock of munitions stowed in this dangerous magazine consisted of about 80 per cent old powder. [92]

The Monis report was accused of being flimsy and hasty in reaching its conclusions. In fact, the results of these commissions were by no as means as definitive as the navy had hoped and did nothing to enhance its prestige, making what had become known as 'La catastrophe du *Iéna*' an event with significant political and military ramifications. Indeed, the future Minister of Marine Théophile Delcassé lost no opportunity to highlight the negligence of the naval authorities to the commission: 'While it is not yet known what caused the first explosion, there can be no doubt that it was the ignition of the Powder B, or the explosion of the black powder, perhaps the two in succession, which were responsible for the catastrophe. With regard to negligence, gentlemen, it is all too clear that the commission has found evidence for it everywhere.'

Already on 6 August 1907 the President of the Republic Armand Fallières had signed a decree setting up an expert commission consisting of the distinguished physicist and engineer Henri Poincaré, the engineer Paul Vieille, the chemist Albin Haller and representatives of the military-industrial complex and the navy. Vieille, who was responsible for developing Powder B in 1884, subsequently declared the conclusions of the Gâvres tests to have been a 'miscarriage of justice', stating that nearly 200 tons of propellant from the forward magazines was currently under analysis, and that Powder B could only be held responsible by invoking as yet unknown properties. [89] In asserting as much Vieille was no doubt relying on the 43°C (110°F) stability trials which governed all directives concerning the inspection of propellant. From these it was concluded that 'It has been established from laboratory experiments that those powders shown to have a total aggregate resistance of twelve hours in the 43°C stability trials can tolerate a constant temperature of 24°C (75°F) over twelve days, or a constant temperature of 4°C (40°F) over twelve months.' These conclusions were cited by the Powders and Saltpetres Service in vindication of its product, but it was soon clear that the 43°C stability trials offered no reliable measure of propellant behaviour, and submission of these before the Haller-Poincaré Commission served only to weaken its case still further among those who saw through this argument.

The press seized on the dossier, stating that 'the Marine wanted above all to economise, that it didn't listen to its officers and that it wanted to put about the notion of sabotage which was both shameful and scandalous.' On 19 October 1908 Minister of Marine Thomson was obliged to tender his resignation the day after a stormy session of the commission. Thomson's downfall was just the beginning. On 25 March 1909 the Chamber of Deputies appointed a grand commission to carry out a full investigation into the state of the navy. Delcassé presided, and during the concluding debates between 1 and 20 July led the final attack against the Prime Minister Georges Clemenceau. Refusing to answer Delcassé's technical questions, Clemenceau resigned on the 24th.

Although no definitive and uncontested explanation has ever been given for the cause of the explosion that destroyed *Iéna*, the evidence for Powder B is compelling. Indeed, the inherent lack of safety in the navy's magazine arrangements had already been recognised in 1905 by one Commandant Charbonnier, assistant director of the navy's central laboratory, who stated that 'No gunner will be surprised the day a catastrophe occurs in a French ship similar to that which befell the *Maine* in Havana', a reference to the spectacular destruction of the US battleship in 1898. [91] His words were prophetic since the destruction of *Iéna* was preceded by an explosion aboard the torpedo boat *Forbin* in February 1907

with the loss of nine men, to be followed by another aboard the gunnery training ship *Gueydon* which killed six in August 1908, one in the protected cruiser *Descartes* which claimed thirteen lives, with six more killed aboard the armoured cruiser *Gloire* in September 1911. Then came the destruction of the battleship *Liberté* whose forward magazines blew up at Toulon on 25 September 1911 leaving 210 dead and 184 injured with consequences comparable to those following the loss of *Iéna*. All these disasters can be attributed to Powder B. More specifically, the navy drew two lessons from the *Iéna* disaster: first, the need to disembark all munitions before a ship was docked, and secondly the need to connect the ship's fire main to the sea.

Aftermath

The day after the catastrophe, 13 March 1906, Minister of Marine Gaston Thomson left Paris for Toulon accompanied by Chief of the Engineering Staff Dupont and his ordnance officer Lt Faucon. Guided by Cdr Van Gaver, Thomson picked his way through the debris to tour the hulk of *Iéna* as ambulances came and went from the dockyard. Next he visited survivors at the 5ème Dépôt as a delegation was appointed to identify the bodies deposited at the hospital. The men carried out this pitiable task until Friday 15th, but the last bodies were not recovered until 16 and 24 May.

President Armand Fallières leads a party of dignitaries aboard to inspect the incinerated hulk. (*Philippe Caresse Collection*)

The top-hatted figures of Prime Minister Georges Clemenceau, President Armand Fallières and Minister of Marine Gaston Thomson lead the funeral procession for *Iéna*'s dead through the streets of Toulon on 16 March 1907. (*Philippe Caresse Collection*)

Iéna's dead had meanwhile become the focus of national mourning. Flags flew at half-mast in Paris and the Élysée ball was cancelled along with an official luncheon hosted by the foreign minister. Tsar Nicholas II of Russia sent a telegram of condolence to the capital. The Vatican hurriedly sent letters of sympathy to the bishops of Fréjus and Toulon and Pope Pius X delivered a special prayer during a mass on 13 March. The Lord Mayor of London and of other cities in Britain sent telegrams of condolence while the Italian parliament and press commented on the frequency with which these tragic events overtook the French navy. On Saturday, 16 March the victims were buried on the Allée du Souvenir Français in Lagoubran Cemetery in Toulon in a ceremony attended by 20,000 people which was less a funeral than an apotheosis. The *cortège de gloire* was led by President Fallières accompanied by Prime Minister Clemenceau together with delegations from the Senate and the Chamber of Deputies. The Marine Nationale was represented by Rear Admiral Manceron and by the Préfet Maritime of Toulon, Vice Admiral Marquis. Also present were the naval attachés of Great Britain, Germany, Russia and Japan. The President, the Minister of Marine, Admiral Touchard, Rear Admiral Manceron and the deputy for Toulon all gave emotional speeches. The funeral service was led by Bishop Guilibert of Fréjus. On 25 July all unidentified remains recovered from the wreck were interred with their shipmates and an imposing monument inaugurated to their memory on 10 April 1908. The families of the victims had to wait six months after the accident to receive compensation but donations were already flooding in: the regional newspaper *Le Petit Var* gave 200 francs to the Préfecture Maritime of Toulon, the Parisian Press Association sent 2,210 francs, the crew of the armoured cruiser *Pothuau* collected 275 francs, the Union des Femmes de France 1,000 francs, while an anonymous Belgian contributed 25,000 francs.

Where *Iéna* herself was concerned, command devolved on the ranking survivor Cdr Van Gaver, Adigard's executive officer. From 17 March it was forbidden for any except flag officers to board the ship or gain access to the dock without special permission. A working party was detailed by Van Gaver to remove all ordnance, personal effects, souvenirs, etc. from the ship and deposit them in a special store. Van Gaver refused to permit access to the magazines until such time as the *capitaine d'artillerie* (supervisor of ordnance) appointed by the Controller Procurement had declared that this could be carried out without danger. Once approval had been given, first the propellant and then the projectiles would be removed. The former was to be loaded into bottom dump barges and the latter into lighters. There was also concern for the status of the ship's confidential papers and of her newly installed Barr & Stroud rangefinders. Van Gaver was able to confirm that the former had all been consumed in the inferno, but the latter had survived intact and were removed for use by the Service Hydrographique. On March 18 Rear Admiral Manceron hauled down his flag and at 1330 he and Admiral Touchard, Commander-in-Chief of the Mediterranean Fleet, bade farewell to *Iéna*'s surviving complement, the ship being struck from the Navy List that same day. Manceron subsequently hoisted his flag in *Saint Louis*, bringing with him a number of *quartiers-maîtres* (leading seamen) and other former crewmen of *Iéna*.

The wreck of the *Iéna* was not only of sentimental but also of professional interest to France's allies, and on 5 April no less than thirty-six British officers were given access to her main deck and 'tween decks. At the end of that month it was the turn of the Japanese naval attaché to request permission for Engineer Inspector Fuiji to come aboard along with Chief Engineers Arisaka and Hoido. This request was granted on the understanding that any attempt to approach the submarines either afloat or under construction in the dockyard was strictly prohibited. The most prestigious foreigner to tour the scene of the catastrophe was King Edward VII who asked to come aboard 'not out of curiosity … but out of a feeling of respect for the victims and to remember the dead.' Steps were immediately taken to scatter disinfectant to counteract the foul stench of decomposition rising from the double bottom and the engine spaces and on 6 April the King came aboard dressed in the uniform of a British Admiral of the Fleet accompanied by Admirals Touchard and Marquis. Having visited the bridge and then the devastation of the senior officers' quarters, he was shown one of the boiler rooms where he uttered these words in parting:

This visit is an act of homage which I wanted to render to the memory of all those brave French sailors who met a glorious death in this terrible catastrophe. By boarding the ship in which they fell victim in the course of their duty I have wanted to make a personal expression of my sympathy. [76]

Where the condition of the ship herself was concerned, Van Gaver was able to send the following report to Paris on 25 March:

Iéna, forward boiler rooms intact, after boiler rooms also seem intact with the exception of boilers 19 and 20. The forward sections of the three engines have suffered little, but the engines abaft the medium-power cylinders have been heavily damaged. Hull in good condition forward. All parts above the armoured deck and abaft that point are in need of reconstruction, and it also seems that all parts of the ship abaft the forward engine room bulkhead below the armoured deck have been heavily damaged. [76]

It was initially believed that *Iéna* would be repaired and re-enter service as a matter of course, but this view had subsequently to be revised in the face of evidence such as this which demonstrated that she was beyond economic repair. On 19 June 1907 the Direction des Constructions Navales (Naval Construction Department) wrote from Toulon informing the Minister of Marine that it would cost 400,000 francs simply to make the ship seaworthy, and a further 7 million and two years' labour to effect a full repair. Its recommendation was that *Iéna* be condemned, a view accepted by the Préfet Maritime. When a subsequent report on 17 July found the ship suffering from '*fatigue générale*' and reassessed the cost of reconstruction at 10 million francs and four years, it was clear that *Iéna* would never be rebuilt. On 9 November the Minister of Marine took the decision to abandon the repair of *Iéna*.

Measures had meanwhile been put in hand to strip all usable fuel, equipment and supplies from *Iéna*, including all guns and munitions. On 10 April the head of the 3ème Section sent a telegram to the Préfet Maritime in Paris, stating that all large-calibre munitions would be unloaded onto barges by the following evening with a view to their being sunk in deep water on the 16th. Only ten 12in and 4in shells remained

unaccounted for, these having almost certainly exploded during the catastrophe; many of the rest were recovered from the floor of the dock. On 14 April the dock was flooded in order to allow the ammunition barges to leave, but causing much of *Iéna*'s lower spaces to be inundated once again. The drying process lasted several weeks and required wood fires to be lit inside the boilers to clear the tubes.

By 19 April all that could be done using onboard facilities had been completed and Van Gaver invited the Service d'Artillerie (Gunnery Branch) to inspect the surviving ordnance. The after 12in turret was beyond repair or salvage, while the base of the forward turret had been damaged by immersion in seawater and had to be completely dismantled. The three salvaged 12in guns were allocated to the army, one destined for service as a railway gun and the other two to the aptly named 78ème Régiment d'Artillerie Lourde à Grande Puissance (Heavy Artillery Regiment). Work continued in May with steps taken to remove the smaller calibre munitions from the ship, including nearly 7,500 1.85in shells which joined their larger counterparts at the bottom of the Mediterranean. By 3 July the ship had been disarmed and the remaining complement, which had dropped to 218 men in mid-April, was paid off on 31 July.

Gunnery Target

Already by June 1907 Vice Admiral Marquis had envisioned the transformation of *Iéna* into a

target ship, and the letter he wrote to the Minister of Marine on the 16th leaves little doubt that the lessons of the Russo-Japanese War of 1904–5 were instrumental in that decision:

Two currents of opinion took hold among officers after the Russo-Japanese War. One of these favoured the view followed by the gunnery branch: very high initial velocities and [armour-]piercing shells; meanwhile, the other group had faith only in shells with a high explosive capacity that, without penetrating, created a vibrant high-temperature atmosphere lethal to those aboard. It was therefore necessary for the trials performed on *Iéna* to shed light on this important matter and leave no stone unturned to ensure that the results of the firings carried out against this target should be conclusive and provide no ground for any controversy. [78]

Further support for the use of *Iéna* as a target came on 19 February 1908, when Senator Monis stated during a meeting of the Commission Sénatoriale de la Marine (Senate Navy Commission) on calculations relating to the penetration of armour plate that actual combat ranges were now estimated at between 6,560 and 8,750yds (6,000–8,000m). Matters gathered pace, and on 6 March 1908 an invitation to tender for sealing the breaches in *Iéna*'s hull in order to refloat her attracted five bids, the lowest of which, from a M. Favre et Cie of Marseilles, eventually received ministerial approval for 328,000 francs. The repair was no small task, since not only had an immense hole been opened up between frames 61 and 84, but the bulkheads had either collapsed or been weakened and punctured by projectiles, while much of the plating had either disappeared or been heavily damaged. However, the work was completed, and *Iéna* was successfully refloated at 0930 on 8 October 1908 after nineteen months in No. 2 Dock. Apart from the reactivation of certain equipment, the opportunity was taken while *Iéna* was still in dry dock to remove her shafts and propellers, one set of which was soon put to good use after her near-sister *Suffren* grounded at Golfe Juan that year. Duly replaced by divers, these spares kept *Suffren* from a lengthy immobilisation.

Already on 12 September 1908 an order from the Préfet Maritime had appointed another commission chaired by Cdr Lanxade, commanding officer of the armoured cruiser *Latouche-Tréville*, entrusted with installing the necessary fittings prior to the gunnery trials. In February of the following year the navy made approaches to the private sector for supplies of cork and ballast, as well as 8,000 francs' worth

Iéna's burnt-out midships section looking forward and showing her secondary armament of 6.5in and 4in guns with a 1.85in weapon visible on the extreme right. It took nineteen months to prepare her for disposal. *(Marius Bar)*

The immense opening in her hull having been patched, *Iéna* is towed away for disposal after nineteen months in the Missiessy Basin on 8 October 1908. *(Philippe Caresse Collection)*

of wooden mannequins which were set up at battle stations throughout the ship. Also installed between 9 April and 15 May were numerous items of equipment including a number of old boats, engine room telegraphs, shell bins of the type fitted in the battleships *Patrie* and *Démocratie*, and several boiler room fans removed from the barbette ship *Magenta* and made serviceable. Sad to relate, these were not the only items placed aboard to make the gunnery trials more realistic, since a number of live animals were included among the installations before the first shots were fired, part of the 700,000 francs expended by the Marine in converting *Iéna* to a gunnery target.

On 5 April 1909 the Préfet Maritime informed the Minister of Marine that: 'Barring unforeseen circumstances, the work necessary to fire the first shots at *Iéna* will be completed on 13 April. We request permission to appear in the Hyères roads on Wednesday 14th to begin the first firings.' However, matters were delayed for budgetary reasons, and it was not until 27 July that *Iéna* was towed to a position between Point Lequin and Cap des Mèdes on the northeastern tip of the Île de Porquerolles, the most westerly of the Îles d'Hyères, to discharge her final duties. Divers were embarked in the netlayer *Polyphème* to prepare four concrete moorings in 30ft (9m) of water with a view to the trials starting in early August.

Meanwhile, an organising committee had been set up in January under Rear Admiral Henri de Faubournet de Montferrand together with a trials committee aimed at testing mélinite-filled

Above: The mannequin crew of one of the casemated 6.5in guns stands in eerie anticipation of the firing in August 1909. *(Philippe Caresse Collection)*

Right: *Iéna* on the receiving end of a 9.5in (240mm) shell on 15 September 1909 during her long calvary as a gunnery target. *(Philippe Caresse Collection)*

shells in the utmost secrecy. Targets in the form of crosses of various sizes were painted on the ship which was repositioned on her anchors to obtain the desired incidence variables. The firing ships were positioned at ranges of between 650 and 6,500yds (600–6,000m), while 9.5in and 6.5in guns were mounted ashore at a range of 275yds (250m). The first vessel to engage was the battleship *Condé* firing high-explosive shells with her 7.6in (194mm) and 6.5in weapons on the morning of 9 August, followed by *Iéna*'s near-sister *Suffren*'s 12in guns, all personally

supervised and assisted by Vice Admiral Augustin Boué de Lapeyrère. Later the armoured cruisers *Latouche-Tréville* and *Jules Michelet* joined the firings which each lasted half an hour, after which experts would board the hulk to photograph and examine the effects on the ship, the mannequins and the animals.

On the 18th Admiral Pierre Le Bris took command of the operations, which now focused on semi-armour-piercing shells. The investigators discovered some spectacular sights, especially during the semi-armour-piercing firings by

Suffren, one of which struck the main belt on the port side forward, cracking the plating and forcing it inboard while scattering the entire complement of mannequins. Another hit on the forward turret dislodged the armour and cut the mannequins to pieces. On 26 October *Iéna* grounded slightly after a storm and had to be refloated. So it went on each day until 5 November when *Iéna* received the last of her thousand cuts. By 2 December, her bows practically submerged and the ship close to foundering, the decision was taken to tow her into deeper water. However, no sooner had the tug got *Iéna* under way in rising seas than she capsized in Alicastre Bay, scarcely a kilometre west of her target position and almost taking the tug with her. At 1050 the Préfet Maritime in Paris received the following telegram from the commander of the 3ème Section: 'High wind from the west and a very heavy sea, *Iéna* took on a sharp list to starboard and her bows went under. I fear she will capsize. Her foremast has collapsed.' [105] At 1110 the Préfet was in receipt of another: 'At 1100 Porquerolles watchman is signalling that *Iéna* has capsized to starboard, wreckage and boats have gone overboard. Tug has abandoned *Iéna*, en route to Porquerolles.' In the event, *Iéna* sank in just 40ft (12m) of water leaving her port side exposed.

Disposal

Within five days, the first private scrap companies were tendering for the demolition of the wreck. Admiral Marquis immediately imposed special conditions on the sale of the hull, stating that unless the ship were destroyed by further explosives, the purchaser would have to be French and employ only local workers bound to secrecy. The wreck was put up for sale in November 1910 but Marquis' conditions meant that it was not until 21 December 1912 that *Iéna* was sold to Lazare Nicolini of Toulon, president of the Chamber of Commerce of Var, for the sum of 33,005 francs, by which time the wreck was estimated to consist of some 10,600 tons, of which approximately 8,600 tons represented salvageable material – this compared with an original standard displacement of over 11,600 tons.

The task proceeded in the traditional manner, with exposed items being removed first while openings were let into the hull to work on the interior. Once the scrapping had reached the waterline divers were called in to recover submerged material in what were usually very favourable conditions. These endeavours were halted with the order for mobilisation on 1 August 1914 but resumed on 18 September 1915, the work continuing in several phases under various companies until July 1927 when l'Entreprise Géré requested permission to use four tons of dynamite on the hulk. This was granted with conditions attached, but it was not until 1957 that the last serious efforts were made to dismantle the wreck.

The pitiful remains of *Iéna* lie at 06° 14' 26" East 43° 01' 36" North, the position marked by a small amount of wreckage protruding above the seabed. With visibility generally good and little current the site makes for an easy if somewhat disappointing dive owing to the absence of recognisable elements. The only major surviving section is part of the starboard side which looks as if it had been parted lengthways. Some distance to the northeast are fragments of the double bottom embedded in the sand, part of an extensive debris field including fire brick, coal and countless shards of metal now impossible to identify. Here then is a ship reduced to its simplest elements, a few steel plates and other fragments being slowly claimed by algae and corrosion, more substantial now in history than in hard reality.

Sources

Unpublished Sources
Musée de la Marine, Paris
Service Historique de la Marine, Toulon
Armament Estimates and Commissioning Estimates
Gunnery. Lectures by Colonel Jacob, 4 vols.
Service Historique de la Marine, Vincennes
Michel Report into the *Iéna* disaster
Monis Report into the *Iéna* disaster, 3 vols.

Bibliography
Caresse, Philippe, 'The *Iéna* Disaster, 1907' in John Jordan, ed., *Warship 2007* (London: Conway, 2007), pp. 121–38
_____, *Histoire des cuirassés d'escadre* Iéna et Suffren : *Genèses, caractéristiques et carrières* (Outreau, Pas-de-Calais: Lela Presse, 2009)
Jordan, John, & Philippe Caresse, *French Battleships of World War One* (Barnsley, S. Yorks.: Seaforth Publishing, 2017)
Roblin, Laurent, & Luc Feron, *La Royale à la Belle Epoque: Photographies d'un marin ordinaire* (Saint-Cyr-sur-Loire: Alan Sutton, 2010)
Ropp, Theodore, *The Development of a Modern Navy: French Naval Policy, 1871–1904* (Annapolis, Md.: Naval Institute Press, 1987)

Armée et Marine
L'Illustration no. 3342 (16 March 1907) & no. 3343 (23 March 1907)
Le Petit Journal, illustrated supplements, 31 March 1907 & 21 April 1907
La Revue Maritime
La Vie Maritime
Le Yacht, 6 September 1898
Revue Historique des Armées

Iéna capsized to starboard and awaiting demolition at Porquerolles with some of the instruments of her destruction seen in the foreground. *(Philippe Caresse Collection)*

Kongelige Norske Marine

The Coastal Battleship *Eidsvold* (1900)

Jacob Børresen

ORDERED BY the Norwegian government from a British yard in 1899, the coastal battleship *Eidsvold* was – as much as any vessel covered in this volume – both a product and a symbol of the recent history of the country which commissioned her, and particularly of its aspirations for independence. This symbolism was as true on the day of her demise as it had been at the time of her commissioning forty years earlier.

Norway and Naval Rearmament

The deep context of the battleship *Eidsvold* dates back eighty-five years to May 1814 when, after 400 years in union with Denmark, Norway emerged from the Napoleonic Wars as an independent state with its own constitution, king, parliament and armed forces, only to be forced by Crown Prince Karl Johan of Sweden into a personal union with the House of Bernadotte in November that year after a brief and decisive summer campaign.[1] Although formally still a separate country with its own parliament (the Storting) and defences, Norway now found herself ruled by a common king with the Swedes who was to be commander-in-chief of the Norwegian armed forces. Moreover, Sweden was responsible for foreign policy and consular representation on behalf of both countries, a reflection of her dominant status in the union.

Inevitably, the passage of years served to accentuate the differences between the two coun-

Eidsvold at anchor. Flying from the jackstaff is the Swedish-Norwegian Union flag, the despised 'pickled herring salad', which dates the picture to the period between *Eidsvold*'s joining the fleet in the spring of 1901 and the instigation of the dissolution of the Union by Norway on 9 June 1905. *(Marinemuseet – Naval Museum, Horten)*

---

[1] Jacob Børresen, *The Norwegian Navy: A Brief History* (Bergen: John Grieg A/S, 2012).

tries. Unlike Sweden, which increasingly owed her wealth to natural resources and industrial production, Norway became a major seafaring nation. Her merchant marine, among the three or four largest in the world, was omnipresent on the seven seas. By the 1890s these differences in outlook and inclination had become a bone of contention between the two union partners. Deeply dissatisfied with the representation of her interests by the Swedish foreign service, on 10 June 1892 the Storting decided to establish an independent consular service to support her merchant marine in foreign ports. Having debated the matter, in 1893 the Swedish government advised King Oscar II not to sanction the Storting's decision. At the same time it suggested that the office of foreign minister could be held by Swedes and Norwegians in alternation and offered to negotiate the question of the consular service. The Norwegian response was to terminate the bilateral Swedish-Norwegian Consular Service Treaty, to which the Swedes replied in May 1895 by threatening war. Norway was left with no option but to back down.

This national humiliation and retreat brought about a complete alteration in Norwegian defence policy, which had hitherto looked to negotiation rather than the use of force in pursuing its aims, and on maintaining neutrality in the event of war between the European powers. Henceforth its policy, first elucidated in a parliamentary debate in July 1895, became one of rearmament, the focus shifting from common defence of the union against a foreign power (implicitly Russia) towards that of a possible attack from Sweden. The Norwegian authorities duly initiated a significant overhaul of the army and navy in support of this new policy, thereby giving Norway the strength and self-confidence to end the union with Sweden unilaterally when the next crisis unfolded, as it did in 1905. This, then, was the atmosphere in which the coastal battleship *Eidsvold* came to be ordered for the Norwegian navy.

The parliamentary debate of July 1895 revealed that the purpose of rearmament was not to match the military strength of Sweden, which was far beyond Norway's means, but instead build a defence force strong enough so that, in the event of a new union crisis, Swedish intervention in Norway would come at an unacceptably high price both politically and militarily. Already in 1891 the Norwegian Defence Commission for the rebuilding of the navy had identified Norway's main strategic priority as the fortification and seaborne defence of the most important fjords in the south of the country, and generally to prevent blockade and maintain lines of communication along a coastline stretching 11,500 nautical miles. An additional consideration, though one less easily implemented, was the need to protect the Norwegian merchant marine on the high seas. Between 1895 and 1905 the Norwegian government therefore voted large sums of money for the acquisition of thirty modern torpedo boats and gunboats and, above all, four coastal battleships, including *Eidsvold*.

Harald Haarfagre, first of the four coast defence battleships built for the Norwegian navy by Armstrong's of Elswick, Newcastle upon Tyne. *(Wilse/Marinemuseet)*

The after 8.2in mounting being installed in late 1900 or early 1901. Looking on are crewmen of the Japanese battleship *Hatsuse*, another foreign order for Armstrong's yard in the process of fitting out. *(Marinemuseet)*

The coastal battleships alone cost 19 million kroner, which at that time constituted 20 per cent of Norway's annual budget, an allocation of money which can only be understood as an expression of that country's powerful urge to freedom and independence during the last years of the union with Sweden.

In the event of war with Sweden, a Swedish attack would almost certainly be aimed at the Norwegian capital Christiania (now Oslo) lying at the head of the Christiania fjord and a mere forty miles from the Swedish border. Christiania was Norway's centre of gravity: if the capital fell, the war would be over. The first line of defence was the army, and the fortifications being built along the Swedish border from Kongsvinger to Halden. Meanwhile, the heavy guns of the coastal battleships, together with the torpedo boats, the coastal batteries and their associated minefields sown in the Christiania and Tønsberg fjords, were seen as key to the defence of the capital. The primary role of the navy was to prevent a Swedish penetration into the Christiania fjord and a subsequent amphibious landing on its eastern shores which would outflank the army. The navy therefore established a forward operating base at Melsomvik in the heavily fortified Tønsberg fjord on the western side of the Christiania fjord including a coal depot, water replenishment facilities and ammunition storage which would be more suitable in time of war than the exposed and largely undefendable main naval base of Karljohansvern at Horten.

The navy had wanted six coastal battleships so that in the event of hostilities two could operate between the southern port of Kristiansand and the Swedish border, two between Stavanger and Bergen in southwestern Norway, and two in the Trondheim area of central Norway, with all three groups supported by torpedo boats and gunboats. It initially got two of these, *Harald Haarfagre* and *Tordenskjold*, which were commissioned in the summer of 1897 and the spring of 1898 respectively. When the purchase of two more was debated in the Storting in June 1898, the navy declared the trials with the new units to have demonstrated the commendable seaworthiness, speed, manoeuvrability and utility of the vessels and urged the acquisition of another pair. The ostensible reason for this second order was the defence of the coast from the Swedish border to Trøndelag in central Norway, but there was as yet no overt naval threat to the southern and western coasts. Anglo-German interest in these waters came later as a consequence of Germany's naval rearmament, then in its earliest stages. The real reason was the threat of Swedish naval rearmament and the expectation of a new union crisis. So it was that *Norge* and *Eidsvold* came into being.

One may wonder why Sweden allowed the Norwegians to acquire coastal battleships for their navy. It may be that the more powerful Swedes felt confident that, coastal battleships or not, Norway was no match either for her army or her navy. Moreover, the Swedes had constantly criticised Norway for not pulling her weight in the common defence of the union since it was instituted in 1814. It was therefore something to be welcomed when the Norwegians finally turned to modernising and strengthening their navy in 1895, not least since Sweden was herself in the process of rebuilding her fleet. The 1890s were in any case the era of navalism in Europe, abetted by the writings of the American theorist Alfred Thayer Mahan who held that possession of a battlefleet and control of the sea lanes was the determining factor in the rise and fall of powerful nations. This theory developed into the conviction that sea power in peacetime generated an undefined political influence which could be translated into military might without recourse to force, a central motivation behind the Anglo-German naval arms race prior to the First World War. Whatever concerns may have been voiced behind closed doors in Stockholm, the Crown neither could nor desired to prevent Norway, like Sweden or any other self-respecting nation, acquiring that most potent symbol of nationhood: a modern navy.

Design

Although Sweden had a significant shipbuilding industry and a long history of warship construction (see *Sverige*), political circumstances made this an option Norway could not take for the updating of her navy, and the government therefore looked across the North Sea to the largest and most experienced builder of oceangoing warships of the day: the firm of Sir W. G. Armstrong of Elswick, Newcastle upon Tyne, England. Already in January 1896 tenders had been placed for two coastal battleships which resulted in *Harald Haarfagre* and *Tordenskjold*, delivered in 1897 and 1898 respectively. These had been designed by Armstrong's chief naval architect, Philip Watts, whose subsequent work included the revolutionary *Dreadnought* of 1906.

Once the Storting had voted funds for a second pair of coastal battleships in 1898, Watts spent the winter of 1898–9 in Norway together with another Armstrong employee, Saxton Noble. The visit resulted in six designs for an improved Harald Haarfagre class of ships to be called *Norge* and *Eidsvold*. The final design legend provided for two 8.2in (208mm) guns and six 6in (152mm) guns on a standard displacement of 3,848 tons (4,233 full load), around 10 per cent larger than the preceding class and distinguished from it with the addition of a second funnel. The hull was 310ft (94.6m) long, 50.5ft (15.4m) in the beam and with a draught of 16.5ft (5m). Two triple-bladed screws gave each vessel a maximum speed of 17 knots. The keel of the second of these ships, *Eidsvold*, was laid at Elswick on 9 May 1899.

Hull and Armour

Eidsvold's hull was built of steel to British Admiralty specifications with the bow strengthened for use as a ram. The vitals of the ship were protected in an armoured citadel consisting of a 2in (51mm) armour deck, a 7in (178mm) belt at the waterline, armoured bulkheads fore and aft, and a double bottom divided into watertight cells. Internally, the citadel was divided into forty-six watertight compartments with thirty-two watertight doors of which thirteen could be operated from outside the citadel. A sample of the armour belt was successfully tested by firing cold 6in (152mm) shells into it at an impact speed of 2,181ft/sec. Horizontal protection was significantly improved by sloping the outer section of the armoured deck downwards, so that it reached the ship's sides at the base of the armoured belt. The space under the main deck, between the sloping sides of the armoured deck and the armoured belt, was used as emergency bunkerage for coal, a feature copied by many navies and whose value in reducing the effect of a hit was confirmed during the Russo-Japanese War in 1904–5. A projectile striking the ship's side had therefore first to penetrate the waterline armour belt, then the coal and finally the sloping sides of the armour deck in order to breach the citadel. Above the armoured deck, the conning tower was protected by 6in (152mm) of plate and the turrets and casemated secondary battery by 8in (203mm) of armour. The training gear and ammunition hoist beneath the turret were protected by a 6in barbette. Away from the armoured belt the ship's sides consisted of 0.4in (11mm) plate.

Armament

The main armament consisted of two 8.2in (208mm) guns in single turrets. Each turret and gun weighed 98.5 tons, the whole resting on a roller path and trained under electrical power. Projectiles weighed 310lbs (141kg) and were propelled by a separate 57lb (26kg) charge at a muzzle velocity of 2,300ft/sec. The magazines contained high-explosive and armour-piercing shells, together with cast-iron practice rounds. The training, elevation and firing of the gun could be performed by a single crewman. The secondary battery consisted of six 6in (152mm) guns amidships, of which four were mounted in casemates while the remaining two were protected by gun shields. Projectiles weighed 121lbs (55kg) and attained a muzzle velocity of 2,300ft/sec thanks to the 26.5lb (12kg) charge. The torpedo boat was considered the main threat to capital ships and *Eidsvold* therefore mounted a tertiary armament of eight 3in (76mm) and six 1.85in (47mm) quick-firing guns.

Eidsvold in dry dock at the Karljohansvern naval base at Horten, her ram bow shown to good advantage. Note the elaborate bow scroll bearing the lion device of the Kingdom of Norway. (*Marinemuseet*)

Calisthenics for crewmen on the quarterdeck.
(Wilse/Marinemuseet)

The primary and secondary armament was fitted with telescopic sights, while the gunnery officer was equipped with a rangefinder in an exposed position on the mainmast aft. The main and secondary gun batteries were provided with electrical firing and target indicators connecting the guns, conning tower and rangefinder. Although the range of the main battery was 11,000yds (10,060m) at an elevation of 11 degrees, the effective range was limited by that of the rangefinder to 5,000yds (4,572m). Nonetheless, in preparing for a possible war

with Sweden in 1905, Rear Admiral Jacob Børresen, then commander of the Norwegian navy's Skagerrak Squadron, was eager to take advantage of the slightly longer range of his guns by comparison with those of his Swedish counterpart. Since the Swedish and Norwegian coastal battleships were of approximately the same size he therefore measured up a range of 11,000yds, marked it with buoys and placed a battleship at either end in order to train the turret crews to estimate that range from the appearance of the target.

Norway's four coastal battleships, *Eidsvold* included, were the first surface vessels in any navy to be armed with underwater torpedo

tubes, each having a single tube in a torpedo compartment forward of the boiler rooms. The 18in (457mm) torpedoes were 'cold', meaning that they were propelled not by a combustion engine but by an engine running on compressed air only. They were straight-running and had a maximum effective range of 1,600yds (1,463m). The warhead was loaded with 155lbs (70kg) of gun cotton. The tubes were disposed at 90 degrees from the bow and consisted of an outer and then an inner tube containing the torpedo, this to permit firing when the ship was at speed. When the torpedo was fired by compressed air, the inner tube containing the torpedo was pushed out through the outer tube in order to shield the torpedo from the immediate effect of the water streaming past the ship's side. No sooner had the torpedo left the inner tube than the latter was forced back in by the water pressure allowing the tube to be closed by a hydraulically operated door and then drained, whereupon the breech could be opened and the tube reloaded.

Propulsion and Auxiliary Machinery

Each of the two screws was propelled by a triple-expansion steam engine designed to yield 2,250ihp for a total of 4,500ihp at 17 knots. The engines, which were built by Hawthorn Leslie on the Tyne, were situated in separate engine rooms within the armoured citadel. They received steam at a maximum pressure of 220.5psi (15.5kg/cm^2) from six coal-fired Yarrow boilers disposed in two boiler rooms, each of which contained two feed water pumps. Eidsvold had bunkerage for up to 590 tons of coal and expended 3.7 tons of coal per hour at 17 knots, giving a range of approximately 2,700 miles.

In addition to the main engines, steam was also delivered to the capstan, the steering engine, to a small steam engine in the ship's workshop for running lathes, drills and other machine tools, to several steam-driven pumps, as well as to two separate auxiliary steam engines to generate electricity. Each electrical power unit had a capacity of 40kW and delivered 80V of direct current for a number of uses, including internal and external lighting, searchlights, gun turrets, ammunition hoists, ventilation fans, fire pumps, bilge pumps, ballast pumps, pumps for flooding shell rooms, etc. The steering engine weighed 3.5 tons and was positioned inside the armour-protected citadel. Hydraulic valves could direct steam to operate the rudder from either the bridge, the armoured conning tower or the steering engine room. The rudder could also be operated manually in an emergency. Substantial contingency was therefore built into all vital systems for propulsion, gunnery and damage control.

Communications and Navigation

In 1901 Eidsvold was equipped with a wireless telegraph system in the form of a spark-gap transmitter manufactured by the German Telefunken company. In reality it was little more than a jammer transmitting broadband noise but capable of producing readable Morse code signals. Obtaining the maximum effect from the aerial required the masts with which Eidsvold was originally rigged to be raised to 130ft (40m). When the coast radio stations on the island of Tjøme off Tønsberg and at Flekkerøya off Kristiansand were established in 1905 they were able to communicate with ships at sea over distances of several hundred miles. This tech- nology preceded the invention of the radio valve (1907) as a generator of high-frequency elec- tronic waves in radio transmitters. Internal communications and the distribution of orders was based on a system of voice pipes and bells.

Inside the cylindrical conning tower was a wheel, magnetic compass, engine-room telegraph and the wireless equipment mentioned above. Although fitted with state-of-the-art navigation equipment at the time of her completion, the newly developed gyrocompass and echo-sounding devices were not installed in Eidsvold until 1908 and 1912 respectively. Following the British style, the bridge was essentially open, a considerable inconvenience in prevailing Norwegian climatic conditions. Nonetheless, it was from here that the ship was navigated and here that the commanding officer took his posi- tion at action stations.

Manning

The manning of the Norwegian navy, including the coastal battleships, was based on a combina- tion of a professional cadre of officers and non- commissioned officers and conscript sailors. The officers were drawn from upper-middle-class families of shipowners, bankers, industrialists, merchants, clergymen and civil servants. Non- commissioned officers were recruited from among the middle and lower-middle classes of craftsmen, smiths, engineers, carpenters, sail- makers and so on. Attempts to recruit non- commissioned officers from the merchant marine were not overly successful, it being recognised that 'The able bodied seaman resents navy disci- pline'.[2] The manning of the navy relied on the conscription of ordinary and able-bodied seamen, stokers and cooks from the merchant marine. Qualification as ordinary seaman required at least twelve months' overseas service between the ages of fifteen and twenty-two. Engineers, stokers and cooks could also be called up for naval service on the condition they were employed as befitted their educational skills. In peacetime a man was avail- able for conscription for sixteen years from the age of twenty-two, but in emergencies or time of war, conscription could be extended to include all qualified men between the ages of eighteen and fifty-five. In 1900 the period of service for conscripts was increased from seventy-two days to six months each year. Each age group was divided into two contingents which were called up for service at six-month intervals.

The men perform their ablutions beside the forward 8.2in turret on the forecastle. Note the 1.85in (47mm) quick-firing gun on the boat deck above and the square spitkid placed to collect discarded items in the foreground. (Wilse/Marinemuseet)

2 Bjørn Terjesen, Tom Kristiansen & Roald Gjelsten, Sjøforsvaret i krig og fred – langs kysten og på havet gjennom 200 år (Bergen: Fagbokforlaget, 2010), p. 163.

In 1910 the period of service was increased from sixteen to twenty years from the age of twenty-two, with initial service time increased from six to twelve months. As before, the actual call-up varied both in size and duration of service, depending on available training and exercise budgets, and normally only lasted during the summer months. However, many were exempted from service by drawing lots as far more conscripts were available than the navy required.

Accommodation Arrangements

Eidsvold had a designed complement of 270 officers, non-commissioned officers and men. Most of the available space on board was taken up by machinery, fuel, weapons and ammunition, but living conditions were nonetheless perfectly adequate. The living spaces were heated by steam and a well-appointed captain's cabin had an open fireplace. Fans, natural ventilation and skylights provided fresh air. There were several washrooms on board, including – most considerately – a separate one for the stokers. Drinking water from the freshwater system was specially filtered. There were several galleys, a drying room for wet clothes, a sick bay, dispensary and a surgery inside the citadel. There was also a detention cell which the ship's logs reveal was in frequent use. The sailors were put up in hammocks on the messdeck. Each man had a seabag, a knapsack and a ditty box kept on a galvanised steel shelf, and each mess had a galvanised cupboard for cutlery, fresh bread, etc. Officers and non-commissioned officers had their own messes and cabins.

When new, *Eidsvold* was a comfortable ship with accommodation standards well above the average Norwegian home around the turn of the century. This held true as long as the vessel was being properly maintained, which she was until shortly after the First World War. By 1939, however, the situation was quite different. The vessel had been allowed to decay, the living spaces were dilapidated and washrooms, heads and the heating and ventilation systems were in a dismal state. The messdecks were cold and damp. In the prevailing cold weather the bulkheads were constantly running with condensation. The ship's company therefore suffered from persistent heavy coughing, though the ship's doctor refused to issue sick reports, stating: 'This is the ordinary battleship cough; you will have to live with it for the rest of your life.'[3]

---

3 Jørgen Sørensen, *Panserskipene 1895–1940* (Hundvåg: Sjømilitære samfund ved Norsk Tidsskrift for Sjøvesen, 2000), pp. 110–11.

Chess, pipes and schnapps in *Eidsvold*'s wardroom in the summer of 1905. Electric lamps light a typically austere man-of-war space. *(Wilse/Marinemuseet)*

Joining the Fleet

Norge and *Eidsvold* were launched in March and June 1900 respectively, and joined the fleet in the spring of 1901. Henceforth two of the four battleships were commissioned year-round. During the winter they either lay idle at Karljohansvern under reduced crews or would deploy on a cadet training cruise. During the summer the battleships formed the main body of the annual exercise squadrons of which two were constituted in 1902, 1903 and 1904, one in the spring and another in the autumn, both lasting about a month. In the event of mobilisation in times of crisis or war, the battleships would be organised into a squadron supported by eleven 1st- and 2nd-class torpedo boats led by the destroyer *Valkyrjen*. The torpedo boats would act as a screen, provide reconnaissance and deliver dispatches. This organisation, named the *Skagerrakeskadren* (Skagerrak Squadron), was to be commanded by the chief of the naval staff, a rear admiral, who was in turn responsible to the commander-in-chief of the navy, a vice admiral in overall charge of the Kongelige Norske Marine. The Skagerrak Squadron was only activated once, during the union crisis of 1905, when it and other task groups in the

Christiania fjord were placed under operational command of the commander-in-chief in the *Heimdal* (usually the royal yacht).

Eidsvold was painted grey on delivery, in marked contrast to *Tordenskjold* and *Harald Haarfagre* which originally had the black hulls and buff superstructure worn by the Royal Navy of the day. By 1901, though, all four battleships were painted grey, in token, no doubt, of the increasingly serious purpose to which they might one day be devoted. Whatever their colour, contemporary accounts leave little doubt that the coastal battleships were the pride both of the navy and the nation, and remained so until they reached obsolescence. Here were real men-of-war, visions of clean scrubbed teak, glistening paint and shining brass. One could find them on postcards and on the wall or mantelpiece of almost every home around the coast.

All four ships were given patriotic names: *Tordenskjold*, named for a Norwegian naval hero from the Great Northern War with Sweden between 1700 and 1721; *Harald Haarfagre*, credited with uniting the greater part of Norway under his kingship in 872, and *Norge*, the name of the country itself. *Eidsvold*, meanwhile, was named for the village forty miles north of the capital Christiania (called Oslo since 1925) where the politician, nobleman and owner of the Eidsvold Ironworks, Carsten Anker, had his stately home. It was here that the Norwegian elites had assembled to write the new constitution which was signed on 17 May 1814, a date which became Norway's national day, and which has made Eidsvold (today called Eidsvoll) a symbol of Norwegian freedom and independence ever since. The first lines in Nordahl Grieg's celebrated poem '17 May 1940' capture this sentiment perfectly. The poem was written while Grieg was fleeing northwards in the face of the German attack on 9 April 1940 which by early May had brought much of southern Norway, including Eidsvold, under occupation. It was broadcast from Tromsø in northern Norway, still under Norwegian control, on 17 May that year. The first lines are these:

Today the flagpole stands naked among Eidsvold's budding trees.

THE ADMIRAL AND HIS MEN

We know relatively little about shipboard life in *Eidsvold* other than that discipline was harsh. However, the mordant diary entries of Rear Admiral Børresen, then commanding the Skagerrak Squadron, contain several anecdotes which give a flavour of conditions aboard at the time and of his relations with those under his command. The summer of 1905 saw intense preparations for war, including manoeuvring in formation and gunnery, torpedo and tactical exercises which extended from early morning until late at night. In the evening the ships either anchored in the exercise area or in Melsomvik. Børresen, who demanded total concentration on preparations for war, one day espied seven sailors busy peeling potatoes on the

A party of sailors fallen in for rifle practice on *Eidsvold's* boat deck during the summer of 1905 with petty officers on either side. Despite the motto of the Kongelige Norske Marine carved into the plaque on the bridge deck beyond (For konge, fædreland og flagets hæder – 'For King, country and the honour of the flag'), Rear Admiral Børresen had scant regard for the commitment of his non-commissioned officers. *(Wilse/Marinemuseet)*

And at this very hour we know what freedom is …[4]

The Union Crisis of 1905

Thirty-five years before Grieg wrote '17 May 1940' it was upon *Eidsvold* and the other three coastal battleships that Norway's aspirations for freedom had, in part, rested. On 7 June 1905, after several failed attempts to reconfigure Norway's place in the union, the Storting passed a unanimous resolution dissolving the union between Sweden and Norway (see *Sverige*). The King of Sweden was no longer sovereign head of Norway, nor commander-in-chief of the Norwegian armed forces. Predictably enough,

forecastle of the *Tordenskjold*. The chief paymaster had put the meat and vegetable stew known as lobscouse (*lapskaus*) on the squadron's menu. 'But the conscript sailors have been sent on board to undergo weapons training, not peel potatoes!' Børresen wrote. 'From now on lobscouse is forbidden!'

After nearly three months of continuous exercises and training the ship's company began to show signs of fatigue. The exercises took place in local waters and many crewmen could see their homes but were not allowed ashore. On 12 June a spurious flag signal was hoisted on board *Norge* declaring 'Shore leave for all.' The guilty parties were three petty officer apprentices who were each sentenced to sixty days' detention under guard. A few days later *Eidsvold*'s entire complement of ordinary seamen applied for shore leave, asking that they be informed of 'the political situation' if the request were not granted. Then there were those non-commissioned officers who each evening requested shore leave until six o'clock

the following morning. 'And the request comes at a time when we are at anchor with steam up every night, with armed pickets at the mouth of the fjord and armed guards around the squadron.' No wonder Børresen confided to his diary that he did not hold the navy's non-commissioned officer corps in particularly high esteem. Impressive though they looked, he doubted whether they would readily sacrifice themselves for the fatherland. 'Their highest ambition is the conjugal bed and perambulator. And wives and daughters run them into debt. […] Moreover, this dump Horten is ruinous to wartime discipline. Everybody is preoccupied with but one thought: to get ashore and fill and push perambulators.'

Where his officers were concerned, the tone was different. 'These fellows have made a good impression on me,' he wrote. He was glad to have his 'band of brothers' with him in the squadron, believing that he could not have received better commanding officers and going on to describe each of them in turn. He singles out Captain Adam Müller of *Harald Haarfagre* who, when the squadron had deployed in line ahead in inverse sequence of numbers, would:

> lead the squadron through the gates of hell if ordered to do so. He will never set the Thames on fire, but what intelligence he has he uses to the full regardless of the situation and is ready to go through fire and water. What is the use in being intelligent in peacetime and in flat seas if one loses one's head in time of war and in heavy weather?

Finally, on 7 and 8 October the squadron put in at Arendal and the ships' companies were given shore leave, which they took with gusto. 'Our sailors have apparently made a proper hullaballoo in Arendal!' the Admiral writes:

> I had to pay a visit to the local newspapers in order to avoid a scandal. The reports from the military police were hilarious. I laughed so much I nearly split my sides when I read them. It was just like a performance at an English variety show where the plot consists of everybody screaming and shouting and hitting each other over the head with pieces of wood.

Officers of the Skagerrak Squadron gathered onboard *Eidsvold* for a briefing on Sunday 14 September 1905, the height of the union crisis. Admiral Jacob Børresen is standing in the centre of the group distinguished by the light-coloured band on his cap. The annotation is in the admiral's characteristic hand, the result of his being obliged to write with his left hand after losing the right in a gun explosion. *(Wilse/Marinemuseet)*

this action brought Norway and Sweden to the brink of a war for which the army and navy of both countries had been preparing for some time.

The Norwegians took the first steps as early as 28 February, when the coastal defence fortresses were instructed that Swedish warships had from now on to abide by the same rules as any other alien warships, and not be given passage without prior permission. Every move of the Swedish navy was closely followed. The Norwegians had agents posted along the Danish Straits, The Sound and The Great Belt with instructions to report all naval movements and any indication that the main body of the Swedish navy was about to deploy from the Baltic to the west coast of Sweden. An agent in the city of Trollhättan would report any transfer of naval vessels by way of the Göta Canal.

In the absence of a king, Prime Minister Christian Michelsen became commander-in-chief of Norway's armed forces in his capacity as acting head of state. Following the resolution of 7 June, Defence Minister Olssøn, acting on behalf of the prime minister, called on all serving generals and admirals to swear allegiance to the Norwegian government. They were informed that the oath of allegiance they had sworn to Oscar II was invalid since he was no longer King of Norway. All accepted. Two days later, at 10am on 9 June, the naval ensign bearing the union badge known derisively as the 'pickled herring salad' was hauled down and the unblemished Norwegian naval ensign hoisted to a twenty-one-gun salute. The ceremony ended with a cry of 'God bless the Fatherland' as opposed to the traditional 'God bless King and Fatherland'. With this the Norwegian navy was ready to carry out whatever duties were assigned it by the government.

On 30 June Rear Admiral Wilhelm Dyrssen commanding the Swedish coastal fleet received orders to deploy to Gothenburg and assume command of the West Coast Squadron. The main body would sail via The Sound while a number of torpedo boats would deploy via the Göta Canal. The following afternoon Norwegian agents reported that six battleships, two torpedo cruisers, a destroyer and eight torpedo boats were steering a northerly course through The Sound. Meanwhile, Sweden's only

The changing of the flag. The new Norwegian naval ensign is hoisted on *Eidsvold*'s quarterdeck on 9 June 1905. (*Marinemuseet*)

submarine and eight torpedo boats were reported heading west through the Göta Canal. The Swedish West Coast Squadron also comprised two torpedo cruisers, two destroyers and six torpedo boat divisions with a total of twenty-three torpedo boats. The Swedish plan was for eight of the newest battleships, together with the entire fleet of thirty 1st- and 2nd-class torpedo boats, to block the departure of the Norwegian fleet from the Christiania fjord while the three remaining battleships would sail for Trondheim in Central Norway.

Rear Admiral Børresen (with white cap band) seen with his officers on *Eidsvold*'s bridge in the summer of 1905. His right hand was maimed in a gun explosion at Horten in 1890 while in the rank of premier-löitnant (lieutenant) at the age of thirty-four. *(Wilse/Marinemuseet)*

Rear Admiral Jacob Børresen, chief of the naval staff, who was to take command of the Norwegian Skagerrak Squadron in the event of mobilisation, was instructed to begin the evacuation of the Karljohansvern naval base at Horten and move all ships to the forward operating base at Melsomvik in the Tønsberg fjord. Mines were laid in the approaches to Melsomvik (covered by the coastal batteries protecting the base) and also in the Glomma estuary to bar the approaches to Fredrikstad harbour on the eastern shore of the Christiania fjord. From 1 July onwards the two countries regarded each other's warships as hostile. Already on 8 May Børresen had taken command of the Battleship Squadron, hoisted his flag in *Eidsvold* and immediately began intensive gunnery exercises. The usual Spring Exercise Squadron was constituted on 29 May. It

consisted of the command ship *Heimdal*, the Battleship Squadron comprising all four battleships and a torpedo-boat division led by the torpedo boat destroyer *Valkyrjen* and consisting of six 1st-class and four 2nd-class torpedo boats. The Commander-in-Chief of the Navy Vice Admiral Christian Sparre directed the exercises from the *Heimdal*.

However, it soon became apparent that the Norwegian navy had a major leadership problem. Rear Admiral Børresen was completely at odds with his superior, Vice Admiral Sparre, as to how best to employ the fleet and take on the Swedish navy. Børresen, a Mahanist at heart, wanted to seek out and confront the Swedish fleet in open waters and destroy its main body in a decisive battle. Sparre, on the other hand, was determined to avoid any loss of battleships which

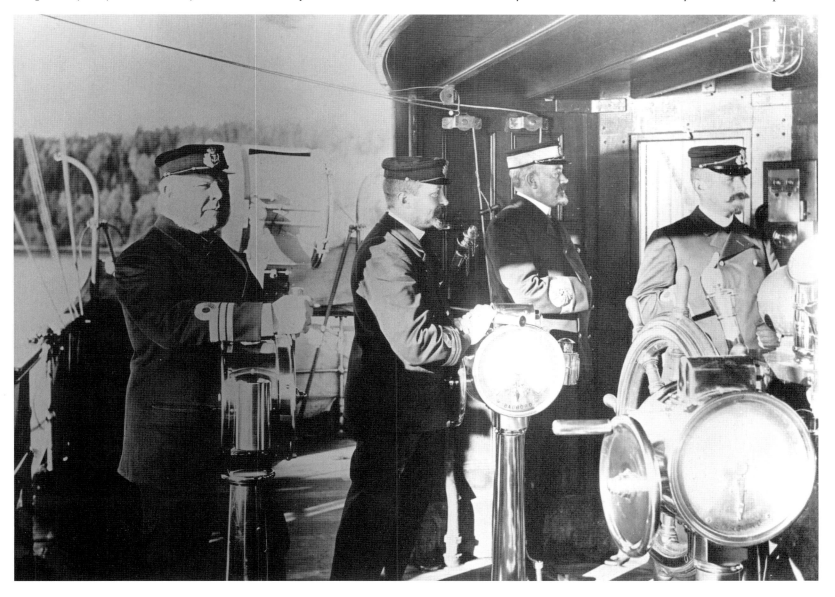

The Skagerrak Squadron steaming in line ahead in confined waters during the summer of 1905. The leading ship is *Harald Haarfagre* followed by *Norge* and *Eidsvold*, from which this photo was taken. Note the two steam pinnaces on *Eidsvold*'s boat deck and the cutter on its davits. *(Wilse/Marinemuseet)*

would leave the fjord open to the Swedes. He therefore insisted on a defensive strategy in which the battleships would remain in their protected harbour at Melsomvik and await a Swedish penetration into the Christiania fjord. When the opportunity arose the Norwegian battleships would sail from their protected anchorage and carry out a swift counter-attack.

Børresen, on the other hand, believed that, taken individually, his battleships were superior to the Swedish ones, both in manoeuvrability

and firepower. As he saw it, Admiral Sparre's approach was tantamount to surrendering this advantage. On leaving harbour his ships would have to manoeuvre in restricted waters in line ahead and be unable to bring the full power of their guns to bear on the enemy, while the Swedes, in open waters, would be able to cross his 'T' and concentrate their entire firepower on the leading ship in his column. Børresen had developed an intricate tactical system for battleships known as the *systemet for støtte* ('system for support') which he hoped would allow him to outmanoeuvre the numerically superior Swedish squadron, isolate individual Swedish units and defeat them piecemeal as Lord Nelson had done at Trafalgar exactly a hundred years before. His system was studied in the French and British navies and Børresen was later to claim

that Admiral Tōgō had used his system in defeating the Russian fleet at the battle of Tsushima on 27 and 28 May that year.[5]

Børresen believed that if the large Swedish battleship squadron attempted to penetrate the Christiania fjord he could defeat it by disposing his battleships across the fjord north of Horten as they advanced in one or two columns. In order to compensate for his inferiority in guns (the Swedish navy had eleven coastal battleships to Norway's four), he wanted to establish a

[5] U. J. R. Børresen, 'A New Tactical System' in *Journal of the Royal United Service Institution* 47, no. 301 (March 1903), pp. 326–38, and 'A New Tactical System Applied to the Russo-Japanese War' in *Journal of the Royal United Service Institution* 50, no. 339 (May 1906), pp. 678–86.

The Skagerrak Squadron in line ahead on manoeuvres in preparation for war with Sweden during the union crisis in the autumn of 1905. Leading the squadron is the flagship *Eidsvold*, followed by *Norge*, *Tordenskjold* and *Harald Haarfagre* with a screen of torpedo boats on the port beam. *(Wilse/Marinemuseet)*

coastal battery at the northern point of the island of Bastøy outside Horten, and another on the southern point of the island of Jeløya off Moss on the opposite side of the fjord. If, however, the Swedish squadron managed to penetrate the Christiania fjord, Børresen would head south to attack the city of Gothenburg and lay mines in the approaches to its harbour, a step he hoped would force the Swedish squadron to abandon the Christiania fjord to defend the city. He would then have a second chance of engaging it in open waters.

His only concern was that the Swedish navy would use his tactical system against him. They knew it well as he had introduced it to the Swedes in a joint Swedish-Norwegian naval exercise in 1903. However, both Admiral Sparre and Defence Minister Olssøn were shocked at what they regarded as his reckless approach and

summarily rejected Børresen's plan, refusing also to place guns on Bastøy and Jeløya. Their over-riding concern was to avoid any posture which could inadvertently lead to war. If war did break out their strategy was to preserve the fleet to prevent the Swedes having a free hand in outflanking the Norwegian army with an amphibious landing on the eastern shore of the Christiania fjord. Børresen's focus was primarily tactical and he had little patience with overall strategic deliberations which would deny him the opportunity of a decisive naval action.

In the event, the Spring Exercise Squadron was dissolved on 29 July and the crews sent home to vote in the plebiscite on the dissolution of the union held on 13 August, a vote which delivered only 184 dissenting voices in the country as a whole. While the Norwegian people stood solidly behind their Storting and

government, opinion in Sweden was divided as negotiations between the two countries began on 31 August.

With tensions rising, Børresen again hoisted his flag in *Eidsvold* on 4 September and resumed command of the Battleship Squadron. On the 13th the rest of the navy and the coastal batteries were mobilised together with the greater part of the army. Meanwhile, the Swedish West Coast Squadron deployed to a forward base just south of Strömstad on the 12th and 13th where preparations were made to embark troops, infantry and artillery for an attack up the Christiania fjord. The Swedish commander Rear Admiral Dyrssen had also been instructed to prepare an amphibious assault against the island of Nøtterøy, south of Tønsberg and lying between Melsomvik and the fjord, in order to destroy the Norwegian fleet in its forward base. Nøtterøy offered a clear line of sight into the anchorage at Melsomvik and the Swedes had good intelligence on the exact location of the various Norwegian units in the base.

Mobilisation meant that Børresen now assumed command not only of the Battleship Squadron but also of the Skagerrak Squadron, the main body of the Norwegian navy, which together consisted of the four battleships, *Valkyrjen* and eleven 1st- and 2nd-class torpedo boats. The main task of the Skagerrak Squadron was to repulse a Swedish penetration into the Christiania fjord leading to the Norwegian capital, thereby protecting the flanks and rear of the army which stood between the Swedish forces and outright defeat. But Børresen was not happy. He had received detailed preliminary orders from Sparre which directed him to stay in port at Melsomvik to await the Swedes' first

move, and only exit Melsomvik when explicitly ordered to do so by Sparre. These orders were not only given to Børresen but distributed directly to his subordinate commanders who, in the event of battle, were instructed to return to Melsomvik on their own initiative the moment they felt at risk of being cut off from the base with its supplies of coal and water. Børresen took this as a sign of mistrust by his superior and for a while contemplated hauling down his flag in protest.

Prime Minister Christian Michelsen not only deplored Børresen's open criticism of his superior at a time of national crisis, but was also critical of the jingoism exhibited by Børresen and other leading military and naval officers which threatened to undermine prudent management of the crisis and disrupt the constructive negotiations he and his Swedish

counterpart Christian Lundberg were engaged in at Karlstad. Nonetheless, Michelsen was wary of relieving him of his command in the circumstances. Not only was Børresen a brilliant and charismatic commander who had worked the Skagerrak Squadron up to a high pitch of efficiency, but he enjoyed the confidence and support of his subordinates.

On 23 September the tension was lifted when agreement was reached at the negotiations in Karlstad. The following day the Swedish West Coast Squadron withdrew to Gothenburg in a reduced state of readiness. On 9 October the Storting accepted the results of the negotiations and the Swedish Riksdag did likewise on the 13th. The crisis was over. Five days later the Norwegian ships were given orders to sail to Karljohansvern at Horten to de-ammunition. On 18 November Prince Carl of Denmark accepted

The Skagerrak Squadron seen from the port quarter on the same occasion. The rear vessel is *Harald Haarfagre*, with *Tordenskjold* and *Norge* ahead and the flagship *Eidsvold* in the van. (Wilse/Marinemuseet)

an invitation to accede to the Norwegian throne and the following June was crowned King Haakon VII of Norway.

Neutrality and Reorganisation: 1905–1914

After the peaceful dissolution of the union with Sweden in 1905 Norway adopted a foreign policy based on neutrality in the event of war in Europe, and the role of the coastal battleships therefore became primarily one of neutrality protection, training and showing the flag at home and abroad, which in *Eidsvold*'s case included the Coronation Review of George V at Spithead in 1911.

In accordance with Article 25 of The Hague Convention of 1907, neutral states had a duty to control their territorial waters, if necessary by force. That same year Britain's First Sea Lord, Admiral of the Fleet Sir John Fisher, confided in Norway's first minister in London, the explorer Fridtjof Nansen, that he had discouraged the Foreign Secretary Sir Edward Grey from signing a treaty to guarantee Norwegian neutrality in the event of war with Germany. Such a treaty could prevent Britain acquiring a Norwegian port as a forward operating base in the event of German attempts to deny the Royal Navy access to the Baltic by blocking the Danish Straits. With Sweden no longer regarded as a threat, the

defence of the North Sea coast therefore became the main focus of concern. The backbone of the mobile defence of the coast was to be the coastal battleships, vessels sufficiently powerful to deliver what was called 'an open protest', in the event of Norwegian territorial integrity being violated. The capital ships were also needed to support the torpedo boats in those areas not covered by coastal artillery. Four battleships were deemed insufficient in view of the extreme length of the Norwegian coastline, and in 1912 the Storting voted to purchase two more coastal battleships from Armstrong's, *Nidaros* and *Bjørgvin*. These were launched in June and August 1914 respectively but requisitioned by the British for war service and commissioned into the Royal Navy under the names *Gorgon* and *Glatton*. In the event, the navy proved capable of covering most of Norway's exposed North Sea coastline during the Great War. To employ the entire navy on coastal patrol and control duties might in any case tempt belligerents to violate Norwegian territorial waters without the risk of encountering a substantial force. The bulk of the navy – a destroyer, three gunboats, seven minelayers and around eighty torpedo boats and leased patrol vessels – was therefore evenly spread along the coast from the Vestfjord in northern Norway to the Swedish border, while the four battleships, including *Eidsvold*, and four

submarines constituted the operational reserve.

These shifting priorities were reflected in the organisation of the Kongelige Norske Marine. In 1899 the coastline between the Swedish border and Bergen in western Norway had been divided into three naval districts: the 1st Naval District based at Karljohansvern in Horten, the 2nd at the Marvika naval station in Kristiansand, and the 3rd at the Marineholmen naval station in Bergen. Prompted by operational needs arising during neutrality guard operations, a preliminary naval district was established in Trondheim in 1915, and another was established for northern Norway at the Ramsund naval base in 1917. However, *Eidsvold* and the other coastal battleships had since 1914 been made subordinate to the naval district commander of the area in which they happened to be operating, regardless of any task group or reaction force to which they had been assigned. The naval district commanders also exercised tactical command over the naval and coastal artillery units attached to them, and were responsible for intelligence and the mobilisation of ships and coast artillery forts within their districts. This organisation, dictated largely by the increased range of reliable radio communications, lasted well into the Cold War.

Neutrality Guard during the First World War

From 1 August 1914 until 21 November 1918 the four coastal battleships were organised as a reaction force on the exposed North Sea coastline, with a primary area of operations extending from Kristiansand to Jærens Rev, a distance of 104 nautical miles. From November 1914 a unit was stationed at Bergen or Trondheim, with the remaining three based on Marvika and the ports of Mandal, Farsund, Flekkefjord and Egersund at irregular intervals. One or two destroyers and four to eight torpedo boats, together with a couple of guardships, were attached to the Battleship Squadron at all times. The battleships were not idle but regularly carried out gunnery and tactical exercises. In 1915, for instance, a major combined exercise was conducted with coastal battleships and submarines, in co-operation with army and coast artillery units. In 1918 an extensive field of 413 mines was laid in the outer Christiania Fjord in an operation covered by the guns of the coastal battleships, while the

A typical spring exercise squadron seen at Leirvik in southwestern Norway in 1912, with the coastal battleships *Tordenskjold* and *Eidsvold* in the background and the torpedo division command ship *Valkyrjen* to the right. Six torpedo boats are moored in the foreground. (S. Konelønning/Marinemuseet)

local coast artillery fortresses were strengthened. Another task was the defence of the main Karljohansvern naval base at Horten.

The First World War was a time of hardship for those among Norway's civilian population who relied on fisheries or the merchant fleet for their income. An entry in the order book of the executive officer of *Eidsvold* in 1915, Kaptein (Commander) Johan Fredrik Ziesler gives an insight into the extent of the hardship and the navy's efforts to alleviate it: 'From now on no waste from the galley will be thrown overboard, but gathered in a bucket and brought ashore … Food that is edible for human beings will not be thrown into the waste, but may be handed out to the small boys who come asking for leftovers.'[6] However, there was privation both ashore and aboard in the last years of the war. Food rations had to be cut, and many fell victim to the Spanish flu epidemic, which resulted in several deaths and a large proportion of the battleship crews going on sick leave.

Between the Wars

The main function of *Eidsvold* and the other coastal battleships between the wars was the education and training of naval cadets, and 'showing the flag' on naval and state visits abroad. But the operational tempo was not high and cruises were few and far between, whether in Norwegian waters or overseas. *Eidsvold*, for instance, made only one foreign voyage after 1918, when she carried King Haakon VII on a state visit to the Netherlands and Belgium in the summer of 1923.

In Norway, as elsewhere, the political reorganisation of Europe following the First World War, including the disarmament of Germany and the establishment of the League of Nations, had the effect of removing any sense of a likely military threat against the country. With minimal political interest in defence, the armed forces including the navy were allowed to decay, and *Eidsvold* was no exception, being commissioned only rarely and receiving no significant refit or modernisation. Threat perceptions did not change until the 1930s, by which time the navy was in a dismal state. The Swedish naval attaché in Oslo was not far wrong when he reported in 1935 that the Norwegian navy was 'to all practical purposes about to leave the surface of the ocean'. That same year the Commander-in-Chief of the Navy

Captain Odd Isaachsen Willoch, *Eidsvold*'s last commanding officer, seen emerging onto his quarterdeck, c. 1940. *(Marinemuseet)*

Rear Admiral Edgar Otto noted that: 'Everything in the navy is in a bad state!' He pointed to the fact that though the ships' hulls had been properly maintained, the navy had not been modernised since 1918 and operational standards were low. There was a shortage of officers and a predominance of elderly ones among those employed. As an indication of the condition of the battleships, in August 1930 the Department of Defence granted permission for radio direction-finders to be dismantled in *Norge* and *Eidsvold* since the equipment was beyond repair. The same happened with the torpedo tubes, the Department of Defence noting that the sale of the resulting scrap might provide a source of income for the navy.

By the time the government began taking steps towards rearmament in 1935 it was too late. Even had the necessary funds been appropriated neither ships nor guns were available on the market. The only solution was to attempt to modernise the existing inventory. The two older battleships, *Harald Haarfagre* and *Tordenskjold*, were considered beyond repair. *Norge* and *Eidsvold*, on the other hand, could be used in a defensive role as floating batteries. Plans were made to increase the range of the main armament from 11,000 to 21,000yds (10,060–19,200m) by converting the turrets to fire at higher elevations

and obtaining modern ammunition. The navy also wanted to replace the obsolete mainmast with a new structure (including a rangefinder) to provide improved communications between the captain, gunnery officer and the gun crews. There were also plans to equip both vessels with a modern director-controlled anti-aircraft armament. But none of these modifications were made. The deck construction was found to be too weak to withstand the recoil pressure at higher elevations and the anti-aircraft guns arrived too late to be of any use.

Neutrality Guard Operations, 1939–40

The task of the Norwegian navy on the outbreak of war in 1939 was the same as it had been in 1914: neutrality guard operations. But while the navy of 1914 had been able to support the neutrality guard with a relatively potent reaction force of coastal battleships, that of 1939 had been neglected to the extent that it was largely without relevant fighting power. The available units were therefore spread along the coast primarily to perform guard duty and report violations of neutrality, though with little ability to interdict them. In the case of *Norge* and *Eidsvold*, these provisions saw them deployed to northern Norway, the strategic importance of which had long been recognised.

Meanwhile, the coastal battleships were not only obsolete but riddled with defects. Not until 30 October 1939, two months after the outbreak of war in Europe, was permission granted for some of these to be rectified in *Norge* and *Eidsvold*. The fire-control equipment in *Tordenskjold* was cannibalised for use in the two newer battleships. Permission was also granted for loudspeaker telephones to be installed in the main and secondary batteries, and the decision taken to mount two 40mm Bofors guns, two 20mm Oerlikon and six machine guns in both vessels. But, as earlier, these decisions came much too late. Neither the telephones nor the bulk of the anti-aircraft guns could be delivered before they sailed for northern Norway. The Oerlikons were on board but had arrived without instruction manuals, mountings, live ammunition or magazines and were therefore quite useless. Moreover, *Norge* and *Eidsvold* were still without gyrocompasses and echo-sounders on the outbreak of war.

The situation is encapsulated in a report prepared by *Eidsvold*'s gunnery officer Kaptein (Commander) Hagbart Thorkelsen on 8 January 1940:

The ships have now been in commission for about four months and I therefore consider it

---

6 Sørensen, *Panserskipene*, p. 92; Ziesler's identity established via Rolf Jensen, *Sjømilitære samfunds kalender 1814–1964* (Horten: Drammen J. Steenberg & Co., 1965), p. 58.

my duty to report the major deficiencies from which they still suffer. This is especially important because the deficiencies are, in my opinion, so grave that I am bound to declare that the value of the vessels as fighting ships is in their present condition so lacking that it can only be characterised as absolutely critical given the grave situation in which we find ourselves ...[7]

He then goes on to detail a number of deficiencies which could easily have been corrected in time. There was still no telephone connection between the commanding officer on the bridge and the gunnery officer in the mainmast where the rangefinding and fire-control equipment was located. A last desperate attempt at improvisation was attempted, but to no avail. In April 1940 the vessels were still without an internal telephone communications system. Worse, the 8.2in battery dating from the turn of the century was also in disrepair. In a letter written on 5 March 1940, while *Eidsvold* was still at Tromsø, Kommandørkaptein (Captain) Odd Isaachsen Willoch stated that it was not certain whether they had been equipped with the correct gunnery scales and range tables for the 101 armour-piercing and 103 high-explosive shells stowed on board. The obsolete electrical training mechanism of one of the 8.2in guns was also out of order. In spite of this they nonetheless packed considerable firepower positioned in a narrow fjord.

Naval Battle at Narvik

The autumn of 1939 found northern Norway in a vulnerable position due to the use of the port of Narvik at the head of the Ofoten fjorden for the export of Swedish iron ore, a strategic resource of vital importance to German arms manufacturing which Britain would surely endeavour to disrupt in the event of war. Moreover, the conflict resulting from the Soviet attack on Norway's northern neighbour Finland threatened to spill over into Norwegian territory. The decision was therefore taken to bolster neutrality guard operations in northern Norway and strengthen the defences of Tromsø by stationing *Norge* and *Eidsvold* in that port. The following spring the two vessels were allocated to the Ofoten Squadron and charged with defending the approaches to Narvik. This force consisted of *Norge* and *Eidsvold*, the submarines *B-1* and *B-3*, and a handful of patrol vessels under the overall command of Captain Per Askim of *Norge*, with *Eidsvold* commanded by

[7] Sørensen, *Panserskipene*, p. 111.

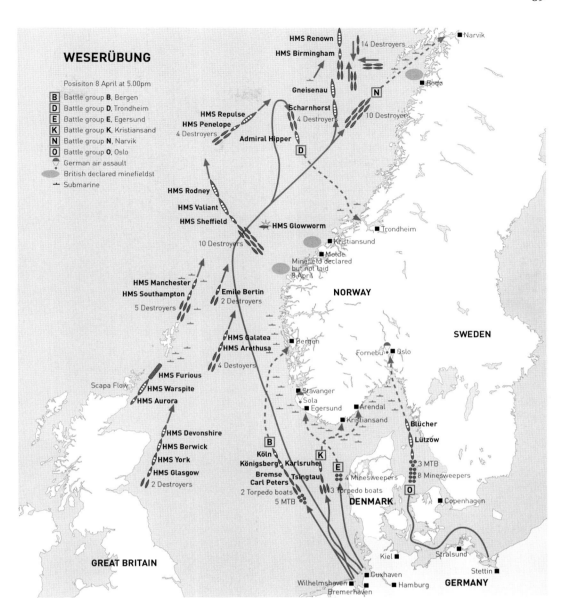

Captain Odd Isaachsen Willoch. On 8 April the squadron was berthed in Narvik, soon to become the scene of fighting on a scale unparalleled in Norwegian history.

Indeed, the German High Command's plans for the occupation of Norway on 9 April, codenamed Weserübung, were well in hand. The occupation of Narvik was assigned to Battle Group N consisting of ten large destroyers covered by the battleships *Scharnhorst* (q.v.) and *Gneisenau* which sailed north from the German Bight on the 7th. Meanwhile, the Royal Navy had deployed the battlecruiser *Renown*, the cruiser *Birmingham* and fourteen destroyers to the area in connection with a minelaying operation in the approaches to the Ofoten fjorden and Narvik. Aware that German naval movements were afoot, the bulk of the British Home Fleet

sailed to intercept any forces interfering with the minelaying operation. However, the Admiralty proceeded in the belief that the Germans were attempting a breakout into the Atlantic rather than an invasion of Norway. On the evening of 8 April the Ofoten Squadron received a signal from the naval staff reporting that German ships had been sighted on a northerly course, but the Commander-in-Chief of the Navy Rear Admiral Henry Diesen still believed that an attack on Norway was unlikely given the strength of the Royal Navy. Nonetheless, Captain Askim ordered the coastal battleships and submarines to double their watches and prepare for war. *Norge* remained at anchor in the inner harbour at Narvik while *Eidsvold* was stationed at its entrance. The submarines were deployed to Bogen, further out on the north shore of the

The last known picture of the coast defence battleships *Eidsvold* and *Norge* at Narvik on 8 April 1940, the day before both were sunk with heavy loss of life. (*Marinemuseet*)

fjord, with the patrol vessels positioned at its mouth.

The Ofoten Squadron was still unclear as to the situation but Captain Askim did not rule out the possibility of a German attack. In the course of the evening he received preliminary orders from the navy staff, and at 0300 on the 9th the patrol vessels reported a German squadron proceeding in line ahead towards Narvik at 30 knots. These were the ten destroyers of Battle Group N which had been observed entering the fjord as the covering battleships steered north-west. The plan was that the latter would distract attention from the landing in Narvik and then return to Germany together with the destroyers once it had been completed. So it was that the destroyers *Wilhelm Heidkamp*, *Bernd von Arnim* and *Georg Thiele* approached Narvik at full speed and in a blizzard. Shortly after 0400 they were sighted from *Eidsvold* which signalled them to stop. When the Germans did not respond *Eidsvold* fired a warning shot. At this the Germans signalled that they intended to launch a boat. Shortly after, a German officer came on board *Eidsvold* and appealed to Captain Willoch to surrender. Having consulted Captain Askim, Willoch informed the Germans that he would rather fight. In keeping with naval tradition, Willoch intended to wait for the negotiator to get clear before opening fire. The latter, however, immediately fired a red flare to indicate that the negotiations had been fruitless. Although *Eidsvold* was cleared for action and had *Wilhelm Heidkamp* at a range of no more than a few hundred yards, she was hit by three torpedoes before she could open fire and immediately broke in two and sank. There were only six survivors of a ship's company of 181 men.

All in *Norge* heard the explosion. The destroyers were sighted a little before 0430 but immediately disappeared into the blizzard. When they reappeared a few minutes later at a range of just 900yds (820m) *Norge* opened fire with her 8.2in main battery and the 6in guns of her starboard battery. While *Georg Thiele* came alongside the harbour jetty, *Bernd von Arnim* attacked *Norge* with torpedoes. The first five missed but the next two struck with effects as disastrous as

with *Eidsvold*. *Norge* sank in a matter of seconds taking 102 of her 192 men with her. The sacrifice of the coastal battleships did nothing to stop Narvik falling later that day.

Sources

Berg, Roald, *Norsk forsvarshistorie*, vol. II: *1814–1905: Profesjon, Union, Nasjon* (Bergen: Eide forlag, 2001)

Bjørgo, Narve, Øystein Rian & Alf Kaartvedt, *Norsk utenrikspolitisk historie*, vol. I: *Selvstendighet og union – fra middelalderen til 1905* (Oslo: Universitetsforlaget, 1995)

Børresen, Jacob, *The Norwegian Navy: A Brief History* (Bergen: John Grieg A/S, 2012)

Børresen, Jacob, & Tom Kristiansen, *Levende breve fra de dødes rige – Admiral U. J. R. Børresens dagboksopptegnelser 1896–1910* (Bergen: Eide forlag, 2005)

Børresen, U. J. R., 'A New Tactical System' in *Journal of the Royal United Service Institution* 47, no. 301 (March 1903), pp. 326–38

_____, 'A New Tactical System Applied to the Russo-Japanese War' in *Journal of the Royal United Service Institution* 50, no. 339 (May 1906), pp. 678–86

Brook, Peter, *Warships for Export: Armstrong Warships, 1867–1927* (Gravesend, Kent: World Ship Society, 1999)

Hobson, Rolf, *Imperialism at Sea: Naval Strategic Thought. The Ideology of Sea Power and the Tirpitz Plan, 1875–1914* (Leiden: Brill Academic Publishers, 2002)

Hobson, Rolf, & Tom Kristiansen, *Norsk forsvarshistorie*, vol. III: *1905–1940: Total krig, nøytralitet og politisk splittelse* (Bergen: Eide forlag, 2001)

Jensen, Rolf, *Sjømilitære samfunds kalender 1814–1964* (Horten: Drammen J. Steenberg & Co., 1965)

Marinens admiralstab, *Tegninger til beskrivelse af panserskibene 'Norge' og 'Eidsvold'* (Christiania: W. C. Fabricius & sønner AS, 1901)

Sørensen, Jørgen, *Panserskipene 1895–1940* (Hundvåg: Sjømilitære samfund ved Norsk Tidsskrift for Sjøvesen, 2000)

Terjesen, Bjørn, Tom Kristiansen & Roald Gjelsten, *Sjøforsvaret i krig og fred – langs kysten og på havet gjennom 200 år* (Bergen: Fagbokforlaget, 2010)

Thomassen, Marius, *90 år under rent norsk orlogsflagg* (Bergen: Eide forlag, 1995)

Ula, Terje, *Flåten som sank* (Oslo: Dreyers forlag, 1946)

Imperial Russian Navy (Российский императорский флот)

The Battleship *Slava* (Слава) (1903)

Sergei Vinogradov with Stephen McLaughlin

SLAVA ('GLORY') was the fifth and final unit of the Borodino-class of battleships, the largest and most tragic in Russian naval history. Completed too late to join Admiral Z. P. Rozhestvenskii's squadron on its ill-fated voyage to the Battle of Tsushima where four of her sisters were lost on 14–15 May 1905, *Slava* nonetheless had plenty of fighting in store and spent three years in the thick of the action during the Baltic naval war from 1915 to 1917.[1] In the course of that campaign she earned the distinction of being the only pre-dreadnought to venture battle single-handedly against not one but two enemy dreadnoughts and of forcing them to retire, albeit briefly. Even after her final battle *Slava*'s shattered hulk served to bar the passage of the enemy in one final act of defiance. This record gives *Slava* a unique place both in the history of the Russian fleets and in that of naval warfare.

Origins and Design

On 20 February 1898 Tsar Nicholas II approved an extraordinary appropriation of 90 million roubles (then about £9 million) for the construction of a powerful squadron to defend Russia's newly acquired ice-free harbour of Port Arthur in Manchuria. With Russian shipyards already at full capacity, the naval ministry turned to France where the firm of Forges et Chantiers de la Méditerranée at La Seyne in Toulon was commissioned to design and build a battleship to Russian specifications. Taking his recently completed battleship *Jauréguiberry* as a basis, the lead designer of the shipyard, Antoine-Jean

Amable Lagane, produced the *Tsesarevich* of 13,105 tons, mounting one 12in turret forward and another aft together with six secondary 6in turrets, three disposed on either beam. Long before she was commissioned in August 1903 *Tsesarevich* had herself become the prototype for the Borodino-class battleships, the design of which was drawn up at the state-owned Novoe Admiralteistvo (New Admiralty) shipyard in St Petersburg under the supervision of Chief Naval Constructor D. V. Skvortsov. While retaining the same general layout as *Tsesarevich* and, like her, mounting both the main and secondary armament in turrets, the Borodino class nonetheless departed from her in several important respects, a consequence of the greater size and weight of Russian-built turrets and machinery. The final design legend of March 1899 provided for a main armament of four 12in (305mm) guns complemented by twelve 6in (152mm) guns, twenty 3in (actually 75mm) guns, twenty 1.85in (47mm) guns, two above-water and two submerged torpedo tubes, all on a displacement of 13,530 tons. With an overall length of 397ft (121m) and a beam of 76ft (23.2m), the intended design draught was 26ft (7.9m) but varied from 27–29ft (8.24–8.9m) as completed. The protection was relatively light by comparison with her contemporaries, the belt, conning tower and main gun turrets receiving 6–7.64in (152–194mm), 8in (203mm) and 10in (254mm) of armour respectively, while the main deck had between 1in and 2in (25–51mm) of plate. The propulsion plant consisted of two sets of vertical four-cylinder triple-expansion engines powered by twenty Belleville water-tube boilers providing 15,800ihp to the twin screws for a designed maximum speed of 18 knots. The ship had stowage for 787 tons of coal at normal load, and 1,350 tons at full load, yielding a maximum range of 2,590 miles at an economical cruising speed of 10 knots.

Construction

Slava was ordered on 18 January 1900 at a cost of 13,840,824 roubles (£1.38 million) and built at the Baltic Shipbuilding and Engineering Works in St Petersburg on the same slip as her sisters *Imperator Aleksandr III* and *Kniaz Suvorov*. No sooner had *Suvorov* been launched on 12 September 1902 than work began to prepare the slip for *Slava*, whose keel-laying ceremony – a more modest affair than that of any of her sister ships – took place on 19 October 1902 after which pre-assembled sections were brought to the slip. The fabric of the ship was almost entirely Russian-made, principally from firms in St Petersburg: steel came from the Aleksandrovskii and Putilovskii works, the main belt plates from the Izhorskii Works and another 1,388 tons of armour came from the Obukhovskii Works. The guns also came from Obukhovskii while their mountings were manufactured by the Metallicheskii Works. The ship's propulsion plant was manufactured by the builder, the Baltic Works. Coming from farther afield were the electrical generators made by the Moscow Electric Company and 490 tons of deck protection ordered from the Nikopolskii-Mariupolskii Armour Works in the Ukraine. The only exception to *Slava*'s all-Russian composition was the armour for the 6in turrets, for which thirty plates totalling 243 tons were supplied by the British firm of Wm. Beardmore & Co. of Glasgow.

At first work proceeded quickly and *Slava* was launched on 16 August 1903 after just 303 days on the slipway – a record for Russian battleships and armoured cruisers despite delays by the Nikolpolskii-Mariupolskii Works in delivering its order of armour plate. At launch she was 67 per cent complete and displaced 6,229 tons. Unlike her subdued keel-laying, the launching ceremony was a magnificent event attended by Tsar Nicholas II and other dignitaries in a display meant to impress on all and sundry – and most

---

[1] All dates are given in the Julian or Eastern calendar used by Russia until January 1918; dates are therefore twelve days before the Gregorian (Western) calendar in the nineteenth century, and thirteen days before in the twentieth century.

Slava awaits launching in the Large Stone Building Shed at the Baltic Shipbuilding and Engineering Works, St Petersburg on 16 August 1903. The attention of the attendees is drawn to the right where Tsar Nicholas II and his entourage are descending from the quarterdeck after pre-launch prayers. *(Sergei Vinogradov Collection)*

especially the foreign representatives present – the extent of Russia's growing naval power and strength on her Pacific coast as relations deteriorated with the Japanese Empire. Although work continued at a steady pace after launch, *Slava* was far from complete by the time the Russo-Japanese War broke out on 27 January 1904. Indeed, Russian war production was only put onto an emergency footing after the death of Admiral S. O. Makarov, lost when the battleship *Petropavlovsk* struck a Japanese mine and sank off Port Arthur on 31 March. After this disaster work went on round the clock to complete the Borodino class, but Russia's limited shipbuilding facilities were already strained to breaking point by the number of vessels under repair or in the process of completion. By the end of March 1904 *Slava* was still awaiting the installation of her main armour plate, turrets, guns, machinery, fittings, boats and rigging. In fact, archival sources make clear that work in many of these areas had been set aside in favour of expediting the completion of her more advanced sisters, including reallocation of some of her auxiliary machinery and even part of the main propulsion plant, leaving virtually no possibility of completing *Slava* in time to take part in the war with Japan. *Slava* therefore remained behind when the Second Pacific Squadron sailed from Kronstadt under Admiral Rozhestvenskii on 17 September 1904.

The departure of the Second Pacific Squadron released hundreds of workers to complete *Slava* and thereafter progress was again rapid despite numerous proposals for alterations. The most curious of these was the idea, subsequently

rejected, of equipping the ship with two midget submarines, but many other improvements were made based on war experience. The most important of these was the installation of longitudinal bulkheads behind the 3in mountings on the middle (battery) deck to limit flooding in the event of hull damage, the addition of a small armoured signal tower to the after bridge, and the elimination of all but four of the twenty 1.85in (47mm) guns, experience having shown these to be ineffectual for repelling torpedo-boat attacks. The above-water torpedo tubes at bow and stern were never installed since they were considered an explosion hazard in a gunnery action. Additional voice pipes were installed

between the central gunnery position and the 12in and 6in turrets. The two 56ft (17m) steam pinnaces, each weighing 21 tons, were replaced by smaller boats of 12 tons each. The bulwark aft was cut away and the conning tower viewing slit reduced from 10.5in to 6in (267–152mm) in width. These changes not only led to cost increases over the contract price but also added weight, the ship's normal displacement rising by some 900 tons to 14,415 tons and increasing her draught to 27ft 4in (8.34m).

On 30 October 1904 – before the winter ice had set in – *Slava* was towed from her builder's yard on the River Neva to Kronstadt, the great naval base and fortress on Kotlin Island lying fifteen miles west of the capital. This was the usual practice for large Russian warships since the shallow waters around St Petersburg required big ships to be completed in the deeper waters at Kronstadt. By this time her machinery had been installed and her funnels and masts erected, but she still lacked turrets, guns, belt armour and boats. Almost all the work was finished during the winter of 1904–5 and *Slava* was prepared for steam trials as the ice began to thaw in early April 1905. On 7 April she was docked to have her bottom cleaned and given three coats of bright red patent paint, the opportunity being taken to cut apertures for the two submerged 15in (381mm) torpedo tubes. The cut-up in the deadwood aft was plated over and the bilge keels shortened to 60ft (18.3m), all these alterations having been made to the other *Borodino*-class ships the previous year.

On 31 May 1905, two weeks after the disaster at Tsushima, *Slava* weighed anchor and put to sea. On trials she drew 4in more than designed, indicating an overload of 216 tons (13,746

Slava fitting out at the Baltic Works in September 1904. To the right of the ship is the facade of the Large Stone Building Shed where the ship's hull was assembled. *(Sergei Vinogradov Collection)*

An early view of the boat deck showing the starboard midships and after 6in turrets. *(Courtesy Philippe Caresse)*

instead of 13,530 tons). Although *Slava*'s normal displacement had increased during construction to 14,415 tons, her trials were run at a displacement as close to the design legend as possible to test the performance of the machinery under the contracted conditions. The ship began her six-hour speed trials in very calm weather, four runs giving a mean speed of 17.64 knots. Despite generating 3 per cent more power than designed, coal consumption was 7 per cent lower than expected and the trials were considered a success despite the ship failing to reach her contract speed of 18 knots. June and July 1905 were taken up with successful completion of the gunnery, auxiliary machinery and other trials and *Slava* was accepted for service late that summer, being allocated to the Baltic Sea Practical Squadron comprising the most modern units in the fleet with which she would undergo training for battle.

Slava's first assignment was to devise methods for centralised long-range fire control. At a time when the Russian navy's range tables were calculated only to 8,600yds (7,860m), *Slava* was ordered to work on methods for shooting out to 20,000yds (18,290m). Barr & Stroud rangefinders were installed and eight days of gunnery exercises began off Reval (now Tallinn,

Estonia) in late September, first at close range and gradually increasing to 9,000yds (8,230m); destroyers towed the targets and a schooner was employed as a target vessel. As one of those present recalled: 'One couldn't say the squadron's shooting was sufficiently accurate at first [...] However, both the targets and the schooner were holed, being repaired in Reval each night.'[2] On 7 November 1905, with winter fast approaching, *Slava* was laid up at Kronshtadt while onboard maintenance continued per the customary winter schedule.

The Ship's Company

Slava was typical of the Russian Imperial Navy as far as her shipboard organisation was concerned. Her company was a microcosm of the empire itself, consisting of a minority of officers (*ofitsery*) and a preponderance of lower ranks (*nizhnie chiny*) separated by a social chasm which, uniquely among Russian capital ships, *Slava* proved able to bridge under the test of war.

According to the 1904 scheme of complement, *Slava* had a crew of 749 petty officers and ratings divided into four divisions (*otdelenie*) composed of two companies (*roty*) in each case, permitting each division to keep a four-hour watch, the first

2 G. F. Tsyvinskii, *50 let v Imperatorskom flote* (Riga: Orient, 1928), p. 260.

of which began at midnight. The eight companies were varied in composition but had roughly the same number of men. Each was led by an officer but authority was wielded by a sergeant-major (*rotnyi feldfebel*), a long-service petty officer responsible not only for work details, leave, pay and clothing allowances, etc. but also for the discipline and loyalty of the men in his charge. No NCO in any other navy can have had such a sweeping range of power and responsibility.

The majority of the lower ranks in the Baltic Fleet were conscripted peasants from Russia's northern and central provinces. By 1906 the term of service was five years, although those with the benefit of a five-year primary school education had to serve only two years. Most men were drafted straight to their ships as ordinary seamen (*riadovie*, from 'rank' or 'line') and served as deckhands, while other conscripts were selected based on their mental or physical abilities for special training in shore establishments as stokers, engine-room artificers, gunners, helmsmen, electricians, signalmen, buglers, etc. In addition to the ordinary seamen, there was a large group of petty officers (*unterofitsery*), a sort of 'sailor aristocracy'. These men were either recent conscripts trained as petty officers in shore establishments, or re-enlistees (*sverkhsrochnosluzhashchie*) who, on the recommendation of their superiors, signed on for extended service at the end of their five-year term. The ratio of petty officers to seamen in *Slava* was about 1:7.

There were significant differences in the pay of petty officers and seamen. First-class seamen (gunners, stokers, machinists, etc.) received 1 rouble per month, second-class seamen 75 kopeks (1 rouble = 100 kopeks; the rouble was equal to about 2 shillings; there were 20 shillings to £1). Petty officers of the deck divisions received 2 roubles per month, second-class specialists received 4 roubles, first-class 5 roubles and boatswains 6 roubles. When cruising in home waters they received a 'sea allowance' which amounted to 75 kopeks per month for ordinary seamen, 3.30 roubles for petty officers of the deck division, 8.25 and 7.50 roubles for specialists of the first and second classes respectively. The boatswain and company sergeant-majors received an additional 14 roubles per month. When serving in foreign waters the sea allowance was increased by about 50 per cent. Moreover, enlisted specialists were entitled to an additional annual payment equivalent to their yearly pay for their 'specialised knowledge', while re-enlistees received an additional annual payment of 200–400 roubles. The Imperial Russian Navy therefore had a well developed system of monetary incentives, and even without the sea allowance a petty officer re-enlistee could receive

Slava soon after completion and seen in her original livery of manila and white funnels on a black hull and superstructure, though soon replaced by an all-grey scheme. Note the elaborate decoration on the bow above the torpedo tube – the imperial double-headed eagle in a richly carved frame, later removed. *(NHHC/NH 60707)*

A group of *Slava* ratings (*nizhnie chiny*) pose in front of the forward 12in turret. The men are dressed in the standard winter uniforms: a cap (*bezkozyrka*) adopted by both the army and the navy in 1811, with a black tally embroidered with the name of the ship in gold letters, and a black double-breasted jacket (*bushlat*) with black trousers. Some of the men are in blue winter flannel shirts (*flanka*) with a turned-down blue collar (*giuis*) with three white tapes along the edges. Under the *flanka* the men are dressed in a flannel shirt with black and white stripes – the *telniashka*. The two mustachioed men in the centre wear caps with visors but no tallies – the one with a notebook is the *feldfebel* (sergeant) of one of the ship's eight divisions, while the other is a chief boatswain (bo'sun). The men with pipes on chains around their necks are junior bo'suns, and those wearing pouches over their shoulders are off-duty members of the ship's guard. (*Sergei Vinogradov Collection*)

an annual pay thirty times greater than an ordinary seaman. For comparison, the annual pay of an industrial worker came to 245 roubles in 1908, increasing to 263 roubles by 1913; the highest wage-earners were metal workers at the St Petersburg Metallicheskii Works, who made as much as 500–550 roubles per year. In addition, sailors did not have to pay for clothing, food (or drink!) or accommodation.

Sailors also enjoyed the best food of all the empire's servicemen. For breakfast they were entitled to 2lb 10oz (1.2kg) of white bread with 1.5oz (43g) of butter (2.8oz/80g on Wednesdays and Fridays) and tea with sugar. Lunch consisted of a hearty soup with meat (about 10.5oz/300g of meat per day) as well as tea and bread (black or rye). Dinner consisted of porridge and tea. There was also the afternoon *poldnik* or *chai* (snack or tea) after the midday rest, consisting of tea with bread and sugar. Bread was baked aboard and was always plentiful. Vodka (40 per cent alcohol; officially called *khlebnoe vino* – 'bread wine') was served before lunch and dinner

Men in summer outfits on *Slava's* forecastle, on galley duty peeling potatoes for dinner. (*Sergei Vinogradov Collection*)

– each man was allotted 1 *charka* (cup) per day (4.3oz/123ml). The vodka was divided into two servings – two-thirds before lunch and a third before supper – dispensed from a large *yendova* (literally 'valley' – an open metal container with a capacity of 1.8–2.6gal/8–12l) by a special petty officer (the *bataler*) who recorded the surnames of each recipient. Non-drinkers were entitled to a monthly payment of 8 kopeks, while non-smokers received 12 kopeks to compensate for the unused tobacco; when at sea these amounts increased by 50 per cent. It is interesting to note that even with the low cost of vodka and the trials of naval service, roughly every other man was a non-drinker or non-smoker.

Slava's extended forecastle made it relatively easy to accommodate the crew. Quarters for the petty officers and seamen were located forward and amidships, while the officers were berthed in cabins aft. Most of the crew slept in hammocks stuffed with crumbled cork, each man being assigned his own berth. According to a witness, 'the crew's quarters in the ships of the Borodino class were not at all bad. Almost all the sailors were accommodated on the upper and battery decks and had good ventilation and lighting through side scuttles. Only a few, mostly stokers, men who worked in the holds and mechanicians, found themselves on the dark lower deck behind the thick armour belt, without natural light.'[3] According to the berthing plan, 229 men were housed on the upper deck, 282 on the battery deck and 213 on the lower deck for a total of 724 men. Another nineteen men were berthed among the crew's lockers, with six more on the lower

---

[3] V. P. Kostenko, *Na 'Orle' v Tsusime* (Leningrad: Sudpromgiz, 1955), p. 133.

deck. Wardroom orderlies were accommodated in two small cabins near the wardroom.

The designed complement of the Borodino-class battleships made provision for twenty-eight officers, including the ship's doctor, his assistant, and an Orthodox priest who had the benefit of a shipboard chapel. Officers were divided into specialisations – gunnery, navigation, torpedoes, engineering, etc. – and deck officers, who acted as watchkeepers and company commanders; in battle they were assigned to specific positions with clearly defined responsibilities. The ship's commander was a captain 1st rank (*kapitan 1-go ranga*, equivalent to an army colonel); his closest aides were the senior (executive) officer (*starshii ofitser*, a captain 2nd rank, i.e. a commander) and the purser (*revizor*, a lieutenant; the Russian navy did not have a specialised paymaster

branch, so the purser was responsible for the ship's cash, disbursement for provisions, repairs, etc.). The officers were educated at the Naval Corps (*Morskoi korpus*), an institution reserved to members of the nobility; entry was almost impossible even for the most talented young men of the lower social orders. In its social composition the Imperial Navy therefore mirrored Russia's division into the 'white bone' of the nobility and 'black bone' of the commoners, a circumstance for which the officers, who were referred to as *drakony* ('dragons') by the lower deck, would pay dearly when revolution came in 1917 (see below).

The officers' cabins were ranged along either side of the upper deck abaft the midships 6in turrets; there were also cabins abaft the after funnel which received natural light through skylights on the forecastle deck. Further aft were the captain's quarters as well as those of the admiral and his staff. The spacious admiral's reception room was at the after end of the superstructure and served as a meeting room when the admiral called his captains together. Nearby were cabins for two orderlies on the centreline abaft the engine room ventilation shaft and separated by the ventilation trunking. There were fifteen officers' cabins located on the deck below, the battery deck, extending aft from the midships 3in battery. The aftermost spaces on the starboard side served as the executive officer's office and cabin. Two more officers' cabins were located inboard, divided by a centreline bulkhead and lacking any natural light. The officers' wardroom was on the battery deck, abaft frame 86. Its after part (abaft frame 91) was taken up by the after 3in battery; the forward section (frames 86–91) contained a long table seating up to thirty officers. The 3in battery, divided by an armoured

Off-duty officers relaxing in *Slava's* wardroom. In the centre reading a newspaper is the ship's Russian Orthodox priest. On the right are three orderlies who were selected from the most presentable men of the lower ranks. (*Central Naval Museum (CNM)*)

Slava's warrant officers (*konduktory*) in their mess under the forecastle. Occupying an intermediary position between the rating and the commissioned officer, the rank of warrant officer was a difficult one in any navy and particularly that of Imperial Russia with its growing social ferment. Note the orderlies standing by on the left. (*Sergei Vinogradov Collection*)

for promotion to sub lieutenant (*michman*) by passing an exam; these men became known as 'wartime sub lieutenants'. The warrant officers' cabins were on the battery deck forward of the 12in turret, with their own mess in the bows of the ship.

Slava's role varied in the course of her career, prompting modifications and improvements to her organisation with a consequent effect on the size of her complement. According to a table of organisation produced on the eve of the Great War, the ship's company consisted of twenty-seven officers, twenty-one warrant officers and 829 lower ranks (108 petty officers and 721 seamen) for a total of 877 men, compared with around 785 in its 1904 equivalent.

centreline bulkhead, was used as a sitting room, with a sofa and several armchairs.

Slava's complement also included nine warrant officers (*konduktory*) who though officially part of the lower deck occupied an intermediate position between ratings and officers. Specialising in gunnery, torpedoes, signals, engineering, etc., the warrant officers often had more expertise in their fields than specialist officers. This expertise was reflected in their officer-style uniforms (albeit made of somewhat cheaper material) and a

higher level of pay than seamen, since most were older men with family ashore. With responsibility for monitoring the work of the seamen and holding them accountable for any negligence, warrant officers were nicknamed *shkuri* ('skins') and were the subject of hostility from ratings, a situation exacerbated by the fact that they were fellow members of the lower orders who were regarded as betraying their own class. A shortage of officers after the outbreak of the Great War resulted in warrant officers being made eligible

Training Ship, 1906–10

By early 1906 the disaster of Tsushima and the unrest which followed it had contributed to a severe shortage of trained officers in the Imperial Russian Navy, leaving nearly one in three posts unfilled. The Admiralty responded by creating a special training squadron of the Baltic Fleet charged with conducting cruises in European waters for newly graduated Naval Corps cadets (*gardemariny*). The aim was to make good this shortage by allowing young officers to complete their preparation for sea duty before promotion

A DAY ABOARD

In peacetime *Slava*'s day began with reveille (usually at 0600, but this could vary as circumstances required), after which the crew stowed their hammocks in open steel racks above deck for airing out. Then came washing and morning prayers. An hour after rising the crew breakfasted before cleaning ship – scrubbing the decks, polishing the brightwork, etc. At exactly 0800 came the flag-raising ceremony; the officers, the guard and band were drawn up in ranks, while crewmen paused from their duties to man the sides at the command 'Attention!' We have a description of this brief and colourful ceremony by A. S. Novikov, a seaman aboard *Slava*'s sister ship *Orël* during the voyage to Tsushima who later found fame as the Soviet writer Novikov-Priboi: 'the flag with its blue cross of St Andrew fluttered as it was slowly hoisted to the gaff by a signalman. The guard presented arms, the officers and crew removed their caps, the buglers and drummers played the march, the petty officers blew an extended trill on their whistles, and the dutyman on the forecastle rang eight bells.'[4] After this the daily routine of training and work resumed. At 1100 a

Men of the ship's guard with their officer (on the extreme left) mustered in full kit on 6 December 1910. (*Sergei Vinogradov Collection*)

whistle signalled the break for 'wine' (i.e. vodka) and lunch, after which the crew rested until 1330. This was followed by tea, then work continued until 1730 when the working day ended and the men prepared for dinner. At sunset the flag was lowered with the

same solemnity as it had been raised, and at 2000 the crew slung their hammocks for the night.

4 A. S. Novokov-Priboi, *Tsusima* (Moscow: Sovetskii Pisatel', 1934), p. 62.

SLAVA AND REVOLUTION

In January 1905, while *Slava* was still fitting out in Kronshtadt, the empire was shaken by a wave of political and social upheaval following the Bloody Sunday massacre in St Petersburg. Before long these events had caused unrest and mutiny in the armed forces, a situation that continued until June 1907. The origins of the 1905 revolution lie deep in the fabric of Russian society but a contributing factor was the series of humiliating reverses suffered by the empire on both land and sea during the Russo-Japanese War which broke out in February 1904. These culminated in the disastrous Battle of Tsushima on 14–15 May 1905 after which Russia sued for peace. On 14 June, while *Slava* was running trials in the Baltic, the crew of the battleship *Kniaz Potëmkin Tavricheskii* mutinied off the Black Sea port of Odessa which was itself in revolt, slaughtering several of their officers and inflaming the disturbances ashore. The *Potëmkin* mutiny ended ignominiously at the Romanian port of Constanza eleven days later, but a succession of uprisings and revolts kept the revolutionary flame burning both in the Black Sea and in the Baltic where a major mutiny broke out at Kronshtadt in October 1905. The continuing unrest touched *Slava* herself the following summer.

In July 1906 *Slava*, now part of the training squadron of the Baltic Fleet (see below), proceeded to Kronshtadt for refitting, but these plans were disrupted when evidence was uncovered of revolutionary agitation by radical elements attempting to fan lower-deck discontent into a co-ordinated fleetwide revolt. Forty-one ratings were arrested on Saturday 8 July but nine days later a mutiny erupted at Sveaborg, the fortress defending Helsingfors (now Helsinki) in what was then the Grand Duchy of Finland. *Tsesarevich* and the protected cruiser *Bogatyr* were sent to help quell the revolt but *Slava* was left

Slava seen in 1905 during a period of major unrest in the Imperial Russian Navy. Note the numerous 3in (actually 75mm) guns on the battery deck and the anti-torpedo nets which were removed that winter. *(Sergei Vinogradov Collection)*

coaling at Kronshtadt, her crew reckoned too unreliable to participate. Only on the evening of the 19th, after shelling by *Tsesarevich* had compelled Sveaborg's mutineers to surrender, did *Slava* receive orders to join the rest of the squadron. The training squadron remained at Helsingfors until 23 July, after which it steamed across the Gulf of Finland to Reval where investigations were carried out into the mutinies at Kronshtadt and Sveaborg and that in the armoured cruiser *Pamiat Azova* during which the ship's captain and six other officers had been killed as the ship lay off Reval. By the time the squadron

weighed anchor and sailed early on 5 August, seventeen men from Kronshtadt, seventeen from Sveaborg and eighteen from *Pamiat Azova* had been tried and executed, a total of fifty-two sailors. No sooner had the squadron reached Kronshtadt than a further sixty undesirables were removed from *Slava*, and only once this had been completed could the squadron begin its first training cruise. An officer in the *Bogatyr* recorded that 'In all these difficult and unpleasant events our squadron of ships took an active part, doing their duty honourably'.[5]

It is interesting to note that the group most

to the rank of sub lieutenant (*michman*). The squadron consisted of *Slava* and two vessels newly returned from the Far East, her near-sister *Tsesarevich* and the protected cruiser *Bogatyr*. In *Slava*'s case these training duties extended not only to cadets but also to petty officers, provision being made to accommodate an additional 150 men on the battery deck.

Arrangements for the first training cruise were overshadowed by the mutinies which affected the Baltic Fleet in July 1906 (see panel) and it was only once these had been suppressed and the culprits brought to justice that planning could be completed and the squadron favoured with an imperial review. This accomplished, on 20

August it sailed from Kronshtadt on the first of a five-year round of foreign cruises which took *Slava* from the Arctic to the Aegean. As one participant of the first cruise optimistically wrote, 'The challenging moral trial sent by fate to this young squadron is over. Joyfully looking forward, the squadron has set forth on its course.'[6] The first cruise combined training with a survey of Russia's Arctic coast in order to identify a suitable location for a future northern naval base. The squadron first visited Kiel, where

it spent a week, then sailed to the Norwegian port of Bergen. Even before departing Bergen on 6 September the barometer had begun falling and the voyage north to the Barents Sea provided a severe test of seamanship. As one participant recorded: 'As soon as we left the fjord and dropped the pilot we began to roll heavily. The sky was overcast with leaden clouds, a sharp piercing northern wind howled dismally. The battleships pitched wildly, showing their red ram bows. The little *Bogatyr* was tossed about like a cork.'[7] On 10 September, after a five-day passage

---

[6] V. Blinov, 'Rol' gardemarinskogo otriada v dele vospitaniia morskikh ofitserov' in *Morskoi sbornik* 10 (1913), p. 47.

[7] L-t B., 'Vospominaniia o pokhode na Murman', p. 2.

inclined to revolutionary ideas was not the ordinary seamen but conscripted petty officers who were more educated and therefore more receptive to radical ideas. Having been put in positions of trust with authority over other men, the betrayal of the established order by mutinous NCOs was seen as especially heinous and the Tsarist judicial system generally punished them very severely. Despite the threat of arrest, imprisonment, execution and transfer, cells of sailor-radicals survived aboard *Slava* as they did in all Russian vessels of the period, but the revolutionary movement temporarily fell into abeyance after the unrest of 1905–7 as the navy made desperate efforts to rebuild and reorganise itself. Even when revolutionary politics returned to the fore during the Great War, its adherents never wielded sufficient influence to incite open revolt in *Slava*. Moreover, the ship's officers generally exercised authority responsibly, taking good care of the men, discharging troublemakers and being generous in the award of decorations to those who had distinguished themselves in battle. Despite the incidents of indiscipline that marred *Slava*'s early career, lengthy peacetime cruises and rigorous combat training under the demanding leadership of the Commander-in-Chief of the Baltic Fleet, Admiral N. O. von Essen, eventually welded her ship's company into something of a rarity in the Tsarist navy, a hardened alloy encompassing practically all those aboard. This unity of officers and men, frequently commented upon by contemporaries, made it possible for *Slava* to endure the many trials that beset her during the Great War.

Midshipmen (*korabelnye gardemariny*) on the quarterdeck during their 'maiden' voyage in *Slava*, 1910. (*S. P. Slavinskii Collection*)

Slava in Naples in February 1909. This photo provides a good overview of the ship's armament, showing a 12in and 6in turret and some of the numerous 1.85in guns in the superstructure. The torpedo nets had been removed before the 1906 navigation season. (*Sergei Vinogradov Collection*)

5 L-t B., 'Vospominaniia o pokhode na Murman' in *Kotlin* 59, no. 4324 (15 March 1911), p. 2.

'in very rough seas', the squadron reached Pechenga Bay on the Murman coast under heavy snow. Here it remained for six days before proceeding to Kola Bay where the ice-free port of Murmansk would be established in 1916.

The return voyage took in the Norwegian ports of Vardø, Hammerfest and Tromsø, but on the next leg the squadron had to weather a Force 11–12 hurricane and the crews were no doubt glad to make Greenock on the Clyde on 10 October. The ships remained there for a week during which the cadets visited Glasgow and Edinburgh where the local authorities arranged visits to various shipyards, 'the management of which very kindly showed both the yards and

ships under construction'.[8] The squadron next passed to Barrow where officers and cadets inspected the large armoured cruiser *Riurik* being built for Russia by Vickers, also taking the opportunity to tour Vickers' River Don armour works in Sheffield. On 26 October the squadron departed Barrow and proceeded to Brest, Vigo, Madeira, Cadiz and Gibraltar, at length reaching Bizerte on 20 December where it spent forty days. It then steamed to Toulon, remaining there three weeks before turning homeward. On 11 March 1907 the squadron arrived at Portsmouth where it was the focus of unprecedented hospitality. Officers and cadets toured the

8 Blinov, 'Rol' gardemarinskogo otriada', p. 48.

dockyard and other shore facilities, as well as numerous warships, including the newly completed HMS *Dreadnought*. The welcome accorded the squadron provided tangible evidence of the growing rapprochement between Britain and Russia in the face of Germany's increasingly aggressive foreign policy, an improvement in relations sealed by the signing of the Anglo-Russian Convention in August 1907.

On 29 March the squadron reached the Latvian port of Libava (Libau, now Liepāja), where an imposing forty-seven-member commission boarded the ships to administer the final exams to the cadets before their promotion to sub lieutenant. No fewer than 133 cadets passed their exams, which the authorities deemed a highly successful outcome. It was therefore decided that another foreign cruise be carried out of what seagoing wits had dubbed the 'squadron of good intentions' (no doubt in reference to Rozhestvenskii's squadron of 1904–5) with the next batch of graduates from the Naval Corps. So it was that on 30 September 1907 the squadron – again consisting of *Slava*, *Tsesarevich* and *Bogatyr* – put to sea with the newly graduated cadets. Having visited Christiania (now Oslo) and Bergen, they again put in at Greenock, the opportunity being taken for officers and cadets to familiarise themselves with the manufacture of coincidence rangefinders at the Barr & Stroud works in nearby Glasgow. They were also able to tour several shipyards, though a visit to a turbine factory was not approved. The ships then visited Brest where tours of inspection were carried out of the latest French construction – the armoured cruiser *Léon Gambetta* and the battleships *Démocratie* and *Vérité* – followed by a cruise of the eastern Mediterranean. After this the squadron set course for the Baltic, calling at Naples, Gibraltar, Vigo and Kiel en route, and reaching Libava on 26 March 1908, *Slava* having steamed 11,500 miles without a single failure of the main machinery.

Slava, *Tsesarevich* and *Bogatyr* were again assigned to a cadet training cruise, their third in as many years, to be carried out over the autumn and winter of 1908–9. The new group of cadets, 164 in number, joined the squadron in June 1908. A cruise of the Baltic followed, including ceremonial visits by King Gustav V of Sweden and President Armand Fallières of France. On 4 October the squadron set off on its winter cruise and after a stormy passage across the North Sea reached Plymouth on the 8th where it spent nine days before heading for the Mediterranean, reaching the Sicilian port of Augusta in late November. At this point routine cruising was interrupted by a major disaster: at midnight on 15–16 December 1908 the city of Messina on the northeastern coast of Sicily was shattered by an earthquake followed by a tsunami. Without waiting for permission from St Petersburg, the commander of the Russian squadron, Rear Admiral V. I. Litvinov, immediately decided to render assistance and was at sea by 0100 on the morning of 16 December. As Cadet V. N. Iankovich recalled, 'None of us had any idea what needed to be done at Messina. But no one slept that night [at sea]. Various materials were used to make stretchers, the machinists made crowbars, picks and axes. Shovels were made ready …'[9] The Russian ships were among the first of what became an international squadron of warships rendering aid to the devastated city. Arriving at the outer roads of Messina at 0600, the entire crew was landed except for those specialists needed to run the ship and her sickbay. V. A. Belli of *Tsesarevich*:

On approaching the Straits of Messina one saw furniture and household items floating everywhere, washed offshore by the waves: cabinets, doors, drawers, tables, etc. The officers and men of the ships went ashore day and night by watches to work at saving people buried in collapsed houses. People worked absolutely heroically, without respite [...] The city was completely destroyed, leaving only the shells of large stone buildings.[10]

Under difficult conditions, amid fires and continuing aftershocks, the crews of the Russian ships cleared away rubble and saved many residents. As Iankovich recalled, 'debris had to be shifted, beams and planks pulled away. Limestone dust burned faces and hands, fingers and palms were rubbed raw and covered in blood. Survivors were put on stretchers or doors and carried to our medical stations on the waterfront.'[11] Rear Admiral Litvinov sent this report to the Naval Ministry:

The King and Queen of Italy, upon arriving at Messina, visited *Slava* and *Tsesarevich* and thanked the crews for their help. A terrible disaster. There are few facilities for saving those buried. Not less than 50,000 people have been lost in Messina, not counting those carried out to sea by the waves. The work of all the personnel of the squadron entrusted to me is beyond all praise.[12]

As darkness fell on 17 December *Slava* and *Tsesarevich* sailed from Messina for Naples with over 700 casualties filling every available space aboard. Having landed the injured they returned to Messina to resume their rescue work and it was not until 26 December that the squadron left the stricken city. After stopping at Augusta the ships proceeded to Alexandria where they stayed until 8 January. Turning west, the squadron reached Gibraltar on the 15th where it encountered the sixteen battleships of U.S. Navy's 'Great White Fleet', then on the final leg of its famous circumnavigation. The Americans hospitably arranged tours of their ships, after which the Russian squadron proceeded to Madeira, Vigo and Portsmouth, reaching Kiel to another warm welcome on 10 March. The cadets were able to

Slava's nine-piece balalaika band poses on the quarterdeck during one of the ship's many visits to Britain between 1906 and 1913 which formed part of the rapprochement between the two countries. The photo shows a range of balalaika styles from descant to base; the round-bodied instrument is the domra. (*The Illustrated War News*)

9   'Russkie moriaki v Messine' in *Voenno-istoricheskii arkhiv* 5 (1999), p. 41.

10 V. A. Belli, *V Rossiiskom Imperatorskom flote. Vospominaniia* (St Petersburg: Peterburgskii institut pechati, 2005), p. 180. The death toll was 90,000–120,000.

11 Iankovich, 'Russkie moriaki v Messine', p. 41.

12 Litvinov's hitherto unpublished report cited in Vinogradov, *Bronenosets 'Slava'*, p. 80.

Warships of the Baltic Fleet's training squadron at Gibraltar in January 1909. Flanking them are the battleships of the U.S. Navy's Great White Fleet, then in the final stage of its world cruise. From left to right, the grey-hulled Russian ships are the armoured cruiser *Admiral Makarov*, the battleships *Tsesarevich* and *Slava*, and the protected cruisers *Bogatyr* and *Oleg*. *(Sergei Vinogradov Collection)*

visit the dockyard and tour the latest battleships during their five-day stay. The squadron then made for Libava, arriving on 17 March having steamed a total of 10,896 miles. *Slava* remained in the Baltic throughout the summer and autumn of 1909, participating in various manoeuvres and training exercises until the navigation season ended on 1 October.

Refit, 1910–11

Extensive repairs were performed during the winter of 1909–10 including replacement of the worn-out 12in guns and installation of improved breech blocks which significantly speeded up the loading process. However, an inspection of *Slava*'s machinery revealed that her boilers were fit only for one or two more years' service, a consequence of inadequate maintenance and the intensive steaming of 1906–9. The installation of new boilers was postponed, but the machinery was given a major overhaul, including hurried installation of the new Belleville-pattern boiler feed pumps. Unfortunately, the work was only completed the night before *Slava* was due to sail so no tests were possible. On 19 July 1910 the squadron, now joined by the armoured cruiser *Riurik*, departed on its fourth cruise carrying another contingent of cadets (thirty-six in *Slava*). It reached Portsmouth on the 24th where tours of the dockyard were again arranged. Having reprovisioned, the Russian ships sailed for Algeria but on the third day at sea it was discovered that only half of the eight feed pumps supplying fresh water to *Slava*'s boilers were working, and of these two were found to be unreliable. As boilers began going out of service, it was first necessary to reduce speed and then stop the engines alto-

gether. The inability of the new pumps to supply the boilers with sufficient water had resulted in overheating, which exacerbated all of the existing problems in her ageing boiler plant. Emergency repairs proved unavailing and *Tsesarevich* had to tow *Slava* the last thirty-five miles into Gibraltar.

The state of the boilers made the long return voyage to Russia unthinkable, so the Naval Ministry decided to send *Slava* to Toulon for the necessary repairs while the rest of the squadron continued its Mediterranean cruise. Makeshift repairs at Gibraltar succeeded in getting all of the feed pumps working and on 20 August she set out for Toulon with twelve out of twenty boilers serviceable. On arrival *Slava* was taken into Forges et Chantiers de la Méditerranée at La Seyne to have her entire boiler plant replaced. An 820,000-franc contract was signed with the firm

of Delaunay Belleville for manufacture of the boilers, while another worth 298,000 francs was signed with Forges et Chantiers for their installation. With *Slava*'s cadets transferred to the other vessels in the squadron and some of the crew discharged to the reserves, the complement was reduced to 528 men, all of whom took an active part in the work which lasted over the winter of 1910–11. By the following spring the refit was nearing completion, with all boilers and both funnels having been replaced. Moored tests were carried out on 4 May, followed by a trial run at low speed on five boilers. On 31 May the ship put to sea for trials of all the boilers and pumps, but problems persisted with the new machinery. A second attempt on 14 June, including a full-power trial, saw a recurrence of the situation, *Slava* being forced to return to the shipyard 'due to the unsatisfactory operation of the boiler pumps and feed tubes'. The defects having been eliminated as far as possible, on 18 July *Slava* again put to sea for final trials during which a speed of 16 knots was reached over a five-hour run. The pumps were still unsatisfactory (one of them did not work at all), and the contracted pump pressure of 500lb/ft^2 (2,441kg/m^2) (as opposed to 250lb/ft^2/1,221kg/m^2 in the boilers) was not achieved. The final reckoning with Forges et Chantiers resulted in some 34,519 francs being deducted from the contracted price due to the delays. On 23 June 1911, nearly a year after she had sailed from the Baltic, *Slava* finally returned to Russia, making only a brief stop at Southampton to coal.

Battleship Brigade, 1911–14

On 14 July 1911 *Slava* was assigned to the Baltic Fleet's newly established Battleship Brigade,

Replacing the 12in guns in *Slava*'s after turret in October 1909. This complex task was carried out at Kronshtadt, main repair base of the Baltic Fleet. Floating cranes and experienced technicians were required to manoeuvre the 43-ton barrels. *(Sergei Vinogradov Collection)*

finding herself in the company of her old companion *Tsesarevich* and two recently completed semi-dreadnoughts, *Andrei Pervozvannyi* and *Imperator Pavel I*. In the Russian navy a brigade usually consisted of four ships, but in this case the Battleship Brigade was host to another veteran of the training squadron, the armoured cruiser *Riurik* which served as flagship of the Commander-in-Chief of the Baltic Fleet, Admiral N. O. von Essen. The brigade began a daily routine of manoeuvres, gunnery practice and other exercises which lasted until the onset of winter. During this time the opportunity was taken to carry out repairs to *Slava*'s main and auxiliary machinery and turrets, and to upgrade her fire-control equipment by the addition of new pattern sights and follow-the-pointer gear for laying the guns.

The navigation seasons of 1912 and 1913 passed off uneventfully with manoeuvres and exercises in company with the other units of the Baltic Sea Squadron, though at a higher pitch in the latter year than formerly. These included brigade and joint evolutions, steaming at night without lights, repelling torpedo attacks, sailing in the wake of minesweepers, and carrying out various tasks among the Finnish skerries lying between Hanko (Hangö) and Helsingfors, culmi-

nating in fleet-wide manoeuvres from 18–25 August 1913. Under ordinary circumstances this would have been the prelude for the winter lay-up, but on 27 August *Riurik*, the Battleship Brigade, four cruisers and four destroyers departed on the first foreign cruise of the major units of the Baltic Fleet since Rozhestvenskii's Second Pacific Squadron in 1904. On 1 September it reached Portland, the main anchorage of the British Home Fleet, where it remained a week. By all accounts the visit with its accompanying entertainments and festivities was a great success, and Admiral von Essen sent this letter of appreciation to the mayor of nearby Weymouth:

Sir, On behalf of the flag officers, captains, officers, non-commissioned officers and men of the squadron under my command and myself I have the greatest pleasure to beg you to accept, and to transmit to the members of the municipality as well as to the citizens of Weymouth and Portland, our sincerest thanks for the cordial hospitality which has been accorded us during our stay in this port. I can assure you that we are carrying away with us a memory which will be a new link in the friendship already uniting the two nations, and which will never fade from our memory.[13]

The Baltic Fleet then proceeded to Brest and another warm reception. In the evening there were 'very impressive fireworks', the ships being illuminated as their searchlights played over the harbour, all of which presented 'a beautiful picture'.[14] The next day the Russian consul in Brest gave a ball in honour of Admiral von Essen and his officers with all the local authorities attending. On the 10th a grand dinner and ball was hosted by the *Préfet Maritime*, while the municipal authorities organised a feast for the seamen of both the Russian and French warships during which over 5,000 men 'fraternised with general joyous gusto'.[15] The officers, meanwhile, took the opportunity to visit France's first dreadnought, the battleship *Jean Bart*. When the fleet sailed for home on 12 September it was sent off by a crowd of thousands. On the 21st the ships reached Reval having steamed 3,520 miles, and on 1 October the fleet was laid up in reserve for the winter in the Helsingfors roads.

The navigation season of 1914 for the Battleship Brigade began on 9 April when it cleared Helsingfors in the wake of the icebreaker *Yermak* before proceeding to Reval. The next two months were spent in the usual round of manoeuvres and gunnery practices. This routine was broken on 4 June with the arrival at Reval of the British 1st Battle-Cruiser Squadron under Rear Admiral Sir David Beatty consisting of HMSs *Lion* (flag), *Princess Royal*, *Queen Mary* and *New Zealand*, accompanied by the light cruisers *Blonde* and *Boadicea*. Repaying the welcome shown at Portland the previous year, each Russian battleship served as host to one of the battlecruisers, *Slava* being paired with *New Zealand*. The two navies vied to outdo the other in hospitality, exchanging visits, dinners, dances and other maritime courtesies.

War in the Baltic

On 15 June the festive summer came to an abrupt end with the assassination of the Archduke Franz Ferdinand in Sarajevo. At midnight on 16 July, only hours after Austro-Hungarian river monitors operating on the Danube had shelled the Serbian capital Belgrade, the Russian ships opened their 'Great Mobilisation Envelopes' and made ready for war. A barge came alongside *Slava* to remove surplus

Slava in the Baltic, c. 1912–13. Included in the Baltic Fleet's Battleship Brigade from its inception on 1 May 1911, *Slava*'s place in the formation was thereafter indicated by her funnel markings – a red band 3ft high halfway up each funnel. *(Sergei Vinogradov Collection)*

13 'End of the Russian Naval Visit. Admiral's Thanks' in *The Times* (London), 20 September 1913, p. 10. The *Times* published accounts of the visit almost daily.

14 'Letopis "Morskogo Sbornika", 1913 god' in *Morskoi sbornik* 12 (1913), pp. 1–16; 10–13.

15 *Ibid.*

equipment and half of the ship's boats were landed. Work also began on the removal of the 3in guns which were considered useless in modern war. On the 17th and 18th the Battleship Brigade put to sea, cruising between Helsingfors and Reval at the entrance to the Gulf of Finland at leisurely speed in expectation of a surprise German assault on the imperial capital, St Petersburg. The battleships were also providing cover for the first of many minelaying operations at the mouth of the gulf. It was here that the 'Central Mine-Artillery Position' was created, a series of dense minefields to be defended by both shore batteries and battleship guns in the event of a German incursion and the keystone of Russia's naval defences in the Baltic.

On 19 July Germany declared war on Russia. Early next morning the brigade weighed anchor and together with the flagship *Riurik* made for Nargen Island fifteen miles northwest of Reval.

There it anchored briefly before steaming for Helsingfors that afternoon along the edge of the newly laid minefield. Upon arrival *Slava*'s crew set to work 'stripping wood, painted brass and iron'. The period between 21st and 23rd July was spent in the Helsingfors roads, ready to weigh anchor at a moment's notice should the German fleet put in an appearance. The Kaiserliche Marine, however, had no intention of storming the Gulf of Finland. Its main goals were protecting the import of high-grade iron ore from Sweden and denying the passage of supplies to Russia through St Petersburg, which was renamed Petrograd shortly after the outbreak of war. Between 2 and 4 August *Slava* completed her preparations for battle which included removing the yards, cutting down the upper after bridgework and compass platform, and reducing the width of the funnel bands from three feet to one. The last of the 3in guns in the midships

battery had by now been landed, together with the twenty-two gunners assigned to them, although their departure was more than compensated for by the arrival of eighty-eight reservists.

Slava and the other heavy ships spent the rest of August cruising between Reval and Helsingfors, with occasional target practice. On 26 August reports of a major enemy force approaching the Gulf of Finland brought Admiral von Essen, still flying his flag in *Riurik*, out of Reval with the main units of the Baltic Fleet, *Slava* bringing up the rear. The ships searched the northern part of the Baltic before making a southward sweep in search of the seven Deutschland-class battleships reported to be in the area. As darkness came on news was received that the enemy force had retired to the south and the search was called off. September was spent exercising in the Gulf of Finland, but after the disastrous loss of the armoured cruiser *Pallada*,

Slava at Helsingfors (now Helsinki), the home base of the Baltic Fleet, during the winter of 1913–14. Note the sentry box on the ice and the Naval Jack flying from the bows of the ship. *(Stephen McLaughlin Collection)*

sunk by the German submarine *U26* with all 597 hands on the 28th, the Battleship Brigade did not venture beyond the Central Mine-Artillery Position and limited its forays to the area east of the Helsingfors–Reval line. The first campaign season of the war ended on 7 December 1914, the ships laying up for the winter in Helsingfors. The brigade commander reported that 'in total during the year the Brigade steamed 6,550 miles in seventy-five days underway'.[16]

The navigation season of 1915 started unusually early for *Slava* and *Tsesarevich*. At dawn on 29 March *Slava* sailed from Helsingfors for Reval escorted by two icebreakers. Here she was joined two days later by *Tsesarevich* to form the 4th Manoeuvring Group as provided in the 1915 fleet reorganisation plan. Admiral von Essen ordered them to southwest Finland to forestall any attempts by the Germans to seize the Åland Islands commanding the entrance to the Gulf of Bothnia and come ashore on the mainland in the vicinity of the Finnish port of Åbo (now Turku). Throughout April, May and June, the ships remained in Jungfrusund (Dragsfjärd) near Åbo, occasionally putting to sea for gunnery practice. On 2 July *Slava* and *Tsesarevich* acted as distant cover for a Russian cruiser thrust into the southern Baltic which led to a confused, fog-bound action with German cruisers resulting in the loss of the minelaying cruiser SMS *Albatross*. *Slava* and *Tsesarevich*, which saw no action during this operation, were subsequently moved first to Reval and then to Helsingfors.

The Battle for the Gulf of Riga, 1915

In May 1915 Admiral von Essen died of pneumonia, being replaced by Vice Admiral (later Admiral) V. A. Kanin as Commander-in-Chief of the Baltic Fleet. The change came at a critical moment on the Eastern Front, coinciding as it did with an offensive by the German and Austro-Hungarian armies which sent the Russian army reeling back in what became known as the Great Retreat. By July the Germans had occupied the province of Kurland (modern Lithuania and western Latvia) and were threatening Lifland and Estland (now eastern Latvia and Estonia), while the western shores of the Gulf of Riga fell into German hands. Futhermore, intelligence reports indicated that the Kaiserliche Marine was preparing an attack on the gulf itself, in which the only naval forces were destroyers, gunboats and minesweepers operating against the enemy's coastal flank. The staff of the Baltic Fleet there-

Slava's commander, Captain 1st Rank O. O. Rikhter, addressing the crew on 19 July 1914, the day Germany declared war on Russia. *(Sergei Vinogradov Collection)*

fore decided to send a heavy warship into the gulf to support the army and defend the minefields being laid at its western entrance known as the Irben Strait. But which battleship should be sent into the gulf? The Sevastopol-class dreadnoughts were the bulwark of the Russian defences in the Baltic and had therefore to be kept in reserve for the day the German navy attempted to break into the Gulf of Finland and attack Kronshtadt and Petrograd. The semi-dreadnoughts *Andrei Pervozvannyi* and *Imperator Pavel I* were also considered too valuable to risk in confined and shallow waters, leaving *Slava* and *Tsesarevich* as the only candidates. Not only were they of inferior value to the new battleships but their draught was significantly less: 27ft 7in (8.4m) at full load as against 29ft 10in (9.1m) for the semi-dreadnoughts. The choice fell on *Slava*, and despite her obsolescence this assignment would make her one of the most

famous ships in the Imperial Russian Navy. On the night of 17–18 July 1915 *Slava*, covered by two battleships and five cruisers, entered the Gulf of Riga via the Irben Strait; the eastern entrance, the Moonsund, would have been safer but was too shallow for *Slava*. Having passed through a swept channel in the defensive minefields (which were immediately replenished after her), *Slava* steamed to her new home at Kuiwast (now Kuivastu), a small port on the island of Moon (now Muhu).

As it turned out, *Slava* had been transferred in the nick of time and within a week she was in action countering a major German operation to break into the Gulf of Riga. The enemy force was formidable: eight dreadnoughts, seven pre-dreadnoughts, three battlecruisers, nine cruisers, fifty-four destroyers and torpedo boats, thirty-nine minesweepers and minelayers, plus auxiliary vessels. This fleet had more than twice the

The battleships of the 1st Brigade frozen in at Helsingfors over the winter of 1914–15. Even at their moorings the ships are disposed as prescribed in the line of battle fighting instructions: from left to right they are *Slava*, *Tsesarevich*, *Imperator Pavel I* and *Andrei Pervozvannyi*. Like all major units of the Baltic Fleet, they have been painted white to reduce their visibility to German air reconnaissance. *(Sergei Vinogradov Collection)*

---

16 Hitherto unpublished Battleship Brigade report for 1914 cited in Vinogradov, *Bronenosets 'Slava'*, p. 127.

Slava as readied for war in late 1914. The yards on both masts have been removed, the after bridgework cut down, the twelve 3in guns of the midships battery eliminated, and the funnel bands painted narrower. (CNM)

strength of the entire Russian Baltic Fleet and immeasurably superior to the naval forces of the Gulf of Riga, which consisted of the pre-dreadnought *Slava*, four gunboats, a division of destroyers, four submarines and the minelayer *Amur*. At dawn on 26 July the Germans began their attempt to force the Irben Strait. The minesweepers led the way covered by the pre-dreadnoughts *Braunschweig* and *Elsass* and the cruisers *Bremen* and *Tethys*. Further out to sea were five more battleships and four cruisers. Having negotiated the first line of mines, the minesweepers came under fire from the Russian gunboats *Khrabryi* and *Groziashchii*. The minesweeper *T52* quickly struck a mine and sank, while *Tethys* and the destroyer *S144* were both damaged on mines and had to be towed to safety. When *Slava* reached the scene at about 1030 *Braunschweig* and *Elsass* immediately took her under fire at a range of 17,500yds (16,000m). *Slava*, whose badly worn guns were now limited to 15,600yds (14,260m) at their maximum elevation of 15 degrees, did not trouble to reply. After the sixth salvo she moved out of range while the German commander, Vizeadmiral Erhard Schmidt, convinced he could not breach the Russian minefields, elected to withdraw. *Slava*'s first encounter with the enemy therefore ended without her opening fire. The expedient was subsequently resorted to of increasing the elevation of her 12in guns by 3 degrees by flooding compartments on the disengaged side of the ship, the list adding 1,600yds (1,460m) to their range. The Germans had meanwhile acknowledged *Slava*'s presence in the Gulf of Riga as a major obstacle to their plans. Kaiser Wilhelm II personally ordered her to be sunk by submarines, with his younger brother Grossadmiral Prince Heinrich of Prussia,

Commander-in-Chief of the Baltic forces, declaring that the destruction of the battleship would have a significant effect on Russian morale.

The next attempt to break into the Gulf of Riga came a week later on 3 August. *Slava* again found herself defending the Irben Strait, but this time she faced far more powerful opposition as the minesweepers were now supported by the dreadnoughts *Nassau* and *Posen*. The Russian destroyers and gunboats were already in action by the time *Slava* entered the Irben Strait, and at 1405 the German battleships opened fire on her as she steamed north and south along the eastern border of the minefield. The initial range was 24,000yds (21,950m), the German shells at first falling short while *Slava* occasionally targeted the minesweepers and their supporting cruisers and destroyers. The action was protracted and the minesweepers, which were beaten back more than once by *Slava*'s fire, made very slow progress, although the latter was periodically forced to retire eastwards by salvoes from the German dreadnoughts. At around 1800 *Nassau* and *Posen* fired their last salvoes at ranges of 21,000–22,000yds (19,200–20,120m) before the entire German force moved off to the west. Despite some near-misses, *Slava* again emerged from the action unscathed, having herself fired thirty-five 12in and twenty 6in shells. However, the Germans were intent on destroying *Slava* and that night sent two large destroyers, *V99* and *V100*, to sink her. Despite penetrating the Irben Strait by a clear channel close to the German-held southern shore, they searched for her in vain. The Germans abandoned the attempt after a few chaotic skirmishes with Russian patrol destroyers but were then intercepted by the destroyer *Novik*. After sustaining numerous hits,

V99 was driven into a minefield where she struck two mines and had to be run aground and abandoned. *V100* escaped.

On the morning of 4 August *Slava* again took up her position in the Irben Strait. There was heavy mist and fog, visibility to the west being no more than 8,000–10,000yds (7,320–9,140m). *Slava* found herself heavily engaged by *Nassau* and *Posen*, and at about 0850 took three 11in hits. The first struck the top of the 6in upper belt, pierced the hull and burst causing significant splinter damage in the vicinity. The second penetrated the upper deck and struck the barbette of the port after 6in turret, pushing in the armour deck and causing a fire which destroyed four officers' cabins on the port side. Not only that, but the shell detonated within 2ft (60cm) of that turret's manual ammunition supply hatch, which was open in accordance with regulations. Splinters and burning debris fell through the hatch causing a fire dangerously close to the turret hoist and the magazine itself. The compartment soon filled with smoke but men came forward to fight the blaze, the magazine was flooded and the possibility of a catastrophic explosion averted. The third shell caused little damage, passing over the upper deck and through a bulwark without bursting. *Slava*, her steering gear out of action, was forced to beat a temporary retreat by manoeuvring on her engines. At 0858 *Slava* moved out of range and the Germans ceased fire after twelve salvoes. The battleship's crew now had a chance to bring her fires under control and repair the steering gear. Miraculously, none of the crew were killed or seriously wounded, though several men suffered burns. This was the second engagement in which *Slava* never opened fire.

Despite the best efforts of the Russian forces the situation in the Irben Strait had reached a critical stage. Fearing that his squadron was about to be overwhelmed, the Russian commander, Captain 1st Rank P. L. Trukhachev, ordered his ships to retreat to the Moonsund Channel. The order to withdraw came just as *Slava* turned west to rejoin the battle some time before 1000. Characteristically impatient to get to grips with the enemy, she initially ignored the order and only withdrew at 1015 after the signal had been repeated, leaving the minefields as the only obstacle to the Germans breaking into the Gulf of Riga. These fields were so dense that, even unopposed, it took the Germans the whole of the following day (5 August) to sweep safe passages, and only on the morning of the 6th did *Nassau* and *Posen* enter the gulf led by the minesweepers.

The Russians had meanwhile fallen back to a second prepared position at the eastern exit of the gulf, the Moonsund. This development put *Slava* in a very precarious position. Not only could she not escape through the Irben Strait, which was now in German hands, but her draught prevented her retreating through the Moonsund. Her only option was to accept an unequal battle with the German dreadnoughts, the outcome of which seemed a foregone conclusion. The grim decision was therefore taken to fight the ship as long as possible before blowing her up. Her commander, Captain 1st Rank S. S. Viazemskii, was particularly insistent on scuttling his ship in such a way as to ensure that she would capsize – he did not want 'the masts of the ship entrusted to him left standing, even though the ship were damaged and lost, lest the Germans dare hoist their flag [in her]'.[17] In the event, no such drastic measures were necessary. On 8 August *Slava* received word from Russian naval intelligence – which was able to decrypt German signals thanks to the recovery of code-books from the stranded cruiser *Magdeburg* a year earlier – that the Germans were abandoning the Gulf of Riga. The eastward advance of the German army along the coast had halted before the city of Riga, without which it had no suitably equipped base for further operations nor consequently much hope of holding the enclosed Gulf of Riga. The Kaiserliche Marine therefore withdrew from the gulf.

Slava's experience in the Irben Strait in the summer of 1915 confirmed that her older 12in guns were outranged by the 11in weapons of her German counterparts of the Deutschland and Braunschweig classes (capable of up to 20,400yds/18,650m) and the Nassau-class dreadnoughts (22,000yds/20,120m) by at least 5,000yds (4,570m). Since *Slava* would remain key to the defence of the Irben Strait minefields and the Gulf of Riga for the foreseeable future, the Commander-in-Chief of the Baltic Fleet, Admiral Kanin, raised the question of improving the range of her guns as quickly as possible. The decision was therefore taken to increase the elevation of her 12in guns from 15 to 25 degrees, though the extent of the alterations meant that these would have to wait until her next refit during the winter of 1916–17. An interim solution was therefore pursued, namely the development of new projectiles with improved ballistic qualities. The existing hollow brass ballistic caps were replaced by more streamlined ones, resulting in a 20 per cent increase in range at

equivalent elevations despite weighing 787lb (355kg) instead of 731lb (332kg). *Slava* received her first batch of the new shells in the autumn of 1915, followed by similarly improved shells for the 6in guns.

Gunnery Support, 1915–16

The withdrawal of the German navy from the Gulf of Riga left *Slava* free to support the northern flank of the Russian XII Army. The front lines followed the course of the Western Dvina which flowed into the gulf at Riga itself. Probably her most dramatic fire-support operation came on the morning of 12 September 1915 when *Slava* moved into position off Cape Ragotsem to bombard German positions in the Latvian town of Tukums. The target lay at the extreme range of her 12in guns and the ship was therefore brought as close inshore as possible, and anchored just 1,600yds (1,460m) off the coast with only a foot of water under the keel. German batteries took *Slava* under fire and soon found the range. A quarter of an hour after anchoring, a German shell (estimated in Russian reports to be of 6in calibre) struck the edge of the viewing slit of the conning tower. Splinters entered the tower, killing the ship's commanding officer Capt. Viazemskii, the flag gunnery officer of the Baltic Fleet Captain 2nd Rank V. A. Svinin and three helmsmen; Lieutenant A. P. Vaksmut, who had been poring over a small chart table while plotting the range was the only survivor in the tower, albeit with splinter lacerations to his back and legs. A second shell killed a petty officer and a third exploded in the galley but caused only limited damage. Fourteen men were slightly wounded. *Slava* slowly turned to port under fire and retreated offshore. Having silenced the German batteries with her 6in guns, she resumed her former position, was inclined to starboard to increase the range of her guns and then opened fire on Tukums.

Then on 23 September *Slava* fought a duel lasting several hours with shore batteries at Cape Ragotsem and Shmarden during which 111 12in and 6in shells were fired. On 8–10 October she supported a landing at Domesnes, making a demonstration off Rohan and firing ninety 6in shells at Cape Messarogotsem. It was largely thanks to the support of *Slava*'s heavy ordnance that the Russian army, which had been badly shaken by the start of a German offensive on 17 October, succeeded in halting the enemy and regaining its positions in almost all sectors by the 24th. On 28 and 29 October *Slava* fired twenty-eight 12in and 250 6in shells against enemy fortifications at Kemmern, followed by a bombardment of Ragotsem on the 29th.

Active operations in the Gulf of Riga came to an end in November with the onset of the winter ice. The campaign of 1915 had demonstrated that the defence of the Irben Strait relied largely on *Slava*'s heavy guns, and the Baltic Fleet command therefore ordered her to winter at the entrance to the Moonsund instead of bringing her back to Helsingfors. *Slava* therefore anchored off the Verder light (now Virtsu) on the Estonian coast and readied herself for repairs during her winter lay-up. Accordingly, in December icebreakers brought transports up to the ship containing coal, provisions and supplies while the crew and workmen from the Putilovskii Works carried out major improvements to the vessel. By the time it was over, all twelve 6in gun barrels had been replaced and three anti-aircraft guns mounted, including two 3in (76.2mm) pieces and a Vickers-pattern 1.6in (40mm) machine gun, together with removal of the underwater torpedo tubes and repairs to the hull and superstructure. The time had also come to recognise the gallantry shown during the recent campaign and on 26 November 1915 a ceremony took place on board during which fifteen men were decorated with the Award of the Military Order (the ratings' equivalent of the Cross of St George for officers), and another fifty-one men received the Medal of St George ('for bravery').

The 1916 campaign began unexpectedly early on 14 April when *Slava*, still lying off Verder, became the target of a new form of attack: two German aircraft which dropped twelve bombs and registered three hits, killing one man and wounding nine more, of whom four subsequently died. *Slava* opened fire on the aircraft but no hits were obtained. This episode marked the beginning of a series of German air attacks on the anchored ship, with ten bombs dropped by a Zeppelin on the night of 18 April and another nineteen by three low-flying aircraft on the 20th, no hits being registered on either occasion.

Slava's main role during the 1916 campaign was providing gunnery support for the coastal flank of the XII Army. Over the course of three days from 19–21 June shore targets were engaged as part of a co-ordinated counter-attack on German army units west of Riga in preparation for an offensive. The Germans responded with nine air raids on *Slava* which defended herself with her anti-aircraft guns. During this episode an enemy shell estimated to be of 9in (225mm) calibre struck the ship's starboard side on the belt but the armour was not penetrated. In early July *Slava* supported the army's large-scale offensive west of Riga, being subjected to return fire from German shore batteries though no hits were scored.

Action continued through late summer and

---

17 K. I. Mazurenko, *Na 'Slavie' v Rizhskom zalivie* (Jordanville, N.Y.: Knigopechatnia prep Iova Pochaevskogo v Sv Troitskom monastyrie, 1949), p. 24.

Splinter damage to *Slava*'s after 12in turret from one of the three aerial bomb hits suffered on 14 April 1916 as the ship lay off Verder at the entrance to the Moonsund. The fitting of additional anti-aircraft guns in *Slava* was expedited as a consequence of this incident. (*Sergei Vinogradov Collection*)

where the heavy guns were replaced and their elevation increased to 25 degrees, the roof of the damaged conning tower repaired, and the hull, machinery and gun mountings refitted. On 17 November she entered the Aleksandrovskii Dock for examination and painting of the hull and repair of her eight bent propeller blades. The ship remained in dock until the end of the month and by mid-December *Slava* was back in Helsingfors for the winter.

The Battle for the Gulf of Riga, 1917

By the winter of 1916–17 the Russian empire was staggering through the last months of its existence. When food riots broke out in Petrograd in late February 1917 troops soon joined the disturbances, which quickly escalated into open revolt against the government. On 2 March Tsar Nicholas II abdicated and a provisional government was established. Lying icebound off Helsingfors for the winter, the Baltic Fleet responded to news of events in the capital with mutiny, and officers were hunted down and lynched in several ships. *Slava*, however, was almost untouched by these disturbances, her crew distinguished by an unusually strong unity

early autumn until 9 October when *Slava* was ordered to prepare to leave the Gulf of Riga for an overdue refit and the replacement of her 12in guns. The Moonsund had been dredged sufficiently during the summer months for her to pass through when her draught was reduced by removal of her coal and ammunition. On 22

October she weighed anchor and was hauled through the narrow channel by tugs, the ship drawing 26ft 8in (7.82m) on an even keel, 8in (20.5cm) less than her normal draught. Next day *Slava* sailed for Helsingfors escorted by the protected cruiser *Diana* and destroyers. Having coaled she headed for Kronshtadt on the 28th

Slava undergoing the exacting task of coaling ship in 1913. In this case the coal is being loaded from the hold of a barge by being piled onto a large piece of canvas before being lifted by the ship's derrick onto the deck for emptying through deck scuttles into the bunkers. Arduous as the work was, humour is not lacking and a rating poses for the camera with a huge chunk of coal on his shoulder in the foreground. Note the starboard forward 6in turret trained on the beam. (*Sergei Vinogradov Collection*)

of purpose shared by officers and men. Nonetheless, as time passed, the corrosive effects of revolution extended even to *Slava* with a gradual erosion of discipline, the formation of sailors' committees and increasing interference in ordinary officer duties. Crews spent less time working and training for battle in favour of endless hours in meetings and political debate.

The German high command elected to adopt a wait-and-see policy as events unfolded in Russia, and for several months the front remained relatively quiet, hostilities only resuming in the summer. Consequently, it was not until June that the Baltic Fleet command decided to send *Slava* back to the Gulf of Riga, an order carried out in the face of considerable resistance on the lower deck. Communist party radicals and anarchist demagogues among the crew tried to persuade others that it was time for other less battle-worn ships to be committed to action; *Slava*, it was claimed, 'has already completely fulfilled her duty to Free Russia and the Revolution'.[18] Only after much urging by the officers did the crew agree to return to the gulf. Waiting for her at Kuiwast, the main base of the Naval Forces of the Gulf of Riga, was her old companion the battleship *Tsesarevich*, now renamed *Grazhdanin* ('Citizen'), together with the minelaying cruiser *Baian*, twenty-one destroyers, three gunboats and an assortment of minelayers, patrol vessels, submarines and transports. The gallant Vice Admiral M. K. Bakhirev, who had commanded the Baltic Fleet Cruiser Brigade in 1914 and then the Dreadnought Brigade from December 1915 to May 1917, was appointed chief of the forces in the gulf.

Meanwhile, the war had taken a decisive turn against Russia. The failure of the Russian summer offensive of 1917 had prompted a German counter-attack; Riga fell on 3 September, once again placing *Slava* in a highly precarious position. The next stage in the German offensive was a major combined operation to capture the Moonsund Islands (Ösel, Dagö and Moon, now Saaremaa, Hiiumaa and Muhu respectively) which formed a screen across the Gulf of Riga. A significant portion of the High Seas Fleet was allocated to the task, consisting of a battlecruiser, ten of the latest dreadnought battleships, nine cruisers, fifty-six destroyers, eleven torpedo boats, six submarines, twenty-six minesweepers and sixty-five motor-minesweepers, fifty-seven anti-submarine patrol motorboats and about twenty auxiliary vessels. This task force enjoyed

Slava at the Baltic Fleet's manoeuvring base at Lappvik (now Lappohja) on the southwest coast of Finland in August 1917. Now on the eve of her last campaign in the Gulf of Riga six 3in (76.2mm) anti-aircraft guns were installed, one atop each 12in turret and four in the superstructure amidships, thereby giving *Slava* the most powerful anti-aircraft battery in the Russian navy. Lying beyond her is the battleship *Andrei Pervozvannyi*. (CNM)

an overwhelming advantage in comparison with the Russian forces in the Gulf, the core of which consisted of the pre-dreadnoughts *Slava* and *Grazhdanin*. The Germans also committed nine Zeppelins and ninety-four aircraft to the operation, opposed by just thirty Russian aircraft.

The German landing force, transported in around forty ships, consisted of 24,600 men with forty guns, 220 machine guns and eighty mortars. Opposing them were the Russian garrisons on Ösel, Dagö and Moon, about 13,400 combatants all told, their resolve much weakened by revolutionary agitation. On the morning of 29 September the Germans began landing at Tagalakht Bay on the northwest coast of Ösel. Although the few Russian shore batteries were quickly suppressed by heavy naval gunfire, the operation was not without cost to the Germans, the battleships *Bayern* and *Grosser Kurfürst* being damaged on mines. However, the German assault forces quickly advanced across Ösel, meeting little resistance as demoralised Russian infantry surrendered in droves, while others fled southeastwards, hoping to escape to the mainland. Even worse for the defence of the Gulf of Riga was the abandoning of Battery No. 43 at Cape Tserel, the southernmost point of the island. These four 12in guns, which had been installed during the winter of 1916–17, covered the entire Irben Strait with their range of 31,200yds (28,530m). The loss of this battery on 2 October made possession of the gulf by the Kaiserliche Marine simply a matter of time, and the Germans were not slow to take advantage of the situation. On the afternoon of 3 October the breakthrough force commanded by Vizeadmiral Paul Behncke and consisting of the battleships *König* and *Kronprinz*, four cruisers and a considerable number of auxiliaries slowly entered the Gulf of Riga through swept passages in the minefields. Mines were not the only threat; two small

British submarines, *C27* and *C32*, were stationed in the Gulf of Riga, and at 1830 that evening *C27* fired two torpedoes at *König* but missed; fifteen minutes later, however, she hit the large auxiliary *Indianola*, badly damaging her.[19] This attack slowed but could not stop the German advance, and Behncke was able to anchor for the night south of the Russian position in the Moonsund.

The Battle of the Moonsund

Slava had so far taken little part in the action. For the first few days after the invasion she had remained at anchor in Kuiwast, protected by torpedo nets but ready to put to sea. From time to time the air defence siren sounded aboard the ship, but it was not until 3 October that *Slava*'s heavy guns spoke for the first time in the campaign. Her targets were enemy destroyers entering the sound between Ösel and Moon to bombard the defending Russian infantry. *Slava*'s 12in guns had to fire over Moon at their extreme range of about 24,000yds (21,950m) and, as in 1915, compartments were flooded to incline the ship by 5 degrees. Because the German ships could not be seen from *Slava*, her fire control was tortuous: spotters on the causeway linking Ösel and Moon telephoned corrections to the transport *Libava* which relayed them by radio to the battleship. Nonetheless, *Slava* drove off the German destroyers, her forward turret firing eighteen 12in shells in two-gun salvoes.

18 A. M. Kosinskii, *Moonzundskaia operastiia Baltiiskogo flota 1917 goda* (Leningrad: Voenno-morskaia akademiia RKKA, 1928), p. 45.

19 A small force of British submarines had been operating in the Baltic since 1915; five large 'E' class boats managed to force the Danish straits (a sixth, *E13*, was stranded in The Sound; see p. 123), while the five small 'C' class boats had been shipped to Arkhangelsk as deck cargo and transported on barges through the Russian river and canal system to the Baltic in 1916.

This, however, was only a temporary respite, and early on the morning of 4 October Vizeadmiral Behncke made his final plans for the coming day's battle. In this he had the further advantage of a captured chart disclosing the locations of the Russian minefields protecting the southern entrance to the Moonsund. This revealed that the deep-water approaches were blocked by two mine barriers arranged north and south of one another, with a gap in between. There were narrow passages to the east and west of the minefields, but the eastern route was hazardous for the dreadnoughts owing to the shallowness of the water, while the western passage was complicated by mines laid earlier by a German submarine. Nevertheless, at 0015 Behncke decided to try the western route, which was estimated to be 2,500yds (2,290m) wide. If he broke through here he could then turn east into the clear waters between two Russian minefields, at which point the 12in guns of his *König*-class battleships would be able to shell the Russian anchorage at Kuiwast. Later that morning he ordered his minesweepers to clear a path on the eastern side of the minefields as an alternative attack route, a piece of foresight which would pay handsome dividends six hours later.

At 0810 on what promised to be a 'beautiful, clear autumn day' the German ships began moving north in two columns, escorted by over forty minesweepers. In the starboard column, protected by eight destroyers, were *König* and *Kronprinz*, and in the port column were the light cruisers *Kolberg* and *Strassburg*. At about 0900 the minesweepers reached the southwestern corner of the minefields and set to work. A few minutes later *König* opened fire on two small Russian destroyers at a range of 17,200–19,400yds (15,730–17,740m); these were *Delnyi* and *Deiatelnyi* which were returning from a patrol toward the southwest. The destroyers made off to the north, zigzagging at full speed, and no hits were scored. At 0955 *Kolberg* and *Strassburg* separated from the group, steering north towards the western channel. Meanwhile the two dreadnoughts, each escorted by two destroyers, slowly turned east in the wake of ten minesweepers.

Vice Admiral Bakhirev had been informed of the German movement at about 0800 and immediately ordered *Slava* and *Grazhdanin*, which had anchored during the night off Shildau Island to the north of Kuiwast, to get underway. At 0900, just as the battleships reached the Kuiwast Roads, Bakhirev hoisted his flag aboard the cruiser *Baian*; at 0912 the masts and smoke of the enemy were sighted and the Russian ships hoisted their battle ensigns. When the German

minesweepers came within 22,000yds (20,120m) Bakhirev ordered his squadron to take up positions at the northern edge of the minefield. At 1000 *Slava* and *Grazhdanin* turned to bring the enemy onto an astern bearing; Bakhirev, whose freedom of manoeuvre was severely hampered by the shoals around the islands of Moon and Verder, hoped to keep the enemy on his port quarter should it be necessary to withdraw to the northwest through the Moonsund. At around 1005 *Grazhdanin* opened fire but soon desisted as the maximum range of her guns was limited to 17,200yds (15,730m). *Slava* opened fire half a minute after her companion, targeting the western group of German minesweepers at the extreme range of 22,500yds (20,570m). The first salvo was over, the second was short and the third straddled. The minesweepers hastily withdrew under cover of a smokescreen and *Slava* ceased fire.

At 1015 the German dreadnoughts, then proceeding eastward at low speed along the southern edge of the minefield, opened fire on the Russian ships. *König*'s first salvo of three shells fell just astern of *Baian*, the southernmost ship in the Russian squadron. At 1018 *Kronprinz* opened fire on *Grazhdanin* with five-gun salvoes which fell somewhat short, fire being checked after five salvoes. At 1030 Vice Admiral Bakhirev ordered the Russian battleships to hold their positions and fire 'at the closest enemy'.[20] By 1050 the German minesweepers had regrouped and were back at work, *Slava* responding by opening fire at them at a range of 19,650yds (17,970m), the enemy being straddled at 19,200yds (17,560m). *Baian* and *Grazhdanin* also fired at the minesweepers which 'worked persistently, despite the fact that our shells were falling around them the whole time'. During this time *Slava* divided her fire, the forward turret shelling the minesweepers while the after turret engaged the dreadnoughts, which returned fire but scored no hits. Despite the efforts of the minesweepers to break the barrier, *König* and *Kronprinz* were in a dangerous position. In the German official history Erich von Tschischwitz records that 'The Russian heavy ships now shifted their fire to [the dreadnoughts] and very quickly established the short bracket. During this bombardment they very skilfully kept at the extreme range of our heavy guns (twelve and a half miles [20,100m]). The Third Squadron found itself in a most unfortunate situation: it

could neither close with the enemy nor evade the hostile fire.' Not wanting to give 'the Russians an easy victory', Vizeadmiral Behncke ordered his dreadnoughts to turn to starboard 'to a position beyond the range of the enemy's guns'.[21]

German efforts at the western border of the minefield, the main sector of the breakthrough attempt, had come to a standstill. Good shooting by *Slava* and *Grazhdanin* had twice forced the minesweepers to withdraw. As von Tschischwitz noted, 'It was evident that a breakthrough between [the Russian] minefield and our submarine mines was impracticable. The attempt was therefore abandoned.'[22] However, it was at this stage, having temporarily driven off the German dreadnoughts, that *Slava* encountered her first major problem when both guns of the forward 12in turret went out of action after firing a total of just eleven rounds. According to her gunnery officers, blame for the failure rested with the Obukhovskii Works in St Petersburg which had installed the guns in November 1916 and had 'negligently manufactured the gearwheels [of the breechblock] from poor-quality metal'.[23]

The German squadron having withdrawn over the horizon (about 30,000yds/27,430m), at 1120 Bakhirev hoisted the following signal in *Baian*: 'The Admiral expresses his pleasure at the excellent shooting of the Half-Brigade of Battleships.'[24] Ten minutes later Bakhirev ordered the ships to anchor; *Grazhdanin* was the southernmost ship, 400yds (365m) north of her was *Baian*, and then *Slava*. However, the Germans had not abandoned their efforts to get at the Russian battleships. The failure at the western edge of the minefield prompted Behncke to activate his alternative plan, namely attacking the Russians via the eastern channel. Nine more minesweepers were assigned to this effort, bringing the total number there to nineteen, 'in order to get through in at least one place'.[25] The success of the German breakthrough of the Moonsund therefore depended on the persistence of the minesweepers. Could they hold out long enough under the fire of *Slava* and *Grazhdanin* to give the dreadnoughts a chance to pass through the swept channel and engage the Russian ships?

20 M. K. Bakhirev, *Otchet o deistviiakh Morskikh sil Rizhskogo zaliva (Morskaia istoricheskaia komissiia 1)* (St Petersburg: Rossiiskii Gosudarstvennyi Arkhiv Voenno-Morskogo Flota, 1998), p. 54.

21 Erich von Tschischwitz, *The Army and Navy during the Conquest of the Baltic Islands in October 1917* (Fort Leavenworth, Kan.: The Command and General Staff School Press, 1933), p. 162.

22 *Ibid.*

23 Hitherto unpublished report by *Slava*'s gunnery officers cited in Vinogradov, *Bronenosets 'Slava'*, p. 155.

24 *Ibid.*

25 Tschischwitz, *The Army and Navy*, p. 163.

Seeing the German minesweepers approaching once again, at 1150 Bakhirev ordered his ships to weigh anchor. *Grazhdanin*, with her shorter-ranged guns, kept to the south. Turning her port side to the enemy, at 1204 she opened fire at the minesweepers with her 12in and 6in guns. *Slava* followed at 1210, firing from her after turret at a range of 23,000yds (21,030m) while keeping the enemy on a bearing of 135 degrees to port. At the same time the German dreadnoughts began their 'dash to the north', moving through the swept channel at 18 knots. They advanced on a line of bearing, *König* leading with *Kronprinz* astern and slightly to port. At around 1215, when they had closed the range to 18,000yds (16,460m), *König* opened fire on *Slava*. Two minutes later *Kronprinz* followed suit. This attack continued as the range decreased until 1222 when the dreadnoughts slowed as they approached the shallows along the coast. Within eight minutes both ships had stopped and, turning to bring their broadsides to bear on the port side, opened fire on *Slava* and *Grazhdanin* with full five-gun salvoes.

No sooner had *Slava*'s lookouts in the foretop reported the approach of the German battleships than the after turret opened rapid fire on them at a range of 22,400yds (20,480m). As her commanding officer, Captain 1st Rank V. G. Antonov, wrote in his report, 'The enemy, having quickly found the range, deluged the ship with shells. Most of the shells fell near the bow. The enemy salvoes consisted of five shells, occasionally of four. We proceeded at slow speed. At 1218, in an effort to throw off the enemy's ranging fire, we increased to medium speed, turning a little to starboard.'[26] The Germans scored no hits during the first ten minutes of the action, but at 1225 *Slava* finally shuddered under the impact of three hits from a single salvo, all of which struck on the port side below the water-line. One struck forward 10ft–11ft 6in (3–3.5m) below the armour, detonating on impact or soon after and making 'a huge hole about 1.5 fathoms [9ft/2.75m] in diameter'. It destroyed the forward dynamo room, knocking out electrical power in that part of the ship. Flooding was immediate and soon reached the battery deck and the forward magazine. The second hit was also forward and flooded several storerooms. Having shipped about 1,130 tons of water, *Slava* took on an immediate list of 4.5 degrees to port, increasing to 8 degrees within ten minutes. Counter-flooding of the starboard compartments from frame 32 aft reduced the list to 3–4 degrees. Although the third shell struck abreast the engine

This extraordinary photograph was taken by Midshipman Nosov in the torpedo boat *Silnyi* at the climax of the action of 4 October 1917. A salvo from *König* has fallen near *Slava* and shell splashes are visible ahead of the ship and off her starboard bow. *Slava*'s forward 12in turret was by this time out of action but her trim by the bow is not yet critical. (CNM)

room, it did so against the armour belt and caused little damage, the engineering staff 'noticing only leaking water and water in the hold, rising so slowly that it could be handled with the pumping facilities'.[27] Nonetheless, between battle damage and damage-control measures, by 1230 *Slava* was flooded forward from the keel to the lower deck as far back as frame 26. The ship had a trim by the head and her draught at the bow had increased by 5ft 6in (1.7m) to 32ft 10in (10m). The bulkheads were holding up well with only a few leaks around the electrical cabling seals. Stability was still adequate since the water had not reached above the armour deck.

The Battle of Moonsund had now reached a tactical climax. The Germans held their position while keeping the Russian ships under heavy and accurate fire; *Grazhdanin* had been hit twice by *Kronprinz*, although she was not so severely damaged as *Slava*. Bakhirev therefore ordered the Russian ships to withdraw to the north. G. K. Graf, a Russian officer, describes the scene: 'Near *Slava* [...] huge columns of water rose up, and several holes could be clearly seen in her side near the forward turret. With a heavy list to port and down by the bows, she proceeded north at high speed.'[28] At 1229, immediately after the order to withdraw, *Slava* received two more shell hits. Although these ignited some fires they were extinguished within fifteen minutes, but at 1239,

Slava burning after being scuttled. The destroyer *Turkmenets Stavropolskii* can be seen to her right. This is another of the photographs taken by Midshipman Nosov in the torpedo boat *Silnyi*. (CNM)

when she was almost beyond the range of the German guns, *Slava* received two more hits. The first shell struck the forecastle and exploded in the chapel; the upper deck was torn up, three men were killed and everything in the vicinity wrecked. The second penetrated the armour and passed through the bulkhead of the side passage to explode near the radio room, badly damaging the bulkheads of the nearby coal bunkers. Fortunately, these hits did not cause major fires and at 1240 the German dreadnoughts ceased fire as *Slava* moved out of range.

Slava's condition, already critical, was not much altered by these last hits. Damaged by several near-misses, the hull was leaking badly and the pumps could barely keep up with the inflow. Water was gaining in the port engine room and required some of the boiler fires to be put out with a consequent drop in steam pressure and in the ship's speed. With half of her heavy guns out of action and 2,500 tons of water in the hull, *Slava* was in no condition to continue the battle. Worse, her only line of retreat was ruled out by the heavy trim by the head, the Moonsund being too shallow for her increased draught even after being dredged. The ship was still moving north slowly and firing occasional shots from her after turret, but it was clear to her officers that it was only a matter of time before *Slava* was lost. At 1245 she ceased fire, her last

[26] Hitherto unpublished report by Captain Antonov, cited in Vinogradov, *Bronenosets 'Slava'*, p. 156.

[27] *Ibid.*

[28] G. K. Graf, *Na 'Novike'. Baltiiskii flot v voinu i revoliutsiiu* (St Petersburg: Gangut, 1997), p. 306.

'The sunken Russian battleship *Slava* in the Moonsund in 1917' reads the German inscription on this photo postcard. *(Sergei Vinogradov Collection)*

shells falling short of the enemy at a range of 23,100yds (21,120m).

At 1247, as *Baian* passed *Slava*, Vice Admiral Bakhirev was given a report on the ship's parlous condition by megaphone. Bakhirev ordered *Grazhdanin* to pass ahead of her, after which *Slava* was to scuttle herself at the entrance to the channel. At 1302 destroyers came alongside and began to take off the crew, at which point discipline finally began to break down and the ship was evacuated in great disorder. At 1320 *Slava* stopped her engines but still had way on and two minutes later Captain Antonov released the helmsmen, signalmen and engine room crew, leaving only five officers and twelve volunteer

seamen aboard the ship. At 1330 *Slava*, still moving slowly, came to the entrance of the channel and ran aground, and ten minutes later the last men, including Antonov, left the ship. With the forward 12in magazine flooded, fuses could only be set in the after magazine, which exploded at 1358 sending up a column of smoke to a height that 'exceeded 100 fathoms' (600ft/183m) and a large blaze was seen aft.[29] A second explosion followed at 1412, with a third at 1420, after which the ship sank to the level of the after 12in turret. To ensure the destruction was complete Bakhirev ordered the destroyers *Amurets*, *Moskvitianin* and *Turkmenets Stavropolskii* to torpedo her. Each launched two

torpedoes, five of which hit *Slava*, but only one detonated, on the starboard side abreast the forward funnel. So ended *Slava*'s gallant career.

Information is lacking on *Slava*'s expenditure of ammunition during her final battle. Based on the rate of fire of her forward turret before it went out of action, she probably expended a total of between thirty-five and forty 12in shells during the entire engagement. This compares with *Grazhdanin* which fired fifty-eight rounds from her 12in turrets, both of which remained in service throughout the battle. Losses among *Slava*'s crew were surprisingly light in the circumstances. Four men were killed during the action with another fourteen wounded, of whom three later died. Had *König* used high-explosive instead of armour-piercing projectiles the losses aboard *Slava* would surely have been far heavier owing to the larger bursting charges.

The Battle of Moonsund on 4 October 1917 had unfolded in a manner none of the designers of the Russian or German battleships involved could have foreseen. Intended for action on the high seas, these ships instead found themselves trading salvoes in shallow coastal waters, surrounded by gravelly shoals and minefields, manoeuvring at low speed behind minesweepers, and periodically enveloped in smokescreens.

Epilogue

There was a curious postscript to *Slava*'s last battle. Unaware that the 'Kaiser's personal enemy' had at last met her fate, the Germans believed she was merely aground in shallow water and would soon be freed and taken away to fight again. Commodore Paul Heinrich, commander of German torpedo forces, therefore ordered three torpedo boats of the 13th Half-Flotilla (*S61*, *S64* and *V74*) to search for *Slava* during the night of 5 October and finish her off. The torpedo boats entered the Moonsund at 2200 but luck did not favour the Germans and a few minutes after midnight the second ship in line, *S64*, fouled a mine laid by the retreating Russians. The explosion killed six men in the forward boiler room and wounded five more. Though still afloat, *S64* had lost power; *S61* took her in tow but shortly afterwards *S64* ran aground and it was decided to abandon her after taking off the crew. In the course of this misadventure *S61* sustained hull damage and began taking water while *V74* damaged a propeller; both were out of service for a time. So it was that *Slava*, even in death, had unwittingly served as a lure and managed to exact a small measure of revenge upon her enemy.

Slava scuttled in shallow water at the entrance of the Moonsund in October 1917. Note that the roof of the after 12in turret has been blown off by the explosion of her after magazines. *(Stephen McLaughlin Collection)*

[29] Vinogradov, *Bronenosets 'Slava'*, p. 162.

Another view of *Slava* aground in the Moonsund, possibly during early salvage operations. *(Stephen McLaughlin Collection)*

Slava and her faithful old companion *Tsesarevich/Grazhdanin* were hostages to an unforgiving fate, and no miracles attended Vice Admiral Bakhirev's final attempts to delay the Germans at the gates of the Moonsund. Outgunned five to one in terms of heavy ordnance, *Slava* and *Grazhdanin* could at best only slow the pace of the German Goliath. In the end *Slava* met her destiny in the very waters she had so stubbornly defended for three years, and where she had been so lucky before. It was a worthy and glorious end to her career, and fully justified her name.

Sources

Unpublished Sources

Rossiiskii gosudarstvennyi arkhiv Voenno-morskogo flota (Russian State Naval Archives), St Petersburg

Documentation on *Slava*'s origin and service, *fonds* 401, 407, 417, 418, 421, 423, 427, 477, 479, 556, 771, 870, 876 & 902

Bibliography

Bakhirev, M. K., *Otchet o deistviiakh Morskikh sil Rizhskogo zaliva 29 sentiabriia–7 oktiabriia 1917 goda (Morskaia istoricheskaia kommissiia 1)* [Report on Operations of the Naval Forces of the Gulf of Riga, 29 September–7 October 1917 (Naval Historical Commission 1)] (St Petersburg: Rossiiskii Gosudarstvennyi Arkhiv Voenno-Morskogo Flota, 1998)

Belli, V. A., *V Rossiiskom Imperatorskom flote: vospominaniia* [In the Russian Imperial Fleet: Memoirs] (St Petersburg: Izd-vo 'Peterburgskii in-t pechati', 2005)

Bengelsdorf, Lutz, *Der Seekrieg in der Ostsee, 1914–1918* (Bremen: Verlag H. M. Hauschild, 2008)

Blinov, V. ,'Rol' gardemarinskogo otriada v dele vospitaniia morskikh ofitserov' [The Role of the Gardemarin Detachment in the Business of Educating Naval Officers] in *Morskoi sbornik* 378, no. 10 (October 1913), Neofitsialnyi otdel' [Unofficial Section], pp. 41–59

'End of the Russian Naval Visit. Admiral's Thanks' in *The Times* (London), 20 September 1913, p. 10

Graf, G. K., *Na 'Novike'. Baltiiskii flot v voinu i revoliutsiiu* [Aboard the *Novik*. The Baltic Fleet in War and Revolution] (St Petersburg: Gangut, 1997)

Iankovich, V. N., 'Russkie moriaki v Messine' [Russian Sailors at Messina] in *Voenno-istoricheskii arkhiv* 5 (1999), p. 41

Kosinskii, A. M., *Moonzundskaya operatsiya Baltiiskogo flota 1917 goda* [The Moonsund Operation of the Baltic Fleet in 1917] (Leningrad: Voenno-morskaia akademiia RKKA, 1928)

Kostenko, V. P., *Na 'Orël' v Tsusime* [Aboard the *Orël* at Tsushima] (Leningrad: Sudpromgiz, 1955)

L-t B., 'Vospominaniia o pokhode na Murman' [Recollections of a Voyage to Murman] in *Kotlin* 59, no. 4324 (15 March 1911), p. 2

'Letopis "Morskogo Sbornika," 1913 god' [Chronicle of *Morskoi Sbornik*, 1913] in *Morskoi sbornik* 379, no. 12

A double-headed eagle salvaged from the wreck of the *Slava* and now in the Maritime Museum in Tallinn. This one may have decorated the sternwalk as seen in the photo on p. 92. *(Stephen McLaughlin)*

(December 1913), pp. 1–16

Mazurenko, K. I., *Na 'Slavie' v Rizhskom zalivie* [Aboard the '*Slava*' in the Gulf of Riga]. (Jordanville, N.Y.: Knigopechatnia prep. Iova Pochaevskogo v Sv. Troitskom monastyrie, 1949)

McLaughlin, Stephen, *Russian and Soviet Battleships* (Annapolis, Md.: Naval Institute Press: 2003)

Novokov-Priboi, A. S., *Tsusima* (Moscow: Sovetskii Pisatel', 1934)

Tschischwitz, Erich von, *The Army and Navy during the Conquest of the Baltic Islands in October 1917* (Fort Leavenworth, Kan.: The Command and General Staff School Press, 1933) [translation of *Armee und Marine bei der Eroberung der Baltischen Inseln im October 1917* (Berlin: Eisenschmidt, 1931)].

Tsyvinskii, G. F., *50 let v Imperatorskom flote* [Fifty Years in the Imperial Fleet] (Riga: Orient, 1928)

Vinogradov, S. E., *Bronenosets 'Slava'. Nepobezhdennyi geroi Moonzunda* [Battleship *Slava*. The Immovable Hero of the Moonsund] (Moscow: Iauza/Eksmo, 2011)

_____, letter to the editor, *Warship International* 52, no. 1 (March 2015), pp. 9–13

Kongelige Danske Marine

The Coastal Battleship
Peder Skram (1908)

◆

Tom Wismann

HER TERRITORY and finances depleted, by the end of the nineteenth century Denmark had settled on a defensive strategy to ward off the threat from the larger powers surrounding her, chiefly Germany. From a naval standpoint this strategy resulted in the construction at the Naval Dockyard in Copenhagen of a succession of coast defence vessels of which the battleship *Peder Skram* was the penultimate expression. Although she and the other units of the Kongelige Danske Marine were sufficient to preserve Denmark's neutrality during the Great War, neglect, supine government and geopolitical realities prevented any such deterrence in the next conflict, during which Germany overran the country in April 1940 with scarcely a shot fired. The Danish navy eventually dissented from the official policy of co-operation with the occupiers by organising a grand scuttle in August 1943, but *Peder Skram* was quickly salvaged and towed away to be pressed into German service before being returned to Denmark in scrapping condition in 1945. Much as her construction was a significant achievement for a small country, *Peder Skram*'s career therefore accurately reflects the fortunes of the Kongelige Danske Marine in the first half of the twentieth century.

From a Major to a Minor Navy

The seafaring heritage of the Danish people needs little introduction, but the Kongelige Danske Marine per se traces its origins to the force founded by King Hans of Denmark on 10 August 1510, making it one of the oldest national navies in the world. For the next 300 years the Royal Danish Navy was a significant power in the Baltic, the North Sea and the North Atlantic, eventually operating warships as far away as India, the west coast of Africa and the West Indies in defence of its overseas colonies and trading interests. Initially, the main antagonist of the Royal Danish Navy was the great trading confederation known as the Hanseatic League, and it was the namesake of the subject of this chapter, Admiral Peder Skram (1503–81), who in the Counts' War of 1534–6 did more than any other to break the power of the Hansa forever, acquiring the nickname '*Danmarks vovehals*' ('Denmark's daredevil') in the process. However, between 1563 and 1721 it was Sweden which represented the principal threat to the territorial integrity and commercial interests of the Dano-Norwegian union and it was against that power that the Royal Danish Navy scored

The coastal battleship *Peder Skram* seen flying the swallow-tailed war ensign known as the *Orlogsflag* during one of her sporadic periods in commission in the 1930s. Her fortunes accurately reflect those of the Danish navy over the course of her long career. *(Bruce Taylor Collection)*

its greatest victories under the swallow-tailed war ensign known as the *Orlogsflag*, first at Køge Bay under Admiral Niels Juel during the Scanian War in July 1677, and then at Dynekilen during the Great Northern War in 1716 under the Norwegian Peter Tordenskjold, at the head of a force which was by now composed largely of his countrymen.

The onset of Denmark's decline as a major naval power dates to the Battle of Copenhagen on 2 April 1801, in which fifteen Danish vessels were captured or destroyed by a British force sailing under the overall command of Admiral Sir Hyde Parker, but led by Vice Admiral Horatio Nelson. However, these losses paled in comparison with the Second Battle of Copenhagen on 2–5 September 1807, during which 30,000 men commanded by Major General Sir Arthur Wellesley (later the Duke of Wellington) came ashore and bombarded the city into submission. The peace terms required Denmark to give up her entire navy to the British, who sailed from Copenhagen on 21 October with sixteen ships of the line, fifteen frigates and corvettes and fourteen minor vessels as prizes, plus equipment and supplies loaded into ninety-two merchantmen. It was a blow from which the Danish navy never recovered. Although Denmark continued the war against the British with a large fleet of gunboats backed by coastal batteries, she went bankrupt in 1813 and the following year was forced to give up the union with Norway at the Treaty of Kiel.

The Royal Danish Navy next saw action in the context of the Schleswig-Holstein Question, the long-standing dispute over the allegiance of the duchies of Schleswig and Holstein to the Danish Crown or to the German Confederation, over which two wars were fought in 1848–51 and

1864. In both of these the role of the Royal Danish Navy consisted largely in blockading ports in the Baltic and the Heligoland Bight. Victories ashore secured Denmark's continued hold over the duchies in the First Schleswig War, but hostilities erupted again in 1864 after the two provinces rebelled to leave the kingdom, this time with the support both of Prussia and Austria-Hungary. The Danish navy initially managed to impose a successful port blockade and beat off an Austro-Hungarian squadron supported by three Prussian gunboats under no less a commander than Commodore Wilhelm von Tegetthoff at the Battle of Heligoland on 9 May 1864. Nonetheless, the blockade was subsequently broken while the land campaign in southern Jutland ended in disaster for Denmark, which had to give up a third of her already much depleted territory. Denmark was thereafter effectively a small state with a minor navy.

The Road to the Coastal Battleship

After 1814 Denmark built eight traditional ships of the line together with a number of smaller warships, but by 1860 the Orlogsværftet (Naval Dockyard) in Copenhagen, which had been responsible for most Danish naval construction since 1690, was struggling to keep up with the rapid pace of technological change. With the Schleswig-Holstein Question looming once more, in 1862 Denmark took the step of ordering the turret ship *Rolf Krake* of 1,350 tons from the Glasgow firm of Robert Napier & Sons. This vessel, built to the designs of the pioneering naval architect Cowper Coles and armed with two centreline turrets each mounting a pair of 68pdr smoothbore guns, was the first warship in

any navy to carry his novel turret and holds the distinction of being the first turret ironclad in Europe. Although *Rolf Krake* could not alter the outcome of the Second Schleswig War, she nonetheless provided the Naval Dockyard's engineers and craftsmen with an invaluable primer in iron warship construction and the manufacture of steam engines. In 1866 the keel was laid of *Lindormen*, the first coast defence vessel designed and built by the Naval Dockyard itself, and six more were constructed to a variety of designs as skills and technology matured over the next thirty years. These ships, ranging from 2,100 to 5,480 tons' displacement and mounting guns of 9in (229mm) to 14in (356mm) calibre, were built as part of a scheme for the defence of the island of Sjælland upon which the city of Copenhagen stands, being subsequently assigned to gunnery support for torpedo boats and submarines in combination with minefields and coastal fortifications.

In 1894 the progressive commissioning by the Imperial German Navy of the eight Siegfried-class coast defence ships mounting three 9.4in (239mm) guns and displacing 3,500 tons prompted the Danish government to propose the construction of a similar vessel for its own navy. Although the Rigsdag (parliament) could not initially be persuaded to vote the necessary funds, the Naval Dockyard continued working on designs for the new vessel, which in consequence benefited from the lessons of the Sino-Japanese War waged over the winter of 1894–5 (see *Chen Yuen*). The designs were prepared by the assistant director H. Vedel and the head of the design office F. L. M. Ortmann under the supervision of the director of the Naval Dockyard J. C. Tuxen, receiving approval on 18 August 1896. Meanwhile, the allocation of funds in the 1896–7 budget opened the way for construction and the keel of what eventually became the coastal battleship *Herluf Trolle* was laid in the Orlogsværftet on 20 July 1897. It is a measure of how limited were the finances of the Danish government that it was not until 1900 that a second unit, *Olfert Fischer*, was laid down, and another five years before construction began on their improved sister *Peder Skram* on 25 April 1905.

Design, Hull and Protection

The design of *Peder Skram* provided for a main armament of two 9.4in (240mm) guns in single

The first *Peder Skram* (right) was laid down as a wooden steam frigate in 1859 but converted on the stocks to an ironclad and launched in 1864. On the left is the first unit of Denmark's armoured fleet, the British-built turret ship *Rolf Krake* of 1863. (*Forsvarsgalleriet – Danish Armed Forces Photo Archive*)

Peder Skram alongside at Aarhus 1910, shortly after joining the fleet. This view shows the forward 9.4in turret, the port forward 5.9in gun in its casemate, a 3in anti-torpedo boat gun on the turret roof and the canvas-covered forward 9.8ft rangefinder aft. Also under canvas are the 35.5in searchlights positioned on either side of the bridge on raised mountings. *(Forsvarsgalleriet)*

turrets and four 5.9in (152mm) guns in casemates on a standard displacement of 3,800 tons. Overall length was 287ft (87.4m), 51.5ft (15.7m) in the beam and with a draught of 16.4ft (5m). The ship was built of steel and the hull divided into ten major compartments by nine watertight bulkheads. There were eighty-two watertight compartments and thirty-one watertight doors all told. The ship was arranged on three decks. First came a forecastle deck running the length of the ship on which the main and secondary armament was mounted. Beneath it was a main deck broken by the boiler and engine room spaces but with sailors (*menige*) and non-commissioned officers (*underofficerer*) accommodated forward

A very rare view of the athwartships torpedo room. It is not known how many torpedoes could be stowed but their effective range was scarcely more than 2,000yds. *(Forsvarsgalleriet)*

Peder Skram: Main and Secondary Armament, 1905

	9.4in (24cm) L/43 M/06	5.9in (15cm) L/50 M/05
Weight of gun	24.1t (24,900kg)	7.6t (7,690kg)
Breech mechanism	Screw	Sliding block
Ammunition type	Separate	Separate
Projectiles	353lb (160kg), HE/AP	112lb (51kg), HE/AP
Shell stowage per gun	80	165
Propellant	89lb (40.4kg)	34.2lb (15.5kg)
Muzzle velocity	2,641f/s (805m/s)	2,723f/s (820m/s)
Maximum elevation	15°	16°
Range at 15°/16°	16,620yds (15,200m)	15,640yds (14,300m)
Firing cycle	3rpm	7rpm

Source: Egil Thiede, *Dansk Søartilleri 1860–2004*, 2 vols. (Copenhagen: Tøjhusmuseet, 2004).

The forecastle in the early 1930s. The 3in high-angle gun atop the turret was fitted in 1916 and removed in 1934. Beyond it is the recently installed 19.7ft rangefinder. The photo shows the base of the spotting top fitted in all units of the class in 1921. *(Forsvarsgalleriet)*

and with the officers' quarters occupying their traditional position aft. Each of these three sections contained a magazine for the 5.9in guns. Then came the lower deck taken up by the engine spaces, the bow, midships and stern torpedo rooms and the main magazines, storerooms and holds. Hull protection consisted of a timber-backed belt with a thickness of between 6.1 and 7.7in (155–195mm) of Krupp cemented armour. The conning tower and the turrets received up to 7.5in (190mm) of plate, with 5.5in (140mm) on the casemates and deckhouse corners. Other vertical protection included bulkheads with up to 6.9in (175mm) and bridge, deckhouse and boiler uptakes with up to 3in (75mm) of armour. Horizontal protection, however, was restricted to 1.8–2.6in (45–65mm) on the main deck, which doubled as the armoured deck.

Armament

Manufactured by the Swedish firm of Bofors, *Peder Skram*'s 9.4in main armament was mounted in single turrets capable of traversing 126 degrees on either beam. Operating under electrical power, the turret could be rotated the full 252 degrees in 32 seconds (80 seconds when traversed by hand). Shells were lifted from the magazines by a chain hoist and moved to the electrically driven main hoist along a traveller under the deckhead. Unlike her sister ships, in which loading was only possible at 0 degrees, *Peder Skram* was capable of all-angle loading with the use of an electrically powered rammer giving her a much improved rate of fire. The increased elevation of the guns of 15 degrees compared to 12 degrees in *Herluf Trolle* and *Olfert Fischer* also significantly improved range. The inside of the turret could be reached either through a hatch in the roof or from the messdeck.

The ship was originally fitted with two 9.8ft (3m) rangefinders, one between the forward turret and the conning tower and the second on the after superstructure, being replaced in the early 1930s by two 19.7ft (6m) units in the same positions. Measured ranges were electrically transmitted to the spotting top, transmitting station and conning tower from where laying and training information could be relayed to the 9.4in turrets and 5.9in casemates. Each heavy gun was fitted with a gyroscopic sight.

Peder Skram's 5.9in secondary armament, also manufactured by Bofors, showed a similar degree of improvement by comparison with those fitted in her sisters, an increase from 43 to 50 calibres and from 12 degrees to 16 degrees in elevation giving improved range. The original armament fit was completed by ten 3in (75mm) guns ranged singly on the boat deck and on each of the

Peder Skram: Weight Distribution in Tons as Designed, 1905

Hull (steel)	875.34
Hull (wood)	39.75
Hull (fixed equipment, accommodation, etc.)	191.94
Armour	1,125.95
Rotating turrets	218.30
Shells and charges	320.94
Main engines	186.00
Main boilers	160.00
Auxiliary machinery	59.26
Masts and rigging	15.67
Torpedo equipment	46.40
Paint and cladding cement	45.00
Electric light apparatus	29.65
Coal	250.00
Crew and personal effects, provisions, consumables, fresh water, feed water	141.51
Total	3,705.71

Source: Forsvarets Bibliotek (Armed Forces Library), Copenhagen: *Panserskibene Herluf Trolle, Olfert Fischer og Peder Skram. Sammenstilling af Hoveddimensioner, Pansertykkelser, Vægte mm.*

turrets to fend off torpedo boats, together with four 1.5in (37mm) weapons, two of which were for use in the ship's boats. There were four underwater 18in (457mm) torpedo tubes, one in the bow, another in the stern and two in an athwartships torpedo room on the lower deck forward of the boiler rooms and below the main steering position. The torpedoes were of the hot air 'e' type with a range of 4,375yds (4,000m) at 31 knots. A torpedo control and sighting position for the stern tube was installed on the quarterdeck abaft the after 9.4in gun.

Peder Skram was not, of course, originally fitted with anti-aircraft armament, the first of which consisted of two high-angle 3in (75mm) guns mounted on the roof of each turret in 1916 to replace the original low-angle weapons, these being replaced in 1934 by 0.303in (8mm) twin or single machine guns. Also fitted in 1934 were twin 0.8in (20mm) guns manufactured by the Dansk Riffel Syndikat in raised mountings on either bridge wing in place of a 35.5in (90cm) searchlight in each case; these were replaced in 1939–40 with single 1.6in (40mm) Bofors guns.

Propulsion

Propulsion consisted of two sets of vertical triple-expansion engines positioned in adjacent engine rooms separated by a longitudinal bulkhead. They were fed by six coal-fired water-tube boilers designed and built by the Orlogsværftet and operating at a pressure of 227.6psi (16kg/cm²). The boilers were divided into two rooms lying

fore and aft, with the plant disposed side by side in each room. The outboard compartments of the engine rooms and boiler rooms were used for

engine stores and coal bunkerage respectively, each of the latter having built-in steam tubes to extinguish fires. A further bunker was positioned immediately forward of the forward boiler room which also contained an auxiliary boiler for harbour use. The 5,400ihp delivered to the twin screws yielded a maximum speed of 15.9 knots. The ship had bunkerage for up to 275 tons of coal giving an endurance of 2,620 nautical miles at 9 knots.

Manning and Organisation

Peder Skram's original complement consisted of 254 officers and men, but by 13 July 1939 had risen to 278, composed in the latter case of nineteen officers (including six engineer, one supply and two medical officers), thirty-eight petty officers, seventy-eight leading, able and ordinary seamen, and 143 conscripts. Unlike her near-sister *Olfert Fischer*, she was not fitted out as a flagship, allowing the captain's and commander's suites to be positioned in the forward superstructure, together with the officers' galley and two cabins for senior petty officers. The remaining officers were accommodated in cabins on the main deck aft, while the balance of the crew lived in an assortment of compartments on the main

One of *Peder Skram*'s two triple-expansion steam engines. To the right is a desk and chair for the watchkeeper to write up the engine room log. The handweel regulates engine revolutions and thus the speed of the ship based on orders passed from the bridge through the large polished voice pipe above. *(Forsvarsgalleriet)*

LAUNCH AND COMPLETION

Peder Skram was launched on 2 May 1908 a little over three years after being laid down at the Orlogsværftet. The major Danish daily *Berlingske Tidende* published this description of what was evidently a memorable occasion in Copenhagen:

From early morning people started making their way towards the Naval Dockyard. Along the streets leading down to Kvæsthusbroen and Toldboden from Nyboder [a residential district reserved for naval families] army and navy officers strode in full-dress uniform towards the harbour and the Naval Dockyard accompanied by their wives. It looked like a veritable migration. Long lines quickly formed at the ferry landings leading from the city to the Naval Dockyard. Public interest was great as it was rare for such a big ship to be launched.

At the entrance to the Naval Dockyard the masses were greeted and checked by petty offi-

cers since the dockyard was usually strictly off limits to unauthorised persons. The large hull of *Peder Skram* could be seen high on the slip, richly painted in red and black with her pointed ram bow hanging in the air.

Around the big hull yard workers went about their business and officers checked the slip which was covered in green grease to induce the hull to slide.

On either side of the ship, to the north and to the south, benches and estrades provided space for navy officers and their wives, sons, daughters and fiancées. There was a crowd of spectators.

The royal marquee was on the south side

Peder Skram launched at the Naval Dockyard in Copenhagen on 2 May 1908. Beyond her and alive with spectators are the decommissioned central battery ship *Odin* of 1872 and then the similarly decommissioned coast defence ship *Tordenskjold* of 1880. Seen at upper right is the paddle-wheel royal yacht *Dannebrog*. (Forsvarsgalleriet)

Peder Skram fitting out at the Naval Dockyard where she was completed in 1909. Next to her is the central battery ship *Odin* and lying across the basin is the monitor *Skjold* of 1896 with *Peder Skram*'s near-sister *Olfert Fischer* bow-on immediately to the right. *(Forsvarsgalleriet)*

beyond the hull. Here petty officer cadets were paraded by Premierløjtnant [Lieutenant 1st Class] Broberg, and army and naval officers congregated together with invited dignitaries. There was a tented grandstand where the prime minister and all the government ministers stood together with the Diplomatic Corps and their ladies. On and in front of the grandstand stood high-ranking officers in full-dress uniform interspersed with ladies in lovely spring dresses which brightened the proceedings.

At exactly 1100 the Sixtus battery began firing the salute, a sure sign the royal party was on its way. From the Copenhagen side of the harbour the royal steam launch made for the Naval Dockyard with the royal party embarked. On arrival the royal party was greeted by Admiral Zachariae and Vice-Admiral Wandel together with much of the navy's officer corps. The crowd issued loud hurrahs and a military band struck up. A full military spectacle unfolded. Her Majesty the Queen was presented with a magnificent bouquet of red and white roses while H.M. King Frederik VIII, resplendent in the full-dress uniform of an admiral, was taken on a quick tour of the slip by the director of the Orlogsværftet to get a close view of the ship.

After this Navy Chaplain Lic. Theol. Fenger stood facing the big ship in front of the royal marquee and uttered powerful and stirring words on the future of *Peder Skram*, declaring that 'this is a day of celebration at the Naval Dockyard, for the old swan's nest has received a cygnet which will defend her home with tooth and claw.' The crowd was silent for a few moments after the chaplain's speech ended. Then one could hear the sound of heavy mallets knocking out *Peder Skram*'s shores. The launching had started!

Peder Skram was the second ship in the Danish navy to bear the name, the first being a wooden steam frigate of 1859 converted during construction to an armoured frigate. After fitting out at the Naval Dockyard she was commissioned into the Kongelige Danske Marine in September 1909.

deck forward. The messdecks followed the usual arrangement of tables and benches capable of being folded away under the deckhead. Officers and senior petty officers slept in bunks, petty officers in bunks or hammocks based on their rate, while sailors were confined to hammocks.

The heads occupied their traditional place right forward on the main deck under the forecastle and the ship was ventilated by electric fans and lit by 400 bulbs.

The crew was divided into three watches and these into two turns of duty called the King's and the Queen's Shift (*Kongens og Dronningens Kvarter*). When the ship was at sea or under daily routine, one watch operated the ship, one engaged in drill or daily tasks and another rested.

The forenoon watch on Saturday was given over to a prolonged inspection of all guns, the engineering department taking the opportunity to carry out general maintenance. That same afternoon the entire crew bathed and changed into clean rig, with personal lockers and all mess gear being subject to a thorough inspection. Sailors would then soak their laundry in a bucket for washing the following Monday before 'clean ship' was piped at 0700, aside from which time

DAILY ROUTINE

0600	Reveille; lash up and stow hammocks; breakfast.
0700	Clean ship followed by half an hour for coffee and preparation of uniform and kit for the morning inspection.
0900	Drill or work.
1130	Lunch and stand easy for the two duty watches.
1400	Exercises and drill.
1645	Inspection.
1700	At the bosun's call 'Tea' the crew changed from working rig to rig of the day. Supper.
2000	Leisure time; hammocks slung; off-duty personnel allowed to turn in unless there was night drill.
2100	Pipe down.

Source: Kai Dahl, *Lærebog for Orlogsgaster* (Copenhagen: Forsvarsministeriet, 1939).

Part of *Peder Skram*'s 250-strong crew gathered on the quarterdeck, the ship lying at the Holmen naval base in Copenhagen. The dome of Frederik's Church can just be seen on the left. *(Forsvarsgalleriet)*

was given over for the crew to mend clothing at least once a week. Once the Saturday routines had been completed the captain might decide to carry out a general inspection of the armament and the ship in general. If this proved satisfactory, shore leave could be granted when the ship was in harbour or at anchor. Sunday morning saw 'clean ship' as usual, but efforts were made to finish this promptly, allowing those who wished to attend divine service aboard to do so. All crewmen not directly involved in the operation of the ship were then excused ordinary duty. Watches were kept as on any other day when the ship was at sea.

There was a small shipboard canteen where soap, razor blades, chocolate, tobacco and postage stamps could be bought. All items had to be paid for in cash. If the ship was on an extended cruise outside Danish waters, it was possible for tobacco and other items to be purchased tax-free, but these were strictly for onboard consumption and could under no circumstances be removed from the ship, on pain of prosecution.

Early Years, 1909–14

Having completed her seakeeping trials in the Skagerrak, *Peder Skram* was commissioned on

A nap on one of the seamen's messdecks during a midday standeasy in 1911 presided over by a petty officer in the rank of *Underkvartermester 1.st. class.* The sleepers on the right are making use of the forms alongside the mess tables. *(Forsvarsgalleriet)*

24 September 1909 with the intention of being ready to join her near sisters *Herluf Trolle* and *Olfert Fischer* in the training squadron in early 1910. In 1911 these duties took her on cruises to the Norwegian port of Bergen and to Stockholm, and the following year *Peder Skram* joined *Olfert Fischer* in the task of repatriating the body of

King Frederik VIII who had unexpectedly collapsed and died in Hamburg on 14 May. In 1913 it was the Netherlands which played host to *Peder Skram*, with visits to the Hook of Holland and Rotterdam before the ship joined *Herluf Trolle* and *Olfert Fischer* as part of the Summer Training Squadron. However, by the time *Peder Skram* visited Kalmar in Sweden in the spring of 1914 the Danish navy was preparing for the outbreak of war in Europe.

Peder Skram's area of operations extended from the island of Bornholm in the Baltic to the Skagerrak in the west, and particularly The Great Belt separating mainland Denmark from the island of Sjælland on which Copenhagen is built, and The Sound separating the latter island from Sweden to the east. The Danish navy's defensive strategy turned on its immemorial experience of navigating these treacherous waters with their shoals, heavy currents and myriad islands and inlets, for which *Peder Skram* with her shallow draught and good manoeuvrability on two propellers was specifically designed. Combined with coastal fortifications, the laying of mine-fields, the extinguishing of lighthouses and removal of other navigational aids in wartime, negotiating Danish inshore waters therefore presented a serious proposition for oceangoing enemy vessels, quite aside from the attentions of the Kongelige Danske Marine itself. This, then, was the defensive strategy adopted by the Danish navy prior to the First World War.

The First World War

The outbreak of the First World War on 1 August 1914 prompted Denmark to establish a

Dhobeying on the confines of *Peder Skram*'s forecastle in 1915. *(Forsvarsgalleriet)*

The 1st Squadron, including *Herluf Trolle* and *Peder Skram* and a variety of torpedo boats, gather off Copenhagen ready to enforce Danish neutrality in August 1914. (*Forsvarsgalleriet*)

Peder Skram's quarterdeck dominated by the after 9.4in turret. The photo shows the ship as completed with one of the original 3in anti-torpedo boat guns mounted on the turret roof; this weapon and its counterpart on the forward turret were replaced in 1916 with a high-angle weapon of the same calibre. Covered in canvas beyond it is the after 9.8ft rangefinder as originally fitted. The structure with the viewing slit placed directly under the 9.4in gun is the armoured director position for the stern torpedo tube. (*Forsvarsgalleriet*)

NEUTRALITY PATROL, 1914–18: THE *E13* INCIDENT

One episode stands out amidst the tedium of the Danish navy's wartime neutrality patrol: the unsuccessful attempt by the British submarine *E13* to reach the Baltic through The Sound on the night of 18–19 August 1915.[1] Her companion *E8* completed the passage successfully during the same operation, but *E13*, commanded by Lieutenant Commander (later Admiral Sir) Geoffrey Layton, ran aground as the result of a faulty gyrocompass on the southeastern tip of the Danish islet of Saltholm, at which point The Sound is only eight miles across. As dawn broke on the 19th, *E13* was sighted by the stationary Danish guard ship *Falster* which reported the incident to the Navy High Command (*Flådens Overkommando*) in Copenhagen. The torpedo boat *Narhvalen* was immediately dispatched to investigate bearing orders from the Chief of Staff of the Navy, Kommandørkaptajn (Commander) H. L. E. Wenck, which leave little doubt as to the sympathies of the Danish authorities:

> If it is a German submarine and other German vessels are able to assist, a protest must be issued but no other measures taken for the time being. If it is a British submarine, German forces must be prevented from seizing or attacking it. First issue a protest and then use the means at your disposal if this is not respected.[2]

At around 0500 *Narhvalen* came alongside *E13*, Løjtnant (Lieutenant) J. A. Thiele informing Lt Cdr Layton that in accordance with neutrality regulations he had twenty-four hours to remove his vessel from Danish territorial waters or else face internment. Learning of this, Commander Wenck followed up his earlier orders to the effect that 'the British submarine should be protected if necessary by force of arms'. As it turned out, this instruction went unheeded.

The 1st Squadron led by *Peder Skram* was at

E13 at Copenhagen in August 1915 after her ordeal. Note the damage caused by German gunfire. Lying beyond her is the coastal defence ship *Iver Hvitfeldt* of 1886. (*Forsvarsgalleriet*)

anchor off Skovshoved about fifteen miles to the north at the time *E13* was first sighted. The squadron was ordered to proceed to her position to bolster Danish forces in the vicinity, not least since German ships had already been sighted to the south, albeit outside Danish territorial waters. The torpedo boats *Søulven* and *Tumleren* were immediately ordered to the scene, reaching it at 0845 together with a third, *Støren*, which had earlier reported a German torpedo boat having closed *E13*, though without manning her guns. However, at 0928 Commander E. Haack of *Søulven* reported that the German torpedo boats *G132* and *G134* were approaching at high speed from the south. Having hoisted signal flags ordering the British to abandon ship, *G132* launched a torpedo at a range of 300yds

(275m) which promptly grounded in shallow water and detonated. *G132* and *G134* then opened fire with their 2in (52mm) guns, quickly scoring hits on the defenceless *E13* which was set on fire. The action lasted under three minutes during which the Danish vessels did nothing to hinder the attack, despite being cleared for action. Only when the British began taking to the water under continued German fire once Lt Cdr Layton gave the order to abandon ship did *Søulven* move to position herself between the torpedo boats and *E13*, by which time the Germans were turning south. The Danes did not open fire on the retiring Germans but launched boats to pick up the British submariners, of whom fifteen out of a crew of thirty were rescued as *Peder Skram* and the protected cruiser *Gejser* arrived on the scene.[3] In the event, the Danish navy had proved itself incapable of upholding either Danish neutrality or protecting the vessel of a friendly power.

[1] 'A deadly morning off Copenhagen in August, 1915' at http://www.navalhistory.dk/English/ History/1914_1918/E13_%20incident.htm.

[2] Flaadens Stab, *Den udrustede Flaades Virksomhed under Sikringsperioden. Kronologisk Oversigt over Neutralitetskrænkelser og andre Forhold vedrørende Neutralitetsbevogtningen*, pp. 163–80; available at http://www.marinehist.dk/orlogsbib/dufvus-2.pdf.

[3] Layton's report is available at http://www.navalhistory. dk/English/History/1914_1918/E13_Layton_report.htm.

Another view of *E13* at Copenhagen in August 1915, this time seen from the starboard side. (*Forsvarsgalleriet*)

combined military and naval entity known as the Sikringsstyrken (Security Force) to guard Danish neutrality and ensure compliance with her obligations as a neutral state. By the end of that month some 65,000 men had been called up in a partial mobilisation. Of these most were soldiers since the total personnel of the Danish navy averaged only 4,000 men throughout the war. Where its material assets were concerned, the frontline strength of the Kongelige Danske Marine consisted of the three coastal battleships (including *Peder Skram*), two minelayers, four minesweepers, fifteen torpedo boats, seven submarines and two seaplanes. In reserve were the monitor *Skjold*, three cruisers, four gunboats, eight torpedo boats and fifteen patrol boats, with a further coastal battleship (*Niels Juel*) and five submarines under construction.

The wartime navy was organised into two squadrons. The 1st Squadron to which *Peder Skram* was initially assigned was stationed in The Sound for the defence of Copenhagen, which was protected on both the landward and seaward sides by a series of fortifications and batteries, together with extensive minefields. The 2nd Squadron, meanwhile, was stationed in The Great Belt for the duration of the war, and only when ships needed repair or maintenance did they come into the Naval Dockyard in Copenhagen. *Peder Skram* herself alternated

between the two squadrons, spending the war on neutrality duty until stood down from the Sikringsstyrken on 12 December 1918.

Between the Wars

Peder Skram spent the first two years after the Great War laid up in harbour, but in October 1920 was recommissioned as command ship of the winter training squadron with its torpedo boats and submarines, their area of operations in the Baltic and Skagerrak unchanged from the pre-war navy. In late November 1920 the squadron paid a visit to the Swedish port of Gothenburg before being stood down in February 1921. Exercises resumed from August 1921 to January 1922 and the Summer Training Squadron that year took *Peder Skram* and *Olfert Fischer* on a cruise to Stockholm and the German port of Danzig, during which both ships embarked a Danish-built Orlogsværftet H-Maskinen HM-1 aircraft for trial purposes.

Peder Skram was thereafter commissioned only sporadically, the result of swingeing cuts in 1922 which beached two-thirds of the naval officer corps. The navy budget was again nearly halved in 1932 with half of its manpower axed, a decision which caused Vice Admiral H. L. E. Wenck, now Chief of the Naval Staff, to resign in protest. *Peder Skram* therefore remained

confined to harbour between the autumn of 1922 and 1929, when she and *Niels Juel* were commissioned as training ships for reserve cadets. However, she spent another five years out of commission once this stint had been completed in the autumn of 1929, briefly hoisting her flag from August to September 1934. In May 1935 the ship was commissioned to escort the royal yacht *Dannebrog* and the torpedo boats *Glenten*, *Hvalen* and *Laxen* to Stockholm to celebrate the wedding of Princess Ingrid of Sweden to Danish Crown Prince Frederik. Such were the financial strictures on the navy that *Peder Skram* was ordered to proceed to a position north of Öland off the Swedish coast at the economical speed of 8 knots before joining the Royal Squadron for the run into Stockholm. The ceremonies completed, no sooner had the squadron cleared the Stockholm archipelago than *Peder Skram* detached and proceeded independently at her 8 knots while the rest of the squadron returned home at 12 knots. After this short spell of activity she was again laid up and it was not until 1939 that the ship was recommissioned, this time in the context of the imminent outbreak of the Second World War.

Neutrality and Occupation, 1939–43

By 1939 *Peder Skram* and *Niels Juel* were the only major ships left in the Royal Danish Navy, *Skjold*, *Herluf Trolle* and *Olfert Fischer* having been stricken in 1929, 1932 and 1936, respectively. With war clouds gathering, in May 1939 they formed the nucleus of a training squadron together with some smaller vessels, *Peder Skram* carrying out a full-power trial during which she matched the 15.9 knots accomplished during her trials thirty years before. However, the commission ended on 7 July with *Peder Skram* laid up at the Holmen naval base in Copenhagen. She was still there when the German army invaded Poland on 1 September, the ship being put at forty-eight hours' notice for steam, with all war provisions embarked. As in the Great War, Denmark established a Sikringsstyrke which *Peder Skram* joined on recommissioning on 20 September, but twenty years of official neglect and public disinterest conspired to make it only a shadow of the force constituted in August 1914. Concentrating off Aarhus, the Kongelige Danske Marine could only muster *Peder Skram* and the coastal battleship *Niels Juel* of 1918, six torpedo boats, up to five serviceable submarines and a handful of mine warfare vessels, patrol boats and

Olfert Fischer seen with *Peder Skram* outboard of her at the Holmen naval base in Copenhagen. They are lying under the Old Mast Crane built in 1742. *(Forsvarsgalleriet)*

Peder Skram carrying out a full-calibre shoot in the summer of 1939 during which she matched the speed of 15.9 knots achieved during her steam trials in 1909. *(Forsvarsgalleriet)*

seaplanes to guard the neutrality of Denmark's long coastline and sow minefields in The Great Belt and The Sound. The scarcity of their resources was not, of course, lost on the men of the Danish navy as they prepared for a second war after twenty years. During the parade ashore at Aarhus which concluded the August manoeuvres the author's grandfather Emil Wismann, then senior engineer of *Peder Skram*, was recognised by the Commander-in-Chief, Vice Admiral Hjalmar Rechnitzer, both having served during the Great War. The following wry exchange ensued: 'Is *Peder Skram* ready for war?' asked Rechnitzer. 'Yes, Admiral,' replied Wismann, '*Peder Skram* is as good as new!' The admiral continued: 'Wismann, have you filled the bunkers with plenty of fuel oil?' To which Wismann, no doubt with a twinkle in his eye, could only reply 'No, Admiral, *Peder Skram* is coal-fired…'

Aside from its material deficiencies, any resistance the navy could have put up when German forces eventually invaded Denmark at 0415 on 9 April 1940 was compromised by the fact that neither it nor the army had been allowed to mobilise for war by a government which reposed its faith in the non-aggression pact signed with Germany the previous May. The German invasion therefore found *Peder Skram* at Frederikshavn in northern Jutland while *Niels Juel* lay at Holmen. The few torpedo boats guarding the minefields in The Great Belt were under strict orders not to open fire except in self-defence or having sought further instructions from the War Ministry, a task complicated by the

fact that not all had been fitted with radio. By 1000 Denmark had capitulated.

The German occupation of Denmark was initially a comparatively benign affair. The Danish government continued to discharge its functions, albeit under German control, in a country the Third Reich regarded as a showcase for peaceful occupation. Germany supplied Denmark with coal, oil and other raw materials essential to supporting her economy, while the bulk of Danish agricultural and industrial output

found its way to Germany. When this enforced co-operation began to unravel in the summer of 1943, it was not on the initiative of the Danish government or parliament but by open defiance among a substantial part of the population, who took to the streets and resorted to strike action and other forms of civilian disobedience. Meanwhile, the Danish Resistance had grown in strength and determination with an increasing capacity for sabotage and disruption. In view of this, on 28 August Hitler gave the Danish government an ultimatum to impose a series of measures to curb personal freedoms or else suffer the imposition of martial law. The government duly handed in its resignation and the following day the German army instituted Operation Safari, the planned neutralisation of the Danish army and navy in response to the end of the policy of co-operation.

Scuttling

The end of co-operation and the expected German response had been anticipated by the Commander-in-Chief of the Kongelige Danske Marine, Vice Admiral A. H. Vedel (son of one of *Peder Skram*'s lead designers, H. Vedel). Accordingly, secret instructions were distributed to all naval vessels to await orders either to attempt to reach Swedish waters (an hour's steaming from Copenhagen) or scuttle their ships

The author's grandfather Emil Wismann seen playing the archlute in the uniform of an engineer sub-lieutenant in 1931. He was *Peder Skram*'s senior engineer on the outbreak of war. *(Lars Wismann)*

The 1st Squadron of the *Sikringsstyrken* (Security Force) including *Peder Skram* lying at Aarhus on 10 March 1940. To the left are three *Dragen* class torpedo boats and lying against the mole is the submarine tender *Henrik Gerner* and three of the four Havmanden class submarines commissioned in 1938–9. (*Ernst Chr. Skabelund/Forsvarsgalleriet*)

in harbour to prevent them falling into German hands, an option facilitated by the covert issue of scuttling charges to most vessels. The morning of 29 August 1943 found *Peder Skram* lying decommissioned but serving as a floating command ship at Holmen in Copenhagen when three German vehicles appeared at the entrance to the naval base at 0359. According to the post-war Danish government report, they were admitted unopposed but another source says that five machine-gun magazines were emptied against the Germans once they had entered the base.[4] Whatever the case, the German column was halted within a few hundred yards by the resourcefulness of a Danish sailor who raised the first of the bridges connecting the succession of five islets upon which the naval base is built. Since the bridge was operated from the far side, the Germans had no option but to turn and select another route to reach the northernmost islet of Nyholm where most of the ships, including *Peder Skram*, were tied up. This enforced detour gave the Danes precious minutes to react.

Meanwhile, the appearance of the first

German vehicle at the entrance to the naval base was promptly reported to the officer commanding operational vessels, Kommandør (Captain) Paul Ipsen in *Peder Skram*, who immediately passed the word to Vice Admiral Vedel at the navy high command in Copenhagen. Vedel unhesitatingly told Ipsen to 'Execute the order', which in this case was for all ships to be scuttled by their crews. At 0408 Ipsen ordered the scuttling signal 'KNU' hoisted by flag and relayed by Aldis lamp from *Peder Skram* to the rest of the fleet, which duly responded by firing their scuttling charges. An exception was *Peder Skram* herself which being decommissioned had failed to receive the charges, requiring her crew to flood the ship by opening the seacocks at 0435. By 0500 she was listing 20 degrees to starboard as she settled on the bottom of the harbour, though with most of her superstructure above water.

Under the Swastika, 1943–5

Of the twenty-seven naval vessels scuttled at Holmen, nine were submarines and eighteen were surface craft, of which eleven were recovered to serve in the Kriegsmarine. Among these was *Peder Skram*, which suffered only slight structural damage in the scuttling and was salvaged with little difficulty. The four 5.9in guns were removed to form part of the Pælebjerg

Battery on the island of Fanø off the southwest coast of Jutland, but the 9.4in guns were left in situ. She was apparently towed to Kiel for conversion in the autumn of 1943, but little more than a refit seems to have been carried out before she was commissioned into the Kriegsmarine as the stationary training and anti-aircraft vessel (*Flakschiff*) *Adler* in 1944. German plans are extant from 1944 showing her fitted with new superstructure and armed with six single 4in (105mm) AA guns, four single 1.6in (40mm) and four quadruple 0.8in (20mm) guns, but this conversion was never completed and seems not to have extended beyond the fitting of some light 20mm mountings. Although German sources reported 'Engines again inoperable' in 1944, it seems most unlikely that she ever sailed under her own power after 29 August 1943.[5] *Adler* was spotted lying at Kiel/Friedrichort by RAF reconnaissance in January 1945 and was reported as damaged in one of the many bombing raids on Kiel in April of that year. Her stern section flooded, she had to be put aground and was found in this condition at war's end in May 1945.

[4] *Generalrapport over Begivenhederne i Søværnet omkring den 29 August 1943*, and Søren Nørby, 'Blev der skudt mod de indtrængende tyskere den 29 August 1943?' available at http://www.noerby.net/pdf/2004/Preuthun.pdf.

[5] Erich Gröner, *Die deutschen Kriegsschiffe 1815–1945*, vol. VII (Koblenz: Bernard U. Graefe Verlag, 1990), p. 214.

Peder Skram lying scuttled at Holmen in October 1943 while the wreck of a torpedo boat is lowered onto the jetty on the right of the photo. The work was carried out by the powerful German floating crane *I/38* known as 'Der Lange Hendrik' ('Long Hendrik') specially brought from Hamburg. *(Courtesy Jørgen S. Lorenzen)*

Peder Skram being towed past Kronborg Castle in Helsingør (Elsinore) on 3 September 1945 on the final leg of her journey home from Kiel to Copenhagen and the scrapyard. *(Forsvarsgalleriet)*

Last Years, 1945–9

In late August 1945 the Danish salvage company of Em. Z. Svitzer dispatched the salvage vessel *Garm* to Kiel to raise and return the hulk of *Peder Skram* to Copenhagen. Three days' work succeeded in refloating and readying her for towing, and on 3 September *Peder Skram* finally sighted the spires of Elsinore at the northern entrance of The Sound, being turned over to the tugs *Gorm* and *Mjølner* to be brought the last twenty miles into Holmen. Here she joined the desultory company of the other vessels salvaged by the Germans after the scuttling of August 1943. Nonetheless, the writing was on the wall and over the winter of 1948–9 the armoured conning tower was landed and positioned to the north of the Naval Academy before being put to use at the nuclear testing facility at Risø in 1961. Then on 1 April 1949 *Peder Skram* was sold to the shipbreaking firm of H. J. Hansen in Odense where she was broken up that summer. However, the opportunity was taken to remove all 50ft of the foremast and spotting top structure which was set up as the company's landmark, in which capacity it continues to preside over Hansen's environmental recycling operations in Odense. One may speculate how many of those approaching Odense by sea realise that this weird-looking structure is all that remains of the Royal Danish Navy's last serving coastal battle-ship, *Peder Skram*.

Sources

Unpublished Sources

Forsvarets Bibliotek (Armed Forces Library), Copenhagen: *Panserskibene Herluf Trolle, Olfert Fischer og Peder Skram. Sammenstilling af Hoveddimensioner, Pansertykkelser, Vægte mm.* [Armoured Ships *Herluf Trolle*, *Olfert Fischer* and *Peder Skram*. Compilation of main dimensions, thickness of armour, weights, etc.]

Flaadens Stab [Naval Staff], *Den udrustede Flaades Virksomhed under Sikringsperioden. Kronologisk Oversigt over Neutralitetskrænkelser og andre Forhold*

Peder Skram's foremast and spotting top structure overlooks H. J. Hansen's recycling yard at Odense, the last vestige of Denmark's coastal battlefleet. *(Courtesy Lars Jordt)*

vedrørende Neutralitetsbevogtningen [Naval Operations during the Security Force Period. Chronological Overview of Neutrality Violations and other Circumstances relating to the Neutrality Patrol] available at http://www.marinehist.dk/orlogsbib/dufvus-2.pdf [accessed June 2017]

Generalrapport over Begivenhederne i Søværnet omkring den 29. August 1943 [General Report on Events Concerning the Navy around 29 August 1943] available at http://www.marinehist.dk/orlogsbib/Generalrap1943.pdf [accessed June 2017]

Bibliography

In collab., *Flaadens virksomhed under verdenskrigen 1914–1919* [Naval Operations during the World War, 1914–1919] (Copenhagen: Marineministeriet, 1920)

Andersen, Chr. I. E., *Bygning og indretning af Flaadens skibe* [Construction and Layout of the Navy's Ships] (Copenhagen: Marineministeriet, 1906)

Christiansen, Henrik, *Orlogsflådens skibe gennem 500 år* [500 Years of Navy Ships], vol. 3 (Copenhagen: Arnold Busck, 2010)

Dahl, Kai, *Lærebog for Orlogsgaster* [Seamen's Handbook] (Copenhagen: Forsvarsministeriet, 1939)

Gröner, Erich, *Die deutschen Kriegsschiffe 1815–1945*, vol. VII (Koblenz: Bernard U. Graefe Verlag, 1990)

Madsen, Kaj Toft, *Danske Torpedoer 1862–2008* [Danish Torpedoes, 1862–2008] (Copenhagen: Arnold Busck, 2008)

Nielsen, M., ed., *Skibsbygning og Maskinvæsen ved Orlogsværftet på Nyholm, Frederiksholm og Dokøen gennem 250 år 1692–6 Oktober 1942* [250 years of Shipbuilding and Engineering at the Naval Dockyard on Nyholm, Frederiksholm and Dokøen] (Copenhagen: Centraltrykkeriet, 1942)

Nørby, Søren, *Flådens sænkning 29 august 1943* [The Scuttling of the Fleet on 29 August 1943] (Odense: Forlaget Region, 2003)

_____, 'Blev der skudt mod de indtrængende tyskere den 29 August 1943?' [Were Shots Fired against the Intruding Germans on 29 August 1943?] available at http://www.noerby.net/pdf/2004/Preuthun.pdf [accessed June 2017]

_____, 'Stabelafløbninger af større Orlogsskibe og kongeskibe 1841–1931' [Launching of Major Warships and Royal Yachts, 1841–1931] available at http://www.noerby.net/pdf/2003/stabel.pdf [accessed June 2017]

Steensen, R. Steen, *Vore Panserskibe 1863–1943* [Our Armoured Ships, 1863–1943] (Copenhagen: Marinehistorisk Selskab, 1968)

Thiede, Egil, *Dansk Søartilleri 1860–2004* [Danish Naval Guns, 1860–2004], 2 vols. (Copenhagen: Tøjhusmuseet, 2004)

Danish Naval History: http://www.navalhistory.dk [accessed September 2017]

Naval History Society: http://marinehist.dk/ [accessed September 2017]

Marinha brasileira

The Battleship *Minas Geraes* (1908)

◆

João Roberto Martins Filho

NAMED FOR the great mining province in southeastern Brazil with its immense deposits of gold and brilliants, the arrival of the battleship *Minas Geraes* in 1910 made the Marinha brasileira the fourth in the world after Britain, Germany and the United States to commission a dreadnought, the ordering of which along with her sister *São Paulo* three years earlier had prompted a naval arms race with Argentina and Chile.[1] Not only that, but the manning and operation of these vast and sophisticated units upset the precarious social balance centred on race which characterised the post-emancipation Brazilian navy, a reminder of the extent to which a capital ship could serve as a microcosm of the social and political fabric of a nation, and which in *Minas Geraes*'s case made her less a ship of war than one of discord.

Context

Much weakened by the abolition of slavery in May 1888, on 15 November of the following year a *coup d'état* led by Marshal Deodoro da Fonseca deposed Dom Pedro II and put an end to the Brazilian empire which dated from 1822. In doing so it ushered in the Brazilian Republic which nonetheless had for some years all the trappings of a military dictatorship. The advent of the Republic augured ill for the Marinha brasileira which had grown out of the Portuguese navy following the removal of the Portuguese monarchy from Lisbon to Brazil in 1808 and enjoyed close ties with the Crown, under whose auspices it became the most powerful in South

America. Not only that but the republican movement was supported mainly by army officers who soon began to starve the navy of funds and personnel and connive in its dissolution. The Marinha responded to this threat with a period of active involvement in Brazilian political affairs eventually known as the *Revoltas da Armada* (naval revolts). The first major expression of this dissent came in November 1891 when the navy rose after Deodoro declared a state of emergency and shut down the National Congress. Led by Admiral Custódio de Melo, the revolt succeeded in overthrowing Deodoro and replacing him by his vice president, Marshal Floriano Peixoto. Peixoto's refusal to vacate office after the statutory term had elapsed two years later prompted the outbreak of a second and far more prolonged naval insurrection on 6 September 1893. Led once again by Custódio de Melo, and this time having the restoration of the monarchy as its ultimate goal, within a week naval units were exchanging fire with army artillery in the coastal forts of Rio de Janeiro, the start of a two-year civil war which left 10,000 dead. Although Custódio de Melo managed to link the revolt with the Federalist Rebellion in the south and enlist the support of the illustrious figure of Admiral Saldanha da Gama, a hero of the Paraguayan War of 1864–70, the campaign ended in defeat for the Marinha in March 1894 with Saldanha da Gama and many of its leaders perishing in the fighting ashore. In the intervening period the Republican government, which enjoyed the support of the United States, found itself obliged to purchase a motley assortment of ships from Europe and elsewhere known as the 'paper fleet', with which it was able to stave off the Brazilian fleet proper.[2] Only when Congress

approved an amnesty law in 1896 were the conditions created in which the Marinha could draw a line under this tumultuous period in its history and begin reintegrating itself into government service.

Although the Revolta da Armada did not succeed in its aims, it did have the effect of bringing a civilian government to power in Brazil which represented the interests of the coffee-exporting bourgeoisie as against those of the military. It was under these circumstances that the opportunity was created for the reconstruction of the Marinha, which in turn prompted an unprecedented debate on the importance of sea power to the Brazilian Republic that drew on the wider navalist thought of the day. The moving spirit in this debate was Senator Rui Barbosa de Oliveira, former Minister of Justice in the Deodoro government and a noted jurist who spent several years as an exile in London after being accused of instigating the 1893 revolt.[3] Still in London, in May 1895 Barbosa published four articles in the *Jornal do Commercio*, one of the country's leading newspapers, which provided the framework for a reassessment of the Marinha brasileira. Under the general title of 'A Lesson from the Far East', Barbosa not only narrated the Japanese victory over the Peiyang Fleet at the Battle of the Yalu River the previous September (see *Chen Yuen*), but presented the material and human reconstruction of the Marinha as the great Brazilian challenge of the late nineteenth century.[4] Influenced by the ideas of Alfred Thayer Mahan, Barbosa regarded

---

[1] The editor would like to thank Marcia Prestes Taft of the Diretoria do Patrimônio Histórico e Documentação da Marinha, Rio de Janeiro, and Zachary Morgan of The Pennsylvania State University for kindly supplying illustrations for this chapter.

[2] Rui Barbosa, *Cartas de Inglaterra* (2nd edn., São Paulo: Livraria Academica Saraiva & C. Editores, 1929), pp. 254–8.

[3] For a brief biography, see Joseph L. Love, *The Revolt of the Whip* (Stanford, Calif.: Stanford University Press, 2012), pp. 9–10.

[4] See the analysis of José Miguel Arias Neto, 'A Marinha do Brasil como imagem da Nação' in *Revista Marítima Brasileira* 121 (2001), no. 7–9, pp. 105–15.

The two architects of the new Brazilian navy, Senator Rui Barbosa de Oliveira (1849–1923) (left) and Admiral Arthur Silveira da Motta (1843–1914), usually referred to as the Baron of Jaceguay. *(Bruce Taylor Collection)*

Minas Geraes taking on coal in c. 1913. The orders placed for *Minas Geraes* and her sister *São Paulo* in February 1907 resulted in the Marinha brasileira being among the first to take delivery of a dreadnought and prompted a naval arms race in South America. *(Library of Congress/13336)*

national strength as a direct product of naval strength.[5] His fundamental point was that the naval revolts had weakened the navy to the point of leaving Brazil open to external intervention; should Brazil be defeated at sea, the army would be incapable of preserving her independence, and fleets, unlike armies, simply could not be improvised:

> Now, history, and our own Brazilian history, is quite familiar with instances of dissolved armies. But to dissolve the Navy would be the greatest of our native innovations. This is because armies can be raised relatively quickly, and can be speedily constituted from the mass of the people at the first sign of danger, while a fleet is something so costly, so complex and technical, a matter of many years, that to extinguish it would be to admit a continuing and irremediable threat to our national existence.

The following year the same journal published a further series of articles on naval organisation by

[5] The *Revista Marítima Brasileira* published a twelve-part serialisation of the main sections of *The Influence of Sea Power upon History* translated by Tenente (Lieutenant) Leão Amzalak in 1895.

REBUILDING A NAVY

In its post-revolt prostration the Marinha brasileira found itself contemplating some of the irreducible elements of which naval power is composed at national level together with the relative importance to be accorded to each in any future reconstruction: *matériel*, the human factor and strategic considerations. Let us take each in turn as they touch on the Brazilian situation.

Matériel

The contributors to the Brazilian naval debate of the turn of the twentieth century wrote in the knowledge that the Marinha was in a deplorable condition where its *matériel* was concerned. As far as Barbosa was concerned, even before the naval revolts the Brazilian navy had been 'reduced to some scattered and inanimate remnants'. To Jaceguay the nation had created a bureaucratic monster hiding a 'Lilliputian navy', what Arthur Dias described as 'no more than a handful of dispersed wrecks'. As he concluded, 'we need everything, we have to rebuild from keel to truck'.

Dias recalled that at the time of the Paraguayan War of 1864–70 the Marinha 'had ninety-four warships of all types, of which sixteen were armoured, with 6,474 officers and men, and 237 guns'. By contrast, thirty years later 'we have fewer than half a dozen serviceable ships, and a confusion of miserable laggardly tubs with no modern guns,

insufficient ammunition, and, worst of all, no officers or sailors'. In 1899, by contrast, the Marinha brasileira possessed two turret ships: *Riachuelo* (launched in 1883 and rebuilt between 1893–5) and *Aquidabã* (1885 and 1897–8 respectively); two coast defence vessels: *Marechal Deodoro* (1898) and *Marechal Floriano* (1899); four protected cruisers: *Tamandaré* (1890), *Benjamin Constant* (1892), *República* (1892) and *Barroso* (1896); in addition to the torpedo gunboats *Tiradentes* (1892), *Gustavo Sampaio* (1893) and *Tupy*, *Timbira* and *Tamoyo* (all 1896). In addition, Brazil had thirteen torpedo boats, eight of slightly over 100 tons and five of 80 tons' displacement. Of these only the eight larger ones had been launched during the 1890s; the others were relics of the empire. Taken as a whole, the fleet itself was a potpourri of assorted provenance:

> Heeding the opinions of the various 'schools' that were established, none of which had been proved in emergency situations, the French supplied us with two coastal defence ships, products of Admiral Aube's *jeune école*, *Deodoro* and *Floriano*; the Germans provided us with the novelty of the

The officer corps represented here by Admiral Penido and his staff in 1925. (*Diretoria do Patrimônio Histórico e Documentação da Marinha (DPHDM)/10808*)

cruiser-torpedo boats *Tupi*, *Timbira* and *Tamoyo*; while from England we were to have received three fast and well-armed cruisers, the *Almirante Abreu*, *Amazonas* and *Barroso*, but were left with just the latter for lack of funds to pay for the first two.[6]

Where manpower was concerned, the Marinha brasileira numbered just 1,792 men in 1899, whereas 'the garrison of the fortress of Villegagnon [off Rio de Janeiro] and the few existing vessels would alone require a minimum of 3,780'.[7]

From a regional perspective, Argentina was Brazil's first point of reference. For the Baron of Jaceguay, 'the superiority of the Argentine fleet is so much greater than ours that it would be impossible for us to dispute command of the sea in the event of a war with the Republic, even if the struggle were a protracted one', a pessimism that seems well founded. Argentina and Chile had by now acquired fast, well-protected and well-armed armoured cruisers, the result of a border dispute which prompted a naval arms race that reached a climax in the first years of the new century (see *Garibaldi*). In Argentina's case, by 1898 she was in possession of four Italian-built armoured cruisers of the latest design and armed with Armstrong 8in or 10in (203–254mm) guns. Although not the product of any pre-existing naval programme, they were all variants of the Giuseppe Garibaldi class, enjoyed good speed and protection, and displaced between 6,840 and 8,100 tons – more than any unit in the Brazilian navy. By the time the dispute was halted by the signing of the so-called Pacts of May in 1902, the Marinha brasileira had fallen well astern of its Argentine and Chilean counterparts.

However, there were two perspectives which put a different complexion on this melancholy picture. On the one hand was the reality of the navy built up by Brazil in the imperial period (1822–89) during which the government had recognised that its geographical and economic conditions required the development of maritime power. On the other hand was the example of such countries as Japan and the United States which had created powerful modern fleets within a few short decades due to sound policymaking.

[6] Hélio Leôncio Martins & Dino Willy Cozza, 'Poderes combatentes' in *História naval brasileira* (Rio de Janeiro: Serviço de Documentação da Marinha, 1997), vol. V 1B, pp. 79–100; p. 79.

[7] Dias, *O Problema naval*, p. 321.

Crewmen of *Minas Geraes* coaling ship on the quarterdeck in *c.* 1913. Note the bugler on the left and *São Paulo* discernible in the distance. *(Library of Congress/13333)*

The Human Factor

'Ships don't make fleets' Barbosa wrote in his 1895 article on the Sino-Japanese War, adding that 'the warship is an increasingly complex machine, but still more complex is the training of the man who gives it life.' As far as he was concerned, the naval problem boiled down to solving the relationship between command, officers and crew, without which 'the delicate complexity of a modern warship would in effect be a constant source of confusion, bewilderment and

feebleness.'[8] To Jaceguay, however, there could be no training of naval personnel without ships, nor could there be crews and officers, without whom there could in turn be no promotion, and it was lack of promotion which had contributed to the apathy of the Marinha in the late imperial period and then to the revolts of 1891 and 1893. More pertinently, Jaceguay posed the following question in 1896: 'With respect to personnel, where are we to find capable and competent men to operate a large number of these highly

complex machines of which modern warships are composed?'[9] To this there was no ready answer.

Where the officer corps was concerned, the Marinha brasileira was a more aristocratic service than the army due both to its social composition and the reduced number of available places, many of which were effectively political appointments. Ships

---

[8] *Cartas de Inglaterra*, p. 267.

[9] Arthur Silveira da Motta [Barão de Jaceguay], *De aspirante a almirante. Minha Fé de Ofício documentada*, 2 vols. (Rio de Janeiro: Serviço de Documentação da Marinha, 1984–5), II, p. 299.

had the atmosphere of government offices. Certain officers in the upper reaches were recognised for their competence, but centralisation and administrative preferment weakened naval organisation. Overburdened by senior officers, opportunities for promotion were few, a fact which served to discourage the young and talented who were obliged to mark time during the first years of their career. No wonder there was little in the way of *esprit de corps* despite efforts to promote morale since the Paraguayan War. Moreover, successive republican governments had not invested in educating or reforming the Marinha, leaving it ill-equipped to operate the new fleet under construction abroad.[10] Officer education was limited to the classrooms of the *Escola Naval* (Naval College) where theoretical training was imparted in the style of a polytechnic institute, although Jaceguay regarded it as capable of producing good cadets for an officer corps lacking only in technical training.

With respect to the lower deck, the navy had, in Jaceguay's opinion, to draw its sailors from a very unsatisfactory pool of men with scant opportunity to recruit from the seafaring community. The answer in the Imperial period had been the establishment of the *Corpo de Imperiais Marinheiros* (Corps of Imperial Sailors) which consisted of eighteen companies of trainees spread about the country. Even when replaced by the *Corpo de Marinheiros Nacionais* (Corps of National Sailors) in 1890, these were so poorly and inefficiently run that the navy's ships were never at full complement. Volunteers were few and far between, requiring impressment of illiterate petty criminals, orphans and the sweepings of Brazil's coastal cities to man the fleet on a three-year engagement.[11] Shipboard conditions were also extremely harsh into the twentieth century, Brazil being 'the last country in the Western world where flogging was still permitted in its navy'.[12] Discipline was enforced by the marines of the *Batalhão Naval* (Naval Battalion), detachments of whom were accommodated aboard in separate quarters. Taken all round, the dominant impression was of sailors as the dregs of society and their ships as floating penitentiaries.

The situation was little better with respect to petty officers. Not until 1910 was the *Escola de Contramestres* (Petty Officers' School) established, by which time many had been drafted to the new battleships. However, on boarding their ships for the first time they found the chief petty officers had little to teach them as they were usually unfamiliar with their own duties.[13]

A group of petty officers pose on the quarterdeck in their starched whites in 1918 as loafing sailors view proceedings from the roof of No. '6' turret. Lack of training and experience among petty officers was among the chief structural problems of the Brazilian navy. *(DPHDM/34490)*

Nonetheless, from Jaceguay's perspective, the key to modernisation lay in technology. As far as he was concerned, the Marinha had two basic challenges: first, how to obtain trained personnel capable of operating the new warships in all their complexity, and secondly how to maintain the efficiency of this *matériel* given that Brazil had no significant state- or privately-owned industrial infrastructure. Were Brazil able to surmount these challenges she would enjoy a significant advantage over her regional rivals, including Argentina.

Strategy and the Necessary Fleet

To Jaceguay writing in 1896, the time had come for Brazil to abandon the emphasis on riverine warfare that had held sway since the Paraguayan War of 1864–70 and focus instead on command of the sea. To do so would require a fleet at least a third of whose vessels had adequate armament and protection, together with a modicum of speed shared by each tactical unit in the battle squadron. It was not necessary for these ships to be excessively large, so long as they were fully armoured and mounted heavy batteries of quick-firing guns. In Jaceguay's opinion this 'front-line squadron' would consist of a dozen ships

consisting of four armoured cruisers, the three protected cruisers currently under construction at Armstrongs in Britain (though only *Barroso* was ever delivered), two scout cruisers, and three torpedo boat destroyers or auxiliary cruisers which could be converted from merchantmen. This ideal squadron would be completed by six torpedo gunboats and eight seagoing torpedo boats.

In Jaceguay's view, timing was of the essence where the procurement of a new fleet was concerned, a task which would require more than a decade to accomplish. What was needed was a naval leader with the political influence, breadth of vision and commitment to Brazil's maritime vocation necessary to realise that endeavour. That moment was not far off.

10 José Eduardo de Macedo Soares [Um Oficial da Armada], *Política versus Marinha* (Rio de Janeiro: Á venda na Livraria H. Garnier, 1911), p. 34.

11 Silveira da Motta, *De aspirante a almirante*, p. 285.

12 Love, *The Revolt of the Whip*, p. 66.

13 Heitor Pereira da Cunha, *A revolta da esquadra brasileira em novembro e dezembro de 1910* (Rio de Janeiro: Imprensa Naval, 1953), pp. 24–5.

Admiral Arthur Silveira da Motta, better known as the Baron of Jaceguay, in which the author concurred with the bulk of Barbosa's arguments while adding a specialist perspective on other key elements in the development of the Brazilian navy. These two noted figures were joined in 1899 by the young journalist Arthur Dias whose writings brought the naval debate to a wider audience, although Dias dissented from Barbosa's view in holding that the real threat to Brazil lay not with her neighbour Argentina but with the United States and the European powers.[14]

The 1904 Naval Programme

It was during the presidency of Francisco de Paula Rodrigues Alves (1902–6) that the political and economic conditions of republican Brazil first began to favour the drafting and approval of a coherent naval programme promoted by the Minister of Marine Admiral Julio César de Noronha. Accordingly, in April 1904 the *Relatório do Ministério dos Negócios da Marinha* (Ministerial Report on Naval Affairs) prepared by Noronha described a construction programme to be carried out over a period of between six and eight years to include three battleships of 12,500–13,000 tons' displacement, three armoured cruisers of 9,200–9,700 tons and six torpedo boat destroyers of 400 tons together with a number of minor vessels.[15] The equal number of battleships and armoured cruisers reflected the influence on Noronha of the Imperial Japanese Navy's evolving 1896 construction programme, while the battleship designs were to be based on those ordered by Chile from Armstrongs and Vickers respectively as *Constitución* and *Libertad* in 1901 but eventually commissioned into the Royal Navy as *Swiftsure* and *Triumph*. Noronha's report also addressed the ongoing debate as to the virtues of the armoured cruiser, which exceeded the protected cruiser in armament, protection and speed and was deemed capable of joining the battle line as a fast wing, thereby breaking the classic squadron division of the eighteenth and nineteenth centuries. Noronha's plan was therefore the first in the history of the Marinha to provide for the acquisition of a homogenous

squadron as first proposed by the Baron of Jaceguay in 1896. In it lay the seed that was to bear fruit as *Minas Geraes*.

On 12 July 1904 the *Comissão de Marinha e Guerra* (Navy and War Committee) of the Chamber of Deputies issued a favourable report on the projected programme. Aside from a few amendments to Noronha's plan, emphasis was placed on the need to provide not only for the construction of a shipyard and expansion of the navy's dry-docking facilities, but also for improved training for officers, stokers and sailors as recommended by Barbosa in 1895. From a budgetary standpoint, it was recommended that construction contracts be issued in three triennial periods ending in 1913. A further argument in support of this arrangement was the impression thus imparted to neighbour states that Brazil had no intention of turning itself into a regional hegemonic power from one year to the next. Moreover, it suggested the advisability of the South American powers uniting their naval forces to defend themselves against 'unjustified pretensions from other continents'.

On 14 December 1904 Noronha's plan for the reconstruction of the Brazilian navy received congressional approval via Legislative Decree 1296. Aside from the procurement mentioned above, provision was made for the acquisition of six 120-ton and six 50-ton torpedo boats, three submarines, a collier capable of transporting 6,000 tons of coal and a training ship with a maximum displacement of 3,000 tons. It was also ordered that construction of the river monitors *Pernambuco* and *Maranhão* be completed as soon as possible. Where the cost was concerned, provision was made for budgetary allocations during each fiscal year. Any amounts not applied would be carried forward to the following fiscal year. By the end of that year Law 1452 had established the national budget for 1906 and authorised the government to implement the programme by signing contracts worth £4,214,550, though expenditure in that particular year could not exceed £1,685,200. This development permitted Noronha to order the *Inspetoria de Engenharia Naval* (Bureau of Naval Engineering) to assess the eleven tenders submitted for the contract, which was eventually awarded to the firm of Sir W. G. Armstrong Whitworth & Co. Ltd of Newcastle upon Tyne. As Noronha recalled, 'It was the outstanding bidder, since not only did it best meet the conditions of the programme, but the stated amount included the complete ship, i.e. including armament, ammunition, etc. on commissioning.'

So it was that on 23 July 1906 a contract was signed with Armstrongs for the construction of three battleships of 13,000 tons. According to

the specifications set forth in a letter from the Brazilian government on 23 June 1905, the approved design provided for twelve 10in guns disposed in six twin turrets, one forward, one aft and two on either beam.[16] Armstrongs was to supply the guns, ammunition and armour, but provision was made for it to subcontract the work to other firms, and the contract stipulated that the engines were to be built by Humphrys, Tennant & Company of Deptford. In the event, Armstrongs made provision for construction of two of the battleships at its Elswick yard, the lead ship to be called *Minas Geraes* under yard number 791 and *Rio de Janeiro* number 792, while subcontracting the third vessel *São Paulo* to Vickers at Barrow-in-Furness as number 347. Not only that, but Vickers was to provide the engine plant for all three vessels. The estimated construction time was twenty-four and twenty-nine months respectively for the first two ships, and twenty-six months for the third.

The 1906 Naval Programme

Despite these developments, the election of Afonso Pena as president in March 1906 and the appointment of Admiral Alexandrino Faria de Alencar as Minister of Marine designate in succession to Noronha resulted in the 1904 programme being halted and communications issued ordering the shipyards to modify the design legend of the battleships. Meanwhile, rumours began circulating about the construction of a revolutionary vessel for the Royal Navy, and Armstrong representatives in Rio de Janeiro, led by the director J. M. Falkner and the head of that company's design office Eustace Tennyson d'Eyncourt, advised the Ministry of Marine to delay its plans until further details were revealed.[17] The vessel in question was of course HMS *Dreadnought* which had been launched at Portsmouth Dockyard on 10 February 1906. This turn of events much aggravated Noronha, but Armstrongs had already recognised that his star was waning and Tennyson d'Eyncourt, who proved as skilled a salesman as he was a naval architect, succeeded in persuading Alencar that Brazil could put herself in the enviable position of building three dreadnoughts while Britain herself had only one.[18] Nor of course was this

---

[14] These and other theses published as Arthur Dias, *O Problema naval. Condições actuaes da marinha de guerra e seu papel nos destinos do paiz* (Rio de Janeiro: Officina da Estatistica, 1899).

[15] Julio César de Noronha, *Programa naval de 1904. Subsídios para a história marítima do Brasil*, vol. 9 (Rio de Janeiro: Imprensa Naval, 1950).

[16] David Topliss, 'The Brazilian Dreadnoughts, 1904–1914' in *Warship International* 25 (1988), no. 3, pp. 240–89; pp. 245–6.

[17] Richard Hough, *The Big Battleship, or the Curious Career of HMS* Agincourt (London: Michael Joseph, 1967), p. 18.

[18] Martins & Cozza, 'Poderes combatentes', p. 83.

solely in Brazil's interest since no sooner had *Dreadnought* appeared than the leading British shipbuilding firms were anxious to incorporate her various innovations into their own construction. With three newly ordered capital ships on its books, the Brazilian navy was the obvious partner for Armstrongs in such an endeavour.

The essence of Alencar's argument was that the vessels approved under Noronha's programme had been outstripped by technological developments in the intervening two years. In July 1906 he defended his plan before Congress, as a result of which the Navy and War Committee of the Chamber of Deputies issued a new report stating that the fleet envisioned in 1904 was already obsolete. On 1 September the matter went to the Senate in connection with the debate on the budgetary allocation for the navy for 1907. One of the senators, Admiral Heráclito Belfort Vieira, a member of the Senate Navy and War Committee and an ally of Noronha, opened the debate by defending his earlier endorsement of the 1904 programme, followed on 17 September by Alencar who rounded on Belfort Vieira in a long and slashing speech. Citing half a dozen British and French naval authorities, Alencar aimed and fired their 'six big guns' in a largely successful effort to 'demolish the fortifications' erected by his critics. Following the latest thinking, he decreed the end of secondary armament, defended the removal of all extraneous superstructure providing an inviting target for enemy guns, proposed the construction of double hulls, stated that a speed of 18 knots was now manifestly inadequate, and declared with utter certainty that armoured cruisers were no longer fit to lie in the battle line. He severely criticised the 1904 programme, declaring it to be 'neither technically advanced nor consistent with experience as revealed by events nor commensurate with the national sacrifice we are bound to make'. Conveniently ignoring the fact that Armstrongs had offered to increase the original displacement of 13,000 tons by nearly 2,000 tons to improve protection without additional charge, he ridiculed the 1904 specifications as 'infelicitous' and even 'haphazard', pointing out that the latest construction was outstripping these vessels by up to 6,000 tons. However, his clinching argument came with respect to gunnery. Addressing Belfort Vieira directly, Alencar not only accused Noronha of having reduced the number of turrets from eight to six, but reminded him that '*Dreadnought* has ten 305mm [12in] guns and ours 254 [10in]. Your Excellency knows that guns of greater calibre have greater penetration and greater range. *Dreadnought* also has greater speed, meaning that our ships would inevitably be destroyed in battle with her.'[19] Alencar had evidently succumbed to the view that it was necessary for Brazil to match the construction not only of its regional rivals but also of the most advanced nations, arguments that were of course enthusiastically supported by the major shipyards for commercial purposes.

On 8 November 1906 Senator Antônio Francisco de Azeredo submitted the draft naval plan to the upper chamber. According to him, the Battle of Tsushima fought the previous year had effectively sealed the fate of the earlier programme, making it essential for modifications to the order placed in Britain. As far as he was concerned, so long as the keels of these vessels remained unlaid it was possible to adjust the 1904 naval programme by 'increasing the

Minas Geraes launched at Elswick by Sra. Regis de Oliveira, wife of the Brazilian minister to Great Britain, on 10 September 1908. Note the ram bow and the scrollwork around the eyes of the ship. *(DPHDM/3429)*

---

[19] Dias, *O Problema naval*, pp. 97 & 93.

Minas Geraes in the final stages of fitting out by Armstrongs at its Walker shipyard on the Tyne in late 1909. *(DPHDM)*

tonnage of the battleships on order to 18,000, thereby converting them to the dreadnought type, which is universally acknowledged as the finest type by the navies of the world'. In fact, the evidence from the Armstrongs archives is that work had already begun on these vessels by the time Azeredo rose to address the Senate, of which Alencar's party could scarcely have been unaware. Whatever the case, the new proposals passed smartly through Congress and within a few days of Alencar finally taking office as Minister of Marine a decree was issued on 24 November annulling the 1904 programme and replacing it with a modified version, increasing the tonnage of the battleships and destroyers, substituting the three armoured cruisers by fast scouting cruisers, and the collier and training ship by a minelayer and hydrographic vessel respectively, all for a total of 67,500 tons. However, the most arresting feature

of the 1906 naval law by comparison with that of 1904 was that none of the specifications of the vessels to be acquired were stipulated beyond the tonnage increases. The decree therefore provided a sort of carte blanche for the ministry and indirectly for the shipyards, and it was no surprise that Alencar had to rebut accusations from Senators Belfort Vieira and Lauro Sodré that the transfer of such sweeping powers to the minister for implementation of the new naval programme constituted a violation of article 48 of the constitution which reserved ultimate authority on all matters relating to the administration of the state to the president himself.

Design and Construction

The revised design for *Minas Geraes* and *São Paulo*, which Alencar had privately shared with President Afonso Pena, had been prepared by

Josiah Perrett and Eustace Tennyson d'Eyncourt, respectively chief naval architect and head of the design office at Armstrongs.[20] The vessels were 543ft (165.5m) long, 83ft (25.3m) in the beam and drew 25ft (7.6m) on a standard displacement of 19,280 tons.[21] Main armament consisted of twelve 45-calibre 12in (305mm) guns disposed in six twin turrets with a super-firing arrangement fore and aft and the remaining two turrets set *en échelon* on either beam. The turrets were electrically powered but all other firing mechanisms operated under hydraulic power delivered from three pump rooms, two forward and one aft. The secondary armament consisted of twenty-two 50-calibre 4.7in (120mm) guns and eight 1.85in (47mm) weapons. With respect to protection, the

[20] In collab., *História naval brasileira*, vol. V 1B (Rio de Janeiro: Serviço de Documentação da Marinha, 1997), ch. 1 & 2.

[21] Topliss, 'The Brazilian Dreadnoughts, 1904–1914', pp. 240–89.

main belt ranged from 4–9in (101–229mm) with bulkheads up to 9in thick. The barbettes and conning tower carried up to 12in of Krupp cemented armour while horizontal protection extended from 1in (25mm) on the lower and upper decks to 2in (51mm) on the main deck. These specifications briefly made *Minas Geraes* the largest and most heavily armed vessel in the

world on completion in January 1910, as well as the first to mount a twelve-gun broadside; she was also the first British-built vessel to carry super-firing turrets, a development introduced in the dreadnought USS *Michigan* of 1908. Here, however, the innovation ended, for *Minas Geraes* was powered by eighteen Babcock & Wilcox boilers with mixed coal and oil firing and two

sets of Vickers triple-expansion reciprocating engines producing 23,500ihp rather than the turbines of HMS *Dreadnought*, though with a matching best speed of 21 knots. There was stowage for up to 2,305 tons of coal and 364 tons of oil. Endurance was approximately 3,600 miles at 19 knots and 8,000 miles at an economical speed of 10 knots.

THE ARMS RACE AND THE BALANCE OF POWER

Needless to say, the signing of the original contract for three dreadnoughts with Armstrongs in July 1906 caused a sensation in Buenos Aires where *La Prensa*, one of the leading dailies, warned that the new Brazilian fleet threatened its Argentine counterpart with technological eclipse: 'We had learned of the decision made by our neighbour country to increase its naval power and had received some information on the new vessels, but we never imagined these would be of such a size as to be classed as the most powerful afloat once completed.' As the moderate Argentine Foreign Minister Manuel Augusto Montes de Oca put it, 'Just one of the battleships ordered by Brazil would be sufficient to destroy the entire Argentine and Chilean fleets.' This development strengthened the position of the Radical party in Argentine politics at the expense of more conciliatory voices, and in September of that year Montes de Oca was replaced as Foreign Minister by Estanislao Zeballos, a sworn enemy of his Brazilian counterpart José Maria da Silva Paranhos, Baron of Rio Branco, the so-called 'Father of Brazilian Diplomacy' who had guided his country's foreign policy since 1902.[22]

In the eyes of her neighbours, the new Brazilian battle squadron was the main instrument in a strategy aimed at positioning her as the hegemonic state in South America, the first stage in cementing an alliance between Brazil and the United States. According to Zeballos, the Baron of Rio Branco was prepared to attack Argentina once the Brazilian squadron had arrived from Britain. On 10 June 1908 Zeballos took advantage of what he described as a 'favourable' diplomatic opportunity to present his government with an extraordinary plan which 'consisted of immediately commencing diplomatic negotiations with Brazil to demand that the latter divide its squadron with us'. Should this be refused, 'we will inform them that we are not prepared to permit the incorporation of two large battleships into their fleet'. According to this stratagem, Argentina would then mobilise its army and navy and give Brazil eight days to comply, while at the same time engaging in diplomacy in Europe to explain its

Minas Geraes showing the flag at Puerto Madero, the port of Buenos Aires, on 20 October 1922. *(DPHDM/24189)*

position to the great powers. Should the impasse remain unbroken, Zeballos posited 'the occupation of Rio de Janeiro, which according to the Ministers of War and Marine represents a carefully planned and straightforward operation given the weakness of Brazilian defences'. Unfortunately for Zeballos, the opposition newspaper *La Nación* immediately published the plans and brought about his downfall before the month was out.[23]

Nonetheless, in December 1908 the Argentine Congress voted funds for the construction of two dreadnoughts intended to meet the Brazilian naval threat. This decision was influenced by rumours, which proved largely accurate, that the third unit ordered from Armstrongs under the Brazilian 1906 naval programme – *Rio de Janeiro* – would be much larger than the first two, displacing 31,000 tons and mounting twelve 14in (356mm) guns; she was later sold to the Ottoman navy as *Sultan Osman-i Evel* and eventually commissioned as HMS *Agincourt* with fourteen 12in (305mm) guns. Predictably enough,

agents of Armstrongs began putting out feelers in the hope of securing further lucrative contracts in the context of the South American naval race. In the event, in early 1910 the Argentine government awarded a contract for the construction of two dreadnoughts (subsequently *Rivadavia* and *Moreno*) to a US consortium composed of the Fore River Ship and Engine Building Co. of Quincy, Massachusetts, and the New York Shipbuilding Co. of Camden, New Jersey following a disingenuous tender process which aroused international condemnation. However, there was consolation for Armstrongs when Chile placed orders with the firm for two battleships (eventually *Almirante Latorre*, q.v., and the carrier HMS *Eagle*) in July 1911.

The frisson caused by the orders for *Minas Geraes* and *São Paulo* was not confined to Brazil's South American neighbours. Further afield there were questions as to her ability to finance the ships and the possibility that she might sell them to one of the great powers, thereby destabilising the delicate equilibrium

On 7 January 1907 work began at Elswick to dismantle the keels of the now superseded Brazilian battleships and clear the slips while the final design was prepared for approval under number 494A. On 20 February a new contract was signed, this time reduced to two units to be known as *Minas Geraes* and *São Paulo*, the first to be built at Elswick and the second at

between rival states. The first of these rumours came in June 1907 when the journal of the British Navy League suggested that construction of the two Brazilian battleships was a stratagem by the Admiralty to gain an advantage over Germany. In early 1908 a *New York Herald* correspondent reported having overheard the Baron of Rio Branco claim that he would sell the first of Brazil's dreadnoughts to the United States in the event of a war between that country and Japan. The Brazilian embassy in Washington immediately denied the report but the rumour reached London, where in March the First Lord of the Admiralty Reginald McKenna was asked in Parliament whether he could give assurances that the government would take measures to prevent the vessels falling into hands of other powers. McKenna answered that he had no cause to give any credence to that theory, and could provide no further information on the vessels under construction for Brazil. While accepting the unusual nature of the situation, he stated that there was no reason to suppose that these vessels were being built with any hostile intention towards Britain, but that the government would certainly follow their careers with considerable interest. The story was perpetuated in a long article published in the journal *The Nineteenth Century and After* in August 1908.[24] Only when Brazil placed orders with Armstrongs and Vickers for the construction of a pair of floating docks to accommodate *Minas Geraes* and *São Paulo* in August 1909 did the matter subside. Nonetheless, the South American arms race unleashed by the orders for *Minas Geraes* and *São Paulo* was real enough.

22 Clodoaldo Bueno, *Política externa da Primeira República. Os anos de apogeu (1902–1918)* (São Paulo: Paz e Terra, 2003), p. 233.

23 Roberto Etchepareborda, *Historia de las relaciones internacionales argentinas* (Buenos Aires: Editorial Pleamar, 1978), p. 47.

24 Gerard Fiennes, 'Dreadnoughts for Sale or Hire' in *The Nineteenth Century and After* no. 378 (August 1908), pp. 207–14.

Barrow.[25] The keel of the former was laid under yard number 791 on 17 April 1907 with *São Paulo* following on 24 September that same year. Progress on the construction of *Minas Geraes* was interrupted by a strike in early 1908 but the vessel was launched on the Tyne on Thursday, 10 September amid great ceremony, *The Times* noting that her displacement was 1,750 tons greater than that of *St Vincent* which took to the water that same day 340 miles away in Devonport. Further delays were caused by the difficulty in obtaining approval for proposals made to Brazilian representatives by Armstrongs, particularly with respect to magazine-cooling options. Nonetheless, the ship was eventually completed on 5 January 1910 and on 17 April *Minas Geraes* made her triumphal entry into Rio de Janeiro to a reception that is remembered as a high point of patriotic fervour in the history of what was still the capital city of the Republic. The newspaper *O Paiz* described the scene as the squadron approached at one o'clock that afternoon: 'the bay was covered with a multitude of vessels of all shapes and sizes from heaven knows where, and a numberless swarm of people thronged the coastline and the nearby hills'. In October she was joined by *São Paulo* with President-elect Marshal Hermes Rodrigues da Fonseca embarked.

25 *Ibid.*, p. 246.

Minas Geraes running speed trials in British waters in early 1910 during which she reached 21.4 knots. Note the exposed compass platform and the brows stowed on either side of the turrets. *(DPHDM/3447)*

British shipyard workers putting the finishing touches to *Minas Geraes* in early 1910. Visible are Nos. '1' to '3' 12in guns and three of the 4.7in guns at various levels abreast No. '2' turret upon which a 1.85in gun has been mounted. The Minas Geraes class was unusual in having the main boat derrick stepped against the foremast rather than the mainmast. Note the large davits abreast the bridge structure and the short-lived anti-torpedo netting stowed against the hull. *(DPHDM/5113)*

From Celebration to Rebellion

Much as the new battleships were marvels of technology, they were far from solving the problems of the Marinha which turned above all on personnel, and specifically on numbers, training, discipline and prospects. The most pressing need was to find sailors to man the ships. A regulation approved on 1 August 1907 dispensed the intake of the *Escolas de Aprendizes* (Apprentice Schools) from the requirement to read and write, stating only that they should be at least sixteen, have adequate physical development and have shown evidence of 'a manifest ability to study' within the first six months of service. Thanks to these provisions the *Corpo de Marinheiros Nacionais* had mustered around 4,000 men by the arrival of *Minas Geraes* in early 1910. Despite new regulations requiring the *Corpo de Marinheiros* to provide companies composed of fifteen unspecialised sailors, ten gunners, five torpedomen, eight stokers and other specialists for a total of approximately forty men, these youngsters were in fact classified as unspecialised, leaving the Marinha facing a severe shortfall of competent personnel.[26] The table on page 142 shows the extent of the problem on the eve of *Minas Geraes* joining the fleet.

To make matters worse, seventy foreign stokers unexpectedly deserted *Minas Geraes* when she put in at Norfolk, Virginia, on the voyage out from England, claiming their contractual obligations to have been fulfilled the moment the ship docked. Meanwhile, as the Chief of Staff of the Marinha Rear Admiral Raymundo de Mello Furtado de Mendonça explained, desperate measures had to be resorted to where manning was concerned: 'To meet the need to man those ships of large displacement then being completed in Europe, individuals were engaged and reengaged who would otherwise never have merited that distinction. This was made worse by the increase in the number of undesirable elements.'[27] What was already a profoundly

---

[26] José Miguel Arias Neto, *Em busca da cidadania: Praças da Armada Nacional, 1867–1910* (PhD thesis, Universidade de São Paulo, 2001), p. 247.

[27] Raymundo de Mello Furtado de Mendonça, *Introdução do relatório apresentado ao Sr. Ministro da Marinha pelo Contra Almirante Raymundo de Mello Furtado em Maio de 1911* (Rio de Janeiro: Papelaria Mendes, 1912), p. 9.

Above: A target shoot by the 4.7in port battery early in *Minas Geraes*'s career. The caption indicates the target range as 2,840yds (2,600m) and the speed of the ship as 10 knots. Note turret No. '4' beyond. *(DPHDM/3928)*

Right: No. '5' and '6' 12in turrets dominate the scene as crewmen go about their duties on the quarterdeck, c. 1913. Note the 1.85in gun positioned atop No. '5' turret. *(Library of Congress/13334)*

Shortfall of specialised crewmen in the Marinha brasileira, 1909

Specialisation	Required personnel	Available personnel	
Gunners	1,180	30	(2.5%)
Stokers	944	491	(52.0%)
Torpedomen	590	70	(11.9%)
Helmsmen	236	28	(11.9%)
Signalmen	118	5	(4.2%)
Artificers	18	0	(0%)
Divers	18	0	(0%)
Total	3,104	624	(20.1%)

Source: José Miguel Arias Neto, *Em busca da cidadania: Praças da Armada Nacional, 1867–1910* (PhD thesis, Universidade de São Paulo, 2001), p. 251.

A *tercero-tenente* (sub lieutenant) poses by the 1.85in gun mounted on the starboard side of the forward superstructure, c. 1913. *(Library of Congress/13335)*

negative impression of Brazilian sailors was enhanced by racial preconceptions. In the racial classification of the day, the Marinha was broken down as 50 per cent black, 30 per cent mulatto, 10 per cent mestizo, and 10 per cent white or 'nearly white'.[28] Moreover, the Marinha retained all the preconceptions and attitudes of the era of slavery:

In contrast to the rapid and dramatic modernization of Rio de Janeiro's economy and urban landscape, the organization of the navy remained hidebound in preemancipation traditions; well into the twentieth century Brazil's navy was a highly stratified and racially segregated institution. [...] In the Brazilian navy,

[28] Macedo Soares, *Política versus Marinha*, p. 85.

Five members of *Minas Geraes*'s Naval Battalion mustered on the quarterdeck in *c.* 1913. Few navies can have had more arduous or discriminatory conditions of service for the lower deck than the *Marinha brasileira* before 1910. *(Library of Congress/13338)*

rank and file sailors, overwhelmingly of African descent, endured such harsh conditions that service was generally avoided whenever possible. In a country that relied so heavily on the labor of enslaved Africans, it followed that Afro-Brazilians were overrepresented among the men pressed into service in the lower ranks.[29]

Indeed, José Eduardo de Macedo Soares, a former naval officer, reserved his especial venom for black crewmen:

The Blacks are sullen runts having all the depressing features of the most backward African nations. Other races submit themselves to the influence of half breeds, but Blacks are always in the majority. Any notion of finesse is totally alien to them, and our sailors are unkempt in their dress and have no idea how to eat or sleep. Shiftless and idle, they carry with them all the inability of their race to progress.[30]

The navy which took delivery of *Minas Geraes* and *São Paulo* in 1910 was therefore marked by extreme contrasts and paradoxes. On the one hand there was undeniable modernisation and progress, but on the other it reflected all the dilemmas of a country which had abolished slavery and proclaimed a republic scarcely twenty years earlier, and had yet to extend basic rights to the most vulnerable sectors of society, including the lower deck of the Marinha where corporal punishment was still meted out. Indeed, although the provisional government had made a priority of abolishing corporal punishment in the armed forces on assuming power in 1889, this measure was reversed with respect to the navy on 12 April 1890 and flogging continued to be applied on an ad hoc basis against sailors ordered to the *Companhia Correcional* (Penal

[29] Zachary R. Morgan, *Legacy of the Lash: Race and Corporal Punishment in the Brazilian Navy and the Atlantic World* (Bloomington, Ind.: University of Indiana Press, 2014), p. 17.

[30] Macedo Soares, *Política versus Marinha*, p. 85.

Some of *Minas Geraes*'s complement of 900 men ranged on the forecastle and forward superstructure on completion of the ship's refit at New York Navy Yard on 12 September 1921. The commissioning of the ship eleven years earlier brought on a collision between the old navy and the new which exploded into mutiny in November 1910. *(DPHDM/3484)*

Company). Moreover, the practice continued even after the issue of a new regulation in 1908 'explicitly prohibiting those punishments not set forth in law and all injurious actions, gestures, words or intentions by a superior to a subordinate'.[31] Such was the case in *Minas Geraes* where at dawn on 16 November 1910 Marcelino Rodrigues Menezes, an Afro-Brazilian sailor, was brought in shackles on deck and subjected to 250 lashes for insubordination before the entire ship's company. It was this incident which, in the context of a long and pervasive tradition of corporal punishment in the Marinha brasileira, provided the immediate trigger for mutiny.

The Revolt of the Lash (1910)

Although Brazil has a long tradition of military insurrection, there are features of the *Revolta da Chibata* (Revolt of the Lash) shared by no other. Not least of these is that it was planned, organised and led entirely by the lower deck and largely by Afro-Brazilian sailors in *Minas Geraes* and directed specifically in protest against

---

[31] Arias Neto, *Em busca da cidadania*, p. 249.

São Paulo seen astern of *Minas Geraes* early in their careers, the former distinguishable by the band around her after funnel; note the deflection scale painted on the latter's No. '5' turret. The ships are lying in Guanabara Bay, the scene of the Revolt of the Lash in November 1910 in which they were the leading protagonists. *(DPHDM/34516)*

corporal punishment in concert with other units of the Brazilian fleet lying off Rio de Janeiro. There are indications that the insurrection was originally intended to coincide with the inauguration of Marshal Hermes Rodrigues da Fonseca as president on 15 November 1910, but it was decided to defer the outbreak until it could be linked with a flogging incident. Subsequent depositions reported *Minas Geraes*'s commanding officer Capitão-de-mar-e-guerra (Captain) João Batista das Neves to be a conscientious officer with an aversion to corporal punishment who attempted to discourage its practice aboard. However, any efforts clearly failed since among his crew was the ship's acknowledged *carrasco* ('executioner'), a sailor by the name of Alípio who flogged Marcelino Rodrigues Menezes on the morning of the 16th and in doing so set in train the Revolt of the Lash.[32]

Shortly after ten o'clock on the night of 22 November, six days after Rodrigues Menezes had been dealt his punishment, Capt. Neves came alongside *Minas Geraes* in his launch after a dinner engagement aboard the French training cruiser *Duguay-Trouin*. Stopping for a brief conversation with the officer of the watch, Segundo-tenente (2nd Lieutenant) Álvaro Alberto, Neves descended the companionway leading to his cabin. Alberto then made his way forward on his rounds where he was set upon by a sailor wielding a bayonet. Although injured, Alberto fought back and beat off his assailant who fled to join a party of sailors gathered by the forward turret screaming 'Long live liberty!' and 'Down with the whip!' Hearing the uproar, Capt. Neves gathered a pair of rifles and came on deck where he found Alberto bleeding profusely. Another lieutenant was ordered to transfer Alberto to *São Paulo* for treatment and then proceed to the Ministry of Marine to report the mutiny. Aboard *Minas* orders were passed for the crew to muster but only sixty sailors complied, and briefly at that, since shots were fired and the remaining officers rushed and overwhelmed by the mutineers. By the time it was over Neves and a lieutenant had been bayoneted and bludgeoned to death, another had saved himself by diving into the water and the rest had been taken captive before being put ashore. By 2250 the vessel and her complement of 900 was in the hands of the mutineers, an achievement signalled by the prearranged firing of a gun, to which *São Paulo* and subsequently the new light cruiser *Bahia* and the coast defence vessel *Deodoro* replied. They were joined by the crew of the protected cruiser

The two leaders of the Revolt of the Lash, Seaman 1st Class João Cândido Felisberto of *Minas Geraes* (left) and his counterpart in *São Paulo*, Seaman 1st Class Manuel Gregório do Nascimento. *(O Malho)*

República who left their ship and dispersed themselves among other vessels in revolt, and of the 5,000 sailors present in Guanabara Bay that night approximately half joined the mutiny. Their counterparts in the light cruiser *Rio Grande do Sul*, the protected cruiser *Barroso* and an eight-strong destroyer flotilla consisting of *Alagoas*, *Amazonas*, *Pará*, *Piauí*, *Rio Grande do Norte*, *Paraíba*, *Santa Catarina* and *Mato Grosso* did not follow suit. Although enjoying a preponderance of numbers, the vessels which remained loyal were comparatively insignificant alongside *Minas Geraes* and *São Paulo* with their combined firepower of twenty-four 12in and forty-four 4.7in guns – even if the hydraulic traversing mechanism of *São Paulo*'s main armament had been immobilised by salt water contamination. Nonetheless, dawn on the 23rd found the mutinous squadron under the red flag at the cost of the lives of three officers and over twenty sailors.

The leader of the mutiny was the lofty figure of Seaman 1st Class João Cândido Felisberto of *Minas Geraes*, soon christened the 'Black Admiral', who took command of the rebel squadron on the night of the 22nd and ordered the ships to get underway and discharge their 4.7in guns periodically as a demonstration of intent. That same night a signal was sent to the presidential palace stating that unless Fonseca and the Minister of Marine issued a public declaration abolishing the lash, the rebels would destroy the city and any vessel which had refused to join the mutiny. When Fonseca responded by issuing orders for any disembarkation to be prevented and radio signals ignored, together with a demand for immediate surrender or face a torpedo attack, the rebels made good on their threat by shelling the city, resulting in the death of two children in the Morro do Castelo district.

This scotched earlier hopes by the authorities that the rebels would be incapable of handling the ships or operating their guns, and daybreak on the 23rd found the Brazilian capital effectively hostage to elements of its most despised underclass. An editorial in the newspaper *O Paiz* left its readers in little doubt as to the immense power of the guns now capable of being brought to bear against them at any time, 'flinging out a mass of metal in such a tremendous discharge, each gun vomiting 385kg [850lb] of steel propelled by 113kg [285lb] of cordite'. To the historian Hélio Leôncio,

> The greatest threat was the presence of those floating fortresses themselves, bristling with guns and powerful turrets training menacingly while cruising at close range off the shores of the city. This terrorising impression assumed even greater proportions thanks to the propaganda that had preceded and accompanied the acquisition of the new Squadron [...]. The news had a devastating effect as it stirred terror in the hearts of the population who now saw all this destructive paraphernalia being turned against them.[33]

The journalist and future diplomat Gilberto Amado provided readers of *O Paiz* with this impression of the tumult which swept the city:

> For the first time I saw panic; wide-eyed faces, trembling lips, all the wretched uproar of a

32 Edmar Morel, *A Revolta da Chibata* (Rio de Janeiro: Pongetti, 1959), p. 32.

33 Hélio Leôncio Martins, *A Revolta dos marinheiros, 1910* (São Paulo: Cia. Editora Nacional; Rio de Janeiro: Serviço de Documentação da Marinha, 1988), pp. 52–3.

stampede. There was practically no one on my street; only tears, recriminations, loud sobbing and the screams of children seeing consternation and disbelief in the faces of their mothers. Every so often cars shot nervously by at unprecedented speeds, laden with baggage and people. It was terror and it seemed like the end of the world. I remembered engravings of earthquakes, utter darkness, pathetic cries of pain, a Dantesque cataclysm of unrivalled proportions. And all of this caused by João Cândido alone.[34]

Losing no time, Cândido and his fellow mutineers formally issued their demands in a memorandum addressed to President Fonseca from *São Paulo*. It read as follows:

We sailors, Brazilian citizens and upholders of the Republic, unable any longer to suffer the slavery practised in the Brazilian navy, neither receiving nor having ever received the protection guaranteed us by this Nation, are now stripping away the dark veil covering the eyes of a patriotic but misled people. With all of the ships under our control [...], we are sending this message so that His Excellency can guarantee Brazilian sailors the sacred rights accorded us by the laws of the Republic, put an end to the unrest and grant us such favours for the betterment of the Brazilian navy as the removal of incompetent and unworthy officers, reform of the immoral and shameful regulations that govern us, abolition of flogging, beating with the ferule and similar punishments; increasing our pay [...], educating those seamen who lack the skills to wear our proud uniform [...], and implementing work routines and ensuring these are respected ...[35]

Although Fonseca refused to deal with the mutineers directly, the retired naval officer and federal deputy Capt. José Carlos de Carvalho, a known proponent of naval reform, was selected to represent the government in negotiations with the mutineers. On the afternoon of the 23rd Carvalho duly made the rounds of the squadron in a launch to parley with the leaders of the revolt in each vessel, being received with full military honours and noting the level of order and discipline in each. Once aboard *Minas Geraes*, Carvalho was taken to examine Rodrigues Menezes prior to his transfer to the naval hospital ashore, Carvalho later reporting

'Admiral João Cândido' says the handwritten inscription on this photo of the chief mutineer and his fellows, the former holding a folded signalling flag and a pair of binoculars. The Revolt of the Lash exerted huge pressure on the Brazilian establishment. *(Bruce Taylor Collection)*

to Fonseca that 'this sailor's back resembles a mullet sliced open for salting'.[36] He also brought this simple message from the mutineers in *Minas Geraes*: 'We don't want anything except to be relieved from barbarous corporal punishment, and to be given the means to work commensurate with our strength', while also demanding 'regular meals and breaks from work'. The account prepared by Carvalho points to the work routine imposed in the dreadnoughts as a significant factor in the outbreak of the revolt. As one of *Minas Geraes*'s crewmen put it,

Powerful vessels like these can't be handled or maintained by half a dozen sailors aboard; there's twice as much work, the food is terrible and badly prepared, and punishments increase unabated. We're in an absolutely desperate situation: without food, overworked, and with our flesh scourged by corporal punishment that reaches the point of cruelty.[37]

Coupled with this was a new sense of dignity and worth accorded to their crews by the symbolic importance of the new vessels, one constantly vitiated by the callous treatment meted out to them.

That same afternoon Congress began debating the passage of a general amnesty for the sailors, but there was significant pressure to end the mutiny by force and lift what was effectively a siege of the city. News of these plans reached the mutineers via a signal from the destroyer *Paraíba* which reported preparations for an attack by loyalist vessels. As on the previous night, the rebel squadron responded by

getting underway with the help of the British electrical engineers embarked and spent the night of the 23rd at sea before steaming back into Guanabara Bay the following morning, a procedure it followed for the duration of the mutiny. By the time the squadron had returned all parties were aware that Congress was drafting a decree of amnesty and the city at large shifted from an air of panic to one of curiosity fuelled by sympathetic coverage in the press. A cabinet meeting summoned by President Fonseca resolved to negotiate and Carvalho made his second visit to *Minas Geraes* late on the morning of the 24th. The upshot of this was a telegram issued by the mutineers expressing regret for their actions and stating that they would submit to the president's orders on the understanding that an amnesty would be granted. In the Senate the opposition leader Rui Barbosa argued the case for amnesty with the same passion he had supported the reconstruction of the Marinha fifteen years earlier. Describing the mutiny as an honest revolt with no political overtones, he cast the rebels as honourable men fighting in a just cause before attributing much of the social ills afflicting Brazil to the pervasive moral degradation of slavery. The amnesty was quickly approved in the Senate and sent down for debate by the Constitution and Justice Committee of the Chamber of Deputies; a favourable opinion on the draft having been issued on the 25th, it was duly passed.

However, even as the amnesty debate began in the Senate, a group of hardliners was formulating quite different plans in an effort to restore the tarnished honour and reputation of the military elite. Not only had the officer corps been assaulted and unceremoniously bundled out of their ships, but it had been excoriated in Congress and condemned as both incompetent and inhumane in the popular press. Moreover, the degree of popular support for the mutineers threatened to exacerbate this situation still further. Plans were therefore drawn up with the tacit support of President Fonseca for the rebel ships to be torpedoed in a concerted attack by the light cruiser *Rio Grande do Sul* and the destroyer flotilla. In the event, this course of action encountered significant opposition, including from the new Minister of Marine Admiral Joaquim Marques Baptista de Leão, which emphasised the likelihood of heavy casualties, destruction of part of the city and significant loss of naval *matériel*.[38] More generally, as Senator Barbosa warned on the 23rd in an echo of his earlier views, such an action not only

[34] 'João Cândido' in *O Paiz*, 29 November 1910.
[35] Morel, *A Revolta da Chibata*, pp. 86–7.

[37] Cited in Arias Neto, *Em busca da cidadania*, p. 263.
[36] *Ibid.*, p. 82.

[38] Martins, *A Revolta dos marinheiros, 1910*, p. 112.

implied a significant waste of public funds but the destruction of resources essential to national defence.[39] Support was lent to this position by the Foreign Minister, the Baron of Rio Branco, who stated that the new dreadnoughts constituted the balance of naval power in South America which Brazil could not afford to lose at any price.[40]

However, President Fonseca remained deaf to these entreaties and in the early hours of the 25th succumbed to sustained pressure from hardline officers by authorising an attack on the rebel ships before the amnesty could be signed. In the event, the Marinha, which had already experienced significant delays in obtaining torpedo warheads, found its plans thwarted by the failure of the squadron to return to Guanabara Bay from its nightly exodus until the afternoon of the 25th, by which time the decree of amnesty was clearing the Chamber of Deputies and the authorisation to attack was revoked. The following afternoon, after another night at sea, the rebel ships entered the bay for the last time, and having conducted further negotiations by radio finally hauled down their red flags and turned themselves over to the authorities at 1900. Before doing so they had received word that Barbosa would shortly submit a bill to Congress abolishing all corporal punishment in the armed forces. The Revolt of the Lash was over.

Aftermath

Much as the mutineers had successfully defied both the navy and the government, and in doing so laid the foundations for sweeping changes in the Marinha brasileira, these victories came at a high price to the instigators. No sooner had the revolt ended than the mutinous crews were allowed ashore and the following day, 27 November, all four rebel ships were disarmed. Losing no time, on the 29th President Fonseca issued a decree permitting the government to dismiss any men reckoned to pose a threat to discipline, and by early 1911 some 1,216 had been ejected from the navy, most of them given one-way rail tickets to their home states with the aim of dispersing seditious elements. Meanwhile, an unrelated uprising among marines of the Naval Battalion on the Ilha das Cobras in Guanabara Bay on 10 December was put down with violence. This episode provided the government with the pretext it needed to declare a state of emergency, and some 600 of the amnestied mutineers were rounded up and incarcerated

Crewmen of *Minas Geraes* gathered on the quarterdeck during the Crossing the Line celebrations on 1 August 1920, the ship en route for refitting in New York. Note the members of the ship's drum and brass band on No. '6' turret. *(DPHDM/34454)*

including João Cândido and other leaders of the Revolt of the Lash. Cândido was eventually released in 1912 but was subject to official harassment for the rest of his life and died in poverty in 1969.

The mutiny and subsequent amnesty had in the meantime unleashed a flood of accusations from both the officer corps and from civilians, the beginning of a controversy which places the Revolt of the Lash among the most studied episodes in Brazilian naval history, one that has elicited contributions from across the social and political spectrum. The resulting corpus of literature can, on the whole, be divided between those which emphasise its non-political nature, its character as a social uprising and the influence of foreign ideas and tactics, acquired either during fitting out in Britain or from the stokers embarked in *Minas Geraes* in the spring of 1910, together with those which regard it as an overtly political event and consequently seek to exonerate the authorities while deploring the laxity displayed in extending an amnesty to the perpetrators. The first major contribution came in 1911 with the publication of *Política versus Marinha* (Politics versus the Navy) by José Eduardo de Macedo Soares, a former naval officer and director of the right-wing newspaper *Diário Carioca*. In it he condemned the effect of political interference on the policy of militarism sponsored by the Marinha, aiming particular criticism at the leader of the oligarchical party, Senator José Gomes Pinheiro Machado, whom he regarded as the author of the amnesty.

Nonetheless, Macedo Soares was not blind to the deficiencies of the navy itself: 'The Marinha has yet to divest itself of the procedures and customs of the Paraguayan War [of 1864–70], of squadrons of sailing ships, and has yet to acquire any technical knowledge of battleships or of the current nature of sea warfare.'[41] It was therefore necessary to condition the navy to the industrial revolution which had transformed modern naval warfare. For the navy to overcome 'unfavourable pathological factors', it was not only essential for a quarter of all officers, sailors and specialists to be replaced by foreigners as part of a naval mission from Britain or Germany, but for the installation of a dictatorship under President Fonseca.

But not all assessments were so extreme. In the report he issued on the revolt in May 1911, the Chief of Staff of the Marinha, Rear Admiral Furtado de Mendonça, declared that the naval policy of the Republic should confine itself 'exclusively to defence, without operating large offensive units better suited to meet the imperialist and commercial interests of countries aiming to extend the export markets for their goods'.[42] What all parties seem to have agreed on is the palpable lack of preparedness of the Marinha to receive the new battleships, a topic which dominated the post-revolt debate. As the Minister of

[39] Arias Neto, *Em busca da cidadania*, p. 270.
[40] *Ibid.*, p. 273.

[41] Macedo Soares, *Política versus Marinha*, p. 154.
[42] Furtado de Mendonça, *Introdução do relatório apresentado ao Sr. Ministro da Marinha*, p. 24.

Marine Admiral Marques de Leão put it in the report he sent to the Senate after the revolt,

> Distracted by a mirage, the Brazilian people participated in the creation of a respectable fleet, supposing that would be sufficient for good naval organisation; however, events have shown that possession of sophisticated and powerful vessels is not the key element for a navy of the first rank.[43]

Decades later Marques de Leão's then chief of staff, Comandante (Commander) Heitor Pereira da Cunha, recorded that the admiral's predecessor Alencar had made no provision whatsoever to select and prepare the crews to 'assimilate what was completely unknown to them so that they might serve in the highly advanced units they were to operate'.[44] Consequently, 'the Marinha do Brasil, without any preparation, any steps, any transitional process, took a leap – a leap into the dark, one might say – from a man-of-war to the *Dreadnought*'.[45] Equally clear is that the incorporation of the battleships into the fleet served to upset the fragile balance in relations between officers and crews. At the same time, it is undeniable that the firepower and symbolic value of those units played a decisive role in the government's decision-making during the revolt. No vessel but a dreadnought could have presented such a dilemma to a government in 1910.

Later Years

The subsequent career of *Minas Geraes* pales by comparison with her lengthy and convoluted political gestation and the explosion of the Revolt of the Lash and its aftermath within months of her joining the fleet. Her first major

---

[43] Cited in Cunha, *A Revolta da esquadra brasileira em novembro e dezembro de 1910*, p. 14.

[44] *Ibid.*, p. 25.
[45] *Ibid.*, p. 19.

A boiler replacement for *Minas Geraes* during her reconstruction at the Arsenal de Marinha (Naval Shipyard) on the Ilha das Cobras, the spiritual home of the Marinha brasileira in Guanabara Bay, Rio de Janeiro, 29 November 1933. *(DPHDM/107893)*

The crew of one of the three twin Madsen 0.79in mountings fitted in *Minas Geraes* during the 1934–7 reconstruction. This one is positioned atop No. '5' 12in turret. *(DPHDM/7733)*

assignment after the unrest of 1910 was to transport the Brazilian Foreign Minister Lauro Müller on a courtesy visit to the United States in 1913. During the first three years of the Great War Brazil pursued a policy of pro-Allied neutrality which was revoked on 1 June 1917 following the German declaration of unrestricted submarine warfare, an action that soon claimed several vessels from her substantial merchant marine. A steady decline in relations with Germany culminated in Brazil declaring war on the Central Powers on 26 October 1917. This development prompted the Marinha to offer *Minas Geraes* and *São Paulo* to the British for service with the Grand Fleet, one politely refused in view of the poor condition of the vessels, the absence of modern fire-control equipment and an acute shortage of coal in the United Kingdom. In the event, the vessels were confined to patrolling the approaches to Rio de Janeiro until the end of the war.

Steps were taken after the end of the First World War to rectify some of the deficiencies recognised by the British, and first *São Paulo* (1918–20) and then *Minas Geraes* (1920–1) were refitted at Brooklyn Navy Yard with the addition of Sperry fire-control equipment and Bausch & Lomb rangefinders for the main armament. Armoured bulkheads were fitted inside the turrets and the 4.7in (120mm) secondary battery reduced from twenty-two guns to twelve by the removal of five casemated guns on each side. This refit also saw the installation of an anti-aircraft armament in the shape of two 3in (76mm) 50-calibre guns mounted on the after superstructure and a number of 1.5in (37mm) weapons positioned near each turret at the expense of the 1.85in (47mm) guns on the turret tops. The main incident of the visit from a human standpoint was the epidemic which swept the ship in August 1920 requiring a large proportion of the crew to be admitted to the Brooklyn Naval Hospital for treatment. The care given by the staff was marked by the presentation of a large statue to the hospital by the Brazilian government in September 1921.

Between June 1934 and April 1937 *Minas Geraes* underwent a major reconstruction at the Rio de Janeiro Navy Yard which focused largely on propulsion. The original mixed coal-oil arrangement in eighteen Babcock & Wilcox boilers was replaced by six Thornycroft oil-fired boilers with the old No. 1 boiler room and all twelve lateral coal bunkers being converted to oil

storage tanks. These measures not only increased output by 27 per cent to 30,000ihp and speed by a knot to 22 knots, but resulted in the trunking of the boiler uptakes into a single funnel. The opportunity was also taken to replace the dynamos with new turbogenerators. With respect to armament, the elevation of the turrets was increased from 13 to 18 degrees and the

Bausch & Lomb rangefinders installed in 1920–1 replaced with Zeiss models. Finally, two additional 4.7in guns were added bringing the total to fourteen, and six Danish-built 0.79in (20mm) Madsen cannon installed. These alterations brought the complement of *Minas Geraes* up to 1,087. Plans to give *São Paulo* a similar reconstruction were abandoned in 1939 in view of the

Crewmen formed up by divisions on *Minas Geraes*'s waist following the 1934–7 reconstruction which resulted in the trunking of the original two funnels into one. Note the 3in guns on the platform abaft the funnel and the canvas-covered Zeiss rangefinder above. The word 'Patria' painted on the screen on the left of the photo completes the ship's motto: 'Tudo pela Patria' (Everything for the Fatherland). *(DPHDM/7729)*

poor state of the ship which foundered off the Azores on 4 November 1951 while being towed to Italy for scrapping.

Like all her South American dreadnought counterparts, *Minas Geraes* spent much of her career inactive, due partly to limited dockyard resources in Brazil and partly to budgetary constraints. Nonetheless, she again found herself drawn albeit peripherally into military insurrection, first with the *Revolução Tenentista* (Lieutenants' Revolution) in July 1922 when she joined *São Paulo* in helping to quell an army revolt at Fort Copacabana in Rio de Janeiro, and then in November 1924 when sympathisers of the Tenentista cause commandeered *São Paulo* in an effort to force the government to release those

convicted after the earlier uprising. On this occasion *Minas Geraes* was at odds with her sister whose call to join the rebellion she failed to heed, the complement of the *São Paulo* expressing their disgust by firing a 2.2in (57mm) shell at *Minas Geraes* which wounded a cook before the rebels shaped course for Montevideo where they disembarked to be granted asylum.

Despite her major refit in the mid-1930s, *Minas Geraes* was in no condition to play any active role in the Second World War during which Brazil again maintained her neutrality until German attacks on merchant shipping prompted a declaration of war in August 1942. This state of affairs caused *Minas Geraes* to be transferred to the port city of Salvador where she

served out the war as a floating battery, her sister doing likewise at Recife. Decommissioned on 16 May 1952, she spent a few months as the inactive flagship of the commander-in-chief of the Brazilian navy until December when she was stricken on 31st and sold to S.A. Cantiere Navale Santa Maria of Genoa for demolition. *Minas Geraes* was taken under tow on 1 March 1954 and reached Genoa on 22 April. By the end of that year the 'ship of discord' was no more.

Sources

In collab., *História naval brasileira*, vol. V 1B (Rio de Janeiro: Serviço de Documentação da Marinha, 1997)

Amado, Gilberto, 'João Cândido' in *O Paiz*, 29 November 1910

Arias Neto, José Miguel, *Em busca da cidadania: Praças da Armada Nacional, 1867–1910* (PhD thesis, Universidade de São Paulo, 2001)

Minas Geraes seen in her final condition in late 1944 or early 1945. *(DPHDM/3520)*

_____, 'A Marinha do Brasil como imagem da Nação' in *Revista Marítima Brasileira* 121 (2001), no. 7–9, pp. 105–15

Barbosa, Rui, *Cartas de Inglaterra* (2nd edn., São Paulo: Livraria Academica Saraiva & C. Editores, 1929)

Brook, Peter, *Warships for Export: Armstrong Warships, 1867–1927* (Gravesend, Kent: World Ship Society, 1999)

Bueno, Clodoaldo, *Política externa da Primeira República. Os anos de apogeu (1902–1918)* (São Paulo: Paz e Terra, 2003)

Cunha, Heitor Pereira da, *A Revolta da esquadra brasileira em novembro e dezembro de 1910* (Rio de Janeiro: Imprensa Naval, 1953)

Dias, Arthur, *O Problema naval. Condições actuaes da marinha de guerra e seu papel nos destinos do paiz* (Rio de Janeiro: Officina da Estatistica, 1899)

Etchepareborda, Roberto, *Historia de las relaciones internacionales argentinas* (Buenos Aires: Editorial Pleamar, 1978)

Fiennes, Gerard, 'Dreadnoughts for Sale or Hire' in *The Nineteenth Century and After* no. 378 (August 1908), pp. 207–14

Furtado de Mendonça, Raymundo de Mello, *Introdução do relatório apresentado ao Sr. Ministro da Marinha pelo Contra Almirante Raymundo de Mello Furtado em Maio de 1911* (Rio de Janeiro: Papelaria Mendes, 1912)

Hough, Richard, *The Big Battleship, or the Curious Career of H.M.S.* Agincourt (London: Michael Joseph, 1967)

Johnston, Ian, & Ian Buxton, *The Battleship Builders: Constructing and Arming British Capital Ships* (Barnsley, S. Yorks.: Seaforth Publishing, 2013)

Livermore, S. W., 'Battleship Diplomacy in South America: 1905–1925' in *The Journal of Modern History* 16 (March 1944) no. 1, pp. 31–48

Love, Joseph L., *The Revolt of the Whip* (Stanford, Calif.: Stanford University Press, 2012)

The forward structure seen in March 1942 showing the alterations to the bridge and compass platform carried out in 1920–1 with further accretions in the 1930s and early 1940s. *(Bruce Taylor Collection)*

Macedo Soares, José Eduardo de, [Um Oficial da Armada], *Política versus Marinha* (Rio de Janeiro: Á venda na Livraria H. Garnier, 1911)

Martins, Hélio Leôncio, *A Revolta dos marinheiros, 1910* (São Paulo: Cia. Editora Nacional; Rio de Janeiro: Serviço de Documentação da Marinha, 1988)

Martins, Hélio Leôncio, & Dino Willy Cozza, 'Poderes combatentes' in *História naval brasileira* (Rio de Janeiro: Serviço de Documentação da Marinha, 1997), vol. V 1B, pp. 79–100

Martins Filho, João Roberto, *A Marinha brasileira na era dos encouraçados, 1895–1910* (Rio de Janeiro: Editora FGV, 2010)

Morel, Edmar, *A Revolta da Chibata* (Rio de Janeiro: Pongetti, 1959)

Morgan, Zachary R., 'The Revolt of the Lash' in Christopher M. Bell & Bruce A. Elleman, ed., *Naval Mutinies in the Twentieth Century: An International Perspective* (London: Frank Cass, 2003), pp. 32–53

_____, *Legacy of the Lash: Race and Corporal Punishment in the Brazilian Navy and the Atlantic World* (Bloomington, Ind.: University of Indiana Press, 2014)

Noronha, Julio César de, *Programa naval de 1904. Subsídios para a história marítima do Brasil*, vol. 9 (Rio de Janeiro: Imprensa Naval, 1950)

O Malho (1910)

O Paiz (1910)

Scheina, Robert L., *Latin America: A Naval History, 1810–1897* (Annapolis, Md.: Naval Institute Press, 1987)

Silveira da Motta, Arthur, [Barão de Jaceguay], *De aspirante a almirante. Minha Fé de Ofício documentada*, 2 vols. (Rio de Janeiro: Serviço de Documentação da Marinha, 1984–5)

Topliss, David, 'The Brazilian Dreadnoughts, 1904–1914' in *Warship International 25* (1988), no. 3, pp. 240–89

Koninklijke Marine

The Armoured Ship
De Zeven Provinciën (1909)

◆

Leon Homburg

THE TURN of the twentieth century found the Koninklijke Marine at the end of a period of technological renewal mirrored in various degrees by the rest of the world's major navies. The wood and sails which in the seventeenth century had made Holland a great naval and trading power had since given way to steel and steam, with torpedoes and breech-loading guns replacing the broadsides of muzzle-loaded cannon of the men-of-war. The armoured ship, the fast protected cruiser and the torpedo boat

now formed the main line of defence against any state moved to challenge either the neutrality or integrity of the Netherlands and her overseas empire. Meanwhile, the same technological advances which had made ships increasingly complex and expensive also kept a country of limited financial resources from building a navy capable of matching those of rival states. Out of the debates centring on the virtues of either a big-gun fleet or a flotilla defence of torpedo boats came a vessel destined to take her place among

the Koninklijke Marine's most famous, even notorious, men-of-war: the *pantserschip* Hr. Ms. *De Zeven Provinciën*.

Context

Tracing its origins to the early seventeenth century, by 1900 the Dutch seaborne empire stretched from the metropolis in Europe westward to Surinam, Curaçao and the Netherlands Antilles in the Caribbean, and finally and most importantly to the Dutch East Indies in Southeast Asia. This immense territory, the forerunner of the modern Indonesia, extended across 735,000 square miles, an area forty-five times greater than the mother country, while its chief city Batavia (now Jakarta) on the north coast of Java lay 7,000 miles from Amsterdam. The East Indian archipelago itself consisted of hundreds of islands with an aggregate coastline in excess of 67,000 miles. Some 3,300 miles separated its westernmost city of Sabang off the island of Sumatra from the easternmost city of Merauke in Papua. In 1900 the population of the Dutch East Indies stood at 35 million, nearly seven times that of the Netherlands. Moreover, for over 250 years the writ of the colonial government was confined largely to major cities and coastal areas, and it was not until 1920 that the pacification of the entire territory had been effected. Despite the extension of colonial authority during the nineteenth century, the East Indies remained largely a trading rather than a settled empire, and as such

De Zeven Provinciën seen in her capacity as flagship of the Dutch East Indies Squadron c. 1920. She wears the flag of the admiral commanding the squadron at her foretop. The bamboo structure amidships is a gunnery practice target. *(Dutch Navy Museum – MMDH)*

Coast defence ships of the Dutch East Indies Squadron at Melbourne on 30 September 1910. Joining *Marten Harpertszoon Tromp* on the left are two of the three units of the Koningin Regentes class. *(MMDH)*

represented one of the chief pillars of the Dutch economy, a dependence which gave the Koninklijke Marine a significant position in domestic affairs.

Although the time when the Netherlands had the resources to build, man and maintain a navy to challenge those of Britain, France or, latterly, Germany in home waters had long since passed, the situation was quite different in the Dutch East Indies, and the Netherlands was the one colonial power whose overseas fleet not only outnumbered, but dwarfed that retained in the metropolis, where the navy played a subordinate role to the army. Indeed, the arrival of the turret ships *Prins Hendrik der Nederlanden* (1866) and *Koning der Nederlanden* (1874), and possession of a major naval base at Surabaya on the northeast coast of Java afforded the Dutch the largest fleet in Southeast Asia at the time. However, within a few decades the regional balance of power had shifted in favour of China, Japan and the United States, while Britain, France and Germany were expanding their spheres of influence in the Far East. The Dutch government responded by taking a number of measures to strengthen its naval power in the East Indies. Where *matériel* was concerned, this initiative resulted in orders for five armoured ships and six protected cruisers which were laid down between 1895 and 1905. The former, comprising the three units of the Koningin Regentes class together with *Marten Harpertszoon Tromp* and *Jacob van Heemskerck*, displaced around 5,000

tons and were armed with two 9.5in (24cm) guns. Meanwhile, the six Holland-class protected cruisers displaced 3,900 tons and were armed with two 5.9in (15cm) guns. In 1900 the navy as a whole numbered 11,000 men, supported by a budget of 22 million guilders (nearly 15 per cent of the national budget), of which roughly a quarter was paid for by the Secretary of Colonial Affairs.[1]

Despite these measures, the Russo-Japanese War of 1904–5 provided a stark demonstration that the Koninklijke Marine would be powerless to defend the East Indies against any but the smallest incursions or *coups de main*, much less a major seaborne attack. This realisation came during the nightmare voyage of the Russian Second Pacific Squadron round the Cape of Good Hope with the intention of lifting the Japanese siege of Port Arthur (now Lüshunkou). Despite the Netherlands' longstanding policy of neutrality, it was feared that this might be challenged should the Russian fleet decide to coal and provision at a port in the Dutch East Indies. Two Dutch squadrons were dispatched to Sabang to act as a deterrent, but their commanding officers knew that their small battleships and cruisers would be no match for

---

[1] These figures are derived from the annual naval budgets published in *Marineblad* between 1890 and 1910, showing an increase of nearly 25 per cent during that period.

the Russian fleet in the event of an engagement. As it turned out, the Russian commander Admiral Zinovy Rozhestvenskii anchored at Nossi Bé in French Madagascar between December 1904 and March 1905, and resumed his voyage eastward to annihilation at the Battle of Tsushima on 27 May without troubling the Dutch East Indies. While this no doubt came as a huge relief to the government and the Koninklijke Marine, it was all too clear that the balance of power in the Pacific had shifted drastically and that the defence of the Dutch East Indies was due for further review.

Parliamentary Debates

The challenge of recasting the Koninklijke Marine was taken up by Minister van Marine (Minister of Marine) William James Cohen Stuart who in 1906 proposed the construction of another four Jacob van Heemskerck-class armoured ships for service in Europe, together with six destroyers and four enlarged Tromp-class armoured ships displacing 7,000 tons for service in the Dutch East Indies. These proposals, however, coincided with the appearance of the revolutionary battleship HMS *Dreadnought* of 21,000 tons, a development which caused the Tweede Kamer (House of Representatives) to veto the Van Heemskercks on grounds of obsolescence but approve the construction of an enlarged Tromp-class vessel. That no designs were reviewed in large measure reflects the concern of the authorities to secure the continued existence of the Rijkswerf, the government dockyard in Amsterdam. So it was that *De Zeven*

Provinciën came into being as a result both of domestic political expediency and the wider diplomatic and naval conjuncture.

For all that, approval did not come without a fight since the big-gun fleet was strongly opposed in both political and naval circles by those who viewed the torpedo as the weapon of choice for smaller navies. Indeed, Cohen Stuart's proposals had been predated by the establishment of a States Commission to address the defence of the East Indies, which in 1907 issued a report recommending that the core of the Dutch overseas fleet be constituted of torpedo boats and cruisers.[2] These conclusions were challenged by those advocates of the big gun who questioned the tactical viability of torpedo boat operations across an immense tropical archipelago. A new States Commission was formed to settle the matter, which on this occasion found in favour of the capital ship, and in 1913 the Tweede Kamer duly approved the construction of a fleet of nine 21,000-ton dreadnought battleships for the defence of the Dutch East Indies.[3] This programme clearly lay well beyond Dutch shipbuilding capabilities and would have made the Netherlands heavily reliant on foreign construction. In the event, the outbreak of the First World War brought a swift end to the programme as the world's major warship builders turned exclusively to domestic requirements.

Design and Construction

De Zeven Provinciën was the culmination of a line of development dating to the turret ship *Koningin Wilhelmina der Nederlanden* of 1892. Usually described as a 'coastal battleship' or 'coast defence ship' in English-language sources, she was never designated as such by the Koninklijke Marine and technically does not answer those descriptions, being neither a battleship in the sense of a vessel designed to form part of an oceangoing battlefleet, nor yet confined to coastal waters either by service or design. Heavily armoured but of slow speed, *De Zeven Provinciën* is best described by the Dutch term *pantserschip* (armoured ship) which is that

Inspection of *De Zeven Provinciën*'s after 11in gun in the Texel Roads near Den Helder, spring 1910. *(Netherlands Institute for Military History – NIMH)*

Hr. Ms. *De Zeven Provinciën* launched at the Rijkswerf in Amsterdam on 15 March 1909. The photo shows the beginning of the stern wave which drenched a number of those gathered around the basin. *(NIMH)*

2 J. Anten, *Navalisme nekt onderzeeboot. De invloed van buitenlandse zeestrategieën op de Nederlandse zeestrategie voor de defensie van Nederlands-Indië, 1912–1942* (Amsterdam: Amsterdam University Press, 2011), p. 126.

3 G. Jungslager, *Recht zo die gaat. De maritiem strategische doelstellingen terzake van de verdediging van Nederlands–Indië in de jaren twintig* (The Hague: Maritieme Historie van de Marinestaf, 1991), pp. 55–7.

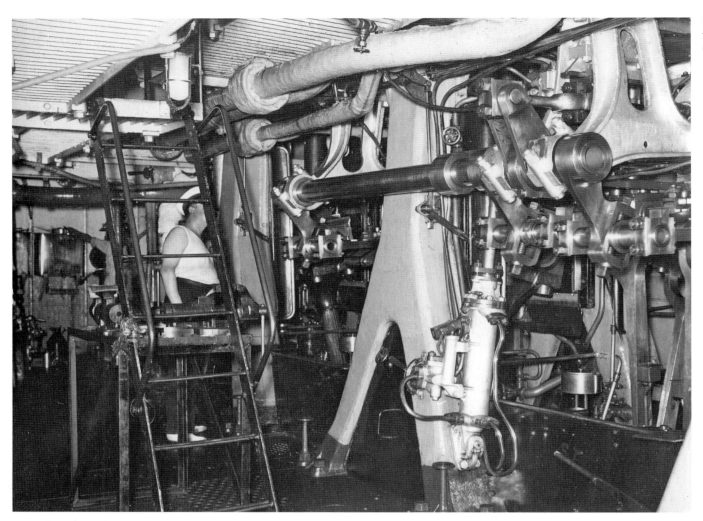

One of the two vertical triple-expansion engines, c. 1930. (MMDH)

favoured in this chapter (see *Sverige* for a similar case). Moreover, although *De Zeven Provinciën* was a small vessel compared to the dreadnoughts of neighbouring states, she was the closest the Koninklijke Marine ever came to commissioning a fully-fledged battleship, and for that alone occupies a special place in Dutch naval history.

De Zeven Provinciën was designed by the Bureau Scheepsbouw Koninklijke Marine (Naval Construction Department) as an enlarged version of the *pantserschip Marten Harpertszoon Tromp* of 5,300 tons which was commissioned in 1906. She had an overall length of 339.5ft (103.5m), a beam of 56.25ft (17.1m) and drew 20.25ft (6.2m) on a standard displacement of 6,530 tons. The main battery consisted of two 11in (28cm) 42-calibre guns in single turrets supplied by Friedrich Krupp AG of Essen. A secondary armament of four 5.9in (15cm) guns mounted on sponsons on either side of the upper deck was completed by ten 3in (75mm) quick-firing guns, six mounted on the upper deck and two pairs disposed immediately abaft and then immediately

forward of the turrets on the forecastle deck.

Where protection was concerned, the conning tower, main gun turrets and belt received 8in (200mm), 8–10in (200–250mm) and 4–6in (100–150mm) of armour respectively, for which Krupp of Essen was again the supplier. The main deck was protected by 2in (50mm) of armour from the Thyssen steelworks of Duisburg. Propulsion consisted of two vertical triple-expansion engines disposed in separate engine rooms and powered by eight Yarrow-type boilers manufactured by the Nederlandsche fabriek van Werktuigen en Spoorwegmaterieel of Amsterdam. These provided a maximum of 8,516ihp to the twin screws giving a top speed during trials of 16.27 knots. The ship had stowage for 872 tons of coal yielding a range of 5,100 nautical miles at an economical cruising speed of 8 knots, but under 2,000 miles at her best speed. *De Zeven Provinciën* was the first ship of the Koninklijke Marine in which wireless communications formed an integral part of her design, and the equipment initially installed

could maintain contact with the radio station at Scheveningen as far as Lisbon, a distance of 1,000 miles.

De Zeven Provinciën was laid down at the Rijkswerf in Amsterdam on 7 February 1908. The size of the hull required the yard to extend the slip beyond the dockyard walls, but subsidence during construction resulted in a permanent sag being imparted to the keel. Moreover, her size necessitated widening the Oosterdoksluizen connecting the dockyard to open water in 1908. Nonetheless, on 15 March 1909 the ship was launched by Queen Wilhelmina's consort, Prince Hendrik van Mecklenburg-Schwerin, in a christening ceremony which attracted a huge crowd to the edge of the basin. From a technical standpoint the launch went perfectly to plan and the hull obediently came to in the middle of the basin, though not before generating a large stern wave which drenched a parade of soldiers mustered from the nearby Oranje Nassau barracks. The name given her that day, *De Zeven Provinciën*, could scarcely

De Zeven Provinciën stranded on a reef off Koendoer Island (Sumatra) in January 1912. She was lifted free after a week. (MMDH)

have had a more distinguished pedigree, since it not only recalled the seven provinces which united to declare independence from Spain in 1581 – the foundation of the Dutch Republic itself – but also the 80-gun man-of-war in which Michiel Adriaenszoon de Ruyter (1607–76) cemented his reputation as one of the great fighting officers in naval history. The new vessel was the sixth to bear the name in the Dutch navy.

Early Years, 1910–14

By May 1910 *De Zeven Provinciën* was ready for acceptance and gunnery trials in the North Sea. These revealed her to have a tendency to pitch heavily and turn into the wind, while the low funnels resulted in the decks being suffused with soot, ashes and fumes. These shortcomings were, however, summarily dismissed as minor inconveniences and the ship duly commissioned in Amsterdam on 6 October 1910. On 21 November she sailed from Den Helder on her maiden voyage to the Dutch East Indies under the command of Kapitein ter zee (Ktz – Captain) Frits Bauduin. Under ordinary circumstances the ship would have made her way east via the Mediterranean and the Suez Canal, but on this occasion *De Zeven Provinciën* sailed down the west coast of Africa to Cape Town where ship

and crew received an enthusiastic welcome on 8 January 1911. The diplomatic overtones of this visit were quite apparent, many years having passed since a vessel of the Koninklijke Marine

had put in at this former Dutch colony, and the mission of the protected cruiser *Gelderland* to fetch Boer President Paul Kruger to exile in the Netherlands from the Mozambican port of Lourenço Marques (now Maputo) in 1900 still fresh in the memory. In the event, the visit passed off in a splendid atmosphere, due largely it was said to the refreshments on offer being changed from 'unlimited beer and gin' to 'lemonade and one glass of local wine'. The voyage continued via Durban and the Seychelles, with *De Zeven Provinciën* reaching Tandjong Priok, the harbour of Batavia, on 25 February 1911. On 13 March she sailed for the main naval base at Surabaya where she dropped anchor a week later. Before long Ktz W. van Voss, commanding the East Indies Squadron, had shifted his flag and staff to the newly arrived vessel.

De Zeven Provinciën now settled into her role as flagship of the East Indies Squadron, a status she retained for the next eight years. As the centrepiece of a force of three or four armoured ships and protected cruisers, her active service invariably consisted of formation exercises,

De Zeven Provinciën in the East Indies, probably at Emmahaven on the island of Padang (Sumatra) in December 1914. The photo shows the scrollwork decorating the stern. To the right is one of the Wolf-class destroyers. (NIMH)

tactical manoeuvres in combination with destroyers and torpedo boats, and gunnery drill. However, the *Zeven*'s career in the Far East began inauspiciously, the ship striking a reef off Koendoer Island northeast of Sumatra on 23 January 1912. Held fast on the rocks for over a week, it was not until her ammunition and coal had been hoisted into locally built lighters that she lifted free at high tide, just as the armoured ship *Hertog Hendrik* appeared over the horizon

to lend assistance. With the ship in need of dry-docking and no facilities capable of accommo-dating her bulk in the Dutch East Indies, the Koninklijke Marine had recourse to the British base at Singapore where she spent the next three months making the necessary repairs. This logis-tical shortcoming was partly remedied by the arrival of a privately owned 14,000-ton floating dock in Surabaya in late 1913, although it turned out not to be immediately serviceable. The

outbreak of the First World War made its avail-ability all the more pressing and urgent requests from the Koninklijke Marine to the owners Droogdok Maatschappij Soerabaja at last brought it into service. By the end of that year the *Zeven* could at last dock in her own base.[4]

The Great War and After

The mobilisation of the Dutch navy in early August 1914 saw *De Zeven Provinciën* readied for battle at Tandjong Priok, the white hull and yellow funnels characteristic of the peacetime East Indies Squadron being overpainted in grey, and all flammable fittings landed. The chief concern of the Dutch government during the Great War was to maintain its neutrality. Aside from non-intervention in Europe, in practice this meant ensuring that the Dutch East Indies did not become a haven for freighters used by belligerent nations to refuel and supply their warships. Any occurrence of this could result in accusations being levelled against the Dutch of aiding the enemy and so risk embroiling her in the war. Predictably enough, the handful of vessels consti-tuting the Dutch East Indies Squadron proved incapable of controlling so vast a coastline, and neutrality violations were not uncommon.

The most notorious of these incidents came in September and October 1914 in connection with the depredations of the German light cruiser SMS *Emden* and particularly two of her supply ships, the converted Hamburg-Amerika liner *Markomannia* and the captured Greek freighter *Pontoporos*, both of which were operating as colliers for the raider.[5] Cruising off northeastern Sumatra on 23 September, the *Zeven* sighted *Pontoporos* just outside territorial waters off the island of Simaloer. *Hertog Hendrik* and two destroyers were brought up to keep her under observation, which they did without incident until she was joined by *Markomannia* to take on coal on 6 October. The presence of the Dutch prevented the Germans anchoring in a sheltered bay to effect the transfer, requiring the entire coaling operation to be painstakingly carried out basket by basket on the open sea. Meanwhile, the Dutch covertly informed the British naval

De Zeven Provinciën in the floating dry dock at Surabaya. (MMDH)

4 F. Bauduin, *Het Nederlandsch eskader in Oost-Indië 1914–1916, benevens eenige beschouwingen over onze marine* (The Hague: M. Nijhoff, 1920), p. 31.

5 Kees van Dijk, *The Netherlands Indies and the Great War, 1914–1918* (Leiden: Koninklijk Instituut voor Taal-, Land- en Volkenkunde, 2007), pp. 187 & 197.

De Zeven Provinciën *on patrol in the East Indies c. 1915.*
(MMDH)

authorities in Singapore of the situation, and early on the morning of 12 October the light cruiser HMS *Yarmouth* hove into sight while the two supply ships were lying side by side. Blocking the route towards Dutch territorial waters, *Yarmouth* took off the crews before sinking *Markomannia* with explosives and gunfire as *Pontoporos* was placed under a prize crew. Of this spectacle the Dutch squadron enjoyed a grandstand view until *Yarmouth* and *Pontoporos* turned for Singapore at 1800.[6]

Much as mobilisation made heavy demands on the fleet, the Koninklijke Marine never saw action during the First World War. No sooner had it ended than *De Zeven Provinciën* was ordered to Holland for a major overhaul, sailing from Tandjong Priok on 11 November 1918, but this time crossing the Pacific and traversing the Panama Canal. The journey home was not uneventful. The commander's report mentions the ship's stock of cigars and cigarettes disappearing during a visit by the Dutch consul and a fifty-strong entourage of family and friends at Balboa in the Panama Canal Zone. However, tobacco was not the only commodity to vanish during this voyage, since courtesy calls at San Francisco in January 1919 and subsequently at New York had resulted in the desertion of thirty-two ratings by the time the *Zeven* sailed from the Hudson for Holland on 11 March, to which the higher wages and standard of living in the United States no doubt contributed. En route, she altered course to assist the leaking coaster SS *Sapinero*, putting thirty sailors aboard her to help dispose of a cargo of engorged grain. Reaching the Den Helder Roads on 1 April, *De Zeven Provinciën* decommissioned and made her way to the Nederlandsche Scheepsbouw Maatschappij in Amsterdam for repairs and a minor refit involving the boilers and ammunition hoists. It would be more than two years before she was recommissioned.

By the autumn of 1921 *De Zeven Provinciën* was ready to return to the Dutch East Indies, sailing from Den Helder on 9 November. On this occasion she took the usual route eastward via the Mediterranean and the Suez Canal, reaching Tandjong Priok on 19 January 1922. Although

De Zeven Provinciën *carries out a practice shoot with her 11in and 5.9in armament. Still in the East Indies, by 1927 she had been reduced to the status of gunnery training ship. (MMDH)*

6 Bauduin, *Het Nederlandsch eskader in Oost-Indië*, pp. 56–8.

quickly resuming her role as squadron flagship, it was quite apparent that she was obsolescent by comparison with the front-line units of other navies, and squadron exercises now used her as a target for destroyers, submarines and aircraft. In March 1924 she escorted the governor general of the Dutch East Indies on a formal visit to the Philippines, but by 1927 had ceased to be a flagship, ceding that honour to the light cruisers Hr. Ms. *Java* and *Sumatra* while being relegated to the status of gunnery training ship. Under ordinary circumstances the *Zeven* would have slipped quietly from secondary duties into the annals of Dutch naval history but it was not to be, and her notoriety, when it came, originated not from without the ship but from within.

Shipboard Organisation

De Zeven Provinciën had a standard complement of 418 men, to which a further twenty-nine were added when the squadron commander and his staff were embarked. As in most navies, shipboard living arrangements for the crew not only reflected practical necessity but also the hierarchical structure which formed the basis of her organisation. In this respect at least, arrangements had changed little since *De Zeven Provinciën*'s seventeenth-century namesake, with the officers accommodated aft, *adelborsten* (midshipmen), *machinisten* (engineers) and *onderofficieren* (petty officers) messing on the main deck amidships, and ratings accommodated

forward on both the upper and main decks.

The captain and the commander were accommodated on the port side of the upper deck aft, the former having a suite consisting of two cabins, a sleeping cabin and a private bathroom. The Koninklijke Marine was among those navies which preserved the convention of reserving the starboard side aft for the flag officer and his staff, these occupying a suite of compartments similar to those of the captain and executive officer on the port side. Situated right aft, immediately abaft the captain's and squadron commander's cabins, was a large compartment used for squadron staff meetings. Joining the two senior officers' cabins was the *westergang* (stern walk), a long balcony stretching round the stern of the ship and to which both had access. Directly beneath these on the main deck was the officers' wardroom, with the sleeping and living quarters of the lower-ranking officers, midshipmen, engineers and petty officers ranged forward. The location of the engineers' cabins reflects their reduced status at the time *De Zeven Provinciën* was commissioned, with even the midshipmen's quarters symbolically located further aft than those of the engineers. In 1910 the members of this branch were only eligible for promotion to officer rank after fourteen years of service, and it was not until 1917 that qualified engineers became officers as a matter of course and the disparity with executive officers removed, a development ruefully referred to as 'the wardroom invasion'.

Located amidships on the main deck was the cabin of the *chef d'équipage*, the senior rating embarked and among the most important members of the ship's company. A Dutch equivalent of the master-at-arms in the Royal Navy and the U.S. Navy or the *capitaine d'armes* in the Marine Nationale, the *chef d'équipage* was not only responsible for shipboard discipline but also occupied a key liaison position between the lower deck and the officers and captain. Holding the substantive rank of chief petty officer, the *chef d'équipage* made it his business to know everything that was going on aboard, and in the words of the petty officers' manual was 'characterised by impartiality, calmness, strength of will, austerity without arbitrariness and benevolence without familiarity'.[7]

The ship's company was divided into five divisions accommodated in two large messes on the upper deck and main deck forward. These consisted of three divisions of seaman ratings, each under a *luitenant ter zee* (lieutenant commander or lieutenant), two divisions of stokers each headed by an engineer officer 1st class, and the forty or so marines commanded by a first lieutenant of the Korps Mariniers. Each division was divided into *bakken* or messes consisting of ten to fifteen men under the authority of a *matroos 1e klas* (seaman 1st class), *marinier* (Marine) or *korporaal* (leading seaman) known as the *baksmeester*. Each *bak* had its own table (*bakstafel*) on the messdeck where the men could eat and relax when off duty. The term *bak* refers to the large bins from which groups of sailors were handed supper in the seventeenth century, and beside each table was a locker in which plates, pots and cutlery were stored. Every evening the tables and benches were folded away and slung to the deckhead to make room for the hammocks, aside from which each man had a small storage locker for his personal effects.

The ship's company was completed by the Marine detachment embarked by the Koninklijke Marine in all larger vessels, descendants of the corps founded by de Ruyter himself in 1665. The Marine complement was not fixed, but generally constituted around 10 per cent of the ship's company; there were fifty-one Marines on board *De Zeven Provinciën* when she sailed for the Dutch East Indies in 1910. Apart from manning

A rare shot of four officers under training in the rank of Adelborst Ie klas (Sub Lieutenant) at work in the ship's wardroom. *(MMDH)*

[7] *Handleiding ten dienste van het onderwijs bij de opleiding tot kwartiermeester zoomede ten gebruike bij den jaarlijkschen cursus voor bootsman en schipper* (Den Helder: C. de Boer, 1929), p. 6.

De Zeven Provinciën in the East Indies, c. 1930. Notice the elaborate scrollwork on the bow denoting the seven provinces from which the ship took her name. *(MMDH)*

sections of the ship's armament, the chief military purpose of the Marines was to form the backbone of a landing party or operation ashore. Aboard, however, Marines acted as the watchful eye of the commander in their role as *baksmeester*, or when filling the important position of *onderofficier van politie* (regulating petty officer), while gymnastics and infantry exercises were usually led by a Marine corporal. The corps was also responsible for passing orders in the ship via drum or bugle. Despite obviously constituting a separate unit, this group had no separate mess, having to content themselves with their own *bakken*.

Although invariably a source of underlying tension, the hierarchical divisions on board *De Zeven Provinciën* were not without their benefits. Telling evidence of this separation comes in January 1922 when the after part of the ship was swept by a throat disorder accompanied by fever. Eight officers, two stewards and two attendants were laid low, but the rest of the crew – hardly any of whom were permitted to venture aft – remained unaffected.

Uniforms and Insignia

Aside from accommodation, hierarchy was also reflected in the uniforms worn by the crew and every man was distinguishable by his rank and trade insignia. Officers wore a variety of coats cut of dark blue wool cloth, of which the most formal was a frock coat with a standing collar. Ordinary dress consisted of a reefer jacket with shirt and tie and dark blue trousers. Rank was indicated by rings of braid around the cuffs, gold with a curl in the case of executive officers and engineers, but with blue velvet between the rings in the case of the latter. Non-combatants such as the officers of the administrative branch and pharmacists wore silver rings without the curl. Doctors also lacked the curl but wore golden rings. An officer's branch was depicted on his coat lapels, showing a crowned anchor for executive and administrative officers, bunched torches and arrows for engineers, and the rod of Asclepius for doctors and pharmacists.

Midshipmen and petty officers wore jackets of the same cut as the officers, but distinguishable by the 'banana skin' pointed braid on the sleeves and, like the ratings, showing their sub-branch insignia on the left arm. These sub-branches included the various subdivisions of the seaman branch, stokers, cooks, police, gunners, carpenters, torpedomen, etc. A sailor's rating was shown on his left upper arm, where two crossed anchors in red, a single anchor or no anchor at all denoted his rating as seaman 1st, 2nd or 3rd class

respectively. Special non-substantive qualifications such as gunner, signalman, rangefinder and diver were denoted by insignia on the right arm.

Although regulations required the wearing of frock coats on formal occasions, in practice officers dispensed with the reefer jacket in the tropics and, together with the petty officers, wore white linen jackets with standing collars, white trousers and matching shoes. The dark blue hat cover was exchanged for a white one. No such concessions were made for engineers and ratings, who continued to wear their heavy sailor's attire of shirt-like jacket for petty officers and white smock for ratings, and it was not until the late 1930s that ratings in the tropics were issued with white singlets as part of new regulations on uniform. Sailors were required to mark every item of uniform and equipment with the service number given them on enlisting in the navy, and it was one of the first tasks of a new rating to mark his blankets, hammocks and uniform during initial training.

Food

As in all other respects, the Koninklijke Marine drew a clear line between officers and NCOs on the one hand, and ratings on the other where provision of food was concerned. The former were granted a subsidy known as the *tafelgeld* (table allowance) to augment their diet with better-quality ingredients, which in the case of the officers was allocated directly to their galley on the main deck. Ratings, however, did not receive this allowance, having to rely on the offerings of the ship's galley, supplemented by purchases of lemonade or other refreshments and cigarettes from the ship's *toko* (the Malayan

word for canteen) out of their own pockets. Although the chief cook presented a sample of the ratings' lunch to the captain, executive officer and *chef d'équipage* at noon each day, the fare must have made for a fairly unappetising *dégustation*. No detailed description of life aboard *De Zeven Provinciën* has yet been found, but the memoir of Petty Officer Signalman K. Twigt of life aboard the protected cruiser Hr. Ms. *Noord*

Brabant in the Dutch East Indies in 1910 was no doubt close to the mark where the provender was concerned:

The main course was pea soup. The top layer, containing lots of floating weevils, was carefully skimmed off. Cooked bacon was added, but having been reheated during cooking it had a slimy and unattractive appearance.

A DAY ON BOARD

At 0530 the order *overal* ('everywhere') was passed, rousing all personnel not already on duty during the morning watch (0400–0800). Hammocks had to be lashed up and stowed and there was a short time for washing and a quick breakfast consisting of a sandwich and a mug of coffee. At 0600 the crew mustered for the orders of the day and to be told off for work (usually cleaning the ship) until the turn of the watch at 0800, when the hands took a second and more substantial breakfast.

This was followed by *vlaggenparade* (colours) at 0900 (0930 on Sunday), the ceremonial hoisting of the Dutch ensign on the quarterdeck while the ship's company stood to attention and saluted. No

sooner was this over than the ship's doctor and *onderofficier van politie* (regulating petty officer) submitted their daily reports to the captain. The daily routine continued with work and exercises until noon when the main meal was served at the start of the afternoon watch. The officers took their lunch somewhat later than the ratings.

After lunch came the afternoon rest until 1430 which ended with the order to clean the upper deck and *lappen en naaien* (make and mend clothes). Twice a week the men were to wash their clothes and then bathe by splashing themselves with distilled water before rinsing off with seawater. The ratings' washrooms were located amidships on the main deck and represented a major improvement on the

open sinks of the protected cruisers in which men had to wash themselves in the open air in all weather conditions. Needless to say, officers' clothing was laundered by servants.

At 1630, half an hour after the start of the so-called *platvoet* (literally 'flatfoot') watch (equivalent to the Dog Watch in the Royal Navy), the evening meal was served. Although known as *theewater* ('tea water'), this usually consisted of white bread and butter and a mug of coffee. The bread could be topped in the Dutch style with sugar purchased from the ship's *toko* canteen.

At 2000 the first watch began. For those who had to turn to during the middle or morning watch this was the moment to climb into their hammocks and get their heads down, while men studying for a certificate or promotion took the opportunity to get their books out. But for the majority of their shipmates it was a time for recreation. At sea this might mean singing, listening to records and tall tales or playing cards and other games, but in harbour the men went ashore to visit local bars, restaurants, cinemas or other entertainments. Boy seamen were frequently confined to the ship or required to be back on board early. On special occasions a film was shown on deck.

The Saturday kit inspection in the waist of the ship, c. 1930. Awnings were kept rigged against the equatorial sun of the Dutch East Indies. *(MMDH)*

The main theme on Saturday was cleanliness, and the entire vessel was scrubbed and washed down in preparation for the weekly kit inspection. A church service was held on Sunday, which varied in content depending on whether the ship was at sea or in harbour. When at sea, the ceremony was led either by a Protestant fleet vicar or, from 1914 onwards, a Catholic fleet chaplain, but in the absence of a clergyman the ranking administrative branch officer or the ship's doctor conducted the service, the ecumenical flavour of which reflected the religions and confessions represented afloat. When the ship was in harbour the crew visited their church of choice, which often meant that five separate church parties went ashore. Regular duties were then carried out, complemented by an afternoon shot of diluted gin for adult ratings.

Ratings taking a meal off the *bakstafels* (mess tables) on one of the messdecks, *c.* 1930. Messes were unsegregated but Dutch and Indonesian ratings partook of different food. *(MMDH)*

When capucijner peas were on the menu, the bacon looked nicer as it was canned raw and then diced and fried, from which both taste and appearance benefited. But here the capucijner peas themselves were the weak point. Like the green peas, they were stored in barrels and were full of beetles. This was not a problem because the insects were washed away when the muddy black cooking water was drained. Worse was the fact that the beans always seemed undercooked. Even if they were cooked long enough, their skins burst, spilling out the insides of the beans. What remained was the shell, which was pitch black and as tough as leather.[8]

There was no shortage of rice in the tropics and this ingredient appeared on the menu on a regular basis. To pea soup or capucijner peas, a rice dish was now added in the form of *rotmok*, a stew consisting of rice, canned beef, chilli, curry and onions. Twigt recalled this being a flavoursome meal which tasted better depending on the amount of caked food remaining at the bottom of the butter tins in which it was prepared. The butter was of good quality, but 'because of the heat it came out of the can like oil. A common joke was to ask the shipmate who had fetched the butter where he had left the butter brush.' Unsurprisingly, the large cohort of Indonesian ratings, amounting to approximately a quarter of the ship's company, detested Dutch cuisine and were allowed to prepare their own meals with ingredients purchased by the supply petty officers. When in port the so-called

kadraaiers (traders) came on board to sell fruit or a refreshing treat of shaved ice with syrup.

Even provision of water for ratings left something to be desired. The drinking of non-purified water was prohibited in the East Indies where outbreaks of cholera were frequent. Recourse was therefore had to seawater distilled in the ship's evaporator, the principal function of which was to produce boiler feedwater. The resulting beverage was often still warm at the time it was dispensed, usually from a barrel positioned on deck complete with a mug on a chain.

Pay

Service on the lower deck of the Koninklijke Marine was by no means a lucrative proposition in the first half of the twentieth century. Indeed, it was accepted that only those rated petty officer or higher could afford to have a family, despite which many leading and ordinary seamen were married. Uniforms, blankets and other consumables supplied by the navy were deducted from pay and had to be replaced at one's own expense when lost or worn out. When it is borne in mind that a skilled labourer in the Netherlands earned about 1,000 guilders per year and a seaman 1st class less than half that, it comes as no surprise that desertion among Dutch ratings was frequent during visits to foreign ports where higher wages obtained.[9] Examination of the paybooks of *De Zeven Provinciën* provides a clear impression of the situation, including much higher pay for European personnel in the tropics.

With such low basic salaries for ratings, additional pay for special conditions and qualifications therefore took on considerable importance.

Naval Pay for European Personnel in Guilders, 1910*

Rank	Home Waters	Tropics
Captain†	4,500	7,500
Lieutenant Commander	1,100	3,500
Sub-Lieutenant	400–600	2,200–2,400
Regulating Chief Petty Officer	2.40	3.65
Petty Officer	2.25	3.30
Boatswain	1.72	2.51
Quartermaster	1.07	1.40
Seaman 1st Class	0.75–1.00	0.99–1.24
Seaman 3rd Class	0.47	0.51

* Amounts are per annum for officers, and per diem for petty officers and ratings. Officers were paid monthly while ratings and NCOs were paid weekly.

† An unemployed captain received 2,900 guilders per year.

8 K. Twigt, 'De Koninklijke Marine in het begin van de 20e eeuw' in *Bijdragen tot de geschiedenis van het zeewezen. Uitgave van het bureau maritieme historie van de marinestaf 7* (March 1972), pp. 66–70.

9 H. Wals, *Makers en stakers. Amsterdamse bouwvakarbeiders en hun bestaansstrategieën in het eerste kwart van de twintigste eeuw* (Amsterdam: Stichting beheer IISG, 2001), p. 111.

Certificates for specialised skills or proficiency, such as those in gunnery, signalling or sharpshooting paid a daily allowance, while encouraging sailors to develop their skills in a particular branch. These extras could amount to as much as 20 cents per certificate per day. Another addition to basic pay came with the award of long-service medals, with efforts to promote discipline resulting in the award of a good-conduct certificate which immediately paid the recipient between 3 and 12 cents per day depending on his rate. The withdrawal of this certificate was a common disciplinary measure which could have significant consequences for the income of the miscreant. Small wonder the early interwar period was notable for a rapid expansion of navy unions.

Mutiny

By 1900 the question was being raised in the Netherlands as to how the metropolis could provide sufficient sailors to man the fleet in the Dutch East Indies.[10] The issue was not simply one of recruitment but also of finance since

European personnel had to be transported to the other side of the world where they received higher wages for service in the tropics. The decision was therefore taken to train native Indonesians as stokers, but this made little impression on the problem and within a few years a number of Dutch politicians were proposing the training of Indonesians as fighting seamen in the executive branches. Despite widespread criticism of the idea the Tweede Kamer gave its assent and in 1915 the Kweekschool voor Inlandse Schepelingen (Training Establishment for Native Ratings – KIS) in Makassar opened its doors to the first classes of Indonesian sailors, signalmen and torpedomen. Trainees received much of their practical experience on board *De Zeven Provinciën*.

When the Netherlands succumbed to the economic depression that followed the Wall Street Crash of 1929, the Dutch government responded with an austerity programme which entailed a succession of pay cuts for civil servants over the next few years. Where the navy was concerned, this involved a cut of 5 per cent in 1931 and again in 1932. In late 1932 the govern-

ment in the Dutch East Indies, which was responsible for covering the wages of all naval personnel in the Indonesian archipelago, proposed a further wage cut of 7 per cent. The naval unions responded by sending a strongly worded telegram to the Minister of Marine in The Hague. The unions were quick to claim victory when the cuts were postponed by the Dutch government, but within a few weeks it became clear that these were going to be implemented regardless, albeit on a somewhat reduced scale. The news hit the Surabaya naval base like a bombshell. On 30 January 1933 over four hundred, mostly European, ratings refused to turn to. The naval authorities eventually managed to persuade them to obey orders, but forty hardliners were arrested. Meanwhile, the East Indies government had seen in the implementation of the cuts by The Hague the encour-

[10] The fundamental study on the causes and effects of the mutiny in *De Zeven Provinciën* is J. C. H. Blom, *De muiterij op* De Zeven Provinciën (Bussum: Fibula-Van Dishoeck, 1975).

Instruction in ropework and flag signalling on the forecastle, *c.* 1930. *(MMDH)*

agement it needed to reduce the wages of Indonesian personnel by the full 7 per cent. Not only that but the news was announced on 30 January, the same day as the protest among European personnel in Surabaya. Predictably enough, some 500 Indonesian ratings came out on strike on 2 February. This time the authorities were unsuccessful in compelling a majority of the men to return to work and over 450 were eventually arrested. However, the focus of the unrest now shifted elsewhere.

A month earlier *De Zeven Provinciën* had sailed from Surabaya for a training cruise off southwest Sumatra. On board were 141 European crewmen (including thirty officers and twenty-six petty officers) and 256 Indonesian ratings (including seven petty officers and eighty students of the KIS). The commanding officer, Kapitein-luitenant ter zee (Commander – Kltz) P. Eikenboom was a man with a gentle disposition who insisted on always being on speaking terms with his crew. By early February, however, news had reached the Indonesian ratings on board *De Zeven Provinciën* that their pay was about to be cut for the third time in three years, and of the hundreds of their comrades who had been arrested while protesting against the reductions. Despite receiving signals from Surabaya warning him against possible agitation and ordering him to arm his officers, Eikenboom thought it unwise to compromise the ship's morale by taking any such precautions, and several times signalled to the effect that all was calm. How wrong he was. Not only were Eikenboom's repeated signals of 'Everything calm and quiet' a source of anger to many crewmen but a small group decided to make a gesture of solidarity with their comrades ashore. They would take control of the ship and sail her back to Surabaya in protest.

The evening of 4 February 1933 found *De Zeven Provinciën* anchored in the Koeta Radja Roads on the west coast of Sumatra. The captain and several of his officers were ashore attending festivities arranged in honour of the newly arrived warship. At 2140 an Indonesian rating with a key to a small-arms locker succeeded in arming himself and several of his comrades who quickly took control of the forward sections of the ship occupied by the crew, the bridge and the engine rooms. Before the remaining officers could appreciate the situation, the ship had weighed anchor and sailed for Surabaya. Despite managing to reach some small-arms lockers they were unable to rush the mutineers as loading of the weapons was thwarted by the tendency of the ammunition box lid handles to snap off in the process of opening them. An attempt by several officers to reach the forward sections of the ship got no further than the wireless room, though they were able to signal the authorities in Surabaya that the ship was no longer under their control before retreating aft to avoid a bloodbath. Having barricaded themselves into the after part of the ship, the officers proceeded to disable the steering gear.

The night of 4–5 February saw the first negotiations between the officers and the mutineers. Korporaal machinist (Leading Stoker) Maud Boshart was the spokesman for the mutineers. He told the officers that the mutiny was directed against the pay cuts and that the mutineers meant to sail the ship back to Surabaya in protest and without malicious intent. A majority of officers believed that while the pay cuts were reprehensible, these did not warrant an effort to

Damage caused by the bomb hit on *De Zeven Provinciën's* forecastle on 10 February 1933 which claimed twenty-three lives and ended the mutiny. *(MMDH)*

retake the ship by force, an action which in any case stood no chance of success and would only result in needless bloodshed. The negotiations ended in a truce, with the mutineers promising to leave the officers unharmed and the latter agreeing to restore the steering gear. Still steaming towards Surabaya, the mutineers signalled the naval authorities to declare that their actions were prompted by the pay cuts and that they had no violent intent. For his part, Kltz Eikenboom had boarded the unarmed government steamer *Aldebaran* and set off in pursuit of *De Zeven Provinciën*. *Aldebaran* fell in with her on 5 February, but predictably enough the mutineers refused to allow Eikenboom to rejoin his ship and the steamer was obliged to keep her distance. The hapless Eikenboom could do nothing but trail his ship, having to trans-ship twice owing to the limited coal supplies in the vessels he boarded.

Meanwhile, tensions were rising both in Batavia and The Hague. The Dutch government was incensed and had not the slightest intention of negotiating with the mutineers. Dr. Hendrik Colijn, chairman of the right-wing Anti-Revolutionaire Partij, declared that the 'mutiny should be suppressed, if necessary by sending the ship to the bottom of the ocean with a torpedo'. The Secretary of Defence Dr. L. N. Deckers of the Rooms-Katholieke Staats Partij concurred and ordered all necessary steps taken to stop the mutineers. So it was that a squadron consisting of the light cruiser *Java*, the destroyers *Piet Hein*

A mutineer is interrogated in the former quarantine camp on Onrust Island in 1933. Sentences averaged over four years per man. *(MMDH)*

De Zeven Provinciën was refitted after the mutiny of 1933 and recommissioned four years later minus a funnel and under the new name of *Soerabaia*. Resuming her role as a training ship, she is seen here putting a landing party ashore somewhere in the Dutch East Indies in c. 1938. *(MMDH)*

and *Evertsen* and the submarines *K VII* and *K XI* was sent to intercept *De Zeven Provinciën* in the Sunda Strait. Moreover, three Dornier Wal flying boats led by Luitenant Th. H. J. Coppers and three Fokker T-IV torpedo bombers were directed to the area to confront the mutineers.

Early on the morning of 10 February two flying boats and three torpedo bombers took off from Oosterhaven near Kaap Vlakke Hoek at the southernmost tip of Sumatra with the intention of being the first to engage since *De Zeven Provinciën* carried no anti-aircraft guns. Sighting her shortly before 0900, Coppers signalled the mutineers to hoist the white flag and surrender or face the consequences. Having transmitted this message three times without response, at 0918 Coppers dropped a 50kg bomb from an altitude of 4,000ft. The bomb struck *De Zeven Provinciën* on the starboard side immediately abaft the bridge and exploded on the forecastle deck with devastating consequences for many of those who had gathered to witness the spectacle. One of the mutineers, Leading Stoker Maud Boshart, recalled the scene:

> I was making my way towards the forecastle deck ... when a bomb struck the ship with a huge impact. A large column of fire raced towards the sky and it struck me like a knife that many men had been standing watching the aircraft at the very spot where the

murderous device had fallen. The blast had thrown me off my feet and I scrambled about looking for cover. Then another three bombers came over. They flew at very low altitude so could hardly have missed had they bombed us. But no more were dropped and when they turned away I went forward. Tears came to my eyes. There they were! Boys, who were in fact still children, with their limbs torn off. Some of them were on fire, others had their guts torn out. One comrade, a *tamboer* [drummer], had a fist-sized hole in his chest from where the remains of his once pounding heart bulged. It was a scene of devastation; steel plates were bent, deck beams were splintered and surrounding all this were these little yellow-blue flames. It was a sad, sad sight.[11]

The explosion killed nineteen men instantly, including an officer and one of the ringleaders of the mutiny. Eighteen more were wounded, of whom four eventually succumbed, bringing the total number of fatalities to twenty-three. The white flag was raised soon after. The mutiny in *De Zeven Provinciën* had ended in a bloodbath.

The mutineers were immediately transferred to other vessels while *De Zeven Provinciën* steamed to Surabaya for repairs. Kltz Eikenboom and most of his officers were relieved of their duties while the mutineers were eventually incarcerated in the former quarantine camps on Onrust Island near Batavia. A series of investigations carried out here resulted in the imprisonment of 166 crewmen (twenty-four Europeans and 142 Indonesians) for a total of nearly 716 years, an average of over four years per man. Virtually all those convicted were also ejected from the navy. Nor were the officers spared, sixteen of whom were given custodial sentences of several months' duration for neglect of duty, with six, including Eikenboom, receiving a dishonourable discharge.

Aftermath

Back in Holland the mutiny and its violent denouement made headline news before the financial crisis regained centre stage in the Dutch press. Nonetheless, the effects of the mutiny were of far-reaching importance from a political standpoint. Those conservative parties which had been vociferous first in condemning the mutiny and then in supporting the bombing won the elections held two months later in April 1933, the beginning of six years in power for

Prime Minister Hendrik Colijn's right-wing coalition. Having spent over a decade advocating a 'restoration of traditional values', Colijn successfully invoked the mutiny to further his anti-revolutionary agenda. In the case of the navy, Secretary of Defence L. N. Deckers ordered a ban on socialist literature and emasculated the naval unions to such a degree that they lost their influence among naval personnel entirely, most having disappeared by the end of 1933. The Koninklijke Marine also took the opportunity to get rid of undesirable elements and established a special commission to promote morale and *esprit de corps*. Far away in Makassar the KIS was closed down. Similar measures were imposed on the army, while the so-called 'civil servant prohibition' barred the latter from joining any left-wing organisations, ranging from political parties, trade unions and even banks and radio clubs.[12] In 1934 the navy published the official report on the mutiny which, however, restricted itself to a chronology of the events during the first two months of 1933, since the Secretary of Colonial Affairs refused to allow inclusion of any information that could be interpreted as justifying the unrest.[13] Meanwhile, the February pay cut was not only retained but followed by another in 1934.

The modernisation of the Koninklijke Marine from 1935 onwards served to dissipate the impact of the mutiny, but it was not until 1937 that *De Zeven Provinciën* herself was recommissioned as *Soerabaia*, the name of de Ruyter's great flagship regarded as having been 'dishonoured' by the events of 1933. In the intervening period she had been refitted at Surabaya, the work involving the removal of most of the secondary armament and its replacement with six 0.50in (13mm) anti-aircraft machine guns, as well as the dismantling of the mainmast and the stern walk. The boilers were converted from coal- to oil-firing and their number reduced from eight to three, a change permitting removal of one of the funnels. However, her role as a training ship remained unaltered, and in June 1937 *Soerabaia* sailed on her first cruise with dozens of European and Indonesian sailors embarked. On 6 September 1938 she participated in the fleet review held in the Surabaya Roads to celebrate the fortieth anniversary of Queen Wilhelmina's accession.

The Second World War

As in August 1914, the outbreak of the Second World War in September 1939 prompted the mobilisation of the Dutch armed forces, and as previously the commencement of hostilities found the Koninklijke Marine in the early stages of an extensive programme of rearmament destined never to be completed, in this case centred on three 28,000-ton battlecruisers as a fleet-in-being to deter Japan. The German invasion of Holland in May 1940 brought this ambitious project to an immediate halt, while the attack on Pearl Harbor in December 1941 settled any lingering doubts about Japanese intentions. Within a few days of the attack Admiraal C. E. L. Helfrich had ordered Dutch submarines to the South China Sea to support the British against the Japanese invasion of Malacca and Singapore.

No sooner had war broken out than *Soerabaia* was ordered to escort 800 Dutch, Australian and British troops of the so-called Sparrow Force charged with occupying East Timor, her 11in guns readied for action should the landing be contested by the Portuguese colonial government.[14] In the event, the Portuguese governor confined himself to issuing a strongly worded protest, but as with most initiatives of the short-lived American-British-Dutch-Australian (ABDA) Command, this operation was to no avail since both West (Dutch) and East (Portuguese) Timor were overrun by Japanese forces in February 1942. Following the Timor landings, *Soerabaia* returned to her namesake port where the ship served as an anti-aircraft battery to defend the naval base and the ammunition factories on the nearby island of Madura. It was while performing these duties on 18 February that a Japanese bomb penetrated the funnel or an armoured grating and detonated in the engine room while the ship was alongside in the Oosterhaven. Several men were killed and twenty-two wounded with more succumbing later in hospital. Sinking in shallow water, *Soerabaia* was largely abandoned except for the AA-gun crews on the quarterdeck.

The destruction of ABDA's naval forces under the command of Schout-bij-nacht (Rear Admiral) Karel Doorman (who had served as a gunnery officer in *De Zeven Provinciën* in 1926–7) at the Battle of the Java Sea on 27 February 1942 and the engagements which followed it, removed the last major obstacle to the conquest of the Dutch East Indies by the Japanese. The capitulation of Dutch forces on 9 March therefore brought the

---

11 Cited on http://www.solidariteit.nl/nummers/66/de_muiterij_op_de_zeven_provincien.pdf.

12 Blom, *De muiterij*, pp. 80 ff.

13 *De ongeregeldheden bij de Koninklijke Marine in Nederlandsch-Indie in den aanvang van 1933* (The Hague: Algemeene Landsdrukkerij, 1934).

14 A. J. van der Peet & J. W. de Wit, *Schepen van gewelt. Acht keer* Zeven Provinciën (Franeker: Van Wijnen, 2002), pp. 79–80.

The wreck of the *Soerabaia* in the Westervaarwater off Surabaya in the late 1940s. *(MMDH)*

sunken *Soerabaia* into the hands of the Japanese who eventually had her raised and pressed back into service as an AA battery ship. However, the tide of war having turned against the Japanese, in December 1944 the ship was towed to the Westervaarwater off Surabaya and scuttled, possibly to serve as an obstruction against an invasion force, and it was in this sorry condition that the half-sunken wreck was found by the Allies in August 1945. The remains were still present in 1949, the year Indonesia gained her independence. Although the wreckage was gradually removed, steps were taken to salvage one of the 11in turrets which is now on display at the Loka Jaya Çrana Navy Museum in Surabaya.

So ended the career of the sixth *De Zeven Provinciën*, though the name was soon revived in the shape of a light cruiser commissioned in 1953 and then in 2002 by an air-defence and command frigate. Only time will tell how many more vessels perpetuate the name.

Sources

Unpublished Sources

Monsterrol (Muster Roll) Hr. Ms. *De Zeven Provinciën* 1910 (Collection Historisch Documentatiecentrum van de Marine Sport en Ontspanningsvereniging, Den Helder)

Harmsen, R., *Pantserschip* De Zeven Provinciën (file 849 in privately-owned database)

Bibliography

Anten, J., *Navalisme nekt de onderzeeboot. De invloed van internationale zeestrategieën op de Nederlandse zeestrategie voor de defensie van Nederlands-Indië, 1912–1942* (Amsterdam: Amsterdam University, 2011)

Bauduin, F., *Het Nederlandsch eskader in Oost-Indië 1914–1916, benevens eenige beschouwingen over onze marine* (The Hague: M. Nijhoff, 1920)

Blom, J. C. H., *De muiterij op* De Zeven Provinciën: *Reacties en gevolgen in Nederland* (Bussum: Fibula-Van Dishoeck, 1975); available at: http://www.zeeuwse-navy-seals.com/files/muiterij-de-zeven.pdf [accessed October 2017]

Boshart, M., *De muiterij op* De Zeven Provinciën (Amsterdam: Bert Bakker, 1978)

Bosscher, Ph. M., *De Koninklijke Marine in de Tweede Wereldoorlog*, 3 vols. (Franeker: T. Wever, 1984–90)

Chambon, A., *Marine gewoonten en gebruiken. Vandersteng serie no. 2* (Den Helder: C. de Boer Jr., 1945)

De ongeregeldheden bij de Koninklijke Marine in Nederlandsch-Indie in den aanvang van 1933 (The Hague: Algemeene Landsdrukkerij, 1934)

Dijk, Kees van, *The Netherlands Indies and the Great War, 1914–1918* (Leiden: Koninklijk Instituut voor Taal-, Land- en Volkenkunde, 2007)

Handleiding ten dienste van het onderwijs bij de opleiding tot kwartiermeester zoomede ten gebruike bij den jaarlijkschen cursus voor bootsman en schipper (Den Helder: C. de Boer, 1929)

Jungslager, G., *Recht zo die gaat. De maritiem strategische doelstellingen terzake van de verdediging van Nederlands-Indië in de jaren twintig* (The Hague: Maritieme Historie van de Marinestaf, 1991)

Mollema, J. C., *Rondom de muiterij op* De Zeven Provinciën (Haarlem: Tjeenk Willink, 1934)

Olling, C. H. L., 'Uit de miljoenenhoek (3): Hr. Ms. *De Zeven Provinciën*' in *Zeewezen: opinieblad voor marine, koopvaardij, visserij, zeetechniek en havens* (March 1984), pp. 56–7

Peer, Harry, 'De muiterij op *De Zeven Provinciën*' in *Tijd en Taak* (18 February 1995), pp. 10–13; available at: http://www.solidariteit.nl/nummers/66/de_muiterij_op_de_zeven_provinciën.pdf [accessed October 2017]

Peet, A. J. van der, & J. W. de Wit, *Schepen van geweld. Acht keer* Zeven Provinciën (Franeker: Van Wijnen, 2002)

Platenatlas Hr. Ms. pantserschip De Zeven Provinciën (1910)

Roseboek van de muiterij (The Hague: Haagsche Drukkerij, 1934)

Twigt, K., 'De Koninklijke Marine in het begin van de 20e eeuw' in *Bijdragen tot de geschiedenis van het zeewezen. Uitgave van het bureau maritieme historie van de marinestaf* vol. 7 (The Hague: Ministerie van Defensie, 1972), pp. 66–70

Wals, H., *Makers en stakers. Amsterdamse bouwvakarbeiders en hun bestaansstrategieën in het eerste kwart van de twintigste eeuw* (Amsterdam: Stichting beheer IISG, 2001)

Westerveld, E. P., 'Onze marine in de Indische Krijgskundige Vereeniging' in *Marineblad* 22 (1907–8), pp. 897–963

Jaarboek van de Koninklijke Marine (1890–1937)

Marineblad (1890–1940)

Hellenic Navy (Ελληνικό Πολεμικό Ναυτικό)

The Armoured Cruiser
Georgios Averof (1910)

Zisis Fotakis

NATIONAL NAVAL HISTORIES constitute complex fields of study which tie together socioeconomic, diplomatic, strategic and operational factors.[1] Notwithstanding their complexity, these histories are occasionally encapsulated by the life of certain fleet units. Such is the case of the centennial life of the Hellenic armoured cruiser *Georgios Averof* which virtually single-handedly challenged the power of the Ottoman navy at a critical juncture in the history of modern Greece and in doing so left an indelible mark both on that country and on the navy for which she fought.

Procurement and Specifications

The procurement of the armoured cruiser *Georgios Averof* resulted from lengthy deliberations regarding the optimum force structure of the Hellenic Navy at the turn of the twentieth century. Given the strategic, operational, economic and technological demands of naval warfare in the Greek seas, it was realised that a fast capital ship could enhance the mobility and firepower of the Greek battlefleet, enabling it to cover various theatres of operations against the Ottoman Empire, from which Greece had gained her independence in 1830.[2] The decision to purchase an incomplete Pisa-class armoured cruiser from Italy was taken by the Minister of Marine, Captain Ioannis Damianos, together with that ministry's Director of Matériel, Capt. Michail Goudas, during the prime ministerial term of Kyriakoulis Mavromichalis.[3] The purchase was opposed both in Greece among those who favoured the acquisition of a dreadnought and in Berlin where it not only came at

Georgios Averof seen shortly after commissioning into the Hellenic Navy in 1911. Few ships can have made such a contribution to the territorial extent of any state. *(Hellenic Maritime Museum, Piraeus – HMM)*

the expense of Greek naval procurement from Germany, but in furthering Greek offensive capabilities against her Ottoman ally also ran counter to German strategy in the Near East.[4] Small wonder the Porte made unavailing efforts in Italy to secure the vessel for the Ottoman navy.

The Pisa-class armoured cruisers, of which *Georgios Averof* was the third and final unit, were designed by Giuseppe Orlando as a scaled-down version of Vittorio Cuniberti's Regina

---

[1] The editor would like to acknowledge the kindness of John Carr in providing photos for this chapter.

[2] Zisis Fotakis, *Greek Naval Strategy and Policy, 1910–1919* (London: Routledge, 2005), pp. 16–17, and Ελληνικό Λογοτεχνικό και Ιστορικό Αρχείο (ELIA), Dousmanis MSS, File 4, Memo 314, Athens, 7 August 1909.

[3] In collab., *Ο Ναυτικός Πόλεμος του 1912–1913* (Athens: Scrip, 1914), p. 12; Nikos Stathakis, *Θ/Κ «Γ. Αβέρωφ» το Χρονικό του Θωρηκτού της Νίκης* (Athens: Hellenic Navy, 1987), p. 61, and Ioannis Theophanidis, *Ιστορία του Ελληνικού Ναυτικού 1909–1913* (2nd edn., Athens: Sakelarios, 1925), p. 30.

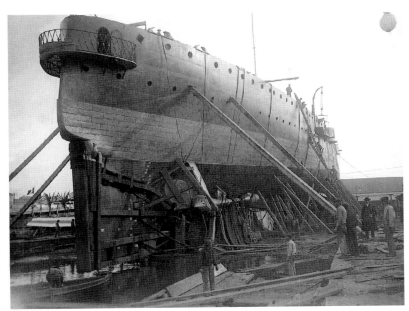

Georgios Averof being readied for launch at Fratelli Orlando of Livorno in 1910 (left) and launched on 12 March that year (right). (Hellenic Maritime Museum, Piraeus – HMM)

Elena-class battleships on which construction had begun in 1901. *Pisa* and *Amalfi* were laid down in 1905 and work had started on a third unit at Fratelli Orlando of Livorno in 1907 before being suspended by the Regia Marina. This decision was due not only to budgetary considerations but also to the completion of HMS *Dreadnought* the previous year which naturally prompted a complete review of naval procurement. However, construction resumed after purchase by the Hellenic government in October 1909, and the ship was launched on 12 March 1910 and completed the following spring, the last armoured cruiser ever to enter service.[5] She was named for the financier Georgios Averof (1815–99) who had made a fortune in banking, property and trade in Egypt and left generous provision in his will for the development of the Hellenic Navy, which in this case covered the deposit required to secure the vessel, amounting to a fifth of the purchase price of 23 million gold drachmae (£950,750). This was 2 million drachmae less than *Pisa* herself despite extensive modifications to meet Greek requirements.

What did the Greek government get for its money? The ship had an overall length of 459.5ft (140.06m), was 69ft (21m) in the beam and drew 23.5ft (7.15m) on a full-load displacement of 10,118 tons (9,956 tons standard). Hull

protection consisted of a belt extending the length of the vessel, with 8in (203mm) of armour between the turrets tapering to 3.25in (82mm) towards the extremities. Turrets and conning tower were protected by 8in (203mm) and 7in (178mm) of armour respectively, with horizontal protection to a maximum of 2in (51mm). Instead of the Italian-built 10in (254mm) guns fitted in *Pisa* and *Amalfi*, the Hellenic Navy opted for the 9.2in (234mm) 46.6-calibre weapon manufactured by the British firm of Armstrongs, of which four were fitted in twin turrets fore and aft. To these were added a heavy secondary armament of eight 7.5in (190mm) 45-calibre guns in four twin turrets mounted two to a side on sponsons amidships. This arrangement allowed *Averof* to fire an eight-gun 9.2in and 7.5in broadside and engage with six guns in pursuit or flight. The armament was completed by sixteen 3in (76mm) quick-firing guns and three 17.7in (450mm) submerged torpedo tubes, one on either beam and one in the stern.

Where propulsion was concerned, *Averof* was fitted with twenty-two French-built Belleville boilers disposed in four rooms, powering two Odero triple-expansion engines generating 19,000ihp for a notional best speed of 23.9 knots. The operational best speed was 20 knots and the ship had a maximum range of 8,416 nautical miles at 14 knots with bunkerage for up to 1,542 tons of coal.

Arrival

Averof was commissioned at Livorno on 16 May 1911 under the command of one of those respon-

sible for her acquisition, Capt. Ioannis Damianos. With Ottoman-Greek relations deteriorating rapidly following the seizure of power by the Young Turks in 1908 and the imposition of an increasingly nationalist agenda in Istanbul, Damianos did not wait to carry out gunnery trials but immediately took *Averof* on her maiden cruise to Britain with the intention of embarking ammunition for her main armament, the opportunity being taken to represent the Hellenic Navy at King George V's Coronation Review off Spithead on 24 June 1911. The visit proved an unhappy one. On 19 June *Averof* ran aground in heavy fog off Spithead requiring her to be refloated with the help of tugs before proceeding to Portsmouth Dockyard for repairs. Once there the first of many mutinies in *Averof*'s long career resulted in the conciliatory intervention of the British naval mission to Greece, Damianos' removal and his replacement by Capt. Pavlos Coundouriotis, scion of a powerful seafaring family from Hydra which had played a leading role in the Greek War of Independence of 1821–30. The leaders of the mutiny were later sentenced to up to twenty-four months of imprisonment.

Not until 1 September 1911 did *Averof* finally sail into the Piraeus from where Rear Admiral Lionel Tufnell, head of the British naval mission to Greece between May 1911 and May 1913, lost no time in leading the fleet on the first of a series of prolonged exercises. It was quickly apparent that there was substantial room for operational improvement, not least since *Averof* was intended to become a model for the internal organisation of the Hellenic Navy. Strenuous

4 Fotakis, *Greek Naval Strategy and Policy, 1910–1919*, p. 23, and Ioannis Metaxas, *Το Προσω-πικό του Ημερολόγιο* 8 vols. (Athens: Govostis, 1972–4), III, p. 40.

5 Myron Matsakis, *Το Σύγχρονον Πολεμικόν Ναυτικόν. Ιστορία και Εξέλιξις* (Athens: privately, 1973), p. 205.

The port waist looking aft showing the forward 7.5in turret together with several of *Averof*'s 3in guns including one of the four anti-aircraft mountings fitted during her 1925–7 refit. A machine gun has been positioned on the turret roof. The photo was taken as the ship lay off Istanbul in October 1937. *(Bruce Taylor Collection)*

Averof dry-docked at Portsmouth after grounding off Spithead on 19 June 1911. The crew, still embarked, have taken the opportunity to do some washing which is hung along the ship's rail. *(HMM)*

efforts were therefore made to improve the war readiness of the Greek battlefleet in the year before the outbreak of the First Balkan War in October 1912.[6] These exercises did not, however, include any heavy-calibre live firing thanks to a shortage of ammunition from British manufacturers. Nor had this deficiency been made good by the outbreak of hostilities, and it was not until late November 1912 that *Averof*'s magazines were fully stowed for war.[7]

Meanwhile, the intensity of *Averof*'s war preparations and the reigning political uncertainty as summer turned to autumn in 1912 prevented her heading to Malta for a much-needed refit.[8] *Averof* together with the bulk of the Hellenic fleet instead covered the mobilisa-tion of the Greek army and on 5 October a signal was sent promoting Coundouriotis rear admiral during the review of the fleet by King George I in Phaleron Bay, hours before it sailed for war.[9]

6 Stathakis, *Θ/Κ «Γ. Αβέρωφ»*, pp. 61–2; in collab., *Ο Ναυτικός Πόλεμος του 1912–1913*, pp. 9–12; Panayiotis Alourdas, 'Τα Ναυπηγικά χαρακτηριστικά του Θ/Κ Αβέρωφ' in Ilias Daloumis, ed., *Γ. Αβέρωφ 100 χρόνια* (Athens: Hipiresia Historias Nautikou, 2011), pp. 56, 61 & 63–4; Ministère des Affaires Etrangères Archives Diplomatiques, Nouvelle Série, Grèce, File 39, Arene to Pichon, Athens, 10 May 1910; Fotakis, *Greek Naval Strategy and Policy, 1910–1919*, p. 34; Bundesarchiv-Militärarchiv, RM 5/1255, Besuch an Bord des griechischen Panzer-

kreuzers *Averoff* an 2 Juni 1912 [Visit aboard the Greek armoured ship *Averoff* on 2 June 1912]; Alexandros Sakellariou, *Ένας ναύαρχος θυμάται. Ναυ-άρχου Αλεξάνδρου Σακελλαρίου Απομνημονεύματα*, vol. 1 (Athens: Giota Sigma Epe, n/d), pp. 39 & 45; see also http://www.averof.mil.gr/index.php?option=com_content&view=article&id=60&Itemid=70&lang=el

7 Fotakis, *Greek Naval Strategy and Policy, 1910–1919*, p. 46; Cambridge University Library, Vickers Ltd MSS, File 1008, Basil Zaharoff to

Vickers, 1 September 1911; in collab., *Ο Ναυτικός Πόλεμος του 1912–1913*, p. 60; TNA, FO 286/549, Sir Francis Elliot to Sir Edward Grey, Athens, 1 July 1912; ELIA, Damianos MSS, File 1.4, Coundouri-otis Report, 3 August 1911; ELIA, Dousmanis MSS, File 5 contains several reports on the defects and weaknesses noted in *Averof* during the fleet man-oeuvres of September 1911 in the Gulf of Volos.

8 Rear Admiral Lionel Tufnell, 'Επιθεώρησις της Σχολής των Δοκίμων υπό του κ. Τώφφνελ' in *Akropolis*, 5 May 1911, p. 3.

Averof sails from Phaleron Bay with the Hellenic fleet for operations in the Aegean on 18 October 1912 on the outbreak of the First Balkan War. The three larger ships in the background and to the right are the French-built barbette ships *Hydra*, *Psara* and *Spetsai* of 1889–90; in the foreground are the Hellenic Navy's British- and German-built destroyers. *(HMM)*

The First Balkan War, 1912–13

In October 1912 the outbreak of the First Balkan War pitted Bulgaria, Serbia, Greece and Montenegro (collectively the Balkan League) in a conflict against the Ottoman Empire which was closely observed by the great European powers, an expression of the labyrinthine and many-layered diplomatic conjuncture that within two years had brought most of the continent to a state of war.[10] Led by Rear Admiral Coundouriotis, the Hellenic Navy took the offensive and on the third day of the war succeeded in capturing the key anchorage of Mudros on the island of Lemnos just forty miles from the Dardanelles, the first in a series of amphibious operations which within a few weeks had occupied many of the islands in the northern Aegean and supported the invasion of Epirus. In the meantime Coundouriotis took steps in unseasonably cold weather to draw the Ottomans out of the Dardanelles.[11] On 14 December the protected cruiser *Mecidiye* sallied forth to make a reconnaissance against erroneous reports that *Averof* was aground off Imbros. Little came of this operation, but it

provided an indication that the Ottoman navy was finally preparing to contest Greek command of the Aegean. So it was that clouds of funnel smoke rising above Gallipoli on the morning of the 16th heralded the emergence of the Turkish

fleet from the Dardanelles.[12] The moment of reckoning had come.

During the Balkan Wars *Averof* constituted the most powerful and modern warship in the north-eastern Mediterranean, a fact acknowledged by the Ottoman navy whose operational plans were restricted to engaging the Hellenic fleet whenever she was reckoned to be out of range, and more generally avoiding being drawn far into the Aegean.[13] For all her many technical advantages, the Greeks were nonetheless acutely aware that

Two of *Averof*'s sixteen 3in guns trained to port during a practice shoot or salute during the First Balkan War. The port forward 7.5in turret can be seen in the foreground. *(HMM)*

---

9 Dimitrios Phokas, *Ο Στόλος του Αιγαίου 1912–1913. Έργα και Ημέραι* (Athens: Hipiresia Historias Nautikou, 1940), pp. 20–1 & 24.

10 For an overview of the Balkan Wars and the involvement of the Great Powers, see, *inter alia*, Ernst Christian Helmreich, *The Diplomacy of the Balkan Wars* (Cambridge, Mass.: Harvard University Press, 1938), and Richard Hall, *The Balkan Wars, 1912–1913: Prelude to the First World War* (London: Routledge, 2000).

11 Phokas, *Ο Στόλος του Αιγαίου*, pp. 29–108 & 125–6, and in collab., *Ο Ναυτικός Πόλεμος του 1912–1913*, p. 75.

12 Phokas, *Ο Στόλος του Αιγαίου*, pp. 130–3.

Averof's armour could be penetrated by the 11in (280mm) shells of the pre-dreadnought battleships *Barbaros Hayrettin* and *Turgut Reis*, but Coundouriotis heeded the advice of Lieutenant Pelopidas Tsoukalas, instructor in naval tactics at the Hellenic Naval Academy during 1910–11, who argued that *Averof* should use her superior speed of 23 knots (approximately 7 knots faster than *Barbaros Hayrettin* and *Turgut Reis*) to engage the enemy at will within the effective range of her armament.[14]

So it was that shortly after 0800 on the 16th the Ottoman navy's Battleship Division consisting of *Barbaros Hayrettin*, *Turgut Reis* and the central battery ships *Mesudiye* and *Asar-i Tevfik* emerged from the Dardanelles under the command of Capt. Ramiz Naman Bey to contest Greek control of the Aegean.[15] Coundouriotis' squadron consisting of the barbette ships *Spetsai*, *Hydra* and *Psara* led by *Averof* was immediately sighted at a range of approximately 14,000yds

(12,800m) and Ramiz turned north to engage the Greek line in a broadside action, opening fire at 0922 at 12,500yds (11,430m). Positioned on *Averof*'s open bridge, Coundouriotis responded first by altering course to starboard to close the range and then by passing the order to open fire at 0926. Aware that *Averof*'s capabilities would be nullified if he remained at 12 knots, Coundouriotis ordered Capt. Sofoklis Dousmanis to work *Averof* up to her best speed and, leaving the rest of the squadron in her wake, proceeded to bring her across the bows of the Ottoman squadron while maintaining a furious rate of fire. Realising that he was in danger of being outflanked, Ramiz ordered the Battleship Division to turn about, but his signal was misinterpreted and several vessels put the helm over immediately rather than doing so in *Barbaros Hayrettin*'s wake. A chaotic scene ensued as *Averof* and the rest of Coundouriotis' squadron kept up a harassing fire while the Ottomans beat

a disorderly retreat to the Dardanelles with *Averof* in hot pursuit. Only when the Ottoman ships were entering the Straits at 1025 did Coundouriotis pass the order to cease fire and alter course to rejoin his squadron.

With this the Battle of Cape Helles ended after an engagement lasting scarcely an hour. *Barbaros Hayrettin*, *Turgut Reis* and *Mesudiye* had been struck repeatedly, suffering heavy damage together with eighteen dead and forty-one wounded.[16] *Averof*, meanwhile, had received just four heavy-calibre hits which claimed the lives of two crewmen, the only Greek fatalities of the battle.[17] Aside from this, the breechblocks of two of her 9.2in guns jammed at the height of the action, a problem not fully rectified until the breech mechanisms were fitted for hydraulic operation at Toulon in 1927.[18] To this was added the inadvertent launch of a torpedo from the stern tube a few hours after the engagement which narrowly missed *Psara*.[19] Despite the satisfactory outcome of the battle, Coundouriotis was criticised for having risked his ship in close pursuit of the Ottoman fleet and was thereafter advised to keep *Averof* at a greater range from the enemy in any future engagement.[20]

That time was not long in coming since the Ottoman navy was determined to reassert its

Capt. Sofoklis Dousmanis, *Averof*'s commanding officer during the Balkan Wars, stands on the quarterdeck at Mudros in 1912. Note the scrollwork bearing the ship's name above the stern walk. *(HMM)*

[13] Bernd Langensiepen & Ahmet Güleryüz, *The Ottoman Steam Navy, 1828–1923* (London: Conway Maritime Press, 1995), p. 21.

[14] In collab., *Ο Ναυτικός Πόλεμος του 1912–1913*, pp. 12 & 255; Pelopidas Tsoukalas, *Μαθήματα Ναυτικής Τακτικής* (Piraeus: School of Naval Cadets, 1910–11), pp. 128–9; Grigorios Mezeviris, *Τέσσαρες Δεκαετηρίδες εις την Υπηρεσία του Βασιλικού Ναυτικού* (Athens: privately, 1971), p. 4; and Cdr C. N. Robinson, 'The Balkan War' in Viscount Hythe & John Leyland, eds., *Naval Annual, 1914* (London: William Clowes & Sons, 1914), pp. 150–68.

[15] For the Battle of Cape Helles, see, *inter alia*, in collab., *Ο Ναυτικός Πόλεμος του 1912–1913*, pp. 242–60; Theophanidis, *Ιστορία του Ελληνικού Ναυτικού*, pp. 150–60; Tsoukalas, *Μαθήματα Ναυτικής Τακτικής*, p. 127; Stathakis, *Θ/Κ «Γ. Αβέρωφ»*, p. 363, and, for the Ottoman view, Langensiepen & Güleryüz, *The Ottoman Steam Navy*, p. 22.

[16] Langensiepen & Güleryüz, *The Ottoman Steam Navy*, p. 22.

[17] Phokas, *Ο Στόλος του Αιγαίου*, pp. 8–9 & 136–48, and Theophanidis, *Ιστορία του Ελληνικού Ναυτικού*, p. 158.

[18] Stathakis, *Θ/Κ «Γ. Αβέρωφ»*, p. 348, and Phokas, *Ο Στόλος του Αιγαίου*, p. 148.

[19] In collab., *Ο Ναυτικός Πόλεμος του 1912–1913*, pp. 248–9.

[20] Phokas, *Ο Στόλος του Αιγαίου*, pp. 164–5.

Part of the 680-strong crew of 'Lucky Uncle George' mustered on the quarterdeck in late 1912, the ship lying off Mudros. The ship's Greek Orthodox chaplain is in the centre and Rear Admiral Pavlos Coundouriotis is to his right. Next to the admiral is Capt. Sofoklis Dousmanis, a telescope under his arm. *(HMM)*

Pavlos Coundouriotis (1855–1935), victor of the battles of Cape Helles and Lemnos and first president of the Second Hellenic Republic (1924–6), seen here in the uniform of a vice admiral. *(John Carr)*

position in the Aegean. The dismissal and court martial of Ramiz Naman Bey was followed by the appointment of a new commander in the person of Capt. Albay Ramiz who conceived a plan to attack the Hellenic fleet at Mudros in the expectation that *Averof* would be anchored there rather than at sea. Ottoman preparations extended to the removal from the National Museum of the immense banner flown by Hayrettin Barbarossa during his defeat of the Holy League at the Battle of Preveza in 1538 and its hoisting to the foremast of his namesake vessel during a ceremony in the Dardanelles on the morning of 18 January 1913.[21] Addressing the crews of his ships before they weighed anchor, Ramiz invoked the glorious past of the Ottoman navy with this Nelsonian call to arms: 'Hayrettin Barbarossa, by defeating the Christian fleets, conquered the whole Mediterranean for the Ottoman Empire; your country expects the same from all of you this day.'

At 0820 the Ottoman fleet consisting of *Barbaros Hayrettin*, *Turgut Reis*, *Mesudiye*, *Mecidiye* and five destroyers emerged from the Dardanelles where they were quickly sighted by the patrolling destroyer *Leon* and the torpedo boat *Aspis* which immediately alerted Mudros.[22] To this news Coundouriotis issued a similarly Nelsonian response, ordering the hands to be given breakfast before putting to sea with *Averof*, *Hydra*, *Psara*, *Spetsai* and seven destroyers. Unaware that his operation had been compromised, Ramiz was therefore astonished when

Mecidiye, then scouting ahead of the fleet, sent a signal at 1055 reporting that the Greek squadron was clearing the coast of Lemnos. Ramiz accordingly altered course to the south to close the enemy and at 1155 *Barbaros Hayrettin* opened fire on *Averof* at a range of 8,800yds (8,000m). Five minutes later Coundouriotis did likewise and, as at Cape Helles, detached *Averof* in an attempt to use her superior speed to outflank the Ottoman squadron. Although Ramiz was able to counter this manoeuvre by a course alteration to the north, *Averof* again proceeded to pound the Ottoman line and at 1255 scored a hit on *Barbaros Hayrettin*'s amidships turret, wiping out the entire crew. Further hits to the superstructure resulted in fumes being drawn into the engine and boiler rooms causing these to be temporarily abandoned and *Barbaros Hayrettin*'s speed to drop to 5 knots. As at Cape Helles a month earlier, the Ottoman squadron turned for home with *Averof* hard on its heels, this time zigzagging astern of Ramiz's line to bring all her guns to bear against the hastily retreating Turks in a scrambling long-range action. Only when *Averof* came within range of the batteries at

Kumkale at 1400 did Coundouriotis turn for Mudros in triumph.

So ended the Battle of Lemnos and with it any pretensions the Ottoman fleet may have had of regaining its position in the Aegean.[23] As the Ottoman Chief of Staff Nâzım Paşa informed the Porte a few days later, 'The fleet has done all it can and nothing further may be expected of the ships.'[24] Meanwhile, it is testament to *Averof*'s stout construction that despite receiving two hits – one near the armoured door of the plotting room and another which caused a fire near the sick bay – the only casualty of the action was the ship's trumpeter, Able Seaman Angelis, who tarried too long after sounding 'Action Stations' and found himself locked outside of the armoured citadel when the ship closed up for battle.[25] *Averof* had also enjoyed her share of good fortune, and the sobriquet 'Lucky Uncle George' applied to her by her ship's company

21 Theophanidis, *Ιστορία του Ελληνικού Ναυτικού*, pp. 164–5, 179 & 182.

22 For the Battle of Lemnos, see, *inter alia*, in collab., *Ο Ναυτικός Πόλεμος του 1912–1913*, pp. 289–307; Theophanidis, *Ιστορία του Ελληνικού Ναυτικού*, pp. 180–96, and, for the Ottoman view, Langensiepen & Güleryüz, *The Ottoman Steam Navy*, pp. 23–4.

23 Fotakis, *Greek Naval Strategy and Policy,*

1910–1919, p. 50, and Phokas, *Ο Στόλος του Αιγαίου*, pp. 188–99. Grigorios Mezeviris, 'Αναμνήσεις από τους Βαλκανικούς Πολέμους' in *Ναυτική Επιθεώρησις* 297 (1963), pp. 7–22; p. 12.

24 Richard Arnold-Baker & Cdr George P. Cremos, *Averof: The Ship that Changed the Course of History* (Athens: Akritas Publications, 1990), p. 36.

25 Phokas, *Ο Στόλος του Αιγαίου*, p. 199.

dates to this engagement. This compares with the Ottoman fleet which suffered forty-one men killed and 104 wounded during the Battle of Lemnos. The decisive nature of *Averof*'s intervention at sea in the First Balkan War, which was concluded by the Treaty of London on 30 May 1913 with significant territorial gains for Greece, could scarcely have been plainer.[26] *Averof*'s only action in the brief Second Balkan War precipitated by a disgruntled Bulgaria two weeks later was the shelling of the port of Amphipolis in Thessaloniki.

The Great War, 1914–18

The fighting qualities of *Averof* and her creditable performance during the Balkan Wars[27] prompted Prime Minister Eleutherios Venizelos to look favourably on the addition of two more of her kind, while Minister of Marine Constantinos Demertzis and Rear Admiral Mark Kerr, Head of the Second British Naval Mission and Commander-in-Chief of the Hellenic Navy, called for the procurement to extend to three armoured cruisers as part of a balanced fleet. However, progress on the two dreadnoughts ordered from British yards by the Ottoman government in June 1911, agitation in Greek naval circles and the prestige attaching to dreadnoughts called for an altogether more imposing solution for the Hellenic Navy, and in

December 1912 a contract was signed with the Vulcan yard of Hamburg for the construction of a battleship armed with eight 14in guns and displacing 19,500 tons which, however, like the other projects was destined never to be completed.

Despite suffering boiler defects and urgently in need of repairs to battle damage, mounting tensions with Turkey over the Northeastern Aegean Islands kept *Averof* out of dockyard hands as they had done prior to the First Balkan War, and she remained the main striking force of the Hellenic Navy until Greece purchased the US pre-dreadnoughts *Mississippi* and *Idaho* (subsequently *Kilkis* and *Lemnos*) in June 1914. The period also saw the creation of the Hellenic Navy's air service and light forces, the development of which was prioritised by Venizelos and Kerr to protect Greece's territorial integrity and strengthen the Triple Entente against both the Ottoman and Austro-Hungarian fleets.[28]

The opening months of the First World War found *Averof* and the Hellenic Navy patrolling the exit of the Dardanelles against a descent by the Ottoman fleet into the Aegean, though neither it nor the Royal Navy squadron performing the same duty could prevent the German battlecruiser *Goeben* (later *Yavuz*, q.v.) and the light cruiser *Breslau* reaching the Straits on 10 August 1914. Nor, in any case, could Coundouriotis have taken any action, since the

policy of neutrality followed by King Constantine I for the first two years of the war confined *Averof* to naval manoeuvres and the transportation of distinguished foreign guests between Corinth and Corfu, a posture much at variance with that of Prime Minister Venizelos who favoured active support of the Triple Entente.[29] The uncontested German-Bulgarian occupation of Eastern Macedonia in August 1916 and the Coup of National Defence led by Venizelos a month later set Royalist Greece on a collision course with the Entente. This came to a head on 19 October 1916 when a French squadron captured the Salamis Arsenal and decommissioned the major units of the Hellenic fleet, *Averof* included. Constantine finally succumbed to Venizelist and Anglo-French pressure and went into exile in Switzerland in June 1917, opening the way for the reunification of Greece under Venizelos and her entry into the Great War on the side of the Entente.[30] The Hellenic fleet was gradually recommissioned but the so-called National Schism between Royalists and Venizelists complicated recruitment and served to delay *Averof* joining the Allied Aegean Squadron at Mudros until 12 July 1918. Even then her high state of efficiency, in which Capt. Clifton Brown's naval mission to Greece had played a hand, could not make up for the incompatibilities in her specifications by comparison with the battleship squadrons

26 Constantinos Svolopoulos, 'Η Συνθήκη του Λονδίνου' in Christopoulos & Bastias, eds., *Ιστορία του Ελληνικού Έθνους. Νεώτερος Ελληνισμός από το 1881 ως το 1913*, pp. 330–4.

27 In collab., *Ο Ναυτικός Πόλεμος του 1912–1913*, pp. 242–60 & 289–307; Theophanidis, *Ιστορία του Ελληνικού Ναυτικού*, and Stathakis, Θ/Κ «Γ. Αβέρωφ», pp. 295–7.

28 Fotakis, *Greek Naval Strategy and Policy, 1910–1919*, pp. 35, 41, 51–65, 78–84 & 87–97, and ELIA, Economou MSS, File 1, Log of Naval Exercises, August–November 1914. TNA, FO 371/1655, Kerr to Admiralty, Athens, 13 November 1913, and FO 286/571, Kerr to Elliot, Athens, 27 January 1914.

29 Fotakis, *Greek Naval Strategy and Policy, 1910–1919*, pp. 102–9, and Stathakis, Θ/Κ «Γ. Αβέρωφ», p. 363, and National Maritime Museum, Greenwich, Francis Clifton Brown MSS, BRO/14, Lecture notes for 'The Naval Mission to Greece, 1917–1919'. For the disagreement between Venizelos and King Constantine I on Greece's position *vis-à-vis* the Entente, see George Leon, *Greece and the Great Powers, 1914–1917* (Thessaloniki: Institute for Balkan Studies, 1974).

30 Fotakis, *Greek Naval Strategy and Policy, 1910–1919*, pp. 129–31 & 134–5.

Averof leads Hydra-class barbette ships on exercises, c. 1920. *(HMM)*

Averof seen after her modernisation at Toulon in 1925–7. (*Courtesy Georgios Averof Museum*)

stationed there, all of which restricted her integration into the Allied war effort.[31]

The Greco-Turkish War, 1919–23

The end of the First World War found Greece on the victorious side and fully expecting to continue the restoration of her historic territories as part of the dismemberment of the Ottoman Empire.[32] Needless to say, this brought significant challenges in its wake both for the Greek state and for *Averof*, which on 31 October 1918 sailed to Istanbul to an enthusiastic welcome from the city's Greek community.

31 Stathakis, *Θ/Κ «Γ. Αβέρωφ»*, p. 297, and Nikolaos Petropoulos, *Αναμνήσεις και Σκέψεις ενός Παλιού Ναυτικού* 5 vols. (Athens: privately, 1978), I, p. 21.

32 Nikolaos Petsalis-Diomidis, 'Το Συνέδριο της Ειρήνης' in Christopoulos & Bastias, eds., *Ιστορία του Ελληνικού Έθνους. Νεώτερος Ελληνισμός από το 1913 ως το 1941*, pp. 85–8.

Here she remained until moving to the Black Sea in early 1919, initially in connection with the Allied intervention in Russia. On 8 April *Averof* anchored off the Odessa lightship on the day the city fell to the Bolsheviks, proceeding first to Sevastopol and then to Smyrna (now İzmir), where on 15 May 1919 she supported the landing of the Greek expeditionary force under the auspices of the Entente, thus marking the beginning of the momentous Greco-Turkish War. Since this conflict had no significant naval dimension, the opportunity was taken between October 1919 and June 1920 to carry out repairs to *Averof*'s engines at Malta. In July 1920 she returned to Smyrna and Istanbul before transporting King Alexander to the newly captured province of Eastern Thrace, where she directed the Anglo-Greek naval forces supporting an attack on the port of Raidestos (now Tekirdağ). Late that year she brought King Constantine back from exile to Athens following Alexander's untimely death and the electoral defeat suffered by Venizelos in November 1920.

Between 1921 and 1922 *Averof* served as flagship of the First Greek Fleet based on Istanbul, with responsibility for policing the Turkish Black Sea coast. These duties found her shelling the port of Samsun on 25 May 1922, with further action in the Sea of Marmara against Panormo on 4 September and the port of Artakis (now Erdek) and the village of Aintintzik next day, while covering retreating troops and assisting in the evacuation of ethnic Greeks in the wake of the collapse of the army in Asia Minor. On 27 September she sailed from Istanbul for the last time, much to the dismay of a majority of her crew, who mutinied. The captain, the executive officer and the master-at-arms were confined in their cabins and the ship taken over by the crew. A few days later the detainees were expelled, command of the ship being assumed by Lieutenant Commander Chatzikyriakos. Between March and July 1923 the Greek fleet exercised relentlessly with the aim of forcing the Dardanelles. Never in all her career was *Averof* a more efficient fighting unit, her gunners setting a record by firing a broadside in under twenty seconds. But it was all for naught, and the signing of the Treaty of Lausanne on 24 July 1923

Averof returns to Piraeus under escort after the failure of the Venizelist coup of 1 March 1935. *(Bruce Taylor Collection)*

confirmed the loss of Asia Minor and Eastern Thrace together with the destruction of their ancient Greek communities and sent the fleet disconsolately back to the Salamis Arsenal.[33]

Between the Wars, 1923–40

The interwar period was one of transition for the Hellenic Navy, with *Averof* no exception.

Although *Yavuz* (q.v.) was in fact *hors de combat* from 1918 until the completion of her own major refit in 1930, the perceived threat to Greek sovereignty presented by the Turkish battle-cruiser led to the retention of *Averof* at the suggestion of Vice Admiral Richard Webb, the British naval adviser to the Hellenic Government between December 1924 and March 1925.[34] Webb's recommendation was contingent on the

ship receiving a thorough refit, including oil-fired boilers, additional armour protection over the magazines, anti-flash protection, improved underwater protection and the installation of director fire control, all at an estimated cost of £260,000.[35] Much to the annoyance of the British Government, the reconstruction when it eventually came in 1925–7 was carried out by Forges et Chantiers de la Méditerranée at La Seyne, during the course of which *Averof* received new boilers (albeit still coal-fired), a new tripod foremast and improved fire control, while eight of the original 3in quick-firing guns were replaced by four 3in AA weapons and the obsolete torpedo tubes removed. The electrical and heating system was overhauled and new boat derricks fitted, but no improvements were made to protection despite the work costing as much as a complete reconstruction.[36]

In the summer of 1931, with *Yavuz* now recommissioned by the Turkish navy, the government voted funds to implement an extended naval programme between 1931 and 1940. This provided for the construction of two flotillas of eight destroyers each, two flotilla leaders, two minelayers, an oil tanker, a floating dock, development of the infrastructure of the Salamis Arsenal, and the procurement of mines and mine barrages, etc.[37] It was also proposed to develop the naval air arm under the supervision of the newly established Greek Air Ministry. However, the implementation of this programme, which came at the expense of the existing battlefleet, was curtailed by the global economic crisis and the ongoing cost of reset-

Averof off Spithead during the Coronation Review of King George VI on 20 May 1937. *(Courtesy Georgios Averof Museum)*

33 Stathakis, Θ/Κ «Γ. Αβέρωφ», pp. 297–8, 310 & 363–4. ACM, 1 7/141, Ministère des Affaires Étrangères to the French Embassies in Rome, Athens and London, Paris, 19 December 1920.

34 The National Achives (TNA), ADM 116/2264, Enclosure I to British Naval Mission Letter no. 1A of 14 February 1925, pp. 8, 10–13 & 18–20.

35 Zisis Fotakis, 'Greek Naval Policy and Strategy, 1923–1932' in Ναυσίβιος Χώρα 3 (2010), pp. 365–93; p. 373, and Dimitrios Phokas, Ἔκθεσις ἐπί τῆς Δράσεως τοῦ Β. Ναυτικοῦ κατά τον Πόλεμον 1940–1944 2 vols. (Athens: Hipiresia Historias Nautikou, 1953), I, p. 25.

36 Stathakis, Θ/Κ «Γ. Αβέρωφ», pp. 310–11, 324–5, 349, 350, 352 & 364; Phokas, Ἔκθεσις ἐπί τῆς Δράσεως τοῦ Β. Ναυτικοῦ, I, p. 62, and Hellenic Ministry of Foreign Affairs, Diplomatic Archive (MFA), File 1925/10a, Roussos to Kaklamanos, Athens; and Historical Service of the Hellenic Navy (HSHN), Kavadias MSS, File 2, Report on the period 1918–41, p. 10.

37 Government Gazette, Series A, Issue 258, Law 5238, 30 July 1931, p. 1999.

tling Greek refugees from Asia Minor.[38] As a result, *Averof*, which had played an important role in naval exercises during the 1920s, spent much of the following decade laid up as her boiler tubes deteriorated and she was destined never to receive the reconstruction she so desperately needed.[39]

Aside from the indignity of grounding less than a mile off Thessaloniki in July 1931 with President Alexandros Zaimis aboard, *Averof*'s activities in the early 1930s were confined to participation in suppressing the pro-Royalist coup led by Generals Leonardopoulos and Gargalidis on 22 October 1923, and in the failed Venizelist coup of 1 March 1935 against the government of Panagis Tsaldaris which was suspected of pro-Royalist tendencies.[40] In the course of the latter she was only prevented from turning her guns on Athens by the presence of Anglo-French naval forces in the Piraeus. She also came under attack from the Greek air force but suffered no serious damage or casualties. The failure of the coup resulted in scores of Venizelist officers and seamen being dismissed from the navy which saw a dramatic reduction in its numbers, while *Averof* herself was placed in reserve. The decision was subsequently taken to use *Averof* as a testbed for a new propellant, the ship being duly towed to a firing range in the Saronic Gulf in December 1935. In the event, a sudden squall parted the tows and left her temporarily ungovernable, and she would have run aground on the coast of Aegina had it not been for timely intervention by the tugs *Taxiarchis* and *Ajax* which managed to bring her in to Salamis Bay. Then in early 1936 the bulk of her ammunition, some 15 million

Averof anchored in the Bosphorus during General Metaxas' historic visit to Istanbul on 22 October 1937. *(Bruce Taylor Collection)*

drachmae worth, blew up in the magazine where it had been landed near the Salamis Arsenal.

Nonetheless, *Averof* was recommissioned in 1936 following the appointment as prime minister of General Ioannis Metaxas and proceeded to make several foreign trips prior to Greece's entry into the Second World War. The first of these was to Brindisi in November 1936 to repatriate the bodies of King Constantine and Queen Sophia. In April 1937 *Averof* sailed to Britain to participate in the Coronation Review of King George VI on 20 May, and later that year conveyed Metaxas to Istanbul on the occasion of his official visit to Turkey, part of a gradual *rapprochement* between the two states prior to the Second World War.[41] However, *Averof* was in poor condition with her best speed restricted to 16 knots thanks to the dilapidated state of her boilers. Her overall combat value had meanwhile fallen by two-thirds, a situation which unavailingly prompted Metaxas to request the British to extend credit for a replacement; the six 1.5in (37mm) anti-aircraft weapons clumsily fitted on the outbreak of the Second World War were the last significant alterations to her fabric.[42]

The Second World War and After

The Italian invasion of Greece on 28 October 1940 found *Averof* anchored in the Salamis Arsenal while serving as the headquarters of the Greek fleet. The bombardment of Salamis by the Italian air force on 1 November prompted her redeployment to Eleusis where she remained for the duration of the Greco-Italian War, carrying out gunnery drills and being used for training and drafting purposes. Things might have been different had the Greeks launched a naval operation to liberate the Dodecanese, which had been under Italian control since 1912, but the operation was vetoed, probably due to British concerns not to antagonise Turkey which aspired to reoccupy the islands. By mid-April 1941, with the German army at the gates of Athens and Capt. Vlachopoulos temporarily away from his ship amidst a welter of contradictory orders, administrative disorganisation and rumours to the effect that *Averof* would be scuttled before the advancing Axis, she was taken over by the gunnery officer Lieutenant Commander Damilatis, Ensign Iliomarkakis and the ship's chaplain. On 18 April *Averof* weighed anchor and cleared Eleusis with the help of the British minesweeping corvette *Salvia* and one of the ship's boats which opened the boom off Psitalia. Her destination was Suda Bay on the north coast of Crete, and manning her were approximately 300 volunteers out of her ordinary complement of 680 men, though Capt. Vlachopoulos at least was able to rejoin his ship later. Within days of her arrival at Suda *Averof* had joined British convoy AS129 with which she reached Alexandria on the 23rd, though not before coming under air attack.[43] This episode not only reflected the chaotic state of the Hellenic government immediately prior to the German occupation of Athens on 27 April, but also the sceptical view taken by the Greek naval high command of the participation of the obsolete *Averof* in the conflict. In the words of Vice Admiral Epameinondas Kavadias, Commander-in-Chief of the Hellenic Fleet, *Averof*'s sole utility was in offering an easy target for air or submarine attack.[44]

During the first two months of her stay in Alexandria *Averof* played host to the Greek Ministry of Marine in exile and consideration was given to sending her to the United States for essential repairs and modernisation.[45] She was

[38] Antonios Sourvinos, 'Το Πρόγραμμα Εξοπλισμού του Πολεμικού Ναυτικού 1824–1989' in *Ναυτική Επιθεώρησις* 459 (1989), pp. 203–24; p. 214, and Ioannis Gianoulopoulos, 'Η Οικονομία από το 1919 ως το 1923' in Christopoulos & Bastias, eds., *Ιστορία του Ελληνικού Έθνους, Νεώτερος Ελληνισμός από το 1913 ως το 1941*, pp. 300–1, and Constantinos Vergopoulos, 'Η Ελληνική Οικονομία από το 1926 ως το 1935' in *ibid.*, pp. 327–42.

[39] Fotakis, 'Greek Naval Policy and Strategy, 1923–1932', pp. 379–80 & 386; Phokas, *Έκθεσις επί της Δράσεως του Β. Ναυτικού*, I, p. 25; and HSHN, Kavadias MSS, File 2, Report on the period 1918–41, p. 52.

[40] ACM, 1 7/148, Compte Rendu de Renseignements [Report of Proceedings] 17, 3 October 1931, and Bulletin de Renseignements [Newsletter], December 1931, p. 30; HSHN, Kavadias MSS, File 2, Report on the period 1918–41, p. 16; and TNA, ADM 116/2810, Capt. Lancelot Holland to Admiralty, Athens, 6 November 1931.

[41] Stathakis, *Θ/Κ «Γ. Αβέρωφ»*, pp. 364–5; Petropoulos, *Αναμνήσεις και Σκέψεις ενός Παλαιού Ναυτικού*, I, pp. 70 & 76–7, Stylianos Charatsis, *1023 Αξιωματικοί και 22 Κινήματα* 3 vols. (Athens: privately, 1987), I, p. 199; ACM, 1 7/169, Compte Rendu de Renseignements 12, Istanbul, 3 August 1936; *ibid.*, Compte Rendu de Renseignements 4, Istanbul, 8 April 1935; and TNA, FO 371/19506, Waterlow to Sir John Simon, Athens, 16 March 1935.

[42] Phokas, *Έκθεσις επί της Δράσεως του Β. Ναυτικού*, I, pp. 25, 62 & 160; Epaminondas Kavadias, *Ο Ναυτικός Πόλεμος του 40* (Athens: Pirsos, 1950), p. 117; and TNA, ADM 116/4200, Waterlow to Halifax, Athens, 16th January 1939.

[43] Stathakis, *Θ/Κ «Γ. Αβέρωφ»*, p. 365, and Phokas, *Έκθεσις επί της Δράσεως του Β. Ναυτικού*, I, pp. 120 & 423–31.

[44] Kavadias, *Ο Ναυτικός Πόλεμος του 40*, p. 254, and Phokas, *Έκθεσις επί της Δράσεως του Β. Ναυτικού*, I, p. 160.

finally ordered to Port Sudan for inspection of her engine plant, and then to Bombay for refitting, docking and degaussing, a decision which caused unrest aboard owing to the desire of the crew to see active service in the Mediterranean and enjoy the warmth of Hellenism in Egypt. This situation was compounded by the removal from the ship by the unpopular Capt. Kontogiannis of the focus of the insubordination, Ensign Iliomarkakis. Nonetheless, on 2 July 1941 *Averof* anchored in Port Tewfik on the Suez Canal where she spent twenty days contributing to its air defence. Her speed limited to 12 knots, on 25 July she reached Port Sudan for the inspection to be carried out, and on 10 September *Averof* made Bombay where she was finally docked. Now wearing a disruptive camouflage scheme, she was assigned to convoy escort and patrol duty from the Indian Ocean to the Persian Gulf.[46]

Averof gradually developed an unenviable reputation for unrest among the Allied forces, the product of an inexperienced crew, left-wing militancy and the fact that she received the sweepings of the Hellenic Navy, both on the lower deck and in the wardroom, since the

cream of the service was appointed to destroyers and submarines. To this was added the severe physical trials of serving in a decrepit coal-fired armoured cruiser on the Tropic of Cancer. The first episode, which lasted from 9 to 15 January 1942 and involved engineering personnel demanding the release of a stoker from detention, was suppressed by *Averof*'s executive officer, Spanidis. Matesis, the new captain, repeatedly requested Vice Admiral Kavadias to see to the removal of undesirable elements, a policy that invited further trouble from those who preferred transfer to Alexandria under punishment to the searing heat of the Arabian Sea. The resulting shortage of stokers required the employment of Sudanese and Indian personnel which brought a number of problems in its train. Not surprisingly, Matesis asked Kavadias to relieve him of his command.[47] His successor Capt. Petropoulos undertook a thorough reorganisation of the ship, introducing a regime of inspection of personnel and *matériel* followed by naval drills, so that by 11 April 1942 *Averof* was ready for her first speed trials and main armament exercises since 1940. However, crew fatigue and the brutal treatment shown by Petropoulos to a sailor under detention resulted in a further outbreak of unrest, quelled only by the intervention of the British naval authorities in Bombay, the replacement of

Petropoulos by his predecessor Matesis, and court martial proceedings against all mutineers. This affair dealt a heavy blow to Greek prestige since the impression had taken hold in Allied circles that the Hellenic Navy was long on unrest but short on action.[48]

Averof eventually made her way back to Port Said on 23 November 1942 where she remained anchored as flagship of the commander-in-chief while being used for training purposes until 26 August 1944; a request by the Greek Admiralty for the transfer of a cruiser of the Regia Marina following the Italian capitulation in the autumn of 1943 proved unsuccessful. It was during this period that *Averof* suffered another of her major mutinies, but on this occasion it was the result of external factors. In early 1944 the Communist-led resistance movement on the Greek mainland known as the National Liberation Front (EAM) issued a proposal to the Greek government-in-exile in Cairo for the establishment of a government of national unity. The urgency of this proposal was not sufficiently appreciated in government circles, resulting in the formation of a Greek revolutionary committee in Cairo at the end of March 1944 which instigated a widespread mutiny among the Greek armed forces in April. The Chief of Naval Operations, the sailor-scholar Rear Admiral Constantine Alexandris, proved unequal to the task of quelling the mutiny, being replaced by Rear Admiral Petros Voulgaris whose past experience of coups and counter-coups served the Hellenic Navy well in its hour of need. By the end of May 1944 the Hellenic fleet was again serving the Allied cause as if nothing had happened in the interim.

Commanded now by Capt. Theodoros Coundouriotis (the admiral's son), *Averof* was the obvious candidate for the repatriation of the Greek government-in-exile and elements of the Hellenic Navy to liberated Athens following the German evacuation in October 1944, the ship anchoring at Phaleron Bay on the 16th. In May 1945 she transported the regent Archbishop Damascinos first to Thessaloniki and then to Rhodes where he solemnly and accurately declared that the union of the Dodecanese with

[45] Phokas, *Έκθεσις επί της Δράσεως του Β. Ναυτικού*, II, p. 18, and Dimitrios Tsalis, *Το «Καταδρομικόν» Αβέρωφ εις την Μέσην και Άπω Ανατολήν κατά την διάρκειαν του Β Παγκοσμίου Πολέμου. Από Μάϊον 1941–Φθινόπωρον 1942* (Athens: privately, 1985), p. 3.

[46] Phokas, *Έκθεσις επί της Δράσεως του Β. Ναυτικού*, II, pp. 38–46, and Stathakis, *Θ/Κ «Γ. Αβέρωφ»*, p. 366.

[47] Phokas, *Έκθεσις επί της Δράσεως του Β. Ναυτικού*, II, p. 94, and Kavadias, *Ο Ναυτικός Πόλεμος του 40*, p. 410.

[48] Phokas, *Έκθεσις επί της Δράσεως του Β. Ναυτικού*, II, pp. 109–11; Stathakis, *Θ/Κ «Γ. Αβέρωφ»*, p. 366, and Petropoulos, *Αναμνήσεις και Σκέψεις ενός Παλαιού Ναυτικού*, vol. IIIα (1978), pp. 57–135; and ELIA, Kyris MSS, File 14, Report on the *Averof*, 31 December 1942.

Greece was approaching. The following year she conveyed the remains of Prince Andrew of Greece and Denmark (father of Philip, Duke of Edinburgh) from Nice to Athens, and *Averof* continued to serve as flagship of the Hellenic Navy until the commissioning of the Italian-built cruiser *Helle* in 1951. She operated as Fleet Headquarters at Salamis until being decommissioned in 1952, remaining there until being towed to Poros where she was docked at the Petty Officers' School from 1957 to 1983. The Hellenic Navy had by this time finally succeeded in persuading the Greek political establishment

of the advisability of towing *Averof* to Phaleron Bay and converting her to a floating naval museum, in which capacity she remains to this day, the last armoured cruiser in existence.[49]

Conclusion

Averof experienced episodes both glorious and inglorious during the course of her long career. The former were products of her early technological excellence, the tactical proficiency of her commanding officers and the stolid seamanship of her ship's companies. Her less glorious moments stemmed from gradual technological deterioration and certain deficiencies in the education and organisation of the Hellenic Navy from the 1920s, together with periods of straitened finances and political and social turmoil, all of which left an indelible mark on the centennial life of the *Averof*. All things considered, her

career is an accurate reflection of the history of twentieth-century Greece herself, whose borders would have been much smaller had it not been for the naval feats of the armoured cruiser *Georgios Averof*.

Sources

Unpublished Sources

Ελληνικό Λογοτεχνικό και Ιστορικό Αρχείο [Hellenic Literary and Historical Archive], Athens (ELIA): Damianos MSS, Dousmanis MSS, Economou MSS, Kyris MSS

Υπηρεσία Ιστορίας Ναυτικού [Historical Service of the Hellenic Navy], Athens (HSHN): Kavadias MSS

Αρχείο Υπουργείου Εξωτερικών [Hellenic Ministry of Foreign Affairs, Diplomatic Archive] Athens (MFA)

Ministère des Affaires Etrangères [Ministry of

---

[49] Phokas, *Έκθεσις επί της Δράσεως του Β. Ναυτικού*, II, pp. 374, 409, 452–6 & 524; Stathakis, *Θ/Κ «Γ. Αβέρωφ»*, pp. 366–8, and MFA, File 1943/35.3, Venizelos to Minister of Foreign Affairs, 2 October 1943.

Averof returns to Piraeus carrying the Greek government-in-exile on 16 October 1944 after an absence of three and a half years. (*Courtesy Georgios Averof Museum*)

Foreign Affairs], Paris: Archives diplomatiques, Nouvelle Série, Grèce, File 39

Archive Centrale de la Marine [Central Naval Archive], Paris (ACM): 1BB7 Série

The National Archives, Kew (TNA): Admiralty Series (ADM) 1 & 116, Foreign Office (FO) Series 286 & 371

Naval Museum of Piraeus, Coundouriotis MSS

National Maritime Museum, Greenwich: Francis Clifton Brown MSS

Cambridge University Library, Cambridge, England: Vickers Ltd MSS

Bundesarchiv-Militärarchiv [Federal Military Archive], Freiburg, Germany: RM 5 Series

Bibliography

In collab., Ο Ναυτικός Πόλεμος του 1912–1913 [The Naval War of 1912–1913] (Athens: Scrip, 1914)

Alourdas, Panayiotis, 'Τα Ναυπηγικά χαρακτηριστικά του Θ/Κ Αβέρωφ' [The Technical Specifications of the Battleship Averof] in Ilias Daloumis, ed., Γ. Αβέρωφ 100 χρόνια [G. Averof: One Hundred Years] (Athens: Hipiresia Historias Nautikou, 2011), pp. 53–65

Arnold-Baker, Richard, & Cdr George P. Cremos, Averof: The Ship that Changed the Course of History (Athens: Akritas Publications, 1990)

Charatsis, Stylianos, 1023 Αξιωματικοί και 22 Κινήματα [1,023 Officers and 22 Coups], 3 vols. (Athens: privately, 1987)

Christopoulos, Georgios, & Ioannis Bastias, eds., Ιστορία του Ελληνικού Έθνους: Νεώτερος Ελληνισμός από το 1881 ως το 1913 [History of the Hellenic Nation: Modern Hellenism 1881–1913] (Athens: Hekdotiki Athinon, 1977)

_____, Ιστορία του Ελληνικού Έθνους: Νεότερος Ελληνισμός από το 1913 ως το 1941 [History of the Hellenic Nation: Modern Hellenism, 1913–1941] (Athens: Hekdotiki Athinon, 1978)

Daloumis, Ilias, ed., Γ. Αβέρωφ 100 χρόνια [G. Averof: One Hundred Years] (Athens: Hipiresia Historias Nautikou, 2011)

Fotakis, Zisis, Greek Naval Strategy and Policy, 1910–1919 (London: Routledge, 2005)

_____, 'Greek Naval Policy and Strategy, 1923–1932' in Ναυσίβιος Χώρα [Maritime Nation] 3 (2010), pp. 365–93; also available at http://nausivios.snd.edu.gr/docs/e4_2010.pdf [accessed April 2016]

Gianoulopoulos, Ioannis, 'Η Οικονομία από το 1919 ως το 1923' [The Economy from 1919 to 1923] in Christopoulos & Bastias, eds., Ιστορία του Ελληνικού Έθνους, Νεώτερος Ελληνισμός από το 1913 ως το 1941, pp. 296–301

Hall, Richard, The Balkan Wars, 1912–1913: Prelude to the First World War (London: Routledge, 2000)

Helmreich, Ernst Christian, The Diplomacy of the Balkan Wars (Cambridge, Mass.: Harvard University Press, 1938)

Kavadias, Epaminondas, Ο Ναυτικός Πόλεμος του 40 [The Naval War of 1940] (Athens: Pirsos, 1950)

Langensiepen, Bernd, & Ahmet Güleryüz, The Ottoman Steam Navy, 1828–1923 (London: Conway Maritime Press, 1995)

Leon, George, Greece and the Great Powers, 1914–1917 (Thessaloniki: Institute for Balkan Studies, 1974)

Matsakis, Myron, Το Σύγχρονον Πολεμικόν Ναυτικόν. Ιστορία και Εξέλιξις [The Modern Navy: History and Evolution] (Athens: privately, 1973)

Metaxas, Ioannis, Το Προσωπικό του Ημερολόγιο [his personal diary] 8 vols. (Athens: Govostis, 1972–4)

Mezeviris, Grigorios, 'Αναμνήσεις από τους Βαλκανικούς Πολέμους' [Reminiscences of the Balkan Wars] in Ναυτική Επιθεώρησις [Naval Review] 297 (1963), pp. 7–22

_____, Τέσσαρες Δεκαετηρίδες εις την Υπηρεσία του Βασιλικού Ναυτικού [Four Decades in the Service of the Greek Navy] (Athens: privately, 1971)

Petropoulos, Nikolaos, Αναμνήσεις και Σκέψεις ενός Παλιού Ναυτικού [Thoughts and Recollections of a Retired Naval Officer] 5 vols. (Athens: privately, 1978)

Petsalis-Diomidis, Nikolaos, 'Το Συνέδριο της Ειρήνης' [The Peace Conference] in Christopoulos & Bastias, eds., Ιστορία του Ελληνικού Έθνους. Νεώτερος Ελληνισμός από το 1913 ως το 1941, pp. 85–8

Phokas, Dimitrios, Ο Στόλος του Αιγαίου 1912–1913. Έργα και Ημέραι [The Aegean Fleet: A Record] (Athens: Hipiresia Historias Nautikou, 1940)

_____, Έκθεσις επί της Δράσεως του Β. Ναυτικού κατά τον Πόλεμον 1940–1944 [Report on the Report on the Activities of the Royal Hellenic Navy during the War of 1940–1944] 2 vols. (Athens: Hipiresia Historias Nautikou, 1953)

Robinson, Cdr C. N., 'The Balkan War' in Viscount Hythe & John Leyland, eds., Naval Annual, 1914 (London: William Clowes & Sons, 1914), pp. 150–68

Sakellariou, Alexandros, Ένας ναύαρχος θυμάται. Ναυάρχου Αλεξάνδρου Σακελλαρίου Απομνημονεύματα [An Admiral Remembers: Memoirs of Alexandros Sakellariou], vol. 1 (Athens: Giota Sigma Epe, n/d)

Sourvinos, Antonios, 'Το Πρόγραμμα Εξοπλισμού του Πολεμικού Ναυτικού, 1824–1989' [The Naval Programs of the Greek Navy, 1824–1989] in Ναυτική Επιθεώρησις 459 (1989), pp. 203–24

Stathakis, Nikos, Θ/Κ «Γ. Αβέρωφ» το Χρονικό του Θωρηκτού της Νίκης [Battleship G. Averof: Chronicle of a Victorious Battleship] (Athens: Hellenic Navy, 1987)

Svolopoulos, Constantinos, 'Η Συνθήκη του Λονδίνου' [The Treaty of London] in Christopoulos & Bastias, eds., Ιστορία του Ελληνικού Έθνους. Νεώτερος Ελληνισμός από το 1881 ως το 1913, pp. 330–4

Theophanidis, Ioannis, Ιστορία του Ελληνικού Ναυτικού 1909–1913 [History of the Hellenic Navy, 1909–1913] (2nd edn., Athens: Sakelarios, 1925)

Tsalis, Dimitrios, Το «Καταδρομικόν» Αβέρωφ εις την Μέσην και Άπω Ανατολήν κατά την διάρκειαν του Β Παγκοσμίου Πολέμου. Από Μάιον 1941– Φθινόπωρον 1942 [The Cruiser Averof in the Middle and Far East during the Second World War: May 1941–Autumn 1942] (Athens: privately, 1985)

Tsoukalas, Pelopidas, Μαθήματα Ναυτικής Τακτικής [Textbook of Naval Tactics] (Piraeus: School of Naval Cadets, 1910–11)

Tufnell, Rear Admiral Lionel, 'Επιθεώρησις της Σχολής των Δοκίμων υπό του κ. Τώφνελ' [Review of the Naval Cadet School by Rear-Admiral Lionel Tufnell] in Akropolis, 5 May 1911, p. 3

Vergopoulos, Constantinos, 'Η Ελληνική Οικονομία από το 1926 ως το 1935' [The Greek Economy from 1926 to 1935] in Christopoulos & Bastias, eds., Ιστορία του Ελληνικού Έθνους, Νεώτερος Ελληνισμός από το 1913 ως το 1941, pp. 327–42

Averof website:
http://www.averof.mil.gr/index.php?option=com_content&view=article&id=60&Itemid=70&lang=el [accessed December 2017]

Kaiserliche Marine/Osmanlı Donanması/ Türk Deniz Kuvvetleri

The Battlecruiser *Yavuz Sultan Selim* (ex-*Goeben*, 1911)

Gökhan Atmaca

THE BATTLECRUISER *Yavuz Sultan Selim* was named for the ninth Ottoman Sultan Selim I whose reign from 1512 to 1520 was notable for a huge expansion of the empire and whose sobriquet *Yavuz* – 'the Resolute' – reflected both to the fratricidal circumstances under which he ascended the throne and the harshness of his rule.[1] Not only that, but Selim's reign saw the beginning of the Ottoman Empire's age of maritime greatness, her navy being instrumental in the conquest of a large part of the Levant and the Maghreb, thereby taking the clash of civilisations which unfolded in the early modern age into the western Mediterranean and even the Atlantic. The name was therefore all too appropriate for a battlecruiser which was not only much the greatest vessel to serve under the *al bayrak* banner in the age of steam, but weathered the eclipse of the Ottoman Empire to form the nucleus of the new fleet established by the Republic of Turkey after 1922. In doing so she became symbolic of an age every bit as momentous as that shaped by her namesake 400 years earlier. However, *Yavuz* owed her existence to quite a different imperial milieu: that of Wilhelmine Germany in the years before the First World War and in the context of the Great Naval Race with Britain.

Origins and Design

During the summer of 1905 news reached Berlin of the construction in Britain of a large vessel which four years later emerged as the world's first battlecruiser: HMS *Invincible* (see *Australia*).[2] The *Reichsmarineamt* (Imperial Navy Office) quickly responded with designs for what it described as a *große Kreuzer* (large cruiser) known as Design 'E' mounting twelve 8.3in (210mm) guns on a displacement of 15,800 tons. The final legend of this vessel was approved in May 1906, but scarcely had the ink dried on those plans than fresh intelligence was received from the German naval attaché in London indicating that the vessel under construction on the River Tyne was a far more powerful unit than had been imagined, mounting as it did eight 12in guns on a displacement approaching 20,000 tons. Although the decision was taken to complete Design 'E' in the shape of the ill-fated large armoured cruiser *Blücher*, this rather shattering development prompted the Kaiserliche Marine to reconfigure its existing *große Kreuzer* plans into a class of fast battleships to which the term *Schlachtkreuzer* (battlecruiser) was eventually given. So it was that the German battlecruiser came into being and with it the subject of this chapter.

The ensuing deliberations resulted in Design 'F' for a vessel mounting eight 11in (280mm) guns, with a standard displacement of 19,370 tons and a best speed of 27.4 knots. This unit, to be named *Von der Tann*, was laid down in March 1908 and completed in May 1910. However, the naval race with Britain dictated a relentless pace of construction and already in December 1908 the keel had been laid of a second battlecruiser to an enlarged design ('G') which was completed as *Moltke* in September 1911.[3] The new vessel had a length of 610ft (186m), a beam of 97ft (29.5m) and a draught of 27ft (8.2m) with a design displacement of 22,979 tons. The main armament consisted of ten 11in guns disposed in five turrets, two forward, one aft, and two *en échelon* amidships, these firing a 666lb (302kg) projectile.[4] Once elevation had been increased from 13.5 to 22.5 degrees, which it had by 1918, the range was 23,730yds (21,700m). Secondary armament included twelve 5.9in (150mm) and twelve 3.5in (88mm) weapons, complemented by four 19.7in (500mm) torpedo tubes. The ship was protected by a belt up to 10.6in (270mm) thick, while horizontal armour ranged from 0.6 to 1.4in (15–35mm) over three decks with bulkheads up to 3in (76mm) thick. The conning tower and turrets were encased in 10in (254mm) and 9in (229mm) of armour respectively. Below decks twenty-four Schulz Thornycroft boilers and two sets of Parsons turbines generated over 85,000shp, giving the ship a best speed in excess of 28 knots, with a range of 4,120 nautical miles

---

[1] The author would like to acknowledge the assistance of Ece Çetin and Berfu Demir of the Istanbul Naval Museum in translating this chapter; the editor does likewise to Steve McLaughlin for his invaluable comments on it, and extends the acknowledgment to Ece Çetin, Thomas Schmid and Lars Ahlberg for generously assisting with photos.

[2] Gary Staff, *German Battlecruisers of World War One: Their Design, Construction and Operations* (Barnsley, S. Yorks.: Seaforth Publishing, 2014), pp. 108–36.

[3] Cem Gürdeniz, ed., *Cumhuriyet Donanması* (Istanbul: Seyir Hidrografi ve Oşinografi Daire Başkanlığı Basımevi, 2000), p. 11.

[4] John Campbell, *Naval Weapons of World War Two* (London: Conway, 1985), pp. 393–4.

at an economical speed of 14 knots. There was bunkerage for up to 3,100 tons of coal. As with all German capital ship construction, *Moltke* had excellent watertight integrity as a result of extensive subdivision on all decks.

It was to this exact design that the battlecruiser *Goeben* – Design 'H' – was laid down at the Blohm & Voss shipyard at Hamburg on 12 August 1909. As with the Kaiserliche Marine's last armoured cruisers and all of its battlecruisers, the ship was named for a prominent military officer, in this case General August Karl von Goeben (1816–80), victor of the decisive Battle of St Quentin in January 1871 during the Franco-Prussian War. Following the tradition of the new German navy, the ship was christened at the launching ceremony on 28 March 1911

not by a woman but by a senior military officer, in this case *Goeben*'s distant successor as commanding officer of the VIII (Rhineland) Army Corps, General Paul von Ploetz.[5]

To the Mediterranean, 1912–14

Goeben emerged from the builders in May 1912, reaching the fleet base at Kiel on the 22nd of that month. On 2 July she was commissioned for trials, though these were interrupted by the autumn manoeuvres of the High Seas Fleet which *Goeben* joined as part of the 2nd Scouting Group.[6] Meanwhile, international tensions were conspiring to draw *Goeben* away from her intended hunting grounds in the North Sea and the Baltic to the body of water destined to make

her one of the most famous warships in history: the Mediterranean.

In October 1912 the outbreak of the First Balkan War pitted Serbia, Montenegro, Bulgaria and Greece (see *Georgios Averof*) against the Ottoman Empire in a conflict closely observed by the great European powers, an expression of the labyrinthine and many-layered diplomatic conjuncture that within two years had brought the entire continent to a state of war. On 1 November 1912 the Kaiserliche Marine responded by establishing an as yet temporary

---

[5] Staff, *German Battlecruisers*, p. 110.

[6] Sinan Avcı, '*Goeben (Yavuz)*' in *Deniz Kuvvetleri Dergisi* 579 (November 2000), pp. 104–13.

Goeben leaving Wilhelmshaven for the Mediterranean in November 1912, never to return. Note the escutcheon of General August Karl von Goeben (1816–80) borne on the bows of the ship, consisting of a rough-hewn tree trunk in silver on a blue field. *(Drüppel)*

Goeben running trials in the summer of 1912. (*Courtesy Philippe Caresse*)

Mittelmeerdivision (Mediterranean Division) to give Germany the ability to project her power in the Mediterranean while protecting her citizens and strategic and economic interests in the region. Three days later *Goeben* and the light cruiser *Breslau* sailed from Kiel for the Mediterranean, the former wearing the flag of Konteradmiral Konrad Trummler and commanded by Kapitän zur See Otto Philipp. Reaching Malta on the 13th, Trummler left *Breslau* behind and pressed on to Constantinople which he reached on the 15th. There the German squadron added its strength to a fleet of foreign vessels which eventually consisted of seventeen French, British, Russian, Italian, Austro-Hungarian, Dutch, Spanish, Romanian and US warships anchored in the Bosphorus under the command of the ranking officer, Vice-amiral Louis Dartige de Fournet in the French armoured cruiser *Léon Gambetta*.[7] With the Bulgarian

army marching on the Ottoman capital, *Goeben*, by now joined by the protected cruiser *Vineta*, put 575 men ashore near Constantinople on the 18th as part of an international intervention force aimed at stabilising the situation.

An armistice was agreed in December but continued unrest kept *Goeben* on station until March 1913 when she led the flotilla of warships repatriating the body of King George I of Greece after his assassination in Salonika.[8] The following month the Mittelmeerdivision was put on a permanent footing,[9] after which *Goeben* and *Breslau* began a round of flag-showing visits to a succession of Mediterranean ports including Venice, the Austro-Hungarian fleet base at Pola (Pula), Naples and Piraeus. By the time *Goeben* docked at Pola for refitting in August 1913 she had underlined her status as the largest, most powerful and influential warship in the Mediterranean. The intervening period saw the outbreak of the Second Balkan War on 29 June and it was in this increasingly charged atmos-

phere that Konteradmiral Wilhelm Souchon assumed command of the Mittelmeerdivision at Trieste on 23 October 1913.[10] *Goeben* and *Breslau* continued to cruise the eastern basin of the Mediterranean, including a five-week tour of the Adriatic in the spring of 1914 escorting the Kaiser in the imperial yacht *Hohenzollern*, and by the outbreak of the First World War these two vessels had made over eighty port visits in support of Germany's evolving Mediterranean naval strategy.

That strategy essentially rested on the Triple Alliance signed between Germany herself, Austria-Hungary and Italy in 1882 against the backdrop of the *Entente Cordiale* forged between Britain and France in 1904 to which Russia was added in 1907, thereby forming the Triple Entente. The immediate context was the withdrawal of the bulk of the British Mediterranean fleet to the North Sea and the strained relations with the Triple Entente

[7] Celalettin Yavuz, *Osmanlı Bahriyesinde Yabancı Misyonlar* (Istanbul: Deniz İkmal Grup K.lığı Basımevi, 2001), p. 236, and Giyasettin Gökkent, 'Balkan Harbi'nde Istanbul'a Gelen Yabancı Harp Gemileri' in *Hayat Tarih Mecmuası*, 8 September 1971, p. 4.

[8] Ersan Baş, *Türk Tarihinde Yavuz Zırhlısının Rolü* (Istanbul: Deniz Basımevi, 2009), p. 67.

[9] *Ibid.*, p. 68.

[10] Sinan Avcı, 'Goeben (*Yavuz*)' in *Deniz Kuvvetleri Dergisi* 579 (November 2000), p. 105, and Redmond McLaughlin, *The Escape of the* Goeben: *Prelude to Gallipoli* (London: Seeley Service, 1974), p. 37.

Rear Admiral Wilhelm Souchon (1864–1946), the inspired commander of the Mittelmeerdivision from 1913–17. *(Library of Congress/LC-B2-3564-10)*

concerned, and it was tacitly understood that the three navies would operate independently in any ongoing conflict.

Aside from the signatories to the Triple Alliance and the Triple Entente, Souchon had of course also to contend with the Ottoman Empire whose steady disintegration had exercised the chanceries of Europe since the 1870s in a phenomenon which came to be known as the Eastern Question. Turkey therefore became a focus of Souchon's diplomacy as the summer of 1914 approached and in May of that year *Goeben* dropped anchor off Dolmabahçe Palace in Constantinople to present the Kaiser's compliments to Sultan Mehmet Reşat V, the latter reciprocating with an invitation to Souchon to dine with him. From *Goeben*'s own standpoint the visit was notable for the parties of Turkish officers who came aboard her, the first of many.[12]

Beset by internal strife and external aggression, the increasingly ramshackle Ottoman Empire had no desire for war, much less with one or more of the great powers, but at the same time there was no confidence in Turkish government circles that she could remain on the sidelines of any future conflict. In this context, with Britain having earlier rebuffed the diplomatic overtures of the Sublime Porte, with Russia as her hereditary enemy and France as the main ally of the latter, it was no surprise that Turkey should respond to cautious German interest in forging what was thus far no more than an informal alliance. In pursuing this policy Germany aimed not only to protect the southern flank of her Austro-Hungarian ally, but also to reap the strategic, military and economic benefits of an Ottoman alliance, while at the same time helping to preserve the latter against complete collapse until the opportune moment. Already in 1903 construction had begun on the 1,000-mile Baghdad railway connecting Berlin with Ottoman Mesopotamia through the Balkans, modern-day Turkey, Syria and Iraq where the Germans planned to establish a port at Basra on the Persian Gulf. There was also interest in establishing a naval base at İskenderun (Alexandretta) on the Turkish Mediterranean coast and, indeed, *Goeben* took the opportunity to carry out surveys of the harbour during her four visits between May 1913 and June 1914. Nor was this rapprochement without precedent from a naval standpoint, since aside from orders already placed with German yards, discussions with the German military attaché in Constantinople in December 1909 had resulted in September of the following year in the transfer of the pre-dread-

Enver Paşa (1881–1922), leader of the 'Young Turks' and a key figure in the decision to permit *Goeben* and *Breslau* to make their way to Constantinople. *(Library of Congress/2002699766)*

nought battleships *Kurfürst Friedrich Wilhelm* and *Weissenburg* to the Ottoman navy. Renamed *Barbaros Hayrettin* and *Turgut Reis* respectively, these vessels saw extensive service against the Royal Hellenic Navy during the First Balkan War (see *Georgios Averof*). However, while the Ottoman army had German advisers, it was the British naval mission in Constantinople which had had the greatest influence on the fleet, and by July 1914 the Turks had the battleships *Reşadieh* and *Sultan Osman-i Evvel* in a state of near completion at Barrow and Newcastle respectively together with a third in the earliest stages of construction.

The shifting patchwork of alliances, understandings, antagonisms and belligerency that characterised European diplomacy in the run-up to the Great War suffered a seismic shock on 28 June 1914 with the assassination of the heir presumptive to the Austro-Hungarian throne, the Archduke Franz Ferdinand, and his wife Sophie, by a Serbian nationalist in Sarajevo. Receiving the news while *Goeben* was lying at the Palestinian port of Haifa, Souchon immediately grasped the significance of this event and

resulting from Italy's aggression in Ottoman North Africa during the Italo-Turkish War of 1911–12. Germany's aim was to secure a degree of mutual co-operation on the outbreak of war, and to this end Admiral Souchon entered into a series of negotiations with the Austro-Hungarian fleet commander Admiral Anton Haus at Pola and his Italian counterparts which resulted in the Triple Alliance Naval Convention signed between these powers in June 1913. In the event of war, Souchon declared that the role of the Mittelmeerdivision would be to intercept French transports bringing troops from Algeria to France while also protecting Italian shores from naval assault. In return it was agreed that the Italians grant him use of the ports of Messina, Naples and Augusta, and that the Austro-Hungarian fleet would sail from its bases in the Adriatic to support the Mittelmeerdivision and the Regia Marina in an engagement with the French fleet.[11] Despite the specific provisions set forth in the convention, there was no effective unity of command where naval operations were

---

[11] Avcı, '*Goeben (Yavuz)*', p. 106.

[12] Baş, *Türk Tarihinde*, p. 70.

hastened to Pola to carry out an overdue refit of the ship's leaking boiler tubes which had reduced her speed to 20 knots. With *Goeben*'s engineers having been sent ahead to prepare for the refit, the battlecruiser entered Pola Arsenal on 10 July where 4,460 of her 9,576 boiler tubes were replaced under the supervision of staff from Blohm & Voss. It had been intended for *Goeben* to effect these repairs at Wilhelmshaven in the autumn with *Moltke* sent to the Mediterranean as a replacement, but these plans were abandoned as Europe spiralled into war. The repairs were carried out under the greatest secrecy in only thirteen days, being completed just as Austria-Hungary issued its momentous ultimatum to Serbia on 23 July.[13]

The previous day the Ottoman deputy commander-in-chief and minister of war, Enver Paşa, a key figure in the Committee of Union and Progress (the 'Young Turks') which had been in the ascendant since 1908, had proposed a defensive alliance with Germany with respect to Russia only, the agreement to take effect once war was declared between that country and the two signatories. This proposal was eventually accepted in Berlin and the resulting treaty secretly signed in Constantinople on 2 August. That same day the Ottoman Empire ordered general mobilisation but immediately announced its neutrality, a decision which not only served Turkish interests but also reflected a lack of consensus at the highest levels of government on the wisdom of the alliance. Already suspicious of Turkish intentions, on 3 August the First Lord of the Admiralty, Winston Churchill, ordered the seizure of the battleships *Reşadieh* and *Sultan Osman-i Evvel* (later commissioned into the Royal Navy as *Erin* and *Agincourt* respectively). Although not unexpected, this decision enraged the Ottoman government which had raised the necessary £7.5 million by public subscription throughout Turkey and had steaming crews in Britain ready to take possession of the two vessels. By 4 August all of the great powers of Europe save Italy were at war; Turkey, meanwhile, did not become a belligerent until November.

Pursuit

Having carried out gunnery exercises off the Istrian port of Pirano and then coaled at nearby Trieste between 27 and 30 July, *Goeben* turned south, meeting *Breslau* at sea off Brindisi on 1 August and exiting the Adriatic en route to Messina, reaching that port on the afternoon of the 2nd, the day Germany mobilised.[14] Once provisions and another 1,580 tons of coal had been embarked from waiting German merchantmen, *Goeben* and *Breslau* sailed from the Messina Roads in the small hours of the 3rd and steamed into the western basin of the Mediterranean with the intention of shelling the French Algerian ports of Bône (Annaba) and Philippeville (Skikda) as agreed in the Triple Alliance Naval Convention of June 1913.[15] That afternoon news reached Souchon of the outbreak of war with France, followed at 0235 on the 4th by a second signal from Berlin stating as follows: 'Alliance concluded with Turkey. *Goeben*, *Breslau* go immediately to Constantinople.' Undeterred, Souchon pressed on for the Algerian coast, detaching *Breslau* to bombard Bône while *Goeben* hit Philippeville with thirty-six 5.9in shells at dawn on the 4th, though there were no French troop transports in either harbour and damage and casualties were slight. No sooner had the Mittelmeerdivision turned for Messina than it was sighted by the British battlecruisers *Indefatigable* and *Indomitable* which were steaming on the opposite course, the two squadrons gliding past each other at action stations. Since Britain's ultimatum to Germany to withdraw from Belgium or face war expired at midnight on the 4th, there was little the Commander-in-Chief of the Mediterranean Fleet, Admiral Sir Berkeley Milne, could do beyond ordering *Goeben* and *Breslau* to be shadowed. Unfortunately for him, even with her reduced speed *Goeben* had the legs on the British and was able to shake off her pursuers to reach Messina on the 5th where Souchon intended to replenish his coal bunkers. This Herculean effort, which cost of the lives of four stokers, had sent all personnel not manning the guns or on bridge duty to the bunkers to trim coal.

However, in an early demonstration of the shortcomings of the Triple Alliance Naval Convention, Souchon found on reaching Messina that Germany's belligerent status and Italy's neutrality prevented him staying longer than twenty-four hours in that harbour. Not only that, but Milne had stationed vessels in the southern approaches to the Straits of Messina. These consisted of the battlecruisers *Indefatigable*, *Indomitable* and *Inflexible* (Milne's flagship) to the west, and the light cruiser *Gloucester* to the east, which as it happened had got on famously with *Goeben* during a pre-war call at the Albanian port of Durazzo (Durrës). Although Souchon was able to secure an additional twelve hours of frenzied coaling, during which the decks of the steamers were ripped up to permit easier extraction, appeals to Admiral Haus at Pola to render the assistance agreed to in the Triple Alliance Naval Convention were rejected as impracticable. Moreover, on the morning of the 6th a signal reached Souchon from Berlin informing him that 'Entry into Constantinople at present not possible on political grounds.' Indeed, not only had the German ambassador in Constantinople, Baron Hans von Wangenheim, failed to report all the provisos under which the Porte had agreed to enter the war, but Turkey was unwilling to compromise her neutrality by allowing two belligerent warships into the Bosphorus. This state of affairs provoked considerable debate in Berlin where it was proposed to order Souchon home to Germany. In the event, Souchon made the personal decision to proceed eastward, and late on the afternoon of 6 August the Mittelmeerdivision sailed from Messina, being quickly sighted by *Gloucester* at the southern end of the Straits.[16] The pursuit of *Goeben* and *Breslau* had begun.

That Milne had only stationed a light cruiser in the eastern approaches to the Straits bears witness to his steadfast belief that Souchon intended either to make a further assault on the French troop convoys or else attempt a breakout into the Atlantic. Certainly, he seems never to have entertained the notion that his German counterpart might be heading irreversibly for Constantinople. So it was that *Goeben* and *Breslau* slipped out of the Straits of Messina and into the Ionian Sea on the evening of the 6th with only *Gloucester* in pursuit. As Souchon feinted towards the Adriatic the task of bringing the Mittelmeerdivision to bay now fell to Rear Admiral Ernest Troubridge with the four armoured cruisers and eight destroyers of the 1st Cruiser Squadron based on Malta. But it was not to be. Despite making contact shortly before 0500 on the 7th, Troubridge passed up the chance of engaging the fleeing Germans, citing 'Being only able to meet *Goeben* outside the range of our guns and inside his.' Aside from his squadron being outranged and outpaced by *Goeben*, this decision owed much to the ambiguous instructions given Milne by the First

---

[13] Matti E. Mäkelä, *Auf den Spuren der* Goeben (Munich: Bernard & Graefe, 1979), p. 42.

[14] Ibid., p. 34, and Rear Admiral Hermann Lorey, *Der Krieg zur See 1914–1918*; *Der Krieg in den türkischen Gewässern*, vol. I: *Die Mittelmeer-Division* (Berlin: S. Mittler & Sohn Verlag, 1928), pp. 9–10.

[15] Lorey, *Die Mittelmeer-Division*, p. 5, and Avcı, 'Goeben (Yavuz)', p. 107.

[16] Lorey, *Die Mittelmeer-Division*, pp. 16–17.

Lord of the Admiralty Winston Churchill and subsequently shared with Troubridge, namely to:

[...] aid the French in the transportation of their African Army by covering, and if possible, bringing to action individual fast German ships, particularly *Goeben*, who may interfere in that action. You will be notified by telegraph when you may consult with the French Admiral. Do not at this stage be brought to action against superior forces, except in combination with the French, as part of a general battle. The speed of your squadrons is sufficient to enable you to choose your moment. We shall hope to reinforce the Mediterranean, and you must husband your forces at the outset.

These instructions had been issued in the context of an attack by *Goeben* on the French troopships and in the event of the Austro-Hungarian fleet emerging from the Adriatic, but were evidently intended by the Admiralty to be interpreted with far greater resolution should the Mittelmeerdivision be intercepted while sailing independently. As it was, not until midnight on the 7th–8th did Milne turn his three battle-cruisers and the light cruiser *Weymouth* eastwards. Even then an erroneous signal from the Admiralty stating that Austria-Hungary had declared war on Britain caused Milne to reverse course until the pursuit was resumed later on the 8th. Meanwhile, *Gloucester* doggedly remained in contact and succeeded in inflicting slight damage on *Breslau* during a brief gunnery

exchange on the morning of the 7th while *Goeben*'s highly efficient radio operators jammed her signals. Still unpersuaded that the Mittelmeerdivision was heading for the Dardanelles, that afternoon Milne ordered *Gloucester* to break off the pursuit at Cape Matapan before opting to guard the exit from the Aegean rather than go in pursuit of *Goeben*, this despite explicit orders from the Admiralty. Small wonder that both he and Troubridge were the subject of courts of inquiry after this debacle, and in the latter case court-martial proceedings; both were exonerated but neither were subsequently employed at sea. For his part, Souchon gratefully disappeared into the islands of the Aegean and on the 9th succeeded in replenishing *Goeben*'s coal bunkers from a steamer waiting off Donoussa.[17] Thus refuelled, Souchon shaped a course for the Dardanelles.

Under the Star and Crescent

Although Souchon had made it into the Aegean almost unscathed, efforts to raise Constantinople by radio proved fruitless and he remained unsure whether the Mittelmeerdivision would be granted permission to enter the Dardanelles. In the event, it was not until 8 August that German diplomacy succeeded in exerting sufficient pressure on Minister of War Enver Paşa to allow the Mittelmeerdivision to traverse the Straits. At 1210 on the 10th Souchon was at sea off the island of Chios when he received a signal ordering him to proceed immediately to the port of Çanakkale, which he did at a speed of

18 knots. So it was that 1700 on 10 August 1914 found *Goeben* and *Breslau* off Cape Helles at the entrance to the Dardanelles. With no Allied warships in sight, Souchon hoisted the pilot flag in *Goeben* and at 1715 the torpedo boat *Kütahya* approached and made the signal, 'Follow me'. By 1935 the squadron was anchored at Nara off Çanakkale and on the 13th it proceeded to the port of Erdek on the southern coast of the Sea of Marmara where it took in coal before sailing to Constantinople on 14 August.[18] The following day the Mittelmeerdivision anchored off Dolmabahçe Palace under the domes and minarets of Constantinople.

Naturally enough, this development caused great consternation not only in Ottoman government circles but also among the signatories to the Triple Entente, particularly Russia, which relied on the Dardanelles for the passage of its Black Sea trade including the grain exports that were vital to its economy, as well as communications with its Western allies. Indeed, Turkey was explicitly bound by treaty to prevent any German warships from traversing the Straits. The Ottoman government came close to yielding to sustained pressure from the British, French and Russian ambassadors in Constantinople for *Goeben* and *Breslau* to be disarmed or ordered to quit the anchorage. However, lengthy discussions between Enver Paşa and other senior figures in the government and a last-minute intervention from Baron Wangenheim resulted on 15 August in the spurious sale of the squadron to the Ottoman navy for 80 million marks, an expedient easy enough to justify in view of the British seizure of *Reşadieh* and *Sultan Osman-i Evvel* two weeks earlier.[19] During a brief ceremony presided over by Enver Paşa the following day, the *Reichskriegsflagge* was lowered for the last time in *Goeben* and *Breslau* and the *al bayrak* banner hoisted in its place. The ships were renamed *Yavuz Sultan Selim* and *Midilli*, the latter for the port of Mytilene on the island of Lesbos which had been lost to Greece in 1912 but which it was hoped could yet be regained.[20] Despite demands from the British that all 1,400 German crewmen be landed, no such disembarkation took place and both vessels remained under German control despite the Ottoman ensign at the masthead and the fezzes worn on the heads of their crews, part of a masquerade which invited ridicule abroad.[21] On

Goeben's 'little sister': the *Magdeburg* class cruiser *Breslau* (renamed *Midilli*), dressed overall and flying the Ottoman flag at Constantinople in 1914. The prominent building on the skyline is the Galata Tower. (*Courtesy Philippe Caresse*)

[17] Mäkelä, *Auf den Spuren der* Goeben, pp. 63–6.
[18] Baş, *Türk Tarihinde*, p. 88.
[19] Lorey, *Die Mittelmeer-Division*, pp. 29–31.
[20] Baş, *Türk Tarihinde*, p. 91.
[21] Yusuf Hikmet Bayur, *Türk İnkılabı Tarihi* (3 vols. in 10 tomes, Istanbul: Maarif Matbaası, 1940–67), II, p. 77.

THE SHIP THAT CHANGED THE WORLD?

Did *Goeben* single-handedly bring Turkey into the war on the side of the Central Powers?[22] The contention that she did has become a commonplace in the historiography on this episode which has attracted more hyperbole than perhaps any other event in the naval history of the First World War. Indeed, within a few years Winston Churchill – who had been First Lord of the Admiralty in 1914 – had expressed the opinion that by forcing Turkey into the war *Goeben* had steamed for Constantinople 'carrying with her for the peoples of the East and Middle East more slaughter, more misery, and more ruin than has ever before been borne within the compass of a ship.'[23]

However, the burden of Churchill's analysis that Souchon's squadron was the sole agent of the Ottoman Empire entering the war on the side of the Triple Alliance ignores the wider strategic and diplomatic conjuncture which had been drawing the Porte inexorably into the German sphere for over ten years. Already in December 1913 the arrival of General Otto Liman von Sanders as head of the German military mission in Constantinople had confirmed the ascendancy within the Turkish government of a hawkish pro-German party led by Enver Paşa. Meanwhile, diplomatic entreaties by more conciliatory elements in Constantinople had been rebuffed in London, of which the seizure at Churchill's behest of two battleships completing for the Osmanlı Donanması in British yards on 3 August 1914 provided conclusive evidence.

Even if it is accepted that *Goeben*'s arrival in the Bosphorus did not inevitably catapult Turkey into war, it is sometimes also contended that she was instrumental in bringing about the Russian revolutions of 1917. Although *Yavuz* and *Midilli* provide a classic example of a deterrent fleet-in-being which, aside from their very real depredations in the Black Sea, enormously complicated Russia's position in the war, it is clear that the Ottoman-German fleet never came close to securing maritime supremacy in those waters until the Soviets sued for peace in 1917, by which time Russia was in the throes of revolution decades in the making and Turkey's strategic position was irretrievable. The notion of *Goeben* as 'the ship that changed the world' is therefore an arch case of historical reductionism which nonetheless detracts not at all from the skilful and resourceful way in which Souchon handled his squadron from the moment he gave Admiral Milne the slip on 6 August 1914 to the time he struck his flag in *Yavuz* on 4 September 1917.

22 See Paul G. Halpern, *A Naval History of World War I* (London: UCL Press, 1994), pp. 58, 62, 64 & 223, and Lawrence Sondhaus, *The Great War at Sea: A Naval History of the First World War* (Cambridge: Cambridge University Press, 2014), pp. 94–5 & 108.

23 Winston S. Churchill, *The World Crisis*, 5 vols. (New York: Scribner's, 1923), I, p. 271.

Goeben sailing from Wilhelmshaven to join the Mittelmeerdivision in November 1912. It is hard to think of any more momentous naval deployment in the dreadnought age. *(Bruce Taylor Collection)*

27 August the British responded by declaring that retention of German personnel aboard would result in the ships being classed as enemy vessels, and added that any Ottoman units in sailing in company with them would be deemed to be acting under German orders and treated accordingly, regardless of the flag they wore. The Porte eventually responded on 29 September by ordering the closure of the Straits to all foreign naval traffic until such time as the British allowed free passage to Ottoman vessels at the western entrance to the Dardanelles.

Flagship of the Ottoman Navy

Although Souchon was appointed Commander-in-Chief of the Ottoman navy (*Befehlshaber der schwimmenden Türkischen Streitkräfte*) in the rank of vice admiral on 23 September, it would be some time before he and particularly the Ottoman navy was ready to go into action. Not only did the fleet remain largely inactive while the empire preserved its neutral status, but Souchon's ability to dispose of units of the Ottoman navy proper was to be decided on a case-by-case basis. Technically speaking,

Souchon became head of a new German naval mission in Constantinople while *Yavuz* and *Midilli* remained ultimately responsible to Berlin, with the architect of these terms, Baron Wangenheim, serving as liaison between Souchon and the Porte. Meanwhile, Souchon embarked on the daunting task of bringing the effective units of the Ottoman fleet to a state of war readiness with the assistance of over 160 officers and technical specialists who reached Constantinople by rail from Germany on 23 August in addition to many officers and senior ratings seconded from *Yavuz* and *Midilli*.[24] Two German liners were moored off Constantinople as depot or accommodation ships and many of the senior positions in the Ottoman fleet were taken over by officers of the Kaiserliche Marine. The intention was for the Germans to return home once the Ottomans were trained to operate their own ships, but that moment never

---

24 Lorey, *Die Mittelmeer-Division*, pp. 41–5, and Bernd Langensiepen, Dirk Nottelmann & Jochen Krüsmann, *Halbmond und Kaiseradler: Goeben und Breslau am Bosporus, 1914–1918* (Hamburg: Mittler & Sohn Verlag, 1999), p. 16.

came while the conflict lasted and it was under these decidedly complicated circumstances that the Ottoman-German fleet waged the war at sea.

After weeks of negotiation, on 14 October the Ottoman government agreed to enter the war on the side of the Central Powers once Germany had facilitated the Turks with a loan of 200 million francs in gold, on receipt of which Enver Paşa and the Navy Minister Cemal Paşa would unleash Souchon on a provocative raid on the Russian Black Sea ports without any formal declaration of war. The aim was to bring about a situation which would propel the Ottoman Empire into war regardless of the reservations of many in government – precisely the situation the Russian government was awaiting in its turn. There was much dragging of feet in government circles even after the lucre had reached Constantinople, but on 27 October Souchon sailed from the Straits with the better part of the Ottoman fleet including *Yavuz*, *Midilli*, the protected cruiser *Hamidiye*, the torpedo gunboats *Berk-i Satvet* and *Peyk-i Şevket*, four destroyers and the converted liner *Nilüfer* as a minelayer.[25] That afternoon the major units gath-

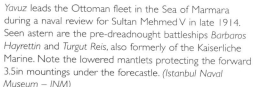

Yavuz leads the Ottoman fleet in the Sea of Marmara during a naval review for Sultan Mehmed V in late 1914. Seen astern are the pre-dreadnought battleships *Barbaros Hayrettin* and *Turgut Reis*, also formerly of the Kaiserliche Marine. Note the lowered mantlets protecting the forward 3.5in mountings under the forecastle. (*Istanbul Naval Museum – INM*)

ered off Kısırkaya on the Black Sea and the commanders came aboard *Yavuz* to receive their sealed orders, which required the fleet to sail eastward along the Anatolian coast on what was ostensibly a training exercise before parting company to attack the Russian ports of Sevastopol, Feodosia, Yalta, Odessa and Novorossiysk on the morning of the 29th. His orders dispensed, Souchon sent them on their way with an exhortation worthy of Nelson: 'Exert every effort and sinew. Turkey's future is at stake.'[26]

Yavuz was charged with attacking Sevastopol in company with the minelayer *Nilüfer* and the destroyers *Samsun* and *Taşoz*, which had been fitted for minesweeping. At 0630 on the 29th *Yavuz* began engaging shore batteries and naval installations, firing forty-seven shells from her main armament at ranges of between 8,500–13,000yds (7,800–12,000m) while her commander Kapt.z.S. Richard Ackermann steered a zigzag course astern of the minesweepers. Fire was returned by the shore batteries and the pre-dreadnought battleship *Georgii Pobedonosets*, *Yavuz* suffering three hits during the action, the most significant of which came after her tenth salvo when two heavy shells struck abaft the after funnel in a hail of splinters which swept the forecastle deck and penetrated the armoured grating to reach the boiler room. With this the bombardment ended but *Yavuz* had next to fend off three Russian destroyers which she did with twelve rounds from her 5.9in battery. The action concluded with the scuttling of the minelayer *Prut* under heavy fire from *Yavuz* and the capture of the steamer *Ida* of 1,708grt which was brought back as a prize to Constantinople.[27] By the time *Yavuz* reached her base at İstinye (Stenia) on the Bosphorus at noon on 30 October, the depredations of the Ottoman-German fleet had resulted in the sinking of at least seven Russian vessels of various types, damage to at least ten more and the capture of another, together with extensive damage to installations and supplies at four ports and the laying of two minefields.[28] As Souchon triumphantly informed his wife, 'I have thrown the Turks into the powder keg and kindled war between Russia and Turkey.'[29]

Meanwhile, Enver Paşa and the other pro-German hawks in the Ottoman government adhered to the fiction that the Russian navy had, in the words of Souchon's prearranged signal on the afternoon of the 29th, 'shadowed all movements of the Turkish fleet and systematically disrupted all exercises,' having thereby 'opened hostilities'. Diplomatic notes were sent to St Petersburg, London, Paris and Rome blaming the Russians and reiterating the desire of the Ottoman Empire to remain neutral, but this cut no ice with the Triple Entente which responded by issuing an ultimatum to the Porte that all German personnel be ordered home. This was refused and on 31 October the Russian ambassador quit Constantinople followed by his British and French counterparts on 1 November. The following day Russia declared war on the Ottoman Empire, and on 3 November a series of incidents culminating in a demonstration bombardment by Allied naval units of the outer fortification line near Çanakkale resulted in Britain and France following suit on the 5th after the Turkish government failed to expel the Germans.[30] However, it was not until 11 November that the Ottoman government declared war on Britain and France, with Sultan Mehmed V proclaiming a jihad against the Triple Entente in his capacity as Caliph of the Sunni Muslim people. As Souchon enunciated it later that month, the primary role of the Ottoman fleet was to defend the Dardanelles and contest any enemy effort to force or seal them, but the fact remained that neither of the belligerents in the Black Sea had a decisive advantage with respect to the other, while Allied command of the Mediterranean confined the Ottoman-German fleet largely to the Straits and the Black Sea where the Russian navy fought gamely and resourcefully until 1917.[31]

A Battlecruiser at War, 1914–15

Despite its rude awakening, the Russian Black Sea Fleet had no intention of allowing the Ottoman navy to assert itself unchallenged, and on 4 November Admiral Andrei Ebergard sailed from Sevastopol with the bulk of his forces to shell the key Turkish coaling and supply port of Zonguldak, sow a minefield across the mouth of the Bosphorus and generally disrupt coastal shipping. Once news reached him of this development, Souchon took *Yavuz* out in the hope of making an interception, but it was not until after Ebergard had shelled Trebizond (now Trabzon) on the morning of the 17th that the two fleets met at sea for the first time. Learning of the Russian attack, at 1300 that day Souchon sailed from the Straits with *Yavuz*, *Midilli*, the protected cruiser *Hamidiye* and the torpedo gunboat *Peyk-i Şevket* with the intention of getting between Ebergard and his base at Sevastopol and thereby forcing an action. *Yavuz* was by now suffering from chronic boiler trouble which kept her to a maximum speed of 22 knots so it was not until noon on the 18th that Souchon overhauled Ebergard's fleet by which time it was just twenty miles off Cape Sarych in southern Crimea. The Russian force consisted of five pre-dreadnought battleships, three light cruisers and twelve destroyers, and no sooner had the Ottoman-German fleet heaved into sight than Ebergard turned and opened fire, his flagship *Evstafi* landing a hit on *Yavuz*'s Port No. '3' 5.9in gun with her first salvo and putting it out of action with the loss of sixteen men. Hampered by poor visibility, *Yavuz* returned fire at a range of approximately 7,700yds (7,000m) and struck *Evstafi* four times in ten minutes, a total of nineteen 11in shells being expended. Recognising that he could not prevent Ebergard making Sevastopol, Souchon decided to break off the action and steered for the Bosphorus.[32] Nonetheless, the episode had provided a further example of the poor radio discipline shown by the Russians who were in the habit of transmitting *en clair* throughout the action thereby giving the Germans an immediate insight into their dispositions and intentions.[33]

Yavuz's next sorties were in support of troop movements on the Caucasian front, including shelling the Georgian port of Batumi on 10 December.[34] However, Admiral Ebergard maintained his aggressive posture and on 21 December succeeded in laying a deep minefield off the Bosphorus into which *Yavuz* blundered five days later. Sailing with *Midilli* to conduct operations off Anatolia, at 1335 on the 26th *Yavuz* detonated a mine on the starboard side abreast the conning tower. The explosion tore a 60-square-yard (50m²) hole in the ship's hull but the torpedo bulkhead held. Two minutes later *Yavuz* struck a second on the port side abreast 'E'

25 Baş, *Türk Tarihinde*, p. 112.

26 Lorey, *Die Mittelmeer-Division*, p. 50.

27 Doğan Hacipoğlu, *Osmanlı İmparatorluğu'nun Birinci Dünya Harbi'ne Girişi* (Istanbul: Istanbul Deniz İkmal Grup Komutanlığı, 2000), p. 135.

28 Bernd Langensiepen & Ahmet Güleryüz, *The Ottoman Steam Navy, 1828–1923* (London: Conway Maritime Press, 1995), p. 44.

29 Cited in Halpern, *A Naval History*, p. 64.

30 Baş, *Türk Tarihinde*, p. 122.

31 *Türk Silahlı Kuvvetleri Tarihi*, 5 vols. (Ankara: Genelkurmay Askeri Tarih ve Stratejik Etüt Başkanlığı, 1964), V, p. 72.

32 Baş, *Türk Tarihinde*, pp. 126–7.

33 Georg Kopp, *Two Lone Ships:* Goeben *and* Breslau, trans. Arthur Chambers (London: Hutchinson, 1931), pp. 127–8.

34 Lorey, *Die Mittelmeer-Division*, p. 69, and Saim Besbelli, *Birinci Dünya Harbi'nde Türk Harbi Deniz Harekatı* (Ankara: Genelkurmay Basımevi, 1976), VIII, p. 81.

wing turret, flooding the ship with 600 tons of water and bringing her 2.5ft (800mm) down by the head with a pronounced list to starboard. Again the bulkheads held and within little more than an hour *Yavuz* was safely anchored in the Beikos Roads behind her anti-torpedo netting and having suffered only two fatalities. With no graving dock large enough to accommodate her in the Ottoman Empire, the task of repairing *Yavuz* posed a significant challenge, requiring advisers from the Werdenburg company to be sent out from Germany. Initial repairs, which

Yavuz seen at her main wartime base, the inlet at İstinye (Stenia) on the Bosphorus, in the early years of the conflict. Only *Midilli* could be accommodated in the floating dock seen beyond her. Note the dense column of smoke issuing from the forward funnel, the result of burning Zonguldak coal from Anatolia. The crew is mustered on deck by divisions. *(Bundesarchiv, Koblenz)*

required the construction of two cofferdams to permit access to the damaged hull, were carried out over a four-month period at İstinye by personnel from the imperial shipyards at Wilhelmshaven and Kiel, but limited facilities meant that this damage would quite literally be a thorn in *Yavuz's* side for the rest of the war and long after.[35]

Gallipoli and After

Despite the severity of the mine damage, the Germans were anxious to dispel any notion that *Yavuz* was not seaworthy and she made several limited forays into the Black Sea in January and February 1915. However, the Allied naval assault on Gallipoli which began on 19 February made

35 Baş, *Türk Tarihinde*, pp. 128–31.

her return to full operational service a matter of urgency. Three days after the completion of preliminary repairs to the port side on 28 March 1915, *Yavuz* sailed with *Midilli* and the protected cruisers *Hamidiye* and *Mecidiye* on a mission to shell Odessa, her starboard side as yet unrepaired and despite a shortage of 11in ammunition. However, the loss of *Mecidiye* on a mine (later salvaged and commissioned into the Russian navy as *Prut*) and the appearance first of the protected cruiser *Pamiat Merkuria* and then the bulk of the Russian fleet off Sevastopol on 3 April caused Souchon to turn for the Bosphorus after a brief engagement with only the sinking of two steamers to show for his efforts.[36] Work immediately resumed at İstinye on *Yavuz's* damaged starboard side, which was completed with extensive use of concrete on 1 May. That same month the Gallipoli offensive prompted the landing of two of *Yavuz's* 5.9in guns and the

Turkish labourers carry out the arduous task of replenishing *Yavuz* with coal as her German crewmen stand by. The poorly developed railway infrastructure of the Ottoman Empire required practically all coal to be transported by sea. *(Courtesy Thomas Schmid)*

formation of machine-gun detachments from among her ship's company for service ashore.

On 9 May a series of Russian seaborne attacks culminating in a prolonged assault on the Anatolian ports of Kozlu and Karadeniz Ereğli again brought *Yavuz* out of the Bosphorus. At 0630 the following morning *Yavuz*, with only the destroyer *Numune-i Hamiyet* for company, sighted *Pamiat Merkuria* scouting ahead of the Black Sea Fleet including five battleships led by the now-familiar profile of Admiral Ebergard's flagship *Evstafi*. At 0735 the Russians formed line of battle and fifteen minutes later both sides opened fire at a range of 17,500yds (16,000m). On this occasion, however, it was *Yavuz* which got the worst of the engagement, taking two high-trajectory hits fired at a range of 15,900yds (14,500m) by the battleship *Panteleimon* (ex-*Kniaz Potëmkin Tavricheskii*) that penetrated the forecastle and the port waist before detonating below the battery deck.[37] Although the ship was not seriously damaged, the second hit put Port No. '2' 5.9in gun and its crew out of action and prompted Souchon to cease fire at 0812 before any of *Yavuz*'s 124 heavy-calibre shells had scored a hit. Having drawn the Russian fleet away from the Bosphorus, *Yavuz* turned for home at 1410 and anchored in the Beikos Roads that evening.[38]

It had been a sobering episode for Souchon who during the first year of the war was made all too aware both of the value of his ships to the Ottoman cause and their vulnerability to harassing attacks by the Russians in the Black Sea and sustained pressure from the Allies in the Dardanelles. This realisation was sharpened after *Midilli* was mined off Constantinople on 18 July and put out of action for eight months. Critical though *Yavuz* was to the Ottoman war effort, Souchon therefore became increasingly reluctant to risk her on convoy escort duty in the Black Sea. As he recorded in his war diary,

> *Goeben* is too valuable to the overall conduct of the war to be risked lightly for the escort of coal transports, and night torpedo-based attacks, submarine attacks and mines must be reckoned with. *Goeben* is a political factor in

this country's conduct of the war and should be fully prepared in the event of the Dardanelles being forced.[39]

Souchon confided to his wife that he was powerless against the depredations of Russian destroyers in particular, and that he spent as much time struggling against Turkish inertia as he did against the enemy.[40] As it was, the blunting of the Allied offensive at Gallipoli in August 1915 and the evacuation of the Dardanelles the following January relieved the pressure from that quarter, but the imminent completion of *Imperatritsa Mariya* and *Imperatritsa Ekaterina II*, Russia's first dreadnoughts in the Black Sea, suggested that the Ottoman-German fleet was far from gaining command of those waters.

Stalemate, 1915–18

Although *Yavuz* remained active during the rest of 1915, not until 21 September did she again get to grips with units of the Black Sea Fleet, this time when three Russian destroyers mistook her for *Hamidiye* and put in an attack before identifying their would-be victim and turning away.

On 14 November Souchon was reminded of the danger of submarine attack when *Yavuz* narrowly escaped two torpedoes fired by the Russian submarine *Morzh* off Cape Burnu. Meanwhile, declining production and the loss of most of its colliers had imposed an acute shortage of coal on the Ottoman-German fleet, and an inventory taken at Constantinople on 7 January 1916 found reserves down to 13,500 tons of 'Cardiff' and 900 tons of Zonguldak fuel. This situation was exacerbated that same evening with the sinking by three Russian destroyers of the collier *Karmen* en route to Zonguldak where *Yavuz* was waiting to provide escort. Once news of this development had been received, Kapt.z.S. Ackermann brought *Yavuz* out of Zonguldak and at 0823 on the 8th sighted the perpetrators and immediately gave chase. At 0915 a thick plume of smoke was spotted to the northwest which was soon identified as belonging to a destroyer and the newly completed dreadnought *Imperatritsa Ekaterina II*. At 0940 both sides opened up at a range of 22,000yds (20,000m) but *Yavuz* ceased fire after just four minutes and five salvos when Ackermann realised that he was both outranged and outgunned by *Imperatritsa Ekaterina II*'s battery of twelve 12in guns. Ackermann turned away with *Imperatritsa Ekaterina II* in hot pursuit, and it was only with difficulty that *Yavuz*, her fouled hull long overdue for docking, managed to pull clear and

36 Besbelli, *Birinci Dünya*, p. 125.
37 Lorey, *Die Mittelmeer-Division*, pp. 130–3.
38 Baş, *Türk Tarihinde*, pp. 142–3.

39 Staff, *German Battlecruisers*, p. 124.
40 Halpern, *A Naval History*, p. 232.

make İstinye that evening. As Ackermann stated in concluding his report, '[*Imperatritsa Ekaterina II*] can run and shoot.'[41] *Yavuz* had therefore ceased to be the most powerful vessel in the Black Sea and as time passed assumed more of the mantle of a deterrent fleet-in-being than an offensive threat.

In early February 1916 *Yavuz* and *Midilli* participated in transporting urgently needed men and *matériel* to Trebizond in the face of a major Russian offensive. It is a measure of how desperate was the Turkish situation that *Yavuz* sailed with aviation gasoline and ammunition stowed on deck, Kapt.z.S. Ackermann steering a course which avoided the collier shipping lanes that were constantly harassed by the Russians. No sooner had these supplies been unloaded than *Yavuz* turned for the Straits, anxious to avoid being bottled up in harbour by the Russian navy.[42] Between March and May *Yavuz* was taken in hand at İstinye for long-overdue maintenance, with further work being carried out on the mine damage inflicted in December 1914. It was not until 6 July that she returned to the fray,

this time shelling the Georgian port of Tuapse on the Caucasus front, during which a steamer and several sailing craft were sunk at their moorings. Maintenance immediately resumed at İstinye, with work on the propeller shafts and the opportunity being taken to install new rangefinding equipment, calibration of which was completed in December.[43]

The depredations of *Yavuz* and, above all, *Midilli* on the Caucasus front meanwhile resulted in Admiral Ebergard being relieved in command of the Black Sea Fleet by Vice Admiral Alexander Kolchak in July 1916, the start of whose tenure was marked by an intensive minelaying campaign off the Bosphorus which soon brought all seaborne coal and food supplies into that city to a complete halt. In other respects, however, the pace of events slackened in the naval war in the Black Sea, a reflection of the internal upheavals besetting the Russian Empire and coal shortages in the Ottoman-German fleet, with *Yavuz* herself destined to spend no less than seventeen months in refit and repair at İstinye. By the time she emerged on 13 October 1917 Souchon had taken up command of the 4th Battle Squadron of the High Seas Fleet, his successor in command of the Mittelmeerdivision and the Ottoman navy, Vice Admiral Hubert von Rebeur-Paschwitz, having hoisted his flag in *Yavuz* on 4 September. Her immediate task on returning to service was to prepare for a visit by Kaiser Wilhelm II who came aboard at Constantinople on 16 October for a return trip to Gallipoli, disembarking after a speech to the ship's company on the morning of the 18th.[44] Within a few weeks the outbreak of the Bolshevik Revolution on 7 November 1917 heralded the momentous exit of Russia from the war, which was completed with the signing of the Treaty of Brest-Litovsk on 3 March 1918.

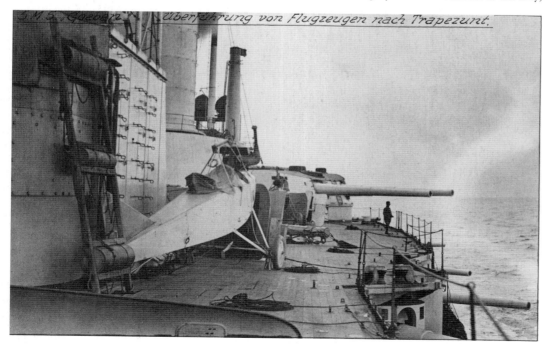

[41] Cited in Staff, *German Battlecruisers*, p. 311.
[42] Baş, *Türk Tarihinde*, p. 149.
[43] Besbelli, *Birinci Dünya*, p. 311.
[44] Baş, *Türk Tarihinde*, p. 150.

The Sundering of the Partnership

The cessation of hostilities with Russia now presented von Rebeur-Paschwitz with the opportunity to attack the Entente Powers in the Aegean in an effort to relieve the pressure on Turkish arms in the Middle East. Aiming to disrupt the Allied supply line to Syria where the Ottoman army was falling back in the face of the British-backed Arab Revolt, the first step in this strategy was to be an attack on the Anglo-French bases on the islands of Imbros and Lemnos in the Aegean.[45] So it was that on 20 January 1918 the Mittelmeerdivision exited the Dardanelles and returned to the waters for which it had been named after an absence of more than three years. Von Rebeur-Paschwitz's force consisted of *Yavuz*, newly under the command of Kapt.z.S. Albert Stoelzel in succession to Ackermann, *Midilli* under Kapt.z.S. Georg von Hippel and the destroyers *Muavenet-i Milliye*, *Numune-i Hamiyet*, *Basra* and *Samsun*. However, despite being in possession of a captured British chart, von Rebeur-Paschwitz had significantly underestimated the danger of Allied minefields of which *Yavuz* was given a first taste shortly after clearing the Straits, the ship striking a mine at 0610. Damage was slight and von Rebeur-Paschwitz pressed on, turning north towards Imbros where at 0742 *Yavuz* began shelling installations and shipping in Kephalo Bay. Challenged by HM destroyers *Lizard* and *Tigress*, *Yavuz* and *Midilli* gave chase towards the north where at 0749, despite unavailing British efforts to lay a smoke-screen, they sighted the monitors *Raglan* and *M28* lying in Kusu Bay. These two were immediately engaged at a range of 10,100yds (9,300m) and succumbed to concentrated fire from both vessels within a few minutes.

There being no further targets in sight, at 0755 von Rebeur-Paschwitz reversed course, with the intention of shelling the harbour at Mudros before proceeding to Lemnos. However, no sooner had the Mittelmeerdivision passed Cape Kephalo than it came under attack from an assortment of British and Greek aircraft, von Rebeur-Paschwitz signalling *Midilli* to move into the van in order to clear his firing arcs. Just as she was passing *Yavuz* to starboard *Midilli* detonated a mine at 0831, the first of five strikes over the course of the next half hour which ended in her loss together with 330 men, the last of the six German light cruisers detached for foreign service before the war. Before this catastrophe had fully unfolded Kapt.z.S. Stoelzel brought *Yavuz* round to take *Midilli* in tow while under persistent though inaccurate aerial bombard-

Another view of the Mittelmeer division at İstinye, this time on 15 June 1916. *Yavuz*, then undergoing refit and repair, is lying alongside in the upper part of the photo with *Midilli* moored beside the floating dock. The most active phase of their involvement in the war was now past. *(INM)*

ment. In doing so he steered her into the same extensive minefield which claimed *Midilli*, and at 0855 *Yavuz* struck her second mine of the day resulting in a 10-degree list to port.[46] Harassed by aircraft from the seaplane carrier HMS *Ark Royal* and with British warships closing in, von Rebeur-Paschwitz reluctantly left *Midilli*'s survivors to be rescued by the destroyers and ordered *Yavuz* to turn for the Straits to preserve his squadron from further disaster. However, not only did she strike a third mine at 0948, but a combination of damaged gyro and magnetic compasses and the misreading of a buoy marking the Nara Burnu bank at the entrance to the

Dardanelles left *Yavuz* aground and at the mercy of Allied air and naval attack. Throwing the engines full astern failed to dislodge *Yavuz*, which over the next six days had to endure incessant aerial bombardment until towed off by *Turgut Reis* and two tugs on the evening of the 26th, reaching Constantinople the following morning. Despite 276 individual attacks, including by seaplanes from *Ark Royal*, just two hits were registered which caused only slight damage owing to the diminutive size of the bombs. So ended the Battle of Imbros and its aftermath, and with it the integrity of the Mittelmeerdivision so carefully husbanded by Admiral Souchon over more than three years of war.

The Central Powers were also concerned to

45 Avcı, 'Goeben (*Yavuz*)', p. 110.

46 Mäkelä, *Auf den Spuren der* Goeben, p. 101.

secure the Russian Black Sea Fleet for possible operations against the Allies in the Aegean as part of the occupation of the Ukraine by German and Austro-Hungarian forces, a campaign which extended as far as the Crimea. It was in support of this strategy that *Yavuz* sailed from the Straits on 30 April 1918 having undergone running repairs at İstinye since January. Two days later

she and *Hamidiye* entered Sevastopol to find it already in German hands, *Yavuz* taking the opportunity to go into dry-dock for the first time since 1912, during which her hull was cleaned and painted. Here she lay under repair and maintenance until ordered to Novorossiysk on 28 June to force the internment of the few surviving effective units of the Russian Black Sea Fleet.

However, she did so in vain because the fleet was found to have been scuttled in the reigning confusion, *Yavuz* returning to the Straits where she spent the rest of the war laid up under ongoing repair at İstinye.[47] Meanwhile, the

[47] *Türk Silahlı Kuvvetleri Tarihi*, V, pp. 387–8; Baş, *Türk Tarihinde*, pp. 161–2.

LIFE ABOARD

Comparatively little has come down to us in print to illuminate life aboard *Goeben/Yavuz* in either her German or Turkish service. Internal arrangements followed those in most capital ships, with ratings messing forward and officers aft. In keeping with Muslim practice, the ship observed Friday as the day of rest rather than Sunday after her arrival in Constantinople. Morale aboard the *Goeben* seems generally to have been excellent, but seaman Otto Runkel who served in her between 1912 and 1916 recalls significant unrest over the quality of food while the ship was lying off Venice in June 1913, some crewmen going so far as to paint the words 'Revolution' on the landward side of the ship, a foretaste of the naval mutiny at Kiel which brought Germany to her knees in November 1918.[48] Tensions remained during *Goeben*'s wartime service, though in this case between German crewmen and their Ottoman counterparts, many of whom were embarked for training. Not only was communication problematic – usually limited to French among the officers – but the Germans had scant respect for the technical ability of the Turkish sailor. The opinion of Otto Runkel was widely shared:

> The Turkish navy was in very poor condition. They had not seen action for a long time and their tech-

nical ignorance was phenomenal. For example, they could not read boiler gauges so chalk was used to mark the point from which the steam pressure was unsafe. This resulted in many burst boilers and casualties.

Moreover, few German officers or men had the slightest interest in Turkish culture and relations were soured by tactlessness and arrogance, particularly with respect to the food, accommodation and amenities in Ottoman vessels, the most serious incidents resulting from disdainful treatment of Turkish officers by German sailors.[49] To that extent, the departure of the German naval mission in November 1918 cannot have come a moment too soon, but there is no doubt that significant improvements had been made to efficiency in the intervening period, a point acknowledged by the Turkish navy.

Yavuz's subsequent career was largely in the capacity of a training ship, Admiral Vehbi Ziya Dümer leaving this record of his time aboard as a cadet at Smyrna (İzmir) in 1924–5:

> There were torpedo parts, cross-sections and engine components on the tables in the classroom. They fitted the classroom with desks. Our teacher was a competent torpedo officer. After

giving us detailed information about torpedoes he provided general technical information about *Yavuz*. An officer in *Yavuz* gave us a lecture on the ship's armament, engines and specifications. [...] In *Yavuz* practical instruction was given in launching a torpedo. On 10 February 1925, the gunnery course began. They provided information on the general features of guns, bores, breechblocks, recoil cylinders, hydraulic mechanisms, fire control, rangefinders and other parts of guns. After these courses we were sent to various ships for training. Most of the cadets remained in *Yavuz*.[50]

The shipboard setting of this education was not altogether satisfactory. Admiral Afif Büyüktuğrul has left this astringent memoir of his days as a divisional commander aboard *Yavuz* when the presence of soldiers exacerbated problems of discipline and morale:

> I arrived at Smyrna to serve in *Yavuz* on 16 March 1927. I was given command of the 4th Division. Our part of ship consisted of quarterdeck, between deck, wardroom, ship's canteen, cabins and chief engineer's cabin, armoured deck cabins, navy band, engineering officers' cabins and passages. There were no scuttles in the junior officers' cabins. Ventilation was provided by large tubes extending to the upper decks. Smells of *rakı* [Turkish anise-flavoured spirit] would issue from the ventilation pipes in the evening because the engineer officers drank alcohol with their meals in their cabins rather than in the wardroom. Since insufficient numbers of men were recruited to man the ship, there were only sixty men in each division which was not enough. They could only clean and take part in the ceremonial duties. The ship wore the flag of a rear admiral but served as a naval headquarters. The exterior of the ship was clean but the interior was not. The soldiers on board used to throw their cigarette stubs on the floor. Whenever I saw a soldier smoking a cigarette in my part of ship, I used to grab his cigarette box and throw it into the sea. We used to stand under the flagstaff and salute the flag

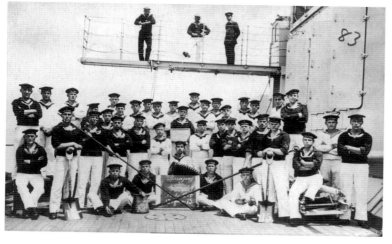

Stokers of *Yavuz*, sorely tried during the first weeks of the war, pose with the tools of their trade and a concertina in 1915. Although Turkish officers and ratings were embarked for training purposes there was little fraternisation between the allies. *(INM)*

Ottoman Empire, assailed from the Balkans and the Middle East, had run out of strategic options, and on 16 October 1918 the new Grand Vizier Ahmed İzzed Paşa sued for peace. Two weeks later on the 30th the Armistice of Mudros was signed aboard the battleship HMS *Agamemnon*. On 2 November von Rebeur-Paschwitz and the entire German naval mission

left Constantinople for Berlin having formally ceded *Yavuz* to the Turks. Under the terms of the Armistice, *Yavuz*, then lying at İstinye, was relieved of her ammunition, breechblocks, gunsights and boiler hatches, and towed to İzmit under escort by a British destroyer, there to remain for five long years with steam and power provided by the gunboat *Zuhaf*.

Yavuz in the Turkish Navy

The successful conclusion of the Greco-Turkish War (1919–23) and the entry of the Turkish army into Istanbul on 6 October 1923 ended *Yavuz*'s long sojourn under British control. Still unable to proceed under her own power, she was towed first to Büyükada and then to Moda Bay where she was cleaned and painted before being

The crew of *Yavuz* mustered on deck by divisions. The *al bayrak* at half mast may date the photo to November 1938 when the ship conveyed the body of Mustafa Kemal from Istanbul across the Sea of Marmara to İzmit for onward journey to Ankara. *(INM)*

morning and evening. Ship commanders and navy commanders were saluted with a boatswain's pipe whenever they came aboard or disembarked. German training methods were not yet used in *Yavuz*. Soldiers were trained only in boat pulling. In

the evenings they were taught reading and writing skills, elementary maths and civics.[51]

[48] http://www.orderfirstworldwar.com/the-salient/2012/02/my-service-on-the-battle-cruiser-goeben.htm

[49] Sondhaus, *The Great War at Sea*, pp. 111–12, and Langensiepen, Nottelmann & Krüsmann, *Halbmond und Kaiseradler*, pp. 15–19.

[50] Vehbi Ziya Dümer, *Amiral Vehbi Ziya Dümer'in Anıları*, ed. Osman Alpay Kaynak (Istanbul: Deniz Basımevi, 2003), p. 82.

[51] Afif Büyüktuğrul, *Cumhuriyet Donanmasının Kuruluşu Sırasında 60 Yıl Hizmet* (Istanbul: Deniz Basımevi, 2005), pp. 124–6.

Yavuz lying in the new 26,000-ton German-built floating dock at Gölcük in 1927. *(INM)*

moored between two buoys off Bebek and opened to visitors for twenty days. On 29 October she greeted the proclamation of the Republic of Turkey by firing a salute off Bebek, being subsequently towed to İzmit where she remained for the next few years. On 3 February 1925 the Turkish government established the Ministry of Marine whose first priority was the repair and recommissioning of *Yavuz*, a point reiterated by the founder of modern Turkey and Prime Minister Mustafa Kemal during a visit to the ship on 21 September:

> This is my first visit to *Yavuz*. Until now *Yavuz* has been a German ship with a Turkish flag. Even though she is damaged, she is more valuable in her current state now than she has ever been. We are going to mould this ship into the strong and powerful battleship the Turkish

Quarterdeck fittings struck in connection with a gunnery exercise in the Sea of Marmara in the 1930s or '40s. 'D' I Iin turret nearest the camera was given the name 'Turgut' in Turkish service in recognition of the great Ottoman privateer and admiral Turgut Reis (1485–1565) known in the West as Dragut. *(INM)*

nation needs. This power will serve you as a weapon and serve us in foreign policy to become a source of pride.[52]

Since Turkey still had no docking facilities capable of accommodating *Yavuz*, an invitation to tender was issued for the construction of a 26,000-ton floating dock and an offer of £225,000 accepted from the German Filander company, which duly delivered in December 1926. A further invitation to tender was made for overseeing the refit at the Gölcük naval shipyard and an offer accepted from Chantiers et Ateliers de St-Nazaire (Penhöet) on 5 December 1926. However, a botched first docking resulted in the collapse of several compartments in the floating dock requiring repairs both to dock and ship, and it was not until 20 August 1927 that *Yavuz* was safely out of the water. An inquiry into the incident resulted in Minister of Marine İhsan Eryavuz being convicted of embezzlement and the abolition of the ministry itself. Long-overdue repairs to the hull, including wartime mine damage, were completed in February 1930, after which the refit continued alongside her old companion the battleship *Turgut Reis*, now reduced to a repair hulk. By the time she recommissioned on 11 August 1930 under the revised name of *Yavuz Selim* (commuted simply to *Yavuz* in 1936), her displacement had increased to 23,100 tons, with modifications to the hull

Yavuz seen after her 1927–30 refit. *(INM)*

having reduced its length by 19.7in (500mm) while increasing the beam by 3.9in (100mm).[53] New coal-fired boilers were fitted and a four-hour trial yielded an average speed of 27 knots.

A French fire-control system was installed for the main battery and two of the casemated 5.9in guns removed leaving a total of eight. However, armour protection was not upgraded and *Yavuz* retained just 2in (51mm) of plating over the magazines.

For *Yavuz* the 1930s were characterised by naval manoeuvres and an increasing number of diplomatic missions in the Black Sea and eastern Mediterranean in her capacity as flagship of the new Turkish fleet. The most momentous of the former came in September 1933 and involved nineteen ships of the battlefleet together with the reserve fleet, submarine fleet, minesweeper fleet and motor torpedo boat flotilla, to which aircraft were added during exercises off the Dardanelles the following year.[54] These manoeuvres grew in complexity as the Turkish fleet was slowly expanded and modernised during the 1930s. Following Mustafa Kemal's injunctions in 1925, the fleet also began projecting this enhanced capability abroad, beginning with a diplomatic

Marshal Kliment Voroshilov (second from the left in the main group) rounds 'B' wing turret during a tour of inspection of *Yavuz* in November 1933. He was in Turkey at the head of the Soviet delegation to celebrate the tenth anniversary of the Turkish Republic. Note the pair of paravanes stowed under the 11in guns. *(INM)*

---

[52] Cited in Baş, *Türk Tarihinde*, p. 185.

[53] İskender Tunaboylu, *Osmanlıdan Cumhuriyete Yavuz Zırhlısı* (Istanbul: Deniz Basımevi, 2006), pp. 77–8.

[54] Baş, *Türk Tarihinde*, p. 203.

Goeben's bell preserved in the Istanbul Naval Museum. (INM)

Yavuz flying the al barak from the stern during the Second World War. Note the stern anchor and the 1.6in Bofors guns mounted on the quarterdeck. (INM)

visit by *Yavuz* to the Bulgarian port of Varna on 23 September 1933 against the backdrop of fears of Bulgarian rearmament. In October 1933 she received King Alexander and Queen Maria of Yugoslavia aboard in Istanbul followed a month later by the Soviet delegation led by Marshal Kliment Voroshilov to the tenth anniversary celebrations of the foundation of the Turkish Republic. *Yavuz* also hosted visits by Rezā Shāh Pahlavi of Iran at Trebizond in June 1934 and

Amir Abdullah of Jordan in 1937. Once finances permitted, *Yavuz* also became the first vessel of the Turkish navy to make a foreign cruise, visiting the British Mediterranean Fleet at Malta and the Hellenic Navy at Phaleron Bay between November and December 1936.[55]

These developments and above all the increasingly aggressive posture of Italy in the eastern Mediterranean resulted in July 1936 in the signing of the Montreux Convention by which Turkey regained control over the Bosphorus and the Dardanelles, which had been demilitarised under the Treaty of Lausanne in 1923. The signing of the convention was marked by a cere-

mony in *Yavuz* which two years later was given the honour of conveying the body of Mustafa Kemal from Istanbul to İzmit following his death on 10 November 1938. It was fitting that the symbolic vessel of the Turkish Republic should transport the Father of the Turks across the Sea of Marmara for onward journey to his final resting place in Ankara.

The Second World War and After

Reflecting the armed neutrality of its government, the Turkish navy responded to the outbreak of the Second World War in September 1939 by assuming a wholly defensive posture, the bulk of the fleet moving from its main base at Gölcük in the easternmost reaches of the Sea of Marmara to Erdek Bay closer to the Dardanelles. *Yavuz*, meanwhile, remained at Gölcük behind anti-torpedo netting as a measure against air-launched torpedoes, her mainmast removed to complicate efforts by a would-be enemy to establish her course.[56] More generally, the Turkish navy responded to the increasing threat of air attack by stationing an army air defence battalion at Gölcük in late 1940, and in the acquisition of modern anti-aircraft armament from the British in 1941. Where *Yavuz* was concerned, this resulted in the mounting of four 3in (76mm) guns, ten 1.6in (40mm) Bofors guns, and four 0.79in (20mm) Oerlikon guns, later increased to twenty-six Bofors and twenty-four Oerlikon guns. The Bofors and Oerlikon procurement involved the dispatch of four naval

The Turkish navy's farewell ceremony for *Yavuz* on 7 June 1973, the date she was towed to the breakers marking the end of a sixty-year career. She had received the hull number B70 on Turkey's accession to NATO in 1952. (INM)

55 Afif Büyüktuğrul, *Cumhuriyet Donanması* (Istanbul: Deniz Basımevi, 1967), p. 76.
56 İ. Bülent Işın, *Cumhuriyet Bahriyesi Kronolojisi 1923'ten 2005'e* (Istanbul: Deniz Basımevi, 2006), p. 44.

officers to Egypt to receive training in these systems from the British.[57] Aside from air attack, the Turkish navy was also much preoccupied with mines, large fields of which it laid in the Straits from 1942 when Turkey came within an ace of going to war with the Soviet Union. This action in turn confined the navy to the Sea of Marmara, and in 1943 degaussing equipment was purchased from Britain and installed in *Yavuz*, *Hamidiye*, *Mecidiye* and other units as a measure against magnetic mines.[58]

The first priority after the end of the Second World War was to clear the Straits of mines thereby allowing the fleet to make a welcome return to Smyrna after many years of absence. The post-war restructuring of the Turkish navy brought it firmly under the influence of the United States Navy, the first manifestation of which came on 5 April 1946 when a US squadron led by the battleship *Missouri* (q.v.) reached Istanbul, she and *Yavuz* exchanging nineteen-gun salutes in the Bosphorus. *Yavuz* continued to participate in the annual fleet manoeuvres each September until 1950 when she discharged her last duties in the Aegean. *Yavuz* was decommissioned on 20 December but received the hull number B70 on Turkey's accession to NATO in 1952. Although stricken from the navy list on 14 November 1954, *Yavuz* remained at Gölcük where she served as the headquarters of Battle Fleet Command and Mine Fleet Command until 1960. An offer to sell her to the West German government for preservation as a museum was declined in 1963 and economic constraints kept the Turkish navy from taking that step on its own account. In 1971 she was sold to the Mechanical and Chemical Industry Corporation for scrapping, and after a farewell ceremony was towed to the breakers on 7 June 1973, the demolition being completed in February 1976. Before doing so two of her propellers were dispatched to Navy Command and a third to the Istanbul Naval Museum together with a large assortment of other smaller items and memorabilia, while her foremast was erected at the naval academy.

Yavuz gave two years' operational service to the German navy and thirty-six to the Ottoman and Turkish fleets. She not only had the distinction of being the last battlecruiser and the last dreadnought in existence outside of the United States, but occupies a special place in the hearts of the Turkish people among whom she has been celebrated in song and verse. Her memory lives on in the shape of the frigate TCG *Yavuz* (F-240)

which, appropriately enough, was completed at the Blohm & Voss shipyard in Hamburg in 1987, seventy-five years after her illustrious forebear.

Sources

Memoir of Otto Runkel: http://www.orderfirstworldwar.com/the-salient/2012/02/my-service-on-the-battle-cruiser-goeben.htm [accessed July 2016]

Avcı, Sinan, 'Goeben (Yavuz)' in *Deniz Kuvvetleri Dergisi* 579 (November 2000), pp. 104–13

Baş, Ersan, *Türk Tarihinde* Yavuz *Zırhlısının Rolü* [The Role of the Battlecruiser *Yavuz* in Turkish History] (Istanbul: Deniz Basımevi, 2009)

Besbelli, Saim, *Birinci Dünya Harbi'nde Türk Harbi Deniz Harekatı* [Turkish Naval Operations during the First World War] (Ankara: Genelkurmay Basımevi, 1976)

Büyüktuğrul, Admiral Afif, *Cumhuriyet Donanması* [The Republican Navy] (Istanbul: Deniz Basımevi, 1967)

_____, *Cumhuriyet Donanmasının Kuruluşu Sırasında 60 Yıl Hizmet* [The Republican Navy: Sixty Years of Service] (Istanbul: Deniz Basımevi, 2005)

Campbell, John, *Naval Weapons of World War Two* (London: Conway, 1985)

Dümer, Admiral Vehbi Ziya, *Amiral Vehbi Ziya Dümer'in Anıları* [The Memoirs of Admiral Vehbi Ziya Dumer], ed. Osman Alpay Kaynak (Istanbul: Deniz Basımevi, 2003)

Gökkent, Giyasettin, 'Balkan Harbi'nde Istanbul'a Gelen Yabancı Harp Gemileri' [Foreign Warships in Istanbul during the Balkan Wars] in *Hayat Tarih Mecmuası*, 8 September 1971, pp. 24–5

Gürdeniz, Cem, ed., *Cumhuriyet Donanması* [The Republican Navy] (Istanbul: Seyir Hidrografi ve Oşinografi Daire Başkanlığı Basımevi, 2000)

Hacipoğlu, Doğan, *Osmanlı İmparatorluğu'nun Birinci Dünya Harbi'ne Girişi* [An Introduction to the Ottoman Empire during the First World War] (Istanbul: Istanbul Deniz İkmal Grup Komutanlığı, 2000)

Halpern, Paul G., *The Mediterranean Naval Situation, 1908–1914* (Cambridge, Mass.: Harvard University Press, 1971)

_____, *The Naval War in the Mediterranean 1914–1918* (Annapolis, Md.: Naval Institute Press, 1987)

_____, *A Naval History of World War I* (London: UCL Press, 1994)

Herwig, Holger H., *'Luxury Fleet': The Imperial German Navy 1888–1918* (London:

George Allen & Unwin, 1980)

Hikmet Bayur, Yusuf, *Türk İnkılabı Tarihi* [A History of the Turkish Revolution] (3 vols. in 10 tomes, Istanbul: Maarif Matbaası, 1940–67)

Hüner, Hans, *Unter zwei Flaggen: Die Lebens und Kampfgeschichte S.M.S.* Breslau-Midilli (Potsdam: Verlag Breslau-Midilli, 1930)

Işın, İ. Bülent, *Cumhuriyet Bahriyesi Kronolojisi 1923'ten 2005'e* [The Republican Spring: A Chronology, 1923–2005] (Istanbul: Deniz Basımevi, 2006)

Kopp, Georg, *Two Lone Ships:* Goeben *and* Breslau, trans. Arthur Chambers (London: Hutchinson, 1931)

Langensiepen, Bernd, & Ahmet Güleryüz, *The Ottoman Steam Navy, 1828–1923* (London: Conway Maritime Press, 1995)

Langensiepen, Bernd, Dirk Nottelmann & Jochen Krüsmann, *Halbmond und Kaiseradler:* Goeben *und* Breslau *am Bosporus, 1914–1918* (Hamburg: Mittler & Sohn Verlag, 1999)

Lorey, Rear Admiral Hermann, *Der Krieg zur See 1914–1918. Der Krieg in den türkischen Gewässern*, vol. I: *Die Mittelmeer-Division* (Berlin: S. Mittler & Sohn Verlag, 1928; typescript translation by H. S. Babbitt available at Naval War College, Newport, R.I.)

McLaughlin, Redmond, *The Escape of the* Goeben: *Prelude to Gallipoli* (London: Seeley Service, 1974)

Mäkelä, Matti E., *Auf den Spuren der* Goeben (Munich: Bernard & Graefe, 1979)

Miller, Geoff, *Superior Force: The Conspiracy Behind the Escape of* Goeben *and* Breslau (Hull: University of Hull Press, 1995)

Mütercimler, Erol, *Destanlaşan Gemiler* [Ships of Destiny] (Istanbul: Kastaş Yayınları, 1987)

Sondhaus, Lawrence, *The Great War at Sea: A Naval History of the First World War* (Cambridge: Cambridge University Press, 2014)

Staff, Gary, *German Battlecruisers of World War One: Their Design, Construction and Operations* (Barnsley, S. Yorks.: Seaforth Publishing, 2014)

Tunaboylu, İskender, *Osmanlıdan Cumhuriyete* Yavuz *Zırhlısı* [The Battlecruiser *Yavuz* and the Ottoman Empire] (Istanbul: Deniz Basımevi, 2006)

Türk Silahlı Kuvvetleri Tarihi [A History of the Turkish Armed Forces], 5 vols. (Ankara: Genelkurmay Askeri Tarih ve Stratejik Etüt Başkanlığı, 1964)

Yavuz, Celalettin, *Osmanlı Bahriyesinde Yabancı Misyonlar* [Foreign Missions during the Ottoman Spring] (Istanbul: Deniz İkmal Grup K.lığı Basımevi, 2001)

---

[57] Erol Mütercimler, *Destanlaşan Gemiler* (Istanbul: Kastaş Yayınları, 1987), p. 154.

[58] Işın, *Cumhuriyet Bahriyesi*, p. 49.

Kaiserliche und Königliche Kriegsmarine
The Battleship *Viribus Unitis* (1911)

◆

Lawrence Sondhaus

AUSTRIA-HUNGARY'S foothold on the Adriatic Sea constituted the smallest coastline of any of the six great powers in pre-1914 Europe.[1] It followed logically that she should traditionally have the sixth largest navy among them, and that the other five powers should ultimately build more dreadnought battleships than the Dual Monarchy. Nonetheless, the Imperial and Royal Austro-Hungarian Navy was the first after the British and German fleets to have a dreadnought in commission in European waters. The vessel in question, SMS *Viribus Unitis* ('with united forces'), took her name from the Latin motto of the Emperor Franz Joseph, reflecting the old monarch's optimism that the multinational character of the Dual Monarchy was a source of strength rather than a fatal weakness.

Mediterranean Ambitions

'We are a Mediterranean power.' So asserted Admiral Count Rudolf Montecuccoli, commander-in-chief of the Austro-Hungarian navy from 1904 to 1913 and father of its dreadnought programme in a speech delivered in October 1912. The occasion was an address to the Delegations, the representatives of the Austrian and Hungarian halves of the Dual Monarchy who convened annually to approve the empire's common budget. By that time the battleship *Viribus Unitis* had completed her sea trials, her three sisters were in various stages of construction, and Montecuccoli had begun to lay the political groundwork for a second class of

Viribus Unitis leading units of the Austro-Hungarian fleet to Trieste on 1 July 1914. The occasion could scarcely be more sombre as she carries the bodies of the Archduke Franz Ferdinand and the Archduchess Sophie, murdered three days earlier in Sarajevo. (*Verein K.u.K. Kriegsmarine – Archiv, Vienna (VKK)*)

four larger dreadnoughts on the reasoning that Austria-Hungary required 'a stronger navy, with which we can assume our proper place among the Mediterranean powers'.[2] In this quest he enjoyed the patronage of the heir presumptive to the imperial throne, the Archduke Franz Ferdinand, who had first embraced the cause of a larger fleet in the early 1890s when he cruised to India, Australia, New Zealand and the Far East including China and Japan aboard the protected cruiser *Kaiserin Elisabeth*. From 1910 the Archduke had served as patron of the Österreichischer Flottenverein (Austro-Hungarian Navy League), an influential political lobby founded six years earlier on the model of the highly successful Deutscher Flottenverein. This

[1] The editor would like to acknowledge Thomas Zimmel and Edwin Sieche of the Verein K.u.K. Kriegsmarine in Vienna for their generous assistance in supplying photos for this chapter, and likewise Steve McLaughlin and Lars Ahlberg.

[2] *Stenographische Protokolle der Delegation des Reichsrathes*, 50 vols. (Vienna: k.k. Hof- und Staatsdruckerei, 1868–1918), XLVI (15 October 1912), p. 903.

organisation brought together a broad coalition of old and new money, aristocrats as well as industrialists, and counted key political leaders from across the multinational empire among its membership. In return for this degree of support, the navy had to build its dreadnoughts in Austria-Hungary entirely from domestic resources and at a far higher cost than if ordered from shipyards in Britain or Germany. In the immediate pre-war years the navy grew to consume one quarter of the Austro-Hungarian defence outlay, a remarkable development for a country which, in a strategic sense, was practically landlocked.

How had this happened? Austria acquired a significant foothold on the Adriatic in 1797 when it was ceded by treaty the territory of the former Venetian Republic together with the vestiges of its fleet. The navy, which traces its institutional origins to the early nineteenth century, remained predominantly Italian in leadership and manpower and was based in Venice until the revolutions of 1848 when much of the fleet deserted. The navy was subsequently rebuilt into a service which more closely reflected the multinational character of the Habsburg domains, with an ethnic German majority in the officer corps and a Croatian plurality on the lower deck, operating from a main base at Pola (Pula) on the Istrian peninsula. During the War of 1866 against Prussia and Italy, Vizeadmiral (Vice Admiral) Wilhelm von Tegetthoff led Austria's first ironclad fleet to victory in the Battle of Lissa (Vis) against a more numerous Italian opponent, but the service subsequently languished until Franz Ferdinand took an interest in it just before the turn of the century. The rapid expansion of the fleet was reflected in the increasing size of its newest classes of pre- and semi-dreadnought battleships, all built in threes: the 5,600-ton Monarch-class (commissioned 1897–8), the 8,300-ton Habsburg-class (1902–4), the 10,600-ton Erzherzog-class (1906–7), and the 14,500-ton Radetzky class (1910–11). The Delegations approved funding for the latter three vessels in November 1906, a month before the commissioning of HMS *Dreadnought* set a new standard for battleship design. Work began on the first two Radetzkys during 1907 but the third unit, *Zrínyi*, was not laid down until January 1909, making her the last pre-dreadnought begun by any navy. Political as well as practical considerations (Austria-Hungary had few slips capable of building vessels so large) therefore conspired to delay Montecuccoli in his efforts to enter the dreadnought race until most of the other European powers already had ships of the type under construction. Nonetheless, the relatively

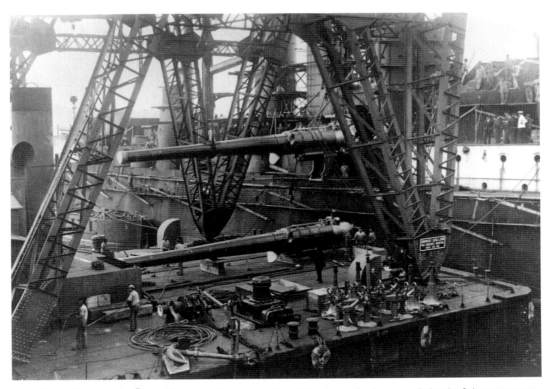

Two of *Viribus Unitis*'s twelve Škoda 12in guns in the course of installation from a floating crane during the fitting-out process at Stabilimento Tecnico Triestino in 1911 or 1912. She was the first capital ship of any nation to be completed with triple turrets. Although foreign technology was used under licence, the Tegetthoff-class battleships were entirely the product of Austro-Hungarian industry. *(NHHC/NH 87185)*

efficient naval-industrial complex which coalesced on Montecuccoli's watch meant that average construction time trailed only that of the dreadnoughts built by the British and Germans.

Since 1882 Austria-Hungary had been joined with Germany and Italy in the Triple Alliance, within which the Dual Monarchy and Italy tolerated each other for the sake of having German support, for the former against Russia in the Balkans, and for the latter against France. But after 1900 the Italians repaired their relationship with the French and the alliance of France with Britain from 1904 onwards left most Italian statesmen doubting the wisdom of their country's German connection. Austria-Hungary already viewed her ostensible ally across the Adriatic as a likely enemy even before 1908, when Italy criticised her annexation of Bosnia-Herzegovina from the Ottoman Empire, causing a further deterioration in relations. In the wake of this crisis Montecuccoli proposed a new fleet plan to Franz Joseph, adding four battleships to the twelve pre- and semi-dreadnoughts already built or under construction as the spearhead of a fleet including twelve cruisers, twenty-four destroyers, seventy-two torpedo boats and twelve submarines. It was as a result of this plan that the subject of this chapter came to be built.

Design

In October 1908, the same month Austria-Hungary annexed Bosnia-Herzegovina, the Naval Section (Marinesektion) of the War Ministry authorised a study of dreadnought designs. By the following spring the Dual Monarchy's naval architects had produced five competing plans, all of which were shelved on the news that Italy was contemplating a dreadnought design (eventually *Dante Alighieri*) with an innovative main battery composed of triple turrets rather than the twin turrets which had hitherto been standard in British and German dreadnought construction. After briefly considering a design modelled on Germany's 24,300-ton *Kaiser* (laid down in December 1909 but then still in the design phase) mounting ten 12in (305mm) guns in five twin turrets, on 27 April 1909 Montecuccoli accepted plans proposed by Siegfried Popper, designer of all twelve of Austria-Hungary's pre-dreadnoughts, for a 20,000-ton dreadnought with twelve 12in guns in four triple turrets.

In the planning stages Popper had preferred a hull length closer to 580ft (177m) to distribute the weight properly, but for budgetary reasons was limited by Montecuccoli to no more than 500ft (152.4m). Popper saved weight and cost by

Above: The turret-mounting shop at the Škoda works at Pilsen in Bohemia showing one of *Szent István*'s turrets in the course of assembly. Note the 2.75in guns mounted atop the turret. *(Courtesy Philippe Caresse)*

Left: A second view of the 12in gun installation process at Trieste, this time those for No. '2' turret. *(VKK)*

reducing the subdivision of the hull which consisted of a centreline bulkhead running from bow to stern flanked by unusually large water-tight compartments. Only the engine rooms and boiler rooms were flanked by lateral watertight bulkheads. Popper also allowed for just 8ft (2.45m) between the exterior armour plating and the interior torpedo bulkhead, well below the German standard of nearly 15ft (4.5m), a provision vindicated in the survival of several battle-ships and battlecruisers of the High Seas Fleet following severe hull damage at Jutland and else-where. This combination of design features left the ship with a metacentric height of just over 3ft (0.98m), less than half that of comparable dread-noughts in other navies, but the dire conse-quences of this flaw would not become apparent until 1918.

Popper's final design called for a vessel 499ft (152.1m) long, 90ft (27.3m) in the beam and having a deep-load draught of 29ft (8.8m) leaving nearly 20ft (6m) of freeboard.[3] The design also included an 11in (280mm) waterline belt along with 11in armour protecting the

turrets, barbettes and conning tower, and an armoured deck of between 1.4in and 2in (36–50mm) of plate from bow to stern. Such protection, slightly heavier than the British stan-dard, also followed the German model. Compared to the most formidable dreadnought in service at the time the design was approved – HMS *Bellerophon* of 18,600 tons commissioned in February 1909 – Popper's dreadnought was shorter, wider and had a deeper draught. Displacing an additional 1,000 tons, she was also a knot slower, but her twelve 12in guns, capable of twenty degrees of elevation, were divided equally among four superfiring centreline turrets in which all twelve guns could be trained to fire a 6-ton broadside on either beam. This was a marked improvement over the first generation of British and German dreadnoughts whose layout included wing turrets capable of firing only forward, aft and on one or other beam. Thus, for example, *Bellerophon* had ten 12in guns in five turrets but could only fire a broadside of eight, while SMS *Nassau*, commissioned as Germany's first dreadnought in October 1909, had twelve 11in (280mm) guns in six turrets but likewise could fire only a broadside of eight. The super-firing arrangement also permitted all six guns in the forward and after turrets to fire ahead and astern respectively by contrast with the Italian

design (the future *Dante Alighieri*) which mounted all four of her triple turrets flush with the forecastle deck thereby preventing her bearing more than three heavy guns either ahead or astern.

Popper's array of secondary armament, some-what excessive by British standards, followed the German preference for a more robust defence against attacks by destroyers or torpedo boats. It consisted of twelve 5.9in (150mm) guns in indi-vidual casemates amidships, six on either side on the main deck, together with eighteen 2.75in (70mm) unshielded guns distributed around the ship on and above the forecastle deck; three 2.6in (66mm) anti-aircraft guns were subsequently mounted on No. '2' and '3' turrets. The arma-ment was completed by four 21in (533mm) torpedo tubes, one each in the bow, stern and on either beam. Propulsion consisted of twelve Yarrow boilers powering four Parsons turbines to turn four screws, providing a best speed of 20 knots. At a full load displacement of 21,595 tons and with nearly 1,850 tons of coal in her bunkers, the ship would have a cruising range of 4,200 nautical miles at 10 knots.

For political reasons, Montecuccoli intended to bring Popper's vision to fruition by having recourse to domestic suppliers only. The San Marco shipyard of the Stabilimento Tecnico Triestino would build the hulls of the dread-noughts, while the same firm's Sant'Andrea works manufactured the Yarrow boilers and Parsons turbines under licence. All guns would come from the Škoda works of Pilsen (Plzeň) in Bohemia, while the Witkowitz (Vítkovice) armoury in Moravia produced Krupp cemented armour, again under licence. Torpedoes were manufac-tured by the famous Whitehead firm in Fiume.

[3] For a sectional plan, see Antony Preston, *Battleships of World War One* (London: Arms and Armour Press, 1972), p. 260.

Delay and Completion

Franz Joseph received his first briefing on the fleet plan, including the dreadnought programme, in January 1909, three months after the annexation of Bosnia-Herzegovina. The ongoing crisis in the Balkans helped Montecuccoli secure the emperor's endorsement, after which he circulated the plan among the appropriate ministries in Vienna and Budapest. The plan had yet to be made public in Austria-Hungary when details of it appeared in the Italian press in April. Italy had included a modest sum in her 1907–8 naval estimates to start a dreadnought programme of her own, but aside from producing the triple-turret design had taken no action by the spring of 1909. News of Austria-Hungary's plans changed that and the Regia Marina laid down her first dreadnought, *Dante Alighieri*, in June, the same month Russia did so in the shape of the four units of the Gangut class, likewise mounting 12in guns in triple turrets. The Italian action increased the urgency for Austria-Hungary to begin work on her own dreadnoughts, but unfortunately for Montecuccoli a political crisis in Budapest left the Hungarian half of the empire without a government between April 1909 and May 1910, thus forcing the cancellation of the October 1909 meeting of the Delegations at which the joint Austro-Hungarian budget for 1910 was to be approved. Meanwhile, the launching of *Radetzky* in July 1909 freed a large slip at the Stabilimento Tecnico Triestino yard whose workers could not be retained for much longer without a new contract. The Witkowitz armoury and the Škoda works faced a similar hiatus in their own lucrative relationship with the navy. To avoid a costly curtailment of their operations, later that month Montecuccoli's partners among Austria-Hungary's leading industrialists offered to undertake the construction of as many as three dreadnoughts 'at their own risk', on the understanding that the government would purchase them as soon as the Delegations reconvened to authorise a budget.[4]

This extra-constitutional arrangement enabled Škoda and Witkowitz to start work on the guns and armour for *Viribus Unitis* and her first sister *Tegetthoff*, while Stabilimento Tecnico Triestino began assembling steel and other materials. On 24 July 1910 the keel of *Viribus Unitis* was finally laid at San Marco, fifteen months after her design was approved, and on 24 September *Tegetthoff* was laid down on an adjacent slip. In

---

[4] Cited in Louis A. Gebhard, Jr., 'Austria-Hungary's Dreadnought Squadron: The Naval Outlay of 1911' in *Austrian History Yearbook* 4–5 (1968–9), pp. 245–58; p. 252.

The spectacle of *Viribus Unitis*'s launch at Trieste on 24 June 1911.
(Library of Congress/LC-B2-2300-14)

the meantime, the resolution of the Hungarian political crisis in May 1910 paved the way for the Delegations to meet that October, at which point Montecuccoli won retroactive approval for the first two dreadnoughts, along with the rest of the navy's budget for 1910. A second session of the Delegations, which convened in December, approved the entire fleet plan of January 1909, including funding to start the second pair of dreadnoughts under the navy's budget for 1911.

Like the recent German fleet programmes, the Austro-Hungarian plan provided for automatic replacement of warships, but the Delegations gave Montecuccoli even more generous terms than the Reichstag had provided Admiral Tirpitz, including a standard service life of twenty years for battleships (rather than twenty-five) and fifteen for cruisers (rather than twenty). In order to win Hungarian approval, Montecuccoli promised to spend in Hungary the proportion of the plan cost equivalent to that country's contribution to the joint Austro-Hungarian budget. The corresponding commitment to spend 36.4 per cent of the construction outlay in Hungary would in time require building dreadnoughts there too, not just in Trieste. After *Viribus Unitis* was launched on 24 June 1911, the slip she vacated was readied for the third dreadnought, to be named *Prinz Eugen*, but the fourth and final ship of the class, called *Szent István* after Stephen, the patron saint of Hungary, was promised to the Danubius shipyard of Fiume (Rijeka), the largest port on Hungary's narrow Adriatic foothold.

By the time Montecuccoli retired in February 1913, *Viribus Unitis* was already in service,

Tegetthoff and *Prinz Eugen* had been launched and *Szent István* was half completed. But the proudest day of his career remained 24 June 1911, the day *Viribus Unitis* was launched. Franz Ferdinand cut short a state visit to attend the coronation of King George V in London to return to Trieste for the most elaborate celebration which ever attended the christening of an Austro-Hungarian warship. The dignitaries included a number of Habsburg archdukes and arch-

duchesses along with most of the empire's leading politicians and industrialists. The Emperor Franz Joseph, then eighty-one, did not make the journey from Vienna to Trieste but used the occasion to award Montecuccoli the prestigious Order of the Golden Fleece which was bestowed upon the admiral by the heir to the throne. The festivities that morning reached a climax when Franz Ferdinand's sister, the Archduchess Maria Annunciata, christened the new dreadnought *Viribus Unitis*, after which the ship slid down the ways into Trieste harbour. A carefully choreographed occasion had almost been ruined by a last-minute strike by local metalworkers, who, with the launch date already set, refused to put in the overtime hours necessary to meet the deadline unless all workers at the San Marco shipyard received a pay rise. Aside from this eleventh-hour glitch, the completion of *Viribus Unitis* had been free of labour problems, the construction of the hull alone having provided steady employment for over 2,000 workers. *Viribus Unitis* was then towed to the arsenal at the Pola naval base for fitting out, setting a precedent followed in the completion of the other units of her class. She began sea trials in August 1912, and on 18 September recorded a best speed of 20.49 knots, slightly faster than any of her sisters

Another view of *Viribus Unitis* during her sea trials in August or September 1912. *(NHHC/NH 87167)*

achieved in their trials. *Viribus Unitis* became fleet flagship on commissioning (5 December 1912), a status she held for the rest of her career.

Arrival

Montecuccoli's political and financial manoeuvres combined with the comparative efficiency of Austro-Hungarian shipbuilding enabled the Dual Monarchy to catch up with her competitors in the dreadnought race. The completion of *Viribus Unitis* in October 1912 made Austria-Hungary the third European power after Britain and Germany to have a dreadnought in service. Italy's *Dante Alighieri*, laid down thirteen months before *Viribus Unitis*, was not commissioned until January 1913, and Russia's first dreadnoughts, begun like *Dante Alighieri* in June 1909, finally entered service in the early months of the Great War. The delays in the Italian and Russian projects therefore gave *Viribus Unitis* the distinction of being the first battleship in the world to mount her heavy guns in triple turrets, but the political requirement that only domestic resources be used had inflated her cost dramatically. Officially listed at 60 million kronen, by some estimates she cost as much as 82 million. By comparison, the 18,500-ton *Nassau*, the first German dreadnought (commissioned in May 1910), cost 37 million marks or 37 million kronen, at the nominal exchange rate of 1:1 between the Austro-Hungarian and German currencies. The last, largest, and most expensive capital ship of the Tirpitz programme, the 26,500-ton battlecruiser *Hindenburg*, would be completed in 1917 at a cost of 59 million marks. When Montecuccoli's successor Admiral Anton Haus hoisted his flag in *Viribus Unitis*, he had in his care not only the summit of Austro-Hungarian industrial technology but also the most expensive warship of any type ever built by anyone, anywhere.

Like all the Austro-Hungarian pre-dreadnoughts, *Viribus Unitis* and *Tegetthoff* (commissioned on 21 July 1913) were initially painted olive green, which colour provided the best camouflage when operating along the Dalmatian coast, but during 1913 the navy piloted a new colour scheme with *Radetzky*, a light blue-grey deemed more suitable for operations on the open waters of the Adriatic and Mediterranean. The trial was deemed a success and the two dreadnoughts were repainted in February 1914. That spring they showed off their new colours during a cruise of the eastern Mediterranean, the only time *Viribus Unitis* ever left the Adriatic. Because *Viribus Unitis* was regarded as the fleet flagship and the preserve of its commander-in-chief, the commander of the navy's active squadron,

NAMING THE SHIP AND THE CLASS

With the approval of Franz Ferdinand, the Naval Section (Marinesektion) of the war ministry initially proposed naming the four dreadnoughts *Tegetthoff*, *Prinz Eugen*, *Don Juan d'Austria* and *Hunyadi*.[5] The first three names (honouring the victor of the Battle of Lissa in 1866, the great imperial commander of the early eighteenth century, and the Spanish victor of the Battle of Lepanto against the Ottomans in 1571) had been used for earlier Austro-Hungarian vessels, and the fourth (commemorating János Hunyadi, the Hungarian military and political leader of the fifteenth century) was added to placate the politicians in Budapest. But Franz Joseph, who normally took little interest in the navy, asserted his right to name the first dreadnought himself and chose *Viribus Unitis* after his personal motto; the second and third dreadnoughts thus received the names *Tegetthoff* and *Prinz Eugen*, displacing *Don Juan d'Austria*, which would probably have been used for one of a second class of four dreadnoughts approved by the Delegations in the spring of 1914 but cancelled on the outbreak of war. Meanwhile, the Hungarian government subsequently made known its preference for *Szent István* over *Hunyadi*.

On 21 March 1912, the day *Tegetthoff* was launched, the Marinesektion issued a proclamation declaring that the dreadnoughts would be collectively known as the Tegetthoff class. The naming of the class after its second ship rather than the first went against naval tradition, but having been overruled by the emperor in naming the first dreadnought the navy was determined to have its way where the class name was concerned.

[5] Wladimir Aichelburg *et al.*, *Die 'Tegetthoff'-Klasse: Österreich-Ungarns grösste Schlachtschiffe* (Munich: Bernard & Graefe Verlag, 1981), p. 3.

The Emperor Franz Joseph (1830–1916), seen here in 1905, who insisted that his personal motto *Viribus unitis* ('with united forces') be taken as the name of Austria-Hungary's first dreadnought. *(Library of Congress/ LC-H25-15512-A)*

Konteradmiral Franz Löfler, had flown his flag in *Tegetthoff* since she had joined the fleet and continued to do so during this cruise. The ships visited Malta from 22–28 May, then proceeded to Smyrna (İzmir), Adalia (Antalya), Mersina (Mersin) and Alexandretta (İskenderun) in Ottoman Asia Minor. Having stopped at Beirut they turned for home, calling at the Albanian ports of Valona (Vlorë) and Durazzo (Durrës) before proceeding up the Adriatic to Pola.

Sarajevo

Within weeks of her return from the eastern Mediterranean in May 1914 *Viribus Unitis* was

given the honour of conveying Franz Ferdinand and his wife Sophie on part of their journey from Vienna to Bosnia, the archduke able to observe army manoeuvres near Sarajevo on 26 and 27 June. Other dignitaries, including the Chief of the General Staff, Franz Conrad von Hötzendorf, made the trip entirely by rail, but the archduke and his consort took the train only as far as Trieste where they boarded Admiral Haus's flagship on the 24th. The voyage down the Adriatic from the empire's primary seaport to the sleepy Dalmatian harbour of Ploccia (Ploče) covered barely 250 miles but it afforded Franz Ferdinand a rare opportunity to indulge his love of the sea. At Ploccia the royal party boarded a small

Viribus Unitis as she joined the fleet in 1912. *(VKK)*

Viribus Unitis lying in one of the Austro-Hungarian navy's floating dry-docks in 1913. Note the anchors characteristically stowed in the aweigh position and the unusual enclosed stern gallery leading off the admiral's suite. *(NHHC/NH 87189)*

steamer which conveyed them up the Narenta (Neretva), navigable as far as Metković fifteen miles upstream where they boarded a train to complete their journey to Sarajevo. The archduke's itinerary called for him to tour the Bosnian capital on Sunday 28th on conclusion of the manoeuvres before retracing his steps to Ploccia where *Viribus Unitis* waited at anchor for the return voyage to Trieste.

Viribus Unitis did indeed transport Franz Ferdinand and Sophie back to Trieste, though in caskets rather than in the admiral's suite. The news that Their Royal Highnesses had been murdered in Sarajevo on the morning of 28 June by a nineteen-year-old Bosnian Serb, Gavrilo Princip, set the navy scrambling to make arrangements suitable for honouring the memory of a man whose patronage had meant so much to the fleet. Haus, who had not accompanied the ill-fated couple on the outbound voyage, arrived from Pola aboard the admiral's yacht *Lacroma* accompanied by *Tegetthoff*, a light cruiser and a flotilla of destroyers and torpedo boats. On 30 June the caskets were embarked in *Viribus Unitis* and placed under a canopy on the quarterdeck attended by a guard of honour. The funeral procession took a longer route back to Trieste, hugging the coast rather than steaming on the open sea. By weaving through the deep channels separating the Dalmatian islands from the coast Haus enabled the inhabitants of Spalato (Split) and other coastal cities and towns to view the sad spectacle and pay their last respects to the deceased. Bells tolled from countless white-washed hillside chapels and village churches as the squadron made its way northward. *Viribus Unitis* dropped anchor in Trieste harbour late on 1 July and the following day the caskets were brought ashore before being taken by train to Vienna for funeral ceremonies on the 3rd.

Uneasy Alliance

The assassination of the archduke sparked a crisis between Austria-Hungary and an invigorated Serbia which within a month had engulfed most of Europe. Officially at least, the navy's war plans assumed the Triple Alliance would hold. After years of deterioriating relations with their partners, the Italians had in 1912 agreed to renew the alliance with the Germans and Austro-Hungarians in light of strained relations with the French and British as a result of the Italo-Turkish

Viribus Unitis puts to sea early in her career. *(VKK)*

War (1911–12). During that same period Britain had responded to the German naval build-up in the North Sea by withdrawing all her dreadnoughts to home waters, an action which weakened the Mediterranean Fleet and made the Italians less anxious about crossing the British. Under the Triple Alliance Naval Convention signed in Vienna in June 1913, in the event of war an Austro-Italian fleet would deploy to the western Mediterranean to disrupt troop convoys from Algeria to France. To get a wary Austria-Hungary to agree to the scheme, the Italians offered to designate Admiral Haus as allied commander, even though their contribution of ships would be the largest. *Viribus Unitis* would therefore be the flagship of the Alliance fleet.

In addition to the latest Austro-Hungarian and Italian pre-dreadnoughts and dreadnoughts, the naval convention also covered any warships Germany had stationed in the Mediterranean. At the time of the archduke's assassination these included the battlecruiser *Goeben* (later *Yavuz Sultan Selim*, q.v.) and her escort, the light cruiser *Breslau*, commanded by Konteradmiral (Rear Admiral) Wilhelm Souchon. The war scare following the archduke's assassination prompted Souchon to bring *Goeben* to Pola for repairs which were completed on 23 July, just as Austria-Hungary submitted her ultimatum to Serbia in

Viribus Unitis seen off Pola while transporting the remains of the assassinated Archduke Franz Ferdinand and Archduchess Sophie to Trieste on 1 July 1914. The caskets were placed on the quarterdeck under the awning. Note the ship's ensign at half-mast and the black mourning bunting. *(VKK)*

A MULTINATIONAL AND SOCIAL MICROCOSM

The ship's company of *Viribus Unitis* and the other larger vessels of the Austro-Hungarian fleet were unique for their ethnic and linguistic diversity, a reflection of the polyglot nature of the empire they served. In its last decades the mechanisation of the fleet brought an influx of Germans and Czechs from the more industrialised areas of the Dual Monarchy, while political motivations prompted the government in Budapest to encourage ethnic Hungarians (Magyars) to volunteer for naval service. These men joined Croatians and Italians from the coastal provinces which had always provided manpower for the fleet, and by 1910 only those nationalities from the predominantly agricultural inland provinces of Austria-Hungary – Romanians, Slovaks and Ukrainians (known as Ruthenians) – had little representation in the navy.

These national divisions were also reflected in the allocation of duties aboard, with Germans and Czechs providing most of the engineers, telegraphists, electricians and those manning the heavy guns, Magyars responsible for the secondary armament, while stoking and boatwork were largely in the care of Croats with the latter also well represented among the deck crews together with the Italians. Prior to the First World War ratings were enlisted for four years followed by eight years in the reserve.

Nationalities of Austro-Hungarian Sea Officers and Ratings, 1910–14

Nationality	Composition of population of Dual Monarchy (1910)	Sea officers (1910)	Ratings (1910)	Ratings (1914)
German Austrians	23.9%	51.0%	24.5%	16.3%
Magyars	20.2%	12.9%	12.6%	20.4%
Czechs	12.6%	9.2%	7.1%	10.6%
Poles	10.0%	2.8%	1.0%	1.8%
Croatians	5.3%	9.8%	29.8%	31.3%
Slovenes	2.6%	4.2%	3.6%	2.8%
Italians	2.0%	9.8%	18.3%	14.4%
Others	23.4%	0.3%	3.1%	
Romanians				1.2%
Ruthenians				0.8%
Slovaks				0.4%

Sources: 1910 data from Lothar Höbelt, 'Die Marine' in Adam Wandruszka & Peter Urbanitsch, ed., *Die Habsburgermonarchie 1848–1918, V: Die bewaffnete Macht* (Vienna: Verlag der Österreichischen Akademie der Wissenschaften, 1987), pp. 687–763; p. 745; 1914 data from Anthony Sokol, *The Imperial and Royal Austro-Hungarian Navy* (Annapolis, Md.: United States Naval Institute, 1968), p. 79.

The Austro-Hungarian navy seems to have had a comparatively flexible promotion system for skilled personnel, with volunteers, mostly from the merchant marine, being eligible for a commission after one or two years on the lower deck, and petty officer graduates of the engineering school eligible to be commissioned as 'officials' after several years' service as mechanicians, with the possibility of promotion to the rank of captain. The pre-war navy was composed of around 1,000 officers including cadets, and 20,000 ratings. During the conflict this eventually increased to 1,500 officers, 1,300 officials and approaching 40,000 ratings.[6]

Like the navy's other larger vessels, *Viribus Unitis* also reflected the gulf-like social divisions of the Habsburg empire backed by severe punishment. Touring the Radetzky-class semi-dreadnought *Zrínyi* off Kaštela near Spalato (Split) in November 1918, Cdr E. E. Hazlett of the U.S. Navy observed that the living spaces were 'constructed with an eye to comfort – for the officers'.[7] Even *Zrínyi*, a vessel of roughly two-thirds the displacement of *Viribus Unitis*, featured 'large, airy rooms with ports of almost window size for even the junior officers', and captain's quarters consisting of 'a magnificent seven-room suite in the stern of the ship'. Surviving photos of Admiral Haus's opulent quarters in *Viribus Unitis* leave little doubt that she was fully up to the same standard.[8] In contrast, 'the crew's quarters [in *Zrínyi*] were cramped, dark, and stuffy, and it was difficult to see how a complement of 1,000 men could be accommodated except in extreme discomfort', a point not lost on the lower deck as the war

Members of *Viribus Unitis*'s ship's company, whose varied national and social composition mirrored that of the Austro-Hungarian Empire. (*Bruce Taylor Collection*)

progressed and privations increased. Then there was discipline. Perhaps no more than deterrent use was made of the paraphernalia Hazlett found in the *Zrínyi*'s large detention quarters, but their inclusion in a vessel completed as late as 1911 is a telling statement of the cast of mind of the pre-war Austro-Hungarian elite:

> Grouped about a dark compartment on the upper platform deck were twelve brigs. In the center of this compartment were several stocks, those instruments of torture so commonly associated with our Puritan fathers, made of strap iron and fitted for both ankles and wrists. A rack on the bulkhead held several wicked-looking whips, with leather thongs and lead pellets – unquestionably the dreaded 'cats'.[9]

Taken all round, the 1,087 men required to operate *Viribus Unitis* no doubt experienced living conditions almost as diverse as their corresponding circumstances in civilian life ashore. Such conditions, exacerbated by the uneven distribution of wartime hardships and sacrifices, would make some of the larger units of the fleet hotbeds of mutiny and revolution in 1917–18. While the unrest, when the time came, had nationalist overtones reflecting the centrifugal forces that were pulling the multinational empire apart, it was social class rather than nationality which remained the main divider within the navy. The Habsburgs being a German dynasty, ethnic Germans traditionally dominated the empire's key institutions, and this was also true of the navy after its post-1848 rebirth. For example, in 1910 Germans accounted for 24 per cent of the Austro-Hungarian population, but 79 per cent of army officers and 51 per cent of naval officers. But because the army was conscripted from territorial districts, leaving few regiments with more than two nationalities, most army officers knew only German and could rely on bilingual NCOs to transmit their orders. In contrast, the navy not only received conscripts from Adriatic coastal districts, but also volunteers from inland provinces whose numbers rose as the age of wood and sail gave way to steel and steam. The warships of the navy were therefore microcosms of the multinational empire as a whole and could only be commanded effectively by particularly well-educated officers; consequently, the four-year curriculum of the naval academy at Fiume required all cadets to study at least five languages; seamen were expected to understand orders in German and have a grasp of the other languages

A pre-war view of the quarterdeck and No. '3' and '4' turrets under an awning. *(VKK)*

generally spoken aboard, Serbo-Croatian and Italian. Thanks to such measures, the navy enjoyed a much better reputation among the leaders of those nationalities most critical of the ethnic German domination of the army. At the meeting of the Austrian Delegation held in May 1914, one Czech politician noted that 'the national intolerance that reigns within the army' had no equivalent in the navy, where 'our people do not complain of nationality troubles'. A Czech colleague seconded these remarks, commenting that 'the officer corps of the navy makes a very favourable impression on all circles of the population', although the reigning inequalities between officers and men were increasingly a cause of deep resentment and eventually mutiny in February 1918.[10]

Two crewmen of *Viribus Unitis* in their working rig. Social inequalities played a major role in the unrest which marked the last two years of the Austro-Hungarian navy. *(Bruce Taylor Collection)*

6 Sokol, *The Imperial and Royal Austro-Hungarian Navy*, pp. 78–80.

7 Cdr E. E. Hazlett. Jr., 'The Austro-American Navy' in *U.S. Naval Institute Proceedings* 66 (1940), pp. 1757–68; p. 1759.

8 Wladimir Aichelburg, *K.u.K. Marinealbum: Schiffe und Häfen Österreich-Ungarns in alten Photographien* (Vienna, Munich & Zürich: Verlag Fritz Molden, 1976), p. 152.

9 Hazlett, 'The Austro-American Navy', p. 1759.

10 Speeches by František Udržal and Josef Kadlčák in *StPD*, XLIX (28 May 1914), pp. 541 & 543.

DAILY LIFE IN THE AUSTRO-HUNGARIAN NAVY

Under peacetime conditions in harbour the naval day in *Viribus Unitis* and the other vessels of the Austro-Hungarian fleet began at 0500 (0400 on Saturday) with the bugle call 'Auspurren!' ('Call the watch!'), repeated on a bosun's call by the petty officers to the traditional refrain 'Die Tagwache und zum Gebet!' (literally 'Rise and pray!').[11] By 0515 the hands had lashed up and stowed their hammocks and the messdeck skylights had been opened, coffee and bread being served at 0530. At 0600, as the supply boat put out to shore to collect the day's provisions, it was time to clean ship, water being pumped by the ship's boys into large open barrels before being poured over the deck with buckets as the men, all barefoot, scrubbed the deck with brushes. This was also the opportunity for laundry to be done on Monday and Friday, clothing and kit being laid on the deck and scrubbed clean with the same brushes before being put out to dry. Individual items were marked in red using purpose-made name stamps. This completed, crewmen performed their ablutions before changing into the rig of the day in time for Divisions at 0730 during which they would be told off for work. The seaman branch was organised into two divisions of two watches each but the engineering department was on a three-watch system. At 0800 came the ceremony of hoisting the ensign on the quarterdeck with which the work of the day truly

Viribus Unitis's anti-torpedo nets deployed during a pre-war exercise. *(Bruce Taylor Collection)*

began, boats being lowered and awnings rigged as applicable. This was followed at 0845 by the cleaning of all guns, weapons and exposed equipment in preparation for inspection at 0945, at which time the ship's executive officer made himself available for requests, complaints and other representations. Between 1000 and 1130 came drill in its various forms, including guns, small arms, boatwork etc., with the exception of Friday when the executive officer delivered an assessment of progress and shortcomings in training, command and drill to the entire crew. At 1130 the order was passed to rig the mess tables for dinner which was collected from the galley at noon.

The standard dinner in the pre-war Austro-Hungarian navy consisted of soup, cooked beef and vegetables, with canned meat being served once a week. Larger vessels such as *Viribus Unitis* had their own bakeries providing bread and fresh pastries even during extended cruises. The barbette ship *Kronprinz Erzherzog Rudolf* (1883) with a complement of approximately 450 men embarked the following provisions for four months: 8 tons of biscuit, 3 tons of cured meat, 14,000 tins of meat, 2.5 tons of rice, 1.4 tons of dried peas, 3 tons of beans, 2 tons of gruel meal, 110lb (50kg) of pepper, 1.5 tons of salt, 1,985lb (900kg) each of coffee and sugar, 330lb (150kg) of sauerkraut, and 220gal (1,000l) each of oil and vinegar. In addition, monthly supplies of 1,320gal (6,000l) wine and 1.8 tons of potatoes were laid in, and 550lb (250kg) fresh bread and 235lb (107kg) of fresh beef were consumed daily. Small wonder that

A large proportion of *Viribus Unitis*'s complement of boats manned for a pulling (rowing) competition or practice. Protected under canvas in the foreground is one of the ship's eighteen Škoda 2.75in guns. *(Bruce Taylor Collection)*

the steady reduction in what was by naval standards generous and balanced fare was a cause of mutiny from 1917.

Work resumed at 1400 with drill and classes as applicable until 1600 when the order was passed to clear up the decks. There followed a period of rest during which the barbers plied their trade until 1745 when the hands were mustered and the ship went to action stations at 1815. Supper was then served including cheese, beans and potato salad helped down by bread and wine. The ensign was lowered at sunset and the ship's riding lights switched on. At 1930 the hands carried out final cleaning duties and secured the ship for the night as orders for the various branches were read out for the following day. Half an hour later the bugle call 'Abpurren!' ('Stand down!') was sounded as hammocks were slung, though the men could remain on deck smoking, singing and making music until pipe down at 2100, compliance being enforced by officers on their rounds.

The same routine based on the four-hour watch-keeping system was followed in winter, albeit with afternoon duty shortened by an hour. Only a quarter of the ship's company was on duty in port, rising to half when the ship was at sea in peacetime. The ship's surgeon inspected the crew on Saturday and the general inspection on Sunday morning was followed at 1000 by a church service, provision no doubt being made for the various denominations and confessions embarked. The rest of that day was reserved for leisure activities which by the early years of the twentieth century were dominated by sport and games. The major recreation of the Austro-Hungarian navy was that of sailing presided over by the prestigious K.u.K. Yachtgeschwader (Imperial and Royal Yacht Squadron) founded at Pola in 1891. The big regattas held off that port each spring and autumn were a highlight of the naval year and attracted spectators from throughout the region. To this was added competitive pulling (rowing), shooting and shipboard gymnastics, while football and roller hockey had been taken up by the outbreak of war. Officers also indulged in water polo, tennis, riding and fencing, and the trials of coaling ship were organised into a competitive regatta. The Austro-Hungarian fleet, in short, had the range and dimension of organisation and activities to be expected of a navy of the first rank.

11 The content of this section is based on Aichelburg, *K.u.K. Marinealbum*, pp. 123–7.

respect of its territorial aspirations. When Haus mobilised the fleet on the 26th, two days before the declaration of war, *Prinz Eugen* (commissioned on 8 July) joined *Viribus Unitis* and *Tegetthoff* as part of the 1st Division at the head of a fleet including twelve pre- and semi-dreadnoughts and ten cruisers of various types. Meanwhile, Souchon made the first move, taking *Goeben* down the Adriatic to meet *Breslau* off Brindisi before steaming to Messina, the assembly point for the Triple Alliance navies designated in the Naval Convention. There Souchon learned that Italy had declared neutrality, making the convention a dead letter. On receiving the news, Haus resolved to assume a defensive posture in the Adriatic while *Goeben* and *Breslau* proceeded to shell the French Algerian ports of Philippeville (Skikda) and Bône (Annaba) at dawn on 4 August, before receiving orders from Berlin to proceed to Constantinople in anticipation of the Ottoman Empire joining the Central Powers.

By the time Souchon returned to Messina on the 5th to take on coal for the voyage to the Dardanelles, Britain had declared war on Germany. Fearful of being blockaded by cruisers deployed from Malta, Souchon signalled Haus at Pola asking for Austro-Hungarian assistance. Within hours the request was relayed directly from Berlin to Vienna. The appeal placed Haus in a dilemma, facing as he did the sobering realities of geography and relative naval strength. The Anglo-French combination had far greater firepower much closer to Messina than he did, putting him in no position to save the German ships. Souchon on the other hand had no interest

Admiral Anton Haus (1851–1917), Commander-in-Chief of the Austro-Hungarian navy, who hoisted his flag in *Viribus Unitis* in February 1913 and died in her four years later. *(Library of Congress/LC-B2-3291-13)*

in spending the war bottled up with Haus in the Adriatic, only that Haus should provide a diversion to allow his ships to escape from Messina. On the evening of 6 August he managed to leave the port and make it to open sea without Austro-Hungarian help, shaping a course which led the British to believe he was heading back to the

Viribus Unitis lies serenely off the Croatian port of Abbazia (now Opatija) in the Adriatic in September 1913. *(Courtesy Philippe Caresse)*

Adriatic. To reinforce the ruse, a second German appeal for help asked Haus to bring his fleet as far as Brindisi at the mouth of the Adriatic to rendezvous with Souchon's ships. Haus responded early on 7 August by putting to sea with *Viribus Unitis* at the head of a formidable force including the three battleships of the dreadnought division, the three Radetzky-class semi-dreadnoughts and the *Sankt Georg*. He had steamed halfway down the Adriatic by the time Berlin informed Vienna that *Goeben* and *Breslau* had altered course and were already in Greek waters en route to Constantinople where they joined the Ottoman navy. Haus had his ships back in port by 8 August.

Italy Enters the War

With the French Mediterranean Fleet maintaining a blockade of the mouth of the Adriatic with nominal British support, Haus focused instead on the neutral Italians, concentrating his three dreadnoughts and nine pre- and semi-dreadnoughts at Pola and ignoring all suggestions that he engage the enemy in the Strait of Otranto. As he explained to his second-in-command, Konteradmiral Karl Kailer von Kaltenfels, in early September, 'so long as the possibility exists that Italy will declare war against us, I consider it my first duty to keep our fleet intact [...] for the decisive struggle against this, our most dangerous foe'.[12] That moment finally came on 23 May 1915 when Italy

Another view of *Viribus Unitis* while transporting the remains of the assassinated Archduke Franz Ferdinand and Archduchess Sophie to Trieste on 1 July 1914 under the quarterdeck awning. (*NHHC/NH 87177*)

declared war on Austria-Hungary after concluding a treaty of alliance and naval convention with the Triple Entente powers. When the news reached Pola late on the afternoon of the 23rd, Haus set in motion a long-standing plan for a punitive bombardment of the Italian coast. Just after sunset Haus put to sea with a fleet including *Viribus Unitis* and the dreadnought division, nine pre-dreadnoughts, six cruisers and a host of destroyers and torpedo boats. Once they were underway he detached the destroyers and most of the cruisers on a reconnaissance sweep to the south to provide warning should Italian or other Allied capital ships came up the Adriatic to challenge them. Nearing the Italian coast, Haus detached *Radetzky* and her sister *Zrínyi* to attack their own targets but kept the remaining ten battleships together for a bombardment of Ancona. The largest Italian city on the Adriatic after Venice, Ancona was an undefended target just 70 miles from Pola whereas Venice, the Italian navy's nearest base, was 150 miles distant. Acutely aware that most of the battleship and cruiser casualties of the war in other theatres had fallen victim to mines and torpedoes in coastal waters, Haus forsook *Viribus Unitis* to lead the attack from the pre-dreadnought *Habsburg* of 8,300 tons, while his erstwhile flagship steamed offshore with *Tegetthoff* and *Prinz Eugen*. Nevertheless, the thirty-six 12in guns of the three dreadnoughts did most of the damage in the bombardment.

Viribus Unitis seen from the air in an undated wartime photo. (*NHHC/NH 87172*)

12 Haus to Kailer, Pola, 6 September 1914, cited in Paul G. Halpern, *The Naval War in the Mediterranean, 1914–1918* (Annapolis, Md.: Naval Institute Press, 1987), p. 30.

The shelling temporarily disrupted Ancona's electricity, gas and telephone services, and set its coal stocks and oil depot ablaze. Buildings damaged or destroyed included the railway station, the police barracks, an army barracks, a military hospital, a sugar refinery and the local branch of the Bank of Italy. A merchantman was sunk in the harbour and three others damaged. Casualties ashore included sixty-eight killed and 150 injured, by far the greatest human toll in any of the places shelled during the raid. While the bulk of the fleet focused on Ancona, *Radetzky* bombarded a railway bridge at the mouth of the Potenza, *Zrínyi* shelled Senigallia and cruisers attacked Rimini, Barletta, Termoli, Campomarino, Manfredonia and Porto Corsini near Ravenna, targets extending some 300 miles along the Italian coastline. In the only naval engagement of the night, the destroyer screen encountered a squadron of Italian cruisers and destroyers off the island of Pelagosa (Palagruža), sinking one destroyer. All of Haus's ships were safely back in port well before dawn on 24 May. Austro-Hungarian casualties included just six dead, all in the light cruiser *Novara* whose daredevil commander Linienschiffskapitän (Captain) Miklós Horthy, later admiral and Regent of Hungary, closed with a coastal battery at Porto Corsini, one of the few defended places on the target list.

The raid of 23–24 May damaged or destroyed three bridges, three stations, and two yards on the Italian coastal railway, causing northbound troop trains heading for the front from central and southern Italy to be diverted for the first days of the Italian army's mobilisation. But because the damage was repaired too quickly to have much significance on the overall Italian war effort, the effect of the raid was mostly psychological – on both sides. An Austro-Hungarian diplomat leaving Italy via the coastal railway after the breach of relations confirmed the 'depressing impact' of the raid on Italian public opinion.[13] Meanwhile, for the officers and seamen of the fleet, if not for Austria-Hungary as a whole, the punitive bombardment of a faithless former ally sparked a mood of euphoria which dissipated amid the inactivity that followed. The Italian, French and British forces at the Strait of Otranto stood at the ready to meet the Austro-Hungarian fleet should it attempt to break out of the Adriatic, just as Haus kept his fleet at the ready to meet the Allied fleet were it to steam northward. More so than the British and Germans in the North Sea, the rivals in the Adriatic accepted the status quo and had little inclination to risk their fleets, especially their battleships, in combat with the enemy. The Italian battlefleet scarcely left harbour while Haus maintained the classic 'fleet in being' at Pola, a naval force sufficiently strong as to compel the enemy to behave with caution by its mere existence, devoting considerable resources to keep it bottled up. For the rest of the war it was the light cruisers, destroyers, torpedo boats and submarines of the opposing fleets which were responsible for practically all of the action in the theatre, supplemented by the occasional raid by seaplanes or airships and in the Italian case by the *Mezzi Insidiosi* (Stealth Units). As late as March 1918 a U.S. Navy memorandum characterised the Adriatic as 'practically an Austrian lake, in which no Allied naval operations of importance are undertaken.'[14]

From Haus to Horthy

With its battleships spending most of the war at anchor, the Austro-Hungarian navy, like the German navy, embraced the submarine as the most effective weapon for a fleet hopelessly outnumbered in surface vessels. Although Austria-Hungary deployed just twenty-seven U-boats to Germany's 335, German submarine operations in the Mediterranean were facilitated by the provision of bases at Pola and Cattaro (Kotor) at the southern tip of Dalmatia. Haus was a strong supporter of unrestricted submarine warfare in 1915 and again in 1917 when Germany decided to risk war with the United States in order to resume it. He accompanied the young Emperor Charles, Franz Joseph's successor, to Germany's Eastern Front headquarters for a meeting to finalise Austria-Hungary's commitment to the resumed campaign on 26 January 1917, only to fall ill with pneumonia on the return trip to Pola. Haus never recovered and died aboard *Viribus Unitis* on 8 February. He was succeeded by Admiral Maximilian Njegovan who proved less capable than Haus at maintaining the navy's morale and discipline, especially once the Dual Monarchy's overall food shortage caused sailors' rations to be cut. Meanwhile, Horthy's tactical victory at the Battle of the Strait of Otranto (15 May 1917), a cruiser action against the Allied barrage line at the mouth of the Adriatic, demonstrated that the smaller, more active vessels of the fleet remained effective, but the same could not be said for the larger warships. In July the first political demonstrations swept the idle battleships at Pola followed by more serious unrest in January 1918. A full-scale

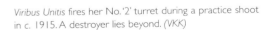
Viribus Unitis fires her No. '2' turret during a practice shoot in c. 1915. A destroyer lies beyond. (VKK)

13 Cited in Hans Hugo Sokol, *Österreich-Ungarns Seekrieg 1914–1918*, 2 vols. (Zürich: Amalthea-Verlag, 1933; reprinted Graz: Akademische Druck-und Verlagsanstalt, 1967), I, p. 218.

14 Cited in Halpern, *The Naval War in the Mediterranean*, p. 439.

mutiny erupted at Cattaro in February 1918 and resulted in the execution of four seamen and the incarceration of nearly 400 more.[15] Charles subsequently replaced Njegovan with Horthy who received an extraordinary promotion to Konteradmiral (rear admiral), a move requiring the eighteen admirals who outranked him to retire or accept posts ashore.

Having hoisted his flag aboard *Viribus Unitis* in March 1918, Horthy ordered a wholesale reassignment of ships, officers and thousands of sailors. Recognising the danger of having too many idle hands unlikely to see action aboard larger warships riding at anchor, he decommissioned the navy's older battleships and cruisers, and assigned much of their complement to roles ashore, especially in support of the U-boat campaign. The battlefleet was reduced to just the dreadnoughts – now four in number since the commissioning of *Szent István* on 13 December 1915 – and the three semi-dreadnoughts of the Radetzky class. During the spring of 1918 Horthy took advantage of an easing of enemy pressure to conduct manoeuvres and gunnery exercises on a scale not seen by the navy since before the war. By late spring he deemed the fleet ready for action.

Horthy planned to provoke a battle with the Allies at the mouth of the Adriatic by repeating the previous year's successful raid on the Otranto Barrage, only this time with a much larger force, including all four dreadnoughts. To avoid attracting attention before the attack on the barrage, which was set for the morning of 11 June, Horthy planned for the dreadnoughts to proceed southward in pairs under cover of the Dalmatian islands, steaming through the deep waters along the coast rather than on the open

sea, and only during the hours of darkness. On the evening of 8 June he sailed from Pola with *Viribus Unitis* escorted by *Prinz Eugen*; *Tegetthoff* and *Szent István* followed late on the evening of the 9th. The first two dreadnoughts were halfway down the coast when the trailing pair were attacked at 0330 on the 10th off Premuda, an island lying forty miles southeast of Pola, by the Italian motor torpedo boats *MAS-15* and *MAS-21*. Two torpedoes from the latter slid harmlessly past *Tegetthoff* but *MAS-15*'s pair struck the starboard side of *Szent István* leaving her in a sinking condition. *Szent István* remained afloat until after 0600 by which time *Tegetthoff* had managed to rescue all but eighty-nine of her crew of over 1,000 men. The detonations which breached the armour belt also compromised the torpedo bulkhead, flooding the large watertight compartments along the starboard side of the ship which coupled with her relatively low metacentric height caused her to capsize. Here was the first tangible evidence of the flaws in Popper's design.

Even with his three remaining dreadnoughts, Horthy still had more than enough firepower to carry out his plan to raid the Otranto Barrage, but the sinking of *Szent István* confirmed that the element of surprise had been lost; to proceed would be to run the risk of being overwhelmed in a counterattack by the much larger Allied fleet. His decision to cancel the operation and return to Pola, though prudent, was a crushing blow to the Austro-Hungarian navy. Facing a superior enemy on a heightened state of alert, Horthy saw no point in repeating the attempt. As late as August 1918 he continued to vouch for the battle-readiness of the fleet but it never sortied again.

Rear Admiral Miklós Horthy, the most distinguished fighting officer in the Austro-Hungarian navy, who was appointed its Commander-in-Chief in February 1918. *(Bruce Taylor Collection)*

The Final Act

During those same August days an Allied breakthrough against the German army on the Western Front set in motion a chain of events that within three months had led to the defeat of the Central Powers, including the collapse of Austria-Hungary and the demise of her navy. In mid-October Germany ended unrestricted submarine warfare in order to improve the prospects of peace negotiations with the United States; in the Dual Monarchy, meanwhile, Emperor Charles issued a promise of self-government for most of the nationalities as part of a last-ditch effort to save his multinational empire, a declaration that inadvertently accelerated the process by which leaders established their own national councils as proto-governments. Horthy was able to maintain discipline in the fleet until 27 October, the day German submariners abandoned their Adriatic bases and headed for home in an undeniable sign that the war would soon be over. Recognising that the disintegration of the

Another view of the same wartime 12in practice shoot, in this case of turrets '2' and '3' firing simultaneously. *(Bruce Taylor Collection)*

---

15 Paul G. Halpern, 'The Cattaro Mutiny, 1918' in Christopher M. Bell & Bruce A. Elleman, eds., *Naval Mutinies of the Twentieth Century* (London: Frank Cass, 2003), pp. 54–79.

empire left most sailors more anxious to return to their homes than take over their ships, the admiral and his officers appealed for calm by promising 'extensive furloughing [...] as soon as hostilities are ended'.[16] Leaving *Viribus Unitis* to make the rounds of Pola on the 28th, Horthy found that most ships were already in the hands of their crews. Committees elected by the sailors presented him with lists of demands similar to those formulated by the Cattaro mutineers in February, including references to Woodrow Wilson's Fourteen Points of 8 January, but also for common messing and conditions of service for officers and men alike. Several mentioned 1 November as a deadline at which time they would abandon their ships and go home.

On 30 October Charles finally acknowledged the impending dismemberment of the empire and decided to turn the fleet over to the Yugoslav (South Slav) national council, a body convened by Croatian leaders in Zagreb which had spent the previous month establishing contacts with Yugoslav émigré groups in the various Allied capitals and laying the groundwork for a new union of Croatia and Dalmatia with Serbia. Slovenian and Bosnian leaders also pledged their allegiance to the Yugoslav concept. On 29 October, acknowledging the reality that a plurality of the fleet's sailors belonged to the South Slav nationalities, the imperial government had appealed to the national council for assistance in restoring calm in the fleet, but it refused to help unless the navy was first placed under its authority. Faced with the alternatives of doing

Manning *Viribus Unitis*'s port 2.75in battery. The danger from the Regia Marina came not from her heavy units but from her small-boat navy. *(NHHC/NH 42830)*

nothing or turning the fleet over to the Yugoslav national council, Charles chose the latter course, instructing Horthy to work through South Slav officers to make the transition as smooth as possible. A Slovenian officer, Capt. Method Koch, who had been elected to a local Yugoslav committee in Pola on 28 October, emerged as the central figure. At 1300 on the 30th Charles signalled Horthy that a 'dispatch concerning the release of crews and transfer of navy to Yugoslav national council will follow shortly'.[17] The Emperor and his advisers then drafted the terms of the transfer, including the provision that all Austro-Hungarian officers, regardless of nationality, could remain with the fleet in Yugoslav

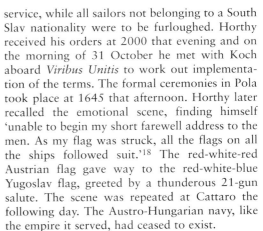

service, while all sailors not belonging to a South Slav nationality were to be furloughed. Horthy received his orders at 2000 that evening and on the morning of 31 October he met with Koch aboard *Viribus Unitis* to work out implementation of the terms. The formal ceremonies in Pola took place at 1645 that afternoon. Horthy later recalled the emotional scene, finding himself 'unable to begin my short farewell address to the men. As my flag was struck, all the flags on all the ships followed suit.'[18] The red-white-red Austrian flag gave way to the red-white-blue Yugoslav flag, greeted by a thunderous 21-gun salute. The scene was repeated at Cattaro the following day. The Austro-Hungarian navy, like the empire it served, had ceased to exist.

At 1700 on the 31st Horthy's Croatian flag captain in *Viribus Unitis*, Konteradmiral Janko Vuković, assumed command of the fleet in what to all appearances was a smooth transition of power. For Croatian and Slovenian sailors, the conclusion of this act just before sunset was the trigger for a night of celebration, assisted by access to the officers' well-stocked shipboard *Weinräume* (wine cellars). For the first time since August 1914 the port of Pola and the ships in its harbour were fully illuminated, and amid the jubilation hardly anyone bothered to stand watch. Taking advantage of this lapse in security, shortly after midnight on 1 November two Italian navy divers began executing a daring and carefully planned operation to infiltrate Pola harbour astride a self-propelled dummy torpedo and lay charges against the enemy shipping moored there. The divers in question were Raffaele Paolucci, a surgeon lieutenant in the Regia Marina, and Raffaele Rossetti, a major in its engineering corps. Having negotiated the harbour defences, at 0445 Rossetti and Paolucci closed *Viribus Unitis* and succeeded in attaching a 400lb (181kg) charge to her hull which was set

Szent István in her death throes two hours after being torpedoed by the Italian *MAS-15* in the northern Adriatic on 10 June 1918. Her demise provided a first inkling of the vulnerability of the Tegetthoff class to underwater damage. *(NHHC/NH 60534)*

16 As authorised in *Armeekommando* to *Flottenkommando*, Baden, 28 October 1918, text in Sokol, *Österreich-Ungarns Seekrieg*, II, p. 719.

17 Richard Georg Plaschka, Horst Haselsteiner & Arnold Suppan, *Innere Front: Militärassistenz, Widerstand und Umsturz in der Donaumonarchie 1918*, 2 vols. (Munich: R. Oldenbourg, 1974), II, pp. 233–4; and Sokol, *Österreich-Ungarns Seekrieg*, II, pp. 728–9.

18 Miklós Horthy de Nagybánya, *Memoirs* (London: Hutchinson, 1956), p. 92.

The end of the *Viribus Unitis*, sunk in fourteen minutes in Pola by the detonation of charges laid by Italian divers on 1 November 1918. Four hundred men went down with her. *(NHHC/NH 87203)*

to detonate at 0630. Having laid their second charge against the hull of the liner *Wien*, they were spotted by a sentry in *Viribus Unitis* and brought aboard at 0600. It was only at this point that Rossetti and Paolucci advised Konteradmiral Vuković to pass the order to abandon ship since *Viribus Unitis* was in mortal danger. This he did, but the evolution was lacking in organisation and many were still aboard when the charge eventually exploded at 0644. The detonation not only breached the hull but compromised the torpedo bulkhead, flooding the large watertight compartments on the starboard side of the centreline, after which the ship's relatively low metacentric height caused her to capsize. *Viribus Unitis* therefore suffered substantially the same fate as *Szent István* after her torpedoing on 10 June, only the hole blown in the hull was in this instance much larger and the sinking consequently much faster, the ship capsizing just fourteen minutes after the explosion and taking around 400 men with her. Vuković was not among the survivors. His tenure had lasted scarcely twelve hours.

Conclusion

At the time of her demise, a month short of six years after entering service, *Viribus Unitis*

retained the distinction of being the most expensive active warship yet built. In over four years of war she had sortied only three times and had never engaged an enemy vessel; indeed, her guns had been fired in anger on just one occasion, the bombardment of Ancona on 23–24 May 1915. Nevertheless, as with the rest of the Austro-Hungarian navy, her contribution to the war effort is best measured by the effect it had on enemy strategy. By the end of 1914 the Allies had elected to concede the Adriatic to the Dual Monarchy for the duration of the conflict, a decision Italy's entry into the war on the Allied side did nothing to alter. France and Britain, along with Italy, expended considerable resources in the Strait of Otranto to ensure the Austro-Hungarian fleet could not break out into the central Mediterranean – resources the Allies could have allocated elsewhere had such countermeasures not been warranted by the mere presence of dreadnoughts in the Adriatic.

SMS *Viribus Unitis* has the broader historical significance of being the first operational battleship with triple turrets, entering service a month before Italy's similarly armed *Dante Alighieri*. Underscoring the innovative nature of her design, three and a half years were to pass before another navy completed a battleship with triple turrets in a superfiring layout, namely USS *Pennsylvania* commissioned in June 1916, albeit on a much larger 600ft (183m) hull and with an improved metacentric height of 7.82ft (2.4m) offering significantly greater stability than *Viribus Unitis* and her sister ships. In the evolution of naval warfare and warship design, navies at times paid a high price for being first, or for the compromises required to attain that distinction. For the men lost in the capsizing of *Szent István* and *Viribus Unitis* that price was paid in full.

Sources

Aichelburg, Wladimir, *K.u.K. Marinealbum: Schiffe und Häfen Österreich-Ungarns in alten Photographien* (Vienna, Munich & Zürich: Verlag Fritz Molden, 1976)

_____, et al., *Die 'Tegetthoff'-Klasse: Österreich-Ungarns grösste Schlachtschiffe* (Munich: Bernard & Graefe Verlag, 1981)

Gebhard, Jr., Louis A., 'Austria-Hungary's Dreadnought Squadron: The Naval Outlay of 1911' in *Austrian History Yearbook* 4–5 (1968–9), pp. 245–58

Halpern, Paul G., *The Mediterranean Naval Situation, 1908–1914* (Cambridge, Mass.: Harvard University Press, 1971)

_____, *The Naval War in the Mediterranean, 1914–1918* (Annapolis, Md.: Naval Institute Press, 1987)

_____, *Anton Haus: Österreich-Ungarns Grossadmiral* (Graz: Verlag Styria, 1998)

_____, 'The Cattaro Mutiny, 1918' in Christopher M. Bell & Bruce A. Elleman, eds., *Naval Mutinies of the Twentieth Century* (London: Frank Cass, 2003), pp. 54–79

Hazlett, Jr., Cdr E. E., 'The Austro-American Navy' in *U.S. Naval Institute Proceedings* 66 (1940), pp. 1757–68

Höbelt, Lothar, 'Die Marine' in Adam Wandruszka & Peter Urbanitsch, eds., *Die Habsburgermonarchie 1848–1918*, V: *Die bewaffnete Macht* (Vienna: Verlag der Österreichischen Akademie der Wissenschaften, 1987), pp. 687–763

Horthy de Nagybánya, Miklós, *Memoirs* (London: Hutchinson, 1956)

Koburger, Charles W. *The Central Powers in the Adriatic, 1914–1918: War in a Narrow Sea* (Westport, Conn.: Praeger, 2001)

Plaschka, Richard Georg; Horst Haselsteiner & Arnold Suppan, *Innere Front: Militärassistenz, Widerstand und Umsturz in der Donaumonarchie 1918*, 2 vols. (Munich: R. Oldenbourg, 1974)

Preston, Antony, *Battleships of World War One* (London: Arms and Armour Press, 1972)

Sokol, Anthony, *The Imperial and Royal Austro-Hungarian Navy* (Annapolis, Md.: United States Naval Institute, 1968)

Sokol, Hans Hugo, *Österreich-Ungarns Seekrieg 1914–1918*, 2 vols. (Zürich: Amalthea-Verlag, 1933; reprinted Graz: Akademische Druck- und Verlagsanstalt, 1967)

Sondhaus, Lawrence, *The Naval Policy of Austria-Hungary, 1867–1918: Navalism, Industrial Development, and the Politics of Dualism* (West Lafayette, Ind.: Purdue University Press, 1994)

_____, *The Great War at Sea: A Naval History of the First World War* (Cambridge: Cambridge University Press, 2014)

Stenographische Protokolle der Delegation des Reichsrathes [Transcripts of the Protocols of the Delegation to the Imperial Council], 50 vols. (Vienna: k.k. Hof- und Staatsdruckerei, 1868–1918)

Vego, Milan N., *Austro-Hungarian Naval Policy, 1904–14* (London: Frank Cass, 1996)

Veronese, Leone, *Imbarcà su la* Viribus Unitis: *Breve storia della Imperial regia Marina da Guerra Austriaca* (Trieste: Luglio, 2003)

Warhola, Brian, 'Assault on the Viribus Unitis' available at: http://www.worldwar1.com/sfvu.htm [accessed August 2016]

Kriegsmarine Archiv, Vienna: http://www.kuk-kriegsmarine.at/ [accessed March 2018]

Royal Australian Navy:
The Battlecruiser *Australia* (1911)

Richard Pelvin

HMAS *AUSTRALIA* was unique in being the only British battlecruiser not to serve in the Royal Navy (RN), operating instead as the flagship of a sparsely populated, newly independent nation on the far side of the world.[1] Her career also reflected a certain tension in the relationship between the fledgling state and its great progenitor – an Australian desire to be seen as independent and as a nation with its own strategic problems, but also one which recognised and took pride in its membership of a great entity in whose governance it desired a voice, a position at variance with the traditional British view of imperial power being indivisible and imperial policy formulated by a centralised authority in London.

Early Australian Concepts of Naval Defence

On 1 January 1901 the six Australian colonies federated to form the Commonwealth of Australia. The naval forces of the former colonies

[1] The author acknowledges the assistance of Rear Admiral James Goldrick RAN (Retd) and Dr David Stevens, Mr John Perryman and Able Seaman Libby Pearce of the Sea Power Centre – Australia at Canberra. The editor does so to Ian Johnston, Ray Burt and Steve Dent for their kindness with photos.

A newly completed *Australia* during her trials on the Firth of Clyde in June 1913. No navy in history can have received a more powerful unit at its inception than that of Australia. *(Crown Copyright/National Records of Scotland (NRS)/UCS1-118-402-83)*

Australia in the fitting-out basin of her builder, John Brown & Co. of Clydebank, over the winter of 1911–12. To the left is the light cruiser HMS *Southampton* with an I-class destroyer alongside *Australia*. Completion of the ship was four months delayed by labour shortages and a boilermakers' strike between September and December 1910. *(Crown Copyright/NRS/UCS1-118-402-91)*

were amalgamated into the Commonwealth
Naval Forces (CNF), a sad collection comprising
a turret ship, several gunboats, harbour defence
torpedo boats and auxiliaries.[2] All were totally
obsolete and unfit for seagoing duties. Australia's
naval defence relied on the Royal Navy which
had stationed a small fleet of cruisers on the
Australia Station since 1859. Local concerns that
the squadron might be caught off station in time
of emergency resulted in 1891 in the establishment of an Auxiliary Squadron of small cruisers
and gunboats which was to be retained for
service on the Australia Station and to which the
Australian colonies contributed a subsidy.

This state of affairs was unsatisfactory to
Prime Minister Alfred Deakin who reached office
in 1903 and served three terms in the first decade
of the twentieth century. As early as 1887
Deakin, then a colonial politician, had expressed
interest in Australia making a responsible contribution to imperial defence but one which would
remain under Australian control. As prime
minister he believed that 'if we do take part in
naval defence, we shall be entitled to a voice in
foreign affairs'.[3] Like all prominent Australians
of the day, Deakin was wary of the growing
power of Japan and mindful of that of Germany
whose colonies (principally German New
Guinea) lay within Australia's sphere of interest
and which was in the process of establishing a
naval presence in Asia. This translated into a
concern that Australia should not be left undefended if imperial forces temporarily lost
command of the sea or were evaded by a raiding
cruiser squadron.

In the early days of Federation a number of
schemes were proposed by the head of the CNF,
Captain W. R. Creswell, a retired Royal Navy
lieutenant who had settled in Australia and
became naval commandant of the Defence Forces
of South Australia before taking up the identical
position in Queensland. He was a strong advocate of an Australian navy but had little experience of naval developments since reaching
Australia in 1879. All his experience was in the
obsolete coastal defence environment of the colonial navies and this was reflected in his proposals
for a local navy. His vision was focused on
coastal defence forces and typical of his thinking
was a 1905 proposal for a fleet equipped with
torpedo boats, destroyers and a type he referred
to as a 'cruiser-destroyer' – effectively an ocean-

[2] For the ships of the various colonial naval forces,
see Colin Jones, *Australian Colonial Navies*
(Canberra, ACT: Australian War Memorial, 1986).
[3] J. A. La Nauze, *Alfred Deakin: A Political
Biography*, 2 vols. (Melbourne, Vic.: Melbourne
University Press, 1965), II, p. 519.

going destroyer – the other vessels being confined to coastal or harbour work.[4] He firmly rejected submarines but in 1907 Deakin included such vessels in the plans for coast defence without consulting him.[5]

Initially both the Admiralty and British officers serving locally discouraged the formation of Dominion navies, believing that these could contribute little to imperial naval defence. However, growing concern at the threat posed to imperial sea communications by enemy cruisers prompted the First Sea Lord, Admiral of the Fleet Sir John Fisher, to encourage the creation of a local flotilla consisting of smaller ships of a type not readily sent out from the metropolis in the event of a crisis, and in early 1909 the government of Deakin's successor, Prime Minister Andrew Fisher, duly ordered three destroyers from Britain.[6]

In April 1909 the Commonwealth's position on naval defence was set out in a letter from the Governor General of Australia to the Secretary of State for the Colonies (the usual channel for communication between London and the colonial governments at the time). In essence, the Commonwealth government proposed to maintain a naval base for the Royal Navy and establish and pay for a local force of torpedo craft to operate around the Australian coast. The force would be under Commonwealth government control but in an emergency would come under the command of the Admiralty. However, redeployment away from Australian coastal waters would require the agreement of the Commonwealth government. The Admiralty would provide officers to assist in the training of the local force and opportunities for the Australian personnel to train with British forces.[7]

The Admiralty had no objection in principle to the proposal and advised that it 'would cordially cooperate in the establishment and organisation of such a force'. However, Their Lordships anticipated there being some difficulties, especially in manning the destroyers, and recommended that a conference between the Admiralty and Australian officials be held to iron these out. 'All

---

[4] G. S. Macandie, *The Genesis of the Royal Australian Navy: A Compilation* (Sydney, NSW: Australian Naval Board, 1949), pp. 123–30.

[5] La Nauze, *Alfred Deakin*, II, p. 528.

[6] David Stevens, *The Australian Centenary History of Defence*. III: *The Royal Australian Navy* (South Melbourne, Vic.: Oxford University Press, 2001), pp. 16–17.

[7] The National Archives, London (TNA), ADM 116/11163, letter from the Governor General of Australia to the Secretary of State for the Colonies, 10 April 1909.

Australia in the final stages of completion at Clydebank in mid-June 1913. Towering overhead is one of Sir William Arrol's Titan cranes while in the foreground workers lay the decking of the Russian Steam Navigation Co.'s liner *Imperator Pyotr Velikiy*, later a hospital ship.
(Crown Copyright/NRS/UCS1-118-402-79)

possible assistance' was to be given to the Commonwealth in the construction of the destroyers.[8]

In the event, other factors combined to shape the force structure of Australia's naval defence in an entirely different way. By March 1909 the British government had become aware of plans to expand the German battleship construction programme, the announcement of which in Parliament by the First Lord of the Admiralty, Reginald McKenna, caused widespread public concern that Britain might lose her naval supremacy. Whipped up by the British press, the concerns led to the 'We want eight and we won't wait' outcry, demanding that eight dreadnoughts be authorised that year.

The call was taken up in New Zealand and Australia, two countries well aware that their defence depended on the maintenance of British sea power. New Zealand quickly offered a battleship. Australia was slower, having just commenced its destroyer construction programme, but the states of Victoria and New South Wales offered to subsidise a major unit. This combined with pressure from conservative sectors of the public and the return of Deakin to power saw the States' proposal subsumed by an offer from the Commonwealth government in June 1909.[9]

The Dominion offers of battleships dovetailed into other British strategic concerns relating to the Pacific. Admiral Fisher was a ruthless driver of reform, the touchstones of which were efficiency and economy. In reply to the rapid expansion of the Imperial German Navy he had scrapped scores of obsolete warships and concentrated the Royal Navy's major fighting ships in home waters. Realising that it could not be strong everywhere, Britain had in 1902 signed an alliance with Japan which protected its interests in the Far East and the Pacific. This had been renewed in 1905 but there were still suspicions of future Japanese intentions despite the Anglo-Japanese Alliance. In June 1909 the Admiralty's attention was drawn to the Pacific by the Committee of Imperial Defence which had concerned itself with the defence of Hong Kong in the event of Japan renouncing the Alliance. The Committee regarded sea power as the colony's main defence and the Admiralty was instructed to strengthen the China Squadron before the termination of the Alliance. The

8 TNA, ADM 116/11163, draft letter, Admiralty to Colonial Office, undated, *c.* April 1909.

9 *Ibid.*, Officer Administering the State of New South Wales to the Secretary of State for the Colonies, 4 April 1909; Governor-General of Australia to the Secretary of State for the Colonies, 4 June 1909.

Committee further recommended study of how Dominion naval forces might contribute to naval defence in the Pacific.[10]

There were also concerns for British trade in the Pacific. A number of nations deployed powerful armoured cruisers in that theatre, including France, the United States and Japan. Of special concern was the Kaiserliche Marine's East Asia Squadron based on the German concession at Tsingtao (now Qingdao) in China. Since 1900 it had included an armoured cruiser, augmented in 1906 by modern light cruisers and some gunboats and by a second armoured cruiser in 1909.[11] Then there was the assortment of territories centred on German New Guinea including New Britain, New Ireland and German Samoa, all of which were in Australia's backyard. Although lacking basing facilities, Blanche Bay on the island of New Britain provided an excellent harbour.

Fisher believed he had the ideal ships to counter such forces. On becoming First Sea Lord in 1904 he pushed through the construction of the revolutionary new battleship *Dreadnought*. Where previous battleships were armed with four 12in (305mm) guns and a secondary battery of between 6in and 9.2in (152–234mm) guns with a speed of 18 knots, *Dreadnought* carried ten 12in weapons with a secondary armament reduced to 3in (76mm) anti-destroyer guns. The uniform-calibre main armament was essential to make the most efficient use of the 12in gun in salvo firing at longer ranges.[12] Meanwhile, the installation of turbines gave her a design speed of 21 knots.

Fisher then introduced a new armoured cruiser along the same principles. Contemporary armoured cruisers had a main armament of between 8in and 10in (203–254mm) guns and secondary batteries of 7.5in or 8in (190–203mm) weapons with maximum speeds in the region of 23 knots. Like *Dreadnought*, Fisher's new armoured cruisers adopted an all-big-gun armament of eight 12in guns and were given a speed of 25 knots to allow them to combine tactically with the dreadnoughts. Fisher saw four roles for his

new armoured cruisers: 1) providing a heavy scouting force; 2) close support for the battlefleet in action; 3) pursuit of a fleeing enemy; and 4) trade protection, with greatest relevance to the Pacific. The last involved hunting down and destroying marauding cruisers on the trade routes. The new cruisers, of the Invincible class, would use their speed tactically to catch raiders and strategically to move rapidly between operational areas.[13] Fisher felt that such ships were suitable for 'colonial imitation'. Smaller cruisers '… like ants will all be eaten up by one 'Indomitable' armadillo, which puts out its tongue and licks them all up!'[14] To these vessels the term 'battle-cruiser' was eventually attached in 1911.

The Fleet Unit Concept

Fisher's concerns led him to advocate a Pacific fleet which would be composed of three fleet units built in each case around one of the new fast big-gun armoured cruisers, supported by three of the new Town- or Chatham-class light cruisers as well as destroyers and submarines. To relieve the British Treasury of much of the cost, Fisher proposed that the Pacific Dominions of Canada, Australia and New Zealand each contribute a fleet unit based around a battle-cruiser. 'We manage the job in Europe. They'll manage it against the Yankees, Japs, and Chinese, as occasion requires out there.'[15]

In April 1909 the British government called an Imperial Conference to bring together these various threads and formalise a scheme of defence for the Pacific.[16] The conference took place in London in late July and early August. Deakin was unable to attend so the Australian government was represented by Colonel J. F. G. Foxton, a loyal follower and 'faithful and effective conduit of Deakin's ideas and wishes'.[17] He

was accompanied by Capt. Creswell and Colonel W. T. Bridges as naval and military advisers respectively. At the conference the First Lord of the Admiralty, Reginald McKenna, tabled a memorandum which reflected Sir John Fisher's strategic concepts and turned Australian naval planning on its head. McKenna noted that some Dominions wished for their own navies. If so,

it is perfectly clear that the first thing you have to consider is personnel. Your navy must be of a kind to offer a career for officers and men. I […] put it to you that it is no use starting with half-a-dozen [flotilla craft] […] which, in the long run, cannot give you all grades of officers and men. If you are going to enlist men in the Navy you must offer them a future, and you will never get men to enlist if they know that when they are over 30 years of age perhaps, the possibility of rising in the service is gone. We therefore have to start on the basis of the smallest fleet unit which will offer both to officers and men a career in life.[18]

McKenna recommended a balanced fleet consisting of an armoured cruiser, three light cruisers, six destroyers and three submarines. The Eastern Fleet then consisted of three divisions – the Australian, China and East Indies Division. Each would consist of a fleet unit and together form an 'Australasian Fleet'. The provision of these units might be 'put on a Dominion basis'. McKenna went on:

To take an illustration, you might in Australia start, according to the extent of the burden which you are willing to bear, by providing part of this unit. I do not now suggest that the Commonwealth Government could provide the whole of this unit, but if the 'Dreadnought' that has been so generously offered to the United Kingdom took the form of an armoured cruiser of the 'Indomitable' type, that could be supplemented as far as the Commonwealth wished to go.

Further discussions with the Australian delegation succeeded in discouraging them from spending money on a scheme which would contribute little either to the protection of Australian trade or to imperial defence. The Admiralty would meet the difference in cost between the maintenance of the fleet of flotilla craft already under construction together with the cost of the offered dreadnought, about

---

10 Nicholas Lambert, 'Economy or Empire?: The Fleet Unit Concept and the Quest for Collective Security in the Pacific, 1909–1914' in Greg Kennedy & Keith Neilson, eds., *Far-Flung Lines: Essays on Imperial Defence in Honour of Donald Mackenzie Schurman* (London: Frank Cass, 1997), pp. 55–84; pp. 60–1.

11 My thanks to Mark E. Horan for information on the composition of the German East Asia Squadron, email correspondence, 24 December 2013.

12 John Roberts, *Battlecruisers* (London: Chatham, 1997), p. 17.

13 *Ibid.*, p. 18.

14 Fisher to Lionel Yexley, 1 August 1909, in Arthur J. Marder, ed., *Fear God and Dread Nought: The Correspondence of Admiral of the Fleet Lord Fisher of Kilverstone*. II: *Years of Power, 1904–1914* (London: Jonathan Cape, 1956), p. 258.

15 Fisher to Lord Esher, 13 September 1909, in *ibid.*, p. 266.

16 TNA, ADM 116/11163, Secretary of State for the Colonies to the Governor-General and Governors [of the self-governing Dominions], 30 April 1909.

17 D. B. Waterson, 'Foxton, Justin Fox Greenlaw (1849–1916)' in Australian Dictionary of Biography, National Centre of Biography, Australian National University, available at: http://adb.anu.edu.au/biography/foxton-justin-fox-greenlaw-6230/text10719

18 TNA, ADM 116/11163, *Proceedings of the Imperial Conference on Naval and Military Defence*.

The after superstructure housing four of the ship's sixteen 4in guns. To the left is the bulk of 'Y' turret. The photo was taken at Clydebank in 1913. (*Crown Copyright/NRS/UCS1-118-402-71*)

£500,000 per annum, and that required to maintain the fleet unit. It would also assist with manning and training until Australia could provide these from its own resources. However, all RN dockyards and shore facilities in Australia would be transferred to the Commonwealth. Creswell had reservations. Noting that a navy 'did not exist to provide careers for the officers', he favoured putting resources into the infrastructure necessary to develop 'a fresh centre of naval strength', in the belief that future officers could aspire to be harbour masters! Foxton, however, found that the Admiralty proposals 'appealed to him strongly' and thought they would find favour with the Commonwealth government, which would have to be consulted.[19] In the end the Commonwealth government elected to pay the full cost of the new vessels.

The details of the proposal were finally worked out at a meeting at the Admiralty on 19 August 1909 and forwarded to Australia for approval. The Australian Fleet Unit would consist of an Invincible-class armoured cruiser, three Bristol-class light cruisers, six destroyers of a type already under construction in Britain for Australia, and three C-class submarines (later modified to two of the more modern E-class vessels). In addition to the financial and manning arrangements already outlined, Australian personnel could avail themselves of training in RN schools and ships and the latter would provide personnel to serve in the Australian fleet. 'Great stress was laid upon the same general standard of training, discipline and general efficiency, both in ships and officers and men.'[20] The proposal was strengthened by New Zealand agreeing that the dreadnought they were contributing, HMS *New Zealand*, should provide the core of another of the fleet units based on the China Station. The Royal Navy would provide the flagship of the Eastern Fleet, although it was hoped, unavailingly as it turned out, that Canada would also participate.

Foxton had Deakin's ear and was aware of the Prime Minister's desire to make a worthwhile contribution to imperial defence and thereby exercise some influence in the formulation of imperial policy. Moreover, ownership of a dreadnought conveyed prestige in the era of navalism. It was far more likely that Deakin would be swayed by Foxton's support than Creswell's reservations and so it proved. Deakin's enthusiasm was shared by the Australian public among whom the scheme 'found wide approval, most factions finding it to

'A' 12in turret and the bridge seen from the forecastle in 1913. (Sea Power Centre – Australia (SPC–A), Canberra)

be attractive and in harmony with their long-held ideas on maritime defence!'[21] The acclaim received by the sixteen battleships of the U.S. Navy's Great White Fleet during its prolonged sojourn in Australian waters in August and September 1908 no doubt influenced this decision on more than one ground, it being approved by the Cabinet on 27 September 1909. On 10 July 1911 King George V accorded the naval forces of Australia the title of Royal Australian Navy.

Design and Construction

The new armoured cruiser would be of the Indefatigable class, which was a modification of the Invincible class with a revised layout enabling the wing turrets to fire across the deck in order to engage targets on the opposite beam. Combined with the speed of the ship, this would notionally allow them to fire a broadside equal to that of a dreadnought battleship carrying two more 12in guns but no cross-deck firing capability.[22] As it turned out, the blast effect of cross-deck firing caused damage to the ship's structure and fittings and was scarcely ever resorted to.

Nonetheless, dreadnought cruiser design had entered a new phase of development by the time *Australia* and *New Zealand* were laid down and the Admiralty has been criticised for proceeding with the construction of these ships when work was about to begin on the new Lion class mounting 13.5in (343mm) guns.[23] It may be that the 12in armament was regarded as more than adequate since both ships were intended to operate against obsolete armoured cruisers in the Pacific, thereby obviating the need to incur the added expense of building larger, more powerful vessels. No consideration seems to have been given to the possibility of other nations commissioning more powerful battlecruisers as the Japanese did with the Kongo class, the first unit of which was built in Britain.

A tender was accepted for the construction of *Australia* from John Brown & Co. of Clydebank on 1 April 1910 and the keel was laid on 23 June.[24] Although there were some delays owing to strike action and labour shortages, construction generally proceeded satisfactorily and the Australian authorities were kept apprised via regular progress reports.[25] The ship was launched on 25 October 1911 by Lady Reid, wife of Sir George Reid, Australian High Commissioner in London and former prime minister, who made a speech in which she emphasised *Australia*'s significance as an earnest of a remote country's desire to maintain its security and one which 'recognises to the full her obligations to the British Empire'.[26] Among those present at the launching was the barrister turned journalist C. E. W. Bean:

She was moving. It was the gentlest thing in motion that ever was. It was slower than the hands of a big clock – but it always increased. The tallow – there were 10 tons of it buttered on the ways, besides oil and soft soap – began to squelch out from beneath the cradles, at first lazily, then like mud under the wheels of a motor-car. [...] Presently the ram passed us, moving as fast as a man could walk – and she always went faster, faster, faster; dwindled as

19 *Ibid.*; also Stevens, *The Australian Centenary History of Defence*, p. 21.

20 TNA, ADM 116/11163, Summary of the results of meetings, 19 August 1909.

21 Stevens, *The Australian Centenary History of Defence*, p. 21.

22 Fisher to Sir Andrew Noble, 14 April 1912, in Marder, ed., *Fear God*, II, pp. 74–5.

23 Roberts, *Battlecruisers*, pp. 29–30.

24 National Archives of Australia (NAA), A4141, AUSTRALIA I Ship's Book. For the contract and construction history, see Ian Johnston, *Clydebank Battlecruisers: Forgotten Photographs from John Brown's Shipyard* (Barnsley, S. Yorks.: Seaforth Publishing, 2011), pp. 36–40.

25 NAA, MP472 16/13/3260.

26 As reported in *The Standard of Empire*, 3 November 1911; clipping in NAA, MP472 16/11/4400

A party of sailors mustered on *Australia*'s starboard waist, the ship lying at Clydebank shortly before her departure for Portsmouth where she commissioned on 21 June 1913. Note the steam picket boat stowed on the midships superstructure and the cutters on their davits abreast the mainmast. The flags decorating the bows of the boats indicate her future status as a rear admiral's flagship.
(Crown Copyright/NRS/UCS1-118-402-75)

Australia's torpedo flat with reloads and handling gear to the left of one of the two torpedo tubes, of which the ship carried one on either beam. (SPC–A)

the tail of a vanishing train disappears. We could see the vacant berth, the sky above, the long thin poles of scaffolding, the little figures of the crowd waving and cheering opposite.[27]

Completed on 21 June 1913, HMAS *Australia* was 555ft (169.2m) long between perpendiculars and 590ft (179.8m) long overall, with a beam of 80ft (24.4m) at launch. Her full-load draught as measured by an inclining experiment on 17 May 1913 was 29ft 4in (8.9m) and full-load displacement was 22,070 tons, and 18,800 standard. She was fitted with Babcock & Wilcox boilers and Parsons turbines designed for 44,000shp driving four three-bladed manganese-bronze propellers. On 7 and 8 March 1914 the ship ran the contractor's thirty-hour trial on the Polperro measured mile in the English Channel during which she recorded 22.5 knots at 31,000shp. Three days later she ran an eight-hour trial at 44,000shp recording 25.841 knots.[28]

Australia was armed with eight 12in Mk-X 45-calibre guns in four twin BVIII* mountings, one forward, two set *en échelon* on either beam and one aft, all manufactured at Vickers, Barrow. The ammunition allowance was eighty rounds per gun in peacetime and 110 rounds per gun in war. Secondary armament consisted of sixteen 4in (102mm) Mk-VII guns on PII* mountings disposed around the superstructure. In March 1915 *Australia*'s anti-aircraft armament was supplemented by a single 3in (76mm) AA gun

followed in June 1917 by a 4in high-angle mounting fitted on the after superstructure.[29] An 18in (457mm) submerged torpedo tube was mounted on each side abreast 'Y' turret with fourteen torpedoes embarked.[30]

Fire control was exercised from spotting tops in the masts connected electrically to a transmitting station on the lower deck. Another spotting platform was fitted under the bridge abaft the conning tower should the upper positions be destroyed in action. The forward turret was also fitted with a 9ft (2.7m) rangefinder and equipped with instrumentation enabling it to serve as a reserve control position for the main armament. Dreyer fire-control tables and director firing were fitted in the ship, probably in early 1916.[31]

Australia was protected by a 6in (152mm) armour belt, thinning to 4in (102mm) abreast 'A' and 'Y' turrets and 2.5in (63mm) forward and abaft of these respectively. Turrets and barbettes were protected by 7in (178mm) of armour with 10in (254mm) on the conning tower. Bulkheads were up to 4in (102mm) thick forward and up to 4.5in (114mm) aft. Horizontal protection consisted of a maximum of 1.5in (38mm) and 2in (51mm) on the upper and lower armoured

deck respectively. The spotting and signal position on the conning tower was protected by 3–6in (76–152mm) of plate.[32]

Commissioning

HMAS *Australia* was commissioned into the Royal Australian Navy at Portsmouth by Capt. Stephen H. Radcliffe RN, an officer with experience of Australian waters, on 21 June 1913.[33] Two days later she hoisted the flag of Rear Admiral George E. Patey RN, formerly commander of the 2nd Battle Squadron, as Rear Admiral Commanding the Australian Fleet.

There was no question of manning the ship entirely from Australian resources, particularly where officers were concerned, so the ship's complement of 1,170 would comprise officers and men of the RN in addition to existing RAN personnel. Members of the RN who transferred to the RAN did so for three years which would count towards their time in British service. For disciplinary matters they remained subject to the Naval Discipline Act and the King's Regulations and Admiralty Instructions, with 'Australian Commonwealth Naval Board' substituted for 'Admiralty' where appropriate. Advancement would be under the same conditions as those obtaining in the RN. They were subject to Australian rates of pay with some differences regarding pensions and deferred pay.[34]

Officers and men were, as far as possible, selected from persons with Australian claims and connections. Some were Australian-born including Lieutenant (T) J. G. Crace, eventually Rear Admiral Commanding the Australian Squadron in the first half of the Second World War and commander of Task Force 17 at the Battle of the Coral Sea. Others had Australian wives or family in Australia.[35] One whose

27 C. E. W. Bean, *Flagships Three* (London: Alston Rivers Ltd, 1913), pp. 280–1.
28 NAA, A4141, AUSTRALIA I Ship's Book.

29 Roberts, *Battlecruisers*, p. 83.
30 Ibid., pp. 82–4; R. A. Burt, *British Battleships of World War I* (London: Arms and Armour Press, 1986), p. 91. For a sectional plan, see Antony Preston, *Battleships of World War One* (London: Arms and Armour Press, 1972), p. 259.
31 Roberts, *Battlecruisers*, pp. 90–2, and email correspondence with Dr John Brooks, 23 December 2013, whose assistance is gratefully acknowledged.

32 Roberts, *Battlecruisers*, pp. 102–4; Burt, *British Battleships of World War I*, pp. 93–5.
33 Henry James Feakes, *White Ensign – Southern Cross: A Story of the King's Ships of Australia's Navy* (Sydney, NSW: Ure Smith, 1951), p. 175n.
34 *Volunteers from the Active List of the Royal Navy for Temporary Service in the Royal Australian Navy – Conditions of Service.* Copy in Australian War Memorial, Canberra (AWM), PR90/109, papers of W. S. Rhoades.
35 NAA, MP472 16/13/144; Chris Coulthard-Clark, *Action Stations Coral Sea: The Australian Commander's Story* (North Sydney, NSW: Allen and Unwin, 1991).

Australian family was fictional was Midshipman Herbert Annesley Packer, then serving in the battleship *St Vincent*. He was persuaded to join *Australia*'s complement to 'circumnavigate the globe' by a fellow midshipman and native of Tasmania, Edward Billyard-Leake who 'lent' Packer an Australian uncle to assist his appointment to the battlecruiser![36] Packer and thirteen fellow midshipmen joined *Australia* on 28 June 1913.

Two days after the arrival of the midshipmen *Australia* received a visit from King George V. Following an inspection, Patey became the first officer to be knighted on his quarterdeck since Queen Elizabeth I dubbed Sir Francis Drake in the *Golden Hind* in 1581. On 30 June Patey hosted a luncheon aboard for the Australian High Commissioner Sir George Reid, First Lord of the Admiralty Winston Churchill and the High Commissioners of the other British dominions. Later that day a firework display entertained 600 Australian expatriates invited to celebrate their new flagship.[37]

Australia sailed for her new home on 25 July 1913, her orders taking her via the Cape. Two days out from Portsmouth she was joined by one of the new light cruisers of the Fleet Unit, HMAS *Sydney*, and the two went on to demonstrate the might of imperial sea power to the Union of South Africa. The ships stayed ten days and concluded the visit by conveying a hundred prominent Capetonians the short distance to the naval base at Simon's Town. However, Lt Cdr Henry Feakes, then serving in *Sydney*, sounded a note of realism regarding *Australia*:

> It was hoped that great results would accrue from the visit of the Australian cruisers in stimulating South African opinion and naval sentiment, but Japan stole the show. Close in the *Australia*'s wake followed the mighty Japanese battlecruiser *Kongo*, greatly minimising the effect the Australian flagship had made. The *Kongo*, a vessel of 27,500 tons, mounting 14-inch [356mm] guns, quite eclipsed memories of the *Australia*, of 18,750 tons, mounting 12-inch [305mm] guns.[38]

Arrival

The new flagship crossed the Indian Ocean to Australia and joined the rest of the Fleet in Jervis Bay 120 miles (200km) south of Sydney on

Australia at the time of her departure for the Antipodes in July 1913. *(Courtesy Ray Burt)*

2 October 1913. On the morning of Saturday 4 October hundreds of thousands Sydneysiders took advantage of the declared public holiday and lined the harbour while small craft dotted the water. *Australia* led the fleet out of a thin mist through the heads and into the harbour. Following were the cruisers *Sydney*, *Melbourne* and *Encounter*, the latter on loan from the RN, and then the destroyer *Warrego* leading her sisters *Yarra* and *Parramatta*. The ships steamed majestically up harbour to cheers, sirens, whistles and the firing of salutes as they were welcomed by the ships of the Australia Station. The flag of the last RN commanding officer on the Station was hauled down and the young nation had her own navy with its powerful dreadnought flagship.

Australia was then dispatched to visit ports around the country, a symbol of the unity of the new nation. The fleet had a problem with local coal as the Australian variety was of poor quality for steam. The best was Welsh steam coal but fortunately a type nearly as good was available from Westport in New Zealand. Modifications were made to *Australia*'s boilers to allow more efficient burning of the Australian product,[39] but

these do not appear to have been effective as the ship was continually arranging for supplies of Westport coal during Pacific operations.[40]

But even as *Australia* commenced her duties in the Australian Fleet the 1909 agreement was starting to unravel. Lord Fisher had left the Admiralty in 1910 and his First Lord McKenna was replaced in October 1911 by Winston Churchill who had little time for basing dreadnoughts in the Pacific, preferring to see them in home waters and in the Mediterranean. The New Zealand government was prevailed upon to bring *New Zealand* to European waters, while lesser ships were to replace her on the China Station.[41] The Australian Government was not informed of the new arrangements but, noting that the 1909 proposals for East Indies and China Fleet units did not appear to be materialising, requested

36 Joy Packer, *Deep as the Sea* (London: Methuen, 1976), p. 4. Bertie Packer retired an admiral, Teddy Billyard-Leake a captain.

37 *Ibid*.

38 Feakes, *White Ensign*, p. 176.

39 NAA, A11085/1 B3C/13, Patey to Governor-General, 18 October 1913.

40 For coaling problems see A. W. Jose, *Official History of Australia in the War of 1914–18*. IX: *Royal Australian Navy* (Sydney, NSW: Angus & Robertson, 1937), pp. 457–60.

41 TNA, ADM 116/1270, Sir William Grahame Greene (Permanent Secretary to the Board of Admiralty), *Naval Policy for the Pacific*; TNA, ADM 116/1270, Governor General of New Zealand to Secretary of State for the Colonies, 1 May 1912.

The passing of responsibility for the Australia Station from the Royal Navy to the Royal Australian Navy, represented by the former flagship HMS *Cambrian*, right, and HMAS *Australia* to the left. A Town-class cruiser, probably HMAS *Melbourne*, can be seen off *Australia*'s port quarter with a River-class destroyer lying on *Cambrian*'s port beam. Gathered in the foreground is part of the huge crowd which lined Sydney Harbour to greet the arrival of the new Australian fleet on 4 October 1913. (SPC–A)

this was overtaken by the outbreak of war. It was obvious that Deakin's ambitions for Australia to be consulted on the formulation of imperial policy were not to be realised.

As much as Churchill might have desired it, the plans for *Australia* did not include her recall to European waters.[44] Perhaps with an eye to the German East Asia Squadron, the War Orders for *Australia* issued on 15 May 1913 and amended on 21 April 1914 called for her to be deployed to the China Station unless there was an enemy 'armoured ship' in Australian waters. It would 'then be the duty of *Australia* to bring her to action before she proceeds on any other service'.[45]

Pacific Operations, 1914

On 28 June 1914 the Archduke Franz Ferdinand and his wife Sophie were assassinated in Sarajevo. News of trouble in Europe travelled fast over the imperial cable network and as early as 29 June, with *Australia* conducting gunnery, torpedo, seamanship and tactical exercises at Palm Island, Queensland, Mid. Bertie Packer was able to write to his father that there 'was a buzz around the ship that there's another critical situation in Europe'.[46] On 28 July the Admiralty sent a signal asking 'Rear-Admiral Commanding what arrangements are necessary to enable him to be prepared to act on his war orders'. Over the next few days the ships were ordered to Sydney for coaling and storing while arrangements were

clarification of current policy.[42] When advised of the new arrangements in 1913, the Minister for Defence noted the Admiralty's bad faith and lack of communication and criticised the new arrangements as inadequate.[43] It was proposed to call a conference to discuss the problem but

'Scrub aft!' Junior ratings scrub the forecastle deck amidships amply supplied with sea water from a deck hose. Behind them 'P' 12in turret, marked as such between the guns, is trained astern. Note the landing gun under a tarpaulin on the right and the paravane stowed on the screen beneath the middle funnel. The polish and attention to cleanliness dates the photo to the pre-war period in *Australia*'s career. (SPC–A)

42 TNA, ADM 1/8375/108, Governor General of Australia to Secretary of State for the Colonies, 16 August 1913.

43 *Ibid., Naval Defence, Memorandum by the Minister for Defence*, 13 April 1914.

44 TNA, ADM 1/8383/179, Battle and Cruiser Squadrons Programme 1914.

45 NAA, MP1049/1 1914/0157.

46 Packer, *Deep as the Sea*, p. 5.

Australia awash with visitors in home waters before the outbreak of the Great War. (*Bruce Taylor Collection*)

made for the supply of Westport coal. Once replenished *Australia* was to proceed to Western Australia in anticipation of deployment to the China Station. Operational control passed to the Admiralty on 10 August.[47]

In the event, *Australia* went neither to Western Australia nor to the China Station. The primitive signals intelligence of the day indicated that *Scharnhorst*, flagship of the German East Asia Squadron commanded by Vizeadmiral Maximilian Graf von Spee was about 300 miles northeast of Papua. In view of the 'armoured ship' provision of her War Orders, Patey decided to take *Australia*, *Sydney*, *Warrego*, *Yarra* and *Parramatta* and proceed north to Rabaul (then Simpsonhafen) on New Britain, which was regarded as the most likely base for the German squadron if it wished to operate in the vicinity of New Guinea and south to Australian waters.[48] The same day he made a general signal of congratulations to the officers and men of the ships, dockyards and naval establishments on their 'splendid work in readying the squadron for sea'. By 4 August the ships were operationally ready in all respects. That day Admiralty advice was received concurring with Patey's plan.[49] The declaration of war came soon after and the RAN sailed on its first wartime operation.[50]

The sailing of the squadron was no secret. Mid. Packer made this entry in his journal for 4 August:

> At 9 pm weighed anchor. Speeded on our way by cheering crowds, cathedral bells, bugles and bands. Darkened ship and when clear of the [Sydney] Heads went to Night Defence. Loaded with Common Shell. Full charges. Orders to fire at once if searchlights came on target. Two prize crews have been told off.[51]

The 4in guns were cleared for action and twenty lyddite shells issued per gun.[52] Exactly eight months after making her triumphal entry into Sydney Harbour HMAS *Australia* was at war.

The squadron arrived off Rabaul on 11 August. Patey doubted that the German cruisers were present but hoped to capture some colliers and the radio station.[53] However, if German ships were present, they were expected to be in nearby Blanche Bay. Patey decided to launch a surprise attack at 2130. The confined waters of the harbour were no place for battlecruisers, so *Australia* remained to the south in support of *Sydney* and the destroyers. If the Germans were found the destroyers were to attack immediately. *Sydney* was to signal *Australia* and, with the destroyers, retire on her.[54] *Australia*'s crew cheered from the rigging as the assault force sailed into the night, perhaps to face an enemy of unknown size but known efficiency. The orders preparing the ship for the night have survived:

> The Ship will be generally at Night Action Stations.
> Officers of Watches and General Control Officers will keep watch as usual, but when off watch will sleep at their Action Stations.
> The same applies to Midshipmen of watch and 4" control officers.
> Turrets' Crews, half will be awake at a time.
> Day Action 4" Guns' Crews will be at their guns, the foremost group being in the rest position, the after group being asleep. The groups will change from aft forward at midnight and 4 a.m.
> Searchlight crews as usual.
> If anything is sighted the ship will turn away; while she is turning, Turrets' and 4" Guns'

Crews that can bear will open fire on the searchlights being switched on or at the order to fire.
> Magazine and Shell Room parties except for the voicepipe men required for watch will sleep at their stations.
> It is anticipated that the after Searchlights only will be used and they will sweep as far forward as possible. The after searchlights will be manned.
> 'P' Turret is limited from Red 60° to Red 150°.
> 'Q' Turret is limited from Green 30° to Green 120°, they will not fire across the deck unless especially ordered.
> Night Action will be sounded at 8 p.m.
> These orders apply only for this night.[55]

These orders suggest that Patey had no intention of engaging in a close-range action and indicate the limitations of the wing turrets, especially in respect of cross-deck firing.

---

47 NAA, MP1049/1 1914/0299; TNA, ADM 137/007.

48 AWM, 35, 2/10, Patey to ACNB, 3 August 1914; TNA, ADM 137/007, ACNB to Admiralty, 3 August 1914.

49 *Ibid.*; TNA, ADM 137/007, ACNB to Admiralty, 3 August 1914.

50 Charts showing this and subsequent operations by *Australia* until January 1915 may be found at: http://www.navy.gov.au/history/feature-histories/charts-showing-hmas-australias-activities-august-1914-january-1915 [accessed February 2018].

51 Packer, *Deep as the Sea*, p. 5.

52 AWM, 1DRL0353, Part 2: Letters and

Miscellaneous Orders of Lt S. C. L. Hodgkinson RAN, HMAS *Australia*, Hodgkinson to his family, 3 August 1914.

53 AWM, 2DRL0795, Patey to his brother and sister, 10 August 1914.

54 AWM, 33 [18], *Admiral Patey's report on the participation by the Australian Seagoing Fleet in the operations in the Pacific*. See AWM, 33 [21], Operation Order No. 1 for the plan of attack; Feakes, *White Ensign*, pp. 243–4; transcript available at http://www.gwpda.org/naval/ranopo1.htm [accessed February 2018].

55 AWM, 1DRL0353, Part 2: Hodgkinson papers, Night Orders, Tuesday, 11 August.

Australia approaching Friedrich-Wilhelms-Hafen on 24 September 1914 ahead the occupation of German New Guinea. The French armoured cruiser *Montcalm* is astern of her. (*AWM/J03326*)

The result was an anticlimax; the harbour was empty, as were nearby Matupi Harbour and Talili Bay.[56] Landing parties were put ashore to destroy the wireless station but it was found to be located well inland. In any case, as Patey noted when reporting the absence of enemy ships to the Navy Office on the 12th, the ease with which they were landed suggested that German settlements could be taken at any time. The following day he reported his intention of reconnoitring Bougainville where the fleet again drew a blank, with which *Australia* sailed for Port Moresby to refuel.[57] In fact, von Spee never had any intention of using Rabaul and the outbreak of war found him a thousand miles north in the Eastern Carolines with his two armoured cruisers and *Nürnberg* before concentrating his forces at Pagan Island in the Marianas. Nonetheless, the attack showed that the RAN was ready for war. Within a week of the opening of hostilities *Australia* and her consorts had deployed over 1,800 miles and planned a faultless night attack in difficult waters.

On 13 August Patey reported that the Senior Naval Officer New Zealand had requested cover for a descent on Samoa. Patey recommended approval as the operation might draw out the German squadron.[58] He expected this operation to take place after the New Guinea expedition, which he advised the ACNB should be under *Australia*'s protection in case of interception by von Spee.[59] He was therefore surprised when on

16 August he was informed by the ACNB that the Admiralty had ordered him to cover the Samoa expedition.[60] He was further surprised to discover that the New Zealand force had already departed, obliging him to split his fleet to cover both expeditions.[61] Leaving *Sydney* and *Encounter* to look after the New Guinea force, *Australia* and the light cruiser *Melbourne* joined the Samoa force at Nouméa in the French colony of New Caledonia on 21 August. The convoy consisted of two transports escorted by the French armoured cruiser *Montcalm* and the British protected cruisers *Pyramus*, *Psyche* and *Philomel*. Having coaled, the ships proceeded to Suva, Fiji, and carried out rehearsals for a landing. In view of Admiralty advice that the German squadron might be off Samoa, Patey drew up his sailing orders with care. The fleet sailed for Samoa in two columns led by *Montcalm* and *Australia*, with *Psyche* stationed ahead as scout. In case of attack, *Australia* would lead out followed by *Montcalm* and *Melbourne* while the three small cruisers would shepherd the convoy away.[62] The expedition arrived off Samoa at 0745 on 30 August. Although Patey did not believe that the island was fortified there were rumours of mines and *Australia*'s steam picket boats swept the approaches without

result.[63] When the wireless station ashore began transmitting the letters 'SG' Patey warned that it would be shelled if it did not cease transmitting forthwith and the threat of *Australia*'s 12in guns was sufficient to ensure compliance.[64]

Samoa was occupied with ease and on 31 August *Australia* sailed for Rabaul to cover operations against German New Guinea. After coaling at Suva she joined the invasion force at 1000 on 9 September which, along with the flagship, consisted of the cruisers *Sydney* and *Encounter*, the destroyers *Warrego* and *Yarra*, the troop transport *Berrima* carrying troops of the Australian Naval and Military Expeditionary Force (ANMEF), and the supply ship *Aorangi*. *Parramatta* arrived later convoying the oiler *Murex* and the collier *Kooronga*. At 1010 Brigadier General William Holmes and the ships' commanders came aboard *Australia* for a conference to discuss further operations. Patey explained his orders for the occupation of Rabaul and Herbertshöhe while Holmes outlined his proposed dispositions. Patey approved of these and stated his intention to give Holmes a free hand in commanding the shore operations. He agreed to the garrisoning of Yap, Angaur, Nauru and Friedrich-Wilhelms-Hafen (now Madang) after the completion of operations on New Britain. With all parties in agreement the meeting broke up at 1115.[65]

Patey sent *Sydney* and the destroyers ahead to reconnoitre Rabaul and assess the suitability of the jetty for landing troops. *Australia* followed at 13 knots with *Berrima*, while *Encounter* and the submarines brought up the slow auxiliaries. The reconnaissance found no enemy warships and the jetty suitable for bringing *Berrima* alongside. *Australia* arrived at Karavia Bay, the southern stretch of Blanche Bay where she again detached her picket boats to sweep the harbour for mines. She then proceeded to sea in time to fall in with the small German steamer *Sumatra* which was boarded and sent to Rabaul.[66] Arriving at Rabaul, Patey sent an ultimatum to the German governor stating that the overwhelming forces at his disposal made resistance pointless and ordering the surrender of 'Rabaul and the dependencies under your control'. Meanwhile, troops had landed and advanced to Bitapaka to

56 Feakes, *White Ensign*, pp. 179–82.

57 AWM, 35 2/10, Patey to ACNB, 12 August.

58 *Ibid.*, Patey to ACNB, 13 August.

59 *Ibid.*, Patey to ACNB, 15 August.

60 TNA, ADM 137/007, Admiralty to ACNB, 15 August; AWM, 35 2/10, ACNB to Patey, 16 August.

61 AWM, 33 [18]; Jose, *Official History*, pp. 54–5; Phillip G. Pattee, *At War in Distant Waters: British Colonial Defense in the Great War* (Annapolis, Md.: Naval Institute Press, 2013), pp. 146–7.

62 Jose, *Official History*, pp. 59–61.

63 AWM, 2DRL0795, Patey to his sister, 29 August 1914; Jose, *Official History*, p. 60.

64 AWM, 33 [18].

65 AWM, 33 [1].

66 AWM, 33 [18].

occupy the wireless station. After a sharp fight it was seized at the cost of six Australian dead and four wounded. While the occupying forces consolidated their position ashore, the naval forces captured two more vessels, the inter-island transport *Madang* and the small auxiliary *Nusa*. At 1500 on 13 September the British flag was raised at Rabaul as *Australia* fired a 21-gun salute. The German Lieutenant Governor capitulated two days later.[67] The following day, reports reached *Australia* that the submarine *AE1* had disappeared while patrolling St George's Channel off East New Britain. Patey ordered searches of the sea area and islands but nothing was found of the submarine and her thirty-four crewmen.[68]

On 15 September *Australia* left Blanche Bay for Sydney where she, *Melbourne* and *Sydney* were to prepare to escort the first Australian and New Zealand troop convoy to Aden. The previous day von Spee's squadron had appeared off Samoa in the expectation of catching imperial units, including *Australia*, at anchor and attacking out of the grey dawn, but withdrew after finding no worthwhile targets and observing the island to be occupied by New Zealand troops.[69] It was feared that the Germans could be off New Zealand at the moment the Dominion's portion of the convoy sailed to rendezvous with the Australian contingent. At the same time, the light cruiser *Emden* had commenced her brief but spectacular raiding career in the Bay of Bengal and posed a threat to the convoy on its voyage across the Indian Ocean from Australia to Aden. Accordingly, the Admiralty ordered *Australia* and the French cruiser *Montcalm* to cover the ANMEF and then search for the German force.[70] Having shifted his flag to *Sydney*, Patey raced back to Rabaul and joined *Montcalm* and *Encounter*. On 22 September *Australia* together with *Montcalm*, *Encounter* and *Berrima* sailed to Friedrich-Wilhelms-Hafen (now Madang) on mainland New Guinea to eliminate the German presence there. This port was occupied on the 24th and the squadron had returned to Rabaul by the 26th.

Other arrangements having been made for escorting the troop convoy to Aden, Patey was free to hunt the main units of the German East Asia Squadron, the armoured cruisers *Scharnhorst* and *Gneisenau*. He had long reckoned they would head eastwards and on 20 August signalled the Commander-in-Chief of

Sir George Patey (1859–1935) who served as the first Rear Admiral Commanding HM Australian Fleet from June 1913 to September 1916 with *Australia* as his flagship.
(Bibliothèque nationale de France, Paris/EST EI-13(392))

the China Station, Vice Admiral Sir Martyn Jerram, that he believed the Germans were collecting coal supplies and concentrating 'somewhere northeast of New Britain' and that they would sail east or southeast visiting Samoa and Tahiti, which is precisely what they did.[71] Still, he was not unaware of the difficulties of running them down. On 5 September he wrote telling his sister that he thought

> [...] they are hiding away amongst some of the more distant Pacific islands or they may be on their way across to America, anyhow they have done no harm to our trade as yet, but I wish we could run them to earth and have done with them, but it is almost impossible in a big place like the Pacific, and with so few warships to do it [...][72]

Patey sailed from Rabaul on 1 October, but just after midnight he received word that the German squadron had shelled the Tahitian port of Papeete on 23 September.[73] *Australia* returned to

Rabaul with a wardroom of officers sick of the toing and froing and champing to get at the Germans.[74] Patey was now confirmed in his belief that von Spee's ultimate destination was South America, especially as the light cruisers *Leipzig* and *Dresden* were understood to be off Chile. However, the Admiralty felt that von Spee might double back to attack Samoa, Fiji or New Zealand and ordered the battlecruiser to cover the Fiji area. Although he believed that Nouméa in New Caledonia would have made a better base, Patey sailed for Suva with *Sydney* and *Montcalm* just before midnight on 3 October followed by *Encounter*, *Warrego*, *Parramatta*, *AE2* and four supply ships on the 4th.[75] *Australia* was darkened at night and steamed with all ports closed making for 'very, very hot' conditions below decks, reaching Suva on 12 October.[76] Three days later the Admiralty dismissed Patey's suggestion that the Marquesas be checked for colliers and flatly stated that '[I]t is decided not to send the Australian Fleet to South America.'[77] Given the improved prospects of obtaining coal in South America and other indications that German ships were already there, it is hard to understand the Admiralty's reasoning. As it was, von Spee sailed for the Marquesas having shelled Papeete, rendezvousing with his colliers and the cruiser *Nürnberg*. Having coaled, he sailed for the South American coast on 2 October just as Patey had predicted a month before.[78]

There now commenced a period of operations where, in the words of the official historian, '*Australia*, like a dog tethered to his kennel, made darts into neighbouring waters and was pulled back before any results could be obtained.' These 'darts' were to Samoa on 20 October and two cruises south of Fiji in late October and early November. At the same time, Patey was repeatedly asked to support a variety of impractical operations.[79] Meanwhile, *Australia*'s men were quite 'fed up at our doing nothing and we are all very sick at not being allowed to cross to America, but still I suppose it is right', complained one officer.[80] Of life aboard Mid. Packer gave this description to his father on 7 November:

> We are now properly cleared for action, every

[67] *Ibid.*

[68] *Ibid.* The wreck of *AE1* was discovered off the Duke of York Islands in December 2017.

[69] Jose, *Official History*, pp. 105–6.

[70] *Ibid.*, p. 100.

[71] AWM, 35 2/10, Patey to HMAS *Penguin* for Commander-in-Chief, China Station.

[72] AWM, 2DRL 795, Patey to his sister, 5 September 1914.

[73] AWM, 35 2/17, Navy Office to Patey, 1 October 1914.

[74] AWM, 2DRL0032, Diary of Capt. G. D. Williams RNR, 30 September 1914.

[75] Jose, *Official History*, p. 104.

[76] AWM, 2DRL0032, Diary of Capt. G. D. Williams RNR, 2 October 1914.

[77] Jose, *Official History*, pp. 122–3.

[78] AWM, 33 [18]; Jose, *Official History*, pp. 108–9.

[79] Jose, *Official History*, p. 123.

[80] *Ibid.*, pp. 123–4.

bit of woodwork gone, all doors, lockers, cupboards, even our sea-chests, and Joanna, the piano. [...] It's wonderful how everyone has settled down to months at sea. It certainly makes a ship a warship and not a species of hotel. In the evening those not on watch have sing-songs. With no Joanna our band is a violin (Billyard-Leake), mandolins, flute and piccolo (me – I borrow the band's). We gather round and make a noise in the Gunroom and Wardroom.[81]

Less pleasantly, 'The ship is alive with cock-roaches, all food, our clothes and I even found one in my pipe yesterday. Of course we are on salt grub – bacon and beans and tinned meat ...'

Gunnery exercises kept the gun crews up to the mark. Sub-calibre firing was held on 24 October for the main and secondary batteries. The 12in guns were controlled from the foretop but with 'A' turret deliberately isolated and firing under local control. Then the armament would be controlled by 'A' turret and finally all turrets exercised in local control. Night action was practised with the guns controlled by turret officers.[82]

On 3 November signals intelligence reported the German ships off the coast of South America and on the 5th word came of the destruction of Rear Admiral Christopher Cradock's squadron at Coronel. *Australia*'s men were disgusted they were not there – 'We regard the *Scharnhorst* etc., as our meat' – but Capt. G. D. Williams drew some comfort from the fact that *Australia* had succeeded in driving the von Spee's squadron 'out of Australasian waters where they could have done immense damage'.[83] This disappointing turn of events was offset somewhat by news of the destruction of the *Emden* by *Sydney* on 9 November, the RAN's first victory.

With von Spee finally located, *Australia* was finally let off her Suva leash and ordered to Magdalena Bay in Baja California from where she could block any attempt by the German squadron to move north to Canada or pursue it through the newly opened Panama Canal. In London Capt. Herbert Richmond, then Assistant Director of the Operations Division at the Admiralty, rejoiced that *Australia* could at last give up 'her puerile duties (which have been the defence of the trade round Fiji!) to come over to the coast of America – a step which should have been taken weeks

ago'.[84] She duly left Suva in company with the fast collier *Mallina* which Patey had kept stocked and ready for just such an eventuality. Her destination was altered en route to Chamela Bay, Mexico, where she met the light cruiser HMS *Newcastle* and a Japanese squadron consisting of the battle-ship *Hizen* and the armoured cruisers *Idzumo* and *Asama*. This fleet came under Patey's command on 26 November.[85] The squadron steamed to search the Galapagos Islands area and was then to sweep the South American coast from the Gulf of Panama to Guayaquil in Ecuador. But on 10 December came the 'worst piece of very good news we have had': von Spee's squadron had been destroyed at the Battle of the Falkland Islands two days earlier. The bitter disappointment was expressed by one of *Australia*'s crewmen:

We are, of course, very glad it has been done; but that we should be disappointed after four months' expectations in the most trying climate and after all these long trips, is very hard. It makes one feel – everyone is alike –

that we have been through a war which is now over, and that peace has been declared without our ever seeing our much-respected enemy.[86]

A long war lay ahead but *Australia* would only sight her 'much-respected enemy' once before 1918.

From the Pacific to the Atlantic, 1914–15

The demise of the German squadron and colonies in Asia and the Pacific by the end of 1914 removed the need for stationing a battle-cruiser there. Accordingly, on 13 December *Australia* was ordered to the Caribbean where, accompanied by *Melbourne* and *Sydney*, she would be in a position to deal with any German cruisers escaping the blockade.[87] This was again a disappointment since the cockpit of the naval war was in the North Sea and *Australia*'s men believed she would be of far more use there than waiting for notional raiding light cruisers.[88]

With the Panama Canal closed to heavy ships,

81 Packer, *Deep as the Sea*, p. 6.
82 AWM, 1 DRL 353, Part 2: Hodgkinson papers, Gunnery Orders for 28 October 1914.
83 Packer, *Deep as the Sea*, pp. 6–7; AWM, 2DRL32, Diary of Capt. G. D. Williams RNR, 10 December 1914.

84 Arthur J. Marder, ed., *Portrait of an Admiral: The Life and Papers of Sir Herbert Richmond* (London: Jonathan Cape, 1952), p. 125.
85 Jose, *Official History*, p. 125.

86 Cited in *ibid.*, p. 126.
87 AWM, 35 2/23, Admiralty to Patey, 13 December 1914.
88 Jose, *Official History*, p. 262.

A quiet evening in *Australia*'s wardroom. A game of table bowls on the wardroom table excites the interest of the ship's dog, known appropriately enough as Bowles, while at least one card game seems to be in progress beyond. Winged collars and flammable furnishings date the photo to the pre-war period. (*NHHC/NH 121018*)

Australia steamed south for the Strait of Magellan via Callao and Valparaíso. She had been at sea since August, and, as indicated by Packer's letter cited above, food was running low. An indication of the dietary needs of the ship is given by the signal sent to the British consul at Callao requesting that he arrange the supply of the following items: 3,000lb fresh meat, 3 tons potatoes, 2,000lb fresh vegetables, 7,000lb tinned meat, 400lb tea, 4,000lb haricot beans, 2,000lb fresh or tinned butter, 1,000lb jam, 2,000lb tinned herrings, 3,000lb sardines, 2,000lb tinned salmon, 100gal lime juice, and, for cleanliness, 2,000lb of yellow soap.[89] Fully replenished at Callao on 18 December, the battle-cruiser reached Valparaíso on Boxing Day. If the recollections of one midshipman were correct, Christmas celebrations had been quite rowdy:

Australia steaming in typical conditions in the North Sea during the Great War. (SPC–A)

> Xmas day – at sea. Service held in the prenoon. The spirit of Xmas; i.e. that of debauch and drunkenness running riot among the young gentlemen. A very good Xmas dinner quite spoiled for me by disgusting exhibitions of inebriation. Roll on the day of release from these despairing circumstances! 1 bottle of beer per man served out – provided out of canteen funds. Glee party at night in gunroom. Some rather good fancy dresses seen. Drink again flowed freely and certain Senior Officers – dead drunk! Messages of welcome from British Colony and French Club at Valparaíso – per wireless.[90]

Others, however, restricted themselves to a quiet day taking a glass of wine with the admiral in the wardroom followed by the noisy fancy dress sing-song in the gunroom in the evening.[91]

On 3 January 1915 the ship developed excessive vibration on the port outer propeller shaft. Divers found that an eddy plate on the fore end of 'A' bracket had carried away, fouling the propeller. The edge of one blade was bent and a piece broken off. Patey informed the Admiralty that a new propeller would be required and that the ship required docking.[92] The same day *Australia* arrived at Port Stanley, Falkland Islands, where she remained until the 5th. Not

until 11 January did the Admiralty order the battlecruiser to proceed to Gibraltar for a new propeller, coaling at São Vicente in the Portuguese Cape Verde islands en route.[93]

Steaming 600 miles north of the Falklands, at 1706 on 6 January *Australia*'s masthead lookout sighted a steamer at a range of twenty-two miles. The strange vessel was steering west-northwest, away from the battlecruiser and far removed from the usual shipping lanes. *Australia* altered course and increased speed to 18.5 knots to intercept. At 1952, with night falling and the suspicious vessel still ten miles off, Capt. Radcliffe fired a shell from 'A' turret to bring her to. This had the desired effect and at 2028 *Australia* closed and illuminated her with searchlights. She was boarded by a party led by Lieutenant Commander H. C. Allen which found her to be the *Eleonore Woermann*, a freighter of 4,624grt which had operated between Germany and her African colonies before the war.[94] She was carrying rice, dressed timber, tobacco, galvanised iron sheets and around 1,800 tons of bagged coal. She also carried extra boats of naval design and had coir matting fenders rigged on one side of the hull. Her master, L. Colmorgen, had destroyed her papers, but Radcliffe had no doubt that she was intended for use as a supply ship to the cruiser *Dresden*. There were also auxiliary raiders still at sea. The boarding party included Acting Sub-Lieutenant Packer who mustered her crew and counted eighty-four Germans, eleven Monrovians and three Krooboys (West African sailors).[95]

Much to the disappointment of *Australia*'s crew, it was decided to scuttle *Eleonore Woermann*, thereby forgoing prize money. She carried little coal in her bunkers, *Australia* could not spare a prize crew, the German was too slow to convoy and there was no other ship available to convoy her. Her officers and men were transferred to *Australia* and at 2200 a scuttling party boarded her to open the sea cocks. In the meantime, Packer and others took whatever souvenirs they could. Upon their return the battlecruiser put two 12in common shells from 'Y' turret and four 4in lyddite shells into her. She started to sink between 2300 and midnight, '… the flames dancing along the decks, the waves lapping her sides creeping higher, and then, without a sound, her bow rose up, her stern sank and she slid out of sight in a tumult of seething water' leaving a small steamboat bobbing on the waves.[96] The remainder of the voyage to São Vicente was uneventful and *Australia* arrived there on 19 January.

Grand Fleet Operations, 1915–18

As *Australia* steamed north the Admiralty changed its mind as to her future deployment. Early in the New Year Lord Fisher, now recalled to the Admiralty as First Sea Lord, informed Vice Admiral Sir David Beatty, commanding the Battle Cruiser Fleet (BCF), that he wished to create a 2nd and 3rd Battle Cruiser Squadron (BCS) for the Grand Fleet. *Australia* was originally earmarked for the 3rd BCS although ended up in the 2nd.[97] Patey was informed of this

89 AWM, 35 2/23, *Australia* to HMS *Newcastle* for the British Consul, Callao, 14 December 1914. One thousand pounds converts to 454 kilos, 100 gallons to 454 litres.

90 AWM, 1DRL0565, Papers of D. A. Sharp, HMAS *Australia*.

91 AWM, 2DRL0032, Diary of Capt. G. D. Williams RNR, 25 December 1914.

92 AWM, 35 2/23, Patey to Admiralty, 3 January 1915.

93 *Ibid.*, Admiralty to Patey, 11 January 1915.

94 http://www.wrecksite.eu/wreck.aspx?58232 [accessed February 2018].

95 AWM, 36 Bundle 1/3/5; Packer, *Deep as the Sea*, p. 7.

96 AWM, 36 Bundle 1/3/5; Packer, *Deep as the Sea*, pp. 7–8.

97 Stephen Roskill, *Admiral of the Fleet Earl Beatty, the Last Naval Hero: An Intimate Biography* (London: Collins, 1981), pp. 106–7.

development as *Australia* left São Vicente on 20 January, the Admiralty signalling that she was to proceed to Devonport Dockyard for repairs to her propeller instead of Gibraltar.[98] She was to arrive 'in the dark hours', taking all anti-submarine precautions and retaining her torpedo net defence on board.[99] Only on 27 January was the ACNB asked its views in respect of *Australia* joining the Grand Fleet as flagship of the new squadron, to which it concurred. *Australia* arrived at Plymouth and entered Devonport Dockyard for refitting on the 28th. She departed on 12 February for further refitting at Rosyth on the Firth of Forth which she reached after a stormy passage, subsequently joining the BCF.[100]

Based in the Forth, the BCF was the fast wing of the Grand Fleet which in turn was based at Scapa Flow in the Orkneys under the command of Admiral Sir John Jellicoe. A seniority problem arose as Patey was senior to Beatty, the BCF commander, but this was resolved by appointing Patey Flag Officer West Indies, as originally intended (although retaining command of the Australian Fleet), while *Australia* became the flagship of Rear Admiral William Pakenham commanding the 2nd BCS. The squadron was completed by *Australia*'s sister battlecruisers *Indefatigable* and *New Zealand*.

The work of the Grand Fleet was essential to the successful Allied prosecution of the war. The British and German fleets attempted to bring the other into a position advantageous to itself – the Germans wishing to trap and overwhelm a portion of the Grand Fleet or draw it over a waiting submarine line, thereby reducing its numerical preponderance; the Grand Fleet, meanwhile, hoped to bring on a general action leading to the destruction of the High Seas Fleet. Neither achieved its object. However, it was sufficient for the British to confine the Germans to the North Sea to obtain their aim of enforcing the blockade that denied Germany its export trade and the import of food and raw materials vital to her war effort. It also prevented the interdiction, at least by surface ships, of shipping bringing vital supplies into Britain while allowing the passage to France of reinforcements, supplies and equipment essential to the prosecution of the war by the Allied armies.

Australia's role as part of the BCF was to scout ahead of the Battle Fleet to contact enemy forces and draw them onto the main fleet. When battle was joined she and her sisters would form a fast division of the main fleet and use their speed to concentrate on part of the enemy's line. However, the High Seas Fleet would prove an elusive enemy, its battlecruisers initially being used to raid East Coast ports with the main fleet acting as distant cover. Only once had the BCF been in a position to bring on an action – at the Battle of the Dogger Bank on 24 January 1915, weeks

before *Australia*'s arrival. However, signalling deficiencies in the BCF allowed the German ships to escape with damage and the loss of the obsolescent armoured cruiser *Blücher*.

For nearly four years *Australia* was involved in a number of unsuccessful attempts by the Grand Fleet to bring the High Seas Fleet to action while at the same time covering operations by light forces or carrying out fleet exercises and gunnery practice in the North Sea. It would be monotonous to detail every one of these so only a representative sample is given.

At the end of January 1916 the Admiralty learnt of the presence of a German minelayer in the Skagerrak. The 1st Light Cruiser Squadron (LCS) was ordered to conduct a sweep to intercept her. On the morning of 26 January *Australia* and the 2nd BCS sailed in support but nothing was found and the squadron returned to the Forth after a sweep of the Norwegian coast.[101] On 10 March 1916 the battlecruisers were again at sea to cover a sweep by light cruisers and destroyers northward up the Norwegian coast from the Naze.[102] In April British destroyers were sent through the Skagerrak and rounded Skagen into the Kattegat to intercept ore ships sailing from Sweden to Germany. To counter any response by German light cruisers, the 2nd LCS would be stationed off Skagen with the 2nd BCS off the mouth of the Skagerrak as heavy support. The 2nd Battle Squadron was dispatched to the area from Scapa Flow in case the High Seas Fleet tried to intervene with its battlecruisers. The British battlecruisers sailed on 21 April. Later that day intelligence was received that the whole High Seas Fleet was stirring. Consequently the destroyer operation was cancelled and the Grand Fleet concentrated in the North Sea on the 22nd. However, once German signals intelligence discovered this mobilisation the High Seas Fleet cancelled its operation, of which the Admiralty became aware at 0900.[103]

Misfortune literally struck *Australia* when the battlecruisers were seventy-five miles northwest

---

[98] The Australian official history states that this decision was made after the Battle of the Dogger Bank on 24 January 1915, but this is incorrect as the signal record shows.

[99] AWM, 35 2/23, Admiralty to Patey, 20 January 1915.

[100] Jose, *Official History*, pp. 262–3.

[101] Jose, *Official History*, pp. 271–2.

[102] AWM, 45 1/72.

[103] Jose, *Official History*, pp. 273–4.

HMS *New Zealand* astern of *Australia* in 1917. A succession of collisions between the two on 22 April 1916 resulted in sufficient damage to *Australia* to require docking and causing her to miss the Battle of Jutland on 31 May. *(Courtesy Philippe Caresse)*

of the Horns Reef. On the afternoon of the 22nd the ships were zigzagging in line abreast five cables apart at 19.5 knots. At 1530 visibility was variable and the next ship to starboard of *Australia*, HMS *New Zealand*, was in sight, but at 1533 the mist 'shut down suddenly' on the fleet, visibility was reduced to fifty yards and *New Zealand* could no longer be seen. At 1540 *Australia* made a scheduled zigzag to starboard. At 1543 *New Zealand*'s bow suddenly loomed out of the fog. Capt. Radcliffe turned *Australia* hard to port and reversed the port engine, but to no avail and the ships breasted together. *Australia* was heavily damaged down her starboard side. Capt. Radcliffe stopped engines, the ships separated and *New Zealand* vanished into the mist. *Australia* proceeded at half speed but at 1546 *New Zealand* was again sighted on the starboard bow, steering a converging course from starboard to port. Again *Australia* attempted to

turn away to port but her stem glanced off *New Zealand*'s side just abaft 'P' turret and the ships breasted together once more. Both ships stopped to assess the damage, *New Zealand* lying hove to just thirty or forty yards off her starboard beam. With no love lost between the two ships, sailors off watch in *Australia* took advantage of a handy potato locker to pelt their opposite numbers in *New Zealand* with tubers accompanied by a barrage of insults.[104] *New Zealand* had again suffered only slight damage but *Australia*'s bulkheads required shoring up after which she proceeded to Rosyth at 12 knots, later increasing to 16.[105]

Australia was ordered to Newcastle to assess

the extent of the damage where further misfortune struck when the pilot conning her into a floating dock fouled the port propellers on the side of the dock. The inner was repaired but the outer had to be replaced. The ship then sailed for Devonport Dockyard to carry out full repairs, arriving on 4 May. This information was included in a letter from Radcliffe to the Australian Naval Representative in London in June, apparently the first official notification received by the Australian authorities as the Admiralty had neglected to inform the ACNB that its flagship had been badly damaged.[106] Meanwhile, the dockyard completed the repairs ahead of schedule and she sailed for Rosyth on 31 May.

104 William Warner, *Onboard HMAS* Australia, *1914–18: A Boy's Recollections of Life on the Lower Deck of the Battle Cruiser* (Seven Hills, NSW: Five Senses Education, 2014), p. 103.

105 NAA, A6108 F51/1/6, Radcliffe to Rear Admiral Commanding 2nd BCS, 28 April 1916.

106 *Ibid.*, Radcliffe to Commonwealth Naval Representative, 6 June 1916.

As *Australia* steamed north to rejoin the fleet news reached her of an engagement in the North Sea during which the High Seas Fleet had finally been brought to action: the Battle of Jutland. She returned to service on 4 June, her company bitterly disappointed at having missed the engagement in which the BCF had been heavily involved. However, the destruction of three battlecruisers which blew up and sank in the course of the action with the loss of all but a handful of their ship's companies revealed serious deficiencies in British battlecruiser design and turret procedures. Among those lost was *Australia*'s sister ship and squadron mate *Indefatigable*, and there can be no doubt that the loss of the former in similar circumstances would have been disastrous to the young RAN. *Australia* was accounted a good gunnery ship

LIFE ABOARD IN THE GRAND FLEET

Shipboard life in the battlecruiser *Australia* as in the Grand Fleet itself was governed by a high degree of organisation which translated into unvarying routine. Boy Seaman William Warner of Sydney recalled it thus:

> We have three distinct jobs: one when we are in harbour; one when we are at sea; and another when the ship is in action. For example, in harbour I am a distributing office messenger, attached to the signal staff to do their bidding. At sea I am a voicepipe man in the for'ard 4-inch gun control; and in action I am personal messenger and voice-pipe man to the gunnery lieutenant-commander. At sea during the day we normally all work at part of ship and are busy with cleaning and other normal duties. The crew is divided into three watches at sea, namely Red, White and Blue. For night defence the voicepipe is manned according to the watches.[119]

Considerable thought and effort was put in to keeping the men of the fleet from boredom between sorties. Films were provided and clubs established ashore. Organised sport was popular, with football and rugby leagues and boxing tournaments being established.[120] Route marches helped keep the men fit. On 10 March, for example, men from *Australia*

Australia coaling ship. Note the trolleys at the ready. Looming over the proceedings is 'Q' turret, trained to port across the deck. The mast and funnel of the collier can be seen beyond. *(SPC–A)*

were landed by steamer at South Queensferry and marched four miles (6.4km) to Dundas Rock, had a breather and marched back again, spending the rest of the day on shore leave.[121] In another scheme to occupy the men, the workshops of the fleet were used to manufacture items useful to the war effort on a voluntary basis. Skilled workers machined parts for shells and fuzes while the unskilled produced cartridge bags and rope grommets or carrying handles. Between the introduction of the scheme in December 1915 and 31 December 1916 *Australia* produced 84,183 grommets for shells of various calibres, 17,349 base plates, 310 slings and 320 gauges.

Thousands more were produced before the end of the war.[122] The men also provided their own entertainment, organising concerts and reviews or playing card games and the traditional pastimes of ukkers (a form of ludo) or shove ha'penny; also resorted to was crown and anchor, although illegally since the men were not allowed to play for money stakes. Writing letters to friends and family on the other side of the world passed more time and mail from home was much prized. There was also ship husbandry to be carried out to maintain equipment in proper order. The bunkers were kept topped up by regular coaling, with about 200–250 tons being taken aboard every few days.

Leave depended on service requirements. Short leave was permitted when the ship was in port, giving the men time for an afternoon, evening and an occasional night ashore. While the ship was refitting long leave allowed the men ten to fourteen days away from the ship, the port and starboard watches into which much of the ship was divided in harbour taking their leave in turn. Unlike the Grand Fleet in the near-desolation of Scapa Flow, the battlecruiser men had the attractions of nearby Edinburgh while two railway warrants per year enabled them to go further afield. *Australia*'s British crewmen could visit families and friends, but native Australians far from home had to settle for the bright lights of London and other cities to provide the pubs and female company so important after long confinement in exclusively male company under naval discipline. Food and accommodation were available at reasonable rates by organisations such as Miss Agnes Weston's Royal Sailors' Rests ('Aggie Weston's'), the YMCA and the Union Jack Club.[123]

Australia was also a training ground for young officers destined to make their names in a future war. The first class of the Royal Australian Naval College at Jervis Bay graduated in December 1916 and five of the midshipmen were sent to *Australia* including Joseph Burnett, subsequently lost in command of the cruiser HMAS *Sydney* in the Second World War, and Rupert Long, the RAN's Director of Naval Intelligence during that conflict. Their conduct was praised by Capt. Oliver Backhouse who had succeeded Capt. Radcliffe on 14 December 1916.[124]

The end of a bout in one of *Australia*'s boxing tournaments, the ship probably lying in the Firth of Forth. *(SPC–A)*

and perhaps her 12in guns would have proved themselves but all such is idle speculation.[107]

Rejoining the BCF, *Australia* resumed her endless routine of North Sea operations. In August Admiral Reinhard Scheer made his last attempt to entice the Grand Fleet into a submarine trap with an attack on Hartlepool. Signals intelligence provided warning of the operation and *Australia* sortied together with the rest of the Grand Fleet on 18 August, but no sooner had Scheer became aware that the Grand Fleet was at sea than he turned for Wilhelmshaven.[108] Throughout 1917 most of the operations in the North Sea were carried out by light forces and

[107] Jose, *Official History*, p. 268n.

[108] *Ibid.*, pp. 275–8.

A further twelve midshipmen arrived in 1918, the opportunity to serve in such a great fleet providing invaluable hands-on training and experience so soon after graduation.[125]

To be sure, much of this experience was humdrum, as in the case of the operations to cover the passage of convoys to Scandinavia against German attack in 1918.[126] The diary of Chief Petty Officer Telegraphist William Powell provides a flavour of the routine nature of these duties:

Monday April 22nd At Sea: Turned out 6.45. Sighted Convoy same time. 22 ships in Convoy proceeding at 8 knots. Arrived off Bergen about 11 am then cruised around at 16 knots until the other one came out. Convoy 'Homeward Bound' came out 3 pm. 36 ships. Sea still smooth. A little warmer today. Altered course 3 points alternative about every 5 minutes. Kept the afternoon watch in Main Office. Read press from Horsea at 1 pm in Type II. Nothing much doing in the evening. Turned in about 9.30.[127]

However, excitement was never far off, even with the enemy nowhere at hand. In May 1918 a possible disaster was averted by the coolness of Lt Cdr F. C. Darley when a 12in shell became wedged in a hoist after its fuze jammed on a projection. Darley cleared the magazine and shell room and undertook the dangerous task of removing the crumpled fuze himself which he then threw overboard before retiring to his cabin for a cigarette.[128] But utter drudgery was never very far off either. William Warner has this memoir of a terrible night at sea in early 1916:

The men on the bridge, fifty feet above the water-line, are drenched and drenched again by wave after wave of water hitting the breakwater and A turret. The icy cold salt water rushes over the bridge and gathers to smash its way onto the after bridges and then pour down the ladders leading below. […] The sounds of retching come out of the blackness. An audible groan follows the retching and can be heard despite the wind and crashing waves. Then there is the smell of vomit.

Crewmen clearing the quarterdeck of snow during a Scottish winter in wartime. Note the scrollwork on the after screen displaying *Australia*'s newly won battle honours and the ship's bell hanging beneath them. (*Royal Australian Navy*)

Even if you don't retch you have an upset belly. Your ears ache; your nose is stuffed up; your eyes are sore from peering into the darkness and howling wind. The funnel chains continue to rattle against the funnels, now throwing off a steamy heat that is discomforting even though we pray for warmth. Midnight comes when the watch is relieved. […] On this night, entering the boys' mess two decks below, we find water swilling from side to side waist high. The water surges fore then aft from side to side, following the movement of the ship as she rises and falls into the mountainous seas and drives ahead. A sea boot floats past me as I gain my mess. Drinking basins the right way up bob about everywhere like toy boats. Hammocks slung high are comfortably clear of the water, but what about my own? How is it faring in the netting? Ah! Some kind and thoughtful friend has slung it for me. How tired we all are! Getting into the hammock is also an ordeal. It is impossible to find dry gear in which to sleep. We have to strip and dry our skin as best we can and then climb naked in between the blankets. This requires much effort, swinging from hammock hook to hammock hook like a chimpanzee to avoid the swirling water.[129]

Under these circumstances the Armistice can only have come as a blessed relief.

[119] Warner, *Onboard HMAS* Australia, p. 62.

[120] Peter Liddle, *The Sailors' War 1914–18* (Poole, Dorset: Blandford, 1985), pp. 125–7.

[121] AWM, PR00435, Papers of William Hope Powell.

[122] AWM, 45 1/74.

[123] Liddle, *The Sailors' War*, pp. 133–6.

[124] NAA, MP472/1 5/17/6248.

[125] Jose, *Official History*, pp. 279n & 475–6.

[126] See for example AWM, 45 1/15 which contains orders for such an operation in February 1918.

[127] AWM, PR00435, Papers of CPO William Hope Powell.

[128] Jose, *Official History*, p. 279n.

[129] Warner, *Onboard HMAS* Australia, pp. 66–7.

Australia leads the 2nd Battle Cruiser Squadron under the Forth Bridge at its anchorage at Rosyth. Following her are *New Zealand* and the *Indomitable*. The occasion is the surrender of the High Seas Fleet in the Forth on 21 November 1918. *(SPC–A)*

2nd BCS *Australia* led the dreadnoughts of the port column as the mighty assembly steamed into the Forth where the Germans dropped anchor at 1430. The 2nd BCS steamed round them to give the crews a grandstand view before dropping anchor. *Australia* was responsible for overseeing the battlecruiser SMS *Hindenburg*. She placed a party aboard the German ship which reported nothing amiss. As CPO William Hope Powell declared: 'We have no fear now as the Hun navy is ours for the time. Censorship removed at midnite.' A few days later *Australia* joined the rest of the Grand Fleet in escorting the High Seas Fleet from the Forth to Scapa Flow where she resumed her duty as guardship of *Hindenburg* and resumed her dull patrols in the North Sea.

Australia's war was over. It had not been a spectacular one. Her sole action, if it can be called that, was against an unarmed merchantman. Through no fault of her own she had never caught up with von Spee and had missed Jutland. Nevertheless, she had been instrumental in forcing von Spee from the South Pacific and had performed duties in the North Sea which though unspectacular and monotonous were vital to maintaining the blockade which hampered Germany's ability to prosecute the war and ensured that Allied trade passed largely unmolested once the U-boat menace had been countered. She had also been a valuable reinforcement for the Battle Cruiser Fleet (redesignated the Battle Cruiser Force in December 1916) whose commanders were concerned to retain a numerical superiority over their German counterparts.[117] Although *Australia* had never come under enemy fire, illness and accident had still claimed the lives of nineteen men during her deployment to Britain.[118]

Unhappy Return: The Mutiny of 1919

Australia's time in Britain ended on 23 April 1919 when she sailed from Portsmouth for home, being

the battlecruisers' seagoing time was mainly spent in exercises between Rosyth and Scapa Flow. There were occasional unsuccessful sorties to intercept raiders, such as that on 3 November 1917 when the 2nd BCS was ordered to a position 120 miles off Rosyth to intercept possible enemy raiding forces.[109] Ten days later there was a major deployment by the battlecruisers when the 1st and 2nd BCS were ordered to rendezvous with the 'large light cruisers' *Courageous* and *Glorious*, the 1st LCS and destroyers with the intention of intercepting German ships returning from a possible raid on the Newcastle area. No enemy vessels were sighted.[110] On 17 November the 2nd BCS was ordered to a position off the Skagerrak to cover the withdrawal of a raid into the Kattegat by the 4th LCS. On 12 December *Australia* was again in collision, this time with *Repulse*, and again receiving sufficient damage to put her in dock until the 30th when she fired on a suspected submarine.[111]

On 23 February 1918 a call for volunteers for special duty resulted in eleven of *Australia*'s crewmen being drafted to the old battleship *Hindustan* for training. They were to take part in an operation to block the canal leading from the German submarine base at Bruges to the North Sea at Zeebrugge. Engineer Lieutenant W. H. V. Edgar was appointed chief engineer of the converted ferry HMS *Iris* which was to accompany the assault ship, the old cruiser *Vindictive*.

Others were part of the assault party in *Vindictive* with more assigned to the blocking cruiser *Thetis*. All performed creditably, Edgar coming on deck when *Iris* was under heavy fire to help activate the ship's smoke apparatus for which he was awarded a Distinguished Service Cross. Three of the assault party were awarded Distinguished Service Medals, one of whom, Leading Seaman D. J. O. Rudd, was included in a ballot to decide which of his unit would be awarded the Victoria Cross. Three others were mentioned in dispatches.[112]

By late July *Australia* was covering minelayers, presumably those working on the Northern Barrage, an exercise repeated on 7 and 27 September and on 3 October.[113] On 28 October she was docked at Rosyth and was there when the Armistice was signed on 11 November, returning to duty the following day. On the 21st she participated in Operation ZZ,[114] the surrender of the High Seas Fleet in the Firth of Forth.[115] The Germans approached in a single column and were met by the Grand Fleet in two columns which turned to conform to the German movements, a column of battleships and battlecruisers on either side. Ensigns were flown from every point and *Australia* flew the Australian flag at the jack.[116] At the head of the

109 Jose, *Official History*, p. 279; AWM, 45 1/43.
110 AWM, 45 1/44.
111 Jose, *Official History*, pp. 279 & 262n.

112 *Ibid.*, pp. 281–2 & 592–3.
113 AWM, PR82/72, Papers of CPO C. F. G. Geary.
114 The orders for Operation ZZ are available at: http://www.gwpda.org/naval/opzz.htm [accessed February 2018].
115 AWM, PR82/72, Papers of CPO C. F. G. Geary.

116 AWM, PR00435, Papers of CPO William Hope Powell.
117 AWM, 45 1/73, Rear Admiral Commanding Battle Cruiser Fleet to relevant BCF commanders, 3 December 1916; on the reinforcement, see for example Roskill, *Beatty*, pp. 96 & 137–8; AWM, 45 1/73.
118 Figures extracted from the AWM Roll of Honour: http://www.awm.gov.au [accessed February 2018].

AUSTRALIA AND AVIATION

Australia made a contribution to the early development of naval aviation. Throughout 1917 the BCF had carried out a number of experiments launching aircraft from its light cruisers and battlecruisers. On 18 December 1917 Flight Lieutenant F. M. Fox took off from the battlecruiser's upper deck into a 25-knot breeze. Rear Admiral Arthur Leveson, who had relieved Vice Admiral William Pakenham as commander of the 2nd BCS (Pakenham now commanded the Battle Cruiser Force), was keen to persist with the experiments by erecting a flight deck on a 12in turret. On 7 March 1918[130] Flight Commander Donald flew a Sopwith 1½ Strutter off a platform on 'P' turret, the first successful launch of a two-seater aircraft from a turret. Noting the possibilities for reconnaissance and gunnery spotting aircraft to be carried aboard the larger ships, Beatty ordered the experiments to be continued.[131] *Australia*'s aircraft was fitted with a wireless set on 17 April and was used for spotting in gunnery exercises two days later.[132] Aircraft were carried in most Grand Fleet capital ships by the end of the war.[133]

130 The official history states 8 March; Jose, *Official History*, p. 281.
131 AWM, 45 1/76.
132 AWM, PR00435, Papers of CPO William Hope Powell.
133 R. D. Layman, *Naval Aviation in the First World War: Its Impact and Influence* (London: Conway, 1989), p. 114.

Flight Commander Donald of the Royal Naval Air Service flies a Sopwith 1½ Strutter (serial number 5644) off a platform on 'P' turret on 7 March 1918, the first successful launch of a two-seater from a turret. *Australia*'s sister HMS *New Zealand* lies beyond. (*NHHC/NH 112864*)

seen off by the Prince of Wales and the First Sea Lord, Admiral of the Fleet Sir Rosslyn Wemyss. Flying his broad pennant from the foremast was Commodore John Saumarez Dumaresq RN, the first Australian-born officer to command the Australian Squadron. Dumaresq had gone to Britain to join the Royal Navy and had shown a technical bent, developing the instrument to measure the rate of change of range which bears his name. He had commanded HMAS *Sydney* in the Grand Fleet and been instrumental in pioneering methods of operating aircraft from ships. The commanding officer was Capt. Claude Cumberlege RN who had served in the RAN throughout the war, commanding the destroyers during the Pacific operations of 1914 and later the cruiser *Brisbane*. Both *Australia*'s gunnery officer, Lt Philip Vian RN, and her First Lieutenant, Lt Cdr Harold Burrough RN, went on to make names for themselves in the Second World War.[134]

134 Feakes, *White Ensign*, p. 197.

Cumberlege, a sun-lover, had that streak of eccentricity for which Royal Navy officers of the era were famous. Vian has this memoir of him:

> On a Sunday morning, divisions were being paraded on the quarterdeck in Number One dress, for his inspection. The Captain electrified everyone, and the Commodore in particular, by appearing on deck in a slip, wending his way through the divisions to the ladder and so into his galley, to picnic ashore in the sun.[135]

For the ship's company the end of the war cannot have come soon enough and there can be no doubt that war weariness set in as 1918 wore on. William Warner:

> Long-term monotony can easily lead to problems for the crew. Tempers are easily frayed;

135 Admiral of the Fleet Sir Philip Vian, *Action This Day* (London: Frederick Muller, 1960), p. 14.

disagreements occur more frequently, both over work matters and at personal levels; wild rumours spread. Jealousies tend to be aroused. This is also the time when insubordination smoulders and efficiency suffers. The crew is stale [...] Many changes had taken place within the ship over the last couple of years. Youngsters have come up from the junior mess deck; older ratings had passed on to high positions; some had left the ship to join the Australian destroyers in the Adriatic Sea; and new crew had joined to take their places. Except for one or two of the old hands, we now messed with strangers. Officers had also been changing frequently. Our old, happy family was disintegrating.[136]

Coupled with the scant information traditionally provided by officers to their crews and the after-

136 Warner, *Onboard HMAS* Australia, pp. 161 & 163.

'A' turret and the bridge with its splinter protection seen from the forecastle in 1918. Compare with the photo on p. 226. *(Courtesy Ray Burt)*

effects of a long and draining war, these circumstances no doubt contributed to the unrest which followed the ship's arrival at the port of Fremantle in Western Australia on 28 May 1919. Feted by the citizens of Fremantle and nearby Perth, it was rumoured that *Australia*, scheduled to depart on 1 June, would delay her departure by a day to allow the hospitality to be repaid. When it became apparent that the rumour was false and the ship would in fact sail on 1 June, a group of ratings, many of whom were in varying degrees the worse for four days' carousing, requested that the departure be postponed so they could entertain their friends aboard. Unsurprisingly, Capt. Cumberlege refused the request and the group dispersed. However, as the ship prepared to sail the stokers on watch were incited to abandon the boiler rooms, delaying the departure of the ship until officers and senior ratings had ordered others to take their places. An internal investigation saw twelve men charged with mutiny, but only five were court-martialled, including Able Seaman Dalmorton Rudd, decorated for his actions at Zeebrugge but subsequently disrated from Leading Seaman for an alcohol-related offence connected with the death of his wife later that year. These men were sentenced to terms of between one and two years' imprisonment.[137]

The case aroused public sympathy and led to calls for clemency in Parliament from both sides of the house. The Admiralty (under whose operational control *Australia* still was at the time of the offences) halved the sentences, not because they were considered excessive but on account of the youth of the offenders. Without consulting the ACNB, the Commonwealth government requested full remission which was acceded to as part of a post-war amnesty for offenders held on disciplinary charges. Already disgusted at the lack of consultation, Dumaresq and the First Naval Member, Rear Admiral Sir Percy Grant, tendered their resignation after reading newspaper reports that the remissions had been granted because the sentences were considered

Australia traversing the Suez Canal in May 1919 on the long voyage home. *(SPC–A)*

137 NAA, MP1049/1 1919/0120; Robert Hyslop, 'Mutiny on HMAS *Australia*: A Forgotten Episode of 1919 Political-Naval Relations' in *Australian Journal of Public Administration* 29 (September 1970), no. 3, pp. 284–96, & David Stevens, 'The HMAS *Australia* Mutiny' in Christopher M. Bell & Bruce A. Elleman, ed., *Naval Mutinies in the Twentieth Century: An International Perspective* (London: Frank Cass, 2003), pp. 123–44.

The last hurrah. *Australia* dressed overall at the Fleet Review for the Prince of Wales in Port Phillip Bay, Melbourne, on 28 May 1920. *(SPC–A)*

too severe. They were requested to withdraw their resignations after it was agreed that it would be widely publicised that the sentences were 'just and necessary' and clemency only extended due to the Armistice.[138] In the meantime, *Australia* continued her return visits, enjoying receptions in Adelaide, Melbourne and Sydney where the crew marched through the city under a celebratory arch.[139]

Last Years

In April 1919 the Admiralty advised that alterations were planned to the armament of certain ships and that *Australia* was consequently to have her 3in and 4in AA mountings replaced by 4in Mk-V guns on HA Mk-III mountings. The guns were duly ordered at a cost of £8720 and received in June 1920, the mountings following two months later.[140] The ship was refitted in Sydney between 15 December 1920 and 23 February 1921 during which the 4in HA guns and their magazines were installed. The same refit revealed her turbines to be in excellent condition, the ship reaching 24.3 knots during a speed trial on 27 September 1919.[141] Between whiles *Australia* resumed normal peacetime activities, highlighted by participation in the RAN's inaugural Fleet Review, held in Port Phillip Bay, Melbourne, on 28 May 1920 with the Prince of Wales taking the salute.

Although *Australia* was in good condition, the ACNB found itself with a large, obsolete warship on its hands. She was expensive to maintain and man at a time when defence budgets were being slashed. Australia had a massive war debt to service and the carnage of the war left scant public enthusiasm for the financing of armaments. Moreover, there was no further realistic role for her in the Pacific. The armoured cruiser danger that had so exercised Sir John Fisher a decade before no longer existed. The German and Russian fleets had been destroyed by war and revolution; France and the United States presented no threat. Japan was now the only possible enemy, especially after the demise of the Anglo-Japanese Naval Treaty in 1921, but an engagement with any of the Imperial Japanese

Australia laid up in reserve in Sydney Harbour in 1923. Her secondary armament has been removed, as has the rangefinder above the control top. *(NHHC/NH 52514)*

138 NAA, MP472/1 5/19/11039, Commonwealth Naval Order 260 of 24 December 1919; Hyslop, 'Mutiny on HMAS *Australia*', p. 292.

139 NAA, MP472/1 1/1919/4290.

140 NAA, MP124 612/202/100.

141 NAA, A4141, AUSTRALIA I Ship's Book.

Navy's new super-dreadnought battleships and battlecruisers would reveal *Australia* to be a death trap, too weak to fight and too slow to run away. The lines of communication could more effectively be patrolled by cruisers.

This was reflected in post-war considerations of the role of the RAN. At a conference held in Penang and attended by the First Naval Member, Rear Admiral Grant, and the commanders-in-chief of the Far East and China Stations, only the Australian light cruisers were considered for a role in the imperial forces in the region in the event of war. Eventually it was decided at the 1921 Imperial Conference in London that future naval policy in the Far East would await the outcome of the naval disarmament conference to be held in Washington later that year.[142] *Australia* was relegated to the role of guardship as tender to HMAS *Cerberus*, the training establishment at Flinders

Naval Depot, Western Port Bay, Victoria.[143] There was no realistic requirement for her guns here and she was effectively a stationary gunnery and torpedo drill ship, a derisory duty for a battle-cruiser. She returned to Sydney and paid off into reserve in December 1921.

The ship's time was now up. Under the terms of the Washington Naval Treaty signed on 6 February 1922 the capital ships of the Royal Navy would be limited to 525,000 tons. Naturally, the Admiralty decided that only the most modern battleships and battlecruisers would be retained – those mounting 13.5in (343mm) and 15in (381mm) guns. Given that she would effectively come under Admiralty control in time of war, the RAN's battlecruiser was included in the RN total and *Australia* was specifically listed as one of the vessels to be disposed of in her entirety – either by sinking or

breaking up. Preservation was not an option. These provisions must have been welcome to the Australian government which was able to rid itself of an obsolete and expensive white elephant while making a public contribution to world arms limitation.

Employment of *Australia*'s eleven 12in guns (eight mounted in the ship and three spares) for coast defence purposes was investigated. The Chief of the General Staff, Lieutenant General H. G. Chauvel, sought advice regarding British Army intentions from Brigadier General T. A. Blamey, the Army's representative in London. Blamey advised that the British intended to use the 9.2in and 15in calibres for long-range coast defence purposes (as eventually installed at Singapore). In addition, the Australian Army anticipated problems finding a sufficiently stout wharf to store the guns and turrets. The ship's turret engines were unsuited for land use and new machinery would have to be constructed at considerable cost. Essentially, Chauvel advised,

---

142 Stevens, *The Australian Centenary History of Defence*, p. 63.

143 Commonwealth Naval Order 123 of 29 March 1921.

The after superstructure bring dismantled prior to scuttling in 1924. The boats and all but the main armament have been removed. *(Courtesy Philippe Caresse)*

Sailors look on as *Australia* capsizes to port off the Sydney Heads minutes after the firing of her scuttling charges on 12 April 1924. *(SPC–A)*

the guns had no role as coastal artillery. They would be sunk with the ship.[144]

When news of the battlecruiser's proposed fate reached the public, reaction was strong, the variety of protests demonstrating how much the flagship meant to a wide cross-section of Australians. The Lord Mayor of Adelaide convened a public meeting and deemed the sinking an 'act of sacrilege'. There was a suggestion that she should be used as a training ship.[145] The Queensland Women's Electoral League asked that the ship be preserved as a museum but were eventually mollified that her destruction was 'consistent with Australia's honour and her part in disarmament as laid down by the Washington Treaty'.[146] The same answer was given to all public proposals to preserve *Australia* or find an alternative use for the vessel such as a breakwater or an 'immigration hostel': that it was necessary for her to be demolished or sunk in deep water for Australia to be in compliance with the Washington Treaty.[147]

Australia was 'stripped to her bare hull and armour, the only section of her fighting or steaming equipment remaining in the ship was her guns […] For months residents of harbour suburbs had been disturbed by mysterious noises at week-ends; explosions by breaking-up gangs, tearing everything of value from within the doomed vessel.'[148] Undersea cable companies were contacted to ensure the wreck would not foul their lines.[149] Anything useful was removed and either recycled for other RAN uses or sold. Items such as pumps saw continued use in industry and her siren signalled the start and close of work at the power station of the new capital city, Canberra. Other items such as a 12in gun breech and one of her screws were passed to the Australian War Memorial where they survive to this day.

On the day appointed for the scuttling of the flagship, 12 April 1924, *Australia* came out of Sydney Harbour towed by four tugs and escorted by the cruiser HMAS *Brisbane* commanded by Capt. Henry Feakes. The battlecruiser looked stunted with her topmasts and fighting tops gone and her middle funnel lying on the deck, to which her three spare guns were lashed. She was

surrounded by a multitude of local steamers and small craft packed with sightseers. Her decks were covered with floral tributes. When the sinking position was reached the sea cocks were opened and scuttling charges fired. *Australia* listed to port and the spare guns broke loose and 'rumbled over the side' as a 21-gun salute was fired by *Brisbane* and an RN light cruiser squadron visiting Australia with the Special Service Squadron led by HMS *Hood* (q.v.). In twenty-one minutes she was gone. The fleet returned to harbour, 'bands playing "A life on the ocean wave", as the traditional naval routine requires on return from a naval funeral'.[150]

Legacy

There were many at the time and after who believed the scuttling was wrong and that *Australia* had a future. Feakes, writing well after the event, considered it a 'tragic blunder'.[151] More surprising is that such views have survived to this day. It has been argued that Australia could have refused to sign the Washington Naval

Treaty and retained the battlecruiser, reclassifying her as an armoured cruiser. She could have been re-engined and her armament and fire control modified. As the 12in gun was becoming obsolete, Australia could have purchased the remaining barrels and ammunition, or even purchased ammunition from Spain or Brazil which operated vessels fitted with the same ordnance. *Australia*, so the argument runs, would then have been superior to any Japanese heavy cruiser at a cost equalling that of a new 'County' class heavy cruiser.[152]

The argument is not only counterfactual but flawed. The subordinate nature of the Australian diplomatic and naval connection to Britain in the early 1920s makes the idea of thumbing the Antipodean nose at the Washington Treaty quite unrealistic. Apart from this, *Australia*, far from becoming a killer of Japanese heavy cruisers, could well have become their victim as the latter were organised in squadrons of four and given a powerful torpedo armament. They were backed up by squadrons of battleships superior in every way even to a rebuilt *Australia*. The stockpiled ammunition would last if properly stored but the

---

144 NAA, B197 1855/1/60; 1865/1/65.

145 NAA, MP124 603/206/205.

146 NAA, MP124 603/206/258.

147 NAA, A458 M376/4.

148 Feakes, *White Ensign*, p. 213.

149 NAA, MP124 606/206/263.

150 Feakes, *White Ensign*, pp. 213–4; a film of the occasion is available at: http://www.abc.net.au/news/2013-10-03/hmas-australia-our-first-flag-ship/4983200 [accessed February 2018].

151 Feakes, *White Ensign*, p. 214.

152 Royal Australian Navy Sea Power Centre, 'A Loss More Symbolic than Material?' in *Semaphore* (May 2004), available at: http://www.navy.gov.au/media-room/publications/semaphore-may-2004

suggested overseas suppliers presented problems: Spain did indeed manufacture 12in ammunition but none would have been available after 1936 (see *Alfonso XIII*), while Brazil did not manufacture her own ammunition at all (see *Minas Geraes*).[153] All in all, *Australia* was better consigned to the deep. The wreck was discovered during a survey in 1990 and inspected by remotely operated vehicle in 2002. It was found that the hull had slid vertically into the water and somersaulted as it sank causing the turrets to fall out. They surround the wreck which lies upside down on the sea floor.[154]

Australia had served as a powerful symbol of a young, confident Federation. She signalled the new nation's determination to take a full part in its own defence while contributing to that of the Empire, being called on to do so far sooner than anyone who watched her lead the new fleet into Sydney Harbour that October day in 1913 could have anticipated. She played a full role in the dismantling of the German position in Oceania and was an important factor in von Spee's move to the eastern Pacific. She then contributed to maintaining the Allied dominance of the North Sea which played a significant role in the defeat of Germany. But by 1919 advances in naval construction and the sweeping changes in the world politico-strategic situation had quite passed her by. Saddled by heavy war debts and with much of her young confidence savaged by the heavy losses suffered by her army, Australia was no longer the country to support the confident navalism of 1913 and the demise of the once proud battlecruiser was symbolic of the passing of an era in Australia's short history.

Sources

Unpublished Sources
The Australian War Memorial, Canberra (AWM)
Official Records Collection
AWM33, AWM35, AWM36, AWM45

---

[153] My thanks to Kent Crawford, Nathan Okun and Adler Homero Fonseca de Castro for clearing up points relating to the storage and supply of 12in ammunition in this paragraph.

[154] Brad Duncan (with Tim Smith & Stirling Smith), *Battlecruiser HMAS* Australia (1) *(1910–1924) Wreck Inspection Report* (Parramatta, NSW: Heritage Branch Office of Environment and Heritage, New South Wales Department of Premier and Cabinet Maritime Heritage Unit, 2011); also available at: http://www.environment. nsw.gov.au/resources/heritagebranch/heritage/ media/hmasaustraliawreckinspectionrpt.pdf

Private Records Collection
1DRL0353, Part 2: Letters and Miscellaneous Orders of Lt S. C. L. Hodgkinson RAN
1DRL0565, Papers of D. A. Sharp
2DRL0032, Diary of Capt. G. D. Williams RNR
2DRL0795, Papers of Admiral Sir George Edwin Patey
PR00435, Papers of CPO W. H. Powell
PR82/72, Papers of CPO C. F. G. Geary
PR90/109, Papers of W. S. Rhoades
National Archives of Australia (NAA)
Canberra: A458, A4141, A6108, A11085/1
Melbourne: B197, MP124, MP472/1, MP1049/1
The National Archives, Kew, London (TNA)
ADM 1, ADM 116, ADM 137

Bibliography
Bean, C. E. W., *Flagships Three* (London: Alston Rivers Ltd, 1913)
Burt, R. A., *British Battleships of World War I* (London: Arms and Armour Press, 1986)
Duncan, Brad (with Tim Smith & Stirling Smith), *Battlecruiser HMAS* Australia (1) *(1910–1924) Wreck Inspection Report* (Parramatta, NSW: Heritage Branch Office of Environment and Heritage, New South Wales Department of Premier and Cabinet Maritime Heritage Unit, 2011); also available at: http://www.environ-ment.nsw.gov.au/resources/heritagebranch/heri tage/media/hmasaustraliawreckinspectionrpt.p df [accessed February 2018]
Feakes, Henry James, *White Ensign – Southern Cross: A Story of the King's Ships of Australia's Navy* (Sydney, NSW: Ure Smith, 1951)
Friedman, Norman, *The British Battleship, 1906–1946* (Barnsley, S. Yorks.: Seaforth Publishing, 2015)
Hyslop, Robert, 'Mutiny on HMAS *Australia*: A Forgotten Episode of 1919 Political-Naval Relations' in *Australian Journal of Public Administration* 29 (September 1970), no. 3, pp. 284–96
Johnston, Ian, *Clydebank Battlecruisers: Forgotten Photographs from John Brown's Shipyard* (Barnsley, S. Yorks.: Seaforth Publishing, 2011)
Jones, Colin, *Australian Colonial Navies* (Canberra, ACT: Australian War Memorial, 1986)
Jose, A. W., *Official History of Australia in the War of 1914–18.* IX: *Royal Australian Navy* (Sydney, NSW: Angus & Robertson, 1937)
La Nauze, J. A., *Alfred Deakin: A Political Biography*, 2 vols. (Melbourne, Vic.: Melbourne University Press, 1965)
Lambert, Nicholas, 'Economy or Empire?: The Fleet Unit Concept and the Quest for Collective Security in the Pacific, 1909–1914'

in Greg Kennedy & Keith Neilson, eds., *Far-Flung Lines: Essays on Imperial Defence in Honour of Donald Mackenzie Schurman* (London: Frank Cass, 1997)
Layman, R. D., *Naval Aviation in the First World War: Its Impact and Influence* (London: Conway, 1989)
Liddle, Peter, *The Sailors' War 1914–18* (Poole, Dorset: Blandford, 1985)
Macandie, G. S., *The Genesis of the Royal Australian Navy: A Compilation* (Sydney, NSW: Australian Naval Board, 1949)
Marder, Arthur J., ed., *Portrait of an Admiral: The Life and Papers of Sir Herbert Richmond* (London: Jonathan Cape, 1952)
_____, ed., *Fear God and Dread Nought: The Correspondence of Admiral of the Fleet Lord Fisher of Kilverstone*, 3 vols. (London: Jonathan Cape, 1952–9)
Packer, Joy, *Deep as the Sea* (London: Methuen, 1976)
Pattee, Phillip G., *At War in Distant Waters: British Colonial Defense in the Great War* (Annapolis, Md.: Naval Institute Press, 2013)
Preston, Antony, *Battleships of World War One* (London: Arms and Armour Press, 1972)
Roberts, John, *Battlecruisers* (London: Chatham, 1997)
Roskill, Stephen, *Admiral of the Fleet Earl Beatty, the Last Naval Hero: An Intimate Biography* (London: Collins, 1981)
Royal Australian Navy Sea Power Centre, 'A Loss More Symbolic than Material?' in *Semaphore* (May 2004), available at: http://www.navy.gov.au/media-room/ publications/semaphore-may-2004 [accessed February 2018]
Stevens, David, *The Australian Centenary History of Defence.* III: *The Royal Australian Navy* (South Melbourne, Vic.: Oxford University Press, 2001)
_____, 'The HMAS *Australia* Mutiny' in Christopher M. Bell & Bruce A. Elleman, ed., *Naval Mutinies in the Twentieth Century: An International Perspective* (London: Frank Cass, 2003), pp. 123–44
Vian, Admiral of the Fleet Sir Philip, *Action This Day* (London: Frederick Muller, 1960)
Warner, William, *Onboard HMAS* Australia, *1914–18: A Boy's Recollections of Life on the Lower Deck of the Battle Cruiser* (Seven Hills, NSW: Five Senses Education, 2014)
Waterson, D. B., 'Foxton, Justin Fox Greenlaw (1849–1916)' in Australian Dictionary of Biography, National Centre of Biography, Australian National University, available at: http://adb.anu.edu.au/biography/foxton-justin-fox-greenlaw-6230/text10719 [accessed February 2018]

Armada de Chile

The Battleship
Almirante Latorre (1913)

Carlos Tromben Corbalán & Fernando Wilson Lazo

THE WAR OF THE PACIFIC waged between Chile, Peru and Bolivia from 1879 to 1883 transformed the Chilean navy into one of the leading naval powers in South America.[1] During the course of that conflict, the Armada gained command of the sea following a succession of naval engagements in which it eventually succeeded in destroying or capturing the bulk of the Peruvian fleet, before launching the Chilean army on a series of amphibious landings which resulted first in the capture of the province of Tarapacá and ultimately that of Lima itself, while permanently severing Bolivia's access to the sea. Eight years later the fleet lent crucial support to the victorious Congressional party in the Chilean Civil War of 1891. Indeed, it was the commander of the Congressional navy, Capitán de navío (Captain) Jorge Montt, who by the end of that year had succeeded the dictator José Manuel Balmaceda as president. The position of the navy in Chilean society was therefore unusually strong, and the determined naval race with Argentina upon which it embarked in the early 1890s served to consolidate its regional position further. The order placed in Britain by Chile in 1911 for a pair of battleships led by *Almirante Latorre*, the southern hemisphere's only super-dreadnought, was the ultimate statement of that naval expansion.

Arms Race

The naval race with Argentina, which originated in a series of border disputes in the northern Puna de Atacama region and particularly at the southern tip of the continent, was settled peacefully via the so-called Pacts of May in 1902 (see *Garibaldi*). Named for the protocols signed in Santiago on 28 May of that year, these documents constitute the first naval arms limitation agreement between two modern states. While Chile secured most of her geographical objectives, including retaining sovereignty over the Magellan Strait and Cape Horn, the Armada viewed the pacts with some frustration since they imposed a five-year moratorium on naval procurement and required the disposal of all vessels already ordered or under construction. Although the terms of the Pacts of May gave the two fleets parity of tonnage – no small achievement given the comparative size of their respective economies – the Chilean navy again found itself at a disadvantage. Whereas for Argentina this implied discarding two Garibaldi-class armoured cruisers (q.v.) it had planned to add to the four units already in service, for Chile this involved abandoning the two pre-dreadnought battleships then in the final stages of construction in British yards, vessels urgently needed to balance the fleet created in spasmodic response to Argentine procurement.[2]

Almirante Latorre unleashes the ten 14in guns which made her the most powerful vessel in the southern hemisphere during the first half of the twentieth century. *(Fernando Wilson Collection)*

[1] The editor would like to acknowledge the generosity and kindness of Piero Castagneto and Cecilia Guzmán of the Museo Marítimo Nacional of Valparaíso, Chile in obtaining photos for this chapter.

[2] Rodrigo Fuenzalida Bade, *La Armada de Chile. Desde la Alborada hasta el Sesquicentenario*, 4 vols. (Valparaíso: Imprenta de la Armada, 1975–8), IV, pp. 1085–6; Guillermo Arroyo, *Adquisiciones navales de Chile. Un estudio crítico* (Valparaíso: Armada de Chile, 1940), pp. 12–13.

In the event, detente was short-lived and the composition of the two fleets remained notionally stable only until 1906 when Brazil, the third naval power of consequence in Latin America, took the unexpected step of ordering a pair of modern capital ships inspired by the revolutionary battleship HMS *Dreadnought*. The design of what became the Minas Geraes class (q.v.) provided for what were then the largest battleships in the world and caused a major upset in the regional balance of power. Faced by this challenge in its long-standing rivalry with Brazil as South America's second Atlantic power, Argentina duly informed Chile that it would resume capital ship construction in order to address this threat once the five-year moratorium had expired.

Argentina promptly set up a naval mission in London and in 1908 issued an invitation to tender for two battleships. The head of the mission, Admiral Onofre Betbeder, took a decidedly unorthodox approach to awarding the construction contracts. Issuing only the vaguest technical requirements, the aim was to give each shipyard the widest latitude to offer its own options and solutions. However, no sooner had the proposals come in than Betbeder declared the competition null and void, before going on to refine his requirements, this time based on a detailed study of the submitted designs. Predictably enough, this action provoked an international furore with numerous claims of violation of trade secrets and several yards refusing to participate in the second phase. Nonetheless, in 1910 a contract was awarded to a US consortium composed of the Fore River Ship and Engine Building Co. of Quincy, Massachusetts, and the New York Shipbuilding Co. of Camden, New Jersey, at a cost of £2,214,000 per unit – £250,000 less than the next best offer. The resulting Rivadavia class proved to be the only dreadnoughts ever built outside of Europe for the export market.[3]

With both Brazil and Argentina having placed orders for classes of dreadnoughts, it was obvious that Chile could not be long in following suit if she were to preserve her regional position. Not only that, but the main units of her fleet were almost completely obsolescent, centred as it was on two British-built armoured cruisers (*Esmeralda* of 1896 and *O'Higgins* of 1897), the French-built 2nd-class battleship *Capitán Prat* of 1890 and five protected cruisers completed between 1892 and 1902. This resulted in

Vice Admiral Jorge Montt (1845–1922), Commander-in-Chief of the Chilean Navy and President of the Republic. *(Museo Histórico Nacional, Santiago)*

Congress approving the Programa del Centenario (Centennial Programme) named in commemoration of the hundredth anniversary of the formation of Chile's first independent government. The Centennial Programme, which was signed into law on 9 July 1910, authorised expenditure of the equivalent of £3.48 million for warship construction including one battleship, £920,000 for coastal defence and £80,000 to improve the naval dockyards. However, this was not all. On 23 October 1911 a second law was passed authorising the securing of a loan of £3.5 million to fund warship acquisition, including a second battleship, for a total procurement of two super-dreadnoughts, six flotilla leaders and two submarines.[4]

Bidding

The Chilean programme was the third of its type in South America and came as the naval race between Britain and Germany was reaching a climax. From the outset it attracted considerable diplomatic and commercial interest since most major warship manufacturers went to great lengths to offer their wares and showcase the virtues of their designs, a marketing effort which complicated the procurement process for the

Chilean authorities. There was, however, a strong and traditional bias towards Great Britain which had not only been a powerful ally and investor since Chile had gained her independence in the early nineteenth century, but had supplied much of her naval construction and technical expertise in the intervening period. A case in point was her long-standing association with the designer Edward Reed which began in 1873 when the latter was engaged as consultant in naval construction to the Chilean mission in London. This resulted in orders for the central battery ships *Almirante Cochrane* and *Blanco Encalada* being placed with Earle's of Hull in 1873, followed by a succession of orders with the firm of Sir W. G. Armstrong of Elswick, Newcastle upon Tyne over the next twenty-five years. In November 1901 Reed visited Chile where he was commissioned to produce designs for a pair of battleships (*Constitución* and *Libertad*) ordered from Armstrongs and Vickers respectively, but which thanks to the Pacts of May were eventually commissioned into the Royal Navy as *Swiftsure* and *Triumph*. Nor did the few deviations towards other suppliers do much to alter this partiality for British construction. This conviction was exquisitely demonstrated during a lengthy conversation between the Commander-in-Chief of the Chilean navy and former president Vice Admiral Jorge Montt, and the German minister in Santiago Hans Freiherr von und zu Bodman, in which the latter extolled the virtues of German naval construction. To this Montt retorted that while he had not the slightest doubt as to the validity of the minister's claims, until such time as the Kaiserliche Marine emerged victorious from a naval conflict he preferred to stick with British vessels which he regarded as the finest in the world.[5]

Anecdotes aside, it was nonetheless incumbent on Chile to preserve a delicate balance between bidders, especially those from two increasingly important trading partners such as Germany and the United States which also had significant investments in Chile. These considerations resulted in the publication of a somewhat elliptical invitation to tender for the new battleships, one that allowed all comers to bid on the hull, but specified that the guns, armour and machinery had to be supplied by British firms.[6] Naturally enough, this placed British yards in an unassailable position in terms of their ability to

[3] Pablo Arguindeguy, *Apuntes sobre los buques de la Armada Argentina, 1810–1970*, 7 vols. (Buenos Aires: Secretaría General Naval, 1972), V, pp. 2192 & 2202.

[4] Vice Admiral Gerald L. Wood, 'El Acorazado "Almirante Latorre"' in *Revista de Marina* 105 (1988), no. 3, pp. 255–86; 258; Fuenzalida Bade, *La Armada de Chile*, IV, p. 1107 *et seq.*

[5] Ricardo Couyoumdjian, 'El Programa Naval del Centenario y el acorazado *Almirante Latorre*' in *Actas del IV Congreso de Historia Naval y Marítima Latinoamericana* (Madrid: Instituto de Historia y Cultura Naval, 1999), pp. 199–221; 206.

[6] *Ibid.*, pp. 204–6.

refine their bids, both for individual ships and for the project as a whole. The British option was, in any case, being pressed by anti-American sentiment in some sections of the Chilean press, possibly stoked by tensions resulting from US concerns over the development of Chile's position in South America which had flared up several times during the last decade of the nineteenth century.[7] After some negotiation, the contracts for the two battleships were finally placed with Armstrongs on 25 July 1911 at a price of £2,339,190 each, in addition to £93,000 in spares and ammunition, which expenditure was authorised on 5 August 1911.[8]

The units were originally named for Chile's main port and for her capital city, *Valparaíso* and *Santiago* respectively, but on the death of the national hero Admiral Juan José Latorre in July 1912 were renamed *Almirante Latorre* and *Almirante Cochrane* respectively. Latorre had been responsible for defeating the Peruvian squadron at the Battle of Angamos in October 1879, an action which effectively settled the naval side of the War of the Pacific in Chile's favour. Meanwhile, the Scotsman Thomas Cochrane, Earl of Dundonald (1775–1860), late and subsequently of the Royal Navy, had from 1818 led the first Chilean naval squadron to victory in the war of independence against Spain. These two figures therefore encapsulated the formative epochs in Chilean naval history and no more illustrious names could have been found for her projected dreadnoughts.

Design and Protection

The Chilean battleships were designed by Josiah Perrett and Eustace Tennyson d'Eyncourt, respectively chief naval architect and head of the design office at Armstrongs. This collaboration resulted on 4 April 1911 in the submission of five designs based on that of HMS *King George V* and reflecting the state of the art of British naval construction.[9] The significance of Chile being given access to the fruit of this technology as the dreadnought race with Germany reached its apogee should never be underestimated, nor has it ever been forgotten in that country. On

Juan José Latorre (1846–1912), victor of the decisive Battle of Angamos against Peru in October 1879 and namesake of Chile's only battleship, seen here in the rank of *capitán de corbeta* (lieutenant commander) in c. 1873. *(Museo Marítimo Nacional (MMN)/151)*

the other hand, the needs of the Royal Navy were necessarily quite different from those of the Armada, requiring Armstrongs to make significant modifications to protection, armament and propulsion in order to meet Chilean requirements.

The selected design, 696A, was 661ft (201.4m) long, 92ft (28m) in the beam and drew 29ft (8.8m) at standard load on 28,600 tons' displacement. The fact that the Chilean battleships were specifically designed to face the two Argentine dreadnoughts of the Rivadavia class then under construction in the United States required them to be protected against 12in (305mm) shells. The 50-calibre guns mounted in the Rivadavias fired projectiles at a relatively high muzzle velocity of 2,900ft/sec (884m/sec), but were comparatively light at approximately 870lbs (depending on shell type). In keeping with tactical ideas current before the First World War, this meant that *Latorre*'s vertical protection could be limited to a maximum of 9in (229mm). This decision was subsequently much criticised in various quarters by commentators who not only overlooked the tactical circumstances under which the vessels were designed to operate, but also the fact that these specifications had been

consciously issued by the Chilean naval high command as far back as 1909. Turrets and barbettes were protected with up to 10in (254mm) of armour but, as with all British construction before the Queen Elizabeth class, horizontal protection was mostly limited to 1in (25mm) of plate, increasing to 4in (102mm) over the magazines.

Armament

Although the Royal Navy had begun mounting 13.5in (343mm) guns in the Orion class of 1909, by 1911 construction was in progress on vessels armed with 14in guns for the US and Japanese navies. These were the New York-class battleships authorised in 1910 and particularly the Kongō-class battlecruisers, the leading unit of which was laid down by Vickers, Barrow-in-Furness, in January 1911 and eventually fitted with eight 14in guns of Vickers' own design and manufacture. Where *Almirante Latorre* is concerned, it has not been possible to establish the origin of this ordnance specification from Chilean sources, involving as it did the design and construction by Armstrongs of a new 14in (536mm)/45-calibre weapon weighing 85 tons. It may tentatively be surmised that it came at Armstrongs' suggestion since this could now be reckoned the standard British export calibre and seemed likely to become the global standard having been adopted by the US Navy. Needless to say, the celebrated 15in Mk-I gun was still in the early stages of design by Vickers, and being shrouded in secrecy did not feature in the negotiations. Meanwhile, it is perfectly clear that Chile was eager to follow the trend for increased calibre in order to maximise the fighting power of her two vessels vis-à-vis her would-be opponents. With a shell weight of 1,400–1,586lb (635–719kg) by comparison with the 850–870lb (386–395kg) of the Minas Geraes and Rivadavia classes, the 14in gun promised a decisive advantage for the Chilean navy. In other respects the main armament arrangements followed contemporary British practice, including wire-wound gun construction, 20 degrees of elevation, all-angle loading, hoists broken at the working chamber, propellant charges in quarters and shell rooms below the magazines having a capacity of 1,106 projectiles.[10]

Where secondary armament was concerned, the original specifications had included twenty-two 4.7in (119mm)/45-calibre guns. However, in line with advances in destroyer design it was decided to replace this arrangement with a

7 William F. Sater, *Chile and the United States: Empires in Conflict* (Athens, Ga.: University of Georgia Press, 1990).

8 Archivo Histórico de la Armada (AHA), *Historial del acorazado* Almirante Latorre, I, p. 2. See also Ian Johnston & Ian Buxton, *The Battleship Builders: Constructing and Arming British Capital Ships* (Barnsley, S. Yorks.: Seaforth Publishing, 2013), p. 281.

9 AHA, Wood, *El Acorazado* (MS), p. 3.

10 John Campbell, *Naval Weapons of World War Two* (London: Conway, 1985), p. 379.

FIRE CONTROL

Canada joined the Grand Fleet in October 1915 with the Mark IV* Dreyer Table as the heart of her fire-control system, to which the gyroscopic Henderson firing gear was added in approximately 1917.[16] These were joined by the earlier Dumaresq and Vickers clock instruments which were standard in the Royal Navy. Rangefinding was provided by 14ft (4.3m) instruments fitted in each of the five turrets and the main director, with fire control available from the main and aloft directors as well as by 'X' turret and the transmitting station. Instructions for training and elevation were relayed to the turrets where they were followed on pointers, with the turrets capable of local control. Modifications made to the Dreyer Table during the refit of 1929–31 at last made Latorre capable of helm-free gunnery, while the opportunity was taken to replace the original 6in directors by new equipment in the maintop which allowed the secondary armament to be aimed by following the pointers in the 14in directors. The same refit also saw the installation of a 4in (102mm) anti-aircraft battery together with the advanced High-Angle Control System (HACS) I fire-control system. In September 1931 this became a matter of concern to the Royal Navy officers advising the Armada in light of reports that Latorre might be disposed of as a result of the naval mutiny the previous month, with fears being expressed as to the possibility of this and other sensitive equipment falling into the hands of a rival power.[17] In the event, these fears proved unfounded.

---

16 See http://www.dreadnoughtproject.org/tfs/index. php/ Mark_IV*_Dreyer_Table; Wood, 'El Acorazado', pp. 277–8; AHA, Wood, El Acorazado (MS), pp. 27 & 29–30.

17 The National Archives (TNA), FO A6120/5655/9, Telegram No. 179 (R) from the British ambassador in Chile to the Foreign Office, 15 October 1931.

The starboard barrel of Latorre's no. '3' (formerly 'Q') turret being cleaned under the supervision of a gunnery chief petty officer in 1921. (Courtesy Piero Castagneto)

Latorre's turrets '4' and '5' as they were known in Chilean service seen trained on the port beam in the 1920s. The structure immediately forward of no. '4' 14in turret is the torpedo control tower with its medium-base rangefinder, removed in 1929–31. *(MMN/555)*

reduced number of heavier weapons, resulting in the mounting of sixteen 6in (152mm)/50-calibre guns at an additional cost of £154,000.[11] These changes in armament required corresponding adjustments to the armour scheme in order to protect the ship against attack from modern destroyers. The resulting modifications to longitudinal stability involved the addition of 213 tons of ballast forward and with it a trimming of a foot by the bows, a problem only corrected when bulges were fitted in 1929–31.[12] With respect to the weapons themselves, it is reported that the improved elevators fitted in *Almirante Latorre* permitted a firing rate of 5.5 6in shells per minute, compared to the three shells per minute which was standard in the Grand Fleet; certainly, as with the main armament, she had stowage for more shells per gun than her Royal Navy equivalents.[13] Secondary armament was completed by two 3in (76mm) anti-aircraft guns fitted by the British on the after superstructure in 1916 and not forming part of the original specification, together with four Hotchkiss 1.85in (47mm) guns.

The design included four Elswick 21in (533mm) submerged torpedo tubes, the forward pair angled at 80 degrees from the centreline and the after pair at 100 degrees.[14] There is no record of these weapons being fired in anger during *Almirante Latorre*'s service in the Royal Navy as HMS *Canada*, and little evidence of their being utilised at all in Chilean service before they were removed during the major refit of 1929–31.[15]

Propulsion

Speed was another area in which the specific requirements of the Chilean navy influenced the fabric of the new battleships, especially in light of the War of the Pacific in 1879 and the Civil War of 1891 during which considerable difficulty was experienced in bringing the enemy to battle. In both conflicts vessels of inferior armament were able to use their superior speed to avoid action,

Latorre's quarterdeck seen from the air during one of her comparatively rare sallies in the late 1920s. (MMN/1305)

as discovered by the Peruvian turret ship *Huáscar* between May and October 1879 and the Congressional auxiliary cruiser *Imperial* in January 1891. This situation had created a preference in the Armada for vessels of high speed, as shown in the designs for the 2nd-class battleship *Capitán Prat* of 1890 and the protected cruiser *Esmeralda* of 1896, as well as the pre-dreadnought battleships *Constitución* and *Libertad* (later *Swiftsure* and *Triumph*) ordered in 1901, which were capable of 19 knots. Where *Almirante Latorre* was concerned, this involved a modification to the original British design from eighteen Yarrow large-tube boilers yielding 31,000shp to twenty-one giving 37,000shp, with a consequent increase in speed from 21 to 24 knots. This redesign, which included four boiler rooms, required lengthening both the hull and the after funnel, the latter adjustment providing a ready means of distinguishing her from the remaining British dreadnought construction. Propulsion was completed by two sets each of Brown-Curtis high-pressure turbines and Parsons low-pressure turbines, built at Clydebank and Wallsend on Tyne respectively. There was provision for mixed firing with up to 3,300 tons of coal and 520 tons of oil, giving a maximum range of 4,400 miles at 10 knots. The Chileans subsequently found the ship's economic speed to be 10.5 knots when using domestic bituminous coal, yielding a maximum range of 3,360 miles; consumption was therefore 25 per cent higher than when anthracite was burnt, of which the

Armada kept a stock at Talcahuano for use in contingencies.[18] There are no records of *Latorre* sailing under oil firing during her Chilean service prior to the refit of 1929–31.

One notable aspect of the design of the Chilean battleships is that their combined boiler capacity was far greater than that required by the engine plant to generate the maximum specified speed. Indeed, *Almirante Latorre* could cruise at 13.5 knots on just 6,540shp. Although no convincing explanation for this state of affairs has been found, the reason may rest in the fact that the efforts of each of the three South American navies to fund the construction of dreadnoughts and other advanced vessels were not always matched by a commensurate logistical organisation to operate and maintain these complex new systems, either with respect to technical personnel or shore facilities. Following this line of thinking, the installation of excess steam capacity would be attributable to a concern to ensure that tactical requirements were met even when some boilers were out of service for maintenance purposes, or even as a result of logistical deficiencies in *matériel* or personnel.

An unexpected consequence of this excess boiler capacity came shortly after the former *Almirante Latorre* had been commissioned into the Royal Navy as HMS *Canada* (see below). As yet largely uninformed as to her specifications and without the Royal Navy having carried out formal acceptance trials due to the circumstances of her transfer, *Canada*'s first commanding

11 AHA, *Historial*, I, p. 13.

12 AHA, Wood, *El Acorazado* (MS), p. 27; Wood, 'El Acorazado', p. 259.

13 Wood, 'El Acorazado', p. 262; Norman Friedman, *The British Battleship, 1906–1946* (Barnsley, S. Yorks.: Seaforth Publishing, 2015), p.168

14 For HMS *Canada*, see: http://www.dreadnought-project.org/tfs/index.php/H.M.S._Canada_(1913).

15 AHA, Letter No. 452 from the Chilean Naval Mission, London, 9 June 1927.

18 Wood, 'El Acorazado', p. 269.

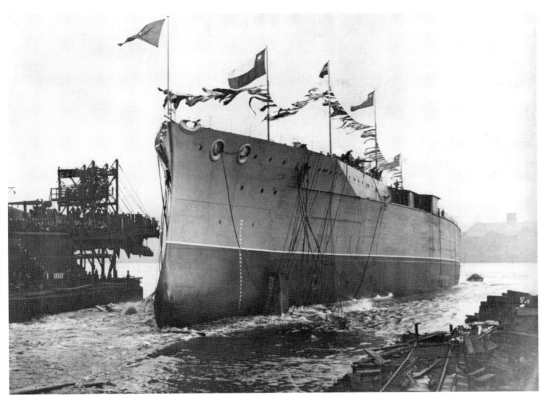

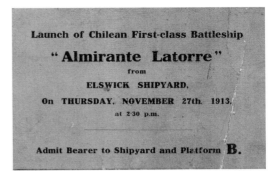

Left: *Almirante Latorre* thunders into the Tyne on 27 November 1913. *(Fernando Wilson Collection)*

Above: Admission to the launch of Chile's 'first-class battleship'. *(Bruce Taylor Collection)*

officer Capt. William C. M. Nicholson took the opportunity of her maiden voyage to the fleet anchorage at Scapa Flow to perform a series of informal trials on 14–15 October 1915. When the order was given for full steam, some 55,410shp was produced, generating 338.5rpm at a pressure of 123psi – more than 50 per cent in excess of the design pressure of 80psi. Small wonder the seals failed in the first expansion of the high-pressure turbines, causing significant damage and loss of power. Naturally enough, the turbine manufacturer John Brown & Co. of Clydebank refused to accept liability for what was a clear breach of design specifications. Although remedial work was done for steam leaks in July and November 1916, the damage was never fully repaired while the ship was in British service, and *Canada* spent the war years with her maximum permitted speed reduced to 21 knots, which was adequate for the Grand Fleet, but not for Chilean tactical needs. The materials allocated to correct these defects were found aboard when Chile repurchased *Almirante Latorre* in 1920, but the speed limitation resulting from the turbine damage of 1915 was not repaired until the refit of 1929–31.

Construction and Sale, 1911–14

The keel of Chile's first dreadnought battleship was laid at Armstrongs yard at Elswick,

Newcastle upon Tyne, on 27 November 1911 and launched exactly two years later by Olga Budge de Edwards, wife of the Chilean ambassador in London, Agustín Edwards MacClure. Capt. Salustio Valdés Cortez was appointed in command.[19] Work on the second battleship had to await the launching of the Brazilian dreadnought *Rio de Janeiro* for the slip to be cleared and did not start until 24 February 1913, by which time Armstrongs was having difficulty obtaining sufficient quantities of steel, a problem which also slowed completion of *Almirante Latorre*. Provision had been made in the contract for *Almirante Latorre* to be delivered in 1915 and *Almirante Cochrane* a year later, but the outbreak of war in August 1914 immediately brought work on both ships to a halt, the former in an advanced state of completion.[20] All vessels building for foreign powers in British yards had previously been earmarked for expropriation on the outbreak of hostilities, which policy was implemented with the two Turkish battleships building at Vickers and Armstrongs, the future *Erin* and *Agincourt* respectively. Where these two were forcibly seized in view of the status of the Ottoman Empire as a likely belligerent (see

Yavuz Sultan Selim), no such action was necessary with *Latorre* since Chile was not only a friendly neutral but also one of Britain's leading suppliers of the nitrate essential to her war effort. The Foreign Office duly approached the Chilean embassy in London offering to purchase the two battleships for a little over £2 million. After several exchanges of notes, it was agreed to limit the transaction to *Latorre* and four destroyer leaders building for Chile at the yard of J. Samuel White of Cowes for a total of £2,036,162. This was approved by the British Cabinet on 5 September and four days later *Latorre* was taken over by the Royal Navy as HMS *Canada*, with *Cochrane* remaining under Chilean control for the time being. Meanwhile, the destroyers entered service in the Royal Navy as the Broke class, the name-ship of which went on to a distinguished wartime career.

Naturally enough, this state of affairs left Chile in an anxious position with respect to her status as a South American naval power at a time when both Brazilian battleships had entered service and the Argentine pair was about to do so. Although Chile recovered her financial outlay with a reasonable rate of interest, her fundamental problem remained unaddressed, since not only would she now fail to receive her battleships on time, but war conditions made it unlikely that *Almirante Cochrane* would be delivered in the near future.[21] These concerns were borne out in 1917 when Britain, by now in her third year of war, approached Chile to enquire about the sale of *Cochrane* on which little progress had been made since August 1914. This time the negotiations were of a different tenor since *Cochrane* was of little use to Chile in her present condition with only her hull and machinery in a state of completion and her armament and armour allo-

[19] AHA, Wood, *El Acorazado* (MS), p. 5.

[20] *Memoria del Ministerio de Marina presentada al Congreso Nacional* (Santiago: Ministerio de Marina, 1913).

[21] Couyoumdjian, 'El Programa Naval', p. 215.

cated elsewhere.[22] The parties therefore agreed that not only would Britain purchase the vessel on the stocks (eventually completed as the carrier HMS *Eagle*), but would also take steps to enhance Chile's military capabilities by way of compensation. It was in this context that fifty military aircraft were transferred to Chile without charge, in addition to five Holland-class submarines being built for the Royal Navy by the Electric Boat Co. of Groton, Connecticut, but which could not be delivered to Britain owing to US neutrality legislation. A sixth submarine of the same type would be sold to Chile for a token sum. In the event, the transfer of this military hardware proved to be of the greatest significance to Chile, since it not only provided the basis for her submarine service but was also instrumental in the development both of Chilean naval aviation and the Chilean air force itself.[23]

Repurchase

As soon as the Great War ended Chile approached Britain with a view to obtaining the modern naval units for which she had been waiting. Initial enquiries were made with several shipyards regarding construction of battle-cruisers, or more nearly fast battleships, armed with 14in guns designed by Armstrongs, but this time lengthened to 50 calibres.[26] However, the fact that no mention of this weapon has been found in Chilean sources suggests that it was only considered very briefly before being abandoned, no doubt on grounds of cost. Negotiations then turned to the reacquisition of those vessels taken over by Britain on the outbreak of war. Of these all were extant save the destroyer leader *Tipperary* which had succumbed at Jutland, the survivors including the three remaining Broke-class destroyers and *Canada* herself representing a mixed bag of virtues and

22 Central to the Royal Navy's interest in the *Cochrane* was the allocation of her armour, manufactured but as yet uninstalled, to the battlecruiser *Repulse* whose protection was inadequate. No time was lost in making this transfer once the purchase was complete; R. A. Burt, *British Battleships, 1919–1945* (2nd edn, Barnsley, S. Yorks., Seaforth Publishing, 2013), pp. 214–15.

23 Carlos Martin Fritz & Pedro Sapunar Peric, *Los Submarinos en la Armada de Chile, hasta el año 1995* (Talcahuano: Comandancia en Jefe de la Fuerza de Submarinos, 2005), pp. 39–74; Carlos Tromben Corbalán, *La Aviación naval de Chile* (Viña del Mar: Comandancia de la Aviación Naval, 1998), pp. 46–52.

26 Couyoumdjian, 'El Programa Naval', p. 254; Norman Friedman, *Naval Weapons of World War I* (Barnsley, S. Yorks.: Seaforth Publishing, 2011), p. 49.

WITH THE GRAND FLEET

No sooner had *Latorre* been taken over as HMS *Canada* in September 1914 than work began to modify her for service with the Royal Navy at Rosyth. Despite the limited nature of the conversion, it was a year before she emerged from this process which involved the removal of the enclosed bridge and chart house in favour of a pair of open platforms as fitted in the battleships of the Royal Sovereign class, rearrangement of the 14in and 6in fire-control positions in the conning tower, improvements to the wireless outfit and removal of the two derrick posts athwart the fore funnel in favour of a single larger post abaft it, together with a number of other alterations including to fire control (see above). The work was completed on 20 September 1915, *Canada* joining the 4th Battle Squadron of the Grand Fleet on 15 October. Her only taste of action came at Jutland on 31 May–1 June 1916, during which she served as part of the 3rd Division of the 4th BS led by Jellicoe's flagship *Iron Duke*. Still under Capt. Nicholson, a total of forty-two 14in and 109 6in shells were fired during that engagement, including two salvoes at the stricken light cruiser *Wiesbaden*, with no hits or casualties being suffered in return.[24] On 12 June 1916 *Canada* was transferred to the 1st BS with which she divided her time between the fleet anchorage at Scapa Flow and fruitless sweeps of the North Sea until the end of the war. Reduced to reserve in March 1919, her final operational voyages under the White Ensign were in a transport capacity carrying relief crews to the Mediterranean and bringing men back for demobilisation in June

HMS *Canada* seen off Portsmouth in 1918 shortly after the end of the Great War. Note the flying-off platforms on 'B' and 'X' turrets, the range clock above the latter turret and the deflection scale painted on 'A' and 'Y' turrets. *(Bruce Taylor Collection)*

and November of that year. She returned to reserve status at Rosyth on 22 January 1920.

Aside from her initial refit, a number of alterations were made to *Canada* during the war.[25] The first of these came at Rosyth from July 1916 and reflects the experience of the Battle of Jutland. This involved the addition of an inch of armour over the magazine crowns and the upper and lower coal bunkers, together with a wholesale rearrangement of the 14in, 6in and 3in magazines, shell rooms and transmitting stations, including upgrading of the ventilation and refrigeration systems. This was followed in 1917–18 by the fitting of range clocks and more and improved 9ft rangefinders, removal of two of the after 6in guns which were found to be susceptible to blast damage from 'Q' 14in turret, and adjustments to the searchlight outfit. Flying-off platforms were added to 'B' and 'X' turrets in 1918 but removed in 1921.

24 For Captain Nicholson's Report of Proceedings, see: http://www.dreadnoughtproject.org/tfs/index.php/H.M.S._Canada_at_the_Battle_of_Jutland

25 Wood, 'El Acorazado', p. 264.

defects. Although these vessels had been modernised during the conflict, all were showing the effects of unremitting war service and were in need of extensive refit and repair. After a series of negotiations, on 12 April 1920 the British government accepted an offer of £1.4 million for *Canada* and *Broke*, *Botha* and *Faulknor*. The reduced price not only reflected wear and tear on the vessels themselves, but also the significant amount of work required on *Canada*'s engine plant which would have to be carried out at Chile's expense. Nonetheless, included in the agreement was the acquisition of large supplies of spare parts and ammunition, including the Royal Navy's entire inventory of 14in shells, as well as facilities to engage the services of British instructors and technical experts to train the Armada in the operation of these ships.

This, however, left pending the issue of Chile's coveted second dreadnought. With *Almirante Cochrane* being completed for British service as the carrier *Eagle*, the Chileans were offered the two surviving battlecruisers of the Invincible class, HM Ships *Inflexible* and *Indomitable*. Unsurprisingly, this raised a storm of protest from naval officers in the Chilean press given the performance of the battlecruisers at Jutland and the offer was turned down. Chile had in any case suffered significant economic hardship during the Great War and was in no financial condition to purchase and maintain a second capital ship. Moreover, it was recognised that both the Brazilian and Argentine navies operated for lengthy periods with only one of their two battleships in commission, the second lying inactive either for mechanical or personnel reasons, sometimes both. On the infrequent occasions that both battleships were in commission simultaneously it was usually at the expense of operational capability elsewhere.[27] Meanwhile, heightened tensions between Chile and Peru made it advisable for the repurchased vessels to reach Chilean waters at the earliest opportunity. Handed over to the Chilean naval mission at Devonport on 1 August 1920 and restored to her original name, *Almirante Latorre*'s first sally under the Chilean ensign came on 16 November, by which time part of her complement of 1,175 men had arrived from South America. In the event, only relatively minor repairs had been carried out by the time *Latorre*, *Almirante Uribe* (ex-*Broke*) and *Almirante Williams* (ex-*Botha*) sailed for the Pacific on the 27th, wearing the flag of Admiral Luis Gómez Carreño; *Almirante Riveros* (ex-*Faulknor*) followed later.

Chilean Waters, 1921–9

Latorre's arrival in Chile was delayed by a planned drydocking at Balboa on the Pacific side of the Panama Canal Zone on 14 January 1921, a measure resorted to because the Armada's existing facility was not of the requisite size. Although funds had been allocated for the construction of a new graving dock at the Talcahuano naval base in southern Chile as part of the Centennial Programme in September 1910 and construction begun in 1912, work was delayed owing to shortage of funds and equipment during the Great War and the new facility was only inaugurated in July 1924, by which time *Latorre* had required a second drydocking in Balboa in April 1922.[28]

Latorre's forecastle and bridge structure shortly after being received into the Armada de Chile in *c.* 1921. It would be several years before *Canada*'s wartime splinter protection was removed from the superstructure. (*Courtesy Piero Castagneto*)

[27] Robert L. Scheina, *Latin America: A Naval History, 1810–1897* (Annapolis, Md.: Naval Institute Press, 1987), p. 286.

[28] *Memoria del Ministerio de Marina presentada al Congreso Nacional* (Santiago: Ministerio de Marina, 1910–13), vii; Wood, 'El Acorazado', p. 267; Tromben Corbalán, *Ingeniería naval*, pp. 246–53.

Nonetheless, the arrival of *Latorre* and the destroyers off Valparaíso on 20 February 1921 was greeted with great jubilation throughout the country, and President Arturo Alessandri was on hand to welcome them to the fleet of which *Latorre* now became flagship. *Latorre*'s first significant contribution came in the aftermath of the earthquake which struck the northern town of Vallenar in November 1922 when she transported Alessandri to the affected area along with an assortment of tents, medical supplies, rations, clothing and 2 million pesos for the victims.[29] In July 1924 *Latorre* embarked the president on a visit to Talcahuano to inaugurate the new naval graving dock there, and in September 1925 Alessandri hosted a shipboard reception for

Edward, Prince of Wales, while the latter was touring South America in the battlecruiser *Repulse*. In the interim *Latorre* had for the first time found herself embroiled in Chile's increasingly strained political situation, being obliged to train her guns on the railway line connecting Valparaíso with Santiago in January 1925 during the provisional military government which pitted elements of the army and navy high command on opposing sides of the conflict. From a purely naval standpoint, however, the reality is that *Latorre* was seldom used in the first years of her service with the Armada, steaming fewer than 9,000 miles in the years between 1923 and 1926 for a total of only thirty-nine days at sea during that period.[30]

As the 1920s wore on the assumption of power by the authoritarian General Carlos Ibáñez del Campo (1927–31) and deteriorating relations with the Peruvians arising from the territorial provisions of the Treaty of Ancón which had concluded the War of the Pacific in 1883 began to recommend the implementation of a new naval expansion programme. Although the Armada had received no less than twelve modern vessels between 1914 and 1921 (six Holland-class submarines, five British destroyers and *Latorre* herself) together with the nucleus of a naval aviation capability, she continued to face many significant doctrinal, tactical and technical challenges. These in turn prompted the arrival of a series of British naval missions first mooted during the visit of the Prince of Wales in 1925.

Meanwhile, the Peruvian navy had in 1927 placed orders for four US 'R'-class submarines, a

---

[29] Fuenzalida Bade, *La Armada de Chile*, IV, p. 1152.

[30] Wood, 'El Acorazado', p. 269.

Part of *Latorre*'s complement of 1,175 men mustered on the forecastle, turrets and superstructure on 4 March 1929 not long before she sailed for her refit at Devonport. *(MMN/934)*

development which initiated a succession of Chilean orders from British yards, beginning with six destroyers specially equipped for anti-submarine warfare from Thornycroft's.[31] To these were added three oceangoing submarines of the British 'O' class and the submarine depot ship *Araucano*, all from Vickers-Armstrongs, Barrow. Whereas the naval programme of 1910–11 had been only partially executed, that of 1927 was to a large extent completed, with only the two heavy cruisers ordered from British yards falling victim to the desperate financial situation in which Chile found herself by 1931. The final element in this naval programme was the overdue refitting of *Almirante Latorre* at Devonport which began in 1929, the year the border dispute with Peru was settled through US mediation under President Herbert Hoover.

Modernisation, 1929–31

Although the Armada was aware that *Latorre* had been modernised during her service with the Royal Navy, she had been left well astern by the major technological advances seen during the brief naval race between Britain, United States and Japan which ended with the Washington Treaty of 1922. To the spectre of obsolescence was added the legion of problems resulting from her hasty commissioning in 1915 and the subsequent failure to carry out a full refit at the end of the Great War, or even prior to her resale to Chile. The solution to this state of affairs as well as the shortcomings in maintenance during the 1920s was a full modernisation at Devonport naval dockyard in Britain, costing £1.4 million and lasting from June 1929 to March 1931.[32] Once again, Britain gave Chile access to the benefit of her expertise and technology, and the selection of a naval dockyard over a commercial shipyard was no coincidence since Devonport had recent experience in modernising the Queen Elizabeth- and Royal Sovereign-class battleships.

The first and most significant work was in connection with the propulsion system which was the most extensive reconstruction of its type yet carried out in any shipyard, though subsequently exceeded in a number of Italian, British and Japanese capital ships. Not only was the number of boilers reduced from twenty-one to eighteen, but these were replaced by oil-fired units and alterations made to the design of the

Latorre seen in dry dock towards the end of her lengthy and extensive refit at Devonport in 1929–31. The new bulges and bridge enclosure have been fitted while the casemated 6in guns have been temporarily removed for alterations to the mountings. *(MMN/562)*

water drums. Moreover, new Parsons high- and low-pressure turbines built by Vickers-Armstrongs were installed at a cost of £162,000. With a simplified gearing system and new generators, the new plant represented a significant improvement in performance, with 56,803shp generating 276rpm during eight hours of trials over the Polperro measured mile on 8 December 1930. Moreover, *Latorre*'s best speed was now increased to 24 knots, half a knot better than her design maximum despite the fitting of bulges and an increase of over 2,000 tons to her standard displacement of 30,837 tons – all in all, dramatic testimony to the advance of engineering technology since the Great War and the basis for a series of similar reconstructions for the Royal Navy over the next ten years.[33]

The main armament was also completely overhauled. The guns were relined and the turret hydraulic systems either modernised or replaced. To the large stocks of 14in ammunition acquired in 1920 a supply of armour-piercing shells of the latest British design was now added, the order being large enough to require the purchase of a steamer to transport it to Chile. However, no

steps were taken to improve the existing elevation of 20 degrees and so take maximum advantage of the range of the 14in gun or the new optical equipment installed in the control tower as part of an upgrade of the ship's fire-control system (see above). This decision, subsequently much criticised in naval circles, was taken on grounds of cost and in view of the fact that *Latorre*'s effective range already exceeded that of the Argentine Rivadavia-class battleships.[34] Nonetheless, the opportunity was taken to install a new anti-aircraft battery, consisting of four single 4in/45-calibre Mk-V mountings fitted on the after superstructure, together with the latest HACS I fire-control and calculator equipment. The original 6in directors were replaced, but it was not possible to increase the range of the 6in armament as had been hoped. The mountings were set at a height to facilitate rapid manual reloading, which at the same time reduced the ability of the gun to elevate sufficiently to engage destroyers firing the latest torpedo designs. Although there are records of the Chilean navy firing to 16,400yds (15,000m)

---

31 Jorge Ortiz Sotelo, *Apuntes para la historia de los submarinos peruanos* (Lima: Biblioteca Nacional de Perú, Asociación de Historia Marítima y Naval Iberoamericana, 2001), p. 82.

32 Wood, 'El Acorazado', pp. 269–72.

33 AHA, *Historial*, II, p. 202, and Wood, 'El Acorazado', p. 285.

34 See AHA, Wood, *El Acorazado* (MS), pp. 29 & 34; Wood, 'El Acorazado', p. 277; Arroyo, *Adquisiciones navales*, p. 34.

with these guns, the usual effective range was 12,000yds (11,000m).[35]

The last significant improvement was the installation of bulges. Although *Latorre* had always been regarded as an excellent gunnery platform, she had a tendency to bury her bows when at sea, a problem aggravated by the trimming forward caused by the installation of the 6in battery (see above).[36] The fitting of bulges went far towards eliminating this problem, allowing her to recover her longitudinal stability despite an increase in topweight, and countering her reputation of being a wet ship forward. Nonetheless, improved stability and comfort were only secondary benefits of the bulges, whose

installation was prompted by increasing concern in Chilean naval circles of the threat posed by submarines, of which the Peruvian navy now operated four units. Not only did the bulges significantly improve *Latorre*'s submerged protection in their own right, but by correcting the trim succeeded in restoring the 9in belt to its designed position in relation to the waterline. Vertical armour was left unaltered, but the improvements made to horizontal protection by the British after Jutland were completed with the installation of additional 2in (51mm) of plating over the magazines, the result being deemed sufficient to withstand 12in shellfire. With improved speed, enhanced protection and greater firepower thanks to her new ammunition and fire control, these modernisations placed *Latorre* among the more modern battleships in the world in 1931.

Latorre spent the final weeks of her Devonport refit undergoing trials and making preparations for the journey home, which included a number of farewell engagements hosted by local dignitaries and widely reported in the press. In February 1931 the mayor of Plymouth presented the ship with a silver salver acknowledging 'the employment for two years given to 2,000 British workers and for the splendid behaviour observed by the ship's crew', this in view of the fact that by the end of 1930 unemployment in Britain stood at 2.5 million – fully 20 per cent of the workforce.[37] On the same occasion the Commander-in-Chief of the

---

[35] Vice Admiral Patricio Carvajal Prado, 'Al servicio de la artillería en el acorazado *Almirante Latorre*' in *Revista de Marina* 108 (1993), no. 1, pp. 7–13; 8.

[36] AHA, Wood, *El Acorazado* (MS), p. 34.

[37] AHA, *Historial*, I, p. 205. 'Chilean battleship final activities in Plymouth' and 'Plymouth Token of Goodwill. Silver Plate for Chilean Battleship', both in *The Naval and Military Record*, 19 February 1931, pp. 18 & 30 respectively.

AVIATION

The flying-off platforms fitted atop 'B' and 'X' turrets in HMS *Canada* in 1918 were dismantled shortly after *Latorre* reached Chile in 1921 and there is no record of their ever being used. However, by 1929 developments in naval gunnery called for spotting and fire control by observers in ship-launched seaplanes, and space was set aside on the quarterdeck for the installation of a revolving air-impulse catapult manufactured by the Italian firm of Ansaldo which allowed the aircraft to be launched into the wind.[38] The intention had been to install this apparatus during the Devonport refit but delays in delivery thwarted this until September 1932 when the equipment was fitted and tested while the ship was at Talcahuano.[39] Where aircraft were concerned, the Chilean naval air arm purchased three Fairey IIIF I seaplanes in 1927 followed by a single Fairey IIIB fitted for catapult launching in 1929.[40] Unfortunately, procurement did not extend to the hydraulic crane designed to recover the aircraft after its flight and for that reason it was necessary for the pilot to head for shore on completion of the operation, although there were instances of planes being hoisted aboard using an improvised rig. Matters were further complicated by the fact that the Armada had lost control of its air arm to the Chilean air force in 1930, meaning that use of an aircraft for spotting purposes had to be requested in advance from the air force even though one of its pilots was permanently embarked. Together with the complexities of handling equipment largely unknown to the Armada, this highly unsatisfactory situation resulted in the catapult being

Latorre's British-supplied Fairey IIIB on one of its rare launchings from the Ansaldo catapult during the 1930s. Use of this capability was shackled by the absence of a dedicated recovery crane and by the Armada having lost control of its naval air arm to the air force in 1930. *(Courtesy Piero Castagneto)*

used only infrequently. Apart from initial trials in the spring of 1932 there are records of only five launches between 1935 and the dismantling of the catapult in late 1942.[41] Gunnery spotting and fire control was therefore usually carried out using land-based aircraft and a number of naval officers were sent to Britain for training as air observers prior to the outbreak of the Second World War.

---

[38] Wood, 'El Acorazado', pp. 272–3.

[39] Fuenzalida Bade, *La Armada de Chile*, IV, p. 1194.

[40] Tromben Corbalán, *La Aviación naval de Chile*, p. 94, confirmed by the research of Professor Ivan Siminic of the Chilean Air Force War College.

[41] AHA, Wood, *El Acorazado* (MS), pp. 22–3.

An undated photo of units of the Chilean fleet lying peacefully at the northern port of Coquimbo including *Latorre*, the destroyers *Almirante Condell*, *Almirante Lynch* and *Almirante Williams*, and on the extreme right the protected cruisers *Chacabuco* and *Ministro Zenteno*, all of British construction. In September 1931 the tranquillity of this anchorage was broken by the outbreak of a mutiny with far-reaching consequences for the Armada. (*Fernando Wilson Collection*)

Portsmouth naval base, Admiral of the Fleet Sir Roger Keyes, took the opportunity to present the ship with a memento subscribed to by the workers of Devonport Dockyard.

The Naval Mutiny of 1931

Amidst the junketings attending *Latorre*'s departure from Devonport in early March 1931, and despite the evident cordiality existing between the Chileans and their hosts, there can be no doubt that her crew was exposed to the strained political climate prevailing in Britain's major ports and dockyards, not least since among those working aboard her were members of the Communist Party of Great Britain.[42] This was particularly true at Devonport where feelings had been running high since the mutiny in the submarine depot ship *Lucia* in early January. The crew of *Latorre* can hardly have remained abstracted from this incident as not only were the papers full of it but *Lucia* was moored not far from their barracks ashore. Not only that, but the increasingly authoritarian regime of President Carlos Ibáñez del Campo had resulted in the exile in Britain of a number of Chilean politicians who made attempts to incite the crew to revolt once *Latorre* returned home.

Latorre reached Valparaíso via the Panama Canal on 12 April where she immediately became flagship of the training squadron under reduced complement. Moreover, the country to which she returned was bankrupt, and seething with economic, social and political unrest, and must in many respects have been scarcely recognisable from the one she left in May 1929. The desperate economic plight, which eventually led the League of Nations to declare Chilean trade as having suffered more during the Depression than that of any other, resulted in July 1931 in the fall of the Ibáñez regime and the beginning of a period of financial retrenchment which led to significant reductions in the salaries of most public employees. This measure, reports of which began appearing in the press in August 1931, came on top of earlier pay cuts of 10 per cent and a halving of the allowance paid for foreign service, a measure which hit the crew of *Latorre* particularly hard. As in the case of the Invergordon Mutiny in September (see *Hood*),

the problem was compounded by the inept job made by the government in explaining the cuts to those affected, which allowed rumours to circulate of universal cuts of 30 per cent.[43] Although many sailors did not earn enough to be affected by the pay cut, in the context of the already pitiful salaries drawn by the military and the decreased purchasing power of the Chilean peso, these developments and the wider political and social conjuncture set the stage for mutiny.

Initially, it seems that news of these events was received with disquiet but nonetheless relatively peaceably by the fleet, nine units of which were lying at the port of Coquimbo, 200 miles north of Valparaíso. Among them was *Latorre* in which the commander of the training squadron, Commodore Alberto Hozven, was embarked. The senior officer present was Rear Admiral Abel Campos commanding the active squadron and flying his flag in the armoured cruiser *O'Higgins*. On 31 August Campos and Hozven were alerted by their subordinates that there was considerable

unrest over pay and that a number of sailors in the destroyers wished to forward a petition asking the government to cancel the pay cuts. To this the already unpopular figure of Hozven responded with contempt. That afternoon Hozven ordered the commanding officers and executive officers of the four destroyers in the anchorage, together with a delegation of twenty men from each, to come aboard *Latorre*. Having cleared lower deck, he proceeded to read out a speech which, far from explaining the reductions ordered by the government, or offering the channel for lodging complaints with the Ministry of Marine provided for in naval regulations, soundly rebuked those who had initiated these actions for their 'unseemly selfishness and utter lack of patriotism'. Hozven concluded by not only refusing to forward the petition, but threatening to eject from the Armada any who attempted to do so.

Naturally enough, this harangue decided elements of *Latorre*'s crew that the time had

---

[42] This climate was also experienced by the crews of the six destroyers being built for Chile at Thornycroft's of Woolston, Southampton, and those of the submarine depot ship *Araucano* and three 'O' class submarines completing at Vickers-Armstrongs of Barrow between 1926–8.

[43] It was not until the end of August that the government finally cleared up the matter. On the 28th *El Mercurio de Valparaíso* published the instructions issued two days earlier by the minister of finance. For the month of August *only*, those receiving salaries under $250 (i.e. Chilean pesos) per month

would suffer a reduction of 12 per cent; those receiving salaries in excess of $250 would be subject to the 12 per cent reduction up to that amount, and then a 30 per cent reduction on salary received in excess of $250. However, any amount deducted could be used to pay up to 50 per cent of housing loans, with a record being made of all deductions with a view to subsequent reimbursement, though with no date specified. On this and the mutiny generally the fundamental study is Carlos Tromben Corbalán, 'The Chilean Naval Mutiny of 1931' (PhD thesis, University of Exeter, 2010), pp. 145–7.

come to act and it was this ship which provided the seat of the Chilean naval mutiny of 1931. Shortly before midnight on the 31st a group of sailors, including several petty officers, surprised the officer corps while they slept, and locked them in their cabins. By 0410 on 1 September 1931 the mutiny had propagated from *Latorre* to both squadrons, though some of the destroyers were only brought round once the battleship trained her 14in guns on them or, in the case of *Hyatt*, after being boarded by armed parties from *Latorre*. Other than two men wounded aboard *O'Higgins*, there were no casualties during the uprising and thereafter adherence to the mutiny was indicated by the burning of a red light on the forward yardarm of each vessel. Effective command of the squadron was assumed by an elected *Estado Mayor de las Tripulaciones* (Crews' General Committee) led by Hozven's secretary in *Latorre*, Suboficial escribiente (Writer Petty Officer) Ernesto González. However, the brains of the mutiny seems to have been Cabo despensero (Supply Petty Officer) Manuel Astica, a product of recent organisational changes in the Armada since *Latorre*'s sojourn in Britain which resulted in the introduction of a new supply system requiring the services of men with accounting experience. Some of these qualified ratings had experience of union movements and activism ashore, including Astica who had engaged in politics and journalism in the nitrate fields of Antofagasta before joining *Latorre* in May 1931.

On the afternoon of the 1st the mutineers signalled a series of demands to the Minister of Marine, Calisto Rogers Ceas, chief among

which was the annulment of the pay cuts and sanctions for those politicians responsible for implementing them. The mutineers made clear that the squadron would remain at Coquimbo until these demands had been met. This was followed around midnight by a second signal extending the mutineers' demands into the political and social sphere, though with a pronounced left-wing slant including land reform and the repudiation of foreign debt which raised suspicions of Communist influence. Support was lent to these suspicions by the sympathy strike ordered by the Chilean Communist Party which immediately brought Santiago's public transport service to a halt. Before long the mutiny had extended to the Maipo regiment in Valparaíso, the air force base at nearby Quintero, and particularly the southern naval base at Talcahuano where, allegedly with the collusion of some officers, armed crewmen ordered officers ashore and expelled others from the shore establishments. At the height of the uprising twenty-three vessels were in the hands of the mutineers, the nine in the north and fourteen at Talcahuano, five of which (minus their officers) sailed for Coquimbo to join the mutiny before dawn on 3 September.

The transitional government of Vice President Manuel Trucco responded by appointing the respected figure of Rear Admiral Edgardo von Schroeders to negotiate with the mutineers. Although von Schroeders was ordered to hold the meetings ashore, these eventually began aboard *Latorre* on the evening of the 2nd. Von Schroeders was treated courteously enough, but despite a promising and even constructive start

which included a promise that the reduction in pay would be rescinded, the discussions ended abruptly on 4 September. In the intervening period, hawkish figures in Santiago were beginning to take a hand in the matter, chiefly the minister of war, General Carlos Vergara. Having issued an ultimatum of unconditional surrender which was flatly rejected by the mutineers, the government decided to end the uprising by force, a decision no doubt precipitated by riots and the calling of a general strike by the Chilean Workers' Federation that same day. Steps were taken to mobilise loyal units of the Chilean army which immediately surrounded those shore establishments in the hands of the mutineers. The naval base at Valparaíso fell without difficulty, but that at Talcahuano was recovered by the government only after heavy fighting on the afternoon of the 5th which, together with sporadic incidents on the following days, eventually claimed the lives of twenty men, with approximately eighty wounded and 700 taken prisoner, aside from significant damage to the destroyer *Almirante Riveros* from shore batteries.

These developments were followed concurrently in *Latorre* and co-ordination made possible thanks to the modern radio equipment fitted at Devonport, but she was nonetheless powerless to intervene in the suppression of the mutiny 450 miles to the south. On the afternoon of the 6th it was Coquimbo's turn to feel the wrath of the government, and between 1500 and 1600 a motley assemblage of twenty-one aircraft of the Chilean air force delivered an attack on the mutinous squadrons with bombs of up to 660lb (300kg). The pilots were ordered to target *Latorre* which, joined by her fellows, went to action stations and opened up with her new anti-aircraft armament. Five aircraft were hit, of which one crash-landed without loss to the crew. Damage to shipping was confined to strafing of the submarine *H-4* which left one man dead and another wounded, but the attack nonetheless succeeded in damaging the increasingly fragile morale of the mutiny. Discussions aboard *Latorre* attended both by destroyer officers and by Rear Admiral Campos himself revealed tensions among the rebels, and that night the mutineers in all four destroyers turned their ships over to the officers, upon which they furtively quit the anchorage and sailed independently for Valparaíso. In *Latorre*, meanwhile, the intention

Stoker petty officers of the *Almirante Latorre* pose for the camera in the 1930s. The naval mutiny of September 1931 was led by educated senior ratings, many of whom had experience of union movements and activism ashore. (MMN/2680)

had been to put to sea at dawn on the 7th in order to meet any further aerial attack in open water with the support of the newly arrived units from Talcahuano. However, the revelation that the destroyers had sailed extinguished the morale of the ringleaders who surrendered the ship to her officers a week after the outbreak of the mutiny, although Commodore Hozven remained locked in his cabin until the ship reached the anchorage at Quintero, 20 miles north of Valparaíso. The Talcahuano squadron followed suit next day.

No sooner had the mutineers surrendered than court-martial proceedings began against a total of ninety-eight defendants, of whom fourteen, including González, were sentenced to death, while thirty-three, including Astica, were given custodial sentences, and the rest acquitted. However, Vice President Trucco first delayed the executions and then responded to widespread pressure by commuting the death sentences to life imprisonment. The case for clemency was boosted by the publication by González's sister of documents showing that no less than ninety officers had signed the mutineers' first signal to the government, confirming suspicions of extensive collusion among the officer corps. In fact, the evidence is that no more than a dozen of the 150 officers present signed letters supporting the mutiny, and the possibility of duress on individuals locked in their cabins under armed guard cannot be discounted in several instances. Whatever the case, in March of the following year the new President Juan Esteban Montero first commuted the life sentences to much shorter terms of imprisonment and then to internal exile. In June 1932 the new socialist government pardoned those still in custody and released the last of the mutineers. Rear Admiral Campos was one of many officers forced into retirement.

Although Communist propaganda subsequently made much capital out of the Chilean naval mutiny, there is no convincing evidence that it had any significant role in its organisation. The most likely explanation for the mutiny is that of a largely spontaneous movement arising from the wider context of Chilean economic, social and political affairs for which the pay cuts of August 1931 provided the immediate motive. In this respect, the events in Chile bear considerable similarity to the Invergordon Mutiny which broke out on 15 September 1931 (see *Hood*). Like their counterparts at Coquimbo, the Invergordon mutineers were acting in response to government decrees affecting their pay. However, the Chilean uprising immediately tapped into a deep wellspring of social and political unrest and unlike the 'quiet mutiny' had eventually to be

President Arturo Alessandri poses with *Latorre*'s officer corps and assorted sailors beside no. '5' turret during a visit on 7 February 1924. The naval mutiny of September 1931 resulted in 30 per cent of the officer strength of the Armada being beached or disciplined. *(MMN/896)*

quelled with recourse to force. Nonetheless, in their different ways, both episodes had a significant effect on the navy and nation in question, a mark of the pervasive importance of naval affairs on the societies of the day.

The Aftermath, 1931–9

The mutiny of 1931 had a devastating effect on the Armada, reducing its prestige both at home and abroad and driving a wedge between officers and men. Moreover, the government took immediate and drastic steps to reduce the size of the fleet both in personnel and ships. Some 2,000 men were expelled from the navy or went into forced retirement – some 23 per cent of all the enlisted personnel in service in 1931. About two hundred officers, 30 per cent of the total, received administrative punishments ranging from expulsion, early retirement, months of unemployment and other more minor sanctions.[44] Meanwhile, a large proportion of the fleet including *Latorre* was sent into reserve at Talcahuano. With the importation of oil

hampered by foreign currency restrictions, the Armada had to curtail the operation of its oil-fired ships, of which only two of the modern Thornycroft destroyers remained in active rotation, leaving the five coal-fired veterans of the Broke class and a flotilla of submarines to bear the brunt of naval operations.[45] The mutiny was therefore only partially responsible for this state of affairs, which also reflected the dire economic situation in which Chile found herself, together with the reigning political instability which resulted in the formation of no less than four governments during 1932.

Meanwhile, settlement of the border dispute with Peru in June 1929 also raised the question as to whether Chile either needed or could afford to avail herself of such a significant unit as *Latorre* at all, and reports appeared in the Chilean press in September 1931 to the effect that the government was considering the sale of the battleship to Japan. In fact, the British embassy in Santiago believed these rumours to have originated a month earlier in Buenos Aires,

44 Tromben Corbalán, *The Chilean Naval Mutiny of 1931*, pp. 221–2.

45 TNA, FO 371/16569, p. 31, British Embassy Annual Report 1932, 6 March 1933; Fuenzalida Bade, *La Armada de Chile*, IV, p. 1193.

where the Argentine government was considering the possibility of joining Brazil in disposing of its battleships as a preliminary gesture before the next disarmament conference.[46] However, the British embassy decided, rightly as it turned out, that Brazil had no inclination to run down its fleet and that Chile would retain her super-dreadnought under

reduced complement.[47] On 30 September the Chilean government duly issued a communiqué denying the rumours.

So it was that *Latorre* spent the next few years anchored in the Talcahuano roads with a skeleton crew, and it was not until February 1935 that the naval budget permitted her and the Armada's other oil-fired vessels to be brought back into full commission. By the end of that year *Latorre* had completed three cruises in company with units of the fleet, including one to the far south of Chile during which a number of tactical exercises were carried out, including catapulting the ship's seaplane for gunnery-spot-

ting purposes.[48] These developments not only improved the morale of the Armada, but also provided evidence that Chile had emerged from the worst of the economic crisis.[49] No doubt the assistance rendered by *Latorre* to the victims of the Chillán earthquake of January 1939, alongside the soon-to-be famous British cruisers *Exeter* and *Ajax* and the French training cruiser *Jeanne d'Arc* helped complete her rehabilitation.

The Second World War and After

The outbreak of the Second World War found the Chilean navy in a period of recovery, with a

[46] TNA, FO 371/15830, p. 18, British Embassy Annual Report 1931, 29 January 1932.

[47] TNA, FO A6832/5665/9, Letter Nos. 217 & 249 from British Ambassador to Chile to the Foreign Office of 26 August 1931 & 30 September 1931 respectively.

[48] TNA, FO 371/19775, p. 58, British Embassy Annual Report 1935, 1 January 1936.

[49] TNA, FO 371/18669, p. 40, British Embassy Annual Report 1934.

SHIPBOARD ORGANISATION

On the outbreak of the Second World War the ship's company of *Latorre* was organised into four brigades subdivided into four divisions each.[50] The first brigade included the divisions responsible for the fo'c'sle, no. '1' and '2' 14in turrets and the starboard 6in battery, while the second brigade comprised those covering the midships, turret '3', the anti-aircraft armament, communications, torpedoes and the ship's boats. The third brigade consisted of those responsible for the quarterdeck, turrets no. '4' and '5', the port 6in battery and the ship's marine detachment, including the ship's band. The fourth brigade covered the principal and auxiliary machinery as well as the electrical installations. To these was added a separate 17th Division consisting of auxiliary and administrative personnel, including cooks, stewards, tailors, shoemakers and storekeepers.

Where wartime cruising stations were concerned, based on operational necessity the ship was either at the first degree of readiness with the entire crew at action stations, the second degree of readiness which brought half of the crew to action stations and the remainder either resting or messing, and the third degree of readiness which had a third of the crew at action stations and the propulsion systems flashed up for economic steaming only.[51] With respect to the naval year, the Armada spent the southern winter off northern Chile, particularly Puerto Aldea Bay, where the mild climate was ideal for seaborne exercises and landing parties, culminating in a full-scale gunnery exercise in August. This was also the opportunity to engage in the Armada's main sporting activities,

A curiosity of the Chilean navy was the presence in larger vessels of a detachment of the Cuerpo de Defensa de Costa (Coastal Defence Corps), seen here formed up on *Latorre*'s forecastle on 9 March 1929, the ship lying at Talcahuano. *(MMN/565)*

including sailing, shooting, athletics, boxing in a ring set up in the armoured cruiser *O'Higgins* and, of course, football. Ships usually spent the month of September at their home ports of Valparaíso or Talcahuano, followed at the end of the year by fleet exercises in southern Chile. Efficiency in gunnery

was denoted by bronze condors affixed to the sides of the turrets, in recognition of Chile's national bird.

[50] Carvajal Prado, 'Al servicio de la artillería', p. 5.
[51] *Ibid.*, p. 11.

Left: The forecastle and bridge structure seen in 1942 showing the alterations made during the 1929–31 refit; compare with the photograph on p. 255 for her pre-refit appearance. *(NA/158-NN-2-1338)*

large proportion of its vessels in commission. Nonetheless, the threat presented by what had become a worldwide conflict was not truly felt until after the Japanese attack on Pearl Harbor. It should at this point be stated that there is no evidence in Chilean sources to support the oft-repeated claim in English-language sources to the effect that the United States approached Chile with a view to purchasing *Latorre*, the submarine tender *Araucano* and the six British-built Serrano-class destroyers, despite the fact that the US did purchase a number of modern merchantmen owned by the Empresa Marítima del Estado (State Shipping Company) in 1942. On the other hand, agreements signed between Chile and the United States facilitated the delivery to the former of a variety of coast defence equipment including artillery, reflectors and fire-control installations, together with a variety of aircraft, but naval supplies were more limited, being restricted to the installation of eighteen 0.79in (20mm) Oerlikon anti-aircraft guns in *Latorre*.[52] To the ten 0.5in (13.2mm) Hotchkiss machine guns installed in single mountings on the turret roofs in the late 1930s a quadruple mounting was now added in place of the catapult aft.[53] Most prominent, however, was the dazzle camouflage consisting of dark grey diagonal bands over the usual light grey paint applied to *Latorre* and the six Serranos after the Chilean government severed relations with the Axis powers in 1943. The ship remained fully manned and at a high state of readiness, with year-round training with the destroyers off Valparaíso culminating in manoeuvres in more distant waters and an exercise before Christmas, usually attended by senior naval and government figures. Among the casualties of these exercises was the decommissioned destroyer *Almirante Riveros* which was expended as a target for *Latorre*'s main armament in 1940. Taken all round, *Latorre* steamed nearly 28,000 miles on Peruvian oil between 1942 and 1945, over three times further than during any comparable period in the 1920s. The period was therefore one of significant activity within the budgetary constraints of the time, though *Latorre*'s battleworthiness had fortunately never to be tested in combat.

Although the Armada did not see action

Latorre drydocked at Talcahuano in 1943. The camouflage was added following the severing of relations with the Axis powers that year. *(Bruce Taylor Collection)*

during the Second World War, the same was not true of several of her officers, who in turn brought the fruit of their experience back to the Chilean navy. The most prominent of these was Teniente de navío (Lieutenant) José Toribio Merino, then commander of *Latorre*'s no. '5' turret and later a member of the military junta, who volunteered for service with the US Pacific Fleet in 1942. Embarked in the light cruiser USS *Raleigh* between April 1944 and September 1945, Merino saw extensive action in the Pacific and on his return to Chile proceeded to write the Armada's damage-control and Combat Information Center (CIC) manuals based on US Navy practice and equipment. Meanwhile, combat experience and courses of study in the United States served to highlight the absence of radar, resulting in the installation of the first sets in *Latorre* in 1946–8, removed from U.S. Navy landing craft and sold to Chile as war surplus. By 1950 examples of SG, SO and SU radar had been fitted, their consoles positioned in the transmitting station where the first CIC was located.[54] Returning to *Latorre* as a Capitán de Corbeta (Lieutenant Commander) in 1950, Merino brought about a complete reorganisation of that ship's damage-control procedures along US Navy

lines, including repairs to the water mains, installation of a system of hoses, 'Y' joints and extinguishers.[55]

Twilight

The end of the Second World War found the victorious powers with an enormous surplus of military *matériel*, which in the case of the United States prompted a diplomatic offensive to extend the various agreements signed with Latin American nations during the conflict for the defence of the western hemisphere. This policy brought about a period of significant US influence in naval affairs, which in Chile's case lasted until 1975, the most tangible result of which was a succession of transfers and acquisitions beginning in 1946, and culminating in the purchase of two Brooklyn-class light cruisers in early 1950. Nonetheless, that same year studies and discussions began on the modernisation of *Latorre* and the four River-class frigates acquired from the Royal Canadian Navy in 1946. Accordingly, in May and June 1950 a party of armament, construction and electrical experts visited Talcahuano from Vickers-Armstrongs with a view to assessing the modifications required to *Latorre*.[56] That such a step should have been contemplated for a vessel with nearly forty years of service behind her is at best questionable, not least since the recent conflict had convincingly demonstrated that submarines and naval aviation had eclipsed the battleship as the principal means of waging war at sea. Not only that, but the rationale for modernisation was based on the perceived threat presented by the five cruisers of the Argentine navy (two Veinticinco de Mayo class, *La Argentina* and two ex-Brooklyn class), whereas that country had already decided to reorganise its fleet around an aircraft carrier, a step financed in part by the sale of her two elderly battleships and the decommissioning of at least one of the cruisers.

Whatever the case, as far as the Armada was concerned *Latorre* remained the nucleus of its naval power and a refitting and modernisation process was called for to keep her in a reasonable state of battleworthiness for the next ten years. The first step in this modernisation would focus on a complete overhaul of her engineering systems, together with the addition of a state-of-the-art anti-aircraft battery. Although the British

[52] Balaresque Buchanan, 'El *Latorre*', p. 220.

[53] Wood, 'El Acorazado', pp. 273–4.

[54] Tromben Corbalán, *La Ingeniería electrónica en la Armada de Chile*, p. 43.

[55] Wood, 'El Acorazado', pp. 275–6.

[56] AHA, vol. 1250, Letters from Gibbs y Cía Ltda, representative in Chile of Vickers-Armstrongs to the Commander-in-Chief of the Armada, 3 & 6 July 1950.

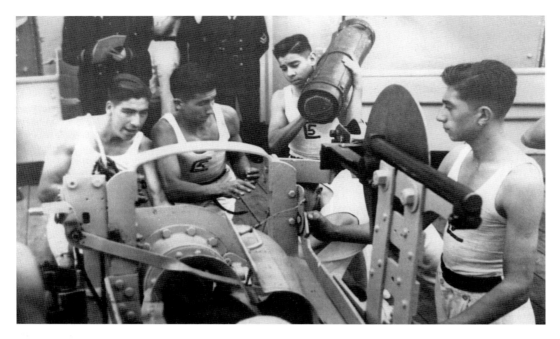

Crewmen manning one of the obsolete 6in guns during a competitive exercise on 20 June 1953. By then it had become obvious that *Latorre*'s long career was drawing to a close. *(MMN/1055)*

embassy in Santiago subsequently concluded that the acquisition of the US cruisers would absorb the financial resources needed to fund the armaments contract to Vickers-Armstrongs, this turned out not to be the case and the contract was duly signed.[57] Nonetheless, while these studies were still in progress an explosion occurred aboard *Latorre* during the commissioning of an electricity generating plant on 11 March 1951, which cost the lives of four

crewmen. Although this provided further evidence that *Latorre* was reaching the end of her useful life, the government nonetheless proceeded to sign a modernisation contract with Vickers-Armstrongs worth £1.2 million, and on 23 August gave authorisation for the work to be carried out in Chile with materials, equipment and technical supervision supplied by that company.[58] This process was to have involved a complete overhaul of the engine plant including

replacement of the boilers, installation of Type-274 gunnery radar and, interestingly enough, a new heavy anti-aircraft battery consisting of six twin 4in (102mm) mountings.[59] Also contemplated was the installation of a number of automatic 1.57in (40mm) Bofors mountings with night fighting fire-control systems. However, by early 1953 it was obvious that not all of this work could be carried out at Talcahuano and that it would be necessary for *Latorre* to make her way to Britain in order to complete the work, something Chile could ill afford at a time of financial stringency. Questions were again raised as to the wisdom of modernising *Latorre* and it was decided to abandon the project and amend the contract in favour of the construction of two modern destroyers instead. This implied payment of £300,000 in compensation to Vickers-Armstrongs, and allocation of the balance of £900,000 towards the construction of the new destroyers, the contract for which was signed in Santiago on 17 May 1955.[60]

Unsurprisingly, this opened the last chapter in the career of *Latorre*, and already in 1954 Fleet Order 1/54 had dispatched her to Talcahuano under her own steam with the intention that she go into reserve from 11 March.[61] Here she

Latorre seen in the 1930s as she has gone down in Chilean naval history, the crew proudly manning the rails in Valparaíso Bay on a national holiday. *(MMN/1463)*

57 TNA, FO 371/90662, p. 4, British Embassy Annual Report 1950, 17 January 1951.

58 Fuenzalida Bade, *La Armada de Chile*, IV, p. 1230; Vickers Company Archive, Quarterly Reports for 31 March and 30 June 1953 cited in Jonathan Wise, 'Securing "The Ripest Plum": Britain and the South American Naval Export Market, 1947–75' in John Jordan & Stephen Dent, eds., *Warship 2013* (London: Conway, 2013), pp. 119–33; 121–2, 133.

59 There has been debate as to whether the guns in question were Vickers Mk XVI or Mk N(R) of the type eventually installed in the new destroyers *Almirante Williams* and *Almirante Riveros*. The fact that the Mk N only became available in 1953 settles the debate in favour of the Mk XVI; see Peter Marland, 'The Vickers 4-Inch Mk N(R) Mounting' in *Warship 2013* (London: Conway, 2013), pp. 174–7.

60 TNA, FO 118/1, Letter of J. J. J. Smith to J. H. Wright of the Foreign Office to the First Secretary, British Embassy in Santiago, 7 October 1954; Wise, 'Securing "The Ripest Plum"', p. 121; Fuenzalida Bade, *La Armada de Chile*, IV, p. 1253.

61 AHA, *Historial*, III, p. 96 *et seq.*

remained, tied up in the approach channel to no. 2 Dock, where she served as a tender, floating workshop, accommodation ship and oil storage vessel, providing technical support for the various units being refitted at Talcahuano. Efforts were made to keep her at a certain degree of combat readiness within the limits of available *matériel* and personnel, with repairs and maintenance extending to her being drydocked on more than one occasion.[62] However, on 14 February 1958 *Almirante Latorre* was finally stricken from the navy list and the process began of removing fuel and usable equipment. Her ensign was lowered for the last time on 1 August, with which she ceased to be a unit of the Armada after a thirty-seven year career. By now sold for scrapping, in May 1959 she was taken in tow by the oceangoing tug *Cambrian Salvor* and departed for her final destination, Tokyo Bay. Despite this, it was several years before she was finally scrapped, during which time part of her fabric found its way to the battleship *Mikasa*, then in the process of restoration as a museum.

The battleship *Almirante Latorre* not only formed the backbone of the Chilean navy for three decades but represented the apogee of naval power in South America during the first half of the twentieth century, a period during which the nations of that continent could acquire capital ships that were equal or even superior to those of any other power in the world. At the same time, Brazil, Argentina and Chile faced huge technical, logistical and financial challenges in operating these ships and keeping them in service. Nonetheless, *Latorre* had an influence on the Armada de Chile greater than that of any vessel in its history and for many years her crewmen regarded themselves as the cream of the service. Her unmistakable silhouette, visible from any point in the immense amphitheatre formed by Valparaíso Bay and now part of that city's rich heritage, ensures that her legacy will survive for successive generations of Chileans.

---

[62] *Ibid.*, p. 106.

Sources

Unpublished Sources

Archivo Histórico de la Armada, Valparaíso (AHA)

Historial del acorazado Almirante Latorre, 3 vols.

Vice Admiral Gerald L. Wood, *El Acorazado* Almirante Latorre, *el último buque de su tipo que combatió en Jutlandia* (unpublished MS)

The National Archives, Kew, London (TNA)

Foreign Office series 118, 371, A6120, A6832

Bibliography

Arroyo, Guillermo, *Adquisiciones navales de Chile. Un estudio crítico* (Valparaíso: Armada de Chile, 1940)

Balaresque Buchanan, Jorge, 'El *Latorre* y los demás acorazados latinoamericanos' in *Revista de Marina* 86 (1967), pp. 208–20

Brook, Peter, *Warships for Export: Armstrong Warships, 1867–1927* (Gravesend, Kent: World Ship Society, 1999)

Burt, R. A., *British Battleships of World War One* (2nd edn, Barnsley, S. Yorks., Seaforth Publishing, 2012)

_____, *British Battleships, 1919–1945* (2nd edn, Barnsley, S. Yorks., Seaforth Publishing, 2013)

Campbell, John, *Naval Weapons of World War Two* (London: Conway, 1985)

Carvajal Prado, Vice Admiral Patricio, 'Al servicio de la artillería en el acorazado *Almirante Latorre*' in *Revista de Marina* 108 (1993), no. 1, pp. 7–13

Couyoumdjian, Ricardo, 'El Programa Naval del Centenario y el acorazado *Almirante Latorre*' in *Actas del IV Congreso de Historia Naval y Marítima Latinoamericana* (Madrid: Instituto de Historia y Cultura Naval, 1999), pp. 199–221

Friedman, Norman, *Naval Weapons of World War I* (Barnsley, S. Yorks.: Seaforth Publishing, 2011)

_____, *The British Battleship, 1906–1946* (Barnsley, S. Yorks.: Seaforth Publishing, 2015)

Fuenzalida Bade, Rodrigo, *La Armada de Chile. Desde la Alborada hasta el Sesquicentenario*, 4 vols. (Valparaíso: Imprenta de la Armada, 1975–8)

Johnston, Ian, & Ian Buxton, *The Battleship Builders: Constructing and Arming British Capital Ships* (Barnsley, S. Yorks.: Seaforth Publishing, 2013)

Memoria del Ministerio de Marina presentada al Congreso Nacional (Santiago: Ministerio de Marina, 1910–13)

Sater, William F., *Chile and the United States: Empires in Conflict* (Athens, Ga.: University of Georgia Press, 1990)

_____, 'Mutiny in the Chilean Navy, 1931' in Christopher M. Bell & Bruce A. Elleman, eds., *Naval Mutinies of the Twentieth Century* (London: Frank Cass, 2003), pp. 145–69

Scheina, Robert L., *Latin America: A Naval History, 1810–1897* (Annapolis, Md.: Naval Institute Press, 1987)

Tromben Corbalán, Carlos, *Ingeniería naval, una especialidad centenaria* (Valparaíso: Dirección de Ingeniería Naval de la Armada de Chile, 1989)

_____, *La Aviación naval de Chile* (Viña del Mar: Comandancia de la Aviación Naval, 1998)

_____, *La Ingeniería electrónica en la Armada de Chile (1953–2003)* (Valparaíso: Dirección de Programas de Investigación y Desarrollo, 2004)

_____, *The Chilean Naval Mutiny of 1931* (PhD Thesis, University of Exeter, 2010); available at http://ethos.bl.uk/OrderDetails.do?uin=uk.bl.ethos.529347 [accessed November 2017]

Wilson Lazo, Fernando, & Rodrigo Moreno Jeria, 'Evaluación de la capacidad táctica del acorazado *Almirante Latorre* con relación a los Dreadnoughts en el cono sur de América' in *Archivum* 2 (2001), no. 2–3, pp. 29–33

Wise, Jonathan, 'Securing "The Ripest Plum": Britain and the South American Naval Export Market, 1947–75' in John Jordan & Stephen Dent, eds., *Warship 2013* (London: Conway, 2013), pp. 119–33

_____, *The Role of the Royal Navy in South America, 1920–1970* (London: Bloomsbury, 2015)

Wood, Vice Admiral Gerald L., 'El Acorazado "Almirante Latorre"' in *Revista de Marina* 105 (1988), no. 3, pp. 255–86

Dreadnought Project: http://www.dreadnought-project.org

Armada Española

The Battleship *Alfonso XIII* (1913)

Agustín Ramón Rodríguez González

THE BATTLESHIP *ALFONSO XIII* was the second of three almost identical vessels of the España class of which she had the longest and most distinguished career.[1] With a displacement of 15,700 tons standard, a main armament of eight 12in (305mm) guns mounted in four turrets, and a range of 7,500 nautical miles at an economical speed approaching 11 knots, these were the only dreadnoughts built in Spain and the smallest vessels answering that description completed anywhere in the world. Although conceived with a clearly defined and hitherto little-known strategic purpose, changes in geopolitical alliances nonetheless deprived the class of the opportunity to carry out the role for which they been intended.

Rebuilding the Spanish Fleet

Defeat at the hands of the United States in the Spanish-American War of 1898 and the consequent loss of the Philippines, Cuba, Puerto Rico and Guam came as a crushing blow to Spain and to her navy, throwing both into a period of crisis. This episode, which marked the end of an overseas empire dating back to the fifteenth century, prompted a period of national soul-searching,

the social, cultural and political consequences of which would be felt for decades in a movement that came to be known as the ''98 Generation'. For the Armada, meanwhile, the one-sided defeats first at Manila Bay in the Philippines on

Alfonso XIII in port in the 1920s with *Jaime I* beyond. She can always be distinguished from her sisters by the single white stripe on the funnel; *Jaime I* had two and *España* none at all. *(Courtesy Camil Busquets i Vilanova)*

1 May and then at Santiago de Cuba on 3 July 1898 were the more painful and humiliating for the fact that the United States was then some way from being the great naval power she subsequently became.[2] Moreover, the obstacles to

---

[1] The author would like to acknowledge the assistance of Juan Luis Coello Lillo and Carlos Alfaro Zaforteza in preparing this chapter. The editor does likewise to Alejandro Anca Alamillo and Elena Casilari with respect to photos.

[2] Agustín R. Rodríguez González, *Política naval de la Restauración (1875–1898)* (Madrid: San Martín, 1988), and *Operaciones de la Guerra del 98: Una revisión crítica* (Madrid: Actas, 1998).

rebuilding Spain's lost fleet in the aftermath of the war were immense, not least of which was the political instability of a country beset with difficulties in the first years of the reign of the young King Alfonso XIII, who reached his majority in 1902. Not only was the Spanish treasury in a parlous state, saddled as it was with the enormous public debt with which it had financed a conflict on two fronts against the colonial Filipino and Cuban rebellions, but it was obvious that many serious errors had been committed where warship procurement and operation were concerned. These ranged from lengthy, costly and often substandard construction of ships in Spanish yards, resulting in many vessels planned before the war being delayed or rendered ineffectual by defects, poor maintenance and deficient training of crews, to a decidedly unimaginative tactical operation and strategic deployment of those vessels which were available. No surprise, therefore, that the immense task of reconstructing the fleet should

be greeted with a palpable lack of enthusiasm in political circles, an undertaking which was not only extremely expensive but reckoned by many to be of secondary importance and well beyond Spain's technical capabilities.

To these problems were added the rapid evolution of warship design and technology during the first decade of the twentieth century, along with the many tactical developments this brought in its train, a situation which in turn prompted debate in Spain as to the most appropriate ship types to defend her national interests. On the other hand, there was no doubting the importance of supporting Spanish shipyards and thereby giving a significant boost to the nation's technical, industrial and economic development, a matter of concern to successive governments and to the navy itself. Despite the efforts of the submarine pioneers Cosme García (1818–74), Narciso Monturiol (1819–85) and particularly Isaac Peral (1851–95), and the destroyer pioneer Fernando Villaamil (1845–98), from a technical

standpoint the Armada therefore recognised herself as having fallen well astern by comparison with the leading naval powers. At the same time, bitter experience had shown that continued dependence on the international market for naval construction and technology – which had in practice meant oscillating largely between British and French designs – was no longer a viable option for the Armada. What was required was a full, continuous and reliable technological transfer of a type which could only be obtained through a concerted diplomatic rapprochement with one of the naval powers. However, this endeavour was complicated by the reality of Spain's international isolation in the Age of Imperialism, during which the great powers vied for markets, colonies and influence in a scramble reflected in an increasingly furious naval race. Spain herself could not possibly ensure the defence of what were still extensive strategic interests – which included the Balearics and the Canaries, Ceuta and Melilla in North

Units of the new Spanish navy c. 1920. Outboard of *Alfonso XIII* is the US-built submarine *Isaac Peral* (1916) and outboard of her the Italian-built *Narciso Monturiol (A-1)* (1917). *(Courtesy Alejandro Anca Alamillo)*

Africa, and the colonies of Spanish Sahara and Equatorial Guinea – against any of these powers, much less an alliance of powers. Indeed, the possibility of sudden aggression and amputation of the type engaged in by the United States was all too apparent to the Spanish government after 1898, not least since such a campaign could be waged at minimal cost to the belligerent. Aside from the prevailing diplomatic conjuncture, the fact that further dismemberment was avoided may only have been due to the unlikelihood of the great powers agreeing on any division of the spoils. In the event, even so powerful a nation as Edwardian Britain proved incapable of shouldering the demands of global defence against aggression from every quarter, having to abandon its policy of Splendid Isolation in a series of strategic alliances between 1902 and 1907.

The immense task of rebuilding the Spanish fleet therefore included many elements to which Spain herself could provide no immediate solution. Unexpectedly, however, a small but active and increasingly influential group of politicians and sailors was able to take advantage of changes in the balance of strategic alliances and accomplish that goal by tenacity and will. Various plans for the reconstruction of the fleet in local yards were tabled between 1898 and 1906 but none received approval, due either to unfortunate timing or excess or lack of ambition, or to a failure to address the structural problems affecting the Spanish shipbuilding industry. However, changed circumstances in international politics eventually made that reconstruction a feasible proposition.[3]

Spain and the Anglo-French Entente Cordiale

Faced by the emergence of the German empire, in April 1904 Britain and France ended a tradition of strategic, naval and colonial rivalry by agreeing to the partition of areas of influence in North Africa. This agreement had important repercussions for Spain, since Article 8 of its terms accorded her the northern part of the Kingdom of Morocco bordering the Mediterranean, but excluding the port of

Tangier, which was to remain neutral under British, French and Spanish administration. Although this arrangement reflected British concerns to prevent any of the great powers establishing a base which could threaten Gibraltar, and with it the chain of ports that stretched from the Rock via Malta, Cyprus and Suez to its empire in India and the Far East, it also gave Spain a modest overseas possession, and in doing so discouraged any temptation she may have had to establish a rapprochement with the Triple Alliance of Germany, Austria-Hungary and Italy. Of course, the Spanish government had little option but to accept this secret agreement given Spain's dependence on British and French trade and investment. Although the commitment thus assumed aroused a certain amount of unease in Madrid once details of the cession of Northern Morocco were announced, there was also satisfaction that Spain had emerged from her isolation and reached an accord with the two powers whose interests were closest to her own. Meanwhile, Germany reacted angrily to the agreement and forced the holding of a conference at Algeciras in 1906 to discuss the Morocco question, an action which served only to strengthen Spain's ties to Britain and France. Already in 1905 Alfonso XIII had made a courtesy visit to England in his yacht *Giralda*, escorted by the armoured cruiser *Princesa de Asturias* and the protected cruiser *Extremadura*. It was during this visit that he became engaged to a granddaughter of Queen Victoria, Princess Victoria Eugenie of Battenberg, whom he married in Madrid in 1906. The new orientation

of Spanish foreign policy was sealed by Alfonso's visit to the Canaries that same year with his entire fleet, an assertion of Spanish sovereignty over the archipelago which put an end to constant German pressure for permission to establish a naval base there.

Apart from the personal support of the monarch, the political climate in Spain was therefore ripe for a major new undertaking in the area of rearmament, and the landslide victory of Conservative Party leader Antonio Maura in January 1907 brought to power not only a firm supporter of the reconstruction of the Spanish fleet and engagement in new foreign commitments, but also an avowed navalist and co-founder of the Liga Marítima Española, the Spanish equivalent of the navy leagues established in so many countries. A series of negotiations culminated in April that same year with the visit to Cartagena of Edward VII at the head of a powerful fleet in which the First Sea Lord, Admiral of the Fleet Sir John Fisher, was also embarked. Receiving them was Alfonso XIII and the minister of marine, Capitán de navío de 1ª clase (Commodore) José Ferrándiz y Niño, the result of which was an Exchange of Notes between Spain, France and Britain signed on 16 May. While stopping short of a formal alliance, this nonetheless constituted a strategic and naval co-operation agreement between the three countries which was aimed at stemming the ambitions of the Triple Alliance both in the Mediterranean and in the Atlantic. From a strategic perspective, the agreement guaranteed the territorial integrity of Spain's coastline and

---

[3] *Id., La Reconstrucción de la Escuadra. Planes navales españoles, 1898–1920* (Valladolid: Galland Books, 2010).

islands with British and French support, thereby eliminating a major concern from her defensive planning.

There was, however, a quid pro quo for Spain, and this was the participation of her navy in maintaining the balance of power in the Mediterranean against the threat posed by the Italian and Austro-Hungarian fleets. Faced by the rise of the High Seas Fleet, it was essential for Admiral Fisher as Britain's chief naval strategist to concentrate the better part of the Royal Navy in the North Sea and the English Channel in order to meet the German threat. Thanks to friendly relations with the United States, the Anglo-Japanese Alliance of 1902, and the addition of Russia to the Entente with France in 1907, Britain had provided for the safety of her global lines of communication with a scattering

Alfonso XIII lying at Cartagena. Agreements between Spain and the Entente powers prior to the Great War accorded the Armada a key strategic role in the event Italy commenced hostilities against France. Note the wind scoops affixed to the scuttles in an effort to bring cool air to the living spaces. *(Courtesy Alejandro Anca Alamillo)*

of older vessels across the major sea lanes of the world. To this, however, there was one critical exception – the Mediterranean – where the French navy could not match the combined strength of the Italian and Austro-Hungarian fleets.[4] Despite the size of her fleet, France had been slow to respond to the latest strategic and technical developments, and it was not until 1912 that she moved the bulk of her naval power to the Mediterranean and 1913 before she completed her first dreadnought, *Courbet*. The intention therefore was that a reborn Spanish fleet would reinforce the Marine Nationale from its strategic ports in the Balearics, especially Mahón on Minorca, and along its lengthy Mediterranean coastline.

Nor was this purely a matter of naval strategy against the Triple Alliance in the Mediterranean, since France's ability to hold the Rhine front against the German army was reckoned to

---

[4] Paul G. Halpern, *The Mediterranean Naval Situation, 1908–1914* (Cambridge, Mass.: Harvard University Press, 1971).

depend on the safe and timely transfer of the elite 19th Army Corps from Algiers and Tunis to Toulon and Marseille. Provision was even made for the transfer of French troops to ports in southern Spain for onward transportation by road and rail to France, an operation which would leave them much less exposed to enemy incursions into the western basin of the Mediterranean. Plans were also considered for Spain to reinforce the French army in the event of an Italian attack in the south, and even for amphibious landings by Spanish troops on the Italian coast, Sardinia and Sicily. In fact, Alfonso XIII offered the Entente the full co-operation of Spanish arms, though no firm undertakings were given since Spain was signatory not to a formal alliance but essentially to a series of agreements. Nonetheless, the advantages to Spain were all too apparent. Not only had she aligned her strategic priorities with those of two of the great powers, but she had secured transfer of the modern naval technology she needed to rebuild her fleet and make good that commitment. This, then, was the strategic context in which the España-class battleships came to be built.

Alfonso XIII sails from Cartagena, c. 1924. The España class restored Spain's status as a significant naval power in the Mediterranean. (*Courtesy Juan Luis Coello Lillo*)

The Ferrándiz Act and the Tender to Rebuild the Fleet

Before 1898 the Armada had favoured armoured cruisers whose extensive range allowed them to be deployed overseas where it was reckoned they would give a good account of themselves against enemy protected cruisers. These units would be complemented by torpedo gunboats or destroyers to see off enemy torpedo boats, supported by a large assortment of colonial avisos and gunboats of scant value in time of war but useful in many other respects. However, defeat in the Spanish-American War and the imposition of what was essentially a European strategic outlook brought about a change of opinion: what Spain now needed was not large numbers of colonial cruisers but capital ships and, more questionably, torpedo boats instead of destroyers. After 1900 the general staff of the Armada therefore held the position that, apart from minor units, the fleet required for Spain to defend herself effectively consisted of twelve battleships which, in view of budgetary constraints, would be ordered in groups of three, each subsequent trio representing an improvement on its predecessor. To this objective the Spanish navy adhered until the summer of 1914.

With regard to type, and despite some disagreement, it was soon made clear that under no circumstances was it intended to build coastal battleships or large monitors, nor vessels designed for a *guerre de course* in the manner of the proto-battlecruisers of the Italian Regina Elena class, but specifically the typical British pre-dreadnought battleship of the era, displacing 12,000 tons, armed with four 12in guns in twin turrets on the centreline and a dozen or more 6in guns, together with a best speed of 18 knots. However, these plans changed decisively under Minister of Marine Commodore José Ferrándiz, a noted technical specialist who had overseen the construction of the barbette ship *Pelayo* at La Seyne in France in the late 1880s, had commanded that ship in 1898 and kept abreast of all the latest innovations. He therefore reacted immediately to the appearance of the revolutionary battleship *Dreadnought* in 1906, taking decisive steps to alter the specifications of the three projected units. With commendable speed, between 18 and 23 March 1907 Ferrándiz secured majority approval from the Junta Técnica de la Armada (Navy Technical Board) for the designs to be overhauled along the lines of Fisher's all-big-gun concept. Of the nine members of the board, six had voted in favour, with two others restricting themselves to proposing a reduction in the calibre of the main armament to 11in or 9.2in guns, and one advocating construction to the design of the Lord Nelson class, the last and most formidable of the British pre-dreadnoughts. As it was, Spain's commitment to the dreadnought concept within six months of Fisher's brainchild being completed could hardly have been more decisive.

On this basis, Ferrándiz went on to propose the passing of a naval act to create a new Spanish fleet which was accepted by the cabinet of Prime Minister Antonio Maura and approved with a significant parliamentary majority on 27 November 1907. Promulgated on 7 January 1908, the Ferrándiz Act as it came to be known not only provided for the construction of the three battleships at a cost of 45 million pesetas each (approximately £1.6 million), but also a total of 40 million pesetas for three 370-ton destroyers, twenty-four (subsequently twenty-two) 180-ton torpedo boats and four 800-ton gunboats for coastal operations off Morocco, together with a number of other vessels and improvements, especially to shipyards, costing an additional 24 million pesetas. Given that Spain's annual budget for 1908 stood at 1 billion pesetas, the total allocation of 199 million (albeit spread over a period of eight years) bears witness to the immense resources the Maura government was prepared to commit to rebuilding the Armada, this at a time when ordinary annual naval expenditure amounted to only 31 million pesetas.

Three months later a royal decree of 21 April 1908 issued a public invitation to tender both for the construction of the new vessels and for a complete restructuring of Spain's naval dockyards. Ceasing to be dependencies of the Armada, control of the dockyards would pass to the winning company or consortium in an effort not only to improve management of these and avoid the errors of the past, but also to provide a stimulus to Spanish manufacturing and technology, both with respect to the dockyards themselves and to ancillary and supply industries. These vessels would no doubt have been completed sooner and more cheaply had they been ordered abroad, as was then standard practice in a number of countries, particularly in South America. But the stated intention was to secure the development and modernisation of Spanish naval construction, an objective which, a century on, seems to have been fully accomplished, while many of those same nations continue to rely on foreign construction. Four consortia eventually responded to the invitation to tender:

– The so-called Anglo-Asturian Group created for the purpose and consisting of a number of industrial, shipping, railway and mining companies from the province of Asturias in northern Spain, together with the British firms of Palmers Shipbuilding and Iron Co. Ltd and William Beardmore & Co. Ltd.
– The French Industrial Group led by Établissements de MM. Schneider et Cie. together with Forges et Chantiers de la Méditerranée and Ateliers et Chantiers de la Gironde.

- The European Group led by the Italian firm of Gio. Ansaldo, Armstrong & Co., backed by a number of companies, chief among which was the Austro-Hungarian Škoda Works.
- A new Anglo-Spanish group, the Sociedad Española de Construcción Naval (Spanish Naval Construction Company – SECN), created for the purpose and backed by the British firms of Vickers, Sons and Maxim Ltd., Sir W. G. Armstrong Whitworth & Co. and John Brown & Co., which together contributed more than 40 per cent of the capital of the new company, along with a consortium of banking, mining, shipbuilding and other Spanish companies. Additional technical support was to be provided by the British Thornycroft and French Normand firms.

On 14 April 1909 it was announced via royal decree that the winning consortium was SECN, which took possession of the Ferrol shipyard on 23 June and that of Cartagena on 25 August. The award provoked an outcry in the Republican and left-wing media following claims of government prevarication by a naval officer, Teniente de navío (Lieutenant) Macías. This resulted in the appointment of a neutral arbitrator to investigate the matter in the shape of the well-known journalist and Republican deputy Luis Morote. Having examined the documentation, the latter declared there to have been no irregularities in the tender process, thereby bringing the controversy and would-be scandal to an end.[5] That said, a certain amount of favouritism must have been shown to the SECN consortium since not only had Ferrándiz been in contact with Vickers for some time, but its first designs for the 'Spanish battleship' (Design no.

336) of September 1907 pre-date the invitation to tender by seven months. Moreover, the other bidders effectively ruled themselves out: the French group had yet to build a single dreadnought, raising significant questions as to its technical expertise. An even less advisable course would have been to entrust such a delicate matter to companies in Italy and Austria-Hungary, countries with which Spain might eventually be at war. Meanwhile, the other British group, that led by Palmers, had fifteen years earlier been involved in the construction of the three Infanta María Teresa-class armoured cruisers by the Astilleros del Nervión shipyard in Bilbao, a venture which ended in bankruptcy for the latter company and its being taken over by the Spanish government as the only means of ensuring completion of the contract. In view of this, there can be little doubt that the winning consortium was not only the strongest in all respects, but also that most competent to take

---

[5] Fernando de Bordejé y Morencos, *Vicisitudes de una política naval* (Madrid: San Martín, 1978).

Alfonso XIII seen *engalanado* (dressed overall) at Cartagena in the 1920s. *(Courtesy Alejandro Anca Alamillo)*

Alfonso XIII in the Bay of Biscay. (Courtesy Manuel Ruiz Sierra)

AN UNBUILT BATTLESHIP PROJECT

The Ferrándiz Act of 1908 was to be but the first stage in the restoration of Spanish naval power within the strategic ambit of the Entente. Once work on the España class was well in hand, plans began to be formulated in 1912 for a second trio of battleships along with a number of minor units. The programme was taken up by the Liberal Party leader José Canalejas, and after his death at the hands of an anarchist assassin by his successor Álvaro de Figueroa, Count of Romanones, and particularly by his minister of marine, Amalio Gimeno. Anxious to underline the commitment of the Liberal government to the naval programme drawn up by its Conservative predecessor, Gimeno lost no opportunity to extol the value of Spain's contribution to the balance of power in the Mediterranean.[6] Where the battleships were concerned, they again consisted of somewhat reduced versions of the latest British designs, trading speed and armour for the same armament, in this case oil-fired vessels in excess of 20,000 tons with a 13.5in (343mm) or preferably 15in (381mm) armament.

Although political instability halted further progress on the programme, it was for the most part picked up by the subsequent Conservative ministry of Eduardo Dato and his minister of marine, Admiral Augusto Miranda, who in 1914 opted for vessels of not less than 25,000 tons in order to accommodate the 15in gun. However, when Italy declared her wartime neutrality and Spain naturally followed suit, Miranda decided, with the approval of the government and parliament, to focus on cruisers, destroyers and, above all, submarines for the new fleet, the latter being deemed the most affordable and cost-effective option for a middle-ranking power not beholden to an alliance. The costly new battleships were therefore surplus to requirements, so the long-planned and much more powerful second generation of Spanish dreadnoughts, apparently to be named the Reina Victoria Eugenia class, remained unbuilt.

---

6 Amalio Gimeno, *El Factor naval de España en el problema Mediterráneo* (Madrid: Imprenta de Juan Pueyo, 1914); Rafael Gay de Montellá, *Diez años de política internacional en el Mediterráneo, 1904–1914. Ensayo de historia política moderna* (Barcelona: Imprenta de la Casa de la Caridad, 1914).

---

charge of the construction and, indeed, of practically the entire Spanish naval and military industrial complex.

Design

Where the design of the new Spanish battleships was concerned, it was stipulated from the outset that under no circumstances were they to have a displacement in excess of 17,000 tons.[7] This was imposed by the limitations of Spanish dock, shipyard and port infrastructure, the expansion of which would have depleted the funds available for warship construction. Aside from this maximum displacement, the navy technical board also specified the mounting of eight 12in guns in twin turrets and a speed approaching 19.5 knots with good endurance. These specifications have frequently been criticised, it being claimed with some justification that any reduction in displacement with a fixed armament would necessarily entail corresponding reductions in protection, propulsion and speed. Leaving aside the infrastructure problem mentioned above, it is therefore argued that Spain would have been better advised to build two larger battleships than three smaller ones. However, these same critics forget that despite having five turrets, *Dreadnought* and the following Bellerophon and St Vincent classes had the same eight-gun broadside as the Españas thanks to a clumsy layout which positioned two turrets abreast of each other. Moreover, the refitting schedules meant that a three-ship squadron would under ordinary circumstances only suffer a 33 per cent diminution of its strength compared with 50 per cent had just two vessels been built. Supposing the Armada had opted for two Bellerophons, this would therefore in practice have reduced her to a single effective unit with an eight-gun broadside, as against two units with a sixteen-gun broadside.

No surprise therefore that a glance at *Alfonso XIII* and her sisters was enough to betray the British origins of their design, albeit on a smaller scale. As it was, the ability of British warship designers to fit a dreadnought into the tonnage and dimensions of the pre-dreadnoughts and armoured cruisers being built just a few years earlier is a mark of how far technology had advanced over the previous decade. The result

---

7 The fundamental work is José Ramón García Martínez, Cristino Castroviejo Vicente & Alejandro Anca Alamillo, *Los Acorazados de la clase España o el resurgir naval hispano (1912–1937)* (CD-ROM, Madrid: Centro Marítimo y Naval Casto Méndez Núñez, 2007; printed edn., Madrid: Real de Catorce, 2012).

was a compact and well-armed design well suited to the needs of the Spanish navy, if somewhat at the expense of protection and propulsion. Of a total standard displacement of 15,700 tons, 36.4 per cent was given over to the hull, 24.8 per cent to armour and 14.5 per cent to armament, with only 7.9 per cent devoted to propulsion, though this is partly explained by the compactness of the design. As a lineal descendant of the *Dreadnought* of 1906, it may be useful to compare the specifications of the España class both with the progenitor of the type and the two succeeding generations of British battleships. Among other things, this data shows how the class bucked the trend for ever larger and costlier battleships, attaining comparable specifications with comparatively little sacrifice in *matériel* or performance.

Armament and Propulsion

The powerful main battery of the España class consisted of eight Vickers Mk H 12in (305mm) guns mounted in four turrets, the selection of 50-calibre ordnance giving shells greater initial speed, range and power than the earlier 45-calibre weapon. Each unit had two turrets manufactured by the Armstrongs-owned Elswick Ordnance Co. and the remaining two by Vickers. Turrets '1' and '4' were positioned on the centre-line while '2' and '3' were set *en échelon* amidships. All turrets were capable of engaging on either beam, though only two could bear dead ahead or astern without damage to the ship herself; the firing arcs were 310 degrees in the

Comparison of Early Dreadnought Designs

Class	Dreadnought	Bellerophon	St Vincent	España
Laid down	1905	1906	1907	1909
Length (overall, ft/m)	527.0/160.60	526.0/160.30	536.0/163.40	459.5/139.88
Beam (ft/m)	82.0/25.00	82.5/25.10	84.0/25.60	78.9/24.00
Draught (standard, ft/m)	26.5/8.10	27.1/8.30	28.5/8.30	26.0/8.08
Displacement (standard)	17,900	18,600	19,250	15,700
Displacement (full load)	21,845	22,100	23,030	16,450
Armour (belt max, in/mm)	11in/279mm	10in/254mm	10in/254mm	9in/254mm
Main armament/calibre	10 × 12in/45	10 × 12in/45	10 × 12in/50	8 × 12in/50
Speed (max)	21	21	21	20
Endurance (nm/knots)	6,620/10	5,720/10	6,900/10	7,500/11
Power (shp)	23,000	24,500	24,500	15,500

case of turrets '1' and '4', and an aggregate of 273 degrees in the case of turrets '2' and '3', composed of 180 degrees on their respective beams and 93 degrees across the deck. These wide arcs in turn placed limitations on the size of the superstructure, which was reduced to a forward and after bridge, two tripod masts with large maintops for the rangefinders, and a single upright and cylindrical funnel. Not only did the reduced silhouette which resulted offer a significant tactical advantage, but the almost symmetrical profile of the class notionally presented enemy gunnery officers with the problem of establishing the heading of their target at the start of an action. The main battery was supplemented by a secondary armament consisting of twenty Vickers Mk E 4in (101.6mm)/50-calibre

guns arranged ten to a side in casemates, the manufacture of which was shared between a handful of Spanish factories. The secondary battery was only 13ft (4m) above the waterline, a feature which rendered it unworkable in heavy seas but was less important in the Mediterranean. Nonetheless, unlike many battleships of the period, the España class had good stability and made excellent gun platforms, even though they were wet ships both forward and aft. This comparatively low freeboard and scant superstructure fairly bristling with armament has no doubt contributed to the impression among some observers and historians that these were effectively large monitors, whereas their specifications could only be equated with those of a battleship. Indeed, seen in retrospect, the España class proved rather more worthy of the sobriquet 'pocket battleship' than the later Deutschland class of the German navy, formidable vessels to be sure, but essentially armoured cruisers rather than battleships.

Meanwhile, the need to reduce superstructure to a minimum in order to clear the firing arcs of the main armament presented a new difficulty: that of shipping the requisite amount of boats, the majority of which had perforce to be stowed on the amidships turrets. However, the greatest limitation on vessels so crammed with armament was the difficulty of modernising them. Although the addition of super-firing guns in the style of the US South Carolina class would have provided greater space and comfort amidships and permitted the installation of a more powerful secondary battery along with an adequate anti-aircraft defence – an increasingly pressing consid-

A busy day on the forecastle of either *Alfonso XIII* or the ill-fated *Jaime I* in the early 1920s. Sheathed in canvas atop no. '1' turret is one of the Škoda 1.85in guns replaced in 1925–6. (*Courtesy Alejandro Anca Alamillo*)

The view forward along *Alfonso XIII*'s port side showing no. '3' and no. '1' 12in turrets together with nine of the ten 4in secondary guns of her port battery. The ship, which is cleared for action, is lying off the Moroccan coast. (*Courtesy Juan Luis Coello Lillo*)

(it took ten hours to bring 600 tons aboard), maintenance of tubing and boilers, and removal of clinker were, of course, no different in this navy than any other.

Steering was by a conventional semi-compensated single rudder which together with *Alfonso XIII*'s reduced hull length gave a tactical diameter at full speed of just 351yds (321m) by comparison with the 471yds (431m) of HMS *Dreadnought*.

Construction and Context

No sooner had SECN gained control of the Ferrol shipyard in June 1909 than it began drafting in British engineers and specialists to assist in the work of upgrading the installations and training Spanish personnel. The keel of the lead ship of the class, *España*, was laid six months later on 5 December 1909. However, the launching and completion dates of her sisters clearly show the stultifying effect of the outbreak of the First World War and Spanish neutrality on the construction and flow of *matériel* supplied by British companies, which first slowed to a trickle and then was suspended altogether. Worst affected was the heavy armament, engine plant,

eration – together with spotter and reconnaissance aircraft, such a redesign would have required a larger hull and consequently a more powerful engine plant to obtain the same speed. Although this was considered for the final and much delayed unit of the class, *Jaime I*, it was ultimately rejected on grounds of cost.

The original gunnery outfit was completed by two Vickers 2.2in (57mm) guns (replaced by Škoda 1.85in (47mm) weapons in around 1920), two Vickers 1.85in guns and a pair of 1.5in (37mm) Maxim guns (later replaced by a varying number of light weapons). Not until 1925–6 was any anti-aircraft armament mounted in the surviving members of the class, when two Vickers Mk FF 3in (76mm)/34-calibre guns replaced the 1.85in weapons atop turrets '1' and '4' at the extremities of the ship. To these were added two Armstrong 3in/17-calibre field guns manufactured under licence in the Basque town of Placencia de las Armas.

Steam was supplied by twelve Yarrow coal-fired boilers powering four sets of ungeared Parsons turbines paired to four screws. Maximum power was 15,500shp, giving a best speed of 19.5 knots, with 20 knots being occasionally exceeded. Assisted by her reduced size, *Alfonso XIII*'s endurance at the economical speed of 10.8 knots was a commendable 7,500 nautical miles. Aside from its efficiency and reliability, the main benefit of the engine plant was

its compact design, which made it possible for the class to be armed out of all proportion to its size while contributing to its reduced silhouette with the single funnel. There was bunkerage for 600 tons of coal, with Welsh steam coal (known in Spain as elsewhere as 'Cardiff') being favoured over domestic production. The trials and tribulations of coal-firing with respect to provisioning

Alfonso XIII running speed trials in the autumn of 1915. She could manage 20 knots. (*Courtesy Lucas Molina Franco*)

España Class: Construction Dates, SECN, Ferrol

	Keel Laid	Launched	Delivered
España	5 December 1909	5 February 1912	8 September 1913
Alfonso XIII	23 February 1910	7 May 1913	16 August 1915
Jaime I	5 February 1912	21 September 1914	20 December 1921

armour and fire-control equipment, so that while *España* took three years and nine months to complete, the second unit, *Alfonso XIII*, required approximately five and a half years, with construction of the third taking no less than nine years and ten months. As it turned out, *Alfonso XIII* was obliged to enter service in 1915 with a fire-control system improvised in part by purchases from neutral countries owing to lengthy delays imposed by British industry, fully stretched as it was by the imperial war effort.

Despite the delays attending completion of the last two units of the class, Spain still compared favourably with many other naval powers in having ordered dreadnoughts at an early stage in the development of the type. Indeed, other more economically and industrially advanced countries delayed considerably in joining the 'great naval race'. Austria-Hungary did not lay the keel of its first dreadnought, *Viribus Unitis* (q.v.), until 24 July 1910, while France waited until 1 September of that year before starting work on *Courbet*. Even powers such as Japan, Italy and Russia only began dreadnought construction a few months before Spain. This fact of not inconsiderable historical significance serves as a reminder that whatever the errors and inadequacies of the Armada, throughout its long history it

Above: *Alfonso XIII* goes down the ways at the SECN yard at Ferrol on 7 May 1913. *(Courtesy Alejandro Anca Alamillo)*

Below: Launch day for *Alfonso XIII* at the SECN yard in Ferrol on 7 May 1913. *Jaime I* seen on the right is sixteen months from launching. *(Courtesy Alejandro Anca Alamillo)*

Alfonso XIII fitting out at Ferrol, c. 1913. Completion was delayed by supply difficulties during the Great War. *España*'s mainmast can be seen on the extreme right of the photo. *(Courtesy Alejandro Anca Alamillo)*

forming the older units into what the British referred to as 'five-minute ships' and providing further incentive for both countries to build dreadnoughts. In the event, the resulting construction turned out to be both larger and better armed than the España class (mounting twelve or thirteen guns in double and triple turrets), though enjoying no improvement in calibre or protection on the Spanish vessels. The outbreak of war in August 1914 therefore found Italy with *Dante Alighieri* (completed in January 1913) along with *Giulio Cesare* and *Leonardo da Vinci* (both completed in May 1914, making it doubtful whether they were fully operational). The Austro-Hungarian navy had *Viribus Unitis* (completed in October 1912), *Tegetthoff* (July 1913) and *Prinz Eugen* (delivered only with great difficulty in July 1914). With *Courbet* and *Jean Bart* away escorting a French presidential visit to Russia, and their two sisters *France* and *Paris* as yet incomplete, the theoretical balance in favour of the Triple Alliance was strengthened by the presence in the Mediterranean of the German battlecruiser *Goeben* (q.v.). Meanwhile, Britain had been obliged to deploy the battle-cruisers *Inflexible*, *Indomitable* and *Indefatigable* to the station, vessels with greater speed than the España class but of inferior protection and even gun power since the first two could only engage a target with six of their eight 12in guns.

has always kept abreast of the latest technical developments and generally given them a favourable and even enthusiastic reception.

More importantly, with the España class Spain was restored to the status of a significant power in the Mediterranean, one she had not enjoyed for over half a century. In 1909 the four largest units in the Armada, the barbette ship *Pelayo* and the armoured cruisers *Carlos V*, *Cataluña* and *Princesa de Asturias* would not have proved a match even for a second-rate Italian squadron of equal size (supposing the latest and most powerful units were engaging the French fleet); now each Spanish battleship would present a serious proposition to a would-be enemy. Indeed, the Spanish factor threatened to erase the Italian and Austro-Hungarian superiority in capital ships in the Mediterranean, trans-

Things might therefore have gone badly for the Entente in the Mediterranean had Italy not declared her neutrality and Austria-Hungary consequently refused to deploy her fleet outside of the Adriatic. Although *España* had only been in service since the previous September and had undergone gunnery trials in June 1914, she was therefore of inestimable value to the Allied cause. Indeed, it is generally agreed that Italian neutrality (and her subsequently joining the Allies) made Spain's own neutrality in the Great War possible, thereby keeping her battleships from participating in the war operations for which they had been designed and built.[8]

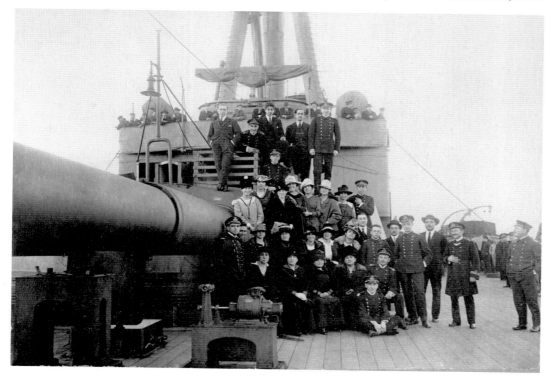

Officers and their guests pose beside no. '4' turret on the quarterdeck of the España in the early 1920s. Class and social distinctions were as pronounced in the Armada as in practically any other navy. (Courtesy Alejandro Anca Alamillo)

8 Paul G. Halpern, *The Naval War in the Mediterranean, 1914–1918* (Annapolis: Naval Institute Press, 1987).

Internal Arrangements

By tradition the officers were accommodated in cabins aft, though in comparatively less comfort than in former times. Right aft, and provided with a balcony around the stern of the ship, was the admiral's cabin and two suites capable of seating up to eighteen guests. Forward of this were the cabins of the captain and the other officers, each with private bathrooms. As in most navies of the day, the decoration, furniture, tableware and other fittings contrasted with the spartan conditions shared by the lower deck. Engineer officers and the most senior *suboficiales* (petty officers) had small cabins amidships, while the more junior were accommodated in the forward casemates, which spaces were also reserved for guests such as *guardiamarinas* (midshipmen) under instruction, musicians, etc.

A total of 372 men were accommodated on two messdecks on the armoured main deck around the barbettes of turrets '1' and '2'. The balance of the lower deck was accommodated in the forward casemates on the upper deck with a notional capacity of between thirty-six and forty-eight men each for a total of 366 men, though conditions aboard and operational necessity kept the total effective complement to approximately 700. These spaces were all arranged in the usual messdeck manner with hammocks and collapsible tables. However, despite having a significantly lower complement than other larger vessels of the era, habitability was not a strong point of the España class, even by contemporary standards. This was due to the low profile of the vessels which yielded only two full decks above the waterline, the absence of scuttles resulting in poor ventilation of the main accommodation spaces making them hot in summer, cold in winter and humid in any season, not least because they shipped a great deal of water both forward and aft in most conditions. In other respects, too, arrangements for the men were less than adequate: there were only thirty-one galvanised steel latrines for the entire complement of seven hundred men, and provision of showers and basins was little better. Where heating was concerned, there were just seven electric radiators aboard, six in the officers' quarters and one in the sickbay.

Despite these shortcomings, it should be remembered that the class was designed to operate in the relatively placid and temperate waters of the Mediterranean and at no great distance from its home ports. Moreover, the men were conscripts and not professional volunteers, meaning that harsher treatment could be meted out without fear of unrest. In any case, the working-class living conditions of the day were extremely harsh, allowing conditions to be accepted without demur which would today

---

JAIME JANER ROBINSON

In October 1913 the President of France Raymond Poincaré paid a visit to Spain with the aim of cementing ties in the event of war in Europe. Having successfully concluded his mission, Poincaré made his way south to Cartagena with King Alfonso XIII to return home in the new but obsolete pre-dreadnought *Diderot*. Lying close by in the harbour was *España* which had joined the fleet scarcely a month earlier. Poincaré and his entourage duly took the opportunity to visit the ship, being given a tour of her armament and systems including its advanced fire control by an engaging young gunnery officer, Jaime Janer Robinson, who had embarked on the career which later earned him the sobriquet of 'Spain's Percy Scott'.[9] Aside from a desire to ingratiate itself with a possible ally, this uncovenanted access to information on new devices and systems was no doubt much appreciated by the French government, Poincaré being sufficiently impressed to confer the *Légion d'honneur* on Janer in January 1914.

Then a mere lieutenant, Janer was with Peral and Ferrándiz, the electrical engineer José Luis Díez, the destroyer pioneer Fernando Villaamil and the torpedo and mine specialist Joaquín Bustamante, one of the luminaries produced by the Spanish navy around the turn of the twentieth century.[10] Son of the Spanish consul in Savannah, Georgia and his Irish-American wife Annie Robinson, Janer was born there in 1884 and joined the Armada in 1899. A precocious and brilliant student, he soon specialised in mines, torpedoes, electricity, wireless telegraphy and radio waves, and by his mid-twenties was the

Spain's Percy Scott: Jaime Janer Robinson seen in the rank of lieutenant, in which he served as *España*'s first gunnery officer. (*Agustín Ramón Rodríguez González*)

leading technical expert in the Spanish navy. However, Janer's main focus was gunnery, and he became a vocal proponent of the adoption of modern fire-control installations for the fleet. His first opportunity in this area came in October 1907 when he successfully tested the installation of advanced fire-control equipment in the gunboat *Nueva España* and the royal yacht *Giralda* in her naval capacity as an aviso. Official inertia and the fact that these innovations relied heavily on British equipment resulted in their being ignored, but Janer's appointment to *España* as gunnery officer in 1913 for the first time gave him the opportunity to install, operate and refine a modern fire-control system – one worthy of impressing the French. Janer went on to establish the Marín college and proving ground in Galicia which also imparted training in the range of naval sciences. Added to this was a flow of technical manuals which for decades served as textbooks for the Armada.

Of the six luminaries listed above, only Ferrándiz (1847–1918) was spared a premature death. Villaamil and Bustamante perished during the Spanish-American War of 1898, while Díez and Peral succumbed to illness in their forties. Janer, meanwhile, was cut down at the age of thirty-nine by a stray Moroccan shell while serving in the armoured cruiser *Cataluña* during the Rif War (see below) on 3 March 1924. Still no more than a *capitán de corbeta* (lieutenant commander), he was busy paying the hands on deck at the time.

---

[9] Admiral Sir Percy Scott (1853–1924) was the apostle of modern gunnery in the Royal Navy.

[10] Agustín R. Rodríguez González, *Jaime Janer Robinson. Ciencia y técnica para la reconstrucción de la Armada* (Madrid: Navalmil, 2012).

seem intolerable – at least under ordinary conditions. Nonetheless, the realities of discomfort, hard work, poor food, harsh discipline and other factors could be and were exploited by political agitators as the Spanish political situation deteriorated with tragic consequences for the Armada.

Shipboard Organisation

The vessel was the responsibility of a *capitán de navío* (captain) as commanding officer, seconded by a *capitán de fragata* (commander) as executive officer. Two *capitanes de corbeta* (lieutenant commanders) were embarked, one responsible for gunnery and electrical installations, and the other for all engineering and administrative services – in other words everything above and below the armoured deck respectively. Eight of the ten *tenientes de navío* (lieutenants) were assigned to the ship's four gunnery sections (no. 1 to 4), each encompassing one of the turrets and the corresponding 4in guns. Of the remaining two, one was the *Director de tiro* (gunnery officer) and the other was the *Ayudante de derrota* (navigating officer). The fifth section consisted of the engineering department under specialist officers.

The ship's company was organised into ten brigades of six *ranchos* (messes) each, with each mess, including its *cabo de rancho* (leading hand), numbering between eight and twelve men. These ten brigades were organised into five sections of two brigades each. Where the majority of shipboard tasks were concerned, the traditional distinction of port and starboard divisions was observed, and four watches were kept. Provision was made for such evolutions as

Transferring a 12in shell aft along the waist of one of the España-class battleships, c. 1920. (*Courtesy Juan Luis Coello Lillo*)

clean ship, port and starboard watch, general quarters, abandon ship, fire stations, clear for action, night and daytime attack stations, night watch, landing party and anti-torpedo nets, though the shortcomings of the Bullivant nets with which the class was fitted soon resulted in their being removed.

When the ship was in harbour routine the day began with the calling of the hands with bugles and pipes known as the *toque de Diana* (an allusion to the Roman goddess) at 0600, giving the sailors three-quarters of an hour to lash up and stow their hammocks and wash and dress themselves. This was followed by breakfast, usually *café con leche* (white coffee) with bread, or sometimes the traditional Spanish garlic, bread and egg broth known as *sopas de ajo*, for which half an hour was allocated. At 0715 the pipe to clean up was called, followed at 0730 by *Asamblea* (divisions) and relief of the watch, together with inspection of the sickbay (two medical officers were embarked), followed at 0800 by the hoisting of the flag, all under the watchful eye of the officers who reported anything of note to their superiors.

At 0900 the call for *Ejercicios* (evolutions) was piped followed half an hour later by *Escuelas* (school) for those under instruction. Then came the *Revista de Policía* (inspection by the ship's police) of kit and personal cleanliness, followed by lunch at noon. As was typical in the Armada, a high proportion of meals consisted of legumes (beans and chickpeas), rice and potatoes, cooked with bacon and small amounts of meat or salted

Petty officers shooting the sun with their sextants under the guns of no. '3' turret in a unit of the España class, c. 1930. Note the boats stowed atop the turret. (*Courtesy Juan Luis Coello Lillo*)

fish. Although somewhat inadequate, particularly in an age which overestimated the nutritional value of meat, this represented a more balanced diet than might at first seem the case. As ever, the weak point lay in the preparation, which could all too easily result in an inedible sludge being served up. There followed an hour of rest except for those under punishment, to whom a range of duties was assigned. Evolutions and school were piped again at 1430, the opportunity also being taken over this two-hour period to perform running repairs and maintenance. The order was then passed to wash and change, with *francos* (libertymen) being permitted to go ashore after another inspection. This always involved boats, since the ship was too large to come alongside in harbour. The day ended with a solemn lowering of the flag and the reading of the *Orden* (order of the day) to the assembled ship's company. This involved a roll call, readings in connection with any historical event or religious feast being commemorated, a listing of those officers and men joining the ship, and the following day's menu. After this came dinner, with *Silencio* (pipe down) following at 2200, by which time the libertymen had returned to the ship and much of the crew was asleep.

The little available spare time was taken up with washing and mending clothing, reading or writing letters for the minority who were literate, or engaging in traditional naval handicrafts such as modelmaking, or playing dominoes, draughts or cards, though with strict prohibitions on gambling for money stakes. The spiritual needs of the crew were met by the ship's chaplain who had the benefit of a small chapel aboard.

The Landing Party

Mindful of its colonial duties in Morocco, the Armada laid great emphasis on the landing party in its shipboard organisation and training. Until 1923 these were spearheaded by the detachment of Infantería de Marina (Marines) embarked in all ships, which under ordinary circumstances not only performed guard duty but also operated part of the secondary armament. Thereafter, all these duties were performed by the seaman complement. At its largest, the landing party of a battleship such as *Alfonso XIII* might include almost half the crew, together with two Armstrong 3in field guns and eight machine guns, the entire force issued with Mauser rifles. However, the party generally consisted of a reinforced infantry company of about 150 men, two field guns and a pair of machine guns under the command of a lieutenant, two or three *alféreces* (sub-lieutenants) and a handful of petty officers. There were three rifle sections, a beach section, a radio station,

a section of sappers and the field gun crews.

The Armada honed its skills with continual marching and firing exercises, culminating in a punishing and fiercely contested annual competition between the gunnery sections of the various vessels of the fleet. In an endeavour reminiscent of the Royal Navy's field gun competition dating from the early twentieth century, teams raced to transport a dismantled field gun and its equipment over an obstacle course including water hazards and walls up to 6ft 6in (2m) high in the shortest time, before reassembling the gun and firing a blank round. However, the naval landing party was often resorted to in earnest by the Spanish authorities, and as related below the time came when *Alfonso XIII*'s detachment was deployed against the coastal towns and cities of the metropolis itself.

Mass being celebrated on *Alfonso XIII*'s quarterdeck in the 1920s. A screen has been rigged before which the ship's chaplain can dispense the sacrament. Note the stern walk bearing the ship's name. *(Courtesy Camil Busquets i Vilanova)*

Early Years, 1915–20

With the leading vessel of the España class bearing the name of the country itself, it was natural that the second unit should be named for the reigning monarch, Alfonso XIII (1886–1941). The subject of this chapter was not in fact the first ship to carry the name, that honour being accorded to a vessel all too typical of the short-comings of Spanish naval construction before the reforms of 1909. Built at Ferrol as a sister of the protected cruiser *Reina Regente* (herself constructed in Britain) and launched in 1891, the first *Alfonso XIII* was found to suffer from chronic defects, especially in her engine plant,

which not only kept her from joining Admiral Pascual Cervera's ill-fated Cuba squadron in 1898, but resulted in her being stricken after extensive but fruitless trials in 1900, and scrapped seven years later. Despite this inauspicious precedent and the king's many personal failings, which ultimately helped cost him his throne, there can be no doubt that he was fully deserving of the accolade of having a battleship named after him. Not only did he help foster the Spanish naval renaissance of the early twentieth century, but his reign saw the Armada recover from the prostration of 1898 to having the fourth largest fleet in Europe by the time of his exile in 1931. The third unit of the class, *Jaime I*, was named for James the Conqueror, King of Aragon and Count of Barcelona from 1213–76 and a leading figure both in the reconquest of the peninsula from the Moors and the expansion of

the Aragonese empire. It has, moreover, been the practice of the Spanish navy to name its leading ships after the monarch and members of the royal family since at least the eighteenth century, a tradition which continues to the present time.

Delivered in August 1915 and, as is traditional in the Armada, formally received into the fleet with the presentation of a battle ensign, *Alfonso XIII* sailed with her sister *España* to Santander to render honours to the king during the court's customary summer holiday there, Alfonso taking the salute from the royal yacht *Giralda*. The following month the fleet sailed for the usual autumn manoeuvres off Galicia but the year came to a climax with the ship winning the Christmas 'Gordo' (jackpot) of the Spanish national lottery. The Lotería Nacional traces its origins to 1763 and it is traditional for members of organisations throughout the country to buy

a stake in a ticket, which in this instance yielded the ship's company of *Alfonso XIII* the princely sum of 6 million pesetas. The lucky number was 48,685 and the winning ball from the tombola has been preserved for posterity in the naval museum at Ferrol. After this excitement *Alfonso XIII* resumed her ordinary routine, until sailing in search of the destroyer *Terror* which had been disabled by a storm in the Bay of Biscay in September 1916, an operation which among other things revealed the aggravations of the Bullivant anti-torpedo nets. The following April *Alfonso XIII* was again called on to assist a vessel in distress, this time the navy tug *Antelo* which had grounded off Cabo Prioriño Chico near Ferrol carrying a dangerous cargo of Sauter-Harlé mines, all of which were transferred to the battleship.

Meanwhile, the economic, social and political consequences of the First World War were beginning to make themselves felt in Spain, which in August 1917 saw the declaration by socialist and anarchist groups of a general strike with pronounced revolutionary overtones. This resulted in *Alfonso XIII* being sent to the major industrial port of Bilbao to help restore order at the request of the local military governor. The ship's landing party was put ashore and charged with guarding several mines together with the railway line between Galdames and Sestao. However, violence was not averted, resulting in the death of a sailor and injuries to several more, while a total of twenty-two revolutionaries were arrested and initially detained aboard. In early 1919 *Alfonso XIII* sailed for Barcelona to participate in the commissioning of the submarine *A-1 Narciso Monturiol*, only to find herself caught up in a further outburst of industrial unrest, in this case directed against the Canadian-owned Barcelona Traction, Light and Power Company. The ship again put her landing party ashore, this time to protect the company's facilities during the violent forty-four-day strike known appropriately enough as 'La Canadiense'.

Showing the Flag, 1920–3

Despite growing domestic unrest, by 1920 the government was ready to project a new image of Spain as embodied by her modern fleet and above all her battleships. Naturally enough, this exercise in showing the flag was focused largely on the Americas, both for historical and cultural reasons, and in view of the wave of immigrants leaving Spain for the New World. As part of this policy, on 14 June 1920 *España* received orders to visit the ports of the River Plate and the Pacific coast before returning to Spain via the Panama Canal, while *Alfonso XIII* would sail

Alfonso XIII enters Havana to a rapturous welcome and a phalanx of Ford Model Ts on 9 July 1920. *(Courtesy Juan Luis Coello Lillo)*

for a prolonged stay in the Caribbean and United States under the command of Captain Honorio Cornejo. Within days *Alfonso XIII* had weighed anchor at Ferrol, and after stopping at Tenerife in the Canaries on 22 June, reached Havana on 9 July to a great reception from the Cuban authorities and people, the first Spanish naval vessel to call there since the sail training ship *Nautilus* in 1908. *Alfonso XIII* then visited Puerto Rico where the reception was scarcely less enthusiastic, a reflection of the special ties linking Spain with this island whose fate in 1898 had been decided not by revolt but by diplomacy. The cruise was completed with a visit to New York in mid-October, the ship returning to Spain in November. This success was followed in April 1921 by a visit to Lisbon to participate in the ceremonies commemorating those Portuguese soldiers who had perished during the First World War.

There was, however, a harder edge to defence diplomacy than simply showing the flag, and by 1923 it was necessary for the Spanish government to wield this power in the context of a significant deterioration in Franco-Spanish relations over the protectorate of Morocco, where a Berber revolt had broken out in the summer of 1921 (see below). This situation focused Spanish diplomacy on Italy where Mussolini was not only frustrated at the lack of booty following the defeat of the Central Powers in the First World War, but had begun to revive long-standing tensions with France over its possession of Tunisia. At the same time, the parliamentary and constitutional disintegration in Spain herself following the disasters of the Rif War had resulted in a *coup d'état* in September 1923 which ushered in the dictatorship of General Miguel Primo de Rivera. Although the Primo de Rivera regime was of a rather different stamp from that of Benito Mussolini, the former lost no time in introducing several Fascist policies to

Spain including dissolving the legislature and suspending the constitution. The time was therefore ripe for the two Latin monarchies, both now under the sway of a dictator, to forge an alliance at the expense of France. This was the backdrop for the momentous visit of the Spanish fleet to Italy in November 1923, a reminder that, as in 1914, the Armada might tip the balance between the French and Italian fleets in the western Mediterranean in the event of war. The fleet, which included *Alfonso XIII* and her newer sister *Jaime I*, the light cruiser *Reina Victoria Eugenia*, two destroyers and four submarines, sailed from Valencia on 16 November. With both the King and Primo de Rivera embarked in *Alfonso XIII*, the itinerary included La Spezia and then Naples from where it weighed anchor for Barcelona on the 28th. However, for all the success of the cruise, relations with France were soon to be restored as a result of events in Morocco.

Fall of the Monarchy and Change of Name

By 1927 *Alfonso XIII* had resumed her peacetime routine, participating in fleet manoeuvres off Arosa in Galicia and attending the annual royal festivities at Santander. Aside from the usual visits and receptions, in September of that year King Alfonso and Queen Victoria Eugenia came aboard for a cruise of the Galician coast. The following month they were aboard again for a visit to the ports of Ceuta, Melilla and others in the recently pacified protectorate of Morocco, escorted by the new cruisers *Reina Victoria Eugenia* and *Méndez Núñez* along with the elderly destroyer *Bustamante*. In 1929 *Alfonso XIII* participated, along with British, French, Italian and Portuguese naval units in the review celebrated off Barcelona as part of the International Exposition held there between May 1929 and January 1930. Meanwhile, and despite the successful outcome of the Rif War, the Primo de Rivera dictatorship was waning in the face of concerted political opposition at home and the economic consequences of the Wall Street Crash of October 1929. On 28 January 1930 Primo de Rivera tendered his resignation having lost the support both of the army and the king whose position as head of the monarchy he had endeavoured to save. It was against a backdrop of deepening political and economic crisis that Alfonso XIII went into exile and the Second Republic was proclaimed on 14 April 1931.

The provisional government of Liberal Party

ALFONSO XIII AND THE RIF WAR, 1921–7

In the autumn of 1920 an ill-conceived attempt by the military governor of the Spanish protectorate of Morocco, General Dámaso Berenguer, to pacify the eastern sector of that territory resulted on 16 July of the following year in an uprising of the Rif Berber tribes led by Abd-el-Krim. Within a period of weeks practically the entire Spanish position in the eastern sector centred on the port of Melilla had collapsed in the so-called 'Annual disaster', with the loss of approximately 10,000 men, a humiliation with far-reaching consequences for the political landscape of Spain herself.

The uprising found *Alfonso XIII* on the Biscayan coast of Spain from where she immediately weighed anchor and, having coaled at Santander on 22 July, reached the beleaguered port of Melilla on 10 August 1921. The following day her ordnance had its baptism of fire, providing support for troop movements, first at Mar Chica and then at Nador and Zeluán (now Salwān), a total of 515 shells being expended. The opportunity was also taken to put the ship's landing party ashore under Lieutenant Pedro Nieto Antúnez, later General Francisco Franco's minister of marine. In September *Alfonso XIII* was again in action, shelling enemy positions on the heights of Mount Gurugú overlooking Melilla. The following year, 1922, was one of constant activity, notably during August when bombardments were carried out of enemy field gun positions threatening coastal shipping and the rocky outcrops of Alhucemas and Vélez de la Gomera. The ship was struck several times in return, suffering neither casualties nor any significant damage, though a section of perforated plating survives in the Ferrol naval museum. Aside from the death of Jaime Janer Robinson (see above), the Armada did, however, suffer a major disaster during the Rif War: the grounding of *España* on Cabo Tres Forcas in thick fog while supporting a landing near Melilla on 26 August 1923. *Alfonso XIII* was on hand to assist in the rescue and steps were taken to lighten her by removing guns, ammunition and stores. A number of foreign salvage companies were consulted and work proceeded for many months but to no avail since the hull, already much damaged in the grounding, was wrecked by a storm on 19 November 1924 when it was only twenty days away from being floated off and salved. There were no casualties at any stage.

España grounded on Cabo Tres Forcas on the Moroccan coast in August 1923. Salvage efforts proceeded for more than a year before the hull was wrecked in a storm. *(Courtesy Alejandro Anca Alamillo)*

By 1925 Abd-el-Krim had brought practically the entire Spanish protectorate of Morocco under his control, which since September 1921 had been formally constituted as the Republic of the Rif, the new entity proclaiming independence both from Spanish occupation and from the Moroccan Sultan. The Rif War had hitherto been confined to Spanish Morocco, but on 13 April 1925 Abd-el-Krim launched an attack on French positions along the River Uarga with consequences scarcely less disastrous for the latter than those suffered by Spanish arms at Annual (Anwāl) four years earlier. This development united the Spanish and French governments in a determination to end the Berber revolt once and for all. The result of this alliance was a carefully planned amphibious landing on the Alhucemas coast, close to the seat of the rebellion, the territory of the Beni Uriaghel tribe of which Abd-el-Krim was a member. Unlike previous efforts, this strategy obviated the need for a slow and costly land campaign across very difficult country. The operation involved 13,000 soldiers disposed in sixteen units of battalion strength, in addition to a Marine battalion. Support was provided by six artillery batteries, eleven Renault FT-17 light tanks and no less than 160 aircraft, a balloon and a dirigible. The invasion fleet included twenty-six 'K'-type lighters, a similar number of transports, four tugs and two water tankers, with support provided by Spain's two surviving battleships, four cruisers, the seaplane carrier *Dédalo*, two destroyers, seven gunboats, six torpedo boats and seventeen coastguard and fishery protection vessels. The French contribution consisted of the battleship *Paris*, two cruisers, two destroyers, two monitors, a tug and six seaplanes, together with a Marine battalion. *Alfonso XIII* served as flagship of the operation with General Primo de Rivera embarked as commander-in-chief. The landings, which began on 8 September 1925, were a complete success and represent the first amphibious operation supported by naval aviation and employing armoured cars. They also marked the beginning of the end of the Republic of the Rif, with the surrender of Abd-el-Krim to the French in May 1926 and the eventual defeat of the Berber cause after savage fighting in 1927.

politician Niceto Alcalá Zamora lost no time in sweeping away all traces of the previous regime, and on 17 April, just three days after the proclamation, a ministerial order provided for *Alfonso XIII* to be rechristened *España*, thereby reviving the name of her ill-fated older sister. Not only that, but the nascent republic ordered a large number of obsolete vessels to be stricken and disposed of, while also removing several newer ones from active duty in an effort to reduce the military budget after the huge expenditure of the Rif War. This cost-cutting policy had an immediate effect on the composition of the fleet, with both *España* (ex-*Alfonso XIII*) and *Jaime I* being consigned to the reserve on 15 June 1931 under the authority of the Ferrol naval district, their complements reduced by half. Then on 15 November *España* was decommissioned altogether, spending the next five years tied up forlornly in the Ferrol naval dockyard, with part of her secondary and anti-aircraft armament

Jaime I and *Alfonso XIII* (centre) at Barcelona in connection with the International Exposition held there in 1929–30. Lying beyond them are the light cruisers *Méndez Núñez* and *Blas de Lezo. (Courtesy Juan Luis Coello Lillo)*

landed and beginning a slow process of deterioration through lack of maintenance. Although less than twenty years old, it was at this time that she became known as *El Abuelo* ('grandfather') given her status as the oldest major unit in the fleet. Meanwhile, her younger sister *Jaime I* enjoyed better fortune, not only preserving her regal name but returning to full commission as fleet flagship on 20 April 1933.

Projected Modernisation

Despite their pacifist inclinations, the leaders of the Spanish Second Republic soon realised that European and world affairs rendered any such an outlook largely untenable. The question of the strategic balance in the Mediterranean again reared its head, and with it the role Spain might play in the evolving Franco-Italian rivalry. However, not only did the political sympathies of the Second Republic lie instinctively with France, but Mussolini's imperialist adventures aroused the misgivings of Spanish diplomats who were quick to condemn them at the League of Nations. Suspicions in Madrid were also raised by the fact that Alfonso and his family had taken

up residence in Rome on going into exile in 1931. The Second Republic had therefore to confront the need for naval rearmament in the face of a new and dangerous enemy, but in the event reserved itself to completing those orders placed in the final years of the monarchy (including the two Canarias-class heavy cruisers), while funding a number of smaller orders to provide work for the naval shipyards at Ferrol and Cartagena, then still under SECN control.

During the 1920s consideration had already been given for the construction of a new class of Spanish battleships, but financial constraints and the heavy burden of the Rif War had made it impossible to fulfil these plans. In the circumstances it was decided to settle for a modernisation of the two surviving units given their continued utility in many tasks. The proposed refit focused mainly on conversion from coal to oil burning, though these plans were set aside once it was realised that the practical benefits were outweighed by the expense involved. However, increased tension with Fascist Italy prompted the formulation of several plans for naval rearmament by the Second Republic in 1935, including the 'Balearics defence plan',

which centred on a flotilla defence of destroyers and submarines, mine warfare and the battleship modernisation project. In the event, implementation of these plans was delayed by political instability and financial constraints, obliging the Ministry of Marine to resort in the spring of 1936 to a refitting policy sufficient to return the ships to service with limited operational capability, although no match for the modernised battleships of the Regia Marina, much less the new Vittorio Veneto class (see *Littorio*). The refit was to consist of the following for each ship:

– Replacement of the secondary 4in battery by twelve 4.7in (120mm)/45 Vickers Mk F anti-aircraft guns, repositioned on the forecastle deck in groups of two or three behind armoured shields.

– Raising of turrets '2' and '3' by the addition of an armoured barbette to open the arc of fire of the new 4.7in armament and permit the former to fire over the latter.

– Increased elevation of the main armament to 25 degrees to improve range, and enhanced protection for turret magazines.

– Installation of anti-aircraft armament based on either five twin 1in (25mm) or four twin 1.6in (40mm) mountings (subject to the results of trials with both types).

– Installation of the best possible fire-control system for both surface and aerial targets.

– General refit of machinery and engines, though not extending to conversion to oil firing on grounds of cost.

– Conversion of the former 4in casemates into crew accommodation.

– Removal of the mainmast to increase the arcs of turret '2' and the new 4.7in armament, and rigging of a signals gaff abaft the funnel.

– Reconstruction of the forward superstructure and foremast to receive new navigation and fire-control equipment.

– Refitting and modernisation of the communication system, both internal and external, as well as provision of remotely controlled searchlights.

– Overhaul of the double bottom and fitting of bulges, budget permitting.

The cost of this refit was calculated at not less than 20 million pesetas for each vessel, and were funds to become available it was estimated that a minimum of two and a half years would be required to complete the work, which was scheduled to begin in early 1937 and be carried out on both ships concurrently. However, these plans were overtaken by the chaos into which Spain descended in the summer of 1936, meaning that

Alfonso XIII lying in the ria of Ferrol in *c*. 1930. Seen atop turrets '1' and '4' is the ship's first anti-aircraft armament, the Vickers Mk FF 3in gun of which two were fitted in single mountings in 1925–6. The light cruiser *Blas de Lezo* lies beyond with her sister *Méndez Núñez* astern. *(Courtesy Lucas Molina Franco)*

España entered the Civil War having benefited only from the measures taken to recommission her in 1935–6, including bringing turrets '1' and '4' back into service ('2' and '3' remained inoperative) and retubing the boilers to restore her speed. For all its limitations, this refit nonetheless turned out to be of considerable significance.

Uprising and Mutiny in Ferrol

Despite these measures, the military uprising against the Republican government on 17 July 1936 found *España* as an accommodation ship at Ferrol. Her commanding officer, Commander Luis Piñero Bonet, was away on official business in Madrid at the time, being relieved by his second-in-command, Lieutenant Commander Gabriel Antón Rozas, who together with six regular officers commanded a reduced company of 400 men, including petty officers, specialist ratings and sailors. Largely as the result of the conservative policies on personnel espoused by the Armada, the gulf between professional officers on the one hand and petty officers and junior ratings on the other was all too apparent on the outbreak of the civil war. It followed that whereas the naval officer corps supported or sympathised with the Nationalist uprising practically to a man, their subordinates remained generally loyal to the Republican government, this in marked contrast to the army in which allegiances were by no means so clearly defined and where adherents to one or other party were to be found in all ranks, even if support for the uprising was more pronounced among junior officers than among colonels and generals. Nor did those naval officers directly involved in the uprising seem to have any clear plans either for the role of the Armada itself, or for co-ordination with the army once the revolt had broken out. The result at Ferrol was an atmosphere charged with mutual suspicion.

This situation was mirrored in the *España*, and it was not until 20 July, three days after the uprising, that orders were given to the ship's company to fall in to form a landing party under the command of Lieutenant Carlos Núñez de Prado. At 1700 the order was passed to disembark, at which point *oficial auxiliar de artillería* (assistant gunnery officer) Dionisio Mouriño González stepped forward and asked Lieutenant Commander Antón Rozas to explain his intentions and the purpose of the landing party. When Antón Rozas refused to do so and ordered him to fall in, Mouriño unholstered his pistol and shot him, an action which immediately incited the landing party to mutiny, proceeding to finish off Antón Rozas, murder Núñez de Prado and his fellow lieutenants Carlos Suances Jáudenes and

Ratings of *Alfonso XIII* pose on the port side of the ship in their best rig, c. 1930. When it finally came in 1936 the Spanish Civil War placed officers and men on opposite sides of a gulf-like political divide. *(Courtesy Alejandro Anca Alamillo)*

Jesús Escudero Arévalo, and take possession of the *España*. The landing party then went ashore to join the Republican fighters attempting to break into the naval dockyard itself, then a stronghold of the uprising. However, on approaching the dockyard gate they were greeted by a fusillade of gunfire from the rebels barricaded inside. Among those killed in the exchange was Mouriño whose death so demoralised the landing party that it returned to the ship, from where the mutineers defended themselves until the 22nd. Following negotiations between Captain Francisco Moreno Fernández and engineer officer Pedro López Amor, the crew laid down its arms and surrendered the ship. As a result of these events, thirty-four of *España*'s crewmen were shot over the next few weeks following formal court-martial proceedings.

To War

Once the rebels had gained control of Ferrol, which like the rest of the province of Galicia remained solidly within the Nationalist camp for the rest of the Civil War, use could be made of the naval base and shipyard to begin the urgent task of bringing *España* to war readiness. Time constraints had only permitted the most important issues to be attended to, so it was in a fairly parlous state that *España* sailed on her first war cruise on 12 August, her no. '2' and '3' turrets still inoperative and the ship mounting only

twelve of her twenty 4in guns; of these, four had been diverted to the cruiser *Canarias* while she awaited her complete 4.7in/45 Vickers Mk F anti-aircraft fit. Where *España*'s complement was concerned, numbers were made up by volunteers and by students and sailors from the nearby Marín naval college and proving ground where the July uprising had been largely uncontested. She was commanded by Captain Luis de Vierna Belando, with Lieutenant Commander Pedro Nieto Antúnez as second-in-command, and four lieutenants and three sub-lieutenants completing the officer corps.

Led by *España*, the light cruiser *Almirante Cervera* (refitting in the naval dockyard at Ferrol on the outbreak of war but also rapidly pressed into service) and the destroyer *Velasco*, the Nationalist navy soon asserted control of the waters off the Cantabrian coast of Spain. The resulting blockade was to prove a decisive factor in the northern theatre of operations, since not only did the Republican territories on the Bay of Biscay have scarcely any naval forces, but they depended on maritime communications for much of their war *matériel*, cut off as they were from the Republican heartlands in central and north-eastern Spain. Escorted by *Velasco*, *España*'s first war cruise therefore took her past Cabo Peñas in Asturias and eastward to the mouth of the River Bidasoa on the French border, earning them the designation of 'pirate vessels' by the Republican government in Madrid on 14 August, which made futile attempts to persuade neutral navies to interdict them. The following day *España* shelled the important industrial centre and Republican stronghold of Gijón, doing likewise against the Santurce oil depots on the 16th. Joined now by *Almirante Cervera*, she next bombarded the fort of Guadalupe in Guipúzcoa which was blocking the advance of Nationalist troops under General Emilio Mola, and over the next few days unleashed 102 12in shells against the Basque coast. By 20 August she was back in Ferrol as the Republicans began installing artillery pieces on the coast to cover the entry of merchant shipping and fishing vessels into their ports, with steps also being taken to arm merchantmen as part of an improvised naval force.

Her turret '3' now in serviceable condition, on 25 August *España* and *Velasco* again sallied forth from Ferrol to harass the Republican coast between Santander and San Sebastián. The following day they captured the Republican steamer *Konstan* (1,857grt) and had snapped up the fishing vessel *Juan Mari* (209grt) off Cabo Peñas by the time they reached Ferrol on 1 September. A third cruise to bombard Gijón on the 14th brought *España* into dry dock in Ferrol for extensive repairs. Naturally enough, the Republicans could not allow the depredations of the Nationalist navy along Spain's northern coast to continue unchecked, and steps were taken to dispatch a flotilla of submarines from the Mediterranean, first *C-4* and *C-5* and then *C-6* and *C-2* which reached El Musel, the port of Gijón, on 6 and 18 September respectively. Also sent north was *B-6* which, however, was sunk by Nationalist forces on the 19th. Indeed, the Republican government deemed the situation sufficiently grave to commit the bulk of its fleet to the Bay of Biscay, and on 21 September *Jaime I*, the light cruisers *Libertad* and *Miguel de Cervantes* and six destroyers sailed from Málaga, reaching Gijón four days later. This movement raised the prospect of a ship-to-ship encounter between *España* and her sister *Jaime I* which had

España (formerly *Alfonso XIII*) lying at the naval dockyard in Ferrol during the Civil War. *(Courtesy Lucas Molina Franco)*

declared for the Republic at Santander in July, but in the event none of the Republican assets accomplished very much and on 13 October the squadron weighed anchor for the Mediterranean leaving only the destroyers *José Luis Díez* and *Ciscar* and the submarines *C-2* and *C-5* to confront the Nationalist navy.

The Nationalists, meanwhile, had no intention of risking *España* against her younger and better maintained sister, and repairs and improvements to her tired fabric continued in Ferrol. She was soon back in the fray, however, and on 21 October captured the fishing vessels *Apagador* (210grt) and *Musel* (165grt) off Cabo Torres, followed on the 30th by the steamer *Manu* (3,314grt). Although it has never been definitively corroborated, it seems that *España* was exposed to mortal danger in the early hours of that same day, *C-5* having hurriedly put to sea from Santander between 0100 and 0200 after the battleship was sighted off nearby Cabo Mayor. A total of four torpedoes were launched in two attacks, the first salvo suffering gyro problems which brought one of the weapons back on a reciprocal course and nearly struck *C-5* herself, while the second pair missed their target; it was later established that *C-5*'s commanding officer had Nationalist sympathies. None the wiser, *España* continued her patrol and the following day collaborated with Nationalist trawlers based on the port of Pasajes near San Sebastián in capturing the steamer *Arrate-Mendi* (2,667grt) north of Cabo Ajo.

In November *España* received the anti-aircraft armament that had become essential in the face of Republican aviation. Entirely of German manufacture, it consisted of four 3.5in (88mm) SK C/30 guns on MPL C/30 mountings, together with the associated EWA fire control. The outfit was completed by two Rheinmetall 0.8in (20mm) C/30 machine guns. December found her harassing the enemy coast once again, especially on the 20th when she was joined by *Velasco* and the auxiliary cruisers *Dómine* and *Ciudad de Valencia* in shelling El Musel in an effort to destroy the Republican units moored there, particularly the destroyer *José Luis Díez*. Ten days later the target was the Cabo Mayor lighthouse near Santander.

The new year began with a Republican air attack on Ferrol which did little damage but served as a diversion for a series of defensive minelaying operations off the Republican coast. On 22 January 1937 *España* stopped the Norwegian freighter *Carrier* (3,105grt) off Gijón and three days later captured the Republican coastal steamer *Alejandro* (345grt). In February she was joined by *Velasco* in another bombardment of Bilbao before going into dry dock at

Ferrol where she remained until 3 March. Five days later she captured the Basque freighter *Achuri* (2,733grt) and on the 30th had a fleeting encounter with *José Luis Díez* before capturing a second merchantman, the steamer *Nuestra Señora del Carmen* (3,481grt), off Cabo Mayor on the 31st, during which she came under attack by Republican aircraft and coastal batteries. On 12 April she was again shelling El Musel, turrets '1' and '4' firing at their maximum range of 21,800yds (20,000m) in another fruitless attempt to destroy or disable *José Luis Díez*. These same weeks in the spring of 1937 had been punctuated by repeated encounters between *España* and British merchantmen attempting to enter Bilbao and Santander, and with units of the Royal Navy determined to secure their free passage. It was during one of these incidents that *España* met her fate.

The Sinking

On 23 April *España* sailed from Ferrol to resume the blockade of Santander and Bilbao. It was to be her final sally. Following further incidents with British vessels, on the morning of 30 April *España* found herself on blockade patrol with her old partner *Velasco* about ten miles off Santander. At about 0700 the British steamer *Knitsley* (2,272grt) was sighted attempting to enter the port, *Velasco* firing several warning shots which caused her to alter course. Eager to support the destroyer, *España*'s commanding officer, Captain Joaquín López Cortijo, ordered a course alteration towards *Knitsley* but in doing so brought his ship into the minefield sown days earlier by the Nationalist gunboat-minelayer *Júpiter*. At approximately 0715 a mine exploded on her port side between the after boiler room and the engine room resulting in a huge inrush of water which soon flooded the engine spaces and the after magazines. Had these detonated, the death toll would no doubt have been much greater; as it was, the victims were initially confined to *maquinista* (mechanic) José Freire Pérez, *cabo fogonero* (leading stoker) José Sanz Serantes and *fogonero* (stoker) Luis Pesqueira Acuña, together with four men suffering the effects of smoke inhalation.

Listing to port, her bulkheads in poor condition and this vessel no better designed to survive underwater attack than any other battleship of her generation, it was obvious that *España* was doomed. *Velasco* was ordered alongside to take off her ship's company, a process which began half an hour after the detonation. By this time *España* and *Velasco* were already in receipt of the first of three attacks by Republican aircraft from the nearby base at La Albericia, each delivered in

España going down off Santander on 30 April 1937, the victim of a mine laid by her own side. *(Courtesy Alejandro Anca Alamillo)*

pairs, but successfully warded off by anti-aircraft fire from both vessels, those in *España* being manned until shortly before she sank. These attacks allowed Republican propaganda to claim responsibility for the sinking, a declaration which until it was found to be untrue caused some consternation in foreign naval circles given the rivalry with advocates of air power. By about 0830 *España* had been abandoned, Captain López being the last to board *Velasco* which promptly got clear of the hulk. Some thought was given to hastening the end with a torpedo but this proved unnecessary as *España*'s decks were soon awash and before long she had capsized to port and sunk. Overloaded with survivors, *Velasco* immediately turned for Ferrol. One of the injured, Stoker Francisco Pantín, succumbed en route bringing *España*'s death toll to four. The ship's company of the *Velasco*, which had not hesitated to enter the minefield to save their fellows, was collectively awarded the Medalla Naval (Naval Medal) for their gallantry.

So ended the career of the second *España*, the former *Alfonso XIII*. She was followed on 17 June that same year by her sister and erstwhile enemy *Jaime I*, which fell victim to what was in all probability an accidental magazine explosion while lying at Cartagena, a disaster that claimed over 200 casualties. The loss of both battleships within the space of six weeks brought a sudden and violent end to what must be reckoned an unfortunate class of vessels, the subject of this chapter having the dubious distinction of being its only member to have been lost in action.

Keel up and breached by a cavernous hole aft, the wreck of the *España* was discovered lying in 60m (200ft) of water by divers of the navy salvage vessel *Poseidón* in May 1984. Despite claims made in official reports prepared after the sinking that *España* had struck a rogue mine, the discovery left no doubt that she had indeed strayed into *Júpiter*'s minefield, placing her among the larger self-inflicted losses in naval history. Several efforts to salvage or scrap the wreck have so far been defeated by cost.

Sources

Unpublished Sources

Archivo General de la Marina 'Álvaro de Bazán', Viso del Marqués (Ciudad Real)

Bibliography

Bordejé y Morencos, Fernando de, *Vicisitudes de una política naval. Desarrollo de la Armada entre 1898 y 1936* (Madrid: Editorial San Martín, 1978)

Diario Oficial del Ministerio de Marina (1908–36)

Estado General de la Armada [Navy Lists] (1900–36)

Fontenla Maristany, Miguel, *Descripción de los servicios del acorazado* España (Madrid: Imprenta del Ministerio de Marina, 1915)

Fontenla, M., J. Carre, J. Cornejo & M. Moreu, *Descripción de las torres del acorazado 'España', su artillería y municiones* (Madrid: Imprenta del Ministerio de Marina, 1917)

Gaceta de Madrid [Official Gazette] (1907–36)

Gantes García, Manuel, *Acorazado Jaime I: el Potemkin español. Memorias de un tripulante superviviente del buque de guerra de la flota Republicana, durante la Guerra Civil* (Madrid: Editorial Arenas, 2012)

García Martínez, José Ramón, Cristino Castroviejo Vicente & Alejandro Anca Alamillo, *Los Acorazados de la clase España o el resurgir naval hispano (1912–1937)*

(CD-ROM, Madrid: Centro Marítimo y Naval Casto Méndez Núñez, 2007; printed edn., Madrid: Real de Catorce, 2012)

Gay de Montellá, Rafael, *Diez años de política internacional en el Mediterráneo, 1904–1914. Ensayo de historia política moderna* (Barcelona: Imprenta de la Casa Provincial de la Caridad, 1914)

Gimeno, Amalio, *El Factor naval de España en el problema Mediterráneo* (Madrid: Imprenta de Juan Pueyo, 1914)

González-Llanos, José María, *El Decenio 1936–1946 en la Factoría de El Ferrol del Caudillo* (Ferrol: privately, 1947)

Gretton, Vice Admiral Sir Peter, *El Factor olvidado: La Marina Británica y la Guerra Civil Española* (Madrid: Editorial San Martín, 1984)

Halpern, Paul G., *The Mediterranean Naval Situation, 1908–1914* (Cambridge, Mass.: Harvard University Press, 1971)

_____, *The Naval War in the Mediterranean, 1914–1918* (Annapolis, Md.: Naval Institute Press, 1987)

Johnston, Ian, & Ian Buxton, *The Battleship Builders: Constructing and Arming British Capital Ships* (Barnsley, S. Yorks.: Seaforth Publishing, 2013)

Libro de régimen de organización interior del acorazado España (Ferrol: Imprenta de 'El Correo Gallego', 1918)

Molina Franco, Lucas, *El Legado de Sigfrido. La Ayuda militar alemana al Ejército y la Marina nacional en la Guerra Civil Española (1936–1939)* (Valladolid: AF Editores, 2005)

Moreno de Alborán y de Reyna, Fernando & Salvador, *La Guerra silenciosa y silenciada. Historia de la campaña naval durante la guerra de 1936–39*, 5 vols. (Madrid: privately, 1998)

Rodríguez González, Agustín R., *Política naval de la Restauración (1875–1898)* (Madrid: Editorial San Martín, 1988)

_____, *La Reconstrucción de la Escuadra. Planes navales españoles, 1898–1920* (Valladolid: Galland Books, 2010)

_____, *Jaime Janer Robinson. Ciencia y técnica para la reconstrucción de la Armada* (Madrid: Ediciones Navalmil, 2012)

Sociedad Española de Construcción Naval, *Resumen de Obras* (Madrid: Imprenta de los Sucesores de Rivadeneyra, various years)

Vega Blasco, Antonio de la, *La Propulsión mecánica en la Armada* (Barcelona: privately printed for Empresa Nacional 'Bazán' de Construcciones Navales Militares S.A., 1986)

Svenska marinen

The Armoured Ship *Sverige* (1915)

◆

Ulf Sundberg

NAMED FOR THE COUNTRY which built her, this is the history of an armoured ship which neither fired her guns in anger nor found herself in a situation in which battle seemed an imminent possibility before being scrapped after thirty years. However, the money spent on *Sverige* and her two sisters was not wasted since all played a role in interwar politics before helping to secure Sweden's territorial integrity and neutrality during the Second World War. Moreover, their design and construction represented a significant technological accomplishment for a nation with limited experience in building warships of this size. Although generally described in English-language sources as a coastal battleship or coast defence ship, these classifications are something of a misnomer since *Sverige* was neither a battle-ship in the fullest sense, nor was she confined to coastal waters either by service or design. The Swedish descriptor of *pansarskepp* – armoured ship – used from *Svea* onwards (1885) is prob-ably the most accurate way of classifying her and is the term used in this chapter (see *De Zeven Provinciën* for a similar case).

Context

The Sweden of 1900 was a relatively minor nation on the northern fringes of Europe, her population having only reached five million in 1897 by comparison with 38 million in the British Isles in 1901. At the turn of the nineteenth century she was a poor agricultural country but by 1900 had experienced significant develop-ment in trade and industry, and it was out of this expertise that *Sverige* and her sisters were forged.

The geopolitical situation of the Baltic region at the close of the nineteenth century found the kingdoms of Sweden and Norway loosely tied in a personal union which dated from 1814 but was entering the final stages of dissolution. Of the

Sverige seen from one of her sisters in the 1930s after reconstruction of the bridge and trunking of the forward funnel during the refit of 1931–3. The product of domestic design and construction, the Sverige class was perfectly adapted to Sweden's strategic outlook in the Baltic. *(Bruce Taylor Collection)*

neighbouring territories, Finland had been part of Sweden since medieval times but was lost to Russia in 1809. Poland had ceased to exist, being partitioned between Russia, Germany and Austria in 1772–95, while the future Baltic states of Estonia, Latvia and Lithuania were as yet part of the Russian empire. Although Denmark stood with Russia as the hereditary enemy of Sweden, the former no longer posed any threat. Indeed, nineteenth-century Europe presented no obvious

challenge to Swedish integrity, a state of affairs confirmed by the Congress of Berlin in 1878 which curbed Russian ambitions following her victory in the Russo-Turkish war. Nonetheless, Russia and Germany remained the chief focus of Sweden's defence strategy in 1900, of which the former was regarded as the most likely enemy.

Although Sweden had a notable belligerent tradition spanning thirty-one wars between 1521 and 1814, including a leading role in the Thirty

Years War of 1618–48 and the conflict with Russia known as the Great Northern War (1700–21), after 1814 she pursued a policy of neutrality backed by a credible military establishment. Sweden's goal therefore became that of maintaining her independence, and the prevailing military doctrine centred on repelling invasion, though exactly how this should be done was a matter of debate. By the early nineteenth century the Swedes had settled on a concept of central defence based on inland fortresses, to which a naval strategy focused on ships of the line was added. Geography dictated that an attack from Russia or Germany would most likely come by sea and the prevailing consideration from this period was that the Swedish navy should be large enough to engage, deplete and even repulse an enemy invasion force in open waters. A related strategy was that of ensuring that any attack on Sweden should be recognised as entailing too high a cost, with significant naval assets having to be diverted to protect the transports in the invasion fleet since reliance on smaller escort vessels would be too dangerous. Underpinning this strategy of deterrence was the belief that any would-be belligerent might either already be at war or courting war with another power. In this scenario, the number of capital ships required for the enterprise would make an invasion of Sweden too costly to warrant contemplation.

The Progress of Capital Ship Construction in Sweden

During the nineteenth century Sweden made efforts to keep up with wider developments in military technology. Occasionally she stood at the forefront of these advances, as with the breech-loading mechanism patented by Martin von Wahrendorff in 1837. However, at mid-century the Swedish navy consisted of a few ships of the line, frigates and corvettes, a fleet which, as with practically all others, was recognised as having been made militarily obsolete by the technology brought to bear in the Hampton Roads engagements in March 1862, during which the Confederate ironclad *Virginia* first destroyed two Union warships and ran a third aground before fighting her counterpart the USS *Monitor* to a stalemate. The latter was the brainchild of the Swedish-born John Ericsson, and within three months of the engagement a series of discussions between Ericsson and his countrymen had resulted in a decision by Sweden to acquire a small squadron of monitors. Matters were assisted by the fact that Ericsson patriotically donated the main armament for the first vessel, which was duly named for him. Moreover, the monitor concept proved well suited to the

The Swedish-American inventor John Ericsson (1803–89) seen in 1862, the year of the engagements of Hampton Roads. Ericsson played a key role in the development of the Swedish armoured fleet. *(NHHC/NH 305)*

Swedish navy. Not only were these vessels small and relatively cost-effective on a limited defence budget, but they fitted well with a strategy which posited a defence system based on mines and monitors among the skerries, islands and archipelagos characteristic of the Swedish coast and not easily navigated by larger ships – as *Sverige* discovered for herself on at least one occasion, striking a rock off Karlskrona in 1935. Defensive in nature, this archipelago-based naval doctrine prevailed for decades, and at 1,500 tons *John Ericsson* and her three sisters remained the largest vessels in the Swedish navy until the country entered a period of naval expansion after 1880.

Aside from the rise of navalist thinking, there are several explanations for this expansion. Although Sweden had not competed with the great powers for over a hundred years, she had regarded herself as the leading nation in Scandinavia since the seventeenth century and it is possible that inter-Nordic rivalry could have influenced this new emphasis on naval capability. While Denmark posed no serious threat to Swedish security, it might not have been satisfactory for Sweden to continue having a fleet inferior to the Danish navy (see *Peder Skram*), quite aside from the increasing friction in the Swedish-

Norwegian Union. More particularly, not only had Sweden made significant progress in naval construction since the 1860s, but as Bertil Åhlund points out, a deeper treasury made the development of the navy a viable financial proposition.[1]

Whatever the reason, Sweden now began a steady if not rapid process of armoured warship construction. The first expression of this was the armoured ship *Svea* of 2,900 tons, approved in 1880 and launched at Gothenburg in 1885. Armed with two Armstrong 10in (254mm) guns in a single turret, *Svea* and her two half-sisters for the first time gave the Swedish steel navy the ability to venture beyond the protected waters of the archipelagos. After the Sveas came another class of three vessels led by *Oden* displacing 3,500 tons, on which construction began in 1893 but was not completed until 1896. Next came *Dristigheten* (launched in 1900) whose armament of 8.3in (210mm) guns was influenced by the lessons of the Sino-Japanese War, during which the Battle of the Yalu River in 1894 highlighted the importance of a high rate of accurate fire (see *Chen Yuen*). This not only required guns to be capable of all-elevation loading, but for the sighting equipment to be fitted away from any recoiling parts, it being supposed that these requirements could be met more satisfactorily with a 8.3in gun than with a 9.8in (250mm) one.

Dristigheten was followed by the three units of the Äran class displacing 3,650 tons and capable of 16.5 knots, together with a half-sister, *Wasa*. Sweden had now built eleven armoured ships to her own designs since 1885, a long journey for a nation in many respects unprepared for the task. However, the ability to build larger and more complex vessels had been enhanced by the incorporation of foreign ideas and components, and the launch in 1907 of a twelfth armoured ship, *Oscar II*, represented a major advance in Swedish naval construction. Displacing 4,270 tons, mounting two 8.3in guns and with a maximum speed of 17.8 knots, she provided much experience that would later be worked into the design and construction of the Sverige class.

The Union Crisis and After

While the Swedish shipbuilding industry and navy honed the skills of building and operating armoured ships, political developments around the turn of the twentieth century began to present Sweden with new challenges to her security and

[1] Bertil Åhlund, *Historia kring Flottans kanoner*, Marinlitteraturföreningen, nr 84 (Stockholm: Marinlitteraturföreningens förlag, 1998), p. 117.

hence calls for stronger defence measures. The most important of these developments was the gradual dissolution of the union with Norway (see *Eidsvold*). The Norwegians had been reluctant partners in the union with Sweden which had been forced on them in 1814, and by the end of the nineteenth century their aspirations for independent nationhood were impossible to ignore. This prospect was not greeted with enthusiasm in Sweden where it was recognised that Britain was a supporter of an independent Norway. Meanwhile, tensions were growing between the British and Germany, a nation with which Sweden had close cultural, social and economic ties. These circumstances together contributed to a heightened sense that Sweden was more subject to the vagaries of diplomatic instability than she had been for many decades.

The Union Crisis, the immediate origins of which dated to 1895, came to a head in June 1905 when the Norwegian parliament unilaterally dissolved the union with Sweden. During the negotiations, which went on until September, the Swedish army massed on the border and forty ships were deployed in the vicinity of Norwegian waters, the largest concentration of Swedish naval power since the war with Russia in 1788–90. Voices were raised in favour of war but this was never a realistic option and Norway left the union peacefully. However, the Union Crisis left Sweden a different nation, one that for reasons which probably owed less to fact than to emotion felt more exposed with an independent Norway along her western and northern flank. Soon there were other factors to be considered. Though much depleted during its disastrous war with Japan (1904–5), the Russian fleet was in the process of rapid reconstruction, while the Germans had created a powerful navy to challenge Britain's command of the sea. The Triple Entente between Great Britain, France and Russia in 1907 came as a severe blow to Swedish security since Britain and France could no longer be relied upon to counter Russia on the international stage. Despite her limited financial capabilities, Sweden had now to consider bolstering her defences.

The Political Battle for Armoured Ships

As became obvious in the years following the Union Crisis of 1905, not all Swedes shared the urgency felt in certain quarters to increase military and naval expenditure, and the armoured ship question was the subject of heated political debate which embraced not only the navy but wider society. In early 1906 the chiefs of the army and navy staff were ordered by the government to hold discussions regarding Sweden's defence requirements. These discussions resulted

in a proposal to build a new class of capital ships which in turn led to the creation of a Navy Designs Committee in the autumn of 1906.

In the first place, the new ships had to fit into Sweden's established naval doctrine of deterrence, with provision to engage an invasion fleet at sea if necessary. This called for the ability to sustain a short battle with the leading enemy ships before attacking the transports. However, should this deterrence prove insufficient, the new ships would have to be capable of engaging more powerful adversaries in prolonged offensive manoeuvres. This was the most complicated part of the Swedish plan, since it not only called for adequate armament but higher speed than any more powerful opponent. As with the identically named *Panzerschiffe* of the Deutschland class twenty years later, the Swedish designs aimed to exploit the gap between slow but heavily armed vessels on the one hand, and fast but lightly armed ones on the other to produce a vessel capable of outrunning anything it could not destroy: 'stronger than the slower and faster than the stronger.'

In the event, the matter came down to gun calibre. On the outbreak of the Russo-Japanese War of 1904–5 the 12in (305mm) gun was the heaviest modern ordnance afloat, while 11in (283mm) armament was considered to be the smallest capable of disabling a major warship of the day. Although the navy was adamant that four heavy guns was the minimum required for effective fire control, no ship mounting four 12in guns could be built within the constraints of the government's budget. The six main design alternatives submitted by the Navy Designs Committee in January 1907 therefore centred mainly on vessels mounting either two 12in guns or four 11in guns:

Although the proposed designs far outstripped any vessel in the Scandinavian navies and could match or outrun the 18 knots of the Andrei Pervozvannyi-class pre-dreadnoughts then building for the Russian navy, each were to varying degrees inferior to the most powerful ships in the world where armament and armour were concerned. Already in 1906 Great Britain

had launched the battleship HMS *Dreadnought* mounting ten 12in guns, protected with vertical armour up to 11in thick and capable of 21.5 knots. Moreover, whereas Designs 'B', 'C' and 'F' would be able to escape from a stronger adversary, this was not the case with Designs 'A', 'D' or 'E'. Nonetheless, these designs together with the committee's recommended 7,500-ton displacement were turned over for review by a second committee, which in November 1909 selected Design 'F', and *Sverige* and her sisters were henceforth often referred to as the 'F-ships'. The committee's deliberations resulted in a bill which was voted through the Riksdag (parliament) in 1911, allocating funds to build a single ship to a displacement of 7,500 tons. The total annual defence budget was approximately 90 million kronor, of which two-thirds was assigned to the army and a third to the navy.

However, no sooner had the navalist government of Arvid Lindman steered the armoured ship bill through the Riksdag than it fell in the autumn of 1911, to be replaced by the avowedly anti-naval ministry of Karl Staaf. On leaving power the outgoing government placed an order for 11in guns from Bofors which the new administration immediately cancelled, followed in January 1912 by the scrapping of the entire programme. This move created a public outcry, with supporters of the programme holding that political developments in Europe pointed ever more strongly to the need for increased defence measures. Faced by government intransigence, a national subscription campaign was started by the Armoured Ship Society led by the Rev. Manfred Björkquist which had raised 17 million kronor by the time it closed later that year. The government had no choice but to accept this gift from the Swedish people, handing the armoured ship lobby a decisive victory and Sweden her greatest vessel. However, continued delays by Staaf resulted in early 1914 in demonstrations in Stockholm to appeal to King Gustaf V, whose speeches brought on the collapse of the government, the dissolution of the Riksdag and a special general election.

Armoured Ship Design Alternatives, 1907

Type	Displacement	Armament	Speed	Armour	Cost in kronor
A	7,500 tons	4 × 11in (283mm)	21.0 knots	7.9in (200mm)	13.45 million
B	7,500 tons	4 × 11in (283mm)	23.0 knots	7.9in (200mm)	13.70 million
C	7,500 tons	4 × 11in (283mm)	23.0 knots	6.7in (170mm)	13.67 million
D	4,800 tons	2 × 10in (254mm)	18.0 knots +	7.5in (190mm)	8.29 million
E	5,650 tons	2 × 12in (305mm)	18.0 knots +	7.9in (200mm)	9.49 million
F	6,800 tons	4 × 11in (283mm)	22.5 knots	7.9in (200mm)	11.61 million

Source: Steckzén, ed., *Klart skepp*, pp. 276–7.

Building Sweden's Greatest Ship

The fundraisers had not only outmanoeuvred the politicians but had created a major challenge for the Swedish shipbuilding industry. Not the least of the issues attaching to the gift was the provision that the ship had to be laid down before the end of 1912. The procurement process duly began that summer. There was, of course, the option of having *Sverige* built abroad, in a British shipyard as *Norge* and *Eidsvold* (q.v.) had been. However, national pride dictated otherwise and the four largest Swedish shipyards were invited to tender: Lindholmens Verkstad AB, Kockums Mekaniska Verkstads AB, Göteborgs Nya Verkstads AB (Götaverken) and Bergsunds Mekaniska Verkstads AB. Nonetheless, the navy's specifications were far from complete and

several features were included in *Sverige*'s design which together made the contract look like a dangerous enterprise. All hesitated, except for Göteborgs Nya Verkstads whose managing director, Hans Hammar, enthusiastically described Design 'F' as 'a feat of Swedish engineering art'. Hammar had benefitted from spending several of his forty-eight years in ship construction building naval vessels, including in British yards, but his board of directors at Götaverken remained sceptical. The yard had yet to build any vessel in excess of 1,200grt and to construct one to naval standards displacing over 7,000 tons entailed significant risk and capital investment the board was unwilling to entertain.

Negotiations stalled and the future of Design 'F' seemed uncertain as autumn approached.

However, at a critical stage Helmer Mörner, head of the Mariningenjörkåren (Navy Corps of Engineers), suggested that the shipyards collaborate in the endeavour. This idea was supported by the chairman of the board at Kockums, and on 2 September 1912 representatives of the yards met and agreed on a scheme of co-operation. Götaverken would be the main contractor. Kockums undertook to deliver the turbines and Bergsunds the boilers and auxiliary machinery.

Sverige seen in her as-built condition prior to the 1924–5 reconstruction, the most visible result of which was the replacement of the light foremast by a heavier construction carrying new fire-control equipment. Note the three crowns device decorating the bows. (Krigsarkivet – Military Archives, Stockholm)

The Svenska marinen's squadron of *pansarskeppet* (armoured ships) at sea during the Second World War while competing for the King's Trophy for gunnery. The modifications to the funnels carried out by 1933 allow them to be readily distinguished: *Sverige* is nearest the camera, then *Gustaf V* and finally *Drottning Victoria*. (*Krigsarkivet*)

Lindholmen would supply steering engines, deck tackle and other equipment. Two weeks later a joint proposal was submitted. The government rejected the bid as too high and a vigorous round of negotiations ensued with the builders. Eventually the bid was lowered and terms agreed on 4 November, the final price for the hull and machinery being a shade over 6 million kronor. Work started immediately at Götaverken and at noon on 12 December Hammar reported the keel as laid and ready for inspection. The Armoured Ship Society's first provision had been met.

According to the contract, construction was expected to last three years, but progress was slowed somewhat by the outbreak of the First World War which cut Sweden off from a number of foreign suppliers. Copper became scarce and the bronze propellers ordered from

A posed shot of one of the starting platforms in an engine room of one of the Sverige-class vessels. (*Krigsarkivet*)

One of the steering positions in *Sverige* with the helmsman keeping a close eye on the compass. The curved tube at head height is a voice pipe. (*Krigsarkivet*)

Britain never arrived, having instead to be manufactured locally in cast steel. However, work continued and *Sverige* was launched on 3 May 1915 in the presence of King Gustav V and other high-ranking dignitaries. The ship was then moved to a quay for fitting out. Mounting the 11in guns presented a challenge since no single crane could take the weight, requiring the use of two in unison.

Sverige was completed in May 1917 at a total cost of 13.5 million kronor, not far off the original 1907 estimate of 11.6 million. Of this the armament had claimed nearly 3 million kronor. *Sverige*'s sisters *Gustaf V* and *Drottning Victoria*, named for the reigning monarchs, were laid down at Kockums in 1914 and Götaverken in 1915 respectively, but progress was slow and the question was raised after the 1918 armistice as to whether they should not instead be completed as civilian ferries. That proposal was rejected, but it was not until 1923 and 1924 that these two joined the fleet, eighteen years after the Navy Designs Committee had first begun its deliberations. By then the shadow of obsolescence had fallen upon the Sverige class.

Hull, Armour and Propulsion

What did the Swedish people get for their money? Displacing 6,852 tons standard and 7,688 tons at full load, *Sverige* had an overall length of 393.4ft (120.0m), with 61.1ft (18.63m) in the beam and a draught of 20.5ft (6.25m). The narrow beam of the ship prevented any extensive subdivision which was restricted to two watertight bulkheads athwart the ship, thirteen compartments below the armoured deck and a double bottom of box-type construction. Unlike her sisters with their deeply cut stems, *Sverige*'s hull was not designed for icebreaking.

Where armour was concerned, the starting point for the design committee of 1906 was that the vitals of the ship should be protected from low-trajectory fire from armoured cruisers, which equated to shells of approximately 8in or 9in (203mm or 228mm) calibre. The resulting protection consisted of a 7.9in (200mm) belt along the waterline, with 6.9in (175mm) for the conning tower and 3.9in (100mm) for the citadel. Horizontal protection consisted of 0.7in (18mm) armour with a 1.1in (28mm) round-down extending to the base of the waterline belt. The main armament was protected by armour up to 7.9in (200mm) thick on the face plates, while the gun shields of the secondary armament had 4.9in (125mm). Waterline and turret armour showed improvement over *Oscar II*, but in other respects protection was either equal to her or of a lesser standard, and the ratio of armour to

standard displacement was 21 per cent in *Sverige* compared with 25 per cent in *Oscar II*.

In 1897 *Turbinia* had dramatically demonstrated the value of turbines by weaving uninvited and with impunity between the lines of battleships gathered to celebrate Queen Victoria's Diamond Jubilee at Spithead. Within ten years *Dreadnought* had been fitted with turbines following extensive testing aboard smaller ships. The first Swedish turbine-driven naval vessels, the destroyers *Hugin* and *Munin*, were launched in 1911 and 1912 respectively, and it was obvious that turbines would be used in *Sverige*, not least since the navy had emphasised that the latest developments in engineering were to be worked into her design. After some deliberation the decision was taken to use Curtis geared turbines operating on four shafts, though *Gustaf V* and *Drottning Victoria* received an improved arrangement consisting of two geared shafts. Employing a mixed coal and oil system, the class was fitted with twelve Yarrow boilers in four boiler rooms calling for two funnels. This plant was required to develop a total of 20,000ihp in order to attain a designed speed of 22.5 knots, which in the event was slightly exceeded during trials. *Sverige* had bunkerage for 665 tons of coal and 100 tons of oil giving her a tactical range of 2,720 miles at 14 knots but just 450 miles at maximum speed. While not impressive, the class was designed to operate within the confines of the Baltic and the distance from Stockholm to the mouth of the Gulf of Finland, from which a Russian invasion fleet could be expected to emerge, is just 170 nautical miles.

This plant remained unchanged until the 1938–40 reconstruction when it was decided to refit the ship entirely for oil firing. Not only were the existing boilers worn out, but the heavy smoke generated by burning coal which had required adjustments to be made to the funnels in every unit of the class was now impairing the effectiveness of the new anti-aircraft armament. The twelve Yarrow boilers were therefore

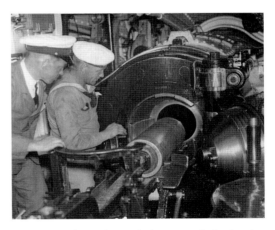

Loading one of the 11in guns in the turret of a Sverige-class vessel, the shell being forced into the breech by the powered rammer. Note the innovative Bofors ogival breech block on the right. *(Bruce Taylor Collection)*

replaced by four Penhoët units, the removal of the coal bunkers representing a considerable saving in space – not to mention expenditure of time and effort by the ship's company.

Main Armament

Although not a dreadnought, the designers of *Sverige* nonetheless subscribed fully to the principle of a comprehensive armament centred on the largest guns which could reasonably be mounted in a ship of her size. These were the four Bofors 11in weapons disposed in a forward and after turret, themselves a major achievement of Swedish design and engineering.

Each gun, which could be laid independently, had a layer seated outboard of the gun beside the turret wall. A third man, seated between the guns, was responsible for training the turret on its roller path. Power to turrets and guns was supplied by electrical motors transferred by hydraulic variable speed gears, an arrangement which allowed for very smooth operation. There were backup motors in the event of main equip-

Sverige: Armament, 1917

Weapon	Number (mounting)
11.14in (283mm) M/12	4 (2 × 2)
6in (152mm) M/12	8 (6 × 1; 1 × 2)
3in (75mm) M/12	4 (4 × 1)
3in (75mm) AA M/15	2 (2 × 1)
0.25in (6.5mm) MG M/14	2
2.25in (57mm) M/16 (landing guns)	2
17.7in (457mm) torpedo tubes M/14	2 (2 × 1)

Sources: Steckzén, ed., *Klart skepp*, p.137, & Krigsarkivet [Military Archives], Inventarium Artilleriuppbörden, Fartyg och Fartygsförband Karlskrona [Karlskrona Ships and Naval Units, Gunnery Inventory], Sv D III, vol. 5.

A schematic illustration showing the interior of the Bofors 11in turret and barbette installed in the Sverige class. The structure is essentially on five levels beginning with shell and propellant handing rooms at the base and a machinery space on the third level. Above that is the working chamber where shells and propellant were transferred from the main hoist to the gun-loading hoist. Finally comes the gunhouse itself with the gunlayer positioned beside the gun and the recoil mechanism with the trainer just visible at the turret faceplate beyond the gun. Seen towards the rear of the gunhouse is the rammer operator, the turret commander in his cabinet with the benefit of a periscopic sight, and the rangetaker above and behind him. The turret, which was electrically powered, was protected by up to 8in of armour. The 11in gun manufactured by Bofors was the largest ever mounted afloat by the Swedish navy. The ships and turrets are long gone but two barrels have been preserved at Karlskrona. (*Krigsarkivet*)

ment failure, but the turret could also be manually operated if necessary. The turret commander occupied an armoured compartment beneath the 10ft (3m) rangefinder at the rear of the turret where he had use of a periscopic sight. Shells were brought from the shell rooms on overhead grabs and trollies, moved to a tray beneath the turret before being manually rolled into a hoist. Two powder cartridges weighing 110lb (50kg) each were brought up to a working chamber along with each projectile in a separate hoist, at which point they changed hoists in an arrangement designed to prevent flash reaching the magazines. Having reached the gunhouse, the shell was placed on a cradle behind the gun and then mechanically rammed into the breech. It was followed by the cartridges which were manhandled into the breech which was sealed by a manually-operated breech block. These loading arrangements allowed for a notional rate of fire of four shells per minute per gun. The ammunition originally consisted of armoured and semi-armoured M/14 shells, the latter holding a larger explosive charge than the former. This ammunition was later supplemented by the M/16 high-explosive shell for use against unarmoured targets.

Secondary Armament

The rate of fire and effectiveness of the secondary gunnery was crucial for a ship designed to engage an invasion fleet including numerous unarmoured targets. As in other navies, the 6in (152mm) gun was selected as firing the heaviest shell which could be manually loaded at speed. Here Bofors was faced with a much simpler task than was the case with the main armament as the company by now had considerable experience in manufacturing

weapons of this calibre. The result was a development of the M/03 weapon known as the M/12 with a muzzle velocity of 2,789ft/sec (850m/sec) giving a theoretical range of 17,500yds (16,000m) at an elevation of 15 degrees. The 6in guns were fitted in six single turrets (three to a side) with a twin turret super-firing the forward 11in turret. The turrets were horizontally supported by ball bearings and vertical roll bearings. The single units were hand-operated, while the twin turret was electrically powered. The secondary armament was commanded by the second gunnery officer (AO2) from the conning tower, in a similar manner to the main armament. The guns were fired by an electromechanical switch operated by the gunlayer.

The rate of fire was limited by the capacity of the electrically-powered ammunition hoists, which could supply six to eight shells per minute to the single turrets, but only four to the twin turret. The major improvement where the 6in gun was concerned lay in the ammunition which had improved ballistic properties. The high-explosive M/14 shell was of an entirely new design, with a high brisant charge. The ammunition was intended to include tracer, though procurement of the latter proved difficult and this contract provision was not met. However, the M/12 was no better than average when compared with foreign weapons, German and Japanese designers having increased the muzzle velocity of 6in guns to 3,051ft/sec (930m/sec).

The 1912 design specifications also called for six 3in (75mm) M/12 guns to ward off attacks by torpedo boats, but the need to provide for the threat from the air was already obvious and in that year the navy requested funds for an experimental anti-aircraft gun. The Riksdag balked at this and funds did not become available until 1914 when Bofors began producing the 3in M/15 anti-aircraft gun, the first in a distinguished line of such weapons by this manufacturer. Two of

Sverige: Final AA armament

Weapon	Number (mounting)	Designed Range	Date Fitted
3in (75mm) M/28	4 (2 × 2)	< 8,750yds (8,000m); altitude: 5,000ft (1,500m)	1931–3
1.57in (40mm) M/36	4 (2 × 2)	1,100–5,500yds (1,000–5,000m)	1940
	2 (1 × 2)*		1942
1in (25mm) M/32	4 (2 × 2)	< 1,100yds (1,000m)	1939
0.78in (20mm) M/40	3 (1 × 3)	< 1,100yds (1,000m)	c. 1940–5
0.31in (8mm) M/36 MG	4 (2 × 2)	< 1,100yds (1,000m)	1940
Total	21		

* Mounting designed for submarines.

Sources: Åhlund (1998), pp. 16ff, & Krigsarkivet, Inventarium Artilleriuppbörden, Fartyg och Fartygsförband Karlskrona, Sv D III, vol. 5.

these guns were fitted on the after superstructure in each vessel of the class instead of two M/12s. They were later modified to M/15-23s with improved mountings and sights. *Sverige* retained this AA armament until her 1931–3 refit when she received four 3in M/28 guns on twin mountings and a 13ft (4m) M/22 stereoscopic rangefinder mounted aft paired with a Hazemeyer electro-mechanical counter. This gave *Sverige* and her sisters an AA fit the equal of any in the world. Also fitted were two 25mm automatic M/32 AA guns in single mountings atop

the forward 6in turrets, later replaced by four guns of the same type in a pair of twin mountings on the AA superstructure aft, positioned diagonally from the 3in guns.

Close-range anti-aircraft defences were further improved during the 1938–40 refit with the installation of four 1.57in (40mm) M/36 automatic AA guns on gyro-stabilised twin mountings in place of the no. '2' 6in turrets on each side, to be followed by two single mountings installed abreast no. '1' 6in turrets in 1942. Finally, three 0.78in (20mm) M/40 automatic AA guns were

installed in single mountings, together with appropriate modifications for 1.57in and 0.78in ammunition stowage and supply. As Ensign John Rumenius noted in 1940, this AA battery was not only the most powerful in the world for a ship of her size, but operated in all conditions – unlike weapons of foreign manufacture.[3]

In concluding this survey of *Sverige*'s secondary armament, mention should be made of the two 2.25in (57mm) guns shipped for use by

---

[3] *Ibid.*, p. 88.

BOFORS AND THE SWEDISH NAVY

In the early 1880s the firm of Bofors-Gullspång AB of Karlskoga began to establish itself as a manufacturer of modern guns. By 1885 the firm was bidding to supply the 6in (152mm) secondary armament for *Svea*, but the Swedish navy thought otherwise. Bofors had experienced difficulties with a 6.3in (160mm) design for the Swedish army and the navy opted instead for ordnance manufactured by the British firm of Sir W. G. Armstrong, as it did for *Göta* of 1889, while *Oden* of 1896 mounted a 10in (254mm) main armament manufactured by Forges et Chantiers de la Méditerranée of La Seyne. Bofors had meanwhile been acquired by Alfred Nobel in 1894, and it was under his auspices that a major investment programme was initiated and the company transformed into a significant player in the field of naval ordnance. When the Riksdag voted funds for *Oden*'s two sisters (*Thor* and *Niord*) in 1896, Bofors once again bid for the contract to manufacture the 10in guns. The navy hesitated. It wanted to support local manufacturing but not at the expense of the quality of its armament, and was as yet uncertain of what Bofors could deliver. However, Bofors had some support in the Riksdag and a compromise was reached: *Thor* was to be armed with French guns and *Niord* with Swedish ones. The French designs were made available to Bofors and work began on the 10in M94/C. As it turned out, the navy was perfectly satisfied with the Bofors weapon and so began a new era in heavy ordnance manufacturing. Bofors went on to design the 8.3in (210mm) M/98 gun for *Dristigheten* which became standard ordnance in the Swedish navy for nearly twenty years.

The decision to arm *Sverige* with 11in (279mm) guns represented a significant challenge to Bofors, which was awarded the contract for designing and building them to navy specifications. Bofors' 8.3in M/98 gun had been the largest modern ordnance manufactured in Sweden and the new weapon was

Unbolting the roof of one of *Sverige*'s six Bofors single 6in turrets during a periodic spell of maintenance. The balance of the ship's 6in armament was contained in a twin turret superfiring the forward 11in turret. (*Krigsarkivet*)

a development of this successful design. After prolonged work the designers settled on a 11.14in (283mm) weapon of 45 calibres. A 672lb (305kg) projectile was fired at a muzzle velocity of 2,822ft/sec (860m/sec) giving a range of 21,430yds (19,600m) at 18 degrees of elevation, which compared unfavourably with German designs having a muzzle velocity of 3,084ft/sec (940m/sec) and commensurately greater range. Plans to increase the elevation to 35 degrees were discussed though never materialised but improved ammunition extended the range to 27,340yds (25,000m). However, Bofors made one major improvement with respect to previous types: an innovative

chamber screw to an ogival design which received international recognition.

Manufacturing the 11in gun was not the only challenge faced by Bofors; no turret had ever been built in Sweden, these having traditionally been ordered from foreign manufacturers. Bofors also supplied the armour plate for the class, some of which they manufactured themselves, with the rest subcontracted to the Carnegie Steel Co. in the United States. In the event, the design and construction of the 11in turret placed a heavy strain on the company which suffered significant losses in meeting its contractual responsibilities for the Sverige class and entered a period of financial crisis in the 1920s.

naval landing parties. Though scarcely mentioned in primary or secondary sources, these pieces were probably Bofors Model 1916 (M/16).

Torpedoes and Searchlights

By the time *Sverige* was designed it was standard practice to fit even the largest vessels of the Swedish navy with torpedoes, a weapon now capable of hitting targets at ranges up to 10,900yds (10,000m) at a speed of 30 knots. In *Sverige*'s case this fit consisted of two 17.7in (457mm) M/14 torpedo tubes located below the waterline forward. However, the installation of a torpedo room created a weak point in the construction of the vessel with only limited tactical advantage in return. Predictably enough, their usefulness was called into question and they were removed during the 1931–3 refit when part of the torpedo room was converted to a fire-control centre. This reconstruction also saw the installation of paravanes to protect the ship against mines.

Sverige was completed with four hand-

FIRE CONTROL

At the turn of the century the navy had tested director firing systems from the German AEG and Siemens & Halske AG firms and the Swedish L. M. Ericsson company, with the AEG centralised control apparatus being selected. Nonetheless, fire control was still in its infancy in Sweden at the time the Navy Designs Committee first sat in 1906, resulting in the establishment of a committee the following year to advise on procurement for the Sverige class. This recommended that each vessel be equipped with a 6.5ft (2m) rangefinder in the gunnery top and a 9ft (2.75m) unit on the searchlight bridge. Initial trials with British and German rangefinders in 1908 proved unsatisfactory, but instruments from the Glasgow firm of Barr & Stroud were eventually selected. That same year trials were carried out with a British range clock, a mechanical device in which data including target range, speed and bearing were entered to provide a continuous calculation of the rate of change of target range and bearing to enable director firing even if the rangefinders failed. The range indicator was a similar though less complex device. These novelties were not fully embraced by the Swedish navy, but it was decided to equip Sverige with three 10ft (3m) rangefinders and one 6.5ft (2m) instrument, together with two range clocks and two range indicators. Of these, a range clock and the range indicators were placed in the conning tower, with the second range clock positioned in the confines of the communications centre, the hub of the ship's fire control.

In 1913 the Marinförvaltningen (Naval Office) produced a classified manual describing fire-control operations in Sverige. The principal gunnery officer (*Artilleriofficer 1*, abbreviated to AO1) would command the main armament from the conning tower, which was fitted with centralised control allowing orders and information to be transferred simultaneously to the two turrets and to the communications centre. The AO1 would also have direct telephone lines to the turrets and the communications centre. Fall of shot would be spotted from the gunnery top and reported to the AO1 by voice pipe. Under special circumstances the AO1 could operate from the gunnery top, communicating via voice pipe to the communications centre from where orders would be relayed to the turrets via centralised control or telephone. The commander of the after turret would take command if necessary, using a direct telephone line to the forward turret, or to the communications centre which would relay the orders to the forward turret. Salvo firing relied on the director apparatus which delivered the fire order simultaneously in both turrets. This arrangement was of course less effective than that of simultaneously firing the ship's main armament from a central position.

Although the Sverige class was intended to represent the state of the art in 1907–12, Swedish designers were denied several important advances in naval technology, particularly in the area of gunnery calculators in which the major powers had made significant strides before and during the First World War. Not until Swedish officers began to study these advances after the armistice did it become apparent how far astern they had fallen. The problem was clear enough. No fighting ship is better than the number of hits it can score on the enemy, and battle ranges and manoeuvrability had increased significantly during the First World War. Not only had a firing solution to be calculated more quickly than before, but the guns aimed and fired simultaneously at ranges up to 22,000yds (20,000m). Much as these problems were understood, it was less obvious how to solve them within technical and financial constraints. An Artillerikommission (Gunnery Commission) was established to find a solution and a series of interim measures taken, beginning with the installation of a 13ft (4m) Goertz rangefinder in 1921–2, to be replaced by a 20ft (6m) Barr & Stroud model under a revolving hood forward of the conning tower in 1923. In 1922 a range table was obtained, providing a continuous paper plot of fire-control data and ending the AO1's reliance on portable range clocks and target indicators, etc. Finally, provision was made for converting the communications centre from a communications hub to an operational fire-control centre.

The obvious solution to the problem of fire control was for the guns to be centrally aimed and fired as part of a synthetic system, but financial considerations put this out of the question. However, a number of solutions were tested, including those from Barr & Stroud and the Italian Girardelli firm, and eventually a bid of 800,000 kronor was accepted from Hazemeyer, the Dutch subsidiary of Siemens & Halske AG, in 1924. The system consisted of a main sight, an arrangement for transmitting instructions to the turrets based on the 'follow-the-pointer' principle, and devices for director firing. Target information would be gathered from the gunnery top and sent to a fire-control centre from where training and laying orders were relayed to the turrets. The new fire-control system called for the replacement of the slender foremast by a heavy tripod structure with a gunnery top in three levels. The lower section contained telephones and director apparatus, surmounted by a revolving middle section housing a 13ft (4m) Zeiss rangefinder and a seat for the AO1. Atop this was the central sight with its periscope, while a new fire-control centre was installed below decks forward. The work, completed in 1925 to the Gunnery Commission's recommendations, restored Sverige's fighting power to an acceptable standard. Indeed, in the memoir of his time aboard in 1940, John Rumenius, then an ensign, records the main armament as very well maintained and capable of hitting targets at a range of 22,000yds (20,000m), despite its age.[2]

This remained the fire-control fit of the Sverige class until the Second Word War when new rangefinders and radar were installed in Sverige in 1945. The latter, however, enjoyed only limited success, the AO1 at the time later claiming that he could not rely on it and would have preferred to direct his fire using established methods.

---

2 John Rumenius, *Klart skepp för minfällning: En reservfänrik berättar från beredskapsåren 1939–40* (Stockholm: Lindfors, 1976), p. 88.

A view of *Sverige*'s quarterdeck in *c.* 1940 providing a summary of the ship's armament at that date. Dominating the scene is the after twin 11in turret traversed to port. Seen on the left and also trained to port is Port no. '3' 6in turret. Positioned on the left above the main armament is one the two 1in M/32 twin mountings fitted in 1939, with one of the two 3in M/28 twin mountings installed during the 1931–3 refit seen on the right. Note the fire-control position and searchlights further forward. *(Krigsarkivet)*

directed 35.4in (90cm) searchlights, the aftermost pair of which were exchanged for centrally-operated 43.3in (110cm) models during the 1938–40 reconstruction. Records of searchlight exercises reflect the Swedish navy's pre-war training in night fighting, though clearly with variable results. Placed under the command of a junior officer known as the light officer (*Lysofficer*, abbreviated to LysO), the 35.4in searchlights had a limited range and firing at night was a complicated operation, calling for illumination as soon as the intended target came within beam range. This would in theory be followed by the first salvo in hair-trigger reaction, an evolution calling for close co-operation between the commander of the ship, the gunnery officer and the LysO. However, it is clear that things could and often did go wrong, with the searchlights coming on too late, too soon or not at all. Not only were the searchlights and the technology for directing them as yet unreliable, but they were manned by galley and supply staff who had them as their battle stations. Inevitably, the blame for failure often fell on the young LysO.

Life Aboard

Sverige was designed with a complement of 443 men. These included the fleet commander with seven executive officers, eighteen non-executive officers, thirty-two *underofficerare* (petty officers), thirty-five *underofficerskorpraler* (leading hands), 258 *sjömän* (seamen), *ekonomister* (supply staff) and *hantverkare* (artisans) in addition to ninety-two *eldare* (stokers). Officers had private or (for the more junior) shared cabins, while petty officers lived in enclosed messes shared by four to six men. The ratings slept in hammocks slung in messdecks on the main deck, though these arrangements were reconfigured during the reconstruction of 1938–40 when an expanded AA fit brought the ship's complement to 540 men. There were bathrooms for officers and petty officers, and washrooms for the

The port 3in (75mm) M/28 twin mounting, one of two installed in *Sverige* during the 1931–3 refit, seen with its crew at action stations. The guns had a range of 8,750yds and could engage aircraft at altitudes of up to 5,000ft. The mountings were equipped to set time-delay fuses on the shells. *Drottning Victoria* is off the port quarter with *Gustaf V* visible just ahead. *(Krigsarkivet)*

ratings. *Sverige* was the first Swedish warship to be fitted with a sauna, and the first to have a reading room for the ratings.

It is difficult at more than fifty years' remove to reconstruct life aboard *Sverige* to any degree. Where general conditions for the ratings are concerned, there is nothing to suggest that life was overly harsh. While it could hardly be taken as representative, the Swedish navy of the period does have a romantic aura around it, enough certainly to dispel any impression of inhuman conditions. Aside from the paucity of sources, any assessment is complicated by the lengthy career of the ship which encompassed fundamental changes in Swedish society between 1917 and 1947, and which found their way into the navy to a greater or lesser degree. While Sweden was by no means untouched by the social unrest sweeping across Europe in the early twentieth century, there was nothing to compare with the circumstances which prompted the mutiny that broke the German navy at the end of the First World War, or the other instances of shipboard unrest treated in this volume. No doubt life aboard for the majority of the crew was more often boring than onerous despite considerable efforts on the part of the navy, ranging from the shipboard facilities mentioned above to sports and various types of entertainment. During the wartime years the effect of cramped quarters and lengthy periods away from friends and family, mostly lying in the bleak Hårsfjärden archipelago, came to be described as *plåtsjuka* – the steel plating disease.

If the tenor of life aboard *Sverige* has so far defied reconstruction, the ledgers of the ship's quartermaster provide us with revealing insights into the nature of shipboard life, especially with respect to daily food consumption. The records from a randomly selected year – in this case 1936 – show this to have been abundant and of good quality. Potatoes are a staple in Sweden and *Sverige* was no different, supplies of between 1.5 and 4 tons being taken aboard every five days. Served with them were Swedish specialities such as meatballs and Falu sausage, and that other local staple, herring. A rich variety of seasonings

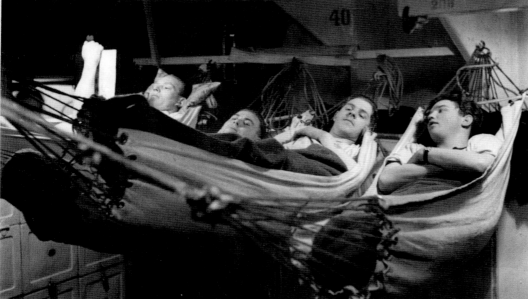

Sailors in their hammocks on one of *Sverige*'s messdecks, perfectly illustrating the cramped quarters experienced by ratings the world over. Note the storage lockers on the left. *(Krigsarkivet)*

One of the two single 1.57in (40mm) M/36 mountings installed in 1942, seen here with its crew at action stations. *(Krigsarkivet)*

and vegetables suggest that the food was far from bland. Large quantities of oats indicate that porridge was often served for breakfast, and vitamin C was provided by ample supplies of dried fruit, mainly pears and apples but also apricots, raisins and prunes.

Sweden has long had a high per capita coffee consumption, one fully reflected in the *Sverige* of 1936. Hundreds of kilos of coffee were consumed aboard every month, along with the pastries much loved by Swedes, including cinnamon rolls and the fluffy Danish pastries known as *Wienerbröd*. The quartermaster's records show that these were served every day, daily deliveries ranging from 800 to 860 pieces when the ship was in harbour, while the large supply of cinnamon stowed aboard suggests that rolls were baked in the ship's galleys when she was at sea. This consumption of patisserie must be set against the dental standard of the *Kustflottan* (Coast Fleet), which an investigation by a navy dentist in 1940 found to be appallingly bad. About 95 per cent of the conscripts had tooth decay and 6.5 per cent of them required a denture. Not surprisingly, the author concluded his report with an appeal for more resources.

The quartermaster's papers leave little doubt as to what the crew drank: milk, of which approximately 44gal (200l) were taken aboard each day. Next came fruit cordial diluted with water, lemon and raspberry being the preferred flavours. Beer was consumed only at Christmas, when each rating received half a litre of special Christmas brew or standard Swedish lager. No sources have been found to shed light on the officers' intake, though it can be assumed that alcohol flowed freely in the wardroom and that most meals would have been three-course affairs, a glass of schnapps always served with the hors d'oeuvre.

Before taking leave of the Sverige class and their crews, mention should be made of Nicke, the ship's dog on *Drottning Victoria* in the 1940s. Assigned ship's number 900, he frequently appears in official records, sometimes recommended for promotion and eventually rated petty officer, but sometimes demoted after going absent without leave. As in most navies, the presence of a pet was both a humorous and irreverent antidote to naval discipline and a reminder of the pleasures of life ashore.

Service Career, 1917–39

The boilers were first flashed up on the morning of 10 May 1917 and five days later *Sverige* sailed from Gothenburg on her maiden voyage. En route to Karlskrona, the main southern base of the Swedish navy, the crew was reminded of the war going on around them in the shape of German minefields stretching to the edge of Swedish territorial waters, sightings of a German battleship and funnel smoke from destroyers and torpedo boats on the horizon. From Karlskrona, *Sverige* proceeded to Stockholm where she was officially handed over to the navy by the board of the fundraising organisation. Following a successful trials and working-up period, *Sverige* became flagship of the Winter Squadron, comprising ships manned and equipped to serve throughout the year.

Although Sweden retained her neutrality during the Great War, the Russian revolutions of 1917 resulted in the outbreak of the Finnish Civil War of January–May 1918, prompting the government to dispatch troops and a naval squadron, including *Sverige*, to protect the ethnic Swedish population of the Finnish archipelago of Åland (Ahvenanmaa) in February. To

Washing up on deck after a meal. Swedish sailors were as wholesomely fed as any treated in this volume. *(Krigsarkivet)*

this Germany responded in early March by sending a large expeditionary force to Åland covered by the battleships *Rheinland* and *Westfalen*, part of a campaign which settled the Finnish Civil War in favour of the Whites and consolidated Finland's independence (see *Väinämöinen*). The Swedes promptly withdrew from Åland, but with the Russian fleet rendered unserviceable by the revolution and the civil war and the bulk of the German fleet first interned and then scuttled at Scapa Flow, the end of the Great War placed the Swedish navy as the most powerful in the Baltic and the newly completed *Sverige* as its major unit.

Joined by her sisters *Gustaf V* and *Drottning Victoria* in 1923 and 1924, *Sverige* settled into the ordered routine of a peacetime fleet punctuated by courtesy visits to foreign ports in the Baltic and beyond. The first of these came in the summer of 1923 with the marriage of Crown Prince Gustaf Adolf to Lady Louise Mountbatten in London in a wedding attended by George V and members of the Swedish and Norwegian royal families. The Pansarskeppsdivisionen (Armoured Ship Division) sailed with two destroyers to bring the couple home. From a naval perspective, the highlight came in the pulling (rowing) regatta arranged by the host navy at Rosyth which pitted Swedish crews against those from seven British battleships. The challenge seemed daunting. Not only did the Royal Navy place pulling at the heart of its sporting activities, but HMS *Valiant* had an undefeated crew. In the event, a crew from *Drottning Victoria* beat *Valiant* into second place with

Sverige coming in third, a famous victory which resonated in the Swedish navy for many years.

The Swedish navy carried out a series of visits to Baltic harbours between the wars, each designed to support the newly-established states and underline its status as the leading naval power in the region. The Latvian capital Riga and Arensburg (now Kuressaare) and Runö in Estonia were visited in 1924. In the same year *Gustaf V* and *Drottning Victoria* sailed for Tallinn in Estonia, culminating in a visit to Helsinki by no fewer than thirty-six ships and five flying boats. In the summer of 1926 *Sverige* and *Gustaf V* visited Copenhagen. The armoured ships also served as hosts for visiting navies. In May 1929 President Gustavs Zemgals of Latvia made a state visit to Sweden, being escorted into Stockholm by *Sverige* and *Drottning Victoria*. Shortly after, King Gustaf V sailed to Tallinn and Riga aboard *Sverige* escorted by *Drottning Victoria*. The visit to Riga offered a dramatic scene. As the squadron prepared to sail at nightfall the searchlights suddenly trained their beams on the Latvian flag flying above the castle. The point was not lost on the 40,000 Latvians gathered around the harbour. When Queen Victoria of Sweden died in Rome in April 1930 her body was brought by train to the German port of Swinemünde on the Baltic and conveyed from there to Sweden aboard her namesake *Drottning Victoria*. Among the last foreign cruises before the war were a series of visits to German Baltic ports in 1937, particularly Kiel where *Sverige* and *Drottning Victoria* received an enthusiastic

welcome, with the latter attending the Coronation Review of George V in May 1937.

Sverige never participated in any of the overseas cruises regularly undertaken by the training ships of the Swedish navy, but in 1933 her sister *Gustaf V* made a cruise of the Mediterranean. Not only was this the first time that a member of the class was tested in heavy weather, *Gustaf V* acquitting herself well with smooth and regular movements in a Force 9 gale in the Bay of Biscay, but she also had occasion to meet the Italian heavy cruiser *Zara* at sea, an encounter which no doubt gave some of the Swedish officers cause to wonder how their ship might stand up against a modern vessel of her type. The question would never be answered.

Obsolescence

There are many criteria for gauging the value of a naval vessel, but it is clear that, though designed to be state of the art for ships of their size, the Sverige class was largely obsolete by the time they entered service. Nonetheless, their position as the most powerful ships in the Baltic remained unchallenged until Germany announced plans to build the *Panzerschiffe* of the Deutschland class (later known as 'pocket battleships') in 1928. These plans were disseminated in an article by the British naval commentator Frank C. Bowen, published in Swedish translation with a commentary by an officer on the Naval Staff, the future Admiral Stig H:son Ericson.[4] The contents made distinctly uncomfortable reading for anyone concerned at the recovery of German naval power, reporting as it did that the new ships would be armed with between six and eight 15in guns of a new design with extremely long barrels and a correspondingly high muzzle velocity, giving them a range similar to the 16in weapons mounted in HM Ships *Nelson* and *Rodney*. Protection was to be of a high standard with an armoured deck, internal bulges and a comprehensive arrangement of watertight compartments. Speed was estimated at 19 knots, but could well be higher. The article concluded by mentioning the Sverige class as its closest Swedish rivals, though any ship-to-ship engagement between these units

Sverige in Stockholm harbour seen from the visiting heavy cruiser USS *New Orleans* in May 1934. *(NHHC/NH 71789)*

4 Frank C. Bowen, with comments by Stig H:son Ericson, 'Det planerade tyska slagskeppet och dess inverkan på svensk flottbyggnadspolitik' [The Planned German Battleship and its Impact on Swedish Naval Construction Policy] in *Tidskrift i sjöväsendet* 91 (1928), pp. 618–21.

could have only one outcome. In the event, the Deutschland class, the nameship of which was completed in 1933, were armed with six 11in guns and had a speed of 26 knots, though Bowen's general conclusions held up.

Not only had *Sverige* and her sisters lost their status as the most powerful vessels in the Baltic, but financial considerations made it impossible for Sweden to reply, since the new German ships cost the equivalent of 75 million kronor each – more than five times that of *Sverige* and well beyond the capabilities of the Swedish defence budget. The only consolation was that the tactical concept underpinning the old armoured ships had not lost its relevance, with any German offensive against Sweden requiring the involvement of at least one of these valuable new ships. The question was whether it could be spared. Until that moment the Swedish navy had to content itself with successive refits of the Sverige class, which in *Sverige*'s case took place from 1931–3 and 1938–40.

Sverige underway in late 1940 or early 1941 showing one of the 1.57in (40mm) M/36 anti-aircraft mountings fitted in place of the no. '2' 6in (152mm) M/12 turrets during the 1938–40 refit. *(Krigsarkivet)*

The Swedish Navy and the Second World War

Like all of Europe's smaller nations, Sweden declared neutrality on the outbreak of the Second World War while frantic measures continued to improve her defences. Although the armed forces soon numbered nearly a million men, acquiring new and modern equipment for the navy and the air force took longer, and many measures were not in place until the end of the war. The main body of the wartime Swedish navy was organised as a striking force known as the *Kustflottan* (Coast Fleet), which in July 1944 consisted of the three armoured ships, three cruisers, eight destroyers, nine submarines, six torpedo boats and sixteen other vessels. A smaller unit operated along the northern coastline and there were local defence squadrons at Stockholm, Karlskrona, Malmö and Gothenburg, each led by one of the older armoured ships supported by destroyers, submarines and smaller vessels. This organisation was completed by two training units. The peacetime Swedish navy had fleet bases at Stockholm, Karlskrona and Gothenburg, but these were easily blockaded so the Coast Fleet operated mainly from improvised anchorages which not only offered ready access to the most likely areas of operations but were difficult to obstruct. The main base was at Hårsfjärden in an archipelago south of Stockholm, with another at Saxarfjärden north of Stockholm, and a third at Orrfjärden in the archipelago lying off the city of Norrköping in eastern Sweden.

If wartime service was frequently tedious for the navy crews, those serving in destroyers and

other smaller units often found themselves overworked with patrol and convoy escort duty while larger units lay quietly at anchor. However, there were moments of high tension. On 30 November 1939 the Soviet Union attacked Finland, the start of a conflict in which Sweden declared nonbelligerency instead of neutrality, a status which allowed her to support the Finns in various ways. As in the Great War, the focus fell on Åland and on 5 December an operation covered by the Sverige class saw the requisitioned ferry *Drottning Victoria* (now christened *Hjälpkryssare 3* – 'Auxiliary Cruiser 3') lay a minefield off Sweden up to Finnish territorial waters. Together with Finnish mining operations, this would effectively bar the northern part of the Baltic to Soviet submarines.

Sweden and the Norwegian Campaign, 1940

The next moment of crisis came with the German attack on Norway and Denmark codenamed Weserübung on 9 April 1940. The events can be followed in the war diary of Rear Admiral Gösta Ehrensvärd, commander of the Coast Fleet from 1939–42, which records his analysis of the general situation. One such entry was written on the night of 8–9 April as it became obvious that German operations were afoot, with reports reaching Ehrensvärd of a convoy sailing north in the Kattegat. Ehrensvärd contemplated three purposes of this convoy: (1) a ruse to draw the British and French fleets into the Skagerrak where they would be attacked, which he considered less likely; (2) an attack on the Swedish west

coast, also considered less likely; and (3) a landing in Norway off which British and French forces were about to lay mines to interdict the passage of iron ore from Narvik to Germany via the Norwegian Indreled (Inner Leads); this third possibility Ehrensvärd considered most likely.

Taking a broader strategic view, Ehrensvärd envisioned a scenario in which Allied and German troops would first clash in northern Norway before the war moved into northern Sweden. Believing that the British would sever German seaborne traffic, he anticipated the latter using Swedish territory for overland access to Norway. Ehrensvärd stated that the Swedish government would not permit any such action, with the implication that war would follow if Germany pressed the matter. He predicted that hostilities would begin with an invasion over The Sound, the narrow stretch of water separating Denmark and Sweden. As Ehrensvärd commented laconically, 'The Coast Fleet cannot help', meaning of course that the Sverige class ships were incapable of contesting command of the sea in the face of enemy air superiority and heavy units of the German navy. He then turned to the Baltic, concluding that the Germans might try to capture Åland in order to open the sea lanes to the north of Sweden, facilitating troop transports by sea to the new front. Here he mused 'The Coast Fleet should stop this. Can we?' Answering his own question, Ehrensvärd pointed out that this depended on the attrition suffered by the Germans in the North Sea. Like his Finnish counterparts, Ehrensvärd therefore viewed Åland as the linchpin of the defence of Sweden since the Germans could block the passage of Allied reinforcements between Norway and northern Sweden if they controlled the waters north of the archipelago. Ehrensvärd's conclusions on the night of 8–9 April were that the Coast Fleet should concentrate its forces to defend Åland and if possible limit the war to southern Sweden. Failing that, the fleet would move to the Orrfjärden archipelago off Norrköping to interdict communications between Germany and northern Sweden. A battle along the lines envisaged by Ehrensvärd might have caused severe attrition to an already overstretched Kriegsmarine, requiring it to divert capital ships it did not have. Though never realised, this scenario provides clear vindication of the Swedish naval strategists at the turn of the century.

As Ehrensvärd suspected, the German movements were directed against Denmark and Norway, with successful landings being made at the Norwegian ports of Kristiansund, Egersund, Bergen, Trondheim and Narvik in the early hours of 9 April. Denmark capitulated immediately and after initial resistance Oslo fell later that day. The evening of the 10th found Ehrensvärd reassessing the situation in the light of these shattering developments. Hearing reports in a radio broadcast of a naval engagement in the Skagerrak (a successful torpedo attack on the 'pocket battleship' *Lützow* by the submarine HMS *Spearfish*) and the sinking of two German steamers, Ehrensvärd formed the impression that the Allies were closing the Indreled and that a German invasion of Sweden was now imminent. Night anti-aircraft stations were ordered and by 11 April Ehrensvärd had no doubt that war was coming to Scandinavia as a whole. Believing that the Kriegsmarine was losing command of the sea off Norway, he presciently concluded that the

Germans would soon need the railroad on the west coast of Sweden to supply their army. Ehrensvärd also concluded that German naval losses had increased the importance of the Swedish fleet and he called for immediate reinforcement of anti-aircraft batteries at naval anchorages. He also assumed that the Allies would land troops in Narvik, as indeed occurred, and that a proportion of these would be directed via rail to northern Sweden to participate in the final battle for Scandinavia. In the event, the collapse of Allied resistance in May and June spared the Sverige class the ultimate test.

Sverige in a War of Neutrality, 1940–5

The German attack on Denmark and Norway on 9 April 1940 found *Sverige* in the final stages of reconstruction at Stockholm and she was sorely missed, Rear Admiral Ehrensvärd calling on 11 April for work on her to be completed 'using all available means'. *Sverige* began working up four days later, a process not completed until 10 May when she sailed from Stockholm for the fleet anchorage at Hårsfjärden. Thereafter *Sverige* settled into a routine which lasted for the rest of the war, her time spent mainly at Hårsfjärden but punctuated by shorter cruises lasting between one and nine days with refitting in Stockholm in winter or spring. To begin with, two weeks between late June to early July 1940 were spent refitting at Stockholm followed by a further spell in October and November. At year's end *Sverige* made a cruise to Karlskrona, spending New Year's Eve there and returning to Hårsfjärden on 9 January 1941 where she spent much of that winter. Late April saw her refitting at Stockholm, including replacement of a propeller damaged by

A bow-on view of Sverige while coming to or weighing anchor. The photo can be dated to 1945 by the wartime recognition stripes on the hull and the new radar fit on the control tower. Note the paravane chains, the degaussing coil running at forecastle deck level with an adjustment over the top of the three crowns device, and also the camouflage in which the ships of the Coast Fleet were painted from July 1943. (*Krigsarkivet*)

ice in January. She then made a short cruise to Saxarfjärden in May before the routine was resumed, spending most of her time at anchor in Hårsfjärden interspersed by a few brief cruises punctuated by gunnery exercises. Most of October and early November 1941 were spent refitting at Stockholm. *Sverige* spent New Year's Eve at Hårsfjärden before docking for repairs at Stockholm on 19 January 1942 after a collision with the submarine *Svärdfisken* off Gotland. No lives were lost and the submarine survived but *Sverige* suffered a punctured hull as *Svärdfisken* slid along her port side.

As *Sverige* was completing her latest refit in mid-March 1942 a new crisis erupted over ten Norwegian merchantmen which had been interned at Gothenburg since 9 April 1940. By January 1942 the matter had become urgent.

Sverige in wartime, her anti-aircraft armament pointing skyward from whence the greatest threat was reckoned to come. The Swedish navy began painting white recognition bands on the hulls of its ships following the German attack on Russia in June 1941. (*Krigsarkivet*)

A wartime view of the Coast Fleet making heavy smoke while proceeding in line ahead in the Baltic. As much as any of Sweden's defences, her armoured ships were essential to preserving her territorial integrity during the Second World War. (*Krigsarkivet*)

Sverige beset at Hårsfjärden in March 1941 where she spent longer during the Second World War than anywhere else – a total of 900 days between May 1940 and April 1945. Note the twin 1.57in (40mm) M/36 mounting installed right aft on the quarterdeck in 1940 and the intricate coat of arms of the Kingdom of Sweden applied to the stern. The swallowtail with tongue ensign was adopted by the Swedish navy in the mid-seventeenth century. (*Krigsarkivet*)

With both Germany and the Allies claiming the ships, Sweden found herself in an awkward position and the armed forces were placed on high alert as it was feared a German attack was imminent. Since several units of the Swedish navy were beset by ice, it was calculated that an attack might begin with an airborne assault on these assets. The navy responded by painting the ships white to hinder detection and barrage balloons were provided for the Coast Fleet in early March. Work on *Sverige* was hurriedly completed and on 23 March she left Stockholm for the icy anchorage of Hårsfjärden, though, as during the Norwegian Campaign, the crisis had blown over by the time she became fully operational. *Sverige* settled into her familiar harbour routine with shorter cruises once or twice a month, the longest of which was a six-day sortie to Sundsvall in northern Sweden. The first two months of 1943 were taken up with docking and repairs in Stockholm but by the end of February she was back in her Hårsfjärden routine, the start of a year of intensive training with the fleet.

On 2–3 November 1943 the navy carried out an ambitious amphibious exercise in collaboration with the army and the air force followed by manoeuvres by the Coast Fleet on 6–8 December, *Sverige* being involved in both operations. The ship then spent Christmas and New Year's Eve 1943 docked in Stockholm. On 3 May 1944 *Sverige* for the first time tied up at one of the moorages built along cliff faces not far from Hårsfjärden. Designed for fast and safe mooring of ships, these wartime moorages also offered improved protection from air attack, a concern which kept the crew busy adding and removing camouflage. A note in the ship's log from 6 July

1944 reports that it took fifty-five minutes to remove the camouflage that day, an indication that this was an evolution in which the crew was well versed. On 29 September 1944 *Sverige* was decommissioned and underwent a major refit in Karlskrona where she remained until 9 April 1945, returning to Hårsfjärden on the 21st. Two weeks later Germany surrendered.

A survey of *Sverige*'s service during the Second World War from the time she emerged from her refit in May 1940 would find that she spent 900 days at anchor in Hårsfjärden, 300 days at sea, a little over 100 days at other anchorages and 500 days in dockyard hands or decommissioned. The most obvious reason for the limited sea time was lack of oil. While the installation of oil-fired boilers in 1938–40 had many advantages, a major disadvantage was that pre-war Sweden relied on overseas imports for practically all her oil needs and relatively few tankers reached Swedish ports after the outbreak of hostilities. This left the navy with an average oil allowance per vessel sufficient for just seven hours' cruising per week, which in turn raised the question as to whether oil stocks should be expended on manoeuvres or preserved

for the day when they might be needed in earnest. The answer was that *Sverige* spent much of her time tied up at Hårsfjärden.

Legacy

The Second World War marked the twilight of the big-gun vessel as the principal means of waging war at sea. Though the Sverige class vessels were at the end of their service lives, none

were immediately stricken and *Sverige* herself remained on the navy list until 1953, though the last crewman left the ship on 12 August 1947. Suggestions that one of the class be preserved as a museum came to nothing, and five years later *Sverige* met her fate largely unnoticed in a scrapyard in western Sweden. *Gustaf V* and *Drottning Victoria* followed in 1959 and 1970, respectively. Some of the ordnance did however survive, with several 6in guns notionally

---

SWEDEN AND THE SOVIET-GERMAN CONFLICT, 1941–5

Perhaps the greatest crisis facing Sweden during the Second World War began on 22 June 1941 with the launch of Operation Barbarossa, the German attack on the Soviet Union. Disruptive enough in itself, matters were complicated by the fact that Sweden again found herself obliged to facilitate German operations, this time with the transit of a German division from Norway to Finland. This breach of her neutrality can be attributed not only to German pressure but to the fact that Germany was Sweden's only source of coal, her most vital commodity, which had to be paid for mainly through iron ore exports to the Third Reich. Her foreign trade already choked off by the war, Sweden could not subsist without German coal, a situation which resulted in the implementation of a convoy system to protect Swedish shipping en route to Germany from Soviet submarine attacks, part of a wider expansion of naval activity which included the laying of a minefield off Öland on 28 June. Already on 5 July a strike force consisting of an armoured ship, destroyers and submarines had been readied at Orrfjärden against any eventuality, *Sverige* taking her turn between 12 and 20 July.

The transit of German *matériel* and troops on leave from Norway continued, but once the war had turned against Germany the Swedish government felt able to respond to Allied and domestic pressure and put a stop to this traffic, a decision it announced in June 1943. The Germans were naturally angered by this decision, and as earlier the Swedish government called up a large proportion of the army and placed the navy on high alert against the possibility of retaliation. *Sverige* now made one of her longest wartime cruises, spending two weeks in July between Hårsfjärden, Orrfjärden and Saxarfjärden before returning to her anchorage and settling back into her routine.

The following year brought new complications as Germany's position on the Eastern Front began to collapse in the face of the Soviet onslaught. The Finns had joined Operation Barbarossa in June 1941,

but by late 1943 military developments were prompting the Swedish government to contemplate the possibility of an armistice between Finland and the Soviet Union. Unsure how Germany might react in the circumstances, orders were passed for the fleet to be ready by early spring, *Sverige* spending January 1944 docked and fitting out before putting to sea on 1 February. Much of that month and March were spent in ordinary routine, but then came a period of uncommonly high activity. On 31 March a German troop convoy sighted between Öland and Gotland brought the navy to high alert the following day. *Sverige* sailed and spent much of April at sea and at various anchorages near Hårsfjärden. The long-awaited Soviet attack on Finland began on 9 June 1944, *Sverige* spending part of July at sea including a visit to the northern port of Härnösand before moving to the eastern anchorage of Orrfjärden in the latter part of August. By the time Finland and Russia signed their armistice on 19 September 1944 any possibility of German intervention had vanished (see *Väinämöinen*).

In early April 1944 the Swedish biweekly *Folk och Försvar* ('People and Defence') published an article on the military situation in the Baltic.[5] The anonymous author considered a situation in which the Red Army, then advancing westwards, had occupied Estonia and Latvia. The Soviet fleet had hitherto been blockaded in Leningrad but the conquest of the southern shores of the Gulf of Finland would no doubt give it access to the open sea. German naval supremacy in the Baltic would then be challenged. The article began with assessments of current German and Russian naval strength. The Germans were reckoned to have two 'pocket battleships' (*Lützow* and *Admiral Scheer*) and two heavy cruisers (*Admiral Hipper* and *Prinz Eugen*) operational in the Baltic, while the battlecruiser *Gneisenau* was out of service. Where the Soviet navy was concerned, there were two elderly battleships of the Gangut class (*Oktyabrskaya Revolutsiya* and *Petropavlovsk*) at Leningrad, though neither was believed to be in

operational condition, while the largest active units were supposedly the cruisers *Kirov* and *Maxim Gorky*. The author remarked that Sweden needed to follow developments with 'great vigilance', and keep navy and air force assets ready to protect Swedish interests in the Baltic, although what these interests were or how they could be protected was not specified.

As it was, the Swedish army had been preparing for military intervention in Norway, Finland and Denmark since at least December 1942, though only the latter involved naval assets. The overriding aims were to forestall a Soviet occupation of Denmark and to counter a last stand by the Third Reich in Norway in the event of Germany being overrun. A secondary consideration was for Sweden to have a say in any post-war settlement. Where Denmark was concerned, this resulted in detailed plans for an amphibious landing at Helsingør (Elsinore) using no less than 1,258 transports covered by around 100 warships – the bulk of the Swedish navy. The armoured ships *Oscar II*, *Tapperheten* and *Äran* were to provide close cover, supported by a destroyer division and a torpedo boat flotilla, with distant cover provided by the Armoured Ship Division (including *Sverige*), the 9th Destroyer Division and the Gothenburg Squadron. Final plans for the attack were submitted on 4 April 1945 and the covering units began mustering at Hårsfjärden for exercises on the 10th.

As military preparations continued, on 27 April 1945 the Swedish Prime Minister Per Albin Hansson announced to a closed session of the Riksdag that 'Changed circumstances could bring new options for Sweden.' However, on 5 May news reached Stockholm that Germany had surrendered unconditionally. There were to be no final battles for Denmark or Norway, nor will we ever know what consequences these might have brought in their train for *Sverige* and her sisters.

---

[5] 'Sck', 'Den militära situationen i Östersjön' in *Folk och Försvar* (April 1944).

remaining in service as fixed gunnery installations in northern Sweden until 1997, and two of the 11in guns having been preserved at Karlskrona in southern Sweden.

By the time she was put into reserve *Sverige* had spent 11,072 days in service between May 1917 and August 1947, including 7,326 days in commission. However, her engines had operated on only 561 days, meaning that no more than 8 per cent of her commissioned service included days at sea – approximately twenty-nine days a year or two and a half days per month. While these statistics say much of shipboard life, they also tell their own story of a warship which had never to face the ultimate test, one no less successful or effective in her designated role for that.

Sverige and her sisters occupy a special place for those Swedes with even a passing interest in their country's naval history. Aside from their unique status of having been funded by public subscription, they were the only modern seagoing capital ships ever built in Sweden. Moreover, they and their 11in broadsides conjure the mystique of 'the old days' for the contemporary Swedish navy with its flotillas of light craft, part of the collective memory of the nation's naval past. With them, too, the Swedish navy definitively left its coastal and archipelagic waters for the Baltic where the clear objective in time of war was to engage the enemy. Although the means have changed, this offensive spirit has infused the Swedish navy ever since, from its light cruisers, destroyers and attack craft to the Visby-class stealth corvettes of today, and also in tactics, training and unit names, including the surface attack flotillas and squadrons of the modern Svenska marinen. The Sverige class can in this respect be taken as an example of how tools shape the mind.

That aside, no one with an interest in Swedish history during the first half of the twentieth century, and especially that of the Second World War, could fail to be aware of the wider significance of the class. Though neither tested in battle nor even the largest ships in the Swedish navy (that distinction is held by the light cruisers *Tre Kronor* and *Göta Lejon* of 7,650 tons standard displacement), the Sverige class was nonetheless a potent diplomatic statement, a declaration that Sweden was ready and able to defend herself *à l'outrance* if necessary. That this conviction was imparted to the men of the Swedish navy is evident in the memoirs of Ensign John Rumenius who, harking back to 1940, recalled 'a sense of

security as I stood on this wide quarterdeck.'[6] As the Sverige class became obsolete that mantle of armed security was gradually assumed by the powerful Swedish air force. However, the smokestacks of the Sverige class in some sense foreshadowed the vapour trails left in the sky by the Draken, Viggen and Gripen supersonic attack aircraft of the second half of the twentieth century, since it was through them that Swedish defence expenditure contributed to stabilising the geopolitical situation on the northern fringes of Europe.

Sources

Unpublished Sources

Krigsarkivet (The Military Archives), Stockholm
Marinberedningens förslag till sjöförsvarets ordnande (Proposal for the Organisation of Maritime Defence from the Navy Study Group), H, CKA, H, E VI:16 b

Beredskapsverket (Sweden during the Second World War), vol. 11, Diverse handlingar (Assorted documents), File M I & M II

Karlskrona örlogsvarv (Karlskrona Naval Shipyard)

ÖVK Varvschefens Militärexpedition (The Military Office of the Shipyard Commandant), vol. 117, Observationsjournaler (Observations Journals), Sv E II

Svenska örlogsfartyg, Fartyg och Fartygsförband Karlskrona (Swedish Naval Vessels, Karlskrona Ships and Naval Units)

Pansarskeppet Sverige: R 1917–1937 Räkenskaper marinen (Accounting)

Sverige Pansarskepp:
Däcksloggböcker (Ship's Logs), 1940–1, 1942–3, 1943, 1943–4, 1945, Sign DI, vol. 18–23

Inventarium Artilleriuppbörden (Gunnery Inventory), Sv D III, vol. 5

Sjöhistoriska muséet i Stockholm (Archive of the Maritime Museum, Stockholm)
H.M.S. *Sveriges* Krönika [The Chronicle of H.M.S. *Sverige*] (written by members of the Wardroom), 1968:372

Bibliography
Åhlund, Bertil, *Historia kring Flottans kanoner*, Marinlitteraturföreningen, nr 84 (Stockholm: Marinlitteraturföreningens förlag, 1998)

Berge, Anders, *Sakkunskap och politisk ratio-nalitet: Den svenska flottan och pansarfartygs-frågan, 1918–1939* (Stockholm: University of Stockholm, 1987)

Borgenstam, Curt, Per Insulander & Bertil Åhnlund, *Kryssare: Med svenska flottans kryssare under 75 år* (Falkenberg: C. B. Marinlitteratur, 1993)

Bowen, Frank C., with comments by Admiral Stig H:son Ericson, 'Det planerade tyska slagskeppet och dess inverkan på svensk flottbyggnadspolitik' in *Tidskrift i sjöväsendet* 91 (1928), pp. 618–21

Campbell, John, *Naval Weapons of World War Two* (London: Conway, 1985)

Forssbeck, Bengt, *Från* Ingegerd *till* Visby: *Svenska örlogsfartyg under 140 år, 1860–2000* (Karlskrona: Abrahamson, 2000)

Glete, Jan, *Kustförsvar och teknisk omvandling* (Stockholm: Militärhistoriska förlaget, 1985)

Harris, Daniel G., 'The Sverige-Class Coastal Defence Ships' in Robert Gardiner, ed., *Warship 1992* (London: Conway, 1992), pp. 80–98

Hofsten, Gustaf von, & Jan Waernberg, *Örlogsfartyg: Svenska maskindrivna fartyg under tretungad flagg* (Stockholm/ Falkenberg: Svenskt Militärhistoriskt Bibliotek, 2003)

Insulander, Per, & Curt S. Ohlsson, *Pansarskepp: Från* John Ericsson *till* Gustaf V (Falkenberg: C. B. Marinlitteratur, 2001)

Lagvall, Bertil, *Flottans neutralitetsvakt, 1939–1945: Krönika av kommendörkapten Bertil Lagvall*, Marinlitteraturföreningen, nr 71 (Karlskrona: Marinlitteraturföreningens förlag, 1993)

Lybeck, Otto, ed., *Svenska flottans historia: Örlogsflottan i ord och bild från dess grundläggning under Gustaf Vasa fram till våra dagar* (6 vols. in 3 tomes, Malmö: Allhems Förlag, 1942–3)

Rumenius, John, *Klart skepp för minfällning: En reservfänrik berättar från beredskapsåren, 1939–40* (Stockholm: Lindfors, 1976)

'Sck', 'Den militära situationen i Östersjön' in *Folk och Försvar* (April 1944)

Steckzén, Birger, ed., *Klart skepp: En bok om Sverigeskeppen*: Sverige, Gustaf V, Drottning Victoria (Stockholm: P. A. Norstedt & Söners Förlag, 1949)

Unger, Gunnar, 'Centralförsvar' in *Nordisk Familjebok: Konversationslexikon Och Realencyklopedi*, vol. 4 (Stockholm: Foerlags Aktiebolag, 1905)

---

[6] *Ibid.*, p. 88.

◆

Royal Navy

The Battlecruiser *Hood* (1918)

Bruce Taylor

FROM THE PERSPECTIVE of the early twenty-first century, the battlecruiser HMS *Hood* stands as the most famous British warship since Nelson's *Victory*. If this seems a bold statement to make of a vessel which gained a single battle honour in the engagement that destroyed her, it alerts us nonetheless to the complexity and range to which a warship's life and legacy may lend themselves with the passage of time. No assessment of HMS *Hood* can fail to contend with this reality, a ship whose fame was as tangible during her lifetime as her loss has retained its symbolic power in the seventy-five years since her destruction.

A Failed Transition

The origins of HM battlecruiser *Hood* can be traced to October 1915 with a request from the Admiralty for designs for a battleship based on the successful Queen Elizabeth class but incorporating the latest advances in seakeeping and underwater protection. Central to the Admiralty's brief was a proportionately higher freeboard and shallower draught than previous construction, features which would not only permit more effective operation under wartime loads but lessen the threat posed by underwater damage. By January 1916 a team led by the Director of Naval Construction Sir Eustace

Tennyson d'Eyncourt had evolved five designs, the most promising of which had a greatly enlarged hull and beam in order to achieve the necessary reduction in draught. However, developments in Germany now took a hand and these studies were rejected by Admiral Sir John Jellicoe, Commander-in-Chief of the Grand Fleet, in light of the large Mackensen-class battlecruisers reported to be under construction for the High Seas Fleet. This at length resulted in a further pair of designs in March of which one was approved by the Admiralty Board on 7 April 1916.

The selected design promised a speed of 32 knots through the use of the new lighter small-tube boilers on a standard displacement of 36,300 tons, over 5,000 more than any other ship in the Royal Navy. An immense hull measuring 860ft (262.1m) – fully 200ft (60m) longer than most capital ships of the day – meant that there would only be three graving docks in Britain capable of accepting her bulk. There were to be eight 15in (381mm) guns in a modified turret design permitting elevation to 30 degrees together with sixteen of the new 5.5in (140mm) mountings and four 4in (102mm) anti-aircraft guns. This armament was to be rounded off by ten 21in (533mm) torpedo tubes, eight above water and two submerged. An 8in (203mm) main belt was reckoned to offer better protection than the 10in (254mm) of the Queen Elizabeth class thanks to the introduction of a sophisticated arrangement of sloped armour. On the other hand, horizontal protection showed no improvement on earlier designs, being restricted to a maximum of 2.5in (63.5mm), and that only

Speed and power. *Hood* in full cry, guns and rangefinders trained to port during a full-power trial in home waters in June 1927. As the visible symbol of a nation's power HMS *Hood* can scarcely have been matched. (*Courtesy Craig Twaddle*)

on the lower deck; elsewhere it was no better than 1.5in (38mm). On 17 April 1916 orders for three (subsequently four) of these vessels were placed by the Admiralty, one, eventually called *Hood*, at John Brown & Co. of Clydebank, Scotland. Then came Jutland.

On 31 May 1916 an action was fought in the North Sea which was to have far-reaching consequences for the Royal Navy. Of these only one need concern us here: the fate of the British battlecruisers. By the time the British turned for home on 1 June three of the nine battlecruisers engaged had been sent to the bottom with all but a handful of survivors, while a fourth, HMS *Lion*, came within an ace of sharing the same fate. It is clear that inadequate measures against flash and poor cordite handling contributed to these disasters, but the stark reality was that the British battlecruiser proved unequal to the demands presented by sustained long-range combat with ships of similar armament. This situation immediately presented *Hood*'s designers with a number of severe challenges. Proposals for increased protection were tabled in June and Tennyson d'Eyncourt submitted a revised design which was eventually accepted in early August. The armament was unchanged from the March legend but belt armour was increased to a maximum of 12in (305mm) and barbettes from 9 to 12in (229–305mm). The angled 12in belt now provided the equivalent of 14 or 15in (356 or 381mm) of vertical armour while a 460ft (140.2m) long bulge offered torpedo protection the equal of any vessel prior to the Second World War. However, horizontal protection saw relatively little improvement and was still no better than 2.5in despite the addition of 3,100 tons to the displacement. This might just have sufficed had the *Hood*'s magazines not been placed over her shell rooms as was the norm in British construction. As it was, this was regarded as inadequate by both Jellicoe and the battlecruiser commander Vice Admiral Sir David Beatty and improvements quickly made both to turret and deck armour which had reached a maximum of 3in (76mm) over the magazines by the time the final design legend was approved in August 1917. The governing criterion was that at least 9in (229mm) of armour would have to be penetrated in order for a shell to reach the magazines, but numerous thin decks offered considerably less protection than one thick one. Put simply, the *Hood* did not have an armoured deck and in this lay the fatal weakness of her design, however superior her arrangements to previous construction. Though occasionally classified as a fast battleship, by later standards HMS *Hood* failed to make the transition from a battlecruiser and ultimately proved incapable of meeting the

requirement that might sooner or later be made of any capital ship: the ability to withstand punishment from vessels armed to the same standard as herself.

Building a Giant

Hood's keel was laid at John Brown's shipyard on 1 September 1916, but construction was slowed by her repeated design alterations, the pressing need for merchant shipping and a shortage of manpower. It was not until 22 August 1918 that Lady Hood, widow of Rear Admiral the Honourable Sir Horace Hood, lost with the battlecruiser *Invincible* at Jutland, shattered a bottle over the bows and the hull slipped stern-first into the Clyde. Even then she retained a remarkably low profile as requests continued for improved protection in the light of test firings and battle experience. These resulted in May and June of 1919 in the removal of four of the sixteen 5.5in guns and then four of the eight above-water torpedo tubes, the last major changes to a design whose construction was by now far advanced. Already in September 1918 the first barbette sections of face-hardened steel had been lowered into place in the fitting-out basin, part of an armour scheme that eventually required 14,000 tons of plate, and by the end of January 1919, five months after launching, the final work was being done to the hull. On 27 February the second funnel was reported as up and the 600-ton conning tower under construction. A month later the armour belt was being fitted and the bridge structure taking shape. The *Hood*'s Brown-Curtis geared turbines, the first such to be fitted in a capital ship, were all *in situ* by May Day and the end of that month saw the mainmast erected and the ship largely decked over. On 29 July the first 15in turret reached Clydebank by sea from the manufacturers, Vickers, Barrow, the ship being hauled out into the river for it to be swung into place by the 200-ton fitting-out crane. Delivery and installation of the turrets went on until the beginning of December. Work proceeded apace with perhaps a thousand men aboard and by the end of October the joiners and electricians were fitting out the living quarters. By November rigging was in progress and on 9 and 10 December basin trials of the engines took place in preparation for her departure for builder's trials in the new year. The work was all but done.

On 9 January 1920 the *Hood* left John Brown's under her own power, the decision having been made to finish the work at HM Dockyard Rosyth in order to clear the fitting-out basin for the urgent completion of merchant contracts. The voyage round Scotland was to

give the crew an early taste of the *Hood*'s seakeeping qualities as a Force 8 gale buried her forecastle and quarterdeck and vibration made life in the spotting top unbearable at speed. Before she departed an experiment revealed her displacement as 46,680 tons at deep load and 42,670 tons at full load – 1,470 tons above the final 1917 legend and no less than 17.5 per cent above the original 1916 design, with most of the increment taken up by armour. The final cost to the British government of its greatest ship was £6,025,000, almost twice that of any previous ship, though wartime inflation and the sheer size of the vessel must be taken into consideration. Needless to say, the concept and above all the expenditure drew criticism from several quarters. Writing in *The Naval Review*, an anonymous officer argued that the *Hood*, whose specifications otherwise compared with the Queen Elizabeth-class battleships, had required an additional £2,030,000 to obtain her 7-knot margin of speed. But there were other concerns, too. Rear Admiral Sir Ernle Chatfield, captain of HMS *Lion* at Jutland, wasn't joking when he quipped at a meeting of the Institution of Naval Architects in March 1920 that 'if the Director of Naval Construction was going to design a ship to-day he would not design the *Hood*'.[1] Certainly, the G3 battlecruisers projected that same year bore little resemblance to her in either appearance, armament or protection. In the memoirs he published in 1948 Tennyson d'Eyncourt, present on that occasion, made plain his own views on the matter:

> The *Hood* had a great deal added to her in the way of protection, but there was more to be done, and [...] the Second World War proved her armour to be still inadequate. [...] It was a terrible tragedy that the *Hood*'s improved protection was not fully carried out between the wars.[2]

But this was over twenty years into the future. For now *Hood* represented the culmination of a stream of British warship design which had begun with *Invincible* and made her the largest capital ship in the world. The cancellation of her three sisters in February 1919 and the limitations on warship construction enshrined in the Washington Treaty of 1922 saw to it that she would hold this status in splendid isolation while peace lasted. That peace was now hers to enjoy.

[1] *The Naval and Military Record*, 31 March 1920.
[2] Eustace H. W. Tennyson d'Eyncourt, *A Shipbuilder's Yarn* (London: Hutchinson, 1948), p. 96.

In a Class of Her Own

The name *Hood* first appears in a communication from the Admiralty to John Brown's on 14 July 1916. Intended as the lead vessel of a class of four, she owed her name to a vicar's son of Thorncombe in Dorsetshire, Samuel Hood (1724–1816). In a career spanning fifty-five years Hood acquired a reputation as a master tactician, making his name against the French at St Kitts, Dominica, Toulon and Corsica before being granted the title of Viscount Hood of Whitley in 1796. Moreover, he was only the first in a line of distinguished sailors from the same family, including his great-great grandson Rear Admiral Horace Hood who perished at Jutland. However, it was the first Viscount whose device and motto Britain's last battlecruiser bore. The badge was of an anchor supported by a Cornish chough, the

The *Hood*'s main deck nearing completion in the autumn of 1917. On the right is the round-down of mostly 2in plating (1in deck plating in double thickness) which constituted an important element in her horizontal protection. Beside it an arrangement of brackets can be seen supporting the rest of the main deck further aft. *(Crown Copyright/National Records of Scotland (NRS))*

rare coastal bird of the crow family, and her motto was *Ventis secundis*: 'With favouring winds'.

Hood was the fourth ship to carry the name, the first being a 14-gun vessel named *Lord Hood* commissioned in 1797, followed in 1860 when the 80-gun *Edgar* was renamed on conversion to screw propulsion. Rendered obsolete by *Warrior* and her successors, the second *Hood* spent a

dismal career first in the reserve and then as a floating barracks at Chatham before being sold out of the Navy in 1888. The next *Hood*, however, was a first-rate unit launched in 1891, though the insistence of another descendant, the First Sea Lord Admiral Sir Arthur Hood, that she carry closed turrets rather than open barbettes greatly reduced her effectiveness in anything other than a flat calm. In 1914 she was expended

Hood in the final stages of fitting out on 2 December 1919. The 15in guns of 'A' and 'B' turrets have been installed but the plating has yet to be completed. The hood is missing from the armoured director and the aloft director remains to be installed. (Crown Copyright/NRS)

One of the first shots of *Hood* in open water, seen off Rosyth on 13 January 1920 and with the aloft rangefinder yet to be fitted to the spotting top. She is riding high in the water, close to her 1916 design legend but showing greater freeboard than would ever be the case again. *(Bruce Taylor Collection)*

a way almost anyone could appreciate. A dozen ships had been fitted with the 15in gun but none ever managed to convey the same synthesis of speed and power within such an immense frame. *Hood*, it turned out, succeeded in marrying the rakishness of a destroyer, the sleekness of a cruiser and the simmering menace of the greatest men-of-war. Appropriately, where others earned nicknames that were by turns jovial, affectionate or even derogatory, there was nothing effacing about 'The Mighty *Hood*', the sobriquet which soon attached to her. For a nation still bitterly disappointed that the Navy had failed to deliver the crushing victory that had so fervently been expected, here was tangible proof that the sinew of Britain's seaborne empire had emerged strong and vigorous from the test of war: 'God that made thee mighty, make thee mightier yet...'. This sense of *Hood* as embodying the survival and perpetuation of the empire was one she immediately acquired and surrendered only in death. The notion is nowhere better or more romantically expressed than in V. C. Scott O'Connor's account of the world cruise of 1923–4:

as a blockship at the entrance to Portland Harbour as a measure against German submarine attack. If the name *Hood* had a ring to it this therefore owed more to famous men than to famous ships. But all that was to change.

Above all else, HMS *Hood* impressed for her appearance. Though her pedigree extended

hardly more than ten years she was by no means the first British dreadnought to excite admiration for the purity of her lines, but the *Hood* was immediately in a different category. More than any British warship before or since, *Hood* captured the power and innovation of her design in a symmetry of grace and beauty, and did so in

> In her mass and speed and perfection of armament, the *Hood* symbolizes the valorous determination of war-weary Britain to maintain intact for the good of mankind the far-flung Empire she has built up through the centuries. It is this symbolism that lifts Hood out of the machine, and irradiates the great grey hulk with a halo of splendour.[3]

Whatever the heady patriotism of the age or the flaws inherent in her design, there is little doubt that Sir Eustace Tennyson d'Eyncourt's last work was a masterpiece of theatre and aesthetic refinement. Beginning with the projected *Incomparable* and continuing through the Renown and Courageous classes and on to *Hood*, Tennyson d'Eyncourt's battlecruiser

'The monstrous anger of the guns.' 'X' and 'Y' 15in turrets engaging in a concentration exercise as part of King George V's Silver Jubilee celebrations on 17 July 1935. Astern is battlecruiser *Renown* and the carrier *Courageous*. *(Bruce Taylor Collection)*

3 V. C. Scott O'Connor, *The Empire Cruise* (London: Riddle, Smith & Duffus, 1925), pp. 258–9.

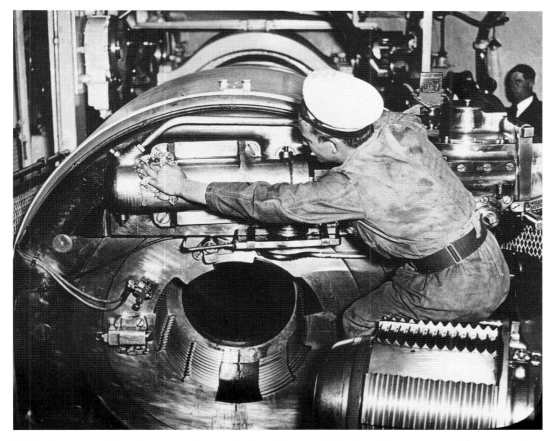

Polishing the breech of the right-hand gun in one of the four 15in turrets. This is the only known photo of the interior of one of *Hood*'s turrets. The Mk-II mounting fitted only in *Hood* represents a high point of British turret design. *(Bruce Taylor Collection)*

A tompion decorating the muzzle of one of the forward 15in guns bearing the ship's chough emblem derived from the crest of Admiral Viscount Hood. Resting on the barrel is a bird of a different feather, the Silver Coquerelle trophy awarded to the winner of the Atlantic Fleet pulling (i.e. rowing) regatta, in this case to *Hood* in 1926, which thereby became 'Cock of the Fleet'. *(Bruce Taylor Collection)*

designs were all characterised by huge forecastles and long quarterdecks with a gentle sheer towards each extremity. Together with her immense size and speed, these features allowed *Hood* to carve her way with majestic ease in heavy weather. But, for O'Connor at least, her power and beauty were never more apparent than when cruising wraith-like through a gentle night in the tropics:

> *Hood* [...] moved upon her course, like the stars themselves, without a sound or murmur. Upon her quarter-deck one stood, for all her greatness, very near the sea. Above its smooth levels there rose, as if to remind one of the ship's dread purpose, her colossal turrets, the long straining muzzles of her guns, like ghosts of Armageddon, her tiers of decks.[4]

Hood indeed was one of those ships with the power to inspire an urge to join the Royal Navy. In 1932 a nine-year-old Ted Briggs, later one of her three survivors, first beheld her from the

sands at Redcar in what was a defining moment in his life:

> I stood on the beach for some considerable time, drinking in the beauty, grace and immaculate strength of her. 'Beauty' and 'grace' seem rather ludicrous words to describe a vessel of such size, particularly one whose primary function was for destruction. But I can honestly say I never could, nor indeed can even today, think of more suitable words to describe her.[5]

But it was as the embodiment of Britain's status as a great naval power that the *Hood* ultimately owed her fame, a point not lost on foreigners who discerned in her forbidding aspect something of the inscrutable quality for which the Royal Navy was known. Here is the report published in the *Diário de Notícias* of Lisbon on

29 January 1925, the height of the Vasco da Gama celebrations at which *Hood* represented the Royal Navy:

> The great *Hood*, the most powerful warship in the world [...] has been lying in the waters of the Tagus for a week, rigid, secret and impenetrable. Until yesterday the sleeping monster had kept her decks closed to the curiosity of all who have been passing round her in boats, seeking to discover what there might be within this extraordinary fortress. It was a hopeless task. The *Hood*, in the usual British manner, remained insensible, unapproachable. Now the curiosity of the people of Lisbon has at last been satisfied. [...] One could at last examine the formidable guns at close quarters, and admire the hidden beauties of the great ship at rest.

So it was that for twenty years the *Hood* dominated every harbour and anchorage from Sydney to San Francisco, a potent reminder that while Britannia might no longer be the one standard of

---

[4] *Ibid.*, p. 37

[5] Alan Coles & Ted Briggs, *Flagship* Hood: *The Fate of Britain's Mightiest Warship* (London: Robert Hale, 1985), p. xii.

power, her ships were still the yardstick by which all others were measured.

The Old and the New

As in other ways, *Hood*'s fabric was a mixture of old and new. She was the last British capital ship to be fitted with the tripod mast and spotting top of the dreadnoughts, and the last to mount a secondary armament of hand-worked guns. On the other hand she was the first to carry an enclosed bridge and two main fire-control positions; the first also to wear a clipper bow since her distant progenitor, the battleship *Warrior* of 1861. It was with *Hood* that the ram bow was finally dismissed from the repertoire of British naval architecture and the result, noted one of her captains, was the most graceful capital ship since the age of sail. Taken all round, the message was quite clear. The *Hood* was an instrument of peace, but if the moment came for war then she would run her enemies down with an irresistible turn of speed and shatter them at long range with her enormous guns.

Where her internal design was concerned, the *Hood* was planned on lines that had become traditional for big ships in the Royal Navy,

though with a somewhat ungenerous allocation of living space where the men were concerned and, being a battlecruiser, a deck less than the battleships. The elongated design that resulted meant that whereas battleships by tradition accommodated their senior officers on the main deck aft, in *Hood* they resided in considerably greater comfort beneath the boat deck and in the bridge structure. Meanwhile, the *Hood*'s seakeeping qualities meant that the rest of her officer complement lived in only moderate comfort on the main deck aft, the after cabin flat being subject to regular flooding when the ship was at sea. The balance of the ship's company messed amidships and forward on the upper deck, with the exception of stokers and boys who were accommodated on the main deck forward.

On completion in 1920 *Hood* enjoyed amenities unmatched by any save the latest US battleship designs, but as time passed and the peculiar conditions of life aboard began to assert themselves these received less frequent or favourable comment. Earlier British capital ship construction had managed to offer natural light and ventilation to a majority of the crew thanks to rows of scuttles along part or all of the upper deck and usually part of the main deck as well.

Renown and *Repulse*, for instance, were ventilated along the full inhabited length of both their upper and main decks. However, this practice ended with *Hood* which accommodated practically her entire lower-deck complement on enclosed messdecks. The absence of scuttles and poor air circulation meant that light and smell deteriorated markedly the further one penetrated into the ship. Although the *Hood*'s ventilation system was a considerable advance on earlier designs it was found to be inadequate in extremes of heat, while the tendency to dampness of a vessel whose messdecks were frequently awash was blamed for the high incidence of tuberculosis in the ship. Moreover, these problems fed on each other because reliance on natural supplies of air drawn in through ventilation fittings on deck made flooding unavoidable in heavy seas, especially on the messdecks forward. At the best of times the crew therefore lived in an environment of recirculated air together with the usual warship smells of oil, paint, polish and bodies, to which a pot-pourri of effluent and funnel fumes might be added when the ship was at sea. This along with the constant whirring of the fans and the occasional rumble of machinery was part of the reality of life afloat, the backdrop against which all served and from which no one was spared.

Life Aboard

The *Hood*'s peacetime complement of over 1,100 men was organised into thirteen divisions based on their trade and the part of the ship for which they were responsible, each numbering about a hundred men. Seamen were gathered into three divisions – Forecastlemen, Topmen and Quarterdeckmen – each of which manned one of the ship's 15in turrets, the fourth being operated by the Royal Marine detachment which formed a

Hood's ship's company mustered by divisions at the climax of King George V's Jubilee Review on 16 July 1935 as the royal yacht *Victoria and Albert* steams through the concourse of ships. *Hood* is lying astern of HMS *Iron Duke*, now reduced to a gunnery training ship, with four 'County'-class cruisers discernible in the line beyond. (*Bruce Taylor Collection*)

The Sick Bay flat on the port side forward of the upper deck, here taken over for use as a messdeck in the late 1930s. This space was home to around thirty seamen whose ditty boxes, cap tins and shoes are ranged outboard. The cage on the left is for stowing hammocks which will later be slung from the kinked bars above. (*Courtesy Brian Withers*)

division in its own right. There were separate divisions for torpedo and communications ratings, along with those for boys, engine room artificers and mechanicians, the Accountant Department and another for Miscellaneous ratings (including artisans such as painters and joiners), ordnance and electrical artificers, cooks, writers and sick berth attendants. Like the seamen, the stoker complement was split into three divisions, in their case by watches: Red, White and Blue. In war a large fourteenth division was added, Hostilities-Only Ratings, bringing the total complement to over 1,400. Each division was placed under a lieutenant or lieutenant-commander who was charged with its discipline, training, clothing and organisation, and who in turn placed the greatest reliance on his chief and petty officers. On this system turned the organisation of the entire ship and its ultimate purpose as a fighting unit of the fleet.

Ranged on the upper and main decks were fifteen enclosed messes for senior ratings and eleven open ones known as 'broadside messes' for the bulk of the ship's company. In a typical open mess, accommodation was provided for about 200 men in a space up to 70ft (21m) long and 30ft (9m) across. The main feature of each was a row of long wooden tables lying athwart the ship and supported on folding legs or suspended from the deckhead by means of a series of highly polished steel bars. On either side wooden forms provided seating for up to twenty men per table. Each of these tables constituted a 'mess' in its own right, one of over sixty in the ship all told, and it was here as in navies the world over that a man ate his meals, read his mail, played games and spent much of his life cheek by jowl with his comrades. Bulkheads and deckheads, kept a brilliant white, contrasted with the red corticene flooring of the decks which a generation of sailors were destined to scrub into a dull brown colour.

On commissioning in 1920 the *Hood* became the first ship in the Navy to adopt the dual systems of General Messing and Central Storekeeping by which the Paymaster and his victualling staff assumed responsibility for all lower-deck catering, undertaking to provide three meals a day to a pre-arranged weekly menu against the deduction of a daily allowance from the men's wages. Though preparation generally improved out of all recognition when compared with the old Canteen or Broadside Messing system, the ingredients remained much as they had been. Breakfasts of bacon, tinned tomatoes, tea, bread and butter, or issued in sandwich form at action stations or after a rough night at sea. A roast or 'pot-mess' stew for dinner or supper with the eternal 'duff' steamed pudding for

dessert. It was surely *Hood*'s misfortune that, having been in the vanguard of General Messing in 1920, she did not survive long enough to savour the next development in naval culinary organisation, the cafeteria-style Centralised Messing introduced during the Second World War.

The naval day was divided into six four-hourly segments marked by the tolling of the ship's bell. It began with the forenoon watch at 0800 when the ship's ensign was hoisted. At midday came

Impedimenta being brought onto the *Hood*'s boat deck at Portsmouth in the summer of 1935, possibly from the heavy cruiser *Shropshire*. The proceedings are under the supervision of a lieutenant-commander while *Hood*'s officer of the watch can be seen with his telescope under his arm near the gangway. Beyond them the operation has drawn the attention of the crew of one of the ship's three steam picket boats. Seen on the far side of the gangway is one of the petrol tanks for refuelling the ship's motorboats which was capable of being jettisoned in action. Stowed on the near side is one of the night lifebuoys, also intended for release in an emergency. (*Bruce Taylor Collection*)

A working party of gunnery ratings cleaning the left-hand gun of 'Y' turret in March 1935. Note the viewing port in the face of the turret. The guns were capable of elevating to 30 degrees. *(Bruce Taylor Collection)*

from compartments or stowage nettings under the deckhead and slung them fore and aft over the mess tables to minimise the effect of the ship's motion on their slumber. The key to messdeck life turned on maintaining respect and comradeliness between men in an environment which was not only fraught and overcrowded but also devoid of privacy. Though truly negative accounts of life aboard are rare, inevitably there were moments when one had had enough of one's messmates, when exhaustion, discomfort and frustration would fray nerves or tempers to breaking point. However, for long-service regulars as much as for wartime conscripts it was the camaraderie and friendship that men remembered from their service. Able Seaman Len Williams of Portsmouth, a torpedoman aboard from 1936–41, puts it eloquently:

> Living as we did, cheek by jowl, in close contact with each other, often led to strong friendships. The sort of relationships not found amongst men in civilian life, where friends meet only occasionally, and where lives are lived in separate houses. Here we lived together as a giant family. We knew each other's failings and weaknesses, and liked each other in spite of them. We slept in close proximity, in swaying hammocks. We even bathed together in the communal bathrooms. In fact we lived candidly with one another, accepting

the afternoon watch and then at 1600 the two dog watches, each two hours long to permit a daily change of watch for a ship working a two-watch routine. These were followed by the first watch at 2000, the middle watch at midnight and finally the morning watch at 0400 with which the cycle was completed. This routine, which the *Hood* observed throughout her career, was called 'watch and watch', and under it the ship's company was divided into two identical watches, known as Port and Starboard, with the exception of the Engineering Department with its three watches. These alternated duties so that every essential function was being attended to by a full complement of men at any given moment. In most cases this provided an individual with an

eight-hour day of work, mostly completed between 0600 and 1600, but rising to twelve hours at sea and probably sixteen or twenty in war as need or circumstance dictated.

At nightfall the men retrieved their hammocks

'Up spirits!' Leading hands of the messes queue for their rum ration on the *Hood*'s forecastle deck, *c.* 1935. The diluted rum known as grog is being dispensed by a petty officer of the Supply Branch. The smaller barrico on the deck contains neat rum as issued to senior NCOs, a number of whom are overseeing the proceedings. The man pointing on the left is a Chief Petty Officer and beside him is a Marine sergeant. Standing behind the barrel and under the paravane stowed against the forward screen is the senior rating in the ship, the Master-at-Arms. Next to him is a petty officer and nearest the camera is a warrant officer. *(Bruce Taylor Collection)*

the rough with the smooth. This sharing and living together, forged a comradeship which one can never find in civilian life.[6]

The open messes were presided over by the 'Leading Hand of the Mess', a leading seaman who was but one promotion away from sharing the enclosed messes of the petty officers. There was a clear hierarchy on each messdeck, the Leading Hand being followed in seniority by those leading and able seamen whose three Good Conduct badges signified at least twelve years' service in the Navy, after whom time on the messdeck was the determining factor when it came to allocation of lockers or a decent berth to sling one's hammock. Responsibility for individual messes was also given to leading seamen who were exempted from the duties of food and mail collection and of course the daily mess cleaning, during which the tables were hoisted to the deckhead and the forms cleared away so that the corticene flooring could be scrubbed and every surface buffed to a gleaming finish. Each mess would then be reassembled and its utensils and equipment laid out in the prescribed manner. These arrangements were replicated for the *Hood*'s 150-strong Royal Marine detachment whose messdeck, known as the barracks, occupied a symbolic buffer space between officers and men on the main deck.

The chief and petty officers lived in enclosed messes which might consist of no more than a curtained-off partition on a larger messdeck or an entirely separate compartment with easy chairs and an adjoining pantry. Whatever their structural arrangements, each mess enjoyed the services of at least two 'messmen' who performed the same duties as the 'cooks of the mess' on the open decks. The food served to chief and petty officers was supposedly the same as that consumed by the rest of the lower deck, but of course in practice this was some way from being the case. Petty officers slung their hammocks with the rest, but there were compensations, not least the privilege of taking their rum issue neat, and consequently of being able to store it illicitly for future consumption if the mood took them. Then there were the warrant officers, the dozen or so men who together with the chief petty officers effectively ran the ship and from whom neither she nor her men held any secrets. In recognition of their status, the warrant officers had a private mess and a separate galley and shared cabins on the main deck aft complete with bunks. As in any navy, it was the endurance, skill

The officers' wardroom looking forward and to starboard in the late 1920s. On the mahogany tables are some of the trophies presented to the ship throughout her career and travels. A pair of skylights, low-slung lamps and naked bulbs illuminate an unexpectedly austere space. *(Sellicks)*

and mordant humour of the long-service rating which moulded a ship's character in peace and stiffened its inmates to the trials that beset them in war. On their shoulders the wartime transformation of the Royal Navy was borne. In quiet expertise and steadying courage they were the finest it had to offer.

No overview of the *Hood*'s complement would be complete without mention of the boy seamen of whom around eighty were embarked. The majority reached the ship at the age of sixteen in drafts from training establishments around the United Kingdom. Rated Boy 1st Class, they constituted the Boys' Division aboard and lived in a segregated mess on the main deck forward under the authority of four Petty Officer instructors, remaining here until promoted Ordinary Seamen on turning eighteen.

Wardroom and Gunroom

The *Hood*'s officer corps numbered around fifty men belonging either to the Executive or the Civilian Branch. The former included specialists

The *Hood*'s officer corps poses for the camera under 'X' turret in the summer of 1920. Capt. Wilfred Tomkinson is seated fifth from the left with Rear Admiral Sir Roger Keyes to his left. Seated sixth from the right is the ship's Navigator, Cdr John Cunningham, later Commander-in-Chief Mediterranean Fleet and First Sea Lord. The midshipmen, including the midshipman of the watch (with telescope), are seated on the deck. *(Bruce Taylor Collection)*

---

6 Leonard Charles Williams, *Gone a Long Journey* (Bedhampton, Hants.: Hillmead Publications, 2002), p. 141.

Part of the ship's peacetime company of c. 1,100 men photographed on the forecastle at Topsail Bay, Newfoundland near the end of the World Cruise in September 1924. Vice Admiral Sir Frederick Field is seated in the centre with Capt. John Im Thurn to his right. Held by a midshipman in the front row is Joey the wallaby who joined the ship at Fremantle, Western Australia. *(HMS Hood Association/Reid Collection)*

in Gunnery, Torpedoes, Navigation and Signals together with those 'salthorse' Seaman officers who made their careers without specialised training in any discipline. This branch of necessity included the Captain and his principal executive officer, the Commander. Officers of the Civilian Branch wore the same uniform as their executive colleagues, though their particular specialisations were distinguished by coloured cloth between the gold stripes on their cuffs: purple for Engineer officers, white for Paymasters, red for Surgeons, green for Dentists, etc. While the *Hood*'s officer complement was remembered as a comparatively friendly and homogenous body throughout much of her career – 'probably as happy as a big ship could ever be' – this cannot disguise the tensions and snobbery that occasionally surfaced, particularly between executive officers and the Engineer sub-branch which was stripped of its executive status by the Admiralty in 1925.

The heart of the officers' world was the large suite on the forecastle deck amidships known as the wardroom which was dominated by four large mahogany tables at which meals were taken. Unlike *Iron Duke*, *London* and *Sheffield*, the *Hood* had never been presented with a great silver service, but in cabinets about the room, on its walls and tables were the mementoes and trophies of her voyages across the world: the silver-mounted elephant's tusk given at Freetown, Sierra Leone and the trophy heads of lion, tiger, bison and moose that followed it during the World Cruise of 1923–4 along with countless cups, salvers and centrepieces in silver and gold. The decor of what by earlier standards was a somewhat austere space was completed by a piano – much used on guest nights – a pair of stoves under mirrored mantelpieces, sundry cupboards and a large buffet from which attendants served food passed through a hatch in the wardroom pantry. The atmosphere in the wardroom, particularly where meals were concerned, had something of the character of an English country house or a gentleman's club ashore with all their quirks and mannerisms. Officers dressed for dinner, which consisted of mess jackets,

winged collars and bow ties in peacetime but no more than reefer jackets in war, though a stiff collar would be added in harbour. As the admiral and the captain usually dined alone there was no special seating at table except for the Mess President and Vice-President who held office for a week at a time. Grace would be said if the chaplain were present, all standing until the mess president had taken his seat. Then came course after course served by a phalanx of attendants in white mess tunics, twice weekly to the accompaniment of a Royal Marine orchestra in the anteroom. In keeping with the tradition of the Royal Navy, the Sovereign was toasted while officers remained seated, followed by a toast to the relevant potentate if foreign guests were aboard.

As with boy seamen on the lower deck, any account of the *Hood*'s officer corps must make mention of her midshipmen, of whom between fifteen and twenty-five were accommodated in the large and austere compartment on the upper deck known as the gunroom. Although the bullying made notorious by the novels of Frederick

Marryat and Charles Morgan was largely a thing of the past, the gunroom remained a spirited community which, like its boarding-school equivalents, deferred to authority yet frequently took pleasure in the misery of its inmates. More particularly, it was often a forcing ground for lifelong friendships between officers. The midshipmen's education, welfare and leave arrangements were entrusted to a lieutenant-commander who had assumed this duty by choice, but his brother officers often regarded midshipmen either as messengers or, in the worst cases, 'as schoolboys and their natural prey'. More often than not the 'snotty' as he was known had to accept his lot with only the lower deck to console him. Looking back on the early 1920s, Capt. George Blundell recalled how 'ships' companies of those days seemed nearly always kind and sympathetic to the "middies"'. While it was never entirely reciprocated, the lasting respect engendered for ratings by those who were later to command them remained one of the greatest strengths of the Royal Navy. Aside from his important duties

afloat, chief of which was that of Midshipman of the Watch, a midshipman's day was filled with classes and study for the Sub-Lieutenants' exam. Until then boys and midshipmen might share duties and instruction, but on promotion the enormous social gap asserted itself and their ways parted forever.

The *Hood* was the most prestigious ship in the Navy and it can come as no surprise that her wardroom and gunroom should have included several whose accomplishments past, present and future place them among the elite of a great service. Naturally, the *Hood*'s officer corps was not without its share of timeservers, failures and non-entities, those who, in Capt. Rory O'Conor's words, lacked 'the spark of leadership, [...] the ability to organise, and the will to carry things through'.[7] Nor could its society very well be

7 Rory O'Conor, *Running a Big Ship on 'Ten Commandments' (with Modern Executive Ideas and a Complete Organisation)* (Portsmouth, Hants.: Gieves, 1937), p. 149.

described as a 'band of brothers'. The 'community of sentiment' preached by Admiral Lord Fisher prior to the First World War would not be realised until the Navy finally embraced the technological realities of its calling in the 1950s. But, as on the lower deck, the *Hood*'s officers and midshipmen were imbued with a certain spirit which they would carry with them in the trials to come – of pride and confidence; above all, a conviction that theirs was the greatest warship in the world.

Glory Ship

Though commissioned with a Devonport crew on 29 March 1920, it was not until 15 May that Capt. Wilfred Tomkinson accepted *Hood* from the builders and she was officially received into the Royal Navy. That a high proportion of her complement should have come from the battlecruiser *Lion* was perhaps no accident. Under Vice Admiral Sir David Beatty the *Lion* had become the most famous ship in the Royal Navy, the battle-scarred veteran of Heligoland, the Dogger Bank and Jutland. Now that *Lion* was passing into the reserve there could be no more fitting vessel to receive her mantle than the *Hood*, the promised flagship of the post-war Navy. Before the year was out the *Hood* had assumed that mantle in full and in doing so had traced the pattern of her next twenty years. As *Lion* had been a great ship of war *Hood* was to prove herself the great vessel of peace.

On 15 May *Hood* weighed anchor at Rosyth and steamed south for the first time. Pausing off Plymouth to hoist the flag of Rear Admiral Sir Roger Keyes, commander of the Zeebrugge Raid in 1918, she made her way to what would be her home port for the next decade. Immediately she was assigned the first in a succession of diplomatic missions on which her peacetime reputation would be built, the Admiralty ordering Keyes to take *Hood*, the battlecruiser *Tiger* and nine destroyers into the Baltic to alert the Soviet fleet at Kronstadt of the consequences of any offensive activity that summer. In the event, the easing of tensions with the Soviets and ongoing negotiations with her neighbours restricted the Battle Cruiser Squadron to the agreeable cruise of Scandinavia which had been planned as cover for the operation.

In retrospect, the Scandinavian cruise seems very much the beginning of a new era of naval diplomacy which, while it lasted, found no greater emissary than HMS *Hood*, the velvet fist of British sea power. In August 1922 *Hood* led the Battlecruiser Cruiser Squadron across the Equator to Brazil to participate in the breathtaking celebrations held at Rio de Janeiro to commemorate the centennial of Brazil's independence, returning home via the West Indies. The following year, after a second cruise to Scandinavia, she led the Special Service Squadron including *Repulse* and the 1st Light Cruiser Squadron on a World Cruise lasting ten months and covering 40,000 miles, the greatest peacetime circumnavigation ever undertaken by the Royal Navy. For the 4,600 men who took part, the 2 million who visited the ships in thirty ports encircling the globe and the millions more who witnessed their passing, the Special Service Squadron left memories and experiences only now fading into oblivion. To these voyages the battlecruiser type was to prove perfectly suited and for a fleeting moment the World Cruise united technology, treasure and organisation in a spectacle never to be repeated, the high point of British sea power between the wars.

Although the *Hood* became known for her great cruises, these were the exception rather than the rule. More often than not the pattern of her life followed the ordered routine of the naval

THE INVERGORDON MUTINY, 1931

In the spring of 1931 the *Hood* emerged from a two-year refit and resumed her exalted status as flagship of the Battle Cruiser Squadron, Atlantic Fleet under Rear Admiral Wilfred Tomkinson who in 1920 had been her first captain. In May she completed to full complement and a month later sailed from Portsmouth for the usual summer spell at Portland. However, it was quite obvious that matters had changed greatly since she had paid off and passed under dockyard control at Portsmouth two years earlier. For one thing she was now a 'Pompey' ship, having exchanged the outspoken Westcountrymen of her first four commissions for the more stolid crews of the Portsmouth Division. But above all, the world to which she returned seemed very much less stable than it had in the summer of 1929. In October of that year the Wall Street Crash precipitated an economic depression which by the autumn of 1931 had put over 2.5 million out of work and brought the National Government of Ramsay MacDonald to power in Britain. With the economy in crisis, on 31 June of that year the Committee on National Expenditure recommended sweeping wage cuts for civil servants including the armed forces. When in September 1931 the Admiralty tamely acceded to a government proposal that the pay of the entire Navy be reduced to the levels obtaining under the 1925 settlement the stage was set for the Invergordon Mutiny. Not only had the Admiralty failed to honour its undertaking with respect to earlier pay settlements, but in sanctioning the government package it had permitted the cuts to be made in inverse relation to rank and seniority. Whereas the basic pay of many able seamen would be cut from four to three shillings a day (25 per cent), that of an admiral of the fleet suffered only by a matter of 17 per cent. Though the proportional cut was in fact rather lower when the allowances earnt by most were included, the inequitable division of the reductions, the manner in which they became known, the speed with which they were to be imple-

mented and the likely impact on the men's families and prospects provided the basis for the Invergordon Mutiny.

Although the mutiny owed its impetus to a spontaneous reaction by the fleet at large, it is clear that the seat of the movement, insofar as there was one, lay in ships of the Devonport Division. Above all, the mutiny owed its support to the 'staid hands', those leading seamen, able seamen, stokers and Marines on the 1919 pay scales who represented the group worst affected by the cuts. However, the practical difficulties of fomenting a mutiny in a dozen or more ships prevented the operation of any central organisation and the degree of participation of individual vessels rested mainly on the morale, convictions and mood of their crews as events unfolded. So it was with the *Hood*, in which the impending cuts were apparently discussed at several illegal meetings before the ship reached Invergordon on Friday 11 September. With Admiral Tomkinson and his staff still oblivious to the unrest on the messdecks, the *Hood* passed quietly into harbour routine, most of those off watch spending the afternoon of Saturday 12th at the Invergordon Highland Games where the ship's Marine band formed one of the attractions. However, the outcome of meetings held ashore that Saturday evening and on the following two evenings was that the fleet would be prevented from going to sea on exercises as planned on the morning of Tuesday 15 September. Indeed, the fleet was not to sail at all until the Admiralty had addressed the reductions in pay, and it was left to an ad hoc committee in each ship to ensure that this was done. The size and composition of *Hood*'s committee, how it came into being and the means by which it influenced events aboard and liaised with those in other ships remains shrouded in mystery. Indeed, virtually nothing of the internal structure and organisation of the *Hood*'s mutiny has survived for posterity. Nor can the atmosphere prevailing on the *Hood*'s decks and messes, in her passageways and spaces public and private during

year. This began with the Spring Cruise in January which required the Atlantic Fleet, or Home Fleet as it became in 1932, to muster at Portland and proceed to Gibraltar for exercises with the Mediterranean Fleet. After what was often a rough crossing of the Bay of Biscay and a welcome pause at Arosa Bay in northwestern Spain, the fleet reached Gibraltar towards the end of January. Although punctuated by sporting and social events, the purpose of this mobilisation was the Combined Fleet exercises

in March which tested the training of the Atlantic and Mediterranean fleets and the tactics of their commanders under battle conditions, the ships darkened and closed up at action stations over a period of days. After a lengthy post mortem and more junketings the fleets would disperse, individual ships making goodwill visits to a Mediterranean or Atlantic port before returning home at the end of March. In *Hood*'s case home was Devonport in the 1920s and Portsmouth in the 1930s, where varying

'The quiet mutiny'. Crewmen gathered on the *Hood*'s forecastle during the Invergordon Mutiny, probably Wednesday 16 September 1931. *(The Illustrated London News)*

those six fateful days be reconstructed in any but the vaguest terms. Both then and later the crew closed ranks to protect the identity of the 'spokesmen' who organised the mutiny and those who succoured and lent it their support, often at the cost of their careers in the Navy. But, for the committee as for the ship herself, the moment of truth was drawing near.

On the night of 14–15 September, in an incident no doubt repeated countless times on the lower deck, R. A. Feltham was roused by a leading hand and told to lash up and stow in the morning but obey no orders thereafter. That morning the crew duly turned

to at 0600 but all eyes were on *Valiant* and *Rodney* upon whose action the success or failure of the mutiny depended. Full muster in the *Hood* encouraged her officers to believe that their ship would remain unaffected by what all now sensed was coming, but in this they were soon to be disabused. Making his way down to the boiler rooms, Stoker Walter Hargreaves found his progress barred by a big stoker who told him to 'get back' and left him in no doubt of the consequences if he didn't. When by 0700 it was obvious that neither *Valiant* nor *Rodney* was being prepared for sea, the forecastles of the eight major vessels left in the

anchorage began to fill with crowds of cheering men. Stoker Charles Wild shut down the hydraulic pumping engine on which he worked, downed tools and headed forward. At around 0745 Cdr C. R. McCrum went forward, climbed onto one of the ship's capstans and implored the men gathered among the shackles to return to work. The request was politely declined and his place taken by a sailor intent on stopping the ship weighing anchor. Four decks below a party of men led by a chief stoker refused to allow the engineer watchkeeper to run the capstan engine. 'Colours' was carried out with due ceremony on the quarterdeck at 0800, but no sooner had the ensign been hoisted than cheering erupted across the anchorage. Only 30 per cent of the *Hood*'s crew fell in for work at 0830 and the howls of derision directed at them from the *Rodney* settled the matter. The Invergordon Mutiny had broken out.

Over the next day a flurry of signals between Invergordon and London finally brought home to the Admiralty the dire consequences that might ensue from its refusal to make the necessary concession. However, by the time the Admiralty relented and agreed to look into the pay scales on Wednesday 16th enormous damage had been done both to the Navy and to the country. The episode not only showed the Admiralty to be out of touch both with the officer corps and with the lower deck, but made apparent its failure to recognise the profound social changes brought on by the Great War. Meanwhile, news of the mutiny had been followed by a run on the pound and within days it was announced that Britain had been forced off the Gold Standard.

Historians will record that the 'quiet mutiny' was in fact less a mutiny than a strike, though it was one which after the frustrations of the Great War and the trials of the 1920s came close to destroying the Navy. Luckily, a new Board of Admiralty proved equal to the task of restoring its fortunes. For the *Hood*, too, a new regime awaited, one that, for a few fleeting years, brought her to the height of her glory.

degrees of refit and repair were needed after the strain of the fleet exercises. This invariably took the form of a month (usually April) refitting at her home port followed in July or August by docking at Portsmouth for the ship's bottom to be scraped and painted and her underwater fittings overhauled. From 1927 this usually preceded the great public spectacle of the year, Navy Week at Portsmouth, Devonport and Chatham when the ship played host to thousands of visitors. Having recovered from this

invasion the *Hood* headed north for the autumn gunnery cruise off Scotland, the most demanding part of the naval year. For two months the fleet carried out practices and exercises in increasingly dismal weather with only sporting competitions and golf on the links to distract it. Then it was back to the Channel for further gunnery and tactical exercises, usually off Portland, before the ships retired to home ports for Christmas leave by watches.

This yearly routine was of course subject to

disruption and over *Hood*'s long career the even tenor of her life was frequently broken by protocol, unrest of one sort or another, and finally by the drift to war. The Rio celebrations of 1922 replaced the autumn gunnery cruise but the World Cruise had kept the *Hood* from her duties for fifteen months by the time she was ready to rejoin the fleet in January 1925. Even then she and the Battle Cruiser Squadron spent a week in Lisbon representing the Navy at the Vasco da Gama celebrations. The General Strike

Hood receiving visitors during Navy Week at Devonport in the late 1920s. Note the flying-off platform on 'B' turret. (*Bruce Taylor Collection*)

had her sitting in the Clyde for nearly two months in the summer of 1926 while the Invergordon Mutiny cancelled the autumn gunnery cruise of 1931 altogether. But much worse was to come. The Spanish Civil War upset the training and manning regime of much of the Navy and after 1936 the *Hood* never regained the rhythm of earlier years.

A Great Commission, 1933-6

The Invergordon Mutiny exposed many failings in naval administration, but in shipboard life it did so in three areas above all: in the widespread disillusion over prospects and promotion; in the strained relations that existed between departments; and finally in the failure of the divisional system in which the Admiralty had reposed such confidence. But where the Admiralty had proved itself incapable of effective leadership in this matter, one officer set himself to influence his peers with a tested paradigm. That officer was Rory O'Conor and his paradigm was HMS *Hood*.

O'Conor's arrival in the *Hood* in August 1933 provided an early indication of how the orchestra of shipboard life was to be tuned for the rest of

the commission. His first act was to tear up the voluminous Standing Orders and substitute his own 'Ten Commandments'. Implicit in these was the notion that every man who gave of his best could expect fairness, respect and consideration

from his superiors; that there were rewards for hard work, and that no one could go very far wrong so long as he kept the interests of the ship at the forefront of his mind; that no ship could be regarded as successful if she were not happy, and that every officer and rating had a share in this endeavour. Never before had such a contract been laid before the lower deck of the Royal Navy, nor was such a system ever sold to her officer corps in such persuasive terms.

The linchpin of the *Hood*'s 'Ten Commandments' was O'Conor himself. What set him apart was his accessibility to the entire crew, of which the outward sign was his celebrated open-door policy. Mindful of Invergordon, O'Conor therefore acted out the central tenet of his ethos: that it was an officer's duty to make himself a conduit for the problems and grievances of those placed under him, and that it was his responsibility to ensure that every man could turn to him for a fair hearing. An essential part of O'Conor's philosophy was what he called 'consideration for the men' on the part of their officers. This extended from reducing the amount of time libertymen had to stand around waiting for boats and drifters to the introduction of a revised weekend routine which at last gave the crew the complete day of rest prescribed in

Hood's marksmen pose with their trophies and weapons on the quarterdeck at Portsmouth, *c.* 1935. With them is Capt. F. T. B. Tower, Cdr Rory O'Conor (holding the telescope) and Judy, O'Conor's West Highland terrier. The battlecruiser *Repulse* lies beyond. (*HMS Hood Association/Clark Collection*)

Cdr RORY O'CONOR'S 'TEN COMMANDMENTS', AUGUST 1933

SHIP'S STANDING ORDERS

The Service. The Customs of the Service are to be observed at all times.

The Ship. The Good Appearance of the Ship is the concern of everyone in *Hood*, and all share the responsibility for this.

The Individual. Every man is constantly required to bring credit to the Ship by his individual bearing, dress and general conduct, on board and ashore.

Courtesy to Officers. The courtesy of making a gangway, and standing to one side to attention when an officer passes, is to be shown by every man. If an Officer passing through men during stand-easy, meal hours, etc., carries his cap under his arm, it will indicate that no attention, other than clearing a gangway, is required.

Execution of Orders. All orders, including those passed by Bugle and Pipe, are to be obeyed at the Run.

Punctual Attendance at Place of Duty. Every man is personally responsible, on all occasions, for his own punctual attendance at his place of duty.

Permission to Leave Work. A man is always to ask permission before leaving his work.

Reporting on Completion of Work. Any man on finishing the work for which he has been told off, is to report to his immediate superior. Parties of men are to be fallen in and reported.

Card-playing and Gambling. While card-playing is allowed at mess-tables and on the upper deck, any form of gambling is strictly prohibited. Gambling includes all games of chance played for money stakes.

Requests. Any man wishing to see the Commander is to put in a request to his Officer of Division. In urgent cases his request is to pass through the Master-at-Arms and Officer of the Watch.

The view from the boat deck forward during the 15in concentration exercise held as part of King George V's Silver Jubilee celebrations on 17 July 1935. Note the Mk-V 0.5in (26mm) pom-pom mounting on the left, one of two fitted in 1931, to which a third was added in 1937. *(Bruce Taylor Collection)*

the King's Regulations. Many of these innovations were no more than the application of common sense to irksome naval tradition, but if this approach contributed to what he called 'the ideal state of every man knowing what is required of him' then it also had the effect of building a sense of community in the ship. That sense of community was assured once a man formed an attachment of pride for her. Indeed, a ship's community need not be confined to her crewmen, but extended to include all their family and friends ashore. In his concern for such matters, in the role and position of a warship in wider society and vice versa, Rory O'Conor was years ahead of his time. But pride was also bound up with the appearance of the ship and O'Conor laid a great, and indeed excessive, stress on smartness, cleanliness and paintwork. Tiresome though his men often found it, under O'Conor's stewardship the *Hood* brought to a pinnacle the art of ship adornment nurtured by the Royal Navy since the age of Nelson.

The effect of O'Conor's approach was not only improved morale and discipline but a far greater and wider degree of involvement in the life of the ship among both officers and men. This was reflected above all in the drive for sporting excellence which O'Conor pursued with unrelenting vigour, and for a few years the *Hood* dominated sporting competition in the Home Fleet. Her record in the fleet Pulling Regatta for the coveted Silver Coquerelle could not match the triumphs of the 1920s when the *Hood* was Cock of the Fleet three years running between 1926–8, but the range of trophies won and competed for gives some idea of the enthusiasm O'Conor brought to the ship. Indeed, within fifteen months of recommissioning the ship had won virtually every trophy available to her. The *Hood* recovered the Cock from *Nelson* in 1935, won the Arbuthnot Trophy for cross-country running from 1933–5 and the Palmer Trophy for bayonet fighting between 1934 and 1936. These and a dozen others O'Conor proudly displayed in his lobby on the forecastle deck.

Although the 1933–6 commission came to a climax with the Regatta victory and then the Jubilee Review in 1935, its final year was overshadowed by events of more lasting significance: the collision with the *Renown* following the conclusion of a gunnery exercise in January 1935 and above all the Abyssinian Crisis which came to a head that autumn. If the former broke the morale of the Battle Cruiser Squadron then the latter set the pattern for the rest of the *Hood*'s peacetime career. A spell in dry-dock at Portsmouth, the Regatta victory at Scapa Flow and the Jubilee Review soon restored the *Hood*'s fabric and fortunes, but the international situa-

Hood, seen here sailing from Portsmouth shortly after the Invergordon Mutiny in late 1931 or early 1932, caught the imagination of the British public like no other ship. Note the newly installed Fairey IIIF seaplane on the quarterdeck, swiftly removed after it was found to be unserviceable at sea. *(Bibliothek für Zeitgeschichte, Stuttgart)*

tion for the first time brought the prospect of war onto her horizon. By early 1936 developments in Germany, the Japanese occupation of Manchuria and the ongoing Abyssinian Crisis had alerted the British political and military establishment to the likelihood of war on a global scale though, as O'Conor's priorities indicate, this point had yet to impress itself on the *Hood*. It was the Commander's principal responsibility to ensure the fighting effectiveness of his ship. Whatever his accomplishment in building a happy and successful community, O'Conor's neglect of the *Hood*'s fundamental *raison d'être* is the one signal failure of his tenure, though here Capt. Thomas Tower must evidently shoulder much of the blame. For all the success of his regime, O'Conor ultimately chose to focus his energies and those of his crew on competition with other ships rather than the fighting efficiency which tradition and circumstance increasingly urged upon him and for which Tower's successor Capt. Francis Pridham never forgave him. The end of the commission must in these circumstances have come as something of a relief for O'Conor, and in June 1936 *Hood* returned to Portsmouth where her Executive Officer saw her pay off with all the pomp and ceremony he could muster. The *Hood*'s greatest commission was over.

Despite his differences with Pridham, O'Conor's performance in the *Hood* earnt him swift recognition and on 30 June 1936 he became, at thirty-seven, the youngest captain on the Navy List. Barely pausing for breath, he immediately set about publishing the fruits of his experience in *Hood* for the wider consumption of the Navy and the result, *Running a Big Ship on 'Ten Commandments'*, remains one of the most influential naval treatises of the first half of the twentieth century. The coming war would change O'Conor's Navy for ever, but the ethos enshrined

in *Running a Big Ship*, that every man was entitled to the understanding and consideration of his officers, was to have a lasting impact on shipboard relations in the Navy. In the final analysis, the ability of men of O'Conor's stature to give practical expression to their convictions is a measure of how far the Navy had come since Invergordon. But for those who study HMS *Hood*, *Running a Big Ship* is above all a record of the halcyon years of the greatest warship in the world, the more poignant for the cruel fate that awaited its author. Capt. Rory O'Conor died following the loss of the cruiser *Neptune* in a minefield off Tripoli in December 1941, a disaster that left just one survivor from her 767 men.

War Clouds, 1936–9

As the 1930s wore on the Royal Navy began to face the nightmare prospect of war on four fronts: with Italy and Germany off Europe, Africa and in the Atlantic, and against Japan in the Far East. Conscious of its weakness, particularly in cruisers and capital ships, the Admiralty was left with no option but to follow the same policy of appeasement and containment pursued by successive British governments over this period. As the ultimate symbol of British sea power it was natural that the *Hood* should feature prominently in this strategy, to which she gave the final years of her peacetime career. If the 1933–6 commission was a highlight in the *Hood*'s career, there can be little doubt that its successor of 1936–9 was more eventful than any which had preceded it. The Spanish Civil War, the Abdication of Edward VIII and Accession of George VI in 1936, the Coronation Review of 1937 and the Munich Crisis of 1938 were played out against the backdrop of continuous service, training and protocol under the mounting threat

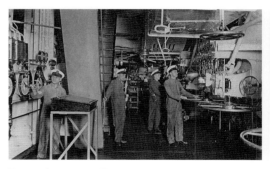

Four engine room artificers on the control platform of the after engine room, c. 1931. Two are on the throttles (ahead and astern) controlling the revolutions of the starboard inner shaft. The desk on the left houses the engine-room register, written up hourly. By the outbreak of war the maintenance of the ship's plant was placing a severe strain on her Engineering Department. (*Sellicks*)

of war. On New Year's Day 1939 the ship's company posed on the forecastle for the traditional valedictory photo as she lay in the Grand Harbour at Valletta. Nine days later the *Hood* sailed from Malta for the last time. The band of the Royal Marines struck up *Rolling Home* and her paying-off pendant caught the sirocco as she passed St Elmo Point into the Mediterranean. Few of those attending can have imagined that they were witnessing the end of an era for the Mediterranean Fleet.

Delayed first by financial restrictions, disagreement over the future of the capital ship and then by international politics, as the 1930s wore on circumstances made it impossible to immobilise the most prestigious warship in the world for a lengthy reconstruction. When the long overdue proposals were finally tabled in 1936, diplomatic considerations, the spectre of war and the urgency of refitting older and weaker vessels meant that neither they nor their successors could ever be put into effect. By the time the *Hood* returned from the Mediterranean in January 1939 the opportunity to make her a truly battleworthy unit had thus long since passed and the Admiralty could only offer another refit before she turned her bows towards the enemy. However, as war became imminent even the year-long 'reconditioning' envisioned in 1936 had to be reduced to a six-month effort pending a complete reconstruction beginning in 1942. Of the original measures, which included the addition of 4in of plating over the magazines, only the installation of two twin 4in (102mm) mountings and a magazine on the platform deck could at this stage be effected. Though this eventually went some way towards rectifying the *Hood*'s woeful anti-aircraft defence, in adding more topweight the 1939 refit placed further strain on an already overloaded hull and aggra-

Hood lies serenely at Toulon on 23 April 1938. Lengthy interludes on patrol and humanitarian duty off Spain and as a tool of diplomacy in the Mediterranean kept her from the reconstruction she so desperately needed. (*Marius Bar*)

Grey Queen of the North. *Hood* at Scapa Flow
on 9 October 1940. *(Bruce Taylor Collection)*

vated a series of existing problems. Moreover, the *Hood*'s boilers and condensers were in a desperate condition. But time had almost run out. Thwarted by the Admiralty in his efforts to have the worst condensers attended to and regarding the ship as neither seaworthy nor battleworthy, her Chief Engineer Cdr (E) Peter Berthon refused to pronounce the Engineering Department 'in all respects ready for war' on being relieved in May 1939. Despite the effort expended it was still a rather dilapidated ship that left for Scapa Flow on 13 August 1939. Although those who lined the shore of Portsmouth and Southsea could not know it, the Mighty *Hood* was sailing never to return.

In view of the international situation it had been decided to retain most of the key ratings, including much of the Engineering Department, and only 500 were drafted to the naval barracks at Portsmouth when the *Hood* docked in January 1939. She recommissioned in June but the mobilisation which followed began to dilute her complement with reservists and eventually Hostilities-Only ratings. By the time the *Hood* sailed for war in August her crew had risen to over 1,400, approximately 15 per cent above peacetime levels. After a week patrolling the Norwegian Sea against the passage of German commerce raiders into the Atlantic, the *Hood* put in at Invergordon to refuel and then made for Scapa Flow on 24 August. At dusk on the 31st, the day the Royal Navy mobilised, *Hood* weighed anchor and sailed from Scapa Flow, going to action stations at 0400 on 1 September as Germany invaded Poland and Britain issued its ultimatum for her withdrawal. On Sunday 3rd, while cruising between Iceland and the Faeroes,

news was received that no response to the ultimatum had been received and at 1120 came Prime Minister Neville Chamberlain's sombre announcement that war had been declared. It was a beautiful morning as men stood down from their action stations to gather beneath the messdeck tannoys or around private radios tuned to the BBC. The news was received with solemn reflection, with optimism, and, in some quarters, with gung-ho enthusiasm for a victory *Hood* would never see.

To War

During the first months of the war the *Hood* settled into a pattern of endless sweeps for enemy raiders and blockade runners in northern waters which, with one or two significant interruptions, would be her lot for the rest of her days. The routine was unwavering. Tanks brimming with fuel, the *Hood* would slip her moorings, gather her destroyer screen and exit the immense anchorage of Scapa Flow through the boom defence between Hoy and Orkney. Moving on to 25 knots, the squadron would begin zigzagging and at length pass into the Atlantic. The departure from Scapa might be enlivened with a practice shoot against a towed battle target at ranges of up to 12,000yds (10,970m) but thereafter came only the strain of maintaining the Navy's lidless eye on the straits through which the German navy had to pass to reach the Atlantic convoys, of remorseless zigzagging in enormous seas and brutal weather, of exhaustion, discomfort and boredom; of being one of the storm-tossed ships that stood between survival and defeat. The *Hood* preserved the four-hour watch

system of the peacetime Navy but circumstances called for a far greater proportion of her crew to be closed up at any given moment. The standard routine for daylight hours at sea was Cruising Stations which required a third of the crew to be on duty. Action Stations at dusk demanded every man in the ship to be closed up for an hour. The hours of darkness were spent at Defence Stations with half the crew at their posts, followed by Action Stations for a further hour around the crack of dawn.

For much of the *Hood*'s wartime career the scale of the Navy's commitments and the attrition to its fleets made her the most overworked capital ship in the world. The sinking of the *Royal Oak* in October 1939, the departure of the *Rodney* for repairs to her steering in November and finally the mining of *Nelson* outside Loch Ewe on 4 December briefly left her as the sole heavy unit at the disposal of Admiral Sir Charles Forbes, Commander-in-Chief Home Fleet. Nor did she escape damage herself, being struck above the port bulge by a bomb dropped by a German Ju 88 while sailing with the Home Fleet to rescue the crippled submarine *Spearfish* on 22 September. Damage to the hull was superficial but the concussion inflicted severe harm on the condensers which came close to leaving the ship dead in the water. Even if the *Hood* had not been crippled as Lord Haw-Haw proclaimed from Berlin, the attack revealed both the inadequacy of her anti-aircraft armament and the ineffectual drill of their crews, a deficiency shared by the rest of the Home Fleet.

By November 1939 the damage suffered during the *Spearfish* episode and the strain of unremitting service in northern waters had brought the *Hood*'s condensers to the brink of collapse. Her best speed was at times down to 25 knots and relentless service in heavy seas was exacerbating other problems. Besides, the burden on the Engineering Department was becoming intolerable, with a routine increasing to eight hours on, four hours off at sea followed by constant maintenance in harbour. On 11 November the *Hood* docked at Devonport for an overdue boiler cleaning and a week's leave for her crew, taken a watch at a time. But no sooner had the second watch departed on 20 November than news of the sinking of the armed merchant cruiser *Rawalpindi* by the battleships *Scharnhorst* (q.v.) and *Gneisenau* caused the *Hood* to recall those on leave and slip her moorings with all despatch. On the 25th, just two weeks after reaching Devonport, the *Hood* sailed

The bleakest of times. *Hood* in the autumn of 1940 with her degaussing coil prominent along the forecastle deck. (*HMS Hood Association/Mason Collection*)

MERS EL KÉBIR, 1940

Early on the morning of 10 May 1940 the German army launched its great offensive in the West. Within two weeks the British War Cabinet, its troops outmanoeuvred and its strategy in disarray, was taking the first steps towards the withdrawal of its troops from the Continent. With the defeat of France sealed by the entry of Italy into the war on 10 June, the Admiralty began taking steps to fill the void created by the collapse of French power in the western Mediterranean with a significant force of British ships. However, once the terms of the Franco-German armistice became known in London, as they had by 25 June, it was plain that this squadron must have a far more urgent remit. Under the terms of the armistice, the French fleet, still largely intact, was to be 'demobilised and disarmed under German or Italian control'. This clause did not satisfy the British government which was already moving to prevent scattered units and squadrons of the French navy falling into the hands of the Axis. The officer chosen to enforce this policy in the western Mediterranean was Vice Admiral Sir James Somerville who assumed command of Force H on 27 June which was transformed into an independent command based on Gibraltar but directly responsible to the Admiralty in London. It was to join this squadron as flagship that the *Hood* was ordered south from Greenock on 18 June, reaching Gibraltar five days later with the carrier *Ark Royal*.

The first task to which Force H was committed was the neutralisation of the French Atlantic Fleet at Mers El Kébir near Oran in Algeria. After two days of deliberations, Force H sailed from Gibraltar on 2 July stiffened by units of North Atlantic Command. There can be no doubt that Somerville's task was among the most unenviable ever assigned to a British commander. His brief from Prime Minister Winston Churchill was to lay before his French counterpart, Amiral Marcel Gensoul, the following options for the disposal of his fleet: that he (a) put to sea and continue the fight against Germany; (b) sail with reduced crews to a British port; (c) do likewise to a port in the French West Indies, or (d) scuttle his ships at their berths. Should these prove unacceptable a fifth was to be offered, namely that Gensoul demilitarise his force at Mers El Kébir. Any measure resorted to would have to be enacted within six hours, a proviso which greatly hindered both admirals' freedom of manoeuvre. In the event of these proposals being rejected Somerville was to present Gensoul with the ultimatum of having his fleet destroyed by Force H.

Shortly after 0800 on the morning of 3 July Force

Hood seen from *Dunkerque* while patrolling in mountainous seas off Iceland in November 1939. Gifts (including this photo) were passed between the two ships as gestures of fraternity; eight months later at Mers El Kébir it was shellfire they exchanged. (*Bruce Taylor Collection*)

H appeared off Mers El Kébir. Somerville had already sent the destroyer *Foxhound* ahead with his emissary Capt. Cedric Holland, but it was not until 1615 that the latter gained direct access to Gensoul. The story of the protracted and ultimately fruitless negotiations between the British and Gensoul, the stirring of the French navy across the western Mediterranean and the mounting pressure from London all lie beyond the scope of this chapter. Suffice to say that by 1730, some three hours after the expiry of his original ultimatum, Somerville found himself with no alternative but to open fire. Within a few minutes Boy Signalman Ted Briggs was hoisting the order for instant action to the starboard signal yard. A little before 1800 it was the order to open fire that he bent on to the halyard. Moments later the harbour at Mers El Kébir was being crucified by the first salvoes of British 15in ordnance. Within three minutes the battleship *Bretagne* had blown up with heavy casualties. Her sister *Provence* and the battlecruiser *Dunkerque* had to be beached after sustaining repeated hits, the latter mainly under *Hood*'s fire. The destroyer *Mogador* lost her stern to a direct hit which left her a smouldering wreck in waters turned black with oil. With the harbour shrouded in a dense pall of smoke, at 1804, nine minutes after the action had commenced, Somerville gave the order to cease fire. Within a few minutes increasingly accurate salvoes from the shore battery at Fort Santon obliged *Hood* to return fire while the squadron sailed out of range under a smokescreen.

This might have been the end of the affair except that at 1818 reports began reaching *Hood* of a battlecruiser emerging from the harbour. Initially dismissed by Somerville and his staff, by 1830 it was apparent that the *Strasbourg*, unscathed by the holocaust enveloping her companions, had negotiated the mine barrage laid by aircraft from *Ark Royal* and was making for Toulon with five destroyers. *Hood* turned to give chase, working up to over 28 knots at the cost of a stripped turbine while *Ark Royal* prepared to launch an air strike in the fading light. The *Hood* again came under attack as the pursuit developed, first from a salvo of torpedoes fired by the light cruiser *Rigauld de Genouilly* and then by a flight of bombers from Algeria. Meanwhile, attacks by Swordfish aircraft failed to slow the *Strasbourg* and at 2020 a dispirited Somerville called off the chase. A second Swordfish strike at 2055 reported two torpedo hits but *Strasbourg*'s speed remained unimpaired and she reached Toulon without damage the following day. Three days later an injudicious announcement by Amiral Jean-Pierre Estéva at Bizerte that 'The damage to the *Dunkerque* is minimal and the ship will soon be repaired' brought Force H back to Mers El Kébir where Swordfish from *Ark Royal* put paid to her operational career.

So ended one of the most regrettable episodes in the history of the Royal Navy. For the *Hood* there was the lingering sadness that her guns had been blooded not only against an ally but, in the case of *Dunkerque*, a companion in arms. The return by the *Dunkerque*'s officers of souvenirs presented to them by members of the *Hood*'s wardroom in happier times made this all the more poignant and unpropitious.

'Still beautiful after all these years.' *Hood* returning to Scapa Flow from Hvalfjord on 5 May 1941 in position 61° 50' N, 16° 98' W. *(HMS Hood Association)*

from Plymouth Sound in mountainous seas, her refit incomplete and 150 ratings drafted from Devonport barracks to make up numbers. It was to be another four months before her condensers received the thorough overhaul they so urgently needed, together with the addition of five 4in mountings and as many of the new UP (Unrotated Projectile) rocket launchers.

The Dark of the Sun

For a month after the Mers El Kébir affair the *Hood* continued in the van of Force H as Somerville took the battle to the Italians in the western Mediterranean. On 8 July Force H sailed from Gibraltar to mount a diversionary attack on the airfield at Cagliari, Sardinia to cover the passage of two convoys between Malta and Alexandria. The following day the squadron came under heavy air attack from Italian S.M.79 bombers. No hits were registered but sticks of bombs fell uncomfortably close. There remained just one more sortie, a second diversionary attack on Cagliari while the carrier *Argus* flew off a

dozen Hurricanes for Malta, before the *Hood* turned her bows northward on 4 August. Her status as Flagship Force H was to pass to the *Renown*. It was with regret that the *Hood*'s company watched Somerville haul down his flag at Scapa Flow to be replaced by that of Vice Admiral William Whitworth.

The autumn of 1940 was among the bleakest periods in the *Hood*'s career. The threat of invasion was past but the Luftwaffe had now turned its attention to the bombing of British cities, placing an added strain on any whose family was on the receiving end. It was a depressing period which not even the raid on Taranto (see *Littorio*) and the collapse of Italian arms in North Africa could lighten. Constant patrolling in terrible weather had left many exhausted and surviving letters home for the first time show that the strain of war was beginning to take its toll on the *Hood*'s company. In December news that she would pass a second Christmas without leave apparently brought part of her stoker complement to the brink of mutiny. But, hard as the circumstances were, the spirit of comradeship never faltered in *Hood*, and the remarkable coming-together of branches and ranks which characterised the Navy at war was echoed in this ship as much as in any other. On Christmas

morning the midshipmen hosted the sergeants of Marines together with the chiefs and petty officers for drinks in the gunroom before lunch, while Capt. Glennie made the traditional tour of the messdecks preceded by a boy seaman dressed as the ship's senior rating, the Master-at-Arms. On New Year's Eve it was the turn of the warrant officers, the Master-at-Arms and the Marine Colour Sergeant to celebrate Hogmanay in the wardroom along with every officer in the ship from Vice Admiral Whitworth to the most junior midshipman. Two short patrols later and the *Hood* found herself at Rosyth for what would be her final refit, her crew dispersed by watches on their first leave in six months.

By the time she emerged on 18 March 1941 *Hood* had received her first radar installations in the shape of a Type-284 gunnery set on the spotting top and Type-279M air-warning equipment on the mainmast. To this was added a change of commanding officer, Capt. Irvine Glennie being succeeded by Ralph Kerr who had made his name in destroyers. Kerr's new command had still to work up after her refit but these plans were again disrupted by news that German raiders had broken out into the Atlantic. On the afternoon of 18 March the *Hood* passed under the Forth Bridge and hastened in search of the enemy, but despite hopes of an interception on 20 March, Admiral Günther Lütjens, the German squadron commander, slipped through the net and reached Brest with *Scharnhorst* (q.v.) and *Gneisenau* on the 22nd. It was at this time that word reached the *Hood* of the commissioning of a new German battleship and the name *Bismarck* was first uttered in her messdecks. Until then much of *Hood*'s company had been glad to regard her as largely invulnerable to German surface vessels, but the *Bismarck* with her displacement of 41,700 tons and eight 15in guns was clearly a very different proposition and no informed crewman can have had much doubt as to the threat posed to his ship in the event of a confrontation between the two.

By early May persistent German aerial reconnaissance between Greenland and Jan Mayen in the Arctic Sea had persuaded the Admiralty that the long-expected appearance of the *Bismarck* was nigh. Already on 28 April the *Hood* had sailed from the dreary anchorage of Hvalfjord in southern Iceland as distant cover for two eastbound convoys against surface attack. For a time it was thought that an attack on Iceland or Jan Mayen might be afoot, but by 18 May the Commander-in-Chief of the Home Fleet Admiral Sir John Tovey and his staff had concluded that a naval breakout was the more likely scenario and on that day the heavy cruiser *Suffolk*, then on patrol in the Denmark Strait, was warned to be on her guard for the appearance of German warships. These fears were confirmed on 20 May with news that a German squadron had left the Baltic. This was the *Bismarck* and the heavy cruiser *Prinz Eugen* which had sailed under Admiral Lütjens from Gotenhafen (now Gdynia) at midnight on the 18th. Their aim was to enter the Atlantic on a commerce-raiding sortie via the Denmark Strait but Rheinübung ('Rhine Exercise') as it was called was compromised from the outset. Even before it had cleared the Kattegat, the body of water separating Denmark and Sweden, the German squadron was sighted by the Swedish cruiser *Gotland* which promptly reported the matter to the naval authorities ashore. By the end of that day, 20 May, the report had reached the Admiralty in London, and the following morning the British learnt through Enigma decrypts that *Bismarck* had reached Grimstadfjorden near Bergen, sending an RAF Spitfire to photograph Lütjens' force from an altitude of 25,000ft (7,620m). That evening, just as *Bismarck* and *Prinz Eugen* put to sea once more, Admiral Tovey ordered the Battle Cruiser Squadron to sail from Scapa to Hvalfjord. Wearing the flag of Vice Admiral Lancelot Holland, at 2356 *Hood* and the new battleship *Prince of Wales* and six destroyers

weighed anchor and exited the Flow shortly after midnight under a veil of rain and mist. By 0100 on the 22nd they were through the Hoxa Boom and out into the Atlantic. The chase from which the *Hood* would not return had begun.

The Denmark Strait

Initially there was nothing to indicate that this sortie would not end as inconclusively as the many that had preceded it. The squadron had been ordered to refuel at Hvalfjord late on 22 May before joining the heavy cruisers *Norfolk* and *Suffolk* on patrol in the Denmark Strait. Meanwhile, the crew viewed the chances of encountering the enemy on this their fifteenth war patrol since returning from Gibraltar the previous summer with some scepticism. The *Hood*, after all, had not laid eyes on an Axis man-of-war since 1938. However, all this changed at around 2030 when the Battle Cruiser Squadron was ordered to abandon its passage into Hvalfjord and make directly for the Denmark Strait. A second RAF reconnaissance flight over Grimstadfjorden that afternoon had found the anchorage empty. Though Tovey and his staff did not know it, *Bismarck* and *Prinz Eugen* had been racing north for twenty-four hours.

For all this, the morning of the 23rd brought a familiar sense of anti-climax in *Hood*. The night had passed off uneventfully; the sun rose to the

Lancelot Ernest Holland seen in the rank of commodore in 1936 or '37. His flag flew just twelve days in *Hood*. *(HMS Hood Association)*

usual routine of action stations and endless vigil, of frigid watches staring into the grey unity of sea and sky. A range and inclination exercise was held during the afternoon watch as the weather began to deteriorate. Those off duty played cards, read and wrote letters destined never to be sent as Vera Lynn echoed across the messdecks, the last woman's voice many of them would ever hear. At 1930 that evening this reverie was abruptly and definitively broken. Ten minutes earlier the *Suffolk*, patrolling 100 miles northwest of Iceland, had sighted *Bismarck* and *Prinz Eugen* as they began the southward leg of their passage through the Denmark Strait. A few minutes later the *Norfolk*, wearing the flag of Rear Admiral W. F. Wake-Walker, strayed too close to the edge of the fog bank shrouding her and immediately got a taste of *Bismarck*'s gunnery, straddled before she could regain cover. Three hundred miles due south Vice Admiral Holland ordered the Battle Cruiser Squadron to work up to full speed and shape an intercepting course of 295 degrees. A little after 2000 a signal from *Suffolk*, now shadowing by radar, confirmed that it was the *Bismarck* and her consort towards which he was heading at an aggregate speed of 50 knots.

Within an hour of the alteration of course Holland's squadron was crashing into a full gale at 27 knots, wind and water forcing *Hood* and *Prince of Wales* to train their forward turrets to port. Shortly after midnight Holland ordered the *Hood*'s immense battle ensign hoisted, but even as it unfurled in the wind events 120 miles to the north were eroding his tactical advantage. By 0030 it was obvious that the *Suffolk*, the only vessel in Wake-Walker's force equipped with effective search radar, had lost contact with the enemy in a blizzard. At this Holland informed his squadron that if contact were not regained by 0210 he would alter course to the south until such time as it had been re-established. In the event, Holland decided not to wait quite that long and at 0203 he hauled *Hood* and *Prince of Wales* round onto a course of 200 degrees, the last reported heading of the German squadron. The men went down to the second degree of readiness.

Until then Holland had intended to close *Bismarck* at speed from her port bow, a tactic which would not only shorten the range between the two squadrons in quick time but minimise the number of guns that could be brought to bear against him as he did so. By the time *Suffolk* had reported regaining contact at 0247 and the *Hood*'s relative bearing on the enemy been determined, the *Bismarck* was thirty-five miles distant and steering a diverging course at 28 knots. This meant that Holland had not only lost bearing on

The lesser known of the two images reckoned to be the last of *Hood* as an effective unit, taken from *Prince of Wales* during the voyage to the Denmark Strait on the afternoon or evening of 23 May. The relative positions of the two ships are almost identical to those they assumed as battle was joined the following morning. (*Bibliothek für Zeitgeschichte, Stuttgart*)

the enemy but had no prospect of regaining it either. Rather than the end-on attack for which he had planned, any approach had now to be made on the *Bismarck*'s port beam and in the teeth of her entire main armament. As at Trafalgar, the Battle Cruiser Squadron would have to endure a prolonged exposure to the full weight of enemy fire before being able to bring its own broadsides to bear.

At 0340 Holland ordered revolutions for 28 knots and brought *Hood* and *Prince of Wales* onto a course of 240 degrees to force the enemy to battle. By 0430 visibility had improved and dozens of pairs of eyes were scanning the north-western horizon where, thirty miles off, *Bismarck* and *Prinz Eugen* were steaming towards their unexpected encounter. Shortly after 0500 Holland passed the order to 'Prepare for instant action', the men rousing themselves to the first degree of readiness. Then they were upon the enemy. At 0535 lookouts in *Hood* and *Prince of Wales* sighted the German squadron at a range of approximately 38,000yds (34,750m). Holland's force was sighted almost simultaneously by the German ships but its presence was by now suspected. At 0515 hydrophone operators in *Prinz Eugen* had detected the sound of high-performance turbines to the southeast and it was on this horizon that two columns of smoke were spotted in the cold light of morning. At 0537 Holland ordered a 40-degree turn to starboard which placed Lütjens' force broadside on and fine on his port bow, his flagship making almost 29 knots. Twenty degrees off her starboard quarter lay *Prince of Wales* at a distance of 800yds (732m).

At 0549 Holland ordered a further turn of 20 degrees to starboard to close the range once

more. A minute later he ordered concentration on the leading ship in the German squadron. This was not *Bismarck* but *Prinz Eugen* which Lütjens had ordered into the van after his flag-ship's radar had broken down while engaging *Norfolk* the previous evening. The error was immediately spotted in *Prince of Wales* and fire redistributed accordingly, but it was against *Prinz Eugen* that *Hood* now brought her forward guns to bear. At 0552 *Hood* fired her opening salvo against *Prinz Eugen* at a range of approximately 25,000yds (22,860m), *Prince of Wales* following against *Bismarck* a few seconds later. Holland had prohibited the use of radar during the approach to battle but it must be supposed that *Hood*'s new Type-284 gunnery set was in action by the time she opened fire. What is certain is that none of her shells registered on their targets. Not only had her firepower been reduced by half by the angle of approach, but the turret rangefinders were being drenched in spray as she thundered into a head sea at 29 knots, the speed at which vibration in the spotting top became 'excessive'. Accuracy must therefore have rested on the 30ft (9.14m) rangefinder in the armoured director, such information as may have been provided by radar and the *Hood*'s inadequate Mk-V Dreyer Table. In view of the conditions, the probable need to shift target and the high rate of change of range as *Hood* closed the enemy, her failure to land a hit is not to be wondered at.

No such difficulty faced *Bismarck* and *Prinz Eugen* and the Battle of the Denmark Strait would provide a further demonstration of the lethal accuracy of German naval gunnery. After a brief delay the German squadron took *Hood* under fire against the morning horizon. Soon their shells were screaming in, *Bismarck*'s first salvo, unleashed at 0555, falling just wide. Her second straddled, the *Hood* pressing on between towering geysers of water. But it was *Prinz Eugen* which drew first blood, a shell from her second salvo striking *Hood* on the boat deck and starting an uncontrollable fire among dozens of ready-use lockers for 4in and UP ammunition that soon began to take a terrible toll of their crews. Mindful of the Mers El Kébir engagement during which *Hood* had suffered splinter damage, orders had been passed for exposed personnel to take cover in the lobby beneath the bridge structure when action commenced, but men were spotted from *Prince of Wales* making futile efforts to control the blaze with deck hoses. The same wind that was dousing the *Hood*'s rangefinders with spray fanned this fire into an enormous conflagration which swept back over the roof of 'X' turret, pulsating in a lurid pinkish flame as ammunition went off like fire crackers.

Bismarck takes *Hood* under fire in the Denmark Strait on the morning of 24 May 1941. Five salvoes destroyed the pride of the Royal Navy and over 1,400 of her men. (*Bibliothek für Zeitgeschichte, Stuttgart*)

But much worse was to come. No sooner had the blaze been reported than a shell landed inside the bridge structure making a terrible execution of the 200 men sheltering there, a slaughter only AB Bob Tilburn lived to relate. On the bridge Holland ordered the fire on the boat deck to be left to burn until the ammunition had been expended. He had, in any case, far more pressing concerns than this. The *Hood* was being hammered and the moment when the squadron's full weight of fire was brought to bear could not be delayed much longer. At about 0555 Holland passed the order for a 20-degree turn to port to open the 'A' arcs of 'X' and 'Y' turrets. On came the *Hood*, shells raining down as her after turrets strained to find bearing on the enemy. His approach completed, at approximately 0600 Holland ordered another 20-degree turn to port. It was just seven or eight minutes since she had opened fire. Even as the *Hood* began to execute her turn *Bismarck*'s fifth salvo was hurtling in from about 16,000yds (14,630m). With it came the death blow, a shell or shells landing abaft the after funnel followed moments later by columns of fire and an immense explosion that wreathed the ship in smoke and engulfed her in an unearthly silence. Listing to starboard, *Hood* righted herself before immediately capsizing to port. Realising that she was finished, those on the compass platform began to abandon ship. Only Holland and Kerr remained, neither making the slightest effort to escape. By the time Ordinary Signalman Ted Briggs began to descend from the compass platform the *Hood* was almost on her beam ends. Halfway down he was washed off the ladder and into the sea. For Midshipman William Dundas, who had spent the battle manning phones and voice pipes on the compass platform, the pitch of the deck prevented him reaching this exit and he was forced to kick his way through a window as the

The boat deck seen from the spotting top in the autumn of 1940. It was here, near the base of the mainmast, that the fatal shell or shells landed. Numerous ready-use ammunition lockers are distributed across the boat deck, the contents of which caused a major conflagration in *Hood*'s last minutes. The grime of a year of war service is everywhere apparent. *(Bibliothek für Zeitgeschichte, Stuttgart)*

The *Hood*'s forward turrets and bridge structure seen from the forecastle in April 1941. The Type-284 gunnery radar fitted at Rosyth a month or so earlier is visible on the aloft director while one of the useless UP launchers is hidden under canvas on 'B' turret. The compass platform from which Briggs and Dundas escaped is the glazed structure above the armoured director. Tilburn sheltered beside Port No. '1' UP mounting (seen on the right) and got clear of the ship from the forecastle just forward of it. *(Bibliothek für Zeitgeschichte, Stuttgart)*

structure met the water. On the boat deck Tilburn looked up to see the bows rising out of the water and immediately dropped down onto the forecastle abreast the compass platform from which Briggs and Dundas were making their escape. There was not a moment to lose. The first waves were lapping onto the decking as the *Hood* began to heel over. He barely had time to strip off his battle helmet and many layers of clothing before being swept into the sea and dragged under like Briggs and Dundas.

In each of these cases the time elapsed between the fatal hit and the moment of abandoning ship seems to have been little more than a minute. Tilburn was clearly the only man in the vicinity capable of separating his destiny from that of his ship, testament to the attrition of her boat-deck personnel once the *Hood* came under fire and the speed of her demise. Distinct as their experiences were, there is one aspect of their ordeal that unites the three survivors: the release of air from collapsing boilers and bulkheads which propelled them to the surface, each swimming away from the towering wreck and eventually selecting one of the numerous biscuit floats with which *Hood* had been equipped during her final refit. So it was that, a little after 0600 on the morning of 24 May, the pitiful remnants of the *Hood*'s company found themselves adrift among the sparse wreckage of their ship in a 15–20ft (4.5–6m) swell as the battle raged on under leaden skies. Beneath them the pride of the Royal Navy and 1,415 of her men were sinking to the bottom of the Atlantic. The three survivors were rescued by the destroyer *Electra* two hours later.

The *Bismarck*, however, was not to emerge unscathed from her moment of triumph. Despite being struck seven times in as many minutes and suffering problems with her turrets which eventually reduced her to only three operational guns, *Prince of Wales* was able to score three hits on the *Bismarck*, one putting a boiler room out of action and the other contaminating two of her oil tanks. With this the battle ended, *Prince of Wales* retiring under a smokescreen while Lütjens turned for Brest. Rheinübung was effectively over but the Royal Navy was to have its revenge. A wrathful Admiralty summoned every unit at its disposal to prevent *Bismarck* reaching harbour. Force H was brought up from Gibraltar and convoys ruthlessly stripped of their escort. Three days later the *Bismarck* suffered her own Calvary under the withering fire of the battleships *Rodney* and *King George V*. After a savage two-hour engagement *Bismarck* disappeared with around 2,100 of her crew.

Aftermath

No one who witnessed the loss of the *Hood* could have had any doubt that it was the detonation of her after magazines which destroyed her. The question, both then and now, was quite how this had occurred. The first board of inquiry convened under the presidency of Vice Admiral Sir Geoffrey Blake (who had flown his flag in *Hood* from 1936–7) on 30 May and submitted its report just three days later. It determined that one or more shells from *Bismarck* had landed in the vicinity of the mainmast and reached the *Hood*'s 4in magazines, which had been doubled in size in 1939–40. The explosion of these had in turn brought on the detonation of the 15in magazines, resulting in an immense deflagration that demolished and incinerated everything in its path, venting through the engine-room exhaust housings on the boat deck and then among the after turrets which were tossed bodily into the sea. Though this conclusion was subsequently endorsed, the inquiry had taken no technical advice, left no minutes, and limited its interviews to a handful of officers; of *Hood*'s survivors only Midshipman Dundas had been called. Above all, it had summarily dismissed what many influential commentators regarded as a likely cause of the explosion: the detonation of the upper-deck torpedoes. A second board had therefore to be convened in August and September under the presidency of the *Hood*'s last peacetime captain, Rear Admiral H. T. C. Walker. This took evidence from 176 witnesses to the sinking including Tilburn and Briggs, while advice was solicited from a range of former officers and technical experts. Dundas was not able to attend but evidence gathered from survivors of the *Bismarck* was taken into consideration. Throughout the proceedings the board took pains to establish whether or not the

Imperial emissary: *Hood* approaching Victoria, British Columbia on 21 June 1924. *(Bruce Taylor Collection)*

boat deck fire and the ship's torpedo armament had any bearing on her loss. Its conclusions, submitted on 12 September 1941, were little removed from those of the first board, namely that *Hood* had sunk as a result of a 15in hit in or adjacent to her 4in or 15in magazines, causing them to explode and wreck the after part of the ship; that the torpedoes were unlikely to have had a hand in her loss; and that the boat deck fire certainly had none. There have been dissenting voices but with these conclusions a majority of expert opinion is now in essential agreement. However, the precise seat of the explosion is probably destined to remain in the limbo of conjecture.

These interpretations were borne out in July 2001 when the wreck of the *Hood* was filmed at a depth of approximately 9,000ft (2,750m). Lying amidst three vast debris fields were the bow and stern sections (*c.* 165ft and 125ft – 50m and 38m – respectively) and, at some remove, an upturned section of the hull some 350ft (107m) long. Missing were approximately 225ft (69m), corresponding to the area between 'Y' turret and the middle engine room inclusive which had disintegrated in the holocaust. The stern section had been seen to break away at the surface, but the real surprise of the expedition was the severed bow section, lying on its port

side wrapped in anchor cable. It seems probable that the break was owed first to structural weakening when the bow rose out of the water and then to implosion damage once the ship left the surface, though arguments have been made for a major explosion in the vicinity. The other revelation was the unprecedented degree of implosion damage inflicted on the hull as *Hood* sank. This field of desolation stretching across a mile of the ocean floor yielded few reminders of the ship as a living entity. One item, however, could hardly have been more poignant: the ship's bell on which the new year had been tolled in on 31 December 1940 and which was recovered in 2015.

On the morning of Tuesday 27 May Churchill was able to announce the sinking of the *Bismarck* to Parliament but nothing could efface the destruction of the *Hood* on, of all days, Empire Day – 24 May. From a material standpoint Germany's loss had been much the greater. One of her few commissioned capital ships had been sunk with huge loss of life including that of the Kriegsmarine's most prominent seagoing commander. But the *Hood* had a symbolic power out of all proportion to her value as a fighting unit and her annihilation had an effect on morale exceeded only by the fall of Singapore in February 1942. Both events raised in the minds of ordinary Britons the spectre of total defeat. And both in their different ways had far-reaching consequences for the prestige of the British

Empire. But that belonged to the future. For now the gleaming sword of the Royal Navy had been unmade, never to be reforged.

Legacy

Completed shortly after the First World War, *Hood* represented not only the survival of the British Empire after the immense human and material losses of that conflict but also a climax of naval technology and design, a ship of superlatives, an aesthetic tour de force of speed and power and sinuous beauty. It was under this mantle that she served as an ambassador for Britain, the Empire and the Royal Navy between the wars, the glittering centrepiece of every naval occasion and the greatest exponent there has ever been of what is now known as defence diplomacy. There was, however, another element which has ceased to be widely appreciated and this is that *Hood* represented the apogee of what the British had evolved into a great national art, namely the operation and manning of warships and fleets, a rich amalgam of seamanship, discipline, ship husbandry and professional pride founded on an unequalled record of victory, a unique culture bound up in language and custom, the work of minutes, the tradition of centuries. No vessel of the Royal Navy ever embodied that culture in her life and loss more completely than HMS *Hood* as Britain's age of greatness drew to a close in the mid-twentieth century. Once she had gone nothing would or could ever be quite the same again and the passage of time has only sharpened that impression.

In the first three years of the Second World War the Royal Navy lost ten capital ships together with dozens of cruisers, destroyers, submarines and escorts. Though these disasters did not alter the outcome of the conflict they encapsulate a loss of power and prestige from which there would be no recovery. And of these blows none fell heavier than the loss of the *Hood*, destroyed with virtually her entire company in a tragedy that has come to stand for the Calvary of the Royal Navy as a whole during that conflict. There is another tragedy, too, and this is that *Hood* went ill-prepared to her moment of reckoning in the Denmark Strait. This circumstance had not only to do with unsatisfactory protection, material shortcomings and the inscrutable turns of Fortuna's wheel. It was also the product of economic decline and financial parsimony, political irresolution and diplomatic incompetence; a result of the strategic and military failure that placed her under *Bismarck*'s guns when she might otherwise have been quietly scrapped or in the throes of reconstruction.

To study the loss of the *Hood* is to appreciate how a great entity many years in the making can be destroyed in the course of a few seconds. But the tragedy is not one of structure so much as of humanity. With *Hood* as with *Bismarck*, *Arizona* and *Yamato*, it was less a ship than a community that was destroyed. From the splendours of Rio de Janeiro to the Stygian waters of the North Atlantic, it was her men who breathed life into her, made her rich in history, character and memory. In *Hood* the notion of the warship as a tool of peaceful diplomacy reached its maximum expression, not only in her graceful form, speed and armament but also in the qualities of her people. The *Hood* was undeniably an engine of war, but as with the greatest weapons her career was as much about preserving life as about taking it. Of her many legacies this shall perhaps prove the most enduring.

Sources

Unpublished Sources

Churchill Archives Centre, Cambridge
Admiral Sir William Davis, memoirs (WDVS 01/002)
National Maritime Museum, Greenwich
Vice Admiral Sir Francis Pridham, *Memoirs* (*c.* 1970) (MSS/76/004)

Bibliography

Bradford, Ernle, *The Mighty* Hood (London: Hodder and Stoughton, 1959)

Burt, R. A., *British Battleships, 1919–1939* (2nd edn, Barnsley, S. Yorks.: Seaforth Publishing, 2013)

Carew, Anthony, *The Lower Deck of the Royal Navy, 1900–39: The Invergordon Mutiny in Perspective* (Manchester: Manchester University Press, 1981)

Coles, Alan, & Ted Briggs, *Flagship* Hood: *The Fate of Britain's Mightiest Warship* (London: Robert Hale, 1985)

Friedman, Norman, *The British Battleship, 1906–1946* (Barnsley, S. Yorks.: Seaforth Publishing, 2015)

Grenfell, Russell, *The* Bismarck *Episode* (London: Faber and Faber, 1949)

Harvey, W. B., *Downstairs in the Royal Navy* (Glasgow: Brown, Son & Ferguson, 1979)

Johnston, Ian, *Clydebank Battlecruisers: Forgotten Photographs from John Brown's Shipyard* (Barnsley, S. Yorks.: Seaforth Publishing, 2011)

Jurens, W. J., 'The Loss of H.M.S. *Hood* – A Re-examination' in *Warship International*, 24 (1987), no. 2, pp. 122–61

Kennedy, Ludovic, *Pursuit: The Chase and Sinking of the* Bismarck (London: Collins, 1974)

Le Bailly, Louis, *The Man Around the Engine: Life Below the Waterline* (Emsworth, Hants.: Kenneth Mason, 1990)

McKee, Christopher, *Sober Men and True: Sailor Lives in the Royal Navy, 1900–1945* (Cambridge, Mass.: Harvard University Press, 2002)

The Naval and Military Record, 31 March 1920

Northcott, Maurice, *HMS* Hood [Man O'War, vol. 6] (London: Bivouac Books, 1975)

O'Connor, V. C. Scott, *The Empire Cruise* (London: Riddle, Smith & Duffus, 1925)

O'Conor, Rory, *Running a Big Ship on 'Ten Commandments' (with Modern Executive Ideas and a Complete Organisation)* (Portsmouth, Hants.: Gieves, 1937)

Roberts, John, *The Battlecruiser* Hood [Anatomy of the Ship] (London: Conway, 1982)

_____, *Battlecruisers* (London: Chatham Publishing, 1997)

Robertson, R. G., *HMS* Hood [Warships in Profile, no. 19] (Windsor, Berks.: Profile Publications, 1972); also as 'HMS *Hood*: Battle-Cruiser 1916–1941' in John Wingate, ed., *Warships in Profile*, vol. II (Windsor: Profile Publications, 1973), pp. 145–72

Taylor, Bruce, *The Battlecruiser HMS* Hood: *An Illustrated Biography, 1916–1941* (revised edn, Barnsley, S. Yorks.: Seaforth Publishing, 2008)

_____, *The End of Glory: War and Peace in HMS* Hood, *1916–1941* (Barnsley, S. Yorks.: Seaforth Publishing, 2012)

Tennyson d'Eyncourt, Eustace H. W., *A Shipbuilder's Yarn* (London: Hutchinson, 1948)

Tute, Warren, *The Deadly Stroke* (London: Collins, 1973)

Williams, Leonard Charles, *Gone a Long Journey* (Bedhampton, Hants.: Hillmead Publications, 2002)

HMS *Hood* Association: http://www.hmshood.com [accessed February 2018]

Imperial Japanese Navy
(大日本帝国海軍 — Dai-Nippon Teikoku Kaigun)
The Battleship *Nagato* (1919)

Hans Lengerer & Lars Ahlberg

NAMED FOR an ancient maritime province lying at the western tip of Honshū and home to one of Japan's most powerful warrior clans, the battleship *Nagato* represents a milestone in Japanese naval construction.[1] The Imperial Japanese Navy had hitherto based not only its organisation but also its warship design on the Royal Navy, and her first eight battleships were all built in British yards. From 1904, indeed, the design, construction and weapon technologies of Messrs Vickers Ltd of Barrow-in-Furness were adopted as standard for Japanese capital ships, a development culminating in the order placed with that yard for the battlecruiser *Kongō* in 1910. Although *Kongō* was the last Japanese capital ship ever built abroad, hull design as well as most fittings and equipment continued to follow British standards up to and including the Ise-class battleships of 1914. With *Nagato*, however, Japanese designers turned away from the British model in several important respects to incorporate a series of bold innovations, the beginning of a truly independent style of capital-ship construction. To that extent, as also from the political and diplomatic perspective, the completion of this immensely powerful ship marks a key moment in the rise of Japanese sea power.

[1] The editor would like to acknowledge the assistance of Arrigo Velicogna for his comments on this chapter.

Nagato running trials in Sukumo Bay off the island of Shikoku on 27 October 1920. Her design, construction and completion was a major achievement for the Imperial Japanese Navy. *(Lengerer/Ahlberg Collection)*

Origins and Design

The origins of the Nagato-class battleships can be traced to the 'Eight-Eight Fleet' concept devised in the aftermath of the Russo-Japanese War (1904–5) as Japan began to shift her expansionist strategy away from Imperial Russia and towards the United States. This programme was, however, subject to constant delay and modification, mainly for budgetary reasons but due also to political considerations and inter-service rivalry with the army, and was never completed as such. The immediate origins of *Nagato* and her sister *Mutsu* therefore lie in the Eight-Four Fleet Nomination Planning submitted by Navy Minister Admiral Yashiro Rokurō to the *Bōmu Kaigi* (Defence Conference) in September 1915 and approved that same month, assisted by the allocation of ¥260,000,000 to the 1917–23 budgets for the construction of eight battleships and two battlecruisers as the nucleus of a new battlefleet. In the meantime, the Naval General Staff had in January 1916 secured approval from the Imperial Diet for that year's naval budget under which vessels could be ordered after 11 May. Losing no time, orders were placed for *Nagato* with Kure Navy Yard on the 12th and for *Mutsu* (under the Eight-Four Fleet Completion Planning) at Yokosuka Navy Yard on 31st July 1917.

Where the design was concerned, completion

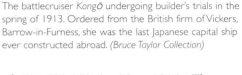

The battlecruiser *Kongō* undergoing builder's trials in the spring of 1913. Ordered from the British firm of Vickers, Barrow-in-Furness, she was the last Japanese capital ship ever constructed abroad. *(Bruce Taylor Collection)*

of ¥26,920,000 in May 1916. Then came Jutland.

The Royal Navy was not the only force whose warship design paradigms were significantly altered by the Battle of Jutland fought on 31 May–1 June 1916, during which the British suffered the loss of three battlecruisers in catastrophic circumstances. In July the Imperial Japanese Navy took receipt of the technical report on Jutland prepared with the assistance of its observers in the Grand Fleet. Meanwhile, on 15 May Constructor Commander (later Vice Admiral) Hiraga Yuzuru had been appointed Superintendent of Shipbuilding in the Naval Technical Department, his first task from Capt. Yamamoto being to revise A-110 to reflect the major lessons from the engagement, particularly in armour protection and speed. That these lessons had been taken on board is evident from the lecture Hiraga delivered to the Crown Prince and future Emperor Hirohito on 18 December 1924 concerning the influence of Jutland on the design of the Nagato class, of which he described himself as the 'chief designer'. As Hiraga related, he had proposed a 2-knot increase in speed to 26.5 knots via the adoption of all-geared turbines. These permitted a 33 per cent increase in engine power to 80,000shp thanks to weight-

of the plans for the Ise-class battleships in June 1914 allowed the *Kaigun Gijutsu Honbu* (Naval Technical Department) to turn its attention to the devising of a more powerful vessel. Its brief was to respond to the international trend for increased gun calibre and the corresponding need for enhanced protection, while at the same time bringing speed into line with that of the battlecruiser. Research into the design of capital ships in ten navies, particularly those of Britain, the United States, Italy, France and Russia, led to a decision to surpass all foreign counterparts both in gun power and speed, while providing the appropriate degree of protection. Seventeen design studies were evolved and rejected before the eighteenth, A-110, was adopted as the prototype of the Nagato class in mid-1915. This design, which was largely the work of Constructor Captain Yamamoto Kaizō under the direction of Asaoka Mitsutoshi, provided for a standard displacement of 32,800 tons and a main armament of eight 16.14in (410mm) guns arranged in four twin turrets distributed forward and aft. In contrast to the crowded upper decks of the Fusō and Ise classes with their six turrets, A-110 offered ample space for mounting additional weapons and equipment, including a casemated secondary battery of 5.5in (140mm) guns on two levels on the upper and boat deck, together with torpedo tubes fitted on the upper deck. Turbines developing a

total of 60,000shp were anticipated to deliver a best speed of 24.5 knots. It was this design which formed the basis of Navy Minister Yashiro's proposal to the Defence Conference in September 1915 and was duly ordered at a cost

The naval constructors responsible for the successive designs which culminated in *Nagato* in 1915–16: Yamamoto Kaizō (left) and Hiraga Yuzuru seen in later years in the uniform of a constructor vice admiral. *(Lengerer/Ahlberg Collection)*

and volume-saving advances in boiler and engine technology, particularly by the Westinghouse Co. of Pittsburgh to which the Japanese navy had access. Hiraga then turned to protection, justifying a reduction in the waterline belt and elimination of the upper belt covering the secondary armament as partial compensation for the addition of 1,300 tons of armour over the magazines and engine spaces. British experience at Jutland was also reflected in extensive alterations to the barbettes to prevent flash reaching the magazines.

The various stages leading up to the final *Nagato* design are somewhat unclear.[2] Although Captain Yamamoto was responsible for the pre-Jutland A-110 design, construction of which was ordered on 12 May 1916 (three days before Cdr

Hiraga was assigned to the Navy Technical Department), a modified post-Jutland design with improved horizontal protection and speed (A-112) was completed in August 1916 and accepted by the *Gijutsu Kaigi* (Higher Technical Committee) in September. The relationship between A-112 and what proved to be the final design – a revision of A-110 carried out by Hiraga and named A-114 – is unclear, but it was A-114 which was approved for construction by the Navy Ministry of 28 October. Whatever the case, the vessel to which the navy minister had appended his signature was 708ft (215.80m) long, 95ft (28.96m) in the beam and had a draught of 29.5ft (9m) on a completed standard displacement of 33,870 tons, making her the largest yet built for the Imperial Japanese Navy.

Protection

Where protection is concerned, the Nagato class adopted the concentrated system, confining both vertical and horizontal armour to the length of the ship's magazines and machinery spaces at the expense of casemate plating for the secondary armament. The waterline belt consisted of 12in (305mm) of Vickers cemented armour to which a new system of underwater protection was added. This consisted of a longitudinal torpedo bulkhead composed of three layers of 1in (25mm) high-tensile steel plates joined together and curved downwards from the base of the main

2 See Abe Yasuo, *Sekai no Kansen*, No. 681 (Tokyo: Kaijinsha, 2007), p. 169; in collab., *Nagato Gata Senkan*, No. 15 (Tokyo: Gakken, 1997), pp. 101–2; Ishibashi Takao, *Senkan·Jun-yōsenkan* (Tokyo: Namiki Shobō, 2007), pp. 319–20; Naitō Hatsuho, *Hiraga Yuzuru Ikō Shū* (Tokyo: Shuppan Kyōdōsha, 1985), pp. 76–7 & 581; Okumoto Gō, *Hachi Hachi Kantai no Shuryokukan* (Tokyo: Kōjinsha, 2011), p. 153; Ōtsuka Yoshifuru, *Hachi Hachi Kantai Keikaku* (Tokyo: Gakken, 2011), pp. 68–72. The authors invite readers to contact them with information on differences between designs A-110, A-112 and A-114.

Nagato soon after completion in November 1920. *(Courtesy Philippe Caresse)*

belt to the double bottom. The resulting scheme was tested with a full-scale model which confirmed its ability to withstand the detonation of 441lbs (200kg) of explosive, then anticipated to be the bursting charge of the next generation of torpedoes.[3] This measure was subsequently enhanced by the addition of a bulge to maintain buoyancy as a result of the increase in weight during the modernisation of 1934–6. Vertical protection was completed by an upper belt of 9in (229mm) of cemented armour above the waterline belt, extending to the height of the middle deck along with transverse bulkheads up to 13in (330mm) thick.

Horizontal protection was disposed on the middle and lower decks, both of which sloped downwards. The main armour deck was the middle deck, with slopes of the same construction as the longitudinal torpedo bulkhead, and extending below the waterline to the base of the

3 Makino Shigeru, Fukui Shizuo *et al.*, *Kaigun Zōsen Gijutsu Gaiyō*, II, p. 204.

lower belt, the thickness of which was reduced to 3in (76mm) from 12in (305mm). The conning tower and turrets were protected by up to 13in and 12in of Vickers cemented armour respectively, the latter increased to a maximum of 18in (457mm) in 1934–6.

Armament and Fire Control

The adoption of the 16in (406mm) gun as the main armament for whichever battleships followed the Fusō class (eventually the Ise class) had been under consideration since 1913. By then the mounting of 15in (380mm) guns in the fast battleships of the British Queen Elizabeth class was a fait accompli, and it was reckoned to be only a matter of time before the U.S. Navy fitted 16in guns in its capital ships. However, no detailed information was available on the larger calibre gun, and the increase from the 14in (356mm) weapon first mounted in *Kongō* to the 16in piece presented significant technical challenges to the Imperial Japanese Navy. The decision was therefore taken to carry out a compara-

tive study into the British 15in gun and a prospective 16in design, with a view to developing a weapon based on analysis of the results. The ballistic requirements were a maximum barrel pressure of 417.17psi (29.33kg/cm^2), together with a remaining projectile velocity of at least 1,900ft/sec (580m/sec) at a range of 8,750yds (8,000m), the study focusing on the requisite balance of calibre and shell weight in reaching its conclusions. After much deliberation, the Japanese settled on a 16.14in (410mm) weapon of 45 calibres firing an intermediate shell weighing 2,249lb (1,020kg). Maximum range at 30 degrees elevation was 33,000yds (30,200m), subsequently extended to 41,885yds (38,300m) at 43 degrees following the 1934–6 modernisation. The flight time of the projectile for 30,000m was given as 59 seconds when fired with a muzzle velocity of 2,559ft/sec (780m/sec). Production by the Ordnance Division of Kure Navy Yard began in 1914 and continued until 1921, though considerable difficulties were experienced in manufacturing the requisite 56ft (17m) tubes, and a high proportion of forgings were

rejected. Nonetheless, *Nagato* and *Mutsu* were the first vessels in the world to adopt a main armament of 16in guns, these arranged in superfiring pairs fore and aft.

The turrets, which were built by the Ordnance Division of Kure Navy Yard and Yokosuka Navy Yard, were essentially scaled-up copies of the Vickers design fitted in the Kongō class. The main improvements introduced by Japanese designers were (1) increased elevation to 30 degrees (from 25 degrees in *Kongō*), (2) all-angle loading to 20 degrees (25 degrees after modernisation in 1934–6), (3) improved flash integrity through the provision of longitudinal bulkheads in the gun house and working chamber, and (4) safer loading cages. The total turret weight was 1,124 tons. Turrets and hoists were hydraulically operated, with a two-stage loading system of the British type capable of supplying 1.5 rounds per minute (later improved to 2 rounds/min following modifications to the rammer stroke).

Secondary armament consisted of twenty 5.5in (140mm) 50-calibre guns arranged in single mountings on the upper deck and boat deck. Anti-aircraft armament came in the shape of four 3.15in (80mm) 40-calibre guns, replaced in 1934–6 by eight 5in (127mm) and four 1.57in (40mm) Vickers weapons, all in twin mountings. The latter were removed in 1939 and replaced by

twenty 1in (25mm) 60-calibre Type-96 guns in twin mountings. These provisions against aircraft were significantly increased during the Pacific War, and by the summer of 1945 *Nagato* mounted twelve 5.5in guns, fifty-two 1in (25mm) weapons, and no less than ninety-six 1in AA guns. Aside from machine guns and saluting guns, *Nagato*'s original armament was completed

Nagato: Armament, 1920–45

Type	As built 1920	As modernised 1934–6	1945
Main guns	8 × 16.14in (410mm) (4 × 2)	8 × 16.14in (410mm) (4 × 2)	8 × 16.14in (410mm) (4 × 2)
Secondary guns	20 × 5.5in (140mm) (20 × 1)	18 × 5.5in (140mm) (18 × 1)	12 × 5.5in (140mm) (12 × 1)
High-angle guns	4 × 3.15in (80mm) (4 × 1)	8 × 5in (127mm) (4 × 2)	4 × 5in (127mm) (2 × 2)
Small-calibre guns	8 × 3.15in (80mm) (8 × 1)	8 × 3.15in (80mm) (8 × 1)	52 × 1in (25mm)
Machine guns	3 × 0.256in (6.5mm) (3 × 1)	3 × 0.303in (7.7mm) (3 × 1)	–
Anti-aircraft guns	–	4 × 1.57in (40mm) (2 × 2)	96 × 1in (25mm)
Torpedo tubes	8 × 21in (530mm)	–	–

Nagato seen from her starboard quarter in 1921. *(Library of Congress/32962)*

by eight 21in (530mm) Armstrong-type torpedo tubes, four submerged and four on the upper deck, though the difficulty of operating the former when the ship was at speed and the inherent danger represented by the latter contributed to their removal in 1934–6.

Fire control was initially restricted to a Type-13 director of Vickers design in the main control position atop the foremast and in the auxiliary control position on the after superstructure, with no gunnery computer beyond a Type-10 range clock. These were replaced by an improved Type-14 system around 1925 which controlled the main and secondary armament; no provision was made for anti-aircraft fire until the Type-31 fire-control director was fitted in 1932. Rangefinding was provided by a Seven-Year 32ft 10in (10m) unit atop the foremast and a 19ft 8in (6m) Barr & Stroud model mounted on each turret. These were replaced during the 1934–6 modernisation by Type-3 32ft 10in double rangefinders on no. '2' and no. '3' turrets and a Type-94 fire director atop the foremast, by which time the Type-92 fire-control computer had been installed in the

TRIPOD TO PAGODA

From the 1920s the Imperial Japanese Navy began fitting foremast structures of increasing size and complexity in its capital ships which were not only novel in themselves but became part of the distinctive aesthetic of its warship design. In this as in so many other respects *Nagato* led the way. To begin with, however, she was to have been rigged with the same British-style tripod masts as those fitted – albeit with progressive modifications – in all Japanese dreadnoughts since *Kongō* in 1913, and it was not until September 1917, more than a year after the design had been completed, that a new multi-post foremast structure was adopted for *Nagato* at the instigation of a specialist ordnance officer, Captain (later Vice Admiral) Kaneda Hidetarō. This consisted of a central post supported by struts aimed at increasing rigidity and reducing vibration to improve the accuracy of the sensitive targeting, measuring, control, command and communication equipment concentrated in the mast. Among this equipment was the main 32ft 10in (10m) rangefinder, the first unit of comparable size to be mounted aloft in a Japanese capital ship. This initiative not only reflected the unexpectedly lengthy ranges at which vessels had engaged each other during the First World War, but also a desire to make the most of the 33,000yds (30,000m) range of the new 16in gun.

Kaneda's design did not, however, come without opposition. Three months after *Nagato* was laid down, a meeting of the Navy Technical Department's Technical Committee on 21 November 1917 was the scene of 'heated arguments', not least over the significant increase in weight implied by the new design, with a corresponding loss of stability to the ship as a whole. In the end, Hiraga accepted the design only after reducing the number of support struts from eight to six, the resulting structure comprising a main post 6ft 3in (1.9m) in diameter, supported by six inclined struts 3ft (91cm) wide. To this hexagonal structure and main post, rising 100ft (30m) from the upper deck to the spotting top, the name *yagura* (pagoda) was given. Provided with an elevator connecting the

The towering pagoda superstructure, seen here in practically its final form in August 1942, was first carried by *Nagato* and became a distinctive feature of Japanese capital ship design. Note the 32ft 10in rangefinder near the top and the two 15ft units two levels below. *(Lengerer/Ahlberg Collection)*

middle deck with the combat bridge, each of the fourteen levels were fitted with a burgeoning array of searchlights, rangefinders or fire-control instruments which eventually obscured the hexagonal structure altogether. Accretions and alterations to the pagoda continued into the Second World War, by which time the Yamato-class battleships had introduced the tower superstructure.

Nagato seen wearing the funnel cap fitted to deflect gases from the bridge structure in 1921. The experiment was not a success and the forward funnel was trunked in 1924 and finally removed in 1934–6. *(Courtesy Philippe Caresse)*

An aerial view of *Nagato* (left) *Mutsu, Ise* and *Hyūga* firing under helm during a gunnery exercise in 1927. *(Lengerer/Ahlberg Collection)*

transmitting station. The 1in (25mm) AA guns were controlled by a Type-95 director, also introduced in 1937. A Type-21 (air search) radar was added in May 1943, followed in late June 1944 by two sets each of the Type-13 (air search) and Type-22 (surface) radar after the Battle of the Philippine Sea, but the lack of effective fire directors was to prove a significant handicap in the Pacific War.

Propulsion

Steam for the main turbines and most of the auxiliary machinery was provided by fifteen Ro gō Kampon-type oil-burning boilers with superheaters generating saturated steam, in addition to six mixed oil- and coal-burning boilers. These twenty-one water tube boilers generated a designed maximum output of 80,000shp, almost double that of preceding Japanese capital ship construction.[4] Advances in boiler technology prompted the replacement of *Nagato*'s outfit by four large and six small boilers in 1934–6, gaining almost 2,150ft^2 (200m^2) of space while increasing output from 81,300 to 82,300shp.[5]

[4] Nihon Zōsen Kikan-shi Henshū Iinkai, *Teikoku Kaigun Kikan-shi*, II, pp. 520–8; Nihon Zōsen Gakkai, *Shōwa Zōsen-shi* (2 vols., Tokyo: Hara Shobō, 1977), I, pp. 664–72; Makino & Fukui, *Kaigun Zōsen Gijutsu Gaiyō*, VII, pp. 1671–2 & 1758.
[5] Fukuda Keiji, *Gunkan Kihon Keikaku Shiryō* (Tokyo: Konnichi no Wadai-sha, 1989), p. 147.

The engine plant consisted of four sets of Gihon all-geared impulse turbines, each incorporating one high-pressure and one low-pressure turbine. The design was based on the Westinghouse triple-flow system and represents the first use of the so-called double-flow system without fitting the cruising turbine stages. Steam passed through the first impulse stage in the high-pressure turbine before being divided three ways, one to the rotor blade set in the HPT casing, while the other two entered the LPT casing in the centre, where they were divided forward and aft to pass through the two sets of counter-rotating blades. This tripartite system delivered economical steaming at low speeds. The speed of both turbines was 2,731rpm, and the maximum design legend of the four propeller shafts was 230rpm for a best speed of 26.5 knots. A range of 5,500 miles at 16 knots could be attained with 3,400 tons of heavy oil and 1,600 tons of coal.

Although doubtless influenced by the Queen

BOW

Nagato's bow was of the so-called 'spoon' type, a reference to the slight double curvature with the large cut of the forefoot. It represented a departure from the clipper bow employed from the armoured cruisers of the Tsukuba class (1904) to the battleships of the Ise class (1914) and became a distinctive feature of the vessels of the so-called Eight-Eight Fleet. This particular shape, which came at the expense of a wet fo'c'sle when steaming into a head sea, was adopted to allow the ships to slide over the ropes of combined (or connected) mine no. I (*Dai ichi*

gō renkei kirai), a classified weapon designed to be laid in numbers in the path of an approaching enemy force. It also had the virtue of providing space for dignified mounting of the imperial chrysanthemum crest (*kikkamonshō*) 48in (1.22m) in diameter which traces its origin to the fourteenth century. In 1927 *Mutsu*'s bow was remodelled to reduce the amount of spray generated over the forecastle, thereby increasing her overall length by 5ft 3in (1.59m) to 713ft 3in (217.39m). The success of this experiment resulted in *Nagato* following suit in 1934–6.

Elizabeth and Francesco Caracciolo classes, the arrangement of the engine rooms was unique and was looked back on by Vice Admiral Hiraga as the most distinctive feature of the design. The four main turbine sets were disposed in three

compartments divided longitudinally, with two sets in the central compartment and one set on either side. Provision was made for three-shaft operation thereby minimising the effect of list in the event of damage and flooding to the wing

Nagato makes a majestic sight in 1928 during the period between the trunking of the forward funnel in 1924–5 and the alteration of the bow in 1934–6. *(Lengerer/Ahlberg Collection)*

compartments. Another unique feature of the Nagato class was the installation of auxiliary turbines for driving the centre shafts at synchronous speed when cruising on the wing shafts. Two rudders of balanced type were fitted. Incidentally, gear cutting for some time presented a problem for the Imperial Japanese Navy, requiring *Nagato*'s double-reduction gears to be manufactured by Westinghouse. Teeth-cutting machines were imported from Britain (David Brown & Sons) and then Germany (Reinecker, etc.), but it was not until the late 1930s that domestic production was deemed satisfactory. Finally, electricity was provided by four 250kW turbine-driven generators and one 25kW diesel-driven generator for a total of 1,025kW. Voltage was 225V using DC current. The ship was lit by the installation of approximately 2,450 electric lamps.

Construction, Arrival and Impact

Nagato was laid down at Kure Navy Yard on 28 August 1917, occupying the same slip as that on which the battleship *Fusō* had been built and where the battlecruiser (eventually aircraft carrier) *Akagi* and the battleship *Yamato* followed (after extension of the slip). Construction proceeded uneventfully, but launching was delayed by almost six months until 9 November 1919 due to difficulties obtaining materials and spiralling costs during the First World War. Thereafter, fitting out progressed at unusual speed for so large a vessel, and *Nagato* was completed on 25 November 1920, followed eleven months later by *Mutsu* at Yokosuka Navy Yard. The emphasis placed on completing *Nagato* and particularly *Mutsu* was due to the impending naval disarmament conference which opened in Washington in November 1921. *Mutsu*, for which a new design incorporating all of the lessons of Jutland had wisely been shelved owing to time considerations, was in fact only nominally complete, the ship lacking part of her armament and equipment and having yet to run trials. Her status was therefore the subject of lively discussion at the conference, not least because the Japanese delegation was determined to retain her as part of a tactical unit with *Nagato*, quite aside from her having been paid for in part by public subscription. The Imperial Japanese Navy ultimately negotiated the retention of *Mutsu*, but in return for agreeing to the completion of two further units of the Colorado class armed with 16in guns (of which one was subsequently cancelled) and the construction of two British battleships (*Nelson* and *Rodney*) under the treaty limitations of 35,000 tons' standard displacement and 16in guns. Failure to

Nagato's keel-laying and naming ceremony at Kure on 28 August 1917. *(Lengerer/Ahlberg Collection)*

Capital ships of the Imperial Japanese Navy in the early 1930s. *Nagato* is closest to the camera with the battlecruiser *Kirishima*, the battleships *Ise* and *Hyūga*, and a Sendai-class light cruiser lying beyond. *(NHHC/NH 111609)*

Nagato seen in July 1927 with her original bow and the chrysanthemum device shown to good effect. Note the aircraft on no. '2' turret, possibly the Yokoshō Ro gō floatplane. *(NHHC/NH 111604)*

secure this concession could have had significant consequences in Japanese government circles, particularly among militarists already incensed at the imposition of the 5:5:3:1.7:1.7 tonnage ratio between Britain, the US, Japan, France and Italy respectively.

Nagato and *Mutsu* were therefore the first and the last battleships of the Imperial Japanese Navy's cherished Eight-Eight Fleet. Japan built no capital ships beyond aircraft carriers during the naval holiday which followed the Washington Treaty of February 1922, leaving these two vessels as the ultimate expression of Japanese naval power and prestige until the commissioning of the battleship *Yamato* in December 1941. This status is captured in the opening line of a popular song of the 1920s and '30s: '*Nagato* and *Mutsu* are our national pride'.

Peacetime Operations, 1920–34

On commissioning both *Nagato* and *Mutsu* assumed the mantle of fleet flagship or divisional flagship and embarked on that round of exercises, training, protocol and foreign visits which, together with refitting and reconstruction, to varying degrees, punctuated the peacetime careers of most of the world's capital ships.[6] On 1 December 1920 *Nagato* was assigned to the 1st Battleship Division flying the flag of Rear Admiral Sōjirō Tochinai, and received her first major visitor in the shape of Crown Prince Hirohito at Yokosuka on 13 February 1921. A year later she conveyed Marshal of France Joseph Joffre from the Naval Academy on the island of Etajima to nearby Miyajima in Hiroshima Bay, and on 12 April hosted Edward, Prince of Wales, and his aide-de-camp Lieutenant Lord Louis Mountbatten at Yokohama during the second of the prince's world cruises in the battlecruiser *Renown*.[7] The arrival of the British squadron was greeted by the entire 1st Fleet flying the White Ensign and a twenty-one-gun salute fired from *Nagato*'s 3in AA guns as

Renown came to her moorings near the flagship. Mountbatten made this entry in his diary:

> Next to our own service I have never seen such fine ships; any one of them could have taken us on, on equal terms. They were spotlessly clean, the men who were manning ship stood rigidly still and somehow I received the impression that here was a power to be reckoned with in a way in which no one who has not been here and seen for himself can possibly conceive. That impression was destined to be strengthened at every minute throughout this day.[8]

The Prince and Mountbatten were given a tour of *Nagato*'s engine spaces before repairing to the wardroom for lunch, followed by a *dégustation* of several cases of specially imported Johnnie Walker Scotch whisky, the Japanese having already acquired a taste for this beverage. Official efforts to procure a more extensive tour of the greatest ships in the Imperial Japanese Navy were rebuffed, a reflection, among other things, of the failure to renew the Anglo-Japanese Alliance that same year. However, Mountbatten succeeded where even the British naval attaché had failed and managed to make an unofficial but thorough inspection of *Mutsu*, due largely to the absence of her commanding officer and Lord Louis having been dismissed as a minor

---

[6] *Nagato* career details from Bob Hackett, Sander Kingsepp & Lars Ahlberg, 'IJN Battleship *Nagato*: Tabular Record of Movement', available on http://www.combinedfleet.com/nagatrom.htm

[7] Richard Hough, *Mountbatten: Hero of Our Time* (London: Weidenfeld & Nicolson, 1980), p. 58, and Philip Ziegler, *Mountbatten: The Official Biography* (London: Collins, 1985), p. 64.

[8] Philip Ziegler, ed., *The Diaries of Lord Louis Mountbatten* (London: Collins, 1987), p. 278.

The forecastle during a standeasy in the 1920s. (*Courtesy Philippe Caresse*)

princeling with scant knowledge of naval affairs.[9] In the event, the tour, which extended to an entire turret and the upper deck torpedo tubes, was an eye-opener for Mountbatten, who not only provided the Admiralty with a comprehensive report of *Mutsu*'s armour and armament, but formed a lasting impression of the power, sophistication and aggressive outlook of the Japanese military establishment. 'This,' he wrote prophetically 'is the war I fear.'

At 1500 on 1 September 1923, while preparing for an inspection following manoeuvres in the Changshan archipelago off Korea, *Nagato* received news of the Great Kantō earthquake which flattened or burnt much of Tokyo, Yokohama and the surrounding area, and claimed over a hundred thousand lives. *Nagato* immediately sailed in the teeth of a typhoon for the southern island of Kyushu where relief supplies were embarked on 4 September and unloaded at Yokohama the following day. In September of the following year she joined with *Mutsu* in sinking the obsolete semi-dreadnought *Aki* during a gunnery exercise in Tokyo Bay under the terms of the Washington Naval Treaty, and on 1 December entered the reserve as a gunnery training ship at Yokosuka, the opportunity being taken to trunk her forward funnel aft to spare the occupants of the pagoda and the main fire director from oppressive funnel gases. In August 1925 aircraft handling and flying-off trials were conducted under the supervision of the aircraft designer Ernst Heinkel and a party of

German engineers with a custom-built platform mounted atop no. '2' turret and employing Heinkel HD 25 and HD 26 prototype floatplanes, together with the Yokoshō Ro gō floatplane. On 1 December *Nagato* became flagship of the Combined Fleet wearing the flag of Admiral Okada Keisuke, in which status she remained until assigned to training duties in December 1928. Before doing so she made one

of her rare foreign visits, on this occasion to Hong Kong in April 1928, and on 4 December led the fleet at the ceremonial review off Yokohama to celebrate the accession of the Emperor Hirohito. The next episode of note was the major fleet exercise carried out north of the Marshall Islands in August 1933, followed by her first major modernisation which began in the spring of 1934.

Life Aboard

On 31 May 1920 internal order no. 164 listed *Nagato*'s complement as 1,331 officers and men. This figure remained largely unchanged even after the reconstruction of 1934–6, the ship's company being recorded as 1,317 men on 23 April 1937, consisting of forty-seven officers, sixteen special duty officers, fourteen warrant officers, 328 petty officers and 912 seamen. The bulk of the crew was divided into the twenty-one divisions (*buntai*) shown below, each commanded by a divisional officer (*buntaichō*):

In 1942 an eighteen-year-old rating had to be at least 5ft 2in (157cm) tall, weigh 104lb (47kg) and have eyesight of at least 20/20 to be accepted into the navy. However, those shorter, smaller or with inferior vision could be accepted so long as they were robust in body and had eyesight

Some of *Nagato*'s ship's company of 1,317 men pictured on the forecastle in 1937. (*Lengerer/Ahlberg Collection*)

capable of being corrected to 20/20. Aviators, however, could only pass with eyesight of 20/16 or better.

The fact that the Imperial Japanese Navy had modelled itself on the Royal Navy since 1870 resulted in considerable similarity in customs, routine and organisation between the two. As a flagship *Nagato* was fitted with suites and cabins for the admiral and his staff, as well as for the captain and senior officers embarked. Officers and warrant officers had private cabins, and there was a gunroom for midshipmen, while

petty officers and ratings lived out of hammocks, kit bags and lockers in the British style in messes ranged on the middle and lower decks. The men ate off tables while seated on forms, but it is probable that these were removed following Japan's entry into the war leaving ratings at least to dine on *tatami* placed on the deck in the Japanese domestic manner. Although the 1929–30 edition of the *Nagato* guidebook reported that 'cool air in summer and warmth in winter are supplied to every corner of the ship', ventilation of the messdecks was no great

priority in the design of *Nagato* and was confined to the senior officers' cabins and critical spaces such as the magazines, conning tower and wireless offices. However, such installations were gradually extended to the crew living quarters and the engine spaces.

The ranks of warrant officer and above were provided with four galleys, while petty officers and ratings were served from three galleys, each capable of feeding four hundred men and purveying a diet of rice, meat, bread, vegetables, pickles and fish. Large vats were used to cook

MODERNISATION, 1934–6

The Imperial Japanese Navy was concerned to keep its two major units in optimum operating and fighting condition, and by the early 1930s the time had come for both vessels to undergo reconstruction. In *Mutsu*'s case this began in November 1933 while work started on *Nagato* at Kure Navy Yard in April 1934, both ships emerging in 1936. The major improvements from which both benefited were a direct product of Japan's decision to end its adherence to the Washington Treaty, which was announced on 29 December 1934 and enacted two years later, thereby giving Japanese designers the freedom to work without tonnage restrictions. The chief alterations to *Nagato* were these:

– Replacement of the original twenty-one boilers

by ten units, thereby permitting the removal of the forward funnel; much weight and space was saved but the opportunity to replace the engines was passed up, resulting in a loss of approximately 2 knots in her best speed.

– Reconstruction of the pagoda-type tower mast and installation of the fire-control and command equipment for the main and secondary armament, high-angle guns, machine guns and also night-fighting facilities including repositioning of searchlights, etc.

– Improvement of horizontal, vertical and underwater protection, increasing the maximum beam from 95ft (28.96m) to 113ft 6in (34.59m).

– Lengthening of the stern by 30ft (9.14m) to 738ft (224.94m) to reduce hull resistance and compensate for the increase in normal

displacement from 33,870 to 39,130 tons.

– Increase of the elevation of the main armament from 30 degrees to 43 degrees in response to extended battle ranges, together with replacement of the turrets by those produced for the Kaga-class battleships prior to their conversion as aircraft carriers.

– Modernisation of the secondary and tertiary armament, including removal of two 5.5in (140mm) guns on the upper deck and mounting of eight 5in (127mm) twin high-angle guns.

– Removal of the torpedo tubes.

– Fitting of an innovative damage-control system consisting of an emergency flooding and pumping system designed to maintain or regain stability.

– Fitting of anti-poison gas equipment for key cabins and compartments.

Nagato seen shortly after emerging from her major refit of 1934–6. The main visual alterations are the new bow and the single funnel. *(Courtesy Philippe Caresse)*

rice, which was available at any time of day for off-duty sailors. Fish was cooked in a similar manner, but could not be eaten freely. Naturally enough, the provender was rather more generous and varied where the officers were concerned. Here are the arrangements during the two and a half years Admiral Yamamoto Isoroku, himself a hearty eater, flew his flag in *Nagato* between September 1939 and February 1942:

Breakfast for the Combined Fleet command was either Japanese-style or – for those who wanted it and told the servant the night before – Western-style with coffee, porridge and so on. The general consensus, however, was that 'one cannot make war on porridge', and most people chose the regulation bean-paste soup and rice.

Luncheon was a full Western meal beginning with soup and ending with dessert, and employing both silver tableware and finger bowls. During the meal, for thirty minutes beginning at 1205, the band would provide music for the C. in C.'s enjoyment on the quarterdeck. This also served as the band's daily practise period, but the repertoire seldom included martial tunes such as the well-known 'Battleship March'; the emphasis, rather, was on sentimental Japanese melodies and popular Western music. [...] The rest of the ship's company would get lunch over quickly in order to go out on the quarterdeck and listen to the music; it provided one of the chief relaxations on board the flagship, but only, of course while the ship was at anchor.

The evening meal, Japanese-style again, included such delicacies as sea bream, either salted or grilled, savoury egg custard, and sashimi, and the galley made a point of employing cooks noted for their skill. The only drawback was that, since naval officers paid their own wardroom expenses, the young officers who occupied the foot of the table found such luxuries a considerable strain on their purses.

At lunch and dinner the C. in C. and all his officers were, in principle, supposed to be present, the rectangular conference table in the C. in C.'s cabin being transformed into a dining table by the addition of a white cloth. On a battleship like the *Nagato* this cabin made great use of teak, in the manner of the first-class saloon in a rather old-fashioned

Nagato: Divisional System (1943)

Battle Organisation (*Sentō hensei*) and **Administrative Organisation** (*Jōmu hensei*)

Department (*Kamei*)	Division Number (*Buntai bangō*) and Battle Station (*Sentō haichi*)
Gunnery (*Hōjutsuchō*)	1: Main armament (*Shuhō hōdai*)
	2: Main armament (*Shuhō hōdai*)
	3: Main armament (*Shuhō hōdai*)
	4: Main armament (*Shuhō hōdai*)
	5: Secondary battery (*Fukuhō hōdai*)
	6: High-angle gun battery (*Kōkakuhō hōdai*)
	7: Machine gun battery (*Kijū hōdai*)
	8: Main armament fire control (*Shuhō shageki kanbu*)
	9: Secondary battery fire control (*Fukuhō shageki kanbu*)
	10: Rangefinding division (*Sokutekibu*)
Communications (*Tsūshin*)	11: Communications (*Tsūshin*)
Navigation (*Kōkai*)	12: Navigation (*Kōkai*)
Internal Affairs (*Naimu*)	13: Daily routine (*Unyō*)
	14: Repair (*Kōsaku*)
	15: Electricity (*Denki*)
	16: Auxiliary engine (*Hoki*)
Aviation (*Hikō*)	17: Aviation (*Hikō*)
Engineering (*Kikan*)	18: Engine (*Kikai*)
	19: Boiler (*Kan*)
Medical Affairs (*Imu*)	20: Medical affairs (*Imu*)
Paymaster (*Shukei*)	21: Paymaster (*Shukei*)

Source: In collab., *Nihon Kaigun Nyūmon* (Tokyo: Gakken, 2007), p. 180.

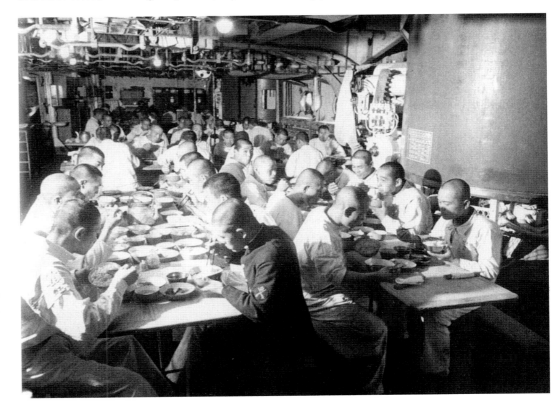

Mealtime on one of the messdecks of *Nagato* or *Mutsu* before the Second World War. The fittings and layout are similar to those in a British vessel with their tables, forms, kinked hammock bars on the deckhead and teapots, in this case no doubt filled with green tea. (*Sekai no Kansen*)

liner, the idea being that any guest at any port anywhere in the world could be welcomed aboard without disgrace.[10]

Although *Nagato*'s evaporators were capable of distilling 48 tons of water each day, the complement had a restricted supply for washing, bathing and laundry, the facilities for which were primitive and exiguous by European and particularly US standards. However, from the Japanese point of view 'much attention is paid to sanitation ... the interior of the ship is cleaned daily ... heads are always disinfected and inspected by the executive officer, chief surgeon and chief paymaster. To keep the crew healthy, a physical inspection is carried out every night and there are fully equipped spaces for medical treatment' with three trained medical officers embarked.

Sport was much practised aboard, including sumo wrestling, judo, archery, fencing, handball, swimming, and even cricket. Other recreational activities included frequent screenings of films, reading (from the ship's library) and listening to 'talking machines' (gramophones).[11] Every ship had its own Shintō shrine but worship was left to each sailor's conscience and the ship's company included practising Buddhists and, as a small minority, Christians. As in all ships of the Imperial Japanese Navy, the portrait of the emperor was guarded and revered much as the colours of a regiment.

Peacetime Weekly Port Routine

	Morning		Afternoon		Remarks
Sunday	Holiday		Holiday		Training, daily routines, drill and maintenance if necessary
Monday	Education	(1) Rounds (2) Moral education	Training	(1) Station training (2) Additional duties	(2) if necessary
Tuesday	Training	(1) Laundry (2) Additional duties	(3) Station training	(2) if necessary	
Wednesday	Training	(1) Station training (2) Additional duties			
Thursday	Training	(1) Station training (2) Additional duties			
Friday	Maintenance	(1) Laundry (hammocks, canvas) (2) Hull, weapons, engine maintenance (3) Additional duties		(1) if necessary	
Saturday	Maintenance	(1) Clean ship (2) Fire drill (3) Tidy all stations and personal effects			

Source: In collab., *Nihon Kaigun Nyūmon*, p. 183.

Discipline was by any standards severe and became more so during the course of *Nagato*'s career, a reflection of the increasingly selective and brutal regime imposed on officer cadets at the Etajima Naval Academy, with statutory corporal punishment complemented by impromptu punching, slapping and beating. These practices were extended by officers to their own kind and to sailors afloat and were in turn visited with ferocity by petty officers on junior ratings in a self-perpetuating culture of violence. Although some no doubt thrived on this, many others suffered from poor morale and took recourse to alcohol, including a lethal brew of diluted ethyl alcohol, the fumes of which may conceivably have contributed to the catastrophic explosion which claimed *Mutsu* at Hashirajima on 8 June 1943; although the seat of the explosion was traced to the magazine below no. '3' turret, the Investigation Committee could not identify the cause which remains uncertain to this day.

To War

No sooner had *Nagato* emerged from her major refit on 31 January 1936 and joined the 1st Battleship Division of the 1st Fleet than she found herself caught up first in the increasingly fraught environment of Japanese domestic politics and then in the military expansionism which brought her into the Second World War. On 26 February an attempted *coup d'état* by junior army officers against the civilian government caused the ship to be ordered to Tokyo Bay where she trained her guns on the Diet which had been taken over by the insurgents, parties of sailors being landed to help quell the revolt. The outbreak of the Second Sino-Japanese War in July 1937 saw *Nagato* pressed into service as a military transport, conveying 1,749 men of the 43rd Infantry Regiment of the 11th Infantry

Sumo wrestling on the quarterdeck during a royal visit to *Nagato* in 1926. Crown Prince and future Emperor Hirohito is seated at the table beyond the sumo ring known as the *dohyō*. (Courtesy Kitamura Kunio)

10 Agawa Hiroyuki, *The Reluctant Admiral: Yamamoto and the Imperial Navy* (Tokyo: Kodansha International, 1979), pp. 14–15. Translation adapted.
11 Uchiyama Mutsuo, email to authors, 24 February 2016.

Division from the island of Shikoku in the Inland Sea to Shanghai in August. Once there, her three Nakajima E4N2 floatplanes bombed targets in the city on 24 August before the ship returned to Sasebo the following day. On 1 December she was assigned to training duties, remaining in this capacity until becoming the flagship of the Combined Fleet on 15 December 1938. By now flying the flag of Vice Admiral Yamamoto Isoroku, *Nagato* still held this distinction on 11 October 1940 when she led an imperial review to celebrate the 2,600th anniversary of the accession of Jimmu, the legendary first Emperor of Japan. Spread across Yokohama Bay for inspection by Jimmu's 123rd successor, the Emperor Hirohito, were ninety-eight vessels, their crews manning ship as the dignitaries took the salute from the fast battleship *Hiei*.

In the spring of 1941 *Nagato* underwent her last pre-war refit involving the exchange of her 16in gun barrels, fitting of an external degaussing coil and filling of the anti-torpedo bulges with crushing tubes. Still Yamamoto's flagship, on 2 December *Nagato* made the momentous signal 'Niitakayama nobore 1208' – Climb Mount Niitaka – to the Carrier Strike Force, then steaming 940 miles north of Midway, thus setting in motion the complex operation by which hostilities were commenced against the United States. Sailing that day from Hashirajima in the Inland Sea for the Bonin Islands with the 1st Battleship Division of the 2nd Fleet, *Nagato*'s first wartime duty was as distant cover for the attack by the Air Fleet on Pearl Harbor on the morning of 7 December. *Nagato* thereafter kept mainly to the Inland Sea until 29 May 1942 when she sailed from Hashirajima with the 1st Battleship Division of the 1st Fleet, including *Yamato* (to which Yamamoto had shifted his flag in February) and *Mutsu* as part of the main force for the invasion of Midway, but never came within 300 miles of the ill-fated Carrier Strike Force and saw no action in the ensuing battle.

The catastrophe at Midway brought about a reorganisation of the fleet, *Nagato* spending over a year in refit at Kure and on exercises in the Inland Sea before steaming for Truk Lagoon in the Caroline Islands in August 1943. Truk was the Imperial Japanese Navy's forward anchorage in the South Pacific theatre and its main base for operations in the Solomon Islands

Nagato and the carrier *Ryujo* (extreme right) off the Chinese port of Tsingtao (now Qingdao) in 1939. An aircraft-handling crane has been installed abreast the after turrets and some of the newly-fitted 1in (25mm) machine gun platforms can just be made out around the funnel. *(Lengerer/Ahlberg Collection)*

The Commander-in-Chief of the Combined Fleet, Admiral Yamamoto Isoroku (left), with his Chief of Staff Rear Admiral Ugaki Matome seen on *Nagato*'s bridge sometime between August 1941 and February 1942 when both flew their flags in her. It was from *Nagato* that Yamamoto planned and commanded the momentous attack on Pearl Harbor in December 1941. *(Sekai no Kansen)*

and New Guinea, and as such was a priority target for Allied aviation. Alerted by signals intelligence to the imminent danger of attack, on 1 February 1944 *Nagato* quit Truk first for Palau and then for Lingga anchorage in Malaya where she carried out exercises interrupted by a brief refit in the King George VI Dry Dock at Singapore in the first half of April. Lingga lies on the equator and the crew of *Nagato* took the opportunity to hold crossing the line festivities on 15 March. The hard-boiled Vice Admiral Ugaki Matome, then commanding the 1st Squadron, took an ambivalent view of these junketings in a ship which had yet to see much action. 'It was good to relax and boost morale but seeing the number of theatrical props they had I couldn't help wondering whether they were really ready for battle.'[12] Nonetheless, this comparatively peaceful interlude was almost over. In May *Nagato* advanced to Tawi-Tawi Island off Borneo and took part in the disastrous Battle of the Philippine Sea on 19–20 June during which the Japanese naval air arm was largely destroyed. *Nagato*, always a lucky ship, escaped with no more than a strafing. Four days later she reached Hashirajima via Okinawa and on the 27th proceeded to Kure Navy Yard where, among other modifications, significant improvements were made to her close-range anti-aircraft defence, with surface and air-search radar being fitted. Emerging from this on 8 July, she conveyed troops and supplies to Okinawa before returning to Lingga for further training and exercises. However, the 'decisive battle' for

which *Nagato* and the remaining battleships of the Imperial Japanese Navy had long been intended was not far off.

Nagato at the Battle of Leyte Gulf

The Battle of Leyte Gulf, perhaps the greatest naval engagement in history, was brought on by Japanese attempts to interdict the US invasion of the Philippines which began on 17 October 1944. Reports that US forces had begun landing on the island of Leyte triggered the activation by the Japanese of *Shō Ichi Gō Sakusen* (Operation Victory One) which had the following aims: (1) commit all available land-based air forces to attacking the enemy invasion fleet, (2) employ the surviving Japanese carrier forces to lure the US battlefleet northward away from the landing area, and (3) use Japanese heavy units to annihilate the unprotected invasion fleet two days after the start of the main landings. *Nagato*'s role in this complex and desperate plan was as part of Vice Admiral Ugaki's 1st Squadron in company with the battleships *Yamato* and *Musashi*, themselves part of the 1st Night Battle Force (NBF), which was in turn part of the Centre Force commanded by Vice Admiral Kurita Takeo. The remaining Japanese assets consisted of the remnants of the carrier fleet known as the Northern Force under Vice Admiral Ozawa Jisaburō, which was to serve in a decoy capacity, and the battleships of the Southern Force under Vice Admiral Nishimura Shōji which was intended to force the Surigao Strait. The 1st NBF

sailed from Lingga at 0100 on the 18th and reached Brunei Bay on the west coast of Borneo for final replenishment at noon on the 20th. Two days later it weighed anchor and steered for its intended destination off the Leyte shore, almost 1,200 miles distant. A tortuous route would take it through the Palawan Passage and the Mindoro Strait, in which it would run the gauntlet of US submarines, followed by the Tablas Strait and then the Sibuyan Sea where it could expect to come under concentrated air attack. Next it had to traverse the San Bernardino Strait, steam along the east coast of Samar, and at length pass into Leyte Gulf itself. This route was favoured because it lay outside the range of US aircraft stationed at Morotai, thereby reducing the possibility of carrier-based aviation being directed onto it until the last stages of the approach. Needless to say, things did not go to plan.

A day after sailing from Brunei Bay the 1st NBF was waylaid by the US submarines *Darter* and *Dace* while heading along the west coast of Palawan on 23 October, suffering the loss of the heavy cruisers *Atago* (Kurita's flagship) and *Maya* and having a third, *Takao*, crippled. Now reduced to three ships and plagued by continual bogus submarine sightings, the 1st NBF rounded the southern tip of Mindoro Island and proceeded into the Sibuyan Sea where at 0800 on the morning of the 24th it was detected by aircraft from Vice Admiral Marc Mitscher's Task Force 38, then operating 200 miles to the north off Luzon. Identified as a heavy cruiser by US observers, *Nagato* was positioned on the left flank of the 1st NBF as part of the first ring anti-aircraft formation, the ship keeping station astern of *Yamato* at 18 knots.[13] At 1015, as the force at large went on to 22 knots, Rear Admiral Kōbe Yūji commanding *Nagato* passed the order for action stations as US aircraft put in the first of five major attacks over the course of the next five hours. In the air command station Chief Gunnery Officer Inoue Takeo ordered 'Main and secondary guns commence fire on the enemy

Nagato off Hashirajima in Hiroshima Bay in August 1942. All nine guns of the port 5.5in secondary battery are trained on the beam. *(Lengerer/Ahlberg Collection)*

---

[12] Ugaki Matome, *Fading Victory: The Diary of Admiral Matome Ugaki, 1941–1945* (Pittsburgh, Pa.: University of Pittsburgh, 1991), p. 339.

[13] See Bōeichō Bōeikenshūjo Senshibu, *Senshi Sōsho*, vol. 56, and Hans Lengerer & Lars Ahlberg, *Capital Ships of the Imperial Japanese Navy, 1868–1945: The Yamato Class and Subsequent Planning* (Ann Arbor, Mich.: Nimble Books, 2014) for maps of this and other formations and track charts based on the war diaries.

Nagato at Brunei Bay on 21 October 1944, the day before she sailed on the operation which culminated in the Battle of Leyte Gulf. *(Lengerer/Ahlberg Collection)*

planes to starboard!' and 'Independent firing!' The air defence buzzer rang and at 1027 *Nagato* opened up, including the firing of Type-3 incendiary shells from the main armament. Taking *Nagato* as their target, four SB2C Helldiver dive-bombers attacked with clusters of bombs, but though two detonated off the starboard bow no hits were obtained. At 1033 *Nagato*'s lookouts reported eight TBM Avenger torpedo bombers to port, Rear Admiral Kōbe manoeuvring accordingly, but the attack was directed mainly against *Yamato* and *Musashi*.

The first air attack ended at 1040, the crew being stood down at 1047, but at 1154 *Musashi* detected an unknown formation of aircraft at a range of 11,000yds (10,000m), and ten minutes later lookouts in *Nagato* sighted thirty-one dive-bombers from the carrier *Intrepid*. Within minutes, *Nagato* was the focus of an attack by a single Helldiver whose bomb was evaded by an emergency turn to port. However, the brunt of this attack fell on *Musashi* which took seven

bomb and torpedo hits. The attack ended at 1218, the 1st NBF making a 90-degree course alteration and reducing speed to 16 knots. Nonetheless, the US Navy was back an hour later, this time targeting the thirteen ships of the

second ring formation in which the battleships *Kongō* and *Haruna* were prominent. Having engaged targets shortly after 1330, *Nagato* found herself the subject of an attack by four Avengers but again succeeded in evading the fish. Twenty

Nagato under attack from aircraft of Task Force 38 during the Battle of the Sibuyan Sea on 24 October 1944. She has just fired a salvo of Type-3 incendiary shells from her forward 16in guns. *(National Archives/80-G-272557)*

minutes later she was attacked by four Helldivers which released eight bombs, but still her luck held. The fourth attack, however, brought *Nagato* her first damage when four near-misses from bomb-armed F6F Hellcat fighters perforated her starboard side forward with about seven hundred holes.

However, it was the fifth and final attack which began at 1514 that ended *Nagato*'s run of good luck and inflicted severe damage on the ship. Kōbe ordered the wheel flung hard to port, the chief gunnery officer once again passing the order for independent fire, but *Nagato* was on this occasion overwhelmed by seven Helldivers and eight Hellcats from the carrier *Franklin*, which scored two hits, probably with 500lb (227kg) bombs. One struck the boat deck amidships, putting three secondary guns out of action and damaging the ventilation system of no. '1' boiler room which had to be temporarily evacuated, reducing *Nagato*'s best speed to 22 knots while emergency repairs were carried out. The explosion dislodged the mounting of one of the 5in HA guns, preventing it being trained, though this was rectified within an hour or so by judicious cutting of deck plates. The second bomb penetrated the seamen's galley and detonated in the after part of the communication room, destroying radio, telephone and encyphering equipment, and disrupting both internal and external communications. Firefighting efforts by damage-control parties resulted in several men being electrocuted

when cables were severed in flooded compartments. Meanwhile, three near-misses added to the number of perforations in the hull. At 1534 the chief gunnery officer gave the order to cease fire as the fifth and final attack of the day subsided. The attack had cost the lives of fifty-two men in *Nagato*, with twenty severely and eighty-six lightly wounded for a total of 158 casualties. It was during this attack, too, that *Musashi* took the last of her thirty-seven bomb and torpedo hits, the ship succumbing that evening.

Nagato, however, steamed on, her crew labouring to plug the holes in the hull while the cooks, their main galley destroyed, struggled to provide sustenance for a ship's company which circumstances had kept unfed and at action stations since before dawn. At 0035 on the 25th the 1st NBF, now reduced from thirty-one ships to twenty-three, passed through the San Bernardino Strait and steered to its intended rendezvous with Vice Admiral Nishimura's Southern Force. In the event, the meeting never materialised because the Southern Force was practically annihilated at the Battle of the Surigao Strait in the early hours of the 25th. Nonetheless, Vice Admiral Kurita pressed on and the predawn found the Centre Force including *Nagato* steaming south off the island of Samar. At 0617, ten minutes before sunrise, the order 'Air attack stations!' was passed and the ships were just beginning to manoeuvre from the night to the ring formation at 0623 when *Yamato*'s air search radar detected a swarm of enemy aircraft at a range of thirty miles. Battle was joined at 0640 but a minute later lookouts in *Nagato* reported masts on the horizon. These were the six escort carriers and seven destroyers of Rear Admiral Clifton Sprague's Task Unit 77.4.3 ('Taffy 3') which had been exposed by Admiral William F. Halsey's questionable decision to leave the San Bernardino Strait unguarded by major units while the bulk of his fleet was successfully decoyed by Vice Admiral Ozawa's Northern Force. *Nagato*'s anti-aircraft battery opened up against four aircraft at 0648, but three minutes later Rear Admiral Kōbe ordered 'Guns engage to port!' and rang down for maximum speed. *Yamato* immediately opened fire from her forward turrets, *Nagato* following suit at a range of 35,000yds (32,800m), initially with Type-3

incendiary shells intended for aircraft formations but subsequently with armour-piercing shells. The initial target for *Nagato*'s gunfire was the escort carrier USS *St. Lo*, but accuracy was spoiled by the intense smokescreens laid by Sprague's force, the limitations of the Japanese Type-22 gunnery radar and harassing attacks by Taffy 3's aircraft and destroyers, *Yamato* and *Nagato* making a subsequently much-criticised ten-mile detour to the north to avoid a torpedo attack from the destroyer *Heermann* at 0700. Two and a half hours after this stern chase had begun, and just when the destruction of Taffy 3 seemed certain, Kurita ordered his ships to break off the action and rejoin the flagship. Although the Japanese claimed that four aircraft carriers, three heavy cruisers and three destroyers had been sunk, the actual US losses during this part of the engagement were the escort carrier *Gambier Bay* and four destroyers. These losses might have been much greater had high-explosive rather than armour-piercing shells been used, the escort carrier *Kalinin Bay* being struck no less than fifteen times by 8in (203mm) AP shells which failed to detonate.

Reassembling the Centre Force, which had suffered the loss of the heavy cruisers *Chokai*, *Chikuma* and *Suzuya* to Taffy 3, took approximately ninety minutes before it turned for the entrance to Leyte Gulf at 1020. Although Kurita was aware from a report received at 0200 on the 24th that eighty US transports were lying in Leyte Gulf, this intelligence was nearly a day and a half old, and his uncertainty as to whether these vessels were still in the anchorage together with his conviction that a decisive engagement with the US fleet to the north would better serve Japanese interests than an assault on the Leyte anchorage – the key goal of Operation Victory One – prompted a change of plan. At 1230 he signalled the Commander-in-Chief of the Combined Fleet, Admiral Toyota Soemu, to the effect that he intended to give up entering Leyte Gulf and instead proceed north along the east coast of Samar with the aim of traversing the San Bernardino Strait following a decisive battle with the enemy. Not even reports from one of *Nagato*'s reconnaissance planes (transshipped from *Yamato*) reporting the presence of forty transports in Leyte Gulf at 1230 and received by

Damage control training aboard *Nagato* before the Second World War. Note the timber, gas masks and hammocks; war would require more stringent measures. *(Sekai no Kansen)*

Nagato: Ammunition expended, 23–25 October 1944

16.14in (410mm)	Type-1 AP Model 4:	45	Type-0 Common:	52	Type-3 Incendiary:	84 **181**
5.5in (140mm)	Capped Common Model 2:	92	No. 2 Common (red):	41	Type-0 Common:	520 **668**
5in (127mm)	Common:	1,502	Incendiary:	38		**1,540**
1in (25mm)	Common:	35,209	Tracer:	12,327		**47,536**
					Total:	**49,925**

Nagato cuts a forlorn figure in Tokyo Bay after the Japanese surrender, the Stars & Stripes flying from the jackstaff and her chrysanthemum crest missing. The secondary armament and portions of the superstructure, funnel and masts had been removed before she was struck by two bombs on 18 July 1945. Within a year she had been expended at the US atomic bomb tests at Bikini Atoll. *(Courtesy Philippe Caresse)*

The end of time for *Nagato*. *(Bruce Taylor Collection)*

Kurita at 1320 just as the Centre Force altered course to the north dissuaded him. Meanwhile, the 1st NBF had at 1245 come under attack from thirty-five Avengers and thirty-five Wildcat fighters, which scored two bomb hits forward on *Nagato*, one of which penetrated the cable deck while the other ricocheted and detonated outboard, further damaging the bows.[14] Harried throughout the afternoon by air attacks, *Nagato* suffered her final casualties of the operation when a violent evasive manoeuvre while avoiding a squadron of dive-bombers resulted in four AA gunners being washed overboard. In the event, Kurita failed to intercept the US fleet and withdrew through the San Bernardino Strait, the 1st NBF suffering further attacks by carrier-based torpedo bombers and Army B-24 Liberators off Panay on 26 October. *Nagato* responded with her main and secondary armament, and claimed several aircraft shot down while suffering no further damage. With this the Battle of Leyte Gulf ended and with it all hope of the Imperial Japanese Navy regaining command of the sea.

In his four-volume *Daitōa Sensō Zenshi* (Complete History of the Greater East Asia War) Colonel Hattori Takushirō levelled severe criticism at Kurita for having passed up the opportunity to fulfil the primary mission of the operation of annihilating the invasion fleet in Leyte Gulf, opting instead to steer north after the 'suppression operation' against Taffy 3 – this despite Vice Admiral Ozawa having sacrificed his carrier force to lure the enemy north.[15] Although Kurita seems subsequently to have acknowledged his error in turning away from Leyte Gulf, many of his ships were heavily damaged and low on fuel and he had by then learnt of the destruction of both the Northern and the Southern Force. The circumstances are not altogether clear but his decision-making may therefore have been influenced by a concern to avoid committing further lives to a war effort he already privately regarded as futile. Whatever the case, Kurita was relieved of his command on 20 December and appointed president of the Etajima Naval Academy.

The End

The remnants of the 1st NBF reached Brunei Bay on 28 October where they immediately refuelled. Nonetheless, the days when the Japanese surface fleet could present a credible threat to the progress of the US Navy across the Pacific were past, and a raid by US Army B-24s on 16 November prompted the removal of the battleship group consisting of *Yamato*, *Nagato* and *Kongō* from Brunei Bay for home waters the following day. Despite an escort of destroyers and the light cruiser *Noshiro*, *Kongō* fell victim to a torpedo attack by the US submarine *Sealion*

II on the 21st, but *Nagato* again rode her luck to reach Yokosuka unscathed on the 25th. Here she was dry-docked for repairs and prepared for service as a floating anti-aircraft battery protected by extensive camouflage and torpedo nets. Although this refit involved the addition of two 5in (127mm) and thirty 1in (25mm) AA guns, her armament was only partially operational for lack of motive power, there being insufficient fuel to flash up the boilers and generators.[16] Steam for the galley was provided by a coal-burning donkey boiler. The fact that *Nagato* was unlikely to put to sea again under her own power was reinforced by the removal of the funnel and the upper part of the mainmast to open the firing arcs.

Half a year passed with *Nagato* stationed as a guard ship at Yokosuka Naval Station before she and the other remnants of Japan's once mighty battlefleet – *Ise*, *Hyūga* and *Haruna* – were assigned to the Special Guard Fleet on 1 June

[14] Ugaki, *Fading Victory*, p. 500.

[15] Hattori Takushirō, *Daitōa Sensō Zenshi* (Tokyo: Hara Shobō, 1953).

[16] US Naval Historical Center (NHC), US Naval Technical Mission to Japan, Report S-06-1, p. 8.

1945. Stripped of her entire secondary armament and half of her 5in high-angle guns for mounting ashore against invasion and air attack, *Nagato* remained at Yokosuka under a reduced crew and heavily reinforced camouflage netting. However, camouflage availed her not on 18 July when TF 58 delivered a succession of massive air attacks on Yokosuka naval base where *Nagato*, the biggest ship in Tokyo Bay, found herself a prime target. Helpless though she was while carrier-based aircraft swarmed overhead, *Nagato* was hit by only two 500lb (224kg) bombs and a single dud 5in (127mm) rocket, although the hull was damaged by no less than sixty near-misses. The first bomb hit the bridge structure and demolished the pilot house and compass platform, killing thirteen men including the commanding and executive officers. A second penetrated the shelter deck abaft the mainmast and detonated near the base of no. '3' turret.[17] There was no fire and fighting efficiency was scarcely impaired, but four 1in mountings were put out of action and a further twenty-two casualties inflicted. The rocket hit the port side of the quarterdeck, passed through the admiral's cabin leaving a gash on the edge of a table before exiting the hull to starboard. As Admiral Kurita had foreseen the previous year, the war had now entered its final stages and *Nagato* was surrendered to the Allies on 30 August 1945 as Japan's only surviving 'operable' capital ship. Appropriately enough, it was men from Admiral Halsey's flagship USS *Iowa* which took possession of her. On 15 September she was stricken from the navy list, twenty-five years after commissioning as the most powerful vessel in the Imperial Japanese Navy.

In March 1946 *Nagato* embarked on her last voyage, being towed to Eniwetok where running repairs were carried out to hull and machinery before proceeding under her own power to Bikini Atoll where she was expended in the Able and Baker atomic bomb tests on 1 and 25 July respectively. The first test left *Nagato* sufficiently intact for a boiler to be flashed up for twenty-four hours but the second severely compromised the hull and she settled and sank in 160ft (49m) of water on 29 July 1946. She remains a remote but prized destination for scuba divers.

Sources

Unpublished Sources

Makino Shigeru, Fukui Shizuo *et al.*, *Kaigun Zōsen Gijutsu Gaiyō* [Outline of Naval

---

[17] *Ibid.*, pp. 8–13 & Plate I.

Shipbuilding Techniques] 7 vols. (1948–54; copy supplied by Capt. (retd.) Tamura Toshio)

U.S. Naval Historical Center, Washington D.C. (NHC): *U.S. Naval Technical Mission to Japan, 1945–1946*. Report S-06-1: *Reports of Damage to Japanese Warships. Article 1, Nagato (BB)*; available at http://www.fischer-tropsch.org/ [accessed October 2016]

Bibliography

In collab., *Nagato Gata Senkan* [Battleships of the Nagato Class], No. 15 (Tokyo: Gakken, 1997)

_____, *Nihon Kaigun Nyūmon* [The Imperial Japanese Navy] (Tokyo: Gakken, 2007)

Abe Yasuo, *Sekai no Kansen* [Ships of the World], No. 681 (Tokyo: Kaijinsha, 2007)

Agawa Hiroyuki, *The Reluctant Admiral: Yamamoto and the Imperial Navy* (Tokyo: Kodansha International, 1979)

_____, *Gunkan Nagato no shōgai* [The Life of the Battleship *Nagato*] (2 vols., Tokyo: Shinchōsha: 1976)

Bōeichō Bōeikenshūjo Senshibu, *Senshi Sōsho* [Military History Series] (102 vols., Tokyo: Asagumo Shimbusha, 1966–80)

Evans, David C., & Mark R. Peattie, *Kaigun: Strategy, Tactics, and Technology in the Imperial Japanese Navy, 1887–1941* (Annapolis, Md.: Naval Institute Press, 2012)

Fukuda Keiji, *Gunkan Kihon Keikaku Shiryō* [Summary of Warship Design Principles] (Tokyo: Konnichi no Wadai-sha, 1989)

Fukui Shizuo, *Nihon no Gunkan: Waga Zōkan Gijutsu no Hattatsu to Kantei no Hensen* [Japanese Warships: Development and Evolution of Naval Engineering] (Tokyo: Shuppan Kyōdōsha, 1956)

_____, *Kaigun Kantei-shi* [Japanese Naval Vessels Illustrated, 1869–1945] (3 vols., Tokyo: KK Bestsellers, 1974–82); I (1974): *Senkan · Jun-yōsenkan* [Battleships and Battlecruisers]

Fukui Shizuo *et al.*, *Fukui Shizuo Chosaku-shū: Gunkan Nanajū-go Nen Kaisō-ki* [The Collected Works of Fukui Shizuo: Seventy-Five Years of Warship History] (Tokyo: Kōjinsha, 1992–2003)

Hackett, Bob, Sander Kingsepp & Lars Ahlberg, 'IJN Battleship *Nagato*: Tabular Record of Movement' available on http://www.combinedfleet.com/nagatrom.htm [accessed October 2016]

Hattori Takushirō, *Daitōa Sensō Zenshi* (Tokyo: Hara Shobō, 1953)

Hough, Richard, *Mountbatten: Hero of Our Time* (London: Weidenfeld & Nicolson, 1980)

Ishibashi Takao, *Senkan · Jun-yōsenkan* [Battleships and Battlecruisers] (Tokyo: Namiki Shobō, 2007)

Izumi Kōzō, *Nihon no Senkan* [Japanese Battleships] (Tokyo: Grand Prix, 2001)

Lengerer, Hans, & Lars Ahlberg, *Capital Ships of the Imperial Japanese Navy, 1868–1945: The Yamato Class and Subsequent Planning* (Ann Arbor, Mich.: Nimble Books, 2014)

Kaigun Hōjutsu-shi Kankōkai, *Kaigun Hōjutsu-shi* [History of Naval Gunnery] (Tokyo: Kaigun Hōjutsu-shi Kankōkai, 1975)

Mayuzumi Haruo, *Kanpō Shageki no Rekishi* [History of Naval Guns and Fire Control Systems] (Tokyo: Hara Shobō, 1977)

Morison, Samuel E., *History of United States Naval Operations in World War II* (14 vols., Boston: Little, Brown & Company, 1947–62); XII (1958): *Leyte June 1944–January 1945*

Naitō Hatsuho, *Hiraga Yuzuru Ikō Shū* [Hiraga Yuzuru Manuscript Collection] (Tokyo: Shuppan Kyōdōsha, 1985)

Nihon Zōsen Kyōkai [Japanese Shipbuilding Association], *Shōwa Zōsen-shi* [History of Ship Construction in the Shōwa Era] (2 vols., Tokyo: Hara Shobō, 1977)

Nihon Zōsen Kikan-shi Henshū Iinkai [Editorial Board for the History of Marine Engineering in Japan], *Teikoku Kaigun Kikan-shi* [The History of Marine Engineering in Japan] (3 vols., Tokyo: Hara Shobō, 1975)

Okumoto Gō, *Hachi Hachi Kantai no Shuryokukan* [The Capital Ships of the Eight-Eight Fleet] (Tokyo: Kōjinsha, 2011)

Ōtsuka Yoshifuru, *Hachi Hachi Kantai Keikaku* [The Eight-Eight Fleet Plan] (Tokyo: Gakken, 2011)

Stille, Mark, *The Imperial Japanese Navy in the Pacific War* (Oxford: Osprey, 2014)

Tully, A. P., '*Nagato*'s Last Year: July 1945–July 1946' available on http://www.combinedfleet.com/picposts/Nagatostory.html [accessed October 2016]

Ugaki Matome, *Fading Victory: The Diary of Admiral Matome Ugaki, 1941–1945* (Pittsburgh, Pa.: University of Pittsburgh, 1991)

Yamamoto Yoshihide *et al.*, *Nihon Kaigun Kansai Heiki Daizukan* [Japanese Naval Shipboard Weapons] (Tokyo: KK Bestsellers, 2002)

Ziegler, Philip, *Mountbatten: The Official Biography* (London: Collins, 1985)

_____, ed., *The Diaries of Lord Louis Mountbatten* (London: Collins, 1987)

Merivoimat

The Coast Defence Ship
Väinämöinen (1930)

◆

Jari Aromaa

NAMED for the central figure in the Kalevala, Finland's great national epic, *Väinämöinen* and her near-inseparable sister *Ilmarinen* were the final expression of a line of Scandinavian coast defence vessels dating back to the 1880s. She was also a major achievement of planning, finance and design for a small country with a limited tradition of naval construction and organisation, and together with *Ilmarinen* formed the nucleus of the independent Finnish navy established after 1918. Although never tested in the roles for which they were designed, the coast defence ships nonetheless played their part in preserving Finland from seaborne invasion and provide a telling example of the fleet-in-being concept.

Finnish Naval Policy between the Wars

After over a hundred years as an autonomous grand duchy of Russia, the outbreak of the Bolshevik Revolution prompted Finland to declare her independence on 6 December 1917. This action, and particularly the civil war between the Whites and the Reds which followed in the spring of 1918, caused most vessels of the former Imperial Russian Navy lying in Finnish ports to evacuate to Kronstadt and Petrograd leaving a collection of small, weak and mostly obsolete vessels to form the nucleus of the new Finnish navy. Unlike Russia proper, in Finland it was the Whites who prevailed in the civil war, a circumstance which, as with other Nordic states, obliged Finland to pursue a defensive strategy

against foreign aggression, in her case by the Soviet Union. With few ships capable of operating on the open sea, Finland's initial seaward defence therefore turned on the development of an extensive coastal artillery system supported by closure of the sea lanes by minelaying vessels. This, however, was a formidable proposition. Although a chain of coastal forts had been established by the Russian Empire to counter attacks from the west and prevent landings in southwest Finland, the only likely threat now came from the east. Moreover, the Tartu Peace Treaty signed between Finland and Soviet Russia in December 1920 resulted in the dismantling of the coastal artillery batteries at Ino and Puumala near the Russian border and the neutralisation of the outer islands of the Gulf of Finland. Then came the Ahvenanmaa (Åland) archipelago lying at the entrance of the Gulf of Bothnia. While the Åland Convention of October 1921 allocated that archipelago to Finland, all fortifications built by Russia between 1914 and 1916 in contravention of the 1856 demilitarisation agreement had to be dismantled. The need to cover this exposed coastline and archipelago together with the limited resources of a nation of just three million people provides the immediate context for Finnish naval policy as it developed over the next twenty years, including the construction of the coast defence ship *Väinämöinen* and her sister *Ilmarinen*.

Several naval programmes were drawn up in the first decade after independence, including plans to provide the navy with big-gun and

Väinämöinen in 1938. She and her sister *Ilmarinen* were instrumental in preserving Finland from seaborne attack during the Second World War. *(Finnish War Museum)*

torpedo vessels in addition to destroyers, submarines and motor torpedo boats. The planning of the new navy fell into three phases. The first ran from 1919 to 1924 during which naval and other service personnel prepared integrated programmes, most of which were rejected on grounds of cost. This was followed by a development phase led by the Ministry of Defence with assistance from private shipyards between 1924 and 1927. The final phase began with the approval by the 1927 Parliament of the Law for the Construction of the Navy for Coast Defence (known as the Navy Act) with a budget of 375 million marks. Detailed planning work was carried out by Finnish navy experts, shipyards and the Ingenieurskantoor voor Scheepsbouw (also I.v.S. or Inkavos), the clandestine German design bureau operating in The Hague. The Navy Act provided for the construction of two 3,800-ton armoured gunboats (eventually completed as *panssarilaivat* – coast defence ships), three 400-ton submarines, one 100-ton submarine and four 15-ton motor torpedo boats. Although only 215 million marks of the original budget was allocated for the construction of these vessels, to be expended over the next four years, the programme was also financed by supplementary budgets in 1926 and 1927 so that a total of 315 million marks was eventually spent on naval procurement. Of this total some

210 million marks was spent on the coast defence ships, constituting approximately 5 per cent of the annual state budget in the early 1930s. Nonetheless, funding did not extend to communications equipment, and provision of armament and ammunition to some of the new ships was delayed.

As the new navy took shape in the 1930s so its role changed from mine warfare to countering the threat to the unfortified coastline extending eastward from Kotka to Helsinki and onward to Ahvenanmaa and to maintaining sea communications with Sweden. Supported by naval units, the task of the coastal artillery was now to repulse landings along the Gulf of Finland. Meanwhile, the Ahvenanmaa archipelago was regarded as the linchpin of Finnish naval defence, being provided with coast defence ships capable of fending off attacks by any warships except modern battleships, mine barrages and large numbers of torpedo vessels intended to contest landing operations supported by cruisers or smaller vessels. With the main units including *Väinämöinen* and *Ilmarinen* in service by 1934, the next step was the construction of destroyers, escorts and additional submarines, but the only other units added to the strength of the Finnish navy before the outbreak of war were the three-masted training ship *Suomen Joutsen* in 1931, the 250-ton submarine *Vesikko* in 1935 and six

Ahven-class motor minesweepers from 1937–8. *Väinämöinen* and *Ilmarinen* were therefore left without supporting units and the Finnish merchant marine without effective escorts. Opinions varied as to the desired strength of the navy, but a third coast defence ship, another two or three medium-sized submarines and up to six escorts, a handful of minelayers and several dozen motor torpedo boats were generally deemed necessary. In the event, these never got beyond the planning stage.

Origins, Design and Construction

Coast defence vessels in various forms (see *Eidsvold* and *Peder Skram*) and the evolution of the type into armoured ships (see *Sverige*) found favour in the Nordic countries with their long and fractured coastlines around the confined waters of the Baltic and the North Sea, and also with the Netherlands for service in the Dutch East Indies (see *De Zeven Provinciën*). Although the armoured ship was fully capable of operating on the high seas, the doctrine of the coast defence ship as originally conceived never included offensive operations in open waters, one reason being a lack of escort vessels. Units of the type generally had an armament of 8.3in or 9.4in (210–240mm) guns, protection to the standard of an armoured cruiser and a speed of around 15 to 18 knots on an average displacement of approximately 4,000 tons. A coast defence ship was therefore slower than an armoured cruiser but better armed, and faster than a monitor though generally mounting smaller guns; *Väinämöinen* lay closer to the monitor than the armoured cruiser on this spectrum and proved to be the last example of the type with the exception of the Japanese-built Sri Ayudhya-class coast defence ships of the Siamese navy which entered service in 1938.

The design of *Väinämöinen* was the product of a compromise between politicians, navy personnel and various shipyards. Politicians tried to keep the size of the ships down while the navy naturally wanted the most efficient and impressive vessels possible. The proposals submitted by shipyard representatives between 1924–5 therefore ran the gamut from the fanciful to the feasible, including designs for 2,450–4,500-ton vessels mounting 8.3–9.4in guns from the Swedish Lindholmen yard, a 3,600-ton vessel with 10.2in (260mm) guns from I.v.S., and a 2,500-ton design mounting 8.3in guns from the Italian Stabilimiento Tecnico Triestino yard. Nor did Finnish firms go unrepresented, with the Kone ja Silta yard of Helsinki submitting six 8.3in gun designs, while Crichton-Vulcan of Turku submitted a 3,900-ton design with an 11in

Väinämöinen alongside during a courtesy visit to Copenhagen on 27 May 1937. Note the 19.7ft rangefinder atop the conning tower and the twin 4.1in mountings in the waist and abaft the forward 10in turret. *(Courtesy Lars Jordt)*

(279mm) main armament. Although Crichton had a track record of construction for the Imperial Russian Navy going back to 1877 and had been awarded the contract for the Vetehinen-class submarines in 1927, it had never built anything on the scale of the coast defence ships. Despite having its tender for the new vessels accepted, in December 1927 Crichton-Vulcan unexpectedly declared itself to have too much work on its books and withdrew from the project. The government had therefore to issue new invitations to tender the following year, but Crichton-Vulcan came back with renewed interest and issued fresh proposals at reduced prices that autumn. These were accepted and the contract for what became *Väinämöinen* and *Ilmarinen* was finally awarded to that yard in December 1928.

These deliberations, tenders and contracts resulted in a pair of coast defence vessels 305ft (93.0m) long and 55.5ft (16.9m) in the beam with a draught of 14.8ft (4.5m) on a standard displacement of 3,900 tons. The main armament consisted of four 10in (254mm) Bofors guns in twin turrets, with a secondary armament of eight 4.1in (105mm) guns by the same manufacturer. Maximum design speed was 14.5 knots. Although Crichton-Vulcan was responsible for construction of the hull and the assembly of the vessel and installation of equipment, the fabric of *Väinämöinen* and *Ilmarinen* was substantially the work of four different companies in as many countries, while I.v.S., then preparing the designs for four Finnish submarines and given responsibility for checking and approving the plans of the coast defence ships, can be said to have designed them. Aside from Crichton-Vulcan's work on the hull, the diesel engines were manufactured by Friedrich Krupp Germaniawerft of Kiel, the generators and propeller motors by Brown, Boveri & Cie of Baden, Switzerland, and the main and secondary ordnance and turrets by Bofors AB of Karlskoga, Sweden. Procurement of weapons, armour, machinery and other equipment and spare parts was in the hands of the Finnish Ministry of Defence.

Väinämöinen's keel was laid at Turku under yard construction number CV 705 on 15 October 1929 and launched on 20 December 1930, though no champagne bottles were broken as the country was still under Prohibition (1919–32). She ran her first trials on 27 July 1932 followed by initial gunnery trials on 8 August, being commissioned as the flagship of the Finnish navy on 31 December that year. *Ilmarinen*, laid down under yard number CV 706 on 2 January 1931, was launched on 9 July 1931 and commissioned on 17 April 1934. The ships were of riveted construction thanks to the

THE BARD AND THE HAMMERER

Väinämöinen and *Ilmarinen* owe their names to Finnish mythology, and specifically to the great national epic compiled by Elias Lönnrot known as the Kalevala of which Väinämöinen is the main character. The son of the god Ilmatar who created the cosmos from the shards of an eagle's egg, Väinämöinen is described in folklore as a wise old man who achieved his ends by magic and ritualised incantation. His name comes from the old Finnish word *väinä*, referring to the deepest and widest part of a river pool. Väinämöinen is presented as the 'eternal bard' who exerted order over chaos and established the land of Kaleva. Another major character in the Kalevala is Ilmarinen. Older tradition represents him as a deity who was the ruler of peace and the weather but he is later represented as a cultural hero, a smith with the knowledge and skill to work with the known metals of the time including brass, copper, iron, silver and gold. Ilmarinen is the 'eternal hammerer', immortal and capable of fashioning practically anything including the mysterious Sampo, but unlucky in love. His name derives from the word *ilma*, meaning weather or air.

Akseli Gallen-Kallela's famous canvas *The Defence of the Sampo* (1896) showing Väinämöinen and his companions slaying Louhi as she attempts to recover the magical artefact known as the Sampo in one of the climactic moments of the Kalevala. *(Turku Art Museum)*

prevailing conviction that welded seams were not as reliable at low temperatures and riveted joints more resistant to sudden changes in pressure, aside from the fact that the Krupp C cemented armour could not be welded. The contract provided for severe penalties for delayed delivery by the builder, as well as for every centimetre of draught in excess of the design draught of 14.8ft (4.5m), and for every tenth of a knot under the specified best speed of 14.5 knots. Although the trials were a success and the technical requirements met, the delivery of *Väinämöinen* was delayed by a year and that of *Ilmarinen* by eight months, though not for reasons attributable to the yard. Neither ship was fully complete on commissioning; *Väinämöinen*'s secondary armament was not fully installed until 1934 and the anti-aircraft rangefinders had to wait until 1939.

Hull, Superstructure and Armour

The coast defence ships were flush-decked with four deck levels in the hull. After the lower deck came the middle deck, the armoured main deck and finally the weather deck. The engine rooms extended from the lower deck to the main deck and the 10in barbettes from the weather deck to the lower deck. Internal subdivision consisted of longitudinal torpedo bulkheads extending from frame 9 to 95, with transverse bulkheads joining

them at frames 20 and 74. All these bulkheads, which were manufactured of 1.2in (30mm) nickel steel plate, extended from the ship's bottom to the main deck with which they formed a citadel measuring 34.1ft (10.4m) by 177.1ft (54m), being divided by transverse bulkheads into fifteen compartments. The citadel housed the engine rooms and control platforms together with fire control, the main radio and navigation rooms (which contained the main gyrocompass), the electricity switchboard room and the damage control and pump compartments ranged on either side of a 10ft (3m) wide passage.

The space between the ship's bottom and the lower deck was largely taken up by oil and water cells, including stowage for up to 200 tons of fuel and lubricating oil, 140 tons of ballast water and 100 tons of fresh water. The rest of the double bottom was divided into cells approximately 3ft (1m) wide and high and 13–23ft (4–7m) long without any pressure division system. This arrangement did not extend above the base of the horizontal belt and ended just below the waterline. The engine spaces were divided longitudinally into paired generator and diesel rooms distributed forward of and abaft the funnel, followed by a pair of propeller motor rooms. The 4.1in magazines were positioned in a space between the diesel rooms. The middle deck contained storage and workshop spaces while the main deck was given over to crew accommodation.

The superstructure consisted of three decks, beginning with the weather deck housing the galleys and the bakery with the junior officers' quarters aft. Next came the bridge deck with a twin 4.1in mounting positioned forward and aft and containing the officers' cabins, a mess accommodating twenty-four petty officers and the sick bay. Last came the boat deck containing the radio rooms and captain's day cabin forward of the control mast together with the forward director surmounted by the main battery 19.7ft (6m) rangefinder, the armoured conning tower and the bridge. The conning tower housed a steering position, engine-room telegraphs, a plotting table and connections to all the internal telephone networks. The conning tower was linked to the navigation room on the lower deck by an armoured shaft. Abaft the control mast and funnel was the admiral's day cabin and the after control position surmounted by a 13.1ft (4m) AA rangefinder.

The heavy control mast was of German design and is similar to those fitted in the vessels built and reconstructed by the Reichsmarine in the 1920s and '30s. The mast stood 100ft (30m) above the weather deck, was 6.5ft (2m) in diameter and extended to the lower deck. The top of the control mast, reached by climbing nearly a hundred rungs through five levels, was in three sections, the lowest of which was a confined lookout platform, followed by that for the aloft 19.7ft rangefinder with the upper level serving for target-spotting purposes. Positioned just below the control sections were two searchlight platforms on either side of the mast, of which one was subsequently moved to the boat deck and the other relocated to the forward face of the control mast.

The armour, either Krupp C or nickel steel, was manufactured by Bofors to Krupp standards and supplied in the correct size and form with ready-drilled perforations for rivets and bolts, often being fixed directly to the frames without any standard plating as backing. The main deck consisted of 1.2in (30mm) of nickel steel while the weather deck received 0.6in (15mm) of plate decked over with 3in (75mm) of Oregon pine. Horizontal protection was

A view from the quarterdeck dominated by the after 10in turret and showing the after 4.1in mounting, two 1.6in Bofors guns trained on either beam, the searchlight shield and the after control position which is trained to port. Note the Maxim machine gun on its simple mounting between the turrets. The officer is Ragnar Hakola, captain of *Väinämöinen* from 1933–8 and reassigned to the ship as Commodore in 1940. The photo was taken at Helsinki on 1 July 1941. *(SA-kuva 22072)*

provided by a 10.6ft (3.25m) high belt of 2in (55mm) nickel steel running from frame 7 to 79 and beginning 40in (1m) below the waterline and extending the same distance above the main deck. The main turret faceplates and conning tower received 4in (100mm) and 4.7in (120mm) of armour respectively.

Distinctive though they were, *Väinämöinen* and *Ilmarinen* looked ungainly with their lofty control mast and bulky main and secondary turrets stacked on a box-like hull whose sloping icebreaker bow was pitched steeper than in the latest Finnish designs. This appearance was in part the result of the unusual sequence in which their dimensions had been worked out. The draught was initially specified at a little over 10ft (3m) in order to make use of safe coastal shipping lanes, including secret military ones. Then the size of the main armament was settled on, involving an increase in the draught. Since the maximum displacement was fixed, it was necessary to increase the beam and decrease the weight of armour. The result was a block coefficient of approximately 0.6, a beam-to-length ratio of 0.19, and a beam-to-draught ratio of 3.7. The metacentric height was between 4.4ft (1.33m) and 5.4ft (1.65m) as the ships were broad in the beam but of shallow draught.

Armament

Väinämöinen and *Ilmarinen* were designed to act as mobile batteries for the defence of areas unprotected by coastal artillery. The emphasis was therefore on mounting the heaviest possible armament and the resulting battery of four 10in (254mm) 45-calibre guns in two twin turrets outgunned the new Soviet Kirov-class 7.1in (180mm) cruisers and at 35,000yds (32,000m) outranged the old Gangut-class battleships with their 12in (305mm) guns.[1] The choice of calibre matched that of the Durlacher guns with which Finnish coastal artillery batteries were equipped and the large reserves of 10in ammunition no doubt contributed to the selection. However, the guns were a new design by Bofors and remained unique to these vessels. Projectile weight was 496lb (225kg) for both armour-piercing and high-explosive shells with a charge weighing 253lb (115kg). There was stowage for 134 shells for each turret. The maximum rate of fire was

Handling a 10in shell in one of the gun turrets on 20 June 1942. The gunhouse was crewed by eighteen men with a further twenty in ammunition supply. (*SA-kuva 93361*)

[1] Kiiskinen, Pekka, & Pasi Wahlman, *Itsenäisen Suomen laivastotykit, 1918–2004* (Helsinki: Typomic, 2003), p. 74.

three shells per minute and the operation of each turret required the services of thirty-eight men: eight in shell supply, twelve in cartridge supply and eighteen in the gunhouse itself.

The initial designs provided for a secondary armament of the old 4.7in (120mm) 50-calibre Vickers twin mountings fitted in the Finnish icebreakers of the 1920s, but during construction it was decided that a dual-purpose weapon capable of engaging aircraft should be carried in the new units. Since the 4.7in gun could not be modified for AA purposes, attention focused on the new 4.1in 50-calibre weapon then being designed by Bofors of which eight were fitted in four twin mountings. The fact that these were not ready until 1934, two years after *Väinämöinen* was completed, resulted in orders to install several old 4in (102mm) Obuhov guns borrowed from coastal artillery and suitable only for surface targets to give the impression of completion. However, the Merivoimat was reluctant to accept any temporary solution which might become permanent and their absence in the earliest photos of *Väinämöinen* shows that it was some time before they were installed. In the event, no meaningful trials of the entire battery were carried out against air targets until the after director had been installed in 1939. Operating a single 4.1in mounting required seventeen men: six in ammunition

Väinämöinen's control mast seen between the barrels of the after 4.1in guns, the ship lying at Helsinki on 1 July 1941. Note the searchlight shield and the extremities of the 13.1ft rangefinder. She is flying the swallowtail with tongue ensign of the Finnish navy. (*SA-kuva 22054*)

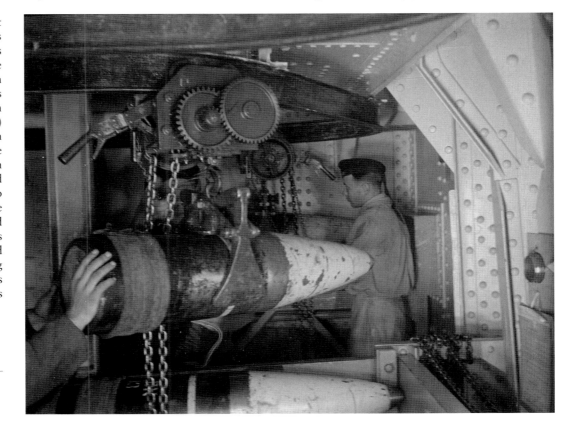

The starboard 4.1in mounting being prepared for action on 1 July 1941. The mounting was crewed by seven men with another ten in ammunition supply. *(SA-kuva 22062)*

stowage, four to bring the ammunition from hoist to gun, and seven at the gun itself.

The anti-aircraft armament was augmented by four 1.6in (40mm) Vickers guns purchased in 1932, albeit the 1918 model. Two were positioned on platforms abaft the bridge and two abreast the after director. Experience demonstrated that the Vickers gun was not only ineffectual against high-level bombers owing to its short barrel and low muzzle velocity, but suffered repeated malfunctions as a result of inefficient water cooling and the tendency of the canvas ammunition belts to jam when wet. They were therefore replaced by one twin and two single 1.6in (40mm) Bofors mountings ordered in 1938 but not delivered until the autumn of 1940. The twin mounting, which was stabilised, was installed on a new platform abaft the bridge following the removal of the compass platform, while the unstabilised single mountings were positioned abreast the after director on the platforms vacated by the Vickers guns. The single mountings required a seven-man crew with eleven needed to serve the twin mounting, to which ammunition supply numbers were added when necessary. Another change was the installation of two Danish-built Madsen 0.79in (20mm) 60-calibre guns in place of the Vickers guns abaft the bridge. These were increased to four in *Väinämöinen* by the spring 1941 and eight by September 1944, the additions being made in the bow and the stern and abreast the funnel. Finally, a single 0.303in (7.62mm) Maxim machine gun was positioned between the barrels of the after 10in turret, though this was removed in 1941.

Target information for the main armament was provided by two 19.7ft (6m) electro-mechanical rangefinders manufactured by the Dutch N.V. Hazemeijers Fabriek voor Signaalapparaten company, one mounted on the forward director and the other high on the control mast; fire solutions were calculated in a transmitting station on the lower deck. The secondary armament was served by a Hazemeijer 13.1ft (4m) rangefinder and fire-control equipment installed in the after director in 1939, this being the only equipment used for anti-aircraft purposes.

The same mounting manned and ready on 21 October 1941. The trainer and layer are visible through the sighting ports and a paravane is stowed on the forward superstructure. *(Finnish Defence Forces Photograph Archive (SA-kuva) 58462)*

The crew of a 1.6in Bofors gun on 1 July 1941. *(SA-kuva 22068)*

Propulsion and Seakeeping

Väinämöinen operated under diesel-electric power and is distinguished as being among the first surface vessels to do so. Her four six-cylinder Krupp diesel engines delivered 875hp each, though this could be increased to 1,200hp with precharging. Each diesel engine operated a 250V DC generator which in turn provided electric power to two propeller motors. The after generators were of double-rotor and the forward generators of single-rotor construction. The ships employed the Ward Leonard propeller motor control system in which the driving motor operates at almost constant speed to power a DC generator. The generator output is then fed into a DC motor; output voltage could be changed by varying the DC generator field current, permitting smooth shifts in the speed of the controlled motor from stopped to full speed. It was assumed

Väinämöinen opens up with her 10in guns in the Gulf of Finland on 18 June 1942. *(SA-kuva 92295)*

that such a configuration would improve manoeuvrability in confined waters and also in ice. Four separate diesel-generator combinations also provided redundancy since both propeller motors could be powered by just one set. With a single diesel engine turning one double-rotor generator, the maximum voltage for each propeller motor was 125V, giving 110rpm for the propellers and 9 knots of speed; with two diesels turning each generator the maximum voltage was 250V, giving 140rpm and 11 knots; and with all four diesels and generators operating the maximum voltage was 500V, giving 180rpm and 14.5 knots. The diesel engines were directly coupled to the generators, but the diesel and generator spaces were separated by bulkheads to protect the latter. The weight of the diesel engines was 75 tons and the electrical equipment 128 tons. Although a steam power plant would have been considerably lighter and occupied less space, fuel consumption would have been two or three times higher. Diesel fuel capacity is variously stated as 93 or 137 tons and fuel consumption is estimated as 180 grams per horsepower per hour, giving a range of 5,000 nautical miles. General electricity needs were supplied by two 60kW diesel generators, with the reserve power stored in two 220V/450Ah Edison-type battery banks positioned on the middle deck forward of the citadel, where lack of protection was exchanged for good ventilation.

Although stability was not an issue, *Väinämöinen*'s seakeeping qualities were by no means good and sometimes made life aboard unpleasant. She and *Ilmarinen* rolled heavily in a slow and wide arc, a motion one merchant skipper who served in them later compared to that of a vessel laden with timber. It has been speculated how this characteristic might have affected gunnery accuracy in a ship-to-ship engagement but this was never tested. In 1933 *Väinämöinen* experienced difficulty in a westerly force 7 gale while making for the naval base of Lappohja on the east side of the Hanko peninsula.[2] Altering course to the north, the rolling became so severe that Cdr A. Wirta decided to resume his westerly course. When the wind veered to the north *Väinämöinen* did likewise and reached the archipelago safely, but the episode prompted the fitting of bilge keels in an attempt to dampen the roll. These were 82ft (25m) long and 18in (0.45m) high and proved effective during the 1935 cruises to the southern Baltic coast. *Ilmarinen* had received bilge keels during her 1934 docking and was found to be much less susceptible to rolling than *Väinämöinen*.

Life Aboard

Väinämöinen was originally designed for a complement of 329 men but crew numbers rose steadily to reach 388 by the end of the Second World War. By March 1947, however, the scheme of complement listed a total of 367 men,

Väinämöinen at full speed in the Gulf of Finland on 18 June 1942. (*SA-kuva 92285*)

2 Eino Pukkila, *Merisotilas – Laivastoelämää 1920- ja 1930-luvulla* (Helsinki: Doseator, 2006), p. 144.

Lieutenant Karmela accompanies Lieutenant Arjomaa in a recital on the wardroom piano on 17 October 1941. Note the Finnish flag on the left of the piano and that of its German ally on the right. *(SA-kuva 57599)*

including twenty-two officers, ninety-nine warrant officers and chief petty officers, and 246 petty officers and men. The ship's company was divided into four divisions: *kansi* (deck), *tykki* (gunnery), *kone* (engineering) and *talous* (supply). Watchkeeping followed the four-hour system with that from 1600 to 2000 divided into two. For operational purposes the crew was separated into port and starboard watches and these into half or quarter watches, with one half watch being comprised of two officers, fourteen petty officers and forty-five men. When the ship was at anchor or in harbour one half watch was responsible for ten deck and eight machinery stations over a twenty-four-hour period, to which more men from the same watch were added when the ship was under way.

Crew accommodation was cramped. The forward section of the main deck was divided into eight messes, two of which were reserved for *alipäällystö* (petty officers). The crew messes accommodated fifty men while their petty officer equivalents held fifteen men, though some of the latter were accommodated on the bridge deck. The messdecks provided daytime living and dining spaces using long tables which were stowed against the ship's side at night as hammocks were slung. Hammocks were later replaced by bunks for most of the men. Due to the sheer of the weather deck the height of the messdecks extended from 6.6ft (2m) to around 10ft (3m) towards the bow. There were only ten toilets, ten urinals, fourteen wash basins and four showers for the 300 men accommodated in the forward section of the ship.

The *upseerit* (officers) and *erikoismestarit* (master chief petty officers, usually engineering specialists) were accommodated on the main deck aft. The after accommodation spaces were accessed along two converging passages with the messes lying between them and the cabins outboard. The twenty master chief petty officers were berthed in two- or four-man cabins, with four showers and a mess seating thirty. Officers were accommodated in two-man cabins with the exception of the executive officer and chief engineer who had their own cabins. The officers had

A quiet evening in the chief petty officers' mess on 20 June 1942. The beverage is probably lemonade, alcohol being permitted in peacetime but taken only at Christmas, Midsummer's Day and on Marshal Carl Gustav Mannerheim's birthday (4 June) during wartime. Note the bunks in which most of the crew slept. *(SA-kuva 93386)*

two bathrooms and two heads. The officers' wardroom was forward of the after 10in barbette. Meanwhile, the admiral and captain had private suites in the stern of the ship, with the admiral's saloon positioned right aft and accessible through a hatch on the weather deck between the after 10in guns, although this was sealed during wartime. Heating for the living spaces was provided by a standard ship's boiler positioned on the main deck close to the funnel and heated by exhaust gas from the main diesel engines or by oil. As the temperature of steam and hot water in the heating system was over 100°C, the crew had to treat the radiators with caution since they were either stone cold or extremely hot.

The ship had separate galleys for officers, master chief petty officers and for the crew. These were equipped with a 132lb (60kg) dough machine, two 77lb (35kg) baking ovens and three 55gal (4.5l) water heaters. The double

bottom had storage for 100 tons of fresh water and there was a 6-ton tank for drinking water on the lower deck, although maintaining sufficient supplies for nearly 400 men in wartime anchorages proved challenging. Severe wartime food rationing in Finland also required the crew to spend time working on farms, fishing and picking berries in the autumn. With coal in short supply, the cutting of firewood was a task in which all shared and in the autumn of 1942 the first communal work parties were organised under the 'Motti mieheen' campaign. Motti is the Finnish term for a cubic metre of wood and the goal of the campaign was the hewing of a million motti, hence its name 'A Motti per Man'.

The coast defence ships were equipped with eight boats, of which two had engines. The latter were stowed on the boat deck and served by powered cranes, being tied to 33ft (10m) booms when the ship was anchored. The finest of these was the 12-knot motor boat reserved for the

personal use of the admiral, the captain or important visitors. The other was a launch used for transporting stores or up to thirty men on shore leave when the ship was at anchor. Two whalers were embarked for rowing competitions, one of which was used for training purposes and the other reserved for the races themselves. Three six-man boats were employed for various tasks, of which two were rigged for the crew to learn sailing. The complement of boats was completed by a dinghy. There were two sets of davits, the starboard one carrying a whaler, the port one carrying a six-man boat for use in emergencies.

Peace, 1933–9

The training of senior officers for service in *Väinämöinen* and *Ilmarinen* began in 1930 when Commanders A. Wirta and Ragnar Hakola and Engineer Lieutenant Commanders A. Aintila and E. Lounela were seconded to the Royal Navy, with Wirta and Aintila subsequently joining the team overseeing the construction of the coast defence ships. Meanwhile, eight candidates selected for training as gunnery officers took a mathematics course at the Helsinki University of Technology from 1930–1. The first commanding officer of *Väinämöinen* was Cdr Wirta, with Lt Cdr R. Göransson and Engineer Lt Cdr S. Aho as executive officer and chief engineer respectively. These three were subsequently transferred to *Ilmarinen*, being replaced in *Väinämöinen* by Cdr Hakola, Cdr J. Koskinen and Engineer Lt Cdr A. Aintila respectively.

The Finnish navy (Merivoimat) was organised into a *Rannikkolaivasto* (Coastal Fleet) established in 1928. By the mid-1930s it was composed of the *Panssarilaivue* (Armoured Squadron: two coast defence ships), the *Sukellusvenelaivue* (Submarine Flotilla: five submarines) and the *Miina- ja varmistuslaivue* (Mine and Escort Flotilla: four gunboats, seven motor torpedo boats and minelayers). The sailing season of 1933 found *Väinämöinen* already working up but *Ilmarinen* was still in the trial phase, making 1934 the first year during which both vessels participated in the Finnish navy's annual training exercises. These involved smaller vessels escorting the larger units against submarine and motor torpedo boat attack. A typical year consisted of ship preparations in April, equipment testing and emergency exercises in May, service aboard in May and June, sea time in July, weapons training in August and September, fleet exercises in September, and refresher training in October and November before the

Scrubbing the port waist. Note the ship's nameplate affixed to the after screen. (SA-kuva 87349)

fleet secured for the winter in late November. The winter months were devoted to maintenance and personnel courses.

When it finally came, the integration of the coast defence ships into the fleet did not go smoothly and three accidents occurred during the 1934 training season which might have had serious implications for the Finnish navy. That summer arrangements were made for the Coastal Fleet to visit the major Finnish ports on the Gulf of Bothnia with exercises to be carried out en route, consisting of submarine and MTB attacks on *Väinämöinen* and *Ilmarinen* while these were sailing under gunboat escort. The first submarine attack, put in off Hanko on 5 July while the fleet was making for the Gulf of Bothnia, resulted in *Iku-Turso* misjudging her approach and having to crash dive when it was realised that a collision with *Ilmarinen* was imminent. The submarine suffered damage to her outer hull and deck plating in the stern but the pressure hull remained intact and there were no leaks. Returning from the north two weeks later, the fleet anchored for the night off Vaasa on 20 July preparatory to visiting the port the following day. In the morning the ships entered a channel 15ft (4.5m) deep but *Väinämöinen* had to anchor unexpectedly due to engine trouble. No sooner had *Ilmarinen* passed her than she ran aground at 12 knots, damaging several cells in the double bottom and requiring the ship to be towed to Turku for repairs. Both the officer commanding the Coastal Fleet (Cdr K. Ikonen) and the captain of *Ilmarinen* (Cdr Wirta) were put into custody and forced to resign a few months later. Another incident followed at Vaasa on the evening of the 20th when smoke was seen issuing from one of *Väinämöinen*'s ventilators, the result of a fire which had broken out in the cobbler's workshop. The blaze was quickly brought under control but the bulkhead separating this compartment from the 10in cartridge magazine was already too hot to touch. Forced ventilation succeeded in cooling the magazine and restoring the situation.

The coast defence ships were the pride of the Merivoimat and were shown in every major Finnish port from Viipuri (now Vyborg) in Karelia to Kemi on the Gulf of Bothnia and eventually throughout much of the Baltic and beyond. In November 1933 *Väinämöinen* made her first foreign visit to the Estonian port of Reval and the following August visited Stockholm in company with a submarine flotilla. Between July and August 1935 she visited Kiel while *Ilmarinen* and the veteran gunboats put in at the Latvian ports of Riga and Libau (now Liepāja). In July 1936 *Ilmarinen* made a visit to the Polish port of Gotenhafen (now Gdynia) and the following May *Väinämöinen* represented Finland at the

Väinämöinen at Copenhagen on 27 May 1937 during her last foreign visit. *(Courtesy Lars Jordt)*

Coronation Review of King George VI at Spithead. The outward journey was made through the Kiel Canal, the opportunity being taken to return through the Danish Straits and put in at Copenhagen. In June 1938 *Ilmarinen* conveyed President Kyösti Kallio on a courtesy visit to Stockholm to celebrate King Gustaf V's eightieth birthday, to which city both vessels returned the following summer. By the time *Ilmarinen* had repatriated the body of Swedish envoy Carl von Heidenstam to Stockholm in November 1939 neutral Finland was on the brink of war.

The Winter War, 1939–40

The outbreak of the Second World War on 3 September 1939 immediately caused the Finnish navy to step up its neutrality patrol operations. The following day the Armoured Squadron consisting of *Väinämöinen* and *Ilmarinen* with an escort of gunboats and patrol boats proceeded to the Archipelago Sea to counter any threat to Ahvenanmaa. Although the Finns regarded it as a key element in their defensive strategy, recent research shows that the occupation of Ahvenanmaa was not a priority in Soviet planning prior to the Winter War. Nonetheless, Finnish fears of Russian aggression were in no way misplaced. In September and October

Estonia, Latvia and Lithuania were obliged to yield to Soviet demands for basing facilities and on 5 October the Finnish government was invited to send delegates to Moscow to discuss a range of territorial concessions. This prompted the mobilisation of the Finnish defence forces and, where the navy was concerned, the start of operations escorting merchantmen to Sweden. In late October minelaying operations began in the context of repeated border incursions by Soviet aircraft as diplomatic efforts faltered. The coast defence ships meanwhile kept to the waters off southwestern Finland and the Armoured Squadron was at Högsåra when news reached it on the night of 29–30 November that diplomatic relations between Finland and Soviet Union had been severed. At 1125 on the 30th two Soviet SB-2 bombers appeared over the anchorage and aimed ten bombs at *Ilmarinen*. All missed and the squadron cleared the anchorage for Lohmi with sufficient speed for the next wave of nine aircraft to find it empty.

The opening gambit of the Baltic Red Fleet was to advance as far as Hanko at the southern tip of Finland and on 1 December the cruiser *Kirov* duly appeared off that port and engaged nearby Russarö fort with her 7.1in guns. The Armoured Squadron was lying off Borstö just thirty miles to the west but arrived too late to affect matters, *Kirov* having broken off the

action after suffering slight shell damage from the coastal guns. This brief sortie did however cause the Armoured Squadron to miss its rendezvous with the transports it was to have covered in the occupation and remilitarisation of Ahvenanmaa, the Finnish navy's first priority on the outbreak of war. In the event, the operation passed off uneventfully and the Armoured Squadron remained in Ahvenanmaa until late December, cruising at low speed during the day and anchoring at night and in poor visibility in an effort to evade Soviet aircraft. In mid-December the Red Air Force began attacking Finland's western harbours, *Väinämöinen* and *Ilmarinen* being moved to the Kihti area between the Ahvenanmaa and Turku archipelagos to provide air defence on the 23rd. On Christmas morning the coast defence ships came under successive air attacks from SB-2 bombers to which they responded by weighing anchor and circling the anchorage at low speed. At 0930 two planes were shot down by 4.1in fire but at 1351 a flight of ten aircraft appeared over the anchorage of which three launched a diversionary attack on *Väinämöinen* while the rest attacked *Ilmarinen* in two groups, the ship suffering a man killed and seven wounded by strafing and near-misses by two 1,100lb (500kg) bombs. Two more aircraft were shot down at 1430 but fire control had been poor with heavy expenditure of ammunition and too much attention paid to secondary aircraft.

At the end of January 1940 the Ahvenanmaa archipelago became icebound and all naval activity ceased. Small vessels were confined to Maarianhamina while the coast defence ships moved east to join the air defence of Turku which eventually became the target of sixty-one raids by approximately 440 aircraft, of which thirty-five attacks were directed against *Väinämöinen* and *Ilmarinen*. Anchored, painted white and their decks covered by a thin layer of snow, the coast defence ships provided an effective 4.1in AA barrage. Meanwhile, despite the extraordinary resistance put up by Finnish troops in the preliminary stages of the Winter War, by early 1940 the strategic situation was becoming desperate and the coast defence ships were readied to counter landings in the Hanko-Porkkala area. It was also planned to send them to support the bitter struggle unfolding around Viipurinlahti (Vyborg Bay) though this plan came to nothing as no icebreaker with smokeless diesel engines was available to open a path for

them, aside from the risk of propeller damage and their depleted stocks of ammunition. On 6 March the Finns sued for peace and hostilities ended a week later.

Väinämöinen and *Ilmarinen* had been confined largely to an anti-aircraft role during the Winter War, but post-Cold War analysis of Soviet records has revealed that plans were in readiness to land 20,000 men on Ahvenanmaa before hostilities ended, including one intended for September 1940.[3] Although this was precisely the kind of threat for which the coast defence ships had been designed, it is unlikely that the Finnish navy could have prevented such a large operation involving two landing areas, five transport groups and thirty vessels in close support, with heavy units and submarines waiting in the open sea, all supported by bomber, fighter and reconnaissance aircraft. As it turned out, *Väinämöinen* and *Ilmarinen* had been spared for a different fate.

Interim Peace and Continuation War

The Winter War ended with the Moscow Peace Treaty signed on 12 March 1940 by which Finland was forced to cede a portion of the province of Karelia, including much of its industrial production centred around the country's second city Viipuri (Vyborg). Among the concessions forced on Finland in the treaty was the lease of the Hanko peninsula to the Soviet Union, a situation which essentially cut Finnish naval forces in two. This resulted in the Coastal Fleet consisting of *Väinämöinen* and *Ilmarinen*, four gunboats, six patrol boats, twelve minesweepers, three minelayers together with a number of escorts and ice breakers being stationed in the Saaristomeri area to the west, and the *Erillinen Laivasto-osasto* (Separate Naval Detachment) consisting of five submarines, two minelayers, five MTBs, eight patrol boats and a number of minelaying and minesweeping vessels keeping to the east. The Moscow Peace Treaty marked the beginning of what became known as the Interim Peace, the fifteen-month period separating the end of the Winter War and the resumption of hostilities between Finland and the Soviet Union following the launch of Operation Barbarossa, the German offensive in the east, on 22 June 1941. This period was spent under constant Soviet economic, territorial and political pressure, a circumstance which naturally drew Finland into the German sphere of influence,

culminating in the secret German-Finnish agreement reached in early June 1941 during which the Finns learnt of the impending attack on Russia. Meanwhile, the German occupation of Norway and Denmark on the one hand and that of the Baltic States by the Soviet Union on the other had left Sweden as Finland's only trading partner aside from the Third Reich. The decision to declare war on the Soviet Union three days after Barbarossa on the 25th was made easier by Soviet bombings of Finnish territory and ships in the wake of the German attack. The Continuation War had begun.

The role of the coast defence ships during the Continuation War was essentially that of a fleet in being and they were a priority target for the Red Air Force while hostilities lasted. The first taste of this came during Operation Kilpapurjehdus, the remilitarisation of Ahvenanmaa on 21–22 June, during which *Väinämöinen* and *Ilmarinen* were attacked by Soviet aircraft on the morning of the 22nd, though without effect. During the failed Soviet assault on Bengtskär near Hanko on 26 July the coast defence ships were ordered to support minor units responding to reports of Soviet destroyers off Örö in the Archipelago Sea. These proved false but the ships were jumped by eighteen Pe-2 light bombers off Bengtskär, two near-misses just astern of *Ilmarinen* resulting in splinter damage, and claiming the life of one man and injuries to thirteen others. *Ilmarinen* was repaired at Turku and sandbag emplacements and splinter shields were installed to protect AA gun personnel. With Hanko still occupied by the Soviets, three bombardment operations were carried out against airfield, harbour and railway battery targets in the area in July and September, though to limited effect, the opportunity being taken during two of the operations to test the 10in Durlacher shells adapted from coastal artillery use.

The *Väinämöinen* Detachment

The loss of *Ilmarinen* left *Väinämöinen* as the last major unit in the Finnish navy and she was to spend much of the next three years in the area between the Seeigel-Rukajärvi and Nashorn minefields laid across the Gulf of Finland to bar the entry of Soviet submarines to the Baltic. In practice, this meant that she remained between 24.4° and 27° E, in the approximate longitude of Porkkala on the Finnish coast and the island of Suursaari (Gogland). In 1942 she became the nucleus of the so-called *Väinämöinen* Detachment consisting, in addition to herself, of six VMV patrol boats and six motor minesweepers based on the coast between

---

[3] Kenneth Gustavsson, 'Åland 1940 – demilitarisering under sovjetisk kontroll, del 2: Den militära linjen' in *Tidskrift i Sjöväsendet* 3 (2014), pp. 241–59.

THE LOSS OF *ILMARINEN*

In early September 1941 came a major exercise in Finnish-German naval co-operation and with it the heaviest blow dealt the Finnish navy during the Second World War: Operation Nordwind, the German landings on the Estonian islands of Hiiumaa and Saaremaa. On 7 September the Commander of Naval Forces, army General Väinö Valve, signalled the Navy Commander in Turku, Commodore Eero Rahola, as follows: 'The Germans will launch an attack on the islands of Hiidenmaa and Saarenmaa on 11 September. Your task is to confuse the enemy. Prepare to muster vessels at Utö [in the Archipelago Sea] and transfer the coast defence ships to the Bengtskär area to attack enemy forces trying to enter Hanko.'

After some discussion it was agreed that a Finnish squadron including *Väinämöinen* and *Ilmarinen* should steam from Utö towards Hiiumaa forty miles to the south as a diversion for the German attack. At 1755 on the 13th Rahola duly sailed from Utö in *Ilmarinen* at the head of the Coastal Fleet. With the squadron steaming thirty miles northwest of Hiiumaa at 10–11 knots, at 2030 Rahola passed the order to reverse course for Utö as planned in position 59° 27' N, 21° 05' E. However, no sooner had *Ilmarinen* altered course 40 degrees to starboard than one or two mines detonated on her port side abreast the after 4.1in gun and 10in turret, lifting her stern as if she had gone aground. She had in fact run onto the Soviet 26-A minefield laid on 5 August, and no provision had been made in operational planning for minesweeping along the intended route. A lookout in *Väinämöinen*, then 850yds (780m) astern of *Ilmarinen*, described two explosions, the first like muffled thunder, which caused foam to boil along waterline, followed by a smart crack like the firing of a gun. A narrow column of fire shot up on the port

Väinämöinen's sister *Ilmarinen* putting to sea on 18 August 1941. Three weeks later she was lost during an ill-planned diversionary exercise in the Archipelago Sea. *(SA-kuva 36669)*

side abaft the after 10in turret after which the ship gave a lurch and began capsizing to port. The bulkhead separating the after diesel room and the propeller motor room had ruptured, flooding six compartments and dooming the ship. Power was lost and within the space of a minute the ship had turned keel-up to reveal a large hole belching smoke in the ship's bottom. Her back broken, *Ilmarinen* disappeared six minutes later.

The escorting patrol boats immediately closed the wreck and *VMV 1* saved fifty-seven men from the capsized hull, some dry shod, while *VMV 14*, *VMV 15* and *VMV 16* picked up another seventy-

five from the water for a total of 132 survivors. Among them were Commodore Rahola and Captain Göransson commanding both the Coastal Fleet and *Ilmarinen* herself, but set against this was the loss of 271 men, with only four members of the ninety-strong gunnery division and fourteen of the eighty-man engineering division surviving to be rescued, so quick was the demise their ship. Meanwhile, *Väinämöinen* and the rest of the squadron turned back to Utö which they reached disconsolately at 2315. Twenty-five miles behind them the fleet flagship was lying at the bottom of the Gulf of Finland.

Helsinki and Kotka. Its intended tasks were anti-submarine operations in the west and the interdiction of Soviet units fleeing Leningrad to neutral countries, implicitly Sweden, though the light forces were only sporadically engaged in anti-submarine duty and no heavy enemy units ever sailed from Leningrad. On 15 November 1941 *Väinämöinen* shelled a railway battery in the Hanko area as part of the successful effort to evict the Soviets from that port, the last heavy shells fired in anger by the Finnish navy. However, fear of air attack and mines kept her in her fastness in the Archipelago Sea and it was not until 24 May 1942 that she received the order to move to the Porkkala area twenty-five

miles west of Helsinki and that evening sailed east of Hanko for the first time in two and half years. Any satisfaction was short-lived since no sooner had *Väinämöinen* passed Hanko than she ran aground, rupturing four of the tanks in her double bottom. The ship floated off early the following afternoon and anchored for her condition to be assessed before continuing to Helsinki, where she docked in the Hietalahti yard on the evening of the 26th. Repairs were completed three days later after which *Väinämöinen* proceeded to the Emäsalo area about twenty miles east of Helsinki. Here she remained under camouflage until November 1942, visiting Helsinki for a few days each month and other-

wise moving only when necessary. The winter months were divided between Helsinki and Turku.

Although the Detachment's main task was to conduct anti-submarine operations east of the Porkkala-Naissaari submarine barrier, *Väinämöinen* herself had settled into the role of a fleet in being by the time the sailing season opened in the spring of 1943. In May she returned to the Emäsalo area where she spent the rest of the year uneventfully at the Djupsundet anchorage with occasional visits to Helsinki. On 17 October she was quarantined for a week due to an outbreak of diphtheria, and her only action that year came in December when she fired a few

Väinämöinen anchoring at Helsinki on 1 July 1941. *(SA-kuva 23616)*

barrages in support of the Helsinki air defences. On 8 January 1944 *Väinämöinen* sailed for Turku where she spent the rest of the winter, but on 24 March was suddenly ordered to proceed at her best speed to a position east of the main island of Ahvenanmaa against the possibility of a German seaborne and airborne attack on the archipelago. The ship sailed on the morning of the 26th and reached Lumparland that afternoon, but no attack materialised and *Väinämöinen* returned to Turku on 24 April where she was briefly dry-docked in early May. The rest of that month was spent training in the Turku and Saaristomeri areas until the 27th when the *Väinämöinen* Detachment sailed for its new base on Strömsö at the westernmost end of Barösund about thirty miles east of Hanko. Here

Väinämöinen at the Barösund anchorage on 29 July 1944 under her cape of spruce and lichen, laid as a measure against air attack. *(SA-kuva 158997)*

she anchored and secured within ten yards of the shore before being placed under an elaborate camouflage netting of spruce and lichen.

The progress of the Second World War of course left little doubt that the true danger lay in the east and on 9 June 1944 the long-awaited Soviet attack began on the Karelian Isthmus which the Finns had recovered by the end of 1941. *Väinämöinen* was however held back as a last line of defence, spending the entire summer hidden at Strömsö but for a brief degaussing in Helsinki between 12 and 14 June and gunnery practice off Hanko on 10 July. New bases were identified in the Sipoo-Pellinki area east of Helsinki in case the ship needed to be brought forward but these were never used. Meanwhile, Soviet air activity was intensifying and on 16 July the Red Air Force claimed to have sunk *Väinämöinen* at Kotka fifty miles east of Helsinki in a well-planned attack involving 132 aircraft. They had in fact accounted for the German anti-aircraft cruiser *Niobe*, formerly the protected cruiser *Gelderland* which had been seized at Den Helder during the occupation of the Netherlands in 1940. Although launched in 1898, the refitted *Niobe* was of comparable size and displacement to *Väinämöinen*, hence the misidentification. The Finns responded by shifting the positions of the *Väinämöinen* Detachment at Strömsö to thwart air-launched torpedo attack and steps were taken to improve camouflage with guidance from Finnish reconnaissance aircraft. On 13 August a 220yd (200m) torpedo net was positioned at a distance of about 100yds (90m) from *Väinämöinen*, but the buoys supporting it increased the likelihood of discovery from the air and she was moved to a new base near Porkkala fifteen miles west of Helsinki four days later. Here she remained except for a brief degaussing at Helsinki at the end of the month.

Although the Finnish defence forces managed to stave off total collapse during the Soviet offensive in the summer of 1944, the country's resources were exhausted and on 4 September nearly eighteen months' intermittent negotiations culminated in a ceasefire. At 0510 that morning a signal was issued by Navy Headquarters to the effect that all hostilities against the Soviet Union were to cease at 0700. The orders to naval vessels included details of new boundaries which should not be crossed, continued defence of the Seeigel-Rukajärvi mine barrage northeast of Suursaari and use of force against any Soviet air and naval incursions. Two weeks later on 19 September Finland signed the Moscow Armistice with the Soviet Union and Britain by which the

Continuation War was brought to a close. Among its terms was a restoration of the 1940 borders including the loss of Finnish Karelia together with the northern province of Petsamo, and the payment of $300 million in war reparations at 1938 prices. This was equivalent to 29 billion marks which equated to Finland's annual budget in 1944. The armistice also required Finland to freeze all German assets including the private property of German citizens and companies under German majority ownership, and to cease debt repayments to Berlin, which assets were to be set against the reparations. The total amount ceded to the Soviet Union was therefore 6 billion marks.

Naturally enough, this unilateral armistice prompted a breakdown in relations with Germany, and the *Väinämöinen* Detachment and Submarine Flotilla were transferred to the Ahvenanmaa-Saaristomeri area when intelligence was received of a German operation to capture Suursaari on 15 September. Within a week the danger had passed and the Detachment was ordered to proceed to Turku, Uusikaupunki and Hanko from where it was ordered to monitor the transfer of Soviet units westwards from Porkkala. *Väinämöinen*, however, remained at the Pansio naval base in Turku and her last sailing season under the Finnish ensign ended on 17 November 1944.

From *Väinämöinen* to *Vyborg*

Väinämöinen remained in Turku after the armistice, being placed under reduced comple-

ment as all available personnel were needed for mine clearance duties. In fact, her days as a unit of the Finnish navy were numbered since the Paris Peace Treaty of 10 February 1947 restricted its size to 4,500 men and 10,000 tons. The navy having no use for a single vessel taking up 40 per cent of its permitted tonnage, an agreement was reached whereby *Väinämöinen* could therefore be used to defray part of the reparations and on 3 March she was sold to the Soviet Union for 265 million marks.[4] The accommodation spaces had to be painted and all defective equipment fixed prior to delivery, the ship being handed over with her remaining inventory of 1,372 10in shells and cartridges, 3,825 4.1in rounds, and 12,000 rounds of AA ammunition. The acceptance inspections were carried out between 10 and 24 March, on which date her Soviet complement came aboard. The flag-changing ceremony took place in Turku on 25 March 1947 by which *Väinämöinen* was symbolically rechristened *Vyborg*, the Russian name for the port of Viipuri in the former Finnish Karelia. Engine and gunnery trials were carried out in Airisto on 29 May and the final act of transfer signed on 6 June 1947. Already, on 5 April *Vyborg* had been classified as a 'coastal armoured ship' in the Baltic

---

[4] See P. V. Petrov, 'Bronenostsy beregovoy oborony "*Väinämöinen*" i "*Ilmarinen*"' in *Taifun* 12 (2000), pp. 2–12, and A. M. Vasiljev, 'Monitor *Vyborg*' in *Gangut* 25 (2000), pp. 41–57. The author and the editor would like to thank Steve McLaughlin for generously producing English translations of these articles.

Red Fleet, the beginning of fifteen years' service under the Soviet ensign.

On 7 July *Vyborg* sailed for the base at Porkkala, twenty-five miles west of Helsinki, which Finland had been obliged to turn over to the Soviets on a fifty-year lease under the Paris Peace Treaty. Well-armed, easily camouflaged against the rocky shoreline and designed for operations in confined waters, the Soviets considered *Vyborg* an extremely valuable addition to their fleet, particularly in the light of the takeover of Porkkala which controlled the entrance to the Gulf of Finland and the approaches to Helsinki. Assigned to the 104th Coastal Vessel Brigade, *Vyborg* was stationed at Porkkala from 1947–52, though less actively from 1949 when she was reclassified as a monitor. Badly in need of refitting, in 1952 she was transferred to Kronstadt where she was docked between January and March for the replacement of approximately 10,000 rivets in the hull and exchange of steel screws for bronze ones. But much more needed to be done, and in March 1953 she was taken in hand for refitting of the hull and replacement of the machinery and electrical plant at Tallinn. By the time she emerged in August 1957 the original Krupp 39/42 main diesel engines had been replaced by Krupp 46A6 units with the same power. The auxiliary diesel generators and emergency batteries were also replaced together with steering, radio and electrical equipment. That the work took so long was due in part to a grounding accident in Tallinn's Mine Harbour on 25 February 1954 which caused severe damage and cracking to the bottom plating in the vicinity of frames 67–68 and required the fitting of a caisson for repairs to be carried out. Four months in the Tallinn Works floating dock during 1956 saw to the replacement of another 10,800 rivets and the welding of 1,200 bolt heads securing the armour belt. This resulted in an increase in displacement to 4,112 tons and draught to 15ft (4.6m) with *Vyborg*'s best speed reduced to 12 knots. The early return of the Porkkala military base to Finland in 1955 meant that *Vyborg* was stationed in Kronstadt from September 1957, being used as a mobile gunnery platform between the southern coast of the Gulf of Finland and the port of Primorsk (formerly Koivisto) on the Karelian Isthmus. After a spell in dry dock in Kronstadt she was transferred to the reserve fleet on 1 November 1959; nothing came of plans to sell her back to Finland and *Vyborg* was removed from active service in 1962.

On 17 September 1965 the staff of the Leningrad naval base issued a report containing a brief summary of the monitor *Vyborg*'s condition. The hull was satisfactory but the weather deck was leaking and much of the deck planking rotted. The main machinery and cabling were in acceptable condition, but the electrical system was otherwise deficient. The main battery was in poor condition with an inventory of only 298 shells, while the secondary and AA armament was by contrast operational but lacking ammunition. Based on this report it was concluded that the ship was obsolete, suffering from major defects and beyond economical repair. *Vyborg* was therefore stricken from the navy list on 25 February 1966 and sent for demolition, being reduced to 2,700 tons of scrap between 18 March and 25 July. The diesel generators, propeller motors and the auxiliary boiler were allocated for other purposes. So ended the last of Finland's capital ships.

Conclusion

The question has often been raised since the Second World War as to whether *Väinämöinen* and *Ilmarinen* were worth the massive expenditure required to build them. The main arguments *in contra* are based on the experience of the Winter War in which Finland lacked field artillery, anti-tank weapons and fighter aircraft. The 210 million marks spent on the two vessels would, it is argued, have been more usefully allocated to the army and the air force. However, the numbers and circumstances tell a different story. Where funding for procurement of equipment and *matériel* is concerned, the army received 1.216 billion marks, the air force 604 million and the navy 564 million between 1919 and 1938. Moreover, the Merivoimat received most of its funding between 1926 and 1931, whereas that of the army and air force increased after 1934 allowing it to benefit from more advanced technology such as the various types of anti-tank weapon selected in 1936–7 and as late as 1939. It must also be pointed out that much army funding in particular was expended on the maintenance and repair of existing *matériel* and that organisational and storage deficiencies during the 1920s resulted in the loss of a large proportion of the booty obtained from the Russians in 1918.

A second argument, specific to the navy this time, is that the money spent on the coast defence ships could have been better used on a number of smaller vessels, such as a pair of modern destroyers and two or three coastal submarines. The answer can be tied to the related question as to whether the coast defence ships fulfilled the roles for which they were designed. *Väinämöinen* and *Ilmarinen* were not intended to fight on the open sea but to act as mobile batteries to repulse landing operations on unfortified areas of coastline. Although it did not affect the outcome, their deterrent value in this role, which *Väinämöinen* discharged alone after the loss of her sister in September 1941, is measured by the fact that no Soviet or German landing operations were attempted on Finland's southern coast or against Ahvenanmaa during the Second World War. Not only that but by constituting a fleet in being both vessels had an appreciable effect on enemy strategy and operations. To that extent the coast defence ships fully justified the expenditure.

Sources

Campbell, John, *Naval Weapons of World War Two* (London: Conway, 1985)

Enkiö, Sulo, 'Laivaston synty ja kehitys 1918–1939' [The Creation and Development of the Navy, 1918–1939] in *Suomen Laivasto 1918–1968* [The Finnish Navy, 1918–1968], vol. 1 (Helsinki: Otava, 1968)

Gustavsson, Kenneth, 'Åland 1940 — demilitarisering under sovjetisk kontroll, del 2: Den militära linjen' [Åland 1940 — Demilitarisation under Soviet Control, Part 2: The Military Dimension] in *Tidskrift i Sjöväsendet* 3 (2014), pp. 241–59

Kiiskinen, Pekka, & Pasi Wahlman, *Itsenäisen Suomen laivastotykit, 1918–2004* [Finnish Naval Guns since Independence, 1918–2004] (Helsinki: Typomic, 2003)

Manninen, Ohto, *Miten Suomi valloitetaan* [How to Conquer Finland] (Helsinki: Edita, 2008)

Niklander, Tauno, *Meidän panssarilaivamme* [Our Armoured Ship] (Jyväskylä: Gummerus, 1996)

Penttilä, Eino, *Panssarilaivat* Ilmarinen *ja* Väinämöinen [The Armoured Ships *Ilmarinen* and *Väinämöinen*] (Helsinki: Mainosteknikot, 1986)

Petrov, P. V., 'Bronenostsy beregovoy oborony "*Väinämöinen*" i "*Ilmarinen*"' [The Coast Defence Ships *Väinämöinen* and *Ilmarinen*] in *Taifun* 12 (2000), pp. 2–12

Pukkila, Eino, *Merisotilas – Laivastoelämää 1920- ja 1930-luvulla* [Sailor: Naval Life in the 1920s and 1930s] (Helsinki: Doseator, 2006)

Vasiljev, A. M., 'Monitor *Vyborg*' in *Gangut* 25 (2000), pp. 41–57

Wihtol, Erik, *Suomen laivaston rakentaminen itsenäisyyden alkutaipaleella* [The Building of the Post-Independence Finnish Navy] (Turku: Turun yliopisto, 1999)

The Finnish Navy in World War II: http://kotisivut.fonet.fi/~aromaa/Navygallery/index.html [accessed September 2017]

Finnish Wartime Photograph Archive: www.sa-kuva.fi [accessed December 2017]

Kriegsmarine

The Battleship *Scharnhorst* (1936)

Thomas Schmid

HEIR TO A NAME made famous during the First World War, the battleship *Scharnhorst* is one of the great warships in history.[1] This reputation is due not only to the aggressive spirit with which she was committed to action but also to the fine leadership and high degree of morale, skill and courage shown by her ship's company during the four years of her war service and for which she became renowned throughout the Kriegsmarine. She was for several years also gifted with the imponderable quality of being a 'lucky ship', in which her crew reposed their confidence to the very end. Appropriately, this chapter not only tells the familiar story of *Scharnhorst*'s origin, fabric, career and avoidable demise, but where possible does so in the words of those connected with her in life and death on both sides. Only by understanding the circumstances and mindset of her officers and men can the circumstances which led to her loss and that of her crew be explained.

Origin, Design and Construction

The origins of the battlecruiser *Scharnhorst* and her sister *Gneisenau* can be traced to the plan tabled by the Reichsmarine in 1933 to replace the pre-dreadnought battleships *Elsass* and *Hessen* with two enlarged versions of the Deutschland-class *Panzerschiffe* ('armoured ships'). With six 11in (280mm) and eight 5.9in (150mm) guns on 11,750 tons, the three Deutschlands of 1928–31 were not only the first capital ships completed for the post-war Reichsmarine, but also the result of an ingenious design which soon earned them the sobriquet of 'pocket battleships' in the British press. Although the armament of the two new vessels was intended to match that of the

Deutschlands, an increase in notional displacement from 10,000 to 20,000 tons allowed for a significant improvement in protection. Orders for these vessels, referred to as Panzerschiff 'D' and Panzerschiff 'E' respectively, were placed in 1934, the first of these at the Reichsmarinewerft at Wilhelmshaven on 25 January. Losing no time, the keel of this vessel was laid three weeks later on 14 February 1934 under yard number 125. However, the navy had never been happy with this design which it regarded as under-armed and unbalanced, and within months the commander-in-chief, Admiral Erich Raeder, had succeeded in persuading Hitler that these vessels would be outmatched by the two Dunkerque-class battleships then under construction or planned in France in response to the earlier Deutschlands. Hitler relented to the extent of permitting the new design to carry a third turret with an additional three 11in guns, but refused to countenance any increase in calibre. On 5 July orders reached the Reichsmarinewerft to stop all construction work and steps were taken to prepare an entirely new design.

Almost a year later, on 15 June 1935 work began at the now renamed Kriegsmarinewerft in Wilhelmshaven on quite a different ship, but under the same yard number 125. The new vessel mounted nine 11in (280mm) 54.5-calibre guns in three triple turrets on a standard displacement of 31,552 tons (well over the declared displacement of 26,000 tons), making her comfortably the largest warship thus far designed for the new German navy. She had a total length of 754ft (229.8m), was 98ft (30m) in the beam and had a standard draught of 32ft (9.9m). Protection consisted of a 13.8in (350mm) belt of Krupp cemented steel extending from the forward to the after turret, tapering to 0.8in (20mm) at the belt ends. Horizontal protection using the new Wotan high-tensile steel was provided by 2in (50mm) on the upper deck and 0.79–2in (20–50mm) on the

[1] The editor acknowledges the kind assistance of Philippe Caresse in the preparation of this chapter.

Right: Commissioning day for *Scharnhorst* at Wilhelmshaven on 7 January 1939 under Kapitän zur See (later Admiral) Otto Ciliax. She went on to become the great German surface vessel of the Second World War. *(NHHC/NH 97536)*

armoured deck, though with 4.1in (10mm) slopes on either longitudinal side. The turrets received between 7.9 and 14.2in (200–360mm) of armour with up to 13.8ins (350mm) on the conning tower, all in cemented steel. The secondary armament consisted of twelve 5.9in (150mm) 55-calibre guns arranged in four twin turrets and four single mountings. Anti-aircraft provision came in the form of fourteen 4.1in (105mm), sixteen 1.5in (37mm) and ten (eventually thirty-eight) 0.79in (20mm) weapons. The armament was completed by six 21in (530mm) deck-mounted torpedo tubes taken from the light cruisers *Nürnberg* and *Leipzig* in 1942. Three Arado Ar 196A reconnaissance seaplanes were embarked in 1939, served by a hangar and catapult amidships. Fire control was provided via a 32in (815mm) FuMO 22 Seetakt radar mounted to the rangefinder on the foretop in December 1939, to be replaced by a 31.5in (800mm) FuMO 27 unit in the summer of 1942.

Where propulsion was concerned, the intention had been to install the same diesel engines as those fitted in the Deutschlands, but industry could not develop units of the shaft horsepower required to guarantee a speed of 29 knots in the available time, so Panzerschiff 'D' was instead equipped with three Brown, Boveri & Cie geared steam turbines generating 159,551 shp. Although these permitted a best speed of 31 knots, not only did the fuel efficiency of the new vessel fail to match that of the diesel-powered Deutschlands (7,100 miles at 19 knots versus 10,000 miles at 20 knots), but the high-pressure turbines were found to be unreliable and gave constant trouble in operational service, even in the hands of *Scharnhorst*'s superb engineering

The forward control tower seen from the port side abreast the funnel. The prominent feature is the 34ft 5in (10.5m) rangefinder, but just visible at top right and receiving the attention of two men is the 32in (815mm) FuMO 22 Seetakt radar installed at Wilhelmshaven in December 1939 and seen here at that time. The destruction of its successor set, the FuMO 27 unit installed in the summer of 1942, was a major turning point early in the Battle of North Cape in 1943. *(NHHC/NH 102544)*

Launch day for *Scharnhorst* at the Kriegsmarinewerft in Wilhelmshaven on 3 October 1936, Adolf Hitler in attendance. Note the straight bow, subsequently reconstructed. *(Courtesy Philippe Caresse)*

department. Steam was supplied by twelve Wagner ultra-high-pressure oil-fired boilers and there was bunkerage for up to 6,000 tons of oil.

Panzerschiff 'D' was launched at Wilhelmshaven on 3 October 1936 in a ceremony attended by Hitler himself. The ship was named in commemoration both of Gerhard Johann von Scharnhorst (1755–1813), the great Prussian military reformer of the Napoleonic Wars, whose armorial device she wore on her bows, and of Vizeadmiral (Vice Admiral) Graf Maximilian von Spee's flagship which had been lost with all hands at the Battle of the Falkland Islands on 8 December 1914. It was the widow of von Spee's flag captain that day, Kapitän zur See (Captain) Felix Schultz, who christened the new vessel. Two months later *Scharnhorst*'s sister *Gneisenau* – named for Scharnhorst's pupil and fellow reformer Graf Neidhardt von Gneisenau (1760–1831) – went down the ways at the Deutsche Werke yard at Kiel in a further nod to the recent battle tradition of the German navy, that vessel having also died gamely off the Falklands under the guns of HM battlecruisers

Invincible and *Inflexible*. With the earlier *Panzerschiffe* bearing the names *Admiral Scheer*, *Admiral Graf Spee* and *Deutschland* herself, the message imparted of Germany's revival as a naval power could scarcely have been plainer. As with their namesakes in the Napoleonic Wars and then in the Great War, the careers of *Scharnhorst* and *Gneisenau* were to be indissolubly linked during the coming conflict.

Arrival

Scharnhorst was eventually commissioned under Kapitän zur See (later Admiral) Otto Ciliax on 7 January 1939, following which sea trials and

One of *Scharnhorst*'s three boiler rooms which contained a total of twelve Wagner ultra-high-pressure oil-fired boilers. The leadership and manning of the ship's engineering department were of a high order. *(Courtesy Philippe Caresse)*

training began immediately. These, however, proved to be a signal disappointment as the ship's low freeboard made her untenable forward at high speed. Oberbootsmannsmaat (Petty Officer 2nd Class) Wilhelm Gödde:

> We carried out numerous speed trails during which maximum engine power was applied to the ship to establish her best speed. We all had to leave the bridge and only the First Officer and Chief Engineer watched the ship as she ploughed on at high speed. In these circumstances water was driven up through the bilge pipes designed to keep the deck dry but which served only to shower it with water. Most of the time the forecastle was completely submerged.[2]

Not only did this constant immersion cause structural damage to the fore part of the ship, but 'A' turret (known as 'Anton' in Kriegsmarine parlance) was itself flooded and unlikely to be operational in high seas. *Scharnhorst* therefore returned to Wilhelmshaven where her straight bow was replaced with a so-called 'Atlantic' bow between June and August 1939, a process requiring the forecastle to be extended by 17ft (5m) giving a total length of 771ft (234.9m). In

---

[2] Thomas Schmid Collection (TSC), transcript of Willi Gödde filmed interview.

Scharnhorst in the final stages of fitting out at the Kriegsmarinewerft in Wilhelmshaven in 1938. Note the armorial device of General von Scharnhorst prominent on the bow. *(Thomas Schmid)*

the event, the reconstruction involved an increase in displacement from 31,552 to 32,358 tons which nullified any improvement the new bow may have given her. Nonetheless, the opportunity was also taken to move the mainmast from a position abaft the funnel to one abaft the seaplane hangar, while the catapult previously on 'C' turret ('Caesar') was re-sited to the roof of the hangar.

The outbreak of hostilities in September 1939 soon pitched the heavy ships of the new German navy into operations against the Royal Navy and the Merchant Navy in an effort to disrupt the seaborne trade upon which the British war effort depended. Not for them the moniker of 'chained watchdogs' that had attached to the major units of the German fleet during the Great War, although the comparatively few ships which were available would require them to be jealously guarded. Mindful no doubt of the mutiny at Kiel which ended Germany's Great War in November 1918, the emphasis of the new German navy was on leadership. As Kapt.z.S. Ciliax told his officers on *Scharnhorst*'s commissioning day on 9 January 1939, 'The important thing to remember is this – that the whole life and character of the ship will rest upon the spirit which you officers are able to inculcate in your men.'[3] Events would show they took good heed of his injunction.

Crew Organisation and Training

As early as possible during construction members of the future ship's company began mustering at the yard, most of them members of the engineering department with orders to supervise the installation of the machinery and begin acquainting themselves with its operation. Meanwhile, other specialised personnel were sent on instruction courses run by the manufacturers of boilers, turbines, shafts, bearings, pumps, diesel engines, generators, gyro compasses, etc. This first phase of training was concluded once the ship had come to full complement and the crew organised into divisions and watches. On the outbreak of war the ship's company was quickly raised from her ordinary complement of fifty-six officers and 1,613 ratings to a wartime complement of sixty and 1,908 respectively, the shortfall drafted mainly from shore divisions.

[3] Fritz-Otto Busch, *The Drama of the Scharnhorst: A Factual Account from the German Viewpoint* (London: Robert Hale, 1956), p. 11.

Divisional Organisation, *Scharnhorst*, September 1939

Divisions 1–4	Seaman branch
Division 5	Supply and secretariat staff, artisans
Division 6	Armourers and ammunition staff
Divisions 7–10	Engineering branch
Division 11	Communications branch
Divisions 12–13	Gunnery branch

Source: Gerhard Koop & Klaus-Peter Schmolke, *Battleship* Scharnhorst (London: Conway, 1998), p. 30.

Scharnhorst running trials in the Baltic in 1939. Structural damage and extensive flooding when cruising at speed or in heavy weather revealed the need for her bow to be replaced, which it was with a clipper design, like many of the Kriegsmarine's larger vessels. *(Courtesy Philippe Caresse)*

This not only involved the arrival of 300 new men, but a redistribution of the peacetime divisional system with the removal of gunnery ratings from Divisions 1–4 and the creation of Divisions 12–13 with sole responsibility for the ship's armament. Division 1 and 4 had hitherto shared responsibility for the secondary armament and 'C' turret (Caesar), with Division 2 responsible for 'B' turret (Bruno) and Division 3 for 'A' turret (Anton).

Once the crew had been organised into divisions and the ship commissioned, full training began with the aim of working the vessel up into a cohesive fighting unit. With so many newly drafted sailors aboard, this initially took the form of guided tours of the ship to familiarise them with her layout. This completed, the crew,

Scharnhorst dressed overall as fleet flagship in Wilhelmshaven on 1 April 1939 to celebrate the launch of the battleship *Tirpitz*. In the foreground is the light cruiser *Nürnberg*. *(Courtesy Philippe Caresse)*

many of whom had only been given basic training ashore, began receiving specialised instruction in their area of expertise. They also learnt how and where to muster at the various stations such as man overboard, fire stations, air attack stations, etc., along with the ship's various states of readiness. Station drill was endlessly repeated during initial trials culminating in the *Gefechtsdrill* (action drill). This first phase in onboard training concluded with a full drill led by the captain. Next came the transitional phase known as *Gefechtsausbildung* (action training) including problem-solving exercises and battle practice. The crew also received training in ship and machinery repair in the event of battle damage, with the final step of closing up under battle conditions. However, training was by no means over, and action drill and action training

continued for as long as the ship remained in commission. A permanent aide-memoire for each member of the crew was the *Rollenkarte* (station card) to be carried at all times and stating each man's ship number, divisional and watch affiliation, and enumerating his action station position and responsibilities, as well as the various station scenarios.

To War

The declaration of war on 3 September 1939 found *Scharnhorst* ready for a further round of sea trials and the following day she and *Gneisenau* anchored at Brunsbüttel-Reede at the mouth of the Elbe as the RAF launched its first raid on the German Bight. However, it was not until 21 November that *Scharnhorst* (wearing the

flag of Vizeadmiral Wilhelm Marschall) and *Gneisenau* sailed from Wilhelmshaven on their maiden war cruise. The aim was to break out into the Atlantic through the Iceland–Faroes gap in order to divert attention from *Admiral Graf Spee*, then reaching the end of her famous commerce-raiding cruise in the South Atlantic. However, it was while traversing this body of water on 23 November that Marschall's force sighted the armed merchant cruiser HMS *Rawalpindi* patrolling against just this eventuality. The ensuing engagement not only accounted for *Rawalpindi* within forty minutes, but in compromising the secrecy of the operation brought the cruise to a premature end. Having steamed towards the Arctic, Marschall's force turned for home via the Shetland Narrows in poor visibility. Despite her new bow, the return voyage at 27 knots in mountainous seas again provided a telling demonstration of *Scharnhorst*'s shortcomings as a sea-boat, the bridge having to be temporarily abandoned and

Kapt.z.S. Kurt-Caesar Hoffmann, *Scharnhorst*'s distinguished commander from November 1939 to March 1942, inspects some of the nearly 2,000 members of his ship's company mustered by divisions on the forecastle in 1940. Note the two decorated Luftwaffe officers standing fourth and fifth from the right, no doubt the Arado seaplane pilots. *(Courtesy Philippe Caresse)*

Scharnhorst seen off Kiel with her newly fitted 'Atlantic' bow in the autumn of 1939. The opportunity had been taken while fitting it to relocate the mainmast aft from its earlier position stepped against the funnel but her sister *Gneisenau* retained the original arrangement, making this the easiest way of distinguishing the two ships in wartime. Note the Arado Ar 196A seaplanes on their catapults. *(NHHC/NH 101558)*

during which *Gneisenau* suffered and inflicted three hits on *Renown* before the engagement ended after nearly three hours. This encounter again revealed the difficulties faced by both ships in heavy seas with the forward turrets flooded and repeated failure of the high-pressure engines. On the morning of the 11th *Scharnhorst* and *Gneisenau* were joined by *Admiral Hipper* off Trondheim and turned for home, reaching Wilhelmshaven the following day.

Operation Juno, 1940

For *Scharnhorst* a spell of maintenance, trials and training ended in early June with a further cruise in company with *Gneisenau*. This was Operation Juno on which the squadron, again flying the flag of Vizeadmiral Marschall, sailed from Kiel on 4 June 1940 with the aim of relieving the pressure on German forces in northern Norway under General Eduard Dietl. In the event, the success of the German offensive in the West which had begun on 10 May and a steady deterioration in the Allied position in Norway itself prompted the British to stage a withdrawal. On the afternoon of 8 June *Scharnhorst* and *Gneisenau* encountered a British squadron making for Scapa Flow,

the forward 11in turrets put out of action due to electrical failures. Both ships reached Wilhelmshaven on 27 November, just six days after they had sailed.

Weserübung, 1940

Between 18 and 20 February 1940 *Scharnhorst* and *Gneisenau* sortied with the heavy cruiser *Admiral Hipper* and eight destroyers in an operation codenamed Nordmark to attack Allied convoys off the Shetland Islands, though none were located. However, events of much greater moment were soon afoot and on 7 April the better part of the Kriegsmarine's surface fleet gathered in the German Bight to participate in Weserübung, the invasion of Denmark and Norway, to which *Scharnhorst* and *Gneisenau* were assigned as distant cover under Vizeadmiral Günther Lütjens. An RAF bomber attack that afternoon was shrugged off without damage, but *Scharnhorst* had shortly to face a far more potent threat in the shape of a full-blown hurricane which caused cracks in the girders supporting the forecastle, serious damage to the superstructure and required speed to be reduced to 9 knots. Despite orders from fleet command that only one boiler per shaft be connected with a second kept at ten minutes' readiness for steam, Kapt.z.S. Kurt-Caesar Hoffmann decided to keep both

boilers running as a safety precaution in mountainous seas after consultation with *Scharnhorst*'s chief engineer Fregattenkapitän (Ing.) (Engineer Commander) Erwin Liebhard. By the time the hurricane abated the after superstructure had also suffered damage and one of the fuel bunkers was contaminated with seawater via a ruptured ventilation tube, requiring the port turbine to be temporarily shut down. Then on the night of 9 April the battlecruiser *Renown* and nine destroyers were picked up by *Gneisenau*'s Seetakt radar off the Lofoten Islands, the prelude to an indecisive action fought in poor weather

Scharnhorst at sea as part of Weserübung, the invasion of Denmark and Norway between 7 and 12 April 1940. Even after the fitting of the new bow the ship was liable to suffer damage in heavy seas. Note the recognition markings on 'B' (Bruno) turret. *(Courtesy Philippe Caresse)*

HM destroyer *Acasta* slides across *Scharnhorst*'s bows in a vain attempt to hide the stricken carrier *Glorious* with a smokescreen, the latter seen burning on the horizon to the right of centre. A few minutes later *Acasta* put a torpedo into *Scharnhorst* at a cost of forty-eight lives. (*Courtesy Philippe Caresse*)

consisting of the aircraft carrier *Glorious* and her escorting destroyers *Ardent* and *Acasta*. Owing to an extraordinary breakdown in relations between the captain of *Glorious* and his air officers, no air patrol was aloft at the time Marschall's force hove into sight, and all three were sunk over the course of the next few hours with the loss of 1,519 lives and only forty survivors. Nonetheless, Marschall's force did not escape unscathed, and desperate attacks were put in first by *Ardent* which scored a 4.7in (120mm) hit on *Scharnhorst* and then by *Acasta* which struck her with a torpedo, flooding the starboard and centre turbine rooms, damaging the starboard propeller shaft and tearing a hole 50ft by 12ft (15 x 3.5m) in the ship's side. *Scharnhorst* reached Trondheim on two of her three propellers under cover of darkness on the 9th where divers assessed the extent of the damage, the beginning of ten days' ceaseless labour by the engineering department under Fregkpt (Ing.) Liebhard and specialist personnel from the repair ship *Huascaran* to restore the centre turbine. Meanwhile, steps were taken to bury the first of forty-eight crewmen, although many of the bodies were in the shaft tunnel and beyond reach until *Scharnhorst* went into dock the day following her return to Kiel on 23 June. Willi Gödde:

> Next morning I and others were ordered to recover the bodies from the stern of the ship to transfer them to the cemetery. This was of course unpleasant work but we had to be prepared for anything. We recovered about fifty bodies and transported them to the cemetery where a mass grave had already been prepared and coffins were provided in which

to place the body parts. The coffins were marked but quite often we were unable to identify our comrade. The mass grave survives in Kiel but today there is a large grave stone provided by the *Scharnhorst* old comrades' association to honour our fifty dead shipmates killed in the battle with *Glorious*.

Nor was the stark courage of the British destroyers forgotten, and during a later sojourn in Brest two of the seamen's messdecks were christened 'Ardent' and 'Acasta' in their honour.

Operation Berlin, 1941

No sooner had the damage been made good than *Scharnhorst* was ordered to Gotenhafen (now Gdynia) in the Baltic to undergo final repairs

safely out of range of British air attack. These completed, on 28 December 1940 *Scharnhorst*, now joined by *Gneisenau*, sailed from Gotenhafen with the intention of breaking out into the Atlantic, but the operation was foiled by heavy damage to *Gneisenau* at sea. Not until 22 January 1941 did the two ships finally sail from Kiel for the Atlantic, once more under Günther Lütjens, now promoted admiral. The resulting cruise, codenamed Operation Berlin, probably represents the high point of the partnership between two vessels the British press had by now dubbed 'Salmon and Gluckstein' after a prominent firm of tobacconists. After an abortive attempt to force the Iceland–Faroes gap, Lütjens decided to steer for the Denmark Strait and on the night of 3–4 February reached the Atlantic, sending this exultant signal from *Gneisenau* at 0030: 'For the first time in history German battleships have succeeded in breaking through to the Atlantic. Now go to it!' Despite Lütjens's injunction, it was some time before his squadron claimed the first of twenty-two merchantmen during the two months of the cruise, which was prolonged by no less than five planned refuellings at approximately eight-day intervals. Lütjens twice declined to engage a convoy in view of the presence of an escorting British battleship, but nonetheless had sunk over 115,000 tons of Allied

Scharnhorst under camouflage netting at Brest in 1941. Prominent in the foreground are the anti-aircraft control towers for the starboard battery. (*Courtesy Philippe Caresse*)

shipping by the time he made Brest on 22 March. Willi Gödde has this recollection of the cruise:

> Eventually we caught twenty-two ships which we were almost always able to warn. If we encountered them in daylight we always sent a warning. The crew was allowed to take to the lifeboats and we then sank the vessel, but there were always captains among them who thought they could engage us with their little guns. Of course we immediately returned fire. On one occasion we had to protect one such captain from the rage of his own crew, whom they were about to kill on board our own ship because they had requested the captain to follow our orders not to signal, not to shoot and to put the crew into the boats, but he instead opened fire on us with his little gun. Naturally, the shell splash fell well short of our ship. We immediately fired a broadside with our 15cm guns into his starboard side.[4]

Aside from the depredations of his own squadron, by signalling the positions of merchantmen to patrolling U-boats for subsequent attack Lütjens succeeded in disrupting the entire North Atlantic convoy system.

Operation Cerberus: The Channel Dash, 1942

In early April 1941 it seemed that *Scharnhorst* and *Gneisenau* might soon be unleashed with the new battleship *Bismarck* and the heavy cruiser *Prinz Eugen* in a catastrophic breakout into the Atlantic. In the event, boiler repairs to *Scharnhorst* made her unavailable before June, while *Gneisenau* was heavily damaged in repeated attacks on Brest by RAF Bomber and Coastal Command from late March. Plans for further operations in the Atlantic were in any case scuppered by the sinking of *Bismarck* on 27 May and the subsequent destruction of seven of her nine supply vessels with the benefit of Enigma decrypts at Bletchley Park. Meanwhile, work continued on *Scharnhorst* which was shifted south to La Pallice for trials on 21 July, though the movement was quickly detected by the British who launched a bombing raid three days later. Willi Gödde describes the outcome:

> A reconnaissance Spitfire came during the day but we camouflaged our ships with big nets.

The ships were also camouflaged with painted windows. As we left the dock we were ordered to move our ship south to La Rochelle. The harbour was smaller with a pretty obvious pier where we were moored. I immediately asked myself 'What will the outcome of this be? We've been served up on a golden platter.' At noon the crew was allowed to leave the ship. I myself was reading but suddenly orders were passed for the AA gunners to stay on board. The message stated that there were fifteen four-engined bombers en route to our position and it wasn't long before we spotted the first.[5] After we started shooting at them the bombers dispersed and attacked from various quarters. A bomber flew directly towards our position but although hit was still was able to drop his bomb load. We were hit five times. This was a shock and to our dismay we realised we had to go back into dock. Three of those five bombs were armour-piercing bombs. They passed right through ship and exited through the bottom without detonating. It was only thanks to this that we were able to make our way back to Brest the following morning.

The constant threat of air attack and acknowledgement that the time had passed for long-range commerce raiding with heavy units prompted the German high command to begin formulating plans to bring *Scharnhorst*, *Gneisenau* and *Prinz Eugen* home. None of the available alternatives was other than extremely hazardous, with a high risk of interception by the British Home Fleet deploying from its bases at Scapa Flow in the Orkneys and Hvalfjord in Iceland should any of the North Atlantic options be taken, or the uninviting prospect of running the gauntlet of the English Channel and through the Straits of Dover whose twenty-one miles were guarded by coastal artillery and minefields and subject to surface, submarine and air attack. On the other hand, the latter alternative offered the benefit of continuous air cover by the Luftwaffe, and it was this option which was favoured by Hitler himself against the advice of Admiral Raeder and other senior naval officers. A major briefing was held in Paris on 1 January in the presence of General Admiral Alfred Saalwächter as group commander, Admiral Otto Schniewind as fleet commander and *Scharnhorst*'s former captain Vizeadmiral Otto Ciliax as squadron commander, together with his successor in command of *Scharnhorst*, Kapt.z.S. Kurt-Caesar Hoffmann, and the captains of *Gneisenau* and *Prinz Eugen*. The final decision to take the

Channel route was made on 12 January at Hitler's headquarters in East Prussia, with which detailed planning began on the aptly named Operation Cerberus, an allusion to the three-headed hound of hell of Greek mythology the Kriegsmarine expected to unleash with its triumvirate of ships.

At Hitler's urging, minimal preparations were made in the ships themselves before the operation began on 11 February 1942 in an effort to preserve secrecy, in contrast to the extensive planning and arrangements along the Channel route, particularly continual minesweeping and close liaison with the Luftwaffe to secure its air umbrella and jam British radar. Other than an air raid which delayed it until 2300 that night, as far as Maschinenobergefreiter (Leading Stoker) Eugen Pfeiffer was concerned, *Scharnhorst*'s departure from Brest, with Vizeadmiral Ciliax embarked, initially seemed no more than a routine exercise:

> We didn't notice any preparations. Once again we were battle-ready, we carried out searchlight and sea target exercises. It had become routine for ships to follow each other out into the bay on exercises. It was 11 February when our turn came. Meanwhile the squadron commander Vizeadmiral Ciliax had come aboard *Scharnhorst*. He had been the first captain of the ship and selected *Scharnhorst* as his flagship. Suspecting that something special was up as we sailed, we tried to find out what course we were steering but the compass was switched off. We suspected that something wasn't right. Nobody told us anything, not even the 1st Gunnery Officer. Only later were the compasses switched on as it was announced we were sailing home. When I glanced at the compass I noticed we were sailing on a westerly course. We continued watching the compass and after a while we steered northward. After a few hours we set an easterly course. We couldn't believe it. Could we possibly go through the English Channel? We couldn't seriously get past their Channel defence guns. But the order was given: 'Sail for home through the English Channel.'[6]

Willi Gödde recalls the mixture of glee and trepidation which greeted the announcement in *Scharnhorst*:

> Eventually our commanding officer Capt. Hoffmann announced: 'We are on our way through the English Channel into the German Bight. Tomorrow evening we will be at

---

[4] The only incident in the cruise which equates to Gödde's description of a merchantman putting up any resistance is that of MV *Chilean Reefer* which was engaged and sunk by *Gneisenau* on 16 March 1941, three of the survivors being picked up.

[5] The attack was carried out by twelve Handley Page Halifax bombers of which two were shot down.

[6] TSC, transcript of Eugen Pfeiffer filmed interview.

Scharnhorst seen leading *Gneisenau* and *Prinz Eugen* from an escorting destroyer during the Channel Dash on 12 February 1942. Not until the battleships struck mines that evening did Operation Cerberus suffer any significant hindrance. *(Thomas Schmid)*

Bight that night, but not for the first or last time her engineering department recovered the situation and brought her safely over the Jade bar and into Wilhelmshaven the following afternoon.

Although the so-called Channel Dash was a tactical defeat for the British and a humiliation in home waters comparable only to the Raid on the Medway by Admiral Michiel de Ruyter in 1667, the operation was in fact a major strategic withdrawal by the Kriegsmarine, one which significantly reduced the pressure on the British in the Atlantic. Not only had both *Scharnhorst* and *Gneisenau* suffered sufficient damage as to require docking at Kiel, but a major British raid on that port on the night of 26–27 February effectively ended *Gneisenau*'s career when a bomb detonated the forward magazine and wrecked the entire forecastle. With it a famous naval partnership was sundered and, it was later reckoned, *Scharnhorst*'s wellspring of luck ran dry.

Norwegian Waters

On 15 February *Scharnhorst* sailed for Kiel where she was docked for repairs until July. As before, she then proceeded to Gotenhafen for final repairs which were completed later that summer. However, in an early sign that her famous luck had deserted her, on 16 September she was in collision with *U523*, again needing dry-docking for repairs. Further exercises and refitting, including the installation of a new rudder at Gotenhafen in October, found her ready for deployment to Norway. After two attempts to break out of the Baltic had been compromised by British aerial reconnaissance, on 6 March 1943 *Scharnhorst* succeeded in escaping undetected and anchored in Bogen Bay near Narvik three days later, to be joined by the battleship *Tirpitz* and the *Panzerschiff Lützow* (ex-*Deutschland*).

Confined to Northern waters by the British blockade, the Kriegsmarine decided to concentrate its heavy surface units in Norway to oblige the enemy to commit a similar array of resources to protect its supply convoys to North Russia and help forestall any attempted invasion. However, shortage of fuel restricted its ability to carry out long-range operations and the German battle group was therefore prevented from capitalising on what was otherwise an excellent strategic position. This left the ships to spend

mother's.' This was his fatherly way of informing us. There were cheers throughout the ship. I was manning the telephone at the time and heard it all. Everyone was happy to finally leave the dockyard which was under constant threat of English air attack, but of course we knew this would be no picnic.

In the event, the 'Channel Dash' proved rather less sternly contested than was feared. Although the British had every reason to believe that a major German sortie was afoot, and even had a contingency plan in place to counter a movement up the Channel, the British response was an extraordinary catalogue of misfortune, confusion, incompetence, disorganisation and lack of co-ordination between the RAF and the Royal Navy, in stark contrast to the meticulous planning and inter-service co-operation which characterised Operation Cerberus. Only once Ciliax's force was past Dover on the afternoon of the 12th did British MTBs put in the first surface attack, though without success. Then came the initial air attack. Nine months earlier in May 1941 a sortie by fifteen Swordfish torpedo bombers from HMS *Ark Royal* had crippled *Bismarck* without loss to themselves. This time, however, an attack of suicidal bravery by six Swordfish was blown out of the sky by the three major units and their escort of six destroyers and numerous minor craft. Willi Gödde:

Between 1000 and lunchtime a torpedo plane squadron appeared. These slow-flying

Swordfish could only launch their torpedoes after flying straight, steady and low for a while. First they had to aim for the ship and it was one plane after another that targeted us. But as soon as they appeared we shot them down. We felt really sorry for them.

Shells from the South Foreland coastal battery fell well astern, and a destroyer thrust and further air attacks that afternoon were beaten off by Luftwaffe air cover. The only tactical consolation for the British came with the mines struck by *Scharnhorst* and *Gneisenau* as the day wore on. Willi Gödde describes *Scharnhorst*'s first:

But then we were hit by a mine. The safety valves in the engine room took over and the ship slowed from 28 knots to almost nothing. Admiral Ciliax had given orders that he be transferred to another ship if his were damaged in order to continue leading the operation. He had to shift from *Scharnhorst* to [the destroyer] *Z29*. The engine room crew was able to repair the damage after around twenty minutes and *Scharnhorst* slowly gathered speed again. Having regained full speed we overtook the destroyer with our admiral on board despite having engine problems. There was a fire in the engine room. Later in Hamburg Admiral Ciliax told me: 'That was my proudest moment as commander when I saw my flagship passing at full speed.'

Scharnhorst struck another mine in the German

Scharnhorst in Norwegian waters in 1943. She is wearing the camouflage scheme applied between March and December that year and replaced by a disruptive pattern shortly before her loss. In the foreground is one of the units of the 4th Destroyer Flotilla. *(Courtesy Philippe Caresse)*

much of their time at anchor between repairs and infrequent exercises. On 8 April *Scharnhorst* suffered a major explosion in the after auxiliary machinery space resulting in death or injury to thirty-four men and prompting the flooding of the magazines for turret Caesar as a precaution against a detonation. A repair ship duly completed work on the vessel in two weeks, and it is a measure of the *esprit de corps* which characterised *Scharnhorst* throughout her career that morale remained high despite such setbacks and months of inactivity as the war turned decisively against Germany. Matrosengefreiter (Ordinary Seaman) Helmut Boekhoff gives a flavour of life aboard as 1943 drew on:

> We were four hours on, four hours off. We had to make our own games, playing chess, cards. We had boxing down below. On our time off we went ashore and had snow fights. We had men dressed up like women in a cabaret. We had a cinema. We had fish in the morning, fish at lunch, fish at night. For sure, I had fish poisoning in the end. We were always ready because morale was very high to go to sea.[7]

As Willi Gödde recalls, the officers were also willing to partake:

In the summer of 1943 we received only two deliveries of provisions in four months. All steamers intended to provide supplies, ammunition and food had been sunk, either by submarine torpedoes or bombs. Finally the fifth ship reached us. One evening 300 red cabbages were delivered and stowed in front of the cold storage adjacent to the pantry. The night watch was supposed to finish stowing the cabbages but as it arrived there were none to be found. Only one small and crumbled cabbage was found in the corner – a cabbage nobody deemed fit to eat. The alarm was

immediately raised and all officers were informed of the situation. An announcement was made that the entire crew was to muster on the quarterdeck next morning. Next morning the crew gathered on the quarterdeck. First Officer Dominik approached the microphone and addressed the crew: Comrades, a horrible theft of a type unprecedented in this ship was committed just last night. Picture this: 300 cabbages disappeared in about half an hour. Then he paused and whispered quietly into the microphone: I got one too and shared it with the communications officer. The entire crew whooped and laughed.

The only operation of note before Christmas 1943 was Operation Sizilien during which *Scharnhorst*, *Tirpitz* and nine destroyers sailed from Alta Fjord on 6 September to destroy the Allied installations on the island of Spitzbergen two days later, paying special attention to the weather station whose reports were essential for planning convoy sailings to North Russia.

The Route to Disaster

After a hiatus during the spring and summer of 1943, in November of that year the Allies resumed the convoy cycle to North Russia.

An informal grouping of officers and men gathered on the forecastle in Norwegian Waters in 1943. The high morale of *Scharnhorst*'s crewmen never faltered despite months of inactivity and the ebbing of Germany's military fortunes. *(Courtesy Philippe Caresse)*

---

[7] Filmed interview in English from 'The Life and Death of the *Scharnhorst*' (BBC, 1971), available at https://www.youtube.com/watch?v=o_LVS-u26no

Konteradmiral Erich Bey (1898–1943), who was overwhelmed by superior tactics and technology at the Battle of North Cape. *(Courtesy Philippe Caresse)*

Kapt.z.S. Fritz Hintze (1901–43), *Scharnhorst's* last captain. *(Courtesy Philippe Caresse)*

Kapt.z.S. Rolf Johannesson (1900–89), the frustrated commander of the battle group destroyer force whose post-war analysis provides a damning indictment of Konteradmiral Bey's leadership. *(Courtesy Philippe Caresse)*

However, recent developments had significantly reduced the ability of the Kriegsmarine to counter this effort with surface ships. With *Lützow* withdrawn to Germany for repairs in September and *Tirpitz* heavily damaged by midget submarines on the 15th of that same month, by the onset of winter 1943 *Scharnhorst* found herself the last operational German capital ship in northern waters. Not only that, but the commander of the battle group, Admiral Oskar Kummetz, was temporarily recalled to Germany while his flagship *Tirpitz* was *hors de combat* and a stand-in appointed in the shape of Konteradmiral (Rear Admiral) Erich Bey. With two of the three destroyer flotillas also withdrawn, Bey reached Alta Fjord under the impression that no offensive operations would be carried out that winter. The commander of the remaining flotilla, Kapt.z.S. Rolf Johannesson, recorded his impressions of Bey in a post-war assessment:

When I reported to him on 8 November 1943 I found him an embittered man. He believed he had been unfairly treated. In his mind he was no more than a stand-in for the commander of the battle group over the winter because the High Command intended no operations to be

carried out. He employed unusually harsh words in describing his promotion. He avoided training his battle group. He did not visit his subordinate units, he did not call staff meetings, he did not share his thoughts, he did not conduct battle simulations, he did not attend any exercises or even visit the destroyers, he did not order signalling exercises involving the participation of all units and did not seek to communicate personally with the Admiral Commanding Northern Waters.[8]

To Johannesson this personal disengagement was typified by the eight-hour return journey he was required to make between the destroyer berth in Lang Fjord and Alta Fjord in order to brief with Bey who had hoisted his flag in *Tirpitz*, this despite the modern means of communication at their disposal. Moreover, neither Bey, who had made his name as a destroyer commander at

---

[8] Bundesarchiv, Koblenz, RM 92/5096, Konteradmiral Rolf Johannesson, Beitrag zum „Scharnhorst" Untergang am 26.12.43, pp. 2–3. The Admiral Commanding Northern Waters (*Admiral Nordmeer*) was Rear Admiral Otto Klüber.

Narvik in April 1940 and during the Channel Dash in February 1942, nor *Scharnhorst*'s new CO Kapt.z.S. Fritz Hintze had any operational experience in heavy ships nor any great knowledge of gunnery. As Johannesson made clear, this situation was in marked contrast to the lengthy seagoing experience enjoyed by their British counterparts, particularly the Commander-in-Chief of the Home Fleet, Admiral Sir Bruce Fraser:

A glance at the admiral's staff handbook shows us who the enemy was. Twelve years as captain of a ship was average. Command of different ships demonstrated their ability to lead and gave them experience and confidence. Admiral Fraser was already a captain when Admiral Bey was still an *Oberleutnant* [lieutenant]. That needn't of itself be an advantage but it definitely wasn't a disadvantage. Bridge experience, training and an effective staff cannot be counteracted by bravery and theoretical knowledge.[9]

Together with loss of the strategic initiative, limitations on the use of his destroyers, poor commu-

---

[9] *Ibid.*, p. 4.

nication with subordinate commanders and Bey's taciturn nature, the result from Johannesson's perspective at least was a significant decline in morale and preparedness.

Although Bey seems not to have anticipated the possibility of any action, circumstances dictated otherwise and during a conference with Hitler on 19–20 December Großadmiral (Grand Admiral) Karl Dönitz, the Commander-in-Chief of the Kriegsmarine, declared that *Scharnhorst* would be deployed against the next Arctic convoy in an effort to relieve the pressure on the eastern front. The convoy in question was JW 55B bound for Murmansk and consisting of nineteen merchantmen carrying approximately 200,000 tons of munitions, armoured vehicles, aviation fuel and other war *matériel*. JW 55B sailed from Loch Ewe in Scotland at 1430 on 20 December with orders to shape a course approximately 400 miles off the Norwegian coast, out of German bomber range but still capable of being spotted by reconnaissance aircraft. Shortly after 1100 on 22 December the convoy, then steaming at approximately 10 knots, was sighted by a Ju 88 weather aircraft at the latitude of Trondheim. German intelligence initially interpreted the convoy as forming part of an assault on Norway, and it was only at 1215 on Christmas Day that *Scharnhorst*'s battle group was put at an hour's notice for steam. Two hours later Dönitz gave orders for the operation to commence and at 1900 *Scharnhorst* cleared Alta Fjord once Bey had transferred with his staff from *Tirpitz*. With her sailed the five destroyers

of Kapt.z.S. Johannesson's 4th Destroyer Flotilla. What did they expect to accomplish?

The departure of the battle group can best be described as hasty and there was no time for so much as a briefing, much less detailed planning between Admiral Bey and his commanders. This was due not only to the logistical obstacles and personal diffidence alluded to above, but also what Johannesson identified as an institutional tendency, shared by Bey, for shore-based command to issue detailed orders instead of general instructions whose execution would be left to the judgement of the force commander based on operational circumstances. As it was, the order was given to implement the contingency plan known as 'Ostfront' which in this case involved three destroyers shadowing the convoy until the time was ripe for *Scharnhorst* and her escort of two destroyers to come up and engage it. However, the shortcomings of a plan which had been drawn up before *Tirpitz* was crippled and two of the three destroyer flotillas withdrawn were all too apparent. Not only was locating the convoy in the darkness of a polar night with just three scouting destroyers improbable without precise intelligence as to position, course and speed, but the reduced size of his force greatly limited Bey's options if they did so. Accordingly, Bey issued the following orders of engagement on 25 December:

I intend to attack the convoy with the strike force on the 26th at dawn at around 1000. If conditions are unfavourable for *Scharnhorst*

(weather, visibility and enemy position), I do not intend to deploy the destroyers against the convoy during daylight hours because there are too few of them.[10]

Beyond this was the likely presence of a powerful covering squadron for which the convoy would essentially serve as bait. Bey's orders leave no doubt that he was fully aware of this possibility:

It must be assumed from past experience that at least one heavy unit will be at sea as distant cover. An unconfirmed signal has reported the presence of a suspected enemy battle group. There is no information as to the composition of any distant cover since reconnaissance over bases in northern England [*sic*] has recently been inadequate. Any British and American battleship, carrier or cruiser type should therefore be expected. A recent signal in connection with the sinking of the minelayer *Ulm* shows that US battleships have been operating undetected in the North Sea since 1942, when our air reconnaissance was much stronger. Enemy carrier aircraft should be expected both by day and by night.[11]

This awareness, which had a significant bearing on the handling of the Kriegsmarine's reduced inventory of heavy ships throughout the Second World War, no doubt influenced the tactics subsequently adopted by Konteradmiral Bey during what became known as the Battle of North Cape. As it turned out, major advances in British radar technology, as yet unsuspected by the Germans, and a preponderance of vessels with highly trained crews were always likely to turn the hunter into the hunted. To that extent, Bey's concerns would prove fully justified.

The Approach

Although the prospect of action was greeted with rejoicing in some quarters, if Willi Gödde's memoir is anything to go by *Scharnhorst* sailed from Alta Fjord not only with Christmas trees swinging from the rigging but under a cloud of foreboding:

The commanding officer Kapt.z.S. Hinze addressed the crew as follows: 'As you know,

Scharnhorst in Alta Fjord from whence she sailed on her last sortie on Christmas Day 1943. *(Thomas Schmid)*

---

[10] *Ibid.*, p. 11.

[11] *Ibid.*, p. 8. *Ulm* was sunk by British destroyers operating with the benefit of 'Ultra' intelligence on 25 August 1942.

Christmas is traditionally celebrated boisterously and with plenty of alcohol in the Kriegsmarine, but we shouldn't do so on this occasion because we don't know who will survive to see next Christmas. It doesn't look good for us. Please let's celebrate Christmas Eve quietly and let's wait and see what the coming hours will bring.

Scharnhorst's departure was immediately reported to the British by Norwegian resistance agents and before long Admiral Fraser, then at sea in the battleship *Duke of York*, was in receipt of Ultra decrypts as the German battle group steered northwest in deteriorating weather. At 2100 Bey broke radio silence and signalled Group North at Kiel as follows: 'Use of destroyers not possible due to weather conditions. Significant impairment of weapons and speed expected.' At midnight Dönitz finally responded with an exhortation to render assistance to the Eastern Front: 'We must help. Press on through the present situation, abort at your discretion, abort if heavy forces appear. I have confidence in your offensive spirit.' *Scharnhorst* therefore steamed on at 25 knots but her destroyers were ordered to reduce speed to 12 knots. Aside from the wretched weather, inadequate communications and lack of sea time imposed by fuel shortages were taking their toll on the destroyers, many of whose crews were debilitated by seasickness.

Based on U-boat sightings, it was reckoned that the battle group would encounter the convoy at around 0700 on the 26th unless it had altered course. In the event, Fraser had rerouted JW 55B north three hours earlier, so no contact was made, to which Bey responded by ordering his destroyers to form a reconnaissance line on the anticipated track of the convoy. This involved a major course alteration to 250 degrees, with *Scharnhorst* intended to keep station ten miles astern and beyond visual range of the destroyers. The difficulty of executing this manoeuvre at night, in heavy seas and with limited visibility, together with Kapt.z.S. Johannesson's uncertainty as to Bey's intentions, conspired to scatter the destroyer force and draw it away from the flagship. By the time the first shell was fired two hours later any opportunity the 4th Destroyer Flotilla had of playing a role in the subsequent engagement had vanished and with it a large share of Bey's tactical flexibility.

Battle Joined

Meanwhile, Admiral Fraser was vectoring his ships to *Scharnhorst*'s position southeast of Bear Island and at 0834 she was picked up on radar

by the first of his two squadrons, Vice Admiral R. L. Burnett's Force 1 consisting of HM cruisers *Belfast*, *Norfolk* and *Sheffield*. At 0924 the cruisers opened fire, catching Bey completely unawares and scoring two hits in quick succession. One of these penetrated the upper deck and came to rest on Division 4's messdeck without exploding, but the other hit proved particularly telling. Willi Gödde:

Scharnhorst was hit once on the port side and we received another more serious hit in our radar system at the foretop, the radar at the highest point of the ship. We had another radar system aft but that one was only about 8 metres [25ft] above the deck. The radar on the foretop was around 30 metres [100ft] above deck.

Although *Scharnhorst*'s radar was kept inactive to prevent detection, the loss of her main FuMO 27 set was a major setback and left her to rely on the after set whose field of view was obstructed by the superstructure and had an effective range of only 12,000yds (11,000m). Thus handicapped, hindsight suggests that Ostfront should at that point have been aborted, but mindful no doubt of Dönitz's injunctions Bey first went on to 30 knots to shake off the cruisers and then turned northwest to attack the convoy at 0945. Burnett broke off the action and fell back on the convoy in the expectation that *Scharnhorst* would return. He was not to be disappointed. At around noon *Scharnhorst* reached her most northerly position, and five minutes later altered course to the southwest in the anticipated direction of the convoy. However, Bey had again been forestalled by Fraser who had issued a second order routing JW 55B further north at 0930. *Scharnhorst* therefore had her second encounter with Force 1 which, reinforced by four destroyers detached from the convoy, now regained radar contact and opened fire at 1221. Willi Gödde, acting as lookout in the port forward searchlight control position, recalled the action:

After another blizzard we spotted the British battle group and immediately opened fire. I instantly reported three larger ships, their positions and ranges. This was confirmed by the gunners who said they had the enemy in their sights. Our 28cm guns fired at once. With my own eyes I saw a big explosion on one of the British cruisers while another was smoking heavily after being hit.

With only her optics and rangefinders to guide her, *Scharnhorst* still managed to put two 11in shells into *Norfolk* and inflicted slight damage on

Sheffield without receiving any hits in return. However, at 1241 Bey mistook one of *Norfolk*'s 8in (203mm) shells as belonging to a heavy unit and, mindful of an unconfirmed though accurate Luftwaffe sighting of *Duke of York* beating up from the southwest earlier that day, decided to abort the entire operation and return to Norway. *Scharnhorst* ended the battle by making off at high speed towards the southeast. Had Bey chosen to turn southwest he would in all probability have again shaken off Burnett's cruisers in the prevailing sea conditions. As it was, they were able to keep *Scharnhorst* within radar range and relay her position to Force 2 which was thundering in from the southwest in the shape of Fraser's flagship *Duke of York*, the cruiser *Jamaica* and four destroyers.

The End of the *Scharnhorst*

With *Scharnhorst* speeding southeast towards North Cape at about 25 knots and lunch being served at battle stations, Kapt.z.S. Hintze felt moved to warn his tired and seasick crew that 'We are not yet out of danger. We have been shadowed for hours. Everyone has to be fully alert.' His words were more true than he can have imagined. At 1617 hours *Duke of York* detected *Scharnhorst* in rising seas on her Type-273Q surface warning radar at 46,100yds (42,150m) when only a few square metres of the latter's control tower were showing above the horizon.[12] Fifteen minutes later her Type-284M(3) fire-control set registered a contact at 35,000yds (32,000m). At 1637 Fraser ordered the destroyers to take up attack positions and ten minutes later *Belfast* commenced firing star-shell, followed at 1648 by *Duke of York*'s first 14in (356mm) salvo at a range of 12,000yds (11,000m). The British found *Scharnhorst*'s turrets trained fore and aft leaving little doubt that, for all Hintze's warnings, she had again been caught completely unawares. As Willi Gödde recalled, 'Suddenly a Christmas tree of flares erupted over us. We were covered with flares from all sides. *Scharnhorst* had been served up on a platter. *Duke of York* immediately fired her heavy guns at us.'

Sporting the finest radar fit in the Royal Navy, *Duke of York* landed a hit with her first full salvo at 1651 which put turret Anton out of action, followed shortly after by a second which accounted for Bruno. Although *Scharnhorst* took as many as thirteen hits from *Duke of York*

---

[12] Derek Howse, *Radar at Sea: The Royal Navy in World War 2* (London: Macmillan, 1993), pp. 181 & 187–90.

The forward 14in turrets of Admiral Sir Bruce Fraser's flagship HMS *Duke of York*. Above them on the bridge structure is her Type-284M(3) fire-control radar with the Type-273Q surface warning set in the round housing beyond, part of the finest radar fit in the Royal Navy which was decisive in detecting and sinking the *Scharnhorst*. *(Bruce Taylor Collection)*

and *Jamaica*, Fraser missed the opportunity to unleash his destroyers for a torpedo attack, and Bey began to pull away from his tormentors at 26 knots, driving his men on by invoking the ship's motto as he did so: '*Scharnhorst* immer voran!' – '*Scharnhorst* ever onward!' By 1820 Fraser was resigned to his prey making good her escape, but at that very moment a last-gasp 14in shell fired from *Duke of York* at a range of approximately 20,000yds (18,300m) penetrated *Scharnhorst*'s starboard side and wrecked No. '1' boiler room, reducing her speed to 8 knots. In a fine display of damage control, Korvettenkapitän (Ing.) (Engineer Lieutenant Commander) Otto König, the ship's chief engineer, succeeded in recovering to 22 knots within half an hour but *Scharnhorst* had lost valuable time together with her crucial margin of speed. Fraser now sent in his destroyers including the Norwegian *Stord* and shortly before 1900 *Scharnhorst*, her secondary armament and their crews already decimated, was struck by a torpedo on the starboard side and three more on the port side, including to one of the boiler rooms. Again *Scharnhorst*'s speed dropped to 8 knots only for Korvkpt. König to bring her back to 22 knots in a supreme feat of naval engineering in the face of the enemy. But it was to no avail and before long *Scharnhorst* found herself surrounded by thirteen warships slavering for the kill. Willi Gödde: 'Wherever we turned the enemy was there. We tried to break through south to Norway. But we were hit by torpedoes and we received another 14in hit in the fore-castle which tore the whole forecastle deck open. The deck was wrapped backwards like the lid of tin can.'

Having ordered the destruction of the ship's confidential books, at around 1915 Bey, echoing Admiral Lütjens's last dispatch from the bridge of *Bismarck* on the morning of 27 May 1941, signalled the naval high command: 'We shall fight to the last shell. Long live the Führer, long live Germany.' To that exhortation his crew responded valiantly while *Scharnhorst* suffered the death of a thousand cuts. Mechanikergefreiter (Mechanician) Ernst Reimann's battle station was at the hydraulic pump of 'C' turret, which was by then operating in local control with ammunition laboriously manhandled from the forward magazines:

We fired until we were out of ammunition. The commander of 28cm turret 'Caesar' ordered the centre barrel to be loaded. We fired the last shell and then evacuated the turret by shutting down all the systems, closing the hatches to the ammunition hoist and squeezing through the hatch at the base of the turret.[13]

Shortly after Kapt.z.S. Hintze was heard urging the last fully operational major ordnance, port No. '4' 150mm turret, to greater effort but his ship was ablaze from stem to stern. By the time *Duke of York* fired her eightieth and final salvo at 1929 *Scharnhorst* was making under 3 knots, her bows submerged and her decks awash, though still keeping up a sporadic fire with her secondary armament, including a 20mm gun on the foretop. John Marsh, a wireless telegraphist in the destroyer *Scorpion*, describes the scene:

Both ships exchanged fire in rapid succession, we could see this clearly. The muzzle flash of *Duke of York* was orange coloured, the muzzle flashes of *Scharnhorst* cherry to dark red. We left the area for a short time and we

weren't sure what had happened. Then we came back because we heard the fire exchange between *Duke of York* and *Scharnhorst*. *Scharnhorst*'s fire became weaker and we found she was in a sinking state.[14]

Fraser ordered *Jamaica* in to finish her off with torpedoes, but it was left to the destroyers to give her the *coup de grâce*, which they did with a further seven hits. At about 1945 an immense explosion was registered aboard *Scharnhorst*, now reckoned to be the detonation of the forward magazine. By the time the British closed to investigate she had disappeared.

Death and Survival

Shortly before the end Matrosengefreiter (Ordinary Seaman) Günter Sträter recalled Hintze instructing the damage-control organisation to 'Execute Measure V', the order to scuttle.[15] However, the destroyers had done their work for them and soon it was the order to abandon ship that came from the bridge as

13 TSC, transcript of Ernst Reimann filmed interview.

14 TSC, transcript of John Marsh filmed interview.
15 RM 134/199, 'Vernehmung des Matrosen Gefreiter Sträter zum Gefecht vom 26 Dez 1943'.

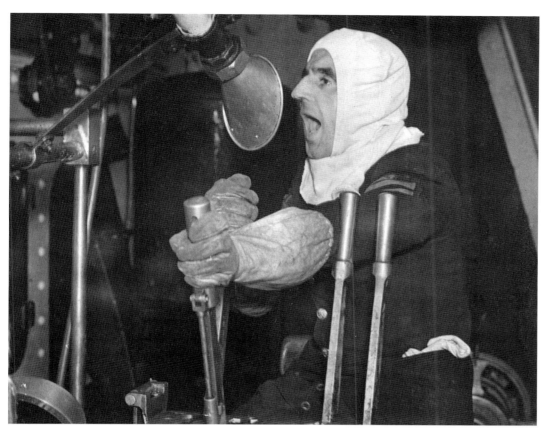

Petty Officer Alex Holgate, Captain of the Gun in one of *Duke of York*'s 14in turrets and a veteran of the Battle of the North Cape, seen operating the cage control levers bringing shells and propellant to the gunhouse from the working chamber below. At 1820 a 14in hit from 20,000yds crippled *Scharnhorst* just as she was on the point of escaping out of range, thus settling the action in favour of the British. This photo was issued on 3 January 1944 following *Duke of York*'s return to Scapa Flow. (*Bruce Taylor Collection*)

2,000 shells and fifty-five torpedoes from thirteen ships:

> I looked back and was able to see directly into the funnel of the ship as the she lay on her side. I could still hear the humming of the turbines as the ship suddenly turned over and gradually disappeared from the surface of the ocean. I felt two underwater explosions after she vanished. The whole scene was lit by the eerie light of the British flares high above us.

The battle now was one of survival. Maschinenobergefreiter (Leading Stoker) Helmut Feifer:

> The starboard side of the *Scharnhorst* was already under water as I slid downwards on the upper deck until I hit a 20mm AA gun. I clung to the gun totally exhausted. I was about to give up. I couldn't control the shivering any longer. It was so cold. A comrade came by and told me to let go of the gun. I did so and was swept away by the icy water. My body quickly became numb and I realised I could not survive. Then a miracle happened. On the crest of a wave I saw a raft. I swam towards the raft and as I reached it I heard comrades saying I was covered in blood. I feared they would throw me overboard so I explained it was not my blood. It was the blood of my friend.[16]

On more than one raft the survivors began singing the German sailor's lament: 'Auf einem Seemannsgrab, da blühen keine Rosen' – 'No roses bloom on a sailor's grave.' Others cried 'Heil Hitler!' and '*Scharnhorst* Hurra!' 'What a waste,' thought Matrosengefreiter Helmut Boekhoff, then clinging to a length of timber.[17] However, rescue was at hand for a pitifully small number of men. Matrosengefreiter Sträter:

> I was on a raft together with six other men for about an hour and a half. The sea was rough

---

Scharnhorst began to capsize. Willi Gödde:

> The captain sent his adjutant, who was always close by him, down to bring him something. He returned with a pistol in his hand and handed it to him. The adjutant said to the captain: 'Please don't.' He thought Kapt. Hintze wanted to kill himself. But Hinze replied, 'My boy, I am not doing what you think. Don't be afraid. I have the weapon only to defend myself in case we get boarded by the English.' This was heard by everyone inside the conning tower.

With that Hintze ordered everyone out of the conning tower and told them to muster on the upper deck where they joined several hundred other sailors gathered in perfect discipline. Once there Hintze handed his lifejacket to the adjutant, assuring him that 'Son, I am a good swimmer.' He then turned to those around him and said: 'If somebody gets out of this mess alive, please tell our relatives at home that we have done our duty. We could do no more than we did.' Hintze and Bey's last act of command was to bid farewell to each crewman by shaking his hand and checking his lifejacket. Some sailors, however, refused to separate their fate from that of their ship. Sträter, a crewman in port No. '4' 150mm turret, was

witness to two such cases. As was traditional in the German navy, his description refers to sailors as *soldaten* ('soldiers'):

> The turret was fully operational until the heavy list to starboard caused the ammunition hoist to jam. The crew of our magazine could not leave the ship any more than anyone else from the lower compartments could. As I left my turret I came across many wounded and dead soldiers on the upper deck. [...] My comrade Wibbelhof and my turret commander Moritz refused to leave the turret. Wibbelhof said: 'I stay where I belong.' Commander Moritz just said: 'I stay in the turret.' Wibbelhof ordered us to leave the turret and shouted 'Long live Germany, long live the Führer' in farewell and we answered with the same farewell. He then lit a cigarette and climbed into the trainer's seat. Both went down with the ship.

Scharnhorst capsized to starboard and sank by the bow with all three propellers still rotating at speed as they rose out of the water. The ship had way on to the very end which no doubt complicated the business of abandoning ship. Willi Gödde watched as *Scharnhorst* went into her death throes following the expenditure of over

---

16 TSC, transcript of Helmut Feifer filmed interview.
17 'The Life and Death of the *Scharnhorst*' (BBC, 1971).

The victor: Admiral Sir Bruce Fraser (1888–1981) seen as Commander-in-Chief of the British Pacific Fleet in 1944, and still flying his flag in *Duke of York*. Beside him is his U.S. Navy counterpart, Admiral Chester Nimitz. *(NHHC/NH 58519)*

scrambling nets and turned away leaving dozens of men screaming in the water after just six had been pulled aboard, while HMS *Scorpion* succeeded in rescuing another thirty.[19] Of a crew of 1,968 officers and ratings, only thirty-six of *Scharnhorst*'s men therefore survived to be rescued of the thousand or so estimated to have got clear of the wreck. Many of the thirty survivors in *Scorpion* wept when they learnt that only six others had been picked up instead of the hundreds they expected.

On the morrow of the sinking, 27 December, the survivors received permission to listen to a German radio news bulletin long enough to hear a broadcast stating that *Scharnhorst* had 'gone down with her battle ensigns flying' and that there was no information on the crew. That afternoon came a visit from Admiral Fraser himself. Willi Gödde:

> As the ranking survivor I was told to command the survivors during this visit. I was also told to listen for a bugle call because that meant the Admiral was about to enter our compartment. I was told to give the command 'attention' and as soon as the Admiral entered the compartment I was to order my soldiers to look at him by the command 'eyes left' or 'eyes right' depending on which side he entered. Once the Admiral and his staff had entered the compartment the door was closed. The Admiral and his staff saluted us for a full minute. Afterwards the Admiral explained that this salute was not for us in person but for our brave ship and all her crew.

The previous evening Fraser had singled out Bey and Hintze for praise while debriefing his officers in *Duke of York*: 'Gentlemen, the battle against the *Scharnhorst* has ended in victory for us. I hope that if any of you are ever called upon to lead a ship into action against an opponent many times superior, you will command your ship as gallantly as the *Scharnhorst* was commanded today.'[20]

Nor did the compliments end there. As Maschinenobergefreiter (Leading Stoker) Helmut

with drifting ice, blizzards and hail. Eventually we drifted towards a stopped destroyer which had lowered a net on its starboard side. We climbed the net to the upper deck. The British did not help those who couldn't climb by themselves because of the cold. Three men from my raft drowned because of this. It was the destroyer *Scorpion*.

Wireless Telegraphist John Marsh of HMS *Scorpion*:

> We turned on the searchlights and could clearly see the men in the water. Our commander brought our ship alongside the men in the water. Our crew had brought nets outside the hull and some of the men in the water were able to clamber up. We grabbed some of them because they were so frozen and couldn't help themselves. They had great difficulty holding onto the lines or netting.

One who survived by the skin of his teeth was Willi Gödde:

> The crew had thrown nets alongside the hull of the ship and if you were still strong enough you could climb them yourself but no one was able to do so. They then tried to get people from the rafts by throwing lassos. Then they threw a lasso towards me but the lasso slipped over my right elbow each time. I hadn't the strength left to fix the lasso under my armpit. I got it under my right armpit but failed to hold on with my left arm and was thrown back into the water again. Once I was half way up when I lost the rope again. This happened four times and I was about to give up because I thought they won't have patience with me, they can't afford to waste so much time with one man. Eventually the same sailor threw the lasso for the fifth time and I was still unable to get it under my arm but at this moment, as I was about to give up, a large wave flung me all the way up onto the destroyer's deck. The sailor immediately grabbed me and threw me on the deck.

However, the rescuing vessels were ordered to withdraw owing to the danger of U-boat attack after only a few men had been pulled out of the water. This did not pass unnoticed among the British. Able Seaman Lou Chappell of HMS *Belfast*: 'I thought we should have picked more survivors up. I saw a signal in the signals office shortly afterwards and it said: "Take a small sample." Well, to me that meant "leave them".'[18]

The same sentiment was echoed by Ordinary Seaman Norman Scarth of HMS *Matchless* which extinguished her searchlight, hauled in the

---

18 TSC, transcript of Lou Chappell filmed interview.
19 Oral history available at http://www.bbc.co.uk/ programmes/p00mb3pp
20 Fritz-Otto Busch, *The Drama of the* Scharnhorst: *A Factual Account from the German Viewpoint* (London: Robert Hale, 1956), pp. 171–2.

Some of the thirty-six survivors of the *Scharnhorst* come ashore at Scapa Flow on 2 January 1944. They are wearing the kit issued to rescued merchant seamen. *(Imperial War Museum, London/A 21202)*

Backhaus recalled, when the survivors were transferred from *Scorpion* to *Duke of York* at Murmansk, the crew of the destroyer paid tribute to them with 'three cheers for the battleship *Scharnhorst*' to which the survivors replied with 'three hurrahs for HMS *Scorpion*'. For Backhaus, however, the bitter moment of incarceration ashore awaited: 'As we arrived in Scapa Flow I endured terrible hours. We were blindfolded and moved from *Duke of York* to a harbour vessel that brought us ashore. We also had to wear white jackets. This was very humiliating.'[21]

Conclusion

The sinking of the *Scharnhorst* was a combina-

---

[21] TSC, transcript of Helmut Backhaus filmed interview.

THE WRECK DISCOVERED

On 10 September 2000 a joint expedition led by Norwegian researcher Alf R. Jacobsen with backing from the BBC, the Norwegian state broadcasting corporation NRK and the Royal Norwegian Navy discovered the wreck of the *Scharnhorst* lying at a depth of 950ft (290m) in position 72° 31' N, 28° 15' E. As Jacobsen makes clear, the extent of the damage was fully consistent with the nature of the ship's demise:

> The main section of the hull lies upside down; the bow section is broken off forward of the bridge structure and is almost completely destroyed. The stern was broken off immediately abaft the rudder. The main section of the hull measures 160m [525ft], the bow section measuring 60–70m [200–230ft] lying to south at an angle of 90 degrees to the main section. It is believed that the forward magazine explosion separated the bow section shortly before she sank. The mainmast was found to the north of the main wreck. A little further off a 10m [33ft] rangefinder was discovered. Parts of the superstructure were located north of the rangefinder and the stern was found north of the superstructure.[22]

---

[22] Alf R. Jacobsen, *Die* Scharnhorst: *Untergang und Entdeckung des legendären Schlachtschiffs* (Munich: Ullstein, 2004), p. 255.

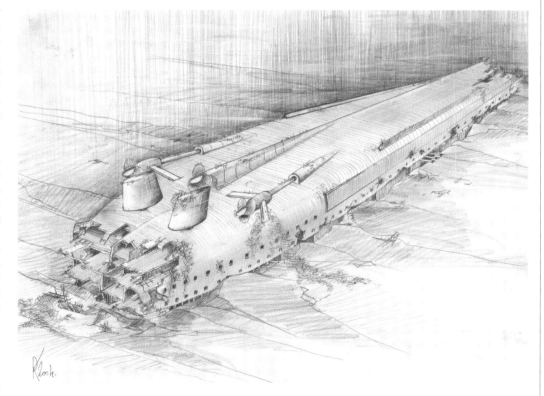

An artist's impression by Pierre Knobloch of the wreck of the *Scharnhorst* as it was discovered in September 2000, hull up and missing her bow and stern. *(Courtesy Philippe Caresse)*

The memorial placed at Wilhelmshaven to the ship and her men. *(Philipp Jakob)*

SCHARNHORSTLIED

Eisiger Sturm, Nebel und Nacht,
Nordlichtshelle, des Ozeans Pracht

Sind stete Begleiter auf jagender Fahrt,
Uns Männern der *Scharnhorst*, trotzig und hart,

Kameraden vom Schlachtschiff, wir trotzen den Tod,
Fahren in leuchtendes Morgenrot

Lachende Augen, sieghafter Blick.
Vorwärts *Scharnhorst*! Nimmer zurück!

THE SONG OF THE *SCHARNHORST*

Ice storm, fog and night,
Northern lights gleaming, the ocean resplendent

As our unfailing companions,
We hunters of the *Scharnhorst*, grim and hard,

We battleship brethren, scorning death,
Sail on into the red aura of dawn

With laughing eyes and the glint of victory.
Onwards *Scharnhorst*! Never retreat!

tion of unpreparedness, mismanagement, poor communication, bad planning, imprudence and ill luck in the context of an increasingly desperate strategic conjuncture for Germany. The Kriegsmarine had also fallen astern of the British in technological development, particularly in the area of radar, which left *Scharnhorst* groping blindly in the polar night off North Cape. Then there was the matter of leadership. As Vizeadmiral Rolf Johannesson put it, 'Last but not least: the British outnumbered us, were better trained and prepared for the task and their leaders were experienced and superior to ours in every way.' These factors combined to end the career of the greatest German surface vessel of the Second World War.

Some ships can in retrospect be defined largely by the circumstances and nature of their demise. Although *Scharnhorst* was one of only two German capital ships destroyed by enemy action on the high seas during the Second World War, succumbing with huge loss of life after a prolonged chase and then a savage engagement lasting two hours, no such definition could ever be hers. Symbolic of the youthful pride and aggression of the Kriegsmarine, in four years of war *Scharnhorst* built a reputation as a thorn in the side of the British and co-author of two spectacular humiliations which have reverberated down the ensuing decades: the sinking of the *Glorious* and the Channel Dash. These and other escapades together with the resources tied down by her made her a priority target, and just as her days of victory encapsulated the Wehrmacht in its pomp, so her immolation reflected the ruin of the Third Reich itself. For that reason, as for her fighting career and high morale, the battleship *Scharnhorst* belongs in very select company.

Sources

Unpublished Sources

Bundesarchiv (State Archive), Koblenz
RM 92/5080, Gefechtsberichte Schlachtschiff „*Scharnhorst*" [Battleship *Scharnhorst* Action Reports]. Bockmühl, Kapitänleutnant (Ing.) und 1. Leckwehroffizier [Engineer Lieutenant and 1st Damage Control Officer].
RM 92/5096, Konteradmiral Rolf Johannesson, *Beitrag zum* „*Scharnhorst*" *Untergang am 26.12.43* [Comments on the sinking of the *Scharnhorst* on 26.12.43], 8 April 1962.
RM 92/5199, „*Scharnhorst*" Gefechtswerte & Erfahrungen [*Scharnhorst* Battle Experience]. (Contains Günter Sträter's report of 6 October 1944 following his repatriation.)
RM 134/199, „Vernehmung des Matrosen Gefreiter Sträter zum Gefecht vom 26. Dez. 1943" [Interview of Ordinary Seaman Günter Sträter concerning the battle of 26 December 1943]
Thomas Schmid Collection (TSC)
Transcripts of filmed interviews (c. 1988–1992):
Scharnhorst: Helmut Backhaus, Helmut Feifer, Willi Gödde, Eugen Pfeiffer, Ernst Reimann; HMS *Scorpion*: John Baxendale, John Marsh; HMS *Belfast*: Lou Chappell

Bibliography

Bredemeier, Heinrich, *Schlachtschiff* Scharnhorst (Jugenheim: Koehlers Verlagsges, 1962)
Busch, Fritz-Otto, *The Drama of the* Scharnhorst: *A Factual Account from the German Viewpoint* (London: Robert Hale, 1956)
Caresse, Philippe, *Le Croiseur de bataille* Scharnhorst: *Son épopée et sa fin tragique* (Outreau, Pas-de-Calais: Lela Presse, 2005)
Garzke, William H., & Robert O. Dulin, *Battleships: Axis and Neutral Battleships in World War II* (2nd edn, Annapolis, Md.: Naval Institute Press, 1990)
Howse, Derek, *Radar at Sea: The Royal Navy in World War 2* (London: Macmillan, 1993)
Humble, Richard, *Fraser of North Cape: The Life of Admiral of the Fleet Lord Fraser (1888–1981)* (London: Routledge & Kegan Paul, 1983)
Jacobsen, Alf R., Scharnhorst (Stroud, Glos.: Sutton, 2004); German trans.: *Die* Scharnhorst: *Untergang und Entdeckung des legendären Schlachtschiffs* (Munich: Ullstein, 2004)
Koop, Gerhard, & Klaus-Peter Schmolke, *Die Schlachtschiffe der Scharnhorst Klasse* (Bonn: Bernard & Graefe Verlag, 1991); English trans.: *Battleships of the Scharnhorst Class* (London: Greenhill, 1999)
_____, *Battleship* Scharnhorst (London: Conway, 1998)
Shoker, Randall S., *Battleship* Scharnhorst: *The Crew Photo Album* (Oxford, Ohio: Oxford Museum Press, 2000)

Oral history of Ordinary Seaman Norman Scarth of HMS *Matchless* (December 2011), available at: http://www.bbc.co.uk/programmes/p00mb3pp [accessed March 2017]
'The Life and Death of the *Scharnhorst*' (BBC, 1971), available at https://www.youtube.com/watch?v=o_LVS-u26no [accessed May 2017]

Regia Marina
The Battleship *Littorio* (1937)

Arrigo Velicogna

FAST, ELEGANT, well armed, well designed and the pride of a generation of sailors, Regia Nave *Littorio* is the most emblematic Italian battleship of the era. She fought in several successful engagements and survived heavier damage than other more famous battleships yet her important role in the struggle for the Mediterranean has often been overlooked, a reflection of the disdain with which the Regia Marina has too often been treated in English-language histories of the Second World War during which Italian ships and sailors fought valiantly on both sides. This chapter seeks to redress that imbalance.

Context

The Regia Marina ('Royal Navy') ended the First World War with ample experience in the operational use of light vessels and small craft but almost none in that of capital ships. In fact, no Italian capital ship had engaged a vessel of her own kind since the Battle of Lissa against the Austro-Hungarian fleet in 1866 which ended in disaster for the Regia Marina. Only the first Italian dreadnought, *Dante Alighieri*, had been employed in anything resembling combat operations. While the Italian *Mezzi Insidiosi* (Stealth Units) had covered themselves in glory by sinking the Austro-Hungarian battleship *Szent István* at sea in June 1918 and then her sister *Viribus Unitis* (q.v.) in Pola hours after the surrender, the Italian battlefleet had remained safely in harbour where two units, *Giulio Cesare* and *Leonardo da Vinci*, had been sunk by sabotage and accident respectively. While the Regia Marina had good reason to preserve her battleship strength, the decision not to risk them at all served to raise questions as to their utility in the immediate aftermath of the war. It also ensured that the navy would have to rely on foreign accounts of battleship combat experience where its own post-

Italian firepower. Probably the most famous picture ever taken of Italian battleships shows a newly completed *Littorio* leading her sister *Vittorio Veneto* during gunnery exercises in the Gulf of Taranto in the summer of 1940. *(NHHC/NH 86134)*

war development was concerned, albeit less wedded to the overriding lessons of Jutland than some of its counterparts.

This state of affairs was compounded by the prevailing diplomatic, economic and military climate, and for nearly ten years after the Great War the Regia Marina showed no active interest in the matter of battleship construction. As in Europe generally, Italy had neither the interest, the resources nor the necessity to pursue any large-scale naval construction programmes. Moreover, of the Regia Marina's two primary adversaries, the Imperial and Royal Austro-Hungarian Navy had disappeared completely

and the French Marine Nationale shared Italy's post-war outlook. The first victims of this climate were the battleships of the Francesco Caracciolo class of which only the name-ship was in a fairly advanced state of completion, her three sisters being still on the slip. The navy and the government initially decided to retain *Caracciolo* and abandon the other three but by 1920 even she had been sold for scrap, to be followed over the course of the next three years by practically all the Italian pre-dreadnoughts and the unrepaired *Leonardo da Vinci*. The Regia Marina in any case regarded the four units of the Conte di Cavour and Caio Duilio classes, along with *Dante Alighieri* (in commission until 1928), as a perfectly respectable battlefleet, leaving it to direct a majority of the resources allocated to it during the 1920s to replacing smaller vessels, especially the aging inventory of light and armoured cruisers and destroyers.[1] Meanwhile, Italy had in 1922 become a signatory to the Washington Naval Treaty, which gave her parity with France by restricting capital ship construction to 175,000 tons. The treaty not only handed Italy a bloodless victory over a traditional rival, but restricted her to a manageable capital ship tonnage in an era of budgetary retrenchment. Moreover, despite the ten-year 'naval holiday' on the construction of new battleships imposed by Washington, Italy was permitted to lay down a pair of capital ships to the 35,000-ton treaty limit to replace those decommissioned or abandoned in 1927 and 1929 respectively. This provision formed the basis of the Littorio-class battleships.

Origins

Circumstances therefore conspired to delay the naval staff showing renewed interest in capital ships until 1927. In September of that year Rear Admiral Romeo Bernotti published a study which laid the foundations for the development of the Regia Marina. Having addressed such topics as war planning, logistics and air-naval co-operation, Bernotti turned to the navy's battleship strength. With *Dante Alighieri*, *Conte di Cavour* and *Giulio Cesare* respectively awaiting decommissioning, disarming and conversion to training duties, Bernotti declared the remaining two units (*Caio Duilio* and *Andrea Doria*) to be obsolete and of limited combat value, and recommended that a class of three battleships be laid down to ensure the availability of at least two vessels at any one time.[2] With 70,000 tons of her quota available under the Washington Treaty, in 1928 the naval staff issued two sets of proposals, the first for three 23,000-ton units with a main armament of six 15in (381mm) guns and capable of 28–29 knots, and the second for three 35,000-ton

The Italian battlefleet between the wars: *Conte di Cavour*, one of four dreadnoughts laid down before the First World War which the Regia Marina subjected to total reconstruction between 1932 and 1937. *(NHHC/NH 111474)*

vessels mounting six 16in (406mm) guns and a speed of 29–30 knots. While the first option could be completed within the available tonnage limitation, the second required two ships to be laid down under treaty limits, with a third to follow on the conclusion of the 'naval holiday' in 1931. Reasonable though these plans were, the Italian Prime Minister Benito Mussolini rejected them on two grounds: not only would a new battleship programme have hampered existing modernisation plans (including construction of the Condottieri-class light cruisers and Zara-class heavy cruisers) but its existence threatened Italy's position at the London Naval Conference due to be held April 1930. The formal plans were therefore shelved by the naval staff.

In the event, it was a change in the diplomatic climate rather than military necessity which prompted Mussolini to support the procurement of new battleships. Despite its various tonnage and armament restrictions, the London Naval Conference failed to address growing French unease that whereas she had been accorded parity with Italy under the Washington Treaty, no consideration had been made of her position with respect to Germany which was in the process of rebuilding its navy. Central to these concerns was the development of the

Panzerschiffe of the Deutschland class, the pet project of Admiral Hans Zenker, whose 'cruiser killers' promised to upset the tactical balance of naval warfare, while posing a major threat to French merchant shipping. The Marine Nationale responded in October 1931 by announcing the construction of the battleship *Dunkerque* with an armament of eight 13in (330mm) guns and a designed speed of 29.5 knots on 26,500 tons (31 knots on trials). However, in providing an effective counter to the Deutschlands *Dunkerque* served to alter the balance of power in the Mediterranean. Even so, Mussolini remained anxious to avoid upsetting the treaty system and had no interest in provoking a naval arms race with France. The initial response from Italy was therefore to order a total reconstruction of *Conte di Cavour*, *Caio Duilio*, *Andrea Doria* and *Giulio Cesare* between 1932 and 1937 which collectively promised to be more than a match for *Dunkerque*. This state of affairs changed abruptly on 16 July 1934 when the French, again in response to German naval construction in the shape of the Scharnhorst class (q.v.), announced plans to build a second unit of the Dunkerque class (*Strasbourg*). This announcement coupled with the failure of talks between Rome and Paris

[1] By way of comparison, the Marine Nationale had the battleships of the Courbet class of 1910–11 (*Courbet*, *France*, *Paris* and *Jean Bart*) which were still lacking director control in 1918, and the Bretagne class of 1912 (*Bretagne*, *Provence* and *Lorraine*). *France* was wrecked on a submerged rock in 1922 and *Jean Bart* was in poor condition.
[2] Erminio Bagnasco & Augusto de Toro, *The Littorio Class: Italy's Last and Largest Battleships, 1937–1948* (Barnsley, S. Yorks.: Seaforth Publishing, 2011), p. 10.

Conte di Cavour as she emerged from her reconstruction at C.R.D.A. Trieste in 1937. The similarity in appearance and layout of the reconstructed battleships with the Littorio class reflects the design leadership of Umberto Pugliese in all projects. (*NHHC/NH 85909*)

forced the hand of the Italian government. Urged on by the chief of the naval staff, Admiral Domenico Cavagnari, on 26 May Mussolini, by now holding both the offices of prime minister and navy minister, announced the construction of two 35,000-ton battleships to be called *Littorio* and *Vittorio Veneto*. The announcement prompted a firm response from the British government which wanted to use the upcoming naval conference in London to propose a reduction in battleship displacement and main-armament calibre. However, such measures were supported neither by Washington nor by Tokyo, and despite a flurry of diplomatic exchanges between Rome and London, and several last-minute attempts by both France and Italy to reach a compromise, the way was clear for the Regia Marina to build the Littorio class.

Design

On 21 and 22 March 1934 a meeting of the *Comitato degli Ammiragli* (Admirals' Committee), the consultative body of the Regia Marina, settled on the four key points which underpinned Italy's future battleship programme including that of the Littorio class:[3]

– From a doctrinal standpoint, battleships remained a fundamental and indispensable part of every fleet.
– From a technical standpoint, only a large displacement could provide reasonable protection against the threat of shellfire, torpedoes and bombs, and it would be a mistake to abandon battleships so long as other nations

either possessed vessels with these features (such as the British Nelson class) or were likely to build them given the uncertain outcome of naval arms limitation treaties.
– From a legal standpoint, Italy was fully within her rights to build battleships to the maximum permitted displacement and armament.
– From a diplomatic standpoint, Italy had made every effort to reach a naval agreement with France which bore sole responsibility for the failure to achieve it, while the preponderance of the Italian 35,000-ton ships over the French 26,500-ton vessels was as justified as the French vessels were with respect to the German 10,000-ton ships.

The selection by the naval staff of a 35,000-ton vessel reflected its commitment to building a fast battleship capable of approximately 30 knots and armed with the largest available ordnance, which meant guns of at least 15in (381mm) and possibly 16in (406mm) calibre of a type already in service with the British, US and Japanese navies. However, unlike the Nelson and Dunkerque classes, in which the main battery was disposed forward of the bridge, the Italian battleships were to have a conventional arrangement of three triple turrets, two forward and one aft. Although the plans drawn up by the *Comitato per i Progetti delle Navi* (Ship Design Committee) in 1928 on the basis of Bernotti's study of the previous September had been shelved, work continued to update them in line with naval staff thinking and in 1932 preliminary designs had been ordered for a 35,000-ton vessel from the naval architect Umberto Pugliese of the *Genio Navale* (Naval Engineering Branch) (see below). Pugliese's instructions from the *Direzione Generale delle Costruzioni Navali e*

Meccaniche (Naval Construction and Engineering Bureau – MARICOST) were the following:[4]

– A main battery greater than (or equal to) that mounted in any potential adversary, the guns to be disposed mainly in the fore part of the ship.
– A speed capable of keeping the standard 10,000-ton Treaty cruisers and capital ships either commissioned or building for other Mediterranean navies within gunnery range.
– A degree of protection sufficient to withstand prolonged combat against similar ships under ordinary conditions.

Preliminary plans were submitted by Pugliese in early 1933 but the final designs were not completed until May 1935, six months after construction of the first two units of the class had begun.

Armament

The emphasis on offensive capability contained in the MARICOST guidelines obliged Pugliese to make a series of fundamental design choices, focusing on the main armament in order to retain a balance of speed and protection while observing the 35,000-ton treaty limit. While MARICOST and, by extension, the naval staff favoured 16in guns, the mounting of these presented a significant challenge on several fronts. The increased weight of the 16in weapon meant that only six could be mounted in three twin turrets or eight in two quadruple turrets (as in *Dunkerque*) if the displacement were to be kept at 35,000 tons, but in the event displacement rose to over 38,000 tons during the design process. Although the *Direzione Generale delle Armi e degli Armamenti Navali* (Naval Weapons and Armaments Bureau – MARINARMI) which was responsible to Pugliese and his team put forward arguments for mounting the 16in gun, namely greater penetrating power and an increase in range of approximately 2,200yds (2,000m), these were offset by reduced rate of fire (due to slower handling of heavier shells) and the fact that the Italian armaments industry had never manufactured naval guns of this calibre.

[3] *Ibid.*, pp. 17–18.   [4] *Ibid.*, p. 29.

Littorio in the final stages of fitting out at Genoa or La Spezia in the spring of 1940. This photo provides an overview of her armament, showing the after 15in turret set on its raised barbette looming over two of the twin 0.79in/65-calibre automatic cannons, the barrels of which were set in a unique echeloned arrangement. On the left is the port after 6in turret. Note the ship's bell affixed to the barbette. (Courtesy Philippe Caresse)

The 16in gun would therefore have to be designed *ab initio*, with a corresponding increase in time and cost. On the other hand, the three major ordnance factories in Italy – Ansaldo, Vickers-Terni (subsequently Odero-Terni-Orlando – O.T.O.) and Armstrong-Pozzuoli – had already manufactured twenty-three 15in 40-calibre guns for the abandoned Caracciolo class. Well-designed, effective and extensively tested, these guns provided a sound basis for the development of a new 50-calibre weapon. Not only that, but nine 15in guns permitted a more balanced arrangement of two turrets forward and one aft, and both MARINARMI and Pugliese settled for that option.

Another discussion, this time once the ships were already under construction, centred on a revised turret arrangement of a quadruple and twin turret forward and a quadruple turret aft, as in the later King George V class. Although this arrangement increased the total weight of fire and, more importantly, allowed a more balanced division of fire should the forward and after batteries engage different targets, there were two important drawbacks. The increased weight of the quadruple turrets would have required a reduction in shell stowage from sixty to fifty per gun, together with the development and construction of two separate designs. In the end, economic and technical considerations prevailed over tactical ones and the triple turrets were retained. The two forward, one aft configuration allowed the ship to maintain a heavy concentration of firepower forward while allowing the main armament to bear during a disengagement situation. Moreover, the after turret was positioned with an unusually wide firing arc of 320 degrees, allowing a full nine-gun salvo to be fired up to 20 degrees off the port and starboard bow. Coupled with a high design speed, this permitted *Littorio* to employ her full battery in an oblique pursuit.

Secondary armament consisted of twelve 6in (152mm) 55-calibre guns mounted in four triple turrets positioned in the waist immediately abaft and immediately forward of turrets '2' and '3' respectively. These were supplemented by twelve high-angle and 3.5in (90mm) dual-purpose guns, twenty-four 1.5in (37mm) guns (in twin and single mounts) and twenty Breda 0.79in (20mm) guns for anti-aircraft defence, all disposed amidships. No torpedo tubes were fitted.

UMBERTO PUGLIESE

Umberto Pugliese was born into a Jewish family in the Piedmontese city of Alessandria in 1880 and joined the Regia Marina as a cadet in 1893. Having graduated from the Naval Academy at Livorno in 1898, he went on to take a degree in naval engineering at the Scuola Superiore Navale in Genoa. In 1902 he duly transferred to the naval engineering branch before serving afloat in the battleships *Vittorio Emanuele* and *Regina Margherita*. Pugliese took a prominent role in the rescue efforts following the Messina earthquake of December 1908 in which the Russian battleship *Slava* (q.v.) also distinguished herself. In 1913 he was assigned to the Ship Design Committee in which he spent the majority of his active career and whose members, like those of the naval engineering branch, held military as against naval rank. Between 1925 and 1931 he was director of the Royal Naval Yard at Castellammare di Stabia near Naples. Pugliese was promoted general on appointment as director of naval engineering and construction in 1931, in which office he remained until 1939. Over the course of those twenty-six years he collaborated first in battleship design and subsequently in the fitting out of the Zara and Armando Diaz-class cruisers. Next he drafted the design of the Montecuccoli and Duca d'Aosta-class light cruisers before taking charge of the reconstruction of *Cavour*, *Duilio*, *Doria*

Persecuted genius: Umberto Pugliese (1880–1961), inventor of the underwater protection system that bears his name and lead designer of the Littorio class who yet fell foul of Mussolini's Racial Laws of 1938. (Bruce Taylor Collection)

and *Cesare*, and then his masterpiece, the Littorio class, all of which received the underwater protection system that bears his name (see below).

Dismissed from active duty in January 1939 as a result of the Racial Laws passed the previous year, Pugliese was nonetheless recalled in November 1940 at the request of the chief of staff, Admiral Cavagnari, to assist in the refloating of vessels damaged during the British raid on Taranto. Although classified as 'non-Jewish' by the Italian authorities and permitted to resume wearing his uniform in 1942, Pugliese was detained in Rome by the Gestapo following the Armistice in January 1944 but paroled, after which he fled to northern Italy. Here he learned that his sister Gemma had shared the same fate as the Jewish Admiral Augusto Capon and been sent to Auschwitz where they both died. Pugliese was buried with full military honours following his death in Sorrento in 1961.

Littorio unleashes a broadside from her main battery during gunnery exercises in the Gulf of Taranto in the summer of 1940. *(NHHC/NH 86135)*

Fire control was based on an integrated suite of stereoscopic rangefinders (39.4ft/12m for the main battery) and computers linking the three main turrets, the majority of the components fitted in *Littorio* manufactured by the San Giorgio firm of Genoa. Auxiliary suites were available in turrets '2' and '3' and similar arrangements were in place for the 6in secondary anti-aircraft batteries. According to the *Direttive e Norme per l'Impiego della Squadra Navale* (Guidelines and Regulations for the Employment of the Naval Squadron), turrets were to engage individually rather than with a full broadside and at no time were more than two turrets to be used simultaneously.[5] Ranging was carried out using the Forcella bracketing method, the turrets firing in quick succession beginning with turret '3'. Although the target was expected to be found quickly under optimum circumstances, the *Direttive* accepted that the system was ineffective in heavy sea when only the fully stabilised 3.5in guns were deemed accurate under automated operation. If the ship were rolling more than 5 degrees, turrets were advised to go over to independent firing with correction based on spotting the fall of shot. No radar installations were included in the designs for the *Littorio* class nor did the Regia Marina succeed in developing a reliable system before the war ended.

Hull and Protection

Littorio had a total length of 780ft (237.7m), was 108ft (32.9m) in the beam and drew 34.5ft (10.5m) at full load. Horizontal protection was concentrated around an armoured citadel extending 394ft (120m) and consisting of between 2.8 and 6.4in (70–162mm) of plate, while the turrets and conning tower received up to 15in (380mm) and 10.2in (260mm) respectively, all in Krupp cemented armour. Total armour amounted to 13,770 tons.

Where underwater protection was concerned, *Littorio* employed the famous Pugliese cylinder system (see below) together with a fractional or composite system for the armoured belt of a type first developed for the French heavy cruiser *Algérie*. Enthusiastically advocated by Pugliese following tests carried out by the Regia Marina, the fractional system as originally conceived consisted of an outer 2.75in (70mm) belt of homogeneous steel separated from an inner main belt of 11in (280mm) cemented armour by a

79in (2m) cavity. The underlying principle was that the external plate would slow down and decap an armour-piercing shell before it struck the main belt. It was also anticipated that the outer layer would disrupt the shell trajectory such as to cause it to fragment rather than explode on contact with the main belt. This system was modified after testing and the version finally installed in *Littorio* reduced the cavity (which was filled with a water-repellent material) to 10in (250mm) while increasing the main belt to 11in (280mm) along the length of the citadel. The resulting structure was manufactured in enclosed boxes which were applied to the hull over a timber backing, part of an innovative and straightforward solution presenting few challenges either to construction or maintenance.

Construction

The contracts for *Littorio* and *Vittorio Veneto* were awarded to private shipyards, the former to Ansaldo of Genoa and the latter to Cantieri Riuniti dell'Adriatico (C.R.D.A.) in Trieste. C.R.D.A. had offered to build both ships but the naval staff favoured dividing the work, not least because Genoa was closer to the main production centres for guns and armour. Initial consultations with industry in the spring of 1934 before the formal announcement in May prompted several unconventional approaches and inducements to Mussolini to secure these lucrative contracts, but the navy stood by its selection of

Ansaldo and C.R.D.A. *Littorio* and *Vittorio Veneto* were laid down on the same day, 28 October 1934, the anniversary of the momentous Fascist march on Rome twelve years earlier which had led to Mussolini's appointment as prime minister. This date was of course no coincidence, the Fascist connotations of which also extended to the name given the subject of this chapter, derived as it was from the Latin *lictor*, the bodyguard of the Roman magistrates who bore the bundle of wooden rods (*fasces*) symbolic of imperial power and authority adopted by Mussolini for his movement. Launched on 22 August 1937, completion of *Littorio* was anticipated in April 1939 and of *Vittorio Veneto* in February 1939, greater efficiency being expected from C.R.D.A., given its recent experience in the construction of the 50,000grt liners *Rex* and *Conte di Savoia*. Although work started in earnest in the autumn of 1934, official contracts were not awarded to Ansaldo and C.R.D.A. until July 1935, resulting in delays in payment and some financial difficulty for the two firms. Payment when it eventually came was made not by the government but by the state-owned *Consorzio per Sovvenzioni sui Valori Industriali* (Consortium for State Aid for Industrial Assets) and guaranteed by the state.[6]

Even then the construction of the two ships did not proceed smoothly. In the first place, the

---

[5] *Ibid.*, p. 92.

[6] *Ibid.*, p. 21.

THE PUGLIESE SYSTEM

In 1917 Umberto Pugliese, then a colonel in the Ship Design Committee, began developing an innovative underwater damage protection system without recourse to those external bulges or accretions which in altering the hull profile of a vessel had the effect of impairing its speed, transverse stability and seagoing qualities. The resulting system consisted of two long but lightly built cylindrical structures running parallel to and just under the armoured belt on either side of the vessel. The inboard edge of the structure rested against the armoured bulkhead comprising the hull proper while the outer layer consisted of a series of lightly constructed dry compartments. The main body of the structure was in two sections: an outer cavity filled with liquid, usually fuel or drinking water replaced by seawater ballast once consumed, and an inner cavity consisting of an empty metal cylinder about 12.5ft (3.8m) in diameter. This lightly built cylinder was held in place by sheet steel diaphragms every three or four frames. When the ship was struck by a torpedo, mine or bomb, the outer compartments absorbed part of the detonation as the bulk of the shock wave was transferred to the liquid-filled outer cavity and thence to the inner cylinder, causing it rather than the armoured bulkhead to collapse. To compensate for the inevitable flooding of the ruptured section, a system of 'automatic balancing

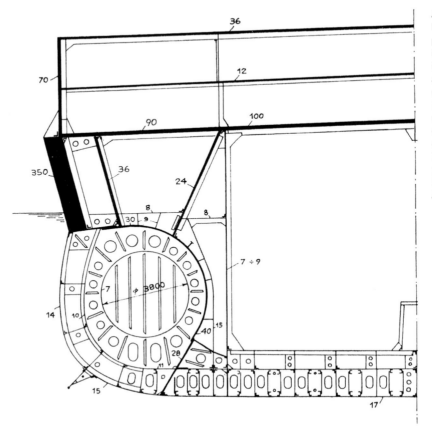

A transverse section of the Pugliese underwater protection system as fitted in *Littorio*. The numbers indicate plate thicknesses and dimensions in millimetres. The 350mm (13.8in) indicated for the main belt is an aggregation of 280mm (11in) of Krupp cemented armour and 70mm (2.8in) of decapping plate. (*Augusto Nani / Ufficio Storico della Marina Militare*)

designs suffered numerous alterations between 1934 and completion in 1940, as a result of which standard displacement rose steadily from 35,000 tons to 38,000 and finally 41,377 tons. Although these increases were approved by the government, this state of affairs was in direct contravention of the Washington Treaty and remained secret. The first of these tonnage increments was the result of major alterations between the preliminary design and final design approved in May 1935, requiring construction to be halted between late 1935 and early 1936 while adjustments were made, mainly in increased armour and the lengthening of the hull to compensate for the additional weight. The second major increase reflected a desire to improve maximum speed from 29 to 30 knots, involving a heavier power plant and adjustments to the hull to obtain the additional speed. Further

Littorio almost ready for launching at Ansaldo's Genova Sestri yard in early 1937, the armour belt yet to be fitted on its timber backing. Attached to the bows for ceremonial purposes are the *fasces* emblems from which Mussolini's Fascist movement took its name. (*Courtesy Philippe Caresse*)

channels' were installed to transfer water from the affected area to empty compartments on the opposite side of the ship. Ballast tanks into which seawater could be pumped were placed above the torpedo protection system as a secondary measure.

The Pugliese system was fitted in two experimental tankers, *Brennero* and *Tarvisio*, and tested extensively as to its seagoing, structural and maintenance capabilities throughout the 1920s. These trials did not however extend to the one area in which its performance was most crucial, that against mines and torpedoes, meaning that experience was confined to theoretical calculation and scale-model testing. In the event, battle experience revealed several issues with the system, chief of which was its inability to cope with magnetic influence torpedoes detonating under the hull. Moreover, the system could only absorb a single hit per section, so that once the outer compartments and cavities had been destroyed and the inner cylinder breached, subsequent damage in the vicinity would be absorbed directly by the hull bulkhead. Finally, while the system did not reduce seagoing performance as much as external bulges, it involved extensive hull modification and was therefore feasible only for new construction or major reconstruction as in the case of the Conte di Cavour and Caio Duilio classes.

problems were linked to the propulsion system. While the Regia Marina wanted two standardised ships, each shipyard had its own plans for the propulsion system. The issue was complicated by the machinations of Senator Giuseppe Belluzzo, a government minister and the leading figure in the Ansaldo-Belluzzo-Tosi (ABT) consortium, Italy's largest turbine manufacturer. Belluzzo lobbied Mussolini to see to the fitting of Belluzzo turbines in all Italian warships. Mussolini agreed in principle, but nonetheless consulted with Admiral Cavagnari on the technical feasibility of such a solution. Cavagnari responded by establishing an advisory committee with naval officers and representatives both of the ABT consortium and the two shipyards, with the effect that each ship ultimately received four Belluzzo turbine sets (including one high-, one medium- and one low-pressure impulse turbine per set) disposed in two rooms forward and abaft the boiler rooms and capable of 130,000shp. They were powered by eight Yarrow boilers arranged in four rooms, and there was notional bunkerage for 3,700 tons of fuel at normal load

Littorio under tow at Genoa following preliminary trials on 23–25 October 1939. *(Courtesy Philippe Caresse)*

and 4,228 tons at maximum load though in practice no more than 3,300 tons were available, giving a maximum range of 4,290 miles at 13 knots.[7] *Littorio* ran 31.2 knots on trials.

Design alterations and typical Italian political and financial tragicomedy aside, an even more critical factor in the construction delays was the shortage of steel both for general use and for armour plate from which Italy suffered after 1935. The main cause was the economic sanctions voted by the League of Nations in response to Italy's military adventure in Abyssinia, which significantly curtailed imports. This situation was exacerbated by Mussolini's retaliatory imposition of a policy of economic autarky which created a severe shortage of raw materials needed for shipbuilding and delayed the commissioning of every Italian warship under construction. A secondary cause was the competing requirements of several construction programmes, particularly the rebuilding of *Caio Duilio* and *Andrea Doria* to allow them to take their place in the new battlefleet alongside the modernised *Conte di Cavour* and *Giulio Cesare* and the Littorios, together with their intended successors of the Impero class. The delays also brought a steady increase in costs in their train. Initially projected at 480 million lire, *Littorio*'s official final cost was 575,833,000 lire, but research suggests that the actual cost of the ship was in the vicinity of 800 million lire.[8]

Fitting-Out and Completion

Although *Littorio* was finally delivered to the Regia Marina at Genoa more than a year late on 6 May 1940 and eight days after *Vittorio Veneto*,

the net effect of these delays was that neither was operational at the time of Italy's declaration of war against France and Britain on 10 June or ready to participate in the first general engagement in the struggle for the Mediterranean, the inconclusive Battle of Punta Stilo (Battle of Calabria) on 9 July. *Littorio* began her sea trials off Genoa on 15 May 1940 before proceeding to the nearby naval base at La Spezia on the 20th where fitting out was completed. Three days later she sailed under destroyer escort for the main Italian naval base at Taranto in Apulia where she encountered her sister *Vittorio Veneto* for the first time, the two ships forming the Regia Marina's 9ª Divisione Navi di Battaglia (9th Battleship Division) under Admiral Carlo Bergamini. Nonetheless, training requirements and the continued presence of Ansaldo workers calibrating and testing the main armament kept *Littorio* and her sister in port for the rest of the summer, although the 9th Division was put on alert on the eve of the Battle of Punta Stilo.[9] Nor was this process trouble-free, and several significant problems were discovered beyond those typical of newly commissioned vessels. The shell rammers in the turrets were underpowered and imperfectly centred, while a fire in turret '1' caused by the carelessness of an Ansaldo employee in early July claimed the life of a worker and put the turret out of action until the end of the month. Officers were also dissatisfied at Ansaldo's shoddy workmanship during the fitting-out process and it was not until late August that *Littorio* and *Vittorio Veneto* first turned their bows towards the enemy.

Organisation

The standard complement of *Littorio* was 1,866 officers and men, though this could increase to over 1,900 if the admiral and staff were

---

[7] *Ibid.*, p. 64.
[8] *Ibid.*, p. 22.

[9] *Ibid.*, p. 166.

Administrative Divisions

1st	*Navigation and Communications* (radio operators, signalmen)	
2nd	*Seamen*	
3rd & 4th	*Gunnery* (gunners, loaders, fire-control specialists and ordnance artificers)	
5th	*Underwater and Aviation* (torpedo and mine specialists were not represented in *Littorio*, but aviation personnel were embarked to operate the IMAM Ro.43 seaplanes and later the catapult-launched Reggiane Re2000 Falco fighters and their associated equipment)	
6th	*Electrical* (electricians, gyrocompass setters and radar operators from the summer of 1941)	
7th & 8th	*Engineering* (stokers, machinists, artificers, mechanicians and shipwrights)	
9th	*Servizio Generale* ('General Service'; a designation for specialised personnel not assigned to the aforementioned divisions)	
10th	*Combined Staff* (if embarked when the ship was acting as a flagship)	

A view from the bridge structure looking aft in the summer of 1940. No. '3' 15in turret is traversed almost to its maximum forward bearing of 20 degrees off the starboard bow and a party of men is standing beside the guns on the starboard after 6in turret. (*Courtesy Philippe Caresse*)

embarked when the ship was serving as division or squadron flagship. The exact breakdown was ninety-two *Ufficiali* (commissioned officers), 122 *Sottufficiali anziani* (chief petty officers), 134 *Sottufficiali* (petty officers) and 1,506 seamen. To these were added twelve civilians usually assigned to the galleys, a mark of the emphasis placed on the quality of food preparation in the Regia Marina which opted to recruit specialist staff from commercial restaurants ashore rather than train its own personnel. If the ship was on the active list the commanding officer held the rank of Capitano di Vascello (captain) and was assisted by a Capitano di Fregata (commander) as executive officer with responsibility for logistical and crew matters. In a large ship like *Littorio* the executive officer was supported by a *Terzo Ufficiale* (third in command) who had charge of administrative affairs. As was customary in the Regia Marina, engineering was in the care of the *Genio Navale* (Naval Engineering Branch) whose members held military rank. In *Littorio*'s case the chief engineer was a Tenente Colonello (lieutenant colonel). Specialist divisions like gunnery, fire control, navigation, electrical, engineering, medical and so on were under the direction of Capitani di

Corvetta (lieutenant commanders) or Maggiori (majors) in the case of the engineering division. The entire complement, with the exception of the commanding officer, the executive officer and his assistant, were distributed into the ten divisions based on specialisation by which the Regia Marina organised its ships (see table above).

These administrative divisions were distributed into the three watches (1st, 2nd and 3rd) by which the ship was run. The officers, some senior NCOs and the civilians did not form part of the watches but could be assigned to them. Each watch was theoretically capable of operating the ship alone, but the whole crew was of course called to stations in action or other emergencies. The daily routine was based on a twelve-hour pattern with a cycle of four hours on, eight hours off, meaning that the first watch was on duty from 0000 to 0400 and then again from 1200 to 1600. In some circumstances the 1600–2000 watch could be split in two and divided between two watches. If cadets from the Naval Academy or other naval schools were embarked, they usually operated on a four hours on, four hours off cycle, though assigned to different watches. The schedule was usually less intensive with watches in daily rotations if the ship were in port, but shore leave was granted only sparingly in wartime and permission to leave the base to which the ship was assigned for more than a day given only rarely.

There were separate wardrooms for senior and junior officers, while senior NCOs had their own messes, food being served at table in each case. Officers had cabins while senior NCOs were assigned cubicles also containing bunks. Junior NCOs and ratings lived on communal messdecks, sleeping in hammocks which had to be stowed by 0800. Tables and benches slung from the deckhead for cleaning purposes were lowered for meals and leisure time. Each mess consisted of between six and ten ratings provided with a single large pot and individual

mess kits. A designated member of each mess was responsible for taking the pot to the galley where it was filled and brought back to the messdeck for serving. Sailors were also responsible for cleaning the pot and their own mess kit as well as the messdeck generally.

The Regia Marina therefore followed the practice of most navies where the living and feeding arrangements of its men were concerned, with the same marked inequalities of rank and disparities in comfort. While these arrangements may have been tolerable during ordinary operational duty either at sea or in port, the three and a half years *Littorio* spent in internment under reduced complement in the Great Bitter Lake between 1943 and 1947 tested them to the limit, especially since contact with the outside world, and even between ships, was restricted to the arrival of Italian vessels delivering mail, supplies or replacement crews.

To War

Littorio's operational career was played out in the context of the naval war in the Mediterranean which pitted the Regia Marina, the Regia Aereonautica, the Luftwaffe and the U-Boot Waffe against the Royal Navy, the Fleet Air Arm and the Royal Air Force. The strategic goals of the Regia Marina between 1940 and 1943 were centred largely on active defence and its chief operational aims were the security of Italian merchant traffic between Italy and Libya, the interdiction of major transfers of British forces and *matériel* between either end of the Middle Sea, including the supply of Malta, and preventing linkage between the Gibraltar-based squadron known as Force H and the Mediterranean Fleet at Alexandria. Although the Italian navy could not alter the outcome of the war in the Mediterranean, research and analysis shows that these goals were largely although not decisively achieved until late 1942. At the tactical

The commissioning ceremony for *Littorio* held on the quarterdeck on 6 May 1940, the ship lying at Genoa and the crew in their dark blue winter uniforms. Four days later Italy entered the Second World War. *(Courtesy Philippe Caresse)*

level the *Supermarina* (the high command of the Regia Marina) instructed the fleet to exploit opportunities to inflict damage on British forces, but this aggressive intent was tempered by a stark realisation that Italian shipyards were incapable of replacing losses in a protracted conflict. Under these circumstances preservation of the Regia Marina as a fleet-in-being was the paramount consideration and extremely cautious orders were issued regarding those situations deemed favourable for engaging the enemy.[10]

By the end of August 1940 *Littorio* had participated in her first operational sortie, an abortive attempt to intercept the major supply convoy from Gibraltar to Alexandria known as Operation Hats. She was at sea again in late September, first in an unavailing attempt to intercept a diversionary sortie by Force H to cover the attempted landings at Dakar, and then in response to Operation MB5, a supply convoy between Alexandria and Malta. These failed interceptions not only revealed the shortcomings of Italian air reconnaissance but also the Supermarina's tendency to issue highly restrictive and risk-averse orders. The operations also highlighted problems in the composition of the Italian battle forces. Although *Littorio* and *Vittorio Veneto* of the 9th Battleship Division were able to operate at speeds in excess of 28 knots

Littorio at speed in the Gulf of Taranto in the summer of 1940. The later Italian battleships were rarely matched for elegance of line. *(NHHC/NH 86136)*

10 Vincent P. O'Hara, *Struggle for the Middle Sea: The Great Navies at War in the Mediterranean Theater, 1940–1945* (Annapolis, Md.: Naval Institute Press, 2009), pp. 5–6.

without difficulty, the modernised battleships *Conte di Cavour* and *Giulio Cesare* of the 5th Battleship Division could only maintain 25 knots for sustained periods. This prompted Admiral Inigo Campioni, commander of the *Forze Navali* (Naval Forces), to recommend that the two divisions henceforth operate independently.

Taranto, 1940

Any immediate prospect of employing these battle tactics was halted by the attack on Taranto by carrier-borne aircraft of the Fleet Air Arm on the night of 11–12 November 1940 which left *Littorio*, *Conte di Cavour* and *Caio Duilio* crippled. The attack was delivered in two waves of Swordfish torpedo bombers. The first comprising twelve aircraft (six armed with torpedoes, four with bombs and two with flares) targeted *Littorio* at around 2315 on the 11th and registered two torpedo hits, one on the starboard side between the forward turrets and another on the port side aft. The Pugliese system absorbed most

of the shock from the forward hit but the detonation aft wrecked the rudder and damaged the steering gear. Shortly after midnight, a depleted second wave of seven Swordfish reached Taranto, including five aircraft armed with torpedoes and two with flares. *Littorio* was again targeted, one torpedo coming to rest in the mud under the hull without exploding while another struck the starboard side forward of turret '1'. Compromised by the earlier hit, the Pugliese system in the starboard bow area proved less effective in absorbing this latest one which caused extensive flooding. Two of the four high-capacity pumps in the forward section failed after the diesel generator compartments were flooded, followed by the remaining pair for the same reason. Pumping in the forward section of the ship had therefore to be carried out by hand and using gasoline-operated mobile pumps, neither of which could keep pace with the flooding. Although the tanker *Isonzo* closed to provide support with her pumps and the damage-control parties succeeded in sealing the breaches in the hull and draining some of the flooded compartments, attempts at correcting the trim by emptying the forward fuel bunker and counter-flooding the after compartments failed to bring the ship back onto an even keel, and by 0315 it was clear that *Littorio* was sinking by the head. At 0400 *Littorio*'s commanding officer Captain Massimo Girosi voiced his concerns to the division commander Admiral Bergamini in the undamaged *Vittorio Veneto*, and the two officers decided to beach her on the Sirena Bank two miles north of the harbour. Steering on auxiliary rudders, *Littorio* covered the distance under her own steam until coming to rest in the mud at 0627. Reconnaissance photographs taken by the British after the attack revealed her forecastle to be submerged as far back as the forward turrets; the death toll in *Littorio* was thirty-two.

By mid-morning on the 12th repair teams were already at work. It was initially intended to make her seaworthy for transfer to a safer and better-

Left: A British reconnaissance photo shows *Littorio* beached on the Sirena Bank the day after the Taranto Raid carried out on the night of 11–12 November 1940. The forecastle is submerged as far back as the forward turrets but salvage work has already begun. *(NHHC/NH 111470)*

Above: A partially camouflaged *Littorio* under repair at Taranto following the raid of 11–12 November 1940 and showing the cylinders used to stabilise her in the salvage effort. The work was completed in March 1941. *(Courtesy Philippe Caresse)*

The Axis Resurgent, 1941–2

The disaster at Matapan had repercussions for the Regia Marina extending beyond human and material losses to inflict severe, albeit temporary, damage to its morale. From a practical standpoint, it was demonstrated that the Regia Marina had little chance of holding its own in a night action against British forces without effective radar. Meanwhile, the continual air attacks delivered by the British against the Italian squadron prompted Mussolini to order the fleet to keep within 110 miles of Axis airbases so that fighter cover could be provided. The immediate consequence of Matapan was that the Regia Marina remained in port while Operation Tiger, a fast convoy dispatched from Gibraltar to Alexandria with a cargo of tanks, was allowed to traverse the Mediterranean unchallenged.

Despite the initial shock and the claims of some historians, the Regia Marina was far from finished. On 14 June 1941 the Supermarina issued *Direttiva Navale Numero 7* (Naval Directive No. 7) restricting the circumstances under which Italian surface forces could engage the enemy and establishing several key doctrines for concerted use of naval and air power. Although Tiger had crossed the Mediterranean unchallenged the next Allied convoys would not be so fortunate. *Littorio*, now rejoined by *Vittorio Veneto*, was at sea in August to contest Operation Mincemeat, a minelaying sortie off Livorno, and then in September against Operation Halberd, one of the major Malta supply convoys during which the Regia Aereonautica scored a torpedo hit on HMS *Nelson*, reducing her speed to 12 knots.

equipped location, but Taranto was ultimately deemed adequate in both respects and work proceeded on the construction of a cofferdam to protect the bow. Once refloated, the ship entered dry-dock on 11 December, a month after the attack. Repairs could now commence on those sections of the hull heavily damaged by the three torpedo detonations, which also involved replacement of internal bulkheads. Repairs had also to be carried out to the stern section, main deck and rudder assemblies, the ship having grounded as the result of a near-miss by a bomb, while the fire-control system had to be cured of the effects of concussion. Finally, extensive modifications were made to the damage-control provisions to avoid a repetition of the sequence of events which required the beaching on 11 November. The loss of pumping in the forward section was due not only to the diesel generators and their control facilities being positioned outside of the armoured citadel, but because secondary power was provided independently for each section of the ship with no means of switching to other sources. It was therefore impossible to connect the intact diesel generators in the after section to the pumps in the forward section once their power supply had been cut.

Most of the work had to be carried out by civilian contractors rather than by naval personnel, but the unhappy experience with Ansaldo employees that summer, and *Vittorio Veneto*'s relatively trouble-free delivery by comparison with that of her sister, prompted Admiral Bergamini to order the bulk of the repairs on *Littorio* to be completed by staff from C.R.D.A. instead. The repairs were given the highest priority and several shortcuts were taken to speed up the work. Complete rudder and fire-control assemblies prepared for the fourth ship of the class, *Impero*, were transferred from Brindisi to Taranto for installation in *Littorio*. Only those repairs and modifications affecting the ship's battleworthiness were carried out while she was in dry-dock, the refitting of the crew accommodation having to wait until she was combat-ready. These measures paid off and *Littorio* exited the dry-dock on 19 March 1941, being declared fit to rejoin the fleet on 1 April. Her return came not a moment too soon since *Vittorio Veneto* had been torpedoed and the heavy cruisers *Pola*, *Fiume* and *Zara* sunk with heavy loss of life during the sortie in the eastern Mediterranean which culminated in the infamous engagement off Cape Matapan on 27–29 March.

Although the Italian *Forze da Battaglia* (Battle Forces) commanded by the newly appointed Admiral Angelo Iachino were in a position to make contact on the afternoon of 27 September, worsening weather and uncertainty as to the strength of the British force prompted the admiral to decline the action.

Littorio was again at sea in December, this time covering a large Italian convoy to Libya, M.41. The operation ended in failure with two merchantmen sunk by HM Submarine *Upright*, two more damaged in a collision and *Vittorio Veneto* struck by a torpedo from HMS/m *Urge* on the 13th. This torpedo salvo was spotted in *Littorio* which managed to comb the tracks in time. The Supermarina reacted by ordering convoys to Libya to be halted, but the personal intervention of Mussolini and the Chief of the General Staff, General Ugo Cavallero, brought about an immediate reversal of this policy and M.42 duly sailed on 16 December. *Littorio* was once more at sea, this time with the bulk of the fleet, including the battleships *Doria*, *Cesare* and *Duilio*. His fleet weakened by heavy attrition off Crete in May, the efforts to resupply Malta and support military operations in North Africa, Admiral Cunningham could only contest M.42 with a force of light cruisers and the anti-aircraft cruiser *Carlisle* which Iachino quickly chased off in a short gunnery action on the evening of 17 December 1941. M.42 was followed by M.43 between 3 and 6 January 1942, again without British opposition and again covered by *Littorio*.

Second Sirte, 1942

Despite the depletion of his forces, Churchill continued to press Cunningham to send more supplies to Malta. Small fast convoys had been successful in January, but Operation MF.5 in February failed completely when a convoy with three merchant ships from Alexandria turned back with the loss of two of its number and damage to a third which was forced to take refuge in Tobruk. Iachino was at sea with the battle force but the convoy had disintegrated under German air attack before he was able to reach it. However, on 20 March 1942 another convoy, MW10, sailed from Alexandria with a force of cruisers and destroyers under Rear Admiral Philip Vian charged with escorting it into Malta as part of Operation MG.1. Informed of this development by Italian intelligence, Iachino put to sea with *Littorio* at the head of a force which eventually included two heavy cruisers and a light cruiser and eight destroyers. At 1422 on the 22nd lookouts in the heavy cruiser *Gorizia* spotted bursts of flak to the southeast. Five minutes later the British cruiser

Euryalus sighted *Gorizia* and the rest of the Italian cruiser division. A confused action ensued in worsening weather as the Italian cruisers resisted engaging decisively in an effort to lure Vian's ships towards *Littorio*. At 1535 Vian signalled Cunningham to the effect that he had driven off the enemy and was resuming his run toward Malta. Although under constant German and Italian aerial attack, Vian had the convoy back in formation by 1630, but seven minutes later four unidentified ships were sighted to the northeast. These were *Littorio* and three destroyers, Iachino having decided to interpose his force between the British and Malta in an effort to engage the convoy. Three minutes later the light cruiser *Giovanni delle Bande Nere* landed a salvo on the bridge of Vian's flagship, the cruiser *Cleopatra*, and *Littorio* hit *Euryalus* shortly after. A prolonged gunnery duel took place in poor visibility compounded by the smokescreens laid by Vian's well-organised forces as Iachino vainly tried to work his way round the British in rising seas. The action ended at 1857 by which time darkness had fallen over the battleground. The outcome of this action was that the Royal Navy had suffered six warships damaged in exchange for a single 4.7in (119mm) shell hit on *Littorio*.

Although the Second Battle of Sirte was over as a purely naval engagement the ordeal of both forces had scarcely begun. The weather worsened to such a degree that the Italian destroyers *Scirocco* and *Lanciere* foundered during the night of the 23rd. Short of fuel and ammunition,

at 1940 on the 22nd Vian had meanwhile detached his force to return to Alexandria and ordered MW10, her escort and some damaged ships to make all speed for Malta. Iachino's interception had however served to delay the convoy which consequently failed to make Malta before daybreak. The results were predictable. The German Fliegerkorps II and the Regia Aereonautica claimed two of the merchantmen at sea on the morning of the 23rd and the last two were bombed and sunk in the Grand Harbour at Valletta on the 26th, meaning that less than 20 per cent of the cargo reached its destination. Added to this was the loss of HM destroyers *Legion* and *Southwold* under the shadow of Malta itself. Admiral Cunningham's description of Second Sirte as 'one of the most brilliant actions of the war, if not the most brilliant' was therefore overshadowed by the near total destruction of MW10.[11] Seen in perspective, the defeat of Operation MG.1 may be regarded as emblematic of Italian naval operations. Acknowledgment of Vian's tactical brilliance at Second Sirte and Iachino's inability to press home his attack in unfavourable weather and given the tactical strictures placed upon him by the Supermarina have served not only to reinforce the real or imagined shortcomings of the Regia Marina, but also to mask his, and by

---

[11] Admiral of the Fleet Viscount Cunningham of Hyndhope, *A Sailor's Odyssey* (London: Hutchinson, 1951), p. 455.

Littorio in the camouflage scheme applied in May 1942. An IMAM Ro.43 reconnaissance floatplane can be seen on its quarterdeck catapult. *(Courtesy Philippe Caresse)*

extension *Littorio*'s, critical role in serving up MW10 for destruction from the air over the following days.

Operation Vigorous, 1942

Starved of supplies and under constant aerial attack, the failure of Operation MG.1 left Malta in an increasingly precarious position and forced the British to renew their attempts to relieve it in the teeth of Axis aerial, surface and submarine attack. What resulted was the conjoined operations known as Harpoon and Vigorous, among the largest British naval deployments of the war. The plan involved simultaneously dispatching two heavily escorted convoys to Malta from each end of the Mediterranean, WS19/Z consisting of six merchantmen assembled on the Clyde and reinforced at Gibraltar (Harpoon), and MW11 from Egypt with eleven merchantmen escorted by Rear Admiral Vian with eight light cruisers, twenty-five destroyers, four corvettes and two minesweepers (Vigorous). Leaving WS19/Z to Admiral Alberto De Zara and his reinforced 7th Cruiser Division, Admiral Iachino turned his attention to MW11. The stage was therefore set for another sortie by *Littorio*, this time accompanied by the entire 9th Battleship Division together with two heavy and two light cruisers and twelve destroyers. The Italian squadron sailed from Taranto early on the afternoon of

Littorio the subject of interest at Taranto in the summer of 1942. The port 3.5in dual-purpose battery is shown to good effect. *(Courtesy Philippe Caresse)*

14 June divided into a battleship group and a destroyer group. British reconnaissance detected this movement at 1745 that day and Iachino's force was attacked at dawn on the 15th by successive waves of British aircraft from Malta and Egypt. Shortly after 0500 an attack by RAF Bristol Beaufort torpedo bombers scored a hit on the heavy cruiser *Trento*, while a second group attacked *Littorio* at 0526. A withering barrage of anti-aircraft fire from *Littorio* succeeded in breaking up this attack, but at 0816 a formation of eight USAAF B-24 Liberator bombers appeared over the 9th Battleship Division and

made three bomb runs out of the sun from an altitude of 13,000ft (4,000m). The attack, which lasted until 0850, put a 500lb (227kg) bomb on *Littorio*'s after turret and obtained several near-misses which dented the hull armour and put the two Ro.43 seaplanes out of commission but otherwise failed to impair her combat effectiveness. Towards the end of the attack a formation of Beauforts depleted by Luftwaffe Bf 109s providing air cover to the Italian fleet appeared on the scene but to no avail.

Although the British succeeded in finishing *Trento* off with a torpedo from HMS/m *Umbra* at 0910 on the 15th, MW11 suffered steady attrition to German and Italian air, submarine and surface attack. Not only was Iachino still steaming to intercept the convoy, but Vian's tactical dispositions were thrown into flux by orders from the new Commander-in-Chief of the Mediterranean Fleet, Admiral Sir Henry Harwood, to perform a series of evasive manoeuvres during which so much fuel and ammunition was expended that the goal of reaching Malta had eventually to be abandoned at 1953. However, if 15 June served to dash any hopes the British may have had of MW11 reaching its destination, it was also a frustrating day for Iachino who failed to make contact with the convoy despite numerous sightings from the air. Air–sea communication difficulties, poor co-ordination between the Regia Aereonautica and the Luftwaffe over long-range cover, the loss of his floatplanes during the Liberator attacks that

morning, and a course alteration to the east ordered by the Supermarina at 1300 in response to reports that the convoy had turned for Alexandria, all conspired to keep Iachino from making an interception. The tactical situation had improved for Iachino by evening on the 15th, but shortly before midnight the Regia Marina came under attack from six Wellington torpedo bombers supported by others dropping flares. Despite anti-aircraft fire, smokescreens and violent evasive manoeuvres, at 2340 *Littorio* received a hit forward on her starboard side. Some 1,600 tons of water were shipped but her combat effectiveness remained unaffected and she was able to keep station and maintain her speed. At 0045 on the 16th, however, the Supermarina signalled confirmation that MW11 had turned definitively for Alexandria and Iachino duly steered for Taranto. Ten days later *Littorio* entered dry-dock where she spent two months under repair. By the time she rejoined the 9th Battleship Division on 26 August it had been reinforced by the third unit of the class, the ill-fated *Roma*.

The Beginning of the End, 1942–3

Although Operation Vigorous had been defeated and a further demonstration provided of the ability of Italian surface forces to disrupt Allied plans even when no contact was made, it also represents the high-water mark of the Regia Marina and for *Littorio* which had carried out her last combat sortie. Henceforth attrition and particularly shortage of fuel kept the battle force in port, a situation already apparent at the time of Harpoon and Vigorous during which *Caio Duilio* had been under sailing orders but ultimately stayed in harbour. This situation was in part due to the Regia Marina's policy of maintaining an untouchable reserve of fuel for use in a fleet action or major contingency such as an Allied descent on the mainland. Although understandable enough, in practice this policy not only aroused the ire and suspicion of some German officers, but kept the Italian battlefleet in harbour for other than training as against operational purposes until September 1943. Moreover, by relieving the pressure on the Allies it made the circumstances for which the fleet was being preserved more likely.[12] Consequently, the Regia Marina's contribution to the last of the heavily contested Malta supply convoys, Operation

Pedestal (10–15 August 1942), was restricted to minor surface craft and submarines together with a force of cruisers and destroyers. Indeed, no major operations were carried out by Italian surface forces after Pedestal.

The withdrawal of the Regia Marina from surface operations in the Mediterranean coincided with the transfer of the Littorios from Taranto, initially to Naples and then to La Spezia. The shift from the eastern to the western coast of Italy was part of a strategy to oblige the Allies to commit greater naval resources to counter the Italian fleet-in-being during the expected landings in North Africa which took place in November 1942. However, in doing so it made *Littorio*, *Vittorio Veneto* and *Roma* priority targets for Allied air power, and between September 1942 and June 1943 several attempts were made to sink them first in Naples and then in La Spezia by massed formations of RAF and USAAF bombers. On the night of 13–14 April *Littorio* was struck by a British 2,000lb (907kg) armour-piercing bomb in La Spezia; she was, however, soon repaired, but *Vittorio Veneto* and *Roma* were heavily damaged by a USAAF raid on that port on 5 June 1943 which forced them to go into dry-dock in Genoa. *Littorio* was therefore the only battleship available to contest the US, British and Canadian landings on Sicily on 10 July. In the event, the Supermarina regarded a sortie against Allied shipping off Sicily as tantamount to a suicide mission and resisted pressure to commit her from the *Comando Supremo* (the

Italian joint chiefs of staff), a decision condemned by Admiral Karl Dönitz in Berlin but supported by the local Kriegsmarine command.

Armistice

On 25 July 1943 the collapse of Italy's military position resulted in King Victor Emmanuel III dismissing Benito Mussolini as prime minister and ordering his arrest. The new government headed by Marshal Pietro Badoglio promised to prosecute the war with renewed vigour, while at the same time making 'de-fascistification' of the armed forces a priority. Among the first expressions of this policy was the renaming of *Littorio* as *Italia* on 30 July, but confusion reigned as to the aims of the new government and the battle force commander, Admiral Carlo Bergamini (who had replaced Iachino on 5 April), requested further instructions while warning that prolonged inactivity was causing growing unrest in the fleet. In fact, with the exception of the navy minister, Admiral Raffaele de Courten, and Rear Admiral Giuseppe Fioravanzo commanding the 8th Cruiser Division, no senior officer in the Regia Marina had any inkling that the Italian government had been in secret negotiations with the Allies regarding the possibility of changing sides in the war since August.[13] De Courten, meanwhile, was anxious to preserve the core of

12 Bagnasco & de Toro, *The Littorio Class*, p. 228.

13 *Ibid.*, pp. 270–2.

the fleet and its three fast battleships, optimistically demanding that the three Littorios had not only to be prevented from falling under either German or Allied control but were to remain under Italian control. Mindful no doubt of the French battleship *Richelieu*, then completing a refit at New York Navy Yard for service in the Allied cause, he advanced the suggestion that the Littorios could be sent to the Far East to join the war against Japan, a notion he brought up again after the Kingdom of Italy formally declared war on her on 15 July 1945. However, the Allies, and particularly Admiral of the Fleet Sir Andrew Cunningham who had now resumed command of the Mediterranean Fleet, had no concern beyond neutralising the Regia Marina. Cunningham therefore saw to the drafting of terms by his chief of staff, Commodore Royer Dick, which reflected his decided sense of an Italian surrender rather than an armistice. Indeed, the so-called 'Dick Memorandum' was so insulting that it had to be kept from Italian naval officers to avoid extreme measures such as the scuttling of the fleet.

These differing objectives, together with the secrecy surrounding the Armistice negotiations, set in train a series of misunderstandings and half-measures which brought a tragic end to the Regia Marina. Not only was Bergamini excluded from any detailed discussions on the Armistice, but the Allied representatives kept the Italian

government in the dark about the exact date of implementation, intending to issue an announcement to that effect in conjunction with an amphibious assault on the mainland. On 6 September 1943 Italian intelligence alerted the government that Allied invasion convoys were in the process of being assembled, but again secrecy prevailed. De Courten failed to mention the Armistice or the Dick Memorandum in a meeting with senior naval officers on the 7th, but did discuss plans prepared by the Comando Supremo on public order measures in the event of a German coup to restore Mussolini (Memo Number 1), a tacit indication of what was to come. Bergamini was therefore instructed to prepare the fleet for action and be ready to mobilise at short notice to secure bases in Sardinia when instructed. At 1730 on the 8th the Italian government received a note from General Dwight D. Eisenhower, Commander-in-Chief of Allied Forces in the Mediterranean, announcing his intention to broadcast the implementation of the Armistice at 1830. However, these plans had not only been leaked beforehand but found the Germans in a high state of preparedness and Hitler immediately activated Operation Achse, the German takeover of Italy.

At La Spezia, home of the naval forces and the battle force, the hours following the declaration of the Armistice were hectic and confused to say the least. Between 1700 and 1800 de Courten

ordered Bergamini by phone to transfer the fleet to the Algerian port of Bône in accordance with the terms of the Armistice. However, Bergamini refused to surrender the fleet to the enemy and threatened to scuttle it instead. During a second call at 2030 de Courten instead ordered Bergamini to proceed to the island naval base of La Maddalena off Sardinia where he was to meet the king and the government. At 2200 Bergamini called a meeting with his division and ship commanders, several of whom were unwilling to follow de Courten's orders and favoured scuttling the fleet. A third and heated phone call with de Courten followed at 2300 during which Bergamini relented and agreed to sail to La Maddalena, eventually managing to persuade every officer to follow suit. At 2345 the Supermarina formally issued the order and Bergamini relayed it to the fleet at 0138 on the 9th. The fleet, including *Italia*, quickly made ready to sail and all ships had cleared La Spezia by 0340. However, its arrival off La Maddalena that afternoon coincided with the capture of that base by German forces. At 1441 Bergamini ordered a simultaneous turn to port into the Gulf of Asinara and an hour later received orders from the Supermarina to make for Bône after all.

Now came the last act in the tragedy. At 1535 twenty-three German Do 217 bombers based in Provence and equipped with the new PC 1400X guided glider bomb approached the formation at an altitude of 20,000ft (6,100m). The Italian anti-aircraft batteries opened fire but three bombs reached their targets, including two against *Roma* which succumbed to the detonation of her forward magazines and went down with at least 1,253 men including Admiral Bergamini. *Italia* was struck by a single bomb on the forecastle which passed through the hull and exploded in the sea beside the ship. The hit was in approximately the same position as that of the first torpedo strike at Taranto three years earlier. As then, the Pugliesi system saved her and she kept her station with her speed and seakeeping unaffected. However, Bergamini's death not only deprived the fleet of its commander but also of its ability to decipher any highly classified signals from Rome or the Supermarina. The ranking officer, Admiral Romeo Oliva of the 7th Cruiser Division, assumed command but was without clear orders and Admiral Luigi Biancheri of the 8th Cruiser Division proposed that the fleet

Commodore Royer Dick of the Royal Navy receives Admiral Alberto Da Zara at Customs House Steps in Valletta after the arrival of the Italian fleet off Malta on 10 September 1943. Frustrating and humiliating terms awaited the Regia Marina. *(NHHC/SC 188573)*

return to La Spezia. The Supermarina eventually reiterated its order to proceed south, later emphasising that the ships should not be handed over but remain manned and under the Italian ensign. On 10 September the fleet fell in with HM Ships *Warspite* and *Valiant* with eight destroyers off North Africa and steered for Malta, reaching it on the 11th.

Internment and Disposal, 1943–54

No sooner had the Italians grasped the nature of the internment to which they would be subjected under Cunningham's orders, including the removal of torpedo pistols, scuttling charges and breech blocks from all except anti-aircraft guns, and the posting of British armed sentries aboard, than the idea of a grand scuttle resurfaced. Biancheri was the most vocal proponent of this measure but Oliva elected to follow orders, a decision confirmed on the 11th by Admiral De Zara, the new commander of naval forces, who had reached Malta with his ships from Taranto the previous day. Instead of the active participation in the war for which they had hoped, *Italia* and *Vittorio Veneto* were instead ordered to sail for Alexandria on the 14th where they were interned under British control on the Great Bitter Lake for two and a half long years until February 1947.

As in the case of the German High Seas Fleet after the First World War, the surviving units of the Italian navy were regarded as booty by the Allied powers, particularly the Soviet Union and France, while the Marina Militare (as the Regia Marina was called after Italy became a republic in June 1946) did everything in its power to retain her modern battleships. The fate of the Littorios was critical to the negotiations that preceded the Paris Peace Treaty of 10 January 1947, the Marina Militare preferring to scrap them rather than turn them over to another power, especially France, which battled to secure one or both Littorios in the teeth of Italian resistance. In the event, both parties were to be disappointed, with only the older *Caio Duilio* and *Andrea Doria* being retained for the Marina Militare while the Soviet Union was allocated *Giulio Cesare*. Where the Littorios were concerned, *Italia* was to be handed over to the United States and *Vittorio Veneto* to Britain, but the Italian government still explored every conceivable way of retaining *Italia*, even as a training vessel. Failure to save her and her sister prompted Admiral de Courten's resignation first as navy minister on 14 July and then as chief of the general staff on 31 December 1947, but the Italian government and the Marina Militare would not give up, and made one last effort to prevent the handover. In the end, *Italia* was spared that humiliation and the United States agreed to have her demilitarised.

It was under this provision that *Italia* finally quit the Great Bitter Lake for the Sicilian port of Augusta on 5 February 1947. She was still seaworthy despite the unrepaired hole in her bow and the crew went to battle stations for one last anti-aircraft gunnery exercise as the ship approached Sicily. In October *Italia* moved from Augusta to La Spezia where she was decommissioned on 1 June 1948. Again the navy tried its

Italia seen at Augusta prior to decommissioning in 1948. *(Courtesy Philippe Caresse)*

Their 15in guns truncated by order of the naval armistice commission in 1948, *Italia* and *Vittorio Veneto* quietly await their fate at the Scali quay in La Spezia. *(Courtesy Philippe Caresse)*

best to save her, issuing covert orders to slow the demilitarisation process to a snail's pace and preserve as much equipment as possible. However, these efforts ended by provoking the ire of the naval armistice commission and all four members (USA, Britain, the Soviet Union and France) ordered the cutting of the 15in gun barrels and severing of the steam mains later that year. Turbines and gears were also to be removed and destroyed. On 7 December 1953 *Italia*, or what remained of her, was sold for scrap. By the end of 1954 she was no more, a sad end to a proud and successful ship.

Legacy

Much as *Littorio* was the finest battleship design Italy ever produced and a benchmark in naval technology, her story and that of her sisters is one of sadness, humiliation and misinterpretation. Not only did the appearance of the class coincide with the eclipse of the battleship type, but the wartime record of the Regia Marina was largely ignored in post-war Italy and the field surrendered to the perspective and interpretations of the victors where its performance was concerned. *Littorio* was in many ways an extremely successful ship which not only earned her status as the pride of the Regia Marina but served her

country well both at sea and as part of Italy's fleet-in-being, surviving heavy damage on three occasions and playing a key role in foiling several British operations. After the war her status as a bargaining counter proved instrumental in securing the continued existence of the Regia Marina's successor institution, the Marina Militare. Ultimately, for good or ill, she represented the accomplishments and failures of an entire period in Italian history.

Sources

Bibliography

Bagnasco, Erminio, & Enrico Cernuschi, *Le navi da guerra italiane* (Parma: Ermanno Albertelli Editore, 2003)

Bagnasco, Erminio, & Augusto de Toro, *The Littorio Class: Italy's Last and Largest Battleships, 1937–1948* (Barnsley, S. Yorks.: Seaforth Publishing, 2011)

Bernotti, Romeo, 'Italian Naval Policy under Fascism' in *United States Naval Institute Proceedings* 82 (1956) no. 7, pp. 722–31

Brescia, Maurizio, *Mussolini's Navy: A Reference Guide to the Regia Marina, 1930–1945* (Barnsley, S. Yorks.: Seaforth Publishing, 2012)

Caravaggio, Angelo N., 'The Attack at Taranto: Tactical Success, Operational Failure', in *Naval War College Review* 59 (2006), no. 6, pp. 103–27

Cunningham of Hyndhope, Admiral of the Fleet Viscount, *A Sailor's Odyssey* (London: Hutchinson, 1951)

Garzke, William H., & Robert O. Dulin, *Battleships: Axis and Neutral Battleships in World War II* (2nd edn, Annapolis, Md.: Naval Institute Press, 1990)

Giorgerini, Giorgio, *La guerra italiana sul mare* (Parma: Albertelli, 1972)

Giorgerini, Giorgio, & Augusto Nani, *Le navi di linea italiane, 1861–1961* (Rome: Ufficio Storico della Marina Militare, 1962)

Hattendorf, John B., ed., *Naval Strategy and Power in the Mediterranean: Past, Present and Future* (London: Frank Cass, 2000)

Ireland, Bernard, *War in the Mediterranean, 1940–1943* (London: Arms & Armour Press, 1993)

Jordan, John, *Warships after Washington: The Development of the Five Major Fleets, 1922–1930* (Annapolis, Md.: Naval Institute Press, 2012)

O'Hara, Vincent P., *The US Navy Against the Axis: Surface Combat 1941–1945* (Annapolis, Md.: Naval Institute Press, 2007)

_____, *Struggle for the Middle Sea: The Great Navies at War in the Mediterranean Theater, 1940–1945* (Annapolis, Md.: Naval Institute Press, 2009)

Pellegrini, Ernesto, *Umberto Pugliese: generale ispettore del genio navale (1880–1961)* (Rome: Ufficio storico della marina militare, 1999)

Simpson, Michael, ed., *The Cunningham Papers, vo. 1, The Mediterranean Fleet, 1939–1942. Selections from the Private and Official Correspondence of Admiral of the Fleet Viscount Cunningham of Hyndhope, OM, KT, GCB, DSO and Two Bars* (London: Ashgate, 1999)

_____, *A Life of Admiral of the Fleet Andrew Cunningham: A 20th-Century Naval Leader* (London: Frank Cass, 2004)

Stille, Mark, *Italian Battleships of World War Two* (Oxford: Osprey, 2011)

Vian, Philip, *Action this Day* (London: Frederick Muller, 1960)

United States Navy

The Battleship *Missouri* (1944)

Paul Stillwell

D URING HER LONG CAREER, USS *Missouri* was for a period the most famous ship in the world, naval or commercial; a seagoing diplomat and showpiece; the source of the U.S. Navy's single greatest embarrassment between the Second World War and the Korean War; relegated to the backwaters of the mothball fleet for nearly thirty years; and a relevant protagonist in a war fought almost half a century after she first went into commission.[1] She was the last American battleship to be completed and the last active vessel of her kind in the world. In her current embodiment as a museum and memorial she is a tangible symbol of a time when the United States was omnipotent on the world stage.

Predecessors

Named for the twenty-fourth state to be admitted to the union, the first *Missouri* was a 229ft (60.8m), 3,220-ton side-wheel frigate. Among the earliest steam-powered warships in U.S. Navy service, she was laid down at the New York Navy Yard in 1840. Two years later she became the first American naval vessel to cross the Atlantic under steam. It was the start of a planned voyage to the Far East to secure a trade agreement with China. Unfortunately, *Missouri*'s career came to a sudden end at Gibraltar on 26 August 1843. The accidental rupture of a container of turpentine in a storeroom set her ablaze and led to the explosion of a powder magazine. Divers later removed the hulk to clear the harbour.

The next *Missouri* was a side-wheel ironclad steamer laid down for the Confederate Navy at Shreveport, Louisiana, and launched in April 1863. The choice of name was a nod to a border

Missouri breathes fire from her 16in guns in 1989. A high point of US battleship construction and a symbolic vessel in her own right, *Missouri* was also the last active unit of her kind in any navy. *(Courtesy USS Missouri)*

state that, although ostensibly neutral in the American Civil War, nonetheless allowed slavery. *Missouri* provided substantial numbers of troops to both the Confederacy and the United States. Intended for use as a ram against Union ships, *Missouri* instead served as a troop transport and engaged in mining activities. Her crew turned her over to the Union in June 1865, two months after the Confederate surrender. Because the ship was in poor material condition, the U.S. Navy never

commissioned her for service and instead auctioned her for scrapping.

The second U.S. Navy ship to bear the name was a Maine-class pre-dreadnought battleship built by the Newport News Shipbuilding and Dry Dock Company in Virginia. Displacing 12,362 tons and mounting four 12in (305mm) guns, *Missouri* was launched in December 1901 and commissioned two years later. Between 1907 and 1909 she formed part of President Theodore

---

[1] The editor would like to acknowledge the assistance of David Way with the photographs in this chapter.

Roosevelt's Great White Fleet that circumnavigated the globe. Relegated thereafter to training and transport duties, she was decommissioned in September 1919. She was scrapped in 1922 to meet the provisions of the Washington naval disarmament treaty signed that year.

Origins and Design

The design of the Iowa-class battleships, of which *Missouri* was the third, must be seen in the context of the naval arms limitations treaties of the 1920s and 1930s. The first of these, the Washington Treaty of 1922, required the disposal of older vessels and the scrapping of a number of battleships already under construction. It also imposed a moratorium on new battleship construction. This treaty and those that followed it as a consequence of the London naval conferences of 1930 and 1936 kept the U.S. Navy from commissioning any new battleships between *West Virginia* in 1923 and *North Carolina* in 1941. Moreover, the Second London Naval Treaty of 1936 imposed a maximum of 14in guns on the existing limit of 35,000 tons' standard displacement for battleship construction. However, it also included an escalator clause permitting increases to 45,000 tons and 16in guns by Britain, France and the United

States should Germany or Italy fail to sign the new treaty by 1 April 1937. In the event, Italy never ratified the treaty, while Japan withdrew from the conference before the close of proceedings, evidence of the deterioration in international relations. That act rendered the interwar naval treaties increasingly irrelevant. Indeed, a new naval arms race – which the treaties had been intended to forestall – was already in progress.

The United States had traditionally produced battleships with modest maximum speeds of 21 or 22 knots and extensive armour protection, in anticipation of surface actions against heavy units. New developments in engine technology now permitted the latest generation of ships to make 27 knots, opening the way for a new category of vessel, the fast battleship. In the U.S. Navy, these were the North Carolina and South Dakota classes. Construction on both began in adherence with the 35,000-ton limit, although the North Carolinas traded their designed 14in guns for 16in weapons after Japan withdrew from the London Treaty of 1936. Intelligence reports in any case indicated that Japan was building ships in excess of the old limit.

While these developments were unfolding, planning was in progress for another class of fast battleships, initially to the 45,000-ton limit. In

May 1938 Congress passed a law authorising the construction of three ships that in time became *Iowa*, *New Jersey* and *Missouri*. The Navy Bureau of Construction and Repair had a number of design alternatives under consideration, the most obvious difference over the preceding two classes being size. The resulting vessels were considerably longer at 887ft (270m) than the North Carolinas (729ft/222m) and the South Dakotas (680ft/208m), and with an ultimate design displacement of 52,000 tons as against 42,000 in the earlier vessels.[2] The hull flared out from the bow to a beam of 108ft (32.9m), a tight squeeze for the 110ft locks of the Panama Canal, while *Missouri* drew a maximum of 28.9ft (8.8m) at standard load. The main deck had a dramatic sheer forward of turrets '1' and '2', contributing to the graceful lines of the class. The boiler uptakes led to two huge smokestacks. The forward one merged into the eleven-level foremast structure that included the bridge and conning tower.

Armament, Armour and Propulsion

Missouri's main and secondary batteries were identical to those of the two previous classes – nine 16in (406mm) guns and twenty dual-purpose 5in (127mm) guns. The increase in number of smaller guns came from the generous length of the Iowa class. It provided ample space for a forest of 129 1.57in and 0.79in (40mm and 20mm) anti-aircraft guns. The anti-aircraft guns enabled what became the primary mission of the modern battleship, as a fast escort to carrier task groups. The main armament was of a new type, 16in/50-calibre, compared with the 16in/45-calibre weapons fitted in the North Carolinas and South Dakotas. The guns were surplus from the earlier South Dakota class cancelled in 1922. The benefit was longer range (42,345yds/ 38,720m as against 36,900yds/33,741m) and the ability to fire heavier projectiles. The armoured barbettes extended six decks down into the ship to store projectiles and protect the hoists carrying propellant and shells to the turrets, an arrangement replicated in the 5in gun mounts. One embarrassing aspect of the original scheme was that the Navy Bureau of Construction and Repair's hull designers planned for a barbette with a diameter

Six of *Missouri*'s nine 16in/50-calibre guns at or near their maximum elevation of 45 degrees. The photo was taken off Hawaii during the RimPac '90 exercise in May 1990. *(Department of Defense/DN-ST-91-07903)*

[2] Norman Friedman, *U.S. Battleships: An Illustrated Design History* (Annapolis, Md.: Naval Institute Press, 1985), pp. 307–27.

Firemen monitor the gauges in *Missouri*'s Fireroom no. '1' under the watchful eye of a Petty Officer First Class as the ship steams off California in the spring of 1989. *(Department of Defense/DN-SN-93-04064)*

of 37ft 3in (11.4m) as a means of adhering to the 45,000-ton limit, whereas the Bureau of Ordnance designed them with a 39ft (11.9m) diameter. The matter was resolved in 1938 when the Bureau of Ordnance produced a design to fit the smaller opening by using the lighter 16in weapon. Turrets '2' and '3' were connected by a longitudinal internal passageway known as 'Broadway'. It was fitted with an overhead monorail to facilitate the transfer of ammunition between turrets in the event of battle damage. The class had both optical rangefinders and fire-control radar. For redundancy there were main and secondary battery plotting rooms located both forward and aft deep within the ship.

The effect of firing the guns was impressive. Observing a nine-gun night-practice shoot at the island of Culebra near Puerto Rico from the 011 level high in the superstructure, Naval Academy Midshipman Leonard Seagren recalled the salvo as a loud whoosh of less intensity than was felt on the bridge itself. The ship was enveloped in a huge burning cloud of 'reddish orange and incandescent-like' gases and powder.[3] Once the smoke had dispersed, Seagren could see the nine 16in projectiles soaring off through the night sky in a parabolic arc as they headed towards their target some twenty miles (32,000m) off. The bases of the projectiles stood out distinctly against the blackness of a Caribbean night with their bases glowing cherry red, the colour reminding him of molten steel in a blast furnace.

Where protection was concerned, *Missouri* had a horizontal belt 12.1in (307mm) thick and bulkheads of up to 14.5in (368mm) at the extremities of the armoured citadel. That was an increase of over 3in by comparison with her earlier sisters *Iowa* and *New Jersey*. The massive scale continued with the barbettes, which were protected by between 11.6 and 17.3in (295–439mm) of plate with the turrets receiving up to 19.7in (500mm) of armour. Horizontal protection consisted of a 1.5in (38mm) weather deck, a combined 6in (152mm) main armour deck, and a 0.63in (16mm) splinter deck over the engine spaces, the latter being increased to a 1in (25mm) layer over the magazines. Among the most striking visual reminders of the extent of *Missouri*'s protection is the bridge conning

tower, armoured to a thickness of 17.3in and accessed through doors resembling those of a bank vault.

The engineering plant of *Missouri* consisted of four General Electric cross-compound steam turbine engines, each driving a single shaft and generating a total of 212,000shp (158,000kW). There were eight Babcock & Wilcox M-Type boilers disposed in four firerooms operating at the then U.S. Navy standard of 600psi. This plant produced a maximum speed under standard load of 33 knots, a 6-knot advantage on their predecessors. The speed was intended to equip the class to deal with the Japanese fast cruiser designs. Endurance at the economical speed of 15 knots was 14,890 nautical miles. Fuel expenditure at speeds above 20 knots could reach 180gal (681l) to the mile.

As it turned out, the careers of the Iowa-class battleships bore little relation to the functions for which they had been designed. Despite all the attention given to the armoured conning tower, barbettes and side and deck armour, no member of the class ever engaged in the ship-to-ship gunnery duels for which they were intended. Insofar as the big guns were effectively used in action, it was in shore bombardment. Their 33-knot speed proved its value not for chasing surface raiders, but for keeping up with the fast carriers whose aircraft far outranged the battleships' guns as offensive weapons. Finally, when *Missouri* and her sisters were modernised for further service in the 1980s, the large sturdy hulls provided accommodation for long-range

cruise missiles. Although the U.S. Navy went on to design the Montana class, which was to have carried twelve 16in guns, heavier armour than any predecessor and a top speed of 28 knots, the class was cancelled before construction began since the Navy had higher priorities for ship-building resources during the Second World War. *Missouri* and her three sisters therefore remain the ultimate expression of US battleships in service.

Construction and Arrival

On a bitterly cold day, 29 January 1941, Rear Admiral Clark Woodward, Commandant of the Third Naval District, put the first rivet in the keel of BB-63 as it was laid at the New York Navy Yard in Brooklyn. The first USS *Missouri* had been built there one hundred years earlier. The yard was simultaneously building the lead ship of the class, *Iowa*, which was a year ahead of *Missouri*. The work proceeded steadily in a carefully planned sequence involving the delivery of steel, wiring, armour, guns, telephones, electronic equipment, bunks and tens of thousands of other items. By 29 January 1944 all was in readiness for the hull's trip down the inclined ways to her first wetting down in the East River. She then went through a fitting-out period that included the installation of her 16in turrets and their guns, the anti-aircraft armament and the radio and radar antennas. Still in the yard, the ship was commissioned on 11 June, the start of a long and illustrious career.

3 Paul Stillwell, *Battleship* Missouri: *An Illustrated History* (Annapolis, Md.: Naval Institute Press, 1996), p. 126.

MISSOURI AND THE TRUMANS

Before the Second World War Democrat Harry S. Truman was the relatively obscure junior senator from Missouri. During the war, however, he headed a committee charged with investigating waste, fraud and mismanagement in government contracts. The committee's work not only saved billions of dollars but also brought the senator national attention, including the cover of *Time* magazine in 1943.

It was customary during the battleship era for the Navy to confer on the governor of the state for which she was to be named the honour of selecting a woman to sponsor the ship. However, the incumbent for Missouri was Republican Forrest Donnell, so Democratic President Franklin Roosevelt's Secretary of the Navy Frank Knox bestowed the honour on Senator Truman's twenty-year-old daughter Mary Margaret. The *St. Louis Post-Dispatch* shrewdly opined that the energetic, upcoming senator could do a lot more good for the Navy than the governor in faraway Jefferson City, Missouri.

The launching of the new battleship took place in Brooklyn on 29 January 1944, three years to the day

after her keel-laying ceremony. Margaret Truman went to New York City with two friends who were to serve as her maids of honour for the christening ceremony. On the eve of the event the three of them saw the hit Broadway musical *Oklahoma* and were so excited they stayed up all night. The day of the launching dawned chilly and overcast – typical January weather – as the trio arrived glassy-eyed at the shipyard. Some 30,000 spectators were on hand, as were newsreel cameramen, radio announcers and print journalists. There was even a bit of television coverage, the signal sent to General Electric plants in Schenectady, New York, where components of the ship had been manufactured.

The naval dignitaries scheduled to speak before the christening itself ate into the time allotted for Senator Truman's speech, which he later described as a fifteen-minute talk crammed into three minutes. Among the words he spoke that day were these: 'The time is surely coming when the people of Missouri can thrill with pride as the *Missouri* and her sister ships, with batteries blazing, sail into Tokyo Bay.' The christening in this case involved a bottle of cham-

pagne made from Missouri grapes. The smashing of the bottle drenched Margaret and her companions. Four and a half months later, on 11 June, the Navy commissioned the ship in a sun-drenched ceremony in Brooklyn presided over by new Secretary of the Navy James V. Forrestal. With him on the speakers' platform was a host of admirals, as well as Harry Truman and the keynote speaker at the commissioning, Missouri's senior senator Democrat Bennett Champ Clark. When he was eleven years old, Clark had witnessed the launching of the previous battleship *Missouri* in 1901.

In July 1944 the Democratic Party held its nominating convention in Chicago and chose a reluctant Truman as President Roosevelt's running mate. On 7 November the Roosevelt-Truman ticket prevailed decisively over the Republican nominees, Thomas E. Dewey and John W. Bricker. Roosevelt would have his fourth term – or so it seemed. On 20 January 1945 Chief Justice Harlan F. Stone administered the oaths of office to Roosevelt and Truman in a low-key inauguration ceremony. Because of the wartime atmosphere, it was at the White House instead of the Capitol.

It was while *Missouri* was supporting the campaign to capture Okinawa that President Roosevelt died of a stroke in Warm Springs, Georgia, on 12 April. Vice President Truman was summoned to the White House to take an ad hoc oath. Two days later a signalman on board *Missouri* raised the American flag on her hoist and then lowered it to half-mast in honour of the dead president. For another *Missouri* crewman the changing of the guard at the White House had a much more personal connection. Seaman John C. Truman, an unassuming member of the ship's navigation department, happened to be the son of Harry Truman's brother Vivian. Preserved in the Harry S. Truman Library in Independence, Missouri, are the handwritten letters John Truman sent to the White House from the battleship. Two weeks after his uncle took over Seaman Truman wrote that 'I still find it difficult to realize you are the President.'[4] Though he was expressing that view from the family perspective, the young sailor doubtless spoke for millions of Americans who felt a similar sense of disbelief because Roosevelt had been president for so long.

In early August 1945 President Truman directed the use of atomic bombs against the Japanese cities of Hiroshima and Nagasaki. Within a week, on 15 August, the Japanese had capitulated and ceased hostilities. Truman immediately selected *Missouri* to be the site of the Japanese surrender (see

Margaret Truman, daughter of Senator Harry S. Truman of Missouri and sponsor of the new battleship, prepares to break a bottle of Missouri champagne over the bows of the new battleship at the New York Navy Yard on 29 January 1944. Also present are Rear Admiral Monroe R. Kelly and Rear Admiral Sherman S. Kennedy (Commandant and General Manager of the yard respectively), and Senator Truman himself. *(National Archives (NA) 180-G-44891)*

'This is the happiest day of my life.' So said President Harry S. Truman, seen here examining the newly installed plaque commemorating the Japanese surrender, during his visit to *Missouri* while she was anchored in the Hudson on 27 October 1945. *(Courtesy Harry S. Truman Library/64-472)*

pp. 419–22). His memoirs explain his choice: the ship was named for his home state, and he had a special connection through his daughter as sponsor. After the ceremony on 2 September, the newly developed schedule called for *Missouri* to be in New York's Hudson River as the centrepiece of a large aggregation of warships to celebrate Navy Day. While the ship was under way Seaman Truman sent another letter to Uncle Harry explaining why he would be leaving the battleship's crew in Norfolk rather than staying on to see him: 'I could have postponed applying for discharge until after I arrived in New York, but I did not know how long that would delay me, and I am certain you understand I want to get home as quickly as possible.'[5] His wife and children were waiting for him in Missouri.

While *Missouri* was in Norfolk shipyard workers installed a brass plaque on her 01 veranda deck to commemorate the spot over which the surrender documents were signed. On 27 October President Truman came aboard to have lunch and review the gathering of ships in the river. He toured *Missouri* and stooped over to read the inscription on the circular plaque. To those around him he said, 'This is the happiest day of my life.'[6]

Two years later the entire Truman family embarked in the battleship for a seagoing vacation. They began by flying to Rio de Janeiro for an Inter-

American Conference for the Maintenance of Hemisphere Peace and Security. *Missouri* arrived on the eve of the conference on 30 August 1947, which also marked the 125th anniversary of Brazilian independence. The crew received a week of liberty. On 7 September the Truman entourage came aboard for the twelve-day trip back to the United States. The president made a hit with his down-home manners as he toured the ship and took part in such activities as leading morning calisthenics. He and his wife and daughter joined him in eating in the enlisted crew's mess, going through a cafeteria-style line to get their chow. One perk the family received was immunity from the ceremonies and high jinks that go with crossing the equator in a Navy ship. The battleship's commanding officer, Captain Robert L. Dennison, so impressed Truman during the cruise that he became White House naval aide soon afterwards.

By 1949 the Navy had decommissioned all of its twenty-three battleships except one – that named for the president's home state. Initially relegated to training duties, the ship's complement rose again for a time with the outbreak of the Korean War. *Missouri*

did not long survive Truman's departure from office in 1953. The Navy decommissioned her in 1955. Nearly thirty years later she emerged from the mothball fleet to be reactivated and modernised for further duty. Captain Lee Kaiss drew the envied assignment to be skipper on her return to service. Former President Truman had died in 1972, but her sponsor was on hand when the ship was recommissioned at San Francisco on 10 May 1986. The state threw a reception and dinner at San Francisco City Hall for *Missouri*'s crew. Now in middle age, Mrs Margaret Truman Daniel made a speech in which she recalled her association with the ship she had christened forty-two years earlier. She closed her remarks with these words: 'Captain Kaiss and the men of the *Missouri*, there's one other thing I want to say to you. Please take good care of my baby.'[7] The crew rose and gave her a standing ovation.

---

[4] *Ibid.*, p. 36.
[5] *Ibid.*, p. 260.
[6] *Ibid.*, p. 261.
[7] *Ibid.*

Margaret Truman joins enlisted men for an impromptu lunch in the ship's messdeck during the presidential family's return voyage from Brazil in September 1947. As she later quipped to Captain Robert Dennison, who ate alone in accordance with his rank, 'I know more about the ship than you do, because I eat with the officers and crew and you don't.' *(Courtesy Harry S. Truman Library/66-1258)*

Missouri's superstructure taking shape at New York Navy Yard on New Year's Day 1944. *(NA/19-N-72971)*

Internal Organisation

The commissioning crew of the ship – known as 'plank owners' by Navy tradition – contained a mixture of experienced senior personnel, seasoned middle-level officers and petty officers, and a large group of recruits new to the Navy. Together they comprised a nominal complement of 2,700 men that at times during the Second World War numbered around 3,000 when an admiral and his staff were embarked. The travails of the raw recruits are encapsulated in

the experience of eighteen-year-old Fireman Bob Schwenk, fresh out of boot camp. During the indoctrination period while *Missouri* was still in New York, Schwenk was assigned to man a sound-powered telephone in fireroom '3'. His job was to receive messages from the main control that operated the engineering plant and relay them to Water Tender John DeGroff. When DeGroff asked him what he was hearing, Schwenk replied, 'I don't know. They're speaking in a foreign language, and I can't understand them.'[8] The problem was that Schwenk had

grown up in California and most of the ship's enlisted men were from New York, New Jersey and New England – where the accent is indeed different from that of California. There were culture shocks of another type also. During part of the training process Seaman Herman Leibig of Pennsylvania and some shipmates went ashore for liberty in Norfolk in the segregated southern state of Virginia. When he took a seat near the back of a city bus, the driver yelled at him, 'Hey, swabbie, you get up front. The niggers sit in the back.'[9] Although *Missouri* had a complement of

8 *Ibid.*, p. 14.

9 *Ibid.*, p. 17.

black mess stewards, it was not until the immediate post-war period that black enlisted men were integrated into the crew at large; desegregation in the South had to wait still longer.

On commissioning in 1944 *Missouri* pioneered a new shipboard department, operations, that in later years was adopted Navy-wide. The concept involved putting all sources of operational information into one department that included both visual and radio communications; navigation; combat operations centre (later known as the combat information centre); lookouts; operation and maintenance of all electronic equipment; electronic countermeasures; and aircraft control. The gunnery department comprised a number of divisions to maintain and operate the ship's guns. They included main battery divisions, one for each turret; secondary battery, port and starboard; 40mm and 20mm guns; fire control; an aviation division for the ship's floatplanes; and a division to maintain catapults and ordnance stores. The ship's Marine detachment was also part of the gunnery department and manned some of her guns. The engineering department consisted of divisions operating and maintaining the turbines, boilers, electrical devices and auxiliary equipment. The construction and repair department was responsible for the external upkeep of the ship, damage control and subsidiary activities such as the bands, buglers and master-at-arms force. Other departments included medical, supply and chaplains.

Unlike the US battleships built up to the early 1920s, the three classes of fast battleships did not have enlisted messing and berthing functions in the same compartments. In the older ships mess tables were stowed between meals just beneath the overhead in each compartment. Tables were set up for meals, and mess cooks would then go to a separate galley and bring the food to the messes where it was served family-style. That format created considerable bonding within each division. In later construction men were still berthed by divisions and wherever room could be found – some had bunks inside the turret structures – but enlisted men went to central mess compartments and drew their chow from cafeteria lines. One effect of the centralised general mess was that men often ate and got acquainted with individuals from other divisions. There were also separate messes for chief petty officers, warrant officers and commissioned officers. The executive officer presided over the wardroom mess and the captain had his own separate mess to which he often invited guests, as did the admiral and his staff in a separate flag mess. The various messes were often used for showing movies in the evening.

In the post-war period the rest of the fleet

Berthing arrangements for enlisted men in 1987. Their designation as 'coffin racks' needs no explanation. *(Courtesy Rich Pedroncelli)*

followed *Missouri*'s example in having an operations department. The old construction and repair department disappeared, with its functions being divided. Damage control became the province of the engineering department, and the first lieutenant and ship's boatswain functions of topside maintenance merged into the gunnery department. The number of gunnery divisions dwindled as the 20mm light anti-aircraft guns disappeared in an age of ever-faster air targets. In May 1949 the Norfolk Naval Shipyard removed

Missouri goes down the ways into the East River on 29 January 1944. *(Courtesy Harry S. Truman Library/58-769-17)*

The *Missouri*'s main battery plotting room on
17 September 1950. *(NA/80-G-420319)*

the floatplane catapults from the fantail. The
catapults had launched her Vought OS2U
Kingfisher and later Curtiss SC Seahawk floatplanes used for gunnery-spotting duties. *Missouri*
then served as a landing platform for helicopters,
first receiving them atop turret '1' and later on
the fantail once the catapults were removed. The
helicopters, which performed spotting duties and
also carried cargo and personnel, were supplied
as needed from other commands.

The departmental organisation of the ship
remained largely unchanged during *Missouri*'s
first period in commission, even when the
complement fluctuated. It was greatly reduced in
the demobilisation period following the Second
World War, when every other battleship in the
fleet was decommissioned. The crew size rose
again for a time with Korean War operations,
before dropping as the ship moved towards
decommissioning in 1955. When the much-
modernised *Missouri* rejoined the active fleet in
the spring of 1986, she also had a different
internal organisation. Now with missiles in addition to guns, she had a weapons department in
place of the old gunnery department. Other functions remained unchanged, but her air capability
was restored in the form of a single helicopter, as
well as a number of RQ-2 Pioneer drones
capable of being sent aloft to transmit television
footage of the fall of shot to facilitate fire-control
corrections. She again had a Marine detachment
responsible for manning some of the guns.
During the Gulf War of 1991 the ship also
carried a detachment of explosive ordnance
disposal personnel.

The Second World War

In early September 1944 *Missouri* got under way
for the first time under her own power to test-fire
her guns and perform structural tests to see how
well the hull and superstructure withstood the
concussion produced by the firing. After additional crew training in the protected waters of
the Chesapeake Bay and the Gulf of Paria off
Venezuela, *Missouri* returned briefly to New
York. She headed south on 10 November en
route to the Panama Canal and the Pacific. Her
slab sides were such a tight fit in the canal locks

A Japanese 'Zeke' fighter flown by a kamikaze pilot strikes
Missouri's hull on the afternoon of 11 April 1945. The crews
of no. '9' and '11' 40mm guns and their directors on the
starboard side of the ship take cover. There were no US
casualties and the remains of the pilot were given a burial
at sea the following day. The photo has become one of the
classic images of the Pacific War. *(NA/80-G-315811)*

Admiral William F. Halsey, Commander Third Fleet, and his Chief of Staff Rear Admiral Robert B. Carney conferring in *Missouri* shortly before the Japanese surrender in August 1945. *(NHHC/NG 124405)*

that pieces of dislodged concrete fell onto the main deck. In the Pacific she made stops in San Francisco and Pearl Harbor before joining the fleet on 13 January 1945 in the huge anchorage at Ulithi Atoll in the Caroline Islands. On 16 February *Missouri* went into action for the first time as part of the anti-aircraft screen of Task Group 58.2 as it launched the first naval air strikes against Japan since the Doolittle raid in April 1942. A few days later she was part of the carriers' escort when U.S. Marines invaded the island of Iwo Jima. On 24 March she joined in a big-gun bombardment of Okinawa, which US forces invaded on 1 April. Seaman Tony Alessandro was the powder-hoist operator for the left gun of turret '3'. His main qualification for the job was his size; his 5ft 6in (1.68m) and 138lb (63kg) frame allowed him to fit into the cramped working space. He operated a lever controlling the mechanical hoist bringing cylindrical powder bags from the handling room to the turret. All told, *Missouri* fired 180 rounds on 24 March.

On 11 April Commander Roland Faulk, one of the ship's chaplains, was making his way up a ladder to the navigation bridge on the 04 level in the superstructure. On reaching the top he was nearly trampled underfoot by a group of men hurrying from the starboard to the port side. A Japanese suicide pilot was coming in about 100ft above the water. The left wing of his 'Zeke' fighter slammed into the starboard side, deflecting the nose into the side of the hull, just below the level of the main deck. A ship's photographer clicked his shutter at the moment of impact, capturing one of the most dramatic images of the Pacific War. The pilot was cut in two, the top half of his body landing on the deck along with remnants of the plane. The following day Chaplain Faulk conducted a burial-at-sea service for the pilot's remains. 'A dead Jap is no longer an enemy,' said Faulk in his eulogy.[10]

On 18 May *Missouri* became the flagship of Admiral William Halsey, then serving as Commander Third Fleet, the vast armada of ships that kept up the pressure on Japan. His chief of staff was Rear Admiral Robert B. Carney. One of the Third Fleet staff members was Lieutenant Bob Balfour, a communications watch officer. As Balfour recalled years later, 'I don't know that this is exactly fair to say, but,

generally speaking, I think most of us felt that Halsey was the blood and guts but that Carney was the brains.'[11] Halsey quickly picked up a reputation on board the ship as a sailors' admiral. Radioman Richard 'Moose' Conner was intrigued by this and asked the orderly if Halsey ever chewed out a sailor. The only time, said the Marine, had been once at Pearl Harbor when the admiral had come out of a building and collided with a young seaman. After they separated, the sailor began to walk away, whereupon Halsey asked, 'Wouldn't it be customary to stop and salute an admiral just after you knocked him on his ass?'[12]

By the summer of 1945, with the giant battleships *Yamato* and *Musashi* on the bottom and the Japanese surface fleet effectively eliminated as a threat, there was no longer any real anti-ship mission for *Missouri* and her cohorts. Halsey, who had served in the pre-dreadnought *Missouri* early in his career, pressed his subordinates to come up with a role for the battleships other than protecting the carriers. On the morning of 15 July *Missouri* joined her sisters *Iowa* and *Wisconsin*, plus cruisers and destroyers, in a bombardment of the steel works at Muroran,

Hokkaido, the northernmost Japanese island. This time *Missouri* used full powder charges with her 16in projectiles, because she was firing at much longer ranges than at Okinawa. The shortest range was 29,660yds (27,121m) and the longest was 32,000yds (29,260m). The US task unit encountered no opposition on the beach, but the battleships' spotter planes were under continuous anti-aircraft fire. Accuracy was useful but not essential, as a prodigious weight of fire saturated the target area. *Missouri* alone fired 297 rounds, including three nine-gun salvoes aimed at large hammerhead cranes. The shelling caused fires, explosions and heavy damage to all the buildings in the steelworks. Ensign Jack Barron watched the bombardment through a periscope from inside turret '2', where the sensation of firing was muted because he was encased in armour. He did, however, see the results ashore, when chimneys from the Japanese steel factory toppled over as 16in projectiles slammed home.

In early August Army Air Forces B-29 bombers levelled the cities of Hiroshima and Nagasaki with atomic bombs. The end of the war was nigh. Admiral Halsey was still on board *Missouri* when he received news on 15 August that Japan had surrendered. He sent out a puckish message to the carrier pilots of Task Force 38: 'Investigate and shoot down all snoopers – not vindictively, but in a friendly sort

---

10 *Ibid.*, p. 35.

11 *Ibid.*, p. 40.
12 *Ibid.*, p. 261.

Work and rest on the fantail on 14 July 1945 while *Missouri* steams off Japan as part of Task Group 38.4. The following day she joined in the shelling of Muroran on Hokkaido, the northernmost of the Japanese home islands. Note the Curtiss SC Seahawk floatplanes on their catapults. *(NA/80-G-407103)*

Missouri (left) transferring personnel to her sister *Iowa* while operating off Japan on 20 August 1945, five days after the Japanese ceasefire. *(NHHC/NH 96781)*

of way.' To celebrate the end of hostilities he called for *Missouri* to blow her steam whistle for a period of one minute. The deep-throated sound duly began issuing forth at 1109 but the whistle, which hadn't sounded in months, wouldn't stop once it started. It stuck in the open position and blasted for two minutes. The engineers finally silenced it by cutting off the supply of steam from deep within the ship.

Seaman Joe Vella, member of a 5in gun crew, had joined the ship shortly after leaving high school in his home state of Connecticut. He had ridden thousands of miles in *Missouri* from the United States and had resigned himself to the notion that he would never see home again. When he heard the news of peace, he looked over at a gunner's mate second class whom he knew well. The other man was crying out of his sense of relief. With an expression of wonder in his voice, Vella said to his shipmate, 'Mac, I made it.'[13] The other man, who had survived a torpedoing before reporting to *Missouri*, said quietly, 'Me too'.

The Surrender

The German surrender in May 1945 had been a low-key affair because Allied troops had

[13] *Ibid.*, p. 49.

conquered and occupied that nation. In the Pacific it was different because mainland Japan had not been invaded during combat. President Truman dictated that a public ceremony on board *Missouri*, amidst the Allied armada anchored nearby, would leave no doubt that Japan truly had been vanquished. Holding the ceremony on board ship would also minimise the opportunity for fanatical final attacks.

For several days after 15 August *Missouri* and her consorts steamed off southern Japan, waiting to learn what would happen next. Captain Stuart Murray ordered the crew to begin cleaning and painting their ship as preparations were made for the ceremony. The surrender would be in the admiral's cabin in the event of rain, but the preferred location was the 01 veranda deck on the starboard side, abreast turret '2' and just outside the captain's in-port cabin. After several days of waiting the American armada moved into Japanese waters and prepared to enter Sagami Wan, a bay separated from Tokyo Bay by the peninsula that includes Yokosuka. *Missouri* arrived off the Japanese coast at dawn on 26 August and awaited the arrival of the destroyer *Hatsuzakura* carrying a party of Japanese naval officers and harbour pilots. As per American instructions, the ship's guns were depressed, their breeches open and the torpedo tubes empty.

Once the Japanese were on board, Corporal Joe Drumheller of the ship's Marine detachment gave them a thorough search. Lieutenant Doug Plate watched the frisking of the Japanese and their reaction as they were subjected to this humiliating treatment in front of hundreds of curious onlookers: 'They were a frightened little bunch, I tell you.' All surrendered their swords and other weapons. By late afternoon many of the ships of the Third Fleet had moved in and anchored in an area some called the Japanese Riviera, off Kamakura. In the distance loomed Japan's revered, snow-capped Mount Fuji. That evening, from *Missouri*'s vantage point in the fleet anchorage, the sun seemed to set directly into Fuji's crater. The symbolism was striking. On 29 August *Missouri*'s crew was at general quarters when she and her accompanying armada entered Tokyo Bay, the destination towards which the U.S. Navy had been pointing since December 1941.

General of the Army Douglas MacArthur had specified that he wanted the Japanese delegates on the main deck only briefly before they proceeded up to the 01 deck for the ceremony. That meant numerous rehearsals to see just how long it would take the Japanese to climb the gangway steps, walk across the main deck, then up the ladder to the veranda deck. One sailor stuck a swab handle down his pant leg so he could simulate the slow walk of Shigemitsu

Mamoru, the Japanese foreign minister. The envoy had a wooden left leg as the result of a bomb thrown at him by a Korean revolutionary in Shanghai in 1933.

The big day, 2 September 1945, began before dawn on board the flagship. At 0500 *Missouri*'s bugler blew reveille to rouse all hands except those who had just come off the midwatch a little before 0400. As for the rest, they were soon up and out. The deck hands were out in force, scrubbing the quarterdeck and 01 veranda deck with fresh water. Like the other decks on board *Missouri*, the veranda was painted a dark blue-grey as part of the camouflage scheme. Once the final cleaning was complete, the crew moved to eat breakfast a little before 0600. Afterward Lieutenant Bob Mackey, the ship's disbursing officer, went out on deck. He then made his way to the 01 level and saw the polished mahogany table sent over by the British battleship *King George V* for the signing. It was about 40in square, little bigger than a card table. Mackey talked with Commander Harold Stassen, Halsey's flag secretary, and they agreed the table was clearly too small to accommodate both sets of surrender documents, the green leather-bound copies for the Americans and the black canvas-bound ones for the Japanese. Stassen asked if the supply officer had any bigger tables on board. Mackey told him that one from the general mess would work. The tables there had spindly metal legs, however, so he suggested one could be made presentable by covering it with a green felt cloth of the type used on wardroom tables between meals.

Fleet Admiral Chester Nimitz, Commander-in-Chief Pacific Fleet, boarded *Missouri* shortly after 0800. General of the Army MacArthur arrived at 0843 and his red five-star flag was unfurled on a metal bar so that it was side by side with Nimitz's blue-and-white flag.

Captain Murray was consumed with details on that morning. One had to do with the ship's position. The National Geographic Society had proposed sending representatives to the ceremony to establish the precise location of *Missouri* as she swung on her anchor chain. Murray concluded that he didn't need any more visitors; the ship's own navigation team could do just as well. So he directed that bearings be taken from the bridge at 0900 on six different objects ashore – twice the usual number – and establish a precise fix where the lines of bearing intersected. As soon as the bearings were taken, the

Missouri anchored in Tokyo Bay on 2 September 1945, the day of the surrender ceremony. She is flying the Union Jack bearing a star for every state in the union and worn at the bow when anchored, made fast or alongside. *(NHHC/SC 210649)*

The head of the Japanese delegation, Foreign Minister Shigemitsu Mamoru, signs the Instrument of Surrender on behalf of the Japanese government attended by foreign ministry representative Kase Toshikazu, later Japan's first ambassador to the United Nations. Facing them is Lieutenant General Richard K. Sutherland, U.S. Army, with Fleet Admiral William F. Halsey looking on. The solidity of the table, struck heavily by Shigemitsu's prosthetic leg as he addressed himself to signing the instrument, gave momentary alarm to *Missouri*'s officers. *(NHHC/SC 213700)*

captain ordered that electrical power to all the ship's gyrocompasses be cut off so no one could come along later and claim to have taken a more accurate position at the precise moment of signing. The position from the fix was subsequently enshrined in a brass plaque embedded in the deck. It was 35° 21' 17" N, 139° 45' 36" E.

The Japanese delegation numbered eleven men all told: three each from the foreign office, the army and the navy, and two from the Japanese civil service. A motor launch brought them to the steep side of the battleship. When the boat bearing the surrender party approached *Missouri*, it made a complete circuit of the ship before letting the first of the passengers off at the forward gangway at 0855. Evidently the plan was to impress the emissaries of the defeated nation with the size and power of the ship. Instead of coming aboard at deck level as the Allied dignitaries had done from destroyers, the Japanese had to climb the accommodation ladder. Moreover, these men who had come to the battleship would not have the luxury of surrendering in private as the German leaders had done earlier that year in France.

Once on the veranda deck the Japanese arranged themselves in three rows. They faced the surrender table and its green cloth cover. They stood stoic and mostly expressionless, disguising whatever thoughts were in their heads. The ranks of American officers were more animated. Correspondents and photographers were all around, frantically seeking the best view. Hundreds of sailors and Marines looked down on the scene. One of the Japanese, Kase Toshikazu, probably spoke for all of them when he wrote, 'As we appeared on the scene, we were, I felt, being subjected to the torture of the pillory. A million eyes seemed to beat on us with the million shafts of a rattling storm of arrows barbed with fire. I felt them sink into my body with a sharp physical pain. Never had I realised that staring eyes could hurt so much.'

Having delivered an opening speech, General MacArthur called for Foreign Minister Shigemitsu to come forward. As the leader of the Japanese delegation sat down, his wooden leg bounced off a tie rod that held up the spindly legs of the mess table. Captain Murray, a deck below

on the quarterdeck, heard the sound of rattling metal and was concerned the table might collapse, but it didn't. Shigemitsu took off his silk top hat and put it on the table and removed a yellow glove from his right hand. He fumbled with watches and papers in his pocket before pulling out a pen. Then he seemed to hesitate a bit in finding the correct place on the surrender document, so General MacArthur called to his chief of staff, Lieutenant General Richard Sutherland, and said, 'Sutherland, show him where to sign.' The chief of staff came over from his position by turret '2' and pointed to the assigned spot on the document. Without saying a word, Shigemitsu signed the first surrender document. The line above his name included a space for the time of signing, so he looked up enquiringly at Kase, who was standing next to him. Kase consulted his wristwatch and told Shigemitsu it was four minutes past nine. History was satisfied as the foreign minister wrote on the document the precise time of the official surrender. He then signed the Japanese copy as well. Without a word, General Umezu Yoshijiro, Chief of the Imperial General Staff, nervously came forward and signed on behalf of the Japanese armed forces. He, alone of all that day's signatories, disdained the chair and remained standing, leaning over to write his signature.

Then General MacArthur sat down to sign on behalf of the Allied Powers. Admiral Nimitz followed to sign for the United States. Protocol then demanded that the officers from the other victorious nations sign as well, and so they did. The only hitch came when an aide to Shigemitsu discovered that some of the Allied signatures were on the wrong lines on the Japanese copy of the documents. Colonel L. Moore Cosgrave, the representative of Canada, started the process, and the three subsequent signatories – on behalf of France, the Netherlands and New Zealand – were thus forced out of place and also signed on incorrect lines. Once the miscue was pointed out, a brief conference followed and General Sutherland then corrected the error with his pen.

Photographers were crammed in all over the place, each trying to have the best vantage point from which to take pictures of the ceremony. Carl Mydans of *Life* magazine had been covering MacArthur for several years. On this occasion his access wasn't as free as he was accustomed to – or as free as he wanted. His assigned post was in a 40mm gun tub behind MacArthur as he spoke and as he signed. Mydans thus had face-on shots of the Japanese, but he was looking at the backs of the Americans and other Allies. During the brief interruption while the problem of Cosgrave's misplaced signature was being resolved, Mydans jumped out of the gun tub and ran over to the surrender table. He managed to click the shutter of his camera only once before a huge *Missouri* Marine lifted him up and carried him bodily back to the 40mm mount. General MacArthur watched the episode unfold, his dignified bearing contrasting with the indignity visited upon a noted *Life* photographer. However, as Mydans passed by the general, he noticed that MacArthur dropped his mask of solemnity for an instant – just long enough to wink at his friend.

When the various signings were concluded,

General MacArthur announced, 'Let us pray that peace be now restored to the world and that God will preserve it always.' Then he turned to the Japanese delegation and said, 'These proceedings are now closed.' Back in the United States, where it was still Saturday evening, millions of Americans listened to a radio broadcast of the proceedings on board *Missouri*. After the formal ceremony ended President Truman spoke briefly from the White House. Then the broadcast shifted back to the battleship for statements from MacArthur and Nimitz. The general concluded

his remarks by saying, 'And so, my fellow countrymen, today I report to you that your sons and daughters have served you well and faithfully. […] They are homeward bound. Take care of them.'[14]

Just as the last Allied representative, Air Vice Marshal L. M. Isitt of New Zealand, had signed at 0922, the overcast sky suddenly cleared. Until then the day had been drab, with rolling clouds obscuring the sky in all directions. But now shafts of bright sunlight penetrated breaks in the clouds and danced on the surface of the water. Radioman Richard 'Moose' Conner, allowed by his division officer to watch from high in the superstructure, looked at the rays and was reminded of the rising-sun insignia on the Japanese flag. Then came even more symbolism. Earlier, while Nimitz was signing, two naval officers stood with him. One was Rear Admiral Forrest Sherman, his war plans officer; the other was Admiral Halsey. As they stood there, MacArthur reached over, put his arm around Halsey's shoulders and whispered, 'Start 'em now!'[15] With that a message went out to 450 carrier planes of Task Force 38; they had been circling nearby. Upon receiving the signal, they roared in over the anchorage at low altitude. After that several hundred B-29 bombers of the Army Air Forces flew over the fleet just as the Japanese were going down the accommodation ladder to depart *Missouri*. As Gunner's Mate Walt Yucka looked up at the hundreds of aircraft flying in front of the sunburst a thought passed through his mind – American power was blocking out the Japanese rising sun. Nearly half a century later the memory was so emotional that it gave him chills. As he recalled, 'That was the greatest thrill of my life. The war was over.'

Post-War Missions

Her role as the surrender ship gave *Missouri* celebrity status, known the world over by her

Hanging on the screen overlooking the veranda deck where the instrument of surrender was signed is the flag flown by Commodore Matthew C. Perry in the steam frigate *Mississippi* as he sailed into Tokyo Bay on 8 July 1853. His mission from President Millard Fillmore was to force the opening of Japanese ports to American trade. Eventually preserved at the Naval Academy Museum in Annapolis, the flag was rushed to Tokyo Bay in the care of an officer who braved a 100-hour flight to add symbolism to the surrender proceedings, the prelude to a further US intervention in Japanese affairs. Also seen among the tiers of reporters and onlookers is the ship's tally of enemy aircraft shot down, indicated by the flags and symbols painted on the bridge. (NA/SC 210644S)

[14] *Ibid.*, p. 74.
[15] *Ibid.*

'Start 'em now!' At Admiral Halsey's command 450 carrier
aircraft from Task Force 38 fly in formation over the US and
British fleets assembled in Tokyo Bay, sealing the surrender
proceedings with a staggering display of power. *Missouri* is
on the left and the vessel closest to the camera on the
right is the light cruiser *Detroit*. (NA/80-G-421130)

nickname 'The Mighty Mo'. Homeward bound
from Tokyo Bay, Captain Murray kept a promise
he'd made to the crew when the war ended – that
they could have a beer bash during a stop in
Guam, since the U.S. Navy did not permit the
drinking of alcohol on board. She also served as
a seagoing taxicab, embarking at Guam
hundreds of veterans who had earned sufficient
discharge points to sail home to the United
States. Fleet Admiral Nimitz held a reception on
board when the ship reached Pearl Harbor. The
crew enjoyed fresh milk, fruit and vegetables –
commodities that hadn't been available during
the long months at sea.

Missouri went through the Panama Canal to
the Atlantic and then stopped at Norfolk. There
workmen at the naval shipyard fabricated a
circular plaque that was embedded in the wooden
planks of the 01 veranda deck to mark the spot
where the surrender table had stood. The bronze
plaque was a magnet for tourists for many years
to come. In New York City President Truman
himself came aboard *Missouri* which was moored
in the Hudson River as part of Navy Day celebrations held on 27 October (see p. 413). The ship
then moved in to moor to a pier on the west side
of Manhattan Island to accommodate the thousands of visitors anxious to step aboard. So eager
were some visitors for something from the
famous ship that they used their fingernails to
scrape grease out of gun barrels. Others ripped
plastic or metal identification plates off various
pieces of equipment. Some tried to pry up the
surrender plaque. Others scratched their initials
onto newly painted bulkheads, while the paint of
the 16in guns was gouged to such an extent that
the barrels had to be elevated to get them out of
harm's way. Hands reached in through the portholes to Captain Stuart Murray's cabin and stole
things off his desk, including one of his caps with
gold decorations on the visor.

Once the hoopla had died down *Missouri* was
tapped for a special mission – one of both
substance and symbolism. Diplomatic tradition
called for the use of navy ships to repatriate the
remains of foreign ambassadors who died while
in office. One of these was Ambassador Mehmet
Ertegün of Turkey. He had died in Washington in
1944, and his remains were preserved there. In

Missouri anchored in the Hudson for Navy Day on
27 October 1945. (Courtesy Ted Stone)

early 1946 *Missouri* took his body aboard and conveyed it to Istanbul for permanent burial. However, there was more to her mission than mere protocol. By entering the Mediterranean *Missouri* and her escorts sent a signal that the United States retained a strong interest in the region. Meanwhile, citizens in the various countries – Turkey, Greece and Italy – were enthusiastic about the ship's presence. A contingent of crew members visited the Vatican for an audience with Pope Pius XII. A tangible result of the cruise was that it opened the door for a permanent U.S.

STRANDING

In December 1949 *Missouri* completed a refit at the Norfolk Naval Shipyard and the following month was due to set out for shakedown training for new crew members.[16] The ship had a new commanding officer as well, Captain William D. Brown, who had an excellent war record, notably in destroyers. However, he had not had sea duty in nearly four years. Commander Jack Fisher, one of *Missouri*'s depart-

Missouri seen during one of the unavailing attempts to bring her off the Thimble Shoal in Hampton Roads, Virginia on which she stranded on the morning of 17 January 1950. She was refloated on 1 February. *(NA/80-G-707570)*

ment heads, observed that the new captain attempted to master details himself rather than delegating duties to subordinates. That approach worked well in smaller ships, including the submarine Brown had commanded in the mid-1930s, but the 887ft *Missouri* was another matter.

On 13 January 1950 the officer of the deck handed Captain Brown a package sent by the Naval Ordnance Laboratory. It contained a letter and a chart with markings for a special range the lab wanted the ship to run when she steamed from Norfolk the following week. The lab wanted to use some acoustic cables to record the sound of the ship's propellers, part of an effort to detect and identify warships by their characteristic noises. The captain gave only brief attention to the letter in the package, entirely overlooking the paragraph specifying the test run as optional. It was an oversight he came to regret.

On the morning of 17 January the navigation team mustered. Captain Brown and the ship's navigator, Lieutenant Commander Frank G. Morris, were on the 08 level conning station, which was high enough to afford views of both bow and stern. Also on the 08 level were the ship's executive officer, Commander George Peckham, who had served in the ship for some time, and Captain R. B. McCoy, a civilian employed by the Navy as a harbour pilot.

The officer whose duty it was to plot *Missouri*'s course through the water was the assistant navigator, twenty-three-year-old Ensign E. R. Harris. Like the navigator and the captain, Ensign Harris was new to his job. The ship cast off at 0725 and the pilot, McCoy, gave the course and speed orders until 0749, when he turned the conn over to Captain Brown. Shortly after eight o'clock the captain mentioned the acoustic range to the offgoing and oncoming officers of the deck, neither of whom had been previously informed. He sent them scurrying to the chartroom to look into it, thereby complicating the inexperienced Ensign Harris's efforts to figure out what was happening. The earlier confusion was compounded when the ship went on the wrong side of a buoy marking the port or northern edge of the acoustic range the ship was due to run. Down on the 04 navigation bridge, Commander Peckham was sending up urgent warnings that the ship was standing into danger but Brown took no heed. (Subsequent testi-

Navy presence in the Mediterranean, soon thereafter designated the Sixth Fleet and still in existence today.

In the following years *Missouri* was based in

Norfolk and took part in a number of Atlantic Fleet operations. Among them was a voyage to the Davis Strait off Greenland to test the fleet's cold-weather capability in the event the Soviets

mounted an attack in the Far North. At the other extreme, she periodically steamed to Guantánamo Bay, Cuba, to maintain crew readiness and proficiency. In July 1947 she arrived at

Captain William D. Brown, commanding officer of the *Missouri*, who unwisely opened his defence at the court of inquiry by blaming his subordinates but later acknowledged his sole responsibility. He spent the rest of his career on shore duty. Note the seal of the State of Missouri on the bulkhead. *(NA/80-G-413652)*

mony demonstrated some of the bridge telephone talkers to be poorly qualified for their roles, so Brown may not have heard the warnings.)

The petty officer following the captain's rudder orders that fateful morning was Quartermaster Second Class Bevan E. Travis, who had been standing helm watches in *Missouri* since 1946. Now, as the battleship headed on the wrong side of the buoy that marked the acoustic range, Travis was concerned for several reasons. For one thing, she soon became sluggish in answering the helm; for another, she appeared to be slowing down even though there had been no order to the engines to reduce speed. He tried to warn the captain, who rebuffed him by telling him to follow orders. At 0817, *Missouri*'s bow hit sand and she had sufficient way on – about 12.5 knots – to keep going for three

ship lengths (about 2,500ft/760m) until coming to rest on a mudflat.

The resulting salvage effort was led by Rear Admiral Allan E. Smith, Commander Cruisers Atlantic Fleet, the ship's type commander. Another with an important role was Rear Admiral Homer Wallin, commander of the Norfolk Naval Shipyard who had been instrumental in raising the vessels sunk at Pearl Harbor in 1941. As Smith recounted in the book he later co-authored on *Missouri*, the basic salvage plan had five phases: remove as much weight as possible, especially fuel and ammunition; lift the ship by such means as pontoons; remove hard-packed sand from around the ship; use sheer force from pulling tugs to get her moving; and provide a dredged channel so the ship could return to deep water once free from the mud.[17]

The first big pull was on 31 January when the efforts of all the tugs and salvage ships were co-ordinated. Cables made from 2in (51mm) wire rope parted during the pull, the result of an unexpected obstacle. An anchor from an old wreck had punctured the ship's bottom and was stuck there. In addition to clearing out the anchor, the remedy was still more lightening of the ship including the anchors and chains, and the addition of two more pontoons in the expectation that an even higher tide the following day would help. The end of the ordeal came on the morning tide of 1 February. With the tugs applying maximum strain, the mighty battleship finally broke free. It was a joy for those on board to feel movement under their feet once again.

After the stranding came the post mortems. Rear Admiral Milton E. Miles chaired the inevitable court of inquiry. Among the witnesses was Quartermaster Bevan Travis, the helmsman on the day of the stranding. Not surprisingly, his testimony while in uniform was more polite concerning Captain Brown than were his oral history recollections years later. He omitted references to the captain's earlier sarcasm when he informed the court that he knew the ship was going to strand but did not tell Brown 'because it is not my place to give the captain orders. It is my place to take orders, and besides, the captain was quite busy at the time.'[18]

On 18 February Captain Brown himself appeared before the inquiry. His initial approach, which was not well received in naval circles, was to lay the blame on

his subordinates. As he spoke of the stranding, he said that he felt 'utterly alone as far as assistance from my team of officers was concerned'.[19] However, after the court of inquiry had sat for seventeen days Brown did a dramatic about-face on 28 February and accepted the blame he had until then been putting on others. In a statement on the stranding, Brown declared that 'I and I alone bear the sole responsibility.' At his court martial on 30 March Brown pleaded guilty to charges of neglect of duty and negligence and placed himself at the mercy of the court. His sentence was reduction by 250 numbers on the Navy's lineal list of captains. He was not selected for flag rank during the remainder of his active duty, which he spent ashore in Florida.

For the new commanding officer the Navy selected Brown's predecessor, Captain Harold Page Smith. He accepted only reluctantly in the belief that his return would create the perception that the Navy had insufficient trained captains to handle the job. But orders were orders. He reported aboard on 7 February as the dry-dock was being flooded to refloat the ship. In the two months his second tour in command lasted, Captain Smith decided the best remedy was to do some grandstanding with *Missouri*, running her at high speed and manoeuvring her with panache when the opportunity permitted. He conceded having expended a lot more fuel than he needed to, but he believed it was worth it. His approach served two purposes. On the one hand, it helped with the process of rebuilding the crew's confidence and pride in their ship. On the other, it told the rest of the Navy – and the world beyond – that *Missouri* was back in service and none the worse for her unfortunate experience in the mud. As he assessed the effect of his approach, Smith said, 'It was exactly what I wanted – a first-class ship again.'[20]

---

16 See John A. Butler, *Strike Able-Peter: The Stranding and Salvage of the USS* Missouri (Annapolis, Md.: Naval Institute Press, 1995), and Stillwell, *Battleship* Missouri, pp. 145–64.

17 Allan E. Smith & Gordon Newell, *The Mighty Mo. The U.S.S. Missouri: A Biography of the Last Battleship* (Seattle, Wa.: Superior, 1969).

18 Stillwell, *Battleship* Missouri, p. 157.

19 *Ibid.*, p. 158.

20 *Ibid.*, p. 164.

the Norfolk Naval Shipyard to undergo an overhaul of machinery and equipment. Soon, however, orders changed. The ship was to prepare to steam to Brazil to bring President Truman and his family home to the States after attending an international conference (see above). The trip northward would be the first vacation the president had enjoyed since taking office more than two years earlier.

Once the ship settled into an in-port routine in Rio de Janeiro, her liberty parties began fanning out ashore to enjoy the local attractions. Sightseeing attracted many in the crew. For instance, Machinist's Mate Art Albert joined some of his buddies in catching a taxi to the top of Sugarloaf Mountain. It was a chore for the cab, which had to stop several times en route because the engine overheated. The trip was worth it, though, because Albert and his shipmates were afforded a spectacular view of the harbour. Others, such as Seaman Dick Klug, enjoyed sunbathing on Rio's fabulous beaches. Klug took care to order several drinks in advance of noon, so he wouldn't be caught short when the bartenders left for their daily siestas. The nightlife was particularly appealing to Messman Eddie Fletcher. He enjoyed going out to nightclubs, listening to Brazilian music, dancing, meeting local people and having a few beers. It was an exotic, appealing life style, even if only a brief interlude from the shipboard routine.

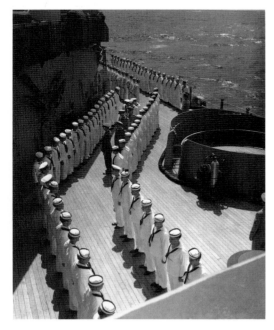

Captain James H. Thach carrying out an inspection forward of turret '3' in 1948. The dark rim on the sailors' hats denotes midshipmen of the U.S. Naval Academy at Annapolis or members of the Naval Reserve Officers Training Corps. (NA/80-G-396323)

of cramped living quarters and early reveille.

After her diplomacy cruises in 1946 and 1947 *Missouri* became a training ship with an understrength crew. In the summer of 1948 she returned to the Mediterranean, this time with a load of Naval Academy and Naval Reserve Officers Training Corps midshipmen on board. Seaman John Williams of the fire-control division watched the midshipmen and mentally divided them into two categories. In one group were those who struck him as hard-working and eager to learn as much as they could about the ship. In the other were those concerned to get through the experience by exerting minimum effort. They knew they would be officers in either a year or three years and were just trying to get by until then. The ones in the latter group treated junior enlisted men as if they didn't know anything and therefore wouldn't listen to them. The ship called at Lisbon, Villefranche in southern France and Algiers in North Africa. The training ended with a shore bombardment of Culebra near Puerto Rico.

In 1949 *Missouri* made two midshipman cruises that included both port calls and war games. Among the stops were Cherbourg, France, and Portsmouth, England. Post-war Britain was still subject to food rationing and the ship entertained hundreds of visitors who willingly scarfed up the refreshments made available. The battleship held a lottery and gave away prizes to locals holding programmes with lucky numbers on them. One young lad won a canned ham. He didn't seem to be with his parents so an officer from *Missouri* followed him to make sure he was all right. Soon the boy joined his mother and the officer said, 'I was wondering if anyone was looking after him.' The boy's mother replied, 'Yes, this is the first ham he has ever seen in his life, and I have to let him carry it.'[21]

The Korean War and Beyond

After the ignominious experience of the stranding at Norfolk in January 1950, *Missouri*'s crew was able to redeem her reputation later that year by getting into combat in the Korean War. In the intervening months she participated in war games in the Caribbean and resumed her training duties, including two midshipman cruises that summer with visits to New York, Boston, Halifax and Panama. Among the battleship's officers was Ensign Lee Royal. He had a girlfriend in New York and one evening they went to see a Broadway musical. Having taken her home, Royal got back to *Missouri* at around 0100. 'Did

'I have returned.' Captain Lawrence E. Kindred, commanding officer of *Missouri*'s Marine detachment, succumbing to the charisma of General of the Army Douglas MacArthur on his return visit to the ship during the Korean War on 21 September 1950. (Courtesy Donald T. Giles, Jr.)

you have a good time?' enquired the duty officer on the forward quarterdeck.[22] 'Yeah' replied the ensign in a happy mood after a pleasant evening. 'Good, because that's the last one you're going to have for some time. Go down to the wardroom. The exec wants you down there.' Despite the late hour, the wardroom was fully lit and people with clipboards in hand were running back and forth. They were making lists of items *Missouri* would need for a major deployment. The ship had received orders to leave at first light for Norfolk. Instead of going to Guantánamo for the planned conclusion of the training cruise, *Missouri* was to head directly back to her home port. There she would land the midshipmen and take on ammunition and supplies for a voyage to the Pacific.

The Korean War had begun with the North Korean invasion of South Korea in June 1950. Now the Navy's only active battleship, *Missouri* was dispatched to the war zone to provide shore bombardment support for General of the Army Douglas MacArthur's planned amphibious invasion of the port of Inchon in mid-September. The ship had the misfortune en route to run into two severe storms that caused some topside damage and delayed her arrival. Having come on station she bombarded the east coast of Korea on

---

[21] *Ibid.*, p. 139.

[22] *Ibid.*, p. 166.

Missouri fires a 16in salvo from turret '2' against the North Korean port of Chongjin on 21 October 1950 in an effort to sever enemy communications. *(NA/80-G-421049)*

15 September, the same day US forces invaded Inchon on the other side of the peninsula. General MacArthur himself came to visit the ship on 21 September while she was anchored at Inchon. Standing stiffly at attention on the quarterdeck, MacArthur saluted during the playing of ruffles and flourishes that were part of the honours rendered to him. While he was doing so, the junior officer of the deck was struck by the fact that the general's right hand was trembling. At seventy MacArthur was old to be a fighting man.

In the days before his arrival MacArthur had been the subject of some rather irreverent discussions from Marines on board *Missouri*.[23] Longstanding references to 'Dugout Doug' the glory hound were thrown back and forth. An eager participant in the discussions was Captain Lawrence E. Kindred, the commanding officer of the ship's Marine detachment. For some years members of the Marine Corps had taken a somewhat jaundiced view of the theatrical army general who was about to return to the ship on whose deck he had accepted the Japanese surrender five years earlier. *Missouri*'s Marine detachment was lined up on the quarterdeck as the general strode aboard through two lines of saluting side boys. He shook hands with Captain Irving Duke, the skipper, and then prepared to inspect the Marine honour guard. As he did so, he took hold of Captain Kindred's arm and pulled him close. Then, in an impressive voice, sounding as if it were emanating from God himself, the general said something like, 'Captain, I have just returned from the far north, where your comrades-in-arms are in close combat with the enemy. And I wish to report to you that there is not a finer group of fighting men in the world than the U.S. Marines.' The general's words rocketed through the ship, endlessly repeated. Captain Kindred's fellow officers began riding him mercilessly, asking him what he now thought of 'Dugout Doug'. Kindred, who had been completely won over by the general's two sentences, was now a MacArthur fan and defender.

Over the next few months *Missouri* was repeatedly called upon to use her 16in guns in support of ground troops on both the east and west coasts of Korea. MacArthur's five stars were tarnished later in 1950 when Chinese forces invaded North Korea despite the general's confi-

dent predictions that they would not come. US troops headed south to escape the onslaught, retreating from the bitterly cold Chosin Reservoir in an action that has become legendary in Marine Corps history. The Americans converged on the port of Hungnam, North Korea, shortly before Christmas, to be evacuated in the face of the advancing Chinese army. *Missouri* received orders to proceed to the area, anchor and take specific co-ordinates under fire in company with other gunfire support ships. Her mission during this operation was to lay down a curtain of exploding projectiles as the Marines' perimeter contracted to protect their rear as they moved into the port. Fire Controlman Warren Lee was impressed, recalling that 'I have never seen such a perimeter of fire as the one set up to protect that particular evacuation.' Since the shooting was at night it provided a spectacular contrast to the surrounding darkness.

After the dramatic troop movements of 1950 the war settled down to a stalemate. The Navy reactivated the other three Iowa-class battleships to take part in the war, sometimes operating with aircraft carriers, but mostly providing shore bombardment support. *Missouri* came home to Norfolk in April 1951 and resumed her role as a training ship. She took midshipmen to France and Norway that summer. Crown Prince Olav,

later to be Norway's king, visited at Oslo on 20 June. *Missouri* returned to Europe for training purposes in 1952 and later that year headed once more to Korea, where she served as flagship of the Seventh Fleet and again fired shore bombardment. During that time Chief Gunner's Mate Jack McCarron went on liberty in Tokyo. Visiting Japan was an interesting experience for McCarron, who on 7 December 1941 had been manning a 5in/25-calibre anti-aircraft gun on the battleship *Arizona*.[24] An explosion blew him over the side and left him badly burned. Now, nearly a dozen years later, he was controlling a battery of 5in/38-calibre dual-purpose guns in another battleship. Unlike a number of Pearl Harbor survivors who harboured an enduring sense of bitterness, McCarron felt no hatred towards the Japanese. He was interested in meeting them and seeing their country. He was impressed by how quickly Tokyo had been rebuilt in the years since the war ended.

In command of *Missouri* during her second deployment to Korea was Captain Warner Edsall. A 1927 graduate of the Naval Academy, the forty-eight-year-old officer had served in submarines, destroyers and on staff duties. At

---

23 *Ibid.*, pp. 172–3.

24 *Ibid.*, p. 203.

0945 on 25 March 1953 *Missouri* completed her last firing mission off Korea. She had fired 3,861 16in and 4,379 5in shells during her deployment. After the last bombardment *Missouri* headed back to Japan so she could pick up her boats that had been landed at Sasebo for the duration of operations off Korea. On the morning of 26 March Captain Edsall was on the 04 level bridge, binoculars strapped around his neck. He gave orders for course and speed as the ship approached Sasebo harbour. The harbour entrance was guarded by anti-submarine nets and the opening through which the battleship was to pass was relatively narrow. The problem

Missouri docks at Norfolk after the Korean War on 27 April 1951. Across the pier are the heavy cruisers Albany and Macon. (NA/80-G-428360)

was complicated by a good deal of traffic as fishing boats darted to and fro. Lieutenant (j.g.) Art Ward had previously noted the captain's tendency to get excited by all these manoeuvres and that he was not his usual self as he tried to avoid the smaller vessels. The passage through the opening in the nets required a large turn. At 0721, just after the skipper had given the order to the helm, he grasped the arm of Commander Bob North, the executive officer, and collapsed to the deck no longer breathing. North quickly took over the conn to bring *Missouri* to a mooring buoy. Medical personnel were summoned but Captain Edsall was pronounced dead of a heart attack at 0730. Captain Robert Brodie took command on 4 April and brought the ship back to the States.

In July of that year negotiations at

Panmunjom led to an armistice concluding three years of hostilities. By then Dwight D. Eisenhower had taken office as president and Harry Truman had retired to Independence, Missouri. No longer did the ship have a protector in the White House and with the coming of peace *Missouri*'s days in full commission were numbered. Meanwhile, operations, summer training cruises for midshipmen and refits continued. In early June 1954 it was time for yet another midshipman training cruise to Europe as part of Task Group 40.1, which consisted of sixteen warships with a total of 3,000 midshipmen embarked. The cruise began as *Missouri* and her three sisters briefly rendezvoused at sea off Norfolk on 7 June and performed a few manoeuvres. It was the only time all four ships of the Iowa class steamed in

formation. Fireman Herb Fahr stood topside on *Missouri* and took in the sight of the huge dreadnoughts steaming together, while an aerial photographer captured pictures of the formation. In the years to come, whenever he saw one of the photos, Fahr remembered with pride that he was present on that occasion

On her return from Europe *Missouri* was earmarked for inactivation at Puget Sound Naval Shipyard in the Pacific Northwest. Although the

MODERNISATION PACKAGE, 1984–6

- Eight armoured box launchers for a total of thirty-two Tomahawk cruise missiles; land-attack version with a projected range up to 700 nautical miles
- Four quadruple canister launchers for a total of sixteen Harpoon anti-ship missiles, each with a projected range up to sixty nautical miles
- Four Vulcan/Phalanx close-in weapon systems for defence against aircraft and missiles
- Advanced communication systems
- SPS-49 air-search radar replacing the less-capable SPS-6
- Aviation facilities, including an enlarged helicopter landing pad on the fantail, parking area, helicopter control booth on the after end of the superstructure and helicopter glide slope indicator
- Conversion of the engineering plant to burn Navy distillate fuel in place of black oil
- A sewage collection, holding and transfer system to comply with upgraded environmental requirements
- Improved habitability for the crew
- Removal of the stern crane to avoid interference with helicopter operations on the fantail
- Refuelling rig on the starboard side to facilitate transfer of fuel to escorting ships
- SLQ-32 electronic countermeasures suite
- Satellite navigation and communication antennae
- Mk-36 super rapid-blooming off-board chaff (SRBOC) launchers
- New tripod foremast; removal of after mast
- Removal of four of the original ten 5in/38 twin mounts to allow for the installation of a missile deck between the smoke-stacks
- Installation of a combat engagement centre in place of the former flag quarters

Two key components of *Missouri*'s 1984–6 modernisation: an armoured box launcher for Tomahawk cruise missiles with one of the Vulcan/Phalanx close-in weapon units on the right, seen here under marine guard in 1987. *(Courtesy Rich Pedroncelli)*

crew dwindled rapidly once that process began, her battle-readiness was already reduced when she made her last summer training cruise since many of the Korean War veterans had departed. In the secondary battery plotting rooms, for example, Lieutenant Willard Clark didn't have enough enlisted crew members to run all the computers at the same time during firing exercises. Men had to move from one piece of equipment to another as an exercise progressed. The Mk-37 directors for the 5in guns were manned, but only one of the four director officers had sufficient experience to do the job properly. The enlisted fire-control personnel were barely qualified as operators. Moreover, the very fact that the crew members knew the ship was going out of commission robbed them of their incentive to master the operation of the equipment.

On 23 August *Missouri* left Norfolk after the summer training, traversed the Panama Canal and put in at Long Beach and San Francisco before reaching Puget Sound. Having offloaded ammunition at Bangor, Washington, she moved into the naval shipyard at nearby Bremerton in mid-September. The next months were dreary ones as the crew gradually departed, storerooms were emptied, and various systems and items of equipment were inactivated. A dehumidification system was installed throughout the ship to minimise rust; gear was cleaned and preservative poured into equipment to ward off oxidation. Dome-like 'igloos' protected the 40mm mounts from the elements. After five months of offloading, mothballing, repairing and inventorying by shipyard workers and ship's crew, the task was complete. The final act came on 26 February 1955, a dismal day of intermittent rain and snow squalls in Puget Sound. Because of the weather conditions, the decommissioning ceremony was held in the wardroom before *Missouri*'s remaining complement of twenty-five officers and 176 enlisted men.

Renaissance

In 1981 Ronald Reagan took office as president with an agenda to build up the US military, which had been allowed to decline during the administration of his predecessor, Jimmy Carter. Reagan's energetic Secretary of the Navy was John Lehman, who pushed hard for the reactivation and modernisation of the four Iowa-class battleships as part of strengthening the fleet. *New Jersey* was recommissioned in 1982 and *Iowa* in 1984. In May 1984 *Missouri* was pulled away from Bremerton after having spent twenty-nine years there in mothballs. A tug towed her south to the Long Beach Naval Shipyard where she underwent a complete overhaul, including being equipped with long-range missiles that restored her offensive capabilities. No longer would she be an anti-aircraft vessel as during the Second World War, or strictly a piece of floating artillery as in the Korean War.

On 10 May 1986 Secretary of Defense Caspar Weinberger presided at San Francisco as *Missouri* was recommissioned and returned to the active fleet for the first time in over thirty years. She combined some of the oldest technology in the fleet in her 16in guns and some of the latest in the electronic support equipment for controlling her newly installed missiles. That summer she underwent a period of refresher training off the coast of Southern California akin to the collective training her original crew had received in the summer of 1944. Finally, on 10 September *Missouri* set off from her new home port of Long Beach for a world cruise to celebrate her restored status as a front-line combatant. Having stopped at Pearl Harbor, she sailed for Australia and then westward into the Indian Ocean. Next was a visit to the US base on the island of Diego Garcia. From there she entered the Red Sea and transited the Suez Canal into the Mediterranean. She anchored at Istanbul which she had first visited in April 1946 bearing the body of the former Turkish ambassador, Mehmet Ertegün. Now, in November 1986, she was back. Among those invited aboard were Ambassador Ertegün's children, including Ahmet Ertegün, the founder of Atlantic Records. He flew to Turkey specially for the occasion. Among the many local visitors was one bearing a set of Turkish postage stamps issued to honour the ship during her earlier call at the city.

During the ship's stay in Istanbul her commanding officer, Captain Al Carney, decided to visit the Hilton Hotel sited on a hilltop position overlooking the Bosphorus. Carney duly settled down to read a newspaper over a drink, periodically looking up to enjoy the majestic view, including his anchored battleship. After a while he looked up to find that *Missouri* had practically disappeared, the only sign of her being her upper works protruding above some trees. Carney was filled with alarm, his first thought being that the anchor had slipped and the ship run aground. Hastily paying his bill, he ran out and climbed into a taxi. Having raced down to the pier he discovered *Missouri* was doing fine; she was still anchored but had swung on her anchor in the opposite direction. Changing currents and the topography of the Bosphorus conspire to produce a little whirlpool there once a week, a phenomenon spelt out in the sailing directions Carney had read en route to Istanbul. Only when he found the ship safe and sound was his memory refreshed and his fears allayed. After further stops in Italy, Spain and Portugal, *Missouri* crossed the Atlantic and then went through the Panama Canal. She arrived home in Long Beach on 19 December, just in time for crew members to celebrate Christmas with their families.

In early 1987 *Missouri* underwent a refit, followed by crew training and fleet exercises. Next on the docket was an operation that went beyond the ceremonial role the ship had performed the previous year. In late August, after wrapping up a multi-ship exercise in the central and western Pacific, *Missouri* set out for the North Arabian Sea and the Gulf of Oman. Already in progress was a tanker war between Iraq and Iran; the hostilities interfered with commercial shipping in the Persian Gulf. To ensure the continued flow of oil, a number of Kuwaiti tankers were transferred to US-flag status and could thus be protected by the U.S. Navy. A convoy system evolved to shepherd the tankers from Kuwait in the northern part of the Persian Gulf to the Strait of Hormuz and safety. *Missouri* remained outside the strait to provide cover and retribution in the event the Iranians attacked the transiting tanker convoys. The arrival of the battleship and a carrier constituted an escalation of US naval presence in the area. As Lieutenant Mark Walker, the ship's public affairs officer, recalled, 'We knew we were sending a very powerful political signal by sending the battleship up there, and that wasn't lost on anybody.'[25] All told, *Missouri* went more than a hundred days without touching port. Her logistical requirements for food, fuel and other consumables were met by underway replenishment from supply ships. *Missouri*'s participation came to an end in late November when the carrier *Midway* relieved her on station and the battleship headed home via Australia and Pearl Harbor.

The years 1988 and 1989 passed with continuing training operations and fleet exercises. In May 1988 *Missouri* fired a Tomahawk missile for the first time and that summer participated in Exercise RimPac '88, mainly in the vicinity of the Hawaiian Islands. That exercise marked the end of a long career for Master Chief Boatswain's Mate John Davidson, who had been in the recommissioning crew in 1986 and then became the ship's command master chief. In that role he was the senior enlisted adviser to both the captain and crew. As a seaman first class, Davidson had been in the crew of *Missouri* when she steamed to Istanbul in 1946. In the intervening years he had been a much-travelled sailor and sported souvenirs of his experience in the form of tattoos injected in such far-flung places as Norfolk, Hong Kong, Pearl Harbor and Yokohama. When the ship was approved for reactivation Davidson received a telephone call from Washington asking if he would like to be in

Bluejackets run aboard as the ship 'comes alive' during *Missouri*'s recommissioning ceremony in San Francisco on 10 May 1986, more than thirty years after she was last decommissioned. (*U.S. Navy*)

25 *Ibid.*, p. 279.

Missouri unleashes her main armament during Operation Desert Storm on 6 February 1991, some of the 783 16in shells fired by her during that conflict. Two of the surviving six 5in mounts can be seen in the foreground. *(U.S. Navy)*

the crew. As he recalled, 'I told them I'd pay them to let me serve,' even though he had been eligible for retirement for some time.[26] The beauty of the situation was that the Navy continued to pay him.

From February to May 1989 the battleship went through a maintenance and overhaul period at the Long Beach Naval Shipyard and for the rest of that year and into mid-1990 continued to take part in fleet exercises and make liberty calls. In early July 1990 *Missouri* made her traditional midsummer visit to San Francisco. Once the ship was back home in Long Beach, Captain Lee Kaiss, reappointed in command after a four-year interval, went to San Diego to attend briefings in connection with *Missouri*'s scheduled deployment to the western Pacific. It was to be a three-and-a-half month cruise that would include liberty ports in Japan, Korea and the Philippines. On the last Friday in July Kaiss received a telephone call from an officer on the staff of the type commander. He told Kaiss that the Pentagon would announce that weekend that it was considering inactivation and decommissioning of the ship. The United States had recently won the Cold War against the Soviet Union and citizens were looking for a 'peace dividend' in the form of reduced defence expenditure. Across the pier from *Missouri* her sister ship *New Jersey* was already beginning the inactivation process. On the East Coast, *Iowa* was nearly ready for decommissioning. The planned fate of *Missouri* would obviously be big news for the crewmen, so Kaiss received authorisation to tell them in advance of the official announcement. On returning to *Missouri* he appeared on the internal television system to report that the ship would probably begin inactivation after she completed her coming deployment. A few days later the situation changed dramatically.

Action in the Persian Gulf

On 2 August President Saddam Hussein of Iraq sent three army divisions across the border into Kuwait and quickly overran it. Of immediate concern was the possibility that Iraqi forces would also invade Kuwait's southern neighbour Saudi Arabia. The United States immediately sent naval forces to the region and began a mobilisation effort, given the name Operation Desert Shield. At the same time President George

H. W. Bush began building diplomatic support, seeking United Nations resolutions and economic sanctions while forging an international coalition ready to take military action if necessary. No sooner had the Iraqi invasion taken place than plans for *Missouri*'s inactivation were put into abeyance.

Missouri arrived in the Persian Gulf on 3 January 1991, waiting for the other shoe to drop. President Bush had given Iraq an ultimatum – leave Kuwait by 15 January or the coalition nations would take steps to remove the Iraqi soldiers by force. On the 16th the president's deadline passed at 0800 Persian Gulf time. At midnight on the 17th Captain Kaiss called for reveille and told the crewmen they had time for a head call. Over the general announcing system he said, 'In approximately ten minutes we will be going to general quarters, and we will be going to general quarters for real. We are currently in receipt of a strike order, and we are making preparations to launch Tomahawks in the next hour.'[27] The ship's navigator, Lieutenant Commander Mike Finn, was one of many on board who felt a great sense of unease. Sending off those Tomahawks would be an act of war and the Americans could justifiably expect the Iraqis to retaliate energetically. The officer of the deck was Lieutenant Wes Carey who didn't believe the ship would actually fire her missiles. But then came the countdown and at 0140 a ball of flame erupted from one of the armoured box

launchers in the superstructure. The first missile flew off into the night towards Baghdad. As Carey recalled, 'I realized then that we were at war. There was no way you could bring it back.'[28] About thirty seconds later Lieutenant (j.g.) Joe Raskin saw another roar off, this time launched by a cruiser or destroyer with a vertical-launch capability. Subsequently one bright blast after another illuminated the area around *Missouri* as she sent half a dozen Tomahawk missiles into the night.

Despite the dread felt by many in the battleship, the weight of firepower raining down on them left the Iraqis in no position to retaliate as yet. The following night *Missouri* fired thirteen more Tomahawk missiles, of which only one failed to operate as intended. A backup missile went off forty-five minutes later to complete the mission. Over the following days, *Missouri* unleashed three more missiles to bring the total to twenty-eight by 20 January. *Missouri* then fired her guns in anger for the first time since the Korean War in 1953. This was a bombardment mission against Iraqi command-and-control bunkers at Khafji, Saudi Arabia. Because of the beach gradient the ship had to steam close to shoal water to bring her 16in guns within range. To spot the fall of shot *Missouri* deployed an unmanned drone that transmitted live television images back to the ship.

In mid-February the ship headed north to provide fire support for a possible amphibious

[26] *Ibid.*, p. 258.

[27] *Ibid.*, pp. 311–12.

[28] *Ibid.*, p. 312.

raid on Faylakah Island lying just off Kuwait City. The manoeuvre was in fact a feint since the actual ground invasion would come from Saudi Arabia in the west. *Missouri*'s presence close inshore lent credence to the idea that a landing would be made on the Kuwaiti beaches in order to tie down Iraqi troops. Although junior to Captain Kaiss, destroyer squadron commander Captain Peter Bulkeley came aboard *Missouri* as officer in tactical command. At 2315 on 23 February Bulkeley directed the ship to fire on Faylakah as soon as she got within range and

targets began appearing. The island itself did not form part of the diversion, but as Bulkeley subsequently explained there were 'enemy troops on there. [...] My job was to attack the enemy, and I did. Simple as that.'[29] *Missouri*'s bombardment was successful. The intelligence reports reaching Bulkeley's embarked staff indicated that the Iraqis were moving corps-level artillery support to the Kuwaiti coast and to the island of Bubiyan to repel the expected invasion.

[29] *Ibid.*, p. 320.

On 25 February the Iraqis finally retaliated by firing a Silkworm cruise missile at *Missouri* and nearby ships. Navigator Mike Finn was on the bridge with the skipper and the weapons officer gazing towards the shore at the scores of oil wells set ablaze by the Iraqis. Then he saw a steady orange glow off the ship's quarter, like the tip of a lighted cigarette, growing larger and larger as it drew nearer. Captain Kaiss recognised the threat and sent the word to the crew to hit the deck. Among the many who felt fear as the Silkworm streaked towards *Missouri* was Ship's

LAST ARRIVAL AT PEARL: A REMINISCENCE

Dawn was just about to break as *Missouri* neared the end of the outward leg of her final cruise as a commissioned vessel. She had steamed out of Long Beach and on the morning of 5 December 1991 was almost at her destination, Pearl Harbor. As she neared the channel entrance, the sun had not yet risen; those of us on board were still in semi-darkness. Arrayed before us were the lights of southern Oahu. The haze-grey battleship steamed west along the south coast of the island, past Waikiki Beach and the mouth of Honolulu Harbor. We saw hundreds of people along the shore, up early to

watch what would be the last time a battleship ever arrived at Pearl under her own power. They flashed cameras and waved to the ship as she passed. Off to the east, the crouching Diamond Head landmark was silhouetted in the gloaming, and then the sun popped up in the distance.

The battleship steamed steadily on, then picked up some tugs to guide her to her berth. The crew, clad in summer white uniforms, manned the rail on the main deck and in the superstructure, each enlisted man standing an arm's length from his shipmate on either side. After *Missouri* passed through the narrow

harbour mouth, I looked off to port and saw Ford Island. Alongside the island were the concrete quays to which the ships of the battle line had been moored on 7 December 1941. Painted on the quays were the names and hull numbers of the battleships of fifty years earlier. First we passed the berth of the *California*. Then came an area filled with concrete pilings where the mooring quays that had been the location of the *Maryland* and *Oklahoma* in 1941 had recently been removed to make room for construction of a new dock. The dock was intended to accommodate *Missouri*, which had been scheduled to be based at Pearl Harbor as part of the strategic home-porting plan. Now we saw only a partially completed dock for a battleship that was about two weeks from the start of the mothballing process that would lead to her final decommissioning.

Missouri continued her journey into the harbour and we could see still more of the mooring quays from long ago, those bearing the names of the *Tennessee* and *West Virginia*. In my mind's eye I could see what those old battleships had looked like, painted in their warlike dark grey with light grey tops. My imagination also recalled the black-and-white newsreel films I had watched so many times; they showed the exploding, burning ships and heavy black smoke billowing skyward from the oil-fed fires. It was an emotional moment as I thought of those long-dead ships and their long-dead crew members.

Looking even farther along the remnants of Battleship Row, I saw the quays for *Arizona* and *Nevada*. The sway-backed white *Arizona* Memorial was gleaming brightly in the morning sun, and as we watched we saw the first boatload of tourists coming aboard shortly after 0730 to pay their respects. The ship that symbolised victory at the end of the Second World War was coming in to moor only a few hundred yards from the ship that symbolised the beginning of the war.

Missouri entering Pearl Harbor on the morning of 5 December 1991 to take part in the fiftieth anniversary commemoration of the attack which brought the United States into the Second World War on 7 December 1941. Beyond her is the USS *Arizona* Memorial. The two ships together symbolise the beginning and the end of America's active participation in that conflict. (*U.S. Navy*)

Paul Stillwell

Serviceman Gregory Green, who lay contemplating a number of outcomes, including damage to the ship or the need to abandon her, being made a prisoner of war, and even wondering what the Iraqis would feed him if they did capture him. With no access to electronic gear or defensive weapons, the weapon he wielded in that circumstance was hope – as if to will the Silkworm away. He had hundreds of helpers in issuing those messages of hope and they were heard. The British guided missile destroyer *Gloucester* shot down the Silkworm with a Sea Dart missile.

The ground war unfolding ashore soon moved beyond the range of *Missouri*'s guns. All told, the battleship fired 611 rounds of 16in projectiles during a sixty-hour period that ended on 27 February, bringing her total for the war to 783 rounds. As *Missouri* drew short on ammunition, Captain Bulkeley shifted his task group flag to *Wisconsin* which took over as duty gunship. Later that day *Wisconsin* unleashed ten or so projectiles to cover the surrender of Faylakah by virtue of which she became the last battleship to fire her big guns in anger. The war ended in victory the following day, 28 February.

The Last Battleship

Once the war in the Middle East was over *Missouri* made the long trek home to Long Beach and joyous family reunions. But the ship's days were numbered. The planned decommissioning, put on hold the previous year because of the invasion of Kuwait, would now take place. In the autumn of 1991 the ship made a farewell cruise of the West Coast, one last go-around for the old warhorse. One stop was for the Seafair festival in Seattle. The ship also took part in Fleet Week in San Francisco, moored at her usual berth near the Oakland Bay Bridge. During the first night or two the local authorities specified that Navy men and Marines on liberty had to be in uniform rather than the customary civilian clothes. With that many servicemen released on the city, it was, said Lieutenant Ross Mobilia, 'a flashback to 1944. The town was just covered with blue uniforms.' The visiting servicemen rode taxis and trolleys free of charge and soaked up the generous hospitality of the cosmopolitan city by the bay.

She had one more mission to perform. *Missouri* steamed to Pearl Harbor, reaching it on 5 December. She moored in sight of the *Arizona* Memorial and on 7 December was present for the fiftieth anniversary commemorations of the Japanese attack that brought the United States into the Pacific War. President George H. W. Bush visited and gave a television interview from the surrender deck. The visit was a relatively brief one, so the president did not have the opportunity to wade in, shake hands and talk with individuals as Harry Truman had done back in the 1940s. The ship then steamed east to Seal Beach, California, to unload her ammunition for the last time. The magazines and projectile decks that had been replenished in the Persian Gulf were now emptied. Here *Missouri* lay at anchor for three days and three nights while the crew manhandled tons of powder and projectiles up from below and over the side into barges.

On the evening of 20 December the ship weighed anchor and made the voyage back to her home port, entering on the evening tide. It was the last time a battleship of any nation steamed on her own power. The executive officer of the Long Beach Naval Station had arranged a tribute. He sent a message to the waterfront that all ships were to sound their whistles when *Missouri* came back in. As she passed through the breakwater and approached the piers, her crew was standing at quarters on deck. It was about 1800 and dusk had fallen on what was almost the shortest day of the year. As the battleship passed by the first pier, the first whistle sounded out, and then another, and then another. More ships joined in the chorus as *Missouri* proceeded into the harbour. Most sailors have a special feeling of pride about their own ship and aren't particularly sentimental about others but this tribute was extraordinary. Finally, tugs pushed the ship in against the pier to be moored. By then it seemed that every ship in the harbour was blasting her whistle in tribute. Now came an announcement over the loudspeaker system: 'The last officer of the deck of the last battleship is shifting his watch to the quarterdeck.'[30] The sense of her being the last in a long and historic line of ships was palpable.

The next three months involved a repetition of the process carried out at Bremerton in early 1955 as *Missouri* reverted to inactivity. On 31 March 1992 hundreds of her former crew members and many others gathered in Long Beach to say farewell. Until then she was the world's only active battleship, *Wisconsin* having already been decommissioned. Now that designation slipped away during the course of an emotional farewell. Near the end of the ceremony Captain Kaiss said to Commander Ken Jordan, 'XO, haul down the colours.'[31] As taps sounded, down came the flags of the state of California, the horizontal red, white and blue-striped Missouri state flag, and that of the United States. As the proceedings closed, the remaining crew members filed off the double brows abreast turret '2'. Captain Kaiss was the last to leave. The officers lined up in a double row at the foot of the brow like side boys so they could shake hands and say goodbye to the captain. It was over.

Missouri remained at Long Beach until 1994, when a tug towed her north to resume her place in the mothball fleet at Bremerton. Once the Navy had concluded that it no longer needed the ship as a mobilisation asset, several ports vied for the honour of having her as a museum and tourist attraction, including Bremerton, San Francisco and Pearl Harbor. Appropriately enough, Pearl Harbor won, and in 1998 the ship was towed to her permanent berth not far from the *Arizona* Memorial. Together they remind us of the beginning and end of America's participation in the Second World War. An army of volunteers set to work to spruce the ship up and on 29 January 1999 she opened as a museum and tourist attraction. To this day she continues to draw visitors to her decks.

Sources

Butler, John A., *Strike Able-Peter: The Stranding and Salvage of the USS* Missouri (Annapolis, Md.: Naval Institute Press, 1995)

Campbell, John, *Naval Weapons of World War Two* (London: Conway, 1985)

Friedman, Norman, *U.S. Battleships: An Illustrated Design History* (Annapolis, Md.: Naval Institute Press, 1985)

Naval History Division, *Dictionary of American Naval Fighting Ships*, vol. IV (Washington, D.C.: U.S. Government Printing Office, 1969); also available at https://www.history.navy.mil/research/histories/ship-histories/danfs/m/missouri-iii.html [accessed August 2017]

Smith, Allan E., & Gordon Newell, *The Mighty Mo. The U.S.S.* Missouri: *A Biography of the Last Battleship* (Seattle, Wa.: Superior, 1969)

Stillwell, Paul, *Battleship* Missouri: *An Illustrated History* (Annapolis, Md.: Naval Institute Press, 1996)

Sumrall, Robert F., *USS* Missouri *(BB 63)* (Missoula, Mont.: Pictorial Histories Publishing Company, 1986)

_____, *Iowa Class Battleships: Their Design, Weapons and Equipment* (Annapolis, Md.: Naval Institute Press, 1988)

Truman, Harry S., *Memoirs*; vol. I: *Year of Decisions* (Garden City, N.Y.: Doubleday, 1955).

---

30 *Ibid.*, p. 341.
31 *Ibid.*, p. 344.

INDEX

Page references in italics are to illustrations; launch dates are provided in parentheses after warship.

A-1 Narciso Monturiol (1917), 283
Acasta (1929), 381, *381*
Achilles (1863), 24
Achuri, SS, 288
Ackermann, Capt. Richard, 191, 193–4, 195
Adigard, Capt. Paul, 62, 63, 63–4, 66, 67, 69
Adler (1908; ex-*Peder Skram*), 127
Admiral Graf Spee (1934), 376, 379
Admiral Hipper (1937), 306, 380
Admiral Makarov (1906), *101*
Admiral Scheer (1931), 306, 376
AE1 (1913), 233
AE2 (1913), 233
AEG AG, 298
AG Vulcan, Stettin, 21, 22–3, 23
Agamemnon (1906), 21, 197
Agincourt (1913; ex-*Rio de Janeiro*, ex-*Sultan Osman-i Evvel*), 13, 138, 186, 187, 188, 253
Ahven-class minesweepers, 358
Ajax (1934), 263
Ajax (tug), 179
Akagi (1927), 345
Aki (1907), 347
Alagoas (1909), 145
Albany (1945), *428*
Albatross (1907), 104
Aldebaran, 166
Aleksandrovskii Works, St Petersburg, 91
Alencar, Admiral Alexandrino Faria de, 135–7, 148
Alessandri, Pres. Arturo, 256, 261
Alfonso XIII (1891), 282
Alfonso XIII (1913; later *España*), 10, 12, 268–89; design, 274–5; construction, 276–7, 277, 278; specifications, 275; protection, 275; armament, 275–6, 276; fire control, 277, 279, 286; propulsion, 276; organisa-tion, 279, 280; life aboard, 279–80, 280–1; see *España*
Algérie (1932), 397
Almirante Abreu (1899; later *Albany*), 132, 134
Almirante Brown (1880), 38
Almirante Cervera (1925), 287, 288
Almirante Cochrane (1874), 38, 248

Almirante Cochrane (1918; ex-*Santiago*), see *Eagle*
Almirante Condell (1912), *259*
Almirante Latorre (1913; ex-*Valparaíso*, ex-*Canada*), 10, 12, 13, 138, 247–67; design, 249; construction, 253, *253*; specifications, 249; protec-tion, 249, 258; armament, 249–52, *250*, *251*, 257–8, 265–6, *266*; fire control, 250, 257; propulsion, 252–3; organisation, 263; life aboard, *15*; mutiny (1931), 15, 18, 250, 259–61
Almirante Lynch (1912), *259*
Almirante Riveros (1914; ex-*Faulknor*), 255, 260, 265, 266n
Almirante Uribe (1914; ex-*Broke*), 255
Almirante Williams (1914; ex-*Botha*), 255, *259*, 266n
Amalfi (1908), 171
Amazonas (1896; later *New Orleans*), 132, 134
Amazonas (1908), 145
Amur (1907), 105
Amurets (1905), 111
Andrea Doria (1913), 394, 396, 399, 403, 406, 407
Andrei Pervozvannyi (1906), 102, 104, *104*, 292
Angamos, Battle of (1879), 249, *249*
Annapolis, U.S. Naval Academy, 25, 29, 411, 426, *426*, 427; Museum, *422*
Ansaldo (Gio. Ansaldo & Co.), Genoa, 41, 42, *43*, 44, 258, 273, 396, 397, *398*, 399, 402
Ansaldo-Belluzzo-Tosi (ABT) consortium, 399
Antelo (tug), 283
Aorangi, SS, 232
Apagador (fishing vessel), 288
Aquidabã (1885), 132
Äran (1901), 291, 306
Araucano (1929), 257, 259n, 265
Ardent (1929), 381
Argentine navy (Armada de la República Argentina), 38–52, 138
Argus (1917), 330
Arizona (1915), 329, *335*, 427, 432, *432*, 433
Ark Royal (1914), 195
Ark Royal (1937), 329, 383
Armando Diaz-class light cruisers, 396
Armstrongs (Sir W. G. Armstrong, Whitworth & Co.), Elswick, High Walker & Newcastle upon Tyne, 26, *35*, 42, *44*, 45, 74, 75, *75*,

75–6, 87, 132, 134, 135–7, *136*, 137, *137*, 138–9, 171, 183, 186, 248, 249, 252, 253, *253*, 254, 273, 281, 297; Armstrong-Pozzuoli, 42, 396
Arrate-Mendi, SS, 288
Asahi (1899), 34
Asama (1898), 234
Asar-i Tevfik (1868), 174
Aspis (1905), 175
Astilleros del Nervión, Bilbao, 273
Atago (1930), 352
Ateliers et Chantiers de la Gironde, Lormont, 272
Aube, Admiral Théophile, 54, 132
Australia (1911), 10, 13, 15, 219–46; design, 226; construction, 220–1, 222–3, 226–8; specifications, 228; protection, 228; armament, 226, 228, *228*; fire control, 228; propulsion, 228; organisation, 228; life aboard, 19, *231*, *232*, 238–9, *238–9*; mutiny (1919), 18, 242–3
Austro-Hungarian navy (Kaiserliche und Königliche Kriegsmarine), 18, 102, 114, 176, 185, 186, 188, 202–18, 271, 393
Averof, Georgios, 13, 171
Awashima, 36

B-1 (1922), 89
B-3 (1924), 89
B-6 (1928), 288
Babcock & Wilcox boilers, 138, 149, 228, 411
Bahia (1909), 145
Baian (1900; later *Aso*), 35
Baian (1907), 108, 109, 111
Bakhirev, Vice Admiral M. K., 108, 109–12
Baltic Shipbuilding and Engineering Works, St Petersburg, 91, 92, *92*
Barbaros Hayrettin (1891; ex-*Kurfürst Friedrich Wilhelm*), 174, 175, 186, *190*
Barbosa de Oliveira, Rui, 129–31, *131*, 132, 133, 135, 146, 146–7, 147
Barr & Stroud, Glasgow, 57, 69, 93, 100, 298
Barroso (1896), 132, 134, 145
Basra (1907), 195
Bausch & Lomb, Rochester, N.Y., 149
Bayern (1915), 108
Bean, C. E. W., 226–8
Beardmore (Wm. Beardmore & Co.), Glasgow, 11, 91, 272
Beatty, Admiral Sir David, 102,

235, 236, 241, 309, 319
Behncke, Vice Admiral Paul, 108, 109
Beikos Roads, 192, 193
Belfast (1938), 387, 390
Belfort Vieira, Admiral Heráclito, 136, 137
Belgrano (1896; ex-*Varese* (ii)), 44, 45, 46, 48, 51
Bellerophon (1907), 204, 274, 275
Belleville boilers, 58, 91, 101, 171
Bengtskär, 369, 370
Benjamin Constant (1892), 132
Bergamini, Admiral Carlo, 399, 401, 402, 405, 406
Bergsunds Mekaniska Verkstads AB, Stockholm, 293
Berk-i Satvet (1906), 190
Berlin, Operation (1941), 381–2
Berlingske Tidende (Copenhagen), 118
Bernardino Rivadavia (1902; later *Kasuga*), 48, 50
Bernd von Arnim (1936), 90
Bernotti, Rear Admiral Romeo, 394, 395
Berrima, SS, 232, 233
Bertin, Louis-Émile, 26, 56
Bey, Rear Admiral Erich, 385–9, *385*, 390
Biancheri, Admiral Luigi, 406–7, 407
Birmingham (1936), 89
Bismarck (1939), 15, 331–2, 332, 333–5, 382–3, 388
Bjørgvin (1914; later *Glatton*), 87
Blanco Encalada (1875), 38, 248
Blas de Lezo (1923), *285*, 286
Blohm & Voss, Hamburg, 184, 187, 201
Blonde (1910), 102
Blücher (1908), 183
Boadicea (1908), 102
Bofors AB, Karlskoga, 88, 116–17, 200–1, 266, 292, 295–8, *295*, *296*, *297*, 359–62, *363*
Bogatyr (1901), 98, 100, *101*
Borodino-class battleships, 91, 92, 96
Børresen, Rear Admiral Jacob, 19, 77, 80–1, *81*, 83–6, *83*
Bostock, Ch. Mech. Charles W., 19
Boston Metals Co., Baltimore, 51
Botha (1914), see *Almirante Williams*
Bouvet (1896), 54, 56, 59, 60, 61, 62
Braunschweig (1902), 105, 106

Brazilian navy (Marinha brasileira), 12, 18, 18–19, 129–52
Breda Meccanica Bresciana, 396
Bremen (1903), 105
Brennero, SS, 399
Brennus (1891), 54
Breslau (1911), see *Midilli*
Bretagne (1913), 329, 394n
Briggs, OSig. Ted, 313, 329, 332, *333*
Brin, Benedetto, 41
Brisbane (1915), 241, 245
Bristol-class light cruisers, 226
Broke (1914), see *Almirante Uribe*
Broke-class destroyers, 253, 254, 261
Brooklyn-class light cruisers, 265
Brown, Capt. William D., 424–5, *425*
Brown, Boveri & Cie, Baden, Switz., 359, 374
Brown-Curtis turbines, 11, 252, 309
Bruix (1894), 60
Buenos Aires (1895), 46
Bulkeley, Capt. Peter, 432, 433
Bullivant nets, 58, 280, 283
Bustamante (1913), 283
Büyüktuğrul, Admiral Afif, 196–7

'C'-class submarines, 108, 108n, 226, 288
Caio Duilio (1919), 393–4, 396, 399, 401, 403, *406*, 407
California (1919), 432
Cambrian (1893), 230
Cambrian Salvor (tug), 267
Campioni, Admiral Inigo, 401
Campos, Rear Admiral Abel, 259, 260, 261
Canada (1913), 250, 252–5, 254, 258, *258*; see *Almirante Latorre*
Canarias (1931), 285. 287
Cândido Felisberto, Seaman 1st Class João 19, 145–7, *145*, 146, 147
Canet gun, 30
Cantieri Riuniti dell'Adriatico (C.R.D.A.), Trieste, 395, 397, 402
Cape Helles, 188; Battle of (1912), 174
Cape Matapan, 188; Battle of (1941), 402
Capitán Prat (1890), 38, 248, 252
Carlisle (1918), 403
Carlos V (1895), 278
Carnegie Steel Co., Pittsburgh, 297

Carney, Capt. Al, 430
Carney, Rear Admiral Robert B., 417, *417*
Carnot (1894), 54, 60
Carrier, SS, 288
Cartagena, 60, 270, *271, 272, 273,* 279, 289
Carvalho, Capt. José Carlos de, 146
Castellammare di Stabia, naval yard, 396
Cataluña (1900), 278, 279
Cavagnari, Admiral Domenico, 395, 396, 399
Cavallero, Admiral Ugo, 403
Cerberus, Operation ('Channel Dash') (1942), 382, *383,* 392
Cerberus, Western Port Bay, Vic., 244
Chacabuco (1898), *259*
Chantiers et Ateliers de St-Nazaire (Penhöet), 199
Chanzy (1894), 61
Chao Yung (1880), 24, 28
Charlemagne (1895), 56, 58, 60, 62
Charles Martel (1893), 54, 57, 59
Chatfield, Ernle, Admiral of the Fleet Lord, 309
Chatham, 311, 321
Chatham-class light cruisers, 224
Chen Hsi (1879), 24
Chen Pei (1879), 30
Chen Yuen (1882; later *Chin Yen*), 10, 12, 13, 15, 18, 20–37; design, 21; specifications, 21; protection, 21; armament, 21; propulsion, 21; organisation, 24–5; life aboard, 25–6
Chih Yuen (1886), 26, 28
Chikuma (1938), 354
Chilean navy (Armada de Chile), 12, 50, 247–67, *263*
Chilean Reefer, MV, 382
Chin Yen (1882; ex-*Chen Yuen*), 33–6
Ching Yuen (1886), 26, 28
Chokai (1931), 354
Chongqing Mutiny (1949), 18
Chosin Reservoir, Battle of (1950), 427
Ciliax, Admiral Otto, *375,* 376, 377, 382–3
Ciscar (1933), 288
Ciudad de Valencia (1930; auxiliary cruiser), 288
Cleopatra (1940), 403
Clyde, River, 99, 309, 404; Firth of, 219
Coles, Cowper, 114
Collar, Operation (1940)
Colorado-class battleships, 345
Colossus-class battleships, 21
Condé (1902), 71
Condottieri-class light cruisers, 394
Conner, Radioman Richard, 417, 422

Constitución (1903; later *Swiftsure*), 135, 247–8, 252
Conte di Cavour (1911), 393, 394, *394, 395,* 396, 399, 401
Conte di Savoia, SS, 397
Convoys: AS129 (1941), 179; JW55B (1943), 386, 387; M.41 (1941), 403; M.42 (1941), 403; M.43 (1942), 403; MW10 (1942), 403–4; WS19/Z (1942), 404; MW11 (1942), 404–5
Copenhagen; Naval Dockyard, *12,* 113, 114, 117, 118–19, *118, 119, 124;* Holmen naval base, *120,* 124, *124,* 125, 126, 127, 128
Coral Sea, Battle of the (1942), 228
Coronel, Battle of (1914), 234
Coundouriotis, Admiral Pavlos, 171–5, *175,* 176
County-class heavy cruisers, 245, 314
Courageous (1916), 240, 312, *312*
Courbet (1911), 271, 277, 394n
Crace, Lt J. G., 228
Cradock, Rear Admiral Christopher, 234
Creswell, Capt. W. R., 221, 224, 226
Crichton-Vulcan, Turku, 358–9
Crickette, Sir Raymond, *319*
Cumberlege, Capt. Claude, 241, 242
Cuniberti, Vittorio, 170
Cunningham, Andrew, Admiral of the Fleet Viscount, 403, 406, 407
Cunningham, Cdr John, *317*
Curtis turbines, 295
Custance, Admiral Sir Reginald, 10

Da Zara, Admiral Alberto, 404, 407, *407*
Dace (1943), 352
Dakar, Battle of (1940), 401
Damianos, Capt. Ioannis, 170, 171
Danish navy (Kongelige Danske Marine), 14, 113–28, *122, 126–7,* 291
Dannebrog (1880), *118,* 124
Dansk Riffel Syndikat, 117
Dante Alighieri (1910), 203, 204, 205, 207, 218, 278, 393, 394
Danubius, Fiume, 206
Dardanelles Campaign (1915–16), 56, 192–3, 193
Darley, Lt Cdr F. C., 239
Darter (1943), 352
David Brown & Sons, Huddersfield, 345
Davidson, John, Master Chief Boatswain's Mate, *16,* 430–1
de Courten, Raffaele, Admiral,

405–6, 406, 407
De Zeven Provinciën (1665), 157, 168
De Zeven Provinciën (1909; later *Soerabaia*), 10, 11, 13, 14–15, 153–69, 358; design, 155–6; specifications, 156; protection, 156; armament, *155,* 156; propulsion, *156;* construction, 156; organisation, 160–1, *160;* life aboard, *17,* 18, 161–4, *162, 163;* mutiny in (1933), 15, 18, 164–8, *165, 166;* sinking, 168–9, *169*
De Zeven Provinciën (1953), 169
De Zeven Provinciën (2002), 169
Deakin, Alfred, 221, 222, 224, 226, 230
Dédalo (1901), 284
Deiatelnyi (1907), 109
Delnyi (1907), 109
Démocratie (1904), 71, 100
Den Helder, *155,* 157, 159, 372
Denmark Strait, 331, 381; Battle of the (1941), 331–4, *332, 335*
Dennison, Capt. Robert L., 413, *413*
Desaix (1901), 63, 64
Descartes (1894), 68
Detroit (1922), *423*
Deutsche Werke Kiel AG, 376
Deutschland (1931), 376; *see Lützow*
Deutschland-class armoured ships (1928), 275, 292, 302–3, 374, 376, 394, 395
Deutschland-class battleships (1902), 103, 106
Devonport, 319, 320, 321; Division, 320, 330; HM Dockyard, 12, 139, 236–7, 257–9, 257, 260, 328–30
Dewey, Thomas E., 412
Diana (1899), 107
Dias, Arthur, 132, 135
Diderot (1909), 279
Dogger Bank, Battle of the (1915), 236, 320
Domecq García, Capt. Manuel, 41, 42
Dómine (1934), 288
Don Juan d'Austria (projected name), 207
Donald, Ft Cdr, 241, *241*
Dönitz, Grand Admiral Karl, 386, 387, 405
Doorman, Rear Admiral Karel, 168
Dousmanis, Capt. Sofoklis, 174, *174, 175*
Dover, 383
Dragen-class torpedo boats, *126–7*
Dreadnought (1906), 11, 50, 75, 99, 135–6, 138, 148, 154, 171, 203, 224, 248, 272, 274–6, 292, 295

Dresden (1907), 233, 235
Dreyer Table, 228, 250, 332
Dristigheten (1900), 291, 297
Droogdok Maatschappij Soerabaja, 158
Drottning Victoria (1917), frontispiece, *294, 295, 300,* 301–2, 306
Dufourq, Cdr Félix, 45–6, 46
Duguay-Trouin (1877), 145
Duke of York (1940), 387–8, *388, 389,* 390, *390,* 391
Dumaresq, Cdre John Saumarez, 241, 242
Dumaresq (instrument), 250
Dumesnil, Lt, 63, 64
Dundas, Mid. William, 332–3, *333,* 334
Dunkerque (1935), 329, 374, *329,* 394, 395
Durlacher guns, 361, 369
Dyrssen, Rear Admiral Wilhelm, 82, 85

'E'-class submarines, 108n, 123, *123,* 226
Eagle (1918; ex-*Santiago*, ex-*Almirante Cochrane*), 138, 249, 253, 253–5
Earle's Shipbuilding and Engineering Co., Hull, 248
Ebergard, Admiral Andrei, 191, 194
Edgar, Eng. Lt W. H. V., 240
Edinburgh, 99, 238
Edsall, Capt. Warner, 427–8
Ehrensvärd, Rear Admiral Gösta, 303–4
Eidsvold (1900), 10, 14, 19, 73–90, 293, 358; ; design, 75–6; specifications, 76; protection, 76; armament, 75, 76, 76–8; propulsion, 78; organisation, 78–9; life aboard, 79, 81–2; sinking, 90
Eikenboom, Capt. P., *165, 166,* 168
El Mercurio de Valparaíso, 259n
Electra (1934), 333
Electric Boat Co., Groton, Conn., 254
Eleonore Woermann, SS, 235
Elsass (1903), 105, 374
Elswick Ordnance Co., 275
Emden (1908), 158, 233, 234
Encounter (1902), 229, 232, 233
Épieu (1903), 62
Ericsson, John, 291, *291*
Erin (1913; ex-*Reşadieh*), 13, 186–8, 253
Erzherzog-class battleships, 203
Esmeralda (1896), 42, 248, 252
España (1912), 268, 276–8, 278, 279, 282–4, *284*
España (1913; ex-*Alfonso XIII*), 18, 285–89, 289; *see Alfonso XIII*

España-class battleships, 13, 271, 274–5, 277–8
Essen, Admiral N. O. von, 99, 102, 103, 104
Eugenio di Savoia (1935), *406*
Euryalus (1939), 403
Evertsen (1926), 166
Evstafi (1906), 191, 193
Exeter (1929), 263
Extremadura (1900), 270

Falkland Islands, 235; Battle of the (1914), 234, 376
Falster (1873), 123
Farfadet (1901), 66
Faulknor (1914), see *Almirante Riveros*
Ferrándiz y Niño, Cdre José, 270, 272, 273, 279
Ferrol, 18, 283, 287, 288, 289; naval district, 285; Naval Museum, 283, 284
Field, Admiral of the Fleet Sir Frederick, 318–19
Filander Co., 199
Finn, Lt Cdr Mike, 431, 432
Finnish navy (Merivoimat), 357–73
First Balkan War (1912–13), 172, 173–6, 176, 184–5, 186
First World War (1914–18), 13, 15, 79, 87–8, 88, 97, 99, 102–12, 113, 121–4, 149, 155, 158–9, 176–7, 183, 185, 186, 187–97, 207, 254, 278, 283, 298, 301–2, 321, 376, 377, 393; naval construction delayed by, 276–7, 294–5, 345
Fisher, Admiral of the Fleet Sir John, 13, 87, 222, 223, 224, 229, 235, 243, 270, 271, 272, 319
Fiume (1930), 402
Forbin (1895), 68
Forcella bracketing method, 397
Fore River Ship and Engine Building Co., Quincy, Mass., 138, 248
Forges et Chantiers de la Méditerranée, La Seyne, 91, 101, 174, *177, 178,* 272, 297; Le Havre, 58
Formidable (1885), 60
Foxhound (1934), 329
France (1912), 278, 394n
Francesco Caracciolo (1920), 344, 394, 396
Franklin (1943), 354
Fraser, Admiral Sir Bruce, 385, 386–90, *390*
Fratelli Orlando, Livorno, 42, 44, 171, *171*
French navy (Marine Nationale), 15, 53–72, 160, 185, 186, 271, 329, 393, 394
Friedrich-Wilhelms-Hafen (now Madang), 232, *232,* 233
Fuji (1896), 33

Fujian Fleet, 20, 21; Naval Academy, 16, 24
Furtado de Mendonça, Rear Admiral Raymundo de Mello, 140, 147
Fusō (1877), 26
Fusō (1914), 337, 339, 345

'G3' battlecruisers, 309
G132 (1906), 123
G134 (1906), 123
Galilée (1896), 62
Gallipoli, 173, 192, 194
Gambier Bay (1943), 354
Gangut-class battleships, 205, 306, 361
Garibaldi (1895; ex-*Giuseppe Garibaldi*), 10, 12, 13, 14, 38–52; specifications, 41; protection, 42; armament, 42, *42*, *44*; propulsion, 41–2
Garibaldi-class armoured cruisers, 38, 41–2, 43–5, 46–8, 52, 132, 247
Garm (salvage vessel), 128
Gaulois (1896), 58, 60, 61, 62
Gejser (1892), 123
Gelderland (1898), 157
General Brown (1865), 50
General Electric, Schenectady, N.Y., 412; turbines, 411
Genoa, 43–4, 47, 51, 60, 63, 399, *399*, *401*, 405; Scuola Superiore Navale, 396
Gensoul, Admiral Marcel, 329
Georg Thiele (1935), 90
Georgii Pobedonosets (1892), 191
Georgios Averof (1910), 10, 13, 15, 16, 18, 170–82; design, 170–1; specifications, 171; protection, 171; armament, 171, *172*; propulsion, 171
German navy: Kaiserliche Marine, 103–12, 114, 129, 183–8, 201, 223, 248, 302; Imperial Navy Office, 183; Navy League, 202; High Seas Fleet, 184, 204, 236, 238, 240, 271, 308, 407; 2nd Scouting Group, 184; Mediterranean Division, 185–97; Surrender of (1918), 240; Reichsmarine, 360, 374; Kriegsmarine, 15, 126, 303–4, 306, 328, 334, 374–92, 405
Gibraltar, 99, 100, 101, *101*, 235, 236, 270, 320, 329, 330, 331, 334, 400, 401, 402, 404, 409
Gihon turbines, 344
Gimeno, Amalio, 274
Giovanni delle Bande Nere (1930), 403
Giralda (1894), 270, 279, 282
Girardelli Co., 298
Giulio Cesare (1911), 278, 393, 394, 396, 399, 401, 403, 407
Giuseppe Garibaldi (1899), 42

Glenten (1933), 124
Gloire (1900), 68
Glorious (1916), 240, 380–1, *381*, 392
Gloucester (1909), 187, 188
Gloucester (1982), 433
Gneisenau (1906), 233
Gneisenau (1936), 89, 306, 328, 331, 374, 376, 379–83, *383*
Gödde, PO Wilhelm, 376, 381–90
Goeben (1911), 12, 15, 183–90; *184*, *185*, *189*, 278; *see Yavuz Sultan Selim*
Gorizia (1930), 403
Gorm (tug), 128
Göta (1889), 297
Göta Lejon (1945), 307
Göteborgs Nya Verkstads AB (Götaverken), 293, 294, 295
Gotenhafen (now Gdynia), 331, 367, 381, 383
Gothenburg, 82, 85, 86, 124, 291, 301, 303
Gotland (1933), 331
Grazhdanin, see *Tsesarevich*
Greco-Turkish War (1919–23), 177–8, 197
Grosser Kurfürst (1913), 108
Groziashchii (1890), 105
Guanabara Bay, 15, *144*, 145–7, *148*
Guangdong Fleet, 20
Gueydon (1899), 68
Gulf of Riga Campaign (1917), 107–8
Gulf War (1990–1), 416, 431–2, *431*
Gurugú, Mt., 284
Gustaf Adolf, Crown Prince, 302
Gustav V (1918), frontispiece, *294*, 295, *300*, 302, 306
Gustavo Sampaio (1893), 132

H-4 (1915), 260
H. J. Hansen, Odense, 128, *128*
Habsburg (1900), 203, 214
Hague (The), 164, 165; Convention (1907), 87
Halsey, Admiral William F., 354, 356, 417, *417*, 417–19, 420, *421*, 422, *423*
Hamidiye (1903), 190, 191, 192, 193, 196, 201
Hanko (Hangö), 102, 364, 367, 369, 370, 371, 372
Hansson, Per Albin, 306
Harald Haarfagre (1897), 74, 76, 79, 81, *84*, *85*, 86, 88
Haruna (1913), 353, 355
Harveyised steel, 56
Hashidate (1891), 30, 34
Hatsuse (1899), 75
Hatsuzakura (1945), 420
Haus, Admiral Anton, 186, 187, 207, 208, 209, 210, 213–16, *213*
Havmanden-class submarines, *126–7*

Hawthorn Leslie, Newcastle upon Tyne, 78
Hazemeyer (N.V. Hazemeijers Fabriek voor Signaalapparaten, Hengelo), 297, 362
Hazlett, Cdr E. E., 18, 210–11
Heermann (1943), 354
Heimdal (yacht), 79, 83
Heligoland Bight, Battle of the (1914), 320
Helle (1935), 181
Hellenic Navy, 15, 170–82, 186
Henrik Gerner (1927), *126–7*
Herbertshöhe (now Kokopo), 232
Herluf Trolle (1899), 114, 116, 121, *122*, 124
Hertog Hendrik (1902), 158
Hessen (1903), 374
Hindenburg (1915), 207, 240
Hindustan (1903), 240
Hintze, Capt. Fritz, 385, *385*, 386–7, 388, 388–9, 390
Hiraga Yuzuru, Constructor Vice Admiral, 337, *337*, 344
Hizen (1900), 234
Hoche (1886), 54
Hoffmann, Capt. Kurt-Caesar, *379*, 380, 382–3
Högsåra, 367
Hohenzollern (yacht), 185
Holland, Vice Admiral Lancelot E., 331–2, *331*
Holland-class protected cruisers, 154
Holland-class submarines, 254, 256
Hood (1848; ex-*Edgar*), 311–12
Hood (1889), 311
Hood (1918), 10, *10*, 14, *14*, 16, 245, 308–35; design, 308–9, *309*; construction, 309, *310*, *311*; specifications, 308; protection, 308–9, 326; armament, 308, *312*, *313*, *316*, *323*, 326, 330, *333*; fire control, 314; radar, 330, 331, 332, *333*; propulsion, 11, 308, 309; organisation, 314–6; Engineering Department, 316, *326*, 328; Marine detachment, 317, 318, 320, 326, 330; life aboard, *18*, 314–9; Invergordon Mutiny (1931), 18, 19, 320–1, *321*, 322, 326; Christmas mutiny (1940), 330; sinking, 15,332–3; inquiry into loss, 334
Hood, Rear Admiral Sir Horace, 309, 310
Horthy, Admiral Miklós, 215, 216, *216*, 216–17, 217
Hozven, Cdre Alberto, 259, 260, 261
Huáscar (1865), 252
Huascaran (1938), 381
Hugin (1910), 295

Humphrys, Tennant & Co., Deptford, 135
Hunyadi (projected name), 207
Hvalen (1930), 124
Hyatt (1928), 260
Hydra (1889), *173*, 174, *176*
Hydra-class barbette ships, *173*, *176*
Hyūga (1917), *343*, *345*, 355

'I'-class destroyers, *220*
I/38 ('Der Lange Hendrik' floating crane), *127*
Iachino, Admiral Angelo, 403–4, *404*–5
Ida, SS, 191
Idzumo (1899), 234
Iéna (1813), 53
Iéna (1898), 10, 15, 53–72; specifications, 56–7; protection, 56; armament, 56, 57–8; propulsion, 57, 58; construction, 58–9; life aboard, *17*, 18, 60–1, *61*; loss, 63–8, *63*
Iffland, D., 25
Iku-Turso (1931), 367
Ilha das Cobras, 147; Naval Shipyard, *148*, 149
Ilmarinen (1931), 15, 357, 358–9, 361, 364, 366–9, *368*, 373; sinking, 370, *370*
Im Thurn, Capt. John, 318–19
Imbros, Battle of (1918), 195
Imperator Aleksandr III (1901), 91
Imperator Pavel I (1907), 102, 104, *104*
Imperatritsa Ekaterina II (1914), 193, 193–4
Imperatritsa Mariya (1913), 193
Imperial (auxiliary cruiser), 252
Imperial Japanese Navy, 18, 20, 26, 27–36, 129, 132, 135, 243–4, 336–56
Imperial Russian Navy, 16, 17, 33, 91–112, 185, 190–4, 357, 359
Impero (1939), 402
Incomparable (1915 battle-cruiser project), 312
Indefatigable (1909), 187, 236, 238, 278
Indefatigable (tug), 60
Independence, Mo., 412, 428
Indianola (auxiliary), 108
Indomitable (1907), 187, 255, 278
Infanta María Teresa-class armoured cruisers, 273
Inflexible (1876), 21
Inflexible (1907), 187, 255, 278, 376
Ingenieurskantoor voor Scheepsbouw (I.v.S.), The Hague, 358, 359
Inoue Takeo, Chief Gunnery Officer, 352, 354
Institution of Naval Architects, 309

Intrepid (1943), 353
Invergordon Mutiny (1931), 15, 18, 259, 261, 320–1, *321*, 322, 326
Invincible (1907), 183, 224, 226,309, 376
Iowa (1942), 356, 410, 411, 417, 429, 431
Iowa-class battleships, 410, 427, 428–9, *429*
Iris II (1906), 240
Iron Duke (1912), 254, *314*, 318
Isaac Peral (1916), 270
Ise (1916), *343*, 355
Ise-class battleships, 336, 339, 344
Isitt, Air Vice Marshal L. M., 422
İskenderun (Alexandretta), 186, 207
Isonzo, SS, 401
Istanbul (Constantinople), 171, 172, 177, *179*, 185, 186, 188, 189, 197, 200, 200, 201, 213, 214, 424, 430
İstinye (Stenia), 191, 192, *192*, 194, *194*, 195, 196
Istrian peninsula, 203
Italia (1930; ex-*Littorio*), 405–8
Italian navy (Regia Marina), 15, 18, 42, 44, 171, 180, 185, 186, 205, 271, 286, 393–408
Italo-Turkish War (1911–12), 186, 208–9
Itō Sukeyuki, Admiral, 27–30
Itsukushima (1889), 34, 35
Iver Hvitfeldt (1886), *123*
Iwo Jima, Battle of (1945), 417
Izhorskii Works, St Petersburg, 91

J. Samuel White, Cowes, 253
Jaceguay, Baron of, Admiral Artur Silveira da Motta, *131*, 131–5, 132, 133, 134, 135
Jacob van Heemskerck-class armoured ships, 154
Jacobson, Alf R., 391
Jærens Rev, 87
Jaime I (1914), 268, *275*, 276, 277, *277*, 283, 285, *285*, 288, 289
Jamaica (1940), 387, 388
Janer Robinson, Lt Cdr Jaime, 279, 279, 284
Jauréguiberry (1893), *53*, 54, 59, 60, 62, 91
Java, 153, 154
Java (1921), 160, 166
Java Sea, Battle of the (1942), 168
Jean Bart (1911), 102, 278, 394n
Jeanne d'Arc (1930), 263
Jellicoe, Admiral of the Fleet Sir John, 236, 254, 308
Jerram, Vice Admiral Sir Martyn, 233

Jeune École, 39, 54, 132
Johannesson, Capt. Rolf, 385–6, *385*, 386, 387, 392
John Brown & Co., Clydebank, *220*, *222–3*, *225*, *226–8*, 227, 253, 273, 309, 310, *310*, *311*
John Ericsson (1865), 291
José Luis Díez (1928), 288
Juan Mari (fishing vessel), 288
Juel, Admiral Niels, 114
Jules Michelet (1905), 71
Júpiter (1935), 288, 289
Jutland, Battle of (1916), 204, 237, 238–9, 240, 254, 258, 309, 337, 338, 345, 393

K VII (1921), 166
K XI (1924), 166
Kaiser (1911), 203
Kaiserin Elizabeth (1890), 202
Kaiss, Capt. Lee, 413, 431, 432, 433
Kalinin Bay (1943), 354
Kamchatka, SS, 34
Kaneda Hidetarō, Vice Admiral, 341
Kanin, Admiral V. A., 104, 106
Karlskrona, 291, 301, 303, 304, 305, 306
Karmen, SS, 193
Kaštela, 210
Kasuga (1902; ex-*Bernardino Rivadavia*), 50
Kavadias, Vice Admiral Epameinondas, 179, 180
Kennedy, Rear Admiral Sherman S., 412
Kephalo Bay, 195
Kerambosquer, Rear Admiral Auguste, 58, 59
Kerr, Rear Admiral Mark, 176
Kerr, Capt. Ralph, 330, 332
Keyes, Admiral of the Fleet Sir Roger, 258–9, *317*, 320
Khrabryi (1895), 105
Kiel, 98, 100, 126, 128, 185, 192, 302, 367, *380*, 381, 383, 387; *see* Krupp, Germaniawerft, *and* Deutsche Werke Kiel AG
Kilkis (1904; ex-*Mississippi*), 176
King George V (1911), 249
King George V (1939), 334, 420
King George V-class battle-ships, 396
Kirishima (1913), *345*
Kirov (1936), 306, 367–9
Kirov-class cruisers, 361
Kısırkaya, 191
Kniaz Potëmkin Tavricheskii (1900; later *Panteleimon*), 18, 59, 98, 193
Kniaz Suvorov (1902), 34, 91
Knitsley, SS, 288
Kobe, 26, 33, 34
Kōbe Yūji, Rear Admiral, 352–4
Kockums Mekaniska Verkstads AB, Malmö, 293, 295

Kola Bay, 99
Kolberg (1908), 109
Kolchak, Vice Admiral Alexander, 194
Kone ja Silta, Helsinki, 358
Kongō (1912), 229, 336, 337, 339, 341, 353, 355
Kongō-class battlecruisers, 226, 249, 340
Kongsvinger, 75
König, Eng. Lt Cdr Otto, 19, 388
König (1913), 108, 109–11, *109*
Koning der Nederlanden (1874), 154
Koningin Regentes-class coast defence ships, 154, *154*
Koningin Wilhelmina der Nederlanden (1892), 155
Konstan, SS, 288
Kooronga, SS, 234
Korean War (1950–3), 413, 416, 426–8
Kotlin Is., 92
Kow-shing, SS, 27
Kozlu, 193
Kristiansand, 75, 78, 87; Marvika, 87
Kristiansund, 304
Kronprinz (1914), 108, 109–10
Kronprinz Erzherzog Rudolf (1883), 212
Kronshtadt, 92, 93, 98, *101*, 104, 107, 320, 357, 373
Kruger, Pres. Paul, 157
Krupp (Friedrich Krupp AG, Essen), 21, 156, 359, 360, 363, 373, 374; Germaniawerft, Kiel, 100–1, 359; cemented armour, 116, 138, 156, 204, 359, 397, 398
Kuang Chia (1887), 28
Kurama (1907), 35
Kure, 33; naval district, 26; Navy Yard, 336, 345, *345*, 348, 351, 352; Ordnance Division, 339, 340
Kurita Takeo, Vice Admiral, 352–5, 356
Kütahya (1906), 188
Kuwait, Invasion of (1990), 431

L. M. Ericcson, 298
La Argentina (1937), 265
La Nación (Buenos Aires), 138
La Pallice, 382
La Plata, 46
La Prensa (Buenos Aires), 46, 138
La Rochelle, 382
La Spezia, 44, 283, 399, 405, 406, 407, *407*
Lacroma (yacht), 208
Lamalgue (tug), 65
Lanciere (1907), 403
Lappohja, 364
Lappvik (now Lappohja), 108
Latorre, Admiral Juan José, 249, *249*

Latouche-Tréville (1892), 61, 70, 71
Laxen (1930), 124
Layton, Admiral Sir Geofffrey, 123
Le Bris, Admiral Pierre, 71
League of Nations, 88, 259, 285, 399
Leão, Admiral Joaquim Marques Baptista de, 145, 146, 147–8
Legion (1939), 403
Leipzig (1905), 233
Leipzig (1929), 374
Lemnos (1904; ex-*Idaho*), 176
Lemnos, Battle of (1913), 175–6
Leon (1911), 175
Léon Gambetta (1901), 100, 185
Leonardo da Vinci (1911), 278, 393
Leveson, Admiral Arthur, 241
Leyte Gulf, Battle of (1944), 352–5
Li Hung-chang, 19, 21, *21*, 23, 24, 25, 26, 27, 31
Liaoning (1988), 36
Libava, SS, 108
Libertad (1903; later *Triumph*), 135, 247, 248, 252
Libertad (1925), 288
Liberté (1905), 68
Liebhard, Eng. Cdr Erwin, 380, 381
Lifland, 104
Lin Tai-tseng, Capt., 24, 26–7, 30
Lindholmens Verkstad AB, Gothenburg, 293, 294, 358
Lindormen (1868), 114
Lion (1910), 102, 309, 319–20
Lion-class battlecruisers, 226
Littorio (1937; later *Italia*), 10, 15, 393–408; design, 395; construction, 397–9, *398*, *399*; specifications, 397; protection, 397; Pugliese underwater protection system, 396, 397, 398–9, *398*, 401; armament, 395–7, *396*; fire control, 397, 400, 402; radar, 397, 400, 402; propulsion, 399; organisa-tion, 399–400
Littorio-class battleships, 19, 286, 394, 395, *395*, 396, 399, 406, 407
Lizard (1911), 196
London; Naval Conference (1930), 394, 410; Naval Conference (1936), 410; Naval Treaty (1936), 410
London (1927), 318
Long Beach; Naval Shipyard, 429, 431; Naval Station, 433
Lord Hood (commissioned 1797), 311

Lord Nelson-class battleships, 272
Lorraine (1913), 394n
Lucia (1907), 259
Lutin (1903), 66
Lütjens, Admiral Günther, 331, 331–2, 334, 380, 381–2, 388
Lützow (1931; ex-*Deutschland*), 304, 306, 383, 385
Lyasse, Constructor, 58

M. Favre et Cie, Marseilles, 70
M28 (1915), 198
McGiffin, Lt Cdr Philo N., 24, 27–8, 28–29, *29*, *29*, 32–3
Mackey, Lt Bob, 420
McKenna, Reginald, 139, 223, 224, 229
Macedo Soares, José Eduardo de, 143, 147; *Política versus Marinha* of, 147
Mackensen class (1914 battle-cruiser project), 308
Macon (1944), *428*
Madang, SS, 233
Madsen, Copenhagen, 149, *149*, 362
Magdeburg (1911), 106
Magenta (1890), 54, 71
Mahan, Alfred Thayer, 39, 75, 83, 129–31
Maine (1889), 39, 68
Maine-class battleships, 409
Majestic-class battleships, 56
Makarov, Admiral S. O., 92
Mallina, SS, 234
Malta, 172, 177, 185, 187, 207, 270, 326, 330, 400, 401, 403–4, 405, 407
Manceron, Rear Admiral Henri-Louis, 62, 63, 63–4, 66, 69
Manila Bay, Battle of (1898), 268
Manu, SS, 288
Maranhão (?), 135
Marceau (1887), 54
Marechal Deodoro (1898), 132, 145
Marechal Floriano (1899), 132
Mariano Moreno (1903; later *Nisshin*), 48, 50
Marín college and proving ground, 279, 287
Marinha Portuguesa, 11, 129
Markomannia, SS, 158–9
Marquis, Vice Admiral René-Julien, 18, 56, 57, 59, 60–1, 62, 64, 66, 69, 70, 72
Marrel-type anchors, 56
Marryat, Frederick, 318–19
Marschall, Vice Admiral Wilhelm, 379, 380–1
Marseillaise (1900), 60
Marten Harpertszoon Tromp (1904), 154, *154*, 156
Maryland (1920), 432
MAS-15 (1916), 216, *217*
MAS-21 (c.1917), 216
mascots, 18, 301, *318–19*, 322

Masdea, Edoardo, 41
Masséna (1895), 54, 63, 65
Matchless (1941), 390
Mato Grosso (1909), 145
Matsushima (1890), 29–30, 34
Matsushima-class protected cruisers, 26
Matupi Harbour, 232
Maxim Gorky (1938), 306
Maxim-Nordenfeldt, 21, *25*, *32*, 42
Maya (1930), 352
Mechanical and Chemical Industry Corp., 201
Mecidiye (1903; later *Prut*), 173, 175, 192, 201
Melbourne (1912), 229, *230*, 232, 233, 234
Melilla, 269, 283, 284
Melsomvik, 75, 80, 83, 84, 85–6, 86
Méndez Núñez (1922), 283, *285*, 286
Merauke, 153
Merino, Admiral José Toribio, 12, 265
Mers El Kébir, Attack on (1940), 329, 330, 332
Mesudiye (1874), 174, 175
Metallicheskii Works, St Petersburg, 91, 95
Michel Henri, 67
Michigan (1908), 138
Midilli (1911; ex-*Breslau*), 176, 185, 187–95, *188*, *194*, *195*, 209, 213, 214
Midway, Battle of (1942), 351
Midway (1945), 16, 430
Miguel de Cervantes (1928), 288
Mikasa (1900), 267
Milne, Admiral Sir Berkeley, 187, 188, 189
Minas Geraes (1905 battleship project), 135
Minas Geraes (1908), 10, 12, 129–52; specifications, 137; protection, 137–8; arma-ment, 137, *140–2*, *149*, *152*; propulsion, 138; construc-tion, *137*, *139*, *139*; organi-sation, 140–4; Revolt of the Lash (1910), *15*, 15, 15–16, 18, 19, 144–8
Minas Geraes-class battleships (1906), 137–9, 248, 249
Ministro Zenteno (1896), *259*
Mississippi (1842), *422*
Missouri (1841), 409
Missouri (1863), 409
Missouri (1901), 409–10, 412
Missouri (1944), 10, 13, 14, 16, 201, 409–33; design, 410; construction, 19, 411, *414*, *415*; specifications, 410; protection, 411; arma-ment, *409*, 410–11, *427*, 429, *429*, *431*; fire control, 411, *416*, 429; radar, 411; propulsion, 411, *411*; organisation, 414–16; life aboard, 18, 415; Marine

detachment, 415, *426*, 427; Stranding (1950), 424–5, *424*

Mitre, Pres. Bartolomé, 49

Mitscher, Vice Admiral Marc, 352

Mjølner (tug), 128

Mogador (1937), 329

Moltke (1910), 183–4, 187

Monarch-class battleships, 203

Monis, Ernest, 66–7, *67–8*, 70

Monitor (1862), 291

Montana class (1940 battleship project), 411

Montcalm (1900), 59, 232, *232*, 233

Montecuccoli, Admiral Count Rudolf, 13, 202, 203, 204, 205, 206, 207

Montt, Vice Admiral Jorge, 50, 247, 248, *248*

Moonsund, Battle of the (1917), 108–12

Moreno (1911), 51, 138

Morzh (1913), 193

Moscow Electric Company, 91

Moskvitianin (1905), 111

Mountbatten, Lt Lord Louis, 346–7

Muavenet-i Milliye (1909), 195

Munin (1911), 295

Murex, SS, 233

Murmansk, 99, 386

Muroran steelworks, 417, *418*

Murray, Capt. Stuart, 420, 421, 423

Musashi (1940), 352, 353, 354, 417

Musel (fishing vessel), 288

Mutsu (1920), 336, 340, *343*, 344, 345, 346–7, 347, 348, *349*, 350, 351

Nagato (1919), 10, 13, 336–56; design, 336–8; construction, 345; specifications, 338; protection, 338–9, 348; armament, 339–41, 348; fire control, 341–3; radar, 343, 352; propulsion, 343–5, 348; organisation, 347, 349; life aboard, 347–50, *349*, *350*; at the Battle of Leyte Gulf (1944), 352–5, *353*

Nagato-class battleships, 336, 337, 338, 345

Naman Bey, Capt. Ramiz, 174, 175

Naniwa (1885), 34

Nanyang Fleet, 20, 21

Narciso Monturiol (1917), *270*

Narvik, Battles of (1940), 89–90, 385

Nascimento, Manuel Gregório do, 145, *145*

Nassau (1908), 105–6, 204, 207

NATO, *200*, 201

Nautilus (sail training ship), 283

Nâzım Paşa, 175

Nederlandsche fabriek van Werktuigen en Spoorwegmaterieel, Amsterdam, 156

Nederlandsche Scheepsbouw Maatschappij, Amsterdam, 159

Nelson (1925), 302, 324, 328, 345, 402

Nelson-class battleships, 395

Neptune (1887), 54

Neptune (1933), 326

Netherlands navy (Koninklijke Marine), 15, 17, 153–69, 185

Neva, River, 92

Nevada (1914), 432

New Admiralty shipyard, St Petersburg, 91

New Jersey (1942), 356, 410, 411, 429, 431

New Orleans (1933), *302*

New South Wales, 223

New York-class battleships, 249

New York Herald, 139

New York Navy Yard, Brooklyn, 19, *144*, 149, 406, 409, 411, 412, *412*, 414, 415

New York Shipbuilding Co., Camden, N.J., 138, 248

New Zealand (1911), 102, 226, 236, 237, *237*, 241

Newcastle (1909), 234

Newport News Shipping and Dry Dock Co., 409

Nicholson, Capt. William C. M., 253, 254

Nidaros (1914; later *Gorgon*), 87

Niels Juel (1918), 124

Nieto Antúnez, Lt Cdr Pedro, 284, 287

Nikopolskii-Mariupolskii Armour Works, 91

Nilüfer (1890), 190, 191

Nimitz, Fleet Admiral Chester W., *390*, 420, 421, 422, 423

Niobe (1898; ex-*Gelderland*), 372

Niord (1898), 297

Nishimura Shōji, Vice Admiral, 352, 354

Nisshin (1903; ex-*Mariano Moreno*), 50

Njegovan, Admiral Maximilian, 215, 216

Noord Brabant (1899), 162

Norfolk (1928), 331, 332, 387

Norfolk, Va., Naval Shipyard, 415, 424–6

Norge (1900), 75, 76, 79, 81, *84*, *85*, 86, 88, 89, *90*, 293

Norge-class battleships, 75–6

Noronha, Admiral Julio César de, 135, 136

Norrköping, 303, 304

North, Cdr Bob, 428

North Cape, Battle of (1943), 19, *376*, 386–90, 392

North Carolina (1940), 410

North Carolina-class battleships, 410

Northeastern Aegean Islands, 176

Norwegian navy (Kongelige Norske Marine), 73–90, 391

Noshiro (1942), 355

Novara (1913), 215

Novik (1911), 105

NRK (Norsk rikskringkasting), 391

Nuestra Señora del Carmen, SS, 288

Nueva España (1889), 279

Nueve de Julio (1892), 38, 48

Numune-i Hamiyet (1909), 193, 195

Nürnberg (1906), 232, 233

Nürnberg (1934), 374, *378*

Nusa (auxiliary), 233

'O'-class submarines, 257, 259n

O'Connor, V. C. Scott, 312, 313

O'Conor, Capt. Rory, 319, 322–6, *322*

O'Higgins (1897), 42, 248, 259, 260, 263

Obukhovskii Works, St Petersburg, 91, 109

Oden (1896), 291, 297

Odero (Odero-Terni-Orlando – O.T.O.), Livorno, 171, 396

Odessa, 98, 177, 191, 192

Odin (1872), *118*, *119*

Oerlikon, 88, 200–1

Okinawa, Battle of (1945), 412, 417

Oklahoma (1914), 432

Oktyabrskaya Revolutsiya (1911; ex-*Gangut*), 306

Oleg (1903), *101*

Olfert Fischer (1903), *12*, 114, 116, 117, *119*, 121, 124

Oliva, Admiral Romeo, 406, 407

Orël (1902), 97

Orion-class battleships, 249

Orlogsværftet, Copenhagen, 12

Oscar II (1905), 291, 295, 306

Ösel Is. (now Saaremaa), 108, 370

Otranto, Strait of, Battle of the (1917), 215

Ottoman navy (Osmanlı Donanması), 12, 15, 170, 173–6, 186, 188–97, 201

Ozawa Jisaburō, Vice Admiral, 352, 354

Pacific War (1941–5), 35, 340, 343, 351–6, 416–22

Packer, Mid. Herbert A., 229, 230, 231, 233–4, 235

Pailhès, Capt., 59

Pakenham, Vice Admiral William, 236, 241

Pallada (1906), 103–4

Palmers Shipbuilding and Iron Co., Jarrow, 272, 273

Pamiat Azova (1888), 98

Pamiat Merkuria (1880), 192, 193

Panama Canal, 159, 234, 259, 283, 410, 416–17, 423, 429, 430

Panteleimon, see Kniaz Potëmkin Tavricheskii

Pará (1908), 145

Paraíba (1908), 145, 146

Paris (1912), 278, 284, 394n

Parramatta (1910), 229, 232, 233

Parsons turbines, 183, 204, 228, 252, 257, 276

Patey, Vice Admiral George E., 228, 229, 230, 231–6, *233*

Patria (1893), 48

Patrie (1903), 64, 71

PC 1400X glider bomb, 406

Pearl Harbor, Attack on (1941), 168, 265, 351, 425, 427, 432, 433

Peder Skram (1864), *114*

Peder Skram (1908; later *Adler*), 10, 14, 113–28, 358; design, 114–15, 117; construction, 12, 114; specifications, 114–15; protection, 116; armament, 114–5, 116–17, *115*, *116*; propulsion, 117, *117*; organisation, 117–21, *121*

Peiyang Fleet, 13, 16, 18, 19, 20–37, 129

Pelayo (1887), 272, 278

Penhoët boilers, 295

Pennsylvania (1915), 218

Pernambuco (1910), 135

Peruvian navy, 247, 256, 258

Petrograd, *see St Petersburg*

Petropavlovsk (1894), 92

Petropavlovsk (1911), 306

Peyk-i Şevket (1906), 190, 191

Philippine Sea, Battle of the (1944), 343, 352

Philomel (1890), 232

Piauí (1910), 145

Piet Hein (1927), 166

Ping Yuen (1889), 24

Piraeus, 61, 171, *178*, 179, *181*, 185

Pisa (1907), 171

Pisa-class armoured cruisers, 170

Placencia de las Armas, 276

Plymouth, 100, 236, 258, 320

Pola (Pula), 185, 186, 187, 203, 206, 207, 208, 209, 213, 214, 215, 216, 217–18, *218*, 393

Pola (1931), 402

Polperro measured mile, 228, 257

Polyphème, 71

Pontoporos, 158–9

Popper, Siegfried, 203–4, 216

Poros, 181

Port Arthur (Lüshunkou), 23, 27, 28, 30, 32, 33, 34, 35, 91, 92

Porto Corsini, 215

Portsmouth, 99, 100, 101, 227, 228, 229, 240, *315*, 320, 321, *322*, *324–5*, 326, 328, 426; HM Dockyard, 135, 171, *172*, 321

Poseidón (salvage vessel), 289

Posen (1908), 105–6

Potëmkin, see Kniaz Potëmkin Tavricheskii

Pothuau (1895), 61, 69

Premuda Is., 216

Presidente Sarmiento (1897), 48, 48, 52

Prince of Wales (1939), 331, 331–2, *332*, 334

Princesa de Asturias (1896), 270

Princess Royal (1911), 102

Prins Hendrik der Nederlanden (1866), 154

Prinz Eugen (1912), 206, 213, 214, 216, 278

Prinz Eugen (1938), 306, 331–2, 382, *383*

Provence (1913), 329, 394n

Prut (1879), 191

Psara (1890), *173*, 174

Psyche (1898), 232

Pueyrredón (1897; ex-*Cristóbal Colón*), 44, 45, *45*, 46, 50, *50*, 51

Puget Sound Naval Shipyard, Bremerton, 429, 433

Pugliese, Gen. Umberto, 19, *395*, *395*, 396, *396*, 398; underwater protection system, 396, 397, 398–9, *398*, 401

Punta Stilo (Calabria), Battle of (1940), 399

Putilovskii Works, St Petersburg, 91, 106

Pyotr Velikiy, SS, 222–3

Pyramus (1897), 232

Queen Elizabeth-class battleships, 249, 257, 308, 309, 339, 344

Queen Mary (1912), 102

'R'-class submarines, 256–7

Rabeur-Paschwitz, Vice Admiral Hubert von, 194, 195, 197

Radcliffe, Capt. Stephen H., 228, 235, 237

Radetzky (1909), 205, 207, 214–15

Radetzky-class battleships, 203, 214, 216

Raeder, Grössadmiral Erich, 374, 382

Raglan (1915), 199

Raleigh (1924), 12

Rapière (1901), 62

Rawalpindi (1925), 328, 379

Reed, Sir Edward, 248

Regina Elena-class battleships, 170–1, 272

Regina Margherita (1901), 396

Reina Regente (1887), 281

Reina Victoria Eugenia (1912 battleship project), 274

Reina Victoria Eugenia (1920), 283
Renown (1916), 89, *312*, 314, 324, 330, 346, 380
Renown-class battlecruisers, 312
República (1892), 132, 145
Repulse (1916), 240, 254n, 256, 314, 320
Reşadieh (1913), *see* Erin
Reverdit, Cdr, 66
Rex, SS, 397
Rezā Shāh Pahlavi, 200
Rheinland (1908), 302
Rheinmetall AG, Düsseldorf, 288
Rheinübung, Operation (1941), 331, 334
Riachuelo (1883), 132
Richelieu (1939), 406
Rigauld de Genouilly (1932), 329
Rikhter, Capt. O. O., *104*
Rio de Janeiro (1905 battleship project), 135
Rio de Janeiro (1913; later *Sultan Osman-i Evvel*), *see* Agincourt
Rio Grande do Norte (1909), 145
Rio Grande do Sul (1909), 145, 146
Riurik (1906), 99, 101, 102, 103
Rivadavia (1911), 51, 138
Rivadavia-class battleships, 50, 248, 249, 257
River-class destroyers, *230*
River-class frigates, 265
Ro gō Kampon boilers, 343
Robert Napier & Sons, Glasgow, 12, 114
Rodney (1925), 302, 321, 328, 334, 345
Rolf Krake (1863), 12, 114, *114*
Roma (1907), 63
Roma (1940), 405, 406, *406*
Rossetti, Raffaele, 217–18
Rosyth, 237, 240, 254, 302, *312*, 320; HM Dockyard, 236, 254, 309, 330
Royal Australian Navy, 17, 219–46
Royal Canadian Navy, 265
Royal Navy, 10, 13, 16, 17, 21, 23, 24, 79, 87, 129, 160, 185, 219, 249, 250, 252, 257, 288, 308–35, 348, 366, 377, 382, 383; Battle Cruiser Fleet, 235, 236; Battle Cruiser Force, 240, 241; Atlantic Fleet, 18, 313, 320; Home Fleet, 89, 102, 320, 328, 385; Mediterranean Fleet, 185, 200, 209, 317, 320, 326, 400, 403, 404, 406; 1st Battle Squadron, 254; 2nd BS, 228, 236; 4th BS, 254; 1st Battle-Cruiser Squadron, 102; 1st BCS, 240;

2nd BCS, 235, 236, 240; 3rd BCS, 235
Royal Oak (1914), 328
Royal Sovereign-class battleships (1889), 56
Royal Sovereign-class battleships (1913), 254, 257
Rozhestvenskii, Admiral Zinovy, 34, 91, 92, 100, 102, 154
Rumenius, Ensign John, 297, 298, 307
Russarö, 367
Russian Steam Navigation Co., *222–3*
Russo-Japanese War (1904–5), 13, 34–5, 36, 50, 70, 92, 98, 154, 292, 336
Russo-Turkish War (1877–8), 290
Ryujo (1931), *351*

S.A. Cantiere Navale Santa Maria, Genoa, 150
S61 (1916), 111
S64 (1916), 111
S144 (?; German destroyer), 105
Saale, River, 53
Saalwächter, General Admiral Alfred, 382
Sachsen (1877), 21
Saikyo Maru, 28, 32
Saint Louis (1896), 60, 62, 69
Salamis Arsenal, 176, 178, 179, 181; Bay, 179
Salvia (1940), 179
Samsun (1907), 191, 195
San Francisco, 159, 313, 413, 417, 429, 430, *430*, 431, 433; City Hall, 413
San Giorgio (1908), 51
San Marco (1908), 51
San Martín (1896; ex-*Varese* (i)), 44, *44*, 45, *45*, 46, 47, 47, 49, 50, 51
Sankt Georg (1903), 214
Santa Catarina (1909), 145
Santiago, Battle of (1898), 268
São Paulo (1905 battleship project), 135
São Paulo (1909), 15, *15*, 15–16, 19, 129, 131, *133*, 137, 138, 139, 143, *144*, 145–7, 149, 149–50, 150
Sapinero, SS, 159
Scapa Flow, 236, 240, 253, 254, 302, *327*, 328, *330*, 331, 380, 382, 391, *391*; Hoxa Boom, 331
Scharnhorst (1906), 233, 234, 376
Scharnhorst (1936), 10, 13, 15, 19, *19*, 89, 328, 331, 374–92; design, 374; specifications, 374; protection, 374; armament, 374; fire control, 374, *381*; radar, 374, *375*, 380, 387; propulsion, 374–5, *375*; organisation, 377–9; life aboard, 384

Scharnhorst-class battleships, 374, 394
Scheer, Admiral Reinhard, 239
Schneerson, Rabbi Menachem Mendel, 19
Schneider et Cie, Le Creusot, 272
Schulz Thornycroft boilers, 183
Scirocco (1934), 403
Scorpion (1942), 388, 390, 391
Scott, Admiral Sir Percy, 279
Sealion (1943), 355
Second Balkan War (1913), 176, 185
Second World War (1939–45), 10, 11, 15, 19, 88–90, 124–7, 150, 168, 350–9, 179–80, 200–1, 263–5, 290, 303–6, 307, 315, 328–35, 350–6, 367–72, 379–92, 400–7, 416–22, 432, *432*, 433
Sendai-class light cruisers, *345*
Serrano-class destroyers, 265
Sevastopol, 177, 191, 192, 196
Sevastopol-class battleships, 104
Sheffield (1936), 318, 387
Shigemitsu, Mamoru, 420, *421*
Shropshire (1928), *315*
Siamese navy, 11, 358
Sibuyan Sea, Battle of the (1944), *353*
Siegfried-class coast defence ships, 114
Siemens & Halske AG, 298
Silnyi (1905), 110
Simaloer Is., 158
Simon's Town, 229
Singapore, 158, 159, 168, 244, 352, 334
Sino-French War (1884–5), 21, 29
Sino-Japanese War, First (1894–5), 11, 21, 25, 27–32, 33, 35, 36, 44, 114, 133
Sino-Japanese War, Second (1931–45), 35, 350
Sir William Arrol & Co., *222–3*
Sirte, Second Battle of (1941), 403–4
Skagerrak, 121, 124, 236, 240, 303, 304
Skjold (1896), *119*, 124
Škoda Works, Pilsen (Plzeň), *203*, *204*, 205, 273, 275, 276
Slava (1903), 10, 13, 14, 15, 16, 18, 91–112; ; design, 91; specifications, 91; protection, 11, 91; armament, 91, *93*; propulsion, 91; construction, 91–2, *92*; organisation, 93–5, *95*; life aboard, 95–7, *96*, *97*; sinking, 110–12, *110–12*
Sociedad Española de Construcción Naval (SECN), Ferrol, 273, 276, *277*, 278, 285, *288*;

Cartagena, 285
Société de Construction des Batignolles, Nantes, 57
Soerabaia (1909; ex-*De Zeven Provinciën*), 168–9
Somerville, Vice Admiral Sir James, 329, 330
Souchon, Rear Admiral Wilhelm, 185–94, *186*, 195, 209, 213
Søulven (1880), 123
South Carolina-class battleships, 275
South Dakota-class battleships, 410
Southampton (1912), 220
Southsea, 328
Southwold (1941), 403
Soviet navy, 306, 320, 367, 372–3
Spanish navy (Armada Española), 185, 268–89
Spanish-American War (1898), 268, 272, 282
Sparre, Vice Admiral Christian, 83–4, 85, 86
Spearfish (1936), 304, 328
Spee, Vizeadmiral Maximilian Graf von, 15, 231, 232, 233, 234, 240, 246, 376
Sperry Corp., Long Island, N.Y., 149
Spetsai (1889), *173*, 174
Spithead, Diamond Jubilee Review (1897), 295; Coronation Review (1911), 87, 171; Silver Jubilee Review (1935), *312*, *314*, 323, 324; Coronation Review (1937), *178*, 179, 302, 326, 367
Sri Ayudhya-class coast defence ships, 358
St. Lo (1943), 354
St Petersburg (later Petrograd, Leningrad), 98, 103, 104, 107, 191, 306, 357, 370
St Vincent (1908), 139, 229
St Vincent-class battleships, 274, 275
Stabilimento Tecnico Triestino, *203*, *204*, 205, *205*, 358; San Marco Yard, 204, 205, 206; Sant'Andrea Works, 204
Stockholm, 75, 124, 295, 301, *302*, 303, 304, 305, 367
Stord (1943), 388
Strasbourg (1936), 329, 394
Strassburg (1911), 109
Suez Canal, 157, 159, 180, 242, 430
Suffolk (1926), 331
Suffren (1899), 60, 63, *63*, 64, 65, 70, 71–2
Sultan Osman-i Evvel (1913), *see* Agincourt
Sumatra (1920), 160
Sumatra, SS, 232
Suomen Joutsen (1902), 358
Surabaya, 154, 157, 158, *158*, 164–5, 165, 168, 169, *169*;

Loka Jaya Çrana Navy Museum, 169
Surcouf (1889), 60
Surigao Strait, Battle of the (1944), 354
Suzuya (1934), 354
Svärdfisken (1940), 304
Svea (1885), 290, 291
Sverige (1915), frontispiece, 10, 13, 15, 156, 290–307, 358; design, 292, *293*; construction, 11, 293–5; specifications, 295; protection, 295; armament, 295–8, *295*, *296*, 297, 299, *300*, *301*; fire control, 297; radar, 297, *304*; propulsion, 294, 295; organisation, 299–300; life aboard, 300–1, *300*, *301*
Sverige-class armoured ships, frontispiece, 13, 290, 291, 292, 295, 296, 302, 307
Svinin, Capt. V. A., 106
Swedish navy (Svenska marinen), 15, 82–6, 290–307
Swiftsure (1903; ex-*Constitución*), 135, 248, 252
Swiftsure-class battleships, 247
Sydney, 229, 230, *230*, 231, 233, 243, *245*, 246, 313
Sydney (1912), 229, 232, 233, 234, 241
Sydney (1934), 238
Szent István (1914), *204*, 206, 207, 216, *217*, 218, 393

T52 (?; German minesweeper), 105
Takao (1930), 352
Talcahuano, 252, 255, 256, 258, 260, 261, 263, 265, 266–7
Talili Bay, 232
Tamandaré (1890), 132
Tamoyo (1932), 132
Tapperheten (1901), 306
Taranto, 399, *402*, 404, *404*, 405, *405*, 406, 407; Raid on (1940), 330, 396, 401–2
Tarvisio, SS, 399
Task Forces: TF17, 228; TF38, *352*, *353*, 417–19, 422, *423*; TF58, 356
Task Groups: TG38.4, *418*; TG40.1, 428; TG58.2, 417
Task Unit: TU77.4.3, 354
Taşoz (1907), 191
Taxiarchis (tug), 179
Tegetthoff, Admiral Wilhelm von, 114, 203, 207
Tegetthoff (1912), 205, 207, 208, 213, 214, 216, 278
Tegetthoff-class battleships, *203*, 207, *217*
Telefunken Co., 78
Tennessee (1919), 432
Tennyson d'Eyncourt, Sir Eustace, 135, 137, 249, 308, 309, 312
Terror (1896), 283

Thetis (1890), 240
Thetis (1900), 105
Thomson, Gaston, 67, 68, *69*
Thor (1898), 297
Thorkelsen, Cdr Hagbart, 88–9
Thornycroft, Woolston, 149,
    257, 259n
Thyssen Works, Duisberg, 156
Tianjin, 23; Naval Academy,
    29
Tierra del Fuego, *40–1*
Tiger (1913), 320
Tigress (1911), 197
Timbira (1896), 132
Ting Ju-chang, Admiral, 23,
    24, 26, 27, 28, 30–33
Ting Yuen (1881), *20*, 21,
    22–3, 23, 24, *24*, 25, 26,
    26, 27, *27*, 28, 29, 33, 37
Tipperary (1915), 254
Tiradentes (1892), 132
Tirpitz, Grand Admiral Alfred
    von, 206, 207
Tirpitz (1939), *379*, 383, 384,
    385, 386
Tōgō Heihachirō, Admiral, 26,
    34, 84
Tokyo; Harbour, 36; Bay, 267,
    347, 350, *355*, 356, 412,
    420–3, *420–3*
Tomkinson, Vice Admiral
    Wilfred, *317*, 319, 320
Tongji, 31
Tordenskjold, Vice Admiral
    Peter, 79, 114
Tordenskjold (1880), *118*
Tordenskjold (1897), 75, 79,
    81, *85*, *86*, 87, 88
Touchard, Admiral Charles, 63,
    67, 69
Toulon, *54–5*, 59, 60, 63–70,
    72, 99, 271, 326, 329
Tovey, Admiral Sir John, 331
Town-class light cruisers
    (1908–11), 224, *230*
Toyota Soemu, Admiral, 354
Travailleur (tug), 60, 66
Tre Kronor (1944), 307
Trento (1927), 404
Trieste, 185, 187, *202*, 206,
    207, 208, *209*
Triumph (1903; ex-*Libertad*),
    135, 248, 252
Tromp-class armoured ships,
    154
Trondheim, 75, 83, 87, 304,
    380, 381, 386
Troubridge, Rear Admiral
    Ernest, 187–8

Truk Lagoon, 351–2
Trukhachev, Capt. P. L., 105
Tsesarevich (1901; later
    Grazhdanin), 34, 91, 98,
    100, 101, *101*, 102, 104,
    108, 109–12
Tsi Yuen (1883), 23, 28
Tsingtao (Qingdao), 34, 36,
    224, *352*
Tsukuba-class armoured
    cruisers, 344
Tsushima, Battle of (1905), 34,
    84, 91, 92, 97, 98, 136, 154
Tumleren (1911), 123
Tupy (1896), 132
Turbinia (1894), 295
Turgut Reis (1891; ex-
    Weissenburg), 174, 175,
    186, *190*, 195, 199
Turkish navy (Türk Deniz
    Kuvvetleri), 15, 178, 196,
    197–201
Turkmenets Stavropolskii
    (1905), 110, 111
Turku, 367, 369, 370, 371,
    372; Pansio naval base, 372

U-4 (1908; K.u.K.), 42
U26 (1913), 104
U523 (1942), 383
Ugaki Matome, Vice Admiral,
    351, 352
Ulm (1937), 386
Umbra (1941), 404
United States Navy, 14, 16–17,
    17, 18, 129, 132, 160, 185,
    201, 215, 249, 265, 268,
    339, 409–33
Upright (1940), 403
Urge (1940), 403

V74 (1915), 111
V99 (1915), 105
V100 (1915), 105
Vaasa, 367
Väinämöinen (1930; later
    Vyborg), 10, 15, 357–73;
    design, 358–9, 359–60;
    construction, 11, 359; speci-
    fications, 359; protection,
    360–1; armament, 359, *360*,
    361–2, *361*, *362*, *363*; fire
    control, 362; propulsion,
    359, 363–4; organisation,
    364–5; life aboard, 365–6,
    365, *366*
Valiant (1914), 302, 321, 407
Valkyrjen (1896), 79, 83, 86,
    87

Valletta, Grand Harbour, 326,
    403
Valparaíso, 235, 256, 259,
    260, 261, 263, 265, 266,
    265
Van Gaver, Cdr Amédée Maire
    Joseph, 63, 68, 69, 69–70
Vasco da Gama (1876), 11
Vedel, Vice Admiral A. H.,
    125, 126
Veinticinco de Mayo (1890),
    38, 48
Veinticinco de Mayo-class
    cruisers, 265
Velasco (1923), 287, 288, 289
Venice, 185, 196, 203
Vérité (1907), 100
Vesikko (1932), 358
Vetehinen-class submarines,
    359
Vian, Admiral Sir Philip, 241,
    403, 404
Vickers (Vickers, Sons and
    Maxim), Barrow-in-Furness,
    99, 106, 135, 138, 186,
    228, 248, 249, 253, 273,
    275, 276, 286, *286*, 287,
    309, 336, *337*, 338, 339,
    340, 341, 361, 362; River
    Don Works, Sheffield, 99;
    Vickers-Terni, 396
Vickers-Armstrongs, Barrow-
    in-Furness, 257, 259n, 265,
    266
Vickers clock, 250
Victoria and Albert (1899),
    314
Victory (1765), 308
Vindictive (1897), 240
Vineta (1897), 185
Virginia (1862), 291
Viribus Unitis (1911), 10, 13,
    18, 202–18, 277, 278, 393;
    design, 203–4; construction,
    204–5; specifications, 204;
    protection, 204; armament,
    203, 204, *204*; propulsion,
    204; organisation, 210–1;
    life aboard, 212; sinking,
    217–18
Visby-class stealth corvettes,
    307
Vitgeft, Admiral Wilgelm, 34
Vittorio Emanuele (1904), 396
Vittorio Veneto (1937), *393*,
    395, 397, 399, 401, 402,
    403, 405, 407, *408*
VMV 1 (1931), 370
VMV 14 (1935), 370

VMV 15 (1935), 370
VMV 16 (1935), 370
VMV patrol boats, 369
Von der Tann (1909), 183
Voulgaris, Rear Admiral
    Petros, 180
Vuković, Rear Admiral Janko,
    217, 218
Vulcan AG, Hamburg, 176
Vulcan/Phalanx system, 429,
    429
Vyborg (1930; ex-
    Väinämöinen), 372–4

Wagner boilers, 376
Wake-Walker, Rear Admiral W.
    F., 331
Walker, Rear Admiral Harold
    T. C., 334
Wangenheim, Baron Hans von,
    187, 188, 190
Ward Leonard control, 363
Warrego (1911), 229, 232, 233
Warrior (1860), 311, 314
Warspite (1913), 16, 407
Wasa (1901), 291
Washington Naval Conference
    (1921–2), 244, 345–6;
    Naval Treaty (1922), 11, *11*,
    244, 245, 257, 309, 345–6,
    347, 348, 394, 398, 410
Weihai (Weihaiwei), 20, 23, 30,
    32, 33, 37; Naval Academy,
    29
Wemyss, Admiral of the Fleet
    Sir Rosslyn, 241
Wenck, Vice Admiral H. L. E.,
    123, 124
Weserübung, Operation
    (1940), 80, 89–90, 303–4,
    305, 380, *380*
West Virginia (1921), 410, 432
Westfalen (1908), 302
Westinghouse Co., Pittsburgh,
    338, 345
Weymouth (1910), 188
Whitehead, Fiume, 204
Wien, SS, 218
Wilhelm Heidkamp (1938), 90
Wilhelmshaven, *184*, 187, *189*,
    192, 239, 376, 378, 379,
    380, 383, 392;
    Reichsmarinewerft (later
    Kriegsmarinewerft), 374,
    376, *376*, *377*
Willoch, Capt. Odd Isaachsen,
    88, 89, 90
Winter War (1939–40), 89,
    303, 367–9

Wirta, Cdr A., 364, 366, 367
Wisconsin (1943), 417, 433
Wismann, Engineer Emil, 125,
    125
Wolf-class destroyers, *157*

Yalu River, Battle of the
    (1894), 21, 24, 27, 27–30,
    28, 29, 33, 34, 35, 129, 291
Yamamoto Isoroku, Admiral,
    349, 351, *351*
Yamamoto Kaizō, Constructor
    Capt., 337, 337, 338
Yamato (1940), 335, 345, 346,
    351, 354, 355, 417
Yamato-class battleships, 341
Yang Wei (1881), 28
Yarmouth (1911), 159
Yarra (1910), 229, 232
Yarrow boilers, 78, 156, 204,
    252, 276, 295, 399
Yashima (1896), 33
Yashiro Rokurō, Admiral, 336,
    337
Yavuz (1985), 201
Yavuz Sultan Selim (1911; ex-
    Goeben, later *Yavuz*), 10,
    12, 15, 18, 176, 178,
    183–201, 209, 213, 214;
    design, 183; specifications,
    183; protection, 183; arma-
    ment, 183; propulsion,
    183–4; life aboard, 196
Yellow Sea, Battle of the
    (1904), 34
Yermak (1898), 102
Yokosuka, 26, 35, 346, 347,
    355, 356, 420; naval
    district, 33
Yokosuka Navy Yard, 33, 56,
    337, 345; Ordnance
    Division, 340

Z29 (1940), 383
Zachariae, Admiral, 119
Zara (1930), 302, 402
Zara-class heavy cruisers, 394,
    396
Zeebrugge Raid (1918), 240,
    242, 320
Zeiss (Carl Zeiss AG), Jena,
    53, 149, *150*, 298
Zonguldak, 191, *192*, 193
Zrínyi (1910), 18, 203,
    210–11, 214
Zuhaf (1894), 197